D0141852

Principles of Economics in Context

NEVA GOODWIN
Tufts University

JONATHAN HARRIS
Tufts University

JULIE A. NELSON
University of Massachusetts Boston

BRIAN ROACH
Tufts University

MARIANO TORRAS
Adelphi University

With contributions by
Frank Ackerman • Synapse Energy Economics
Thomas Weisskopf • University of Michigan, Ann Arbor
James Devine • Loyola Marymount University

M.E.Sharpe
Armonk, New York
London, England

Library of Congress Cataloging-in-Publication Data

Goodwin, Neva R.
Principles of economics in context / Neva Goodwin, Jonathan Harris, Julie Nelson,
Brian Roach, Mariano Torras.
pages cm
Includes index.
ISBN 978-0-7656-3882-3 (cloth : alk. paper)
1. Economics. I. Title.

HB171.G624 2014
330--dc23 2013038498

Printed in Canada

The paper used in this publication meets the minimum requirements of
American National Standard for Information Sciences
Permanence of Paper for Printed Library Materials,
ANSI Z 39.48-1984.

MI (c) 10 9 8 7 6 5 4 3 2 1

Brief Contents

Contents

Preface

For students taking a full-year introductory economics course, *Principles of Economics in Context* lays out the principles of economics in a manner that is thorough, up to date, and highly readable. Whether students take this class simply to gain some understanding of how economics can be useful to them, or go on to further studies in economics or business, this book will equip them with the tools and the critical understanding that they need to succeed.

Principles of Economics in Context stands apart both for its emphasis on real-world context and for its affordable price. Core economic models are presented with reference to key contemporary issues such as equity (especially income distribution), environmental sustainability, rational behavior (how realistic is "Economic Man"?), and history (path dependence and the impact of past choices on present choices). It introduces students both to the standard topics and tools taught in most introductory courses and to a broader and richer set of topics and tools to deepen comprehension of the economic realities of the twenty-first century.

This textbook is written to encourage engaged and critical thinking about topics in economics. While demonstrating the uses of economic theory, it also provides a variety of viewpoints. Woven throughout the book are themes of great importance in everyday life as well as for an understanding of the economy. There is a full treatment of standard neoclassical market theory and related topics, but the text also integrates discussion of history, institutions, gender, ethics, ecology, and inequality throughout the book. Within the broad themes of social and environmental well-being and sustainability, attention is repeatedly given to globalization, poverty and inequality, unpaid work, technology, and the environment as well as the financialization of the economy, the Great Recession, and its aftermath.

The text is priced at $99.95, much cheaper than most competitors, and available at an even lower price if purchased on-line. The price will not rise over the life of this edition. The text is also available as an E-book for $60 or less. The microeconomic and macroeconomic subject matter in *Principles of Economics in Context* is also available in two single-semester texts, *Macroeconomics in Context* (2nd ed.) and *Microeconomics in Context* (3rd ed.), also published by M.E. Sharpe and priced at $59.95 (cheaper on-line).

On pages xxv–xxviii you will find several possible course plans based on different emphases (such as ecological, global, human development, and structural). We hope that this will help in planning the course that will best suit the needs of instructors and students.

What Makes This Book Different from Other Texts?

This text covers the traditional topics included in most economics texts but treats them from a broader, more holistic perspective. The following chapter-by-chapter synopsis shows how this book manages both to be "similar enough" to fit into a standard curriculum and "different enough" to respond to commonly expressed needs and dissatisfactions.

Chapter 0, "Economics and Well-Being" presents graphically illustrated data on 34 variables, including data for the United States as well as international comparisons, using a selected set of countries. The related website www.gdae.org/principles allows users to see the same variables listed in order for all countries in the world where such data are available. The variables have been selected for intrinsic interest as well as relevance to the material in the rest of the book. This chapter is an innovation that teachers and students may choose to use in a variety of ways, including as an introduction to later topics, as a reference for use with other chapters, or as material to draw on in designing research projects.

Chapter 1, "Economic Activity in Context" presents standard economic topics such as the economic goals of living standards and stability—for the present and the future. These subjects are placed in a broader context of concern for well-being. The well-being goals of economics are defined as (1) improvement in living standards, (2) stability and security, and (3) financial, social, and ecological sustainability. Most textbooks discuss three essential activities—production, distribution, and consumption—but we add the activity of "resource maintenance" to draw attention to the importance of maintaining capital stocks, including stocks of natural (environmental) capital. The difference between stocks and flows is explained, and basic concepts of abundance, scarcity, tradeoffs, and opportunity costs are introduced and illustrated with production possibility curve analysis.

Chapter 2, "Useful Tools and Concepts" introduces standard concepts of economic modeling, efficiency, scarcity, and circular flow. It includes a review of graphing techniques and the use of empirical data. In addition to the usual economic "circular flow" diagram, this chapter presents an image of economic activity as embedded in social and physical contexts and relates this approach to issues of economic concern.

Chapter 3, "Markets and Society" discusses the institutional requirements of markets and introduces the concepts of externalities, public goods, market power, transaction costs, information and expectations, and concern for human needs and equity. The early introduction of these topics allows us to demonstrate why markets, while useful, are not on their own sufficient for organizing economic life in the service of well-being.

Chapter 4, "Supply and Demand" includes basic supply and demand analysis, including the slopes of supply and demand curves, factors that shift the curves, equilibrium and market adjustment, and the signaling and rationing functions of prices. Unlike many books that present equilibrium analysis as "the way the world works," we explicitly introduce supply and demand analysis as a *tool* whose purpose is to help a person disentangle the effects of various factors on real-world prices and quantities. Rather than concentrating solely on the efficiency effects of markets, the contextual approach demands that distributional consequences and power issues also be raised.

Chapter 5, "Elasticity" presents definitions and discussions of price elasticities of demand and supply, income elasticity of demand, and the income and substitution effects of a price change.

Chapter 6, "Welfare Analysis" presents standard welfare analysis, including the topics of consumer and producer surplus. It also includes a careful look at different ways of understanding efficiency. Consideration of what is efficient—and for whom—is followed by a first look at policy conclusions that have been drawn from this approach, and a first look at the requirements for "market perfection" that underlie traditional welfare analysis.

Chapter 7, "International Trade and Trade Policy" covers the gains-from-trade story that is now so important in discussing topical issues of global commerce. (The formal theory of comparative advantage and the gains from trade is spelled out in the appendix to the chapter.) We also discuss some possible negative impacts of trade as they may affect both developed and developing countries, and put these in the context of the globalized world, as it differs from the historical example of trade between England and Portugal.

Chapter 8, "Economic Behavior and Rationality" elaborates on the topics of individual choice, rationality, and self-interest. It updates and amplifies standard expositions, drawing on studies of human economic behavior by scholars such as Herbert Simon and Daniel Kahneman, and introduces issues of organizational structure and behavior. The result is a richer picture of the complex motivations and institutions underlying real-world economic activities.

Chapter 9, "Consumption and the Consumer Society" begins by presenting the traditional utility-theoretic model of consumer behavior. The chapter explains the notion of consumer sovereignty, shows students how to graph a budget line, and explains the rule for utility maximization derived from marginal analysis. We also discuss the historical development of the "consumer society" and the psychological models of consumer behavior used in marketing research, presenting views and evidence on the relation between consumption/consumerism and happiness, and the personal and ecological impact of high-level consumption patterns. The Appendix presents a formal theory of consumer behavior, using budget lines and indifference curves to illustrate utility maximization in the standard model.

Chapter 10, "Markets for Labor" includes the traditional derivation of profit-maximizing labor demand by a perfectly informed and perfectly competitive firm. Topics include the upward-sloping and backward-bending individual paid labor supply curves. The chapter then offers additional ways of understanding how wages are determined, including theories of compensating wage differentials, market power, worker motivation, and labor market discrimination. The Appendix sets out in formal terms the standard theory of the firm's hiring decisions.

Chapter 11, "Economic and Social Inequality" introduces Part IV, moving from definitions and measurement of inequality to data on trends in the United States and other countries. The second half of the chapter focuses on what is known about the underlying causes of inequality, and discusses possible policy responses.

Chapter 12, "Taxes and Tax Policy" starts out, like many of the other chapters in the book, with standard theory—in this case, taxes in the supply-and-demand model—and (referring back to the chapter on welfare analysis) it analyzes deadweight losses from taxes. Moving then to discuss taxation specifically in the United States, data are presented on the structure of various federal taxes, and their impacts.

Chapter 13, "The Economics of the Environment" shows how an understanding of externalities makes supply-and-demand analysis more relevant. This topic raises the problem of the valuation of externalities. We draw a distinction between standard and ecological views of the value of natural capital, raising the question of whether a standard cost-benefit framework can reasonably be applied to issues with unpredictable effects over the very long term (given the complexity of natural systems). A section on approaches to nonmarket environmental valuation is followed by a survey of some policy options for dealing with externalities. The Appendix offers a formal analysis of negative externalities.

Chapter 14, "Common Property Resources and Public Goods" differentiates between private and public goods. It relates recent work on this important topic to environmental considerations, contrasting Garrett Hardin's "tragedy of the commons" analysis with Elinor Ostrom's work on common property management. These analyses are then applied to a discussion of the challenge of global climate change.

Chapter 15, "Capital Stocks and Resource Maintenance" is the first of two chapters on production. It begins with a discussion of the activity of resource maintenance—that is, the importance of taking into consideration the effect of flows created by economic activity on the stocks of productive resources that will be available for future use. In a departure from other treatments, this book examines the crucial contributions of natural capital (environmental resources), human capital, and social capital to economic activity and human well-being. It also incorporates treatments of manufactured capital (machinery and physical infrastructure) and financial capital.

In **Chapter 16, "Production Costs"** the discussion of production continues with a focus on the costs of production. We present the traditional model of a firm's cost structure, with a focus on marginal costs. The chapter includes a traditional discussion of fixed and variable inputs; diminishing, constant, and increasing returns; total and marginal costs, and short-run versus long-run issues. We set this model in context in two important ways. First, the chapter encourages students to reflect on the idea that because of externalities, private and social net benefits from production may not be equivalent. Second, the chapter offers examples of cases where other economic actors (besides firms) make production decisions, and cases where other methods of decision making are necessary.

Chapter 17, "Markets Without Power" focuses on the concept of a perfectly competitive market. Its theoretic characteristics are described, and the zero-economic-profit and efficiency outcomes are discussed. It continues the discussion from the previous chapter to explain the profit-maximizing decisions of a perfectly competitive firm. Rather than simply concluding that perfectly competitive markets are always efficient, it balances the perfectly competitive model with a discussion of efficiency and equity, including the topics of path dependence and network externalities. The Appendix offers a formal model of perfect competition.

Chapter 18: "Markets with Market Power" covers traditional models of monopoly, monopolistic competition, and oligopoly. These different market structures are presented along a competitiveness continuum, with perfect competition and pure monopoly the "ideal types" representing the opposite extremes. The chapter provides abundant examples of the different market structures, including a separate section on agriculture and health care.

Chapter 19, "Introduction to Macroeconomics" begins Part VI of the book with a presentation of basic macroeconomic concepts such as recession and inflation. It considers some micro-foundations issues including discussion of price changes that are either too slow (i.e., "sticky") or too volatile (e.g., financial market speculation), leading to macroeconomic instability. A broad view of macroeconomic goals includes stabilization, living standards growth, and sustainability. These issues are placed in historical context, introducing themes related to classical and Keynesian economics that will be developed more fully in subsequent chapters.

Chapter 20, "Macroeconomic Measurement: The Current Approach" presents a fairly standard introduction to national income accounting but emphasizes that the accounts have been created for specific purposes, with conventions that reflect particular assumptions or choices. It notes how the production and investments undertaken in the "household and institutions" and government sectors have historically been deemphasized in national accounting.

Chapter 21, "Macroeconomic Measurement: Environmental and Social Dimensions" gives a more thorough introduction to alternative measures of economic performance than can be found in any other introductory economics textbook. The chapter briefly describes the Genuine Progress Indicator, the Better Life Index, the Human Development Index, and other current approaches for assessing well-being. It includes discussions of issues in the valuation of environmental and household services and of satellite accounts for environmental and household production.

Chapter 22, "The Structure of the U.S. Economy" is unique to this book. It describes key features of production and employment in the U.S. economy, broken down into its primary, secondary, and tertiary sectors. We include this material for several reasons. First, it makes the text more "real world" to students. Second, it provides basic economic literacy that we believe is sorely lacking among most economics students. Finally, it presents the context to illustrate several economic debates, such as the loss of manufacturing jobs, the rising costs of health care, and the meaning of the trend toward an ever-growing service sector, especially financial services. While this chapter is written with a U.S. focus, its description of sectoral shifts is relevant to many economies around the world.

Chapter 23, "Employment, Unemployment, and Wages" discusses standard macroeconomic labor topics such as the definition of the unemployment rate, the different types of unemployment, and theories of the causes of unemployment. In addition, there is a special focus on labor market institutions. The chapter discusses changes in labor force participation rates, different theories of wage determination, and the sources of wage differentials and inequalities.

Chapter 24, "Aggregate Demand and Economic Fluctuations" introduces the analysis of business cycles, presents the classical theory of savings-investment balance through the market for loanable funds, and develops Keynesian aggregate demand analysis in the form of the traditional "Keynesian cross" diagram. Our treatment of these topics is fairly standard, although our contextual approach places more emphasis on the possibility of persistent unemployment than do many other current textbooks—a perspective that is important in the light of the very slow recovery from the Great Recession.

Chapter 25, "Fiscal Policy" balances formal analysis of fiscal policy with real-world data and examples. Analysis of fiscal policy impacts is presented in fairly simple terms, with an algebraic treatment of more complex multiplier effects in appendices. While the basic analysis presented here follows the Keynesian model, the text also discusses classical and supply-side perspectives. The section on budgets and deficits should give students a basic understanding—developed further in Chapter 16—of deficits, debt, and how these affect the economy. The difference between automatic stabilizers and discretionary policy is made clear, and recent fiscal policies are discussed.

Chapter 26, "Money, Banking, and Finance" presents the basics of money and the banking system, including inflation, deflation, liquidity, and the different aggregate measures of money. Students are introduced to asset and liabilities tables, different banking institutions, and the process of money creation through the fractional reserve system. The chapter concludes with a discussion of non-bank financial institutions, financialization, and financial bubbles—topics of great relevance following the financial crisis of 2007–8.

Chapter 27, "The Federal Reserve and Monetary Policy" focuses on the role of the Federal Reserve and the implementation of monetary policy. Here we discuss the Federal Reserve's structure, functions, and monetary policy tools that it employs to create money. The chapter also spotlights the monetary economy in the United States over the past 12 years, with particular attention to the role of monetary policy in the 2007–8 financial crisis, and the nature of the monetary response to the crisis. The chapter also contains an appendix that explains in detail the indirect effect that the Federal Reserve can have on interest rates through the workings of the market for Treasury bonds.

Chapter 28, "Aggregate Supply, Aggregate Demand, and Inflation: Putting It All Together" addresses the tricky problem of how to teach the relationship between output and inflation to introductory students in a way that is simple yet intellectually defensible. The model presented in this chapter has many features that will be familiar to instructors. But unlike *AS/AD* models that put the price level on the vertical axis, this model has the inflation rate on the vertical axis, which makes it more relevant for discussing current events.* Unlike many new classical theory–influenced textbooks, our basic presentation is not centered on a notion of long-run full-employment equilibrium output. We emphasize, instead, how the macroeconomy adjusts dynamically in the short and medium term to often-

*Regarding the theoretical underpinnings of our model, our downward-sloped *AD* curve is based on the *AD* curve developed by David Romer ("Keynesian Macroeconomics Without the LM Curve," *Journal of Economic Perspectives* 14:2 [2000]: 149–169) and adopted by other introductory textbooks writers, including John B. Taylor (*Principles of Macroeconomics,* Houghton Mifflin, various editions). Our curved *AS* is based on the notion of an expectations-augmented Phillips curve, translated into inflation and output space. The idea of a dynamically evolving economy, rather than one always headed toward settling at full employment, is an approach based on Keynes' own (rather than new Keynesian) thought, as explained in the appendix to Chapter 13.

unpredictable economic events. This also makes relating the model to current events more realistic. (Classical theory is not, however, neglected. It is also discussed in the chapter and the Appendix.)

Chapter 29, "The Global Economy and Policy" adds the foreign sector to the circular-flow picture, which now includes savings, investment, taxes, government spending, exports, and imports. This chapter provides a more detailed treatment than most books of the factors that influence currency exchange rates worldwide. Chapter 29 also highlights the increasingly important links between fiscal and monetary policies and the global economy. Finally, in introducing students to the World Bank and the International Monetary Fund, the chapter addresses the real-world political economy of international economic relations.

Chapter 30, "The Financial Crisis and the Great Recession" is another unique feature of this book. In treating a topic that, as of early 2014, continued to affect the lives of millions, the chapter helps adds current relevance to the discussion of macroeconomic policy. Rather than develop a theoretical framework, Chapter 15 applies many of the insights introduced in earlier chapters to explain some of the likely causes and consequences of the financial crisis that led to the Great Recession. The chapter supplies an ideal context for extensive discussion of how the "real" economy relates to the financial economy, and the potential problems with an imbalance toward finance. It highlights the role of the housing bubble and subprime lending, as well as financial deregulation more generally, in creating the conditions for crisis. The latter part of the chapter discusses financial reform—efforts as well as new ideas—and asks some of the "big" questions that must be addressed if we are to avoid such crises in the future.

Chapter 31, "Deficits and Debt" is distinctive in a number of ways. First, it provides a current focus for the discussion of fiscal policy, allowing for greater elaboration on deficits and debt. Second, in an effort to alleviate the common confusion over the definition of the debt, the chapter includes a detailed classification of public and private debt types. Third, Chapter 16 analyzes the debate over stimulus versus austerity, including a contrast between how the United States and the eurozone have addressed their recent economic downturns, and considering the issue of sovereign debt. Finally, the chapter offers a survey of policy responses to the problem of long-term debt.

Chapter 32, "How Economies Grow and Develop" presents basic concepts related to economic growth, such as the Rostow and Harrod-Domar models, which emphasize the importance of investment in manufactured capital. But the chapter also provides examples of how investment in other types of capital—e.g., human or natural capital—can be equally, if not more, important, and distinguishes between growth and development. It also explores in detail the question of whether most poor countries have been "catching up" with the industrialized world ("convergence") or falling behind. Country diversity is a recurrent theme; the chapter emphasizes that the "one size fits all" approach to economic development emphasizing structural reforms—such as those embodied in the Washington Consensus—has produced disappointing results, and that different approaches are required in response to the circumstances in individual countries.

Chapter 33, "Growth and Sustainability in the Twenty-First Century" is an unusual chapter for an economics textbook—but a crucially important one, in terms of economic education for intelligent citizenship. It examines a number of ecological challenges and includes a section on global climate change. While it covers standard theories such as the environmental Kuznets curve, it raises serious challenges to the belief that economic growth and markets on their own can solve this century's social and environmental problems. More directly, it asks whether the traditional macroeconomic goal of continued economic growth is compatible with the long-term goal of sustainability. Finally, the chapter presents ideas for alternative approaches at the local, national, and global level that, while sustainable, do not detract from well-being.

SPECIAL FEATURES

Each chapter in this text contains many features designed to enhance student learning.

- *Key terms* are highlighted in boldface throughout the text, with sidebar definitions for easy comprehension and review.
- *Discussion Questions* at the end of each section encourage immediate review of what has been read and relate the material to the students' own experience. The frequent appearance of these questions throughout each chapter helps students review manageable portions of material and thus boosts comprehension. The questions can be used for participatory exercises involving the entire class or for small-group discussion.
- *End-of-Chapter Review Questions* are designed to encourage students to create their own summary of concepts. They also serve as helpful guidelines to the importance of various points.
- *End-of-Chapter Exercises* encourage students to work with and apply the material, thereby gaining increased mastery of concepts, models, and investigative techniques.
- Throughout the chapters, boxes enliven the material with real-world illustrations drawn from a variety of sources regarding applications of economic concepts and recent economic developments.
- In order to make the chapters as lively and accessible as possible, some formal and technical material (suitable for inclusion in some but not all course designs) is carefully and concisely explained in chapter appendices.
- A glossary at the end of the book contains all key terms, their definitions, and the number of the chapter in which each was first used and defined.

CONTENT AND ORGANIZATION

Some of the innovative features of this text are apparent in even a quick scan of the table of contents, the sample course outlines on pp. xxv–xxviii, or Chapter 0 and Chapter 1. Although this textbook takes a broader and more contextual approach to economic activities, it fits these within a familiar overall organizational strategy.

Part I, "The Context for Economic Analysis" presents the themes of the book and the major actors in the economy. Students are introduced to a range of economic questions and goals, to basic empirical and theoretical tools, and to the basic activities and institutions of a modern economy.

Part II, "Basic Economic Analysis" introduces basic supply and demand analysis, elasticities, and welfare analysis. It also includes a chapter on international trade. Most of this material will look very familiar to teachers of economics, although this text gives greater recognition than is typical to real-world market institutions and the limitations of traditional welfare analysis.

Part III, "Economics and Society" considers the economic roles that will be familiar to all readers throughout their lives: as workers and as consumers. These roles are illustrated with examples that depart from the standard models—for example, household production is recognized throughout. This part is introduced by a chapter on economic behavior, based on the latest studies in behavioral economics. It also includes a chapter on the topic of consumerism, and one on labor markets.

Part IV, "Essential Topics for Contemporary Economics" puts the economy in a social context, with one chapter on distribution, inequality, and poverty, and another on government roles, with an emphasis on taxes. The ecological context for the economy is then examined in two chapters that take up issues such as pollution, externalities, common property, and public goods.

Part V, "Resources, Production, and Market Organization" goes more into depth on market topics by describing the idealized model of perfect competition, presenting models of market power including monopoly, monopolistic competition, and oligopoly, and analyzing various resource markets.

Part VI, "Macroeconomic Basics" introduces basic macroeconomic definitions and accounting methods, including gross domestic product (GDP), inflation, aggregate demand, and unemployment. These are supplemented with a discussion of how new accounting systems are being developed to measure the economic contributions of the natural environment, unpaid household labor, and other previously uncounted factors. The second half of Part VI brings these abstractions down to earth with a description of the structure of the U.S. macroeconomy and discussion of the labor market and unemployment.

Part VII, "Macroeconomic Theory and Policy" explores the issue of macroeconomic fluctuations. The first chapters clearly present Keynesian and classical theories of the determination of aggregate demand (AD) and aggregate supply (AS) and the effects of fiscal and monetary policies. This section develops a dynamic AS/AD model of output and inflation that, with inflation rather than price level on the vertical axis, is designed to be comprehensible and usefully representative of the real world. It concludes with a chapter discussing macroeconomic issues in the global economy.

Part VIII, "Macroeconomic Issues and Applications" addresses the contemporary issues of financial crisis, the Great Recession, debt and deficits, economic development, and the environment. While the first two chapters here are presented from a largely U.S. perspective, the second half of this Part widens the lens to explore current global issues of poverty and inequality, economic growth, human development, and environmental challenges.

In order to focus on "contextual" discussions, formal instruction in algebraic modeling techniques is placed in optional appendices to the chapters. While this book reviews the basics of supply and demand and includes "new classical" economics among the theories discussed, it devotes fewer pages to the concept of efficient markets than many books do and certainly less than recent books that have adopted a strongly "new classical" slant. Instead, this text gives prominent consideration to new thinking in behavioral economics, analysis of financial instability and market bubbles, social and environmental issues, and policy responses to problems of unemployment, inequality, and environmental damage.

SUPPLEMENTS

The supplements package for this book provides a set of teaching tools and resources for instructors using this text. The authors have worked closely with our associate Dr. Patrick Dolenc to create an *Instructor's Resource Manual* and Test Bank to accompany *Principles of Economics in Context.* To access these electronically, send a request via e-mail to gdae@tufts.edu that contains sufficient information for us to verify your instructor status.

For each chapter, the *Instructor's Resource Manual* includes an introductory note and answers to all review questions and end-of-chapter exercises. In addition, the "Notes on Discussion Questions" section provides not only suggested answers to these questions but also ideas on how the questions might be used in the classroom. Sections titled "Web Resources" and "Extensions" provide supplementary material and links to other passages in the book or other materials that can be used to enrich lectures and discussion.

The Test Bank includes multiple-choice and true/false questions for each chapter. The correct answer for each question is indicated.

PowerPoint slides of figures and tables from the text and a Student Study Guide that provides ample opportunity for students to review and practice the key concepts are available for free download at www.gdae.org/principles.

ACKNOWLEDGMENTS

Principles of Economics in Context was written under the auspices of the Global Development and Environment Institute (GDAE), a research institute at Tufts University. All contributors of written materials were paid through grants raised by the Global Development and Environment Institute. By agreement with the authors, all royalties from sales of the book will go to support the work of the institute. We greatly appreciate the financial support that we have received from the V.K. Rasmussen Foundation, Spencer T. and Ann W. Olin, and the Ford, Island, and Barr Foundations.

This text has been a long time in the making, and many people have been involved along the way. First, we would like to thank Wassily Leontief, who initially urged us to write a book on economic principles for students in transitional economies. He provided inspiration and encouragement during those early years. We also are enormously grateful to Kelvin Lancaster, who allowed us to use *Modern Economics: Principles and Policy* (a textbook that he and Ronald Dulany wrote in the 1970s) as a jumping-off point for our work.

GDAE Research Fellow Anne-Marie Codur contributed to Chapter 33 on growth and sustainability, including updating the demography appendix; Dr. Nathan Perry of Colorado Mesa University contributed to Chapter 31 on deficits and debt; Ben Beachy contributed to Chapter 30 on fiscal crisis; and Dr. James Devine of Loyola Marymount University, Los Angeles, contributed to the macro modeling chapters.

We thank a number of instructors who were exceptionally generous in giving us detailed comments on the previous and the new edition, including Alison Butler, Willamette University; Gary Flomenhoft, University of Vermont; Robin King, Georgetown University; Dennis Leyden, University of North Carolina, Greenville; Valerie Luzadis, SUNY-ESF, Syracuse; Eric Nilsson, California State University San Bernardino; Chiara Piovani, University of Utah; Rebecca Smith, Mississippi State University; Saranna Thornton, Hampden-Sydney College; Marjolein van der Veen, Bellevue Community College; and Thomas White, Assumption College.

David Garman, of the Tufts University Economics Department, arranged an opportunity for us to class-test a very early draft of the micro portion of the text. Other faculty who assisted in the developmental stage of this text include Steven Cohn (Knox College), Julie Heath (University of Memphis), Geoffrey Schneider (Bucknell University), Robert Scott Gassler (Vesalius College of the Vrije Universiteit Brussels), Julie Matthaei (Wellesley College), and Adrian Meuller (CEPE Centre for Energy Policy and Economics).

Among the many faculty who provided valuable comments on earlier editions of the micro and macro sections, we would like to thank Sandy Baum (Skidmore College), Jose Juan Bautista (Xavier University of Louisiana), Gary Ferrier (University of Arkansas), Ronald L. Friesen (Bluffton College), and Abu N. M. Wahid (Tennessee State University), Fred Curtis (Drew University), James Devine (Loyola Marymount University), Richard England (University of New Hampshire), Mehrene Larudee (Bates College), Akira Motomura (Stonehill College), Shyamala Raman (Saint Joseph College), Judith K. Robinson (Castleton State College), Marjolein van der Veen (Bellevue Community College), Timothy E. Burson (Queens University of Charlotte), Will Cummings (Grossmont College), Dennis Debrecht (Carroll College), Amy McCormick Diduch (Mary Baldwin College), Miren Ivankovic (Southern Wesleyan University), Eric P. Mitchell (Randolph-Macon Woman's College), Malcolm Robinson (Thomas More College), June Roux (Salem Community College), Edward K. Zajicek (Kalamazoo College), Steve Balkin (Roosevelt University), Ernest Diedrich (College of St. Benedict/St. John's University), Mark Maier (Glendale Community College),

Ken Meter (Kennedy School of Government), Sigrid Stagl (University of Leeds), and Myra Strober (Stanford University), David Ciscel (University of Memphis), Polly Cleveland (Columbia University), Judex Hyppolite (Indiana University), Bruce Logan (Lesley College), Valerie Luzadis (SUNY-ESF), and Maeve Powlick (Skidmore College).

Early drafts of the micro section also formed the basis for editions designed for transitional economies, which were translated and published in Russia (Russian State University for the Humanities, 2002) and Vietnam (Hanoi Commercial University, 2002). Economists who contributed ideas to the transitional economies texts included Oleg Ananyin (Institute of Economics and Higher School of Economics, Moscow), Pham Vu Luan and Hoang Van Kinh (Hanoi Commercial University), Peter Dorman (Evergreen College); Susan Feiner (University of Southern Maine); Drucilla Barker (Hollins College); Robert McIntyre (Smith College); Andrew Zimbalist (Smith College); Cheryl Lehman (Hofstra University); and Raymond Benton (Loyola University).

Essential support work on research and manuscript preparation, including data analysis for Chapter 0, was provided by GDAE Research Coordinator Josh Uchitelle-Pierce, who took on a wide variety of tasks, solving many technical problems and maintaining a high quality of presentation throughout the volume. He was ably assisted by Mitchell Stallman, Reid Spagna, Nicholas Lusardo and Lauren Jayson. Administrative and outreach support at the Global Development and Environment Institute was provided by Casey Kennedy and Erin Coutts.

We also thank the staff of M.E. Sharpe, particularly Irene Bunnell, Angela Piliouras, and Laura Brengelman, for their enthusiasm and meticulous work in getting this book to press. Our editors, George Lobell and Patricia Kolb, contributed support and helpful suggestions throughout the process.

Finally, we would like to thank the many students we've had the privilege to teach over the years—you continually inspire us and provide hope for a bright future.

Sample Course Outlines

Providing both standard and innovative materials for introductory economics, *Principles of Economics in Context* can be used as the basis for a variety of approaches, depending on which topics and approaches are of particular interest.

To help identify the chapter assignments that make the most sense for a particular class, we have put together some ideas for course outlines below. Arranged in terms of broad selections and more specific emphases, they are designed to help instructors choose among chapters when there is not enough time to cover everything in this textbook.

We understand that in many departments one primary objective of the introductory course is to teach in some detail "how (neoclassical) economists think." For instructors who choose to focus exclusively on neoclassical content, the most traditional combination of the selections described below—the Base Chapters, combined with some or all of the Basic Microeconomics and Basic Macroeconomics Selection and the Neoclassical Emphasis and Macro-Modeling Emphasis chapters—will provide what you need. This combination of chapters does not come close to exploiting fully the richness of *Principles of Economics in Context,* but the contextual discussions (a hallmark of this text) that are woven into the standard material will broaden the students' understanding of economic theory and provide tools for critical thinking.

Many instructors have somewhat more leeway and can combine coverage of traditional neoclassical ideas with other material. Addressing such users of *Principles of Economics in Context,* we suggest that you make use of the special structure of the book, which enables you to introduce traditional concepts in your introductory course while still reserving class time for other areas of interest. Ecological sustainability, for example, is an issue of increasing importance and is deeply linked to the functioning of the economy. For this focus, the Base Chapters Selection and most of the Basic Microeconomics and Basic Macroeconomics Selection could be combined with the "Ecological Emphasis" Selection.

Some instructors and students may have less interest in the formalities of economic modeling, in which case it might make sense to cover the Base Chapters Selection, some material from the Basic Microeconomics and Basic Macroeconomics Selection, and much more material from the topical emphases such as "Human Development" and "Poverty/Inequality/Social Justice." For coverage of alternative and critical perspectives, the "Critiques of Neoclassical Economics" and "Keynesian/Post-Keynesian/Institutionalist" selection will be useful.

The data presented in Chapter 0 cover a wide variety of topics and applications, and it may be appropriate to refer back to this chapter for almost any of the selections below.

BASE CHAPTERS SELECTION

- Chapter 1, "Economic Activity in Context"
- Chapter 2, "Useful Tools and Concepts"
- Chapter 3, "Markets and Society"
- Chapter 4, "Supply and Demand"

BASIC MICROECONOMICS SELECTION

- Chapter 7, "International Trade and Trade Policy," Sections 1 and 2
- Chapter 10, "Markets for Labor," Sections 1 and 2
- Chapter 16, "Production Costs"
- Chapter 17, "Markets Without Power," Sections 2–4
- Chapter 18, "Markets with Power," Sections 1–5

BASIC MACROECONOMICS SELECTION

- Chapter 19, "Introduction to Macroeconomics"
- Chapter 20, "Macroeconomic Measurement: The Current Approach"
- Chapter 23, "Employment and Unemployment"
- Chapter 24, "Aggregate Demand and Economic Fluctuations"
- Chapter 25, "Fiscal Policy"
- Chapters 26 and 27, "Money, Banking and Finance," and "The Federal Reserve and Monetary Policy"
- Chapter 28, "Aggregate Supply, Aggregate Demand, and Inflation: Putting It All Together"
- Chapter 32, "How Economies Grow and Develop"

NEOCLASSICAL EMPHASIS

- Chapter 7, "International Trade and Trade Policy," Appendix
- Chapter 8, "Economic Behavior and Rationality," Section 1
- Chapter 9, "Consumption and the Consumer Society," Section 1 and Appendix
- Chapter 10, "Markets for Labor," Appendix
- Chapter 17, "Markets Without Power," Appendix
- Chapter 18, "Markets with Power," Appendix

EMPHASIS ON CRITIQUES OF NEOCLASSICAL ECONOMICS

- Chapter 1, "Economic Activity in Context," Section 2
- Chapter 2, "Useful Tools and Concepts," Section 2
- Chapter 3, "Supply and Demand," Section 5
- Chapter 7, "International Trade and Trade Policy," Section 3
- Chapter 10, "Markets for Labor," Section 5
- Chapter 17, "Markets Without Power," Sections 1 and 5

WELFARE ANALYSIS EMPHASIS

- Chapter 6, "Welfare Analysis"
- Chapter 12, "Taxes and Tax Policy," Section 1
- Chapter 13, "The Economics of the Environment," Section 1 and Appendix

APPLIED MICROECONOMICS/POLICY EMPHASIS

- Chapter 5, "Welfare Analysis," Section 5

- Chapter 7, "International Trade and Trade Policy," Section 4
- Chapter 9, "Consumption and the Consumer Society," Section 5
- Chapter 10, "Markets for Labor," Sections 3 and 4
- Chapter 11, "Economic and Social Inequality," Section 4
- Chapter 12, "Taxes and Tax Policy," Sections 2 and 3
- Chapter 13, "The Economics of the Environment," Sections 2 and 3
- Chapter 18, "Markets with Market Power," Section 5

ECOLOGICAL EMPHASIS

- Chapter 9, "Consumption and the Consumer Society," Section 4
- Chapter 13, "The Economics of the Environment"
- Chapter 14, "Common Property Resources and Public Goods," Sections 3–5
- Chapter 15, "Capital Stocks and Resource Maintenance," Section 2
- Chapter 21, "Macroeconomic Measurement: Social and Environmental Dimensions"
- Chapter 22, Section 1, "The Three Major Productive Sectors in an Economy," and Section 2, "The Primary Sector in the United States"
- Chapter 33, "Growth and Sustainability in the Twenty-First Century"

GLOBAL EMPHASIS

- Chapter 7, "International Trade and Trade Policy"
- Chapter 29, "The Global Economy and Policy"
- Chapter 32, "How Economies Grow and Develop"
- Chapter 33, "Growth and Sustainability in the Twenty-First Century"

HUMAN DEVELOPMENT EMPHASIS

- Chapter 21, "Macroeconomic Measurement: Environmental and Social Dimensions"
- Chapter 32, "How Economies Grow and Develop"

STRUCTURAL EMPHASIS

- Chapter 22, "The Structure of the U.S. Economy"
- Chapter 30, "The Financial Crisis and the Great Recession"
- Chapter 31, "Deficits and Debt"

BEHAVIORAL ECONOMICS EMPHASIS

- Chapter 8, "Economic Actors and Rationality," Sections 2 and 3
- Chapter 9, "Consumption and the Consumer Society," Sections 3 and 5

KEYNESIAN/POST-KEYNESIAN/INSTITUTIONALIST EMPHASIS

- Chapter 19, "Introduction to Macroeconomics," Sections 2 and 4
- Chapter 28, Appendix A3, "Post-Keynesian Macroeconomics"
- Chapter 30, "The Financial Crisis and the Great Recession"
- Chapter 31, "Deficits and Debt"
- Chapter 33, "Growth and Sustainability in the Twenty-First Century," Section 5

MACRO-MODELING EMPHASIS

- Chapter 24, Appendix, "An Algebraic Approach to the Multiplier"
- Chapter 25, Appendix, "More Algebraic Approaches to the Multiplier"
- Chapter 28, Appendix "More Schools of Macroeconomics"

- Chapter 29, Section 4, "Macroeconomics in an Open Economy"
- Chapter 32, Section 1, "Development and Economic Growth"

Money and Finance Emphasis

- Chapters 26 and 27, "Money, Banking and Finance," and "The Federal Reserve and Monetary Policy"
- Chapter 30, "The Financial Crisis and the Great Recession"
- Chapter 31, "Deficits and Debt"

Poverty/Inequality/Social Justice Emphasis

- Chapter 9, Consumption and the Consumer Society," Section 3
- Chapter 10, "Markets for Labor," Sections 4 and 5
- Chapter 11, "Economic and Social Inequality"
- Chapter 21, Section 2, "Why GDP Is Not a Measure of Well-Being," Section 3, "Some Leading Approaches to Measuring Well-Being," and Section 4, "Measuring Household Production"
- Chapter 23, Section 3, "Theories of Employment, Unemployment, and Wages"
- Chapter 32, Section 3, "Understanding Poverty" and Section 4, "Inequality"

Contrasting Schools of Thought Emphasis

- Chapter 19, "Introduction to Macroeconomics," Section 4
- Chapter 28, Section 4, "Competing Theories," and Appendix, "More Schools of Macroeconomics"
- Chapter 33, "Growth and Sustainability in the Twenty-First Century," Section 5, "Are Stabilization and Sustainability in Conflict?"

PART I

The Context for Economic Analysis

0 Economics and Well-Being

What comes to your mind when you think of the word "economics"? Perhaps you think about things like money, the stock market, globalization, and supply-and-demand. These things are definitely important to our study of economics, and we will spend much of our time in this book studying these concepts.

But the goals of economics are about much more than these. As we will see in Chapter 1, economics is: *the study of how people manage their resources to meet their needs and enhance their well-being.* The term "well-being" can mean different things to different people. We take an inclusive approach to well-being in this book. Well-being depends on traditional economic indicators like our income and material standard of living. But our well-being also depends on many other issues, such as the quality of our environment, our leisure time, and our perceptions of fairness and justice. Our study of economics will help you better understand many of the outcomes that we observe and think about ways that we might be able to improve things. Many of the topics that we will study relate to current economic and political debates, such as economic inequality, the environment, taxes, and globalization.

The purpose of this introductory chapter is to provide an overview of some of the topics that we cover in more detail later in the book. Good data are essential for informed debates about how to enhance well-being in our communities. In this chapter, for each topic we provide a graphical representation of important data. We have tried to be as objective as possible by presenting a wide range of data from reliable sources. You may find some of this information surprising, as the results may differ from common perceptions and media representations.

The information in this chapter is divided into three sections: time trends, showing how a particular variable changes over time; bar graphs, showing data for different sections of the population or different industries; and bar graphs showing international comparisons. While we focus on the United States here, and in much of the rest of the book, it is important to see individual country data within the global context. If you are interested in the performance of specific countries we have not included here, detailed tables are available on the book's companion website: www.gdae.org/principles.

The graphs that appear in this chapter are:

Time Trends

1. U.S. GDP per Capita
2. U.S. Unemployment Rate, 1960–Present
3. U.S. Inflation Rate, 1960–Present
4. Taxes as a Percentage of GDP
5. Stock Market Performance
6. Median Home Prices
7. Median Worker Earnings vs. Corporate Profits
8. Global International Trade
9. Global Carbon Dioxide Emissions

Bar Graphs for United States

10. Income Inequality
11. Unequal Income Growth
12. Gender-Based Earnings Inequality
13. Educational Attainment
14. Industrial Concentration Ratios

International Comparisons

15. GDP per Capita
16. Recent Growth Rate of GDP per Capita
17. Net National Savings
18. Government Debt
19. Labor Productivity
20. Average Annual Hours Worked
21. Unemployment Rate (Percent of Total Workforce)
22. Inflation
23. Total Tax Revenues (Percent of GDP)
24. Trade Balance (Percent of GDP)
25. Income Inequality (Gini Coefficient)
26. CEO Pay vs. Worker Pay: International Comparisons
27. Absolute Poverty
28. Foreign Aid
29. Internet Users
30. Educational Performance
31. Life Expectancy
32. Subjective Well-Being
33. Carbon Dioxide Emissions per Capita
34. Local Air Quality

International comparison rankings are based on the available data, including the highest and lowest values for each variable. While there are over 200 countries in the world, data are not available for all countries for each variable, so the number of countries ranked for each variable differs. The United States is shown in a different color. The rankings are presented with the "highest" at the top and the "lowest" at the bottom. However, this does not always mean that it is best to be at the top. For example, one of the graphs shows the percentage of people living in absolute poverty. Obviously, it is not a good thing to be ranked #1 for this variable.

1. U.S. GDP per Capita

What it is: GDP, or Gross Domestic Product, is a measure of the total value of goods and services produced in a country. As discussed in Chapters 20 and 21, there are controversies about exactly what is covered, or not covered, by GDP, but the measure is used very widely as an index of the status and growth of an economy. GDP can be seen both as a measures of product and of income. GDP per capita, shown here, is GDP divided by the country's population, and the time trend of GDP/capita shows how average income changes over time.

The results: U.S. GDP per capita has increased nearly threefold since 1960. The progression has not been entirely smooth, with pauses and declines especially during periods of economic recession, but the overall trend is upwards. One of the largest breaks in this trend was the recent recession of 2007–9, discussed in detail in Chapter 23, 25, 28, and 30. As the graph shows, GDP/capita started to recover after 2010, but remained below its 2007 peak through 2012.

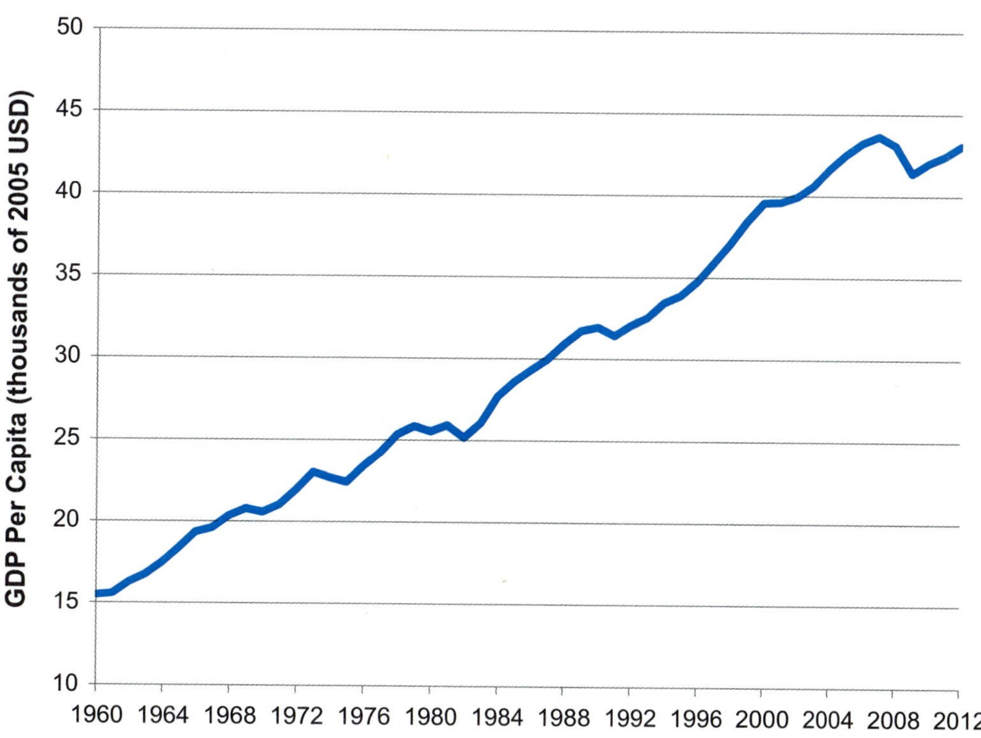

Source: World Bank, World Development Indicators database.

2. U.S. Unemployment Rate, 1960–Present

What it is: The unemployment rate is a measure of the proportion of people in the labor force who are seeking jobs but unable to find them (discussed in detail in Chapter 23). The measure does not include people who have part-time work but would like full-time work, nor does it include "discouraged workers" who have given up looking for work. The unemployment rate typically falls during economic expansions, and rises during and immediately after economic recessions.

The results: U.S. unemployment has varied since 1960 between about 4 and 10 percent. In expansionary periods such as the late 1960s and the late 1990s, it was between 4 and 5 percent. In recessions it has typically risen above 6 percent, with peaks of between 8 and 10 percent in 1975, 1982, and 2010, resulting from severe recessions.

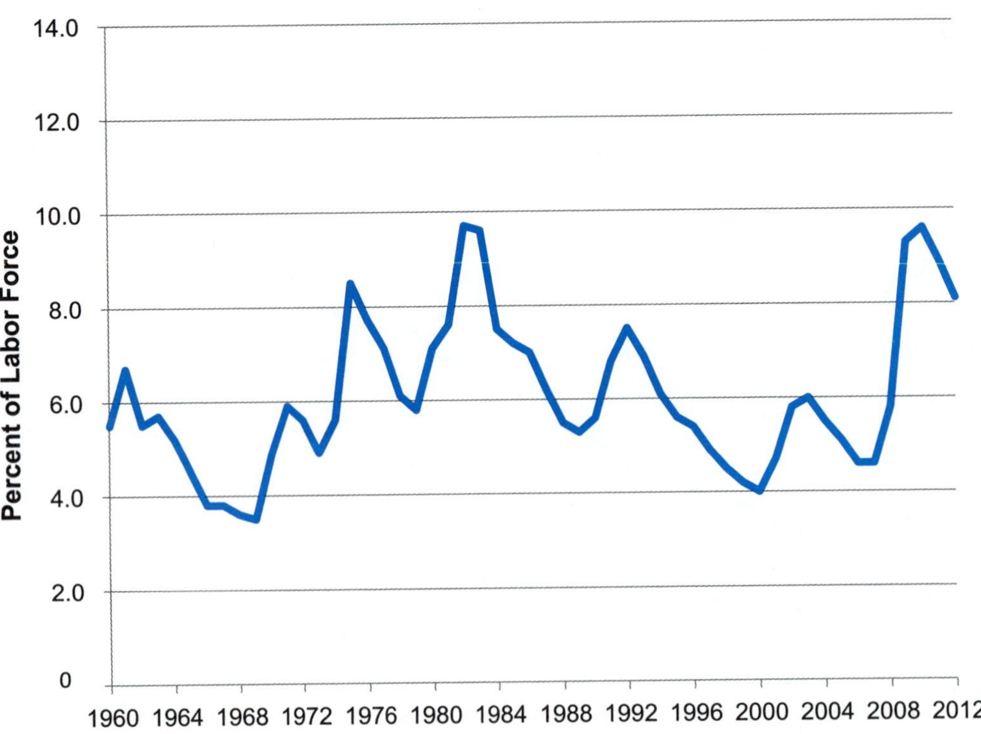

Source: U.S. Bureau of Labor Statistics, Current Population Survey, 2013.

3. U.S. Inflation Rate, 1960–Present

What it is: The inflation rate is a measure of the average increase in prices between one year and the next. It is measured by the change in the Consumer Price Index, discussed in Chapter 20. There are various versions of the Consumer Price Index (CPI); the graph below is based on the CPI-U, which measures the cost of living in urban areas.

The results: The U.S. inflation rate has varied considerably since 1960, with noticeable peaks in the late 1970s and early1980s. At these times, the inflation rate rose above 10 percent (referred to as "double-digit inflation). This level of inflation is considered significantly harmful to an economy, as discussed in Chapters 26-28. Since 1990, inflation rates in the United States have generally been fairly low, not rising above 4 percent, and averaging around 3 percent. During the 2007–9 recession, inflation briefly fell to zero, arousing concern about deflation—negative inflation or generally falling prices. (Although some might think that falling prices would be a good thing, sustained deflation can be very damaging to businesses and reduce employment, as occurred during the Great Depression of the 1930s.)

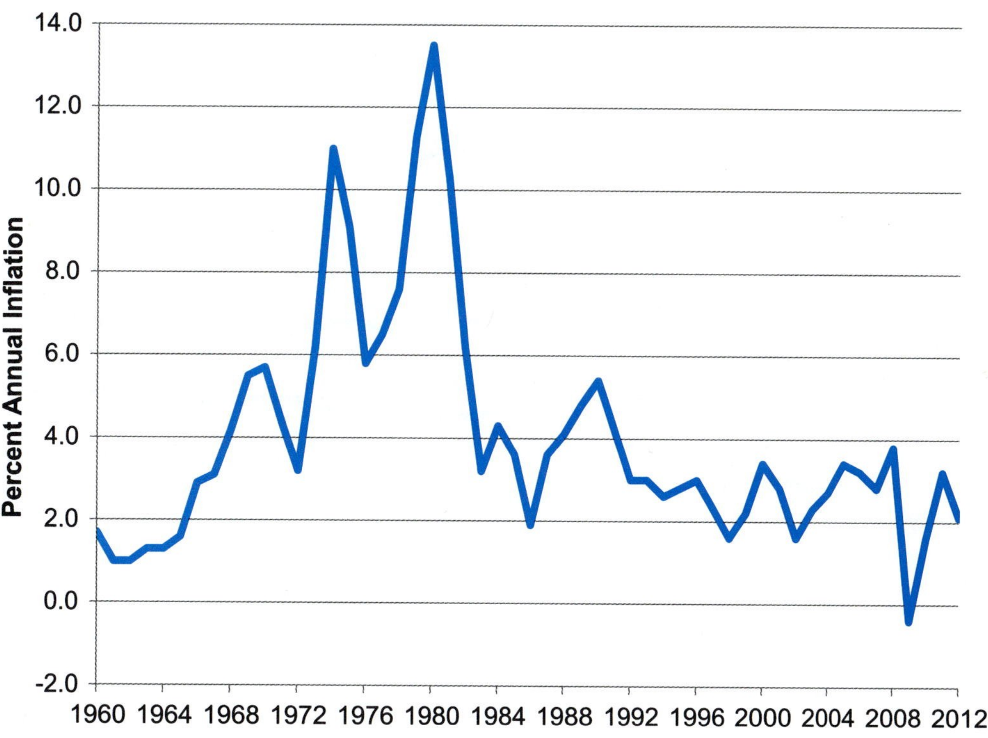

Source: U.S. Bureau of Labor Statistics, Consumer Price Index (CPI-U), 2013.

4. Taxes as a Percentage of GDP

What it is: The graph below shows tax collections in the United States over the period 1950–2012, measured as a percentage of gross domestic product (GDP). Total taxes are divided into federal taxes and state and local taxes.

The results: Total tax collections in the United States gradually increased from about 25% of GDP in the 1950s to close to 35% of GDP in the late 1990s. Since then, state and local tax collection has remained relatively constant, while federal tax collection has generally declined. Although in surveys many Americans say they believe taxes have increased in recent years (particularly federal taxes), the opposite is true. We discuss taxes in more detail in Chapter 12.

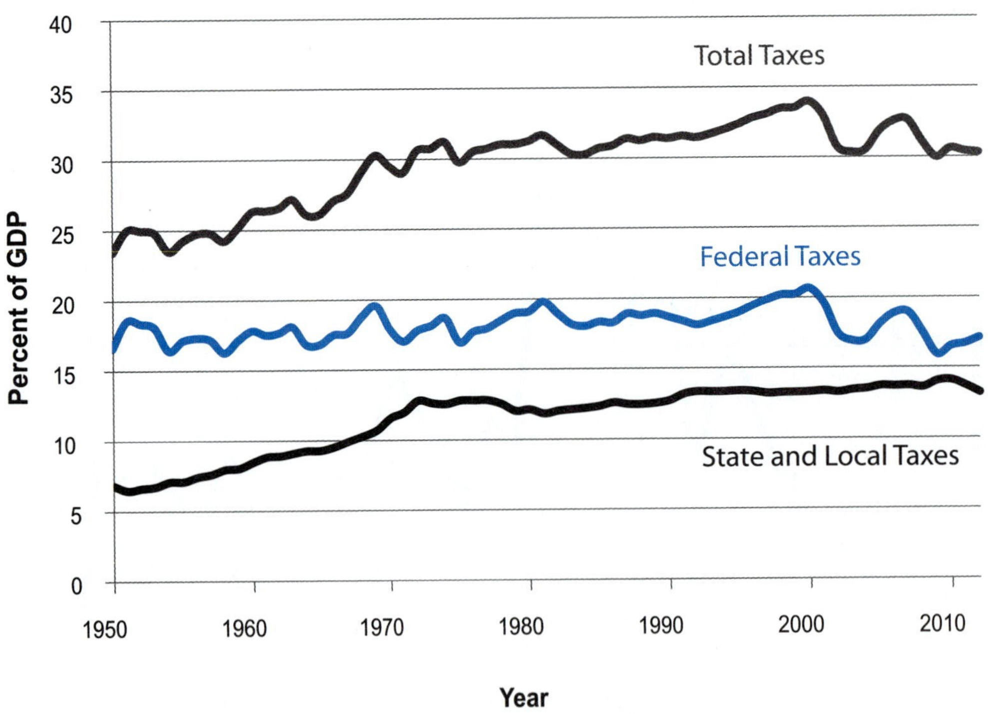

Source: U.S. Bureau of Economic Analysis, online database.

5. Stock Market Performance

What it is: Media stories about the economy often focus on the performance of the stock market. Several common stock indices, such as the Dow Jones Composite, the Nasdaq Composite, and S&P (Standard & Poor's) 500 Index, provide a broad overview of stock market prices. The graph below shows the value of the S&P 500 Index from 1965 to mid-2013. The S&P 500 Index is calculated based on the stock prices of 500 large, mostly American, companies.

The results: From 1965 to 2000, the S&P 500 Index rose from about 100 to more than 1,500. Since 2000, two major "crashes" have taken place in the U.S. stock market. In each crash, the S&P 500 lost about half its value and then recovered to previous levels over several years. Although we do not discuss the stock market in much detail in this book, we spend considerable time discussing how markets operate, including the factors that lead to price fluctuations.

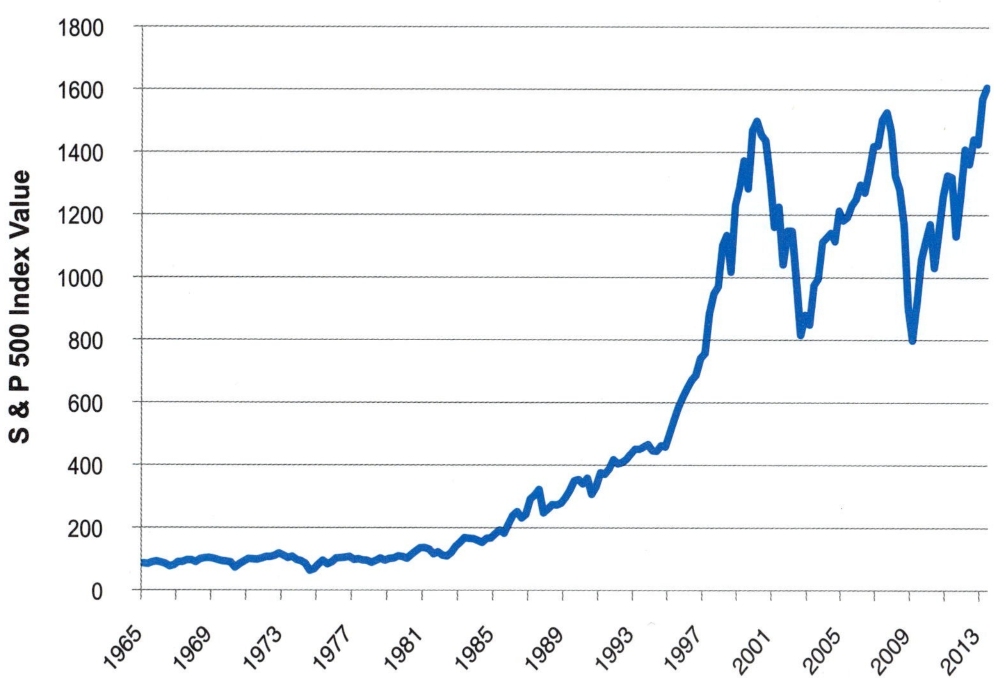

Source: St. Louis Federal Reserve Bank, S&P 500 Stock Price Index (SP500), http://research.stlouisfed.org/fred2/series/SP500/downloaddata.

6. MEDIAN HOME PRICES

What it is: The "median" price of home sales is the price at which half of homes sell for more than this price, and half sell for less. The graph below shows median home price in the United States over the period 1987 to mid-2013. The prices have not been adjusted for inflation.

The results: The median price of houses in the United States increased by a factor of three between 1987 and 2007. Then the housing bubble burst, and home prices fell by about one-third. Since then home prices have remained relatively low. Our discussion of markets, beginning in Chapter 2 and covering many of the chapters in this book, will help you understand how markets operate.

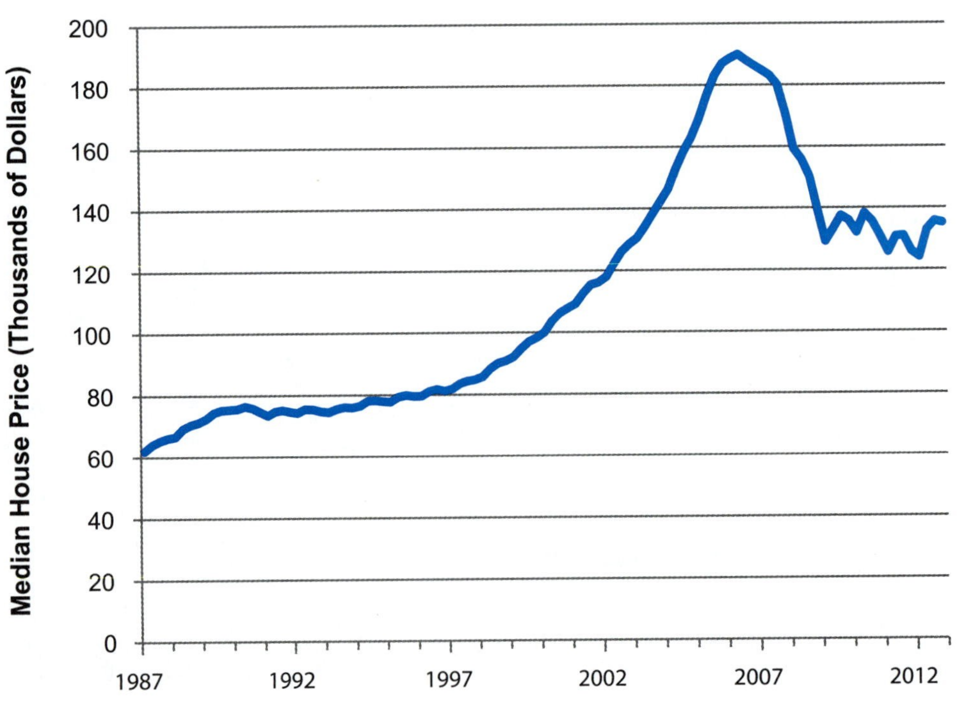

Source: S&P Dow Jones Indices, Case-Shiller Home Price Index, National; www.spindices.com/indices/real-estate/sp-case-shiller-us-national-home-price-index.

7. MEDIAN WORKER EARNINGS VS. CORPORATE PROFITS

What it is: The graph below shows the change in two variables over the period 1980 to 2012 in the United States:

1. Total corporate profits, measured in billions of dollars
2. Median weekly earnings for American workers, measured in dollars

The data for both variables have been adjusted for inflation. Note that the vertical axis is measured in dollars for median worker earnings and billions of dollars for corporate profits.

The results: Corporate profits have fluctuated based on the health of the overall economy, but we see that profits reached a record high in 2012. Corporate profits in 2012 were over three times the level they were at in 1980. Meanwhile, the median wages of U.S. workers have essentially not changed at all since 1980. We will discuss wages in more detail in Chapter 10, including the reasons why wages have not risen in proportion to corporate profits.

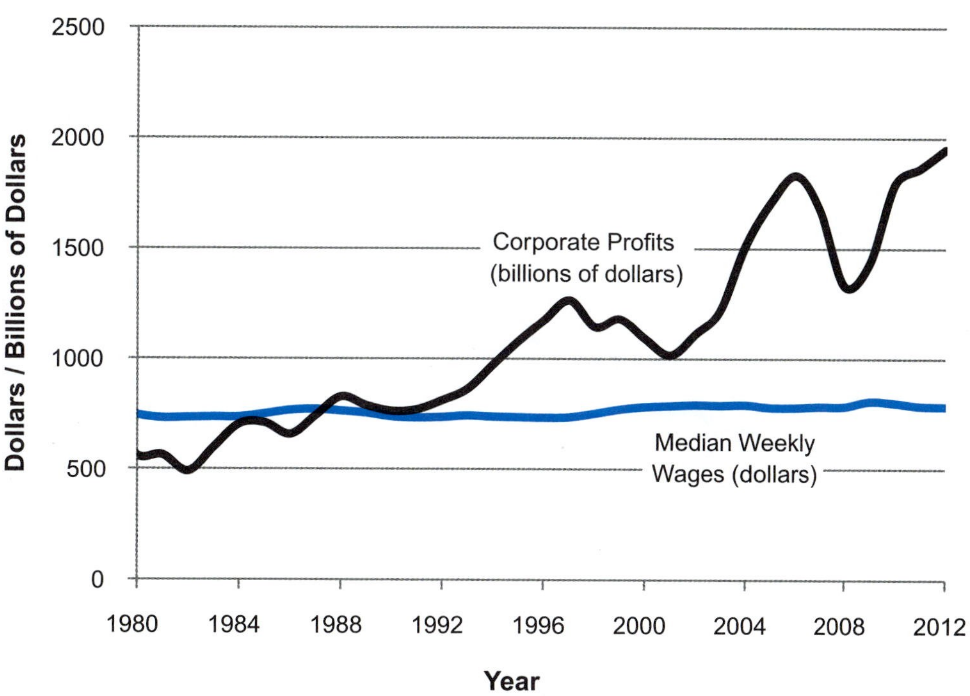

Sources: U.S. Bureau of Economic Analysis, National Income and Product Accounts Tables; U.S. Bureau of Labor Statistics, Weekly and Hourly Earnings Data from the Current Population Survey.

8. Global International Trade

What it is: The graph below shows the percentage of world economic production (called "gross world product") that is traded across international borders, over the period 1960 to 2011. This is one way to get a quick snapshot of the degree of "globalization."

The results: At least as measured by international trade, the world is clearly becoming more globalized. About 12 percent of all goods and services produced in the world were traded across international borders in 1960. Currently, about 30 percent of world production is traded internationally. We can see that the global financial crisis of 2007–8 temporarily reduced international trade but that it has since recovered to previous levels. We discuss international trade further in Chapters 7 and 29.

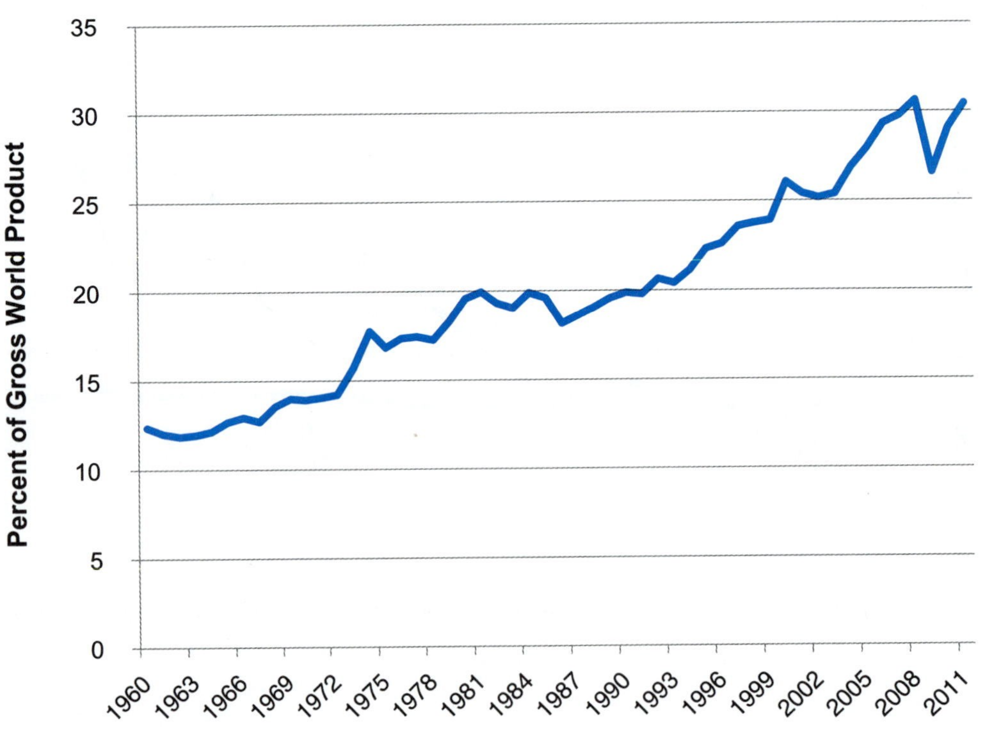

Source: World Bank, World Development Indicators database.

9. Global Carbon Dioxide Emissions

What it is: The vast majority of scientists believe that human activities are affecting the global climate. Carbon dioxide emissions, which result when oil, coal, and natural gas are burned, have been identified as the primary cause of global climate change. The graph below shows global carbon dioxide emissions from 1960 to 2010, measured in gigatons (a gigaton is a billion metric tons).

The results: We see that global carbon dioxide emissions increased from about 10 gigatons in 1960 to over 30 gigatons in 2010. Although most projections indicate that global carbon dioxide emissions will continue to increase in the future, scientists indicate that emissions must decrease substantially in the next few decades to avoid significant negative consequences to the global ecosystem and to human societies. We discuss global climate change in more detail in Chapters 14 and 33.

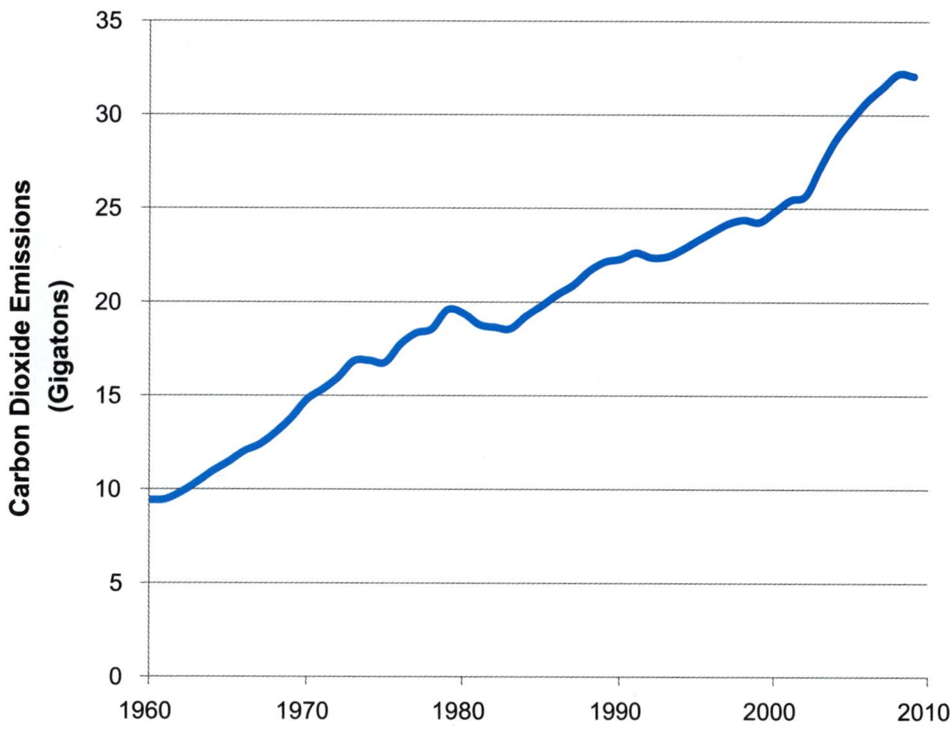

Source: World Bank, World Development Indicators database.

10. Income Inequality

What it is: The graph below shows the average household income for different income groups in the United States, based on 2011 data. Each group represents one-fifth of American households, except for the last group, which includes only the top 5 percent.

The results: For households in the bottom fifth of Americans, average income in 2011 was only about $11,000. For those in the middle fifth, household income averaged about $50,000. Those in the top fifth had an average household income of nearly $180,000. Average household income was more than $300,000 for the top 5 percent. Note that these are average values, so some households in each group made less than these income values, while some made more. We discuss income inequality, including its causes, in more detail in Chapter 11.

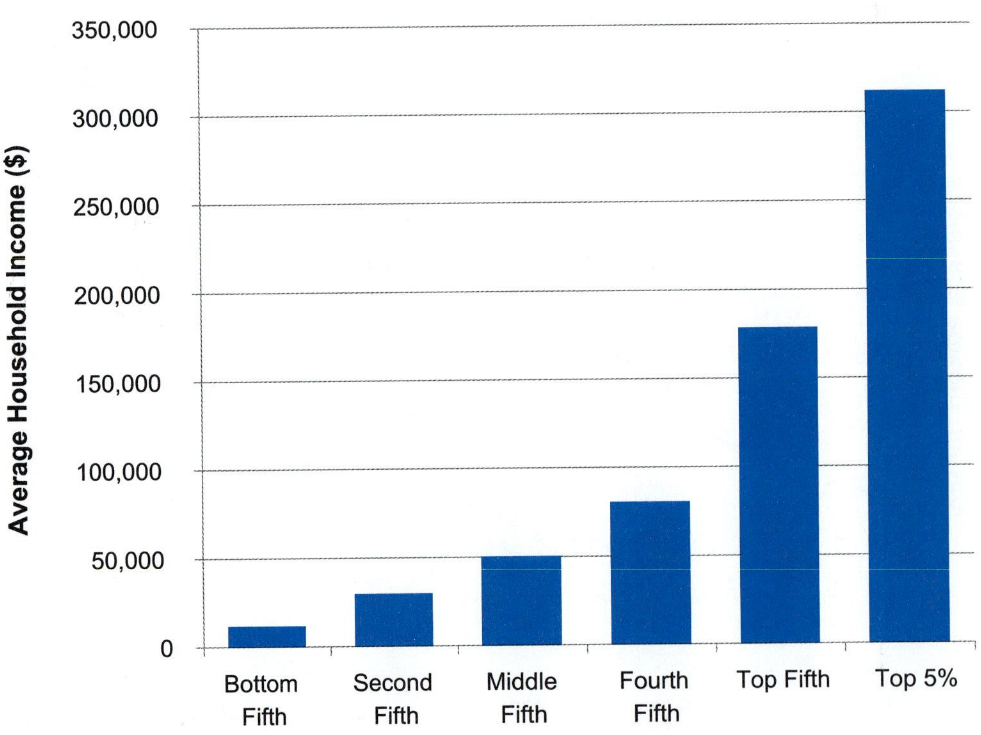

Source: U.S. Census Bureau, Historical Income Tables: Income Inequality, Table H-3.

11. Unequal Income Growth

What it is: The graph below shows the growth in household income for different income groups in the United States, over the period 1968–2011. As in the previous graph, each group represents one-fifth of American households, except for the last group, which includes only the top 5 percent. The data have been adjusted for inflation.

The results: You have probably heard the saying: "The poor get poorer and the rich get richer." That is close, but not quite true. We see that those at the bottom of the income distribution did see small income gains in recent decades. Those in the middle did a little better. But the largest gains, by far, were obtained by those at the top, particularly those in the top 5 percent. The graph tells us that income inequality has increased considerably in recent decades. We discuss trends in income inequality in more detail in Chapter 11.

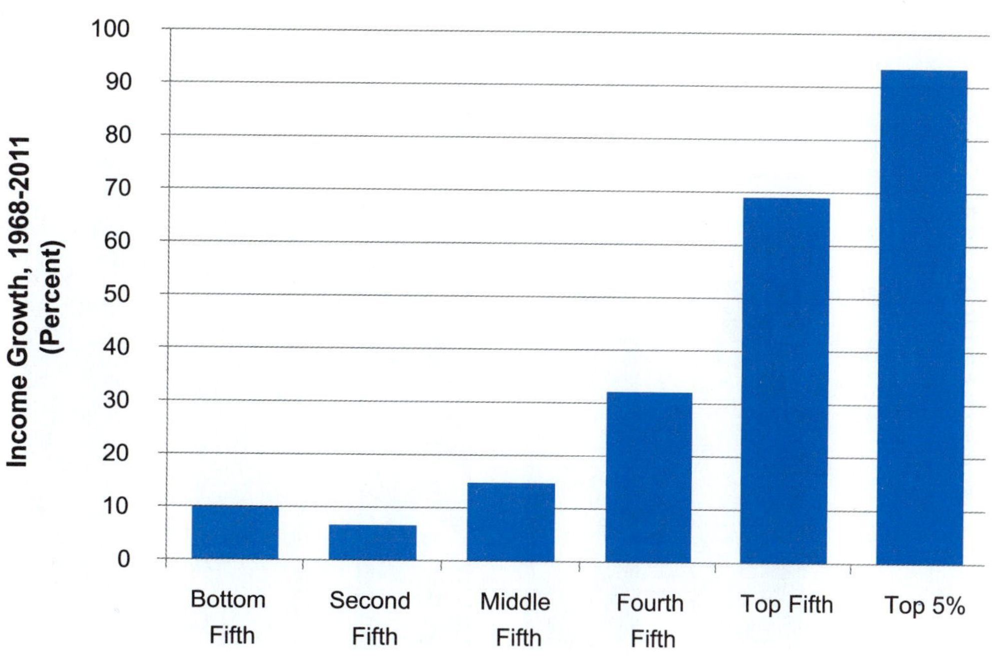

Note: We use 1968 as the starting year in this analysis because it is the year in which income inequality in the United States started to increase, as we will discuss in Chapter 10.

Source: U.S. Census Bureau, Historical Income Tables: Income Inequality, Table H-3.

12. Gender-Based Earnings Inequality

What it is: The "gender wage gap" is the difference in median earnings between men and women who work full time. The graph below shows women's median earnings in the United States as a percentage of men's median earnings, over the period 1979 to 2011.

The results: In 1979, women working full time in the United States earned only 62 percent of what men earned. During the 1980s the gender wage gap closed considerably. By the early 1990s, women working full time earned more than 75 percent of what men earned. Since then, the wage gap has continued to close, but more slowly. In 2011, women earned 82 percent of what men earned. Is this clear evidence of gender discrimination? We discuss this topic in more detail in Chapter 10.

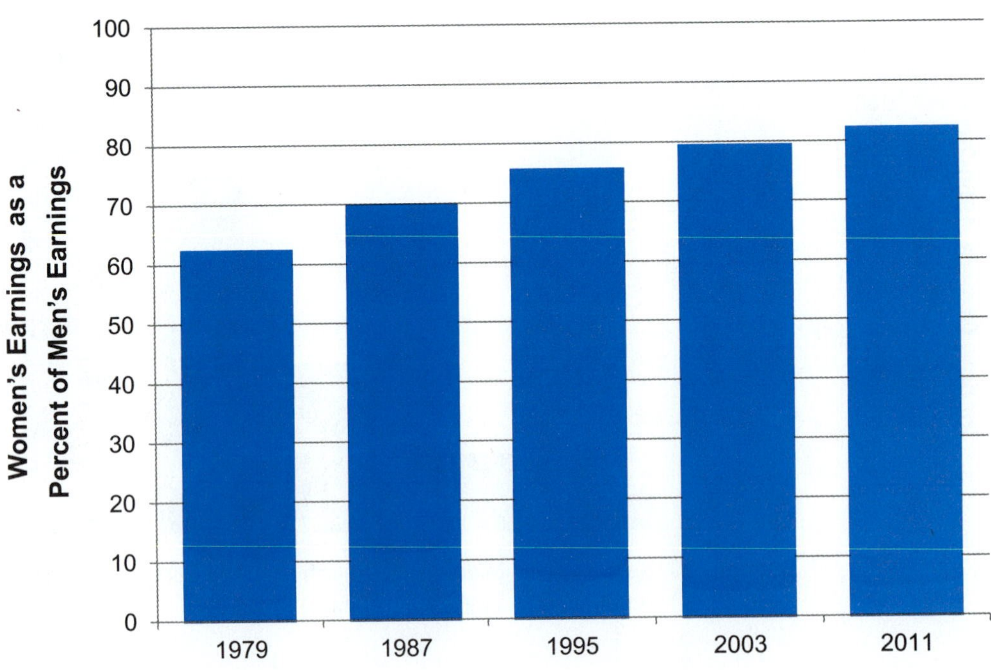

Source: U.S. Bureau of Labor Statistics, Women's Earnings, 1979–2011, www.bls.gov/opub/ted/2012/ted_20121123.htm.

13. Educational Attainment

What it is: Education is an important type of "human capital"—a term that economists use to describe the knowledge and skills people possess that allow them to engage in production activities. The graph below shows the maximum educational attainment for Americans age 25 and older in 1960, 1970, 1980, 1990, 2000, and 2012. Each column adds up to 100 percent, but the percentage falling into each education category varies with changes in educational attainment.

The results: In 1960, about 58 percent of Americans age 25 and older had not graduated high school, and less than 10 percent had a college degree or higher. We see that educational attainment has increased each decade but still only about 30 percent of adult Americans have a college degree or higher. We discuss the relationship between education and wages in Chapter 10 and education as a form of human capital in Chapter 15.

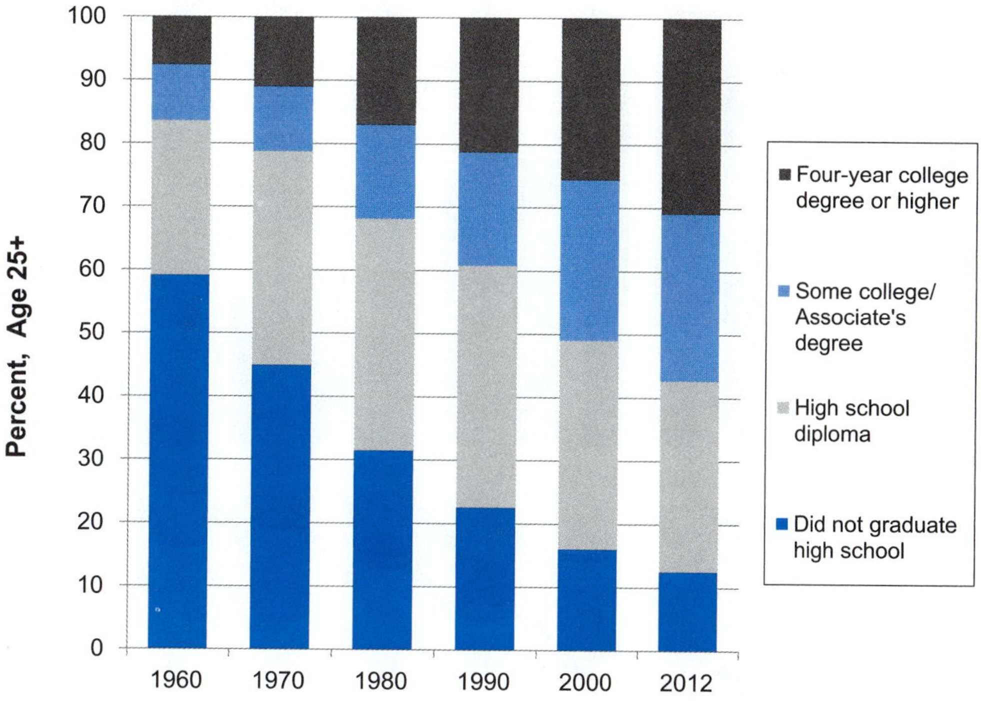

Source: U.S. Census Bureau, Educational Attainment, CPS Historical Time Series Tables, Table A-1.

14. Industrial Concentration Ratios

What it is: An industrial concentration ratio measures the percentage of all sales in a particular industry that are received by the largest firms in that industry. The figure below shows four-firm concentration ratios—the percentage of all sales received by the largest four firms in each industry. Industrial concentration ratios provide information about the degree of market power held by large firms in a particular industry.

The results: Some industries in the United States are dominated by a few firms, while other industries are more competitive. Examples of industries with a few dominant firms include discount department stores (e.g., Walmart and Target) and home centers (e.g., Home Depot and Lowe's). Examples of industries that are not dominated by a few firms include convenience stores and gasoline stations. We discuss market power in more detail in Chapter 18.

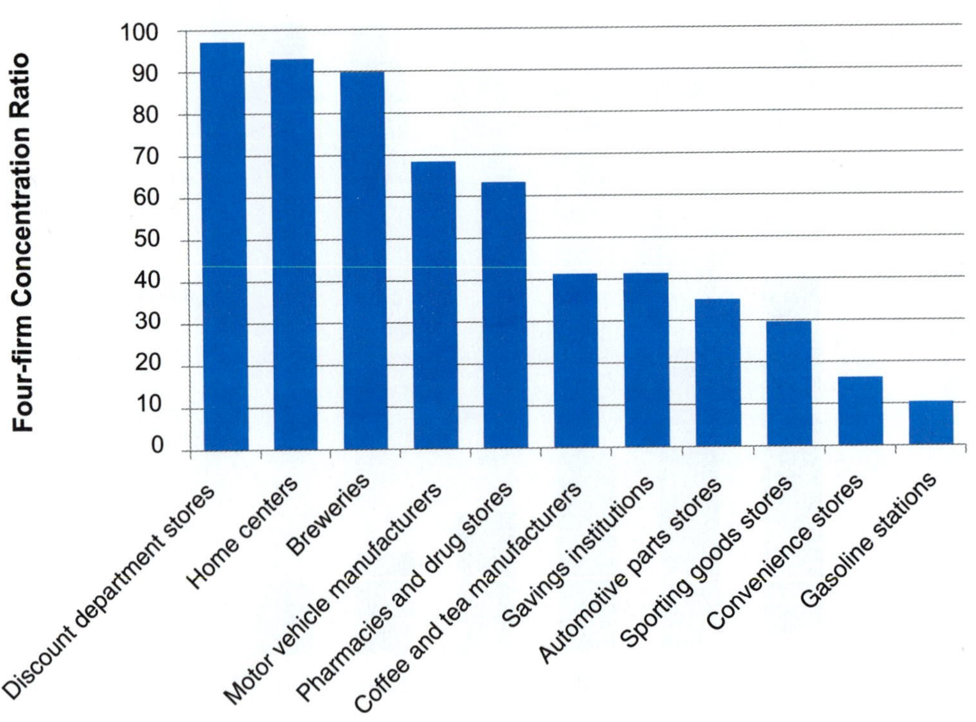

Source: U.S. Census Bureau, 2007 Economic Census.

15. GDP per Capita

What it is: Media stories of economic performance frequently refer to gross domestic product (GDP). A country's GDP per capita measures economic production per person per year, which gives us an idea of the average material living standards in the country. While GDP is perhaps the most commonly used macroeconomic metric, it does not necessarily measure well-being. We discuss how GDP is calculated in Chapter 20 and about the limitations of, and alternatives to, GDP in Chapter 21.

The results: The United States ranks tenth, with a GDP per capita of around $48,000. Luxembourg has the world's highest GDP per capita at around $90,000, and the Democratic Republic of the Congo has the lowest, at only $370.

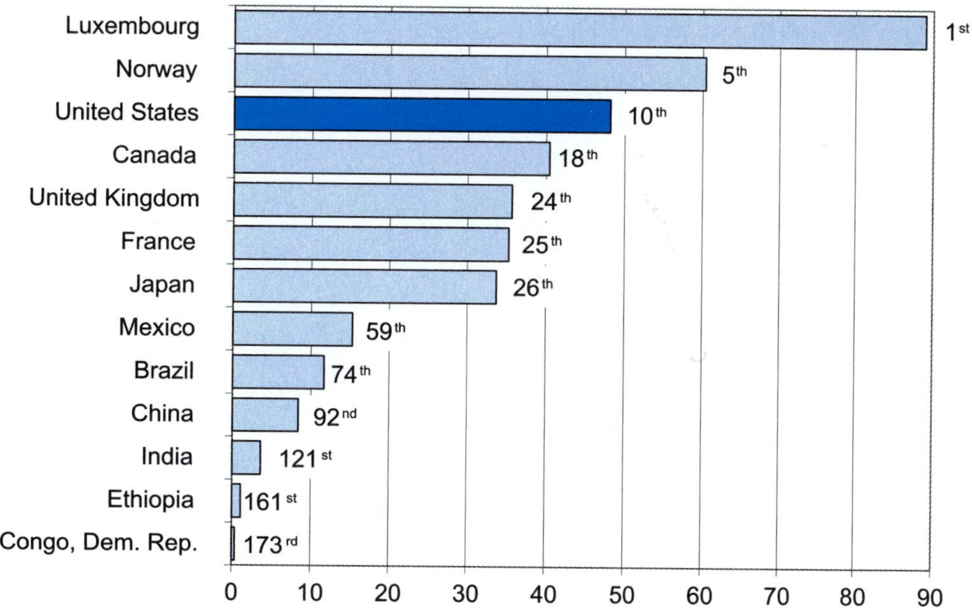

Source: World Bank, World Development Indicators database.

Data are adjusted for purchasing power differences across countries (e.g., a dollar in India buys more than a dollar in the United States).

16. Recent Growth Rate of GDP per Capita

What it is: In macroeconomics, we seek to explain not only why some countries have a higher GDP per capita but also what conditions lead to strong GDP growth rates. In this graph we compare the growth in GDP per capita, after adjusting for inflation, across countries over the ten-year period 2002–2011. We discuss measuring GDP growth rates in Chapter 20 and theories of GDP growth in Chapter 32.

The results: GDP per capita over 2002–2011 grew rapidly in some countries, slowly in others, and even declined in several countries. The highest growth in GDP per capita occurred in Azerbaijan, primarily from oil and gas development, with high growth also in China, Argentina, Ethiopia, and India. The fastest growth among developed countries took place in Sweden. Countries with declines in GDP per capita include Italy, Haiti, Iraq, and the Bahamas.

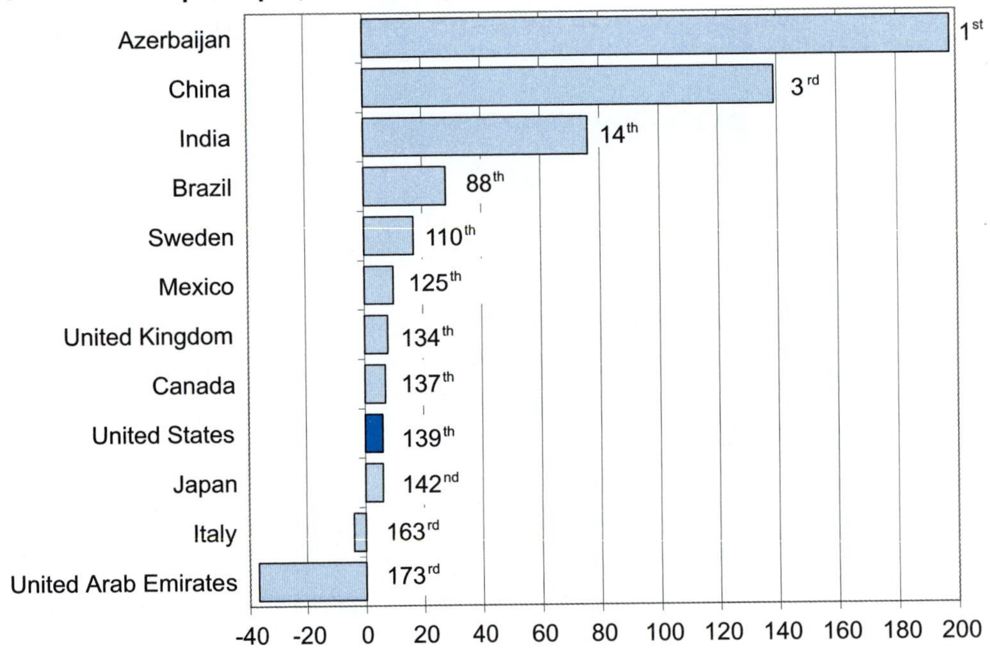

Source: World Bank, World Development Indicators database.

Data are adjusted for purchasing power differences.

17. Net National Savings

What it is: How much a country saves and invests is widely considered an important factor in explaining differences in GDP growth rates. Here we present data on net national savings rates, which equal total national savings minus the depreciation of productive capital such as factories and machinery. A negative net national savings rate implies that a country's productive capacity may be declining. We discuss saving, investment, and growth in detail in Chapter 33.

The results: In 2010, China had the highest net national saving rate. Other countries with high savings rates include India, Singapore, Vietnam, and Thailand. Fourteen countries (among those with data) had a negative net savings rate in 2010, including the United States, Portugal, Greece, and Iceland. (The economy of Iceland was especially badly damaged in the crash of 2007–8; this history is still apparent in the 2011 data.)

Net National Savings Rate, 2011 (Percent of GNI)

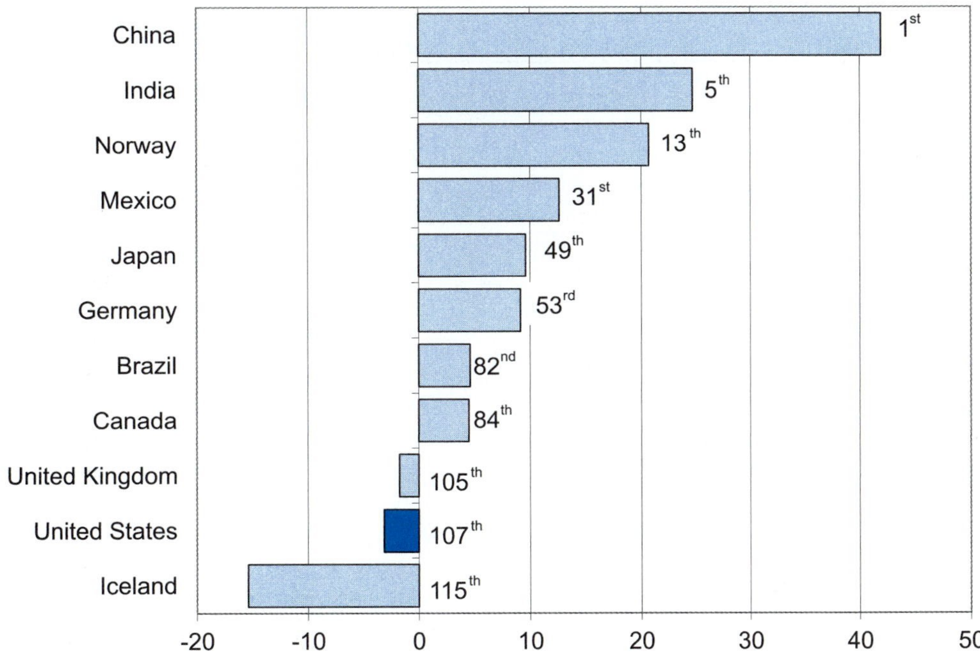

Source: World Bank, World Development Indicators database.

GNI is gross national income, a measure similar to gross domestic product.

18. Government Debt

What it is: The level of government debt has been a focus of media stories in recent years. What matters is not so much the size of debt in dollars but government debt relative to a country's GDP. This variable considers the amount of debt owed by the governments of different countries, including debts owed to domestic and foreign entities. What level of debt is a problem is a topic we discuss in more detail in Chapter 31.

The results: Japan has the highest government debt in the world, measured as a percentage of GDP, followed by Zimbabwe and Greece. The United States has the thirty-fifth-highest debt, but many other developed countries have higher debt, including Singapore, France, Canada, and Germany. Most developing countries have relatively low government debt.

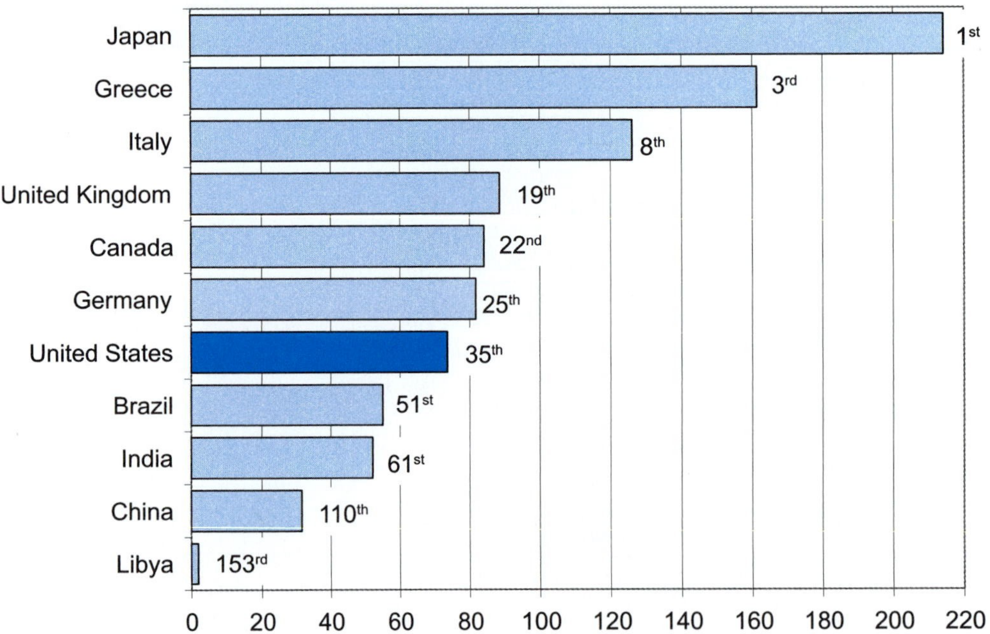

Source: United States Central Intelligence Agency, *CIA World Factbook.*

Data are mostly 2012 estimates.

19. Labor Productivity

What it is: One measure of the economic efficiency of a country is labor productivity. This is calculated by dividing a country's GDP by an estimate of the total number of hours worked. Thus labor productivity tells us how many dollars of GDP are generated for each hour worked. We present more about labor productivity in Chapter 10.

The results: Data on labor productivity are available for only 35 countries. Norway has the highest labor productivity in the world. The United States ranks fourth, behind Luxembourg and Ireland. Productivity is slightly lower in France and Germany. Less developed countries have lower labor productivity. We see that productivity in Mexico is only about one-third of the U.S. level.

Labor Productivity, 2011 (GDP per Hour Worked)

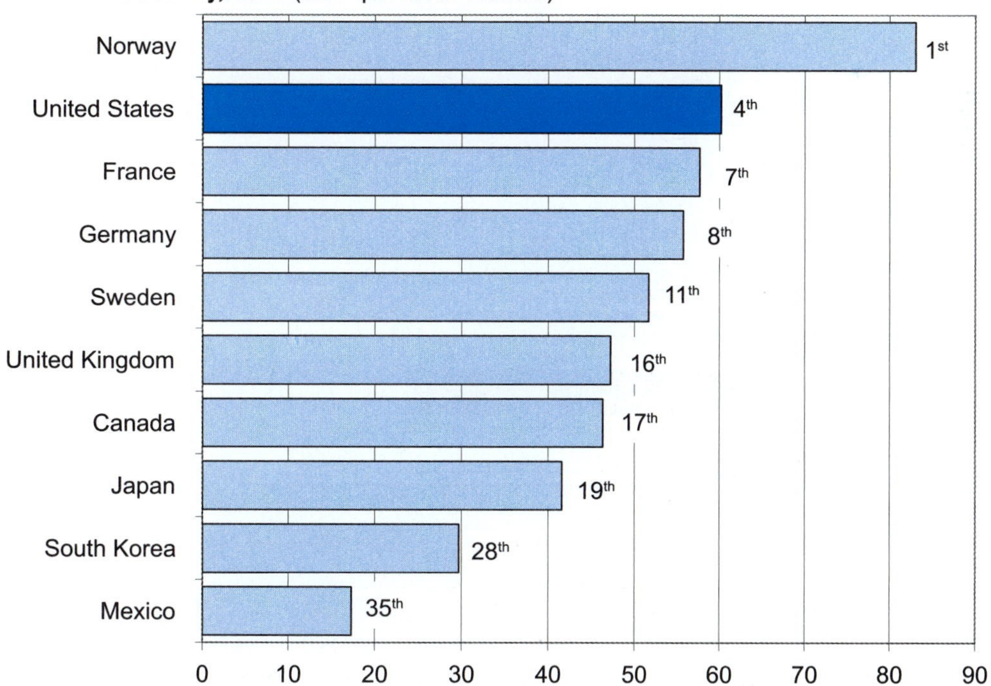

Source: Organisation for Economic Co-operation and Development, OECD online statistical database.

20. Average Annual Hours Worked

What it is: Even if two countries have the same labor productivity, their GDP will differ if the number of hours worked are different. This graph shows the average number of hours worked each year by full-time employees. Note that this includes only hours actually worked; vacations, holidays, and sick days are excluded. Thus the average annual hours worked in a country may be high if work expectations are more stringent and time off is limited. Work hours may also be high if workers choose to work long hours. We discuss work hours further in Chapters 10 and 23.

The results: Data on hours worked are available for only 34 countries. The average annual hours worked per full-time employee are lowest in the Netherlands. Other countries with relatively low annual work hours are Germany, Norway, France, and Denmark. One reason for the low work hours in these countries is federal laws that mandate minimum vacation times and paid holidays. In the United States, where such laws do not exist, average work hours are higher. Work hours tend to be highest among countries with lower levels of GDP per capita.

Average Annual Hours Worked, 2011 (Lowest to Highest)

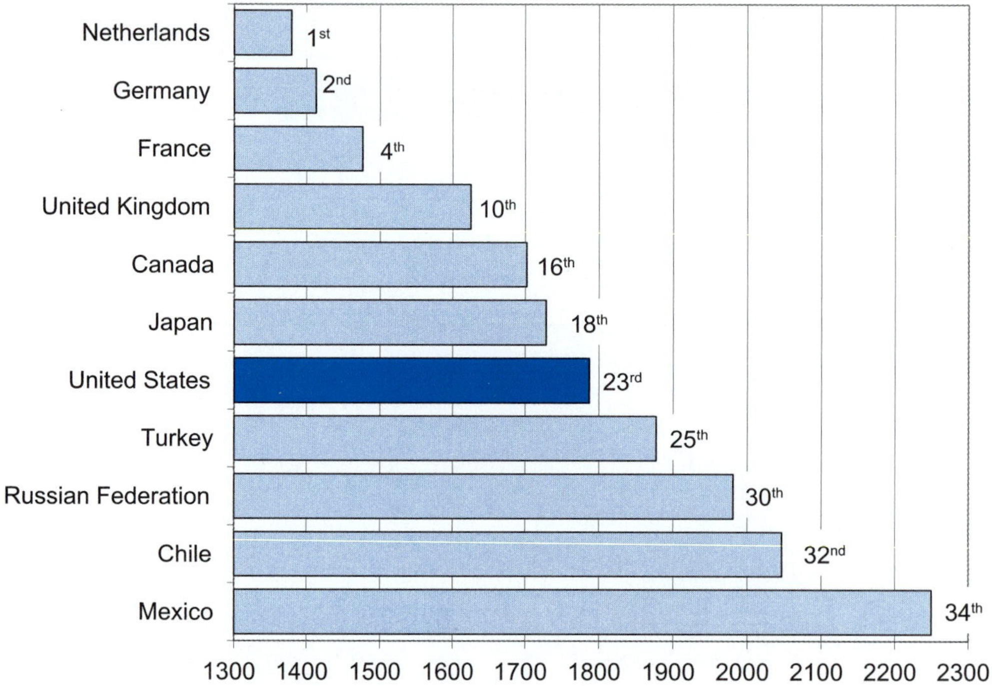

Source: Organisation for Economic Co-operation and Development. OECD online statistical database.

21. UNEMPLOYMENT RATE (PERCENT OF TOTAL WORKFORCE)

What it is: The unemployment rate in a country is an important macroeconomic metric. Not only does having a job provide a source of income, but it also provides a sense of identity and contributes to overall well-being. Estimating the unemployment rate is somewhat complex. In Chapter 23 we discuss issues involved in estimating the unemployment rate including defining what it means to be in the workforce.

The results: Unemployment rates vary tremendously across countries. Cambodia has the lowest official unemployment rate at 0.2 percent. While many poor countries, such as Zimbabwe, Haiti, and Kenya, have very high unemployment rates (30 percent or more), other poor countries such as Cuba and Bhutan, have rather low unemployment rates, at around 4 percent. The unemployment rate in the United States, usually in the range of 4–6%, rose considerably in the 2007–9 recession, and has since declined only slowly.

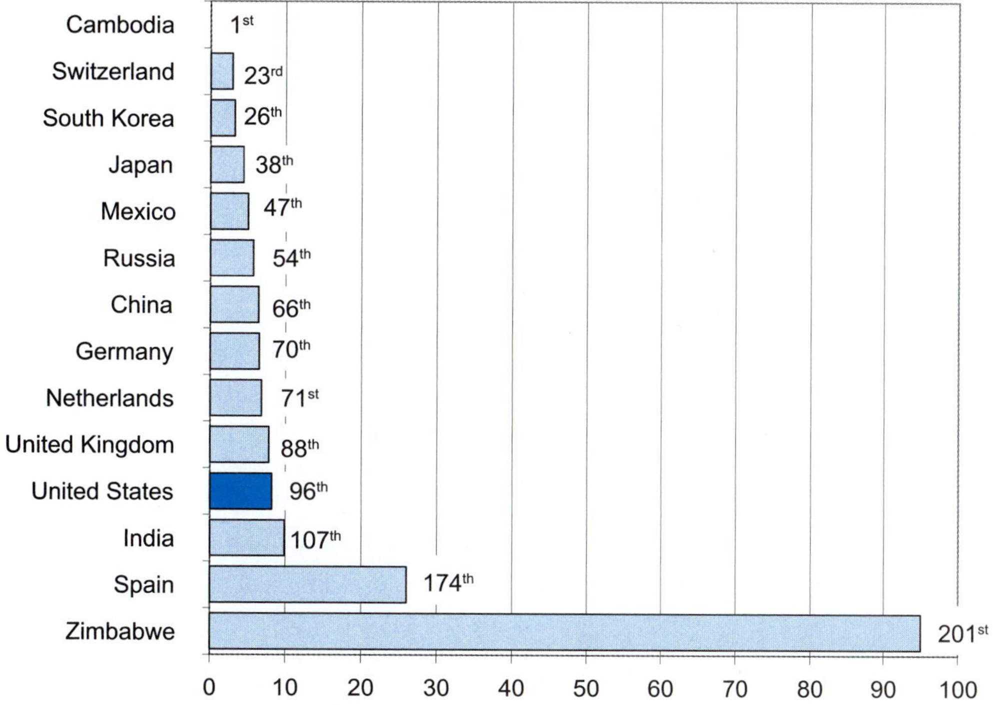

Source: Central Intelligence Agency, *CIA World Factbook.*

22. Inflation

What it is: The rate of inflation summarizes how average prices change in a country in one year. For example, an inflation rate of 5 percent means that average prices increased by 5 percent that year. We discuss how to adjust data from different years for inflation in Chapter 20 and then focus on macroeconomic theories of inflation in Chapters 26 and 27.

The results: Over the period 2002–2011, Japan had the lowest inflation rate in the world, with prices actually declining slightly during this time. However, this is not necessarily a good thing, as we see later in the book. A low and stable—but not negative—inflation rate is generally considered one of the main macroeconomic policy goals. Most developed countries have generally been successful in controlling inflation in recent years. High and fluctuating inflation rates in a country are a sign of macroeconomic instability.

Average Annual Inflation Rate, 2002–2011 (Lowest to Highest)

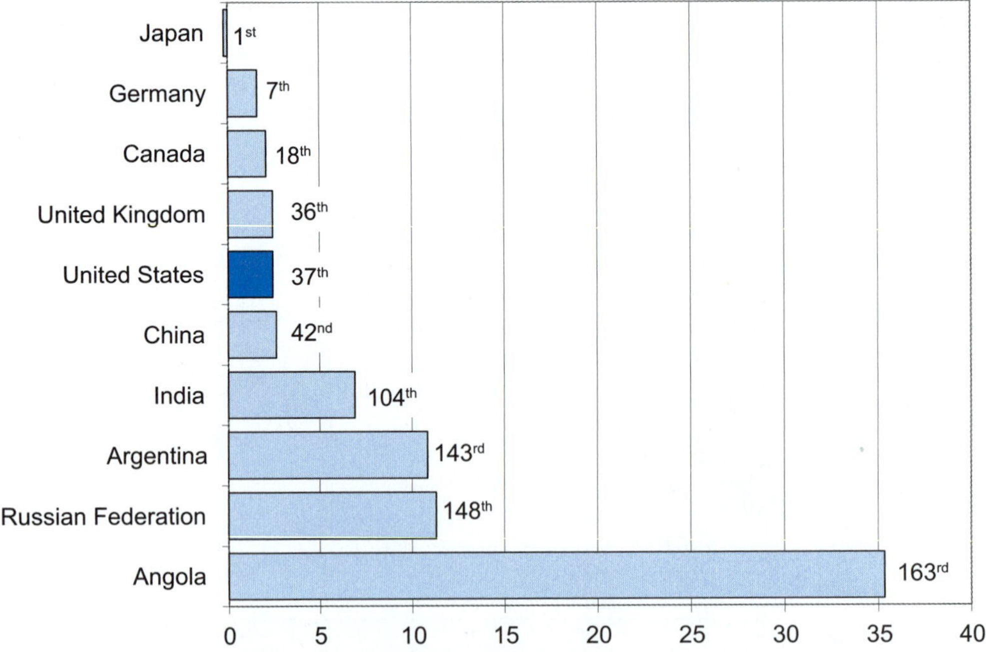

Source: World Bank, World Development Indicators database.

The average inflation rate is calculated as the average of the inflation rate for each year from 2002 to 2011.

23. Total Tax Revenues (Percent of GDP)

What it is: Tax policies are among the most significant ways a government can influence the well-being of the citizens, as we discuss in Chapters 12 and 25. The overall rate of taxation, expressed as a percentage of GDP, includes taxes collected at the federal, state, and local levels.

The results: Overall tax revenues vary significantly across countries. While Western European countries tend to have relatively high taxes, some other countries with surprisingly high taxes (more than 40 percent of GDP) include Iraq, Bolivia, and Bhutan. The United States has one of the lowest overall tax rates in the world—by far the lowest of any major industrialized country. The countries with the lowest tax revenues (less than 15 percent of GDP) tend to be relatively poor countries in Africa and Asia.

Total Taxes, 2012 (Percent of GDP)

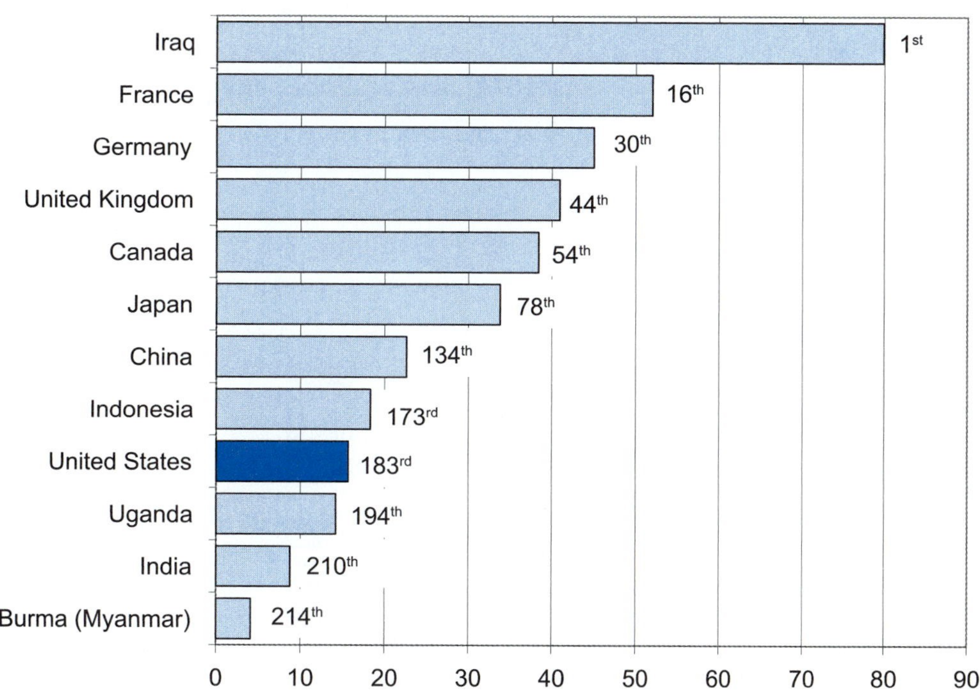

Source: Central Intelligence Agency, *CIA World Factbook.*

24. TRADE BALANCE (PERCENT OF GDP)

What it is: The trade deficit of the United States is often considered a cause for concern in media stories. A trade deficit means that a country imports more than it exports. Economists refer to a country's trade balance as the dollar value of its exports minus its imports, normally expressed as a percentage of GDP. Thus a negative trade balance indicates a trade deficit. A positive trade balance indicates a trade surplus. We discuss trade balances, and other trade issues, in more detail in Chapters 7 and 29.

The results: Of the 153 countries with available data, 49 have a positive trade balance (exports exceed imports) and 104 have a negative balance. Those countries with the largest trade surpluses tend to be smaller countries (such as Luxembourg and Singapore) or oil-producing countries (such as Saudi Arabia and Kuwait). The U.S. trade deficit is about 4 percent of GDP, with other developed countries, such as the United Kingdom, France, and Canada, in a similar range. The countries with the largest trade deficits tend to be poorer countries, although some poor countries do have trade surpluses.

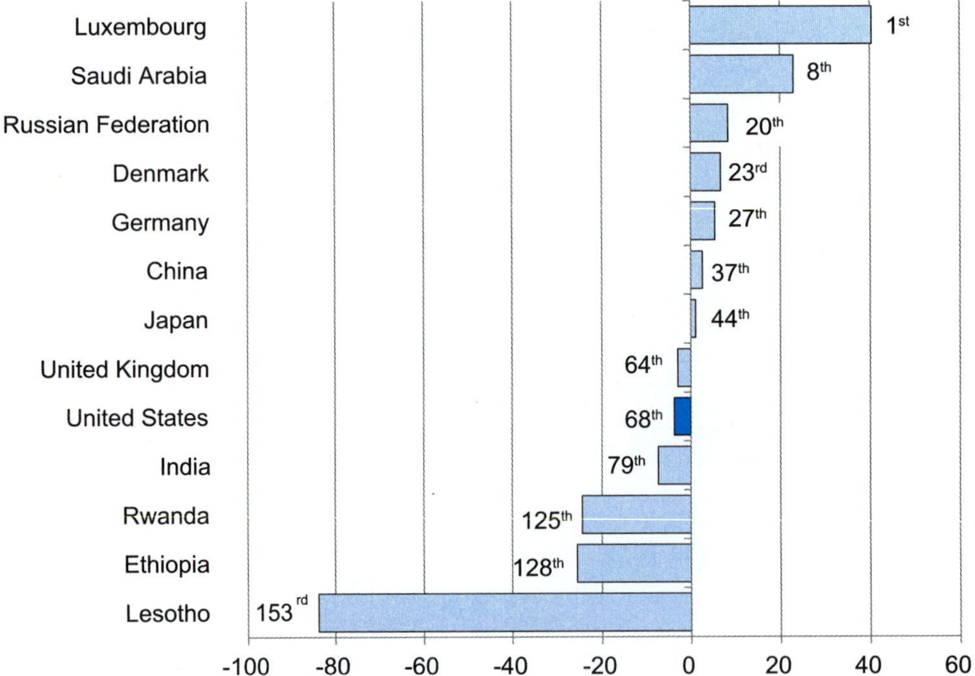

Source: World Bank, World Development Indicators database, and authors' calculations.

25. INCOME INEQUALITY (GINI COEFFICIENT)

What it is: A Gini coefficient is a measure of economic inequality in a country. It is most commonly applied to the distribution of income, but it can also be apply to wealth distribution or other variables. It can range from 0 (everyone in the country has the same exact income) to 1 (one person receives all the income in a country). We learn more about Gini coefficients and economic inequality in Chapters 11 and 32.

The results: Scandinavian countries such as Sweden, Norway, and Finland tend to be the most equal countries in the world, by income. Japan is also in this group, in a number of equality measures (not all shown here, but discussed in Chapter 32). The United States is the most economically unequal developed country. Several African countries, including Botswana, Lesotho, Sierra Leone, and South Africa are the most unequal countries in the world.

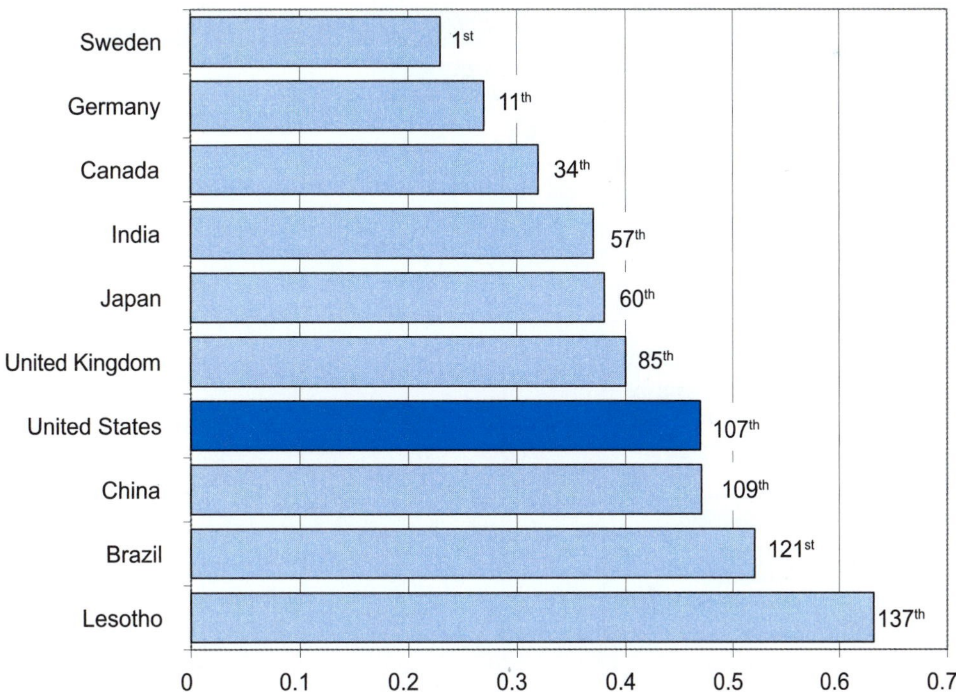

Source: Central Intelligence Agency, *CIA World Factbook.*

26. CEO Pay vs. Worker Pay: International Comparisons

What it is: In addition to comparing corporate profits to worker pay, we can look at the pay difference between chief executive officers (CEOs) and workers. The graph below shows the ratio of average CEO compensation to the average pay of "rank-and-file" workers, in several industrialized countries. The ratios are based on data from 2011 and 2012.

The results: In the United States, average CEO pay is more than 350 times higher than average worker pay. (This difference has rapidly increased in the past 50 years—in the mid-1960s average CEO pay was only about 20 times that of the average worker.) In other industrialized countries, CEOs today make significantly more than rank-and-file workers, but pay differences are not as pronounced. For example, in France CEOs make, on average, 100 times more than workers, while in Denmark CEOs make about 50 times worker pay.

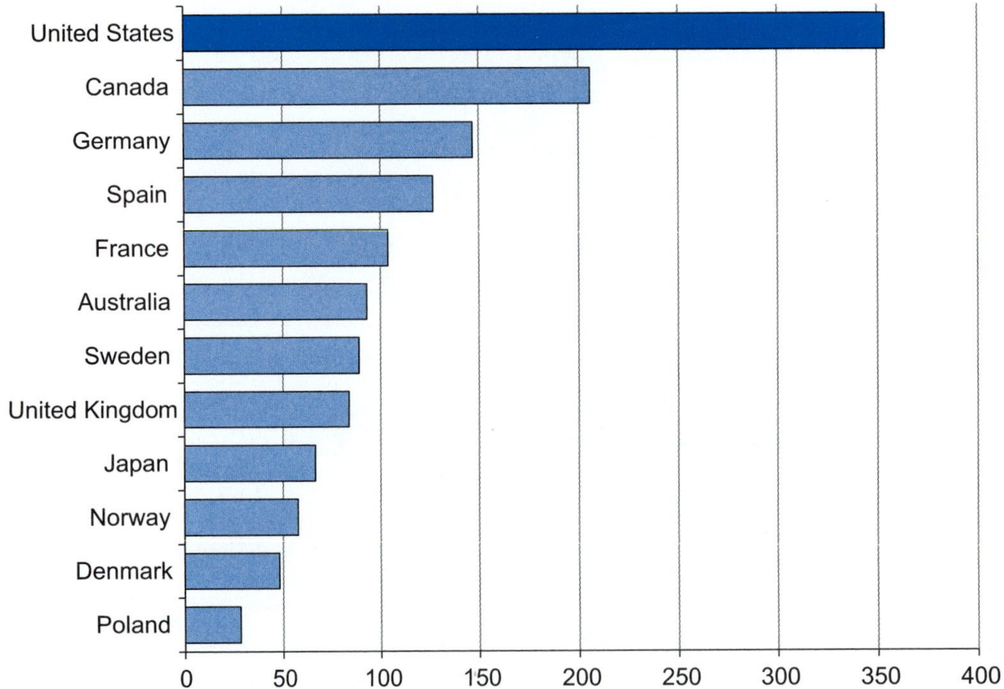

Source: AFL-CIO, Executive Paywatch, CEO-to-Worker Pay Ratios Around the World.

27. Absolute Poverty

What it is: The $1-per-day poverty line has been defined by the United Nations as a measure of absolute poverty. One of the Millennium Development Goals set by the United Nations is to halve the number of people in the world living below this poverty line between 1990 and 2015. This goal has already been met, mainly due to progress in China and India. We discuss poverty and economic development in Chapter 32.

The results: Note that this is the only graph in this chapter that does not include the United States or any other developed countries (essentially no one in developed countries lives below the dollar-a-day poverty line). A majority of people do live below that poverty line in 12 countries, including Rwanda, Nigeria, Mozambique, and Mali. About one-third of India's population and 13 percent of China's population still live below the dollar-a-day poverty line. A small portion of the population lives in absolute poverty in Argentina, Hungary, Poland, Thailand, and Uruguay.

Percent of Population Living Below $1/day Poverty Line

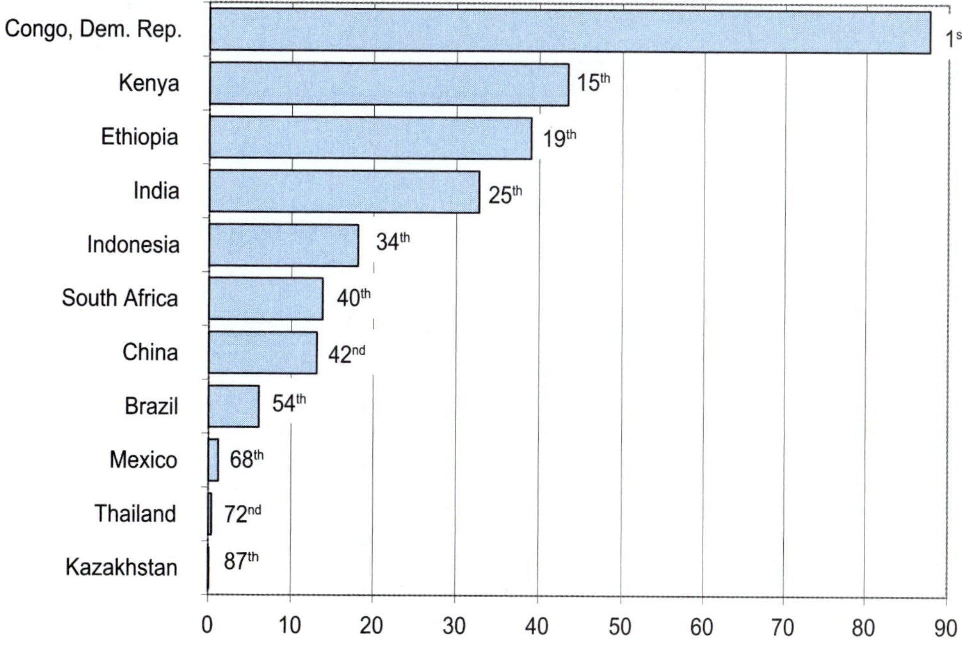

Source: United Nations, Millennium Development Goals Indicators database.

Data are for the most recent year available, generally 2008 or 2009.

28. Foreign Aid

What it is: In 1970, the "economically advanced" countries agreed to a United Nations resolution on foreign aid to developing countries. The resolution set a target for official development assistance (ODA) of 0.7 percent of gross national income (GNI). ODA is defined as government flows to promote economic development and welfare in developing countries. The 0.7 percent target has been reaffirmed at subsequent international meetings. We discuss the role of foreign aid in promoting economic development in Chapter 32.

The results: In 2012 only five countries met the 0.7 percent target: Luxembourg, Sweden, Norway, Denmark, and the Netherlands. ODA from the United States was 0.19 percent of GNI. Italy and Greece had the lowest ODA percentage, at 0.13 percent. Note that ODA does not include private charity donations or non-governmental organizations, only official aid given by governments.

Official Development Assistance, 2012 (Percent of GNI)

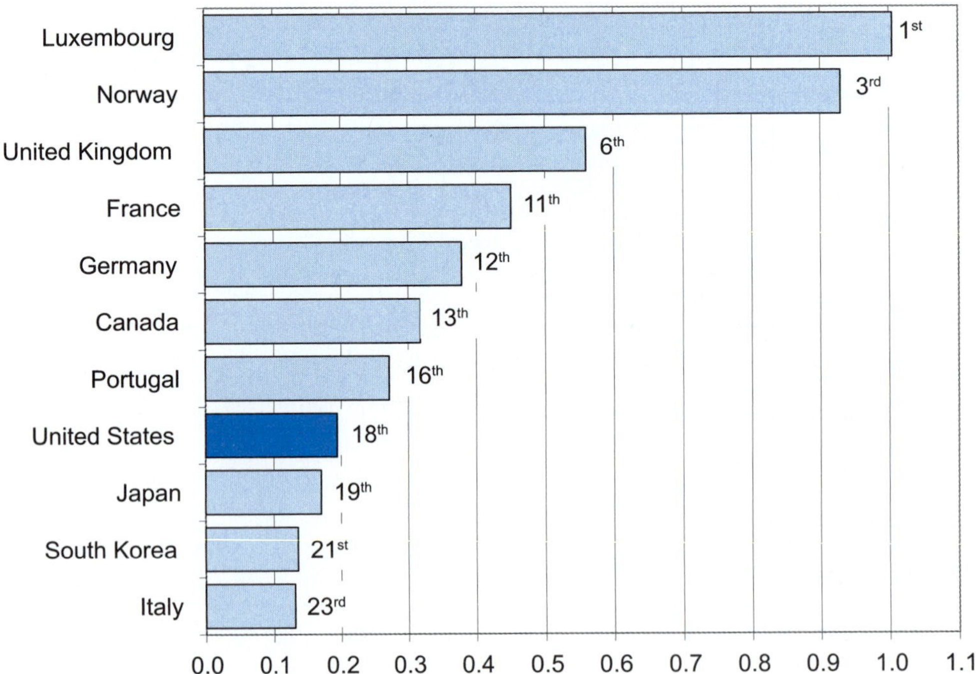

Source: Organisation for Economic Co-operation and Development, Official Development Assistance—2013 Update.

29. INTERNET USERS

What it is: The percentage of people who have access to the Internet provides an indication of a country's level of technological development. As we discuss in Chapter 32, technology has long been recognized as one of the drivers of economic growth.

The results: Access to the Internet may not be as widespread as you think. While near-universal access occurs in a few countries, such as Iceland, Norway, and the Netherlands, in most developed countries access rates are about 70–85 percent. Middle-income countries generally have access rates around 30–50 percent. Forty countries, most of them poor African countries, have access rates of less than 10 percent.

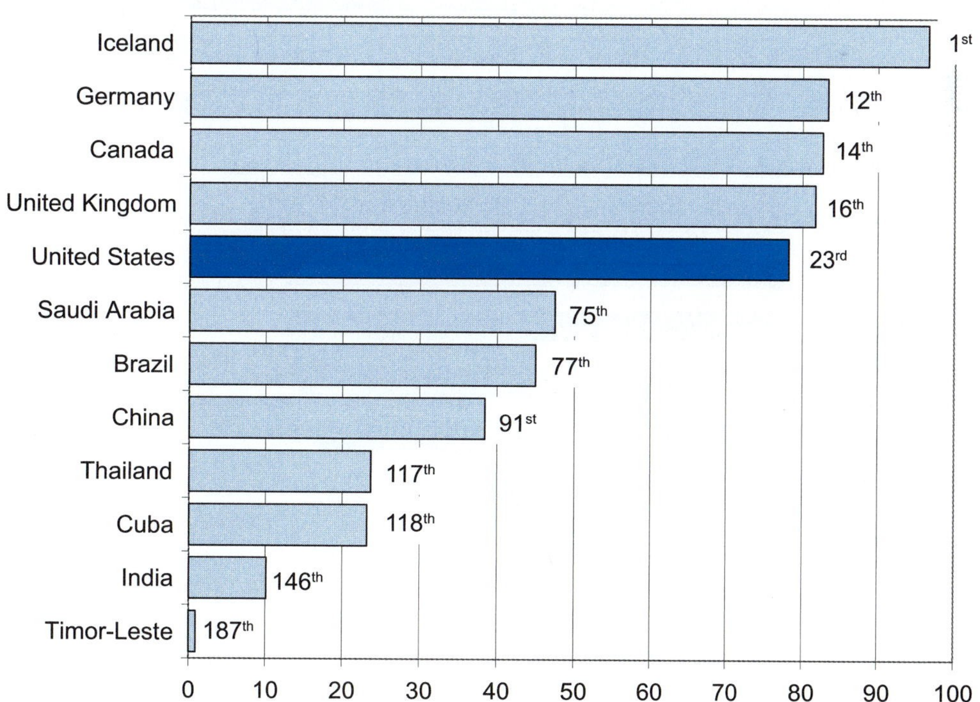

Source: World Bank, World Development Indicators database.

30. Educational Performance

What it is: Next we look at the educational performance of students in different countries. To compare across countries, we present data from the Programme for International Student Assessment, which administers standardized math, science, and reading tests to 15-year-olds in over 60 countries every three years. The graph below provides results from the science test. The country rankings were relatively similar for the math and reading tests, with some variations (e.g., the United States ranked seventeenth on the reading test and thirty-first on the math test).

The results: Students in Asian countries tended to achieve the highest test scores, including China, Singapore, Japan, and South Korea. Among European countries, students received high scores in Finland, the Netherlands, and Germany. The scores from the United States were average for developed countries. For less developed countries, scores tended to be lower.

Average PISA Science Test Score, 2012 (15-year-olds)

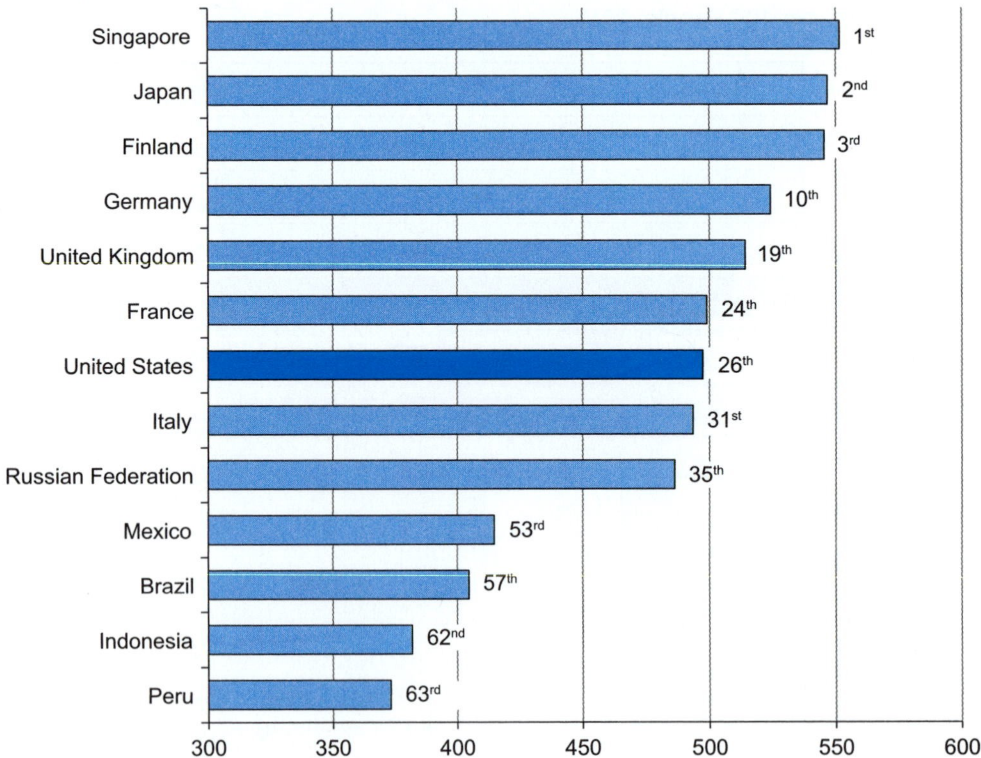

Source: Organisation for Economic Co-operation and Development, Programme for International Student Assessment, PISA 2009 Key Findings.

31. Life Expectancy

What it is: Average life expectancy at birth is a common measure of health outcomes in a country. We discuss health as one component of well-being indices in Chapter 21 and as a topic of economic development in Chapter 32.

The results: Life expectancy at birth now exceeds 80 years in over 20 countries, including Japan, France, Spain, and Greece. For a developed country, the United States has a comparatively low life expectancy, even lower than some middle-income countries such as Costa Rica, Cuba, and Chile. Life expectancy is the lowest, below 50 years, in several African countries, including Zambia, Sierra Leone, and Lesotho.

Life Expectancy at Birth, 2010

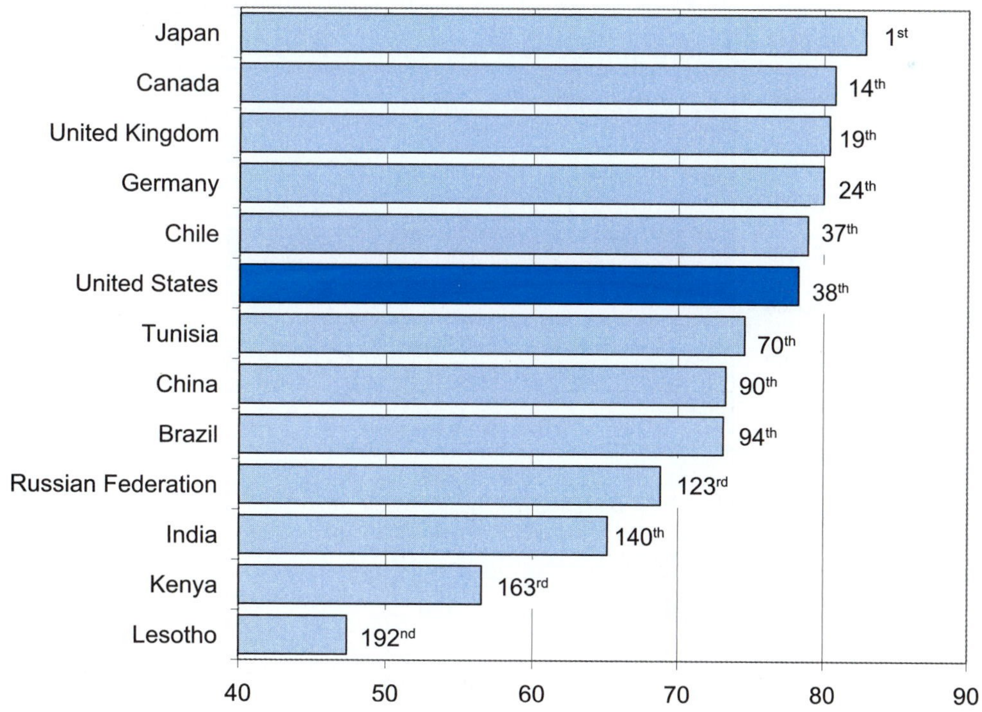

Source: World Bank, World Development Indicators database.

32. Subjective Well-Being

What it is: Researchers are increasingly using surveys to measure well-being or happiness directly. The most common approach is to ask people to rate their overall satisfaction with their lives, on a scale from 1 (dissatisfied) to 10 (satisfied). The responses are referred to as "subjective well-being." We discuss subjective well-being in more detail in Chapter 21.

The results: According to the most recent data, which cover 57 countries, Colombia has the highest level of average subjective well-being. Other relatively happy countries include Norway, Mexico, Canada, and Guatemala. Happiness levels in the United States are about average for a developed country. Happiness levels are relatively low in the poorest developing countries, such as Iraq, Zambia, and Rwanda, as well as Eastern European countries, such as Bulgaria, Ukraine, and Romania.

Average Life Satisfaction, 2005–2008 Results (1 = Dissatisfied, 10 = Satisfied)

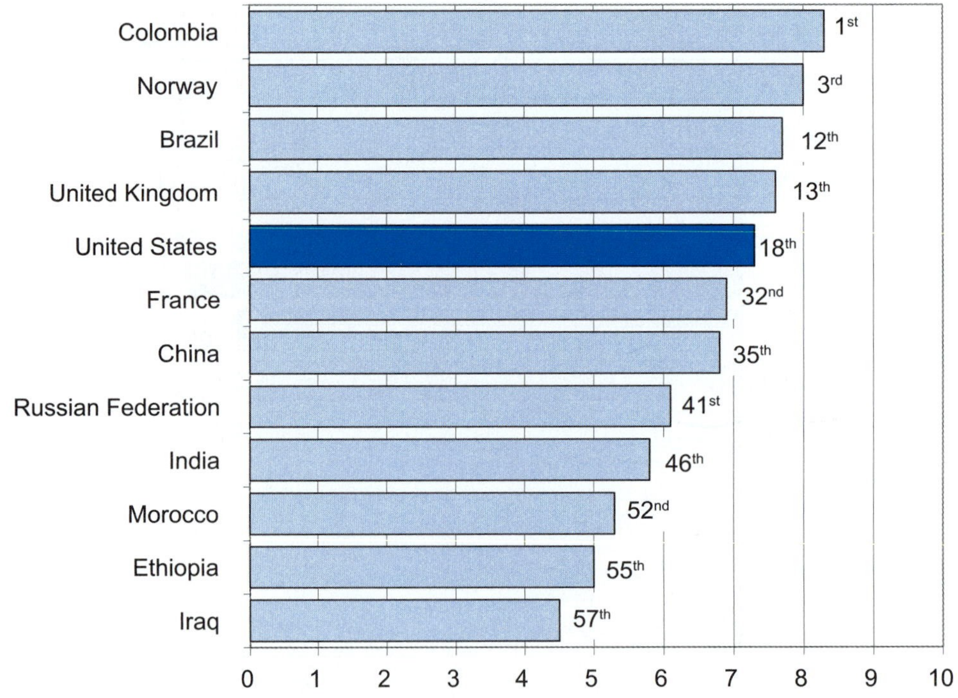

Source: World Values Survey, online database.

33. Carbon Dioxide Emissions per Capita

What it is: Carbon dioxide (CO_2) is the most important gas responsible for global climate change. CO_2 is emitted whenever fossil fuels are burned. Scientific analysis indicates that the accumulation of CO_2 in the atmosphere is raising global temperatures, leading to negative impacts on human societies and ecosystems. CO_2 per capita gives us an idea of how much the average person in a county is affecting the environment. We learn more about CO_2 and climate change in Chapter 33.

The results: The countries with the highest CO_2 emissions per capita are several oil-producing countries, including Qatar (the highest, at 44 tons per person), Kuwait, and Bahrain. The United States has the tenth-highest emissions per capita, around 17 tons per person. Emissions per person in European countries such as the UK and Germany are less than half of U.S. levels. While China is the world's largest emitter of CO_2 overall, on a per-capita basis its emissions are only one-third of those in the United States. CO_2 emissions are negligible in the world's poorest countries.

Carbon Dioxide Emissions per Capita, 2009 (Metric Tons per Year)

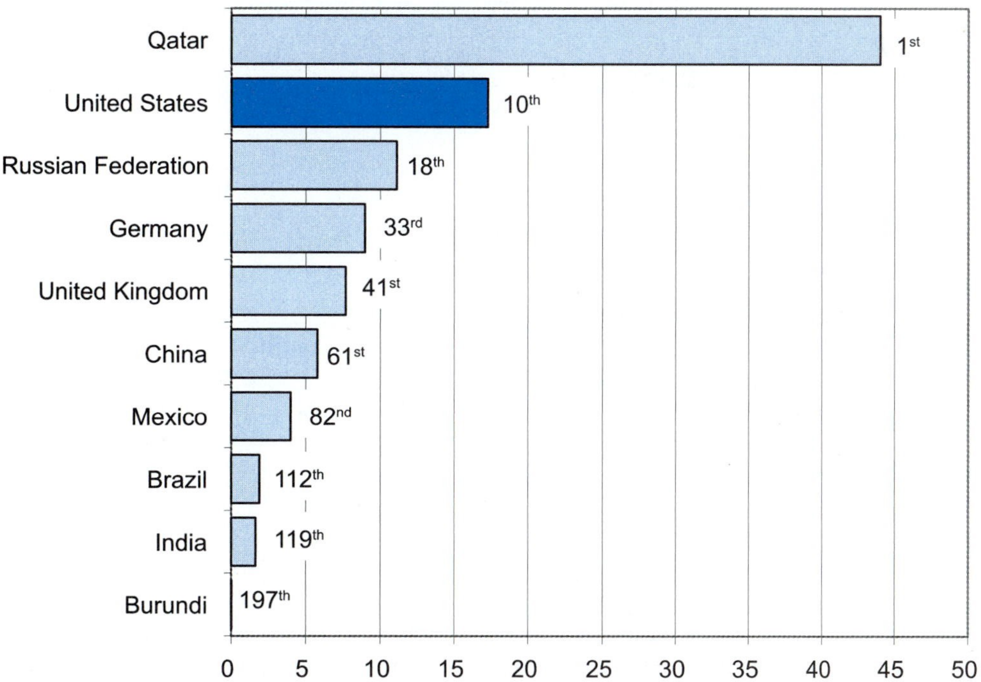

Source: World Bank, World Development Indicators database.

34. Local Air Quality

What it is: While CO_2 emissions contribute to climate change, breathing air with elevated levels of CO_2 does not cause any adverse health effects. Local air pollutants, on the other hand, can cause numerous health effects, including asthma, lung cancer, and heart problems. One of the most important local air pollutants is particulate matter, which is emitted from power plants, industrial factories, motor vehicles, and other sources. Particulate matter pollution can be reduced through effective environmental regulations and technology. We discuss pollution further in Chapters 13 and 33.

The results: A country with high CO_2 emissions does not necessarily have poor local air quality. The United States is a prime example—CO_2 emissions are high, but local air quality is relatively good due to environmental laws and modern technologies. Other developed countries have as good, or better, local air quality. Developing countries can have good or poor local air quality, depending on their level of development, regulations, and technologies.

Average National Particulate Matter Concentration, 2011 (Micrograms per Cubic Meter)

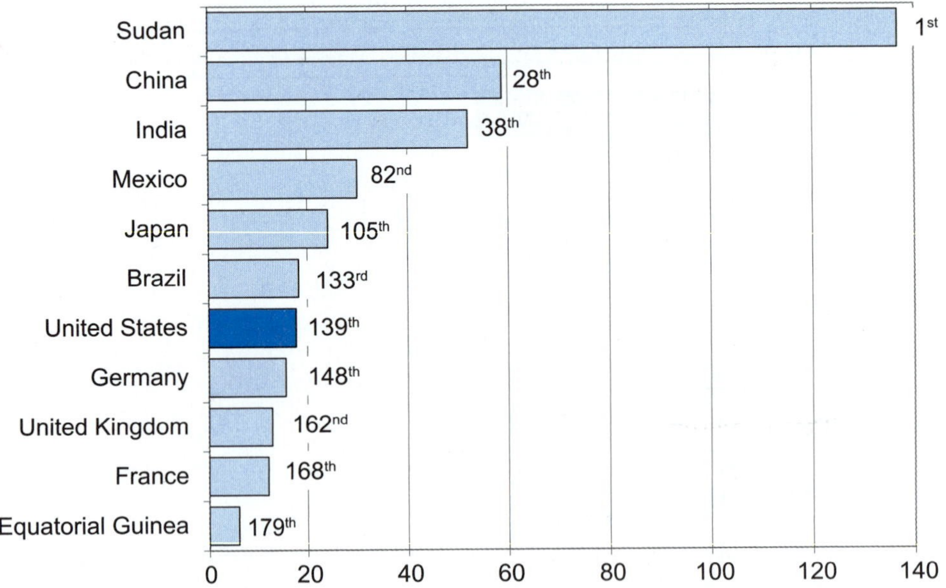

Data are for particulate matter smaller than 10 micrometers, referred to as PM10. For reference, the European Union pollution standard for average PM10 is 40 micrograms/cubic meter (μg/m3); California has a stricter standard of 20 μg/m3.

1 Economic Activity in Context

There are many reasons to take an introductory economics course. One reason might be to satisfy a course requirement. Another is that some knowledge of economics may help you get a rewarding job. More broadly, studying economics can help you understand a variety of issues that are likely to be important in your life, such as taxes, the environment, and health care.

The overall goal of this book is to give you tools and insights to help you understand how the economy works—and, to some degree, to encourage you to think about what a "better" economy might be, and how it could be achieved. Of course, different people will have different ideas about what they want in an economy. Questions that will elicit a wide variety of answers include the following:

- Should a "good" economy produce as much as possible?
- How important is inequality of income, or of wealth?
- Should a goal of the economy be to sell goods to consumers at the lowest possible cost?
- Should production and consumption be limited when we perceive that these activities are degrading the environment?
- Would a good economy ensure that there is a job available for everyone who wants one?
- How should pay and other job characteristics be determined?
- What about work that is now normally done without pay, such as taking care of homes and families, or volunteer work—should this be considered an economic issue?
- If there are trade-offs among achievement of various outcomes—such as good jobs, cheap consumer goods, and environmental protection—how should the economy operate to set and implement priorities?
- When you have decided on the priorities for a good economy, are these only relevant for the present, or should the future also be taken into account?

These are all difficult questions, and one of the objectives of an introductory economics course is to provide some new ways of thinking about them. The study of economics can help us to achieve our goals as individuals, and to create a society in which we are satisfied to live.

One of the things the list of questions asks you to think about is goals, and tradeoffs among goals. As an individual you are familiar with this idea: You surely want to get good grades, but you also want to have spare time to spend with your friends and family. Societies also operate in relation to goals, and are often required to make choices to come up with the proper balance—which frequently requires making trade-offs.

If we want better health care *and* a clean environment *and* national security *and* confidence that present policies are not creating serious future economic problems, how can we first define what tradeoffs exist, and then negotiate among them? Economics has much to teach us about this. Some of the tradeoffs we will consider are measured in dollars, but, as we will soon see, economics is about much more than money.

1. OUR STARTING POINT

economics: the study of how people manage their resources to meet their needs and enhance their well-being

microeconomics: the subfield of economics that focuses on activities that take place within and among the major economic actors and organizations of a society

macroeconomics: the subfield of economics that focuses on the economy as a whole

Although this book is divided into two parts, it is helpful to start with an overview of the whole. **Economics** is the study of how people manage their resources to meet their needs and enhance their well-being. For convenience (and for other reasons, related to the history of economic thought), the field of economics is normally divided into two subfields.

Microeconomics is the subfield that focuses on activities that occur within and among the major economic in a society, such as individuals, households and communities, governments and nonprofit organizations, and for-profit businesses. **Macroeconomics**, the other main subfield of economics, adopts an overview, focusing on understanding national and international trends and fluctuations in economic activity taken as a whole.

The dividing line between micro- and macroeconomics is not always sharp. The first half of this book focuses mainly on microeconomics, while the second half presents macroeconomics, using many of the concepts developed in the first half as well as new concepts and analyses. In this introductory chapter we will discuss some over-arching issues that concern the whole field of economics.

We will begin by looking carefully at the definition of economics that was just given. The "resources" mentioned there include natural resources such as trees, coal, and air, as well as human-made productive resources such as factories, vehicles, computers, and roads. Our resources also include our knowledge and skills, financial resources, and even the social relationships that improve the quality of our lives. Economists refer to these as different types of capital (as discussed in the next section).

Our "needs" obviously include our basic requirements for food, shelter, and physical security. Beyond that, different people may have different views about what constitutes a "need." Some people may think that having their own car is a "need," while others may see it as a luxury. We discuss this issue in more detail below.

well-being: a term used broadly to describe a good quality of life

Finally, we use the term **well-being** to broadly describe a good quality of life. Beyond meeting our "needs," virtually everyone desires such things as adequate food and shelter, sufficient leisure time, good friends, and various kinds of freedom.

Discussion Questions

1. In which social issues are you most interested? How do you think that economics might help you understand these issues?
2. Thinking further about the social issues in which you are interested, do you see economics as part of the problem or part of the solution? Is it possible that economics can be both—responsible for social problems yet also potentially part of a solution?

2. THE GOALS OF AN ECONOMY

It is not an exaggeration to say that the study of the economy—what you are now embarking on—can make a significant difference in how the economy actually functions. In recent history, economic beliefs, advice, and policies have indeed been very influential in shaping the kind of world we live in. Behind the advice and policies that are proposed by economists, and assessed by politicians and citizens, there is the question of goals. In order to understand what goals (overt or hidden) may be pursued by economists we need to ask a deeper question: What is the goal, or the purpose, of the economy itself?

In the definition of economics given earlier you can find an implicit answer to this question: the purpose of the economy is to enable people to manage their resources to meet their needs and enhance their well-being. The remainder of this section will look at what is involved in raising such questions, to start with, and will then go on to discuss a variety of ways of understanding the goals of an economy.

2.1 POSITIVE AND NORMATIVE QUESTIONS

positive questions: questions about how things are

normative questions: questions about how things should be

Social scientists often make a distinction between two kinds of questions. **Positive questions** concern issues of fact, or "what is." **Normative questions** have to do with goals and values, or "what should be." For example, "What is the level of poverty in our country?" is a positive question, requiring descriptive facts as an answer. "How much effort should be given to poverty reduction?" is a normative question, requiring analysis of our values and goals. In our study of economics, we often find that positive and normative questions are inevitably intertwined. For example, both of the questions just posed require that we start with a definition of poverty. To achieve this, we need to combine facts about income and wealth with a normative assessment of where to draw the poverty line. Life rarely offers us a neat distinction between "what is" and "what ought to be." More often, we have to deal with a combination of the two.

Positive statements also sometimes carry normative implications. Consider the statement: "The total share of federal taxes paid by the top 1 percent of households, by income, has risen from 14.2 percent in 1980 to 22.3 percent in 2009."[1]

This is a positive statement, but it seems to suggest that taxes on the top 1 percent have increased rather dramatically and that further tax increases might be unfair. But is this really true? As we discover in more detail in Chapter 12, a more complete analysis reveals that the main reason that the share of taxes paid by the richest 1 percent has risen so much is that this group is now receiving a much larger share of all income. So we need to be careful about coming to normative conclusions based on incomplete or misleading positive statements.

Although much of this textbook is concerned with positive issues, we have, in defining the objective of economics as enhancing well-being, begun with a normative statement. People disagree about what it means to "enhance well-being." Economic actions that we take are all significantly affected by our goals and values. When we study, for example, how business decisions are made, we need to understand what might motivate all the people involved—business owners, workers, and their customers. Thus it is helpful for us to think further about our goals.

2.2 INTERMEDIATE AND FINAL GOALS

intermediate goal: a goal that is desirable because its achievement will bring you closer to your final goal(s)

final goal: a goal that requires no further justification; it is an end in itself

A useful way to look at goals is to rank them in a kind of hierarchy. Some are **intermediate goals**—that is, they are not ends in themselves but are important because they are expected to serve as the means to further ends. Goals that are sought for their own sake, rather than because they lead to something else, are called **final goals**. For example, you might strive to do well in your courses as an intermediate goal, toward the final goal of getting a good job. Of course, we might also think of the goal of "getting a good job" as itself intermediate to other final goals, such as satisfaction, status, or well-being.

2.3 TRADITIONAL ECONOMIC GOALS

wealth: the net value of all the material and financial assets owned by an individual

Before taking this course, you probably thought that economics is mostly about money and wealth. Although it is true that many economists spend their lives studying these topics, in this book we take the position that these are intermediate, as opposed to final, goals. We first consider the goals that economics has traditionally emphasized and then go on to consider how those relate to our final goals.

Adam Smith and the Goal of Wealth

assets: property owned by an individual or company

Adam Smith (1723–1790) emphasized the word *wealth* in the title of his famous book *An Inquiry into the Nature and Causes of the Wealth of Nations* (published in 1776). **Wealth** is often defined as the net value of all the material and financial **assets** owned by an individual. Is wealth really what economics is about? Those who seek to enhance their country's wealth generally do so because they have a notion that a wealthier country is in some way stronger, better, safer, or happier. Here, the relevant final goals might be strength, virtue, safety, or happiness. Similarly, an individual might seek wealth, or a good job, as an intermediate goal leading to such final goals as security, comfort, power, status, or pleasure.

The variety of final goals held by different individuals is sometimes used as a reason for viewing the accumulation of wealth as the sole purpose of economics. Implicitly or explicitly, this position rests on the normative argument that material wealth is a nearly universal intermediate goal because it can be used to pursue so many final goals.

In Smith's time, the vast majority of people lived in conditions of desperate poverty. Although about a billion people on earth still struggle with poverty on a daily basis, economic advancement in the past couple of centuries allows many people to focus on goals other than acquiring more wealth. Moreover, we are coming to recognize that the continual expansion of human economies in a finite material world has costs as well as benefits. Looking at the complex fallout of our achievements—including environmental degradation, stresses felt by families, and other social ills—it is clear that promotion of material wealth without concern for the ends to which wealth is used, or for the consequences of the manner in which wealth is pursued, may in fact work *against* the final goals that we most desire to achieve.

Recent Trends and the Goal of Efficiency

economic efficiency: the use of resources, or inputs, such that they yield the highest possible value of output or the production of a given output using the lowest possible value of inputs

Most economists have focused on **economic efficiency** as a key goal in economic policy-making. An efficient process is one that uses the *minimum value of resources* to achieve a desired result. Or to put it another way, efficiency is achieved when the *maximum value of output* is produced from a given set of inputs. Given this focus, many economists have seen their role as advising policymakers on how to make the economy as efficient as possible.

One appealing aspect of the goal of efficiency is that apparently everyone can agree on it. Who in his right mind would argue for using more resources than necessary or having less of something good when more is possible at the same cost? Because it seems so obvious that efficiency is a good thing, aiming for it is often thought of as a purely technical and scientific exercise, one based on positive analysis. This is not actually the case, however, because regarding efficiency as a goal involves a very important normative judgment: A standard of *value* must be adopted before the definition of efficiency can be applied.

Money is the standard of value that has traditionally been used in economics. Specifically, the commonest economic definition of value has been that of *market* value—that is, price. Using this standard, an economist would say that resources are being used most efficiently when the market value of the resulting outputs is maximized. "More is always better," it is assumed, where the "more" is composed of things that people are willing to pay for.

This definition of efficiency is not a simple matter of positive fact; when examined, it clearly includes some normative assumptions. First, it is based on an implicit acceptance of the current distribution of wealth and income. Because a person's *willingness* to pay for something is obviously influenced by his or her *ability* to pay, in general those with the most money will disproportionately determine what is an economically "efficient" allocation of resources. For example, if the aggregate willingness to pay of high-wealth households for luxury cars exceeds the willingness to pay of lower-income households for basic health care, then the efficient allocation would tilt toward production of luxury cars over provision of basic health care.

Second, this definition of efficiency assumes that nothing has value unless humans are willing to pay for it. In other words, nothing has intrinsic value and should exist for its own sake regardless of whether people place monetary value on it. But perhaps certain things should have intrinsic value, such as the right of nonhuman species to exist or goals like freedom or fairness.

Other standards could be used instead to measure value. Many things that we value are *not* bought and sold in markets: Health, fairness, and ecological sustainability are examples. Policies directed toward producing the highest value of *these* outputs from given inputs may be quite different from policies designed simply to maximize the market value of production. Likewise, focusing only on minimizing the monetary costs of inputs may lead to actions with high social and environmental costs. Thinking of efficiency only in terms of market value can lead to neglect of other, perhaps more urgent considerations (see Box 1.1).

Box 1.1 Goals Beyond Efficiency

The point that efficiency defined in terms of market value is rarely the only important goal is vividly illustrated in a story that a now-eminent economist always tells at the first session of a new class.

After he finished graduate school, this young man's first job was to advise the government of a rice-growing country where it should put its research efforts. He was told that two modern techniques for rice milling had been developed elsewhere and was asked to calculate which of these two technologies should be selected for development. The young economist analyzed the requirements for producing a ton of rice under each of the two competing technologies. Each of them used a mixture of labor, machinery, fuel, and raw materials. He calculated the monetary costs for these inputs, and, finding that Technology A could produce a ton of rice at slightly less cost than Technology B, he recommended that the government invest in the more "efficient" Technology A.

Returning a few years later, the economist was horrified to discover what had happened when the country implemented his suggestion. It turned out that the traditions of that country included strict norms for the division of labor: specifically, what work women were allowed to do and what was defined as men's work. Technology B would have been neutral in this regard, maintaining the same ratio of "male jobs" to "female jobs" as had existed before. Technology A, however, eliminated most of the women's work opportunities. In a society where women's earnings were a major contributor to food and education for children, the result was a perceptible decline in children's nutrition levels and school attendance.

Charged with determining which technology was best, the young economist had not asked, "Best for what?" Instead, he made an implicit assumption that the only final goal was maximizing output and that the only intermediate goal he had to worry about was efficiency in resource use. He has subsequently told several generations of economics students, "Nobody told me to look beyond efficiency, defined in terms of market costs—but I'll never neglect the family and employment effects again, even when my employer doesn't ask about them."

2.4 Components of Well-Being

We define economics in terms of enhancing well-being, but what exactly do we mean by this? We have mentioned that well-being is about a good quality of life, recognizing that this concept has many normative components. But we suggest that some components of well-being are common to all living things. Evolution has instilled in all living creatures a preference for survival, along with an aversion to pain, hunger, thirst, and other sensations that signal a threat to survival.

Evolution has operated not upon individuals but upon gene pools. Thus the survival imperative works to motivate behavior that will enhance group, as well as individual, survival. In the human species, the group survival imperative is expressed through culture, values, and goals. Thus it is normal for human beings to hold values that would lead us to preserve the health of the society in which we live as well as the health of the environment, on which, ultimately, the future survival of our species depends.

We can distinguish between the things that make life possible (our true "needs," or survival issues) and the things that we feel make life worth living (quality-of-life, or well-being, issues). Even this distinction involves some normative judgments. Some evidence indicates that when the things that make life worth living are removed, many individuals go against the dictates of survival and even risk their own lives for a higher purpose (see Box 1.2).

In Table 1.1, we present one possible list of the final goals of economic activity, summarizing the careful reflection of a number of thinkers but not attempting to represent a final consensus. The first five goals on the list are related to individual concerns; the last five are related to social concerns. Some of the goals (such as the first one) involve making life possible, some (such as the third) involve making life worthwhile, and yet others involve both types of concerns. You may believe that some of the elements on this list are less important than others or could even be omitted, or you may believe that other important goals should be added. Normative analysis is not something that is set in stone forever; rather, it develops with reflection, discussion, experience, and changing circumstances. In any case, it is clear

Box 1.2 GOALS BEYOND SURVIVAL

A simple view of evolution might suggest that the individual survival imperative would always prevail over any other motives. Yet even among animals this is not true, as illustrated by stories of dogs that lie down and die when they have lost their master or of birds courting danger as they try to lure a predator away from the young in their nest.

Many famous stories of human heroism also illustrate human choices for quality of life over life itself or the sacrifice of present survival for the sake of future generations. A true story of such a choice occurred during World War II, when Leningrad (now St. Petersburg) was under siege and starvation was widespread. A researcher at the university who had been developing improved strains of seeds locked himself in his laboratory. At the end of the war, his starved body was found there, among the containers of seed corn that he had protected for future generations.

Table 1.1 **A Potential List of Final Goals**

Satisfaction of basic physical needs, including nutrition and care adequate for survival, growth, and health, as well as a comfortable living environment

Security: assurance that one's basic needs will continue to be met throughout all stages of life, as well as security against aggression or unjust persecution

Happiness: the opportunity to experience, reasonably often, feelings such as contentment, pleasure, enjoyment, and peace of mind

Ability to realize one's potential in as many as possible of the following dimensions of development: physical, intellectual, moral, social, aesthetic, and spiritual

A sense of meaning in one's life—a reason or purpose for one's efforts

Fairness in the distribution of life possibilities, and fair and equal treatment by social institutions (fairness is a universal goal despite cross-cultural differences in how it is defined or assessed)

Freedom in making personal decisions (limited by decision-making capacity, as in the case of children); also, not infringing on the freedom of others

Participation: opportunity to participate in the processes in which decisions are made that affect the members of one's society

Good social relations, including satisfying and trustful relations with friends, fellow citizens, family, and business associates, as well as respectful and peaceful relations among nations

Ecological balance: preserving natural resources, and where needed, restoring them to a healthy and resilient state

that any reasonable discussion of the quality of life must go beyond the simple notions of wealth or efficiency.

2.5 ECONOMICS AND WELL-BEING

Economic activity is not, of course, the only ingredient that goes into creating well-being. Economics cannot make you fall in love, for example, or prevent you from being in a car accident. But economic factors can help to determine whether your job leaves you with the time and energy to date, whether your car has advanced safety features, and whether you have access to medical treatment. A well-functioning economy is one that operates to increase the well-being of all its members.

In Table 1.1, we have suggested for your consideration one plausible list of final goals to be taken into account in guiding economic activity. Economic activities are often necessary to promote our final goals, but economic activities can also sometimes create "ill-being" instead of well-being, whether because of conflicts among goals or because of unintended consequences. However, some economic activities directed toward one goal have consequences that *enhance* the achievement of other goals. For example, doing work that is believed to contribute something positive in the world can add significantly to people's happiness and their ability to realize their potential, at the same time as it brings in the income that permits the satisfaction of their basic needs.

Conflicts Among Goals

If the goal of immediate enjoyment is given too much emphasis, economic activity can actually decrease health and long-term happiness. A supermarket checkout counter offers a good example. Appealing displays of unhealthy snack foods may offer short-term satisfaction, but the temptation of immediate gratification may lead us, even if we are fully informed about the consequences, to make decisions that are unhealthy in the long term.

In addition to tradeoffs between immediate and longer-term impacts, we often also face conflicts among our goals. For example, a current public health debate concerns whether people with contagious, antibiotic-resistant tuberculosis or dangerous new illnesses such as bird flu should be *required* to accept hospital services—in locked wards, if necessary. In this case, we see that the social goal of a physically healthy population and the goal of freedom seem to demand opposite approaches. Likewise, an employer may need to decide between trying to pressure workers to produce the largest possible quantity of some product and wanting to help employees realize their intellectual and social potential on the job.

economic actor (economic agent): an individual or organization involved in the economic activities of resource maintenance or the production, distribution, or consumption of goods and services

Unintended Consequences: An Introduction to Externalities

negative externalities: harmful side effects, or unintended consequences, of economic activity that affect those who are not directly involved in the activity

positive externalities: beneficial side effects, or unintended consequences, of economic activity that accrue to those who are not among the economic actors directly involved in the activity

An **economic actor**, or **economic agent**, is an individual or organization engaged in one or more of four economic activities (explained in detail below)—resource maintenance, and the production, distribution, or consumption of goods and services. Although aimed at achieving a goal, such activity may also produce unintended side effects. Some of the impacts are harmful, such as air pollution that is emitted in the course of production. Negative consequences of an economic activity that affect those who are not directly involved in the activity are called **negative externalities**. In the case of a negative externality like air pollution, neither the firm emitting the pollution nor the consumers buying its products is likely to take the externality into account. But as economists, we need to consider the impacts of the externality on the broader well-being of society. We discuss negative externalities, particularly in relation to environmental issues, in more detail in Chapter 13.

Some of the unintended consequences of economic activity increase well-being. **Positive externalities** are the beneficial effects of an economic activity that accrue to those who are not directly involved in the activity. A college education is an example of an economic activity that generates positive externalities. Although education can be viewed as an economic transaction between the educational institution and the student, society as a whole benefits because college-educated people are likely to be more productive and more informed as citizens in the democratic process.

Discussion Questions

resource maintenance: preserving or improving the resources that contribute to the enhancement of well-being, including natural, manufactured, human, and social resources

1. You have evidently made a decision to dedicate some of your personal resources in time and money to studying college economics. Which of the goals listed in Table 1.1 was most important to you (and perhaps to your family or community, if they were involved) in making this decision? Did any of the other goals figure in this decision? If you were to write up a list of your own final goals, how would it differ from Table 1.1?
2. Certain drugs such as heroin act on the brain to produce intense, temporary feelings of euphoria or pleasure. Some of them are physically addictive and cause people to lose interest in everything except getting another dose of the drug. Do these drugs add to well-being? Discuss.

3. The Issues That Define Economics

In discussing goals, we have addressed the question of what economics is *for*—what its purpose is. Now we summarize what economics is *about:* what activities it covers, and which questions it addresses.

3.1 The Four Essential Economic Activities

We think of an activity as "economic" when it involves one or more of four essential tasks that allow us to meet our needs and enhance our well-being.

Resource maintenance means preserving or improving the resources that contribute to the enhancement of well-being. As we mentioned earlier, these resources may be physical, as in the case of natural resources and manufactured products, but they also include the knowledge and skills of individuals and the social relations and institutions that underpin economic activity. Forestry projects that plant trees for future use are one common example of resource maintenance, but there are many others. Child care and education prepare people for future economic activity as well as directly improving well-being. Other examples of resource maintenance include figuring out how much oil to extract from an oil field now and how much to leave for later; maintaining the transportation infrastructure (subways, roads, etc.) of a city; and, in a factory, keeping the machinery in good repair and maintaining the necessary knowledge, skill levels, and morale of the employees.

production: the conversion of resources into goods and services

inputs: resources that go into production

outputs: the results of production

waste products: outputs that are not used either for consumption or in a further production process

distribution: the sharing of products and resources among people

exchange: the trading of one thing for another

transfer: the giving of something, with nothing specific expected in return

Production is the conversion of some of these resources into usable products, which may be either goods or services. Goods are tangible objects, such as bread and books; services are intangibles, such as TV broadcasting, teaching, and haircuts. Popular bands performing music, recording companies producing CDs and MP3s, local governments building roads, and individuals cooking meals are all engaged in the economic activity of production.

The economic activity of production converts some resources, which we call **inputs**, into new goods and services, which we refer to as **outputs**. This conversion is a flow that takes place over a period of time (See Box 1.3). Some goods, such as machines and computers, are produced to assist in the production of other goods and services. The way in which production occurs depends on available technologies. Production processes can also lead to undesirable outputs, such as **waste products**. We consider only *useful* outputs to be economic goods and services.

Distribution is the sharing of products and resources among people. In contemporary economies, distribution activities take two main forms: **exchange** and **transfer**. When you hand over money in exchange for goods and services, you are engaging in exchange.

Box 1.3 Stocks Versus Flows

When noneconomists use the term "stock," they usually mean ownership shares in enterprises that are traded on the "stock market." To an economist, however, the concept of a **stock** refers to something as it is measured at a particular point in time. For example, the amount of water in a bathtub can be measured at one particular instant, and that quantity would be considered a stock. The number of computers in an office at ten o'clock on Tuesday morning is a stock, as is the number of trees in a forest at two o'clock on Saturday afternoon.

stock: something whose quantity can be measured at a point in time

In contrast to stocks, **flows** are measured over a period of time. For example, the water that goes into a bathtub from a faucet is a flow; its quantity can be measured per minute or per hour. The number of computers purchased by an office over the course of this month or this year is a flow. So is the number of computers sold or junked over a period of time. As trees grow or are cut down or felled by lightning, these flows add to or subtract from forest resources.

flow: something whose quantity can be measured over a period of time

Flows are like a movie; stocks are like a still photograph. Flows can either add to stocks or decrease them. Figure 1.1 is a generalized **stock-flow diagram**, which shows how flows change the level of a stock over time, either by adding to it or taking away from it.

stock-flow diagram: an illustration of how stocks can be changed, over time, by flows

For example, the balance in your checking account at the beginning of the month is a stock value. The deposits and withdrawals you make to your checking account are flows; your bank statement will tell you what the various flows were during a month. The "ending balance" listed on the statement is a stock value.

Figure 1.2 gives an alternative representation of the relation of stocks and flows, this time showing a stock at only *one* point in time. Like water flowing through the tap (additions) and the drain (subtractions) of a bathtub, flows raise or lower the level of the water in the tub (stock).

Figure 1.1 **The General Stock-Flow Diagram**

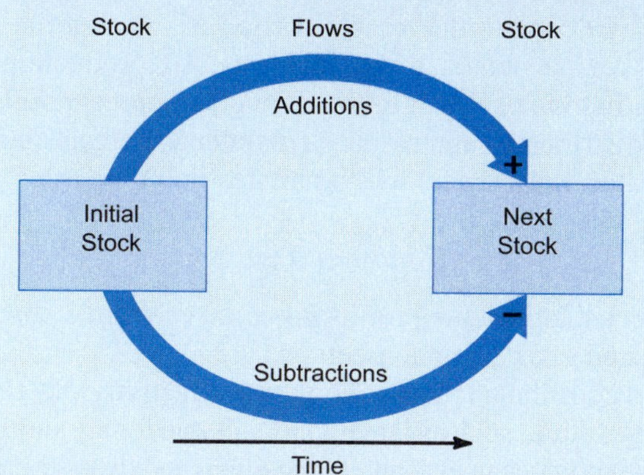

Starting from an initial quantity of a stock, flows into and out of the stock determine how great the quantity is the next time the stock is measured.

Figure 1.2 **A "Bathtub"-Style Diagram**

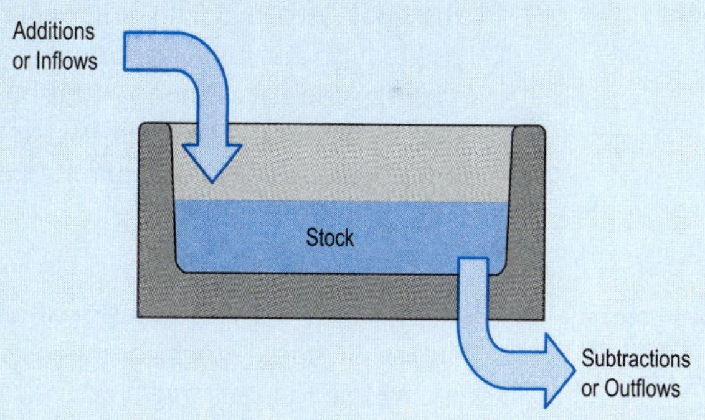

Like water flowing into a bathtub, flows that add to a stock will tend to raise its level over time. Like water flowing out of a bathtub, flows that subtract from a stock will tend to lower its level over time.

People are generally much better off if they specialize in the production of a limited range of goods and services and meet most of their needs through exchange than if they try to produce everything that they need themselves. (We study this in more detail in Chapter 7 of this book.) Distribution also takes place through one-way transfers, in which something is given with nothing specific expected in return. Local school boards, for example, distribute education services to students in their districts, tuition-free (although public education is, of course, supported by tax revenues).These sorts of nonmonetary transfers are called **in-kind transfers.**

in-kind transfers: transfers of goods or services

consumption: the final use of a good or service to satisfy current wants

Consumption is the process by which goods and services are, at last, put to final use by people. In some cases, such as eating a meal or burning gasoline in a car, goods are literally "consumed" in the sense that they are used up and are no longer available for other uses. In other cases, such as enjoying art in a museum, the experience may be "consumed" without excluding others or using up material resources.

saving: refraining from consumption in the current period

In macroeconomics, the activity of consumption is frequently contrasted with the resource-maintenance activity of *investment.* The two activities, production and investment, are linked by the activity of **saving**, or refraining from consumption today in order to gain benefits in the future.

Most real-world economic undertakings involve more than one of the four economic activities. The trucking industry, for example, can be seen as "producing" the service of making goods available, physically distributing produced goods, and consuming large amounts of fuel—as well as a variety of mechanical inputs required to keep the trucks on the road.

Resource maintenance in particular often overlaps with production, consumption, and distribution. For example, the production of paper using recycled materials can be classified as both production, because a good is being produced, and resource maintenance, because the impact on natural resources is minimized. As another example, you may decide to distribute a memo to your coworkers via e-mail to save on paper, thus engaging in resource maintenance as part of the distribution process.

A final point on the relationship between resource maintenance and the other economic activities is that sometimes resource maintenance means *not* engaging in production, consumption, or distribution. For example, people who make voluntary decisions to minimize their unnecessary consumption are maintaining resources. Although this may look like *inactivity,* including resource maintenance as an economic activity implies that minimizing some kinds of consumption can contribute to well-being. Throughout this textbook you will find many examples and analyses of the four basic economic activities listed above. The first half of the book, dealing with microeconomics, will contain the largest portion of the material on production and consumption. However, as we have noted, a particular aspect of production—savings and investment—will be covered in greater depth in the second, macroeconomics, part of the text. The other two activities, distribution and resource maintenance (especially, but not exclusively, the maintenance of natural resources) will be treated in both parts.

3.2 The Five Kinds of Capital

capital stock: a quantity of any resource that is valued for its potential economic contributions

natural capital: physical assets provided by nature

manufactured capital: physical assets generated by applying human productive activities to natural capital

human capital: people's capacity for work and their individual knowledge and skills

A **capital stock** is a quantity of any resource that is valued for its potential economic contributions. Capital stocks are also often referred to as "capital assets."

We can identify five types of capital that contribute to an economy's productivity. **Natural capital** refers to physical assets provided by nature, such as land that is suitable for agriculture or other human uses, fresh water sources, healthy ocean ecologies, a resilient and diverse stock of wild animals and plants, and stocks of minerals and fossil fuels that are still in the ground. **Manufactured capital** means physical assets that are generated by applying human productive activities to natural capital. These include such things as buildings, machinery, stocks of refined oil, transportation infrastructure, and inventories of produced goods that are waiting to be sold or to be used in further production. **Human capital** refers to individual people's capacity for productive work, particularly the knowledge and skills each can personally bring to his or her work. **Social capital** means the existing institutions and the stock of trust, mutual understanding, shared values, and socially held knowledge that facilitates the social coordination of economic activity.

Lastly, there is a fifth sort of resource, **financial capital**, which is a fund of purchasing power available to economic actors. While financial capital is not part of any physical production activity, it indirectly contributes to production by making it possible for people to produce goods and services in advance of getting paid for them. It also facilitates the activities of

social capital: the institutions and the stock of trust, mutual understanding, shared values, and socially held knowledge that facilitates the social coordination of economic activity

financial capital: funds of purchasing power available to economic actors

investment: actions taken to increase the quantity or quality of a resource over time

distribution and consumption. An example of financial capital would be a bank checking account, filled with funds that have been either saved up by the economic agent who owns it or lent to the agent by a bank.

Notice that economists' description of "capital" is different from what you might hear in everyday use. In common usage, sometimes people take "capital" to mean *only* financial capital. We hear this in everyday references to "capital markets," "undercapitalized businesses," "venture capital," and so on. Economists take a broader view (discussed further in Chapter 15).

Capital stocks may increase or decrease as a consequence of natural forces, as in the case of a natural forest; or they may be deliberately managed by humans in order to provide needed inputs for the production of goods and services. When people work to increase the quantity or quality of resources in order to make benefits possible in the future, this is what economists mean by **investment**. Advances in technology also expand or improve the stocks of capital, including manufactured, human, and social capital, thereby increasing the productivity of economic activity.

One way to understand resource maintenance is that it is about making sure that investments are sufficient to provide an economy with a good asset base for future years and future generations. You, right now, are investing in your "human capital" by studying economics.

3.3 THE THREE BASIC ECONOMIC QUESTIONS

The four economic activities that we have listed give rise, in turn, to the three basic economic questions:

1. *What* should be produced, and *what* should be maintained?
2. *How* should production and maintenance be accomplished?
3. *For whom* should economic activity be undertaken?

For example, a family faces the problem of how much of its economic resources (money, credit, and so on) to use now and how much to preserve for future use. Suppose that members of a family decide to spend some of their money on a dinner party. They will have to decide "what" foods to prepare. The "how" question includes who is going to cook and what recipes to use. Answering the "for whom" question means deciding who will be invited for dinner and how to take into account the food preferences and needs of the various individuals.

The complexity of decision making and the number of people involved rise steeply as we move to higher levels of economic organization, but the questions remain the same. Businesses, schools, community groups, governments, and international organizations all have to settle the questions of *what, how,* and *for whom.*

Discussion Questions

1. Identify which kinds of capital are being maintained in the following examples of resource maintenance:
   a. figuring out how much oil to extract from an oil field now and how much to leave for later
   b. saving some of the profits from a business to reinvest
   c. child-care and education.
   d. maintaining the transportation infrastructure (subways, roads, etc.) of a city;
   e. starting a savings account for your children's education
   f. in a factory, keeping the machinery in good repair and maintaining the necessary knowledge, skill levels, and morale of the employees
   g. a forestry project that plant trees

2. Classify each of the following according to which economic activity, or activities, it involves, from this list: production, resource maintenance, distribution, and consumption. If any seem to include aspects of more than one activity, name the activities and explain your reasoning.
   a. Harvesting a crop of corn
   b. Attending college
   c. Building an addition onto a factory
   d. Receiving a Social Security payment
   e. Sewing a button onto your jacket—or someone else's jacket

4. ECONOMIC TRADEOFFS

Tradeoffs are a central concept in economics. When we have limited resources, we have to decide how to allocate them to meet competing goals. If we allocate more resources toward one objective, then less are available to meet other goals.

4.1 ABUNDANCE AND SCARCITY

When you think of all the abundant natural resources in our world, all the human knowledge that exists, all the investments that have been made in organizing human societies, and the massive stock of machinery and other productive resources that have accumulated, you realize that the world is wealthy indeed. When you are well fed, comfortably warm, engaged in interesting activities, and close to those you care about, you can appreciate these benefits. Although the distribution of resources is far from even, either across countries or among people within countries (a topic that we take up again in Chapters 15 and 32), contemporary human society as a whole still has a rich resource base on which to build. It is no wonder that many world religions and ethical teachings encourage gratitude for life's **abundance**.

abundance: resources are abundant to the extent that they exist in plentiful supply

scarcity: the concept that resources are not sufficient to allow all goals to be accomplished at once

It may seem odd, then, that when discussing society's choices concerning *what, how,* and *for whom,* many economists emphasize the notion of **scarcity**—that is, the notion of insufficiency. What this really means is that even with all the available resources, not all of our goals can be accomplished, at least not at the same time. The current capacity of a particular hospital, for example, may allow it to increase the number of heart transplants that are performed there *or* increase the amount of care that can be provided there for the severely mentally ill, but not both. If a given resource, such as an hour of your time, is dedicated to one activity, such as studying, then it will be unavailable for certain other activities, such as relaxing with your friends. Choices have to be made.

This book presents some key tools and language that can be helpful in understanding how choices can best be made about what to produce, how, and for whom, when current resources are insufficient for meeting all possible current well-being goals, and also when choices need to be made between meeting well-being goals now and meeting them in the future.

4.2 SOCIETY'S PRODUCTION-POSSIBILITIES FRONTIER

production-possibilities frontier (PPF): a curve showing the maximum amounts of two outputs that society could produce from given resources, over a given period

Economists use the model of a **production-possibilities frontier** (PPF) to illustrate several important economic concepts. To make matters simple, let us assume that society is considering only two possible choices of what to produce over the coming year from its available resources. The classic example is to take "guns" as one output and "butter" as the other. In more general terms, the guns-versus-butter tradeoff can refer to the general choice of a society between becoming more militarized ("guns") and becoming more civilian- or consumer-oriented ("butter").

Figure 1.3 shows a PPF for this case. In this graph, the quantity of "butter" produced over a year is measured on the horizontal (or *x*-) axis. The quantity of "guns" is measured

Figure 1.3 Society's Production Possibilities Frontier

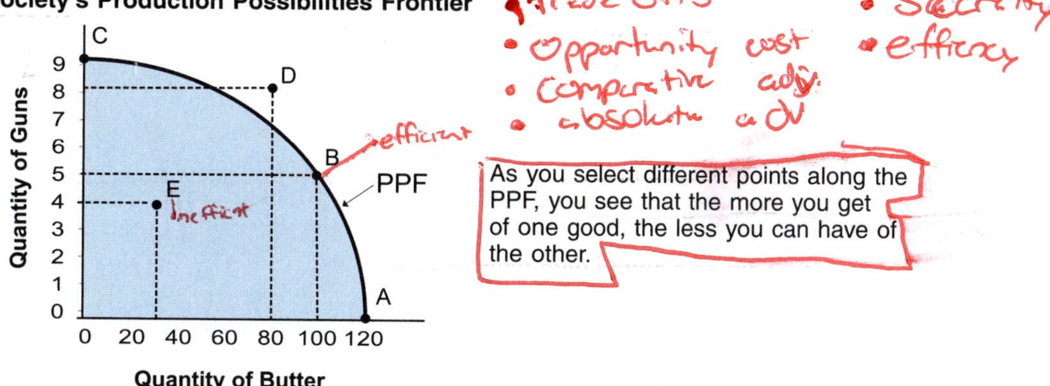

on the vertical (or *y*-) axis. The points on the PPF curve illustrate the maximum quantities of guns and butter that the society could produce. For example, point A, where the curve intersects the *x*-axis, shows that this society can produce 120 units of butter if it does not produce any guns. Moving up and to the left, point B illustrates production, over the year, of 100 units of butter and 5 units of guns. (At this level of abstraction, it is not necessary to be specific about what is meant by "units." You may imagine these as kilos of butter and numbers of guns, if you like.) Point C illustrates that the society can produce 9 units of guns if it decides to produce no butter. While it may seem odd to think about a society that only produces two goods, this figure is nevertheless helpful for illustrating several important economic concepts.

Scarcity. Point D in Figure 1.3 represents a production combination (80 units of butter and 8 units of guns) that is not attainable given existing resources (or, as we will see, the present state of technology). To produce at that point would take more resources than the society currently has. The PPF is specifically defined so that only those points on or inside it (the shaded region) represent outputs that can actually be produced.

Tradeoffs. All the points that lie on the PPF illustrate the important notion that scarcity creates a need for tradeoffs. Along the frontier, one can get more of one output only by "trading off" some of the other. Figure 1.3 illustrates the important concept of **opportunity costs**. Opportunity cost is the value of the best alternative to the choice that one actually makes. In this case, the cost of increasing gun production is less butter. For example, suppose the economy is at Point A, producing 120 units of butter and no guns, but then decides that it needs to produce 5 guns. Point B illustrates that after some resources have been moved from butter production into producing the 5 guns, the maximum amount of butter that can be produced is 100 units. The gain of 5 guns comes at a "cost" to the economy of a loss of 20 units of butter. Likewise, starting from a point where the economy is producing only guns, the "cost" of producing more butter would be fewer guns.

opportunity cost: the value of the best alternative that is forgone when a choice is made

Efficiency. Resources are used efficiently as long as the process by which they are used does not involve any waste. Points that lie *on* the PPF illustrate the maximum combinations that a society can produce from its given resources, if these are used efficiently. But what about points *inside* the frontier, such as point E? At point E, the economy is not producing as much as it could. It is producing 30 units of butter and 4 guns, even though it *could* produce more of one or the other, or even more of both. Some resources are apparently being wasted at point E. This could occur for at least three reasons:

1. The resources may be wasted because they are being left idle. For example, workers may be left unemployed, or cows could be left unmilked.

2. Even if resources are fully employed, the technology and social organization applied to the resources may not be optimal. For example, suppose that the gun factory is poorly designed, so a lot of the workers' time is wasted moving parts from one area to another. In this case, a better, more efficient organization of the work flow could increase production, with no increase in resources.
3. The allocation of resources between the two production activities (i.e., guns and butter) might not be optimal. For example, if gun factories are built on the best pasture land when they could just as well be built on poorer land, the ability of the economy to graze cows and produce butter would be hampered.

When an economy is imagined to be *on* the PPF, and thus producing efficiently, the only way to produce more of one good is to produce less of the other. If an economy is *inside* the PPF (producing in the shaded region), however, it is producing inefficiently, and improvements in the employment of resources, the application of available technology and social organization, or allocation of resources among production activities could allow it to move toward the frontier (i.e., to produce more of both goods).

The bowed-out shape of the curve comes from the fact that some resources are likely to be more suited for production of one good than for the other. We can see, for example, that the society can get the first 5 guns by giving up only 20 units of butter production. Workers, for example, can be pulled out of butter production and set to work on relatively plentiful supplies of the materials most suited for guns, such as easily tapped veins of iron ore and minerals for gunpowder. Gun manufacturing plants can—if allocation decisions are made wisely—be built on land unsuitable for pasture. To produce 4 more guns (to go from point B to point C along the PPF), however, comes at the cost of the remaining 100 units of butter! Why is this? In order to produce more guns, we must pull workers off of the most productive dairy land and direct them toward increasingly less-accessible veins of mineral ores or to the now-crowded gun assembly lines.

Of course, we could put on the axes many other pairs of outputs, besides guns and butter, and still illustrate these concepts. We could look at soda and pizza, cars and bicycles, or health care and highways. This classic example, however, is a good one. In the real world, such guns/butter or militarization/peacetime tradeoffs can be crucially important (see Box 1.4).

Box 1.4 The Opportunity Cost of Military Expenditures

What do military buildups and wars really cost? One way to look at this is to consider what else could have been bought with the money spent on armaments.

World military expenditures in 2013 totaled $1.75 trillion, or 2.5 percent of world GDP. The United States is by far the biggest spender, accounting on its own for 46 percent of the global total. The United Kingdom, France, China, and Japan are the next biggest military spenders. Smaller and poorer countries spend less, but some of the poorest countries—including Eritrea and Burundi—spend more on the military than they do on public services such as health care and education. Where do such countries get their weapons? The United States and Russia are the leading suppliers of military goods to international markets.

Meanwhile, about 10 million children every year—over 27,000 every day—die before they reach the age of 5, most of them from malnutrition and poverty. The Millennium Development Goals set out by the United Nations include eradicating extreme poverty, achieving universal primary education, reducing child mortality rates, and improving maternal health, gender equity, and environmental sustainability in the poorest areas of the world. All this comes at a cost, of course. The amount of money that would be needed to achieve these goals has been estimated to be in the range of $145 to $270 billion per year, that is, about 8–15 percent of what is currently spent on arms. This level of funding has not been forthcoming, however, and indications are that some of the goals will not be met.

As U.S. president Dwight D. Eisenhower said in 1953, "Every gun that is made, every warship launched, every rocket fired, signifies in the final sense a theft from those who hunger and are not fed, those who are cold and are not clothed."

Sources: Stockholm International Peace Research Institute, *SIPRI Military Expenditures Database,* www.sipri.org/; United Nations Millennium Project, www.unmillenniumproject.org/reports/costs_benefits2.htm.

What precise combination of outputs, such as guns versus butter or health versus highways, should society choose to produce? The PPF does *not* answer this question. All points along the PPF are efficient, in the sense that there are no wasted resources. But among the different efficient points, such as A, B, or C, which one would produce the most social well-being? To determine this, we would have to know more about the society's requirements and priorities. Is civilian satisfaction a high priority? Then the society would lean toward production of butter. Does the society fear attack by a foreign power? Perhaps then it would choose a point closer to the guns axis. For good social decision making, this production question would have to be considered alongside a full array of questions of resource maintenance, distribution, and consumption, because all have effects on well-being. In a society with free speech and democratic discussion, there is wide room for disagreement about what the best mix of goods might be. The PPF provides a rubric for thinking about scarcity, tradeoffs, and efficiency but does not, itself, tell us how to choose among the various economically efficient possibilities.

4.3 Tradeoffs Over Time

We have said that a PPF reflects possible production combinations for a given set of resources. This idea deserves more investigation. Do we mean that society should look at *all* the resources it has at a point in time and then strive to employ them to produce the *maximum quantity* of valued outputs over the coming year?

If we consider that achieving well-being also involves questions of *how* and *for whom,* as well as activities of resource maintenance, distribution, and consumption, then the question becomes more complex—and more interesting. For example, we generally want to conserve resources so that we can produce goods not only right now but also later in our lives. And we have an obligation to future generations to include them in our considerations of *for whom.*

Some production activities are also resource maintenance activities, of course, and these activities can add to the stock of resources available for the future. Investments in plant and equipment can provide productive capacity not just for a few months but, often, for years. Production of goods and services that protect the environment or that encourage the development of new forms of knowledge and social organization also lead to an improved resource base. **Technological progress**, in which new methods are devised to convert resources into products, can lead to long-run improvements in efficiency and productive capacity. Thus some kinds of production can *add* to the production possibilities for the future. The PPF may expand over time, out and to the right, making previously unobtainable points obtainable, as shown in Figure 1.4. With the initial PPF, points A, B, and C are attainable, but points D and E are unattainable. With technological progress and an expanded PPF, points D and E could become attainable.

technological progress: the development of new methods of converting inputs (resources) into outputs (products or services)

Some productive activities create an ongoing flow of outputs without drawing down the stock of capital resources, such as organic farming that maintains the nutrient levels in soil. Many other productive activities, however, lead to resource depletion or degradation. The intensive use of fossil fuels is now depleting petroleum reserves, degrading air quality, and contributing to global climate change. Production processes that destroy important watersheds and wildlife habitats are also resource depleting. Mind-numbing drudgery, work in dangerous circumstances, or excessively long hours of work can degrade human resources by leaving people exhausted or in poor mental or physical health. These kinds of productive activities are at odds with resource maintenance.

Taking a longer-term view, then, it is clear that getting the absolute most production, right now, out of the available resources is not an intelligent social goal. Decisions such as our guns versus butter example need to be accompanied by another decision about *now* versus *later.* What needs to be currently produced, what needs to be maintained, and what investments are needed to increase future productivity?

Figure 1.4 **An Expanded Production Possibilities Frontier**

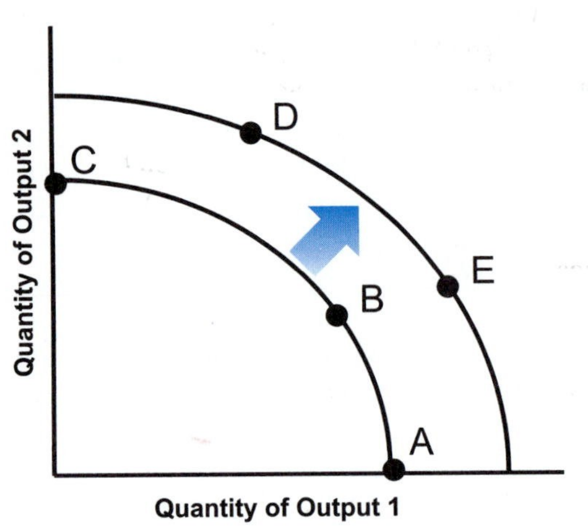

When the PPF moves "out" (away from the origin), we can obtain previously unattainable production choices, such as points D and E.

Figure 1.5 **Society's Choice between Current Production and Resource Maintenance**

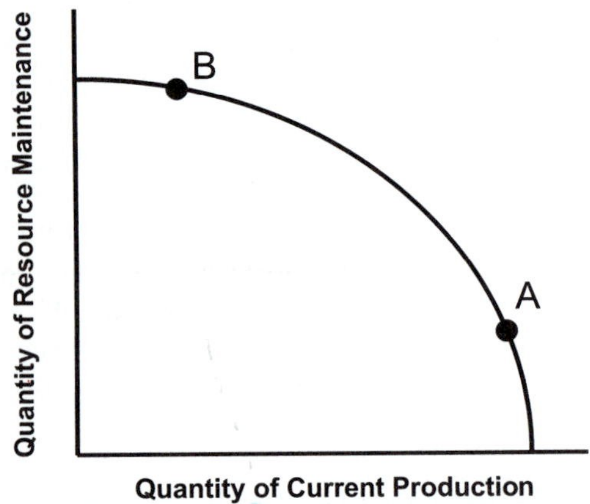

Society also faces a tradeoff between current production and resource maintenance for the future.

The choice between current and future production can be presented in terms of a different PPF, as shown in Figure 1.5. In this case, the tradeoff is between current production and resource maintenance for the future. If society chooses point A, current production is high but resource maintenance for the future is low. However, choosing point B reduces current production but results in significantly higher resource maintenance.

The consequences of choosing between points A and B are illustrated in Figure 1.6, where once again we portray a two-output PPF (such as that for guns versus butter). Now, however, the graph illustrates how future conditions are affected by the current choice between A and B. As Figure 1.6 shows, a decision to maintain more for the future, by choosing point B in Figure 1.5, leads to a larger set of production possibilities in future years. A decision to engage in less resource maintenance, shown by point A in Figure 1.5, leads to the smaller future PPF shown in Figure 1.6.

Of course, some will argue that advances in technology will *always* push out the PPF (as in Figure 1.4) and make up for low current resource maintenance. But this is no more than an assertion of belief. If this belief turns out not to be warranted, then acting on the basis of it may lead to large-scale, unfortunate, and irreversible consequences.

Figure 1.6 **Possible Future Production Possibilities Frontiers**

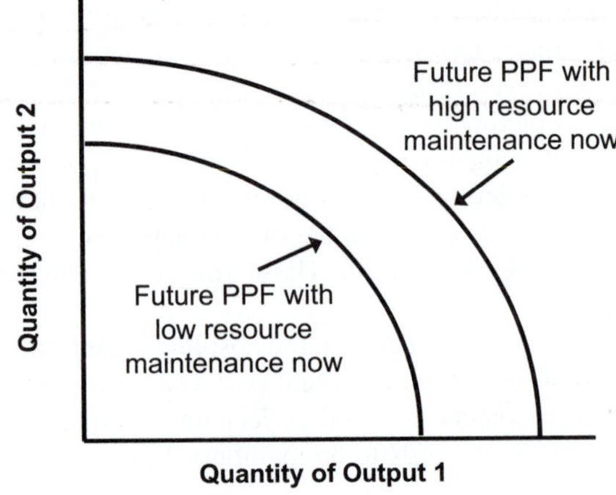

Current decisions about how to produce will affect our options for future production.

Discussion Questions

1. Suppose that your "resources" for studying can be devoted to either or both of two "outputs": knowledge of economics and knowledge of the subject matter of another class you are taking. Would the PPF for your "production" have the shape portrayed in Figure 1.3? Discuss.
2. Consider the following possible productive activities. Which ones do you think will tend to expand the PPF in the future? Which ones will tend to contract it? (There may be room for disagreement on some points.)
   a. Increasing educational opportunities ↑
   b. Manufacturing lawn mowers ↓
   c. Building a nuclear power plant ↓
   d. Restoring wetlands ↑
   e. Building a new interstate highway ↑
   f. Expanding Internet capacity ↑

REVIEW QUESTIONS

1. What is the definition of economics?
2. Name the four essential economic activities.
3. What is the difference between positive and normative questions? Give a couple of examples of each.
4. What is the difference between final and intermediate goals?
5. Is the attainment of wealth a final goal?
6. What is the goal of efficiency?
7. What are some examples of final goals?
8. What is an economic actor?
9. Define negative and positive externalities, and give examples of each.
10. How do abundance and scarcity create the possibility of, and the necessity for, economic decision making?
11. Draw a societal PPF, and use it to explain the concepts of tradeoffs (opportunity cost), attainable and unattainable output combinations, and efficiency.
12. What kinds of decisions would make a PPF expand over time? What kinds of decisions would make it contract over time?
13. What is the relationship between a society's PPF and resource maintenance?

EXERCISES

1. In each of the following, indicate which of the four essential economic activities is taking place.
   a. Ms. Katar, an executive at Acme Manufacturing, directs the cleanup of one of the company's old industrial waste dump sites.
   b. Mr. Ridge plants a garden in his yard.
   c. Ms. Fuller hands an unemployed worker a bag of groceries at a local food pantry.
   d. Mr. Hernandez eats lunch at a cafeteria.
2. The notion of scarcity reflects the idea that resources cannot be stretched to achieve all the goals that people desire. But what makes a particular resource "scarce"? If a resource seems to be in greater supply than is needed (like desert sand), is it scarce? If it is freely open to the use of many people at once (like music on the radio), is it scarce? What about resources such as social attitudes of trust and respect? Make a list of a few resources that clearly *are* scarce in the economic sense. Make another list of a few resources that are *not* scarce.
3. How is the concept of efficiency related to the concept of scarcity? Consider, for example, your own use of time. When do you feel that time is more, and when less, scarce? Do you think about how to use your time differently during exam week than you do when you are on vacation?
4. Suppose that society could produce the following combinations of pizzas and books:

Alternative	Quantity of pizzas	Quantity of books
A	50	0
B	40	10
C	30	18
D	20	24
E	10	28
F	0	30

a. Using graph paper (or a computer program), draw the PPF for pizza and books, being as exact and neat as possible. (Put books on the horizontal axis. Assume that the dots define a complete curve.)
b. Is it possible or efficient for this society to produce 25 pizzas and 25 books?
c. Is it possible or efficient for this society to produce 42 pizzas and 1 book?
d. If society is currently producing alternative B, then the opportunity cost of moving to alternative A (and getting 10 more pizzas) is ________ books.
e. Is the opportunity cost of producing pizzas higher or lower moving from alternative F to E than moving from alternative B to A? Why is this likely to be so?
f. Suppose that the technologies used in producing both pizzas and books improve. Draw one possible new PPF in the graph above that represents the results of this change. Indicate the direction of the change that occurs with an arrow.

5. Match each concept in Column A with an example in Column B.

Column A	Column B
a. Negative externality	1. You should spend more time studying economics.
b. An essential economic activity	2. A fair and just society
c. A final goal	3. If you spend more time studying economics, you will have less time to sleep.
d. An intermediate goal	4. The current unemployment rate is 7 percent.
e. A normative statement	5. You are studying economics in order to get a good job.
f. A positive statement	6. Producing this book resulted in pollution.
g. An opportunity cost	7. Resource maintenance

NOTE

1. Data from tax reports published by the Congressional Budget Office, www.cbo.gov.

2 Useful Tools and Concepts

In order to study economics we need various analytical approaches for understanding economic actors and their behavior. This chapter will describe three major ways to investigate and understand economic realities: empirical, theoretical, and historical. As part of the discussion of the empirical approach, Section 1 includes a review of how to use graphs as visual images of abstract ideas. In applying the theoretical approach, we will also discuss the use of economic models. It is sometimes useful temporarily to isolate certain aspects of economic behavior from their larger historical and environmental context, in order to examine more closely the complex elements involved. This simplification is a necessary part of economic models, which will be used in many places in this book.

In Section 2 we will examine two models that take different approaches to defining and understanding the economy. Section 3 will go into more depth regarding types of economic activity, discussing the economic roles played by businesses, households and communities, governments, and non-profit organizations.

1. Our Tools for Understanding

Here we will outline the three main modes of investigation for explaining economic phenomena: empirical, theoretical, and historical.

1.1 Empirical Investigation

empirical investigation: observation and recording of the specific phenomena of concern

time-series data: observations of how a numerical variable changes over time

Empirical investigation is observation and recording of specific happenings in the world. In economics, empirical investigation often involves numerical data. However, useful empirical investigation of a specific item of interest may also be represented in words or images.

When the observations take the form of showing how a variable changes over time, we call them **time-series data**. We saw important examples of time-series data in Chapter 0, in graphs that showed how GDP and atmospheric carbon dioxide (CO_2) emissions have grown over time.

We will be seeing many such graphs in this book—for price levels, employment, exchange rates, and other economic variables. The accompanying Graphing Review Box (Box 2.1) will help you refresh your skills in working with data and graphs.

It is tempting to think that if two economic variables seem empirically related to each other, changes in one variable are *causing* changes in the other. Sometimes this is true. In the case of the upward trends over time that we saw for both GDP and CO_2 emissions, as shown in Chapter 0, there *is* causality: Growing industrial production has led, over time, to increasing accumulations of CO_2. There are good scientific reasons to believe that the rise in CO_2 emissions is a direct result of years of fossil fuel–intensive economic growth.

Box 2.1 Graphing Review

Empirical analysis involves collecting and interpreting numerical data. This review covers the two most common ways that economic data are presented in this book. The first way is in a table, such as Table 2.1, which presents time-series data for the U.S. economy over the period 2000–2012. The table provides data each year for two variables: the annual real growth rate of GDP and the annual average unemployment rate. So we can determine from the table, for example, that in 2004 the unemployment rate was 5.5 percent and real GDP grew at a rate of 3.5 percent.

Table 2.1 **Unemployment Rate and Real GDP Growth Rate, United States, 2000–2012** (in percent)

	Unemployment rate	Real GDP growth rate
2000	4.0	4.1
2001	4.7	1.1
2002	5.8	1.8
2003	6.0	2.5
2004	5.5	3.5
2005	5.1	3.1
2006	4.6	2.7
2007	4.6	1.9
2008	5.8	–0.3
2009	9.3	–3.1
2010	9.6	2.4
2011	8.9	1.8
2012	8.1	2.2

Sources: U.S. Bureau of Economic Analysis, http://bea.gov/iTable/index_nipa.cfm ;U.S. Bureau of Labor Statistics, http://bls.gov/cps/cpsaat01.htm.

While tables can present detailed numerical data, it is not always obvious what is really happening by simply looking at a table. We could carefully study Table 2.1 to determine when unemployment is rising and when it is falling, but this is normally not the easiest way to observe trends over time. Instead, we can commonly present data in visual form, using graphs, to quickly "see" what is happening in an economy.

Figure 2.B1 presents a time-series graph of the unemployment rate. Graphs have a horizontal axis (also called the "x-axis") and a vertical axis (also called the "y-axis"). It is common practice to present time-series data with the time intervals on the x-axis. Presented this way, we can easily see that unemployment rose from 2000 to 2003, then fell for a few years, then rose significantly to nearly 10 percent by 2010, then fell somewhat in 2011 and 2012.

You can test yourself by using the data in Table 2.1 to construct a time-series graph for the GDP growth rate. You can do this using graph paper or a spreadsheet application such as Microsoft Excel.

Figure 2.B1 **Unemployment Rate, United States, 2000–2012**

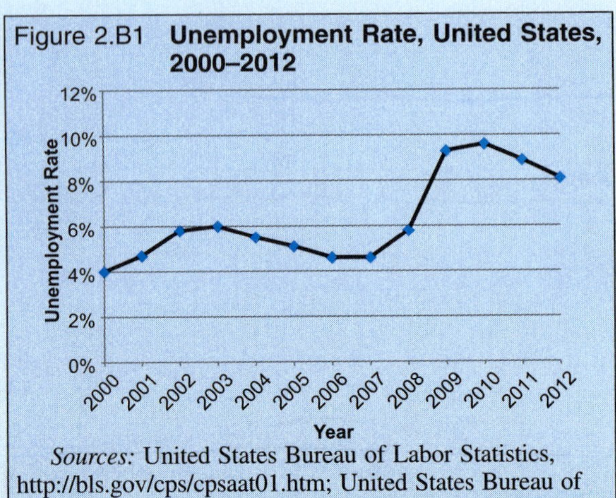

Sources: United States Bureau of Labor Statistics, http://bls.gov/cps/cpsaat01.htm; United States Bureau of Economic Analysis, http://bea.gov/iTable/index_nipa.cfm.

In addition to using graphs for time-series analysis of a single variable, we can also use graphs to explore the relationship between two different variables. This is important because it provides a way to test specific economic hypotheses. Referring back to Table 2.1, we might form the hypothesis that unemployment rates tend to be higher when GDP growth rates are lower. We call this a **negative, or inverse, relationship**—when an increase in one variable is associated with a decrease in another variable (or, vice versa, when a decrease in one variable is associated with an increase in another variable).

Negative (or inverse) relationship: the relationship between two variables if an increase in one variable is associated with a decrease in the other variable (or vice versa)

Figure 2.B2 plots the relationship between unemployment rates and GDP growth rates. Each "data point" on the graph tells us the values of *both* variables for a specific year. In the graph we have kept the unemployment rate on the y-axis, but the x-axis now indicates the GDP growth rate. So the data point for 2008, for example, indicates that the unemployment rate was 5.8 percent (by reading across to the y-axis), and the GDP growth rate was –0.3 percent (by reading down to the x-axis). Note that there is one data point for each year. You can test yourself by figuring out which data points match which years.

A visual inspection of Figure 2.B2 can help us determine whether our hypothesis of an inverse relationship between unemployment and GDP growth rates is correct. We can see that when GDP growth rates were at their highest, 3 percent or higher, unemployment rates were relatively low. In general, the graph seems to support our hypothesis, but there are some exceptions.

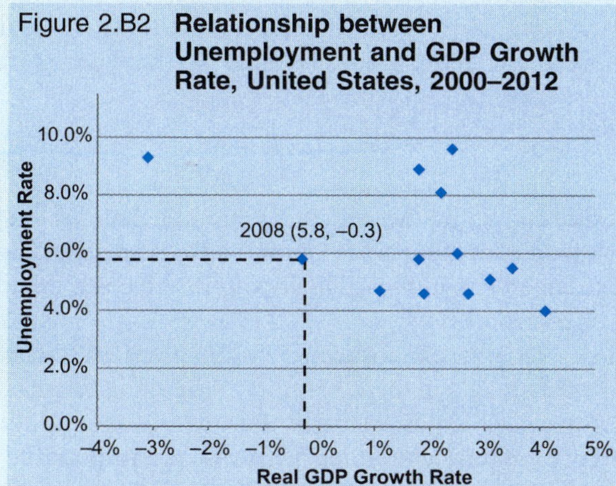

Sources: United States Bureau of Labor Statistics, http://bls.gov/cps/cpsaat01.htm; United States Bureau of Economic Analysis, http://bea.gov/iTable/index_nipa.cfm.

For example, in the year when unemployment was at its maximum, in 2010, GDP growth was about average at 2.4 percent. To determine more accurately whether our hypothesis is supported by the data, we would need to undertake statistical analysis, often called "econometrics." If you are an economics major, you will likely take a future course on econometrics.

Figure 2.B2 can tell us whether our two variables are related, or "correlated," but as mentioned in the text we cannot determine whether there is a causal relationship between the two variables. While we suspect that low GDP growth causes high unemployment, we cannot prove it using a graph. The causality could potentially be in the opposite direction—that high unemployment causes low GDP growth. Even if the variables seem related in a graph, the relationship could be random, or "spurious." For example, you may have read stories about how the outcome of sporting events can predict the performance of the stock market or the winner of presidential campaigns. However, it seems highly unlikely that such relationships are causal.

The opposite of an inverse relationship is a **positive, or direct, relationship**. In this case, an increase in one variable is associated with an increase in another variable—or a decrease in one variable is associated with a decrease in another.

Positive (or direct) relationship: the relationship between two variables if an increase in one variable is associated with an increase in the other variable

A good example of a positive relationship is between the growth rate of GDP and the growth rate of greenhouse gas emissions, such as carbon dioxide and methane. When the economy is growing, manufacturing industries tend to produce more goods, people tend to fly and drive more, and construction activity tends to increase. All these factors tend to increase greenhouse gas emissions.

The relationship between GDP growth and the growth of greenhouse gas emission is shown in Figure 2.B3, which includes data for 1990–2012. In this case, we see a reasonably clear positive relationship—when the economy is growing rapidly greenhouse gas emissions also tend to increase. Again, we can undertake a more sophistical statistical analysis of the positive relationship, and we cannot demonstrate causality just by looking at a graph, but the graph provides strong support in favor of a positive relationship between the two variables.

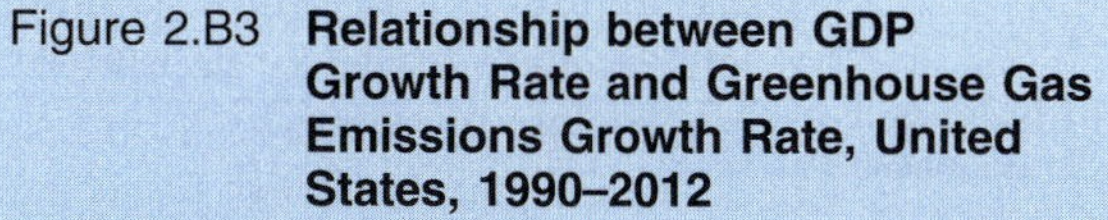

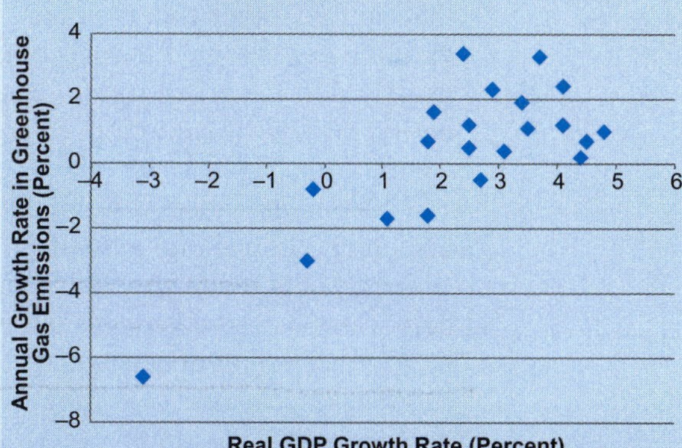

Source: Greenhouse Gas data from United States Environmental Protection Agency, http://www.epa.gov/climatechange/ghgemissions/usinventoryreport.html.

But two variables may be related empirically (or be "correlated" with each other, to use the statistical term) *without* there being a well-defined causal relationship between them. For example, countries with higher GDP tend to have higher reported levels of cancer. Does this mean that higher GDP causes cancer? No, the true relationship is between GDP and life expectancy. Higher GDP is broadly associated with longer life expectancy, and people who live longer are more likely to develop cancer at some point in their lives. The specific causes of cancer include genetics, environmental exposure, diet, and other factors. This provides an excellent example for the warning that "correlation does not necessarily imply causality." In other words, the existence of an observable relationship between two economic variables does not imply that changes in one variable *cause* the changes in the other.

Empirical investigation creates the foundation for macroeconomic analysis. Looking at the data on unemployment and GDP growth, we can see, however, that more tools are clearly needed if economists are to try to *explain,* rather than simply describe, macroeconomic phenomena.

1.2 Theoretical Investigation

theoretical investigation: analysis based in abstract thought

The adjective "empirical" is usually contrasted with "theoretical," where the latter refers to statements made on the basis of abstract thought, making assumptions and logical deductions. **Theoretical investigation** is essential to macroeconomics. This book introduces a number of theories of how the macroeconomy operates.

Many economic theories are based on "thought experiments." In the physical sciences, much theorizing is based on controlled experiments in the laboratory. While it is sometimes possible for economists to carry out controlled experiments at the microeconomic level (creating a relatively new field of "experimental economics"), this is rarely possible in macroeconomics. Thus economists tend to create theories based on assumptions about economic agents and institutions, from which, with careful reasoning, they draw out potential implications for economic behavior.

model: an analytical tool that highlights some aspects of reality while ignoring others

ceteris paribus: a Latin phrase meaning "other things equal" or "all else constant"

In order to make it possible to build a theory, it is sometimes useful to isolate certain aspects of economic behavior from their larger historical and environmental context, in order to examine more closely the complex elements involved. A **model** is an analytical tool that highlights some aspects of reality while ignoring others. It can take the form of a simplified story, an image, a figure, a graph, or a set of equations, and it always involves simplifying assumptions. We look at some examples of economic models later in this chapter when we examine the basic neoclassical model and the contextual model. Other models appear throughout this course.

An important part of many models is the assumption of **ceteris paribus**, a Latin phrase that means "other things equal" or "all else constant." In order to focus on one or two variables, we assume that no other variables change. Of course, in the real world, things usually don't stay constant. Usually after a basic model is constructed, we can vary the *ceteris paribus* assumption, to see how changes in other variables will affect the model's conclusions.

Theories and models essentially simplify reality. Is this justifiable? It is if it gives us greater insight into how things actually work. A model plane, for example, cannot carry passengers or freight, but it can give aerodynamic engineers insights into how a real plane works and help them to design better features for real aircraft. In the same way, simplified models can help economists to understand the working of very complex real-world economies. Of course, economists may disagree about which models to use and as a result may come to different policy conclusions. In this text we try to make clear what simplifying assumptions we are using to build models and to indicate when there are different economic theories that may lead to conflicting policy recommendations.

1.3 Historical Investigation

historical investigation: study of past events

Throughout the book, we also include a crucial third mode: **historical investigation**, which uses our knowledge of historical events to help explain macroeconomic phenomena. The Great Depression of the 1930s, major wars, the invention of computers, changing roles of women in the workforce, the financial crash of 2007–8 and the severe recession that resulted, sometimes called the Great Recession—all are examples of historical events that have had a significant macroeconomic impact.

These events will receive more attention in Parts VI–VIII of this book, dealing with macroeconomics, but there are many issues normally studied within microeconomics that are also hard to understand without some historical reference. One example is the way we define different kinds of competition, or lack of it, in markets: We will see this in Chapter 18, which deals with monopoly and oligopoly.

Economists have become increasingly aware that, while gathering and analyzing data and thinking theoretically about what *could* be true are valid and important tasks, knowledge of the real-world evolution of political, economic, and social life is indispensable to understanding macroeconomics.

Discussion Questions

1. Consider the following examples of investigation. For each one, indicate which mode of investigation it most closely represents—empirical, theoretical, or historical.
   a. A biologist tries to determine the number of different species of plants found on a plot of rainforest
   b. Albert Einstein develops his theory of relativity
   c. An economist measures how GDP varies across countries
   d. A sociologist examines the impact of movements for equal pay for women on women's social and economic status
   e. An economist states that a rise in investment will lead to a fall in unemployment
2. Model building is sometimes compared to map making. If someone asks you how to get to your house, what will you put on the map you draw for them? What if the question asked has to do with the location of the highest point in town, the town's political boundaries, the public transit system, or how your dwelling links up to the local sewer system? Is it possible for a single, readable map to answer every possible question? Does the goal you have in mind for the map affect what you put on it?

2. DIFFERENT ECONOMIC THEORIES: EXAMPLES OF TWO BASIC MODELS

basic neoclassical (traditional microeconomic) model: a model that portrays the economy as a collection of profit-maximizing firms and utility-maximizing households interacting in perfectly competitive markets

The discipline of economics, like most other areas of academic and public discussion, has a long history of varying approaches, beliefs, and conclusions. There are many different schools of economic thought, and we will deal with many of them in later chapters of this text,* but here we present two overall theoretical approaches for understanding the economy: the neoclassical model, which has dominated much of standard economics, and the contextual economics model, which is the approach taken in this text. These approaches are not mutually exclusive, and have some overlap, but they have different scope and emphasis, and can lead to different understandings of economic theory and policy.

2.1 THE BASIC NEOCLASSICAL MODEL

The **basic neoclassical model**, traditionally taught in detail in most microeconomics courses at the introductory level, is a model of market exchange that—while abstracting away from many real-world factors, some of which are discussed below—portrays in a simple and elegant way some important aspects of markets. Neoclassical economics arose during the late nineteenth and early twentieth centuries. It took the eighteenth-century classical idea that economies can be thought of as systems of smoothly functioning markets and expressed this idea in terms of formalized assumptions, equations and graphs. (The prefix "neo-" in "neoclassical" means "new.")

utility: the level of usefulness or satisfaction gained from a particular activity such as consumption of a good or service

In this model, the world is simplified to two kinds of economic actors. Households are assumed to consume and to maximize their **utility** (or satisfaction). Firms are assumed to produce and to maximize profits. Households are considered the ultimate owners of all

*The sub field of History of Economic Thought is a valuable one; students who intend to pursue economics in more depth would do well to find a course, or at least a good book, by which to orient themselves in this history. *The Worldly Philosophers* by Robert Heilbroner is one of the outstanding books for this purpose.

Figure 2.1 **The Circular Flow Diagram for the Basic Neoclassical Model**

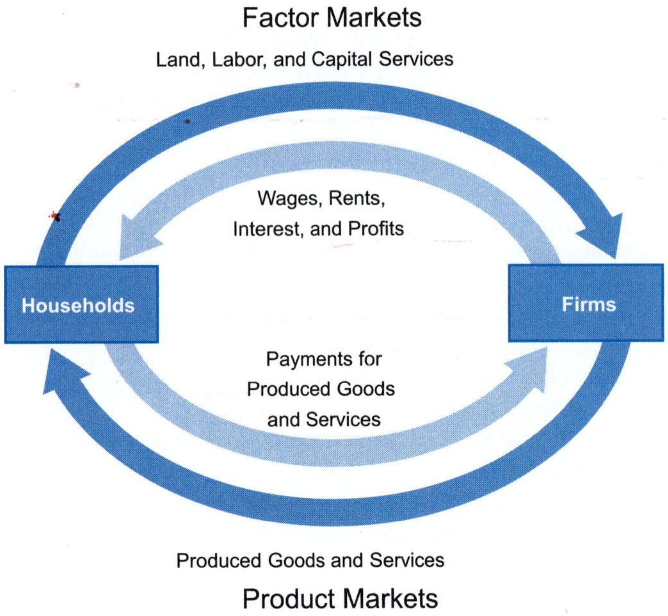

Factor Markets

Land, Labor, and Capital Services

Wages, Rents, Interest, and Profits

Households

Firms

Payments for Produced Goods and Services

Produced Goods and Services

Product Markets

The neoclassical circular flow diagram represents a model in which there are only two kinds of economic actors, interacting through markets.

factor markets: markets for the services of land, labor, and capital

product markets: markets for newly produced goods and services

circular flow diagram: a graphical picture of an economy consisting purely of households and firms that are engaging in exchange

resources of land, labor, and capital. They rent the services of these to firms through **factor markets**, receiving monetary payments in return. Firms produce goods and services, which they sell to households on **product markets** in return for monetary payments. This model can be portrayed in the **circular-flow diagram** in Figure 2.1. The two economic actors (households and firms) are represented by rectangles, and the activity of exchange by arrows. Flows of goods and services create the clockwise flow of the outer circle. Flows of monetary funds, exchanged for these goods and services, move in the opposite direction around the inner circle. The model further assumes that there are so many firms and households involved in the market for any good or service that a situation of "perfect competition" reigns, in which prices are determined purely by forces of supply and demand.

In this idealized world, goods and services are produced, distributed, and consumed in such a way that the market value of production is as high as it can be. The model combines important observations about markets with assumptions about human values and human behavior, as both producers and consumers. (In reading the following statements about the neoclassical model, see if you can recognize which parts are "positive" observations of facts, and which are assumptions, which may include a "normative" slant, toward "the way things ought to be.") Full social and economic efficiency is said to arise because:

- The prices set by the forces of supply and demand in smoothly functioning markets carry signals throughout the economy, coordinating the actions of many individual decision makers in a highly decentralized way
- The profit motive gives perfectly competitive firms an incentive to look for low-cost inputs and convert them into highly valuable outputs. Production decisions are thus made in such a way that resources are put to their most (market) valuable uses
- Consumption decisions made by individuals and households are assumed to maximize the "utility" or satisfaction of consumers
- Maximizing the market value of production is assumed to be a reasonable proxy for maximizing human well-being

The circular flow diagram is useful in portraying in a very simplified way two of the major actors (households and firms) and three of the major activities (production, exchange, and consumption) involved in economic life. However, it is important to recognize that the model leaves out some key actors and activities.

For example, while "land" is included as a factor of production, the fact that natural resources can be used up or polluted is not portrayed. Because of this, the circular flow diagram is a little like a "perpetual motion machine"; the economy it portrays can apparently keep on generating products forever without any inputs of materials or energy. The necessity of resource maintenance activities is not included.

Also, the diagram only takes into account flows of goods or resources that are paid for through the market (the inner, gray arrows show these payments). This ignores unpaid work and free use of natural resources, among other things. You will also notice that there is no role for government in this diagram. While this oversimplification has some value, in allowing us to focus only on the workings of specific markets, we also want to present a broader picture.

2.2 THE CONTEXTUAL MODEL

In reality, economic activities take place within *environmental* and *social contexts.* Thus we need a more inclusive, and more realistic, model than the one presented in Figure 2.1. This is illustrated in Figure 2.2.

The *environmental context* for economic activities includes the built environment as well as the natural world, but its fundamental processes are ecological. Economic activity brings natural resources into the economy and transforms them for human use. In the process, pollution and waste materials are generated, and these in turn affect the flow of natural inputs that are available. In addition to negative externalities such as pollution and waste materials, economic activity can also generate some positive externalities, such as care for soils and forests that make them more fertile over time.

The economy also operates in a *social context,* one that is created and operated by human beings, even when they are not consciously designing it as a system. The social context includes history, politics, culture, ethics, and other human motivations. This social context

Figure 2.2 **Economics in Context**

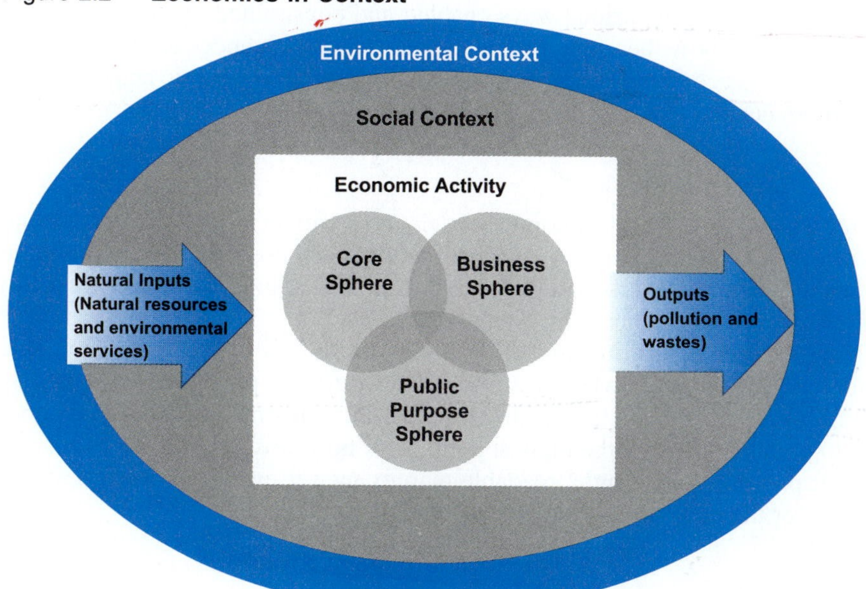

Economic activity always occurs within a broader social and environmental context.

Non factors that impact economy

determines what constitutes acceptable economic activity. For example, we do not allow legal markets for human organs or certain drugs. It also determines the relative weight that a society attaches to the different goals discussed in Chapter 1, such as how to identify and assess a potential tradeoff between improving material living standards and ecological sustainability. As we will see in the Chapter 3 discussion of markets, much economic activity would become impossible without aspects of the social context such as laws, norms, trust, and honesty. In Figure 2.2 we show the social context as existing inside the environmental context because all human activities—not only those of the economic system—are ultimately completely dependent on the environmental context.

Instead of showing economic activity as occurring between just two actors, households and firms, as in Figure 2.1, our contextual approach presents economic activity as occurring within three "spheres." These spheres provide a basic classification of the major types of economic actors.

core sphere: households, families, and communities

business sphere: firms that produce goods and services for profitable sale

public purpose sphere: governments as well as other organizations that seek to enhance well-being without making a profit

1. The **core sphere** includes households, families, and communities. Traditionally, economists have focused on the core sphere as consumers and workers, in their interactions with businesses. But important economic activity occurs *within* the core sphere. For example, the core sphere is where people generally raise children, prepare meals, maintain homes, organize leisure time, and care for mildly ill individuals.
2. The **business sphere** includes firms that produce goods and services for profitable sale. It is often thought that businesses operate only to obtain profits. But the final goals of many businesses may extend beyond simply maximizing profits.
3. The **public purpose sphere** includes governments as well as other organizations that seek to enhance human well-being without making a profit. These may be anything from the United Nations down to a local homeless shelter.

Individuals may move among these three spheres in their economic activities. A woman may be a wife and mother in the core sphere, a business executive in the business sphere, and a volunteer for an environmental group in the public purpose sphere.

Economic activity within and between these three spheres always occurs within the social and environmental contexts. At the same time, our economic actions often have important impacts on the larger physical and social contexts. A useful understanding of economics must take into account the most critical interactions between the economy and its contexts, showing how the economy is in various ways enabled and constrained by the contexts in which it is embedded, and how these environmental and social influences *on* the economy are in turn affected *by* the economy. In the next section, we discuss economic activity in the three spheres in more detail.

Discussion Questions

1. Describe three situations in which economic behavior could affect its physical context and three ways in which economic behavior could affect its social context. How might these influences that the economy exerts on its contexts result in changing how the contexts, in turn, affect (either support or constrain) economic activity?
2. Model building is sometimes compared to map making. If you wanted to give people directions for reaching the place where you live, what would you put on the map that you drew for them? What would you put on the map you drew if someone asked you about good places to go hiking, where the highest point is, or how close you are to your town boundary? Is it possible for a single, readable map to answer every possible question? Does your goal for the map affect what you put on it?

3. THE THREE SPHERES OF ECONOMIC ACTIVITY

As we mentioned above, economic activity takes place in three major spheres, which we designated as the core, public purpose, and business spheres. In other economics writings, the terms used are "household," "government," and "business." In this text, we use the term "core" instead of "household" to emphasize the importance of communities, in addition to households, in the "core" activities described below. (Think of the maxim "It takes a village to raise a child.") We use the term "public purpose" instead of "government" to include both government organizations and the nongovernmental nonprofit organizations whose activities are of growing importance in modern societies. Many economic activities are conducted through markets, but some activities, especially in the core sphere, take place outside of markets. In this chapter, we give an overall view of the three spheres and then focus on the nature and workings of markets in more detail in Chapter 3.

1.1 THE CORE SPHERE

Long before the invention of money, organized markets, and systems of government, human societies organized themselves along lines of kinship and community to undertake the economic activities essential to maintaining and improving the conditions for human life. The **core sphere** is made up of household, family, and community institutions that undertake economic activities, usually on a small scale, and largely without the use of money. Even in modern societies, the core sphere is still the primary site for raising children, preparing meals, maintaining homes, taking care of the mildly ill, and organizing activities among family members, friends, and neighbors.

core sphere: households, families, and communities

One distinguishing characteristic of the core sphere is how work activities are rewarded: Instead of earning money, work tends to be rewarded directly by what it produces. For example, work in a home garden is rewarded with tomatoes, and the reward of good child care is a happy and healthy child. People may volunteer their services to their community because they recognize that living in a healthy community is important. People play cards, softball, or music together because they find these activities intrinsically enjoyable. Another distinguishing characteristic is that activities in the core sphere are organized to respond not only to *wants* but also, importantly, to *needs*—unlike market activities, which respond to what people are able and willing to pay for (regardless of need).

The core sphere is obviously critical for subsistence economies, where extended families and villages may raise or make for themselves most of what they consume, with little outside trading. Although reliance on the core sphere has to some extent been reduced in the United States and many other countries by the increasing use of prepared foods, child-care centers, restaurants, commercial forms of entertainment, nursing homes, housecleaning services, and the like, it remains of central importance for the maintenance and flourishing of any economy.

Core sphere activities, however, have been—and sometimes still are—often described as noneconomic or nonproductive because they generally do not produce goods and services for trade through a market. However, consider just one activity that takes place in the core sphere: the help provided by relatives, friends, and neighbors that enables seniors to remain in a home setting rather than entering a nursing facility. If we were to value the actual unpaid time invested in these activities in the United States at a low wage of $8–$9 an hour, we would find that each year about $300 billion to $400 billion worth of elder care is provided in the core sphere—without being recorded in gross domestic product (GDP) statistics.* For comparison, this amount exceeds the total annual expenditures on nursing-care services, including both private and public spending.

*Estimates of unpaid elder care in "Valuing the Invaluable: A New Look at the Economic Value of Family Caregiving," AARP Policy Brief, http://assets.aarp.org/rgcenter/il/ib82_caregiving.pdf.

According to one estimate, between a third and half of all economic activity in industrialized countries consists of unpaid labor that is not counted in GDP.[1] Recognizing the value of unpaid work is important if we are to make a comprehensive assessment of well-being. To quote from a recent report:

> Unpaid work contributes not only to current household consumption (e.g., cooking) but also to future well-being (e.g., parental investments in raising children) and to community well-being (e.g., voluntary work). In all countries, women do more of such work than men, although to some degree balanced—by an amount varying across countries—by the fact that they do less paid work.[2]

When the core sphere is working effectively to support the quality of life, important goods and services are provided to many people, even if the scale of production in each specific case is quite small. Because most core sphere activities involve face-to-face interaction, the core sphere is the primary location in which the ability to form good social relations is developed.

Of course, core spheres can also work badly or inadequately. For example, responsibilities for children, the elderly, and ill people may be inequitably assigned between women and men. Such responsibilities may also overwhelm the personal resources of impoverished families and communities. There are limits to what can be accomplished within small-scale, largely informal networks of personal relations. For many economic goals, more formal and larger-scale organizations are also needed. The public purpose sphere is uniquely capable of meeting certain well-being needs.

3.2 THE PUBLIC PURPOSE SPHERE

public purpose sphere: governments as well as other organizations that seek to enhance well-being without making a profit

The **public purpose sphere** includes governments and their agencies, as well as nonprofit organizations such as charities, religious organizations, professional associations, and international institutions such as the World Bank and the United Nations. They may be as large as a national government or an international scientific organization or as small as a Cub Scouts group or an organization whose only goal is the protection of a landmark building. The distinguishing characteristic of these institutions is that they exist for an explicit purpose related to the public good—that is, the common good of some group larger than a household or informal community—and they do not aim at making a profit.

Some of the larger public purpose organizations often associated with some level of government, are charged with purposes such as defending a country's borders, relieving poverty, providing formal health care and education, protecting the natural environment, and stabilizing global financial markets. Religious organizations are other well-known public purpose organizations, associated with governments in some countries but not in the United States. Small nonprofits may be found working on local issues such as the preservation of a particular park or providing homeless people with shelter.

Organizations in the public purpose sphere tend to be more formally structured than those in the core sphere, and usually they are more monetized, though a public purpose organization can lie anywhere on a spectrum of those that rely entirely on voluntary work to those that pay for all work done to achieve their ends. Even in the latter case, however, people will often accept pay for jobs in the public purpose sector that is lower than the going wages for comparable work in the business sphere.

The reason for this is twofold. First, public purpose organizations are often scraping by with financial resources too small to achieve their goals and are therefore more careful to watch every dollar than is necessary in some businesses. In addition, many people are willing to accept lower salaries in public purpose work because they receive an additional psychic benefit in the feeling that their work is meaningful.

In some instances public purpose organizations offer goods and services for sale as businesses do, but this is generally not their primary focus. They usually raise much of their support by soliciting monetary contributions or, in the case of governments, requiring such contributions in the form of taxes or fees. Your college or university, for example, may be either a nonprofit or government entity (i.e., operated by the city, county, or state). As another example, public (that is, government-supported) hospitals in the United States provide emergency medical care to the poor and uninsured.

public good: a good whose benefits are freely available to anyone, and whose use by one person does not diminish its usefulness to others

The public purpose sphere is able to provide goods and services that cannot, or would not, be adequately provided by core sphere institutions and businesses alone. Some of the goods and services that it provides are what economists call public goods. A **public good** (or service) is freely available to anyone (or some people could be excluded from using it only with difficulty), and use of a public good by one person does not diminish the ability of another person to benefit from it.

For example, when a local police force helps to make a neighborhood safe, all the residents benefit. Public roads (at least those that are not congested and have no tolls) are also public goods, as is national defense. Education and quality child care are in a sense public goods because everyone benefits from living with a more skilled and socially well-adjusted population. A system of laws and courts provides the basic legal infrastructure on which all business contracting depends. We discuss public goods in more detail in Chapter 14.

The public purpose sphere is a substantial contributor to U.S. economic activity. In 2010, the value of the production by nonprofit organizations was 5.5 percent of GDP, and federal, state, and local governments contributed 12.3 percent of GDP—for a total share of about 18 percent.[3]

The main strength of public purpose institutions is that (like core institutions) they provide goods and services of high intrinsic value, but (unlike core institutions) they are big enough to take on jobs that require broader social coordination. The provision of goods and services itself, and not the financial results of these activities, remains the primary intended focus of public purpose organizations, in contrast to the business sphere.

Overall, a larger amount of the work that is undertaken by governments in other industrialized countries is taken care of by either the business or the nonprofit sector in the United States. Canada and countries in most of Europe, for example, put more government resources into health and social welfare than is the case in the United States. However, the United States has traditionally been a leader in charitable and philanthropic support for private, nonprofit organizations in this sphere.

The public purpose sphere has its weaknesses, of course. Compared to the core sphere, the government, in particular, is often criticized as cold and impersonal. Some parents prefer to home school, for example, rather than accept what they characterize as "one size fits all" public education. Compared to for-profit businesses, not-for-profit institutions and governments are sometimes accused of being rigid, slow to adapt, and crippled by inefficiency through impenetrable regulations and a bloated bureaucracy. Organizations can lose sight of the goal of providing "public service" and become more interested in increasing their own organizational budgets. Public purpose organizations are commonly supported by taxes or donations that are often not tightly linked to the quality of their services. For this reason, they may not have a *financial* incentive to improve the quality of what they provide. Many current debates about reforms in both governments and nonprofits concern how efficiency and accountability can be improved without eroding the commitment of these organizations to providing valuable goods and services.

Public purpose organizations respond to the demands of their "public," whether voters, members, or other participants. Nonprofit organizations frequently offer services related to religion, education, health, and welfare. Sometimes, they offer these services only within a particular community (such as to members of a certain religion); at other times, they work more widely and may receive subsidies from the government. Some such organizations may have goals that are directly at odds with other public purpose organizations; for example, organizations working to support gay families seek outcomes that differ from those sought by organizations that aim to maintain exclusively the traditional family headed by a married man and woman.

Because definitions of the public good vary, some people will reject the "public purpose" of some of these organizations. For example, a few nonprofit organizations are thinly disguised hate groups. Trade organizations and labor unions promote the interests of (some of) their own members, while other members of society may disagree with their agendas. A continuing issue with government institutions is the question of *whose* interests are represented. Majority groups? Outspoken minority groups? Special interests who donate money to campaigns? Yet, because of the nature of public goods and the general interests of social welfare, the question cannot be *whether* to have a public purpose sphere but only *how* to allow it to function well.

3.3 The Business Sphere

business sphere: firms that produce goods and services for profitable sale

The U.S. government defines businesses as "entities that produce goods and services for sale at a price intended at least to approximate the costs of production."[4] The **business sphere** is made up of such firms. A business firm is expected to look for opportunities to buy and manage resources in such a way that, after their product is sold, the owners of the firm will earn profits.

Whereas the core sphere responds to direct needs, and the public purpose sphere responds to its constituents, business firms are responsive to demands for goods and services, as expressed through markets by people who can afford to buy the firms' products.

Private for-profit enterprises in the United States and many other countries fall into four main legal forms: proprietorships, partnerships, corporations, and cooperatives. Proprietorships are businesses owned by single individuals or families. Partnerships are owned by a group of two or more individuals. Corporations are business firms that, through a process of becoming chartered by a state or federal government, attain a legal existence separate from the individuals or organizations who own it. Individual owners can come and go, but the corporation remains. If the corporation goes bankrupt and is forced to dissolve, the owners of a corporation cannot lose more than their investment. On the other hand, there is no legal limit to the profit they can make if the corporation is successful. This asymmetry, along with its other legal advantages, makes the corporation the preferred structure for major business activities in most countries.

Corporations that issue stock are governed by shareholders according to the principle of "one share, one vote." In principle, shareholders elect a board of directors, who in turn hire professional managers to run the day-to-day operations of the corporation. (In fact, shareholders often lack the power to propose directors other than those put forward by the existing board or management. There are ongoing struggles about how or whether to increase the investors' control in this respect.) Cooperatives, in contrast to corporations, cannot issue stock and are governed by a different ownership principle. Each member of the cooperative, no matter what his or her position, has one and only one vote. In practice, cooperatives are owned by one of three groups: their workers, their suppliers, or their consumers.

It is sometimes thought that maximizing profits is the *only* goal of businesses. But firms may not always aim for the highest profit for two main reasons.

First, some business managers cite being a good "corporate citizen," with regard to their workers, communities, or the environment, as a motivation for some of their actions. Businesses organized on a cooperative model (including large food-marketing organizations such as Land O'Lakes for dairy products and Ocean Spray for cranberries) explicitly state their purpose in terms of providing services to their members, rather than in terms of profit. Still, making enough profit to stay afloat is a goal of all well-run businesses. Some businesses may set a certain goal for profits while also pursuing other goals. Mindless profiteering, however—going after the last bit of profit at all costs, neglecting social and even ethical concerns—need not be how businesses are run.

Second, within a modern business corporation of any size, the activities of "the firm" are made up of the activities of many people, including its stockholders, board of directors, chief executive officer (CEO), mid- and top-level managers, and employees. The interests of the various individuals and suborganizations may be in conflict. Sometimes, top officers and managers may act, for example, not in the profit-making interest of the owners but according to their *personal* self-interest. That is, they may seek to maximize their own prestige and incomes, even when this goes against the interests of everyone else involved in the firm, including those who have invested in it. Profits, and even the long-term survival of the company itself, may be sacrificed in a race for individual high salaries and lucrative bonuses.

One strength of business organizations is that because they have at least one clear goal—making a profit—their efficiency in operating to reach that goal may be greater than the efficiency of activities in the other two spheres. A profit orientation is commonly thought to drive firms to choose the most (market) valuable outputs to produce and to produce them at the least possible cost—where, again, costs are determined by the forces of the market. (In Chapter 3 we begin a much closer look at how markets determine prices; ability to pay is just one of the relevant forces.)

Another advantage of the profit motivation is that it encourages *innovation:* People are more motivated to come up with clever new ideas when they know that they may reap financial rewards. We all benefit, in terms of our material standard of living, from business efficiency and from innovations when they bring us improved products at lower prices.

The relative weakness of the business sphere comes from the fact that business interests do not necessarily coincide with overall social well-being. Firms *may* act to enhance social well-being—for example, by making decisions that consider all the needs of their customers and their workers and take into account externalities, including those that affect the natural environment. They *may* be guided in these directions by the goodwill of their owners and managers, by pressure from their customers or workers, or by government regulation.

Production for market exchange, however, has no *built-in* correction for market externalities; this is, indeed, a way to remember the meaning of the term "externalities"—it refers to things that are external to the interests of the firm (or of any other economic actor in question). We will discuss externalities in more detail in Chapter 13. Moreover, sometimes "innovation" can take a perverse form. In the late 1990s, for example, Enron boosted its reported earnings primarily by inventing unusual and "innovative" accounting practices, which served to hide the extreme weakness of its financial situation from investors. Similarly, "innovative" investment and accounting practices were a major cause of the financial crisis of 2008, as will be discussed in Chapter 30. In fields such as health care and education, where it can be difficult to define clear goals, businesses may increase profits by "innovatively" cutting corners on the less-measurable and less-often-marketed aspects of quality of life.

The potential for social harm grows when firms gain excessive market power—that is, when they come to dominate the market in their area. They may then be able to charge socially inefficient prices (as we discuss in Chapter 18) or to squelch socially advantageous innovations by competing firms. Industrialized countries also have considerable power to harm the natural environment on which they ultimately depend. Thus market economies today face a major conundrum: How can societies continue to benefit from the strengths of the business sphere while ensuring that this sphere supports the kind of world that will sustain the livelihoods and the well-being of future generations? For one example of the debate over the allocation of certain economic activities to the business sphere, see Box 2.2.

BOX 2.2 PRIVATE PRISONS

The United States has more prisoners than any other country, not only in absolute numbers but also on a per-capita basis. Up until the 1980s, prisons in the U.S. were operated exclusively by state and federal government agencies. But since 1984, a growing share of U.S. prisons are being operated by for-profit companies. Currently, around 130,000 prisoners in the United States, or 9 percent of the prison population, are housed in prisons operated by private companies. The main argument in favor of prison privatization is that for-profit companies will have an incentive to identify economic efficiencies, and thus reduce prison operation costs to taxpayers.

However, a 2011 report on private prisons reported that most studies indicate little or no cost savings when prisons are turned over to for-profit companies. Analysis of private prisons in Arizona found that per-prisoner costs were actually *higher* in private prisons. The report concluded that:

> the supposed benefits (economic and otherwise) of private prisons often fail to withstand scrutiny. The view that private prisons save taxpayer money, fuel local economies, and adequately protect the safety of prisoners helps to feed mass incarceration by making privatization appear to be an attractive alternative to reducing prison populations. But the evidence for such benefits is mixed at best. Not only may privatization fail to save taxpayer money, but private prison companies, as for-profit institutions, are strongly incentivized to cut corners and thereby maximize profits, which may come at the expense of public safety and the well being of prisoners. (ACLU, 2011, p. 18)

For example, a 2007 audit of a private prison in Texas found deplorable conditions, with prisoners denied medical care, refused access to their lawyers, and forced to live in their own wastes due to a lack of toilets. One study found that private prisons hire fewer guards than public prisons, leading to higher rates of violence.

Another implication of prison privatization is that companies that operate prisons lobby legislators for higher incarceration rates and longer prison terms. The largest prison company, Corrections Corporation of America, hired 199 lobbyists in 32 states between 2003 and 2011. Prison companies are normally paid on a per-prisoner basis, so they have an incentive to house as many prisoners as possible. A 2013 article on private prisons concluded that:

> unless authorities implement significant changes, including regular inspections and holding private institutions to humane standards, private prisons are not a solution. Corporations which benefit from longer prison stays must also be removed from discussions of sentencing and drafting legislation.

Sources: American Civil Liberties Union, *Banking on Bondage: Private Prisons and Mass Incarceration* (New York, 2011); Paul, Samakow, "Private Prisons: The Worst of the American Dream," *The Washington Times*, July 7, 2013.

3.4 THE SIZE OF THE THREE SPHERES

Figure 2.3 presents estimates of the monetary value of the annual production of goods and services in the United States by the three spheres in 2010, in dollar and percentage terms. The business sphere contributed 58 percent of production, the core sphere contributed 32 percent, and the public purpose sphere contributed 10 percent. The dollar figures add up to more than GDP in that year ($14.7 trillion) because an estimate of the value of unpaid household labor as equal to one-third of the value of GDP has been included. This differs from government estimates of GDP, which do not currently include the value of household production.

3.5 A COMPARATIVE NOTE: LESS INDUSTRIALIZED COUNTRIES

Many less industrialized countries have large **informal spheres** of small market enterprises operating outside government oversight and regulation. Although this sphere could be classified as business because it involves private production for sale, it is also similar to the core sphere in that the activities are very small-scale and often depend on family and community connections. Like activities in the core sphere, informal business activities are often excluded from government-compiled accounts. In the United States, illegal drug trades and house-cleaning services provided "off the books" are two examples of the informal sphere. In less

Figure 2.3 **Estimated Size of the Three Spheres of Economic Activity in the United States, 2010**

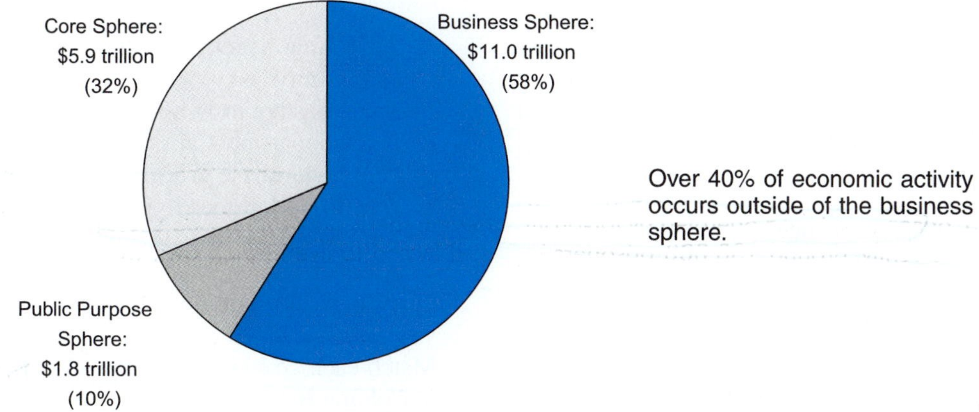

Sources: U.S. Census Bureau, *Statistical Abstract of the United States, 2012* (Washington, D.C.: GPO, 2011); Katie Roeger, Amy S. Blackwood, and Sarah L. Pettijohn, *The Nonprofit Almanac 2012* (Washington, D.C.: Urban Institute Press, 2012); and authors' calculations.

industrialized countries, however, it is sometimes the case that *most* people are employed in small-scale agriculture, trade, and services, which often go uncounted.

If this textbook were being written for use in developing countries, it would be necessary to pay a great deal more attention to the complicating reality of informal economic activity and perhaps to discuss it as a fourth sphere. However, in a text for use in industrialized countries, we can deal with this issue by simply noting, as we have just done, that informal economic activity could legitimately be classified as occurring within either the business sphere or the core sphere, leaving open the question of which of these classifications is more appropriate.

Discussion Questions

1. Education is sometimes provided within the core sphere (at-home preschool activities and home schooling), is often provided by the public purpose sphere (public and nonprofit schools), and is occasionally provided by for-profit firms ("charter schools" or firms offering specific training programs). Can you think of some possible advantages and disadvantages of each of these three ways of providing education?
2. Make a list of several things that, over the past few days, you have eaten, drunk, been entertained by, been transported by, been sheltered by, or received other services from (e.g., "dinner at Gina's," "my apartment," and "the health clinic"). Then, using the definitions in this section, determine which of the three spheres of economic activity provided each item.

Review Questions

1. What are the three main modes of economic investigation? Describe each.
2. What is a positive (direct) relationship? What is a negative (inverse) relationship?
3. What is a model? How does the *ceteris paribus* assumption simplify the creation of a model?
4. What are some of the assumptions of the basic neoclassical model? Why are markets said to be efficient according to this model?
5. What does a contextual economic model take into account that is not present in the basic neoclassical model?
6. What are some major characteristics of the core sphere?
7. What are some major characteristics of the public purpose sphere?
8. Why do businesses find it difficult to supply "public goods"?
9. What is a public good? Why might it be difficult for private businesses to supply public goods?
10. What is the informal sphere? Where is it most significant?

EXCERCISES

1. Consider the following data, taken from the *Economic Report of the President* 2013. Perform the graphing exercises below using either pencil and graph paper or a computer spreadsheet or presentation program.

Year	Unemployment rate (%)	Inflation (% per year)
2005	5.1	3.4
2006	4.6	2.5
2007	4.6	4.1
2008	5.8	3.8
2009	9.3	–0.4
2010	9.6	1.6
2011	8.9	3.2
2012	8.1	2.1

   a. Looking at the data listed in the chart, can you detect a trend in the unemployment rate during these years? In the inflation rate? If so, what sort of trends do you see?
   b. Create a time-series graph for the unemployment rate during 1992–99.
   c. Create a scatter-plot graph with the unemployment rate on the horizontal axis and inflation on the vertical axis.
   d. Using your graph in part (c), do the two variables seem to have an empirical relationship during this period, or do the points seem to be randomly scattered? If there appears to be an empirical relationship, is it inverse or direct?

2. Identify the sphere in which each of the following activities takes place. Could some involve more than one sphere?
   a. Recycling is picked up at curbside in a community
   b. Tomatoes are grown in a home garden
   c. A fire department answers an emergency call
   d. People purchase groceries at a supermarket
   e. A fifth-grader goes to public school
   f. A ninth-grader goes to a private high school
   g. An environmental protection group lobbies for stronger pollution control laws

3. Match each concept in Column A with an example in Column B.

Column A	Column B
a. Theoretical investigation	1. U.S. GDP from 2001 to 2010
b. A core sphere activity	2. Perfectly competitive markets
c. Time-series data	3. A city park
d. A public purpose sphere activity	4. Einstein develops the theory of relativity
e. A public good	5. Police Services
f. An assumption of the basic neoclassical model	6. An economists studies the Great Depression
g. Ceteris paribus	7. Home care for the elderly
h. Historical investigation	8. All variables except one are held constant

NOTES

1. Miranda Vreel, "Cooking, Caring, and Volunteering: Unpaid World Around the World," OECD Social Employment and Migration Working Papers, No. 116, 2011.
2. Ibid., p. 30.
3. Katie L. Roeger, Amy S. Blackwood, and Sarah L. Pettijohn, The Nonprofit Almanac 2012 (Washington, D.C.: Urban Institute Press, 2012); U.S. Census Bureau, The Statistical Abstract of the United States, 2012 (Washington, D.C.: GPO, 2011).
4. www.bea.gov/scb/account_articles/national/0398niw/maintext.htm.

3 Markets and Society

An important area of interest—and dispute—among economists concerns how markets function. As we saw in the previous chapter, the basic neoclassical model is based on the idea that market systems function fairly smoothly, are largely self-regulating, and if mostly left alone will produce the most efficient economic outcomes. Others believe that without some important modifications through government policy or regulation, as well as from other forces of culture and ethics, market economies may serve only some people, and some goals of human well-being, while endangering others.

Beyond noting that markets really do bring about some good and some bad results, there is no simple way to resolve these differences. Economists who worry about negative results, such as extreme inequality, or concentrations of power that can work against democracy, nevertheless recognize the importance of markets, while seeking to moderate some of their negative effects.

Before we address these debates more specifically, it will be essential to understand what, in fact, economists mean by markets.

1. Three Definitions of Markets

When people talk about markets, they may be referring to a number of different meanings of the word, from very concrete to very abstract. The language of economics has at least three different uses of the word "market," and the appropriate meaning must be judged from the context in which it appears. We will start with the most concrete and move toward the more abstract definitions.

1.1 Markets as Places to Buy and Sell

market (first meaning): a place (physical or virtual) where there is a reasonable expectation of finding both buyers and sellers for the same product or service

The most concrete and commonsense definition of a **market** is that it is a place where people go to buy and sell things. Historically markets have been physical locations. For example, the Grand Bazaar in Istanbul, Turkey, is one of the world's oldest and largest covered markets in the world, dating to the fifteenth century. The Grand Bazaar now has more than 3,000 shops and attracts hundreds of thousands of visitors every day. The Grand Bazaar and produce stands in African villages have flourished for ages as meeting places for people who wish to engage in exchange transactions.

In the context of the contemporary world, many different kinds of physical markets have these same functions. They can be a single store, a shopping mall with many retail stores sharing one structure, or a livestock auction. A market, as suggested by these examples, can be defined as a physical place where there is a reasonable expectation of finding both buyers and sellers for the same product or service.

But in modern societies, markets do not necessarily need to be physical places. One can now easily make purchases online that in the past required physically going to a store. Amazon and eBay are modern examples of "places" where buyers and sellers can also come together.

1.2 Markets as Social Institutions

market (second meaning): an institution that facilitates economic interactions among buyers and sellers

institutions: ways of structuring human activities based on customs, habits, and laws

The term "market" can also refer to economic activity that is not confined to a single place such as a shopping mall or a Web site. A more general definition is that a market is an "institution" that facilitates economic interactions among buyers and sellers.

To understand this definition of a market, we first have to understand what we mean by an **institution**. Once again, we have a word that can be understood in several ways. An institution can be a physical location, such as penal institutions (prisons), mental institutions (psychiatric hospitals), or institutions for housing parentless children (orphanages). This meaning is, in fact, incorporated into the U.S. Census in a number of instances in which the people being counted are specified as the "noninstitutionalized population"—meaning that they are neither in prisons nor in long-term hospital care.

However, an institution in an economic sense is more than a physical structure. The term refers to the ways of structuring economic activities based on customs, habits, and laws. Thus we can speak, for example, of the institutional structure of health care in the United States as one that is based on private care for many working-age adults, Medicare for older adults, and Medicaid for low-income children, families, and people with disabilities. This institutional structure also includes the federal and state laws regarding health care, the rules of health insurance companies, customary procedures about doctor visits, and so on.

When we view markets as institutions, we can see that they not only bring buyers and sellers into communication with each other but also structure and coordinate their interactions. Specific market institutions come in many types. Credit cards are a type of market institution that facilitates purchases when a consumer does not have enough cash readily available. Consumer protection laws are a market institution that defines certain exploitative business practices and makes them illegal. The ability to return purchased products for a refund can also be viewed as a widely accepted market institution.

market (third meaning): an economic system (a "market economy") that relies on market institutions to conduct many economic activities

Thinking of markets as institutions, rather than places, leads to definitions of markets for particular goods and services or categories of goods and services. For example, we can speak of the "real estate market" in a particular city or even the entire country. We can define the market for used cars, the market for wind turbines, or the market for luxury goods. Speaking of the "stock market" in a broad sense is another common example of a market as an institution, whereas the New York Stock Exchange would be a market according to our first definition, as a place where buyers and sellers come together.

We can define markets at various levels of detail depending on our interests. Thus we can analyze the wheat market or be more specific and study the market for No. 2 dark winter wheat or No. 1 dark northern spring wheat. Or we might delineate a market based on geographic location, such as the New England market for home heating oil.

1.3 "The Market" as an Economic System

In the most abstract terms, people sometimes refer to markets as an economic system, for example, describing the United States as having a "market economy" or indicating a preference for "free markets." In this macroeconomic sense, a market economy is one that relies on markets (as social institutions) to conduct economic activities, rather than relying on other institutions.

When you think of an alternative to a market economy, you might think of a system that relies on central planning to conduct economic activities, as was the case in the Soviet Union. But we should realize that, even in modern market economies, many economic activities are not structured by markets. For example, decisions about resource maintenance are not always made based on markets, but often on scientific evidence or political preferences. The distribution of economic resources within the core sphere is normally made based on social or family relationships rather than market forces.

The view of markets as an economic system underlies some of the most heated current debates in economics; one side takes a "pro-market" view, and the other side takes an "anti-market" view. Market advocates claim that "free markets" and a **laissez-faire economy** (one with very little government regulation) lead to economic growth and prosperity. Others believe that markets can provide social benefits in many cases, but that unchecked and unregulated markets can contribute to problems such as poverty, inequality, environmental degradation, and an erosion of social ethics. As we examine different issues throughout this book, we frequently refer to these perspectives and this continuing debate.

laissez-faire economy: an economy with little government regulation

Discussion Questions

1. In what sense is the term "market" being used in each of the following sentences? "Go to the market and get some bananas." "The market is the best invention of humankind." "The labor market for new Ph.D.s is bad this year." "The advance of the market leads to a decline in social morality." "The market performance of IBM stock weakened last month." Can you think of other examples from your own readings or experience?
2. Do you think the U.S. economy can be described as a free market? Why or why not?

2. Institutional Requirements for Markets

Contemporary markets do an amazing thing: They allow many separate decision makers, acting in a decentralized manner, to coordinate their behavior, resulting in highly complex patterns of economic activity. However, in order for markets to operate smoothly, they depend on a number of even more basic institutions. We classify these in four broad groups:

1. individualist institutions related to property and decision making
2. social institutions of trust
3. infrastructure for the smooth flow of goods and information
4. money as a medium of exchange.

2.1 Individualist Institutions of Property and Decision Making

Before people can begin to think about making a market transaction, they have to be clear about what belongs to whom. Ownership is usually defined through systems of property rights set out in law and enforced by courts and police. These rights define what is **private property** and how economic actors can manage their property. Markets require that economic actors be free to make decisions about voluntarily trading their private property (including their financial assets) for others' property. Also, prices must not be under the complete control of a central planning agency but are generally determined by the interactions of market participants themselves.

private property: ownership of assets by nongovernment economic actors

The institutions of private property and individualist decision making exist both formally, in codes of law, and informally, in social norms. For example, some Western economists expected markets to grow quickly in the former republics of the Soviet Union after communism was dismantled and market opportunities opened up. However, many people living in these countries were accustomed to being told by the state where to work and what to do. Norms of individual entrepreneurship, it turns out, do not just arise naturally. Nor did other sorts of market infrastructure appear quickly, and the post-Soviet Russian economy went into a severe decline for some time.

2.2 Social Institutions of Trust

A second critical institutional requirement for markets is that a degree of trust must exist between buyers and sellers. When a buyer puts down her payment, she must trust that the seller will hand over the merchandise and that it will be of the expected quality. A seller must be able to trust that the payment offered is valid, whether in the form of currency, personal check, credit card, or online payment. Consider that the online auction site eBay could not operate unless winning bidders were confident that they would receive their products.

One way in which trust is built up is through the establishment of direct, one-to-one relationships. If you have dealt with some people in the past and they treated you fairly, you are likely to choose them when it comes time to trade again. Even in sophisticated contemporary economies, this kind of confidence plays an important role. Companies know which suppliers they can count on to come through on time, and consumers patronize stores where they feel comfortable.

Reputation also can be important in creating trust. A buyer might be fleeced by a seller in a transaction, but if that buyer spreads the word, the seller may suffer a damaged reputation and a loss of customers. Online reviews provide useful information about which products and merchants are reliable. Marketers try to capitalize on the tendency of buyers to depend on reputation by using advertising to link certain expectations about quality and price to a recognizable brand name and thus creating "brand loyalty" among repeat customers.

Cultural norms and ethical or religious codes can also help to establish and maintain an atmosphere of trustworthiness. The functioning of markets is facilitated by having enough members of a society subscribe to a common moral code and not betray one another's trust.

explicit contract: a formal, often written agreement that states the terms of an exchange and may be enforceable through a legal system

implicit contract: an informal agreement about the terms of a market exchange, based on verbal discussions or on traditions and normal expectations

In addition to broad cultural ethics, markets depend on specific legal structures. A "contract" is a general set of terms that structure a market exchange. **Explicit contracts** are formal, usually written, contracts that provide a legally enforceable description of the agreed-on terms of exchange. Explicit contracts can be quite complex, including many clauses to cover a multitude of contingencies (such as "If goods are not delivered by June 1, the price paid will be reduced to . . . "). They may involve many parties, as in a contract between a union and an employer. For formal contracts to work, there must be laws that state the parties' legal obligation to honor contracts and establish penalties for those who fail to do so.

An **implicit contract** is said to exist when the parties have agreed informally about the terms of their exchange. Such agreement may be based on verbal discussions or on traditions and normal expectations.

In modern societies, many market encounters take place between strangers who are unlikely ever to meet again and may not even share the same traditions and moral codes. In such cases, the formal institutions of explicit contracts are often needed. Even with a system of formal contracts, however, social norms are still essential. Detailed formal contracts are costly to write and costly to enforce. It is not practical to police every detail of every contract, and it is impossible to cover every conceivable contingency. The legal system can work smoothly only if most people willingly obey most laws and believe that it is dishonorable to cheat.

In effect, relationships, social norms, and the government-created apparatus of law are institutions that must exist side by side, reinforcing one another. None of these alone can carry the whole burden of making complex contracts work and, hence, make markets possible.

2.3 Infrastructure for the Smooth Flow of Goods and Information

physical infrastructure: roads, ports, railroads, warehouses, and other tangible structures that provide the foundation for economic activity

A third set of institutions needed for market functioning has to do with making possible a smooth flow of goods and information. Most obviously, a **physical infrastructure** is needed for transportation and storage. Such infrastructure includes roads, ports, railroads, and warehouses in which to store goods awaiting transport or sale. This sort of infrastructure can be most noticeable when it is absent, as in economies ravaged by war or natural diseaster.

In addition, an infrastructure must be in place for information to flow freely. Producers and sellers need information on what and how much their customers want to buy. At the same time, consumers need to know what is available and how much of something else they will have to give up (i.e., how much they will have to pay) to obtain the products that are on the market. Ideally, in fact, consumers should be able to compare *all* potential purchases as a basis for deciding what to acquire and what to do without. Although this ideal is unlikely to be attained, access to the Internet, as well as more traditional sources of information such as newspapers and radio, have greatly expanded the flow of market information.

2.4 MONEY AS A MEDIUM OF EXCHANGE

The final basic institution required to facilitate the operation of markets is a generally accepted form of money. Many different things have been used as money in the past. Early monetary systems used precious or carved stones, particular types of seashells, or other rare goods. Gold, silver, and other metal coins were the most common choice for many centuries. More recently, paper currency has become important. Today, the use of checks, credit cards, and debit cards further facilitate making payments for goods and services.

What makes something **money**? Three criteria are necessary for something to be defined as money in a market economy.

money: a medium of exchange that is widely accepted, durable as a store of value, has minimal handling and storage costs, and serves as a unit of account

1. One obvious criterion is that money must be widely accepted as *a medium of exchange.* In other words, money is whatever everyone accepts as money. In this sense, money is a social institution of trust.
2. Money must provide *a durable store of value.* Imagine the problems that would occur if heads of lettuce were proposed as money. A form of money that starts to rot within a week or two would be difficult to use! The value of money must be relatively stable over time. In addition, money *must have minimal handling and storage costs.* By this criterion, paper currency is generally better than coins, and electronic transactions are better still.
3. Money must be accepted as a *unit of account.* When people say that something is worth $1,000, that does not necessarily mean that they are proposing to buy or sell the item. Money serves as a way of valuing things, even if no market exchange takes place.

In most cases, money is created or sanctioned by national governments. However, this is not essential. For example, cigarettes are often used as a form of money by prisoners. Also, communities smaller than national governments can create their own money. In recent years, local "time-banking" currencies have appeared in some communities in the United States and elsewhere. People earn time dollars by performing valuable services for others or for the community as a whole, such as child care, tutoring, or building repairs. Time dollars can then be used to pay for other services or used instead of "normal" dollars to purchase products from local merchants (see Box 3.1).

Discussion Questions

1. When you shop on-line, how do you know that you can trust the seller to deliver the goods as promised? What is necessary for the social institution of trust to work, and how might in break down, in on-line transactions?
2. Are you aware of situations in some countries or regions where physical and communications infrastructure is lacking, or poorly maintained? How do you think this affects economic development in these regions?

3. TYPES OF MARKETS

Markets take a wide variety of forms. They can be classified according to what is sold, how prices are determined, and the period covered.

3.1 MARKETS DEFINED BY WHAT IS SOLD

Recall from last chapter that we defined two basic market types—product and factor markets—in the traditional model of economic activity. In this section we further classify different types of markets.

retail markets: markets where goods and services are purchased by consumers from businesses, generally in small quantities

The most obvious and well-known product markets are those in which people buy goods and services from businesses. Such **retail markets** deal in food, books, clothes, haircuts, and so on. Some retail markets sell, instead of tangible objects, services such as banking or repairs for your car. Retail markets may be supplied directly by producers, but more often

Box 3.1 Time Banking

Time banking is a core sphere activity that uses a creative system to bring together unused human resources with unmet human needs. It is of interest because it is so closely related to *all* the spheres of economic activity. Time banking is a system of computerized credits operating within a defined location (it might be a hospital or nursing home, or a city, such as Portland, Maine). If you join a time bank system, you are initially issued a small number of credits; each one is a claim on one hour of time offered by someone else in the system. You list, in the central computer, the services that you can offer—from doing errands or cooking to carpentry or music lessons—and whenever you provide an hour of such service to someone else in the system, you receive a credit. Some interesting characteristics of the system include:

- It is a little like barter, only the person who receives your service does not need to be the same one who provides something for you in return.
- It is strictly non-monetized. However, it has been learned that it is usually necessary to have a small amount of money to pay an individual who will ensure that the central computerized system is operating smoothly.
- Some people join time banks who are not keen to do traditional volunteer work, because in the latter they sometimes feel that their time is valued at zero.

Time banks often have to grapple with an unexpected fact: Many people are more eager to give services than to receive them—as long as their service is recognized in some formal way. The resulting "balance of payments" problems have been solved in a variety of ways, such as asking people to donate their excess time dollars to day-care centers (which can call on time bank members to read to the children) or places where the residents are too ill to be able to offer anything in return. However, even in the latter case, there are often examples of receivers finding something that they can offer in return.

Time banks—more than 300 of them—exist in 23 countries. The largest one in New York City is the Visiting Nurse Service of New York Community Connections TimeBank. It has more than 2,000 members and is most active in three places—Upper Manhattan, Lower Manhattan, and parts of Brooklyn. Members come from all over New York City, but exchanges are easiest when people live in the same neighborhood. One example is Elayne Castillo-Vélez, who earns a credit for each hour she spends tutoring immigrant students who are having trouble learning English. She coordinates with the students' teachers to help focus her efforts. The students she has worked with have seen improvements in their grades and even won certificates for academic achievement. She spends her accumulated credits to take art classes.

Source: Tina Rosenberg, "Where All Work Is Created Equal," *New York Times,* September 15, 2011.

wholesale markets: markets where final goods are purchased by retailers from suppliers, normally in large quantities

intermediate goods market: a market for an unfinished product

resale market: a market for an item that has been previously owned

commodity market: a market for a raw material

labor market: a market in which employers interact with people who wish to work

they are supplied by distributors and brokers who trade in **wholesale markets,** which act as intermediaries between producers and retailers and tend to involve transactions in larger quantities. For example, Walmart and most other discount retailers don't actually produce the products they sell, but purchase them from suppliers in wholesale markets.

We can differentiate between wholesale markets and **intermediate goods markets**, which involve sales of unfinished products between businesses, such as the purchase of sheet metal by an automobile company. **Resale markets** are product markets for items that have been previously owned. Used-car markets are resale markets, as are markets for antique furniture. Most shares traded in stock markets are also being resold, having been previously owned by other investors. In **commodities markets**, raw materials such as agricultural products, minerals, or petroleum are bought and sold.

The **labor market** is a type of factor market, defined as the set of institutions through which people who wish to work offer to sell their services to employers: businesses, public agencies, nonprofit organizations, and households other than their own. Unlike a physical object, labor cannot be produced first and then handed to the buyer; rather, the worker promises to do something in return for a promised payment of wages. Labor markets are sufficiently different from other types of markets that this topic warrants separate treatment (in Chapter 10).

financial market: a market for loans, equity finance, and financial assets

Financial markets, also classified as factor markets, are markets for loans, equity finance, and financial assets such as stocks and bonds. An economic actor who needs money may get a loan from a bank. Businesses may sell shares of stocks—that is, small holdings that represent ownership rights in the firm—as a way to raise funds via "equity financing." Although corporations sometimes issue new shares of their stock to raise funds, as just noted nearly all the activity on stock markets is resale of existing stocks.

underground market: a market in which illegal goods and services are sold or legal goods and services are sold in an illegal way

Some markets operate outside the law. **Underground markets** (also sometimes called shadow markets or black markets) are illegal markets, normally for a type of product. It might be that the good or service itself is illegal, as are heroin, smuggled antiquities, and murder for hire. Or the markets deal in legitimate goods but in illegal ways. For example, smugglers may sell cigarettes or imported perfume at prices that do not include payment of required taxes.

3.2 Markets Defined by How Prices Are Determined

At first glance, it might seem as if many consumer retail markets violate one of the institutional requirements for markets that we mentioned above: that prices must generally be allowed to be set by the interactions of market participants themselves. In an old-fashioned open-air bazaar or flea market, buyers and sellers haggle about prices. But in a typical retail setting in an industrialized society, you do not "interact" so directly with the retailer to determine the price of bread or a shirt. The price is listed on the shelf, a tag, or directly on the product. Either you pay the **posted price** set by the seller, or you do not buy the item.

posted prices: prices set by a seller

Even though you do not haggle with the cashier at The Gap or at the supermarket, the fact that you *can* decide whether to buy is itself a form of interaction. Over time, retailers will take note of what moves off the shelf most quickly and will then order more of it and may also raise its price. They will also take note of what does not sell so quickly and will then reduce their order from wholesalers or mark the items down. The retailers' purchases from the wholesalers, in turn, give the suppliers information that they can use in deciding how much to order or produce and how to set *their* prices.

So while you may not be able to bargain directly, your actions, in combination with the actions of other customers, ultimately affect the prices and quantities offered in the market. These adjustments should tend, at least in theory, to lead posted prices to reflect what economists call the market-determined value, or **market value**, of the item. Market value, discussed in detail in Chapter 4, is the price as freely determined by voluntary interactions of buyers and sellers. The posted price is most likely to move to the market value if markets are competitive, the flow of information is good, the adjustment process is given enough time, and no big changes in market conditions occur in the meantime.

market value: the price for an item as freely determined by the voluntary interactions of buyers and sellers

auction market: a market in which an item is sold to the highest bidder

Auction markets are markets in which an item is sold to the highest bidder. Auction markets are used when the appropriate price for an item is relatively unknown and there are many possible buyers or sellers. Although in the past auction markets were commonly limited to goods such as antiques and artwork, the advent of online auction sites such as eBay have made auction markets much more prevalent. Real-world auctions offer interesting opportunities to observe how market values are determined.

open auction: an auction in which the opening price is set low and then buyers bid it up

Auction markets come in different types. In an **open auction**, an opening price is set low, and then potential buyers top one another's bids until only one bidder remains. This is what many people first think of when they think of an auction, and it is the main type of auction used on eBay.

Dutch auction: an auction in which the opening price is set high and then drops until someone buys

In a **Dutch auction**, an opening price is set high and then drops until a buyer offers to purchase the item. The name comes from its use in the Dutch wholesale cut-flower market. You can find numerous Dutch auction sites online, and stores that follow the practice of taking an extra 10 percent or 20 percent off the prices of unsold items each week are following a Dutch auction procedure.

sealed-bid auction: an auction in which bids are given privately to the auctioneer

Sealed-bid auctions get their name from the fact that the bids are given privately to the auctioneer, who then selects the winning bidder. In contrast to an open auction, the bidders are not supposed to know how much others value the item. Sealed-bid auctions are often used to sell commercial real estate (where the high-price buyer wins) and to allocate construction contracts (where the low-price seller of construction services wins).

double auction: an auction in which both the buyers and sellers state prices at which they are willing to make transactions

In a **double auction**, both buyers and sellers state prices at which they are willing to make transactions. The New York Stock Exchange is a double auction market. When you see pictures of traders on the stock exchange floor, they are shouting out bids either to buy or sell, and a sale can occur when the "bid" and "ask" prices become the same (although most stock transactions now occur electronically).

bargaining: an activity in which a single buyer and a single seller negotiate the terms of their exchange

Finally, in markets with **bargaining**, a *single* buyer and a *single* seller negotiate the price of an item, for which no definitive market value has been established. Residential real estate, for example, is generally sold by using such negotiated agreements, as are used cars. (Sometimes there is also a posted price, but both parties understand that it is merely a starting point for negotiation.)

Salaries of high-level managers, professionals, and unionized employees—and, notably, of sports and entertainment stars—are commonly set by bargaining. The presence of *potential* other buyers and sellers, however, is obviously important in determining the relative bargaining strength of the two parties. A seller who knows that he can easily find other eager buyers, for example, will quickly walk away from an unfavorable deal. A seller with fewer options will have less ability to hold out for good terms.

Discussion Questions

1. Reviewing the different types of markets outlined in this section, think about whether you have ever directly participated in a market of each type. If so, describe specific instances.
2. The Internet has opened up a whole new set of markets for everything from antiques to airplane tickets. Pool your knowledge with that of others in the class, and, for the types of markets listed in this section, think of as many examples as possible that are online.

4. Advantages and Limitations of Markets

In the previous chapter, we talked about the strengths and weaknesses of each of the three economic spheres—core, public purpose, and business. As we conclude this chapter with a discussion of the advantages and limitations of markets, it will be evident that these topics overlap, especially the strengths and weaknesses of the business sphere. The reason for this is obvious: The business sphere operates entirely through markets. But how does this differ from the core sphere, from which are drawn the people who are hired to work in businesses and which must purchase goods and services to serve the needs and wants of families, households, and communities? Or, indeed, from the public purpose sphere, which also hires workers through labor markets and purchases goods and services through other markets?

The essential characteristic that is common to businesses and to markets is the dominant role of the profit motive—as distinct from the motives of the other two spheres. We noted in the earlier discussion that this is not the *only* motive for businesses; however, in individual companies, as in the market as a whole, this motive affects many decisions and outcomes. Let us review the more and less desirable results of this fact.

The many advantages of markets as a way to conduct economic activities include how they allow a steady flow of information, in terms of prices and volumes of sales, that encourages producers to respond flexibly to consumer desires. Profits provide feedback to sellers about whether resources are being transformed in ways that individuals are willing (and able) to pay for. Markets also give people a considerable amount of freedom in deciding which activities to engage in, and they encourage some beneficial forms of innovation and social cooperation. Markets promote economic efficiency, and encourage technological innovation and entrepreneurship. But as we have noted, the idealized model of a completely free private market (as in the basic neoclassical model) rarely exists in practice. Actual market-oriented economies always include a mixture of decentralized private decision making and more public-oriented decision making.

This is not because voters and government officials are unaware of the advantages that markets can have in helping an economy run efficiently. Rather, it is because real-world economies include a number of important, complex factors that are not taken into account in the basic neoclassical model. We have already mentioned the issues of externalities and public goods, which will be discussed in detail in Chapters 13 and 14. Some other issues that we will briefly define and discuss here are transaction costs, market power, questions of information and expectations, and concerns over human needs and equity.

4.1 Transaction Costs

transaction costs: the costs of arranging economic activities

Transaction costs are the costs of arranging economic activities. In the basic neoclassical model, transaction costs are assumed to be zero. If a firm wants to hire a worker, for example, it is assumed that the only cost involved is the wage paid. In the real world, however, the activity of reaching a hiring agreement may involve its own set of costs.

The firm may need to pay costs related to searching, such as placing an ad in print or on the web or paying for the services of a recruiting company. The prospective worker may need to pay for preparation of a résumé and transportation to an interview. One or both sides might hire lawyers to make sure that the contract's terms reflect their interests. Because of the existence of such costs, some economic interactions that might lead to greater efficiency, and that would occur in an idealized, transaction cost–free, frictionless world, may not happen in the real world.

4.2 Market Power

market power: the ability to control, or at least affect, the terms and conditions of a market exchange

In the basic neoclassical model, all markets are assumed to be "perfectly competitive," such that no one buyer or seller has the power to influence the prices or other market conditions that they face. In the real world, however, we see that many firms have **market power**. For example, when there is only one firm (a monopolist) or a few firms selling a good, they may be able to use their power to increase their prices and their profits, creating inefficient allocations of resources in the process. Workers may also be able to gain a degree of market power by joining together to negotiate as a labor union. A government, too, can have market power, for example when the Department of Defense is the sole purchaser of military equipment from private firms.

Businesses may also gain power by their sheer size—many corporations now function internationally and have revenues in the tens of billions of dollars. The decisions of individual large corporations can have substantial effects on the employment levels, economic growth, living standards, and economic stability of regions and countries. Governments may need to factor in the responses of powerful business groups in making their macroeconomic decisions. National leaders may fear, for example, that raising business tax rates or the national minimum wage may cause companies to leave their country and go elsewhere. Corporations frequently also try to influence government policies directly, through lobbying, campaign contributions, and other methods. We explore the implications of corporate size at more length in Chapter 18.

4.3 Information and Expectations

static analysis: analysis that does not take into account the passage of time

In the basic neoclassical model, in which purely decentralized decisions lead to efficient outcomes, people are assumed to have easy access to all the information that they need to make good choices. This analysis is **static**; that is, it deals with an idealized case in a timeless manner. The model does not consider the time that it might take for a person to make a

dynamic analysis: analysis that takes into account the passage of time

decision or that it might take for a factory to gear up to produce a good. In the real, **dynamic**, world, obtaining good information may be difficult, and planning for an uncertain future is a big part of anyone's economic decision making.

A manufacturing business, for example, might be considering whether to borrow funds to build an additional factory. If the company's directors were able to know exactly what the demand for its products will be like in the future and what interest rates will be—along with additional information about things such as future wages, energy costs, and returns on alternative investments—the decision would be a simple matter of mathematical calculation.

But the directors will have to guess at most of these things. They will form expectations about the future, but these expectations may turn out to be incorrect. If their expectations are optimistic, they will tend to make the new investment and hire new workers. Often optimism is "contagious," and if a lot of *other* business leaders become optimistic, too, then the economy will boom. If, however, people share an attitude of pessimism, they may all tend to cut back on spending and hiring.

Because no one business wants to take the risk of jumping the gun by expanding too soon, it can be very difficult to get a decentralized market economy out of a slump. How people get their information, how they time their actions, and how they form their expectations of the future are all important topics that are not addressed in the basic neoclassical model. Taking these factors into account suggests why markets sometimes do not work as smoothly as that model suggests.

4.4 Human Needs and Equity

Another important issue concerns distribution of income and the ability to pay for goods and services. In the basic neoclassical model, the only consumer demands for goods and services that can affect the market are those that are backed up by a consumer's ability to pay. This has several implications.

First, there is nothing in the model that ensures that resources are distributed in such a way that people can meet their basic human needs. If a few rich people have a lot of money to spend on diamonds, for example, while a great number of poor people lack the money to pay for basic health care, "free markets" will motivate producers to respond to the demand for diamonds, but not to the need for basic health care.

For this reason, governments often adopt more deliberate policies of economic development, government provision, subsidies, or income redistribution, to try to ensure that decent living standards become more widespread. These policies can sometimes incorporate market mechanisms and sometimes replace them.

Second, the model does not take into account nonmarketed production, such as the care given to children, the sick, and the elderly by family and friends. There is nothing in the basic neoclassical model that ensures that these sorts of production will be supplied in adequate quantities and quality.

Lastly, it is also the case that problems such as unemployment and inflation tend to affect some people more than others, so how a country deals with these problems also has distributional consequences.

4.5 Conclusion

market failure: a situation in which markets yield inefficient or inappropriate outcomes

Clearly, although market systems have strong advantages in some areas, they cannot solve all economic problems. Economists sometimes use the term **market failure** to refer to a situation in which a market form of organization would lead to inefficient or harmful results. Because of the existence of public goods, externalities, transaction costs, market power, questions of information and expectations, and concerns for human needs and equity, macroeconomic systems cannot rely on "free markets" alone if they are to contribute effectively to present and future human well-being.

To some extent *private* nonmarket institutions may help remedy "market failure." For example, a group of privately owned factories located around a lake may voluntarily decide to restrict their waste emissions, because too much deterioration in water quality hurts them all. Likewise, a widespread custom of private charitable giving may help alleviate poverty. But sometimes the problems are so large or widespread that only government, *public* actions at the national or international levels seem to offer a solution. Exactly how much government action is required, and exactly what governments should do, however, are much-debated questions within contemporary economics.

Discussion Questions

1. On a sheet of paper, draw two columns. In one column, list some historical and contemporary advantages of market exchanges, and in the other, list some disadvantages. Can you give examples beyond those listed in the text?
2. "Indeed, it has been said that democracy is the worst form of government," said British Prime Minister Winston Churchill (1874–1965), "except all those other forms that have been tried from time to time." Some people make the same claim about more market-oriented forms of economic systems. What do they mean? Do you agree or disagree?

REVIEW QUESTIONS

1. Give three different meanings of the term "market."
2. Describe four main categories of institutional requirements for markets.
3. Give several examples of ways in which trust can be established.
4. Give several examples of the infrastructure necessary for markets to function.
5. List eight different types of markets in terms of what is sold.
6. List three major types of markets in terms of how prices are set.
7. What are some of the major advantages of markets?
8. How do transaction costs affect the workings of markets?
9. What are some of the implications of market power?
10. What is the difference between static and dynamic analysis?

EXERCISES

1. Give an example of each of the following:
   a. A retail market
   b. A commodity market
   c. A resale market
   d. A financial market
   e. An underground market
   f. An auction market
   g. A market with bargaining
2. Imagine trying to run a contemporary market economy without each of the following. What problems do you think would arise? What might people have to do to get around the lack of each one?
   a. Money
   b. The expectation that most people will not cheat
   c. An organized way of keeping people from adulterating foods or selling medicines that do not work
   d. A system of roads, canals, or railways
   e. Phone and computer connections
   f. An expectation that individuals will take the initiative in decision making
3. Match each concept in Column A with an example in Column B.

Column A	Column B
a. Explicit contract	1. Failure to account for environmental externalities
b. A strength of markets	2. A signed lease for an apartment
c. Implicit contract	3. An auction in which prices start high and go lower
d. Transaction cost	4. The expectation that roommates will contribute to rent
e. A drawback of markets	5. Legal services to draw up a contract
f. Dutch auction	6. An auction in which the price is bid up
g. Open auction	7. Effective information flow
h. Double auction	8. An auction in which both buyers and sellers state prices

Basic Economic Analysis

4 Supply and Demand

Prices are among the things considered central to any economy. Many people in the United States have been painfully affected by changes in housing prices, as the median price of a new house increased from about $170,000 in 2000 to about $250,000 in 2007, then fell to less than $220,000 at the bottom of the housing bust in 2009—and is now on the rise again, signaling, for many, the beginning of the end of the recent Great Recession (see Box 4.1).

To give a more relevant example for most students, textbook prices have risen over the past three decades, from an average of about $25 for an introductory economics textbook to an average of more than $200 in 2012. In other parts of the world, corn tortilla prices in Mexico doubled over several months in 2006–7, leading to mass protests. Between 2000 and 2002, coffee prices were cut in half, bringing hardship to many coffee growers—after 2005 they rebounded and in 2012 were higher than in 2000, but in 2013 they fell again to about 2000 levels.

Closely related to *prices,* as variables of economic interest, are *quantities* of things that are bought and sold in markets. When people dramatically decrease their purchases of goods and services, the businesses that had hoped to sell those things suffer—and so do the people working for those businesses, as falling sales result in lay-offs and reduced work hours. The U.S. automobile industry went through some miserable years in 2008–9, when employment fell from more than 1 million to only 650,000. China, in contrast, saw the quantity of new automobile sales increasing from only about 2 million per year in 2000 to more than 20 million by 2012.

To understand fluctuations in prices, and in the quantities of goods and services sold, it is necessary to understand the basics of market functioning. This chapter introduces the famous relationships between supply and demand, which go a long way toward explaining the workings of markets.

The basic concept, as you will see, is quite simple: In general, sellers (on the "supply" side) will want to supply more of what they sell if they can get higher prices, while on the "demand" side, buyers will generally be willing to buy more when prices are lower. Sellers and buyers thus want to see prices move in opposite ways. Some sort of balance, or equilibrium, has to be established between supply and demand.

demand: the willingness and ability of purchasers to buy goods or services

supply: the willingness of producers and merchandisers to provide goods and services

Note that as we continue to discuss this supply/demand relationship we use the term **demand** to indicate the willingness and ability of purchasers to buy goods and services, while **supply** means the willingness of producers to produce, and merchandisers to sell, goods and services.

BOX 4.1 RECOVERY IN THE HOUSING MARKET

The housing market is considered an important indicator of the overall economy. In the wake of the Great Recession, the average house price in the United States fell by about one-third between 2006 and 2011. Finally, in 2012 the housing market began to show signs of recovery. By the end of 2012 prices were rising at an annual rate of over 7 percent.

The rising prices are a function of both supply and demand factors. The number of homes sold nationally in 2012 was up by about 30 percent compared to the previous year. At the same time, the supply of homes for sale reached its lowest level since 2005.

The increase in house prices varied significantly across regions of the country. The biggest gains were found in areas hit the hardest when the housing bubble burst in 2007. Prices increased by 23 percent in Phoenix, 14 percent in Detroit, 13 percent in Las Vegas, and 10 percent in Miami. Of the 20 major metropolitan markets, only New York City saw further declines in house prices in 2012.

The reasons housing prices have increased recently include an improvement in the overall economy, lower unemployment rates, very low mortgage rates, and the tight supply. Richard Green of the USC Lusk Center for Real Estate, said the recovery in housing prices hasn't been even across all the different price segments. He said the upper end of the market has done well as wealthier families' earnings have recovered and foreign buyers have come into the market. The lower end of the market has recovered due to purchases by investors looking for bargains.

"It's the middle market that needs help—particularly in the form of higher income—if it is going to have a sustained recovery," Green said.

Source: Chris Isidore, "Housing Recovery Gains Strength," CNN Money, February 26, 2013.

1. INTRODUCTION TO THE MICROECONOMIC MARKET MODEL

In this chapter, we present the basic microeconomic model of how markets operate and adjust. This model forms the foundation for much of our discussion for the remainder of the book, as we extend it (in the next two chapters) and apply it to different types of markets (in later chapters). The roots of this model can be traced back to Adam Smith and the nineteenth-century school of classical economics (discussed further in Chapters 8 and 19). It was further refined in twentieth-century neoclassical theory, as discussed in Chapter 2, and has become an essential tool for much of economic analysis. The basic microeconomic market model is relatively simple, and, therefore, like all simple models, it inevitably misses many of the subtleties of what really happens in the world. But its great strength is that it summarizes in a concise and tidy way many valid observations about the workings of markets, which is why it has proved to be such an enduring contribution to economic theory.

As we go on to examine applications of the supply/demand model throughout this book, you will have plenty of opportunities to become an intelligent critic of basic economic theory, noticing when the model does and does not explain or predict events. First, however, it is necessary to go into considerable detail about how the simple model works.

The model considers two "market outcomes":

market price: the prevailing price for a specific good or service at a particular time in a given market

- **Market price:** the prevailing price for a specific good or service at a particular time in a given market. In our basic model, we assume that the good or service is narrowly defined such that we can speak of "the" current price, without any variation. For example, we could say that the market price for a can of soda on campus is $1.00. In this case, we have defined "the market" as "the market for cans of soda on campus." Although this price can change over time, it does not vary at any single point in time. Of course, in reality, there may be more than one place to buy soda on campus, and different places may charge different prices. We consider the impact of competition in a market in later chapters.

market quantity sold: the number of "units" of a specific good or service sold in a given market during a particular period

- **Market quantity sold:** the number of "units" of a specific good or service sold in a given market during a particular period. In the example above, "units" are cans of soda. Other markets may measure quantity sold in terms of "tons of wheat," "number of haircuts," or "gallons of gasoline." Note that we also need to define a particular time frame and location in our analysis. So we would define the market quantity as, say, "number of cans of soda sold on campus per week." Again, market quantities can vary over time, but we assume that market activity is constant within each time unit. So by defining the market quantity as "number of cans of soda sold on campus per week," we are not concerned about variation in quantity on a daily basis.

The basic microeconomic model involves the interaction of two economic actors, buyers (or consumers) and sellers (or producers and merchandisers). We can think of consumers as individuals, households, or even businesses buying supplies or raw inputs. Sellers are normally thought of as businesses, but this is not always the case. For example, the "sellers" in labor markets are individuals offering their labor services.

Another important feature of the microeconomic model is that both buyers and sellers are acting voluntarily. The model assumes that potential buyers are acting to enhance their own well-being. For example, you may be willing to voluntarily trade $1 for a can of soda because you believe that the transaction enhances your well-being. (In some real-world cases, it may not always be true that buyers always act in the interests of their own well-being—we will explore this issue further in Chapter 8.) The model also assumes that potential sellers are also acting to enhance their well-being, primarily by earning profits. However, sellers may act on the basis of other motivations, even at the expense of lower profits, such as a desire to conduct business with suppliers that treat their workers with certain ethical standards.

We now consider in more detail the behavior of buyers and sellers in markets. Specifically, we look at the relationship between market prices and quantities from each perspective, first from the point of view of sellers and then from the consumer perspective. After that, we see what happens when buyers and sellers interact in markets.

2. THE THEORY OF SUPPLY

About 40 percent of college students drink coffee on a daily basis. With more than 13,000 Starbucks locations in the United States, plus 13,000 McDonald's locations, 7,000 Dunkin' Donuts stores, and numerous other coffee shops and restaurants, there is no shortage of places to buy coffee. We introduce the microeconomic market model by considering how it applies to coffee markets. Coffee is a good example to use because, as you will see as we go through the chapter, we can use it to illustrate several important features about how markets operate.

First, let's define what we mean by "the coffee market" in this example. Let's assume we are looking at the market for a basic cup of regular coffee in the vicinity of your college campus. Although there may be several different locations on and around campus to buy coffee, for simplicity we also assume that all these businesses offer the same basic regular cup of coffee and sell it at the prevailing market price. Of course, in reality each business could set its own price for coffee, but for now we keep our model as simple as possible, assuming that individual sellers have no power over market prices. Let's define the period of our analysis as a week. We consider how the market changes week to week, but within each week the price does not vary.

At the beginning of each week, each coffee business must make a decision about how much coffee it will offer to sell in the coming week—buying the appropriate quantity of coffee supplies, establishing employee work schedules, and so on. How would we expect changes in the prevailing market price of a cup of coffee to influence the quantity of coffee offered for sale each week? In particular, if the market price rises, would we expect more coffee, or less coffee, to be offered for sale? Or conversely, if market prices are falling, how would we expect the quantity offered for sale to change?

It is important to realize that we are asking this question, for now, only from the perspective of coffee sellers. Coffee sellers are most likely either already selling other products, such as hot chocolate, doughnuts, or sandwiches, or could sell these other products if they thought switching would offer more profit than selling coffee. So if the selling price of coffee is rising, it seems reasonable that these sellers will want to sell *more* coffee relative to selling other items. Conversely, if the market price for coffee is falling, sellers will be less interested in selling coffee and some may decide to stop selling coffee altogether.

positive (or direct) relationship: the relationship between two variables when an increase in one is associated with an increase in the other variable

Thus common sense tells us that sellers should offer more coffee when prices are relatively high and less coffee when prices are relatively low. We call the relationship between the market price and the quantity supplied a **positive (or direct) relationship**—increases in the value of one variable (price) tend to be associated with increases in the value of another variable (the quantity supplied).

individual supply: the supply of one particular seller

market (or aggregate) supply: the supply from all sellers in a particular market

Note that we can talk about the quantity supplied at the individual level or the market level. The **individual supply** is the quantity supplied by one particular seller. The **market (or aggregate) supply** is the quantity supplied by all sellers in the market.

2.1 THE SUPPLY SCHEDULE AND SUPPLY CURVE

supply schedule: a table showing the relationship between price and quantity supplied

We have been talking about the relationship between price and the quantity of coffee supplied only in abstract terms so far. Now let's suppose that we have studied the coffee market around campus by speaking with different coffee sellers and can estimate how the quantity supplied will vary with price. We can present our results as shown in Table 4.1. We call a table representing the relationship between price and the quantity supplied a **supply schedule**. In the case of coffee, we have the supply schedule for a physical good. But we can also think of a supply schedule for a marketed service, such as housecleaning, babysitting, or a college education.

Table 4.1 **Supply Schedule for Cups of Coffee**

Price of coffee ($/cup)	0.70	0.80	0.90	1.00	1.10	1.20	1.30	1.40	1.50	1.60
Cups of coffee supplied per week	300	400	500	600	700	800	900	1,000	1,100	1,200

As we expect, the quantity of coffee supplied increases with higher prices. For example, at a price of $0.80 per cup, only 400 cups would be supplied per week. But if the price rises to $1.00 per cup, then 600 cups would be supplied. Note that Table 4.1 shows only the cups supplied at $0.10 increments. We can interpolate to estimate, for example, that 550 cups would be supplied at a price of $0.95 per cup.* The supply schedule in Table 4.1 shows the market supply, which is an aggregation of the individual supply schedules in the local coffee market.

supply curve: a curve indicating the quantities that sellers are willing to supply at various prices

From a supply schedule, we can graph a **supply curve**, as shown in Figure 4.1. This is simply the same relationship between price and quantity supplied in graphical form. It is standard in economics to place the quantity on the horizontal axis (also called the *x*-axis) and the price on the vertical axis (also called the *y*-axis). We see, for example, that at a price of $1.00 per cup, coffee sellers are willing to supply 600 cups of coffee per week.

*"Interpolate" means to estimate a relationship between known data points.

Figure 4.1 **Supply Curve for Cups of Coffee**

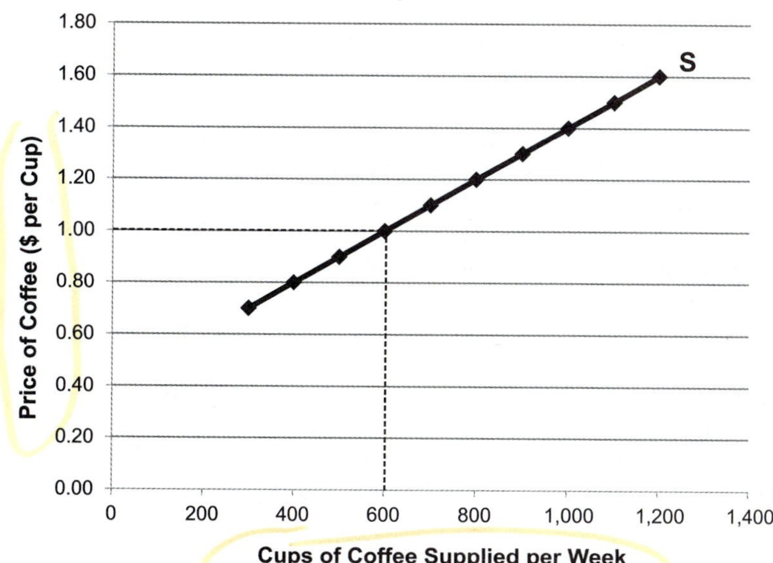

A supply curve shows the same information as the supply schedule. At higher prices, more cups of coffee are offered for sale.

Note that the supply curve in Figure 4.1 slopes upward. This is another illustration of a positive relationship—as price goes up, the quantity supplied also goes up. (Sometimes this positive relationship between price and the quantity supplied is referred to as the "law of supply." Such a choice of words may reflect a somewhat misguided attempt to make economics sound more scientific. As we see in later chapters, especially the one about labor, this "law" does not hold everywhere.)

We now need to introduce an important distinction in market analysis. When price changes, we say that we move *along* a supply curve. So if the price increased from $0.80 to $1.00 per cup, we would move up from a quantity supplied of 400 cups to 600 cups. Another term for movement along a supply curve is a **change in the quantity supplied**. We *would not* say that this is a "change in supply" because that occurs when the entire supply curve shifts—a topic that we address in the next section.

change in quantity supplied: movement along a supply curve in response to a price change

Test yourself by answering this question with reference to Table 4.1 or Figure 4.1: By how much does the *quantity supplied* change when the price changes from $1.20 to $1.40 per cup?*

It is very important when going through this example to imagine that the price is the *only* thing changing. Economists sometimes use the Latin term **ceteris paribus** as shorthand for "all else constant" or "other things equal." This is a basic research technique used in other disciplines as well. For example, when medical researchers try to determine the effect of diet *alone* on a disease, they usually choose as research subjects people whose sex, age, and level of exercise ("all else") are nearly identical ("constant"). If we were to try to estimate a real-world supply curve, we would ideally try to hold everything else in the market constant while varying just the price and observe how the quantity supplied changes. Of course, this cannot be done in the real world, and economists normally have to rely on statistical techniques to try to isolate the effect of price alone. We discuss the issue of estimating actual supply curves in Chapter 5.

ceteris paribus: a Latin phrase that means "other things equal" or "all else constant"

---

*The quantity supplied increases by 200 cups per week, from 800 to 1,000.

2.2 Changes in Supply

change in supply: a shift of the entire supply curve in response to something changing other than price

In contrast to a "change in quantity supplied," which is a response to a price change, we say that there has been a **change in supply** when something else changes and the whole supply curve shifts.

Why might the whole curve shift? In our coffee example, one potential factor that could shift the supply curve is a change in the number of coffee sellers. Starbucks, for example, was founded in 1971 by two college professors and a writer, in Seattle, Washington. If a new coffee seller enters the market, then at any given price, more coffee would be supplied, as shown in Figure 4.2. The addition of a new coffee supplier shifts the entire supply curve from S_1 to S_2. So if the prevailing price of coffee was $1.00 per cup, the change in supply would result in 1,000 cups of coffee being offered for sale each week instead of 600, as shown in the graph.

We can describe this increase in supply by saying either that "supply has increased (or risen)" or that "the supply curve has shifted out." (Some students may find it confusing that a supply *increase* shifts the supply curve *down.* Always start by reading across horizontally from the price axis. Then you will notice that the shift goes out toward *higher* numbers on the quantity axis.)

Figure 4.2 **An Increase in Supply**

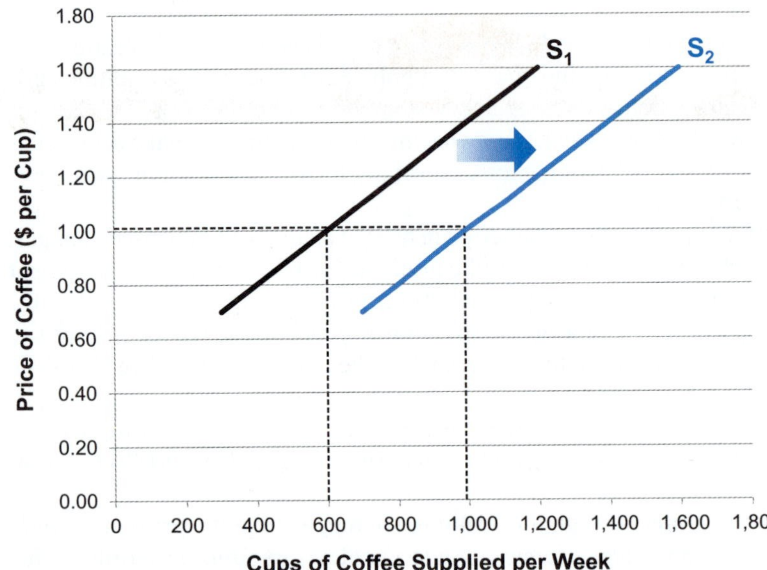

A supply curve shifts outward (to the right) when sellers decide to offer a higher quantity for sale at the same price (or charge less for a given quantity).

2.3 Nonprice Determinants of Supply

nonprice determinants of supply: any factor that affects the quantity supplied, other than the price of the good or service offered for sale

A change in the number of sellers is not the only factor that can shift the entire supply curve. We can define six potential **nonprice determinants of supply** that would shift the entire supply curve:

1. a change in the number of sellers
2. a change in the technology of production
3. a change in input prices
4. a change in seller expectations about the future
5. a change in the prices of related goods and services
6. a change in the physical supply of a natural resource

Consider, for example, a change in the technology used to make coffee that allows coffee to be produced at lower cost. A decrease in production costs suggests that sellers may be willing to accept a lower price for coffee. In Figure 4.2, we see that with the original supply curve at S_1, sellers would be willing to supply 1,000 cups of coffee at a price of \$1.40. Now suppose a decrease in production costs means that sellers would be willing to supply 1,000 cups of coffee at a price of only \$1.00 per cup. This technological change would also shift the supply curve to S_2 in Figure 4.2. (Note that in this case it may be easier to think of the supply curve shifting downward because sellers are willing to accept a lower price for their product. But we would still say that "supply has increased" or that "the supply curve has shifted outward.")

A change in input prices (nonprice determinant #3 in our list) includes the price of coffee beans, labor, milk, sugar, coffee cups, electricity, rent, and any other resource that is an input into the coffee production process. Let's suppose that the price of coffee beans increases, which actually occurred in 2010–11 as a result of extreme heat in Brazil and Colombia (two of the top three coffee-producing countries), causing the price of coffee beans to double. In this case, sellers would need to charge higher prices per cup in order to cover the increase in their input costs. We see this in Figure 4.3. With the original supply curve, S_1, sellers were willing to offer 600 cups of coffee at a price of \$1.00 per cup. With higher coffee bean prices, sellers now require a price of \$1.40 per cup in order to supply 600 cups per week. We would refer to this shift as a "decrease in supply" or that "the supply curve has shifted back."

Figure 4.3 **A Decrease in Supply**

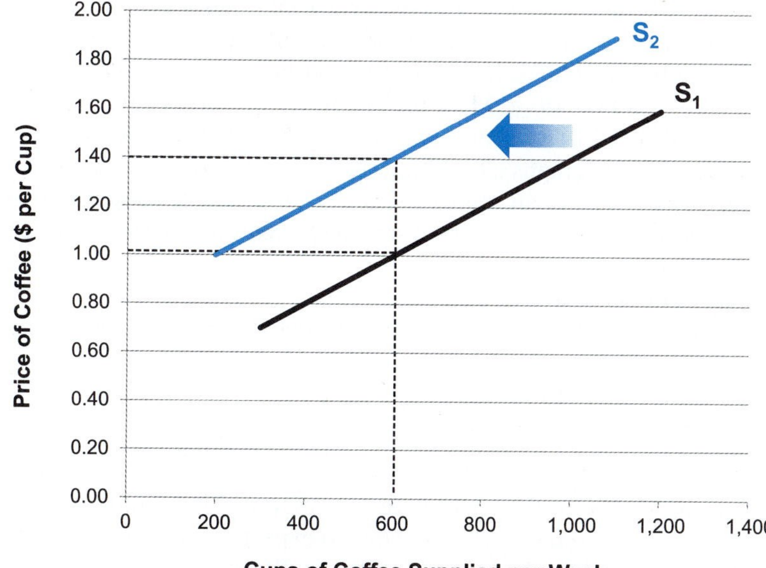

A supply curve shifts backward (to the left) when sellers decide to offer a lower quantity for sale at the same price (or charge more for a given quantity).

The effect of seller expectations about the future (nonprice determinant #4) can be tricky. If a coffee seller expects that coffee bean prices will increase soon (perhaps he or she has been following the news on weather conditions in South America), he or she might hold back some coffee bean inventory for now, to sell later when coffee prices increase. However, if he or she hears that a new technology has been adopted by other coffee sellers that lowers production costs, he or she might be eager to sell as much coffee as possible now before the price is driven down.

Suppose that a coffee seller notices that many people are switching from coffee to tea and are willing to pay high prices for gourmet teas. He or she may decide to supply more tea and less coffee. In this case, the price of a related good (nonprice determinant #5) has induced the firm to reduce its output of coffee, causing a decrease in the supply of coffee similar to what is shown in Figure 4.3.

Finally, in markets for natural resources such as agricultural crops, oil, or minerals, the supply curve may shift as a result of physical supply factors like weather conditions or absolute availability. So a drought that decreases crop yields would directly cause a reduction in supply. Supplies of recoverable oil are ultimately limited and may someday lead to reductions in supply. Note that this nonprice determinant differs from nonprice determinant #3 in that supplies are directly reduced as a result of natural factors, rather than indirectly through a change in input prices.

Discussion Questions

1. Verbally explain the difference between a change in "quantity supplied" and a change in supply. Considering the supply side of the market for lawn-mowing services, what kind of change (*increase* or *decrease,* in *quantity supplied* or *supply*) would each of the following events cause?
   a. There is a rise in the price of gasoline used to run power mowers.
   b. There is a rise in the going price for lawn-mowing services.
   c. More people decide to offer to mow lawns.
   d. A new lawn mower is invented that is cheap and makes it possible to mow lawns at a lower cost.
2. Sketch a supply curve graph illustrating a student's willingness to sell his textbooks from all his classes right now. Assume that the student will receive offers of this sort: "I'll give you [a fixed number of dollars] apiece for all the books you want to sell." Carefully label the vertical and horizontal axes. Suppose that, at an original offer of $30 per book, the student will be willing to sell three books, because he knows he can replace these three for less than $30 each at a local bookstore. Mark this point on your first graph. Assume further that at $40 he would be willing to sell four books, at $50 he would supply five books, and so on. Now, on separate graphs labeled (a), (b), and (c), show this line and his offer at $30 and the precise new *point* or an approximate new *curve* that illustrates each of the following changes in conditions. Consider them separately, returning to the condition of no Internet resources in part (c).
   a. He is offered $70 per book instead of $30.
   b. He discovers that the textbook materials for many of his classes are available free on the Internet.
   c. The local bookstore raises its prices substantially.

3. THE THEORY OF DEMAND

We now turn to the coffee market from the perspective of coffee buyers. Unlike sellers, consumers find low prices attractive. So it seems reasonable to expect that people will want to purchase more cups of coffee per week when prices are lower. We now work through the theory of demand using our coffee example. While the consumers in this example are individuals, realize that demand can also arise from, for example, businesses looking to purchase raw materials or government agencies looking to hire employees.

demand schedule: a table showing the relationship between price and the quantity demanded

3.1 THE DEMAND SCHEDULE AND DEMAND CURVE

demand curve: a curve indicating the quantities that buyers are willing to purchase at various prices

Just as with supply, we can present a **demand schedule** showing the relationship between price and the quantity demanded. In Table 4.2, we see that as the prevailing price of a cup of coffee goes up, the quantity demanded goes down.

From the demand schedule, we can graph a **demand curve**, as shown in Figure 4.4, which shows the quantities that buyers are willing to purchase at various prices. So we see,

Table 4.2 **Demand Schedule for Cups of Coffee**

Price of coffee ($/cup)	0.20	0.50	0.80	1.10	1.40	1.70	2.00	2.30
Cups of coffee demanded per week	1,000	900	800	700	600	500	400	300

Figure 4.4 **Demand Curve for Cups of Coffee**

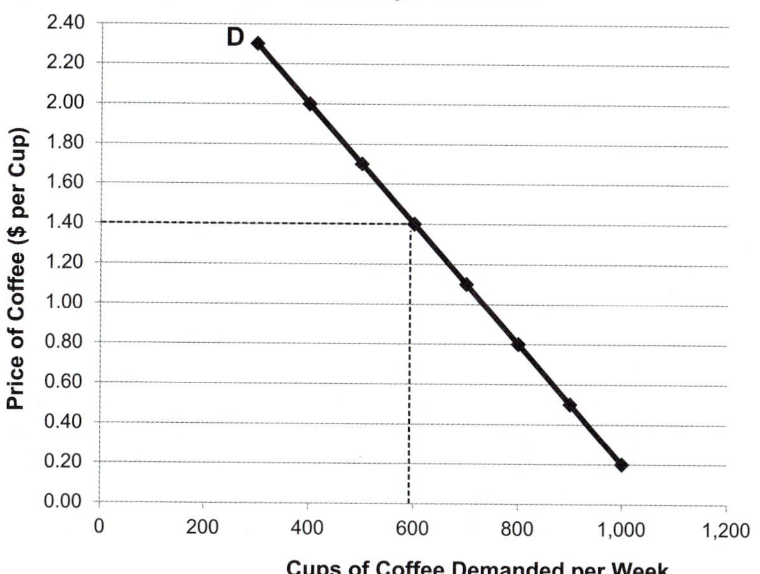

A demand curve shows the same information as the demand schedule. At higher prices, fewer cups of coffee are demanded.

for example, that at a price of $1.40 per cup, consumers would demand 600 cups of coffee per week.

It is important to keep in mind that someone's willingness to buy a good or service is not only a function of his preferences but also of his income or wealth. Economists sometimes use the term "effective demand" to stress that they are talking about demand backed up by enough money to pay the prevailing price. However, you should remember that virtually anywhere that the economic term "demand" is used, it refers to this specific meaning, that is, both a willingness *and* an ability to pay.

Some people who might want to buy a cup of coffee every day may decide not to because they do not believe that they can afford it, and decide instead to make their own coffee. Although the inability of people to pay for daily cups of coffee at a coffee shop may not be a cause for public concern, the inability of people to pay for things such as health care, sufficient nutrition, or a college education may create sufficient motivation for government involvement. Markets do not, by their nature, take into account wants or needs that are not backed up by the ability to pay.

Note that the demand curve in Figure 4.4 slopes downward. Again, this should be common sense that, generally, the higher the price of a good, the fewer that people will want to buy. If a book is very expensive, you might look for it in the library rather than buying it. If an accounting firm raises its rates, some of its clients may consider hiring a different accountant. Price and quantity have a **negative (or inverse) relationship** along a demand curve. That is, when price rises, the quantity demanded falls. (This is sometimes called the "law of demand." Like the "law of supply," it does not always hold. Sometimes, for example, a smart marketer will find that buyers will want more of a good if it is sold as a "prestige" good at a high price.)

negative (or inverse) relationship: the relationship between two variables if an increase in one is associated with a decrease in the other variable

market (or aggregate) demand: the demand from all buyers in a particular market

individual demand: the demand of one particular buyer

The curve that we have drawn is the entire **market (or aggregate) demand** curve in our local market for coffee. As was the case with supply, the market demand is obtained by aggregating the **individual demand** of each consumer in the market.

Again we need to differentiate between movement *along* a demand curve and a *shifting* demand curve. Movement along a demand curve is always referred to as a **change in the quantity demanded**. So if the prevailing price of coffee rises from $1.40 per cup to $1.70, we would say that the quantity demanded declines from 600 cups to 500 cups per week.

Check yourself by answering this question with reference to Table 4.2 or Figure 4.4: By how much does the "quantity demanded" change when the price changes from $1.10 to $0.50 per cup?*

3.2 CHANGES IN DEMAND

change in quantity demanded: movement along a demand curve in response to a price change

change in demand: a shift of the entire demand curve in response to something changing other than price

As with supply, we distinguish between a change in "quantity demanded" and a **change in demand**. When there is a change in demand, the whole demand curve shifts due to a change in some factor other than a change in price.

Why might the whole demand curve shift? Suppose that our demand curve in Figure 4.4 is based on buying patterns at the beginning of a semester. During final exams, we might expect the overall demand for coffee to increase. Such a change in demand is presented in Figure 4.5. Our initial demand curve is D_1, with a quantity demanded of 600 cups per week when price is $1.40 per cup. But during the final exam period, the demand curve shifts to D_2, with a quantity demanded of 900 cups per week at the same price of $1.40. In this case, we would say that "demand has risen (or increased)" or that "the demand curve has shifted out." (Because of the curve's negative slope, in this case shifting out also means shifting up, but again the normal approach in economics is to refer to curves moving horizontally rather than vertically.)

Figure 4.5 **An Increase in Demand**

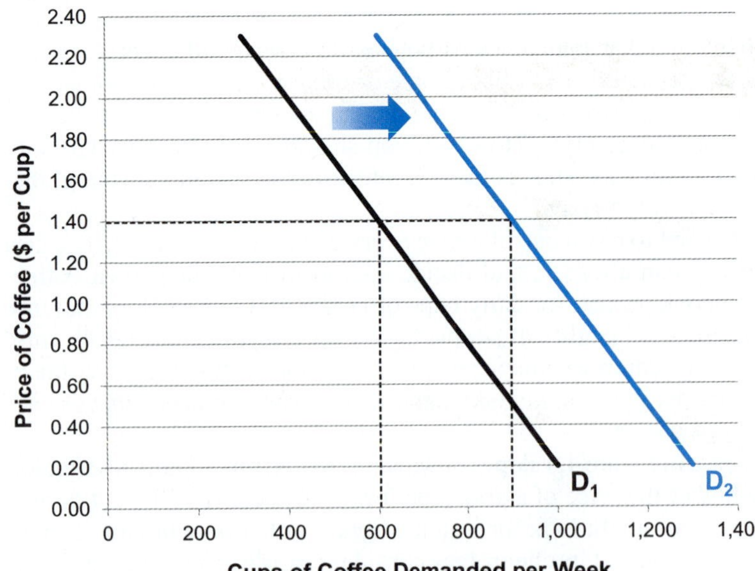

A demand curve shifts outward (to the right) when a higher quantity is demanded at the same price (or people are willing to pay more for a given quantity).

*The quantity demanded increases from 700 cups to 900 cups per week.

3.3 NONPRICE DETERMINANTS OF DEMAND

nonprice determinants of demand: any factor that affects the quantity demanded, other than the price of the good or service being demanded

We can identify five **nonprice determinants of demand** that can shift the entire demand curve:

1. changes in buyers' tastes and preferences
2. changes in buyers' income and other assets
3. changes in the prices of related goods and services
4. changes in buyers' expectations about the future
5. a change in the number of buyers in the market

Suppose that a news story comes out that says drinking more than one cup of coffee per day is harmful to your health. This could lead to a decrease in demand as coffee drinkers decide to cut back on their consumption. Such a decrease in demand is illustrated in Figure 4.6. In this case, the demand curve shifts back (to the left) to D_2, and the quantity demanded falls from 600 to 400 per week. Marketers seek to increase demand through advertising campaigns, such as the ads for new Apple products that can lead to many consumers waiting in line to buy something the day that it becomes available.

A change in buyers' income can shift market demand curves. For example, the 2007–9 recession in the United States reduced income for many households and thus their demand for various products such as restaurant meals and new automobiles.

substitute good: a good that can be used in place of another good

We can define two types of "related" goods and services (nonprice determinant #3). First, there exist **substitute goods** for most market products, that is, a good that can be used in place of another good. For coffee, substitutes include tea and caffeinated energy drinks. If the price of tea were to increase significantly, say as a result of poor weather conditions in tea-exporting countries such as Sri Lanka and India, we would expect the demand for coffee to increase. Meanwhile, if the price of tea were to fall, we would expect the demand for coffee to decrease as some coffee drinkers switch to tea instead.

complementary good: a good that is used along with another good

The other type of related goods are **complementary goods**, or goods that tend to be used along with other goods. Examples of complementary goods for coffee include cream and doughnuts. If someone frequently purchases coffee along with a doughnut, a significant increase in doughnut prices may cause that person to reduce his demand for coffee.

Figure 4.6 **A Decrease in Demand**

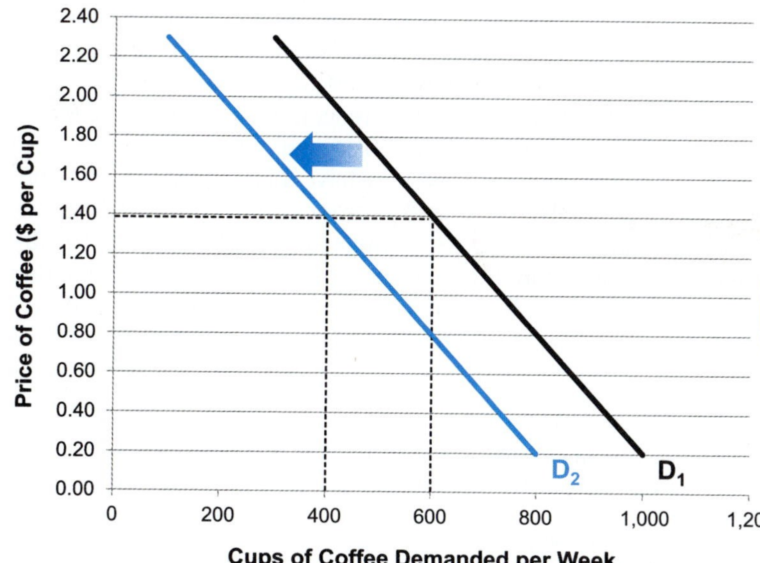

A demand curve shifts backward (to the left) when a lower quantity is demanded at the same price (or people are willing to pay less for a given quantity).

Like suppliers, buyers can adjust their behavior based on future expectations (nonprice determinant #4). If you expect several days of late-night studying for final exams in several weeks, you might temporarily reduce your demand for coffee so that it will have a greater effect on you when you really need it to study.*

The last nonprice determinant of demand is the number of potential buyers in the market. Obviously, the demand for coffee will shift depending on whether we are looking at the summer months when many students are away or the normal school months.

Discussion Questions

1. Explain verbally why the demand curve slopes downward.
2. Verbally explain the difference between a change in "quantity demanded" and a change in demand. Considering the demand side of the market for lawn-mowing services, what kind of change (*increase* or *decrease,* in *quantity demanded* or *demand*) would each of the following events cause?
   a. A new office park, surrounded by several acres of lawn, is built.
   b. A drought is declared, and lawn watering is banned.
   c. The going price for lawn-mowing services rises.
   d. A more natural, wild yard becomes the "in" thing, as people grow concerned about the effects of fertilizers and pesticides on the environment.

4. The Theory of Market Adjustment

Now that we have considered sellers and buyers separately, it is time to bring them together. We will see how the interaction of supply and demand can determine what the price of coffee will be and how much coffee will be sold. Remember that with our relatively simple model, we assume that all coffee in our market will sell for the same price. But what will that price be?

4.1 Surplus, Shortage, and Equilibrium

surplus: a situation in which the quantity that sellers are prepared to sell at a particular price exceeds the quantity that buyers are willing to buy at that price

Using the original supply and demand curves, reproduced here in Figure 4.7, we can look for the answer. Let's suppose, for whatever reason, that the price of coffee is initially $1.40 per cup. As we see in Figure 4.7, at this relatively high price, coffee sellers are prepared to sell 1,000 cups of coffee per week, but buyers are interested in buying only 600 cups. (You can check these numbers in Tables 4.1 and 4.2.) Economists call a situation in which the quantity supplied is greater than the quantity demanded a **surplus**. This is illustrated in the upper part of Figure 4.7, where there is a surplus, or excess supply, of 400 cups of coffee.

If a market is in a situation of surplus, what would we expect to happen? Imagine that at the start of the week, coffee sellers are equipped to sell 1,000 cups of coffee. At the end of the week, they find that they have sold only 600 cups, and they have a large leftover inventory of coffee supplies. Coffee sellers realize that they need to attract more customers, so they will respond to the surplus by lowering their price. Assuming that all sellers respond equally (which is unlikely in the real world, but it simplifies our model at this point), the prevailing price will be somewhat lower the next week. We do not necessarily know how much lower it will be, but there will be downward pressure on prices whenever there is a surplus.**

*There is surprisingly little research on whether the consumption of caffeine actually is associated with improved academic performance. It is clear, however, that excessive use of caffeine is associated with several negative health effects including increased blood pressure, seizures, and headaches.

**If one particular coffee seller lowers his price in response to the surplus, pressure will be created on other sellers to lower their prices as well. Thus the most likely outcome in response to the surplus would be lower prices.

Figure 4.7 **The Market Adjustment Process**

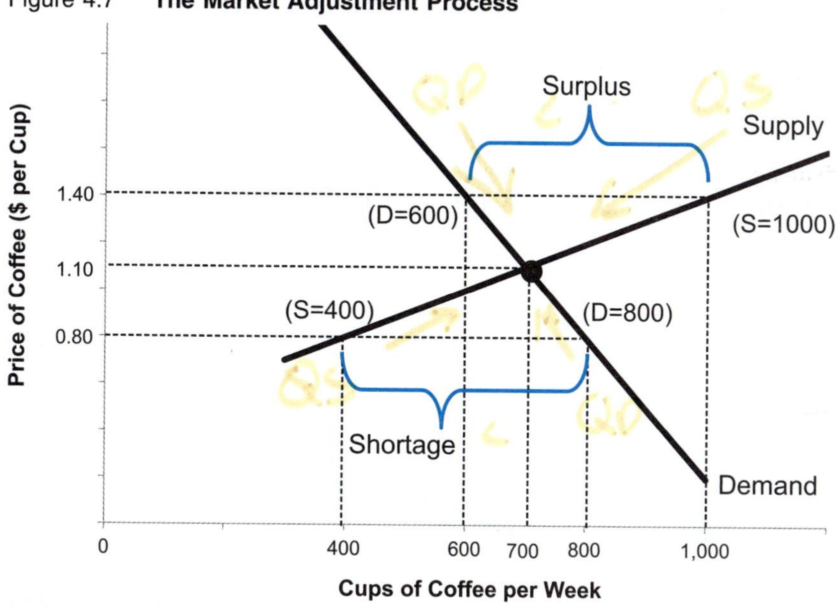

At a price of $1.40 per cup, we have a situation of surplus (the quantity supplied exceeds the quantity demanded), and there is downward pressure on price. At a price of $0.80 per cup we have a situation of shortage (the quantity demanded exceeds the quantity supplied), and there is upward pressure on price.

Let's say that the next week the prevailing price is lowered from $1.40 to $1.30. Looking at Figure 4.7, we see that there would still be a surplus (the quantity supplied exceeds the quantity demanded), but the surplus would be a little smaller. Thus there would still be downward pressure on prices as long as a surplus existed.

Now let's consider the opposite situation. Assume that the initial price of coffee is relatively low, at $0.80 per cup. As shown in Figure 4.7, at this price sellers are prepared to sell only 400 cups per week while the quantity demanded is 800 cups. A situation in which the quantity demanded exceeds the quantity supplied is referred to as a **shortage**.

shortage: a situation in which the quantity demanded at a particular price exceeds the quantity that sellers are willing to supply

What would we expect to happen in a market with a shortage? Before we even get to the end of the week, the suppliers' inventory will be depleted and they will end up turning away customers who want to buy coffee. Realizing that there is excess demand for coffee, sellers will conclude that they can probably charge a little more for coffee and still have a sufficient number of customers. So whenever there is a situation of shortage, there will be upward pressure on prices.*

So if the prevailing price is "too high" (a surplus), there will be downward pressure on prices, and if the price is "too low" (a shortage), there will be upward pressure on prices. Where will prices be "just right"? Starting from either a surplus or shortage, we see in Figure 4.8 that market adjustments will push the price toward $1.10 per cup. At this price, the quantity demanded equals the quantity supplied at 700 cups of coffee per week. (Check Tables 4.1 and 4.2 to confirm this.)

market equilibrium (market-clearing equilibrium): a situation in which the quantity supplied equals the quantity demanded, and thus there is no pressure for changes in price or quantity bought or sold

Economists call this a situation in which the "market clears" and a **market equilibrium (market-clearing equilibrium)** is reached. "Equilibrium" describes a situation that has reached a resting point, where there are no forces to acting to change it. (Economists borrowed this term from natural science.) In a market situation, equilibrium is reached when the

*Because there are many buyers who are willing to pay more than $0.80 for coffee, it is easy for some sellers to raise prices. So even if everyone does not raise prices immediately, the overall tendency will be toward higher prices in a situation of shortage.

theory of market adjustment: the theory that market forces will tend to make shortages and surpluses disappear

market disequilibrium: a situation of either shortage or surplus

quantity supplied is equal to the quantity demanded. The price will stop falling or rising and the quantity sold will stay constant as long as there are no other changes.

The **theory of market adjustment** says that market forces will tend to make price and quantity move toward the equilibrium point. Surpluses will lead to declines in price, and shortages will lead to rises in price. Surplus and shortage are both instances of **market disequilibrium**. Only at the equilibrium price and quantity is there no tendency to change. In this example, the equilibrium price is $1.10 per cup and the equilibrium quantity is 700 cups per week (Figure 4.8).

Figure 4.8 **Market Equilibrium**

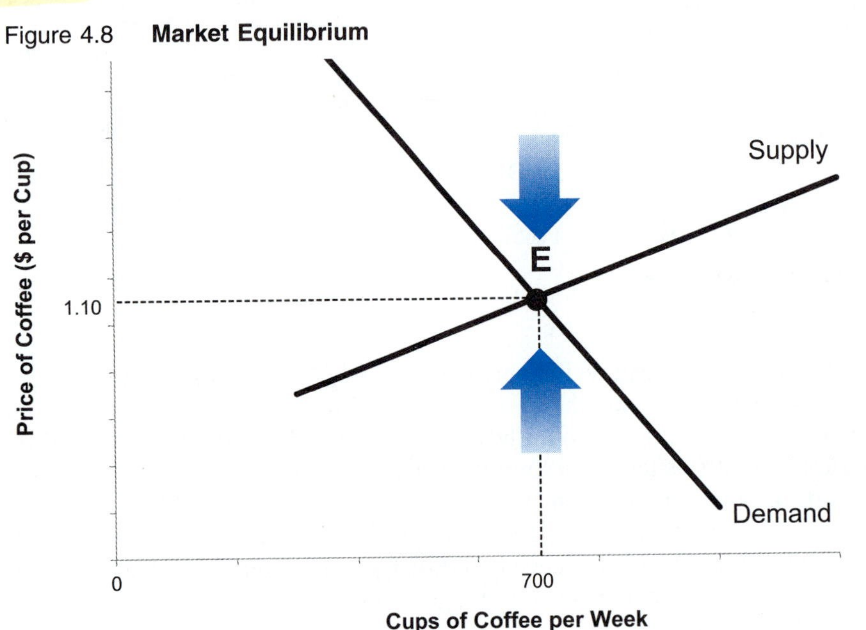

Equilibrium occurs when the quantity demanded equals the quantity supplied. At this point there is no upward or downward pressure on price.

4.2 Market Forces and Other Forces

We know that market forces will tend to push the price of coffee toward the equilibrium price, but how long will this adjustment process take? Just a couple of weeks, a month, maybe longer? We do not know, as our simple model doesn't address this issue.* In the real world, some markets have adjustment processes that lead rapidly to equilibrium. In highly organized stock markets and other auction-like markets, thousands of trades may take place every minute, as buyers and sellers find each other and quickly negotiate a price. Such a market can probably be thought of as in equilibrium, or moving quickly toward equilibrium, nearly all the time. (When we look at stock markets, it is evident that the price/quantity combinations that constitute equilibrium now may be quite different from the conditions for equilibrium tomorrow—or even 15 minutes from now.)

In other markets, however, adjustment to equilibrium may take months or years—if it happens at all. The market forces that we have just examined are not the only forces in the world. For example, hospital administrators complained for decades about a shortage of nurses. The obvious solution, from the point of view of labor supply and demand, would be for hospitals to offer higher wages, thus increasing the incentives for people to enter (and

*More advanced market models do consider the period required for adjustments.

stay in) nursing careers while also reducing the quantity demanded. As in Figure 4.7, market forces would then move us from shortage to equilibrium.

If you study the strategies used by hospitals to combat the shortage, however, you will note that offering higher wages is rarely one of them. Instead, larger training programs, signing bonuses, and forced overtime (which reduces the quality of life for workers and the quality of patient care) have often been used to try to fill the gap. Various explanations have been suggested as to why the nursing wage is not rising to clear the market. On the demand side, hospital management may discount the importance of nurses to patient well-being, preferring to devote financial resources to high-tech medicine. On the supply side, unionizing and fighting for higher wages can be emotionally and ethically difficult for health-care personnel, because striking can mean refusing help to people in need (special features of labor markets are discussed further in Chapter 10).

More generally, the forces that can work against quick movement toward equilibrium include such human characteristics as habit or ignorance. Slow production processes and long-term contracts may also slow down or stop adjustment. A seller may keep a good at its accustomed price long after it has failed to clear, or the back orders have begun to mount up, simply because she is slow to change. A common reason for slow adjustment is a lack of information. To be sure, the corner grocer knows which products are or are not moving; increasingly, sophisticated computerized systems are feeding this information back up the supply chain, to speed up price adjustment. However, in many parts of the world, and in some industries even in industrialized countries, information is slow to get to those who make some of the essential pricing decisions. Consumers, too, often lack information or behave on the basis of habit.

Equilibrium analysis is limited by the reality of constant change in the world, and nonmarket forces may effectively combat the equilibrating tendency of market forces. Market adjustment analysis can, however, tell us what to expect from normal market forces. Most generally, disequilibrium situations create forces that tend to push prices toward an equilibrium level.

4.3 SHIFTS IN SUPPLY AND DEMAND

Our model predicts that after we reach equilibrium, the price will stay the same. In the real world, however, we observe that prices change quite frequently. For example, consider the change in housing prices in the United States over the past few decades, as noted in the introduction to this chapter. Constantly fluctuating prices are also common in fossil-fuel markets, minerals such as gold and copper, and consumer electronics. And as we noted at the beginning of this chapter, coffee prices have varied significantly over time.

Many price changes can be explained, and in some cases even predicted in advance, by using our microeconomic market model. We can determine how a shift in one (or both) of our curves, as a result of a change in one or more nonprice determinants, will lead to a change in the equilibrium price and quantity.

Returning to our coffee market, let's suppose that a new seller enters the market. As we discussed earlier, this is a change in a nonprice determinant of supply and will shift the supply curve out (to the right). This is shown in Figure 4.9 with the supply curve shifting from S_1 to S_2. Our initial equilibrium is point E_1 with a price of \$1.10 and a quantity of 700 cups per week. But note that with the entry of the new coffee seller shifting the supply curve to S_2, and assuming that initially price stays at \$1.10, we go from equilibrium to a situation of surplus (as shown in Figure 4.9). At a price of \$1.10 per cup, the quantity supplied exceeds the quantity demanded with the new supply curve of S_2.

Just as before, a situation of surplus creates downward pressure on prices. But realize that as sellers lower their prices, the quantity demanded increases as we move along the demand curve. As long as a surplus continues to exist, there is downward pressure on prices, leading

Figure 4.9 **Market Adjustment to an Increase in Supply**

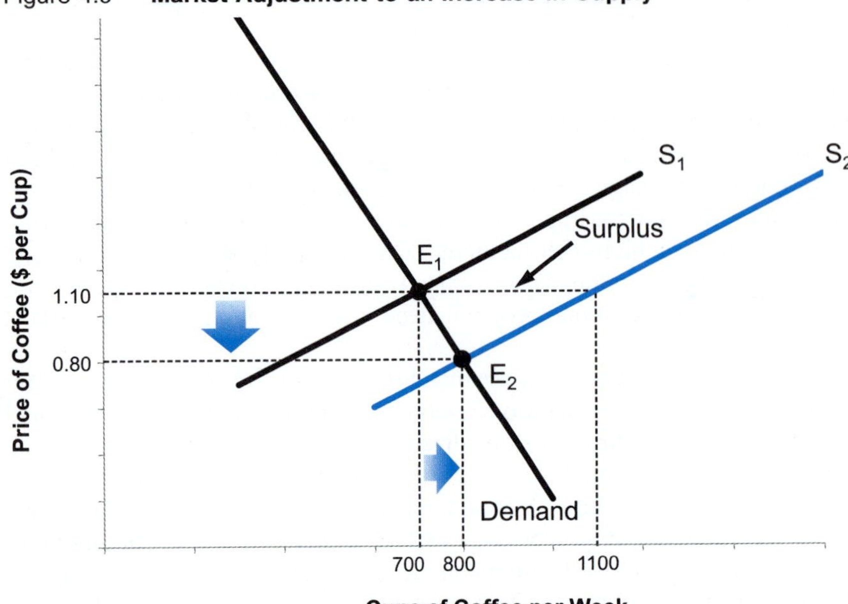

An increase in supply creates a surplus, and downward pressure on price. The new equilibrium occurs at point E_2, with a lower price and a higher quantity sold.

to further movement along the demand curve. The surplus is eventually eliminated when we reach point E_2, the new equilibrium. The increase in supply has resulted in:

- a decrease in the equilibrium price
- an increase in the equilibrium quantity

What if, instead, we have a decrease in supply? Suppose one coffee seller decides to stop selling coffee. In this case, the supply curve would shift to the left. The new equilibrium would result in a high price and a lower quantity sold. (Try this yourself by drawing a graph similar to Figure 4.9 but with the supply curve shifting in the opposite direction.)

Now let's consider what happens when the demand curve shifts. Suppose we have an increase in demand in the campus area as a result of a large incoming freshman class. Figure 4.10 shows an increase in demand (the demand curve shifts to the right) from D_1 to D_2. This creates a temporary situation of a shortage, in which the quantity demanded exceeds the quantity supplied. Sellers perceive the shortage and respond by slightly raising prices. With the higher prices, we move along the supply curve as sellers are willing to supply more coffee.

As long as the shortage persists, we have continued upward pressure on prices and further movement along the supply curve. The shortage is eventually eliminated when we reach point E_2, the new market-clearing equilibrium. The increase in demand has resulted in:

- an increase in the equilibrium quantity
- an increase in the equilibrium price

Note that with an increase in supply or an increase in demand, the equilibrium quantity increases. But the effect on price differs—prices rise with an increase in demand but fall with an increase in supply. This should align with your expectations even before you took this class. If people want more of a product, it makes sense that prices should rise. An increase in the availability (supply) of something should drive prices down. Our microeconomic

Figure 4.10 **Market Adjustment to an Increase in Demand**

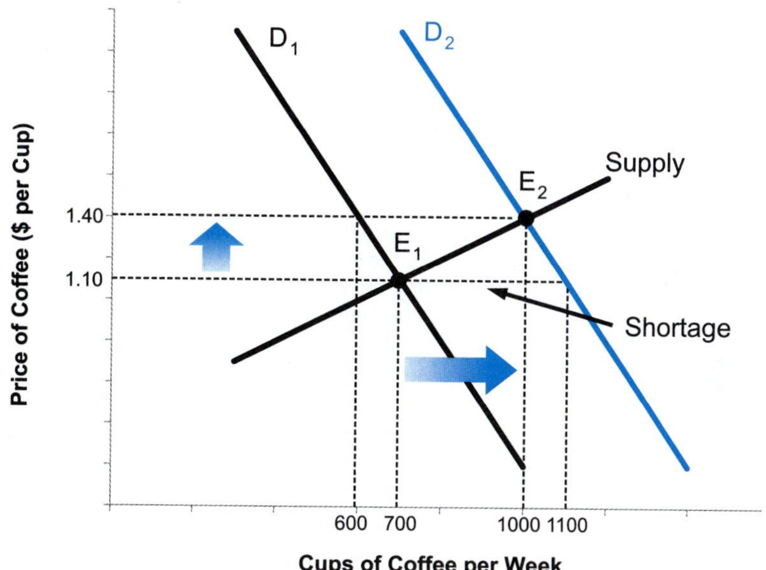

An increase in demand creates a shortage, and upward pressure on price. The new equilibrium occurs at point E_2, with a higher price and a higher quantity sold.

model tells a common sense story about market adjustment, although perhaps in a somewhat complex manner.

What would we expect if demand instead decreases, say due to a news story that indicates that drinking coffee is harmful to your health? The demand curve would shift inward (to the left), and we would expect a lower equilibrium price and a lower equilibrium quantity.

Note that when the supply curve shifts, the resulting change in equilibrium price and quantity are in the *opposite* direction. But when the demand curve shifts, price and quantity change in the *same* direction. We summarize what happens when one of the market curves shift in Table 4.3.

Table 4.3 **Summary of the Market Effects of Shifts in Supply and Demand**

Market change	Effect on equilibrium price	Effect on equilibrium quantity
Increase in supply	Decrease	Increase
Decrease in supply	Increase	Decrease
Increase in demand	Increase	Increase
Decrease in demand	Decrease	Decrease

What if *both* curves shift at the same time? What if, for example, there is a concurrent increase in the number of sellers of coffee and an increase in the number of potential buyers of coffee? We analyze this situation in Figure 4.11. Supply increases from S_1 to S_2 and demand increases from D_1 to D_2. The initial equilibrium is E_1, and the new equilibrium, once the market fully adjusts, is E_2. Both shifts tend to increase equilibrium quantity (see Table 4.3), so we can unambiguously state that the overall result will be an increase in the quantity of coffee sold, as shown in Figure 4.11.

But the effect on price is more difficult to discern. Although an increase in demand tends to increase the equilibrium price, an increase in supply tends to decrease prices. Looking at Figure 4.11, we cannot tell whether the net effect is an increase or decrease in

Figure 4.11 **Market Adjustment with an Increase in Both Supply and Demand**

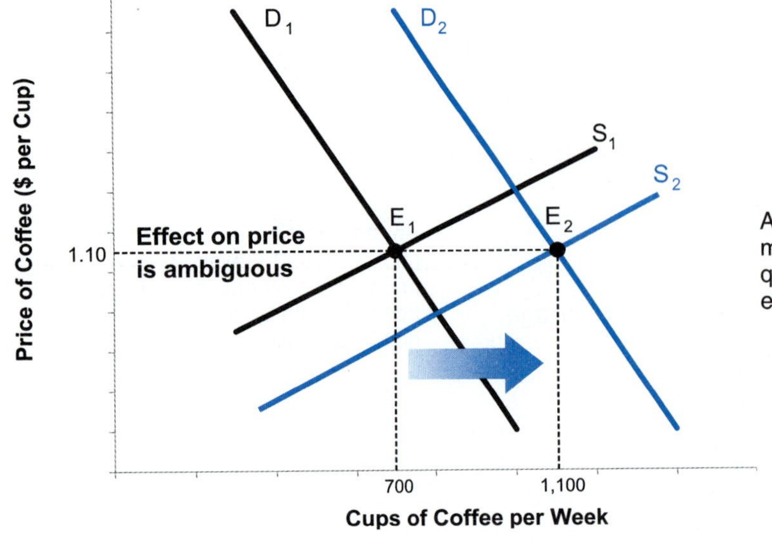

An increase in both supply and demand moves the equilibrium to point E_2. The quantity sold has clearly increased but the effect on price is ambiguous.

price. Although it looks as if price has stayed about the same, note that if we shifted one of the curves a little more, or a little less, the net result could be a price increase or a price decrease.

Whenever both curves shift at the same time, we can make an unambiguous statement about how one of our market variables (price or quantity) will change, but not the other. The net effect on one variable will depend on the relative magnitudes of the shifts in the curves. Table 4.4 summarizes the market results if both curves shift. You should confirm these conclusions based on your own market graphs. See Box 4.2 for a real-world application of our market model to the international coffee market.

Table 4.4 **Summary of the Market Effects When Both Supply and Demand Shift**

Market change	Effect on equilibrium price	Effect on equilibrium quantity
Increase in supply, increase in demand	Ambiguous	Increase
Increase in supply, decrease in demand	Decrease	Ambiguous
Decrease in supply, increase in demand	Increase	Ambiguous
Decrease in demand, decrease in demand	Ambiguous	Decrease

Discussion Questions

1. Think about the market for basketballs. In each of the following cases, determine which curve will shift and in which direction. Also draw a graph and describe, in words, the changes in price and quantity. (Treat each case separately.)
   a. A rise in consumers' incomes
   b. An increase in wages paid to the workers who make the basketballs
   c. A decrease in the price of basketball hoops and other basketball gear
   d. The country's becoming obsessed with soccer

2. Have you ever found yourself shut out of a class that you wanted to take because it was already full? Or has this happened to a friend of yours? Analyze this situation in terms of surplus or shortage. Are classes supplied through "a market" similar to what has been described in this chapter?

Box 4.2 Coffee Markets in the Real World

After reaching a 14-year high in May 2011, wholesale coffee bean prices began to tumble. By July 2013 prices for arabica beans, the most-consumed coffee in the world, had fallen over 60 percent. How can our market model provide insights into changing coffee prices in the real world?

Our model suggests that falling prices can occur either due to an increase in supply or a decrease in demand, or both. According to data from the United States Department of Agriculture, global coffee supplies increased over this time period. At the same time, consumption in coffee-growing countries and coffee exports both increased. So these data suggest that the main reason prices fell so much over 2011–13 was an increase in the supply of coffee.

In the 2012/2013 growing season Brazil, the world's largest coffee producer, had a bumper crop with production up 14 percent over the previous year. Vietnam, the world's second-largest producer, has been scaling up its coffee production in recent years. Between 2010 and 2012 production there increased nearly 30 percent. Other major coffee-producing countries, including Colombia and Indonesia, also had production gains.

With coffee bean prices so low, you may wonder why in June 2013 Starbucks announced that it was *increasing* its prices. According to a Starbucks spokesman, the reasons for the price increase included higher costs for labor, raw materials, and rent. The cost of the actual coffee beans represents a minor portion of the total cost of producing a retail cup of coffee. So Starbucks raising its coffee prices can be explained by an increase in input prices, which would be modeled as a shift of their supply curve. The price increase could also reflect a response to an increase in the demand for Starbucks coffee.

Sources: U.S. Department of Agriculture, "Coffee: World Markets and Trade," Foreign Agricultural Service, June 2013; Parija Kavilanz, "Next Week You'll Pay More for a Starbucks Latte," CNN Money, June 21, 2013.

5. Topics in Market Analysis

Now that we understand the basic functioning of microeconomic markets, we can begin to assess markets in terms of their ability to explain real-world economic outcomes and their ability to produce conditions that truly enhance well-being. As we proceed through this book, further developing and analyzing our market model, we seek to gain insights into where markets currently function well, where markets can be made to function better, and where markets do not offer the best way to allocate society's resources.

5.1 Real-World Prices

The workings of markets in the real world may differ in some ways from the assumptions in the model constructed above. We discuss this in detail in later chapters, but here are three cases in which individuals or businesses may manage prices in ways that are not predicted by the simple model of supply and demand.

The Cost of Changing Prices

First let's revisit the coffee example, noting that, in reality, the price of coffee in your college's neighborhood probably does not change very often. This contradicts the expectation that the market demand curve should shift at the start of each semester when students return (demand should increase) and at the end of the semester when they leave (demand should decrease). Even though the quantity sold surely fluctuates depending on whether college is in session, prices are rather stable.

One reason is that steady, long-term customers (who are local residents, not students) will be offended by seeing prices "opportunistically" go up when the students arrive. This can give a shop a bad name—and reputation is important for most sellers. Another reason is that changing prices entails costs. For example, a restaurant with printed menus may keep prices fixed even though demand increases because the cost of printing new menus would offset the additional revenue.

markup (or cost-plus) pricing: a method of setting prices in which the seller adds a fixed percentage amount to his or her costs of production

In fact, rather than responding according to each change that might affect them, retailers like the ones where you buy your morning cup of coffee commonly set prices using **markup (or cost-plus) pricing**. Using this method, they determine how much it costs them to make or supply a product and then set its price including a percentage increase over their costs. Markups can vary from as low as 10–15 percent for some goods to 200 percent or more for products such as high-end jewelry or art.

Taking a Loss on One Item to Promote Sales of Other Items

To give another example, during the annual holiday season in December, the demand for electronic products such as televisions and computers increases significantly. According to our model, the increase in demand should lead to an increase in prices. But most retailers *lower* their electronics prices during the holiday season. One reason is that competition among retailers heats up at this time of the year (many retailers in the United States expect that 30–60 percent of total annual sales take place between late November and early January). A retailer that raised the price of its most popular item during this time could lose out if other businesses are lowering theirs. In fact, during the holiday season, some retailers lower their prices on some products so much that they actually lose money on each sale. The rationale is that even though they lose money on sales of those items (called "loss leaders") customers will be attracted to the stores and end up buying other, nondiscounted products so that overall profits will increase.

Taking Advantage of Differences Among Consumers' Willingness and Ability to Pay

A real-world market that seems to follow our predictions more closely in some respects is the market for air travel during the holidays. Here we have an increase in demand that usually produces the predicted price increases: A quick check online reveals that the price of a round-trip ticket between Boston and Los Angeles costs about $250 in early December, but rises to over $700 a few days before Christmas! Why is this different from the electronics case? Why doesn't one airline decide to keep its prices low and increase its ticket sales? One reason is that airlines cannot offer loss leaders because they do not have another product to sell to make up for lower-priced ticket sales. Moreover, as long as an airline can fill its planes at relatively high prices during the holidays, it has no incentive to lower its prices. (We explore the role of competition in markets in more detail in Chapters 17 and 18.) At the same time, however, airlines do attempt to create "brand loyalty" by giving various advantages to "frequent flyers."

5.2 MARKETS AND EQUITY

Markets can be viewed as rationing mechanisms—they determine who gets what. Usually, people think of rationing in terms of government action in times of shortage. For example, during World War II people were issued ration cards indicating how much of certain foods and gasoline they would be allowed to buy.

Freedom of choice is often emphasized as an outstanding characteristic of markets, so it may seem strange to view markets as a way to ration society's resources. But note in our coffee example that there are people who want coffee (or more coffee) but do not get it. The section of a demand curve to the right of the equilibrium quantity consists of potential consumers who are willing and able to pay prices *lower* than the equilibrium price for the good or service. So if the equilibrium price of coffee is $1.10 per cup, as in Figure 4.8, there are more people who would buy coffee if the price were reduced to, say, $0.70 per cup. Has the rationing function of the market resulted in the "right" amount of coffee being produced and sold?

Of course, this is a normative question, involving one's values and beliefs. In the market for coffee, society probably is not too concerned that some people who want coffee do not buy it at the equilibrium price. Some of these people may simply not like coffee all that much. Others might believe that they cannot afford to buy coffee from a retailer every day, preferring to make their own at a lower cost. Given the availability of alternatives and the fact that coffee is not necessarily an essential good, we may conclude that the amount of coffee sold is approximately the "right" amount.

The fact that markets produce about the "right" amount of many goods and services, such as television sets, backpacks, haircuts, and pencils, is a rather amazing accomplishment. No central authority is telling manufacturers how much of these products to offer. Private sellers act in a decentralized, voluntary manner. Motivated by profits and responding to consumer demands, they produce quantities of these goods and services that many would consider about right.

But do markets produce "too much" of some goods and services, and "too little" of others? As mentioned before, markets respond to *effective demand,* backed by a willingness and ability to pay. Billions of dollars are spent every year on luxury yachts, presumably enhancing the well-being of those who buy them. Companies that build yachts are responding to consumer demand. If there were a greater demand for, say, public transportation, then such companies might be making buses or trains instead. But companies will prefer to build yachts as long as they are more highly valued in markets.

market value: the maximum amount that economic actors are willing and able to pay for a good or service (i.e., effective demand)

social value: the extent to which an outcome moves us toward our final goals

But we can differentiate between market value and social value. **Market value** is defined according to effective demand—the maximum amount that economic actors are willing and able to pay for something. Market value can, in theory, be measured positively, without normative judgments. **Social value** is more difficult to define and measure. We broadly define the social value of an outcome according to the extent to which it moves us toward our final goals. So if "fairness" is one of our final goals, then it should be part of how we assess the social value of an economic outcome. But even if we had an accepted way to measure fairness, we would still need to make a normative judgment about how much fairness is appropriate.

Although yacht production may maximize the market value of production, it may not maximize social value. Devoting yacht-building resources to public transportation, basic health care, or public education may yield greater social value.

5.3 SHORTAGE, SCARCITY, AND INADEQUACY

In thinking about the fairness of market outcomes, it is important to distinguish between conditions of "shortage," "scarcity," and "inadequacy." These different terms have distinct meanings in economic analysis.

We have seen that a *shortage* is a situation in which willing and able buyers are unable to find goods to buy at the going price. We usually think of this as the result of disequilibrium, but it may also be deliberately created. Sometimes producers intentionally choose a production and pricing strategy that will create shortages, such as the one used for selling luxury cars. The shortage could be eliminated, and equilibrium achieved, if producers raised the price enough. However, they have calculated that their long-run profitability will be higher if they permit a shortage to create a mystique around their product.

Economists think of *scarcity* as a more general condition. As we discussed in Chapter 1, a fundamental scarcity of resources relative to everything that people might need or want is what requires individuals and societies to make choices. Scarcity is about an imbalance between what is available and what people would *like* to have, regardless of what they can afford. Many people would *like* to have a Rolls-Royce or a Lamborghini, but these luxury cars are scarce because not everyone can buy one. But even cups of coffee are scarce in that price acts as a rationing mechanism in which some people decide not to buy all the coffee that they might theoretically want.

Not all kinds of scarcity are alike. We tend to feel differently about the scarcity of Rolls-Royces or Lamborghinis (there are still plenty of other cars that people can purchase to meet their transportation needs) and the scarcity of affordable housing. We use the term **inadequacy** to refer to scarcity when it involves something that is necessary for minimal human well-being but is not obtainable by everyone who needs it. Food, shelter, and basic health care, for example, can be in inadequate supply relative to needs.

inadequacy: a situation in which there is not enough of a good or service, provided at prices people can afford, to meet minimal requirements for human well-being

While markets can eliminate shortages, and general scarcity is a fact of life, markets normally do not address problems of inadequacy. However, if economics is truly about meeting needs and enhancing well-being, then we need mechanisms to supplement markets to reduce problems of inadequacy, such as provision of some goods and services by governments or other public purpose actors.

5.4 Precision Versus Accuracy

Returning one last time to our coffee example, recall that the initial equilibrium price was exactly \$1.10 per cup (Figure 4.8). We assumed that this price would be the same at all coffee shops in the area. In the real world, one coffee shop might sell coffee for \$0.99 per cup, another for \$1.10, while a third charges \$1.25. Does this observation conflict with our basic model?

One response is that each coffee shop faces a *separate* demand curve for its coffee. So the equilibrium price at one shop may differ from the equilibrium price at another, depending on such factors as their relative labor costs, the quality of their coffee, or the ambiance of each shop. (This situation is discussed further in Chapter 18.) But even if market conditions are similar for different coffee shops, we may still observe some variation in prices.

The model presented here is **precise** because it describes outcomes exactly, such as our equilibrium price being exactly \$1.10 per cup. The advantage of precision is that we have eliminated uncertainty. Another example of precision is making an economic prediction that the unemployment rate at the end of next year will be exactly 6.0 percent. However, when we are being precise we run the risk of being inaccurate. Our unemployment rate prediction will likely turn out to be wrong. A prediction that stands a better chance of being **accurate** is saying that the unemployment rate will be between 5 percent and 7 percent. An accurate prediction is one that is correct, even if only in a general way.

precise: describes something that is exact (though it may be unrealistic)

accurate: describes something that is correct (even if only in a general way)

Often there is a tradeoff between accuracy and precision. Rather than saying that the equilibrium coffee price is precisely \$1.10 per cup, it may be more accurate to say that the equilibrium price is between \$1.00 and \$1.20 per cup. The distinction between precision and accuracy is one that we face frequently. The statement "He is middle-aged" is untrue of a 20-year-old and a 70-year-old and perhaps clearly true of a 45-year-old. But middle age does not begin abruptly at 40 or 43, nor does it end abruptly some years later. Rather, it is a more or less appropriate description of people at varying ages. "He is middle-aged" may be perfectly accurate, without being precise.

Ideally, we would like our economic analyses to be characterized by both accuracy and precision—but sometimes we have to choose between these qualities. How should we decide which to choose?

Precision often has the virtue of simplicity. For example, it is easier to contemplate a single point than it is to deal with ranges of various possibilities. Precision and simplicity together are qualities that are often helpful—sometimes essential—to translate economic concepts into readily understood mathematical representations and graphs.

In contrast, accuracy is especially important when we are attempting to understand the real world. We keep the theory "in our head" to help us understand economic activity, but what we actually observe is often more messy and complicated than a simple graph could represent, as our discussion of electronics and plane tickets suggested.

If we mistakenly confuse precision with accuracy, then we might be misled into thinking that an explanation expressed in precise mathematical or graphical terms is somehow more rigorous or useful than one that takes into account particulars of history, institutions, or business strategy. This is not the case. Therefore, it is important not to put too much confidence in the apparent precision of supply and demand graphs. Supply and demand analysis is a useful, precisely formulated, conceptual tool that helps gain an abstract understanding of a complex world. It does not—nor should it be expected to—also give us an accurate and complete description of any particular real-world market.

Discussion Questions

1. In Chapter 1 we discussed the three basic economic questions: *What* should be produced, and *what* should be maintained? *How* should production and maintenance be accomplished? *For whom* should economic activity be undertaken? Discuss how the workings of markets provide some answers to these questions.
2. Explain which of the three situations—shortage, scarcity, or inadequacy—is illustrated by each of the following, and why.
   a. You go to a store to buy a certain computer game and find that it is sold out.
   b. Jasmine cannot afford to go to a doctor.
   c. Rafe can think of dozens of music CDs he would like to buy, but he also would like to buy a lot of new clothing.

REVIEW QUESTIONS

1. Define and sketch a supply curve.
2. Illustrate on a graph:
   (a) a decrease in quantity supplied; and
   (b) a decrease in supply.
3. Name six nonprice determinants of supply for a product sold by firms.
4. Define and sketch a demand curve.
5. Illustrate on a graph:
   (a) a decrease in quantity demanded; and
   (b) a decrease in demand.
6. Name five nonprice determinants of demand for a product purchased by households.
7. Draw a graph illustrating surplus, shortage, and equilibrium.
8. Explain the difference between market value and social value.
9. Name three ways in which supply can be inadequate.
10. Explain the difference between precision and accuracy.

EXERCISES

1. Explain in words why the supply curve slopes upward.
2. Explain in worlds why the demand curve slopes downward.
3. Suppose that the supply and demand schedules for a local electric utility are as follows:

Price	17	16	15	14	13	12	11
Quantity supplied	9	7	5	3	1	–	–
Quantity demanded	3	4	5	6	7	8	9

The price is in cents per kilowatt hour (kWh), and the quantity is millions of kilowatt hours. The utility does not operate at prices less than 13 cents per kWh.

   a. Using graph paper and a ruler, or a computer spreadsheet or presentation program, carefully graph and label the supply curve for electricity.
   b. On the same graph, draw and label the demand curve for electricity.
   c. What is the equilibrium price of electricity? The equilibrium quantity? Label this point on your graph.

d. At a price of 17 cents per kWh, what is the quantity supplied? What is the quantity demanded? What is the relationship between quantity supplied and quantity demanded? What term do economists use to describe this situation?

e. At a price of 14 cents per kWh, what is the relationship between quantity supplied and quantity demanded? What term do economists use to describe this situation?

f. Sometimes cities experience "blackouts," in which the demands on the utility are so high relative to its capacity to produce electricity that the system shuts down, leaving everyone in the dark. Using the analysis that you have just completed, describe an *economic* factor that could make blackouts more likely to occur.

4. Continuing on from the previous problem, suppose that new innovations in energy efficiency reduce people's need for electricity. The supply side of the market does not change, but at each price buyers now demand 3 million kilowatt hours fewer than before. For example, at a price of 11 cents per kWh, buyers now demand only 6 kWh instead of 9 kWh.

a. On a new graph, draw supply and demand curves corresponding to prices of 16 cents per kWh or less, after the innovations in efficiency. Also, for reference, mark the old equilibrium point from the previous exercise, labeling it E_1.

b. If the price were to remain at the old equilibrium level (determined in part (c) above), what sort of situation would result?

c. What is the new equilibrium price? The new equilibrium quantity? Give this point on your graph the label E_2.

d. Has there been a change in demand? Has a change in the price (relative to the original situation) led to a change in the quantity demanded?

e. Has there been a change in supply? Has a change in the price (relative to the original situation) led to a change in the quantity supplied?

5. Using your understanding of the nonprice determinants of supply and of demand, analyze each of the following market cases. Draw a graph showing what happens in each situation, indicate what happens to equilibrium price and quantity, and explain why, following this example: Market for gasoline: A hurricane hits the Gulf of Mexico, destroying many refineries that produce gasoline from crude oil.

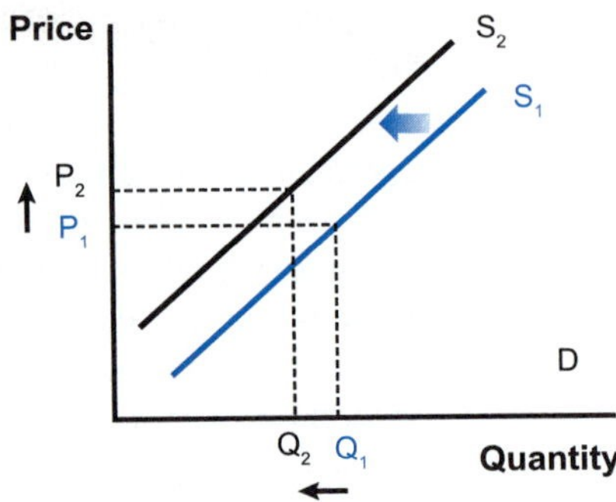

S shifts back; *P* rises; *Q* falls; the hurricane reduces the number of producers.

a. Market for bananas: New health reports indicate that people can gain important health benefits from eating bananas.

b. Market for shoes: A new technology for shoe making means that shoes can be made at a lower cost per pair.

c. Market for Internet design services: Several thousand new graduates of design schools enter the market, ready to supply their services.

d. Market for expensive meals: A booming economy raises the incomes of many households.

e. Market for grapes *from California:* A freeze in Chile, usually a major world provider of fresh fruit, raises the price of Chilean grapes.

f. Market for salsa dance lessons: The only nightclub featuring salsa music triples its entrance fee.

g. Market for bottled water: A rumor circulates that the price of bottled water is about to triple. (Think only about the demand side.)

h. Market for Internet design services: Several thousand new graduates of design schools enter the market, ready to supply their services, *at the same time* that many firms want to create new Web sites.

i. Market for bananas: New health reports indicate that people can gain important health benefits from eating bananas, while *at the same time* an infestation of insects reduces the banana harvest in several areas.

6. At a price of $5 per bag, William is willing to supply 3 bags of oranges, Marguerite 2 bags, and Felipe 5 bags. At a price of $7 per bag, William is willing to supply 5 bags, Marguerite 4 bags, and Felipe 7 bags. Graph and carefully label the individual supply curves, and then graph the market supply curve for oranges (at these two prices).

7. At a price of $8 per ticket, Shalimar goes to 2 movies per month, Wen goes to 1 movie per month, and Adam goes to 3 movies per month. At a price of $10 per ticket, Shalimar goes to 1 movie, Wen goes to 0 movies, and Adam goes to 2 movies. Graph and carefully label the individual demand curves, and then graph the market demand curve for movie tickets (at these two prices).
8. Suppose that a newspaper report indicates that the price of wheat has fallen. For each of the following events, draw a supply-and-demand graph showing the event's effect on the market for wheat. Then state whether the event could explain the observed fall in the price of wheat.
   a. A drought has hit wheat-growing areas.
   b. The price of rice has risen, so consumers look for alternatives.
   c. As a consequence of increasing health concerns, tobacco farmers have begun to plant other crops.
9. Match each concept in Column A with an example in Column B.

	Column A	Column B
a.	Substitute goods	1. Price and quantity along the supply curve
b.	A nonprice determinant of demand	2. Tea and coffee
c.	A nonprice determinant of supply	3. A change in technology
d.	Mark-up pricing	4. Hunger
e.	Positive relationship	5. Shoes and shoelaces
f.	Negative relationship	6. Consumer income
g.	Inadequacy	7. Price and quantity along the demand curve
h.	Complementary goods	8. Setting price equal to cost plus 20 percent

Note

1. See Gary E. McIlvain, Melody P. Noland, and Robert Bickel, "Caffeine Consumption Patterns and Beliefs of College Freshman," *American Journal of Health Education* 42(4) (2011): 235–244.

5 Elasticity

In 2012 the Massachusetts Bay Transportation Authority (MBTA), which operates buses, subways, and commuter trains in the Boston area, raised its fares in order to address major budget deficits. Based on what we learned in Chapter 4, we would expect overall ridership to decline when fares are raised (a decrease in the quantity demanded). So we have two market forces affecting the MBTA's revenues, working in opposite directions:

- The fare increase would bring the MBTA more revenue for each ride taken.
- The fare increase would reduce the number of rides taken.

Whether the MBTA's total revenue increases as a result of the fare increase depends on how responsive riders are to price changes. In order to plan properly, the MBTA needed to estimate how much the quantity demanded would decline with an increase in fare prices. If ridership decreases only a little, then total revenue would probably increase. However, if the fare increase causes ridership to decline significantly, then perhaps revenues would actually decrease.

This is one example in which economists, businesses, or policymakers require information about the responsiveness of the quantity demanded, or the quantity supplied, to price changes. For example, a restaurant may wish to know how its customers will respond to higher prices. A state government may need to estimate how its revenues will change if it increases taxes on cigarettes or another product. Agencies that monitor traffic patterns may want to know how much vehicle travel will respond to changes in gas prices.

elasticity: a measure of the responsiveness of an economic actor to changes in market factors, including price and income

In this chapter, we introduce the concept of **elasticity**. Elasticity measures the responsiveness of economic actors to changes in market factors, including price and income. The most common kinds of elasticity are those related to changes in the quantity demanded or quantity supplied with changes in price (i.e., movement along a demand or supply curve). But we can also measure elasticity with respect to changes in income or other nonprice determinants (i.e., shifts in demand or supply).

1. The Price Elasticity of Demand

price elasticity of demand: a measure of the responsiveness of the quantity demanded to a change in price

When the MBTA raised its prices in July 2012, by an average of 23 percent, do you think ridership declined a little or a lot? It depends on the **price elasticity of demand** (often just called the "elasticity of demand"), which is the responsiveness of the quantity demanded to a change in price. Elasticity of demand is the particular elasticity most studied by economists. Businesses can use information on the elasticity of demand for their products to set prices. Governments can use elasticity of demand estimates to determine how much revenue they will raise with a tax on a particular product.

1.1 PRICE-INELASTIC DEMAND

price-inelastic demand: a relationship between price and quantity demanded characterized by relatively weak responses of buyers to price changes

Demand for a good is **price inelastic** if the effect of a price change on the quantity demanded is fairly small. Demand might be price inelastic for three main reasons:

1. There are very few good, close substitutes for the good or service.
2. The good or service is something that people need, rather than just want.
3. The cost of the good or service is a very small part of a buyer's budget.

For example, gasoline has no good, close substitutes for powering nonelectric motor vehicles. When gas prices rise, most drivers still need to use their vehicles to get to work, run errands, and so on. So gasoline is an example of a good that is price inelastic because of the lack of any good substitutes and because people believe that they need it. Other examples of goods that tend to be price inelastic for these reasons include water for basic needs, essential health care, and electricity.

Some goods are price inelastic because expenditures on them represent such a small portion of people's incomes that most consumers are not affected much by a change in prices. Consider that a 50 percent increase in the price of dental floss is not likely to reduce the quantity demanded significantly.

1.2 PRICE-ELASTIC DEMAND

price-elastic demand: a relationship between price and quantity demanded characterized by relatively strong responses of buyers to price changes

Conversely, demand for a good is **price elastic** if the effect of a price change on the quantity demanded is fairly large. Demand may be price elastic for three main reasons:

1. The good has a number of good, close substitutes.
2. The good is merely wanted, rather than needed.
3. The cost of the good makes up a large part of the budget of the buyer.

An example of a good that is likely to be price elastic is orange juice. This product is not necessary for most people, and various substitutes exist, such as apple juice or other fruit juices. Although gasoline is a price-inelastic good, the elasticity of demand for a particular brand of gasoline is likely to be very elastic. Gasoline may not have readily available substitutes, but the gasoline from Exxon-Mobil or BP does. For another example of elastic demand, see Box 5.1.

To the extent that a good is merely wanted (e.g., ice cream), rather than needed (e.g., essential medicines), demand for it will tend to be more elastic. Studies typically find that demand for airline travel is more elastic for people going on vacation than for business travelers. Demand also tends to be more price elastic when the good makes up a large part of the budget of the buyer, because then the buyer will be more motivated to seek out substitutes when prices increase.

1.3 MEASURING PRICE ELASTICITY

To obtain useful economic forecasts, we need to be more precise than simply stating that quantity demand changes "a little" or "a lot" in response to a given price change. The elasticity of demand is mathematically calculated as:

$$\textit{Price elasticity of demand} = \left| \frac{\textit{\% change in quantity demanded}}{\textit{\% change in price}} \right|$$

where the vertical bars indicate absolute value. As we discussed in Chapter 4, price and the quantity demanded normally change in opposite directions (an inverse relationship), so the

BOX 5.1 GYM MEMBERSHIPS AND ELASTICITY

The city of New York operates dozens of recreation centers, which offer facilities such as indoor pools, weight rooms, basketball courts, and dance centers. These centers offer a low-cost alternative to expensive private gyms.

In an effort to raise revenue, in 2011 the city doubled its recreation center adult membership fees, to $150 per year for centers with pools and $100 per year for those without pools. The Parks Department projected that the fee increase would result in a 5 percent drop in memberships, but a $4 million increase in revenues. In other words, their analysis concluded that demand for the recreation centers was rather inelastic.

Instead, the fee change resulted in a 45 percent drop in membership, and a $200,000 decline in revenues! The demand for the city's recreation centers turned out to be much more elastic than the city anticipated. In January 2013 the Parks Department Commissioner, Veronica M. White, acknowledged that the plan to increase revenues had backfired.

One change that she suggested was to make memberships available to those age 18–24 for only $25 per year, the same rate charged to seniors. Memberships for those under age 18 are free, so those turning 18 had to suddenly pay at least $100 per year. Membership among this age group dropped by the highest percentage after the fee change, by 55 percent. The Parks Department hopes that the new lower membership fees will encourage young adults to exercise, as 52 percent of young adult males and 31 percent of young adult females in New York City are overweight or obese.

Many of the clientele of the recreation centers are low-income individuals. Thus the fee increase posed a particular hardship for them. Holly Leicht, executive director of New Yorkers for Parks, a nonprofit advocacy group, noted, "Thirty percent of Bronx residents alone are living at or below the poverty rate of $23,021 per year for a family of four. For these families, an extra $50 or $75 is often prohibitive."

Source: Lisa W. Foderaro, "Public Recreation Centers Looking to Stem Exodus," *New York Times,* February 15, 2013.

fraction inside the vertical bars tends to be a negative number. For example, if price increases (a positive sign in the denominator of the fraction), we would expect the quantity demanded to decrease (a negative sign in the numerator of the fraction). So after dividing, we would end up with a negative number. Taking the absolute value turns the negative number into a positive number.

The reason we take the absolute value is so that when we talk about a "large" responsiveness to price, we can represent this using a "larger" number. If we did not take the absolute value, we would have to talk about –2 being "bigger" than –1, which would be confusing.*

An example illustrates how we calculate the price elasticity of demand for a particular good. Suppose that executives at Braeburn Publishing are trying to decide what price to charge for a new book of poetry. Although the firm competes with many other firms in the market for books in general, it has sole rights to sell this particular book, so it has some power over the price that it sets. In order to see how responsive demand for the new poetry book is to variations in price, Braeburn decides to test-market it in three locations that are very similar in terms of consumer preferences and incomes but are far enough apart geographically so that the company can set a different price in each location. Table 5.1 and Figure 5.1 show the data the marketing department has collected on prices and the quantity sold during the month of the test. As in this example, real empirical data on prices and quantities are generally limited to specific points along a demand curve without knowing data points for the entire demand curve. For simplicity, we have assumed that the demand curve is a straight line between the three known data points.

*If you look at economic studies that estimate the price elasticity of demand, sometimes the elasticity estimates are presented as negative numbers (i.e., they do not take the absolute value). Remember that price and quantity demanded almost always change in the opposite direction. So you can safely make this assumption, unless information is presented to the contrary.

Table 5.1 **Relationship Between Price and Quantity Demanded for Braeburn's Poetry Book**

Book price	Quantity of books sold
$12	720
$10	800
$5	1,000

Figure 5.1 **Demand Curve for Braeburn's Poetry Book**

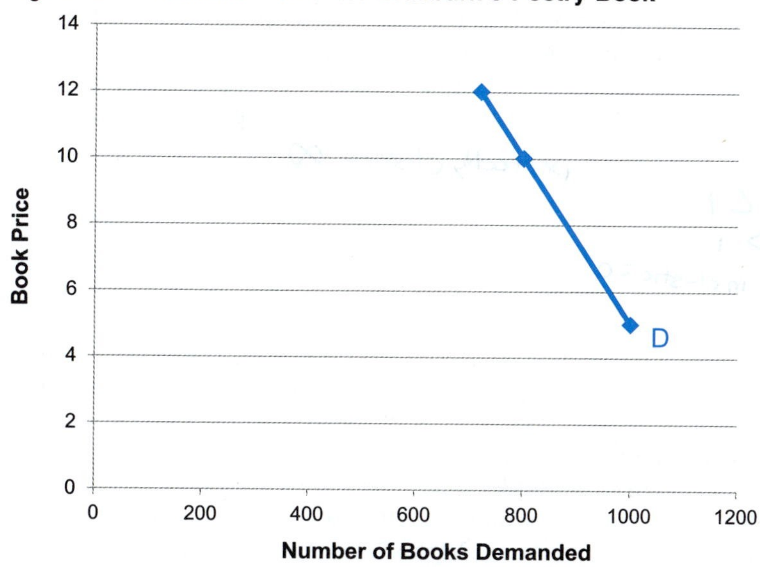

We can use a demand curve to calculate the price elasticity of demand.

We can now calculate the price elasticity of demand for Braeburn's poetry book. We work our way "up" the demand curve starting at the lowest price, $5. To calculate the percentage change in a variable, we define one number as the starting, or "base," value and the other as the ending, or new, value. So, working up the demand curve, $5 would be our base value and $10 would be our new value. A percentage change is calculated as:

$$\textit{Percent change} = \left[\frac{\textit{New value} - \textit{Base value}}{\textit{Base value}}\right] \times 100$$

So, going from a base of $5 to a new value of $10, the percentage change is:

$$\begin{aligned}\textit{Percentage change in price} &= [(\$10 - \$5)/\$5] \times 100\\ &= [\$5/\$5 \times 100]\\ &= 1 \times 100\\ &= 100\%\end{aligned}$$

For the percentage change in quantity demanded, our base is 1,000 and our new value is 800. So the percentage change is:

$$\begin{aligned}\textit{Percentage change in quantity} &= [(800 - 1{,}000)/1{,}000\ ] \times 100\\ &= [-200/1{,}000\ ] \times 100\\ &= -0.2 \times 100\\ &= -20\%\end{aligned}$$

We can then calculate the elasticity of demand as the absolute value of the percentage change in quantity demanded divided by the percentage change in price, or:

$$\begin{aligned} \textit{Elasticity} &= |-20\%/100\%| \\ &= |-0.2| \\ &= 0.2 \end{aligned}$$

price-inelastic demand (technical definition): the percentage change in the quantity demanded is smaller than the percentage change in price. The elasticity value is less than 1

In this example, notice that the percentage change in the quantity demanded is less than the percentage change in price. Whenever this is the case, the elasticity value will be less than 1. This is the **technical definition of price-inelastic demand**.

The **technical definition of price-elastic demand** is that the percentage change in the quantity demanded is larger than the percentage change in price. With price-elastic demand, the elasticity value will be more than 1.

1.4 Two Extreme Cases

Perfectly Inelastic Demand

price-elastic demand (technical definition): the percentage change in the quantity demanded is larger than the percentage change in price. The elasticity value is more than 1

perfectly inelastic demand: the quantity demanded does not change at all when price changes. The elasticity value is 0

Perfectly inelastic demand means that quantity demanded does not respond at all to price changes. Suppose that you are on medication, and you must take exactly three pills a day to survive. Would a 10 percent increase in the price of the medication change the quantity that you demand? Chances are your demand would be perfectly inelastic in the range of that price change, because you unquestionably need the medicine.

Think about what a demand curve would look like for a good with perfectly inelastic demand. For any price level (i.e., any point on the vertical axis), the quantity demanded would be unchanged. Thus a perfectly inelastic demand curve would be a vertical line at the quantity demanded, as shown in Figure 5.2. As the quantity demanded is constant (i.e., percentage change is 0), the elasticity value for a good with a perfectly inelastic demand would be 0.

For a good with perfectly inelastic demand, such as lifesaving drugs and basic foodstuffs, profit incentives may be at odds with social well-being. Because a seller of such a good could raise prices without reducing the quantity demanded, by continually raising prices, up to the absolute maximum that people could afford, the seller would maximize profits.

For this reason, in markets for certain kinds of health-care commodities or basic foodstuffs, governments sometimes regulate prices to give the seller a fair return but not an excessive

Figure 5.2 **Perfectly Inelastic Demand and Perfectly Elastic Demand**

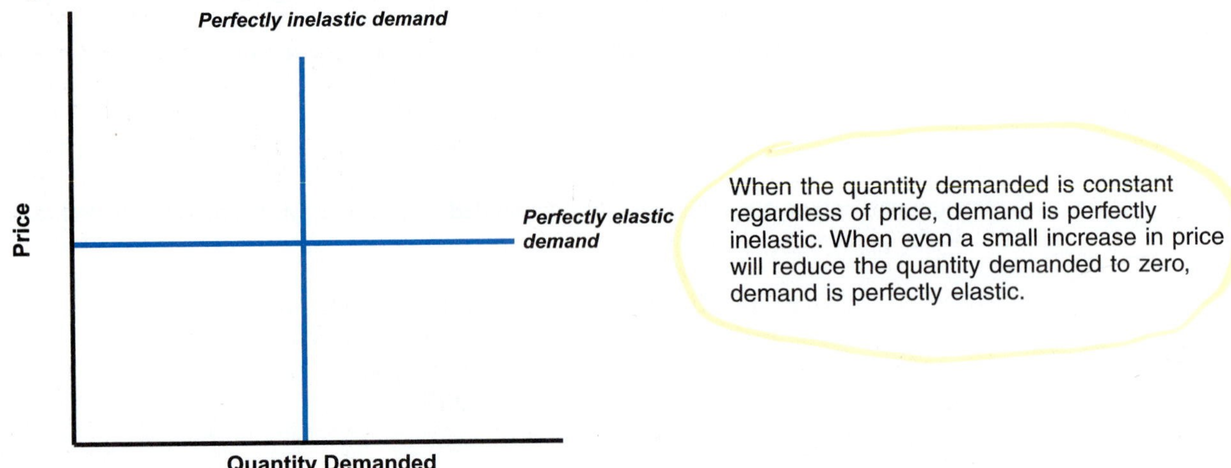

one while ensuring that many people will get what they need. Controversies have recently arisen in the United States over whether prices for pharmaceuticals and hospital stays are reasonable or are out of line with actual production costs and human needs.

Sometimes, sellers themselves are guided by notions of what is a "fair" price. Economists have noticed that, for example, few stores raise the price of umbrellas during rainstorms. The stores could almost certainly get away with charging higher prices to people whose only alternative is to get soaking wet. However, the sellers also know that if they want repeat business from their customers, they should not ruin their reputation for fair dealing by engaging in such price gouging.

Perfectly Elastic Demand

perfectly elastic demand: any change in price leads to an infinite change in quantity demanded. The elasticity value is infinity.

Perfectly elastic demand, by contrast, means that any price change, no matter how small, leads to an "infinite" change in quantity demanded. This occurs when there is a "going price" for a particular good or service and any attempt to charge above that price will eliminate all demand for it. One case in which demand tends to be very elastic in the real world is in the market for general-skilled labor, when general-skilled workers are plentiful. Employers are the buyers, or demanders, in this case. If all you had to offer on the labor market were general skills, such as flipping burgers or sweeping floors, then you and all workers similar to you would be the sellers, or suppliers. Chances are that you would face a demand curve for your labor that would be horizontal at the going wage. Competing against many other sellers, all with the same basic skills, you would have very little or no ability to affect the wage that you would get in the market.

A perfectly elastic demand curve would be horizontal at the "going price," as shown in Figure 5.2. Almost any quantity can be sold at the going price, but charging even slightly above this price will reduce demand to 0. Because even a slight change in price will result in an "infinite" change in quantity demanded, the elasticity value for a good with a perfectly elastic demand is essentially infinite.

In reality, examples of perfectly elastic or perfectly inelastic demand curves are rare. However, actual demand curves may come close to these two extremes, at least for some portion of the demand curve.

1.5 DEMAND CURVES AND ELASTICITY

The Shape of a Demand Curve and Elasticity

Let's take another look at Figure 5.1. We have already calculated the elasticity of the demand curve when the price increased from \$5 to \$10, which was 0.2. Given that the demand "curve" is a straight line, you might think that the elasticity would also be 0.2 if the price increased further from \$10 to \$12. Let's see if this is true, inserting the appropriate values from Table 5.1.

$$\textit{Elasticity} = \left| \frac{[(720 - 800) / 800] \times 100}{[(12 - 10) / 10] \times 100} \right|$$

$$= \left| \frac{0.1 \times 100}{0.2 \times 100} \right|$$

$$= 0.5$$

The elasticity value within this range of the demand curve is higher (more elastic) than it was previously. This result will be true for any straight-line, or linear, demand curve: As we

Figure 5.3 **Elasticity Varies Along a Straight-Line Demand Curve**

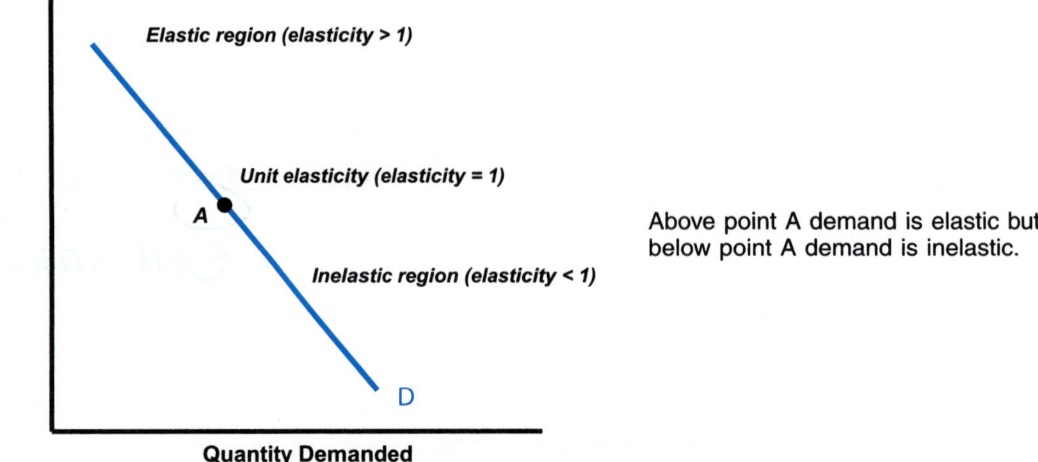

Above point A demand is elastic but below point A demand is inelastic.

unit-elastic demand: the percentage change in the quantity demanded is exactly equal to the percentage change in price. The elasticity value is 1

move "up" the demand curve (to the left), the elasticity value will increase. Often a linear demand curve will have both an elastic region (with an elasticity value greater than 1) and an inelastic region (with an elasticity value less than 1).*

This is illustrated in Figure 5.3. Note that at some point along this linear demand curve, the elasticity value is exactly 1. Economists call this **unit-elastic demand,** when the percentage change in the quantity demanded is exactly equal to the percentage change in price. This is shown as point A on the demand curve. (Note that the point of unit elasticity does not necessarily occur in the "middle" of a linear demand curve.)

Elasticity and the Direction of the Price Change

Next, let's consider another question: Does the direction of the price change matter when calculating elasticity?

Referring again to our data in Table 5.1, let's calculate elasticity with price decreasing from \$10 to \$5, instead of increasing from \$5 to \$10. Inserting the appropriate values, we get:

$$Elasticity = \left| \frac{[(1000 - 800) / 800] \times 100}{[(5 - 10) / 10] \times 100} \right|$$

$$= \left| \frac{0.25 \times 100}{0.5 \times 100} \right|$$

$$= 0.5$$

So while the elasticity value was 0.2 when price increased from \$5 to \$10, it is 0.5 when price decreases from \$10 to \$5, even though we are moving along the same exact segment of the demand curve! So when we quote an elasticity value for a particular good or service, do we also need to indicate whether this elasticity applies to a price increase or a price decrease?

Fortunately, this problem can be avoided. As explained in Box 5.2, we can use the "midpoint" formula to obtain the same elasticity value regardless of whether the price increases or decreases along the same segment of a linear demand curve.

*Economists often work with "constant-elasticity" demand curves, where the elasticity value is the same at any point along the demand curve. Constant-elasticity demand curves are actual curves, not straight lines, that bow in toward the origin. Constant-elasticity demand curves tend to be more realistic representations of demand for many goods and services.

BOX 5.2 THE MIDPOINT ELASTICITY FORMULA

The reason that the direction a price change matters when we calculate an elasticity value is that the denominators change when we calculate the percentage change in each variable. The denominator used to calculate the percentage change is the "base" value. But by changing the direction of the change, the base value can be the higher or the lower number. So the key to obtaining the same elasticity value regardless of the direction of the price change is to obtain the same denominators when calculating the percentage changes. We can do this by using the "midpoint formula."

Consider our example of price changing from \$5 to \$10 (or vice versa). The percentage change is either 50 percent or 100 percent depending on the direction of the change. To use the midpoint formula, instead of using the base value as the denominator when calculating the percentage change, we use the midpoint, or average, of the two values:

$$\textit{Midpoint} = (\textit{new number} + \textit{base number})/2$$

So for the price change between \$5 and \$10, in either direction, the base value for the denominator when calculating the percentage change in price is now 7.5. For the quantity change, the midpoint between 800 and 1,000 is 900. Thus the elasticity value for a price increase from \$5 to \$10 using the midpoint formula would be:

$$\begin{aligned} \textit{Elasticity} &= |[(-200/900) \times 100]/[(5/7.5) \times 100]| \\ &= |-22.22/66.67| \\ &= 0.3333 \end{aligned}$$

You can test yourself by proving that you get the same elasticity value if the price decreases from \$10 to \$5. Note that the elasticity value here, 0.3333, is between our two previous elasticity estimates (0.2 and 0.5) based on prices of \$5 and \$10. However, realize that the elasticity obtained using the midpoint formula is *not* the midpoint of the two elasticity values using the conventional approach.

Elasticity and Slope

You may recall from a math class that the equation for a straight line is:

$$y = b + m\,x$$

where m is the slope of the line and b is the intercept term. The slope defines the numerical change in the y value every time the x value increases by 1.

Some students mistakenly think that elasticity is the same thing as the slope of a linear demand curve. But note that the slope of the line in Figure 5.3 does not change. As we have already seen, the elasticity value differs as we move along a linear demand curve.

Although a "steeper" slope generally suggests a less elastic demand curve than a "flatter" curve, we can make any demand curve look flatter or steeper depending on how we draw (i.e., scale) the two axes. Compare Figure 5.4 to Figure 5.1. At first glance, the demand curve in Figure 5.4 appears flatter than the curve in Figure 5.1, suggesting that it is a more elastic demand curve. But the underlying data are exactly the same in the two figures—the x-axis in Figure 5.4 has merely been adjusted to start at a quantity of 700 rather than 0, making the curve appear flatter. Thus we cannot determine elasticity, even approximately, simply by looking at a demand curve without making the necessary calculations.

1.6 ELASTICITY AND REVENUES

Important to look out for self-interest

A common application of elasticity estimates is predicting how a company's revenues will change in response to a price change. A business, such as Braeburn Publishing, can use an elasticity estimate to determine what price it should charge to maximize its revenues. Recall the example from the beginning of the chapter regarding the MBTA's raising fares to eliminate a budget deficit. If the MBTA had a reliable estimate of the elasticity of demand for public transportation, it could calculate how much revenues would be expected to change with different fare levels. Other government agencies can rely on elasticity estimates to determine how different tax rates will affect revenues.

Figure 5.4 **Changing the Scale of Braeburn's Demand Curve**

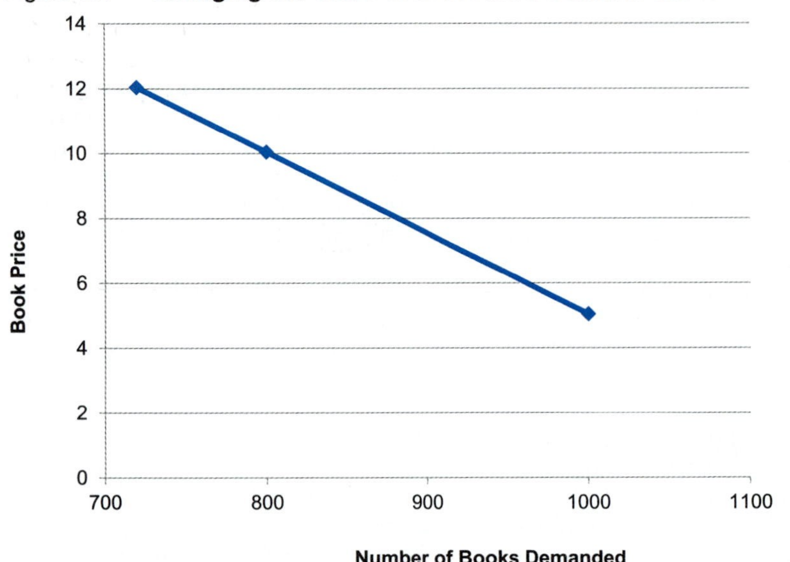

We cannot make conclusions about elasticity simply by looking at a demand curve. By changing the scale of the axes we can make a demand curve "look" more or less elastic.

The revenues that a business (or government agency) will receive from selling a good or service at a specific price is simply that price multiplied by the quantity sold:

$$\textit{Revenues} = \textit{Price} \times \textit{Quantity Sold}$$

So in the case of Braeburn, the revenue that it obtains from selling 1,000 books at a price of \$5 per book is:

$$\textit{Revenue} = \$5 \times 1{,}000 = \$5{,}000$$

We can also represent revenues graphically based on a demand curve. First, recall that the area of a rectangle is its height multiplied by its length. Thus the revenue obtained at any point on a demand curve can be shown as a rectangle equal to its height (price) multiplied by its length (quantity sold). This is illustrated in Figure 5.5, which is the same demand curve presented in Figure 5.1. At a price of \$5, book revenues are equal to area A plus area B, which is \$5,000.

Figure 5.5 **Braeburn's Book Revenues**

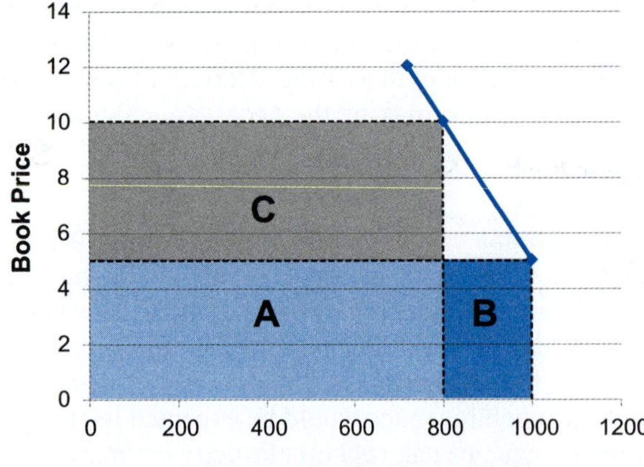

Braeburn's book revenues equal areas A+B at a price of \$5 per book. Revenues equal areas A+C at a price of \$10 per book.

Now suppose that price is increased to \$10—will revenues increase or decrease? We can see in Figure 5.5 that if the price is \$10, revenues will be equal to area A plus area C. So increasing the price from \$5 to \$10, Braeburn loses area B in revenues but gains area C (Braeburn obtains area A at either price). From looking at the figure, it seems apparent that area C is greater than area B. So we can conclude that Braeburn's revenues will increase as a result of a price increase. We can confirm this by calculating revenues at a price of \$10 as \$8,000 (\$10 × 800 books).

What does this have to do with elasticity? When we calculated the elasticity of demand moving from a price of \$5 to a price of \$10, we found that demand was price inelastic (with a value of 0.2). Whenever demand is price inelastic, increasing price will have a relatively small effect on quantity demanded. Thus a business will be able to sell almost the same quantity but at a higher price, earning higher revenues. In other words, whenever demand is price inelastic, increasing the price will increase revenues. Conversely, with inelastic demand, decreasing price will decrease revenues.

But if demand is price elastic, then increasing price will lead to a relatively large decrease in the quantity demanded. A business will receive more revenue per unit sold, but the quantity sold will decrease substantially, earning lower overall revenues. So whenever demand is price elastic, increasing prices will lower revenues. Decreasing prices will increase revenues if demand is price elastic.

If the elasticity value for a good or service is 1, then the percentage changes in price and quantity demanded are the same magnitude (but in opposite directions). For example, doubling price would reduce the quantity demanded by half. Selling twice as many of something at half the price will result in the same exact revenue. So if the elasticity value for a good or service is 1, changing the price will have no effect on revenues.

The effects of price changes on revenues for different elasticities are summarized in Table 5.2. As mentioned previously, a demand curve may be elastic for one range of prices but inelastic over a different range. Thus revenue changes may vary considerably as one moves along a demand curve.

Table 5.2 **Effects of Price Changes on Revenues**

Elasticity value (e)	Elasticity description	Effect of a price increase on revenues	Effect of a price decrease on revenues
$e = 0$	Perfectly inelastic	Increase	Decrease
$0 < e < 1$	Inelastic	Increase	Decrease
$e = 1$	Unit elastic	No change	No change
$1 < e < \infty$	Elastic	Decrease	Increase
∞	Perfectly elastic	Revenues fall to zero	Decrease

1.7 PRICE ELASTICITY OF DEMAND IN THE REAL WORLD

Economists have estimated the elasticity of demand for many goods and services. In order to estimate an elasticity, one needs information on the quantity demanded at different prices. In some cases, variations in prices commonly occur over time. Gasoline is a good example of a product whose price fluctuates. In other cases, price variations may occur across geographic regions. For example, different electric utilities charge different electricity rates.

However, estimating elasticity is not as simple as tracking how the quantity sold responds to price variations. Remember that elasticity measures movement along a demand curve as price changes, ceteris paribus. Thus an accurate measurement of elasticity requires that none of the nonprice determinants of demand have caused the demand curve to shift and that the supply curve has not shifted either. Although economists cannot prevent these changes from occurring, they can use statistical techniques to attempt to isolate the effects of price changes on the quantity demanded.

We normally cannot speak of "the" elasticity of demand for a particular good. Different economists may obtain different elasticity values for the same product because of variations in the statistical techniques that they use or the region studied. For example, the elasticity of demand for cigarettes has been found to vary between developed and developing countries. As we discuss further later in the chapter, elasticity can change depending on the time allowed for consumers to adjust their behavior. See Box 5.3 for more on how the elasticity for a product can vary.

For these reasons, many economic analyses present a range of elasticity values for a particular good. Thus the effect of a price change on revenues will commonly be difficult to predict accurately, but we hope that the actual result will fall within our forecasted range. This is another illustration of the tradeoff between precision and accuracy, as discussed in Chapter 4.

Table 5.3 presents the range of elasticity values found for some products. In air travel, for example, we see that demand is inelastic for first-class travelers, who might either be on business trips or wealthy enough to disregard some price changes, but that demand is elastic for pleasure travelers, who might decide to take a road trip instead for vacation if air fares rise significantly. Note also that elasticity tends to be higher in developing countries, where lower incomes tend to make people more sensitive to price changes.

Table 5.3 **Some Estimated Price Elasticities of Demand**

	Price elasticity of demand	
Good or service	*Low range*	*High range*
Cigarettes	0.4 (developed countries)	0.8 (developing countries)
Gasoline	0.1 (short term)	0.3 (long term)
Residential water	0.1 (lower estimates)	0.7 (higher estimates)
Air travel	0.3 (first-class travelers)	1.4 (pleasure travelers)
Soft drinks	0.8 (soft drinks in general)	4.4 (specific drink brands)
Eggs	0.1 (United States)	0.6 (South Africa)
Rice	0.3 (United States)	0.8 (China)

Box 5.3 The Shifting Demand Elasticity for Gasoline

Gasoline is perhaps the good whose demand elasticity has been most studied by economists. Numerous estimates of the demand elasticity for gasoline have been published going back to the 1960s. Because so much data are available, economists have been able to explore whether the demand elasticity for gasoline has changed over time.

A 2008 paper compared gasoline demand in the United States in the late 1970s with data from 2001–6. The results indicated that the elasticity value had decreased significantly over time, from about 0.30 in the 1970s to only 0.05 in the 2000s.

What may be responsible for such a large decrease in the demand elasticity for gasoline? The authors propose several explanations, including:

- American drivers have become more dependent on their vehicles over time. In particular, an increase in suburban development has increased the travel distances between where people live and where they work and shop. Thus alternatives such as walking and biking are less viable now than in the past.
- As incomes have increased over time, gasoline purchases comprise a smaller share of overall expenses. Thus consumers may be less responsive to increases in gas prices.
- Vehicles have become more fuel efficient over time. Consumers with relatively fuel efficient vehicles may be less responsive to gas price increases.

The authors conclude that attempts to reduce gas consumption significantly by increasing gas taxes are likely to be ineffective. Instead, they suggest that higher fuel-economy standards for new vehicles are likely to be both more effective and more politically acceptable.

Source: Jonathan E. Hughes, Christopher R. Knittel, and Daniel Sperling, "Evidence of a Shift in the Short-Run Price Elasticity of Gasoline Demand," *Energy Journal* 29(1) (2008): 113–134.

Going back to our MBTA example, what did it estimate for the elasticity of demand for public transportation? The MBTA obtained elasticity estimates based on analysis of the impacts of previous fare increases. It estimated separate elasticity values for different types of public transportation, such as buses, subways, and commuter trains. Moreover, it differentiated between riders who purchase monthly passes and those who pay for each ride.

As one example, the MBTA estimated that the elasticity of demand for commuter rail passengers with monthly passes was about 0.1 but for "single-fare" riders of the commuter trains it was 0.35. In either case, demand is inelastic, meaning that MBTA revenues would increase with a fare increase. But why would demand be relatively more inelastic for those with monthly passes? A likely explanation is that those with monthly passes use the commuter trains for daily transportation to their workplace. Although car travel is a potential alternative, the cost of parking and the hassle of traffic jams may make the commuter rail a better choice, even with a modest fare increase. Alternatively, single-fare riders may only take the commuter train occasionally, for work or pleasure, and might have viable transportation alternatives or decide just to stay home.

The MBTA also estimated that demand would be less elastic for students than nonstudents. Again, this seems a reasonable result, given that students are less likely to have their own vehicles as a transportation alternative. The MBTA decided on an average fare increase of 23 percent in July 2012. According to its analysis, it expected that overall ridership would decline by about 5.5 percent. Because public transportation demand is inelastic, revenues were expected to increase.

How accurate was the MBTA's prediction? It turned out that in the immediate months after the fare increase, overall ridership actually increased slightly! Does this result refute the basic inverse relationship between price and quantity demanded? Not necessarily. Remember, elasticity only estimates movement along a demand curve. The increase in ridership after the fare increase may have been the result of an increase in demand (i.e., a shift in the demand curve), which more than offset a decrease in the quantity demanded as a result of the fare increase. The increase in demand may have been due to improving economic conditions, an increase in gas prices, the weather, or some other factor. It may also suggest that the actual elasticity of demand is almost perfectly inelastic. This example demonstrates that economic forecasting is not an exact science and that human behavior is difficult to predict. (See Box 5.1 for another example of the problem with economic predictions.)

Discussion Questions

1. Consider the goods and services for which estimated elasticity values are given in Table 5.3. Can you think of some reasons why demand for cigarettes, eggs, and rice is inelastic? Can you think of an explanation for the two different elasticity values for soft drinks?
2. Suppose that when Winged Demons Athletic Shoes offers a 15 percent discount on its latest model of shoe, it finds that it sells 20 percent more of them. Calculate the price elasticity of demand for these shoes. Describe whether demand is price elastic or price inelastic, and describe what happens to the company's revenues after it offers the discount.

2. THE PRICE ELASTICITY OF SUPPLY

price elasticity of supply: a measure of the responsiveness of quantity supplied to changes in price

Just as movements along a demand curve can be described by elasticity, so can movements along a supply curve, which reflect the **price elasticity of supply**. The price elasticity of supply measures the responsiveness of quantity supplied to changes in price.

Suppose, for example, that a manufacturing company is having trouble getting adequate supplies of a needed component that is an input to its production process. Only a limited number of companies have the equipment to make this particular component, and those companies are not willing to produce more of it at the going price. The company's buyer might consider offering the suppliers a higher price. By how much will the buyer need to sweeten his firm's offer to induce suppliers to supply the quantity of components that the company needs? What the company's buyer needs to know is the responsiveness of quantity supplied to price.

If the suppliers will significantly increase the quantity that they sell with a modest increase in price, then we would say the supply curve is price elastic. Meanwhile, if it takes a considerably higher price to induce suppliers to increase quantity, then we would say the supply curve is price inelastic.

The company's dilemma is illustrated in Figure 5.6. It is initially able to purchase a quantity of Q_0 of the components at a price of P_0. Then suppose that it wishes to increase the quantity it purchases to Q_1. If supply is relatively elastic (represented by the supply curve S_e), it can induce suppliers to increase supply to Q_1 with a price of only P_e. However, if supply is relatively inelastic (such as supply curve S_i), it will need to pay a higher price, say P_i. Obviously, the company needing the components will hope that the supply curve is relatively elastic, such as S_e, which means that it will have to pay less to obtain Q_1. Note that the known starting point, at a price of P_0 and a quantity supplied of Q_0, lies on both supply curves. The elasticity of supply determines how the curves diverge from the known starting point.

Figure 5.6 **The Price Elasticity of Supply**

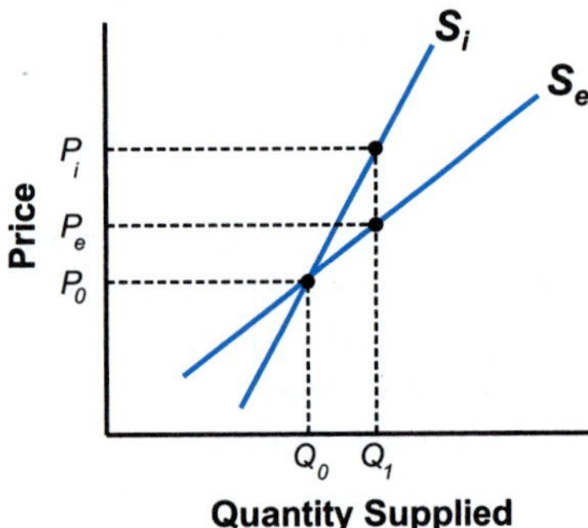

Supply curve S_e is more elastic than supply curve S_i. Thus with supply curve S_e a company can entice their supply to increase the quantity supplied to Q_1 with a smaller price increase.

As in the equation for the price elasticity of demand, the price elasticity of supply is calculated as:

Elasticity = % change in quantity supplied / % change in price

Given that supply curves normally slope upward, price and quantity supplied change in the same direction and thus taking the absolute value is not required. If the price elasticity of supply is greater than 1, we would say the supply curve is price elastic. If the price elasticity of supply is less than 1, we would say the supply curve is price inelastic. A price elasticity of supply equal to 1 is "unit elastic."

A perfectly inelastic supply curve is vertical and indicates that supply is completely fixed. The supply of authentic 1940 Chevrolets, for example, can no longer be increased, no matter what the price. A perfectly elastic supply curve is horizontal, indicating that buyers can buy all they want at the going price. As individual consumers, for example, each of us makes up such a small part of the total market for things like supermarket groceries and mass-produced clothing that such a horizontal curve is a reasonable representation of what we face. We generally pay the same price, no matter how many units we buy of a good.

Hundreds of economic studies have estimated the elasticity of demand, but relatively few estimate the elasticity of supply. Several studies have estimated the elasticity of supply for housing, primarily in the United States. The results indicate that the supply of housing is normally, but not always, price elastic. Estimates of the elasticity of supply for housing range from below 1.0 (inelastic) to as much as 30 or higher.[1] The elasticity of supply for labor, however, is generally found to be price inelastic. The U.S. Congressional Budget Office uses a value of 0.40 for the elasticity of supply for labor in its analyses.[2]

Discussion Questions

1. Suppose that a government alternative-energy program is having difficulty hiring enough engineers to work on a project, and so it raises the wage that it offers to pay by 15 percent. Who are the buyers in this case? Who are the sellers? What does the wage represent, in terms of a supply-and-demand framework? If the program finds that employment applications then increase by 30 percent, what can you conclude about the price elasticity of supply of engineering labor?
2. Economists draw supply curves as upward sloping. But sometimes, as consumers, we notice that the price per unit goes down if we buy more of something, not up. For example, a liter bottle of Pepsi costs less per ounce than a can of Pepsi, warehouse stores sell breakfast cereal in "jumbo size" for a low per-unit price, and clothing stores offer "buy one, get one free." Why might sellers offer such prices?

3. INCOME ELASTICITY OF DEMAND

income elasticity of demand: a measure of the responsiveness of demand to changes in income, holding price constant

The final kind of elasticity that we consider in this chapter is the **income elasticity of demand**. This measures how much the quantity demanded changes when income changes, but holding price constant. Recall from Chapter 4 that income is a nonprice determinant of demand that shifts the entire demand curve.

Figure 5.7 illustrates the concept of income elasticity. Suppose that D_0 represents an initial demand curve. At a price of P_0, the quantity demanded is Q_0. Now suppose that consumer incomes increase. At higher incomes, demand will normally increase (i.e., shift to the right). Income elasticity indicates how much demand shifts. If demand for the good is relatively income inelastic, then demand might only shift slightly, say to D_i. At D_i and with price constant at P_0, the quantity demanded increases to Q_i. The demand curve D_e represents a relatively elastic response, with the quantity demanded increasing to Q_e.

Figure 5.7 **Income Elasticity of Demand**

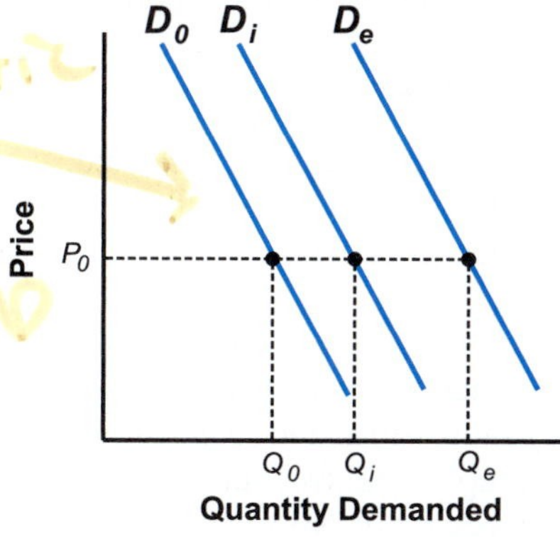

An increase in income shifts the demand curve outward (to the right). The greater the income elasticity of demand, the greater the shift.

As in the equations for price elasticity, income elasticity is calculated as:

income elasticity of demand = % change in quantity demanded / % change in income

normal goods: goods for which demand increases when incomes rise and decreases when incomes fall

inferior goods: goods for which demand decreases when incomes rise and increases when incomes fall

For most goods, when income increases, demand also increases. Thus income elasticity is positive. Goods for which demand rises when a household's income rises are called **normal goods**. As people can afford more, they tend to buy more.

However, demand for some goods may fall when incomes rise; these goods are called **inferior goods**. Individuals and families tend to buy less of goods like ramen noodles or second-hand clothes as incomes rise. For an inferior good, the income elasticity of demand is negative.

When income elasticity is positive but less than 1, demand is called income inelastic. Spending rises with income, but less than proportionately. For example, when income rises by 10 percent, spending on a particular good may rise by only 5 percent. When the income elasticity is positive and greater than 1, a good is called income elastic. In this case, expenditures on that good will take up a greater share of total spending by the buyer. For example, income may rise by 10 percent, but spending on the good rises by 20 percent. (If some goods are income elastic, then other goods must be income inelastic—or a buyer would end up exceeding his or her budget!)

Income-elastic goods are referred to as "luxuries," because the rich spend proportionately more on them than do the poor. By the same token, goods for which demand is inelastic are sometimes called "necessities." These labels, however, are only economists' shorthand for specifying ranges of income elasticity and have nothing to do with human well-being. For example, studies of consumer demand usually find cigarettes to be, by this definition, "necessities" because poorer people (who are more likely to smoke) spend a greater proportion of their income on them.

Households are not the only economic actors that have to work within a budget. Divisions of businesses, branches of government, and other organizations also find that the budgets for their operations may vary. Thus we can also speak of income elasticity for these economic actors. Businesses that make high profits often spend more on holiday parties and other perks. Offices with tight budgets may spend more on low-grade copier paper, an inferior good. As discussed in Chapter 4, income changes—or, more generally, changes in any overall ability to pay—shift the demand curve, changing the quantity demanded at any price.

Discussion Questions

1. Suppose that your income increases. Which goods and services would you buy more of (i.e., normal goods)? Which goods and services would you buy less of (i.e., inferior goods)?
2. Which goods might be normal goods at some income levels but inferior goods at other income levels? (Hint: You might think of a household that is desperately poor, then becomes moderately poor, and eventually becomes middle income.)

4. Income and Substitution Effects of a Price Change

Returning to the impact of price changes on the quantity demanded, we can think further about the motivations of consumers. It makes intuitive sense that consumers will buy more of a good when prices fall and less of it when prices rise. But we can define two underlying reasons for these responses.

First, a change in the price of a particular good or service changes how consumers evaluate that good or service relative to other goods and services. Specifically, if the price of something falls, it becomes relatively more attractive to consumers. If the price rises, it becomes relatively less attractive. For example, suppose that the price of apples and oranges start out at $1.00 and $1.50 per pound, respectively. Now suppose the price of oranges rises to $2.00 per pound while the price of the apples remains at $1.00. The oranges are now twice as expensive as apples, instead of 1.5 times as expensive. Oranges have become relatively more expensive, and apples relatively cheaper.

substitution effect of a price change: the tendency of a price increase for a particular good to reduce the quantity demanded of that good, as buyers turn to relatively cheaper substitutes

Economists refer to changes in consumer behavior as a result of changes in relative prices the **substitution effect of a price change**. When one good becomes more expensive relative to others, people will reduce the quantity demanded of that good and turn toward the relatively cheaper substitutes. If you think that apples and oranges are good substitutes for each other, then the rise in the relative price of oranges will tend to make you buy fewer oranges and more apples. If the price of natural gas water heating rises relative to the price of solar water heating, one can expect any household or organization that uses hot water to lean more toward solar than before, when the time comes to replace its system.

Note that a substitution effect occurs only when relative prices change. For example, if the price of apples rose to $2.00 per pound at the same time that the price of oranges rose to $3.00 per pound, then their relative prices would remain unchanged (oranges are still 1.5 times more expensive than apples). In this case, there is no substitution effect.

income effect of a price change: the tendency of a price increase to reduce the quantity demanded of normal goods (and to increase the quantity demanded of any inferior goods)

In addition to a substitution effect, economists also speak of the **income effect of a price change**. The income effect arises because an increase in the price of any good that a buyer purchases reduces her or his overall purchasing power (given a set income or budget). For example, suppose that you could buy 12 apples and 5 oranges at their initial prices, but then the price of oranges rise. Given your limited income, you can no longer afford 12 apples and 5 oranges. In other words, the effect of the rise in the price of oranges is essentially the same as a decrease in your income. Any price rise for a good that you usually purchase makes you, in a sense, poorer. Similar to a decrease in income, the income effect indicates that people will respond to a price increase by reducing the quantity of normal goods that they buy (and increase the quantity demanded of any inferior goods).

Because you are now poorer, your response to the price increase will depend, in part, on which goods are normal and which (if any) are inferior, as defined earlier in the chapter. If both apples and oranges are normal goods, you, now being poorer, will tend to buy less of each. If, however, apples are inferior goods to you, which you buy only because you cannot afford more oranges, you will tend to buy even more apples (but fewer oranges) when you are made poorer by a rise in orange prices. (What if, instead, oranges were the inferior good?)

When the price of a good or service changes, the income and substitution effects act together:

- If the good is a normal good and its price rises, both the income effect and the substitution effect will tend to reduce the quantity demanded of the good. The quantity demanded falls with a price rise, both because the buyer is poorer and because other goods now look relatively more attractive.
- If the good is inferior and its price rises, the income effect will encourage greater expenditures, at the same time that the substitution effect pushes toward lower expenditures. In general, though, we expect that the substitution effect will be stronger than the income effect in the case of inferior goods, so the demand curve will still be downward-sloping.

The exception, where a price rise for an inferior good leads to such a large income effect that quantity demanded increases, is called the case of a "Giffen good." It is rare in practice, especially in industrialized countries. In very poor countries, however, it is sometimes the case that the poorest of the poor spend a large proportion of their income on a basic foodstuff, such as low-quality rice or starchy root vegetables, and tiny amounts of income on more expensive vegetables and protein-rich foods. If the price of the basic foodstuff rises, survival may demand that they stop purchasing the more expensive foods entirely and make up for these lost calories by buying more of the basic foodstuff. In terms of market analysis, the demand curve for the basic foodstuff will slope upward (and the price elasticity will be positive, even before taking the absolute value). In terms of well-being, of course, the situation represents a human disaster; the starchy food will not supply the vitamins or protein needed for healthy functioning and development.

Discussion Questions

1. Which of the following might be inferior goods? Could they be normal goods at some portion of the income scale and inferior goods at others?
   a. A community college education
   b. Cigarettes
   c. BMW cars
   d. Supermarket food
   e. Restaurant food

2. Suppose that the prices of all goods and services available to a particular buyer go up by 20 percent, all at the same time, while the buyer's income (or budget) remains unchanged. What is the effect on the buyer's purchase of normal goods? Of inferior goods? Is there a substitution effect?

5. Short-Run Versus Long-Run Elasticity

So far, our analysis has essentially assumed that adjustment from one equilibrium point to another equilibrium point happens without any lapse of time. In the real world, the time taken for adjustments is important. For example, we noted how the price elasticity of demand for a good depends on the availability of substitute goods. If substitutes are readily available, demand for the good in question will tend to be more price elastic than it would be if substitutes were hard to get. But what if substitutes are hard to get right away but easier to get over time?

short-run elasticity: a measure of the relatively immediate responsiveness to a price change

long-run elasticity: a measure of the response to a price change after economic actors have had time to make adjustments

It is possible for a good to be highly price inelastic in the short run but more price elastic as people can make adjustments over time. We can distinguish **short-run elasticity**, which measures relatively immediate responses to a price change, from **long-run elasticity**, which measures how much quantity responds after economic actors have had some time to adjust.

Gasoline is a good example for which the passage of time is important in determining the elasticity of demand, as we saw in Table 5.3. In the short run, when gas prices increase, consumers are mostly unable to reduce the amount of gas that they use for commuting and shopping. But over time they may be able to purchase a more fuel-efficient vehicle, rely more on public transportation, consider carpooling, and even move closer to where they work. We see in Table 5.3 that the long-run elasticity of demand for gas is still inelastic at 0.3, but it is more elastic than the short-run elasticity of 0.1.*

Discussion Questions

1. Maria rents on a month-to-month basis an apartment that she can barely afford, in a market where apartments are hard to find. Her landlord announces that she is doubling the rent, effective immediately. What is likely to be Maria's short-run response (say, over the next few days or weeks)? What might be her likely long-run response (over the next few months)?
2. Suppose that new technological breakthroughs make solar water heaters extremely cheap to run, compared with water heaters that use fossil fuels, and only moderately expensive to install. Illustrate on a graph what you might expect the short-run and long-run demand adjustments to this price drop to be. What sorts of factors affect how long, in real time, it might take for the "long-run" situation to occur?

Review Questions

1. List three reasons why the demand for a good or service may be elastic. List three reasons why the demand for a good may be inelastic.
2. What is the formula for the price elasticity of demand?
3. What is the "technical definition" of a price-elastic demand? What is the technical definition of a price-inelastic demand?
4. What does a perfectly inelastic demand curve look like? What does a perfectly elastic demand curve look like?
5. How does elasticity change along a linear demand curve?
6. Is elasticity the same thing as the slope of a curve?

*The difference between the short run and the long run, as specific periods, is rather vague. In the case of gasoline demand, the short run might be only a few months. A period of a year or more would probably be considered the long run.

7. What is the relationship between elasticity and how a firm's revenues change as it changes its prices?
8. How can we represent revenues on a graph?
9. Describe quantity and revenue responses to price changes when the price elasticity of demand takes on the following values: (a) 0, (b) between 0 and 1, (c) 1, (d) greater than 1.
10. What are examples of goods that are price elastic? What are some examples of price inelastic goods?
11. Sketch, on a single graph, a relatively price-elastic supply curve and a relatively price-inelastic supply curve. (Make sure that they go through the same point.)
12. What is the equation for calculating the price elasticity of supply?
13. What is the income elasticity of demand?
14. Give one example of a normal good and one example of an inferior good.
15. Can you illustrate the income elasticity of demand using a single demand curve? Why or why not?
16. Explain how a price change has both "income effects" and "substitution effects" on buyer behavior.
17. Explain why the long-run elasticity of demand for a good may differ from the short-run elasticity.

EXERCISES

1. For each of the following items, discuss whether you think the demand that the seller faces will be price inelastic or price elastic, and explain why.
   a. A new CD by an extremely popular recording artist
   b. One share of stock, when there are millions of shares for that company outstanding
   c. Bottled drinking water, at a town in the desert
   d. Your used textbooks, at the end of the term
2. Calculate the price elasticity of demand for the following cases:
   a. When price rises by 5 percent, quantity demanded drops by 10 percent.
   b. When price rises by 10 percent, quantity demanded drops by 2 percent.
   c. When price rises by 0.05 percent, quantity demanded drops by 99 percent. (Which extreme case is this approaching? Note that the price rise is a fraction of 1 percent, not 5 percent.)
   d. When price rises by 99 percent, quantity demanded drops by 0.05 percent. (Which extreme case is this approaching?)
   e. When price falls by 10 percent, quantity demanded rises by 2 percent.
3. Calculate the percentage change in revenue that would result from each of the actions in Exercise 2 above. Assume that the initial price in all cases is $100 per unit, and the initial quantity demanded is 1,000 units.
4. Braeburn Publishing decides to try to cut its costs of printing books by cutting the price that it offers to companies that supply it with paper.
   a. Suppose that the supply is perfectly price inelastic (at least in the short run), because Braeburn buys the entire output of the Morales Paper Company. Because it has no other customers (for now), Morales has no choice but to sell to Braeburn. Illustrate on a graph what will happen to the quantity that Braeburn buys, the price that it pays, and the amount that it will spend on paper.
   b. Suppose, instead, that the supply of paper is very (but not perfectly) price elastic, because all the companies that sell paper to Braeburn can easily sell their paper elsewhere. Illustrate on a graph what will happen to the quantity that Braeburn will be able to buy, the price that it will pay, and the amount that it will spend on paper, if it follows through with its plan to offer a lower price.
5. Use the formulas for elasticity to answer the following questions.
   a. When Mariba's income rises by 10 percent, her expenditures on carrots rise 12 percent. What is Mariba's income elasticity of demand for carrots? Are carrots, for her, a normal or an inferior good?
   b. Suppose that the price elasticity of demand for milk is 0.6. If a grocer raises the price of milk by 15 percent, by what percentage will milk sales decrease as a result of the price increase? Will the grocer's revenue from milk sales go up or down?
   c. Suppose that the price elasticity of supply for paper is 1.5. You notice that the quantity of paper supplied decreases by 6 percent as the result of a change in the price of paper. Determine by what percentage the price of paper must have declined.
6. Clark Marketing Services has found, through market tests, that the demand for Sonya's Peanuts has

a price elasticity of 0.5 and an income elasticity of 1.8. You, an economist employed by Sonya's Peanuts, have been asked by the executives of the company to explain what this means for its pricing policy and choice of sales outlets. Company executives have been thinking of lowering the firm's prices and concentrating on selling to discount stores. What do you advise? Explain in a paragraph.

7. Many environmentalists think that an increase in the price of petroleum products to consumers would be a good thing. Many policymakers believe that an increase in the price of higher education (say, through increased tuitions), however, would be a bad thing. Discuss why these beliefs might be held, using the concepts of "externalities" (discussion in Chapter 1) and "substitution effects of a price change."
8. Look at the estimated price elasticity of demand for cigarettes in Table 5.3. If the government raises taxes on cigarettes, the price to consumers goes up. The extra revenue collected from the higher price goes to the government. Describe in a few sentences the effectiveness of taxing cigarettes as (a) part of a campaign to stop people from smoking and (b) a way of raising revenue.
9. Match each concept in Column A with the corresponding fact or example in Column B:

Column A	Column B
a. Price-inelastic demand	1. Income elasticity of 1.4.
b. Inferior good	2. A 12% rise in price is associated with a 12% fall in quantity demanded.
c. Income effect of a price change	3. Dining out more often because your landlord reduced your rent.
d. Perfectly price elastic supply	4. Expenditures on a good increase when your income rises.
e. Unit price elasticity of demand	5. Any rise in price will cause quantity demanded to fall to zero.
f. Perfectly inelastic supply	6. Buying fewer muffins, and more donuts, because the relative price of muffins has risen.
g. Normal good	7. Revenues rise as a seller increases her price.
h. Perfectly elastic demand	8. What you face when buying milk at the grocery store.
i. Substitution effect	9. The acres of land in downtown Chicago.
j. Income-elastic demand	10. People spend less on this as they get richer.

Notes

1. See Sock-Yong Phang, Kyung-Hwan Kim, and Susan Wachter, "Supply Elasticity of Housing," in *International Encyclopedia of Housing and Home* (Oxford: Elsevier Science, 2012).
2. Felix Reichling and Charles Whalen, "Review of Estimates of the Frisch Elasticity of Labor Supply," Congressional Budget Office Working Paper 2012–13, Washington, DC, October 2012.

6 Welfare Analysis

Adam Smith's *An Inquiry into the Nature and Causes of the Wealth of Nations,* published in 1776, laid down the theoretical framework for modern capitalist economies. In perhaps the most famous passage from the book, Smith asserted that a seller interested only in maximizing his own gain would be

> led by an invisible hand to promote an end which was no part of his intention. . . . By pursuing his own interest he frequently promotes that of the society more effectually than when he really intends to promote it.

Thus Smith suggests that an economic system based on markets can effectively promote the general welfare of society. In the eighteenth century, this was a new, even radical, idea. Until Smith's time, societies tended to be authoritarian and hierarchical. For the average person, individual freedoms were few and opportunities for economic advancement were virtually nonexistent. Many thinkers worried that if people were free to pursue their own self-interest, then the rigid organization of society might break down, leading to a chaotic situation in which nothing would get done. But Smith detailed how the self-regulating features of markets could not only impose order on society but even potentially create the best outcome for society as a whole.

But what do we mean by the "best" outcome? And how can we measure the general welfare of a society in a meaningful way? In this chapter, we extend our understanding of markets to consider their implications for social welfare. We see that under certain conditions and assumptions, markets do, indeed, produce an outcome for society that may be considered "best." But in the real world, these conditions and assumptions rarely apply, and a more accurate assessment of markets requires us to consider the benefits of markets in a broader social and environmental context.

1. Welfare Economics

welfare economics: the branch of microeconomics that seeks to estimate the social welfare of different scenarios in order to determine how to maximize net social benefits

In Chapter 1, we stated that a central objective of economics is enhancing the well-being of society. **Welfare economics** is a branch of microeconomics that seeks to estimate the social welfare of different scenarios in order to determine ways to maximize net social benefits. Welfare economics can be studied from both a theoretical perspective and a quantitative applied perspective.

As a theoretical approach, welfare economics provides insights into situations in which markets produce desirable outcomes as well as other situations in which markets either require policy interventions or are ineffective at meeting our final goals. As a quantitative approach, welfare economics seeks to measure social costs and benefits numerically so that different policy scenarios can be compared. Ideally, we can then choose the policy that produces the greatest social welfare.

social welfare: total benefits to society minus total costs, or total net benefits

Welfare economics offers an appealing feature—the possibility of measuring the quantitative costs and benefits of different policy scenarios. If this can be done reliably, it should then be possible to simply choose the option that results in the greatest social welfare, where **social welfare** is defined as total benefits minus total costs, or total net benefits.

Some economists use such terms as "social welfare" and "social well-being" interchangeably. However, the two concepts have a subtle, but critical, distinction. As defined above, social welfare is something that can potentially be measured quantitatively, although this approach has numerous limitations. Well-being, which we regard as the final goal of economics, is a broader concept that cannot be measured in quantitative terms. Well-being includes such objectives as fairness, participation, and social relations (recall Table 1.1 in Chapter 1). A particular outcome may maximize social welfare in a quantitative sense but not necessarily be the best outcome from the perspective of social well-being.

The goal of maximizing social welfare is sometimes viewed as a positive framework, which does not require normative judgments. In particular, it may seem that simply adding up all benefits and costs and choosing the option that yields the greatest net benefits avoids the influence of value judgments. But explicit and implicit value judgments are almost always involved in stating that a particular policy is "best." For example, in a highly unequal society, would it be better to add $20 billion to the income of those who are already rich or $10 billion to the income of those who are currently poor? The former option offers the greatest net benefits in monetary terms, but the latter might be considered preferable on social and ethical grounds.

Welfare economics considers the costs and benefits of three basic economic actors:

1. consumers
2. producers
3. the rest of society (including, for this discussion, future generations and the ecological context)

third-party effects: impacts of an economic transaction on those not involved in the transaction, such as the health effects of pollution

Consumers obtain benefits when they can voluntarily purchase a desired product at an acceptable price. Producers obtain benefits when they profitably sell products. Often a market transaction results in costs or benefits to those not directly involved in the transaction, that is, the "rest of society." For example, the production of paper can generate pollution that is harmful to the health of local residents. Such impacts on people not involved in the transaction were identified as externalities in Chapter 1, also sometimes called **third-party effects.** In this chapter, we focus mainly on the costs and benefits to consumers and producers. However, we should be aware that any analysis that focuses exclusively on the consumers and producers involved in a market is likely to be incomplete. In Chapter 13, we study impacts on the "rest of society" in more detail, with a particular focus on environmental impacts.

We next turn to how to estimate market benefits to consumers. Then we consider market benefits to producers. Section 4 combines our results to determine the overall social welfare arising from market transactions, both in equilibrium and in cases of surplus or shortage. The final section makes some initial policy inferences based on welfare analysis.

Discussion Questions

1. Do you believe, in principle, that the costs and benefits of various policies can be quantified in monetary terms? Do you believe that some impacts cannot be fundamentally measured in dollars? How would you suggest that we evaluate these impacts?
2. Think of a government policy that is currently being debated in the news. Describe how you would evaluate the costs and benefits of this policy differently if you were concerned primarily about social welfare or social well-being.

2. CONSUMER SURPLUS

In order to understand what our market model tells us about benefits to sellers and buyers, we need to reconsider supply and demand curves. In this section, we take a closer look at demand curves, and in the next section we apply a similar approach to supply curves. The analysis requires some detailed thinking, but after you grasp the concepts in this chapter, you will have a solid foundation for much of microeconomic analysis.

2.1 QUANTIFYING CONSUMER BENEFITS

We will see in Chapters 8 and 9 that consumer decision-making is a complex process—one that appears reasonably rational in some cases but quite irrational in others. For now, we assume that consumers make rational choices that effectively move them toward their final goals.

Every time you contemplate buying something, you have to make a decision about whether you should part with a particular amount of money in exchange for a certain good or service. For example, say that you are considering whether you should spend $1.10 for a cup of coffee. You must decide whether the cup of coffee is worth $1.10 to you. If you decide to buy the coffee, then presumably the loss of $1.10 is more than offset by the amount of welfare that you get by consuming the coffee. Economists use various terms to describe the benefits that people get from their purchases, including utility, welfare, and well-being. As discussed above, we use the term "welfare" here to represent a concept that can be quantitatively measured, as opposed to well-being that cannot be reduced to a single number.

The benefits that people gain from their purchases are mainly "psychic" benefits—they are somehow happier as a result of their purchases. So how can we take this vague notion of a psychic benefit and measure it quantitatively? And in what units should it be measured?

As you might guess, economists tend to prefer to measure this benefit in monetary terms, in dollars in the case of the United States. This allows us to compare these benefits directly with the cost of a product. So, if a cup of coffee costs $1.10, and you decide to purchase it, then those psychic benefits must in some sense exceed $1.10. A rational consumer who buys a cup of coffee is willing to part with $1.10 for it, while a rational consumer who does not buy the coffee does not believe that it is worth $1.10.

But obviously some consumers realize more personal benefits from the same cup of coffee. In other words, the welfare that someone gets from a cup of coffee can vary considerably from one consumer to another. Some people's "happiness" might increase only a little, while others may obtain a big increase in their happiness from the coffee. According to welfare economics, these differences in consumer preferences are expressed in differences in their willingness to pay for something.

maximum willingness to pay (WTP): the maximum amount that a rational consumer will pay for a particular product. In welfare economics, consumers' maximum WTP represents the total benefits that they expect to obtain from a product, expressed in monetary terms.

The key to measuring consumer benefits using welfare analysis is to identify consumers' **maximum willingness to pay (WTP)** for something. Welfare economics assumes that consumers' maximum WTP represents the total benefits that they expect to obtain from a product, expressed in monetary terms. A rational consumer is someone who buys a product as long as the actual price is not greater than her maximum WTP for it. Imagine that the price of coffee increases from $1.10 per cup to, say, $1.40. Some people who were willing to buy coffee at $1.10 would not be willing to pay $1.40. Theoretically, every consumer has a maximum amount that he is willing to pay for a particular product, given the fact that he has alternative choices, for example, purchasing another product or just saving his money.

Suppose that a particular consumer, Luis, is willing to pay a maximum of $1.40 for a cup of coffee, and not a penny more. If the price of coffee is $1.40, then Luis would view trading $1.40 for the coffee as essentially an equal trade—he gives up $1.40 and obtains an equivalent value in welfare from the coffee.

Now suppose that a different consumer, Madeleine, is willing to pay a maximum of $1.75 for the same cup of coffee. Thus $1.75 represents the welfare that she would get if she buys the same cup of coffee. Given that Madeleine has to pay only $1.40 for it, she is willing to

consumer surplus: the net benefits obtained from a purchase, equal to the difference between a consumer's maximum willingness to pay and the price

buy the coffee. In fact, she is getting a bargain in a sense because she can buy the coffee for \$0.35 less than the maximum amount she is willing to pay. Welfare economics defines the difference between a consumer's maximum WTP and the price one must actually pay as the net welfare benefit from the purchase, referred to as **consumer surplus**. Consumer surplus represents the "extra benefits" received from buying something above what is paid for it.

So, in Madeleine's case, she obtains a consumer surplus of \$0.35 from buying a cup of coffee, calculated as her maximum WTP of \$1.75 minus the price of \$1.40:

Consumer surplus = \$1.75 *(maximum WTP)* – \$1.40 *(price)* = \$0.35

Suppose that a third consumer, Emma, is willing to pay a maximum of \$2.00 for the same cup of coffee. Note that this may reflect either Emma's greater appreciation for coffee or her higher disposable income, a point to which we return later. Emma's consumer surplus would be \$0.60. Finally, suppose that a fourth potential consumer, Tom, is willing to pay a maximum of only \$1.00 for a cup of coffee. Because the market price is \$1.40, Tom would choose not to buy the coffee, assuming rational behavior. Of course, anyone who is not willing to pay the going price will not receive any consumer surplus.

2.2 Consumer Surplus and Demand Curves

Of course consumers are rarely required to think about the exact maximum amount that they would be willing to pay for something. In the real world, consumers are normally presented with a price, and either they buy the product or they don't. So, at first glance, it seems that estimating consumer surplus quantitatively is not a realistic option.

But if we think about a demand curve in more detail, we see that it actually provides us with the information that we need to estimate consumer surplus, not only for an individual but for the entire market. Let's go back to our demand curve for coffee. Figure 6.1 repeats Figure 4.4. We know that at a price of \$1.40 per cup, 600 cups of coffee will be demanded per week, as shown at Point A in Figure 6.1.

Next, imagine that we look at a demand curve with a magnifying glass, zooming in on a single point like Point A. This is shown in Figure 6.2.* Note that the *y*-axis now covers

Figure 6.1 **Demand Curve for Cups of Coffee**

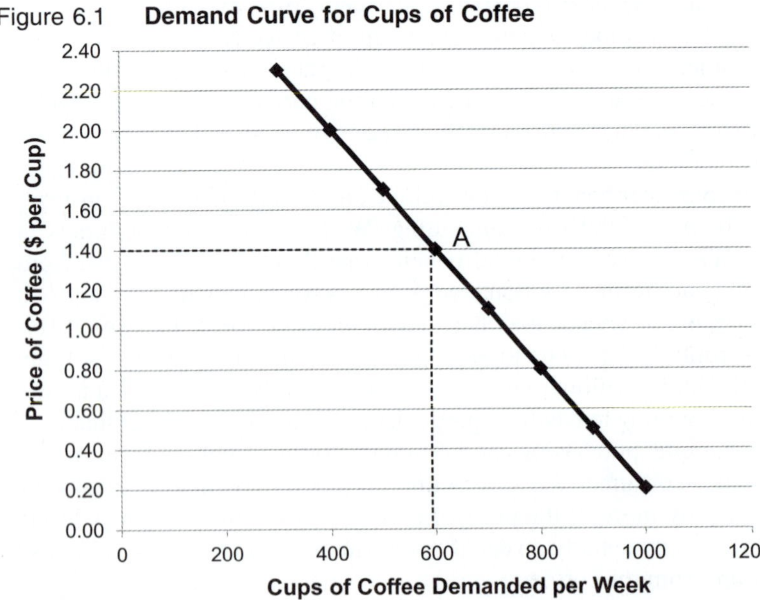

This figure shows the same demand curve for coffee we presented in Chapter 4.

*The "magnified" demand curve in Figure 6.2 is not actually the same as the one in Figure 6.1; in Figure 6.2 we use a different slope, in order to focus on a price change that causes the quantity demanded to decrease by 1.

Figure 6.2 **Detailed Demand Curve for Coffee**

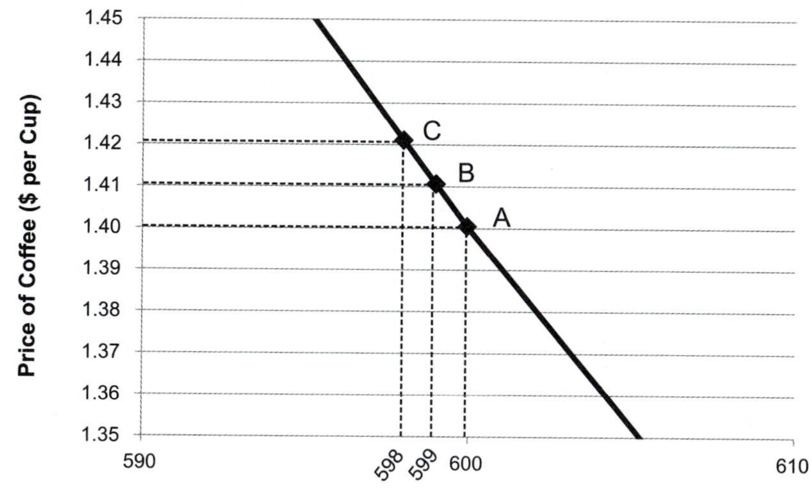

By "zooming in" on the demand curve we can associate marginal price changes with marginal changes in the quantity demanded.

only the range between $1.35 and $1.45, and the *x*-axis covers only the range between 590 and 610 cups of coffee. Point A shows that once again at a price of $1.40, exactly 600 cups of coffee are demanded per week. Now suppose that the price of coffee were increased slightly, by only a penny, from $1.40 to $1.41 per cup. We see in Figure 6.2 that the quantity demanded decreased from 600 to 599 cups per week, as shown by Point B. In other words, one person in our market was willing to pay $1.40 for a cup of coffee, but not $1.41. That one person is the reason that the quantity demanded decreases by 1 when the price rises from $1.40 to $1.41.

Going back to the idea of consumer surplus, Point A represents the maximum willingness to pay ($1.40) of that one person. So we can actually determine the consumer surplus for this person by comparing this point on the demand curve to the price. If the price of coffee were, say, $1.10, then we can conclude that this person's consumer surplus would be $0.30.

If price rises by another penny, from $1.41 to $1.42, then the quantity demanded decreases by 1 again, from 599 to 598 cups (Point C). This is because one other person was willing to pay $1.41, but not $1.42. Again, we can calculate the consumer surplus for the person represented by Point B (the point at which this person is still willing to buy coffee) as the difference between his maximum WTP ($1.41) and price. So if the price of coffee were $1.10, the person at Point B would receive a consumer surplus of $0.31.

The point of this detailed look at a demand curve is to emphasize that a demand curve is not really a smooth line, but a collection of points that represent the decisions of many individuals. Every time the quantity demanded decreases by 1, it is because the price has increased sufficiently for one person to switch from being willing to pay for the product to being not willing to pay.

marginal change: a change of one unit (either an increase or a decrease)

Much economic analysis involves considering **marginal changes**, which means very small changes, either an increase or a decrease; often this is modeled as a change of one unit, as when (above) we add *one* penny to a price, or subtract *one* customer from a large number. We go into this important topic in more detail in relation to production decisions (Chapters 16 and 17).

marginal benefit (for consumers): the benefit of consuming one additional unit of something

In the case that we have been discussing, for each one unit increase in quantity, the corresponding point on the demand curve represents the maximum WTP of the individual (or other economic actor) now willing to buy the product. Another way to understand this is that the points on a demand curve indicate the **marginal benefits**, measured in monetary

marginal benefits curve: a curve showing the additional benefit from each unit consumed. Another name for a demand curve, as applied to welfare economics.

units, of each additional unit of the product to those demanding them. We can say that a demand curve is actually a **marginal benefits curve**, because it tells us the benefits of each additional unit to consumers.

Note that there is a difference between the benefit of consuming a product, which is defined as the maximum WTP, and the **net benefits**, which are the benefits minus any costs. Consumer surplus is a measure of *net* benefits because the price of the product is subtracted from the maximum WTP.

Going back to our demand curve, we can show consumer surplus for any individual by subtracting his maximum WTP (his point along the demand curve) from the price. This is shown in Figure 6.3. Here Luis's maximum WTP is at Point A; he is willing to pay a maximum of $1.40 for a cup of coffee. This is the vertical distance between his point on the demand curve and the *x*-axis. If the price of coffee is $1.10, then the difference ($0.30) is his consumer surplus. This is the net benefit that he obtains from buying a cup of coffee.

Figure 6.3 **Consumer Surplus and a Demand Curve**

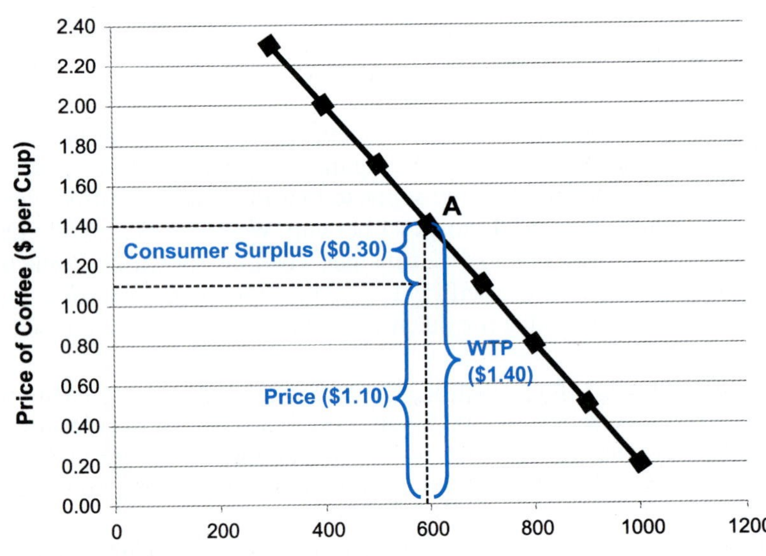

Consumer surplus is the difference between price and someone's maximum willingness to pay (i.e., the demand curve).

2.3 CONSUMER SURPLUS IN AN ENTIRE MARKET

net benefits: benefits minus any costs. Consumer surplus is a measure of net benefits because it is equal to the difference between the maximum willingness to pay and price.

aggregate (or market) benefits: the benefits to all consumers in a market

Now we are ready to take the final step in our analysis of consumer benefits. We have just seen that a demand curve tells us the marginal benefits of each additional unit of a product to consumers. But what really interests us is the benefits of a product to the entire market. Welfare economics assumes that the **aggregate (or market) benefits**, or the benefits to all consumers, is simply the sum of the benefits to each individual consumer. For example, if the entire coffee market consisted of just Luis, Madeleine, and Emma, market benefits would be the sum of the benefits of these three consumers.

The same logic applies to consumer surplus. Aggregate consumer surplus, or aggregate net benefits, is simply the sum of the consumer surpluses for all individuals who buy a product.

Although an individual's maximum WTP is shown by a single point on the demand curve, aggregate benefits can be represented by areas under a demand curve.* So, the area under a demand curve represents the total WTP for all consumers, or the aggregate benefits for all

*If you have studied calculus, you can use integration to determine areas under demand (and supply) curves. This is done in more advanced economics courses.

consumers. The consumer surplus for all consumers in a market is the difference between their aggregate benefits and the aggregate costs that they must pay.

We can illustrate these concepts in another graph, as shown in Figure 6.4. This is the same demand curve for coffee, but in this case extended all the way back to the y-axis. The price of coffee is \$1.10 per cup, and at this price the quantity demanded is 700 cups per week. The amount that consumers must pay for these 700 cups of coffee is the gray rectangle equal to the price multiplied by the quantity sold. This is also the revenue that coffee sellers receive.

market consumer surplus: the difference between aggregate costs and aggregate benefits, or net benefits obtained by all consumers in a market. On a supply-and-demand graph, it is equal to the area under a demand curve but above the price.

Aggregate benefits are the area under the demand curve, up to the quantity actually sold (700 cups). Of course, no benefits are obtained for cups of coffee that are not sold. The **market consumer surplus** is the difference between aggregate costs and aggregate benefits—the blue-shaded triangle in the graph. In other words, market consumer surplus is the area under the demand curve but above the price. According to welfare economics, this area represents the net benefits consumers receive from a market. Thus we can now use a supply-and-demand graph to estimate the quantitative welfare benefits that accrue to consumers—measured as the area below the demand curve but above price. This approach allows us to convert the aggregate psychic benefits of consumers, a rather vague concept, into something we can actually measure. We now turn our attention to the benefits of producers.

Figure 6.4 **Market Consumer Surplus**

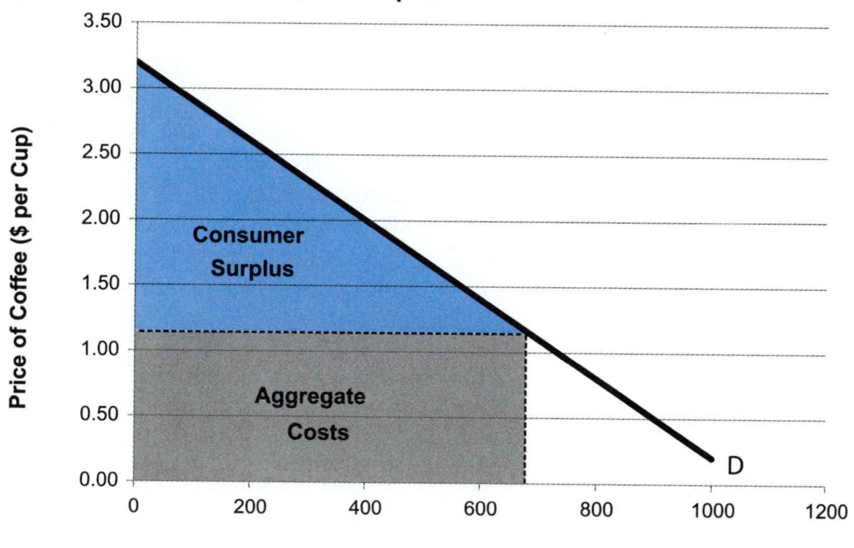

Market consumer surplus is the area below the demand curve but above the price.

Discussion Questions

1. Think about a good or service that you have purchased recently. Try to estimate the maximum amount that you would have been willing to pay for it. What factors influenced your WTP decision? How do you think your willingness to pay might differ from that of other consumers?
2. Do you think that the concept of consumer surplus is an effective tool for converting "psychic" benefits to a monetary value? Do you have any reservations about the concept?

3. Producer Surplus

Now that we understand welfare analysis from the perspective of consumers, we can apply much of the same logic to producers. In particular, we will take a closer look at supply curves to determine how we can use them to understand the benefits producers receive from markets.

3.1 Quantifying Producer Benefits

producer surplus: the net benefits that producers receive from selling products, equal to the difference between the selling price and the marginal costs

marginal cost: the cost of producing one additional unit of something

Whereas the benefits to consumers were defined somewhat vaguely as "psychic" benefits, the benefits that producers receive from markets are much more concrete. So, while consumers seek something vague like happiness or well-being, economists assume that producers seek profits. This makes our analysis of producer benefits relatively straightforward. Rather than needing to convert consumer psychic benefits to monetary units based on their WTP, profits are already measured in dollars.

Welfare economics uses the term **producer surplus** to indicate the benefits that accrue to producers from selling products. For the purpose of our analysis, we essentially assume that producer surplus and profits are the same thing.* The producer surplus for any unit of a product is the difference between its selling price and the cost of producing that particular unit, that is, its **marginal cost**. (We examine the concept of marginal cost more closely in Chapter 16.)

Are sellers really interested only in profits? We consider this issue later in the book. For now, we can note that sellers are also people who seek to enhance their well-being. Making a healthy profit is, of course, a component of their well-being, but they may have other motivations and goals as well. But producer surplus considers only sellers' financial benefits. Again, we must realize that welfare, as defined in economics, is different from well-being.

3.2 Producer Surplus and Supply Curves

In order to estimate producer surplus, we need information on sellers' production costs. You might think that we need to come up with some new curves to illustrate production costs, but that is not necessary. In fact, a supply curve is actually a marginal cost curve. In order to understand why, we need to reconsider how a supply curve relates to the decisions of individual suppliers.

We start with our supply curve from Chapter 4, shown here as Figure 6.5. We can see, for example, that at a price of $1.00 per cup, 600 cups of coffee are supplied. But at that price, why are exactly 600 cups of coffee supplied, and not 601 or more?

Welfare economics assumes that sellers will offer a given unit of a product for sale *only* if they can make a profit on that unit. In other words, if the price they can receive by selling

Figure 6.5 **Supply Curve for Cups of Coffee**

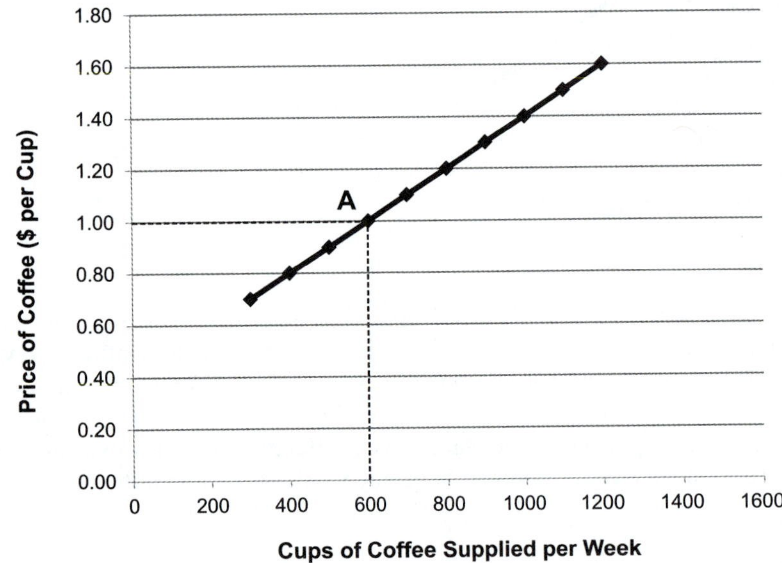

This figure shows the same supply curve for coffee we presented in Chapter 4.

*Technically speaking, this is not quite true. From a marginal perspective, producer surplus is the difference between the price of a product and its marginal cost. Some of this surplus, however, may be used to pay fixed expenses and thus not represent profit to the producer.

is higher than their production costs, they will produce that unit and offer it for sale. If the price is less than their production costs, they will not produce it.

Just as we did with a demand curve, we can zoom in on a supply curve to understand why exactly 600 cups of coffee are offered for sale at a price of $1.00 per cup. We do this with Figure 6.6. The graph shows us that in order for more than 600 cups of coffee to be offered for sale, the price must rise from $1.00 per cup to $1.01 per cup.* So assuming that sellers will offer a product only if they can make a profit on it and will not offer a product if they cannot make a profit on it, we can make the following statements:

- The seller *does* make a profit on the 600th cup of coffee when price is $1.00, because it *is* offered for sale (Point A).
- The seller *does not* make a profit on the 601st cup of coffee when price is $1.00, because it *is not* offered for sale.
- If the price rises to $1.01, then the 601st cup of coffee then becomes profitable and is offered for sale (Point B).

Now ask yourself: How much does it cost the seller to produce the 601st cup of coffee? Realizing that it is not profitable at a price of $1.00, but is profitable at a price of $1.01, we can conclude that the production cost must be more than $1.00 but less than $1.01. In other words, the marginal cost of producing the 601st cup of coffee is slightly more than $1.00.** Looking at Figure 6.6, that is exactly what the supply curve indicates—moving from 600 cups (Point A) to 601 cups (Point B) of coffee, the corresponding price is between $1.00 and $1.01. The supply curve is telling us the marginal cost of producing coffee.

At a price of $1.01, the seller offers 601 cups of coffee, but not 602. Again, it would take a further price increase, from $1.01 to $1.02, to induce the seller to offer the 602nd cup of coffee (Point C). So we conclude that the marginal cost of supplying the 602nd cup is between $1.01 and $1.02. Again, this is exactly what the supply curve indicates.

Now that we know that the supply curve tells us the marginal cost of producing each unit, all we need to do to obtain producer surplus is to compare the supply curve to the price. If the

Figure 6.6 **Detailed Supply Curve for Coffee**

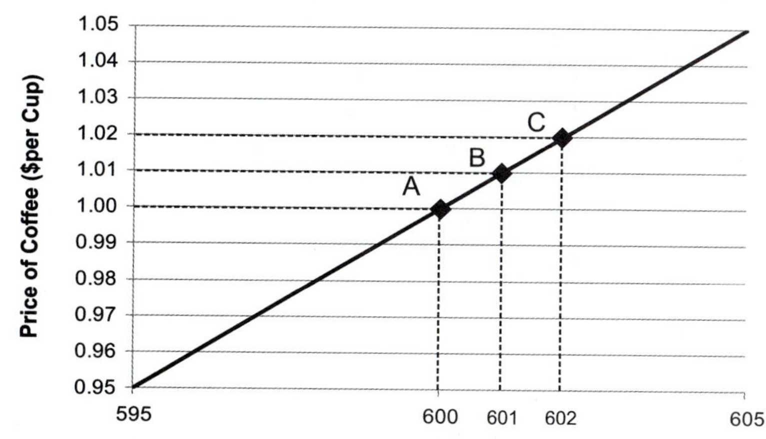

By zooming in on the supply curve we can associate marginal price changes with marginal changes in the quantity supplied.

*We have again adjusted the slope of the curve in order to focus on a change in quantity of one.

**Note that there may be points where the marginal production cost exactly equals the price. Thus the producer would not increase profits by offering the unit for sale but would not lose money either. In this case, we would say that the producer is indifferent between selling and not selling the unit.

price of coffee is $1.40, then the producer surplus on the 600th cup of coffee is the difference between the production cost and the price, as shown in Figure 6.7. So the seller obtains a producer surplus, or profit, of $0.30 on the 600th cup of coffee.

Figure 6.7 **Producer Surplus and a Supply Curve**

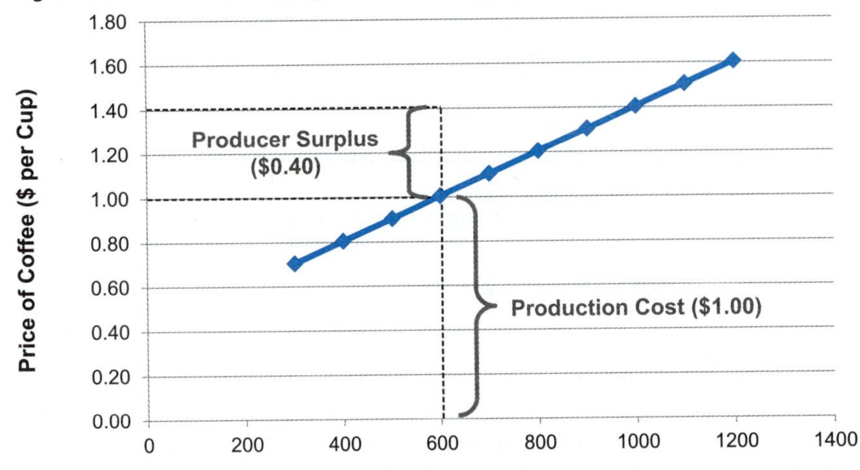

Producer surplus is the difference between price and the production cost (i.e., the supply curve).

3.3 Producer Surplus in an Entire Market

The final step in our analysis of producer benefits is to determine the producer surplus for the entire market. As with market consumer surplus, we need to extend our analysis from points *along the supply curve* to *areas above the supply curve.* Note that we are focused on the area *above* the supply curve because the supply curve represents the marginal costs to producers. It is only the revenue above costs that represents producer surplus, or profits.

market producer surplus: the net benefit (profits) obtained by all producers in a market. On a supply-and-demand graph, it is the area below price but above the supply curve.

Figure 6.8 shows the same supply curve shown above but now extended back to the *y*-axis. Given that the supply curve represents the marginal production costs, the aggregate production cost for the entire market is the area under the supply curve, up to the quantity that is produced. So if the price of coffee is $1.10 and a quantity of 700 cups is offered for sale at this price, the aggregate production cost equals the gray-shaded area under the supply curve. The difference between price and the supply curve, for each unit produced, is producer surplus. Thus **market producer surplus** is the blue-shaded area below price but above the supply curve. This is the net benefit obtained by all producers in the market.

Figure 6.8 **Market Producer Surplus**

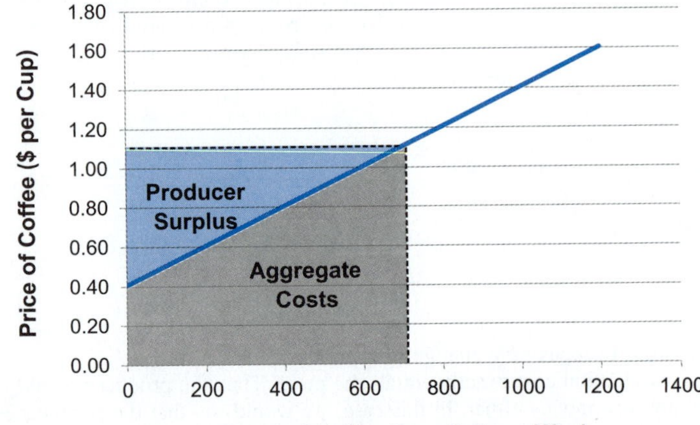

Market producer surplus is the area above the supply curve but below the price.

Discussion Questions

1. Do you think that the concept of producer surplus accurately represents the benefits that producers obtain from selling goods and services? Do you have any reservations about the concept?
2. Have you ever operated a business, even a small one, such as a lemonade stand when you were younger? If so, what factors motivated you to start a business? Do you think that your profits (producer surplus) overstated or understated your benefits? Does your answer have any implications for welfare analysis?

4. SOCIAL EFFICIENCY

social efficiency (in welfare economics): an allocation of resources that maximizes the net benefits to society

Recall that in Chapter 1 we defined efficiency as the use of resources in a way that does not create waste. In welfare economics, efficiency is defined more precisely. Specifically, **social efficiency (in welfare economics)** means an allocation of resources that maximizes the net benefits to society.

This is normally what modern economists mean when they say that a certain result is "best" or "optimal." But we must emphasize that this definition of optimality is a normative one, and it does not mean the same thing as maximizing well-being. A result may be "socially efficient" but fail to address final goals such as fairness, justice, or environmental sustainability.

Even with such caveats in mind, our study of social efficiency is worthwhile because it helps us understand when markets work well and when markets fail to produce efficient results. We reach two conclusions in this section:

1. Under certain conditions, a private market in equilibrium results in the socially efficient outcome.
2. When these conditions are not met, private markets fail to produce the socially efficient outcome. When this occurs, market interventions may be justified in order to increase social efficiency.

Current economic debates are often centered around whether private markets produce socially efficient outcomes. Conservative economists tend to believe that private markets, without regulations, produce efficient outcomes. Liberal economists are more likely to believe that market outcomes can be improved with some regulations, either because regulation will increase social efficiency or to achieve final goals other than efficiency.

Whether a market outcome enhances overall well-being is a normative question, dependent on one's final goals and, especially, on the question of whose welfare is given more weight and how the weighting is done. For example, if the weighting is purely according to willingness to pay, then more weight is given to the desires, happiness, or well-being of those with more money. Whether a market outcome is socially efficient is mostly a positive question, estimated by calculating the size of the consumer and producer surpluses. Even then, however, normative value judgments may be involved.

Later chapters explore in more detail under what conditions markets fail to produce socially efficient outcomes. For example, Chapter 10 focuses on market outcomes and inefficiencies in the labor market. Chapter 13 considers the effects of pollution and other negative externalities. Chapter 18 looks at how concentration of power in a small number of producers can be inefficient.

However, before we can analyze situations in which markets fail to produce efficient outcomes, we must first understand how markets can lead to social efficiency. To do this, we can combine our knowledge of consumer and producer surplus to determine the net benefits of a market to those involved in it. At this point, we are considering market benefits *only to the market participants.* As mentioned earlier, the impacts of markets on the "rest of society" are also relevant to social welfare. So the analysis below is an incomplete, preliminary analysis. We extend our model to consider impacts on the rest of society in Chapter 13.

Figure 6.9 **Social Welfare at Market Equilibrium**

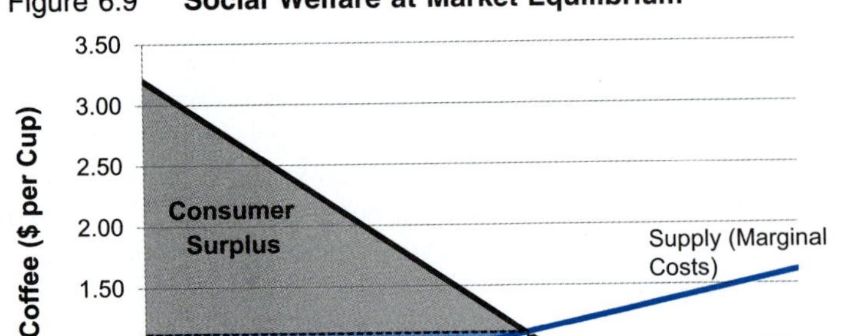

Net welfare benefits are the sum of consumer and producer surplus.

4.1 Market Equilibrium and Social Efficiency

Figure 6.9 shows the consumer and producer surplus of a market in equilibrium. This is the same equilibrium outcome that we obtained in Chapter 4, with a coffee price of $1.10 per cup and 700 cups sold per week. Consumer surplus is the area below the demand curve but above the price. Producer surplus is the area below the price but above the supply curve. The net benefits to the market participants (buyers and sellers) are simply the sum of consumer and producer surplus.

In this example, consumer surplus is larger than producer surplus. This is a result of the relative elasticity of the two curves. You can easily imagine situations in which the majority of the market benefits accrue to producers rather than consumers. An important point is that social welfare considers only the aggregate benefits in the market, *not the distribution of benefits*. So whether the majority of benefits accrue to buyers or sellers, social efficiency seeks only to maximize total benefits. Of course, this ignores the final goal of fairness. Again, social efficiency is not a final goal and is not the same thing as well-being.

Another way to visualize the net benefits in a market is to recall that a demand curve can be considered a marginal benefits curve, and a supply curve can be considered a marginal cost curve. The difference between these two curves at any point represents the gap between the maximum willingness to pay of consumers and the production costs of suppliers. Although some of this difference is "captured" by producers as profits, the rest is consumer surplus. As long as the demand curve is higher than the supply curve, society receives net benefits by producing that unit of a product. However, if the supply curve is higher than the demand curve, then marginal costs exceed marginal benefits, and society would actually be worse off if that unit were produced. So, as long as the demand curve is higher than the supply curve, it makes sense (from the perspective of social welfare) for society to produce each unit, to the point where marginal benefits equal marginal costs. Note in Figure 6.9 that this is true up to the equilibrium quantity of 700 cups of coffee. However, when the supply curve is higher than the demand curve, marginal costs exceed marginal benefits and society should not produce these units. Any production above 700 cups of coffee would decrease social welfare. Thus the market equilibrium is the outcome that maximizes social welfare.

We now test this result by considering what happens when the market is not allowed to reach equilibrium—when a regulation is enacted that sets a price different from the equilibrium price.

4.2 Price Ceilings

Sometimes, governments intervene in markets to set price limits, either above or below the market equilibrium price. Somewhat confusingly, a price set *below* the market price is called

Figure 6.10 **A Price Ceiling**

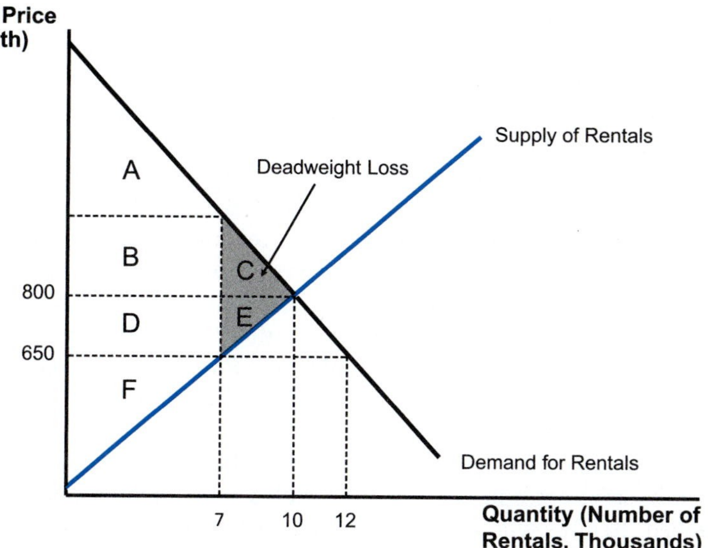

A price ceiling sets a maximum allowable price, which creates a deadweight loss.

price ceiling: a regulation that specifies a maximum price for a particular product

a **price ceiling,** or price control (it is a "ceiling" because it establishes a maximum allowable price).

Price ceilings are usually set with a goal of helping certain groups of consumers by keeping prices low. A classic example is rent control, which specifies maximum prices for rental units. A welfare analysis of a rent control is shown in Figure 6.10.

In the absence of rent control, the market equilibrium rent would be \$800 per month and the quantity of rental units would be 10,000 apartments. Consumer surplus to renters would be areas (A + B + C) and producer surplus to landlords would be areas (D + E + F). Total social welfare would be the sum of these two areas. This graph also portrays a situation in which rent control limits the amount of rent that a landlord can charge, to no more than \$650 per month. At this price, we have a shortage—the quantity demanded (12,000) exceeds the quantity supplied (7,000). Without regulation, market forces would push prices up and eliminate the shortage, but this cannot happen with rent control.

In the case of a price ceiling, the quantity is determined *only by the supply curve* (because producers will react to the price set by the government in deciding how much to supply). So, the market quantity at a rent control price of \$650/month is 7,000 rental units. Note that this leaves many potential renters unable to find a rental unit at a price of \$650/month (5,000 in this example).

The intention of rent control is normally to help renters. Their consumer surplus would still be the area above the price and below the demand curve up to the quantity sold. At a quantity supplied of 7,000, this is equal to areas (A + B + D). Because consumer surplus was areas (A + B + C) before rent control, renters have lost area C and gained area D. The question of whether consumer surplus has increased thus depends on the relative sizes of areas C and D. The way the graph is drawn, it appears that consumer surplus has indeed increased, since D is larger than C. But this may not always be the case. You can try to draw a different graph such that consumer surplus would decrease as a result of a price ceiling.

We can be more definitive with the change in producer surplus. Producer surplus with rent control is only area F, which is clearly smaller than areas (D + E + F). Producers have lost (D + E). Of this amount, D has been gained by consumers, so we can say that it has been *transferred* from producers to consumers.

Note than in addition to this transfer from producers to consumers, two areas, C and E, have been lost completely. This loss, which benefits no one, decreases total social welfare. Before

deadweight loss: a reduction in social welfare as a result of a market regulation

rent control, total social welfare was (A + B + C + D + E + F). With rent control, it is areas (A + B + D + F). Economists call the net loss of (C + E) a **deadweight loss**, a reduction in social welfare as a result of a market regulation. This seems to indicate that from the point of view of total social welfare, rent control is a bad policy, implying a loss of economic efficiency. In more commonsense terms, the reason for the deadweight loss is that at the enforced lower price, less housing is available overall.

But this conclusion can be controversial. Sometimes, for example, in wartime or during other emergencies, many people favor price controls on essential goods. Many apartments in New York City and other cities in New York State are subject to rent control, and, of course, it is very popular with tenants who benefit from it, so it has proved politically resilient. Can this be justified economically? Many economists would say no, for the reasons discussed above. But note that the conclusions above are affected by the elasticity of the supply and demand curves. In particular, if supply is inelastic, the deadweight loss will be small (visualize this, or draw another set of inelastic supply and demand curves to see how areas C and E shrink).

The deadweight loss may be small in the case of apartments in New York City, where there is little room for new construction (i.e., an inelastic supply curve). In addition, not all apartments are covered by rent control, so, where possible, new, uncontrolled apartment buildings can be developed. To those who sympathize with the original goal of rent control—to help renters and keep at least some apartments affordable—the benefits to renters justify the relatively small efficiency loss.

But in other cases, especially where elasticity of supply is high, price controls can be disastrous. One example was in Zimbabwe, where extensive price controls were imposed in 2007 with the goal of keeping prices for food and other essential goods low. As our example leads us to expect, the result of enforced low prices was to destroy the incentive for farmers and other suppliers to produce, leading to severe shortages. So, the poor people whom the policy was supposed to help were instead hurt by unavailability of food and other basic goods, while farmers and other merchants were forced into bankruptcy. The price controls had to be abandoned after they forced the economy into virtual collapse.

4.3 Price Floors

price floor: a regulation that specifies a minimum price for a particular product

Governments also sometimes intervene in markets with the opposite goal—to keep prices from falling. A price set above the market price is called a **price floor** or price support (because it establishes a minimum allowable price).

Why would governments want to keep prices at higher levels? The obvious reason is to aid producers. In the agricultural sector, price supports are common. Governments commonly specify minimum prices for agricultural products such as grain or milk. Of course, this also pushes up prices to consumers. The goal is to help farmers, who often have considerable political influence.

The economic effect is the opposite of a price ceiling. Rather than creating a shortage, price floors create a *surplus,* as producers increase their output to take advantage of profitable higher prices, but the same higher prices cause consumers to cut back their purchases. In general, the government will have to buy up the surplus in order to maintain the price floor. From an economic point of view, this is clearly inefficient, because it encourages excess production and involves both higher prices to consumers and large government expenditures. A more efficient approach would be to give direct aid to farmers if this is considered necessary but to leave market prices alone.

Another classic example of a price floor is the minimum wage. Most governments have minimum wage laws specifying that hourly wages must be at least a given level. The United States has a federal minimum wage of $7.25 per hour (as of 2013), although about 20 states have set higher minimum wage rates. Most other developed countries have higher minimum wage rates. For example, the minimum wage is equivalent to about $10/hour in Canada, about $13/hour in France, and $16/hour in Australia.

Figure 6.11 **A Price Floor**

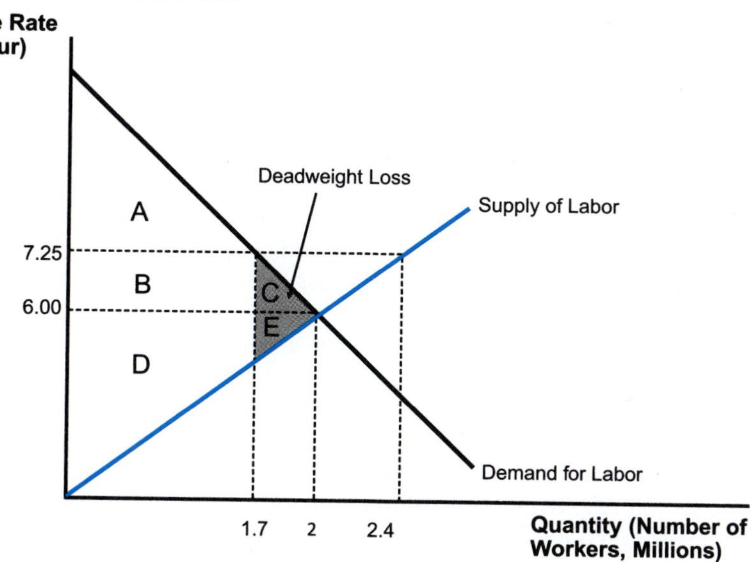

A price floor sets a minimum allowable price, which creates a deadweight loss.

The impact of a minimum wage is illustrated in Figure 6.11, which illustrates a hypothetical labor market for unskilled workers such as cashiers or manual laborers. In this case, the demand curve represents the willingness to pay of employers for workers. The "sellers" are potential workers willing to supply their labor in exchange for pay. (We discuss labor markets in more detail in Chapter 10.)

If the labor market were allowed to reach equilibrium, the market-clearing wage rate would be $6.00 per hour and employment would be 2 million workers. But the minimum wage of $7.25/hour prevents market forces from pushing the wage rate any lower than $7.25/hour. The minimum wage is called a price floor because it prevents the wage rate from moving lower. Note that if the minimum wage were set below the equilibrium wage, say at $5.00/hour, it would have no effect on the market price.

At $7.25/hour, the graph tells us that the supply of labor is 2.4 million workers and the demand for labor is 1.7 million workers. Although an equilibrium quantity is determined by the interaction of supply and demand, in the case of a price floor, the market quantity is determined *only by the demand curve.* In other words, the situation of surplus (excess supply) cannot be eliminated with a price decline, so demand limits the amount that is sold. Thus the presence of the minimum wage, relative to the equilibrium outcome, reduces employment from 2 million to 1.7 million. (Again, these are only hypothetical numbers.)

What does this price floor mean in terms of social welfare? Presumably, a minimum wage law is intended to benefit workers, rather than employers. In a labor market, producer surplus represents the social welfare benefits to workers—they are the suppliers. Remember that producer surplus is the area above the supply curve and below the price, up to the quantity sold. We see in Figure 6.11 that if the market were allowed to reach equilibrium (a wage rate of $6.00/hour), consumer surplus would be areas (A + B + C) and producer surplus would be areas (D + E). Total social welfare would be the sum of both surpluses, or (A + B + C + D + E).

But with the minimum wage set at $7.25 producer surplus becomes areas (B + D). Without the minimum wage, producer surplus was (D + E). The way the graph is drawn, it appears that producer surplus has increased (i.e., area B, which has been gained, is larger than area E, which has been lost). However, this is not necessarily always the case. To test this, try to draw a market in which a price floor decreases producer surplus. (Hint: Make the price floor even further above the equilibrium price.)

We also need to see what has happened to consumer surplus (keeping in mind that in this story the "consumers" are employers). Recall that consumer surplus is the area above price but below the demand curve, up to the quantity sold. So, with the minimum wage in place, consumer surplus is only area A, instead of (A + B + C). We can definitively conclude that consumer surplus has decreased, by the area (B + C). This is *always* the case with a price floor.

Returning to Figure 6.11, we see that total social welfare with the minimum wage is the sum of areas (A + B + D); it has decreased by areas (C + E). Area C used to be part of consumer surplus, and area E used to be part of producer surplus. Also note that area B represents a transfer of benefits, from consumers (employers) to producers (workers). As in the rent control example above, there is a deadweight loss of areas (C + E), representing a loss of economic efficiency.

So on the basis of economic efficiency, a price floor such as a minimum wage law seems to be a bad idea. In theory, at least, it reduces both social welfare and employment. Although workers who have jobs earn higher wages, the theory predicts that more workers will be unable to find jobs.

But as we discussed earlier, economic efficiency is just one of many societal goals. Figure 6.11 shows that the minimum wage law did benefit workers (i.e., producer surplus has increased). If we believe that employers are exploiting low-wage workers, then perhaps the loss in economic efficiency could be justified on the basis of social justice. For example, we might conclude that benefits to the workers whose salary rises to at least a "living wage" are so significant that they outweigh the other losses, in profits and in number of jobs.

Another important question in weighing the merits of minimum wage laws is how much they actually do reduce employment. It is an empirical question whether raising the minimum wage increases unemployment by a significant amount. If demand for labor is relatively inelastic, the effect on unemployment will be relatively small. Indeed, empirical research has found that in some cases there is no detectable effect of increased unemployment as a result of a higher minimum wage! (See Box 6.1 for details on this surprising result.)

Given these findings, you might wonder why the empirical reality does not necessarily support the predictions of the theory. This example reminds us that it is important to both learn the theory and, at the same time, to be cautious in its application. The minimum wage example raises important issues of social justice; it also emphasizes the fact that wages are in many ways not standard prices. Markets for labor, as discussed further in Chapter 10, make it clear that economics is a social science—about people—and the behaviors of people cannot be predicted with mathematical precision.

Discussion Questions

1. Think of another real-world example of a price floor or a price ceiling, not discussed in the text. Based on what you read in this section, as well as your own views, do you think that price regulation is a "good" policy?
2. Do you think that social efficiency is an appropriate tool for analyzing the net impact of different policies? Can you think of some policy situations in which social efficiency is a sufficient measure for determining which policies should be enacted? Can you think of other policy situations in which social efficiency would be an inappropriate goal of policy decisions?

5. POLICY INFERENCES FROM WELFARE ANALYSIS

A simple conclusion from basic welfare analysis is that private unregulated markets, bringing together self-interested consumers and producers, can produce an outcome that is the "best" overall for society, where best is defined as maximizing economic efficiency (i.e., social welfare). But as we have already seen, this simple conclusion often needs to be qualified or questioned in terms of real-world effects. Bearing this in mind, we now look at some of the policy implications of welfare analysis.

Box 6.1 The Debate over the Impact of Minimum Wage Laws

The model presented in this chapter illustrates that a minimum wage, a type of price floor, will reduce employment. The only question, it seems, is how much.

In the most referenced research on the topic, two economists, David Card and Alan Krueger, took advantage of a real-world experiment to try to answer this question. In 1992 the minimum wage in New Jersey was raised from $4.25 to $5.05 per hour. In the neighboring state of Pennsylvania, the minimum wage remained at $4.25/hour. Card and Krueger then collected employment data from fast-food restaurants, which paid many workers the minimum wage, in New Jersey and eastern Pennsylvania. According to economic theory, fast-food restaurant employment should have decreased in New Jersey relative to Pennsylvania.

Instead, Card and Krueger found that employment at fast-food restaurants in New Jersey actually *increased*—the opposite of what the theory predicted! This result initiated a lively debate among economists, with some arguing that it was simply impossible based on the market model. Research subsequent to Card and Krueger's 1994 paper has produced mixed results. Some studies have identified a negative employment impact from minimum wage laws, while others have found no discernible impacts. A 2006 article in *The Economist* notes: "Today's consensus, insofar as there is one, seems to be that raising minimum wages has minor negative effects at worst." However, the article does note that raising the minimum wage is not a very effective tool for reducing poverty. For example, many people paid the minimum wage are teenage workers who are not from poor families. The article suggests that tax credits paid to low-income workers, such as the Earned Income Tax Credit in the United States, are more effective at reducing poverty.

There may also be a difference between the United States and Europe. In the United States, the minimum wage may be fairly close to the equilibrium wage, and thus its impact on employment is relatively small. In Europe, minimum wages are much higher and consequently are more likely to be a significant cause of unemployment among low-skilled workers.

Sources: David Card and Alan B. Krueger, "Minimum Wages and Employment: A Case Study of the Fast-Food Industry in New Jersey and Pennsylvania," *American Economic Review* 84(4) (1994): 774–793; "The Minimum Wage: A Blunt Instrument," *Economist*, October 26, 2006.

5.1 Laissez-Faire Economics

laissez-faire: the view that government intervention in markets should be limited to what is absolutely necessary. The term is French and means "leave alone"

The type of analysis presented in this chapter is the reason that some economists are supportive of a **laissez-faire** (pronounced lays-say fair) approach to regulation. We saw above that government intervention in markets, such as price floors and price ceilings, generally decreases social welfare, defined strictly in terms of economic efficiency. In this analysis, total benefits are maximized *only when the market is allowed to reach equilibrium.* Laissez-faire advocates thus believe that government intervention in markets should be limited only to what is absolutely necessary to ensure that markets function smoothly. For example, proponents of laissez-faire recognize that regulations are needed to protect private property rights.

But defining the "best" outcome for society as maximizing economic efficiency obviously implies that economic efficiency is a paramount goal. As we saw in Chapter 1, numerous other social goals, such as fairness and ecological sustainability, may be as important, or more important, than efficiency.

One justification often given for a focus on efficiency is that it is considered an objective way to assess policy options. Maximizing efficiency is concerned only with increasing overall social benefits, not the allocation of those benefits. So, by looking only at total benefits, in principle we avoid making subjective judgments about who receives those benefits.

As in our discussion of positive and normative statements in Chapter 1, we need to look further to understand any subjective inferences from this viewpoint. In particular, an emphasis on efficiency implicitly views the current distribution of economic resources as acceptable. In order to understand this, we need to expand our notion of efficiency. Although we have been discussing efficiency as it applies in a single market, we can also define efficiency as maximizing social benefits across the totality of markets.

Consider that markets allocate resources across different markets based on consumers' willingness to pay. In one sense, markets are democratic in the sense that everyone is free to participate in them and can thus make their preferences known. But unlike in the democratic principle of "one person, one vote," markets operate according to a "one dollar, one vote" principle. In other words, those with more economic resources have a greater say in determining what a society produces. So whether a society allocates resources at the margin to luxury cars or school lunches depends to some extent on the relative willingness to pay for each.* If the demand by wealthy consumers for luxury cars exceeds the demand by other consumers for school lunches, then that society's production will shift toward producing more luxury cars and fewer school lunches.

So, while at first glance it seems that a focus on efficiency avoids having to make subjective assessments, we see that efficiency cannot be separated from questions about fairness. Whether the existing distribution of wealth and income in the United States is fair is a question that we consider in more detail in Chapter 11.

5.2 Market Failure

Can we conclude from welfare analysis that unregulated markets are always efficient and that the only justification for government intervention is to further other social goals such as justice or ecological sustainability? No, because economists also recognize situations in which unregulated markets *are not efficient*. In these cases, government intervention may be justified solely to increase economic efficiency.

market failure: situations in which unregulated markets fail to produce the socially efficient outcome

Situations in which unregulated markets fail to maximize social efficiency are referred to as **market failure**. In response to market failure, we may be able to design policies that "correct" the market failure—an intervention that then allows the outcome to be socially efficient.

We consider several instances of market failure in later chapters. These examples include:

- In Chapter 9 we look at how consumer behavior can lead to inefficient market outcomes. These outcomes may be due to irrational consumer behavior, as discussed in Chapter 8, arising from either decision-making limitations or external factors that lead consumers to make inefficient choices, such as advertising.
- In Chapter 10 we look at labor markets, which may also be subject to market failure. For example, employers may have significantly more power than workers, or institutional arrangements may prevent an efficient outcome.
- Situations in which there are significant impacts on "the rest of society" (including the natural environment, and people of the future). Costs and benefits to "the rest of society" should be included in a complete welfare analysis of any market. In Chapter 13, we consider the importance of these impacts, particularly with regard to environmental policy.
- Not all products can be efficiently allocated using private markets. In extreme cases, no private market will arise at all, as no potential for profits exists. The provision of some goods and services directly by public sphere entities is addressed in Chapter 14.
- In Chapters 17 and 18, we consider different market structures based on the degree of producer competition. We see that insufficient competition is another common example of market failure.

Going beyond the theoretical model presented in this chapter, to a more real-world perspective on economics in these future chapters, we see that unregulated efficient markets are more the exception rather than the rule. Yet this does not mean that government intervention is always justified in situations of market failure. We must consider the details of individual markets to determine whether intervention is justified. If an intervention is justified, we must

*The allocation will also depend on the cost of production. For example, even if the willingness to pay for luxury cars exceeds the willingness to pay for school lunches, if producers cannot make equal or greater profits selling luxury cars, they will not have an incentive to produce them.

decide what type is appropriate—a tax, a subsidy, or some other regulation. We must also decide the magnitude of the intervention. For example, if we institute a tax on gasoline to correct for a market failure, should it be 10 cents a gallon, $1.00 per gallon, or more?

We also have to be clear whether the justification for intervention is based on increasing efficiency or achieving another goal. In some cases, increased efficiency may be possible while also making progress on other social goals. In other cases, we must assess whether we should place a higher priority on economic efficiency or on another objective.

Discussion Questions

1. Do you think that the current level of government regulation is too high or too low? Do you generally support a laissez-faire approach to regulation or more active regulation? Does your answer change depending on the policy issue under consideration?
2. Considering everything that we have covered so far in the book, have you changed your mind about any policy issues in your country? What lessons from the book do you find particularly relevant to current policy debates?

REVIEW QUESTIONS

1. What is the difference between social welfare and well-being?
2. Define consumer surplus.
3. What do different points on a demand curve represent?
4. What is a marginal change?
5. What is another name for a demand curve, in reference to welfare analysis?
6. What does each point on a demand curve represent?
7. How is consumer surplus for an individual consumer represented in a supply-and-demand graph?
8. How is market consumer surplus represented in a supply-and-demand graph?
9. Define producer surplus.
10. What is another name for a supply curve, in reference to welfare analysis?
11. What does each point on a supply curve represent?
12. How is producer surplus for an individual transaction represented in a supply-and-demand graph?
13. How is market producer surplus represented in a supply-and-demand graph?
14. What is social efficiency? What are some limitations of this concept?
15. Why is a market equilibrium socially efficient?
16. What is a price ceiling? How can it be represented in a supply-and-demand graph?
17. What limits the quantity sold with a price ceiling: supply or demand?
18. How does a price ceiling affect consumer and producer surplus?
19. What is a deadweight loss? How is it represented in a supply-and-demand graph?
20. What is a price floor? How can it be represented in a supply-and-demand graph?
21. What limits the quantity sold with a price floor: supply or demand?
22. How does a price floor affect consumer and producer surplus?
23. What is the laissez-faire approach to government regulation?
24. What is market failure?

EXERCISES

1. Consider the following demand schedule for umbrellas at a local store:

Price	Quantity demanded per day
$20	0
$18	5
$16	10
$14	15
$12	20
$10	25

   a. Draw the demand curve for umbrellas. Be sure to label the axes.
   b. Suppose the price of umbrellas is $14. Indicate the area of market consumer surplus in your graph. Also indicate the area that represents the total amount that consumers spend on umbrellas.
   c. Next, assume that Rebecca is willing to pay a maximum of $18 for an umbrella. What is Rebecca's consumer surplus if she purchases an

umbrella? Show her consumer surplus on your graph.

d. Another consumer, Andy, is willing to pay a maximum of $10 for an umbrella. What is his consumer surplus in this market?

e. If the demand schedule above represents demand on a normal summer day, what would you expect to happen to market consumer surplus if the forecast is for a heavy rainfall? Assume that the store does not raise its price. Draw a graph to support your answer.

2. Suppose the maximum willingness to pay for a new iPhone by the different consumers in a market is given in the table below.

Consumer	Maximum Willingness to Pay
#1	$550
#2	$530
#3	$490
#4	$440
#5	$420
#6	$370
#7	$350
#8	$310

a. If the price of iPhones is $420, how many iPhones will be sold?

b. What is the total consumer surplus in the market?

c. Suppose the price of iPhones decreases to $390. Now how many iPhones will be sold? What is the new consumer surplus?

3. Consider the following supply schedule for apartments in a local market.

Rent (per month)	Quantity of apartments supplied
$800	100
$700	80
$600	60
$500	40
$400	20
$300	0

a. Draw the supply curve for apartments. Be sure to label the axes.

b. Suppose the going rental price for apartments is $550 per month. How many apartments will be supplied? (Assume the supply curve is a straight line between the points in the table above.)

c. Indicate the area of market producer surplus in your graph. Also indicate the area that represents the total cost of supplying apartments.

d. Next, assume that a particular landlord is willing to supply an apartment only if the rental price is at least $450 per month. What is her producer surplus in this market? Use a graph to support your answer.

e. Suppose that the price for condominiums in the area increases. This creates an incentive for apartment owners to sell their apartments as condominiums, thus removing them from the rental market. What would you expect to happen to producer surplus in the apartment market as a result of this change? Draw a graph to support your answer.

3. Suppose that the market equilibrium price for a basic medical check-up is $50, in a market in which there is no health insurance. To encourage more people to get a check-up, the local government mandates that the price of a check-up cannot be more than $40.

a. Is this a price floor or a price ceiling?

b. Draw a graph to illustrate the implementation of this government policy.

c. What happens to the number of check-ups in this market? Show this in your graph.

d. What happens to consumer surplus in this market? What happens to producer surplus? Show these changes on your graph.

e. Was the government's policy successful? What has happened to social welfare? Show this in your graph.

f. Can you think of a different policy that would likely be more successful at encouraging more people to obtain check-ups?

g. Is this a typical market? Is there any reason to suppose that producers of health care would respond differently to price regulation than, say, producers of umbrellas? What does the producer's responsiveness have to do with the cost of providing health care? What other factors might be involved?

4. Consider the market for wheat. Suppose that the demand for wheat decreases because of dietary concerns.

a. How does the decrease in the demand for wheat affect total net social welfare in the wheat market? Use a graph to support your answer, and indicate the area that represents the change in social welfare.

b. Can we clearly say what happens to producer surplus as a result of the decrease in demand? Use a graph to support your answer.

5. Consider the market for electricity. Suppose that the price of producing energy decreases due to lower fuel costs.
   a. How does the decrease in electricity production costs affect total net social welfare? Use a graph to support your answer and indicate the area that represents the change in social welfare.
   b. Can we clearly say what happens to consumer surplus as a result of the decrease in energy production costs? Use a graph to support your answer.

6. Match each concept in Column A with an example in Column B:

Column A	Column B
a. Consumer surplus	1. Profits
b. The government mandates that the price of milk must be at least $3 per gallon.	2. A price ceiling
c. Marginal change	3. An increase in demand of one unit
d. Producer surplus	4. A loss in social welfare that occurs when a market is not in equilibrium
e. Deadweight loss	5. Part of the psychic benefits of buying something
f. The government mandates that the price of gas can be no higher than $4 per gallon.	6. A school of economics that opposes government regulation
g. Laissez-faire economics	7. A price floor

7 International Trade and Trade Policy

What does the United States export more of than anything else on the global market? The answer might surprise you (hint: think food). And which country purchases more U.S. exports—China or Mexico? In fact, the United States exports twice as much to Mexico as to China in terms of value. Are there similar surprises to be found when we look at Japan, for example, or Brazil? More generally, what factors determine which goods a country produces for trade with other countries? Classical economists Adam Smith and David Ricardo noticed that countries will tend to produce an abundance of goods that they are especially good at producing and trade their surplus for other goods that they are not as skilled at producing. Smith and Ricardo also believed that such trades would always benefit both countries. Yet, as we see, the world has grown increasingly complex over the past two centuries, and, despite obvious advantages to free trade, there are also reasons for caution. This chapter considers some of these issues and discusses ways in which national governments have addressed them.

1. Trade, Specialization, and Productivity

As we saw earlier, Adam Smith is generally credited with the idea that leaving decisions of production and distribution to a market system is superior to having the government impose its will. Many recognize this as the meaning of "laissez-faire" as discussed in Chapter 6. Here we look at what it is about free markets that, in theory, produces desirable outcomes in terms of trade, both within and between countries.

In *An Inquiry into the Nature and Causes of the Wealth of Nations* (1776), Smith made a connection between specialization and efficiency. We have seen that one way to define "efficiency" is to say that efficient production allows us to obtain the maximum product from a given amount of resources, *or* conversely to require the least possible resources to produce a given amount of a product. This is a fundamental economic goal because it has very important consequences for the well-being of individuals, groups, and countries. What Smith argued was that specialization (he called it "division of labor") would make people more efficient, because focusing our time on one task (or a few tasks) instead of many would make us learn it more quickly and become better at it.

Smith then noted that the *extent* of the specialization achieved in a society would be governed by the extent or size of the market. If, for example, the market for shoes were tiny, it would make no sense for you to devote all your time to shoe production, as you would not make enough money in such a small market to support yourself. If, however, the market were large, specialization would make sense—and the larger the market, the more that you would want to specialize. Nobody speaks more eloquently on this subject than Smith himself:

> As it is the power of exchanging that gives occasion to the division of labour, so the extent of this division must always be limited by the extent of that power, or, in other words, by the

> extent of the market. When the market is very small, no person can have any encouragement to dedicate himself entirely to one employment, for want of the power to exchange all that surplus part of the produce of his own labor, which is over and above his own consumption, for such parts of the produce of other men's labour as he has occasion for.[1]

Taking this logic to its extreme, economic productivity in all areas would be maximized if all markets were extended around the world. It is for this reason that Smith advocated not only a system of free markets for a specific economy but also free and unfettered trade among countries. Although the same logic applied at any scale of participation—that is, the logic of mutual gains for both parties—it seemed perfectly reasonable that under globalized markets *more would be gained* because of the maximized productive efficiency that results from maximum specialization.

In Smith's view, specialization at the national level would lead each country to become so efficient in the production of some things that it would enjoy an "absolute advantage" over other countries in their production. Other countries would enjoy such an advantage in the production of other goods, and because each country would produce far more than it needed because of its remarkable productivity, there would be ample opportunity for mutually beneficial trade between countries.

As we mentioned in the last chapter, Smith's book was considered revolutionary. He was writing at a time when the so-called mercantilist philosophy prevailed—a philosophy that supported strong involvement by the state in economic affairs and was highly skeptical of free trade. Even today, more than two centuries later, debate over the benefits and drawbacks of free trade continues. But the influence of Smith's book is indisputable; today, his pronouncements in favor of free trade are about as far as one could imagine from "revolutionary," having been widely accepted by many economists and policymakers.

Discussion Questions

1. Does it make sense that the larger or more extended a market is, the greater would be the incentive to specialize in supplying that market? What if everyone decided to specialize in shoemaking because the shoe market went global? What would Adam Smith say?
2. Do you currently "specialize" in something? If not, what do you plan to do after college? Do you hope to develop knowledge or expertise in only one area or more than one? Why?

2. Gains from Trade

free trade: exchange in international markets that is not regulated or restricted by government actions

Economists and policymakers have argued for centuries about whether it is better for a country to engage in free trade with other countries or to place some limits on such trade. Adam Smith presented the argument for free trade in general terms, as we have discussed. Many who argue for "**free trade**"—exchange in international markets that is not regulated or restricted by government actions—often appeal more specifically to David Ricardo's 1817 book *On the Principles of Political Economy and Taxation* to demonstrate that a country that engages in trade can reap significant welfare gains. In this section, we present Ricardo's basic model, along with other arguments in favor of free trade.

2.1 The Theory of Comparative Advantage

In Chapter 1, we discussed the production-possibilities frontier (PPF), which illustrates how a society might make tradeoffs between the production of two different goods, reaching higher output levels when it uses its resources efficiently. We showed how some points, which represent combinations of the two outputs (guns and butter), would be unattainable. But to take our analysis only that far, it turns out, would be misleading.

Points outside a societal PPF represent unattainable levels of *production* for the society on its own. However, they may not reflect unattainable levels of *consumption.* The key to this apparent magic trick is in the benefits that can arise from a system of exchange. Economists call these benefits the "gains from trade," and they are actually *efficiency* gains. People also often point to other important advantages derived from a system of exchange, as well as to important disadvantages, and we elaborate on these as the chapter progresses.

Ricardo's model relies on a trade example with two goods—wine and cloth—and two countries—Portugal and England. Although here we give a simple numerical version of his story, using PPFs, the point is more general. The principles might be applied to any pair of economic actors—for example, housemates, companies, governments—that produce and exchange goods or services at any level of organization—local, regional, national, or global.

Returning to Ricardo's story, suppose that, given its resources or productive factors, Portugal can produce a maximum of 200 bottles of wine if it devotes all its resources to wine production or 100 units of cloth (a unit of cloth is a "bolt") if it devotes all of its resources to cloth production. In Figure 7.1 we have assumed constant opportunity costs, so the PPF is just a straight line.* Meanwhile, England can produce a maximum of 200 bottles of wine or 400 bolts of cloth, as illustrated in Figure 7.2.

Figure 7.1 **Portugal's Production-Possibilities Frontier**

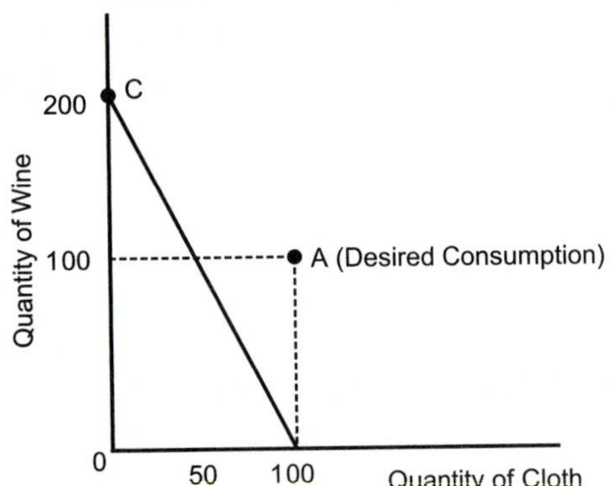

Portugal can produce 200 units of wine if it specializes in wine, or 100 units of cloth, if it specializes in cloth. Or it can produce any combination on the line between these two points. However it would like to consume a larger bundle—represented by point A.

Figure 7.2 **England's Production-Possibilities Frontier**

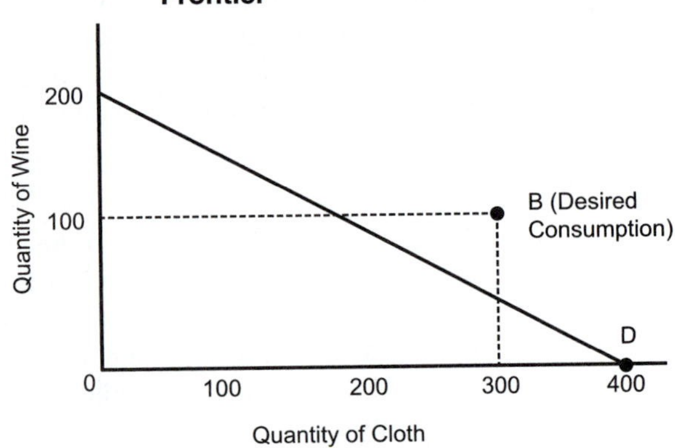

England can produce 200 units of wine if it specializes in wine, or 400 units of cloth, if it specializes in cloth. Or it can produce any combination on the line between these two points. However it would like to consume a larger bundle—represented by point B.

Suppose that the Portuguese would like to be able to consume 100 bottles of wine and 100 bolts of cloth, as represented by point A, and the English would like to be able to consume 100 bottles of wine and 300 bolts of cloth, represented by point B. As we can see, if each relies only on its own production possibilities, points A and B are unachievable.

But suppose that Portugal produced only wine and England produced only cloth. This production combination is illustrated in the "Production" section of Table 7.1 and by points C and D in Figures 7.1 and 7.2. Total production would be 200 bottles of wine and 400 bolts of cloth.

*This means that, contrary to our earlier guns vs. butter example, Portugal does *not* give up more and more of, say, wine as it increasingly specializes in the production of cloth. Here we are simplifying in order to more easily illustrate the advantage of trade.

Table 7.1 **Production, Exchange, and Consumption of Wine and Cloth**

	Country	Wine	Cloth
Production:	Portugal	200	0
	England	0	400
Total production		*200*	*400*
Exchange:	Portugal	sell 100	buy 100
	England	buy 100	sell 100
Consumption:	Portugal	100	100
	England	100	300
Total consumption		*200*	*400*

Further, suppose that Portugal and England were to agree to *exchange* 100 bottles of Portuguese wine for 100 bolts of English cloth, as listed in the "Exchange" section of Table 7.1. Now Portugal and England could each *consume* the quantities listed in the "Consumption" section of Table 7.1. Note that their total consumption does *not* exceed the total amount produced of each good. Yet Portugal would consume at point A and England at point B—the desired points that they could not each reach on their own!

The "magic" behind this result is that Portugal and England differ in their opportunity costs of production. For every bolt of cloth that Portugal produces, it forgoes production of 2 bottles of wine. You can see this by examining the slope of the PPF in Figure 7.1. Comparing the two endpoints, moving from left to right, we can see that a fall (or negative "rise") of 200 bottles of wine is accompanied by a "run" of +100 bolts of cloth. Because the curve is straight, the slope is therefore –200/100 = –2 throughout. At any point, then, reducing wine production by 2 bottles (i.e., a fall or "negative rise" of 2) is needed to increase cloth production by 1 bolt (that is, to create a "run" of 1 unit to the right). However, for every bolt of cloth that England produces, it forgoes production of only half a bottle of wine (check this yourself using Figure 7.2). We say that England has a **comparative advantage** in cloth production, because cloth costs less in terms of the other good (wine) in England than in Portugal. In other words, England has a lower opportunity cost associated with its cloth production.

comparative advantage: the ability to produce some good or service at a lower opportunity cost than other producers

The above example is undoubtedly a product of the geographical reality in Ricardo's time. England had energy resources (coal) that made it relatively good at industrial production such as spinning and weaving and a relatively cool and cloudy climate that was not suitable for growing grapes. Portugal, by contrast, enjoyed a comparative advantage in production of wine, owing to its relatively warm and sunny climate—good for growing grapes—but lacked the necessary energy sources to produce cloth as efficiently as England. In our example, an additional bottle of wine comes at the cost of half a bolt of cloth when produced in Portugal but requires giving up 2 bolts of cloth when produced in England, as noted in Table 7.2.

Put simply, the principle of comparative advantage says that one should *specialize* in what one does best. This means that even if it turned out that one of the countries was more efficient at producing *both* goods, it would still pay for that country to specialize. Indeed, it is on this

Table 7.2 **Opportunity Cost and Comparative Advantage**

Country	Opportunity cost of 1 unit of cloth	Opportunity cost of 1 unit of wine
Portugal	2 units of wine	½ unit of cloth
England	½ unit of wine	2 units of cloth

point especially that Ricardo goes further than Smith. While Smith had earlier expounded on the benefits of trade, in his view the benefits existed only if each country possessed an *absolute* advantage in the production of at least one good. To Smith, if a country did not produce at least one good more efficiently than its trading partner, the latter would have no incentive to engage in trade with it.

Ricardo recognized that even in such a circumstance both countries gain. He would say that a country has a comparative advantage in the good that it produces *less relatively inefficiently*. Both countries gain by having the economically "stronger" country produce only what it produces *most* efficiently and then trading. Regarding our example above, Ricardo would have said that even if England produced wine *and* cloth more efficiently (i.e., using fewer resources per unit), it would still face a higher opportunity cost than Portugal for the good that it was *relatively* less efficient at producing—so there would still exist mutual gains from trade. Only if both countries faced exactly the *same* opportunity costs (an exceedingly rare phenomenon in the real world) would there be no possible gains from trade.

The source of comparative advantage in the above example is climate and other resource endowments, which differed between England and Portugal. It is not hard, by extension, to understand why, for example, bananas are currently exported by Ecuador, while Sweden finds it advantageous to import bananas rather than grow them in greenhouses. But comparative advantage can also be created by human action. Countries can become more efficient at producing particular goods by investing in the physical capital needed to produce them. Sometimes, technological advances or changes in the social organization of work can change the pattern of comparative advantage, and the evolution of comparative advantage over time may thus be unpredictable.

Ricardo's example concerned trade between countries, but the principle of comparative advantage has also been used to show how other economic actors can reap gains from trade. Organizations seek gains from trade when they specialize in a particular area—say, production of training workshops—while contracting with other companies to provide support services—say, transportation or advertising design. You may reap gains from trade in your household if, instead of splitting all chores 50–50, you put the person who is relatively more "efficient" (i.e., better) at shopping in charge of shopping and the person who is relatively efficient at cleaning in charge of cleaning.

The mere fact that some companies, or some people, *could* be self-sufficient in producing everything that they need does not mean that they *should* provide everything for themselves. The story of specialization and gains from trade is a powerful one.

labor-intensive production: production using methods that involve a high ratio of labor to capital

capital-intensive production: production using methods that involve a high ratio of capital to labor

factor-price equalization: the theory that trade should eventually lead to returns to factors of production that are equal across countries

Economists often make a distinction between countries that are thought to be more suited for **labor-intensive production** processes, such as stitching clothing or making handicrafts, and others that specialize in relatively **capital-intensive production**, such as the manufacture of airplanes or automobiles. The fact that the United States has more manufactured capital per worker than does Bangladesh, for example, is considered an explanation for Bangladeshi exports of clothing. Bangladesh presumably has a comparative advantage in relatively labor-intensive industries. Clothing production, meanwhile, has nearly disappeared from the United States.

The economic theory of **factor-price equalization** predicts that free trade should tend to equalize the returns to capital (profits) and labor (wages) across countries. For example, to the extent that the United States is rich in capital and relatively lacking in labor power, in the absence of trade, returns to capital are theorized to be relatively low and returns to labor relatively high. The logic of this is that a scarce factor commands a higher return—higher demand for a factor, relative to available supplies, increases the price that must be paid for it. Because factor endowments in Bangladesh are the opposite, capital investments there would be expected to receive high returns in the absence of trade, while workers receive low wages compared to those in the United States.

After the two countries start to trade, however, the demand for capital in the United States should rise (because the country now has a larger market for selling its capital-intensive goods), increasing the return on investments there. The demand for labor, however, will fall, because the United States will now be importing labor-intensive goods from Bangladesh. Meanwhile, the demand for labor in Bangladesh should rise (because it now exports labor-intensive goods), putting upward pressure on wages in that country, while returns to capital there fall. According to this theory, in a (hypothetical) world of perfectly free trade, we would expect wages to converge eventually, so that workers in the United States and Bangladesh would be paid about the same. Returns to capital investments would also be equalized.

Of course, in the real world wages are much higher in the United States than in Bangladesh—about 30 times higher. The theory of factor-price equalization merely states that wages should *eventually* converge, yet it says nothing about how long this process may take.

We find evidence of factor-price equalization in other cases, such as economic growth in Asia over the past 50 years. It is hard to remember now that Japan (in the 1950s) and then South Korea were the first two Asian countries that "bootstrapped" their economic growth by depending heavily on the export of very cheap goods made with very cheap labor. We could use factor-price equalization to explain how wages in those countries have risen to the levels of other industrialized countries—although it is evident that this did not just happen automatically but was urged in the right direction by a combination of factors, including government policies of industrial support and strong support for economic equality. It is now possible to see substantially rising wages in China. Will the same happen in Bangladesh, for example? The theory of factor-price equalization does not say what institutions or policies are necessary for this to happen.

The theory of factor-price equalization also disregards the possibility that, instead of an international equalization of wages, higher unemployment would result. This has, in fact, been a far more common outcome in countries like the United States; internationally as well as locally, wages seem to rise with some ease, while being "sticky" downward (as we will discuss in Chapter 10). More often than not, rich country labor markets "adjust" by seeing capital move overseas to take advantage of lower wages in other countries. The result is that wages remain relatively high in the United States, but some people lose their jobs.

Another reason that the theory can mislead is that investments in *human* capital—health, skills, and education—blur the distinction between "labor" and "capital." Some studies suggest that the comparative advantage of the United States is now tilted toward goods that require production by an *educated and skilled* workforce and away from production that involves lower-skilled work or heavy machinery. When production is intensive in *human* capital, the earlier two-way classification is harder to apply. Meanwhile, studies of factor prices are mixed in their support of the theory of factor-price equalization. Ongoing changes in technology, skills, and the composition of production, as well as deliberate government policies that limit and shift patterns of trade, make it difficult to test the theory.

2.2 Other Benefits of Free Trade

Specialization and trade can lead to improvements in economic efficiency, as the story of comparative advantage points out. Trade allowed Portugal and England to organize their use of resources more efficiently for producing wine and cloth. The result was a more highly valued combination of outputs than the countries could have achieved through self-sufficiency. Yet many also point to additional advantages of systems based on exchange.

Exchange relations, for example, give economic actors (whether countries, businesses, or workers) clear incentives to be productive: Because these relations are *quid pro quo,* in order to get something, you must have something to give! Unless you happen to be sitting on a pile of wealth, it means that you have to do or make something that other people value before you can participate in exchange. If you see something that you want, and exchange is the only way to get it, exchange relations provide a strong extrinsic motivation to participate in productive activities.

In particular, *decentralized* exchange through markets is thought to have advantages, in terms of incentives, that lead to efficiency even in the case of changing conditions. In decentralized market exchange, individual actors make agreements to trade at a particular moment in time or for some span of time specified by a contract. When that particular trade is completed, each partner can choose to try to continue this trading relationship or can look for new ones.

Suppose that after trading with England for some time, Portugal discovered that it could get more cloth (or other valuable goods) by growing table grapes for Germany than by producing wine for England. In a system of decentralized, or "free market," unregulated exchange, it could freely move resources into producing the more highly valued product. A system of market exchange gives producers incentives to produce the goods that command the highest market value. Such an incentive therefore has the potential to encourage competition and innovation, to the ultimate benefit of all consumers.

Another desirable consequence of free trade or exchange is technical. A production process is characterized by "economies of scale" (we'll discuss this topic in more detail in Chapter 16) if the cost per unit of production falls as the volume of production rises. With trade, the volume of a country's production of a good can be substantially higher than its internal (domestic) market can use, increasing the opportunity for economies of scale to be realized. A larger market means that goods can be produced more cheaply, a fact related to Smith's earlier point about specialization.

In addition to the incentive to generate greater value and economies of scale, many economists also believe that exchange is a morally praiseworthy form of distribution because of its *noncoercive* nature. People enter into exchanges *voluntarily.* As we noted in Chapter 1, freedom is among the final goals that you might hope for in an economic system. Presumably, if what you are offered in exchange does not meet your idea of what you think your item is worth, you can refuse to make the trade.

Finally, some argue that exchange relations encourage economic actors to think in terms of their common interests. Rather than each actor watching out for just him- or herself or close kin, exchange relations bind actors together in a sort of cooperative venture. Classical economists like Ricardo and Smith often argued along these lines. Indeed, writers of that era often waxed eloquent on the moral and community-building advantages that they saw in a system of exchange. A seventeenth-century business textbook, for example, claimed that

> [Divine Providence] has not willed for everything that is needed for life to be found in the same spot. It has dispersed its gifts so that men [*sic*] would trade together and so that the mutual need which they have to help one another would establish ties of friendship among them. This continuous exchange of all the comforts of life constitutes commerce and this commerce makes for all the gentleness of life. [2]

If England and Portugal came to rely on each other for trade, such thinking goes, they might think twice about engaging in a war with each other. Citizens of any city, such writers argued, would likewise be motivated to act more respectfully to each other when they shared commercial interests.

You can find real-world cases in which this appears to be true. For example, after World War II the United States acted beneficently toward the devastated countries of Europe. It gave them significant aid for rebuilding their industries and infrastructure though a program called the Marshall Plan. Why? The actual name of the act that created the Marshall Plan was "The Economic Cooperation Act of 1948." U.S. policymakers realized that their own economy would not prosper unless the economies of its major trading partners prospered as well.

In contemporary times, as well, some invoke the image of a market-based "global village," in which countries, linked by economic interdependence, also enter into harmonious mutual understanding and cultural exchange. Advocates of free trade argue that increased globalization of economic activity, free of barriers set up by governments, will lead to greater good for all.

Discussion Questions

1. Suppose that in a one-hour period, you can buy six bags of groceries *or* clean three rooms. Your housemate, however, is slower moving and can buy only three bags of groceries or clean only one room in an hour. You clearly have an absolute advantage in production of both these services. Does this mean you should do all the work?
2. Ricardo's model discusses benefits to countries at an aggregate level. But what if you were a Portuguese cloth maker or an English winemaker? Might you have a different view about the benefits of trade? Which factors might influence what you think about your country's trade policies?

3. Drawbacks of Free Trade

David Ricardo's simple example of two countries and two goods neglects some political, social, and environmental issues that can sometimes offset "gains from trade" or eliminate them altogether. Because rational thinking about the role that societies should allow exchange to have as a mode of distribution requires weighing both benefits and costs, we must also examine the drawbacks of organizing distribution by exchange. The potential disadvantages of exchange as a form of distribution, and of the specialization that often accompanies exchange, include increased vulnerability, becoming locked into disadvantageous production patterns, abuse of power, and the destruction of community.

3.1 Vulnerability

One obvious potential problem with specialization and exchange is that each party becomes more vulnerable to the actions of its trading partners. Supplies of the things that you need, and markets for what you sell, could deteriorate or be cut off at any time. This is as true for individuals and businesses as for countries. If you let your housemate specialize in shopping and cooking, for example, you may find yourself hungry if the exchange relationship suddenly breaks down. Businesses may find themselves unable to obtain needed inputs when the source of the inputs is not under their direct control. If Portugal and England were to go to war, to continue the earlier example, or if Portugal were to find a better buyer, England might temporarily find itself with an excess of cloth and no wine to drink.

For many nonessential goods for which substitutes exist, the issue of vulnerability may seem relatively unimportant. But vulnerability is a more serious issue at the national or international level when the goods in question are resources such as oil, minerals, food, or water, the lack of which would seriously weaken an economy or country. In the United States, for example, some of the same people who argue for "free trade" in most goods also argue for increased development of domestic energy resources, on grounds that excessive reliance on petroleum imports decreases economic self-sufficiency and military preparedness.

Vulnerability is also a serious issue for countries that rely heavily on sales of a single, or a few, export goods for much of their national income. In Ethiopia, for example, producing coffee for export is currently the vastly dominant source of cash income for about one-quarter of the population. When the price of the export commodity is high in international markets, such national economies do well. When prices weaken—or plummet, as coffee prices did in 1989—economies dependent on single exports are subjected to major crises that are beyond their control.

Besides making an economy vulnerable to the whims of its trading partners, widespread monoculture (growing of a single kind of crop) carries other risks as well. It can make agricultural economies more susceptible to crises arising from events such as drought, an agricultural pest, or disease. In a more diversified economy, some sectors and crops may do well while others are hard hit; in a very specialized agricultural economy, the entire economy may spin into crisis from one adverse event.

Thus, although the "gains from trade" argument appears logically correct, the benefits of specialization and trade must be weighed against its costs. When *diversification* increases national security, economic stability, or ecological diversity, then a decision *not* to rely on trade for certain things may be better than pure specialization.

3.2 Lock-In

Some production processes are characterized by increasing returns: The more of something that you do, the more efficient you become. In dynamic economic systems, patterns of comparative advantage can change over time as a consequence of learning by doing.

To draw a personal analogy, during your early years of school, it may have seemed more efficient for you, when you were first doing simple arithmetic problems, to use a calculator. Chances are that your teachers told you that you could not use a calculator, however. They demanded that you not use the easy (and, in the short run, more efficient) method and, instead, build up a base of cognitive skills (for greater long-run efficiency). They did not want you to become locked into an arithmetic "production technology" that was dependent on the presence of a calculator.

Similarly, an important question for a company deciding which lines of business to enter, or for a country trying to build a healthy national economy, is whether it should engage in some kinds of production that may seem inefficient now but have the potential to improve with time and growth. Should a country, for example, stay locked into its current pattern of comparative advantage—for example, by importing cars and not even thinking of building a domestic auto industry? Or should it, at least temporarily, restrict automobile imports (as Japan did), while developing its own auto industry past the start-up stage?

The critical issue here is that people, companies, or countries should not become "locked in" to specializing in what they do well today if doing so prevents them from developing their future potential in other, more rewarding, pursuits. If, in other words, workers stood to eventually gain from producing cars and electronics instead of bananas and coffee, specializing and getting "locked into" banana and coffee production would likely be harmful to future development prospects.

3.3 Coercion and Power Differentials

Our simple story of England and Portugal also ignored the real-world political context of exchange relations. Some element of voluntariness is always present in exchange, but real-world exchange relations are also heavily influenced by the relative power of the parties involved.

For example, we described England and Portugal as exchanging 100 bottles of wine for 100 bolts of cloth—a 1:1 ratio. But what if England were more powerful and could demand different terms, more in its own favor? England might have such a power advantage if it were the only seller of cloth or the only buyer of wine, or through its military might, or through controlling important financial institutions or access to technology.

Whatever the source of its power, suppose England were to demand that Portugal give it 100 bottles of wine in exchange for only 60 bolts of cloth instead of 100. Under such a deal, production, exchange, and consumption would be as described in Table 7.3. England would end up consuming more, and Portugal consuming less, than in the consumption outcome described earlier.

Table 7.3 **A Different Outcome of Exchange and Consumption**

	Country	Wine	Cloth
Production:	Portugal	200	0
	England	0	400
Total production		*200*	*400*
Exchange:	Portugal	sell 100	buy 60
	England	buy 100	sell 60
Consumption:	Portugal	100	60
	England	100	340
Total consumption		*200*	*400*

Would Portugal *voluntarily* accept such an exchange? Looking back at Figure 7.1, you can see that a consumption pattern of 100 bottles of wine and 60 bolts of cloth is still outside of Portugal's own PPF. Thus Portugal might, indeed, still find it advantageous to trade rather than go it alone. (Note that if England offered only 50 bolts of cloth or less, Portugal would not want to trade, because it could do at least as well on its own.)

England does not need to coerce Portugal directly into trading: Portugal's trade is still voluntary. But if England had more power than Portugal, it could force Portugal to accept terms of trade that favor England. In fact, it was England's superior military power that led to the opening of Portuguese cloth markets to English manufactures (see Box 7.1). If, instead, Portugal had been the country with more power, it might have been able to enforce terms of trade that were more in its own favor (say, 100 bottles of wine for 150, rather than 100, bolts of cloth). Similarly, if you and your housemate engage in specialization and exchange of your services, a variety of equitable and inequitable distributions of tasks are possible, based on your relative bargaining power. Just because an exchange is *voluntary* does not mean that it is fair or that differences in power are irrelevant.

Similar struggles for power go on *within* countries that are considering engaging in world trade. Countries in the real world are not simple, unitary decision makers but, rather, are made up of a diversity of citizens, workers, companies, and so on. Although importing wine may be to the advantage of England as a whole, in the sense shown in our graphs and charts, it could be disastrous for *part* of England—namely England's previous wine producers, who would lose their livelihood.

Box 7.1 England, Portugal, and the Treaty of Methuen

When Ricardo wrote about trade between England and Portugal in 1817, it was indeed true that England exported cloth to Portugal in return for wine. But this was not pure "free trade," and it had not come about simply due to the impersonal forces of economic efficiency and comparative advantage.

Before the Treaty of Methuen in 1703, Portugal had severely restricted the importation of cloth from abroad, and England had imported wine primarily from France. But England lost much of its access to French wine during the War of the Spanish Succession (1701–1714). Portugal, meanwhile, was pressured to join a military alliance with England by displays of England's superior naval power. The 1703 treaty cementing their alliance also contained economic terms: Portugal would admit English cloth without charging any tariffs at all, while England would reduce its tariffs on Portuguese wine to two-thirds of what it collected on French wine. Some commentators argue that this was a crucial—and negative—turning point for the development of Portuguese manufacturing.

A concern for human well-being, rather than just for efficiency per se, demands that such distributional considerations be taken into account. When increased trade threatens a major industry, the negative effects on certain people and regions can be deep and prolonged. This happened in Detroit, formerly a bustling industrial city, which became economically depressed—part of the U.S. "rust belt"—as auto manufacturing gradually moved overseas. In parts of Africa during the late twentieth century, increases in export agriculture, run largely by men, caused hardships for those engaged in subsistence agriculture, primarily women and children. It may be that efficiency gains for the country as a whole outweigh local losses. But the local losses, and the costs of redistribution policies designed to alleviate hardship and move people to new occupations, must be properly weighed when the benefits and costs of exchange relationships are considered.

3.4 Other Social and Political Impacts

Is it appropriate to establish trade in anything? There is reasonable resistance to the idea of "commodifying" certain things that society does not generally treat as commodities. Most agree, for example, that kidneys, votes, and babies should never be a part of exchange relations. Treating such things as though they were on a par with shoelaces or cars is thought to destroy the bonds of respect necessary for social life. Potentially life-saving kidney operations, for example, might become available based on ability to pay rather than medical urgency.

Current tensions between government and corporate interests are another area for controversy. In Ricardo's time, it was natural to think about international trade in terms of the actions and policies of countries such as England and Portugal, but in the twenty-first century, discussing trade in terms of multinational corporations such as Microsoft and Daimler-Benz might be at least as appropriate. Corporations have grown ever larger and have become able to move their financial capital and their physical production facilities across international boundaries with increasing ease.

This leads to a dilemma for governments. Traditionally, democratic governments have been able to enact policies perceived to be in the public interest, even though they were not always in the interest of business. Minimum standards for pay and safety on the job, for example, or environmental standards and taxation to support public projects, are widely considered necessary for a healthy, just society. Yet members of the business sphere often oppose such policies because they generally increase costs and decrease profits.

Because capital is increasingly mobile, businesses exclusively concerned with profits are able to move their operations to countries with lower labor and environmental standards and taxes. Countries or states that want to hold onto their business base may therefore find themselves drawn into a "**race to the bottom**," in which they compete to attract businesses on the basis of their *lack* of attention to social and environmental concerns. This is a serious concern for cities and states, as well as for countries; some regions, in their eagerness to compete for businesses that will bring jobs, have offered to soften environmental regulations, while providing other incentives—tax holidays, building infrastructure, and so on—that have, in some cases ended up costing the region hundreds of thousands of dollars per job created. For an example of this from the United States, see Box 7.2.

race to the bottom: a situation in which countries or regions compete in providing low-cost business environments, resulting in deterioration in labor, environmental, or safety standards

Powerful corporations can also attempt to influence international organizations and agreements directly. These issues began to receive more public attention in the United States after the 1999 "anti-globalization" demonstrations at the Seattle meetings of the World Trade Organization. The ability of people to make democratic decisions about the direction of their society is threatened when the power of democratic governments is overshadowed by the power of nondemocratic economic interests.

These political and social impacts need to be considered as we evaluate the impacts of trade. They do not necessarily invalidate the basic message of Ricardo regarding the great benefits to be gained from freer trade. But they must at least be considered as economists and policymakers try to formulate appropriate trade policies.

Box 7.2 The High Cost of Competing for Jobs

Politicians commonly talk about the need to "create jobs," but often the competition among different regions for jobs can come at a high cost to taxpayers. In the United States, individual states often find themselves courting companies to locate a new production facility or other large employment center in their state. The winning state in such competitions is normally the one that offers the largest financial incentive to the company.

One notable example of this competition for jobs occurred in the 1990s, as the states of North Carolina, South Carolina, and Alabama vied to become the location of the first Mercedes-Benz factory in the United States. As each state sweetened its offer, Mercedes eventually requested that the winning state pay some of the workers' wages. The apparent frontrunner, North Carolina, balked at this request, which allowed Alabama to win the competition for the factory. Alabama additionally agreed to purchase the land for the factory for $30 million, with public funds, and lease it to Mercedes for only $100. On top of that the state provided tax breaks valued at about $300 million. Ultimately, it is estimated that the cost to taxpayers for each job created was between $153,000 and $220,000.

Some economists believe Alabama's offer was economically irrational. Joel Kotkin, an economic analyst who has followed various competitions among states for corporate investment, said "They went crazy. This is lunatic stuff." Noting Alabama's need for improved education, he added, "The question is, what have you taken out of your economy in order to do this? Most studies show it doesn't work. You're essentially giving away three-quarters of what you're going to gain."

Now that the factory is operating, employing about 3,000 workers, it is unclear whether Alabama's investment has paid off. According to economic analysis by Mercedes, the factory has added $1.3 billion annually to the state's economy. But academic economists remain divided.

Annette Watters, assistant director for the Center for Business & Economic Research at University of Alabama, has noted, "Some of the benefits are so difficult to measure. There are still strongly held opinions in the academic community that it's good and that it's bad."

Sources: Donald W. Nauss, "Bids by States to Lure Businesses Likely to Escalate," *Los Angeles Times*, October 1, 1993; Adam M. Zaretsky, "Are States Giving Away the Store? Attracting Jobs Can Be a Costly Adventure," *The Regional Economist*, Federal Reserve Bank of St. Louis, January 1994; "Ten Years after Mercedes, Alabama Town Still Pans for Gold," *Savannah Morning News*, October 9, 2002.

Discussion Questions

1. Think of a recent situation in which you bought something that you could, if you had wanted to, have produced for yourself (a restaurant meal that you could have cooked, a bus ride when you could have walked, or the like). Do any of the advantages or disadvantages of exchange discussed up to now apply to your case?
2. What do you suppose Smith or Ricardo would have had to say about the disadvantages of free trade discussed in this chapter? Do you agree with them? Why or why not?

4. Globalization and Policy

globalization: the extension of free trade and communications across the entire world, leading to a great increase in the volume of traded goods and services, and in expanded interconnections among different regions

As the global scope and volume of trade has increased, we need to consider the realities of globalization rather than simply of trade between two countries such as England and Portugal. **Globalization** involves increasing trade and communications among all parts of the world, leading to a great increase in the volume of traded goods and services. These interconnections turn up in a large variety of ways, including:

- a global audience for music, films, fashion, and other aspects of culture;
- expanded communications through the Internet, regardless of distance;
- exchanges of scientific, medical, and technical knowledge;
- inspiration regarding the possibility of freedom from hunger and want and from repressive government;
- shared images of a "good life," often based on images of material affluence associated with the West; and

- trade relationships that allow those who have money to purchase goods and services from virtually anywhere in the world—and that attract poor people into jobs producing for global consumers.

Although many of these developments are conducive to increased well-being overall, globalization can also accentuate some of the problems with free trade discussed above. Trade does create winners and losers; how is one to determine the relative importance of each group—for example, consumers, workers, citizens, children, and businesspeople? Are the wishes of consumers for lower prices as important as workers' fears of losing their jobs to foreign competition? Chapter 6, on welfare analysis, supplied some tools for measuring gains and losses in social welfare, but, as emphasized there, those tools depended entirely on market valuations. Thus, for example, if the workers' wages are low to begin with, their loss will not be counted as heavily in a standard welfare analysis as it would be if the "social loss" came out to a larger dollar figure.

In addition to economic threats, globalization is sometimes also criticized for its political and cultural effects, as people feel as if they are losing control over their local customs and livelihoods in a globalized world. This has often led to some degree of popular and government resistance to free trade and globalization.

4.1 Trade Protectionism

protectionism: the use of government policies to restrict trade with other countries and protect domestic industries from foreign competition

Exchange, as we have noted, has the potential to produce mutually beneficial outcomes for the parties involved, whether countries, companies, or family members. Yet we have also considered some reasons to be wary of too much reliance on exchange. National governments have always been aware of these problems and have historically tried, through a variety of policy tools, to control the degree to which their markets were "free." The use of such policies is often referred to as **protectionism**.

tariffs: taxes (or duties) charged by national governments to the importers of goods from other countries; tariffs can also be placed on exports

One example of protectionism, probably the most commonly used throughout history, is a **tariff** (sometimes called a "duty"). Tariffs are taxes charged by national governments to importers of merchandise from other countries. They often reduce trade to some degree, because the tariff raises the price of the good sold in the importing country, thereby reducing the import quantity demanded. The tariff can also have the effect of raising the price of domestically produced goods that compete with the imported good. Tariffs therefore tend to benefit domestic producers while raising prices to consumers. They also provide the government with often critically important tax revenue; indeed, this has often been the primary motivation for tariffs through history. Finally, tariffs sometimes even force foreign producers to lower their prices in order to remain competitive with domestic producers who do not pay the tariff.

trade quota: a nationally imposed restriction on the quantity of a particular good that can be imported from another country

Another example of protectionism is a **trade quota**, which is a limit on the quantity of a good that can be imported from another country. By restricting supply, a quota generally has the effect of increasing the price of the good. Like a tariff, it helps domestic producers by shielding them from lower-price competition, and it hurts consumers by making them pay a higher price. Unlike tariffs, quotas generally do not provide monetary benefit to the government, except when the quotas are sold or auctioned to the importers (this may be done out in the open or "unofficially"). The effect on the exporting foreign country is, however, more ambiguous than with a tariff. On the one hand, the quota may hurt foreign producers because it limits how much of a particular good they can export. On the other hand, they may obtain some benefit from extra revenues from the artificially higher price. Which effect prevails depends on, among other things, the elasticity of demand (discussed in Chapter 5) for the imported good.

trade-related subsidy: payments given to producers to encourage more production, either for export or as a substitute for imports

Imposing either tariffs or quotas or both has historically been the most frequently method of engaging in protectionism. But a few others, while less direct, have gained in importance in recent decades. One of these is the **trade-related subsidy**, which, unlike a tariff or quota, may be used to either expand or contract trade (and therefore cannot always precisely be regarded as

import substitution: a policy undertaken by governments seeking to reduce reliance on imports and encourage domestic industry. These often include the use of industry subsidies as well as protectionist policies.

"protectionist"). Trade expansion is facilitated through subsidies to exporters, since such payments reduce their production costs and therefore help exporters price their goods more competitively in foreign markets. Such payments can also be granted to domestic producers to encourage the production of certain goods for domestic markets, with a goal of reducing the quantity of imports. This is achieved to the extent that the demand for imports can be diverted to the domestic product (which is nothing more than a substitute for the imported product). Such subsidies fall into the more general policy of **import substitution**, which refers to government promotion of greater economic independence by decreasing the country's dependence on imports.

administrative obstacles: use of environmental, health, or safety regulations to prevent imports from other countries under the pretext of upholding higher standards

A final category of protectionism is subtle and often not easy to detect. It is when countries use **administrative obstacles** such as regulations relating to the environment, consumer protection, and labor standards to block importation of goods from foreign countries. They are difficult to detect because most of the time the pretext seems legitimate—and often it *is*. But in some cases it is clear that the standard being upheld is nothing more than a form of protectionism. In 1984, for example, the European Union (EU) struck down the German "beer purity" law—in effect for more than 300 years—a law that required all beer sold in Germany to use only a select few ingredients. The EU overturned the law because it found that it was motivated less by true concerns about "purity" than by the desire to keep beer imports out of the country. Another more amusing example occurred in the 1980s when Japan sought to ban imports of European ski equipment on grounds that Japanese snow was "unique" and that only Japanese-manufactured equipment was suitable for skiing on it.

Countries do not necessarily choose sets of policies that consistently lead toward "openness" or consistently toward "closedness." Often there is a mix—policies are chosen for a wide variety of reasons and can even work at cross-purposes. Nor do countries choose their policies in a vacuum. Policymakers need to take into account the reactions of foreign governments to their policies. Increasingly, they also need to pay attention to whether their policies are in compliance with international agreements.

4.2 International Trade Agreements

Many countries remained quite closed to trade up through the early decades of the twentieth century, charging high tariffs or imposing strict quotas on imported goods. It was only after World War II that this began to change. Despite Smith and Ricardo's famous pronouncements in favor of free trade, throughout history countries have seldom reduced their barriers to trade unilaterally. But starting in the 1940s, many countries became more interested in negotiating mutual reductions in tariffs and quotas.

Some trade agreements are "bilateral," meaning that two countries negotiate directly with each other. Other agreements are "multilateral," involving a group of countries. In 1948, 23 countries joined the General Agreement on Tariffs and Trade (GATT), which sought to set out rules for trade and enhance negotiations. The GATT has sponsored eight subsequent negotiation "trade rounds," some of which led to significant reductions in average tariff rates among participating countries over the next several decades.

World Trade Organization (WTO): an international organization that provides a forum for trade negotiations, creates rules to govern trade, and investigates and makes judgment on trade disputes

In 1995, the Uruguay Round of GATT trade negotiations led to the creation of a new forum for multilateral negotiations, the **World Trade Organization (WTO)**. As of 2013, the WTO has 159 member countries. In addition to being a forum for trade negotiations, the WTO attempts to set out rules about trade and is charged with investigating and making rulings on trade disputes between member countries. Many believe that its rulings are not without bias, because the WTO tends to rule in favor of the party in the dispute that is upholding free trade principles. In 2009, for example, the United States appealed to the WTO over dozens of subsidies that China was granting to its apparel, agriculture, and electronics industries. Anticipating the WTO's unfavorable ruling, China voluntarily ended the subsidies.

Some critics argue that, because of its bias toward free trade, the WTO's scope is too narrow. Yet in its assiduous pursuit of universal free trade, the WTO is also seeking to ensure that global trade is "fair." In other words, to the extent that it can create a world free of trade restrictions, the WTO is "leveling the playing field." The goal is for no country to be able to display favoritism toward or discriminate against others by subjecting them to different tariff levels or quota restrictions.

Can the WTO so easily impose its will on other countries? Well, not exactly; it technically has no sovereignty over countries that wish to ignore its rulings. Yet the loser in a dispute almost always has strong reasons for abiding by the WTO's decision. For one thing, the WTO considers it fair for the injured country to retaliate against its adversary if the latter ignores the judgment. So a country that wishes to breach WTO regulations must seriously consider the possibility of a trade war, in which each country keeps retaliating against the protectionist acts of the others, leading to escalating losses for both countries.

What if a country enjoys disproportionate economic power and therefore has little reason to fear retaliation? One might, for example, believe that the United States has the ability to impose tariffs on all (or at least most) imports from, say, Mozambique with impunity, because any attempted retaliation would likely just shift U.S. demand from Mozambique's markets to those of its neighbors. Yet the United States also must be concerned with its international image. As a leading global advocate of free trade, it would probably suffer diminished goodwill from its allies if it were seen to be flouting WTO rulings simply because it could. Consequently, trade dispute rulings from the WTO are almost always binding.

In addition to being members of the WTO, many countries have also entered into regional trade agreements with their neighbors. Leading examples of such attempts to integrate trade within a geographic area include the European Union (EU), formed in 1992, which now counts 27 countries as members; the North American Free Trade Agreement (NAFTA), entered into in 1994 by the United States, Canada, and Mexico; and Mercosur (Southern Cone Common Market) in South America, established in 1991, which now has five full members and five associate members. Although each of these regional agreements is unique regarding its specific policies, they all share a general commitment to reducing trade barriers such as tariffs or quotas.

There is some debate over whether such regional integration promotes "free trade" or retards it, because it promotes both trade *expansion* (within the region) and trade *diversion* (away from trade with other regions). To some degree, regional trade agreements have the same objective as the WTO—to lower tariffs and other barriers to trade. At the same time, these regional agreements can implicitly promote trade discrimination against countries outside the membership in any particular trade agreement.

4.3 Why Countries Follow Protectionist Policies

One very important reason that many policymakers have, historically, restricted trade is that they believe it is necessary to "protect" domestic industries and jobs from foreign competition. The United States, for example, still engages in protection of a variety of industries including Southern cotton, Northwestern timber, and Midwestern sugar beets. Without government protection, these industries would lose market share to lower-cost foreign producers. Such adjustment to global competition can be very painful. When U.S. automakers began to lose out to foreign competition, for example, a swath of the Midwest became so economically depressed that it became known as the "rust belt."

Sometimes protectionism is called a "beggar-thy-neighbor" approach, because each country is, in effect, trying to gain at the expense of other countries. Each country wants to *raise* its own production levels while simultaneously *reducing* the access of foreign producers to its market. Even after decades of trade negotiations—and encouragement by economists to "liberalize" their trade regimes—many countries continue to employ protectionist policies, at least of a modest, piecemeal sort. Although simple economic theory ignores the power differentials between countries and assumes that labor and capital resources can immediately and smoothly adjust to new patterns of commerce, in real life things can be quite different. Trade relations continue to be an arena in which countries try to exert dominance over one another. Policymakers continue to be concerned about the job losses and industrial dislocations that global competition can cause. Policies to ease unemployment may help, but there is no sign that—at least in democratic countries—policymakers will completely abandon protectionist tendencies any time soon.

A particular weakness of Ricardo's two-country, two-good model is that, like many economic models, it is a "static" model that does not take into account the passage of time. Patterns of comparative advantage can, after all, change. Should a country simply follow whatever comparative advantage it happens to have at a given time, or should it explore policies that might *change* its comparative advantage? If the country could end up better off in the long run by deliberately changing its mix of productive capabilities, it might achieve "dynamic efficiency" overall—that is, efficiency-based welfare gains over a sustained period of years—even if "static efficiency" is sacrificed over the short run.

In fact, many countries that have achieved high rates of industrialization—including the United States, the United Kingdom, Japan, and South Korea—did so by erecting substantial tariff barriers. If these countries had maintained their natural comparative advantages as they had existed in the past, the United States might still be known mostly for its production of wheat and raw cotton and the UK for its wool, while South Korea and Japan would still import all their cars. Policies that excluded foreign imports of manufactured textiles or automotive parts helped these countries to shift their economies away from less-processed goods toward a more industrial economic base. Now they all compete in global markets for sophisticated manufactured goods.

infant industry: an industry that is not yet globally competitive, but receives government support with the expectation that it may become so

The **infant industry** argument claims that sometimes governments should "protect" domestic industries from foreign competition until they become better able to compete on world markets. Usually, the government subsidizes the industry or places tariffs or quotas on imports of the good. Many industrializing countries have engaged in such import substitution policies in attempts to diversify their (earlier, often agriculture- or mining-based) economies. Sometimes, an entire package of industry-promoting policies is referred to as "industrial policy," and the goal is stated as the creation of a superior "*dynamic* comparative advantage."

The downside of deliberate, comparative-advantage-shifting industrial policy is that current potential "gains from trade" are sacrificed. The upside is that, over the long run, the country might be able to increase its national productivity and competitiveness and thus avoid getting locked into a disadvantageous pattern of production and trade.

Whether the gains from protectionist policies outweigh their costs is a matter of dispute. Many analysts point to long-term government protection of persistently high-cost production in India and some countries in Latin America as evidence that, once started, infant-industry policies tend to serve political special interests, rather than the interests of rational economic development. However, many economic historians point out that, into the early twentieth century, industries in France, Germany, the UK, and the United States all developed by erecting stiff tariff protection. These early industrializing countries bought raw materials from colonized or previously colonized areas, while refusing, as also noted earlier, to open their markets to imports of many manufactured goods. Japan, Taiwan, and South Korea are more recent examples of countries in which some varieties of protectionist policies were important in the history of their industrial development.

But even an advanced industrialized economy can become too specialized, which can sometimes lead to an unhealthy dependence on other countries for important goods like food and energy. Japan, for example, at the forefront when it comes to electronics and other manufactured goods, is heavily dependent on food imports, which could make the country vulnerable in the event of a war or other disruption in trade. Japan has long used quotas and tariffs to limit rice imports, providing protection for its domestic rice producers. Energy security is another important concern. In recent years, the United States has been pushing, through the use of generous subsidies to domestic producers, to develop alternatives to petroleum—most notably natural gas, with the attendant controversy over the manner in which it is extracted. Developers of renewable energy like solar and wind power have also been receiving subsidies, albeit at a smaller scale. The goal of U.S policymakers is reduce dependence on petroleum imports from other countries.

Another important reason that some countries engage in protectionism is perceived lack of "fairness" by trading partners. Companies that are not required by their governments to abide by certain labor, safety, or environmental laws or regulations receive an indirect subsidy in that they face lower production costs, ceteris paribus, than foreign competitors. So we can say, for example, that clothing made in countries that are hostile to labor unions are likely to be priced more competitively than clothing made in countries where workers enjoy more rights and benefits (which tend to be more costly to employers). It is a "fairness" issue in that countries that observe higher standards believe themselves to be unjustly penalized.

One way in which countries can try to avoid such a "race to the bottom" is to ban both the domestic manufacture and importation of goods that are considered hazardous to consumers, have been made under labor standards considered inhumane, or were made using production processes that cause serious damage to the environment. In this way, at least the domestic market is reserved for producers who follow higher standards. The setting of standards may also encourage potential trading partners to raise their environmental, labor, or safety standards, so that their goods can be admitted.

At the same time, setting standards may provoke strong resistance. For example, in 1994, the United States sought to ban tuna imports from Mexico, an act generally prohibited by the GATT. Its claim was based on its higher environmental standards: The United States accused Mexico of using nets that tended to inadvertently catch and drown dolphins—nets that were also much cheaper to use than "dolphin-friendly" nets. Mexico appealed to the GATT, which ruled in its favor and required the United States to lift the ban. Since then, numerous other instances of protectionism have occurred on the basis of asymmetric (unequal) standards for, among other things, labor, the environment, safety, and health.

Another justification for protectionism, mentioned earlier, is the need for government revenue. This has without a doubt been one of the greatest motivators for such policies over the years, specifically in the case of tariffs. Until 1913, for example, the United States had no income tax, and the federal government relied heavily on tariffs to run its operations. Of course, this is no longer the case, as the U.S. federal government today obtains a tiny fraction of its revenue from import tariffs. Yet in many poor countries, it is, even today, very difficult to collect taxes on income and property. People may be spread over wide areas, and much of the economy may not be monetized. Because tariffs are taxes on monetized transactions at harbor facilities or airports, they are, as a rule, relatively easy to collect. Tariffs can therefore be an important source of revenue for health, education, defense, and other government activities.

4.4 When Is Limiting Trade "Unfair"?

When should a restriction on trade be considered legitimate, and when should it not be? This complicated question is a topic of vigorous, ongoing debate. Most countries staunchly defend their right to restrict trade for purposes such as military security or consumer safety, so international trade agreements tend to stop short of banning all restrictions.

But beyond agreement on a few principles, debates become heated. Consider three examples.

GMO Products. The EU has banned the importation of products containing genetically modified organisms (GMO), on grounds that they present a threat to public health and the environment. The United States and other grain-producing countries have contested this at the WTO, arguing that GMO products are safe and the real reason for the ban is that the EU simply wants to protect its farmers. The WTO ultimately ruled that the ban was illegal, a ruling entirely consistent with its pro–free trade bias. But the ruling has only intensified the debate.

dumping: selling products at prices that are below the cost of production

Dumping. The United States has accused China of subsidizing the production of many of its products and **dumping** them on the U.S. market. "Dumping," the selling of products on foreign markets at prices that are unfairly low (that is, below the cost of production), is forbidden in international agreements. The United States argues that it has the right to retaliate by levying quotas and tariffs on Chinese goods. But China, of course, can argue that it simply is blessed with a low-cost production environment and that the United States is engaging in protectionism.

Labor Standards. In some extreme cases, such as the use of slave labor, restrictions on trade are usually considered permissible. But should countries be allowed to use trade restrictions to punish unfair labor practices? Some poorer countries have accused richer countries of imposing unreasonably high labor standards. Under the pretext of trying to protect global workers, they say, the richer countries are just trying to protect their workers from fair competition. But the lack of such standards can have disastrous consequences, for example, the death of hundreds of workers in Bangladesh in factory fires and building collapses (see Box 7.3).

Questions of what will be ruled "fair" or "unfair" by the WTO—and whether such rulings can be enforced—often come down to questions of political economy. Large, powerful countries and corporations use the WTO negotiations and dispute resolution mechanisms as ways to advance their own interests. Smaller and less powerful groups have a more difficult time having their voices heard. Many labor, environmental, and social justice groups, for example, charge that the WTO primarily serves the interests of powerful multinational corporations. They worry that WTO negotiations have served to speed up the "race to the bottom" and have reduced national sovereignty. Observers concerned about economic development believe that WTO rules disadvantage countries that are still relatively poor, by forbidding the use of the sorts of industrial policies that helped other countries achieve economic growth at an earlier time. In other words, in its zeal to support the elimination or reduction of trade restrictions, the WTO appears to be forgetting the economic path that today's wealthier countries followed during their own rise.

In 2001, the WTO officially launched the Doha Round of negotiations (also officially called the Doha Development Agenda), which was, in its official statements, intended to take into account the needs and interests of poorer countries. Now, even a dozen years later, the Doha Round remains at an impasse. Many poorer countries pushed for richer countries to reduce their tariffs and subsidies, particularly on agricultural goods. At the same time, top priorities for richer countries included persuading poorer countries to open their service sector

Box 7.3 Labor Standards, Tragedy, and Reform in Bangladesh

The Rana Plaza complex was built on swampy ground outside Dhaka, Bangladesh. Code violations included the building of several illegal floors. The building's collapse on April 24, 2013, ranked among the world's worst industrial accidents, killing more than a thousand garment workers. A fire at another garment factory in Bangladesh the previous year killed 112 people.

Low wages in Bangladesh, along with tax concessions offered by Western countries, have helped turn the country's garment sector into its largest employment generator. Annual exports from the sector are worth $21 billion, with 60 percent of these exports going to Europe. After the recent industrial accidents, the European Union, which gives preferential access to the Bangladeshi garment industry, threatened punitive measures if worker safety standards were not improved.

In July 2013, Bangladesh approved a new labor law to boost worker rights, including the freedom to form trade unions. The legislation puts in place provisions including a central fund to improve living standards of workers, a requirement for 5 percent of annual profits to be deposited in employee welfare funds, and an assurance that union members will not be transferred to another factory of the same owner after labor unrest.

The legislation is seen as a crucial step toward curbing rising cases of exploitation in a country with 4 million garment factory workers. But activists said it failed to address several concerns and blamed the government for enacting the law in a hurry to please foreigners.

Source: Nandita Bose, "Stronger Labour Law in Bangladesh after Garment Factory Collapse," Reuters, July 15, 2013.

(including banking and airline transportation) to foreign companies and to abide by stricter rules on intellectual property (e.g., to stop making less expensive versions of patented drugs). Because the wealthier countries showed little willingness to reduce protection of their domestic agricultural industries, Doha Round talks were suspended in July 2006. Negotiations again broke down in 2008, and since then no notable progress has been made to restart them.

Discussion Questions

1. What international trade issues have been in the news recently? What views are presented by different interest groups in trade debates? Are there any issues that particularly affect your community?
2. Debates between advocates of "free trade" and advocates of "protectionism" have gone on for hundreds of years. How aware are you of current debates, which are now often framed in terms of pro- and anti-"globalization"? Do you have more sympathy for one side than for the other? What do you think you need to know more about—in terms of theories or real-world facts—to be able to decide with confidence whether increased world trade, in a specific situation, is a good idea?

5. CONCLUSION

We have seen that the observations made by Adam Smith and David Ricardo in support of free trade have an almost unassailable logic based on economic efficiency. And one could argue that their logic has been borne out in practice, because much of what they observed two centuries ago has since played out at a much greater scale. Yet if there is a lesson in our experience with trade, it is that theory often does not account for what practice later reveals.

The world was a much simpler place during the time of Smith and Ricardo. Large multinational corporations did not yet exist for the most part, and businesses could not readily pick up and migrate to another country if they found conditions more favorable there. Indeed, in those days such actions might even have been considered treasonous. The simple comparative advantage model discussed earlier was more suited to the relatively simple world that existed during that time. The far greater complexity in today's world is much more difficult—if not impossible—to capture in a simplified model.

This is a good time to remind ourselves once again that models best serve us as simplifications of reality that grant us some basic insight into the functioning of real-world systems. The original insights about the advantages of free trade—that is, that it can be of substantial benefit to both parties to an exchange—appear no more contestable today than during Smith and Ricardo's time. Yet beyond this important insight, numerous complicating factors should cause us to be cautious in interpreting the model.

Here we briefly list and review three such factors, though the list is far from exhaustive. First, as noted above, the logic of unfettered free trade does not account for the fact that today capital can easily migrate across borders. What this means is that countries do not have to conform to mutually beneficial exchange. Recalling an earlier example, let us assume that the United States has a comparative *dis*advantage in clothing production compared to Bangladesh. Instead of trading with Bangladesh, U.S companies today can move there and hire local workers—at a relatively low wage—to produce clothes for global markets. Easy capital mobility could, in such cases, reduce opportunities for mutually beneficial trade.

Second, in Smith and Ricardo's time, the economic landscape consisted of only about a dozen economic powers at a more or less similar level of development. The "playing field" was, in other words, more or less level. Today, because former colonies have achieved political independence over the past 50 to 60 years, the world is far more imbalanced. One danger facing poor countries today is that they will follow the "logic" of comparative advantage and continue to specialize in simple primary goods that offer them scant hope of someday becoming stronger, more diversified economies.

Third, there is the role of the WTO. It might appear that Smith and Ricardo would have supported an agency empowered to promote global free trade. Yet because inequality between countries is so much greater today than it was then, it seems increasingly doubtful, the WTO's mission notwithstanding, that today's brand of "free trade"—meaning a wholesale dismantling of protectionist policies—is always mutually beneficial. It is indeed quite possible that by making it more difficult for developing countries to actively nurture their fledgling industries, some WTO policies may worsen inequality around the world. This is especially true because more powerful countries can often win exceptions to the rule for their products in certain areas, notably agriculture.

Perhaps the greatest controversy exists over asymmetric "standards"—whether motivated by labor, environmental, safety, or other concerns. There is no question that rigid adherence to, say, labor standards might result in trade restrictions against countries that do not place a high priority on workers' rights. For this reason alone, the WTO is likely to disallow their use as a basis for blocking trade, except in extreme cases such as child or slave labor. Yet such a case vividly illustrates how in some cases the "gains from trade" might mask social or environmental losses resulting from the "race to the bottom" that the WTO's pro-trade policies might foster.

The question arises as to how to balance the "gains" to importers and consumers against the potential losses to workers, domestic industry, and the environment. And, again, although economics can provide some concepts and methods to use in reaching for answers, important decisions in these areas often require ethical judgments that go beyond the discipline of economics.

REVIEW QUESTIONS

1. How does specialization lead to greater productivity?
2. Explain how more extensive markets tend to produce a higher degree of specialization.
3. Was Adam Smith a revolutionary? Explain.
4. Describe the Ricardian model of trade.
5. What is meant by the "principle of comparative advantage"?
6. On what does a country's comparative advantage depend?
7. What does it mean to say that a particular country is labor intensive (or capital intensive)?
8. What is the theory of "factor-price equalization"?
9. How does free trade produce an incentive to work hard?
10. What are some other advantages of free trade?
11. Explain how the concepts of vulnerability and "lock-in" are related. How do they weaken the case for free trade?
12. What is "protectionism," and why do countries often engage in it?
13. List and describe four types of protectionist policies.
14. What is import substitution?
15. What are some international organizations and agreements that involve trade relations?
16. What does the World Trade Organization do?
17. What is the "infant industry" argument?
18. How does the notion of "dynamic comparative advantage" explain some countries' adoption of "infant industry" policies?
19. How can international openness cause a "race to the bottom"?
20. Give some examples of recent controversies in trade policy.

EXERCISES

1. Hereland and Thereland are two small countries. Each currently produces both milk and corn, and they do not trade. If Hereland puts all its resources into milk, it can produce 2 tanker truckloads, while if it puts all its resources in corn production, it can produce 8 tons. Thereland can produce either 2 loads of milk or 2 tons of corn. (Both can also produce any combination on a straight line in between.)
   a. Draw and label production-possibilities frontiers for Hereland and Thereland.

b. Suppose that Hereland's citizens would like 1 truckload of milk and 6 tons of corn. Can Hereland produce this?
c. Suppose that Thereland's citizens would like 1 load of milk and 2 tons of corn. Can Thereland produce this?
d. What is the slope of Hereland's PPF? Fill in the blank: "For each truckload of milk that Hereland makes, it must give up making ___ tons of corn."
e. What is the slope of Thereland's PPF? Fill in the blank: "For each truckload of milk that Thereland makes, it must give up making ___ tons of corn."
f. Which country has a comparative advantage in producing milk?
g. Create a table similar to Table 7.1, showing how Hereland and Thereland could enter into a trading relationship in order to meet their citizens' consumption desires as described in (b) and (c).
h. Suppose that you are an analyst working for the government of Hereland. Write a few sentences, based on the above analysis, advising your boss about whether to undertake trade negotiations with Thereland.
i. Would your advice change if you knew that unemployment in Hereland is high and that retraining corn farmers to be dairy farmers, or vice versa, is very difficult to do?
j. Would your advice change if Thereland insisted in trade negotiations that 1 truckload of milk be exchanged for exactly 4 tons of corn?

2. Continuing the Ricardian story from Section 2.1 of this chapter, suppose that England were, after a while, to put a tariff on imports of Portuguese wine. Since we only have wine and cloth in this story, we will have to (somewhat unrealistically) express this tax in terms of units of goods rather than units of currency. Say that England demands that Portugal "pay a tariff of 40 units of cloth" if it wants to sell 100 units of wine. Or, in other words, England now says that it will give Portugal only *60 units of cloth* instead of 100, in exchange for 100 units of wine.
   a. With production unchanged, what would exchange and consumption be like under these modified terms of trade? (Create a table like Table 7.1.)
   b. Does England benefit from instituting this tariff?
   c. Would Portugal voluntarily agree to continue trading, with these changed terms of trade? (Assume that Portugal has no power to change the terms of trade—it can only accept England's deal or go back to consuming within its own PPF.)
   d. If trade is voluntary, does that mean it is *fair?* Discuss.

3. Match each concept in Column A with a definition or example in Column B.

Column A	Column B
a. Tariff	1. Economic weakness resulting from too much import dependence
b. Import substitution	2. When a region competes by providing a low-cost business environment, resulting in deterioration of labor, environmental, or safety standards
c. Vulnerability	3. An organization charged with facilitating international trade
d. Race to the bottom	4. Getting trapped into the long-term production of primary goods for export
e. Dumping	5. The theory that trade should eventually lead to returns to factors of production that are equal across countries
f. Quota	6. A tax levied on an internationally traded item
g. Dynamic comparative advantage	7. Changes in the opportunity cost of production over time
h. WTO	8. The use of environmental, health, or safety regulations to prevent imports from other countries under the pretext of upholding higher standards
i. Factor-price equalization	9. The deliberate promotion of domestic goods production to reduce reliance on imports
j. Comparative advantage	10. An industry that needs protection until it is able to compete
k. Lock-in	11. Selling goods abroad at a price that is below the cost of production
l. Administrative obstacles	12. Putting a quantity limit on imports or exports
m. Infant industry	13. Putting a tariff on orange juice imports to help Florida orange growers
n. Protectionism	14. A country is relatively more efficient in the production of some good(s)

NOTES

1. Adam Smith, *An Inquiry into the Nature and Causes of the Wealth of Nations* (London: Methuen, 1930), pp. 6, 7.

2. Jacques Savary, *Le parfait négociant* (Paris, 1675), quoted in Albert O. Hirschman, *The Passions and the Interests* (Princeton: Princeton University Press, 1997), pp. 59–60.

APPENDIX: A FORMAL THEORY OF GAINS FROM TRADE

Here we explore in more detail the "gains from trade" example given in the text. There, for simplicity, we explored a case in which both countries completely specialize, because their level of desired total consumption just happens to match each country's total production level with complete specialization. Graphing a *joint* PPF for the two countries enables us to relax this assumption, while also exploring more fully the concepts of opportunity costs and comparative advantage.

Recall that in this example, Portugal can produce a maximum of either 200 bottles of wine or 100 bolts of cloth. Portugal's PPF was shown in Figure 7.1. Examining its slope more closely reveals that, moving left to right starting at the (0, 200) point, a fall (or negative "rise") of 200 bottles of wine is accompanied by a "run" of +100 bolts of cloth. Because the curve is straight, the slope is therefore –2 throughout. At any point, then, reducing wine production by 2 bottles (i.e., a negative "rise" of 2) is needed to increase cloth production by 1 bolt (i.e., to create a "run" of 1 unit to the right).

England can produce a maximum of 200 bottles of wine or 400 bolts of cloth, as was shown in Figure 7.2. The slope of its production possibilities frontier is –0.5 (= –200/400). For each additional bolt of cloth, England gives up producing half a bottle of wine.

In Figure 7.3, we create a *joint* PPF for the two countries. Suppose that they both start out producing only wine. Adding Portugal's 200 bottles to England's 200 bottles, we find that jointly they can produce 400 bottles if they produce no cloth, as shown at the point (0, 400). Now suppose that they would like to consume *some* cloth, and they make a joint decision about where it should be produced. They see that if Portugal produces the first bolt of cloth, it will cost them 2 bottles of wine. If England produces the first bolt of cloth, it will cost them only half a bottle of wine. Clearly, England should produce it. This kind of reasoning will tell England to produce not only the first bolt of cloth but also every succeeding bolt of cloth, as long as possible. Portugal will keep producing only wine, at its maximum level of 200 bottles.

Figure 7.3 **Joint Production Possibilities Frontier for England and Portugal**

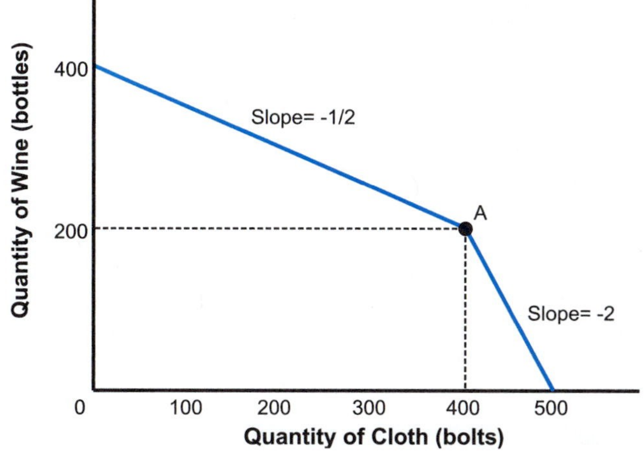

By specializing efficiently, England and Portugal together can produce these combinations of wine and cloth.

The possibility of exploiting England's relatively low-cost cloth production runs out when these two countries reach point A. At point A, England produces the maximum amount of cloth it can—400 bolts—and Portugal still produces only wine (200 bottles). This was the point used as an example in the text, for simplicity. Now if they want to continue to have even more cloth (and less wine), Portugal will have to produce it. Each extra bolt of cloth will now cost 2 bottles of wine, up to the point (500, 0), where they both produce only cloth.

What if, instead, the countries were to follow their comparative *dis*advantages, having Portugal change to cloth production first, and England only after Portugal was producing at capacity? Figure 7.4 contrasts the efficient PPF with this case. With inefficient full specialization represented by the point where Portugal produces 100 bolts of cloth and England produces 200 bottles of wine, the PPF bends *inward.* The bold line is the efficient production possibilities frontier, and the lighter line reflects the most inefficient production choices. As you can see, following the rule of comparative *advantage* leads to a much larger PPF than doing the reverse! A similarly inefficient result would follow if you were better at cleaning, and your housemate at shopping, but you tended to shop and your housemate tended to clean.

Figure 7.4 **Efficient and Inefficient Joint Production Possibilities Frontier**

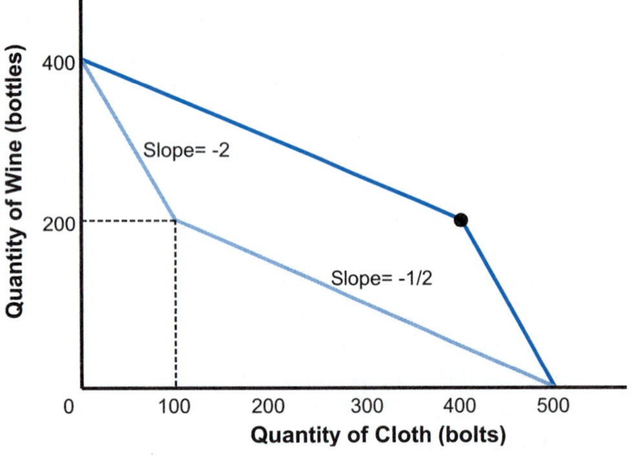

If England and Portugal specialized in an inefficient way, the joint production possibilities frontier would bow in rather than out.

Along with the concept of comparative advantage, economists also discuss the concept of absolute advantage. A producer has an absolute advantage when, using the same amount of some resource as another producer, it can produce more. Usually, labor hours are the resource considered. For example, suppose that in a one-hour period you can buy enough groceries for six days *or* clean three rooms. Your housemate, by contrast, moves more slowly and can buy enough groceries for only three days, or clean only one room, in an hour. You clearly have an absolute advantage in production of both these services. Does this mean you should do all the work?* (See whether you can figure out the answer before looking at the footnote.)

*No. Comparative, not absolute, advantage should guide the assignment of tasks. Although you have an *absolute* advantage over your housemate in both activities, your housemate has a *comparative* advantage in shopping. That is, to get enough groceries for six days would "cost" only two rooms' worth of cleaning if your housemate does it (taking two hours). But if you shop for six days' worth of food, the opportunity cost is more—the three rooms you could have cleaned. Therefore, on efficiency grounds at least, your housemate should shop and you should clean. (You can also come to the same result by examining your own comparative advantage—in cleaning.)

PART III

Economics and Society

8 Economic Behavior and Rationality

In Chapter 1, we defined economic actors, or economic agents, as people or organizations engaged in any of the four essential economic activities: production, distribution, consumption, and resource maintenance. Economic actors can be individuals, small groups (such as a family or a group of roommates), or large organizations such as a government agency or a multinational corporation. Economics is about how these actors behave and interact as they engage in economic activities. In this chapter we explore the behavior of individual economic actors—people. We look at contemporary research on this topic, and, where it seems relevant, compare this with older approaches.

1. Economic Understandings of Human Motivations

Economics is a *social* science—it is about people and about how we organize ourselves to meet our needs and enhance our well-being. Ultimately, all economic behavior is human behavior. Sometimes institutional forces appear to take over (witness the tendency of some bureaucracies to expand over time), but if you look closely at all economic outcomes, you will find that they are ultimately determined by human decisions or behavior. Thus economists have traditionally used, as a starting point, some kind of statement about the motivations behind economic actions.

1.1 Classical Economic Views of Human Nature

In Chapter 6, we mentioned Adam Smith's concept of the invisible hand, according to which people acting in their own self-interest would, through markets, promote the general welfare of society. The concept of the invisible hand has become very famous, but it is often taken out of context to mean that if people *only* behave with self-interest, they will do what is best for the entire society.

This interpretation would have astonished Smith, who, before writing *An Inquiry into the Nature and Causes of the Wealth of Nations,* had written another long book, *The Theory of Moral Sentiments,* in which he examined with care how people are motivated. His emphasis there is on the desire of people to have self-respect and the respect of others. He assumes that such respect depends on people acting honorably, justly, and with concern and empathy for others in their community. Smith recognizes that selfish desires play a large role but believes that they will be held in check both by the "moral sentiments" (the universal desire for self-respect and the respect of others) and also by the fortunate accident by which "in many cases" (not all!) selfish acts can "promote the public interest."[1]

Thus Smith's vision of human nature and human motivation was one in which individual self-interest was mixed with more social motives. Rather than starting with Robinson Crusoe, who lived alone on an island, he perceived that the behavior of any one person always had to be understood within that person's social context.

classical economics: the school of economics, originating in the eighteenth century, that stressed issues of growth, distribution, and markets

Smith was followed by other economists, such as the trade theorist David Ricardo and the philosopher/economist John Stuart Mill. These theorists of **classical economics** held similarly complex views of human nature and motivations. In 1890 Alfred Marshall tried to codify these ideas in a very influential text called *Principles of Economics,* which was published in eight editions, the last published in 1920. Marshall viewed the motives of human actors in an optimistic light—including those of economists, whom he assumed were motivated by a desire to improve the human condition. He specifically focused on the reduction of poverty so as to allow people to develop their higher moral and intellectual faculties, rather than being condemned to lives of desperate effort for simple survival.

1.2 The Neoclassical Model

neoclassical model: a model that portrays the economy as a collection of profit-maximizing firms and utility-maximizing households interacting through perfectly competitive markets

In the twentieth century, the approach that came to dominate economics was known as the **neoclassical model**. This approach took a narrower view of human motivations. The basic neoclassical or traditional model builds a simplified story about economic life by assuming that there are only two main types of economic actors and by making simplifying assumptions about how these two types of actors behave and interact. The two basic sets of actors in this model are firms, which are assumed to maximize their profits from producing and selling goods and services, and households, which are assumed to maximize their utility (or satisfaction) from consuming goods and services. The two kinds of agents are assumed to interact in perfectly competitive markets (the subject of Chapter 17). Given some additional assumptions, explored later in this book, the model can be elegantly expressed in figures, equations, and graphs.

Some benefits can be gained from looking at economic behavior in this way. The assumptions reduce the actual (very complicated) economy to something that is much more limited but also easier to analyze. The traditional model is particularly well suited for analyzing the determination of prices, the volume of trade, and efficiency issues in certain cases.

The neoclassical model was introduced to generations of students in 1948 with the publication of Paul Samuelson's textbook *Economics: An Introductory Analysis*, which went on to become the best-selling economics text ever. Samuelson's text promoted the idea that economics should be "value free" (i.e., it should be developed without reference to any human goals or values) and that it should be largely or purely deductive, meaning that it should derive conclusions from the simple assumptions stated above, about the motivations of market actors.

rationality axiom: the statement that "rational economic man maximizes his utility (or self-interest)"

In addition to the claim of being value free, through the second half of the twentieth century, many economists used another belief to assert that their discipline was more scientific than other social sciences. They claimed that the entire system of economic theory is so purely deductive that everything in it can be deduced from one essential axiom.* This, the **rationality axiom**, states that "rational economic man maximizes his utility." (Some economists substitute for "utility" another term such as "self-interest," or "well-being.") This statement has often been interpreted to mean that pursuit of self-interest is the *only* thing that is done by rational economic actors—and that anything else is *irrational.*

The statement that the subject of economics is "completely axiomatized" (i.e., everything in it can be deduced from this single basic axiom) has come under considerable criticism. To discuss that in depth, however, would be to get into issues of methodology that are beyond the scope of an introductory textbook. Instead of addressing these arcane matters, we describe some real-world tests that have been applied in recent years to a model of human behavior that states that all that economics needs to know about human behavior is that people are rational and self-interested. We return to the issue of selfishness in Section 3 of this chapter. Section 2 first focuses on the assumption that people are rational in those portions of human

*An axiom is a statement that is considered to be self-evident, without need of proof.

behavior that are related to the economic activities of production, distribution, consumption, and resource maintenance.

Discussion Questions

1. Do you agree with the assumption of the neoclassical model that human behavior is rational and self-interested? Can you think of some examples of economic behavior that might contradict these assumptions?
2. Do you believe economics should strive, as much as possible, to be value free? What do you think are the advantages and disadvantages of this approach?

2. ECONOMIC BEHAVIOR

Recent economic theory has explored views of human nature and decision-making that go beyond the simple axioms of the basic neoclassical model. In this chapter, we examine other models of economic behavior that consider people's (1) choice of goals, (2) the actions they take to achieve these goals, and (3) the limitations and influences that affect their choices and actions.

As we learned in Chapter 2, any model highlights some aspects of reality while ignoring others. In this case, we employ the term "model" to mean a description of human behavior that emphasizes what is most important to understand about how people act most of the time when engaging in economic activities. Such a model obviously cannot explain all human actions, but it should be sufficient to provide a general outline of what to expect. We work our way gradually toward such a descriptive model.

2.1 BEHAVIORAL ECONOMICS

behavioral economics: a subfield of microeconomics that studies how individuals and organizations make economic decisions

In the past few decades, the neoclassical view of human behavior has been challenged by a strong alternative called **behavioral economics,** which studies how individuals and organizations make economic decisions. Studies in this area suggest that a more sophisticated model of human motivations is required to explain behaviors such as those that lead to stock market swings, the ways that people react to good and bad fortune, and why people often seem to act against their own self-interest.[2]

Rather than making assumptions about human behavior, behavioral economics relies heavily on scientific experiments to determine how people behave in different situations. Consider the insights from one such experiment, which concerns a three-hour seminar class that has a short break in the middle, when the professor offers the students a snack. Every week, the professor provides the students with a list of possible snacks, and the students vote on which snack they want. Only the snack with the most votes is then provided. The results of this experiment show that every week students tend to pick the same snack—the one that is their favorite.

With a different group of students, who are also taking a three-hour seminar class with a break, the students are instead asked in advance which snacks they will prefer for the next three weeks. In this case, students tend to vote for variety, thinking that they will not want the same snack every week. But this is precisely what students actually do want when they get to vote every week! When planning ahead, students think they will want variety, but when the time comes to consume a snack students tend to stick with their favorite each time. Similar experiments have shown that people who go grocery shopping infrequently also tend to think that they will want variety, but in reality they tend to want their favorite foods more often.

Another illustration of behavior that does not fit older, rigid definitions of rationality concerns the way that we process information. Perhaps the most famous contemporary behavioral economist is not an economist by training. Despite being educated as a psychologist, Daniel Kahneman won the 2002 Nobel Memorial Prize in economic science. Kahneman's

availability heuristic: placing undue importance on particular information because it is readily available or vivid

research has found that people tend to give undue weight to information that is easily available or vivid, something he called the **availability heuristic**. ("Heuristic" means a method for solving problems.) For example, suppose that college students are deciding which courses to take next semester, and they see a summary of evaluations from hundreds of other students indicating that a certain course is very good. Then suppose that they watch a video interview of just one student, who gives a negative review of the course. Even when students were told in advance that such a negative review was atypical, they tended to be more influenced by the vivid negative review than the summary of hundreds of evaluations, even though such behavior seems irrational.

framing: changing the way a particular decision is presented to people in order to influence their behavior

Kahneman has also shown that the way a decision is presented to people can significantly influence their choices, an effect he referred to as **framing**. For example, consider a gas station that advertises a special 5-cent-per-gallon discount for paying cash. Meanwhile, another station with the same prices indicates that they charge a 5-cent-per-gallon surcharge to customers who pay by credit card. Although the prices end up exactly the same, experiments suggest that consumers respond more favorably to the station that advertises the apparent discount. For one of Kahneman's famous experiments on the importance of framing, see Box 8.1.

A common area of seemingly irrational economic behavior is personal finance. Some companies offer their employees the option of matching contributions to their retirement plans; for each $1 the employee voluntarily contributes to his or her retirement plan, the employer matches it with an additional contribution. For example, with a 50 percent matching program, for each $1 an employee contributes, the employer contributes 50 cents. This amounts to an instant 50 percent rate of return on the employee's investment.

Although most financial advisers suggest taking advantage of matching contributions, many employees do not enroll in such programs, voluntarily forgoing the opportunity to garner thousands of additional dollars for retirement. This is not necessarily irrational, as some employees may have pressing current economic needs. However, one research study

Box 8.1 The Effect of Framing on Decisions

Suppose that you are presented with the following question:

> Imagine you are a physician working in an Asian village, and 600 people have come down with a life-threatening disease. Two possible treatments exist. If you choose treatment A, you will save exactly 200 people. If you choose treatment B, there is a one-third chance that you will save all 600 people, and a two-thirds chance you will save no one. Which treatment do you choose, A or B?

Kahneman and Tversky found that the majority of respondents (72 percent) chose treatment A, which saves exactly 200 people. Now consider the following scenario:

> You are a physician working in an Asian village, and 600 people have come down with a life-threatening disease. Two possible treatments exist. If you choose treatment C, exactly 400 people will die. If you choose treatment D, there is a one-third chance that no one will die, and a two-thirds chance that everyone will die. Which treatment do you choose, C or D?

In this case, they found that the majority of respondents (78 percent) chose treatment D, which offers a one-third chance that no one will die. But if you compare the two questions carefully, you will notice that they are exactly the same! Treatments A and C are identical, and so are treatments B and D. The only thing that changes are the way the options are presented, or framed, to respondents.

According to Tversky and Kahneman people evaluate gains and losses differently. Thus while treatments A and C are quantitatively identical, treatment A is framed as a gain (i.e., you save 200 people) while treatment C is framed as a loss (i.e., 400 people die). It seems people are more likely to take risks when it comes to losses than gains. In other words, people prefer a "sure thing" when it comes to a potential gain but are willing to take a chance if it involves avoiding a loss.

Source: Amos Tversky and Daniel Kahneman, "The Framing of Decisions and the Psychology of Choice," *Science* 211(4481) (1981): 453–458.

looked at what happened when a large company changed its policy from a matching program that required employees to sign up for it (an "opt in" program) to a similar program in which employees were automatically enrolled but could opt out if they wanted to.[3] Under the new (opt-out) program, 86 percent of employees stayed in the program. For comparable employees prior to the change, the participation rate was only 37 percent. The economic advantages were the same in either case, and the huge difference in participation rates is difficult to justify on the basis of the paperwork needed to sign up for the program. Again, the results demonstrate that framing can have a significant influence on people's choices.

anchoring effect: overreliance on a piece of information that may or may not be relevant as a reference point when making a decision

An effect similar to framing is known as **anchoring**, in which people rely on a piece of information that is not necessarily relevant as a reference point in making a decision. In one powerful example, graduate students at the MIT Sloan School of Management were first asked to write down the last two digits of their Social Security numbers.[4] They were then asked whether they would pay this amount, in dollars, for various products, including a fancy bottle of wine and a cordless keyboard. Assuming rational behavior, the last digits of one's Social Security number should have no relation to one's willingness to pay for a product. However, the subjects with the highest Social Security numbers indicated a willingness to pay about 300 percent more than those with the lowest numbers; apparently they used their Social Security numbers as an "anchor" in evaluating the worth of the products.

In a real-world example of anchoring, a high-end kitchen equipment catalog featured a particular bread maker for $279. Sometime later, the company began offering a "deluxe" model for $429. Although they did not sell too many of the deluxe model, sales of the $279 model almost doubled because now it seemed like a relative bargain.

2.2 The Role of Time in Economic Decisions

The retirement program example cited above suggests that in making their decisions people might not appropriately weigh the future. In other words, people seem to place undue emphasis on gains or benefits received today without considering the implications of their decisions for the future. Further evidence of this is the large number of people who have acquired significant high-interest credit card debt; indeed, about 6 percent of Americans are considered "compulsive shoppers," who seek instant gratification with little concern for often very troublesome consequences of running up a great deal of debt.[5] But you do not need to be a compulsive shopper to fall short of the ideal "rational consumer" who knows and weighs all the relevant costs and benefits.

time discount rate: an economic concept describing the relative weighting of present benefits or costs compared to future benefits or costs

You may know someone who does not pay much attention to the future consequences of his or her actions. Economists would say that this person has a very high **time discount rate**, meaning that in his or her mind, future events are very much discounted or diminished when weighed against the pleasures of today. (The technical meaning of "discount rate" is discussed in Chapter 13.)

On the other hand you might also know people who seem to have the attitude "I've got to work hard and prepare now; enjoying myself will have to wait for later." Economists would say that people like this have low time discount rates if by their current work they are gaining benefits for tomorrow. The later benefits loom large (i.e., are *not* "discounted") in their decisions.

Time discount rates are important in all sorts of situations. Economists usually assume that people who invest in a college education have a relatively low time discount rate, because they are willing to forgo current income or relaxation to study for some expected future gain. (Of course, this is not true for individuals who enjoy college or regard it as more appealing than the prospects for postcollege experience.)

Company leaders with high time discount rates may concentrate on making this quarter's financial statement look good, whereas those with more concern about the future will look toward longer-term goals. In deciding on environmental regulations, people who work at government agencies are forced to make decisions about how much weight to give the well-being of future generations. The lower their discount rate, the more important safeguarding the well-being of future generations appears.

2.3 THE ROLE OF EMOTIONS IN ECONOMIC DECISIONS

The potential conflict between our reasoning and our emotions has long been studied by philosophers and writers. The conventional view is that emotions get in the way of good decision making, as they tend to interfere with logical reasoning. The American author Marya Mannes once wrote: "The sign of an intelligent people is their ability to control their emotions by the application of reason." This implies that excessive reliance on emotions to make economic decisions could result in irrational behavior.

But again, research from behavioral economics suggests a more nuanced reality. It does not seem to be true that decisions based on logical reasoning are always "better" than those based on emotion or intuition. Instead, studies suggest that reasoning is most effective when used for making relatively simple economic decisions, but for more complex decisions we can become overwhelmed by too much information.

The 2010 book *Predictably Irrational*, by the psychologist Dan Ariely, describes how people consistently tend to procrastinate, overpay in certain situations, and fail to understand the role of emotions in our decision making. The book also reveals that we often place an above-market value on what we possess because we are "irrationally" attached to our possessions and that we use price as a "signal" in selecting among medicines, to the point that the placebo effect is stronger for more expensive drugs.

Research by Ap Dijksterhuis, a psychologist in the Netherlands, has shed some valuable insight on the limits of reasoned decision making. In one experiment, he and his colleagues surveyed shoppers about their purchases as they were leaving stores, asking them how much they had thought about items before buying them. A few weeks later, they asked these same consumers how satisfied they were with their purchases. For relatively simple products, like small kitchen tools or clothing accessories, those who thought more about their purchases tended to be more satisfied, as we might suspect. But for complex products, such as furniture, those people who deliberated the most tended to be *less* satisfied with their purchases. Dijksterhuis and his colleagues conclude:

> Contrary to conventional wisdom, it is not always advantageous to engage in thorough conscious deliberation before choosing. On the basis of recent insights into the characteristics of conscious and unconscious thought, we [find] that purchases of complex products were viewed more favorably when decisions had been made in the absence of attentive deliberation.[6]

Even for relatively simple decisions, there is such a thing as "thinking too much." Another experiment with college students involved their tasting five brands of strawberry jam.[7] In one case, students simply ranked the jams from best to worst. The student rankings were highly correlated with the results of independent testing by *Consumer Reports,* suggesting that the students' rankings were reasonable. But in another case students were asked to fill out a written questionnaire explaining their preferences. As a result of the additional deliberation, students' rankings were no longer significantly correlated with the *Consumer Report* rankings. The researcher concluded:

> This experiment illuminates the danger of always relying on the rational brain. There is such a thing as too much analysis. When you overthink at the wrong moment, you cut yourself off from the wisdom of your emotions, which are much better at assessing actual preferences. You lose the ability to know what you really want.[8]

Discussion Questions

1. Why do you think economists are so interested in questions of how decisions are made?
2. Discuss how one or more conclusions reached by behavioral economists helps you to understand an experience that you have had.

3. ECONOMIC RATIONALITY

"Rationality" has become a loaded word in economics, bringing with it the baggage of earlier models that did not anticipate the findings of behavioral economics or take into account other everyday observations. In this section we formulate an alternative view of human behavior that is more realistic.

3.1 CHOOSING GOALS AND TRYING TO ACHIEVE THEM

Economists generally proceed from a belief that people should be free to choose their own goals, even if their chosen goals differ from those of most others. However, what can be considered a rational goal has limits, especially considering that people usually have more than one final goal. Some goals that people pursue may be unachievable. People may also choose reasonable goals, but engage in irrational behavior that leads them *away from* their achievement rather than toward it. A reasonable definition of rational behavior includes (1) selecting goals that are consistent with present and future well-being, and (2) pursuing the goals in a manner that can reasonably be assumed to lead to their achievement.

3.2 THE ROLE OF CONSTRAINTS AND INFORMATION

It is important to note that economic decisions are always made subject to constraints, including limits on income and other resources and on physical or intellectual capacities. A universal constraint is time. Every day you face the choice of how to allocate 24 hours among competing activities such as sleeping, studying, going to class, eating, and entertainment. You cannot decide to allocate 10 hours each day to sleeping, 5 hours to studying, and 10 hours to hanging out with friends because you do not have 25 hours available. To put this in terms that we introduced in Chapter 1, your "production possibilities frontier" has only 24 hours per day.

Another important factor in an economic model of rationality is *information.* In assessing their options, economic actors make use of their existing knowledge but often need to collect additional information. Consider the decision to purchase a new automobile. Numerous factors go into such a decision. Should you buy a new car or a used one? What is the relative importance of fuel economy, safety, and luxury features? What about resale value and maintenance costs? Making a rational decision requires that you obtain information on these various factors.

optimizing behavior: behavior that achieves an optimal (best possible) outcome

The neoclassical approach tends to assume that rational behavior is **optimizing behavior**, based on the further assumption that rational economic actors have "perfect information." A slightly more modest version says that people will collect information until the perceived costs of acquiring additional information exceed the perceived benefits. However, there is no way of guaranteeing either that people can know enough to make that "cost/benefit" calculation (i.e., to make an informed decision about when to stop gathering information) or that, when they do stop gathering information, they will know enough to make an optimal or even a good choice.*

One challenge to the traditional assumption of rationality comes from Herbert Simon, another psychologist who received a Nobel Memorial Prize in economic science (in 1978). Considering the matter of whether it is indeed possible for people to identify the optimal

*The uses of cost-benefit analysis, and some issues with this approach, are examined in Chapter 13.

point at which one should cease gathering additional information, Simon logically showed that, in fact, one first needs to have complete knowledge of all choices in order to identify that optimal point! Moreover, determining what additional information might be out there and then gathering it can be very costly in time, effort, and money. Accordingly, Simon maintained, people rarely optimize. Instead they do what he called **satisficing**; they choose an outcome that would be satisfactory and then seek an option that at least reaches that standard.

satisfice: to choose an outcome that would be satisfactory and then seek an option that at least reaches that standard

Given constraints of time and so forth, satisficing seems to be a reasonable behavior. If an individual finds that the "satisfactory" level was set too low, a search for options that meet that level will result in a solution more quickly than expected or perhaps even multiple solutions. In this case, the level may then be adjusted to a higher standard. Conversely, if the level is set too high, a long search will yield nothing, and the "satisficer" may lower his or her expectations for the outcome.

Another deviation from rational behavior as traditionally defined has been called **meliorating**—defined as starting from the present level of well-being and then taking any opportunity to do better. A simple example is a line fisherman who has found a whole school of haddock but wants to keep only one for his supper. When he catches the second fish, he compares it to the first one, keeps the larger, and releases the other. Each subsequent catch is compared to the one held in the bottom of the boat. At the end of the day, the fish that he takes home will be the largest of all those caught.

meliorating: starting from the present level of well-being and continuously attempting to do better

One result of using melioration as the real-world substitute for theoretical optimization is its implication that *history matters:* People view each successive choice in relation to their previous experience. It is commonly observed, for example, that people are reluctant to accept a situation that they perceive as inferior to previous situations. This psychological **path dependence**—the idea that where you are going depends on where you have been—is relevant to feelings about rising prices and even more so to attitudes about declining wages.

path dependence: situations in which what is possible, or what is chosen, in the present depends on what has happened in the past

Satisficing and meliorating may both be included under the term **bounded rationality**. The general idea is that, instead of considering all possible options, people limit their attention to some more-or-less arbitrarily defined subset of the universe of possibilities. With satisficing or meliorating behavior, people may not choose the "best" choices available to them, but they at least make decisions that move them toward their goals.

bounded rationality: the hypothesis that people make choices among a somewhat arbitrary subset of all possible options due to limits on information, time, or cognitive abilities

3.3 The Role of Influence

The discussion above cautions that in modeling human behavior, it is necessary to recognize that there is no known decision rule within human capabilities that guarantees an entirely satisfactory conclusion, let alone the "best of all possible" conclusions.

A very important aspect of decision making relates to the outside influences on us. In the discussion of behavioral economics, we saw examples of ways that others can affect our decisions by setting a "frame" or providing extra emphasis on one conclusion at the expense of others. Available information is, of course, a critical feature, and actors other than the decision maker may have a strong influence on which information is available. The literature in behavioral economics provides a wide array of other ways that decision making can be distorted by influences not related to the goals of the particular actor.

These realities have long been well known to politicians and advertisers, who, since the early part of the twentieth century, have often based their successes on assuming *irrational* consumers and voters. For example, food companies are well known to cater to the innate physical preference for sugar, fat, and salt. These three elements are crucial for health when eaten in appropriate amounts, but they were rarely available in sufficient quantity during most of human evolution. We are all therefore born with some degree of craving for these substances; learning is required to recognize when we have had "enough." Makers of potato chips and other sweet, salty, fatty, prepared foods would prefer that this learning *not* take place. And just as corporations gravitate toward behavior that fattens profits, even if their products do more harm than good, politicians also often find it hard to resist the easy appeal to emotions of greed, even fear, rather than offering sound information on which voters can make good decisions.

As we go through this book, applying microeconomic principles to different issues, we continue to explore whether economic actors are making rational decisions and whether there are policies that could encourage decisions that enhance both individual well-being and the well-being of society.

3.4 SELF-INTEREST, ALTRUISM, AND THE COMMON GOOD

We have referred to the neoclassical model of economic behavior that is deduced from the axiom: "Rational economic man acts so as to maximize his utility." This could be—and often has been—interpreted by teachers, students, and practitioners of economics to mean: "Rational people try to get what they want." That in turn was often understood as saying, "Rational people are only self-interested—*any non-self-interested acts are irrational.*"

Many students found this approach so unappealing that they dropped economics as their major, while others who stayed with these courses more or less bought in to the lesson that "Only self-interested behavior is rational." This probably explains a good deal of why economics students (and economics faculty) have frequently been shown, in tests, to be less altruistic than others (see Box 8.2).

altruistic behavior: actions focused on the well-being of others, with no thought about oneself

The opposite of pure self-interest is **altruism**, which means a concern for the well-being of others, with no thought about oneself. Although it would be excessively idealistic to assume that altruism is the prime mover in human behavior, it is reasonable to assert that some elements of altruism enter into most people's decision making—contrary to the simple neoclassical model of "rational" selfishness.

BOX 8.2 ECONOMICS AND SELFISHNESS

Are people who have studied economics more likely than other individuals to behave selfishly? For more than 30 years, various research studies have explored this question. In one example, economics students expressed a lower willingness than other students to contribute money to pay for public goods. The same was found of economics faculty, though their average pay was higher than that of the faculty in the other disciplines to which they were compared.

Another study found that economics students offered less to others in the Ultimatum Game (see Box 8.3 for a description of the Ultimatum Game). Although most studies have found that economics students tend to be relatively more selfish, one study found that students in upper-level economics classes were more likely than students in other upper-level classes to return a lost envelope containing cash. According to the authors of one research study, "We . . . found evidence that the giving behavior of students who became economics majors was driven by nature, not nurture: Taking economics classes did not have a significant negative effect on later giving by economics majors."

The same study did find, however, that taking economics classes did reduce the generosity of students who did not go on to become economics majors. These non-majors may have experienced a "loss of innocence" as a result of being exposed to economic theories such as efficiency and profit maximization. The authors conclude:

> Our research suggests that economics education could do a better job of providing balance. Learning about the shortcomings as well as the successes of free markets is at the heart of any good economics education, and students—especially those who are not destined to major in the field—deserve to hear both sides of the story.

Source: Yoram Bauman and Elaina Rose, "Selection or Indoctrination: Why Do Economics Students Donate Less Than the Rest?" *Journal of Economic Behavior and Organization* 79(3) (August 2011): 318–327; Yoram Bauman, "The Dismal Education," *New York Times*, December 16, 2011.

the common good: the general well-being of society, including one's own well-being

Especially relevant to economics is the fact that much economic behavior may be motivated by a desire to advance **the common good**—the general good of society, of which one's own interests are only a part. Striving to advance the common good means seeing your own well-being as connected to the larger well-being of society. That is, people are often willing to participate in the creation of social benefits as long as they feel that others are also contributing.

Economists are increasingly realizing that a well-functioning economy cannot rely only on self-interest. Without such values as honesty, for example, even the simplest transaction would require elaborate safeguards or policing. Imagine if you were afraid to put down your money before having in your hands the merchandise that you wished to purchase—and the merchant was afraid that as soon as you had what you wanted, you would run out of the store without paying. Such a situation would require police in every store—but what if the police themselves operated with no ethic of honesty? Without ethical values that promote trust, inefficiencies would overwhelm any economic system.

If all those in business cheated whenever they thought they could get away with it, business would grind to a halt. If everyone in the government worked only for bribes, meaningful governance would disappear. In addition, people have to work together to overcome problems from externalities. And it is hard to imagine how the human race could survive if altruism was not common enough that people would be willing to make sacrifices of time, convenience, and resources to meet the needs of those who cannot take care of themselves, such as children or sick people.

Fortunately, recent experiments on human behavior demonstrate that people really *do* pay attention to social norms, and they are willing to reward those who follow these norms and to punish people who violate them, even when this has a cost in terms of their narrow self-interest. (See Box 8.3.)

3.5 The Model of Economic Behavior in Contextual Economics

Many real-world problems would be difficult, if not impossible, to solve in the absence of a reasonable number of people willing to work for the common good. These people are often especially concentrated in the public purpose sphere, while individual altruism is most often evident in the core sphere of the economy. Does that mean that business is the sphere that operates only on self-interest? From about 1970 to the end of the twentieth century, economists, especially from

Box 8.3 The Ultimatum Game

A famous behavioral economics experiment is known as the "Ultimatum Game." In this game, two people (who are in situations in which they cannot communicate with each other) are told that they will be given a sum of money, say \$20, to share. The first person gets to propose a way of splitting the sum. This person may offer to give \$10 to the second person or only \$8 or \$1 and plan to keep the rest. The second person cannot offer any input to this decision but can only decide whether to accept the offer or reject it. If the second person rejects the offer, both people will walk away empty-handed. If the offer is accepted, they get the money and split it as the first person indicated.

If the two individuals act only from narrow financial self-interest, then the first person should offer the second person the smallest possible amount—say \$1—in order to keep the most for himself or herself. The second person should accept this offer because, from the point of view of pure financial self-interest, \$1 is better than nothing.

In fact, researchers find that deals that vary too far from a 50–50 split tend to be rejected. People would rather walk away with nothing than be treated in a way that they perceive as unfair. Also, whether out of a sense of fairness or a fear of rejection, individuals who propose a split often offer something close to 50–50. In the context of social relations, even the most selfish person will gain by serving the common good and thus walking away with somewhere around \$10, rather than just looking at his or her own potential personal gain and quite possibly ending up with nothing.

what was known as the "Chicago School," pressed this case. Even early in this period concern arose that individuals who acted solely to achieve their *personal* goals could not be counted on to operate a business in ways that would be good for the business itself. This concern resulted in various efforts to reward business leaders for the success of their business.

These efforts had the unintended consequences of escalating compensation of top management in the United States to levels that were many times greater than anything that had previously been considered normal (or were normal in other countries). They also resulted in an increasingly short-term vision on the part of business leaders, whose compensation was set up to provide large rewards for quick profits. Large-scale frauds, Ponzi schemes, tax evasion, and environmental and human costs that businesses externalized during this period have made it increasingly evident that society cannot afford to encourage a definition of economic activity in which normal human motivations are stripped down to selfish pursuit of personal gain.

Modern research in behavioral economics suggests that the neoclassical rationality axiom does not stand up to tests of logic, experience, or the needs of society. (And some feminist economists have pointed out that the reference to "rational economic *man*" may be related to this one-dimensional view of human nature.)[9] With that said, the following statements concerning motivations and behavior may provide a better grounding for economic theory.

- We start with a definition of rationality that includes
  1. *choosing goals* such that (a) when the actor achieves the goals, she or he will be glad to have done so; or (b) the pursuit of the goal itself contributes to well-being; and
  2. *pursuing those goals* in a manner that the actor expects will lead toward their achievement.
- This definition does not insist that the goals be either entirely *self-interested* or entirely *altruistic*. Rather, based on common experience and observation, it appears that most people operate with some mixture of these kinds of goals.
- Our model then posits that *most adults attempt to act rationally*. However, sometimes lack of information, the influence of conflicting emotions, or influence from others who are pursuing different goals may cause rational actors to choose goals that are not consistent with well-being or to do things that lead away from their goals.

Although, compared to the rationality axiom, these statements are obviously much more inclusive, and closer to reality, they are also much looser and cannot be used in the same, deterministic manner. For example, because they do not claim that people optimize or maximize, they provide less opportunity for developing mathematical models based on simple axioms about behavior. Nor is there any claim that these statements are all that the economist needs to know about human behavior. Explanations or predictions of economic phenomena sometimes require individual judgment, experience, or inputs from other social sciences. Thus they do not conform to the ideal of "scientific" social science pursued by neoclassical economists.

However, many people have come to believe that neoclassical economics, which achieved many fruitful insights in its early decades, has explored all the territory that it initially opened up and has contributed less and less value as time has gone on. Moreover, its narrow view of human nature and lack of contextual awareness are criticized for leading to some of today's problems. Neoclassical economists almost uniformly failed to see the growth of the financial and real estate bubbles that led to the Great Recession, beginning in 2007. More broadly, some people believe the emphasis on selfishness has been used to justify a "culture of greed" (see Chapter 9), the dramatic increase in income and wealth inequality in recent decades (see Chapter 11), and ever greater concentration of economic and political power in ever larger corporations (see Chapter 18).

Once again, we face tradeoffs. If we are to develop economic theories equipped to deal with the critical issues of the twenty-first century, we probably need to give up a degree of tidiness, amenability to mathematical modeling techniques, and the appearance of completely value-free objectivity. As you proceed through this book, you will be the judge of how well the view of human nature developed in this chapter supports a useful approach to understanding the economy.

Discussion Questions

1. Under what circumstances can you imagine making poor decisions because of lack of information? Which economic actors might affect your decision making, and how?
2. Is "satisficing" always a rational way of behaving? What about "meliorating"? For example, recall the example of the fisherman who compares each fish that he catches to the one in the boat, keeping the larger one and throwing the others back into the water. What might be wrong with an attempt to perform the same exercise with choosing friends, instead of fish? Have you ever heard of anyone who selected a spouse in this manner?

REVIEW QUESTIONS

1. What is the invisible hand?
2. What is the neoclassical model?
3. What is the rationality axiom?
4. How does "framing" affect decision making?
5. What is the anchoring effect?
6. What is the effect of time discounting?
7. Do people typically engage in optimizing behavior?
8. Explain the concept of bounded rationality.
9. Why is self-interest not sufficient as a social organizing principle?
10. Discuss various ways of defining rationality. Which do you think is best as a basis for economic theory?

EXERCISES

1. Which of the following is consistent with the view of human behavior as purely self-interested? Which may indicate broader motivations?
   a. Michael sells his car on eBay.
   b. Jane joins a community clean-up group.
   c. Ramon studies to become a doctor.
   d. Joe buys a birthday present for his daughter.
   e. Susan buys a new pair of shoes for herself.
2. Consider the process of applying to college and choosing a college to attend if admitted. Would you say that this process involves:
   a. Optimizing behavior
   b. Satisficing behavior
   c. Meliorating behavior
   d. Path dependence
   e. Bounded rationality

   Could it involve a combination of them? Could this differ from person to person?
3. How does time discounting affect your own decision making? Do you do things today with a view toward future benefits, or do you look mainly for short-term satisfaction? Does your time discount rate differ in different areas of your life?
4. Consider a rational, profit-maximizing business firm. What motivations might the firm have that are not directly related to making a profit? For example, what if the firm made a donation to a community organization or voluntarily cleaned up pollution resulting from its production process? Why might it do this? How about if it offered employees a good health-care plan or subsidized day care? Are these actions all ultimately directed at making more profit, or could there be something else involved?
5. Match each concept in Column A with an example in Column B.

Column A	Column B
a. Self-interest	1. Finding a restaurant that is close by and has food that is "good enough"
b. Altruism	2. The study of how economic actors make decisions
c. Satisficing	3. You buy a $500 watch because it seems inexpensive compared to a $1,000 watch
d. Path dependence	4. Looking for a job that's better than your current job
e. Meliorating	5. Volunteering at a homeless shelter
f. Anchoring	6. Choosing a college because your older brother or sister went there
g. Behavioral economics	7. How households act in the neoclassical model

NOTES

1. A. Smith, *Correspondence of Adam Smith (Glasgow Edition of the Works and Correspondence of Adam Smith)* (Oxford: Oxford University Press, 1982), vol. 2a, p. 456.

2. Material from this section is drawn from Barry Schwartz, *The Paradox of Choice* (New York: HarperCollins, 2005).

3. Brigitte C. Madrian and Dennis F. Shea, "The Power of Suggestion: Inertia in 401(k) Participation and Savings Behavior," *Quarterly Journal of Economics* 16(4) (November 2001): 1149–1187.

4. Example from Dan Ariely, *Predictably Irrational: The Hidden Forces That Shape Our Decisions* (New York: Harper Perennial, 2010).

5. Lorrin M. Korna et al., "Estimated Prevalence of Compulsive Buying Behavior in the United States," *American Journal of Psychiatry* 163 (2006): 1806–1812.

6. Ap Dijksterhuis, Maarten W. Bos, Loran F. Nordgren, and Rick B. van Baaren, "On Making the Right Choice: The Deliberation-Without-Attention Effect," *Science* 311(5763) (February 17, 2006): 1005.

7. Example from Jonah Lehrer, *How We Decide* (Boston: Mariner/Houghton-Mifflin, 2009).

8. Ibid., pp. 142–143.

9. See Marianne A. Ferber and Julie A. Nelson, ed., *Beyond Economic Man: Feminist Theory and Economics* (Chicago: University of Chicago Press, 1993).

9 Consumption and the Consumer Society

We have defined the economic activity of consumption as the process by which goods and services are put to final use by people. But this rather dry, academic definition fails to capture the multifaceted role of consumerism in our lives. As one researcher put it:

> For a start, it is immediately clear that consumption goes way beyond just satisfying physical or physiological needs for food, shelter, and so on. Material goods are deeply implicated in individuals' psychological and social lives. People create and maintain identities using material things. . . . The "evocative power" of material things facilitates a range of complex, deeply ingrained "social conversations" about status, identity, social cohesion, and the pursuit of personal and cultural meaning.[1]

Until recently, most economists paid little attention to the motivations behind consumer behavior. As we discussed in Chapter 8, economic theory in the twentieth century simply assumed that the vast majority of people act rationally to maximize their utility. But as suggested in the quotation above, perhaps no other economic activity is shaped by its social context more than consumption. Our consumption behavior conveys a message to ourselves and others about who we are and how we fit in with, or separate ourselves from, other people.

Modern consumption must also be placed in a historical context. When can we say that "consumer society" originated? Furthermore, is consumerism as experienced in the United States and other countries something that is ingrained in us by evolution, or is it something that has been created by marketing and other social and political forces?

Finally, it is impossible to present a comprehensive analysis of consumption without considering its environmental context. Specifically, ecological research suggests that consumption levels in the United States and many other developed countries have reached unsustainable levels. According to one recent analysis, if everyone in the world had the same living standard as the average American, we would need at least four earths to supply enough resources and process all the waste.[2] So any serious discussion of sustainability must consider the future of consumption patterns throughout the world.

1. Economic Theory and Consumption

1.1 Consumer Sovereignty

Before focusing on the historical, social, and environmental contexts of consumption, we present the economic theory on the topic. Adam Smith once said, "Consumption is the sole end and purpose of all production and the welfare of the producer ought to be attended to, only so far as it may be necessary for promoting that of the consumer."[3]

consumer sovereignty: the idea that consumers' needs and wants determine the shape of all economic activities

The belief that satisfaction of consumers' needs and wants is the ultimate economic goal and that the economy is fundamentally ruled by consumer desires is called **consumer sovereignty**.

Consumer sovereignty suggests that all economic production and distribution are ultimately driven by the preferences of consumers. For example, consider the fact that sales of sport utility vehicles (SUVs) in the United States approximately doubled during the 1990s, while sales of cars decreased. The theory of consumer sovereignty would suggest that the primary reason for the growth of SUV sales is that consumers began to prefer larger vehicles over cars. Referring to Chapter 4, we would say that a change in consumers' tastes and preferences increased the demand for SUVs and decreased the demand for cars. The idea that the shift in demand was driven primarily by automakers' marketing efforts to sell large vehicles with higher profit margins would not be consistent with consumer sovereignty.

The notion of consumer sovereignty has both positive and normative components. From a positive perspective, we can consider whether consumers really do "drive the economy." In Chapter 8, we briefly mentioned the possibility that consumers can be swayed by advertising. We consider the impact of advertising in more detail in this chapter.

living standard (or lifestyle) goals: goals related to satisfying basic needs and getting pleasure through the use of goods and services

Consumer sovereignty can also be viewed from a normative perspective. *Should* people's preferences, as consumers, drive all decisions about economic production, distribution, and resource maintenance? People are more than just consumers. Consumption activities most directly address **living standard (or lifestyle) goals**, which have to do with satisfying basic needs and getting pleasure through the use of goods and services.

But people are often interested in other goals, such as self-realization, fairness, freedom, participation, social relations, and ecological balance. To some extent, these goals may be attained through consumption, but often they conflict with their goals as consumers. People also often obtain intrinsic satisfaction from working and producing. For many people, work defines a significant part of their role in society. Work can create and maintain relationships. It can be a basis for self-respect and a significant part of what gives life purpose and meaning.

If the economy is to promote well-being, all these goals must be taken into account. An economy that made people moderately happy as consumers but absolutely miserable as workers, citizens, or community members could hardly be considered a rousing success. We evaluate the relationship between consumption and well-being further toward the end of this chapter. But now we turn to the formal economic theory on consumption.

1.2 The Budget Line

budget line: a line showing the possible combinations of two goods that a consumer can purchase

The choices that we make as consumers illustrate yet another example of economic tradeoffs. In this case, consumers are constrained in their spending by the amount of their total budget. We can represent this in a simple model in which consumers have only two goods from which to choose. In Figure 9.1 we present a **budget line**, which shows the combinations of two goods that a consumer can purchase. In this example, our consumer—let's call him Quong—has a budget of \$8. The two goods that are available for him to purchase are chocolate bars and bags of nuts. The price of chocolate bars is \$1 each, and nuts sell for \$2 per bag.

If Quong spends his \$8 only on chocolate, he can buy 8 bars, as indicated by the point where the budget line touches the vertical axis. If he buys only nuts, he can buy 4 bags, as indicated by the (4, 0) point on the horizontal axis. He can also buy any combination in between. For example, the point (2, 4), which indicates 2 bags of nuts and 4 chocolate bars, is also achievable. This is because $(2 \times \$2) + (4 \times \$1) = \$8$. (We draw the budget line as continuous to reflect the more general case that might apply when there are many more alternatives, although here we assume that Quong buys only whole bars and whole bags, not fractions of them.)

A budget line is similar to the concept of a production possibilities frontier, which we discussed in Chapter 1. A budget line defines the choices that are *possible* for Quong. Points

Figure 9.1 **The Budget Line**

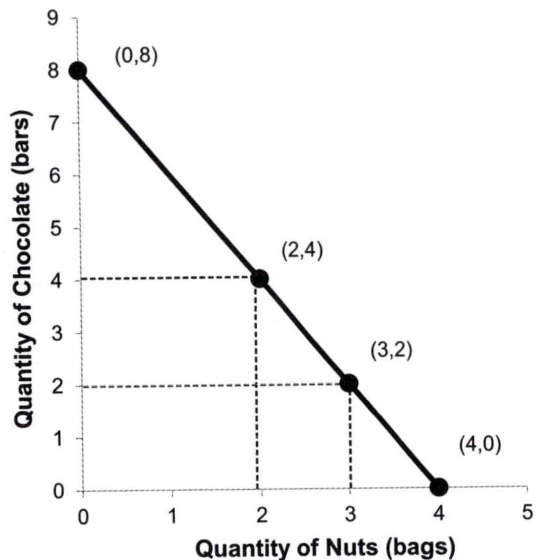

The budget line shows the combination of goods that a consumer can buy with a given income.

above and to the right of the budget line are not affordable. Points below and to the left of the budget line are affordable but do not use up the total budget. In this simple model, economists assume that people always want *more* of at least one of the goods in question. Consuming below the budget line would hence be inefficient; funds that could be used to satisfy Quong's desires are being left unused. Therefore, economists assume that consumers will choose to consume at a point *on* the budget line.

The position of the budget line depends on the size of the total budget (income) and on the prices of the two goods. For example, if Quong has $10 to spend, instead of $8, the line would shift outward in a parallel manner, as shown in Figure 9.2. He could now consume more nuts, or more chocolate, or a more generous combination of both.

If (starting at the original income of $8) the price of nuts dropped to $1 per bag, the budget line would rotate out, as shown in Figure 9.3. Now, if Quong bought only nuts, he could buy

Figure 9.2 **Effect of an Increase in Income**

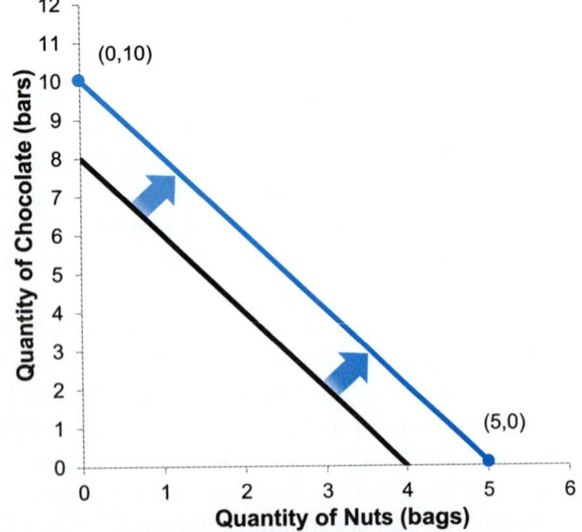

With an increase in income the budget line shifts out in a parallel manner. The consumer can now buy more of either good, or more of both goods.

Figure 9.3 **Effect of a Fall in a Price**

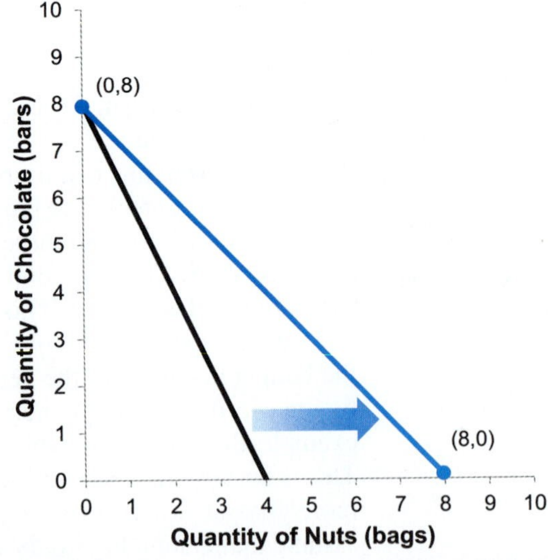

With a decrease in the price of one good, the budget line rotates out to indicate that the consumer can afford more of that good (or of both goods).

8 bags instead of 4. With the price of chocolate unchanged, however, he still could not buy more than 8 chocolate bars.

A budget line tells us what combinations of purchases are possible, but it does not tell us how the consumer will decide *which* combination to consume. To get to this, we must add the theory of utility.

1.3 CONSUMER UTILITY

utility: the pleasure or satisfaction received from goods, services, or experiences

Economists have traditionally defined consumers' "problem" as how to maximize **utility** given their income constraints. Utility is a somewhat vague concept, similar to the idea of welfare defined in Chapter 6. However, although economists attempt to measure welfare quantitatively, utility is generally recognized as something that cannot be measured quantitatively and cannot be aggregated across individuals.* We define utility as the pleasure or satisfaction that individuals receive from goods, services, or experiences. Furthermore, we assume that individuals make consumer decisions to increase their utility. But as discussed in Chapter 8, we recognize that consumers often do not always make the best decisions, because they sometimes act irrationally or are unduly influenced by certain information (or misinformation). We discuss the implications of this further in the next section.

Economists have developed a model of utility that, like many economic models, is an abstraction from reality that is useful for illustrating a particular concept. So despite the fact that we just said that utility cannot be measured quantitatively in the real world, for the purposes of our model we assume that we actually can measure utility in some imaginary units of "satisfaction." Thus Table 9.1 presents the total utility that Quong obtains from purchasing different quantities of chocolate bars in a given period, say a day.

Table 9.1 **Quong's Utility from Chocolate Bars**

Quantity of chocolate bars	Total utility	Marginal utility
0	0	—
1	10	10
2	18	8
3	24	6
4	28	4
5	30	2
6	29	-1

utility function (or total utility curve): a curve showing the relation of utility levels to consumption levels

diminishing marginal utility: the tendency for additional units of consumption to add less to utility than did previous units of consumption

We can then plot Quong's total utility from consuming chocolate bars in Figure 9.4. This relationship between utility and the quantity of something consumed is called a **utility function**, or a **total utility curve**.

Quong's utility curve levels off as his consumption of chocolate bars increases. This is generally expected—that successive units of something consumed provide less utility than the previous unit. In other words, consumers' utility functions generally display **diminishing marginal utility**. This is shown in Table 9.1. We see that Quong obtains 10 units of "satisfaction" from consuming his first chocolate bar. While his utility increases from 10 to 18 units by consuming his second chocolate bar, his marginal utility is only 8 units. Consuming his third chocolate bar, he obtains a marginal utility of 6 units. This is shown in Figure 9.4, where his utility is shown as increasing from 18 to 24 units. Eventually, Quong's consumption of chocolate becomes much less pleasurable, and when he consumes his sixth chocolate bar, his utility actually starts to decline. Assuming that Quong is rational, he would never consume more than five chocolate bars in a day.

*Some economists in the 1800s, such as William Stanley Jevons (1835–1882) actually did believe that utility was something that could eventually be measured numerically.

Figure 9.4 **Quong's Utility Function for Chocolate Bars**

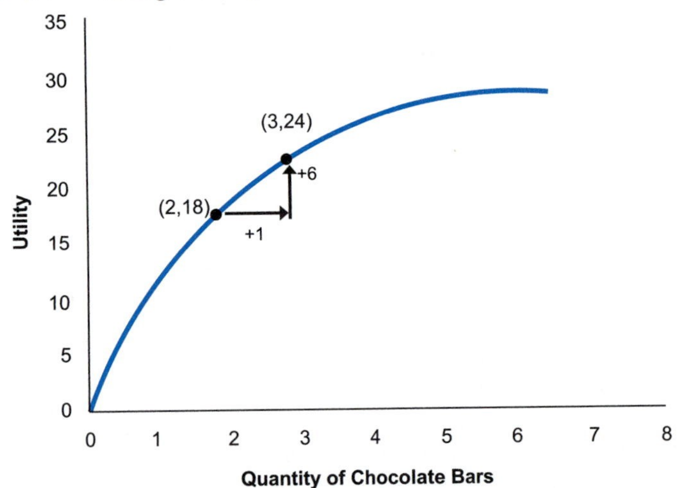

Utility rises steeply for the first few chocolate bars and then more slowly as Quong gets sated.

Now we can apply the concept of utility to the budget line that Quong faces. Realize that Quong will also have a utility function for bags of nuts, which will display a similar pattern of diminishing marginal utility. Let's assume that his first bag of nuts provides him with 20 units of utility, his second bag with 15 units, and each successive bag with less units of utility. How can Quong allocate his limited budget to provide him with the highest amount of total utility?

We provide a formal model of utility maximization in the appendix to this chapter, but we can easily see how Quong might approach his problem in a purely rational manner using marginal thinking. Suppose that Quong is thinking about how he will spend his first $2. With $2 he can buy either two chocolate bars or one bag of nuts. If he buys two chocolate bars, he will obtain 18 total units of utility, as shown in Table 9.1. If he buys one bag of nuts instead, he will obtain 20 units of utility. Thus Quong will receive greater utility by spending his first $2 on a bag of nuts.

What about his next $2? If he spends this on his *second bag of nuts,* he obtains an additional 15 units of utility. But if he instead purchases his *first two chocolate bars,* he will obtain 18 units of utility. So, by spending his next $2 on chocolate bars, he increases his utility by a greater amount. After spending $4 Quong has purchased one bag of nuts and two chocolate bars, thus obtaining a total utility of 38 units. Quong can continue to apply marginal thinking to maximize his utility until he has eventually spent his entire budget. The basic decision rule to maximize utility is to allocate each additional dollar on the good or service that provides the greatest marginal utility for that dollar.* Again, see the appendix for a formal presentation of utility maximization.

1.4 Limitations of the Standard Consumer Model

We suspect that you have never thought about how to spend your money in a manner similar to Quong's marginal analysis of chocolate and nuts. It is less important that people behave exactly as a model suggests than it is to consider whether people generally act *as if* they are always trying to increase their utility as much as possible. There are several reasons to be skeptical about this. First, the utility model assumes that people are rational, but as we saw in Chapter 8, this is not always the case. The model also assumes that all the benefits from consumption can be identified, compared, and added up.

*As most goods and services are not available in $1 increments, such as bags of nuts, consumers will not always be able to allocate every single dollar in a way that maximizes utility.

While comparing the utility from chocolate and nuts may be relatively easy to imagine, consumers' decisions become much more complicated when they are faced with a wide variety of options.

Economists have traditionally assumed that having more options from which to choose can only benefit consumers, but recent research demonstrates that there is a cost in trying to process additional information. In fact, having too many choices can actually "overload" our ability to evaluate different options. Consider a famous example demonstrating the effect of having too much choice.[4] In one experiment, researchers at a supermarket in California set up a display table with six different flavors of jam. Shoppers could taste any (or all) of the six flavors and receive a discount coupon to purchase any flavor. About 30 percent of those who tried one or more jams ended up buying some.

The researchers then repeated this experiment but, instead, offered 24 flavors of jam for tasting. In this case, *only 3 percent* of those who tasted a jam went on to buy some. In theory, it would seem that more choice would increase the chances of finding a jam that one really liked and would be willing to buy. But, instead, the additional choices decreased one's motivation to make a decision to buy a jam. A 2010 article from *The Economist* addressed this topic:

> As options multiply, there may be a point at which the effort required to obtain enough information to be able to distinguish sensibly between alternatives outweighs the benefit to the consumer of the extra choice. "At this point," writes Barry Schwartz in *The Paradox of Choice*, "choice no longer liberates, but debilitates. It might even be said to tyrannise." In other words, as Mr. Schwartz puts it, "the fact that *some* choice is good doesn't necessarily mean that *more* choice is better."
>
> Daniel McFadden, an economist at the University of California, Berkeley, says that consumers find too many options troubling because of the "risk of misperception and miscalculation, of misunderstanding the available alternatives, of misreading one's own tastes, of yielding to a moment's whim and regretting it afterwards," combined with "the stress of information acquisition."[5]

Another important point is that when consumers make a decision to purchase a good or service, they are essentially making a prediction about the utility that the purchase will bring them. Daniel Kahneman, whom we encountered in Chapter 8, distinguishes between *predicted* utility and *remembered* utility. Predicted utility is the utility that you expect to obtain from a purchase (or other experience), whereas remembered utility is the utility that you actually recall after you have made a purchase. In other words, Kahneman considers whether people actually receive the benefits they expect in advance of their purchases. According to the standard consumer model with rational decision makers, these two utilities should match relatively closely.

Once again research from behavioral economics suggests that people's predictions can often turn out to be incorrect. In one well-known experiment, young professors were asked to predict the effect of their tenure decision on their long-term happiness. Although being granted tenure essentially ensures a professor lifetime employment, being denied tenure means he or she must find a new job. Most young professors predict that being denied tenure will have a long-term negative impact on their happiness. Yet surveys of professors who actually have and have not been granted tenure indicate that there is no significant long-term effect of tenure decision on happiness levels. A similar experiment showed that college students overpredicted the negative effects of a romantic breakup.[6]

These findings have implications for welfare analysis, as discussed in Chapter 6. Realize that a demand curve is an expression of predicted utility. Welfare analysis measures consumer surplus based on demand curves, thus implicitly assuming that predicted utility matches well with remembered utility. But if predicted and remembered utility differs, any welfare implications based on demand curves will be an inaccurate estimate of the utility that people actually receive from their purchases.

We must also recognize the potential for consumers to be swayed by advertising and other influences into making poor consumer decisions, as we discussed in Chapter 8. Advertising expenditures in the United States totaled about $250 billion in 2012, equivalent to close to 2 percent of the entire national economy, or about $800 per person.[7] Of course, the purpose of advertising is not necessarily to assist consumers to make the best choices. We further discuss the impact of advertising later in this chapter.

Discussion Questions

1. Budget lines can be used to analyze various kinds of tradeoffs. Suppose that you have a total "time budget" for recreation of 2 hours. Think of two activities you might like to do for recreation, and draw a budget line diagram illustrating the recreational opportunities open to you. What if you had a time budget of three hours instead?
2. Explain in words why the total utility curve has the shape that it does in Figure 9.4.

2. Consumption in Historical and International Context

Perhaps the greatest limitation of the standard consumer model is that it does not really tell us anything interesting about *why* consumers make particular choices. For example, why might Quong purchase so many chocolate bars that it has a negative impact on his health? Can someone who smokes cigarettes truly be acting in a utility-maximizing manner? Why do people acquire huge credit card debts by making seemingly frivolous purchases? Why would someone spend $60,000 or more on a new car when a car costing much less may be perfectly adequate for all practical purposes?

consumer society: a society in which a large part of people's sense of identity and meaning is found through the purchase and use of consumer goods and services

To answer such questions, we must recognize the historical and social nature of consumption. We are so immersed in a culture of consumption that we can be said to be living in a **consumer society**, a society in which a large part of people's sense of identity and meaning is achieved through the purchase and use of consumer goods and services. Viewing consumption through the lens of a consumer society is quite different from looking at consumption from the standard economic model of consumer behavior.

We first consider the historical evolution of consumer society, along with the institutions that allowed consumer society to flourish. Then we take a brief look at consumer society around the world today.

2.1 A Brief History of Consumer Society

consumerism: having one's sense of identity and meaning defined largely through the purchase and use of consumer goods and services

When can we say that consumer society originated? Historians have placed the birth of the consumer society variously from the sixteenth century to the mid-1900s.[8] To some extent, the answer depends on whether we consider **consumerism**, understood as having one's sense of identity and meaning defined largely through the purchase and use of consumer goods and services, as an innate human characteristic. In other words, does consumerism come naturally to humans or is it an acquired trait?

Of course, for thousands of years a small elite class has existed that enjoyed higher consumption standards and habitually bought luxury goods and services. One story of the birth of consumer society says that it is human nature to want to acquire more goods, so all that is needed for the birth of consumer society is for a significant portion of the population to have more money than is necessary for basic survival. However, this explanation is incorrect or at least a vast oversimplification.

Before the eighteenth century, families and communities that acquired more than enough to meet basic needs did not automatically respond by becoming consumers. Religious value systems generally taught material restraint. Patterns of dress and household display were dictated by tradition, depending on the class to which one belonged, with little change over time. Unlike the norm in modern times, in the past emphasis was more often placed on community spending, such as for a new church, as opposed to private spending.

The historical consensus is that the consumer society as a mass phenomenon originated in the eighteenth century in Western Europe. Although it is no coincidence that this time and location coincides with the birth of the Industrial Revolution, consumer society was not solely the result of greater prosperity. The Industrial Revolution clearly transformed production. It is less obvious, but equally true, that it transformed consumption, as much through the social changes it produced as through the economic changes.

> The arrival of consumerism in Western Europe involved truly revolutionary change in the way goods were sold, in the array of goods available and cherished, and in the goals people defined for their daily lives. This last—the redefinition of needs and aspirations—is the core feature of consumerism.[9]

The large-scale emigration of people from the agricultural countryside to cities in search of work brought significant social disruption. Instead of finding personal and social meaning in tradition and community, people sought new ways to define themselves, often through consumer goods. Also, shopkeepers for the first time began to create window displays, engage in newspaper advertising, and use other methods to attract customers. Furthermore, the breakdown of strict class lines meant that common people had the freedom to express themselves in new ways, including displays of wealth that would have been discouraged, or even illegal, in the past.

Yet although consumerism took root in the eighteenth century, it took some time before it fully blossomed. At the dawn of industrialization, it was not at all clear that workers would or could become consumers. Early British industrialists complained that their employees would work only until they had earned their traditional weekly income and then stop until the next week. Leisure, it appeared, was more valuable to the workers than increased income. This attitude, widespread in preindustrial societies, was incompatible with mass production and mass consumption. It could be changed in either of two ways.

At first, employers responded by lowering wages and imposing strict discipline on workers to force them to work longer hours. Early textile mills frequently employed women, teenagers, and even children, because they were easier to control and could be paid less than adult male workers. As a consequence of such draconian strategies of labor discipline, living and working conditions for the first few generations of factory workers were worse than in the generations before industrialization.

Over time, however, agitation by organized workers, political reformers, and civic and humanitarian groups created pressure for better wages, hours, and working conditions, while rising productivity and profits made it possible for business to respond to this pressure. A second response to the preindustrial work ethic gradually evolved: As workers came to see themselves as consumers, they would no longer choose to stop work early and enjoy more leisure; rather, they preferred to work full-time, or even overtime, in order to earn and spend more. In the United States, the "worker as consumer" view was fully entrenched by the 1920s, when the labor movement stopped advocating a shorter workweek and instead focused on better wages and working conditions.

Other historical developments were important to the spread of consumer society. One was the invention of the department store, in the mid-nineteenth century in England. Department stores quickly spread to other European countries and the United States. Featuring lavish displays, department stores presented shoppers with the opportunity to purchase an entirely new lifestyle, all under one roof. Department stores introduced the idea of shopping as "spectacle," with entertainment, elaborate interiors, seasonal displays, and parades.[10]

> The department store was a permanent fair, a dream world, a spectacle of excessive proportions. Going to the store became an event and an adventure. One came less to purchase a particular article than to simply visit, to browse, to see what was new, to try on new fashions and even new identities.[11]

Modern shopping malls originated in the United States in the early twentieth century. Suburbanization in the United States in the mid-twentieth century was supported by the construction of large shopping malls far from city centers but easily accessible by automobile. By the 1980s and 1990s enormous shopping malls, such as the Mall of America in Minnesota, were being constructed with entertainment options including indoor roller coasters and aquariums.

Another institution created to support the consumer society was expanded consumer credit, particularly the invention of credit cards in the 1940s. In 2012, nearly three-fourths of U.S. households had at least one credit card. Although some cardholders use them only for convenience, paying off their balances in full each month, about half of cardholders use them as a form of borrowing by carrying unpaid balances, on which they pay interest, with annualized rates that can exceed 30 percent.

Figure 9.5 illustrates the growth of revolving debt in the United States over the past several decades, adjusted for inflation.* We see that revolving debt, which consists almost entirely of credit card debt, increased by a factor of 100 from 1968 until about 2007, when the Great Recession caused households to reduce their debt, as spending declined and credit became less available. In early 2013, total outstanding credit card debt in the United States was about \$830 billion, equivalent to more than \$7,000 per household. However, given that about half of households do not carry an unpaid monthly balance on their credit cards, those households that do carry a balance had an average credit card debt of around \$15,000.

2.2 Limits to Modern Consumerism

Can we say, at the start of the twenty-first century, that consumerism has become a global phenomenon? It is true that people all over the world are increasingly exposed to similar

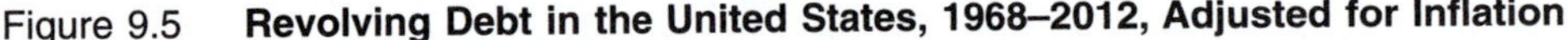

Figure 9.5 **Revolving Debt in the United States, 1968–2012, Adjusted for Inflation**

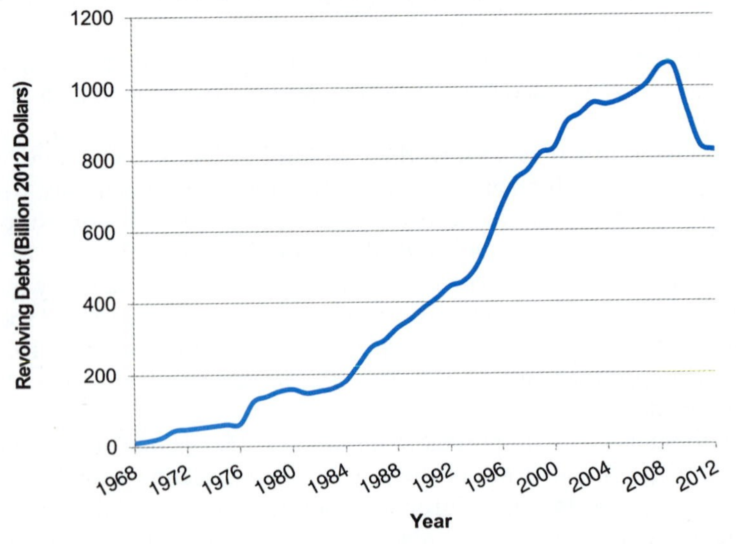

Revolving debt rose steeply from the late 1960s up until the Great Recession starting in 2007. The Great Recession resulted in many households reducing debt as spending declined and credit became less available.

*Revolving debt allows consumers to borrow money against a line of credit, without the requirement that the amount borrowed be fully paid off each month. Thus the balance from one or more months can carry over, or "revolve," to the next month. The vast majority of revolving debt is credit card debt.

commercial messages and images of "the good life," but consumer society is not yet universal for two main reasons. First, about 2.4 billion people around the world (about one-third of humanity) live in absolute poverty, defined by the World Bank as living on less than $2 per day. Obviously, consumerism is not an option for the global poor. Second, in numerous places around the world cultural and religious values exist that seek to restrain, or even reject, the consumer society. We first discuss global poverty and then turn to a brief discussion of nonconsumer values.

Insufficient Consumption: Poverty

absolute deprivation: severe deprivation of basic human needs

One-third of the global population lives in extreme poverty, or **absolute deprivation**. What constitutes absolute deprivation? The United Nations has defined it as "a condition characterized by severe deprivation of basic human needs, including food, safe drinking water, sanitation facilities, health, shelter, education and information. It depends not only on income but also on access to services."

The poorest of developing countries, particularly in sub-Saharan Africa and Southern Asia, are simply too poor to lift their entire populations out of absolute deprivation. Increasingly, however, the more economically successful developing countries in Asia and Latin America have sufficient resources to provide everyone with basic necessities; the fact that absolute deprivation still exists for the poor in these countries reflects inequality in the distribution of income. Absolute deprivation may also vary with factors such as race and ethnicity and even within a household on the basis of age or gender.

Because insufficient consumption is not simply a matter of having a low household income, even in regions that could be generally characterized as middle or high income, examples of absolute deprivation can still be found. Some people—particularly young children and the ill and handicapped—have **dependency needs** for care that may be unmet. Even people with a fairly high household income may sometimes, then, find themselves lacking basic necessities. Advocates for the elderly, the sick, and children, for example, often claim that the United States has an inadequate system of care.

dependency needs: the need to receive care, shelter, or food from others when unable to provide these for oneself

Absolute deprivation is only one type of insufficiency. Modern communication technology means that nearly everyone has some exposure to the "lifestyles of the rich and famous." The result is the creation of widespread feelings of **relative deprivation**, that is, the sense that one's own condition is inadequate because it is inferior to someone else's circumstances. The richest man in a small village may be quite content with traditional clothing and diet, an outdoor latrine, and water drawn from a communal well, so long as that way of life is consistent with honor and self-respect. However, after he begins to compare his circumstances with those in the city, he may begin to feel that they are less than they should be.

relative deprivation: the feeling of lack that comes from comparing oneself with someone who has more

The government-defined poverty level in the United States was $23,550 for a family of four in 2013. This income would be at or above the national average in many countries; in most developing countries, a family income of $23,550 would be considered wealthy. It may be possible to buy the bare physical necessities of life for this sum, even in the United States—at least in areas of the country with low housing costs. Yet it is likely that most of the Americans who fall below the poverty level (15 percent of the population in 2011) do not feel able to enjoy a "normal" American lifestyle. They clearly do not have the resources to buy the kinds of homes, cars, clothing, and other consumer goods commonly shown on American television. They may need to rely on inadequate public transportation and wait in long lines for health care. People with sufficient physical means of survival may still feel ashamed, belittled, and socially unaccepted if they have much less than everyone around them. The 22 percent of U.S. children who live in poverty do not start out on an "even playing field" with nonpoor children, in terms of nutrition, health care, and other requirements. The fact that people who cannot afford to consume at "normal" societal consumption levels feel relative deprivation suggests that poverty, even relative poverty, is not conducive to promoting well-being and self-respect.

Nonconsumerist Values

The spread of consumerism has met considerable resistance in some societies, usually because it conflicts with existing values, either religious or secular. For example, the Muslim concept of *riba* prohibits charging interest on loans. Buddhism teaches a "middle path" that emphasizes material simplicity, nonviolence, and inner peace. Various passages of the New Testament of the Bible emphasize the spiritual dangers of wealth, such as the saying that it is easier for a camel to pass through the eye of a needle than for a rich man to enter heaven.

Traditional cultural values in some countries have restrained the spread of consumerism. In some countries, consumerism is associated with foreign, typically American, values.

> Consumption expansion thus tends to lead to some level of global homogenization of culture among consumers, an effect that gives rise to negative responses to globalization. As consumer goods are always also cultural goods, expansion of consumption of imported products and services often gives rise to an exaggerated sense of "panic," of cultural "invasion" which, supposedly, if left unchecked will result in the demise of the local culture.[12]

Social norms and government policies in various European countries aim to promote nonconsumerist values. For example, many retail stores in France, Italy, and other European countries are normally closed at lunchtime and on Sundays. European policies on vacation time, parental leave, and flexible working hours emphasize a work–life balance.

Even in the United States, the spread of consumerism has not been an even, uninterrupted process. The history of consumer society in the United States reveals periodic movements against consumerism. The Quakers in the eighteenth century, the Transcendentalists of the mid-nineteenth century (most famously, Henry David Thoreau), the Progressives at the turn of the twentieth century, and the hippies of the 1960s all espoused a simpler, less materialistic life philosophy.[13] More recently, starting in the 1980s the idea of voluntary simplicity, which we discuss further later in the chapter, has attracted a following among Americans motivated by objectives such as reducing environmental impacts, focusing more on family and social connections, healthy living, and stress reduction.

Discussion Questions

1. Considering what you know about the societies in which your grandparents or great-grandparents grew up, would you say that they lived in a "consumer society"? How do you think their views on consumerism as young adults might have differed from those of you and your friends?
2. What do you know about views on consumerism in other countries, either from what you have read or what you have observed from traveling? Which societies, if any, do you find too focused on consumerism? Which societies, if any, do you think have appropriate views on consumerism?

3. CONSUMPTION IN A SOCIAL CONTEXT

As mentioned at the beginning of this chapter, in modern consumer societies, consumption is as much a social activity as an economic activity. Consumption is tied closely to personal identity, and it has become a means of communicating social messages. An increasing range of social interactions are influenced by consumer values.

> Consumption pervades our everyday lives and structures our everyday practices. The values, meanings, and costs of what we consume have become an increasingly important part of our social and personal experiences. . . . [Consumption] has entered into the . . . fabric of modern life. All forms of social life—from education to sexual relations to political campaigns—are now seen as consumer relations.[14]

3.1 Social Comparisons

As social beings, we compare ourselves to other people. Our income and consumption levels are some of the most important ways in which we evaluate ourselves relative to others. As discussed above, whether people consider themselves poor often depends on the condition of those around them.

You have probably heard of the saying "Keeping up with the Joneses." This saying refers to the motivation to maintain a material lifestyle that is comparable to those around us. A **reference group** is a group of people who influence the behavior of a consumer because the consumer compares himself or herself with that group. Most people have various reference groups, traditionally including our neighbors, our coworkers, and other members of our family. We also are influenced as consumers by **aspirational groups**, groups to which a consumer *wishes* he or she could belong. People often buy, dress, and behave like the group—corporate executives, rock stars, athletes, or whoever—with whom they would like to identify.

reference group: the group to which an individual compares himself or herself

aspirational group: the group to which an individual aspires to belong

Economist Juliet Schor argues that the nature of social comparisons related to consumption has changed in the past few decades. She suggests that in the 1950s and 1960s the idea of "Keeping up with the Joneses" emphasized comparisons between individuals or families with similar incomes and backgrounds. Because prosperity was broadly shared in the postwar decades, people did not want to feel left out as new consumer goods and living standards emerged. More recently, however, she has observed a different approach to consumption comparisons.

> Beginning in the 1980s, those conditions changed, and what I have termed the new consumerism emerged. The new consumerism is more upscale in the sense that there is more aggressive, rather than defensive, consumption positioning. The new consumerism is more anonymous and is less socially benign than the old regime of keeping up with the Joneses. In part, this is because reference groups have become vertically elongated. People are now more likely to compare themselves with, or aspire to the lifestyle of, those far above them in the economic hierarchy.[15]

Schor presents the results of a survey to support this view, which indicates that 85 percent of respondents aspire to become someone who "really made it" or is at least "doing very well." But the survey results also show that only 18 percent of Americans are members of these groups based on income.[16] If 85 percent of people aspire to be in the top 18 percent, obviously most will end up disappointed.

Changes in economic inequality, which we discuss further in Chapter 11, are also relevant to her hypothesis. During the 1950s and 1960s, economic inequality in the United States was decreasing—that is, the gap between different levels of the income hierarchy was generally shrinking. However, beginning in the 1970s economic inequality began to increase, thus making it difficult to maintain even the existing distance between an individual and his or her aspirational group.

Media representations of wealthy lifestyles also became more common. In the 1950s and 1960s, most television shows depicted middle-class lifestyles. But starting in the 1980s, television shows as well as advertisements increasingly depicted upper-class lifestyles. Exposure to media representations of wealth influences people's values and spending patterns. Schor's own research indicates that the more television a person watches, the more he or she is likely to spend, holding constant other variables such as income. Higher rates of television watching have also been associated with having materialistic values.[17] Other research has found that heavy television watchers are likely to overstate the percentage of the population that owns luxury items, such as convertibles and hot tubs, or that have maids or servants.[18]

Schor's conclusion is that identifying with unrealistic aspirational groups leads many people to consume well above their means, acquiring large debts and suffering frustration as they attempt to join those groups through their consumption patterns but fail to achieve the income to sustain them. As people tend to evaluate themselves relative to reference and aspirational groups, with increasing inequality some may feel as if they are falling behind even if their incomes are actually increasing.

> The more our consumer satisfaction is tied to social comparisons—whether upscaling, just keeping up, or not falling too far behind—the less we achieve when consumption grows, because the people we compare ourselves to are also experiencing rising consumption. . . . The problem is not just that more consumption doesn't yield more satisfaction, but that it always has a cost. The extra hours we have to work to earn the money cut into personal and family time. *Whatever* we consume has an ecological impact. . . . We find ourselves skimping on invisibles such as insurance, college funds, and retirement savings as the visible commodities somehow become indispensable. . . . We are impoverishing ourselves in pursuit of a consumption goal that is inherently unattainable. In the words of one focus-group participant, we "just don't know when to stop and draw the line."

3.2 ADVERTISING

Although advertising has existed as a specialized profession for only about a century, it has become a force that rivals education and religion in shaping public values and aspirations. We already saw that advertising spending in the United States totals about $800 per person annually. According to various estimates, arrived at before the widespread use of the Internet, Americans are exposed to between 200 and 3,000 commercial messages per day.

About one-third of global advertising spending takes place in the United States (see Figure 9.6). Japan is the world's second-largest advertising market, followed by China. Advertising is

Figure 9.6 **Global Advertising Expenditures, by Country/Region, 2011**

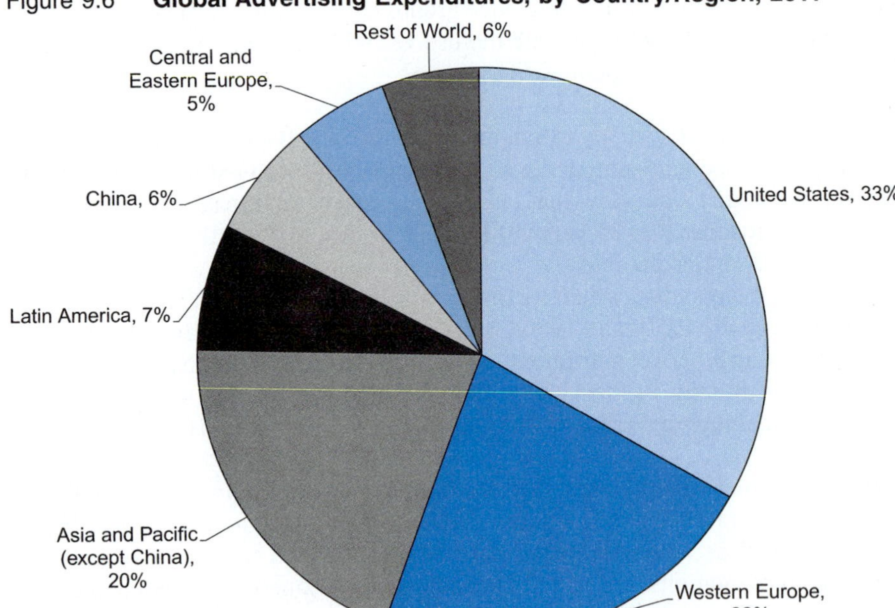

One-third of global advertising expenditures are made in the United States.

Source: Advertising Age, December 5, 2011.

increasing most rapidly in China and other emerging markets. Per-capita advertising spending in China increased from just 9 cents in 1986 to $22 in 2011.

Advertising is often justified by economists as a source of information about products and services available in the marketplace. Although it certainly plays that role, it also does much more. Advertising appeals to many different values, emotional as well as practical needs and a range of desires and fantasies. The multitude of advertisements that we encounter carry their own separate messages; yet on a deeper level, they all share a common, powerful cultural message.

> What the vast amount of advertising really sells is consumer culture itself. Even if advertising fails to sell a particular product, the advertisements still sell the meanings and values of a consumer culture. As Christopher Lasch writes, "The importance of advertising is not that it invariably succeeds in its immediate purpose, . . . but simply that it surrounds people with images of the good life in which happiness depends on consumption. The ubiquity of such images leaves little space for competing conceptions of the good life."[19]

According to one estimate, the typical American will spend about three years of his or her life watching television ads.[20] We have already mentioned how watching television can influence people's spending behavior and values. Other research details how television, and advertising in particular, is associated with obesity, attention deficit disorder, heart disease, and other negative consequences. Furthermore, advertising commonly portrays unrealistic body images, traditionally for women but more recently for men as well. (See Box 9.1 for more on the effects of advertising on girls and women.)

BOX 9.1 WOMEN AND ADVERTISING

A 2007 report by the American Psychological Association concluded that advertising and other media images encourage girls to focus on physical appearance and sexuality, with harmful results for their emotional and physical well-being. The research project reviewed data from numerous media sources, including television, music videos and lyrics, movies, magazines, and video games. The report found that 85 percent of the sexualized images of children were of girls.

The lead author of the report, Dr. Eileen L. Zurbriggen, said, "The consequences of the sexualization of girls in media today are very real and are likely to be a negative influence on girls' healthy development. We have ample evidence to conclude that sexualization has negative effects in a variety of domains, including cognitive functioning, physical and mental health, and healthy sexual development."

Three of the most common mental health problems associated with exposure to sexualized images and unrealistic body ideals are eating disorders, low self-esteem, and depression. It is estimated that 8 million Americans suffer from an eating disorder—7 million of them women. About 20 percent of anorexics will eventually die from the disorder. According to a 2012 article, most female models would be considered anorexic according to their body mass index. Twenty years ago the average model weighed 8 percent less than the average woman; now it is 23 percent less.

Jean Kilbourne, an author and filmmaker who holds a Ph.D. in education, has been lobbying for advertising reforms since the 1960s. She has produced four documentaries on the negative effects of advertising on women, most recently in 2010, under the title *Killing Us Softly*. Kilbourne notes that virtually all photos of models in advertisements have been touched up, eliminating wrinkles, blemishes, extra weight, and even skin pores. She believes that we need to change the environment of advertising through public policy. Dr. Zurbriggen concludes, "As a society, we need to replace all of these sexualized images with ones showing girls in positive settings—ones that show the uniqueness and competence of girls."

Sources: Jean Kilbourne Web site, www.jeankilbourne.com; Edward Lovett, "Most Models Meet Criteria for Anorexia, Size 6 Is Plus Size: Magazine," ABC News, January 12, 2012; "Sexualization of Girls Is Linked to Common Mental Health Problems in Girls and Women," *Science Daily*, February 20, 2007; South Carolina Department of Mental Health, Eating Disorder Statistics, www.state.sc.us/dmh/anorexia/statistics.htm.

3.3 Private Versus Public Consumption

The growth of consumerism has altered the balance between private and public consumption. Public infrastructure has been shaped by the drive to sell and consume new products and the availability of public and private options, in turn, shapes individual consumer choices.

In the early 1930s, for example, many major U.S. cities—including Los Angeles—had extensive, relatively efficient, and nonpolluting electric streetcar systems. Then, in 1936, a group of companies involved in bus and diesel gasoline production, led by General Motors, formed a group called the National City Lines (NCL). They bought up electric streetcar systems in 45 cities and dismantled them, replacing them with bus systems that also tended to promote automobile dependency. U.S. government support for highway construction in the 1950s further hastened the decline of rail transportation, made possible the spread of suburbs far removed from workplaces, and encouraged the purchase of automobiles.

Many of the choices that you have, as an individual, depend on decisions made for you by businesses and governments. Los Angeles would look much different today—more like the older sections of many East Coast and European cities—if it had been built up around streetcar lines rather than cars and buses. Even today one can see tradeoffs between public (or publicly accessible) infrastructure and private consumption. As more people carry cell phones and bottled water, pay telephones and drinking fountains come to be less well maintained in some cities, leading more people to need to carry cell phones and bottled water.

Discussion Questions

1. What are your reference groups? Describe why you consider these your reference groups. What are your aspirational groups? Why do you aspire to be a member of these groups?
2. Think about at least one fashion item you own, such as an item of clothing, jewelry, or accessory, that you think says a lot about who you are. What do you think it says about you? Do you think others interpret the item in the same way that you do? How much do you think that you were influenced by advertising or other media in your views about the item?

4. Consumption in an Environmental Context

The production process that creates every consumer product requires natural resources and generates some waste and pollution. However, we are normally only vaguely aware of the ecological impact of the processes that supply us with consumer goods.

> The problem is that we do not often see the true ugliness of the consumer economy and so are not compelled to do much about it. The distance between shopping malls and their associated mines, wells, corporate farms, factories, toxic dumps, and landfills, sometimes half a world away, dampens our perceptions that something is fundamentally wrong.[21]

Most of us are unaware that, for example, it requires about 600 gallons of water to make a quarter-pound hamburger or that making a computer chip generates 4,500 times its weight in waste.[22] (For another example of the ecological impacts of consumption, see Box 9.2.)

4.1 The Link Between Consumption and the Environment

In quantifying the ecological impacts of consumerism, most people focus on the amount of "trash" generated by households and businesses. In 2011, the U.S. economy generated about 250 million tons of municipal solid waste, which consisted mostly of paper, food waste, and yard waste.[23] Although the total amount of municipal solid waste generated has increased

BOX 9.2 THE ENVIRONMENTAL STORY OF A T-SHIRT

T-shirts, along with jeans, are perhaps the most ubiquitous articles of clothing on college campuses. What is the environmental impact of each of these t-shirts?

Consider a t-shirt constructed of a cotton/polyester blend, weighing about four ounces. Polyester is made from petroleum—a few tablespoons are required to make a t-shirt. During the extraction and refining of the petroleum, one-fourth of the polyester's weight is released in air pollution, including nitrogen oxides, particulates, carbon monoxide, and heavy metals. About *10 times* the polyester's weight is released in carbon dioxide, contributing to global climate change.

Cotton grown with nonorganic methods relies heavily on chemical inputs. Cotton accounts for 10 percent of the world's use of pesticides. A typical cotton crop requires six applications of pesticides, commonly organophosphates that can damage the central nervous system. Cotton is also one of the most intensely irrigated crops in the world.

T-shirt fabric is bleached and dyed with chemicals including chlorine, chromium, and formaldehyde. Cotton resists coloring, so about one-third of the dye may be carried off in the waste stream. Most t-shirts are manufactured in Asia and then shipped by boat to their destination, with further transportation by train and truck. Each transportation step involves the release of additional air pollution and carbon dioxide.

Despite the impacts of t-shirt production and distribution, most of the environmental impact associated with t-shirts occurs *after purchase*. Washing and drying a t-shirt 10 times requires about as much energy as was needed to manufacture the shirt. Laundering will also generate more solid waste than the production of the shirt, mainly from sewage sludge and detergent packaging.

How can one reduce the environmental impacts of t-shirts? One obvious step is to avoid buying too many shirts in the first place. Buy shirts made of organic cotton or recycled polyester or consider buying used clothing. Wash clothes only when they need washing, not necessarily every time you wear something. Make sure that you wash only full loads of laundry and wash using cold water whenever possible. Finally, avoid using a clothes dryer—clothes dry naturally for free by hanging on a clothesline or a drying rack.

Source: John C. Ryan and Alan Thein Durning, *Stuff: The Secret Lives of Everyday Things* (Seattle: Northwest Environment Watch, 1997).

in recent decades (an increase of nearly 200 percent since 1960), the portion recycled has increased from around 6 percent in the 1960s to about one-third today.

But most of the waste generation in a consumer society occurs during the extraction, processing, or manufacturing stages—these impacts are normally hidden from consumers. According to data from 2000, the U.S. economy required about 30 billion tons of material inputs, which is equivalent to more than *100 tons per person.*[24] The vast majority of this material is discarded as mining waste, crop residue, logging waste, chemical runoff, and other waste prior to the consumption stage.

ecological footprint: an estimate of how much land area a human society requires to provide all that the society takes from nature and to absorb its waste and pollution

Perhaps the most comprehensive attempt to quantify the overall ecological impact of consumption is the **ecological footprint** measure. This approach estimates how much land area a human society requires to provide all that it takes from nature and to absorb its waste and pollution. Although the details of the ecological footprint calculations are subject to debate, it does provide a useful way to compare the overall ecological impact of consumption in different countries.

We see in Figure 9.7 that the ecological footprint per capita varies significantly across countries. The United States has one of the highest per-capita ecological footprints (the per-capita footprints of some oil-producing countries are higher). The average European has a footprint about half the U.S. level, while the typical Chinese has a footprint one-quarter the U.S. level.

Perhaps the most significant implication of the ecological footprint research is that the world is now in a situation of "overshoot"—our global use of resources and generation of waste exceeds the global capacity to supply resources and assimilate waste, by about 50 percent according to recent estimates. The situation is much worse when we consider whether everyone in the world can consume at a level equivalent to the typical American. In that case, we would require four to five earths to provide the needed resources and assimilate the waste.

Figure 9.7 **Ecological Footprint per Capita, Select Countries, 2007**

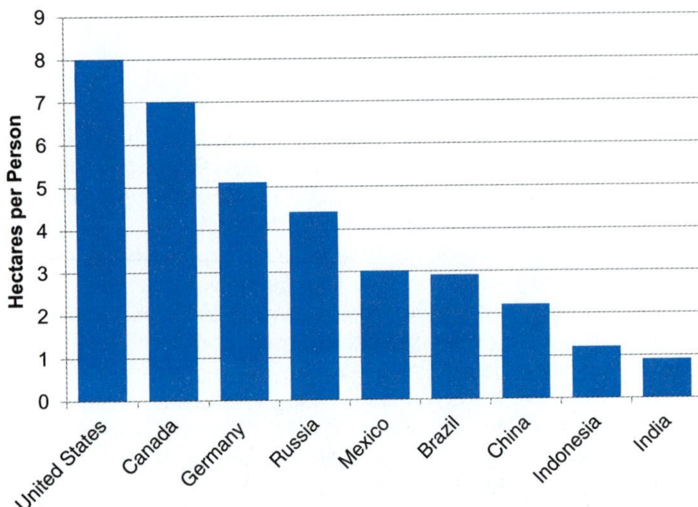

The ecological impacts of consumption are relatively high in the United States, with a per-capita impact about twice as high as most European countries and four times as high as China.

Source: Global Footprint Network, www.footprintnetwork.org/en/index.php/GFN/page/footprint_for_nations/

4.2 Green Consumerism

green consumerism: making consumption decisions at least partly on the basis of environmental criteria

Green consumerism means making consumption decisions at least partly on the basis of environmental criteria. Clearly, green consumerism is increasing: More people are recycling, using reusable shopping bags and water containers, buying hybrid cars, and so on. Yet some people see green consumerism as an oxymoron—that the culture of consumerism is simply incompatible with environmental sustainability.

Whether green consumerism is an oxymoron depends on exactly how we define it. Green consumerism comes in two basic types:

1. "shallow" green consumerism: consumers seek to purchase "ecofriendly" alternatives but do not necessarily change their overall level of consumption
2. "deep" green consumerism: consumers seek to purchase ecofriendly alternatives but also, more importantly, seek to reduce their overall level of consumption

Someone who adheres to shallow green consumerism might buy a hybrid car instead of a car with a gasoline engine or a shirt made with organic cotton instead of cotton grown with the use of chemical pesticides. But those who practice deep green consumerism would, when feasible, take public transportation instead of buying a car and question whether they really need another shirt. In other words, in shallow green consumerism the emphasis is on substitution while in deep green consumerism the emphasis is on a reduction in consumption. Note that people who buy so-called ecofriendly products such that their overall consumption increases, or as status symbols, could hardly be said to be practicing green consumerism.

ecolabeling: product labels that provide information about environmental impacts, or indicate certification

Ecolabeling helps consumers make environmentally conscious decisions. An ecolabel can provide summary information about environmental impacts. For example, stickers on new cars in the United States rate the vehicle's smog emissions, on a scale from one to ten. More commonly, ecolabels are placed on products that meet certain certification standards. One example is the U.S. Environmental Protection Agency's Energy Star program, which certifies products that are highly energy efficient. The Forest Stewardship Council, headquartered in Germany, certifies wood products that meet certain sustainability standards.

In addition to environmental awareness by consumers, many businesses are seeking to reduce the environmental impacts of their production processes. Of course, some of the motivation may be to increase profits or improve public relations, but companies are also becoming more transparent about their environmental impacts. The Global Reporting Initiative (GRI) is a nonprofit organization that promotes a standardized approach to environmental impact reporting. In 2011 more than 2,300 companies used the GRI methodology, including Coca-Cola, Walmart, Apple, UPS, and Verizon.

Discussion Questions

1. Think about one product you have purchased recently that is not mentioned in the text. Try to list the environmental impacts of this product, considering the production, consumption, and eventual disposal of it. What steps do you think could be taken to reduce the environmental impacts associated with this product?
2. Do you think that green consumerism is an oxymoron? Do you think that your own consumer behaviors are environmentally sustainable? Why or why not?

5. CONSUMPTION AND WELL-BEING

If the goal of economics is to enhance well-being, as we discussed in Chapter 1, then we need to ask whether current levels of consumerism are compatible with well-being goals. If not, then what should we do about it?

5.1 DOES MONEY BUY HAPPINESS?

subjective well-being (SWB): a measure of welfare based on survey questions asking people about their own degree of life satisfaction

Earlier in the chapter, we mentioned that utility is a somewhat vague concept, one that cannot be easily measured quantitatively. But a large volume of scientific research in the past few decades suggests that we actually can obtain meaningful data on well-being rather simply—just by asking people about their well-being. Data on **subjective well-being (SWB)** can provide insight into social welfare levels and the factors that influence well-being.

Collecting data on SWB involves surveying individuals and asking them a question such as: "All things considered, how satisfied are you with your life as a whole these days?" Respondents then answer based on a scale, say, from 1 (dissatisfied) to 10 (satisfied). How much credence can we give to the answers to such questions?

> Research has shown that it is possible to collect meaningful and reliable data on subjective as well as objective well-being. Quantitative measures of [SWB] hold the promise of delivering not just a good measure of quality of life per se, but also a better understanding of its determinants, reaching beyond people's income and material conditions. Despite the persistence of many unresolved issues, these subjective measures provide important information about quality of life.[25]

One of most interesting questions that SWB research can address is the relationship between income level and life satisfaction. We can ask whether the higher-income individuals in a society tend to have higher average SWB. A 2010 paper, based on the results of more than 400,000 surveys conducted in the United States, found that higher income does tend to be associated with higher SWB, but at a decreasing rate.[26] This finding is consistent with the concept of diminishing marginal utility; additional income does increase utility, but each additional dollar tends to result in smaller utility gains. It is also consistent with the idea that people evaluate themselves relative to others.

The paper went on to measure well-being in a different way, referred to as "emotional well-being," which asks people to describe the positive and negative emotions that they feel on a daily basis. In this case, higher income was associated with more positive, and fewer negative, emotions, again at a decreasing rate, *but only up to a point.* At an income level of around $75,000, further increases in income did not improve emotional well-being. The authors conclude that "high income buys life satisfaction but not happiness, and that low income is associated both with low life evaluation and low emotional well-being."

Other research has explored how people's values and goals affect their well-being. Psychologist Tim Kasser and his colleagues have studied the mental and physical consequences of holding materialistic values. They have used surveys to determine how strongly oriented different people are toward financial and material goals, by asking whether it is important that, for example, they "be financially successful," "have a lot of expensive possessions," and "keep up with fashions in hair and clothing." Respondents were also asked about their SWB, as well as questions about how often they experience negative mental and physical symptoms such as depression, anxiety, headaches, and stomachaches. Based on results for both college students and older adults, their results were clear:

> [Those] who focused on money, image, and fame reported less self-actualization and vitality, and more depression than those less concerned with these values. What is more, they also reported experiences of physical symptoms. . . . This was really one of the first indicators, to us, of the pervasive negative correlates of materialistic values—not only is people's psychological well-being worse when they focus on money, but so is their physical health.[27]

Additional research by Kasser and others finds that people who hold materialistic values tend to be less happy with their family and friends, have less fun, are more likely to abuse drugs and alcohol, and to display antisocial symptoms such as paranoia and narcissism.

For some individuals, consumerism itself can be addictive. According to a 2006 paper, about 6 percent of Americans are considered compulsive shoppers.[28] This is similar to the percentage of Americans considered alcoholics. People are classified as compulsive shoppers based on their answers to questions about whether they went on shopping binges, bought things without realizing why, had financial problems as a result of their spending, or frequently bought things to improve their mood. Compulsive shoppers were just as likely to be men as women, but they tended to be younger than average and have a lower income than the average. Compulsive shoppers are more likely to experience depression and anxiety, suffer from eating disorders, and have financial problems.

5.2 AFFLUENZA AND VOLUNTARY SIMPLICITY

Economists have traditionally assumed that more income and more goods are always better, holding all else constant. But we can never hold all else constant. One of the main lessons of economics is that we should always weigh the marginal benefits of something against its marginal costs. In the case of consumerism, these costs include less time for leisure, friends, and family, greater environmental impacts, and negative psychological and physical effects. In short, there can be such a thing as too much consumption—when the marginal benefits of additional consumption are exceeded by the associated marginal costs.

As we have seen, people tend to evaluate themselves relative to other people. The situation of rising consumption levels has been compared to one in which one row of a crowd of spectators stands up in order to see a show better. Then, the row behind them has to stand up, just in order to see as well as before. The same with the row behind them, and so on. Eventually, everyone is uncomfortable standing up, and no one is really seeing any better. Everyone would be better off just sitting down.

Economist Robert Frank discussed this problem in his 1999 book *Luxury Fever.* He suggests that the lavish spending of the superrich, whose incomes have increased dramatically in recent decades, creates pressure on the merely rich to ratchet up their spending as well. This pressure then eventually trickles down to middle- and even low-income individuals. Again, we must consider the cost of this competitive spending.

> Even among those who can easily afford today's luxury offerings, there has been a price to pay. All of us—rich and poor alike, but especially the rich—are spending more time at the office and taking shorter vacations; we are spending less time with our families and friends; and we have less time for sleep, exercise, travel, reading, and other activities that help maintain body and soul. . . . At a time when our spending on luxury goods is growing four times as fast as overall spending, our highways, bridges, water supply systems, and other parts of our public infrastructure are deteriorating, placing lives in danger.[29]

Two public television specials, as well as a book,[30] refer to the problem of "affluenza"—a "disease" with symptoms of "overload, debt, anxiety and waste resulting from the dogged pursuit of more." The use of reference groups creates a paradox in consumption: We can apparently never have enough to be satisfied, because (unless we are Bill Gates) there is always someone who has more than we do.

Some people see the solution to affluenza as rejecting consumerism as a primary goal in life. The term **voluntary simplicity** refers to a conscious decision to live with a limited or reduced level of consumption, in order to increase one's quality of life.

voluntary simplicity: a conscious decision to live with limited or reduced level of consumption, in order to increase one's quality of life

> [W]e can describe voluntary simplicity as a manner of living that is outwardly more simple and inwardly more rich. . . . Simplicity in this sense is not simple. To maintain a skillful balance between the inner and outer aspects of our lives is an enormously challenging and continuously changing process. The objective is not dogmatically to live with less, but is a more demanding intention of living with balance in order to find a life of greater purpose, fulfillment, and satisfaction.[31]

The motivations for voluntary simplicity vary, including environmental concerns, a desire to have more free time to travel or raise a family, and to focus on nonconsumer goals. Voluntary simplicity does not necessarily mean rejecting progress, living in the country, or a life of poverty. Some people ascribing to voluntary simplicity have left high-paying jobs after many years, while others are young people content to live on less.

Perhaps the unifying theme for those practicing voluntary simplicity is that they seek to determine what is "enough"—a point beyond which further accumulation of consumer goods is either not worth the personal, ecological, and social costs, or simply not desirable. Unlike traditional economics, which has assumed that people always want more goods and services,* voluntary simplicity sees these as only intermediate goals toward more meaningful final goals. (For more on voluntary simplicity, see Box 9.3.)

5.3 Consumption and Public Policy

It is unrealistic to expect that a majority of people in rich countries will become adherents of voluntary simplicity. If we accept that overconsumption is problematic, for reasons of ecological impacts, social cohesion, or personal well-being, then we must consider whether government regulations are needed to curb consumerism.

Of course, some people will argue that government intrusion into personal consumption decisions is unwarranted. But current government regulations already influence consumer decisions, for instance, high taxes on products such as tobacco and alcohol and limits on advertising. Rather than dictating consumer behaviors, thoughtful regulations can encourage people to make choices that better align with social and personal well-being. A 2009 book titled *Nudge* proposes that changing the "choice architecture"—how choices are presented to people—can have a dramatic influence on people's behavior.[32] Often this relates to changing

*Economists use the term "nonsatiation" to describe the tendency to always want more.

Box 9.3 Voluntary Simplicity

Greg Foyster had a good job in advertising, creating television commercials and print ads in Australia. But in 2012 he and his partner Sophie Chishkovsky decided to give up their consumer lifestyles and bicycle along the coast of Australia, interviewing people who have decided to embrace voluntary simplicity and eventually write a book about their experience.

Voluntary simplicity is a growing movement in Australia, with a popular Web site (www.aussieslivingsimply.com.au) and a regular column on the topic in the *Australian Women's Weekly*. Foyster explains,

> The overall idea is that you should step out of the consumer economy that we're all plugged into and start doing things for yourself because that is how you'll find happiness. The best way to think of it is as an exchange. In our society people trade their time for money, and then they spend that money on consumer items. . . . It's really about stepping back and deciding what's important to you in your life.

Foyster found that his career in advertising conflicted with his personal sense of ethics. His "eureka" moment came during an advertising awards event when he saw colleagues being praised for their efforts to sell people products they didn't need or even want. He realized that most of the world's environmental problems stem from overconsumption, not overpopulation. He was so overwhelmed that he left the event and sobbed. He says,

> When I worked in advertising, I had a decent income, I had a prestigious job, and I was miserable. I chose to leave the industry because it wasn't making me happy; it wasn't my purpose in life. And now I have a much lower income; I work as a freelance writer, which isn't the most prestigious job. But I am so much more happy because I know what is important to me and I'm doing what I love and I have everything I need.

Source: Michael Short, "Seeking a Simple Life," *The Age* (Australia), July 9, 2012.

the default option for a particular choice. For example, employees' retirement savings increase significantly when they are automatically enrolled in a 401(k) savings program, with the option of dropping out if they so choose (an opt-out program), as opposed to a policy that requires them to sign up for the savings program (an opt-in program). People are still entirely free to decide whether to participate in the savings program, but the opt-out option results in more savings for retirement.

Flexible Work Hours

One specific policy to reduce the pressure toward consumerism is to allow for more flexibility in working hours. Current employment norms, particularly in the United States, create a strong incentive for full-time employment, if available. Employees typically have the option of seeking either a full-time job, with decent pay and fringe benefits, or a part-time job with lower hourly pay and perhaps no benefits at all. Thus even those who would prefer to work less than full time and make a somewhat lower salary may feel the imperative to seek full-time employment. With a full-time job, working longer hours with higher stress, one may be more likely to engage in "retail therapy" as compensation.

Europe is leading the way in instituting policies that allow flexible working arrangements. Legislation in Germany and the Netherlands gives workers the right to reduce their work hours, with a comparable reduction in pay.[33] An employer can only refuse such requests if it can demonstrate that the reduction will impose serious hardship on the firm. A Dutch law also prohibits discrimination between full-time and part-time employees regarding hourly pay, benefits, and advancement opportunities. Some government policies encourage part-time employment particularly for parents, such as a Swedish law that gives parents the right to work three-quarter time until their children are eight years old. Norwegian parents also have the right to work part-time or combine periods of work with periods of parental leave.

Such policies encourage "time affluence" instead of material affluence. Economist Juliet Schor also argues that policies to allow for shorter work hours are one of the most effective ways to address environmental problems such as climate change.[34] Those who voluntarily decide to work shorter hours will be likely to consume less and thus have a smaller ecological footprint.

Advertising Regulations

A second policy approach is to focus on the regulation of advertising. Government regulations in most countries already restrict the content and types of ads that are allowed, such as the prohibition of cigarette advertising on television and sporting events. Additional regulations could expand truth-in-advertising laws, ensuring that all claims made in ads are valid. For example, laws in the United States already restrict what foods can be labeled "low fat" or "organic."

Children are particularly susceptible to advertising, as they generally cannot differentiate between entertainment and an ad intended to influence consumers. Again, European regulations are leading the way. Sweden and Norway have banned all advertising targeted at children under 12 years old. Regulations in Germany and Belgium prohibit commercials during children's TV shows.

Another option is to change the tax regulations regarding advertising expenditures. In the United States, companies are generally able to fully deduct all advertising costs. Restricting the amount of this tax deduction (or eliminating the deduction entirely) would create an incentive for companies to reduce their advertising.

Consumption Taxation

Economics tells us that one of the ways to reduce the extent of any activity is to tax it. One option is to impose luxury taxes on specific goods that are seen as representing conspicuous consumption—consumption primarily for the display of high economic status. For example, from 1992 to 2002 the United States imposed luxury taxes on new automobiles that cost more than $30,000. Australia still collects a luxury tax on new vehicles that sell for more than about $60,000.

Rather than classifying particular goods and services as luxuries, some economists prefer broader tax reforms. In *Luxury Fever,* Robert Frank proposes replacing the current emphasis in the United States on taxing income with taxes on consumption. Under his proposal, the tax on a household would be determined by the amount it spends each year. Rather than saving receipts, taxpayers would calculate their annual spending simply as the difference between total income and savings. A certain amount of spending would be exempt from taxation so that low-income households would be exempt from the tax—Frank suggests $30,000 per family. Beyond that, consumption would be taxed at successively higher rates. For example, while the first $30,000 of spending would be nontaxable, he suggests that the next $40,000 of spending be taxed at a 20 percent rate. Then the next $10,000 of spending might be taxed at a 22 percent rate. In his example, consumption tax rates on spending above $500,000 rise to 70 percent.* He argues that such high tax rates on conspicuous consumption are necessary:

> If a progressive consumption tax is to curb the waste that springs from excessive spending on conspicuous consumption, its rates at the highest levels must be sufficiently steep to provide meaningful incentives for the people atop the consumption pyramid. For unless their spending changes, the spending of those just below them is unlikely to change either, and so on all the way down.[35]

Frank notes that both conservatives and liberals have expressed support for a shift from taxation of income to taxation of consumption, although they disagree on the details.

*A progressive tax imposes higher tax rates with higher income levels. We discuss progressive taxation in more detail in Chapter 12.

Exempting all savings from taxation would increase savings rates, which he suggests is reason enough for the shift. But the main objective would be to reduce the pressures toward consumerism and promote true well-being.

> We currently waste literally trillions of dollars each year as a result of wasteful consumption patterns. Much of this waste can be curbed by the adoption of a steeply progressive consumption tax. Taking this step would greatly enhance every citizen's opportunity to pursue independent visions of the good life.[36]

Discussion Questions

1. In what ways do you think money can buy happiness? In what ways can having a lot of money decrease one's happiness? How does money enter into your own conception of what happiness means?
2. Do you believe that the government has a right to influence or otherwise interfere in consumer decisions? What additional policies, if any, do you think are needed regarding consumer behaviors?

REVIEW QUESTIONS

1. What is consumer sovereignty?
2. What is a budget line? How can we show one on a graph?
3. How does a budget line change when one's income changes?
4. How does a budget line change when the price of one of the items changes?
5. What is a utility function? How can we represent one on a graph?
6. What is diminishing marginal utility? What does it imply about the shape of a utility function?
7. What are some of the limitations of the standard consumer model?
8. What is the consumer society?
9. What were some of the key developments in the history of the consumer society?
10. What is the difference between absolute and relative deprivation?
11. What are reference and aspirational groups?
12. About how much is spent annually on advertising in the United States, on a per-person basis?
13. What is the ecological footprint approach to quantifying environmental impacts? What are some of the findings of ecological footprint research?
14. What is green consumerism? What is the difference between "deep" and "shallow" green consumerism?
15. What is subjective well-being?
16. What are the results of research on the relationship between subjective well-being and happiness?
17. What are the results of research on the relationship between materialistic values and well-being?
18. About what percentage of Americans are considered compulsive shoppers?
19. What is voluntary simplicity?
20. What policies might reduce levels of consumerism?

EXERCISES

1. Monifa plans to spend her income on concert tickets and movie tickets. Suppose that she has an income of $100. The price of a concert ticket is $20, and the price of a movie ticket is $10.
   a. Draw, and carefully label, a budget line diagram illustrating the consumption combinations that she can afford.
   b. Can she afford 6 movie tickets and 1 concert ticket? Label this point on your graph.
   c. Can she afford 2 movie tickets and 6 concert tickets? Label this point on your graph.
   d. Can she afford 4 movie tickets and 3 concert tickets? Label this point on your graph.
   e. Which of the combinations mentioned just uses up all her income?
2. Continuing from the previous exercise, suppose that Monifa's income rises to $120. Add her new budget line to the previous graph.
3. Next, suppose that Monifa's income stays at $100, but the price of concert tickets drops from $20 to $12.50 each.
   a. Draw and carefully label both her original and her new budget lines.

b. Can she afford 2 movie tickets and 6 concert tickets after the price drop?

4. Suppose that Antonio's total utility from different quantities of snacks per day is given by the table below.

Quantity of snacks per day	Total utility	Marginal utility
0	0	
1	20	
2	40	
3	60	
4	75	
5	85	
6	90	
7	85	
8	75	

a. Draw and label Antonio's utility function for snacks.
b. Fill in the last column of the table above, calculating Antonio's marginal utility from snacks.
c. Does Antonio always display diminishing marginal utility in his satisfaction from snacks?
d. Assuming Antonio is rational, what is the maximum number of snacks that he could choose to consume per day?

5. Various U.S. government agencies, among them the Food and Drug Administration (FDA) and the Environmental Protection Agency (EPA), include "consumer protection" as one of their goals. The FDA, for example, decides whether drugs that pharmaceutical companies want to sell are safe and effective, and the EPA decides whether particular pesticides are safe for consumer use. Some people believe that such government oversight unnecessarily interferes with companies' freedom to sell their goods and with consumers' freedom to buy what they want. Indicate how you think each of the following individuals would evaluate consumer protection policies, in general.

a. Someone who believes strongly in consumer sovereignty
b. Someone who believes strongly that consumers make rational choices
c. Someone who believes that consumers sometimes have less than perfect information about what they are buying
d. One who believes that consumers can be overly influenced by marketing campaigns

6. Match each concept in Column A with an example in Column B.

Column A	Column B
a. Diminishing marginal utility	1. Janet hopes to become a CEO someday
b. Reference group	2. You decide that you have enough clothing and do not need any more
c. Aspirational group	3. Your income increases
d. Absolute deprivation	4. You feel poor because you cannot afford the same designer clothing as your classmates
e. Relative deprivation	5. The price of one good that you purchase increases
f. Deep green consumerism	6. You start getting bored after watching your third TV show in a row
g. Shallow green consumerism	7. You buy clothing made with organic cotton instead of cotton produced with pesticides
h. Your budget line rotates	8. You compare your car to those of your neighbors
i. Your budget line shifts	9. You cannot afford basic medical care

NOTES

1. Tim Jackson, "The Challenge of Sustainable Lifestyles," in *State of the World 2008* (Washington, D.C., Worldwatch Institute, 2008), p. 49.

2. Living Planet Report 2012, WWF, Global Footprint Network, and Zoological Society of London, 2012.

3. Adam Smith, *An Inquiry into the Nature and Causes of the Wealth of Nations* (London: Methuen, 1930), p. 625.

4. Sheena S. Iyengar and Mark R. Lepper, "When Choice Is Demotivating: Can One Desire Too Much of a Good Thing?" *Journal of Personality and Social Psychology* 79(6) (2000): 995–1006.

5. "The Tyranny of Choice: You Choose," *Economist,* December 16, 2010.

6. Daniel T. Gilbert, Elizabth C. Pinel, Timothy D. Wilson, Stephen J. Blumberg, and Thalia T. Wheatley, "Immune Neglect: A Source of Durability Bias in Affective Forecasting," *Journal of Personality and Social Psychology* 75(3) (1998): 617–638.

7. Bradley Johnson, "Big U.S. Advertisers Boost 2012 Spending by Slim 2.8 Percent with a Lift from Tech," *Advertising Age,* June 23, 2013, http://adage.com/article/news/big-u-s-advertisers-boost-2012-spending-slim-2-8/242761/.

8. Material from this section is drawn primarily from Peter N. Stearns, *Consumerism in World History: The Global Transformation of Desire* (New York: Routledge, 2006).

9. Ibid., p. 25.

10. George Ritzer, *Enchanting a Disenchanted World: Revolutionizing the Means of Consumption* (Thousand Oaks, CA: Pine Forge Press, 1999).

11. Douglas J. Goodman and Mirelle Cohen, *Consumer Culture* (Santa Barbara, CA: ABC-CLIO, 2004), p. 17.

12. Ibid., p. 68.

13. See David E. Shi, *The Simple Life: Plain Living and High Thinking in American Culture* (Athens, GA: University of Georgia Press, 2007).

14. Goodman and Cohen, *Consumer Culture,* pp. 1–4.

15. Juliet Schor, "What's Wrong with Consumer Society?" in *Consuming Desires: Consumption, Culture, and the Pursuit of Happiness,* ed. Roger Rosenblatt (Washington, DC: Island Press, 1999), p. 43.

16. Juliet B. Schor, *The Overspent American* (New York: Harper Perennial, 1998).

17. See, for example, L.J. Shrum, James E. Burroughs, and Aric Rindfleisch, "Television's Cultivation of Material Values," *Journal of Consumer Research* 32 (2005): 473–479.

18. Thomas C. O'Guinn and L. J. Shrum, "The Role of Television in the Construction of Consumer Reality," *Journal of Consumer Research* 23(4) (1997): 278–294.

19. Goodman and Cohen, *Consumer Culture,* pp. 39–40.

20. Debra J. Holt, Pauline M. Ippolito, Debra M. Desrochers, and Christopher R. Kelle, "Children's Exposure to TV Advertising in 1977 and 2004," Federal Trade Commission, Washington, DC, 2007.

21. David Orr, "The Ecology of Giving and Consuming," in *Consuming Desires,* pp. 145–146.

22. John C. Ryan, and Alan Thein Durning, *Stuff: The Secret Lives of Everyday Things* (Seattle: Northwest Environment Watch, 1997).

23. U.S. Environmental Protection Agency, "Municipal Solid Waste Generation, Recycling, and Disposal in the United States: Facts and Figures for 2011," EPA530-F-13–001, Washington, DC, 2013.

24. Donald Rogich, Amy Cassara, Iddo Wernick, and Marta Miranda, "Material Flows in the United States," World Resources Institute, Washington, DC, 2008.

25. Joseph Stiglitz, Amartya Sen, and Jean-Paul Fitoussi. "Report by the Commission on the Measurement of Economic Performance and Social Progress," www.stiglitz-sen-fitoussi.fr/documents/rapport_anglais.pdf, p. 16.

26. Daniel Kahneman and Angus Deaton, "High Income Improves Evaluation of Life but Not Emotional Well-Being," *Proceedings of the National Academy of Sciences* 107(38) (2010): 16489–16493.

27. Tim Kasser, *The High Price of Materialism* (Cambridge, MA: MIT Press, 2002).

28. Lorrin M. Koran, Ronald J. Faber, Elias Aboujaoude, Michael D. Large, and Richard T. Serpe, "Estimated Prevalence of Compulsive Buying Behavior in the United States," *American Journal of Psychiatry* 163 (2006): 1806–1812.

29. Robert H. Frank, *Luxury Fever: Why Money Fails to Satisfy in an Era of Excess* (New York: Free Press, 1999).

30. John de Graaf, David Wann, and Thomas H. Naylor, *Affluenza: The All-Consuming Epidemic* (San Francisco: Berrett-Koehler, 2005).

31. Duane Elgin, "Voluntary Simplicity and the New Global Challenge," in *The Consumer Society Reader,* ed. Juliet Schor and Douglas B. Holt (New York: New Press, 2000).

32. Richard H. Thaler and Cass R. Sunstein, *Nudge: Improving Decisions About Health, Wealth, and Happiness* (New York: Penguin Books, 2009).

33. See Anders Hayden, "Europe's Work-Time Alternatives," in *Take Back Your Time: Fighting Overwork and Time Poverty in America,* ed. John de Graaf (San Francisco: Berrett-Koehler, 2003).

34. See Juliet B. Schor, *Plentitude: The New Economics of True Wealth* (New York: Penguin Press, 2010).
35. Frank, *Luxury Fever,* p. 216.
36. Ibid., p. 224.

APPENDIX: A FORMAL THEORY OF CONSUMER BEHAVIOR

A1. THE ASSUMPTIONS

This appendix presents in more detail the standard economic model of consumer behavior. In this model, the consumer is seeking to maximize his or her utility. The consumer is assumed to be well informed and rational and to consider only his or her own preferences, budget, and prices in making a consumption decision. For simplicity, we assume there are only two goods, good *X* and good *Y.*

A2. THE BUDGET LINE AND ITS SLOPE

The combinations of *X* and *Y* that are available to the household are shown by a budget line, like that in Figure 9.8. The budget line arises because the sum of the consumer's expenditures must add up to—not exceed—the consumer's income. Mathematically:

$$P_x x + P_y y = Income$$

where x and y denote the quantities purchased of each good, and P_x and P_y are their respective prices. This equation can be rearranged, algebraically, into slope-intercept form (i.e., $y = a + bx$, where the intercept a gives the value of y when x equals 0, and b is the slope of the line). This yields:

$$y = \frac{Income}{P_y} - \frac{P_x}{P_y} x$$

For example, in Figure 9.8, income could be \$40, the price of *X* could be \$10, and the price of *Y* could be \$5. The budget line crosses the *y*-axis at 40/5 = 8 units of *Y* and has a slope of −10/5 = −2. In general, we note that the budget line has a slope equal to $-P_x / P_y$.

Figure 9.8 **The Budget Line and Its Slope**

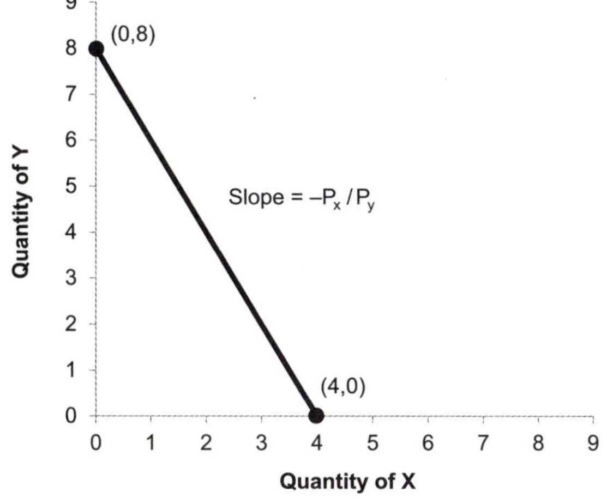

The slope of the consumer's budget line is $-P_x / P_y$.

A3. INDIFFERENCE CURVES

indifference curve: a curve consisting of points representing combinations of various quantities of two goods, such that every such combination gives the consumer the same level of utility

The consumer's preferences concerning the two goods can be illustrated on the same graph by using the concept of **indifference curves** pioneered by the economist Paul Samuelson.

Indifference curves show combinations of the two goods with which the consumer would be equally satisfied (i.e., has the same utility). Indifference curves are generally thought to have the bowed-in-toward-the-origin shape shown in Figure 9.9. This shape arises because we assume that the consumer experiences diminishing marginal utility for both *X* and *Y*.

Suppose the consumer starts out at point A, with a large amount of *Y* (7 units) but relatively little of *X* (only 1 unit). At point A, the consumer has a fairly low marginal utility of *Y*, because she is already consuming a lot of it, and a fairly high marginal utility of *X*, because she has only a little of it. (Refer to the shape of Figure 9.4 if necessary. Utility flattens out if you have a lot of a good and rises steeply if you have little.) She will be willing to give up some of the *Y*—marginal units from which she is getting relatively little utility, anyway—to get more of *X*, a good that still has fairly high marginal utility. If she is just willing to give up 3 units of good *Y* to get 1 additional unit of good *X*, then she is indifferent between point A and point B. The slope of the indifference curve can be mathematically shown to be equal to $-MU_x/MU_y$, where MU_x is the marginal utility of *X* and MU_y is the marginal utility of *Y*. As we see on the graph, the slope of the indifference curve between point A and point B is –3 (rise/run on a straight line between the points = –3/1). The ratio of marginal utilities, MU_x/MU_y is called the **marginal rate of substitution**, which tells how much of one good the consumer is willing to give up to get more of the other.

marginal rate of substitution: how much of one good the consumer is willing to give up to get more of another

However, at point B, the consumer's marginal utility from good *Y* will have risen from what it was at point A, because she is consuming less of it. Meanwhile, her marginal utility from *X* will have fallen, because she is consuming more of it. She will be more reluctant to give up more units of *Y* in exchange for further units of *X*. Likewise, because she is now consuming more *X*, she is less eager to get more of it than she was before. This means that if she is presented with further opportunities to trade, she will demand *more X* to compensate her for giving up any more *Y*. If forced to give up 2 more units of *Y*, Figure 9.9 shows that she will now require 3 more units of *X* to keep her just as happy. The slope of the indifference curve between point B and point C is –2/3, and the marginal rate of substitution is now 2/3. Indifference curves tend to be steep at low levels of consumption of *X* and then flatten out as you move to the right, as a consequence of diminishing marginal utility. Thus we have a falling marginal rate of substitution.

Figure 9.9 **An Indifference Curve**

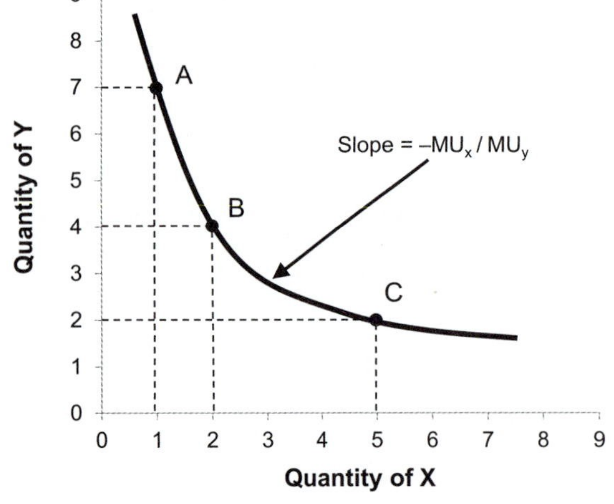

An indifference curve shows all combinations of goods that give the consumer the same level of utility. Its slope is $-MU_x/MU_y$.

A4. UTILITY MAXIMIZATION

Different levels of utility are represented by different indifference curves. Because the standard economic view assumes that consumers always want more of at least one good (and usually of both goods), this "more is better" assumption means that utility rises as you move upward and to the right on the graph. Figure 9.10 shows three examples of indifference curves, corresponding to three different levels of utility.

The consumer's problem, then, is to get to the highest level of utility possible, given her budget. This problem and its solution are illustrated in Figure 9.11. The consumer can afford many points on the lowest indifference curve—much of the curve lies below and to the left of the budget line. If she chose to consume at point C, she would use up all her budget. But this is not the best that she can do. Points A and B would both give her more utility than point C, and point D would give her even more. Points B and D are unobtainable, however, because they are above the budget line.

Figure 9.10 **Different Levels of Utility**

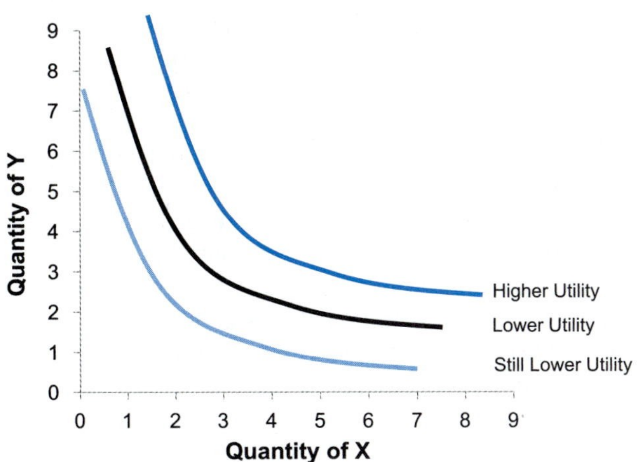

Moving above and to the right, indifference curves represent higher levels of utility.

Figure 9.11 **Utility Maximization**

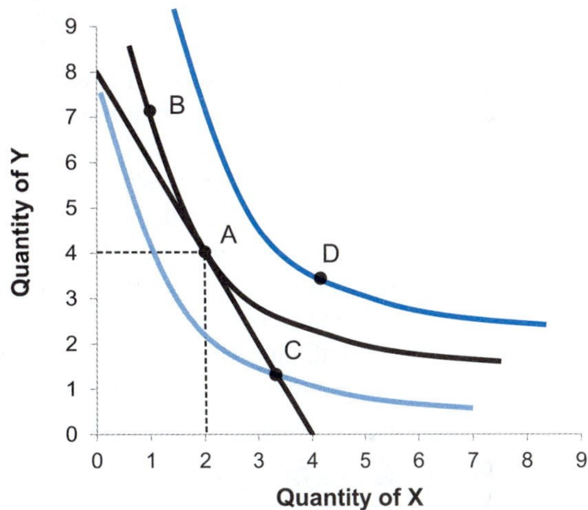

The consumer's utility is maximized by choosing a consumption point on the highest achievable indifference curve. This happens at point A.

The best the consumer can do is get onto the indifference curve that just touches his budget line, at point A, purchasing 4 units of Y and 2 units of X. At point A, the two curves just touch and have the same slope. That is:

$$-\frac{MU_x}{MU_y} = -\frac{P_x}{P_y}$$

which can be algebraically rearranged into:

$$\frac{MU_x}{P_x} = \frac{MU_y}{P_y}$$

This equation states that the consumer will maximize her utility when the marginal utility per dollar spent on X is equal to the marginal utility per dollar spent on Y. If this were not true, and the last dollar spent on good X produced more utility than the last dollar spent on good Y, the consumer could increase her utility by switching a dollar from Y to X. She can continue to increase her utility in this manner until the last dollar spent on each good provides similar marginal utility.

If we add a third good, *Z*, or as many as we want, the rule remains the same. To maximize utility, a consumer should equate the marginal utility per dollar spent for all goods, or:

$$\frac{MU_x}{P_x} = \frac{MU_y}{P_y} = \frac{MU_z}{P_z} = \ldots$$

A5. RESPONSE TO VARIATIONS IN PRICE

We can also use a utility theory graph to theorize about consumer response to a price change. For example, Figure 9.12 shows what might happen if the price of *X* drops from \$10 to \$5 (with income held constant at \$40). Now the budget line is higher at all points, except where it meets the *y*-axis. The consumer is thus able to afford more of the goods than before and to reach a higher indifference curve. The consumer portrayed in Figure 9.12 will now choose to consume at point B.

Given the assumptions of this model, it is clear that the consumer has higher utility after the fall in price. Generally, it will be true that consumers will buy more of a good when its price falls. In Figure 9.12, we see that point B is farther to the right than point A.

This is one of the rationales for the downward-sloping demand curve discussed in Chapter 4 on supply and demand. By no means, however, is it the only explanation. First, downward-sloping demand curves may be a useful tool for analyzing the behavior of many other kinds of buyers, such as businesses, nonprofits, and governments. The foregoing is not an explanation for their behavior. Second, the tool of utility theory is not necessary for deriving demand curves. In a 1962 article, economist Gary Becker showed that market purchases of a good will tend to rise when prices fall, even if consumers act only impulsively or out of habit.

What happens to the level of purchases of good *Y* when the price of good *X* falls? This is hard to predict without knowing more about the particular goods. This question was discussed under the topics of "substitutes" and "complements" in Chapter 4.

Figure 9.12 **Response to a Change in Price**

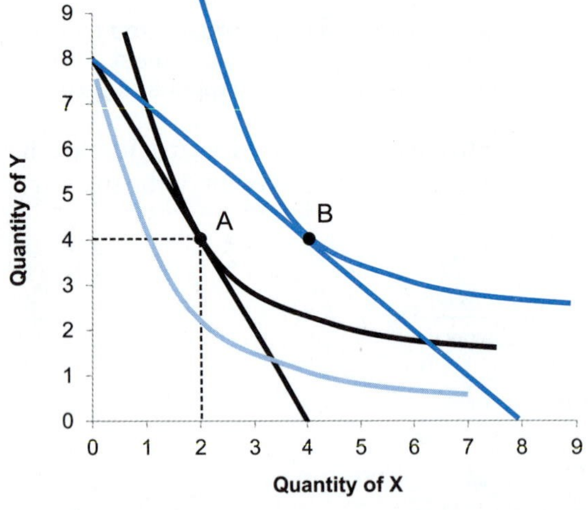

If the price of good *X* falls, the consumer will be able to reach a higher utility level.

10 Markets for Labor

When you next look for a job—during the summer, perhaps during the school year, or after you graduate from college—what characteristics will you be seeking in your job? Some possibilities include: good pay, opportunities for advancement, opportunities for learning, doing a variety of interesting activities, a feeling that you are contributing something of value, and a comfortable and congenial work environment.

And what will you want to avoid? Studies of human happiness find that one of the leading causes of dissatisfaction in modern life is a long commute. Other things that are generally not preferred include work that is dangerous, dirty, or physically uncomfortable, mindlessly repetitive, or exhausting. Low pay is generally a disincentive, as is a lack of benefits such as health care and paid vacations.

Traditionally, economics has been most concerned with understanding the compensation attached to different jobs. We will see that some of the other characteristics of work just mentioned may have some impact on compensation—and are of importance in their own right as well.

1. Labor in the Traditional Neoclassical Model

"The labor market" is a familiar phrase, but markets for labor are different from other markets in many ways. For a start, consider what is sold in a labor market. It is not human beings; slavery, one of the worst practices in human history, is illegal everywhere in the world (although it still exists, even in developed countries). Rather, what is sold in labor markets is what is sometimes called "labor power"—that is, what a given person is able and willing to do in a given amount of time. An employer who hires a certain amount of labor power (X number of people working for Y hours) expects that it will produce a certain level of output. But it is not the actual output that is being purchased in this market—it is the contribution that employees make toward the production of output. This makes labor markets somewhat more abstract than markets for the things that labor can directly produce, such as sweaters, jet planes, or a sales pitch over the telephone.

We examine some unique characteristics of labor markets and some of the factors that determine the level of earnings for different kinds of jobs. However, we start with a familiar supply-and-demand picture as a point of reference. The very simple neoclassical model that we discussed in Chapter 8, for the most part, treats the demand for and supply of labor very much like other things that are bought and sold on markets. Labor, in this model, is demanded by profit-maximizing firms and is supplied by utility-maximizing households. The stylized utility-maximizing consumers who were described in Chapter 9 are now simply dressed in overalls or suits and sent into the workplace, with the single goal of earning the money that will allow them to be consumers.

On the side of the demander—the firm—this model assumes a number of characteristics that are not usually found in the real world: for example, that all firms are powerless entities forced by competition to maximize profits and minimize costs; that productivity can be easily measured; and that historical and social contexts can be ignored. (Markets with powerless firms are described in Chapter 17; more realistic markets are described in Chapter 18.)

The traditional model, which we quickly survey, describes how these sets of actors make decisions about *how much* labor will be supplied and purchased, and at *what price (wage)*.

1.1 Labor Demand

On the demand side of the labor market, consider a firm seeking to hire a specific type of labor. What should guide the firm's decisions about how much labor to hire? From the viewpoint of a profit-maximizing firm, an additional person-hour of labor will be desirable if it increases profits, but not otherwise. Hiring an additional person-hour does two contradictory things to the firm's profit position:

- Costs are raised by the amount of the additional wages paid.
- Revenue is increased by the value of the increase in output produced by the additional hour of work.

Clearly, as long as the firm gets *more* additional revenue than it has to pay out in additional wages, it should keep hiring workers. But if it is getting *less* in additional revenue than it is paying out in additional wages, it should reduce the number of workers that it hires. The profit-maximizing decision rule for the firm can thus be expressed as:

$$MRP_L = MFC_L$$

marginal revenue product of labor (MRP_L): the amount that a unit of additional labor contributes to the revenues of the firm

marginal factor cost of labor (MFC_L): the amount that a unit of additional labor adds to the firm's wage costs

where MRP_L is the **marginal revenue product of labor,** or the amount that an additional unit of labor contributes to revenues, and MFC_L is the **marginal factor cost of labor,** or the amount that the additional unit of labor adds to the firm's wage costs.*

In other words, the firm should hire additional units of labor until the marginal benefits just equal the marginal costs. We will see very similar reasoning in Chapter 17, concerning a firm's decision about how much to produce—for exactly the same reasons. A formal derivation of this rule is described in the appendix to this chapter.

If the firm buys labor services in a competitive market, MFC_L will simply be the competitively determined market wage, and the rule will simplify to:

$$MRP_L = Wage$$

The traditional neoclassical model offers an elegant solution for this simplified case. It gives a formalized statement of the intuitive sense that workers should be rewarded in relation to their contribution to the organization. However, actual measurement of productivity is difficult. Moreover, the market valuation of a production process—its direct outputs and its side effects—can differ from social valuations because of externalities and distributional issues. Hence, you must be careful about inferring that, in the real world, any observed wage accurately represents the worker's contribution to society's well-being.

1.2 Labor Supply

The traditional model of consumer behavior presented in Chapter 9, in which consumers seek to maximize their utility, can be extended to decisions about labor supply. Specifically, we can consider how much time an individual is willing to work, given different wage levels.

*Note that hiring an additional unit of labor may increase other costs, such as energy and supplies. These costs would be subtracted from the MRP_L to determine the net increase in revenues associated with an additional unit of labor.

In this model, the potential labor market participant is assumed to have perfect information and to be free to vary his or her hours of paid work. However, the labor market model differs from the model of consumer choice in that here the "budget line" is defined according to the number of *hours* that the individual has available to "spend" on activities, rather than according to the amount of money that he or she has to spend on goods.

The model imagines essentially three kinds of activities:

- paid work
- unpaid work
- leisure

Hours "spent" on paid labor result in wages, which in turn give opportunities for consumption. Hours spent on other activities yield utility either directly (as in the case of leisure) or indirectly through unpaid production. (In this model, paid work is generally assumed to yield no direct utility.) According to the model, the potential labor market participant will choose the level of labor market participation that maximizes his or her utility.

Two forces govern the supply of factors of production: the total quantity available at any point in time and the willingness of their owners to actually supply them. Labor is fundamentally "owned" by the individual, who may be thought of as renting out his or her services when working for pay. In many cases, actual decisions about supplying paid labor are made not by individuals but jointly with other household members, as part of a general plan for family support and investments for the future. Continuing with the simple model, however, for now we discuss paid labor supply as though an individual person is making the decision. Also, because this chapter discuses labor *markets,* we focus on labor that is performed in exchange for a wage or salary.

The Opportunity Cost of Paid Employment

In general, the willingness of an individual to supply work may be analyzed in terms of the wages and other benefits that he or she can get, compared to the benefits to him or her of not supplying it or supplying it elsewhere. An individual weighing these decisions is assessing the opportunity cost of labor supply. This idea may be applied broadly; the "costs" and the "benefits" of supplying labor may be seen in terms of money but also reflect any other gains or losses that are valued by the individual.

Most of the alternatives facing an able-bodied adult who is considering going out to work for a wage or salary fall under the following headings:

- *Household production:* A paid job may reduce the time that can be spent in productive but unpaid work at home—raising children, caring for elderly or sick relatives, cooking, keeping house, gardening, and the like.
- *Education:* As an alternative to seeking paid work immediately, individuals may decide to stay in school or return to school—either to prepare for better-paid future employment or simply to enjoy the process of education or the life of a student.
- *Self-employment:* People can work for themselves in household enterprises, making crafts, providing personal services (such as day care or yard work), writing, painting, or starting another home-based business. (The income of self-employed proprietors tends to be a mix of returns to labor, returns to capital, and profits. In this chapter, we do not discuss the nature of their labor compensation because we are focusing only on people who work *for wages or salaries.*)
- *Leisure:* Work cuts into the time available for playing music, fishing, camping, reading novels, playing or watching sports, hanging out with friends, playing computer games, traveling, and other pleasurable activities.

To the extent that you value any of these pursuits and reduce the hours you devote to them when you take a paid job, that job has a "cost." The cost is the lost opportunity for other activities. In addition to the opportunity costs associated with your time, you may incur direct monetary costs when taking a paid job, such as the costs of work-related clothing and transportation. You may incur increased monetary expenditures for things that otherwise might have been home-produced (using your time resources), such as child care and meal preparation.

The Benefits of Paid Employment

At the same time, of course, paid jobs have many benefits. Most obvious is the fact that they are *paid.* In a contemporary industrialized economy, households need some money income to survive and to participate in society. Even if paid work is unpleasant, boring, stressful, or even demeaning, wages and salaries are strong extrinsic motivators that encourage individuals to supply their labor.

In addition, however, paid work itself has great intrinsic significance in most people's lives. Evidence from state lotteries in the past few decades, for example, illustrates this point. In a number of cases, winners of large lottery prizes have decided *not* to quit their jobs entirely, even when they could easily have done so. They usually cite their friendships on the job and the sense of identity that they have found in their work as reasons for continuing at least some of their usual work activities. For billions of people, the nature of the work experience is a decisive part of the quality of life: The work process determines whether a major part of life will be boring or interesting, lonely or companionable, comfortable or filled with bodily discomfort, tranquil or full of anxiety, stunts personal growth or offers opportunities to develop mental or physical capacities.

Household production and self-employment can also supply many of the same intrinsic rewards, though often with less companionship and social interaction. Sometimes, people who only work at unpaid household production activities feel marginalized due to a social perception that only work for wages or salaries is "real work." Again, we focus on paid work in this chapter, but we recognize that many people provide valuable contributions to society without being paid.

1.3 The Individual Paid Labor Supply Curve

We look at the decision of an individual to supply various amounts of hours over a week or year, assuming, for the moment, that the worker can find part-time, full-time, or overtime paid jobs that satisfy his or her desires. For now, we also abstract from a worker's choices among different kinds of paid jobs, focusing only on the decision about how much time to put into paid work. As in many other supply curve thought experiments, we abstract from all considerations *other than* the relationship between price and quantity. In this case, we look only at the effect of different wage levels on the individual's willingness to supply labor to the market.

In Figure 10.1 we show an upward-sloping supply curve like those presented for markets for coffee in Chapter 4. The "wage," which we use as a shorthand term for the price paid for an hour of labor, is on the vertical axis. In practice, many blue-collar and service jobs pay an hourly *wage,* whereas professional and managerial jobs tend to pay a weekly or monthly *salary* independent of how many hours they actually work. Jobs may also pay in the form of tips, bonuses, or stock options, and they may provide fringe benefits such as health insurance. For our simple supply-and-demand analysis, we include all these in the concept of a "wage." The quantity of labor, which might be thought of as the number of hours that the individual works in a week or a year, is on the horizontal axis.

Does this "usual" curve apply to labor? Following one line of reasoning, we can see that in many cases it does. From the perspective of an individual, the upward-sloping supply curve reflects the *substitution effect* of changes in prices: Individuals decide whether to substitute the benefits of paid work for the benefits of other activities. When offered a very low wage,

Figure 10.1 **Upward-Sloping Labor Supply Curve**

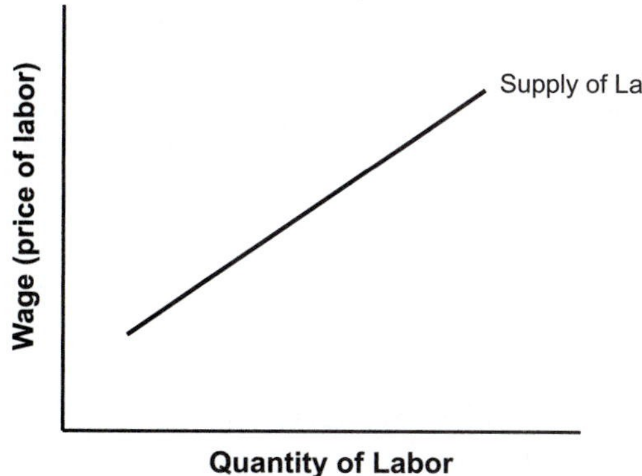

Like other supply curves we have discussed, the labor market supply curve may be expected to be upward-sloping.

an individual may be reluctant to join the labor market, or to supply many hours of work, because he or she may get more benefits from self-employment or other activities. The higher the market wage rate, the more attractive it is to engage in additional paid labor instead of unpaid household work, education, self-employment, or leisure.*

However, one of the important reasons that an individual works is to earn an income, which in turn is used to buy goods and services that he or she can then enjoy. As the wage gets higher and higher, will the person *always* want to work more and more? Probably not. Economists explain this in terms of the fact that leisure (and perhaps other unpaid activities) are usually "normal goods," in the sense explained in Chapter 5. As people earn higher incomes, they may also want more time to enjoy the fruits of their labor. The rising wage also has an *income effect:* The higher the market wage, the more leisure (and other unpaid activities) that people might want to "buy." Because "buying" leisure means reducing work hours, the paid labor supply curve will be *downward*-sloping if the income effect is dominant.

backward-bending individual paid labor supply curve: a pattern that arises because, beyond some level of wages, income effects may outweigh substitution effects in determining individuals' decisions about how much to work

People may have a target level of income in mind, beyond which they have less need for additional money. As we saw in Chapter 9, workers early in the industrial era often had such income targets. Increases in wages above the traditional level led individuals to take longer weekends and offer fewer hours of work the next week. Today such extreme cases of income "targeting" are rare, but there still is a tendency for some people to reduce their hours of work as their income rises. In such a case, the substitution effect may dominate at low wage levels, but the income effect dominates at high wage levels. The result is a **backward-bending individual paid labor supply curve,** as shown in Figure 10.2.

Figure 10.2 **Backward-Bending Individual Labor Supply Curve**

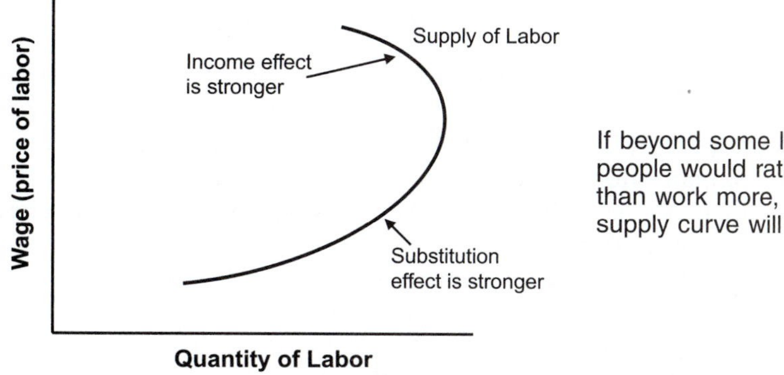

If beyond some level of income people would rather do other things than work more, the individual labor supply curve will bend backward.

*We are assuming that the potential worker can enjoy at least a minimal standard of living from activities other than market work when the wage is too low to make market work attractive. In situations of dire poverty, however, this may not be the case, and people may need to work two or three jobs at very low wages just to get by.

The presence of the income effect makes individual paid labor supply different from the usual supply curves of businesses or other economic actors. As businesses or nonprofits rarely have a target level of revenues, they will display no income effect. Usually, even if high revenues allow some employees to enjoy more leisure (e.g., the founder might cut back on his or her work hours), the organization as a whole will expand its operations, perhaps by hiring more people.

1.4 How the Standard Model Explains Variations in Wages

Among the things that economists are especially eager to understand about labor markets are the reasons for differences in wages. Why do star basketball players make so much more than aerospace engineers, who earn so much more than preschool teachers? In addition, within the same job definition it is possible to find workers who receive very different compensation, even though they seem to have equivalent qualifications. Are such patterns of wage differentials determined solely by the logic of markets? If not, what other forces affect them?

Some economists stress productivity differences as nearly the sole source of wage variation over the long run. This emphasis requires a number of assumptions: that people behave in a rational, purely self-interested way, that market forces are strong, and that markets are fully competitive. A high wage, in this view, is merely a sign that an individual is making a highly valued contribution.

The demand for labor—the employers' willingness to pay for different types of labor services—is related to just *how productive* workers are. Employers generally are not willing to pay their workers more than the value that each one contributes to what the employer finally sells—what we have called marginal revenue product of labor. Employers who can get away with paying workers less than their MRP_L are motivated to do so in order to minimize costs and therefore to maximize profits. Theoretically, this should not be possible, if the labor market is truly competitive. In that case, workers who do not receive a "fair" wage in one place (a wage equal to their MRP_L) can find another employer who will offer the wage that actually represents the worker's contribution to the value of output.

Human Capital

In the standard model, the main reason for variations in labor productivity and, hence, in wages is human capital. This consists of people's knowledge and skills. It is affected by:

- formal education and job-related training
- informal education and job-related experience
- innate talents
- the physical and mental health of the worker*

Obviously, different kinds of jobs require different kinds of human capital. Different levels of human capital often result from different levels of investment, in terms of education and training. The wages for skilled occupations, such as aerospace engineers (e.g., compared to farm manual laborers), reflect in part the fact that aerospace engineers have normally engaged in formal training to acquire skills and credentials, whereas farm laborers largely use more common skills that, it is assumed, most people possess.

We can see the impact of education levels in Figure 10.3, which shows median earnings by education level in the United States. Those with a master's degree earn about 22 percent more than those with just a bachelor's degree, and those with a bachelor's degree earn 63 percent more than those with just a high school diploma.

---

*The last determinant of human capital is sometimes overlooked; however, malnourishment and mental or physical ill-health can seriously affect a worker's energy, motivation, and general capacity to use her or her knowledge and skills.

Figure 10.3 **Median Weekly Earnings of U.S. Workers, by Educational Attainment, 2012**

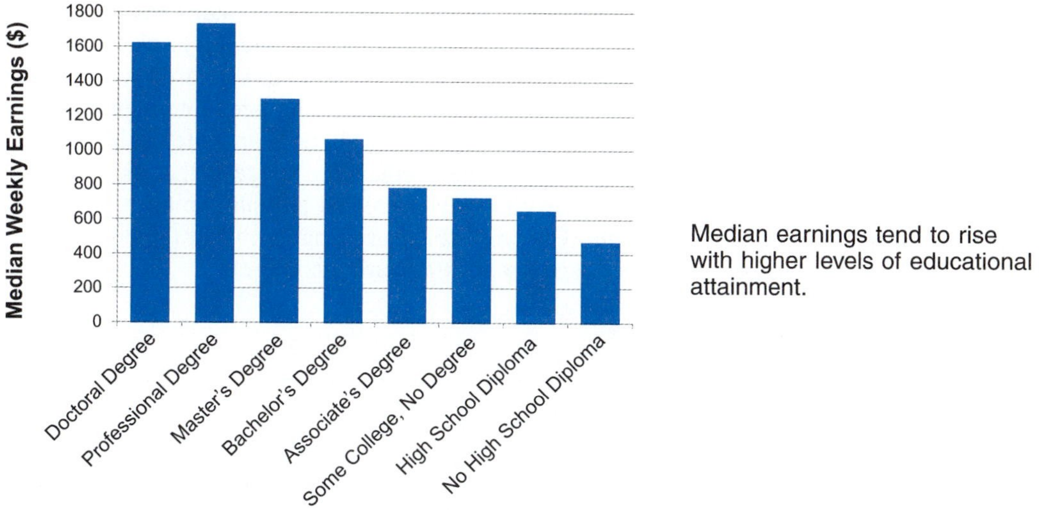

Median earnings tend to rise with higher levels of educational attainment.

Source: U.S. Bureau of Labor Statistics, "Employment Projections," www.bls.gov/emp/ep_chart_001.htm, May 22, 2013.

The income benefits associated with education have increased in recent decades. For example, between 1975 and 1999 the ratio of average earnings of those with advanced degrees to those with a high school diploma increased from 1.8 to 2.6. According to analysis by the U.S. Census Bureau, the increase in the economic benefits of education

> may be explained by both the supply of labor and the demand for skilled workers. In the 1970s, the premiums paid to college graduates dropped because of an increase in their numbers, which kept the relative earnings range among the educational attainment levels rather narrow. Recently, however, technological changes favoring more skilled (and educated) workers have tended to increase earnings among working adults with higher educational attainment, while, simultaneously, the decline of labor unions and a decline in the minimum wage in constant dollars have contributed to a relative drop in the wages of less educated workers.[1]

general human capital: knowledge and skills that workers can take with them as they move from one employer to another

employer-specific human capital: knowledge and skills that have been gained on a particular job and are useful only as long as a worker remains with the same employer

screening methods: approaches used by employers to limit their job search to specific candidates

In addition to formal education, human capital may also be accumulated through on-the-job training. For example, a more experienced farm laborer can do some of the work faster, or to a higher standard, and might therefore be paid more than a new hire. Human capital acquired on the job may be either general or employer-specific. **General human capital** consists of the knowledge and skills that workers can take with them if they leave one organization and go to work for another. **Employer-specific human capital** consists of knowledge and skills that are valued only by a particular employer. For example, many farming and engineering skills may be general, but knowledge about a specific piece of land or crop, or a specific engineering project, may be useless away from a particular employer.

How do employers judge the human capital embodied in a prospective worker? Ideally, before offering a wage, they should be able to assess which skills the worker possesses and how much these skills will contribute to productivity. Because this assessment is often difficult to make, employers may use credentials, such as educational degrees or training certificates, as proxies for observed skills. A firm that is seeking to employ an aerospace engineer would look for someone with the appropriate degree. A college degree is a common **screening method** that employers use to limit their job search to specific candidates. Other screening methods used by employers include requirements that applicants have a minimum number of years of work experience, or certification that they have been trained to do specific tasks.

signaling theory: a theory of the value of an education that suggests that an educational credential *signals* to an employer that a potential worker has desired character traits and work habits

In a subtler, but also common, example, firms may require credentials such as a college degree, or even a graduate degree, not because they are convinced that the undergraduate or graduate education has directly provided essential knowledge or skills but because the possession of the degree *signals* that the person is a certain kind of worker. Educational credentials such as these are used by employers as reassurance that the applicant possesses desirable characteristics such as self-discipline, patience, and the ability to work under pressure. The **signaling theory** of the value of education suggests that the value of a college education may be not so much in the way it creates human capital as in how it solves information problems for employers, revealing, or signaling, what type of worker a person already was before starting college (or became during college).

Other Factors Affecting Productivity

A worker's productivity may also depend on several factors that are at least somewhat under the control of the employer. These include:

- *The level of effort with which workers work:* The workers' level of effort on a job includes the pace at which they work, as well as how careful they are to do the job right. The level of work effort depends on employer management practices, such as rewards and punishments, but it may also depend on historical, cultural, personal, or other circumstances beyond the manager's control.
- *The efficiency with which workers apply their skills:* Management is also an important contributor to worker efficiency; a good manager can put each worker in the job that best suits his or her abilities, can see to it that work groups are organized in more rather than less efficient ways, and can try to organize an optimal interaction of workers with the technology available to them.
- *The quantity and characteristics of the resources available to each worker:* In the simplest terms, those who work with more, newer, and better technology and equipment, energy resources and materials, are more productive. A lack of the appropriate quantity or quality of resources can make even the most skilled and motivated worker unproductive.

Discussion Questions

1. Think of a job that you have held. Describe how your productivity on the job was affected by:
   a. your skills
   b. the organization of the workplace (whether it encouraged efficiency)
   c. your level of effort (and what it was about the job that encouraged this specific level of effort)
   d. the resources you had available to work with
2. In any production process, when one factor limits what can be produced and other factors are in abundant supply, that one factor is called the *limiting factor.* Continue to reflect on the job that you considered in Question 1. Which contributor to productivity would you identify as the "limiting factor" in that case? What change would have been most effective in bringing about increased productivity?

2. LABOR SUPPLY AND DEMAND AT THE MARKET LEVEL

labor force participation rate: the percentage of the adult, noninstitutionalized population that is either working at a paid job or seeking paid work

In order to think about labor markets in terms of supply and demand, we need to consider how labor supply at the individual level translates into labor supply at the market level. We start with a bit of history.

Since the early twentieth century, industrialized countries have shown a striking trend toward an increase in the (paid) **labor force participation rate** (defined as the percentage of the adult, noninstitutionalized population that is either working at a paid job or seeking paid work). In most countries, this increase has been accounted for entirely by the increasing labor force participation of women. The increase in women's participation in the labor force has been partially offset by a small decline in men's participation; most of the change for men has resulted from decisions to stay in school longer or to retire earlier.

If we think about these social trends in "opportunity cost" terms, we can see that they involve changing perceptions of the costs and benefits of entering the paid labor market. The cost of this choice has declined as improved technologies for the home and the increased availability of substitute services (such as child care and prepared meals) have reduced the number of hours of household work strictly necessary to maintain a household. The benefits have risen in societies where activism and changes in social norms and laws have opened a greater variety of paid occupations to women. The perceived benefits have also risen to the extent that increased consumerism (discussed in Chapter 9) has encouraged people to focus more on making money at the expense of time for household production or leisure.

2.1 MARKET LABOR SUPPLY

The supply of labor to a particular market, such as the national market for aerospace engineers or the market for restaurant wait staff in Chicago, can be thought of as the horizontal sum of the supply curves of those individuals who could participate in the market. Although the supply curves of some individuals might bend backward, the supply curve for a particular market can generally be assumed to have the usual upward slope shown in Figure 10.1. This is because employers can obtain a larger quantity of labor in two ways. The first is by persuading workers already in the market to supply more hours, in which case income effects could become important. The second way, however, is to attract more workers to enter the particular market, either by drawing them away from other jobs or by drawing them into the paid labor force from other activities. For most of these workers, we can assume that this substitution effect dominates, and so the aggregate supply curve will slope upward.

Market labor supply is relatively wage elastic if a variation in the wage brings a large change in the quantity of labor supplied. This could occur if the (upward-sloping sections of) individual worker's supply curves are elastic. It also occurs when a rise in the wage readily draws more workers into the particular market. Markets for types of labor that use general or more easily acquired skills generally tend to have relatively elastic supply curves. If the wage for local restaurant wait staff rises, for example, people may leave jobs as salesclerks and delivery truck drivers in order to offer their services to restaurants. If the wages paid by restaurants fall, wait staff may fairly readily look for jobs as salesclerks and drivers.

Market labor supply is relatively wage inelastic, however, if a variation in the wage brings little change in the quantity of labor supplied. At the extreme, the supply of labor might be "fixed" for some occupations, at least in the short run. For example, there are only so many aerospace engineers in the United States at any point in time. (What slope would the supply curve have?) Raising the wage might draw a few engineers out of retirement or self-employment, but it cannot instantly produce a large quantity of new engineers, because obtaining the skills necessary for this job requires many years of education. A drop in the wage, similarly, might not much decrease the quantity of labor supplied in the short run, because the engineers' specialized skills are not valued nearly as much in other markets. Changes in the quantity supplied will occur only over the long run, as high wages attract more students to train for the job or low wages cause more engineers to become dissatisfied and retrain for something else. The United States has also used immigration policies to increase the quantity of labor supplied in certain high-skilled areas where there are labor shortages. (For a real-world example of a labor shortage, see Box 10.1.)

So far, we have discussed the responsiveness of quantity to price *along* a supply curve. Market labor supply curves can also *shift,* in response to nonprice factors, just like the shifts in other supply curves that we studied in Chapter 4. For the economy as a whole, for example,

BOX 10.1 A SHORTAGE OF DOCTORS

Nevada is experiencing a shortage of doctors. According to a 2013 study by John Packham, a health policy researcher at the University of Nevada, the state has one of the lowest numbers of primary care physicians per capita in the United States. Packham also notes a shortage of orthopedic and general surgeons, which will become more critical as the state's population ages. The impacts of the doctor shortage include longer wait times to get an appointment, higher costs, and lower-quality health care.

Many other regions of the United States are also experiencing a shortage of doctors, with this problem forecast to increase. According to the Association of American Medical Colleges, in 2015 the doctor shortage will reach 30,000. By the mid-2020s, the shortage will approach 70,000. One reason for this is that doctors have migrated to specialized, high-paying fields such as dermatology and cardiology, instead of primary care and general surgery. Also, the demand for health care has increased due to an ageing population. Expanded health-care coverage under the Affordable Care Act (i.e., Obamacare) will also increase the demand for doctors.

On the supply side, the number of doctors is relatively fixed in the short term. It commonly takes about 10 to 15 years from the time an undergraduate student decides to pursue a career as a doctor to the time he or she can actually start practicing. Thus the labor market for doctors is an example of a market that can persist in a condition of disequilibrium for many years.

In Nevada it is particularly difficult to attract doctors to rural areas, particularly those with high minority populations. Trudy Larson, director of community health sciences at the University of Nevada, Reno, says, "There are plenty of students who apply to medical school, but we need to diversify the physician workforce. We need to provide an outreach for people who are interested in health care [so they can] know the pathway."

Source: Editorial Board, "Nevada Must Get Creative Solutions for Doctor Shortage," *Reno Gazette-Journal,* August 3, 2013.

labor supply curves tend to shift outward over time because of population growth. Changes in laws and norms and in household technology caused the supply curve to shift outward in many areas when women joined men seeking employment in many high-skill markets such as law and medicine.

Changes in one labor market may also have repercussions in other markets. For example, a rise in the wages of salesclerks (a movement *along* the supply curve for salesclerks) might decrease the supply of wait staff (that is, *shift* the supply curve for wait staff back), as people exit the wait staff market in order to take advantage of the higher wages now being offered for salesclerks.

2.2 MARKET LABOR DEMAND

For the most part, the demanders of labor (i.e., potential employers) are organizations, including businesses, nonprofits, and governments. A very small fraction of employers are households or individuals, who may directly employ people for tasks such as in-home child care and domestic service.

The demand curve for paid labor—whether for an individual organization or for an entire market—can generally be thought of as downward sloping, like the demand curves we examined in previous chapters. The reason for the downward slope is as follows. When wages are high, employers have incentives to economize on the use of labor. They may cut back on their activities or try to substitute other inputs (e.g., another type of labor, machinery, or computerization) for the type of labor whose wage is high. But when wages are low, employers may be able to expand their productive activities or substitute relatively cheap labor for other inputs.

Labor demand will tend to be relatively wage elastic if there are good substitute inputs available and if the wage bill is a large proportion of total production costs (so that the employers are motivated to seek out substitutes). Labor demand will tend to be relatively inelastic if no good substitute inputs are available and the wage bill is a small proportion of total costs.

The labor demand curve may shift if there is a change in the demand for the good or service that it is used to produce, if technological developments alter the production process, if the number of employers changes, or if the price or availability of other inputs changes. For example, when an organization experiences a fall in demand for its products, its labor demand curve will shift back as well.

2.3 MARKET ADJUSTMENT

Still using the same simplifying assumptions as in Chapter 4 about how markets work, we can examine how market forces might influence wage rates and the quantity of labor employed.

For example, let Figure 10.4 depict a stylized market for e-commerce Web site designers. In the late 1990s, e-commerce was booming, and demand for the services of such designers was high, as depicted by demand curve D_1. The short-run supply curve was fairly inelastic, because the job required a certain amount of specialized education and talent. Stories in the newspapers at the time touted the fat salaries being offered to talented, self-taught computer experts just out of high school and told of people being aggressively recruited by businesses, with large signing bonuses.

In 2000, however, many investors decided that e-commerce was not going to be the money maker that they had expected, and investment funds for e-commerce dried up considerably. Many firms went out of business, and others laid off many of their employees. The market for Web site designers went from boom to bust. We can think of this as the demand curve shifting to D_2.

Comparing equilibrium E_1 to equilibrium E_2, we can see that the model predicts that the number of Web site designers will fall and that the wage will fall as well. In fact, many Web site designers became unemployed and had to search for other types of jobs, while signing bonuses and premium wage offers became a thing of the past. Students who had been training to enter the field found that they had to make other plans.

Labor market adjustment takes time—the movement from E_1 to E_2 is not instantaneous. It takes time for workers to change their career plans and for employers to adjust wages and salaries, which may be set by labor contracts. Given that labor market conditions are constantly changing, it may be unclear whether a particular labor market is in equilibrium. Much of the recent labor economics research has focused on the persistence of "friction" in labor markets, which slows the transition of workers from one job to another. In particular, unemployed workers may spend considerable time searching for a job that meets their specific requirements.

Figure 10.4 **The Market for Website Designers**

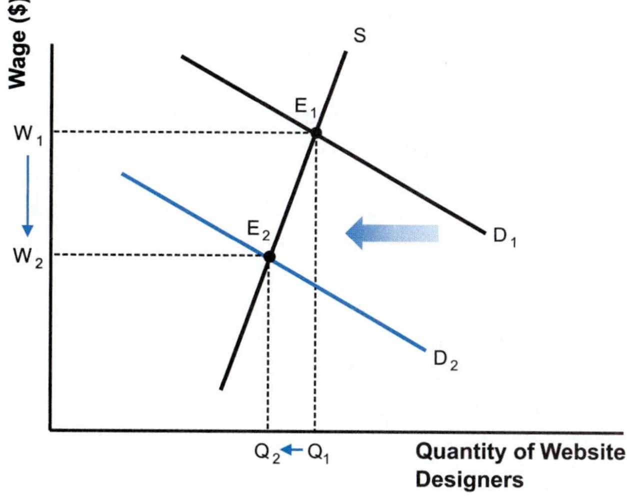

A drop in the demand for website designers leads to lower employment and a fall in wages.

The existence of labor market friction means that a significant number of jobs are commonly available, even when unemployment is high. For example, in June 2013 unemployment was 7.6 percent, and 11.8 million people were unemployed, but there were also 3.9 million job openings. Discussion of labor conditions at a national level is an important topic in macroeconomics.

Discussion Questions

1. Suppose that your college or university substantially raises the wages that it offers to pay students who tend computer laboratories, monitoring the equipment and answering questions. What do you think would happen to the quantity of labor supplied? Why? Where would the extra labor hours come from? Do you think the supply of this kind of labor is elastic or inelastic? Why?
2. Opticians fit people who have poor eyesight with glasses or contact lenses, prescribed by an optometrist. Beginning in the 1990s, technological developments in laser eye surgery made surgery an increasingly popular way of correcting bad eyesight. What effect do you think this development had on the market for opticians? Draw a graph, carefully showing whether the shift is in demand or supply and showing the resulting predicted changes in the quantity of labor demanded and in the wage.

3. Changes in Jobs and in the Labor Force

For the remainder of this chapter, we move away from the idealized world of perfect competition and equilibrium markets, to paint a more realistic portrait of paid work in the United States. We start with a reminder that what we see today is not exactly the way that things were in the past—and is not necessarily the way that things will be in the future, either. In 1933, when unemployment was widespread because of the Great Depression, the U.S. Senate voted overwhelmingly to establish a 30-hour workweek. The House of Representatives voted down this measure, but in 1938 the Fair Labor Standards Act became law, establishing the 40-hour workweek as the legal norm. By the 1960s U.S. workers were regarded with envy in much of the rest of the world, as having legal protection for relatively less time spent in paid work. This is no longer the case. What happened?

3.1 Employment Flexibility

For most of the twentieth century, Americans generally thought of "a job" (or at least a good job) as something that you typically did Monday through Friday, 40 hours a week, for a wage or salary and benefits (such as health insurance and pension plans). People often expected to stay in the same job for years or even decades. In recent years, however, it has become popular to talk about how employment is becoming more "flexible." But the term "flexibility" has two very different meanings, depending on whether it is considered from the point of view of the worker or the employer.

One meaning of "flexible" work is that it is more suited to workers' varying needs. Some workers—especially professional and managerial workers—now enjoy "flextime" or the ability to set their daily starting and ending times. Job sharing and part-time work allow employment to be more easily combined with family care, studying, or leisure pursuits. However, many jobs remain inflexible and are not "family friendly." The United States is practically alone among industrialized countries in lacking a federal law that mandates paid parental leave for new parents. According to a 2013 book that studied nearly 200 countries, 180 of those mandated paid leave to new mothers, and 81 require paid leave to fathers.[2] In the United States, a two-parent family is entitled to 24 weeks of parental leave but without pay. In most other industrialized countries, families receive 52 or more weeks of parental leave (as much as 318 weeks in France!), with 22 weeks of that with full-time pay.[3] The effects of insufficient parental leave fall disproportionately on women:

> In the absence of paid parental leave policies, traditional gender roles that involve women as "caregivers" and men as "providers," and the typically lower earnings of mothers (relative to fathers) in the labor market, create strong incentives for women to reduce their employment and take on a large majority of child care responsibilities. The most obvious problems associated with such outcomes are that women bear a disproportionate burden of child care responsibilities and pay both a short- and a long-term penalty in the labor market.[4]

"Flexibility" can refer to people's ability to change jobs when they want to or retrain for new careers. However, the term "flexibility" has also been used to refer to policies that make things easier for employers—and often make life more difficult from a worker's perspective. Many employers would like to have complete discretion over setting their workers' hours and pay, to offer few or no benefits, and to be able to terminate employees quickly and without fuss. Increasingly, some firms have hired "independent contractors," "consultants," or part-time workers to avoid having to extend the benefits that they provide to their regular full-time employees. More people now work nonstandard workweeks, regardless of whether they want to, in an economy that is increasingly "24/7."

To some extent, "flexibility" from the employee's perspective is also in the interest of employers. Workers who are better rested and less stressed about their families, thanks to accommodating schedules and expectations, can be more productive. And to some extent, "flexibility" from the employer's perspective is also in the workers' interest. An overly rigid labor market, in which workers are too expensive and difficult to fire, could cause employers to try to minimize the number of workers that they hire, thus reducing the number of jobs. From a well-being perspective, the question is how to achieve a good balance in this aspect of work organization.

3.2 Work Hours

Another important labor issue is weekly work hours and the availability of paid time off for vacations and illness. Although some workers may wish to work long hours for financial or personal reasons, recent surveys suggest that one-third to half of American workers would prefer to work shorter hours with an equivalent reduction in pay.[5]

The average number of hours worked each week by employed Americans has stayed relatively constant since the mid-1970s, at around 39 hours. The percentage of workers working long hours (49 or more hours) generally increased from the 1970s to the 1990s, but has generally declined since then (to about 16 percent of workers in 2010).

International comparisons generally look at average annual work hours, instead of weekly work hours, to account for differences in vacation time. Average annual work hours among employed Americans have stayed relatively constant since the 1980s at around 1,800 hours.[6] This differs from the situation in most other industrialized countries, where average work hours have declined in recent decades. For example, over the period 1980 to 2006 average annual work hours declined by 18 percent in Germany, 15 percent in France, and 7 percent in the United Kingdom.

Figure 10.5 shows the average annual work hours in several OECD countries in 2012. The average work year in the United States was 1,790 hours, compared to 1,728 in Australia, 1,654 in the United Kingdom, and 1,479 in France. We used to think of hard-working Asian populations as suffering much longer work hours than Americans, and, of course, this is still true for the poorer countries in Asia. However as of 2000 Japan, a former leader in long hours, had reduced its annual work hours to below the U.S. level. The difference of 400 hours per year between American and German workers is the equivalent of having American workers put in an additional 10 full-time weeks per year!

Movements in Europe toward shorter standard working hours have often been motivated by stronger labor unions and by macroeconomic considerations, with the goal of reducing

Figure 10.5 **Average Annual Hours Worked, Select OECD Countries, 2012**

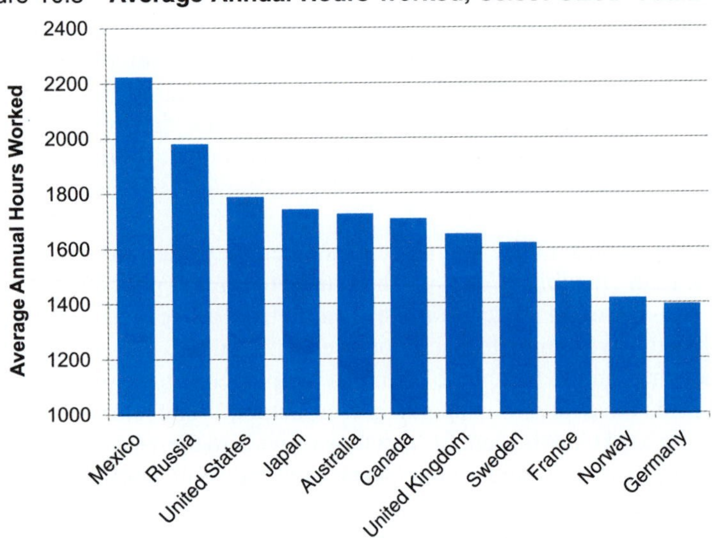

Average annual hours worked varies significantly across countries.

Source: OECD Employment Outlook 2013, Statistical Annex, Table K.

unemployment. Other goals are to encourage strong families and to reduce consumption for ecological reasons. Most European countries have legal limits on the number of hours per week an employee is allowed to work, and paid vacation time of at least one month per year is standard—even for workers who are just starting. European employers are also normally required to provide several holidays, with pay. The United States is the only industrialized country that does not require employers to provide any paid vacation days or holidays.[7]

3.3 Immigration and Labor Markets

One of the most controversial topics in discussions of labor markets and wages is the impact of immigration, particularly the immigration of workers seeking low-wage jobs. According to the traditional neoclassical labor model, an influx of unskilled workers willing to work for relatively low wages will clearly drive down equilibrium wages in markets for unskilled labor and displace some domestic workers. But as in any economic analysis, we must consider all the costs and benefits of immigration to determine its overall impact on society.

Economists generally agree that immigration, both legal and illegal, does decrease the wages of unskilled workers, mainly those without a high school diploma. But they disagree on the magnitude of this impact. According to one study, between 1980 and 2000 immigration to the United States reduced the wages of men without a high school diploma by 7 percent. However, another study found that the wage reduction was only about 1 percent, and decreased over time as education levels increased.[8]

Other research has estimated the impact of immigration to the United States differently, depending on whether workers were born in the United States.[9] The results indicate that due to immigration from 1994 to 2007 wages fell for foreign-born workers in the United States by about 5 percent but slightly *increased* for U.S.-born workers, by 0.4 percent. These findings suggest that new immigrants compete for jobs mostly with previous immigrants, rather than taking jobs away from U.S.-born workers. Meanwhile, U.S.-born workers may benefit as new immigrants increase the demand for goods and services.

Despite common media representations to the contrary, a National Research Council study found that U.S. immigrants collectively pay more in taxes than they consume in public services and benefits. According to economist Michael Clemens, the net effect on American society of immigration is "definitely positive." He notes that immigration led to a massively more prosperous economy. Everyone across the board is way, way better off now. The whole economy is the richest and most powerful in the world, and of all time, and that's the effect that quadrupling our population, largely through immigration, had.[10]

Discussion Questions

1. What evidence have you seen—in your own family, or through the media—of increasing "flexibility" in labor markets? Do you think that these changes have been beneficial, harmful, or both?
2. Do you think that all employees should receive paid vacation? What are the advantages and disadvantages of mandated vacation time?

4. Alternative Explanations for Variations in Wages

The standard model of labor markets assumes that they operate in such a way that everyone is paid exactly the amount of his or her contribution to revenues. We saw that discussions of wages in this model focus on human capital, but with some allowance for the idea (emphasized especially in business schools) that the employer also has some responsibility for getting the best out of the workers. They may do so by providing appropriate management, a motivating and efficient work environment, and complementary factors of production that will maximize the workers' productivity.

The idea of the employer's responsibility complicates the simple story because it blurs the question of which factors should receive which part of the compensation. If a new manager can get increased productivity out of the same group of workers, should the increased revenue that results all be assigned to the manager? Should it be shared with the workers?

Consider another scenario, in which one group of workers is provided with new equipment that makes them more productive, while another group stays at a lower level of productivity, using the older equipment. What should be done with the increased revenue resulting from the more productive work group? Some of it, clearly, can be used to pay for the equipment (maybe repaying a loan that was taken out to purchase it), but after that cost has been covered, then should it go to the workers in that group? Or should it be shared among both groups, on the grounds that they are all putting in the same amount of time and effort? Or should it go to the manager who had the idea to introduce the new equipment? As we continue to look at variations in wages, we see that issues of fairness and justice frequently combine with the economic issues.

4.1 Compensating Wage Differentials

Early economic thinkers put forth the idea that extra pay is required to attract workers to take jobs that are especially unappealing, compared to other work that is available for people at the same skill level. Apart from the wage, what would make one job either less or more appealing than another? A short list would probably include:

- *Working conditions.* These include physical discomfort or danger, stress, whether the job is interesting, how the worker is treated, degree of autonomy, flexibility of hours.
- *Nonwage benefits.* Some firms provide nonwage benefits such as more vacation time, educational benefits for the worker's children, meals at company cafeterias, and subsidized housing.
- *Opportunities for advancement* either within the firm or by moving to a new firm.
- *Social contribution.* Many workers will ask not only whether the job is good for themselves but also whether it contributes to society and is consistent with their beliefs.
- *Job security.* Because there are costs to being unemployed or searching for work, the likelihood that a job will continue is an important characteristic.

It is possible to find some real-world examples in which people demand, and get, a higher wage to take on jobs with less appealing characteristics. For example, because most people prefer to work days, night-shift work generally pays slightly more than day-shift work, even though the skills needed and the tasks accomplished are identical. In some cases, people accept a lower-than-necessary wage to perform an especially appealing job. The example that professors usually give is the job of being a professor: For those who like the intellectual life, it may be a very rewarding job, even though the pay is often below what professors believe that they could earn elsewhere. The idea that workers will demand higher wages for jobs with unappealing characteristics, and be willing to accept lower wages for jobs with better characteristics, is known as the theory of **compensating wage differentials**.

compensating wage differentials: the theory that, all else being equal, workers will demand higher wages for jobs with unappealing characteristics, and be willing to accept lower wages for jobs with better characteristics

At the same time, you have probably noticed that many of the least attractive jobs in a society—such as garbage collection, agricultural work, and boring and repetitive work in clothing manufacture or meat processing—are found at the lowest end of the pay scale. This is partly because they require relatively little in the way of formal qualifications. To the extent that this is true, the low wages do not violate the theory of compensating wage differentials; this theory compares only jobs of equal skill. But even within the class of jobs that require few qualifications, some unpleasant jobs pay particularly badly, and one tends to find that the workers here belong to particular groups—usually minority or female, nonunionized, and often immigrants.

For the theory of compensating differentials to operate in reality, it is necessary for workers to have good information about job conditions and risks and to be able to move freely to alternative jobs for which they are qualified. It turns out that, especially when unemployment is high, the effect of compensating differentials within jobs in the same skill class can be swamped by other factors, such as bargaining power or discrimination.

4.2 Social Norms, Bargaining Power, and Labor Unions

In any society it is usually possible to find a set of norms about how much most types of jobs *should* be paid. A norm is an expectation, usually based to some degree on experience, but sometimes lagging, as when, for example, employers find that they can get a certain type of work done more cheaply by machines than by people. According to the standard labor model, we would expect that the wage rate would fall to a level that allows people to be competitive with cheaper machines. In fact, employers are usually slow to offer lower wages, and people will resist taking the offers if made, because each side is aware that this would be contrary to existing norms.

In addition to norms, an essential aspect of any labor market is the bargaining power on each side. One obvious situation that allows a firm to bargain down wages, below what is the norm in other places, is if it is the only employer to whom a certain group of workers can look for work. This is called a condition of **monopsony**—with only one buyer but many sellers. In the 1900s, for example, some manufacturing companies (including Hershey's for chocolate and Pullman for railway cars) set up "company towns" in which they were the sole major employer. Remote mining towns and logging camps are other examples. In such cases, employers have more discretion in setting wages than if workers could easily choose between working for them and working for other employers. The workers may have to accept the company's demands as the price of keeping their jobs—unless they have the ability and the determination to leave the area.

monopsony: a situation in which there is only one buyer but many sellers. This situation occurs in a labor market in which there are many potential workers but only one employer.

In other situations, workers have market power in the sale of their services. This can happen if they have unique talents. It can also happen if a strong union represents all the workers in a particular occupation or region, so employers have to bargain with one organization representing a number of sellers. Then employers may have to accept union demands as the price of remaining in business; the only limit is that if wages exceed a certain level, an employer may find it more profitable to close its local operation and reopen in a region where labor is cheaper.

bilateral monopoly: the situation in which there is only one buyer confronting only one seller

oligopsony: the case of a relatively small number of buyers

labor unions: legally recognized organizations that collectively bargain for their members (workers) regarding wages, benefits, and working conditions

These examples—a single employer, on the one hand, and a single "star" or union federation, on the other—represent the extremes of concentration of power in the labor market. If a single employer (buyer) faces a single seller, the case can be described as a **bilateral monopoly**. In this case, results will be determined by bargaining, rather than by any kind of auction procedure. The outcome depends on the strength, cleverness, and perhaps political power of the parties and on the skills of professional mediators and litigators.

More common in labor markets are cases of **oligopsony**, in which there are a relatively small number of buyers. For example, in the U.S. music-recording industry, oligopsonistic record label *buyers* of music face uniquely talented but as yet unorganized *sellers* of musical work.

Labor unions are legally recognized organizations that collectively bargain for their members regarding wages, benefits, and working conditions. Unions first appeared in the mid-nineteenth century, but they were not legally recognized in the United States until 1935. As seen in Figure 10.6, membership in labor unions in the United States increased until the mid-1950s, when about one-quarter of the labor force was unionized. Since then, membership in unions has gradually but steadily declined. In 2012, only about 11 percent of workers in the United States belonged to a union. Labor union membership is much higher in the public sector than the private sector. About 36 percent of public sector employees belong to a union, but only 7 percent of private sector workers.

One of the reasons for the decline in union membership in recent decades has been an anti-union regulatory environment. Perhaps most famously, in 1981 President Ronald Reagan responded to an illegal strike by air traffic controllers, who were federal employees, by giving them 48 hours to return to work or face termination. More recently, since 2011 states such as Wisconsin and Indiana have passed new laws limiting the power of labor unions. Another reason for the decline of labor unions has been a shift in employment from traditional unionized occupations such as manufacturing to service occupations in which it is more difficult to unionize, such as retail and restaurant workers.

Union membership rates are higher in most other industrialized countries. For example, union membership is 18 percent in Australia, 26 percent in the United Kingdom, 29 percent

Figure 10.6 **Union Membership in the United States, 1940–2012**

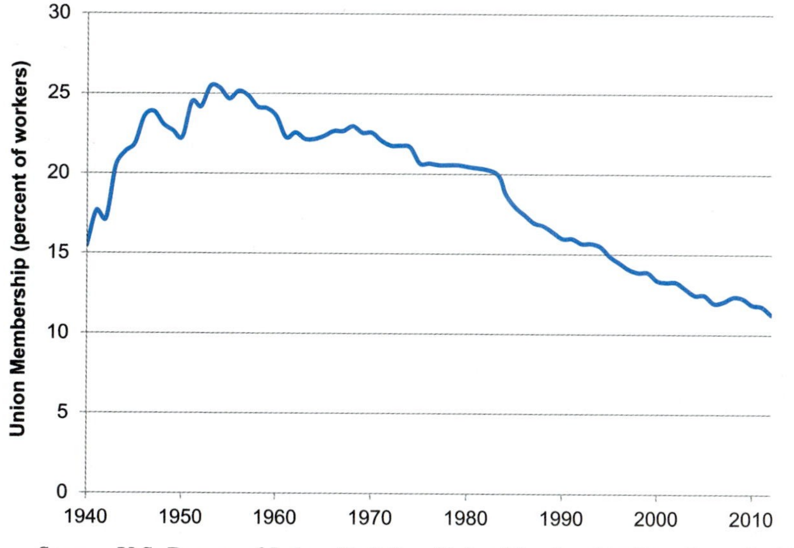

Union membership reached a peak of around 25 percent of the labor force in the 1950s, but has declined since then to only 11 percent in 2012.

Source: U.S. Bureau of Labor Statistics, Union Membership Data from the National Directory Series and Union Affiliation Data from the Current Population Survey.

in Canada, 55 percent in Norway, and 70 percent in Finland.[11] However, in most countries union membership rates have been declining in recent years.

Labor unions have generally been effective at providing good-paying jobs for their members. According to the U.S. Bureau of Labor Statistics, the average weekly earnings of unionized workers in 2012 were $943 per week, compared to average earnings of $742 for non-union workers. Union workers are also more likely to have employer-provided benefits such as health insurance and paid vacations.

Some economists see the decline in labor union membership as a positive development, arguing that unions had pushed wages to above-market levels.[12] This argument concludes that while unions were probably necessary to counter the excessive power of corporations in the first half of the twentieth century, they had become a source of market inefficiency by the end of the century.

Other economists see labor unions as a necessary way for workers to bargain on an equal footing with management. The decline of unions is widely considered to be a contributing factor in the rise of economic inequality in the United States, which we discuss in more detail in Chapter 11. Also, the benefits of unions may extend beyond those who actually belong to them.

> [Unions] affect nonunion pay and practices [by instituting] norms and practices that have become more widespread throughout the economy, thereby improving pay and working conditions for the entire workforce. . . . Many fringe benefits, such as pensions and health insurance, were first provided in the union sector and then became more commonplace. Union grievance procedures, which provide due process in the workplace, have been adapted to many nonunion workplaces. . . . [Unions] remain a source of innovation in work practices (e.g., training and worker participation) and in benefits (e.g., child care, work-time flexibility, and sick leave).[13]

4.3 EFFICIENCY WAGES AND EMPLOYEE MORALE

efficiency wage theory: the theory that an employer can motivate workers to put forth more effort by paying them somewhat more than they could get elsewhere

Economists have theorized that employers may sometimes pay wages somewhat above the market-determined level as a way of motivating and retaining workers. **Efficiency wage theory** proposes that workers will work harder and "smarter" when they know that their present employer is paying them more than they could receive elsewhere. Because these wages are above the market-clearing level, there is likely to be a queue of potential workers who would like to get the relatively high wages. This fact adds to employee motivation, because they understand that if they were to shirk and be fired there would be plenty of applicants for their position.

In a perfectly competitive labor market, the workers, knowing they could get a job elsewhere at the same wage, would be fairly indifferent about whether their current employer wants to keep them on. If an employer pays more than the going wage, however, the employee has an incentive to try to hold on to their particular job. He or she may be motivated by the fear of losing the current "good" job and having to take one that pays less. The extra effort may also be motivated by a sense of gratitude, or identification with the firm, because we tend to like people who treat us well. Thus it is theorized that efficiency wages can be profit maximizing: The cost to the firm of the extra wages may be more than made up for by the superior work effort and loyalty that they elicit. (See Box 10.2 for more on the potential benefits of efficiency wages.)

employee morale: the attitude of workers toward their work and their employer

Researchers have found that **employee morale**—the attitude of workers toward their work (and toward their employer)—can be very important in explaining productivity variations among workers who have the same skills and are using identical equipment. Morale is a subtle thing that can be analyzed in relation to many factors, including particular personalities, work organization and management, traditions within a firm or a culture, and relative pay.

Box 10.2 Good Jobs Are Good for Business

According to research by Zeynep Ton at Massachusetts Institute of Technology (MIT), providing employees with "good" jobs and paying efficiency wages can frequently be good for business, too. She notes that this idea runs counter to prevailing notions of cost minimization.

The conventional wisdom is that many companies have no choice but to offer "bad" jobs—especially retailers whose business models entail competition by offering low prices. If retailers invest more in employees, customers will have to pay more, so the assumption goes.

She studied several businesses that provide their employees with good jobs, including Trader Joe's and Costco. Trader Joe's starting salary of around $40,000 per year is about twice what many of its competitors offer. Costco's wages are about 40 percent higher than those of their main competitor, Walmart's Sam's Clubs. Both Trader Joe's and Costco also offer good opportunities for advancement. Turnover at these companies is low, and employee morale is relatively high. They are both also known for high-quality customer service.

Ton finds that, rather than hurting these firms' profits, they actually financially outperform their competitors. For example, annual revenues per square foot are $986 at Costco, but only $588 at Sam's Club. Sales rates at Trader Joe's are about three times that of a typical U.S. supermarket. She notes that companies offering well-paying jobs also institute policies that promote worker efficiency, including training workers for a variety of tasks and allowing them to make relatively small decisions on their own. Ton concludes:

> Today many retail managers believe that there is a tradeoff between investing in employees and offering the lowest prices. That is false. Retailers that persist in believing in it forgo the opportunity to improve their own performance and contribute the kind of jobs the U.S. economy urgently needs. When backed up with a specific set of operating practices, investing in employees can boost customer experience and decrease costs. Companies can compete successfully on the basis of low prices and simultaneously keep their customers and employees happy.

Source: Zeynep Ton, "Why Good Jobs Are Good for Retailers," *Harvard Business Review* (January–February 2012): 124–131.

In some cases, employers try to increase good feelings through direct means, such as by hosting parties, giving nonmonetary honors to let employees know that they are appreciated, or having "team-building" activities designed to increase cooperation among coworkers and identification with the organization.

A key factor in morale is perceived equity: whether the workers feel that they are being treated fairly by management, especially compared to expectations raised by history and by the wider culture. For example, people have expectations about the relative wages of different jobs. If the wage for one job goes up, there is strong psychological pressure for the wages of what are seen as related jobs (whether they are paid more, less, or the same) to rise enough to keep the wages in about the same relation.

4.4 Dual Labor Markets

dual labor markets: a situation in which *primary* workers enjoy high wages, opportunities for advancement, and job security, while *secondary* workers are hired with low wages, no opportunities for advancement, and no job security

The theory of **dual labor markets** also presents a different picture from the standard labor model, based on the idea that there can be different segments within a labor market. Although not all economists agree with the theory, it is useful for explaining some real-world labor outcomes.

The theory describes labor markets in which the "primary" portion of a workforce is motivated by high wages, opportunities for advancement, job security, and perhaps other favorable working conditions. Employment in the "secondary" workforce, by contrast, is more closely driven by market conditions. These workers receive generally lower wages, have minimal opportunities for advancement (even if they increase their human capital), and have low job security. Obviously, many workers in the secondary sector would prefer to work in primary sector jobs. Secondary sector workers could be assumed to be willing to accept something less than the normal wages in primary sector jobs; yet those employers do not jump on the chance to lower their wage bill.

Such labor market segmentation may take place across firms. A primary sector of large, established firms (or entrenched government agencies), which use some of their surplus revenues to pay high wages, may exist side by side with a secondary sector of smaller organizations that are more subject to competitive pressures.

Dual labor markets may also exist within a single organization. For example, a firm may employ regular workers with health and retirement benefits and, alongside them, hire temporary workers on short contracts with no benefits. In many colleges and universities, tenured faculty constitute the "primary" workforce. Then lecturers, adjuncts, and research associates, who constitute a secondary workforce, are hired as the need arises—and let go when the need falls. Such a structure allows an employer to keep a loyal core of employees *and* to avoid making new long-term commitments in times of temporary high demand. But for an individual worker, moving from the secondary to the primary labor force may be difficult indeed. Workers in the secondary sector have fewer opportunities to build up human capital and may quickly develop an "unstable"-looking work history.

An extreme type of dual labor market is what some economists call a "winner-take-all" market, such as the ones for star athletes, famous actors, and top managers. In such markets, the rewards for being in first place are vastly greater than the rewards for being a step down, even if the actual difference in talents and skills between the top tier and the next is negligible. Welfare analysis applied to such markets would find significant inefficiency. Very few people can actually get into the top tier in, for example, Olympic sports or an acting career; yet the rewards for winning are so appealing that many individuals devote huge amounts of time and effort to trying to "reach for the gold." Except in cases in which the effort to "be the best" is rewarding in itself, those who unsuccessfully devote their lives to the effort would probably have happier, more productive lives working toward different goals.

4.5 Discrimination

labor market discrimination: a condition that exists when, among similarly qualified people, some are treated disadvantageously in employment on the basis of race, gender, age, sexual preference, physical appearance, or disability

Not all social norms and customs that influence the labor market can be considered benign. **Labor market discrimination** exists when, among similarly qualified people, some are treated disadvantageously in employment on the basis of race, gender, age, sexual preference, physical appearance, or disability. Workers who belong to disfavored groups may be paid less for the same work, may be denied promotions, or may simply be excluded from higher-paying and higher-status occupations.

Historically, much labor market discrimination, particularly against African Americans and other minorities, was based on racist beliefs that certain groups were innately inferior. Some discrimination against women was similarly based on sexist notions of inferiority. However, sexual discrimination was also historically rooted in social norms that reserved better-paying jobs for men (who were assumed to be supporting families), while making women (who were assumed to have husbands to rely on) solely responsible for providing unpaid household labor and family care.

Discriminatory attitudes may be held by employers, who discriminate on the basis of their own biases, expectations, and beliefs. They may also be held by customers or coworkers. This case poses a dilemma for employers, even if they themselves are not prejudiced. For example, suppose that a law firm hires a skilled minority lawyer, but clients feel more confident being represented by European-American lawyers. The firm may find that the new lawyer attracts little business to the firm. A construction firm that hires a female forklift driver or a preschool that hires a male teacher may find that the morale of its other workers sinks, as the workers react badly to seeing someone of the "wrong" sex in "their" jobs. More insidiously, discriminatory attitudes can become self-fulfilling prophecies: Even though the minority lawyer, the female construction worker, and the male preschool teacher are all fully qualified in a technical sense, their contribution to the firm can be low, and perhaps even negative, if social norms create an environment in which their skills go unused or work group cooperation is jeopardized. Employers concerned with immediate productivity may therefore fail to hire disfavored groups, even if they themselves do not harbor discriminatory beliefs about racial differences or gender roles. Such discrimination can be eliminated only by socially coordinated—and even courageous—action.

In Figure 10.7 we compare median weekly earnings in the United States of full-time, year-round workers in various groups, using government data from 2013. *Median* earnings are at a level where half the people in the group make more and half less. We see that median earnings vary significantly by both race and gender. The median earnings of black male workers were about 77 percent of the earnings of their white male counterparts, and the median earnings of Hispanic male workers were only 67 percent of white male earnings. Disparities among female workers of different races also exist, although the differences are somewhat less pronounced. White female workers only earn 82 percent of the earnings of their white male counterparts. Sexual disparities are also evident among male and female workers of other races.

We must realize that the data in Figure 10.7 are not necessarily evidence of wage discrimination. Some variations in wages may be due to other factors such as differences in experience, education, and occupational choice (although some of these differences may also be a result of discrimination). For example, we saw earlier in the chapter that educational attainment can have a significant impact on earnings. Education levels vary by race. About 30 percent of white individuals have a bachelor's degree or higher, but only 20 percent of black and 14 percent of Hispanic individuals have at least a bachelor's degree.[14] So differences in education levels may explain the variation in wages by race, rather than discrimination. But again, differences in educational attainment may be a result of past, and current, discrimination.

Educational attainment does not vary significantly by gender in the United States. So the differences in earnings between male and female workers in Figure 10.7 cannot be attributed to differences in education. Part of the explanation for women's lower earnings is that women have traditionally had less work experience than men, on average. Men as a group have tended to work more continuously at their jobs, whereas, given social norms and, sometimes, individual preferences or requirements concerning family responsibilities, many mothers participate in the labor market less than full time when their children are young. To the extent that time on the job can contribute to productivity, this could explain some of the difference.

occupational segregation: the tendency of men and women to be employed in different occupations

Another important factor in explaining earnings differences by gender is **occupational segregation**—the tendency of men and women to be found in different kinds of jobs. For example, in the United States, jobs like bookkeeper, dental hygienist, child-care worker,

Figure 10.7 **Median Weekly Earnings, Select Groups of U.S. Workers Age 25–54, 2013**

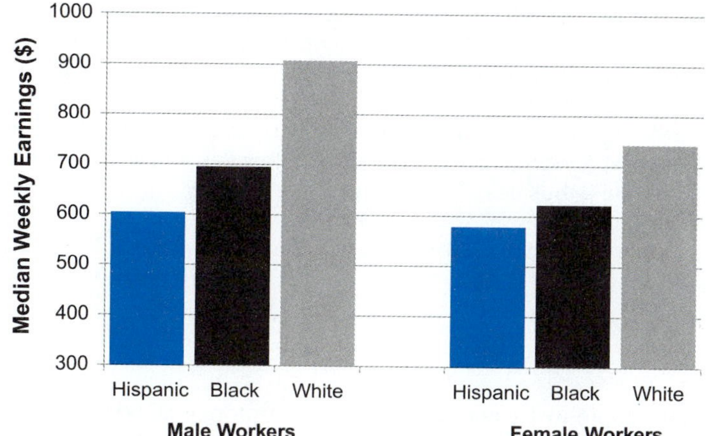

Median earnings vary based on race and gender.

Source: U.S. Bureau of Labor Statistics, "Usual Weekly Earnings of Wage and Salary Workers," Economic News Release, July 18, 2013.

registered nurse, and teacher of young children are held overwhelmingly by women. Meanwhile, men notably dominate in occupations such as construction, metal working, truck driving, and engineering. Occupational segregation could be a result of differences in preferences, or it could also reflect discrimination. For example, existing stereotypes may lead more women to become nurses while doctors are more likely to be men.

Statistical studies suggest that about a third of the differences between men's and women's pay in the United States can be associated with differences in occupational choice. Various reasons have been offered to explain why the sorts of jobs women tend to work at pay less on average. One explanation is that, because women were historically "crowded" into a narrow range of occupations, the supply curve in these job markets was artificially shifted outward, thus lowering the wage. Some have suggested that the average difficulty level of the job or the skill required might be less for "female" jobs. Others argue that differences in preferences between male and female workers could lead women to trade high wages for other beneficial job characteristics (such as flexibility in working hours). And still others argue that entrenched wage norms systematically devalue certain kinds of work (e.g., work involving emotional empathy or work with children).

Even after accounting for differences in education, experience, *and* type of job, however, over a third of the difference between men's and women's earnings in the United States remains unexplained. That is, even comparing men and women with equal qualifications who hold the same jobs, differences in pay remain. In the United States, discrimination by sex and race in hiring and wages was made illegal by Title VII of the Civil Rights Act of 1964. (This act also covered discrimination by "color," religion, and national origin. Later acts have addressed discrimination according to age and disability, and various states and localities have passed laws concerning employment treatment on the basis of sexual preference.) Enforcement, however, has proved difficult. Evidence suggests that bias, both blatant and subtle, still plays a significant role. (See Box 10.3 for more on labor discrimination.)

Box 10.3 Labor Discrimination by FedEx

In March 2012 the delivery company FedEx reached a settlement with the U.S. Department of Labor over allegations that the company discriminated against more than 20,000 job seekers. As part of the settlement, FedEx agreed to pay $3 million in back wages and offer jobs to about 2,000 rejected applicants as new openings become available. The company also agreed to revise its hiring practices to avoid future discrimination.

The allegations were brought against FedEx by the Labor Department's Office of Federal Contract Compliance Programs. The office said it found evidence of discrimination in hiring on the basis of sex, race, and national origin based on a regular audit of hiring practices. Such audits are conducted for all companies that contract with the federal government for services and goods.

Of the rejected applicants, 61 percent were female and 52 percent African American—percentages that were disproportionate to the number of applicants. As one example of discrimination, it was found that women were automatically excluded from certain positions that required the lifting of heavy objects. Hiring rates for Hispanics and Native Americans were also significantly lower than hiring rates for whites.

Labor Secretary Hilda L. Solis commented on the settlement: "When you do business with the government, we expect you to do the right thing. That includes giving all Americans an equal shot at a good job. It's about more than just the law—diversity is smart for business."

Source: Steven Greenhouse, "FedEx Agrees to Pay $3 Million to Settle Bias Case," *New York Times,* March 21, 2012.

Discussion Questions

1. "Economists assume that people just want to make as much money as possible." Is this statement correct or incorrect? Of the nonwage working conditions listed in the text, which ones are most important to you as you think about your future career?

2. Think about your current job or the last job that you held. Would you say that it is in a "primary" or "secondary" labor market? To what extent do you think that the factors discussed above—human capital, market power, compensating wage differentials, or discrimination—explain the wage and working conditions you experience(d)?

5. WAGES AND ECONOMIC POWER

In Section 4, we considered various explanations for why wages vary among different groups of employees. In this final section, we look at changes in overall wages over time, based on data for the United States. In order to understand how wages have changed over time, it is necessary to address the topic of economic power. In particular, how much of total revenues must firms pay their workers versus how much do they allocate in other ways, including to profits and taxes?

5.1 WAGE TRENDS

Figure 10.8 repeats a graph that we presented in Chapter 0, showing the time trend for real (inflation-adjusted) median weekly wages and corporate profits in the United States from 1980 to 2012. After adjusting for inflation, median weekly wages in 2012 were nearly the same level they were in 1980. Meanwhile, corporate profits, also adjusted for inflation, nearly tripled.

Historical data indicate that American workers fared much better earlier in the twentieth century. According to the U.S. Census Bureau, real average annual earnings increased by a factor of about four between 1900 and 1970.[15] During the 1970s real earnings essentially stopped increasing. *Household* income continued to increase slightly beyond the 1970s, only because more people per household entered the labor force.

Figure 10.8 suggests that corporations have effectively been able to dramatically increase their profits in the past few decades without having to pay their workers higher wages and salaries. Meanwhile, the incomes of management executives, particularly those at the very top, have soared. As we also discuss in Chapter 11, the pay of chief executive officers (CEOs) of large U.S. corporations in 1965 was 20 times the pay of an average worker. But in 2012, CEO pay stood at 273 times the pay of an average worker!

Are CEOs really worth so much more today than they were 50 years ago? It would require the use of very questionable assumptions to make the case that either the supply of CEOs has greatly diminished or the demand for them has greatly increased, relative to the supply and demand for

Figure 10.8 **Real Median Weekly Wages Versus Real Corporate Profits, United States, 1980–2012**

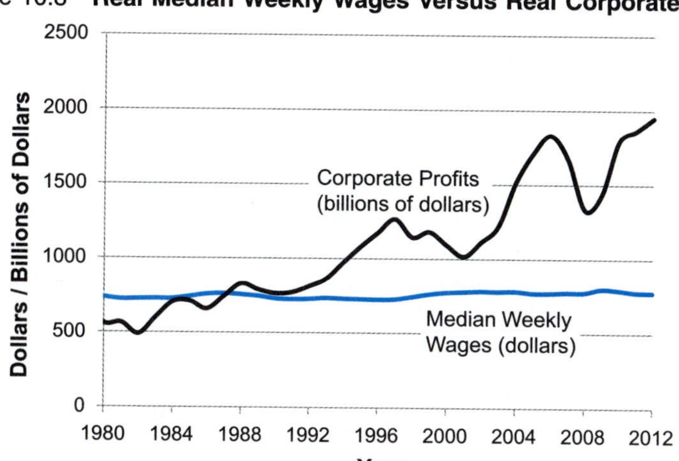

While median wages, adjusted for inflation, have stayed virtually constant since 1980, corporate profits have tripled.

Sources: U.S. Bureau of Economic Analysis, National Income and Product Accounts Tables; U.S. Bureau of Labor Statistics, Weekly and Hourly Earnings Data from the Current Population Survey.

workers. However, American culture has evolved along with the rise in executive pay so that the lack of protest has suggested that people accepted these relative valuations for different kinds of work, at least until the emergence of the Occupy Wall Street movement in 2011.

These trends indicate a shift in economic power, away from workers and toward corporate profits and executive compensation. American workers have lost economic power as a result of various factors, including globalization, technological change, and the decline of labor unions (which we also discuss further in Chapter 11). (For a real-world illustration of the relative fortunes of workers, CEOs, and corporations, see Box 10.4.)

Box 10.4 Wage Cuts and Record Profits

Caterpillar, maker of bulldozers, backhoes, and other construction machinery, is widely seen as one of the most aggressive companies in seeking steep concessions from employees during labor negotiations. In 2012 the company pressed its long-term workers to accept a six-year wage freeze, while also instituting a two-tier wage system, so that new hires are put on a significantly lower wage scale than those who had been there longer. Wages for those employed at Caterpillar for at least seven years average $26 per hour. However, new employees are typically given an initial wage of only $13 per hour.

The company has stated that such concessions are necessary so that they can remain competitive. Rusty L. Dunn, a Caterpillar spokesman, said the company's stance is that wages should reflect market conditions, and that such adjustments would help Caterpillar "keep competitive when times are bad." But Caterpillar reported profits in 2012 of $5.7 billion. If Caterpillar's 2012 profits had been divided among all employee salaries, each worker would have earned an *additional* $45,000. If even a third of the profit had gone to additional employee salaries, they could each have received an additional $15,000 that year.

Meanwhile the compensation of Caterpillar's CEO, Douglas Oberhelman, increased by 113 percent between 2010 and 2012; his total compensation in 2012 was $22.4 million. Only $6 million of this was in direct salary, with the rest in stock options and other incentives. (A large part of the compensation of top management in large modern corporations comes in the form of gifts of stock and/or stock options. The latter are often, in effect, permissions to buy the company's stock at a relatively low price, and sell it at a higher price.)

Timothy O'Brien, president of an Illinois union that represents Caterpillar workers, notes, "A company that earned [record profits in 2011 and 2012] should be willing to help the workers who made those profits for them. Caterpillar believes in helping the very rich, but what they're doing would help eliminate the middle class."

Sources: Steven. Greenhouse, "At Caterpillar, A Test Case for U.S. Unions; Despite a Record Profit, Heavy Machinery Giant Is in Cost-Cutting Vanguard," *International Herald Tribune,* July 24, 2012; "Compensation for Cat's Oberhelman Jumps 60%," *Chicago Tribune,* April 11, 2012; Executive Profile, Caterpillar, Inc., Bloomberg Businessweek, 2013.

5.2 An Alternative Framework: Worker Cooperatives

Much of the discussion in this chapter has assumed a working arrangement in which the goals of the "employee" do not necessarily align with those of the "employer." For example, we discussed how the relative bargaining power of employees and employers can influence wages and how "flexibility" can mean very different things to employees and employers. A typical for-profit corporation is owned by those who hold shares of the company's stock, in proportion to the amount of stock that they own. Top executives answer directly to shareholders and manage subordinate workers with the goal of maximizing profits. From the perspective of shareholders and top executives, maintaining (or increasing) worker productivity while lowering wage costs is desirable, as it leads to higher profits. From the perspective of workers, however, increases in wages are seen as desirable, and workers may have little concern for the profitability of the company.

worker cooperatives: a labor arrangement in which the owners of an enterprise are the workers themselves

Worker cooperatives, an alternative labor framework, seek to reduce or eliminate the potential for labor conflicts by specifying that the owners of the enterprise are the workers themselves. Worker cooperatives are sometimes viewed as a "third way" of labor organization, in contrast to standard for-profit companies and government-run enterprises. The organizational structure of worker cooperatives can vary, but in a typical cooperative every worker is also an owner. Worker cooperatives normally do seek to make a profit, and any profits are distributed among the worker-owners (in addition to receiving wages or a salary). Some workers may hold more ownership shares than others and thus receive a greater share of profits, say perhaps because of seniority, but in many cooperatives all workers have equal ownership shares. Important decisions are generally voted upon by all worker-owners, including decisions about wages, working hours, and benefits. Despite any differences in ownership shares, decisions are typically made on a "one person, one vote" basis.

Worker cooperatives arose as an alternative labor framework during the Industrial Revolution. Cooperatives are found throughout the world, the most famous being the Mondragón Cooperative Corporation in the Basque region of Spain, founded in 1956. Mondragón, which consists of more than 250 separate cooperatives with a total of about 85,000 worker-owners, is the seventh-largest company in Spain. Some of the differences between Mondragón and a typical capitalist company were described as follows:

> One of the co-operatively and democratically adopted rules governing [Mondragón] limits top-paid worker-members to earning *6.5 times* the lowest-paid workers. Nothing more dramatically demonstrates the differences distinguishing this from the capitalist alternative organization of enterprises. . . . [I]ts pay equity rules can and do contribute to a larger society with far greater income and wealth equality than is typical in societies that have chosen capitalist organizations of enterprises. Over 43 percent of members are women, whose equal powers with male members likewise influence gender relations in society different from capitalist enterprises.[16]

Italy has about 8,000 worker cooperatives, and France has nearly 2,000. In India, the India Coffee House is a cooperative restaurant chain with nearly 400 locations. In the United States, the U.S. Federation of Worker Cooperatives, whose membership comprises more than 100 cooperatives, works to promote cooperative formation, advocacy, and development. One example of a successful worker cooperative in the United States is Evergreen Cooperatives in Cleveland, OH, based in a low-income neighborhood and providing living wage jobs. The cooperative's main business is an environmentally conscious laundry facility that provides service to local hospitals.

Based solely on economic performance, such as worker productivity, the scientific evidence suggests that worker cooperatives can perform at least as well as traditional capitalist companies.[17] According to a 2011 paper that studied Mondragón, cooperative member-owners tend to be better paid than their peers in comparable firms, with greater opportunities for involvement and training. Although the cooperative labor framework is a "viable and possibly even superior alternative" to the traditional capitalist firm, it is not a "universal panacea" either. For example, job satisfaction was lower in cooperatives than in traditional firms, perhaps a reflection of higher worker expectations. Obviously, estimating the overall impact of worker cooperatives on well-being requires a multifaceted analysis in which all factors cannot be easily quantified.

5.3 How Are Revenues Allocated?

Workers are one group that lays a claim on the revenues of firms, while their executives are another claimant. We now briefly consider other groups that also expect to share in the revenues of corporations and how allocations among these groups affect wages.

Government

The claims that governments make on businesses most often come in the form of taxes, though they may also at times levy fines on firms that are found to be disobeying a law. This money allows governments to supply much of the institutional and physical infrastructure necessary to operate businesses and to try to keep their activities somewhat in line with the social good. Businesses generally dislike paying taxes and complying with regulations and reporting requirements. However, without tax revenue governments cannot maintain services on which businesses depend, such as emergency call centers, firefighters, and police. Businesses as well as citizens depend on these services, as well as on roads, communications infrastructure, and the legal and other infrastructure that supports commerce. Moreover, all of society depends on government to monitor and regulate businesses to ensure safety in food, pharmaceuticals, and other products as well as a degree of honesty in claims made about the goods and services that they provide.

Suppliers of Physical Capital

Suppliers of physical capital include individuals or firms that supply both natural resources and manufactured capital. The price at which natural resources are sold depends to some extent on the cost of extraction, but also on economic power. For example, owners of oil wells have sometimes colluded to hold the selling price of this valuable commodity well above the cost of extraction and transportation. Owners of mines that produce gems or precious metals similarly have a long tradition of "fixing" prices, in part by strictly controlling the amount that is produced in a given time frame.

In other cases, scarcity is a critical factor in the price of the resource, as may be seen in the case of renewable resources such as some wood species or nonrenewable ones such as bauxite, oil, or copper. Some analysts predict that increasing scarcity of certain important natural resources will drive up the cost of production of many goods. This prediction, if true, is especially important in relation to wages; the same wage will be able to purchase less of the products that have become more expensive. On the other hand, "technological optimists" predict that human ingenuity will stay ahead of this trend, so that the prices of most natural resources will not affect the relative prices of wages and goods.

Prices of manufactured capital are more likely to be set according to our familiar supply-and-demand models. Their supply curve reflects the costs of producing the equipment (including what the producers had to pay for the natural resources used in their intermediate products). This interacts with the quantities demanded and the prices offered in the market.

Suppliers of Financial Capital

From the point of view of the firm, these can be divided into those whose claim can be considered part of "the necessary cost of doing business" and those that are the "residual claimants." When a firm takes out a loan, the payments of interest and principal are considered part of the necessary cost of doing business. They are taken out of revenues, along with taxes and the cost of purchasing inputs (including labor services), *before* anything remains that can be called a profit.

Investors, as distinct from lenders, are generally considered residual claimants; their return comes out of profits—what is left over after the firm has covered all necessary costs to sustain its activity. There is no clear law that states who else is a residual claimant, but top management often receive part of the profits, in one form or another.

A Useful Image

To summarize, the necessary costs of doing business include payments to factors of production (labor, financial capital, and material inputs) as well as taxes. The commonest uses for corporate profits include paying dividends to shareholders, investing in buildings and equipment, purchasing other companies, and buying stock shares from shareholders, to be held by the company. (The last of these actions increases the company's power when it is confronted by proposals from outside shareholders, on subjects such as environmental protection, employee rights, or obligations of the board of directors.)

One image that you can take away from this discussion is of a very fancy kind of sprinkler hose, which is filled by the revenues generated by the sale of a firm's products. As you look along the hose, you can see places where it sprinkles out appropriate payments for the necessary inputs to production—wages, salaries, payments for physical inputs, and taxes or fees. Finally, you come to the end of the hose; what is left—whether it be a trickle or a fountain—is considered profit.

The salient word in the preceding paragraph is "appropriate"—what is the appropriate amount of revenue to allocate to each factor of production? The analysis in the first half of this chapter gives us the simple, neoclassical answer: Every factor should be compensated according to its marginal revenue product—the amount contributed to the market value of the product by the last unit of that factor. And the assumption of perfect competition (which we discuss in more detail in Chapter 17) further insists that firms must set wages exactly equal to MRP_L, just as the returns to capital must be set exactly equal to the marginal revenue product of capital.

Box 10.4 suggests that diverting all or part of the company's profits could have prevented the wage freeze at Caterpillar, or even significantly increased worker compensation. Is this realistic? It is, in principle, possible. For comparison, consider for a moment another factor of production: raw materials. Supposing that the cost of some critical raw material were to rise, so that at least in the short run, before it could find any alternative, Caterpillar would be forced to pay a great deal more for these materials. This would be expected to cut immediately into profits. For a comparable thought-experiment, imagine that a very strong union is formed, and it is joined by all of the types of workers that Caterpillar requires. Imagine, additionally, that this union is able to make a credible threat of a strike, unless Caterpillar raises workers' salaries by an amount that cuts its profits by a third. Again, in the short run, the necessary cost of doing business would rise. Unless the firm decided to simply shut down, it would have a smaller profit left over at the end of its metaphorical sprinkler hose.

The second of these imaginary scenarios is not about to happen for at least two reasons: Unions have greatly dwindled in the United States, to the point that it is hardly imaginable that they would have this kind of power; and globalization allows even a maker of heavy, expensive-to-transport machinery to threaten to move to another country where labor is cheaper. The world has shifted in such a way that it is hard for workers to make credible threats and relatively easy for employers to do so. The relative loss of worker power is one of the explanations for the growing inequality that we discuss in Chapter 11.

Discussion Questions

1. Do you think that the relative wages of average workers and top executives reflect their respective marginal revenue product? Do you think that the relative wages of average workers and top executives should be regulated by the government? What, if any, specific regulations do you propose?
2. Do you believe that worker cooperatives can become a widespread alternative to traditional firms? Do you know of any worker cooperatives in your area?

REVIEW QUESTIONS

1. In the traditional neoclassical model, how does a firm decide on the quantity of labor to hire?
2. What are some of the opportunity costs of paid employment?
3. Why might the individual labor supply curve bend backward?
4. How is human capital important in explaining wage variations?
5. What is signaling theory in relation to labor markets?
6. In what types of labor markets might labor supply be relatively wage elastic? In what types of markets might labor supply be relatively wage inelastic?
7. In what types of labor markets might labor demand be relatively wage elastic? In what types of markets might labor demand be relatively wage inelastic?
8. How can we use a supply-and-demand graph to illustrate the operation of a labor market?
9. What is employment flexibility from the perspective of workers? From the perspective of employers?
10. How have annual work hours changed in recent decades in the United States and other industrialized countries?
11. What are compensating wage differentials?

12. What is monopsony?
13. What is oligopsony?
14. What is efficiency wage theory?
15. What are dual labor markets?
16. How can we identify labor discrimination?
17. What is occupational segregation?
18. What has been the trend in median wages in the United States in the past few decades? How does this compare with the trend in corporate profits?
19. What are worker cooperatives, and how do they differ from traditional firms in terms of labor organization?
20. In addition to workers and management executives, who are some other claimants on business revenues?

EXERCISES

1. Reviewing Chapters 4 and 5 if necessary, illustrate on a labor market graph the following examples that were described in the text.
   a. A relatively elastic supply curve for wait staff.
   b. A virtually "fixed" supply of aerospace engineers, in the short run.
   c. The effect on the supply of lawyers of the reduction of barriers to women's participation in the practice of the law.
   d. The effect on the market for wait staff of a rise in the wage of salesclerks.
2. Draw labor market graphs illustrating the following examples that were mentioned in the text.
   a. A labor demand curve, when very good substitutes for labor in the production process exist.
   b. The effect of a drop in demand for the organization's product.
   c. The effect of a rise in the price of other inputs that have been used as substitutes for labor.
3. Suppose that you observe that the wages for accountants in your town have gone up and that the number of accountants employed has also gone up. Which one of the following conditions could explain this? Illustrate your answer with a graph and explain in a brief paragraph.
   a. Businesses are failing, reducing the need for accountants.
   b. Many accountants are leaving the field in order to train to become financial analysts instead.
   c. A rash of business scandals has increased the demand for auditing services performed by accountants.
   d. The local university has just graduated an unusually large group of accountants.
4. The U.S. Bureau of Labor Statistics keeps track of the average wages and number of workers involved in various occupations over time and also makes projections about what jobs may show the most growth in the future. Using data available at the bureau's Web site, www.bls.gov, try to look up information on an occupation that interests you. How does it pay, compared to other jobs? Is demand projected to rise in the future?
5. Match each concept in Column A with an example in Column B.

Column A	Column B
a. An alternative to wage employment	1. "Insurance adjustor" jobs are traditionally given to men while "insurance representative" jobs go to women
b. The income effect on individual labor supply	2. Isabella cuts back her hours at her job after she gets a raise
c. A cause of a shift in the demand for professors	3. Many professors reach retirement age
d. A cause of a shift in the supply of professors	4. Acme Corp. hires only college graduates for sales jobs, but doesn't care about their majors
e. Using education as a "signal"	5. Acme Corp. pays above prevailing market wages to motivate and retain its employees
f. Labor market monopoly	6. Westinghouse is the major employer in the county
g. Labor market monopsony	7. Marshall is the only person who knows how to run his company's antiquated database
h. Compensating wage differential	8. Household production
i. Occupational segregation	9. Resident assistants get a rent-free apartment but little pay
j. Efficiency wages	10. A rising college-student-age population

Notes

1. Jennifer Cheeseman Day and Eric C. Newburger, "The Big Payoff: Educational Attainment and Synthetic Estimates of Work-Life Earnings," U.S. Census Bureau, Current Population Reports, P23–210, 2002.

2. Jody Heymann, *Children's Chances: How Countries Can Move from Surviving to Thriving* (Cambridge: Harvard University Press, 2013).

3. Rebecca Ray, Janet C. Gornick, and John Schmitt, "Parental Leave Policies in 21 Countries," Center for Economic and Policy Research, Washington, DC, 2009.

4. Ibid., pp. 1–2.

5. Lonnie Golden and Tesfayi Gebreselassie, "Overemployment Mismatches: The Preference for Fewer Work Hours," *BLS Monthly Labor Review* (April 2007): 18–27.

6. Susan E. Fleck, "International Comparisons of Hours Worked: An Assessment of the Statistics," *BLS Monthly Labor Review* (May 2009): 3–31.

7. Rebecca Ray, Milla Sanes, and John Schmitt, "No-Vacation Nation Revisited," Center for Economic and Policy Research, Washington, DC, 2013.

8. Nell Henderson, "Effect of Immigration on Jobs, Wages Is Difficult for Economists to Nail Down," *Washington Post,* April 15, 2006.

9. Heidi Shierholz, "Immigration and Wages: Methodological Advancements Confirm Modest Gains for Native Workers," Economic Policy Institute, EPI Briefing Paper 255, Washington, DC, 2010.

10. Dylan Matthews,"Immigration's Effect on Wages: 'Definitely Positive, Without Any Doubt Whatsoever,'" *Washington Post,* April 17, 2013.

11. OECD Employment Database, "Trends in Union Density, 1960–2011," http://stats.oecd.org/Index.aspx?DataSetCode=UN_DEN.

12. See, for example, Michael Watchner, "The Rise and Decline of Unions," *Washington Post,* July 18, 2007.

13. Lawrence Mishel, "Unions, Inequality, and Faltering Middle-Class Wages," Economic Policy Institute, Policy Brief 342, Washington, DC, 2012.

14. Educational attainment data from the *Statistical Abstract of the United States 2012,* table 231.

15. U.S. Census Bureau, *Bicentennial Edition: Historical Statistics of the United States, Colonial Times to 1970,* Series D 722–727, 1976; U.S. Census Bureau, *Statistical Abstract of the United States 1982–1983*, table 667, 1982.

16. Richard Wolff, "Yes, There Is an Alternative to Capitalism: Mondragon Shows the Way," *The Guardian,* June 24, 2012.

17. Chris Doucouliagos, "Worker Participation and Productivity in Labor-Managed and Participatory Capitalist Firms: A Meta-Analysis," *Industrial and Labor Relations Review* 49(1) (1995): 58–77.

Appendix: A Formal Model of a Firm's Hiring Decision

marginal physical product of labor (MPP_L): the amount that a unit of additional labor contributes to the physical product of a firm

Suppose that a firm produces disposable razors. Holding all other inputs fixed, the relationship between the number of workers (the "quantity of labor") hired and the number of razors that can be produced in a day is given in the first two columns of the table on the following page. From these first two columns, the **marginal physical product** of each additional worker **(of labor)** (MPP_L) can be computed. For example, one worker can produce 5 razors, but adding an additional worker makes possible the production of 12 razors, so the *marginal* physical product of the second worker is 7 razors. Note that the marginal physical product of labor first rises and then falls.

We further assume that the firm sells razors in a competitive market and that the price received per razor is constant at \$3. Hence the marginal revenue product of labor (MRP_L), the monetary value of the additional physical production, is always just \$3 × MPP_L. We assume that the firm buys labor in a perfectly competitive labor market, at a constant wage of \$12. Hence the marginal factor cost of labor (MFC_L) is constant at \$12.

Quantity of labor	Quantity of razors	MPP_L	MRP_L	MFC_L
1	5	5	15	12
2	12	7	21	12
3	18	6	18	12
4	23	5	15	12
5	27	4	12	12
6	30	3	9	12
7	32	2	6	12
8	33	1	3	12

The MRP_L and MFC_L curves are graphed in Figure 10.9. The MRP_L curve has an initial hump, because the MPP_L initially increases and then declines. For all workers up to the fifth worker, hiring the additional worker adds more to revenues than to costs. The profit-maximizing firm should stop hiring workers when $MRP_L = MFC_L$, at an employment level of five workers.

Figure 10.9 **Marginal Revenue Product of Labor and Marginal Factor Cost of Labor**

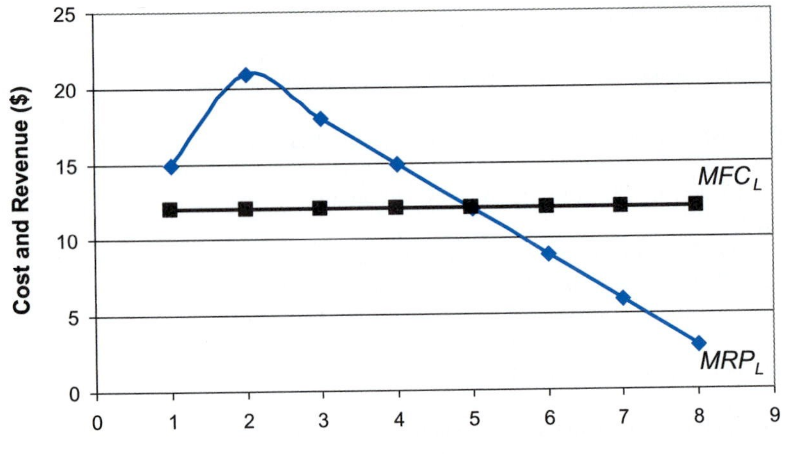

The optimal amount of labor for a firm to hire occurs where the marginal revenue product equals the marginal factor cost.

PART IV

Essential Topics for Contemporary Economics

11 Economic and Social Inequality

Which do you think is a more important dimension of human well-being: the quantity of goods and services that an economy produces or the ultimate distribution of those goods and services within society? Many economists believe that only the first is a meaningful goal—the second should just take care of itself through market allocation. Or if markets result in an unacceptable distribution, some economists suggest that politicians can always step in and make whatever redistributions are necessary. But what are the consequences of a distribution of income and assets that is highly unequal? How does economic policy relate to inequality? Because of growing inequality, both in the United States and abroad, it is an issue to which many more economists than in the past have been paying attention.

1. Defining and Measuring Inequality

We can think of social equality as a "goal" in economics, just as efficiency is an important goal. But there is an important difference. Few would argue that we could be "too" efficient. As long as efficiency is carefully defined and is not pursued in ways that are destructive to other goals, the more efficient we are, the better. The same does not hold for equality. Whether we are talking about income, opportunities, or education, it is possible to be "too equal." Few desire a society in which everyone earns the same exact income or where everyone is a carpenter or a Ph.D. Our goal should be to strive to be a society that is neither "too equal" nor "too unequal."

How do we know whether we are successful? This is a more complex issue than dealing with efficiency because, as we will see, it is impossible to prescribe a degree of inequality that works ideally for everyone. Compounding the problem is that inequality, unlike efficiency, presents a problem that has both an ethical *and* an economic dimension.

1.1 Inequality of What?

When the subject of inequality is raised, most people think of income or wealth inequality. Because this is an economics textbook, we also emphasize these, especially inequality of income. But it is important to recognize that inequality is a broader concept that extends beyond the realm of money.

Let us consider a few examples. Public health is an area in which vast inequality exists. Preventable or treatable diseases in numerous tropical countries (such as malaria, measles, and tuberculosis) cause average life expectancy to be significantly shorter than in the United States or in other rich countries. There is also significant health inequality within many countries. Increasingly, access to adequate medical care can make a difference in terms of whether one can obtain effective treatment for a particular ailment. This is generally not much of a problem in advanced industrialized countries that have a "single payer" system, but in countries that lack universal health insurance one's health condition can be dictated by whether one can reliably see a doctor, which often depends on whether one has adequate insurance coverage.

There is also a considerable imbalance in education, both nationally and internationally. The majority of adults in the United States lack a college education, which today is regarded as almost indispensable to economic success (as we saw last chapter). However, most Americans do have a high school degree. Although this is true in other rich countries, it is not the case in most others. Primary and secondary education are not a priority in many parts of the world, where poverty and hunger are widespread—not to mention violence or civil war, as well as gender discrimination, which makes it especially hard for girls to go to school in some countries. Even where families want to send their children to school, national governments often lack the funds to support basic education. Without a proper education, many millions are inadequately prepared for competing in today's global economy.

Related to both health and education is what Nobel laureate Amartya Sen has famously referred to as "capabilities." By his reckoning, money is only one dimension—albeit an important one—of an individual's "capability" to function in his or her economic environment. To Sen, what matters most is that people possess the necessary tools—for example, money, health, education, friends, social connections—to provide them with realistic economic *choices*. As Sen has pointed out, there is considerable inequality of capabilities in the world, not just in the poor countries.

Inequality is also manifest in certain environmental outcomes. Proponents of "environmental justice," generally studying the United States, point out that polluting industries and toxic waste disposal sites tend to be located disproportionately near poor and minority communities. This effect is even more pronounced in countries like Ecuador and Brazil. Tribal residents in Ecuador confront widespread pollution from petroleum extraction in the remote areas where they live as well as extensive harm to their local habitat. Native Brazilians suffer from the environmental toxicity of the gold-mining process as well as from the alteration of their landscape resulting from deforestation. These effects are generally associated with inequality—not of income but of land ownership or property rights. People who reside in these areas often lack the legal power to keep the miners or timber companies out.

One also sees considerable inequality when confronting the issue of climate change. Countries with sizable portions of land near sea level—for example, Egypt and Bangladesh—are likely to be affected by climate change in the coming decades more adversely than, say, the mountain kingdom of Bhutan. Some of the most northern countries, like Canada and Russia, may actually benefit, at least in the short term, from climate change, in that warmer global temperatures would lengthen the agricultural season and potentially allow these countries to produce crops that they formerly could not. In addition to these specific effects, however, a critical fact about climate change, as well as other environmental damage, is that the rich can protect themselves much better than the poor can.

1.2 Measuring Inequality

To illustrate one approach for measuring inequality, we begin by looking at the distribution of household income in the United States in 2011 (Table 11.1). The data are arranged in order of income, and the share of the total income "pie" that accrues to each twentieth percentile (or quintile) is in the second column. To understand what this table means, imagine dividing up U.S. households into five equal-sized groups, with the poorest households all in one group, the next-poorest in the next group, and so on. The last group contains the richest quintile among all households. The poorest quintile, with household incomes below $20,262, received only 3.2 percent of all the household income in the country. The richest quintile, those with incomes of $101,582 or more, received 51.5 percent—in other words, more than half—of all the income received in the United States.

Table 11.1 **Distribution of U.S. Household Income in 2011**

Group of households	Share of aggregate income (%)	Income range
Poorest fifth	3.2	Below $20,262
Second fifth	8.4	$20,262 – $38,519
Middle fifth	14.3	$38,520 – $62,433
Fourth fifth	23.0	$62,434 – $101,581
Richest fifth	51.1	Above $101,582
Richest 5%	22.3	Above $176,000

Source: U.S. Census Bureau, Table A-2 of "Income, Poverty, and Health Insurance Coverage in the United States," 2011.

Suppose that we further separate the richest group into two groups: those with income of less than $176,000 and those with income higher than this. The group with household income above $176,000 constitutes the richest 5 percent, or one-twentieth, of the population. As we can see, this richest 5 percent earned 22.3 percent of national income, close to the amount earned by all of those in the fourth quintile. (See also figures illustrating similar points in Chapter 0.)

Based on these data, we can now construct many different measures of inequality. For instance, we could calculate the ratio of the income share of the richest fifth to that of the poorest fifth of the population; in this case, we obtain 51.1/3.2 = 16.0—that is, a household in the richest quintile has about 16 times the income, on average, of a household in the poorest quintile. We can then see how this ratio has changed over time to track changes in inequality. For example, in 1979 this ratio was only about 7, indicating an increase in inequality between the richest and poorest fifth of the population.

Lorenz curve: a line used to portray an income distribution, drawn on a graph with percentiles of households on the horizontal axis and the cumulative percentage of income on the vertical axis

However, a simple ratio is somewhat arbitrary, focusing on some parts of the income distribution while ignoring others. Economists frequently prefer to use a more comprehensive measure that reflects the shape of the entire income distribution. This measure first involves creating a graph of the income distribution, referred to as a **Lorenz curve**—named after Max Lorenz, the statistician who first developed the technique. A Lorenz curve for household income in the United States is shown in Figure 11.1. In this graph, the horizontal axis represents households, lined up from left to right in order of increasing income. The vertical axis measures the *cumulative* percentage of all income received by households up to a given income level.

Figure 11.1 **Lorenz Curve for the United States**

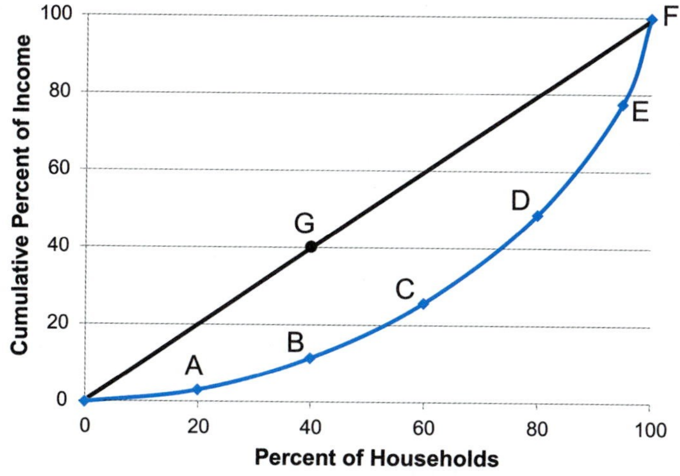

A Lorenz curve shows the cumulative amount of all income obtained by different percentiles of households, ordered from those with the lowest incomes to those with the highest incomes.

Source: U.S. Census Bureau, Historical Income Tables, Households, Table H-2.

We use the data in Table 11.1 to draw the Lorenz curve in Figure 11.1. Point A represents the fact that the poorest 20 percent of households received 3.2 percent of all income. To obtain Point B, we need to calculate the cumulative percent of income received by the bottom 40 percent of households. So we add the income received by the bottom 20 percent to the income received by the next 20 percent. Thus the cumulative percent of income received by the bottom 40 percent is 3.2 + 8.4 = 11.6 percent of total income. For point C, we need to calculate the cumulative percent of income received by the bottom 60 percent of households, which is 3.2 + 8.4 + 14.3 = 25.9 percent of total income. Similarly, point D shows that the income share of the bottom 80 percent is 48.9 percent of all income. Finally, point E shows that the bottom 95 percent received 77.7 percent of all income (everyone except the top 5 percent). The Lorenz curve must start at the origin, at the lower left corner of the graph (because 0 percent of households have 0 percent of the total income) and must end at point F in the upper right corner (because 100 percent of households must have 100 percent of the total income).

The Lorenz curve provides information about the degree of income inequality in a country. Note that the 45-degree line in Figure 11.1 represents a situation of absolute equality. If every household had the same exact income, then, for example, the "bottom" 40 percent of households would receive 40 percent of all income. This is shown by point G in Figure 11.1. Imagine the other extreme—a situation in which one household received all the income in a country. In this case, the Lorenz curve would be a flat line along the horizontal axis at a value of zero until the very end, where it would suddenly shoot up to 100 percent of income (at point F).

Of course these two extremes do not occur in reality, but they indicate that the closer a country's Lorenz curve is to the 45-degree line, the more equal its income distribution. This is illustrated in Figure 11.2, which shows the Lorenz curve for three countries: Sweden, the United States, and Bolivia. Income is distributed relatively equally in Sweden; its Lorenz curve is closer to the 45-degree line of absolute equality than the U.S. Lorenz curve. Bolivia is an example of a country which has greater income inequality than the U.S.; its Lorenz curve bows further from the line of absolute equality.

The more the Lorenz curve bows away from the line of absolute equality, the greater is the extent of inequality in the income distribution. This observation led a statistician by the name of Corrado Gini to introduce a numerical measure of inequality that came to be known

Figure 11.2 **Lorenz Curves for Sweden, the United States, and Bolivia**

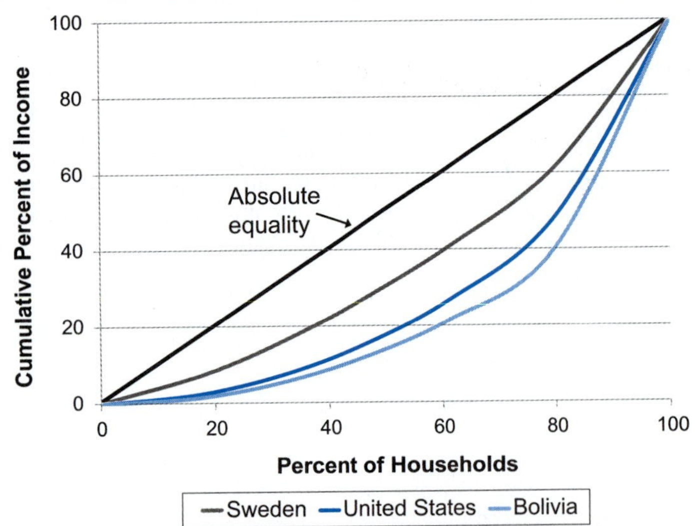

The closer the Lorenz curve is to the line of absolute equality, the lower the degree of economic inequality.

Sources: Statistics Sweden, online database, Disposable Income in Deciles 2011–2014; U.S. Census Bureau, Historical Income Tables, Households, Table H-2; World Bank, World Development Indicators database.

Figure 11.3 **The Gini Coefficient: A/(A+B)**

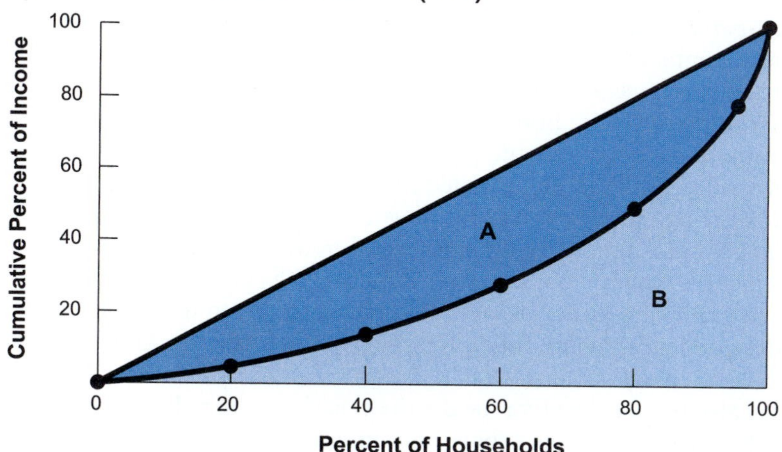

The larger area A is, the greater the deviation from absolute equality, and thus the higher the Gini coefficient.

Gini ratio (or Gini coefficient): a measure of inequality, based on the Lorenz curve, that goes from 0 (absolute equality) up to 1 (absolute inequality). Greater inequality shows up as a larger area between the Lorenz curve and the diagonal line of absolute equality.

means-tested programs: programs designed to transfer income to recipients based on need

as the **Gini ratio** (or "Gini coefficient"), which is defined as the ratio of the area between the Lorenz curve and the diagonal line of equality to the total area under the diagonal line.

Referring to areas A and B in Figure 11.3, the Gini ratio is A/(A+B). Clearly, the Gini ratio can vary from 0 for absolute equality (since in such a case area A would equal zero as the Lorenz curve overlaps the line of absolute equality) to 1 for absolute inequality (where area B would equal zero). According to U.S. Census Bureau calculations, the Gini ratio for U.S. household income in 2011 was 0.477. We will present international comparisons of inequality, along with data trends, later in the chapter.

You might be wondering about some details of the measure of income we are using. Higher-income people, after all, pay more taxes, so they really do not have control over all the money income that they have been counted as receiving. Meanwhile, poor people may qualify for **means-tested programs**, including noncash programs such as food stamps, or for subsidized housing and medical care, and arguably the value of these programs should be included as part of income.

On the basis of considerations like these, the U.S. Census Bureau has experimented with at least 15 different definitions of income. One definition, for example, is meant to approximate what the distribution of income would be if—hypothetically—the impact of government activity were excluded. For this definition, the Census Bureau starts with the measure of pretax money income that we have been working with until now and subtracts government cash transfers (such as welfare payments). Then it adds the value of health insurance fringe benefits paid by businesses for their (often middle-class or higher) employees and the value of net capital gains (usually earned by the relatively wealthy). Under this definition, the Gini ratio, not surprisingly, rises, showing greater inequality. The share of the bottom fifth drops considerably, while the share of the top fifth rises.

Adjusting that measure of income for the effects of the tax system causes some change at the top, but little at the bottom. When the Census Bureau further adds in the effects of both cash government transfer programs and noncash programs (such as food stamps, Medicare, and Medicaid), the distribution becomes somewhat less unequal. Government tax and transfer policies—and especially the transfer side—have significant effects on the U.S. household income distribution. Even with the most thorough accounting for aid to low-income households from transfer payments, however, the income of the top fifth of the population is still roughly ten times that of the bottom fifth.

How much importance should we place on income inequality and the Gini index? Many important goods and services are, after all, obtained without the use of cash income. Many families prefer to produce at least some services (such as child care and cooking) for themselves. In addition, many of the things that we enjoy—such as pleasant parks, safe roads, or clean air—add to our well-being without requiring payments out of our cash income (although some of these things are financed through taxes). If we were to look at the distribution of *well-being* rather than just the distribution of income, we would need to take account of these nonincome sources of important goods and services. Some of these goods may contribute to lessening inequality—for example, everyone, rich or poor, can enjoy a public park or use a public library. Evidence suggests, however, that at least in some cases the distribution of such nonpurchased goods may accentuate, rather than lessen, measures of inequality. For example, as noted earlier, proponents of "environmental justice" point out that polluting industries and toxic waste disposal sites tend to be located disproportionately near poor and minority communities. Moreover, considerable evidence indicates that families that are money-poor are also time-poor; they cannot devote the time that they would wish to child care and cooking, often being forced to use the television as the babysitter and to depend on fast foods for meals—with serious known health consequences.

Gini coefficients may also be calculated for the distribution of wealth rather than income. This distribution, which depends on what people own in assets, tends to be much more unequal than income distribution. Most people own relatively little wealth, relying mainly on labor income and perhaps government or family transfers to support their expenditures. It is even possible to have *negative* net wealth. This happens when the value of a person's debts (e.g., for a car, house, or credit cards) is higher than the value of her assets. For people in the middle class, the equity that they have in their house is often their most significant asset. By contrast, those who *do* own substantial wealth are generally in a position to put much of it into assets that increase in value over time or yield a flow of income and dividends—which can in turn be invested in the acquisition of still more assets.

The distribution of wealth is, however, less frequently and less systematically recorded than the distribution of income—in part because wealth can be hard to measure. Much wealth is held in the form of unrealized **capital gains**. A household realizes—turns into actual dollars—capital gains if it sells an appreciated asset, such as shares in a company, land, or antiques, for more than the price at which it purchased the asset. An asset can appreciate in value for a long time before it is actually sold. No one, however, will know exactly how much such an asset has really gained or lost in value until the owner actually *does* sell it, thus "realizing" the capital gain. Another reason that it is harder to get information on wealth is that although the government requires people to report their annual *income* from wages and many investments for tax purposes, it does not require everyone to regularly and comprehensively report their asset holdings. Finally, wealth consists not only of financial assets but also commodities, paintings, real estate, and the like. Such disparate forms of wealth make estimating aggregate wealth statistics reliably much more cumbersome.

capital gains: increase in the value of an asset at the time it is sold compared to the price at which it was originally purchased by the same owner

These caveats notwithstanding, estimates of the U.S. Gini ratio for the distribution of wealth are in the neighborhood of 0.8, and those for most other countries are also considerably higher than the corresponding income Gini ratios. Should we be concerned about such a global concentration of wealth?

To be sure, ownership of wealth is usually a very good thing, because it can help households maintain their accustomed consumption patterns, if income temporarily becomes low. But contemplating such vast wealth inequality brings us back to the question of opportunity. Are there sufficient compensatory assets available to those with little or even negative wealth? It is critically important not to ignore wealth inequality because it bears heavily on the much more advertised income inequality. And the effect is cumulative: To the extent that income is unequally distributed, it will further concentrate wealth.

Perhaps most important, great wealth confers its owners with both economic and political power. When the ownership of wealth is highly uneven, the power to direct the operations of businesses and to influence government policy through campaign contributions and the like may become concentrated in the hands of relatively few. We return to this point below.

Discussion Questions

1. What is the difference between inequality of incomes and inequality of "capabilities"? How are the two related? Which one do you think deserves more attention from policymakers?
2. What do you think is the minimal amount of annual income that an individual, or a small family, would need to live in *your* community? (Think about the rent or mortgage on a one- or two-bedroom residence, etc.) What does this probably mean about where the average level of income in your community fits into the U.S. income distribution shown in Table 11.1?

2. Data and Trends

We now have a quantitative method to use for comparing inequality, both across different populations and over time. Yet it is important to fully understand that, although Gini coefficients help us measure the extent of inequality that exists, they do *not* help us decide whether the inequality is acceptable or excessive. This will always be a judgment call, and different people will render different judgments.

2.1 Inequality in the United States

No one disputes that income inequality in the United States has generally increased in recent decades. We can see this in Figure 11.4, which shows the Gini coefficient in the U.S. from 1967 to 2010, based on data from the U.S. Census Bureau. The Gini coefficient reached a record low of 0.386 in 1968. After that, the Gini coefficient increased in 31 of the next 42 years. In 2010 the Gini coefficient reached a record high of 0.469.

While comparable government data are not available for the years prior to 1968, academic researchers have estimated longer trends in income inequality by focusing on the share of total income going to the top income groups. Figure 11.5 shows the income share of the top 10 percent and the top 1 percent from 1917 to 2012. After the Great Depression, the share of income going to the top income groups generally declined, suggesting that income inequality was decreasing. The share of income going to the top 10 percent remained low at around 32 percent from 1950 until the early 1970s. The share of income going to the top 1 percent reached a low of less than 8 percent in the

Figure 11.4 **Gini Coefficient in the United States, 1967–2010**

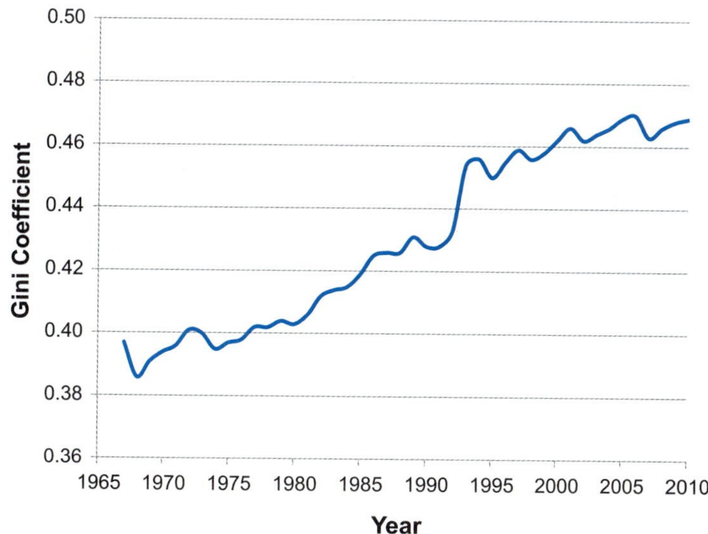

Since the late 1960s income inequality in the United States has tended to increase.

Source: U.S. Census Bureau, Historical Income Tables, Households, Table H-2.

Figure 11.5 **Income Share of the Top 10 Percent and Top 1 Percent in the United States, 1917–2012**

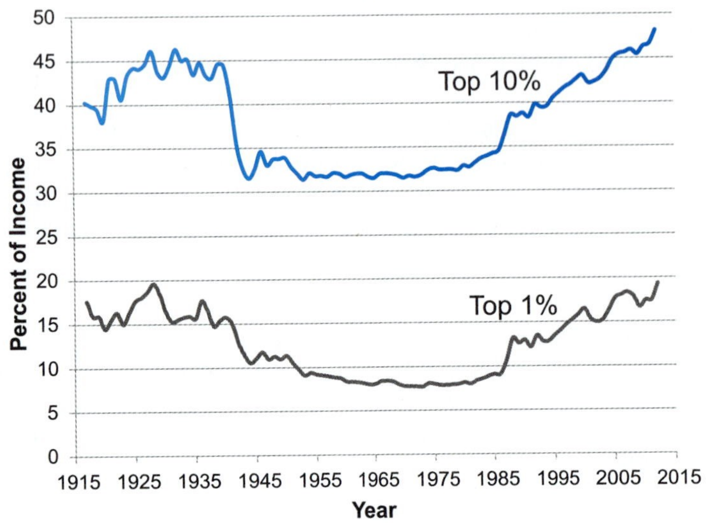

The share of income going the highest income groups generally decreased from the Great Depression until the early 1970s. Since then, the share of income going to the top groups has increased, reaching levels even higher than those prior to the Great Depression.

Source: Emmanuel Saez, income inequality database updated to 2012, University of California, Berkeley, http://elsa.berkeley.edu/~saez/.

early 1970s. Since the early 1970s, the income share going to these top groups has increased, surpassing the high levels that occurred prior to the Great Depression.

As mentioned earlier, inequality of wealth tends to be even higher than inequality of income. This is illustrated in Figure 11.6, which shows the distribution of wealth in the United States in 2009. We see that the top 1 percent own more than a third of all wealth in the U.S., and the top fifth (the 80th percentile and above) own 87 percent of wealth. Collectively, the bottom 80 percent own only 13 percent of all wealth. Analysis of wealth data suggests that wealth inequality has also increased in recent decades. For more on wealth inequality, see Box 11.1.

We can look at inequality from several other perspectives. For example, inequality is clearly evident across race in the United States, as shown in Table 11.2. Asian households have the highest median annual income, about $69,000, while black households have the lowest at only $33,000. Married couples, with the potential for two adult workers, have higher incomes than households with just one adult male or female. Among households with just one adult, male

Figure 11.6 **The Distribution of Wealth in the United States, 2009**

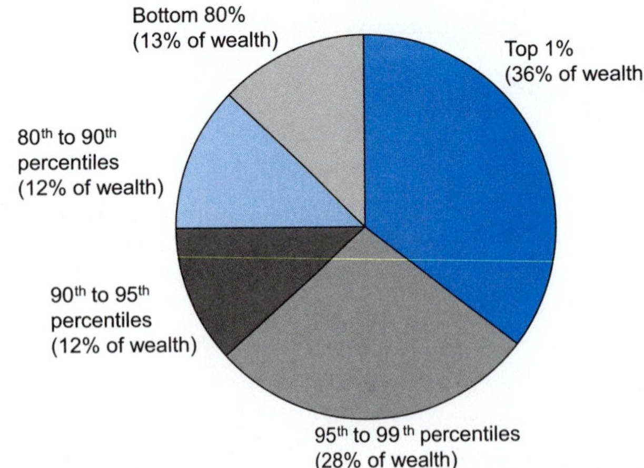

The top 1 percent owns over one-third of wealth in the United States and the top 20 percent own 87 percent of wealth. The bottom 80 percent own only 13 percent of wealth.

Source: Sylvia A. Allegretto, "The State of Working America's Wealth, 2011," Economic Policy Institute, EPI Briefing Paper #292, March 23, 2011.

Box 11.1 Wealth Inequality in the United States

Figure 11.6 presented data on the actual distribution of wealth in the United States. However, political debates about inequality are often based upon perceptions rather than facts. In a 2011 paper, researchers Michael Norton and Dan Ariely surveyed people regarding their perceptions of wealth inequality in the U.S. Specifically, respondents were asked to estimate what percentage of total wealth was owned by each wealth quintile. Further, they also asked people to construct their ideal distribution of wealth, again assigning a percentage of total wealth to each quintile.

The results are presented in Figure 11.7, along with the actual distribution of wealth in the U.S. We see, for example, that the top quintile actually own 84 percent of all wealth in the U.S. according to the paper. (Note that the "actual" distribution of wealth in Figure 11.7 differs from the distribution given in Figure 11.6—the two figures rely upon different data sources and apply to different years.) However, respondents estimated that the top quintile only owned 59 percent of all wealth. But most respondents thought that this estimated concentration of wealth was excessive. On average, their ideal wealth distribution allocated only 32 percent of all wealth to the top quintile.

Looking at the other end of the wealth spectrum, the bottom quintile actually owns only 0.1 percent of wealth in the U.S. Respondents estimated that the bottom quintile owns about 3 percent of wealth. According to their ideal distribution, the bottom quintile should own about 11 percent of all wealth.

The results clearly illustrate the difference between reality, perceptions, and subjective preferences. Norton and Ariely draw two primary messages from the results:

> First, a large nationally representative sample of Americans seems to prefer to live in a country more like Sweden than like the United States. Americans also construct ideal distributions that are far more equal than they estimated the United States to be—estimates which themselves were far more equal than the actual level of inequality. Second, there was much more consensus than disagreement across groups from different sides of the political spectrum about this desire for a more equal distribution of wealth, suggesting that Americans may possess a commonly held ''normative'' standard for the distribution of wealth despite the many disagreements about policies that affect that distribution, such as taxation and welfare.

Source: Michael I. Norton and Dan Ariely, "Building a Better America—One Wealth Quintile at a Time," *Perspectives on Psychological Science* 6(1) (2011): 9–12.

Figure 11.7 **Actual, Estimated, and Ideal Distribution of Wealth in the United States**

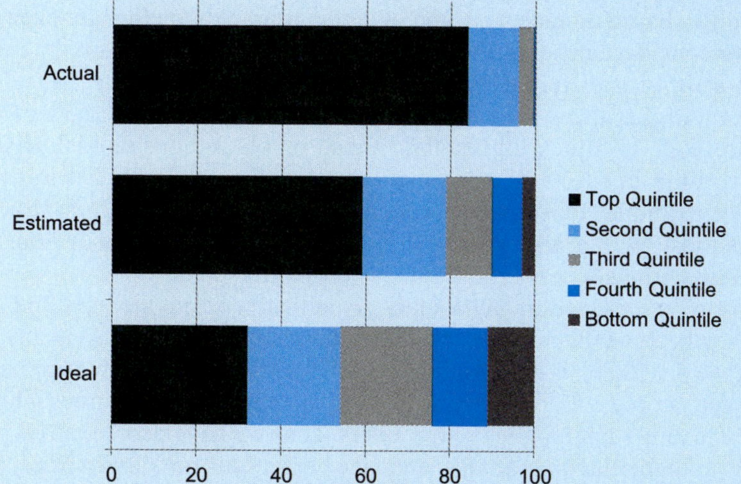

According to a 2011 paper by Michael Norton and Dan Ariely, Americans tend to significantly underestimate the degree of wealth inequality in the United States. The ideal distribution of wealth, according to most Americans, is even more equal than their incorrect estimates.

Source: Michael I. Norton and Dan Ariely, "Building a Better America—One Wealth Quintile at a Time," *Perspectives on Psychological Science* 6(1) (2011): 9–12.

Table 11.2 **Median Household Income in the United States by Select Characteristics, 2012**

Group	Median Household Income
All households	$51,017
Households by Race	
Asian	$68,636
Black	$33,321
Hispanic	$39,005
White	$53,706
By Type of Household	
Married Couples	$75,694
Female householder, no husband	$34,002
Male householder, no wife	$48,634
By Age of Householder	
Age 15 – 24	$30,604
Age 25 – 34	$51,381
Age 35 – 44	$63,629
Age 45 – 54	$66,411
Age 55 – 64	$58,626
Age 65 and older	$33,848
By Residence Area	
Metropolitan area	$52,988
Outside of metropolitan area	$41,198

Source: Carmen DeNavas-Walt, Bernadette D. Proctor, and Jessica C. Smith, "Income, Poverty, and Health Insurance Coverage in the United States: 2012," U.S. Census Bureau, Current Population Report P60-245, September 2013.

households have higher incomes than female households. Median incomes increase with age up until age 55, and then decline as people retire. Finally, households in metropolitan areas have higher incomes than those outside of metropolitan areas.

Economic inequalities based on race, age, and other demographic factors are even more pronounced when we consider household wealth. Table 11.3 presents data on the median value of household assets for different types of households. While white households' incomes are 61 percent higher than the incomes of black households, the assets of white households are more than 17 times higher than those of black households! Hispanic households also have little in assets. We see that education has a significant impact on household assets. For example, those with a college degree have about three times the household wealth as those with a high school diploma. The median value of household assets also tends to rise with age.

Some inequality is to be expected in any society given that people's incomes and assets tend to increase as they become older and more established in their careers. So at any point in time in a country, we are likely to have younger people with relatively low incomes and few assets, middle-aged people with higher incomes and more assets, and retirees who tend to have relatively low incomes but relatively high assets. Thus we have people moving from lower income groups to higher income groups, and vice versa. This possibility of people or households to change their economic status, for better or worse, is called **economic mobility**. For a given level of economic inequality, we may be more tolerant if economic mobility is higher because it implies that people have the opportunity to improve their economic condition.

economic mobility: the potential for an individual or household to change its economic conditions (for better or worse) over time

A common way to measure economic mobility is to track the frequency with which individuals or households move into different income groups. A study by economists at Harvard University

Table 11.3 **Median Value of Household Assets in the United States by Select Characteristics, 2011**

Group	Median Household Assets
All households	$68,828
By Race of Householder	
White	$110,500
Asian	$89,339
Hispanic	$7,683
Black	$6,314
By Type of Household	
Married Couples	$139,032
Female householder, no husband	$22,184
Male householder, no wife	$27,310
By Age of Householder	
Less than 35 years	$6,676
Age 35–44	$35,000
Age 45–54	$84,542
Age 55–64	$143,964
Age 65 and over	$170,516
By Education Level of Householder	
No high school diploma	$9,800
High school diploma	$43,945
Some college, no degree	$49,082
Associate's degree	$56,512
Bachelor's degree	$147,148
Graduate or professional degree	$240,750

Source: U.S. Census Bureau, Survey of Income and Program Participation, 2008 Panel, Wave 10, Table 1, Release date March 21, 2013.

and the University of California at Berkeley found that, overall, the chance that a child in the United States from the bottom fifth (with household income below $25,000) could get into the top fifth by age 30 was about 8 percent.[1] They found that economic mobility in the U.S. varied considerably across metropolitan areas. The chances of moving from the lower fifth to the highest were as high as 11 percent in Salt Lake City and San Francisco, and as low as 4 percent in Atlanta and 5 percent in Detroit.

2.2 Cross-Country Comparisons

The Gini ratio for the United States is higher than that of all other major industrialized countries, signifying that the country has a higher degree of income inequality. Figure 11.8 shows the range in income inequality across different countries. Sweden, with a Gini ratio of 0.23, has the lowest degree of income inequality of any country. Income inequality is also low in Germany and Canada. While many of the countries with the lowest income inequality are also high-income countries, inequality is also low in Hungary, Belarus, Ethiopia, and Pakistan, among others.

Patterns across geographic regions are fairly consistent. Latin American countries, for example, tend to have relatively high degrees of inequality. In addition to Brazil and Mexico, Guatemala has a Gini coefficient of 0.55, Honduras 0.58, and Haiti and Colombia 0.59. Asian countries, in contrast, appear, by this measure, to be more economically equal. Most countries in the Asian continent have Gini coefficients between 0.3 and 0.4. Sub-Saharan Africa appears to have the greatest variability, ranging from 0.30 (Ethiopia) to 0.63 (South Africa and Lesotho).

Figure 11.8 **Income Gini Coefficients for Select Countries**

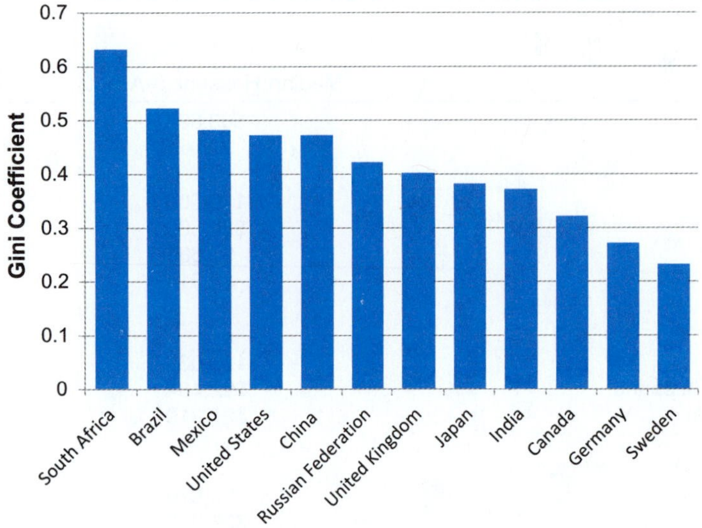

Country-level Gini coefficients range from a low of 0.23 (Sweden) to a high of 0.63 (South Africa). Among developed nations, the United States has the most inequality.

Source: United States Central Intelligence Agency, *CIA World Factbook* online database.

In the related area of mobility, a variety of studies have shown that economic mobility in the United States is lower than in a number of other rich countries, including Japan, Canada, Australia, France, Germany, and the Nordic countries.[2] A 2008 paper surveyed international research on economic mobility, looking specifically at how children's incomes fare relative to their parents' incomes. The results indicated that:

> a growing number of economic studies have found that the United States stands out as having less, not more, inter-generational mobility than do Canada and several European countries. American children are more likely than other children to end up in the same place on the income distribution as their parents. Moreover, there is emerging evidence that mobility is particularly low for Americans born into families at the bottom of the earnings or income distribution.[3]

We have seen that from around 1930 until the late 1960s inequality diminished in the United States. The relatively recent intensification of inequality is not limited to the United States. According to a recent OECD study, income inequality has been increasing over the past few decades in most, if not all, rich countries. Inequality may not be automatically self-perpetuating, but there is some evidence of a consistent pattern of increased inequality in rich countries. To what can this be attributed? The next section explores some possible causes and consequences.

Discussion Questions

1. Were your parents better off economically than their parents? Do you believe that you will be better off than your parents? Do you think that this is true of most of your friends?
2. Do you think the fact that the United States is more unequal than other rich countries is an advantage or disadvantage? Why?

3. Causes and Consequences of Inequality

The question of why inequality has been increasing in the United States and many other countries is a source of much debate. We now consider several of the explanations proposed by economists, recognizing that rising inequality is something that cannot be attributed to a single cause. We then turn to a discussion of the consequences of a high degree of inequality in a society.

3.1 CAUSES

One point on which economists appear to agree is that some of the increase in inequality is due to changing demographics. As people worldwide live longer on average, the proportion of the population that is elderly increases. This trend, coupled with an increase in the rate of single parenthood, has tended to drive down incomes at the low end. People too old to work and people in single-parent households (where paid work and caring activities compete for a limited resource—the adult's time) often lack economic resources. About 23 percent of U.S. children live in poor families. (A household is defined as poor if its income falls below a poverty threshold based on its family size. In 2013, the poverty threshold for a family of four was $23,550.) Meanwhile, the increasing number of women entering the labor force has helped boost the income of married-couple households at the top of the income range.

labor income: payment to workers, including wages, salaries, and fringe benefits

capital income: rents, profits, and interest

rent: payments for the direct or indirect use of any capital assets

Another factor that helps explain growing inequality is that the wage "share" of the income "pie" has diminished over time. Wages and salaries make up the majority of **labor income**, which includes the implicit value of fringe benefits. **Capital income** includes rents, profits, and interest. "**Rent**," as economists use the term, refers not just to rent for housing but to payments for the use of any capital asset, such as machinery or an e-mail list. (See Box 11.2 on "rent-seeking.") In general, higher-income households receive a larger portion of their total income from capital income.

The shrinking of wages as a share of total income over time suggests that inequality is intensifying because it means that the 60 or 70 percent of the population with the lowest incomes are falling behind, relative to those who count on profits and rent—as interest payments and dividends—as major sources of income. Generally, a declining wage share over time suggests that wage growth, if present, is not keeping up with overall economic growth. This has, in fact, been the case over the past four decades or so, and is partially responsible for rising inequality. Since 1970, the share of total income that comes from wages in the United States has fallen from about 72 percent to less than 64 percent.

Similar trends have been observed in most of the other rich countries. The critical question is *why* this has been happening, and on this there is no universal agreement. In what follows, we look at some of the more likely causes.

The first likely factor in increased inequality is globalization and the growth in trade that it produces. Because markets are increasingly interconnected, domestic producers of certain goods encounter greater competition from imports from other countries. In many instances,

BOX 11.2 RENT SEEKING AND INEQUALITY

"Rent seeking" refers to the act of expending time or other resources in the hope of obtaining value that already exists somewhere else instead of using those resources to produce new economic value. In other words, a rent seeker will try to provoke redistribution of existing wealth in his or her favor instead of generating new wealth.

One example of rent seeking is when lobbyists try to convince government officials to adopt policies favorable to their interests, at the expense of other economic actors. This is considered rent seeking because, even though such lobbying can produce benefits for the lobbyists' employers, it does not generate new economic value. One could even make the case that it subtracts from value creation in an "opportunity cost" sense: by diverting potentially useful or productive resources for the purpose of some zero-sum gain.

The effect of rent seeking can be to exacerbate inequality, because those who are already rich and powerful are most effective at directing government support and subsidies to themselves. The economist Mancur Olson has proposed a depressing scenario in which countries tend to grow less competitive and efficient over time, as organized interest and lobby groups gain in importance, and are increasingly able to influence government.

Clearly, the motivation of groups such as the Occupy Wall Street movement and other critics of inequality and the dominance of the top "1 percent," is based on a perception that much of the wealth of those at the very top is based on rent-seeking activities rather than genuine economic productivity.

the price of such imports is significantly lower than that for the domestically produced good, compelling the producer either to lower prices (and therefore wages, too) or simply leave the business. Competition from imports has indeed eliminated many industrial jobs—in textiles and automobiles, for example—that formerly fell in the middle of the U.S. wage distribution. The replacement of such jobs by lower-income service and retail jobs has probably contributed to the increase in inequality, although economists generally do not consider it a major factor, as it may explain only 10 percent of the increase.

It is worth noting that, while job opportunities and wages in certain sectors are decreasing in countries like the United States, they are increasing in many poor countries that previously lacked opportunities to produce for a global market. In this sense, freer trade may *reduce* inequality *across* countries.

The second, perhaps more important, factor has been the advent of rapid technological change. New technologies related to computers and biotechnology have become more important, increasing the income of skilled workers who understand and use the new techniques and equipment, while leaving behind the less-skilled workers who remain in low-technology occupations. The income of the skilled workers has risen relative to those of the less skilled simply because their skills are relatively scarce. Recalling our discussion of the labor market in Chapter 10, labor resembles other commodities in the sense that the more scarce it is (i.e., there is less supply), the higher its "price." The less-skilled workers are, in contrast, relatively abundant, depressing their average wage or "price."

Technological change has also, especially in the long run, led machines to replace human workers for certain types of jobs (especially in services), making workers at the "low-skill" end of the spectrum especially abundant. It has contributed substantially to what we defined in Chapter 10 as labor market segmentation, which is a polarization of the labor market into groups of "high-skill" jobs at one end and many more "low-skill" jobs at the other end. A defining feature of a segmented labor market is its inflexibility; it is extremely difficult, if not impossible, to move from one segment to the other.

The third likely cause of rising income inequality is the progressive weakening of labor unions, especially in the United States. Government policy has become decidedly less supportive of unions and low-wage workers, and the rate of participation in them has declined markedly, as discussed in Chapter 10. Recall that labor union membership in the United States declined from a peak of around 25 percent in the 1950s to only about 11 percent today.

The final reason proposed to explain rising inequality is that policies have been instituted that, intentionally or unintentionally, have led to higher inequality. There have, for example, been a series of tax cuts—starting in the 1980s under President Ronald Reagan, but continuing during George W. Bush's presidency—that primarily reduced the tax burden on the wealthiest groups. (The Bush tax cuts were partially reversed by the Obama administration in January 2013.) The primary consequence for the distribution of income has been this: For the past few decades, rather than providing tax revenue to the government, the richest households have increasingly been *lending it money at interest* through government bonds (the loans were necessary as a result of the shortfall in tax revenue), thus allowing the wealthy continued access to their capital. Economists such as Paul Krugman maintain that tax policy over the past four decades has indeed increased income inequality by enabling far greater access to capital for the wealthiest Americans than for lower-income ones.

Another policy change has been reduction in welfare expenditures, starting in the 1990s, with the phasing out of programs such as Aid for Families with Dependent Children (AFDC). The federal minimum wage ($7.25 as of 2013) has fallen significantly behind inflation, lowering the purchasing power of the lowest-income workers. In addition to directly reducing such subsidies to the poor, the diminished generosity of the welfare state also adversely affects workers' bargaining power, hence their wage. With less government benefits on which to rely, employees threatened with unemployment are more likely to accept a wage cut. Researchers have found a direct relationship between a reduction of the welfare state in the European

Union—where, because of its greater initial size, cuts have been more dramatic—and the increase in inequality that has resulted in most EU countries.

As noted earlier, many of these policy changes have a political as well as economic component. A major problem associated with increased inequality is that those who gain a greater share of total wealth are able to translate it into greater political power. This plays out through the U.S. system of campaign finance, in which candidates for political office can accept disproportionate donations from wealthy individuals or large corporations with an interest in, say, keeping taxes low for the rich or minimizing regulations on the financial sector. Well-endowed individuals or companies may also hire representatives (or lobbyists) to seek private interviews with influential politicians, in hopes of ensuring favorable legislation. This is another example of "rent-seeking" activity that does not produce any economic value but, rather, redistributes it, accentuating other trends towards greater income inequality.

3.2 CONSEQUENCES

Recall from Chapter 9 that consumers' marginal utility of successive units of a good tends to decrease. Economic evidence suggests the same is true of income. For example, an additional $1,000 in income when one is making $20,000 per year tends to provide greater marginal utility than when one is making $50,000 per year. While some economists avoid making interpersonal comparisons of utility, a reasonable implication of this principle is that overall welfare may be lower in a society with a high degree of inequality as opposed to a society with a low degree of inequality, assuming the same amount of total income. So from a social welfare perspective too much inequality may be economically inefficient as well as unfair.

Many researchers have studied the relationship between economic status and other measures of well-being. Intuitively, it seems reasonable that those with low incomes and little assets tend to have reduced access to quality education, adequate health care, and other resources. And the facts do support this view, see Box 11.3.

BOX 11.3 INEQUALITY IN THE UNITED STATES

While most attention regarding inequality in the United States has focused on income, inequality is evident in many other ways. Despite being one of the richest countries in the world, the United States has the highest level of infant and maternal mortality among developed nations. Life expectancy in the U.S. is one of the lowest among developed nations. Richer households in the U.S. generally have access to adequate, if not excellent, health care. Thus the main reason that the U.S. ranks so poorly according to these measures is that those at the bottom fare so poorly.

The same is true with education. Richer households can afford to send their children to high-quality schools, while most students from disadvantaged families attend school with lower-quality resources. Consider that the gap between American students at the top and those at the middle, according to standardized tests, is equivalent to the gap between the average scores of the U.S. and Azerbaijan.

While inequality in the U.S. has been increasing for decades, so far the policy response has been negligible. Proposals by President Barack Obama to reduce inequality include raising the minimum wage, improving infrastructure, and universal preschool for 4-year-olds. However, in a highly partisan environment, such proposals seem unlikely to meet approval in Congress.

> You would think Americans must be tiring of their lack of progress. The disposable income of families in the middle of the income distribution shrank by 4 percent between 2000 and 2010, according to data compiled by the O.E.C.D. In Australia, by contrast, it increased 40 percent. Middle-income Germans, Dutch, French, Danes, Norwegians and even Mexicans gained more ground.
>
> And indeed Americans are tiring of it. Over half—52 percent—say that the government should redistribute wealth by taxing the rich more, according to a Gallup poll in April, the highest share since Gallup first asked the question in 1998.

Source: Eduardo Porter, "Inequality in America: The Data Is Sobering," *New York Times*, August 1, 2013.

But going even further, we consider whether a high degree of inequality imposes broad costs on society—impacts that not only affect the poor, but all members of society. One of the most studied issues is the relationship between inequality and health. Imagine two countries with the exact same average income levels. However, one of these countries has a high degree of economic inequality, while the other has low inequality. Are health outcomes better in the country with lower inequality?

In their 2009 book *The Spirit Level,* Richard Wilkinson and Kate Pickett (both epidemiologists) argue that higher inequality, ceteris paribus, is indeed associated with reduced health. They reason that economic and social inequality creates stress and anxiety, which increases one's susceptibility to disease and also leads to destructive behaviors like substance abuse. They support their position by presenting data showing that rich countries with greater inequality tend to have lower life expectancy, higher rates of infant mortality, and higher rates of mental illness. In addition to the relationship between inequality and health, Wilkinson and Pickett also find that higher inequality is associated with various social problems, including homicide rates, teenage pregnancy, and school dropout rates.

The findings of Wilkinson and Pickett that many social problems are a result of inequality are controversial. For example, a 2010 article in the *Wall Street Journal* criticized *The Spirit Level* for presenting selective data.[4] Also, a 2003 journal article by health economist Angus Deaton concluded that "it is not true that income inequality itself is a major determinant of public health."[5]

There seems to be greater acceptance among economists that excessive inequality can lead to reduced economic growth. One reason is that economic reforms may be more difficult to institute in unequal countries with concentrated political power. Also, if economic mobility is low, those at the bottom have little incentive to invest in their own productivity, and thus overall growth suffers. A 2011 study published by the International Monetary Fund found that greater equality is associated with longer periods of sustained economic growth.[6] The paper concludes that "attention to inequality can bring significant longer-run benefits for growth."

In the 2001 book *Bowling Alone: The Collapse and Revival of American Community,* Robert Putnam argues that an inverse link exists between income inequality and social cohesion. He notes that greater equality causes people to trust one another more, and trust is a cornerstone of social welfare. Putnam has traced the relationship through the twentieth century and found that during periods when the United States had a more equal income distribution (such as the 1950s), there was much more community engagement in general, and that there has been much less over the past few decades as inequality has become more pronounced.

Finally, inequality tends to perpetuate itself. We often prefer to believe that success in our society is based on individual merit, but in fact the family situation in which we start out tends to matter a great deal. Economic mobility is more difficult in a more unequal society because the change in income needed to move to a higher income quintile becomes larger. Again, this maintains existing concentrations of political power, which reduces the possibility for broad-based economic and social reforms. Policies tend to be instituted which benefit a powerful minority, while the preferences of the majority are not heard.

Discussion Questions

1. If you could change a single one of the "causes" of inequality described above, on which would you choose to focus? Why?
2. People are often ashamed of coming from a relatively poor family, even if it is poor only relative to its immediate neighbors (and might appear wealthy to someone in another community, or another country). Why do you suppose this is? Do you think this psychological factor is relevant to the perpetuation of inequality in society?

4. Responding to Inequality

As we mentioned at the beginning of the chapter, there is no consensus regarding the "right" amount of inequality in a society. So before we consider what policies might be instituted to respond to inequality, we first consider various philosophical perspectives on the topic of inequality.

4.1 Philosophical Perspectives on Inequality

Unlike the goal of efficiency, which has a specific technical meaning that we have discussed in earlier chapters, there is no single standard of equity or fairness. Yet to many people, there is something disturbing about the current degree of income and wealth inequality in the United States. What are some standards that can be used to judge the kind and degree of equity in a society?

Several philosophical standards of equity have been suggested; we will focus on five standards here:

1. Equality of outcomes
2. Equality of opportunities
3. Equal rewards for equal contributions
4. Equal rights
5. The basic needs approach

Equality of outcomes is an easily stated—but rarely adopted—standard of equity which says that everyone should achieve the same level of well-being. The idea of everyone being equally happy has a certain appeal, but no country has ever tried to translate this into practice by precisely equalizing economic outcomes such as wealth or income. In all existing economies, at least some degree of inequality of outcomes is thought to serve as an important incentive for people to develop skills, to work, and to innovate.

Although complete equality is not a feasible goal, governments frequently seek to reduce the *inequality* of outcomes, and this has historically been done through redistribution. The most common example is the practice of taxing those who earn high incomes and redistributing some of the tax revenue to the most needy groups. The effectiveness of such a policy in reducing inequality has, however, varied considerably over time and across regions.

Equality of opportunity is another popular standard of equity, based on the thinking of, among others, the philosopher John Rawls. According to this principle, all individuals should have the same opportunity to create a life and a livelihood for themselves that will allow them to acquire the things that they value. After they have been given the same opportunities, people who are ambitious and want to work hard to acquire wealth should be able to do so. People who choose not to take as much advantage of these opportunities can accept a lesser economic standing. This standard has the appeal of rewarding effort, while putting everyone on a presumed "level playing field."

Unfortunately, this is much simpler and appealing in theory than it is in practice. Although a society can try to *approach* this standard through programs like public education and antidiscrimination laws, it is a hard standard to apply in any precise sense. If opportunity is to be equal in each generation, then no material wealth should be passed along by inheritance. It is not equitable for some children to be able to start out in safe neighborhoods with parents who encourage them, while others grow up surrounded by crime or indifference. Thus creating equal opportunity for the next generation would mean great changes in this one.

And what does it mean to create "equality of opportunity" if some people are naturally endowed with greater intelligence or talents than others? Should a society allow those endowed with more talent to realize more economic gain for less work effort? The essential point is that when we speak of equality of opportunity, what we really mean is equality of the "wherewithal to conduct a prosperous, happy, and meaningful life," and this "wherewithal" really comes down to *assets,* whether financial, social, mental, physical, or other (recalling Amartya Sen's concept, mentioned above, of "capabilities"). It is an essential point because, as we see, income inequality stems from asset inequality. If we address the latter, we go a long way toward correcting the former. This is not an easy thing to do because, while relatively few would object to a philosophy based on "equality of opportunity," many more would strongly oppose "equality of total assets."

The "equal rewards for equal contributions" principle is similar to the "equality of opportunity" concept, but it is more of an exchange-based standard that tends to conform to traditional economic logic. According to this standard, those who contribute the most to an economy should be entitled to receive the most in return. Discrimination should not be allowed among individuals who do the same work, according to this principle, but market outcomes, even fairly unequal ones, are acceptable, whether they are due to differences in work effort or innate talents. In support of this view, there is a long-standing belief that people are entitled both to the products of their labor and to the fruits of their property (where property is viewed as the product of past labor).

The fourth perspective on equality focuses on equal rights as opposed to a focus on income or wealth. Societies often specify certain rights to which each individual should have an equal claim (e.g., liberty, the pursuit of happiness). As another example, modern democracy usually assumes the principle of "one person, one vote." This means that all eligible citizens have an equal right to cast a ballot and be fairly represented in the electoral system. Sen has suggested a rather direct link between democracy and economic outcomes. He points out that famines in which thousands or even millions of people die of hunger tend to occur in dictatorial states—even, sometimes, in the face of plentiful food supplies—and have not arisen in democratic ones, where those in power are accountable to the people.

A rights-based interpretation of equality assumes that equal rights are more fundamental to well-being than a particular level of material goods. There is no universal agreement, however, on just what these rights should include or on how they should be related to economic issues. Among the things that have been thought to belong to everyone by right, in some (but not all) countries, are free education, free health care, and easy access to resources for family planning.

Finally, attention to the least fortunate presents a different interpretation of equity. Sometimes referred to as the "basic needs" approach, it also echoes positions traditionally taken by many religions. According to this principle, the success of a society should be judged not by its members' average, or total, well-being (if such a thing could be calculated) but, rather, by its treatment of those who are worst off. While some philosophers such as Rawls support this perspective, others are critical of it because it places disproportionate attention on the poorest groups. Focusing exclusively on the poorest groups ignores the fairness (or lack thereof) of the distribution over the middle and upper-income ranges.

Which definition of equity should an economist use? There is no simple answer; different people have strongly held political and ethical preferences for one or another concept of equity. It should be clear from our description that in particular situations, different concepts might have conflicting implications.

Yet few if any advocate either extreme inequality or complete equality. For many economists the question is *how much* inequality is tolerable, or desirable, and what policies are appropriate to achieve this desirable level. We turn to policies that can affect the degree of inequality in a society.

4.2 Tax and Wage Policies

One way of reversing the trend toward greater inequality is through the tax system. By shifting more of the overall tax burden to high-income households, after-tax income inequality can be reduced. As we will see in more detail in Chapter 12, federal income tax rates on the highest-income households in the United States have changed significantly over time, from above 90 percent in the 1950s to as low as 28 percent in the 1980s. The maximum federal income tax rate is currently 39.6 percent. However, the tax rate that wealthy people actually pay is often considerably less than this due to tax provisions that allow them to claim many deductions, such as the mortgage interest on a second home. Also, income from investments, such as stocks and mutual funds, are taxed at a lower rate—a maximum of 20 percent.

Tax rates on those at the highest income levels have tended to decrease in recent decades. For example, a 2007 paper found that the top 0.01 percent in the U.S. paid over 70 percent of their income in federal taxes in 1960, but only about 30 percent in 2005.[7] Some politicians have suggested reversing this trend by increasing tax rates at the top of the income spectrum, not necessarily to the levels of the 1950s but to ensure that wealthy households are not able to lower their taxes excessively through deductions. Specifically, in 2012 President Barack Obama proposed the "Buffet Rule," named for billionaire investor Warren Buffet, who in 2011 publicly stated that it was unfair that wealthy people like himself were able to pay a lower overall tax rate than many middle-class people. President Obama's proposal was that households making more than $1 million per year should have to pay at least 30 percent of their total income in taxes regardless of how many deductions they could claim. This proposal, however, was unable to pass the U.S. Congress.

Another approach for reducing inequality is to increase the federal minimum wage, which is now $7.25 per hour. Although the federal minimum wage has been increased at times over the years, it has not kept up with inflation. If the minimum wage in the late 1960s is adjusted for inflation, in current dollars it comes to approximately $10 per hour. Many believe that the current $7.25 minimum is insufficient even to provide for the basic necessities of a family. In several U.S. states, "living wage" campaigns have advocated passing legislation at the state level that requires a minimum wage higher than the federal standard. About 20 states have a higher minimum wage than $7.25, the highest minimum wage being $9.19 in Washington state.

4.3 Spending Priorities

Another area where reforms have the potential to redress inequality is government spending. There is little question that government spending priorities have long been skewed in a way that does not favor a more equitable distribution of income. Two important examples are military spending and debt financing.

Defense expenditures have been estimated to be between one-fourth and one-third of the total federal budget. Critics suggest that this level of this expense is a relic of the cold war and that we could easily do with less. Because the military accounts for a sizable share of the budget, even a modest cutback would make a considerable amount of funds available in other areas that could increase economic opportunities for low-income households, such as better access to education and health care.

Debt financing is another way that the federal budget effectively helps transfer income from the poor and middle classes to the wealthy. In recent years, between 6 percent and 12 percent of the federal budget is devoted to paying interest on existing debt. (Recently it is on the low end, because of historically low interest rates). Because it is overwhelmingly the wealthy who own government bonds, they are the ones who receive these flows from the government. To the extent that the government is able to reduce its relative debt burden—raising taxes would be an effective way of doing this—doing so would contribute to reducing income inequality.

As for areas in which the government could spend more to address inequality, education stands out. As we saw in Chapter 10 and earlier this chapter, education levels are highly correlated with economic outcomes. According to the U.S. Department of Education, educational inequalities are increasing—meaning that the gap in education access and affordability between high and low income households is increasing.[8] Under President Barack Obama, Pell grants to college students based on economic need have increased, but the Department of Education notes that the benefits of more Pell grant money are likely to be more than offset by tuition increases. Policy recommendations of the Department of Education include further increasing need-based financial assistance, expanding loan forgiveness for student debt, and promoting the ability of students to transfer from 2-year to 4-year colleges.

4.4 CONCLUDING THOUGHTS

It is increasingly evident that income and wealth in the United States are increasingly concentrated. As noted earlier, as wealth becomes concentrated in fewer hands, it also becomes more of a challenge to pursue countervailing reforms. Nonetheless, both economic theory and practical policy analysis suggest that policy reform can make a difference in reducing inequality.

In the aftermath of the Great Recession of 2007–9, much more attention has been focused on inequality, in the United States and in other countries. It is possible that this will lead to policy changes such as those discussed above. The high degree of inequality in the years leading up to the Great Depression (recall Figure 11.5) helped usher in the New Deal policies of the 1930s. Now that inequality has returned to, and even exceeded, the levels that existed prior to the Great Depression, many concerned citizens feel the time has finally come to address the issue. Thus the economic analysis both of inequality, and of policies to respond to inequality, is likely to be of great relevance in the immediate future.

Discussion Questions

1. Do you generally believe that raising taxes on the rich is an appropriate approach for reducing economic inequality? What level of taxation on the rich do you think is fair? (Note that we will also consider this topic in the next chapter.)
2. Do you think the spending priorities of the government should be changed in order to reduce economic inequality? Beyond the suggestions in the text, can you think of any other ways that government spending priorities could be changed?

REVIEW QUESTIONS

1. About what share of aggregate income does each quintile of households receive in the United States?
2. How is a Lorenz curve constructed? What does it measure?
3. What is the Gini ratio? What does a higher value of the ratio signify?
4. What effect do taxes and transfer payments have on the distribution of U.S. household income?
5. What tends to be more unequal—the distribution of income or wealth?
6. How has income inequality in the United States changed in recent decades?
7. How does income and wealth vary by race?
8. What is economic mobility?
9. How does economic inequality in the United States compare to other countries?
10. What are some of the causes of growing inequality in the United States?
11. What are some of the consequences of inequality?
12. Describe the five different philosophical perspectives on inequality.
13. How can tax and wage policies be used to reduce inequality?
14. How are government spending priorities related to inequality?

EXERCISES

1. Statistics from the government of Thailand describe the household income distribution in that country, for 2000, as follows:

Group of households	Share of aggregate income (%)
Poorest fifth	5.5
Second fifth	8.8
Middle fifth	13.2
Fourth fifth	21.5
Richest fifth	51.0

Source: National Statistics Office Thailand, "Household Socio-Economic Survey," table 6, http://web.nso.go.th/eng/en/stat/socio/soctab6.htm.

   a. Create a carefully labeled Lorenz curve describing this distribution. (Be precise about the labels on the vertical axis.)
   b. Compare this distribution to the distribution in the United States. Would you expect the Gini ratio for Thailand to be much higher or lower or about the same? Why?

2. How does inequality vary across countries? Choose two countries not mentioned in the text, and write a paragraph comparing their performance on the Gini ratio and according to income share by quintile. Which country seems to have a more unequal distribution of income? For data, consult the World Bank's *World Development Indicators* online database or the CIA's *World Factbook*, also available online. Note which data source you used.

3. Match each concept in Column A with a definition or example in Column B.

Column A	Column B
a. Economic mobility	1. A very unequal income distribution
b. Equality of outcomes	2. Wages, salaries, and fringe benefits
c. Capital gain	3. Focuses on the well-being of the least fortunate
d. Quintile	4. Rents, profit, and interest
e. Labor income	5. A very equal income distribution
f. A Gini ratio close to 1	6. A group containing 20 percent of the total
g. Equality of opportunities	7. Changes in one's economic status over time
h. A Gini ratio close to 0	8. An increase in the value of an asset at the time of sale
i. Capital income	9. Everyone has the same income level
j. Basic needs approach	10. Everyone has access to the same quality of education

NOTES

1. Raj Chetty, Nathaniel Hendren, Patrick Kline, and Emmanuel Saez, "The Economic Impacts of Tax Expenditures: Evidence of Spatial Variation across the U.S.," Harvard University, Department of Economics, 2013, http://scholar.harvard.edu/hendren/publications/economic-impacts-tax-expenditures-evidence-spatial-variation-across-us/.

2. For example, Marcus Jäntti et al., "American Exceptionalism in a New Light: A Comparison of Intergenerational Earnings Mobility in Nordic Countries, the United Kingdom, and the United States," IZA Discussion Paper 1938, Bonn, Germany January 2006; Linda Levine, "The U.S. Income Distribution and Mobility: Trends and International Comparisons," Congressional Research Service, Washington, DC, November 29, 2012.

3. Julia B. Isaacs, "International Comparisons of Economic Mobility," The Brookings Institution, Washington, D.C., www.brookings.edu/~/media/research/files/reports/2008/2/economic%20mobility%20sawhill/02_economic_mobility_sawhill_ch3.pdf.

4. Nima Sanandaji, Tino Sanandaji, Arvid Malm, and Christopher Snowdon, "Un-Level Ground," *Wall Street Journal*, July 9, 2010.

5. Angus Deaton, "Health, Inequality, and Economic Development," *Journal of Economic Literature* 41(1) (2003):113–158.

6. Andrew G. Berg and Jonathan D. Ostry, "Inequality and Unsustainable Growth: Two Sides of the Same Coin?" International Monetary Fund, IMF Staff Discussion Note SDN/11/08, April 8, 2011.

7. Thomas Picketty and Emmanuel Saez, "How Progressive Is the U.S. Federal Tax System? A Historical and International Perspective," *Journal of Economic Perspectives* 21(1) (2007): 3–24.

8. United States Department of Education, "The Rising Price of Inequality," Advisory Committee on Student Financial Assistance, Washington, D.C., June 2010.

12 Taxes and Tax Policy

Albert Einstein reportedly once said: "The hardest thing in the world to understand is income taxes." It is true that taxes can be complicated. The United States federal tax code is more than 70,000 pages long. Browsing the tax code's table of contents offers a glimpse into the vast complexity of federal taxation. Entire sections of the tax code apply specifically to the taxation of vaccines (Sec. 4131–4132), shipowners' mutual protection and indemnity associations (Sec. 526), specially sweetened natural wines (Sec. 5385), and health benefits for certain miners (Sec. 9711–9712).

Fortunately, one need not comprehend the imposing complexity of tax laws to understand the crucial role of taxes in modern societies. Taxation is an important topic for students of economics. Tax policies have important economic consequences, both for a national economy and for particular groups within the economy. Tax policies are often designed with the intention of stimulating economic growth—although economists differ significantly about which policies are most effective at fostering growth. Taxes can create incentives promoting desirable behavior and disincentives for unwanted behavior. Taxation provides a means to redistribute economic resources toward those with low income or special needs. Taxes provide the revenue needed for important public services such as social security, health care, national defense, and education.

Taxation is as much a political issue as an economic issue. Political leaders have used tax policy to promote their agendas by initiating various tax reforms: decreasing (or increasing) tax rates, changing the definition of taxable income, creating new taxes on specific products, and so forth. Of course, no one particularly wants to pay taxes. Specific groups, such as small business owners, farmers, or retired individuals, exert significant political effort to reduce their share of the tax burden. Tax codes are packed with rules that benefit a certain group of taxpayers while inevitably shifting more of the burden to others.

In this chapter, we take a look at taxes and tax policy. First, we consider taxes from a theoretical perspective based on the economic models already discussed. Second, we summarize the different types of taxes, with an emphasis on the United States. Third, we present an international comparison of tax policies. Finally, we address current tax debates, including the distribution of the tax burden.

1. Economic Theory and Taxes

1.1 Taxes in the Supply-and-Demand Model

excise tax: a per-unit tax on a good or service

The supply-and-demand model we presented in Chapter 4 can be used to gain insights into the effects of taxation on consumers and producers. To incorporate taxes into our model, we consider a per-unit tax on a product or service, referred to as an **excise tax**. Let's suppose that an excise tax is imposed on cups of coffee—$0.30 per cup. In this section, we use our model to answer the following two questions:

1. How will the tax affect the price of cups of coffee?
2. How will the tax affect the quantity of coffee sold?

Common sense provides part of the answer to these questions. It seems reasonable to expect that taxing a product will increase its price. It also seems reasonable that the tax will reduce the quantity of coffee sold, given that the quantity demanded will decrease if the price rises.

But our model helps us to answer questions that we might not be able to answer with common sense alone. In particular, how much will the price of coffee increase as a result of the tax? You might think that a tax of $0.30 per cup should increase the equilibrium price by $0.30 per cup. In other words, the tax would be "passed on" to the consumer. Our model determines whether this logic is correct.

To determine how to incorporate an excise tax into our supply-and-demand model, we can recall our discussion of marginal costs and marginal benefits from Chapter 6. We stated then that a supply curve is a marginal cost curve and a demand curve is a marginal benefit curve. A tax is essentially an additional cost. We assume for simplicity that the $0.30 excise tax is paid by coffee suppliers directly to the government. So, in addition to the production cost of actually making a cup of coffee, the coffee supplier must pay the government $0.30 per cup. Effectively, the tax increases the marginal cost of supplying coffee.

We express an increase in the marginal cost of supplying coffee due to a tax just as we express an increase in input prices—the supply curve shifts upward.* The upward shift would be exactly equal to the amount of the tax. In other words, the marginal supply cost of each cup of coffee increases by $0.30 as a result of the tax.

This is shown in Figure 12.1, which presents our market for cups of coffee. The supply curve without any tax is $Supply_0$, with equilibrium at E_0—a price of $1.10 per cup and a quantity sold of 700 cups per week. Instituting the excise tax raises the supply curve upward by $0.30 per cup to $Supply_{Tax}$. Note that $Supply_{Tax}$ is parallel to $Supply_0$ because the cost of supplying each cup of coffee has increased by the same amount of $0.30.

Suppliers will seek to recoup the cost of the tax by raising their prices. You might think that they will increase their price by $0.30, to $1.40. But notice that at a price of $1.40 (the dashed blue line in Figure 12.1) the quantity supplied exceeds the quantity demanded—a situation of surplus. As we discussed in Chapter 4, this creates a downward pressure on prices.

The new equilibrium with the tax occurs at E_{Tax}, at a price of $1.33 per cup and a quantity sold of 625 cups per week. As we expected, the price has risen and the quantity sold has decreased. However, the price has not risen by the amount of the tax. The $0.30 per cup tax led to a $0.23 increase in the price. Most of the cost has been passed on to consumers, but the suppliers also bear some burden of the tax.

How much of the tax burden is borne by consumers and producers depends on the elasticity of demand. In Figure 12.2 we see the impact of a tax when demand is highly inelastic, such as the demand for gasoline or cigarettes. Before the tax, the supply curve is $Supply_0$, and the equilibrium price is P_0 and quantity is Q_0. The tax shifts the supply curve upward to $Supply_{Tax}$, and the equilibrium price rises to P_{Tax} and quantity falls to Q_{Tax}. The vertical distance between P_{Tax} and P_1 is the amount of the tax—the distance between the two supply curves. In this case, we see that the price has risen by nearly as much of the tax. Thus when demand is inelastic, most of the tax is passed on to consumers. An inelastic demand curve implies that consumers' quantity demanded will change little when prices rise.

*We could also visualize the supply curve shifting "back" instead of "up." But in the case of a tax, it is easier to think of the curve shifting upward—an increase in the marginal cost of supply.

Figure 12.1 **The Impact of a Tax on the Market for Cups of Coffee**

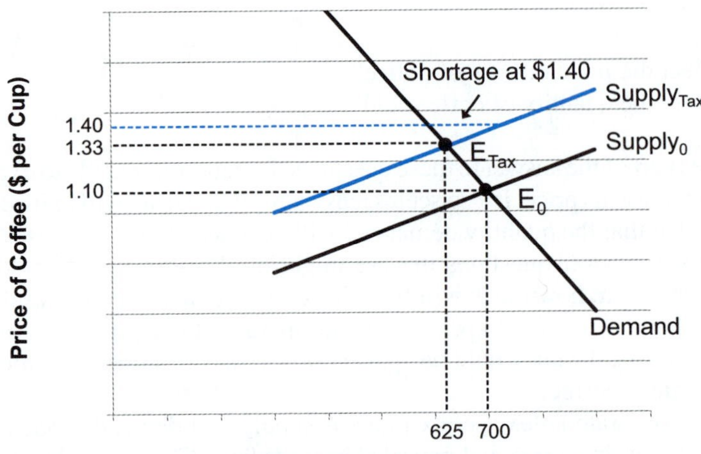

An excise tax on a product results in a higher price and a lower quantity sold.

Figure 12.2 **The Impact of an Excise Tax with an Inelastic Demand Curve**

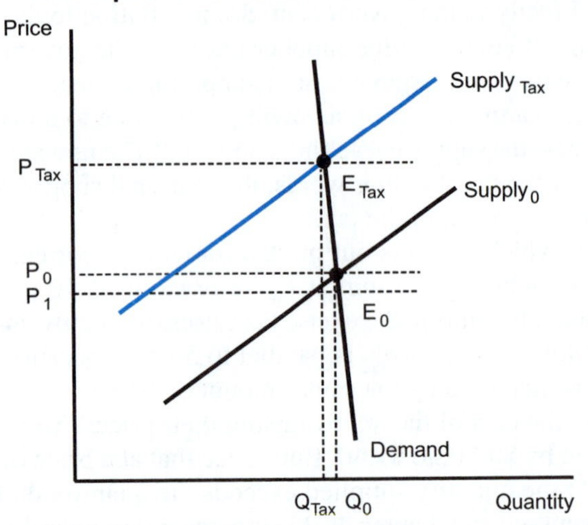

When demand is highly inelastic, most of the burden of an excise tax will fall on consumers. In other words, producers will be able to pass on most of the cost of the tax by raising price.

At the extreme, if demand is perfectly inelastic, the demand curve is a vertical line and the quantity demanded does not change when prices rise. With a perfectly inelastic demand curve, the price rises by the exact amount of the tax and the full burden of the tax is borne by consumers.

However, if demand is highly elastic most of the burden of the tax is borne by producers. This is shown in Figure 12.3. Again, the supply curve before a tax is $Supply_0$, with an equilibrium price of P_0 and quantity of Q_0. The supply curve with the tax is $Supply_{Tax}$. We see that as producers raise their prices, the quantity demanded falls significantly, from Q_0 to Q_{Tax}. Recall that an elastic demand curve means that consumers have many alternatives or consider the good nonessential. Producers are able to raise prices only slightly, to P_{Tax}, which is much less than the per-unit tax, which is again the vertical distance between P_{Tax} and P_1.

The elasticity of supply also affects the distribution of the tax burden. It is a little more difficult to see why this is so, but in general if supply is very elastic, more of the tax burden is passed on to consumers. This might be true, for example, in a very competitive industry in which it is not possible for producers to accept a lower price without going out of business. If supply is very inelastic, by contrast, suppliers can accept a price reduction without affecting the quantity supplied by much. (Try varying the elasticity of supply in a graph like Figure 12.3 to see this effect.)

Figure 12.3 **The Impact of an Excise Tax with an Elastic Demand Curve**

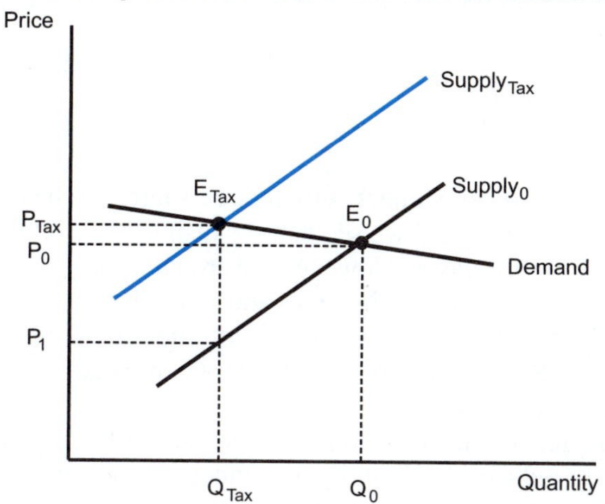

When demand is highly elastic, most of the burden of an excise tax will fall on producers. Price will rise slightly, but the quantity sold will decline significantly.

1.2 TAX REVENUES

We now consider using our supply-and-demand model to explore how much revenue is generated from a tax. The tax revenue from a per-unit tax is simply:

$$\textit{Tax revenue} = \textit{Per-unit tax} * \textit{Quantity}$$

So if the tax on cups of coffee is \$0.30 per cup and 625 cups of coffee are sold per week, then the tax revenue collected by the government each week is:

$$\textit{Tax revenue} = \$0.30 * 625 = \$187.50$$

We can represent this tax revenue in Figure 12.4, which again shows our market for coffee with a tax of \$0.30 per cup. The vertical distance between the two supply curves is \$0.30, as shown in the graph. So the shaded rectangle, with a height of \$0.30 and a length of 625 cups, represents our tax revenue of \$187.50 per week. Being able to represent tax revenues on our supply-and-demand graph is important as in the next section we analyze the welfare effects of a tax.

Figure 12.4 **Tax Revenues from a Tax on Cups of Coffee**

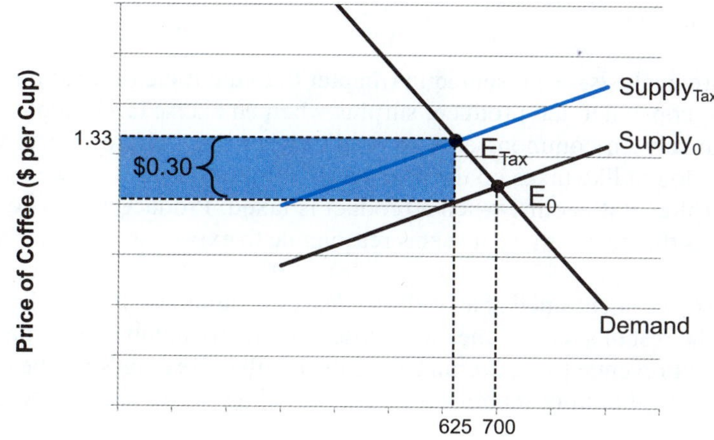

We can represent the revenue from an excise tax as the shaded area in the graph.

But first consider a government's decision about which goods and services to tax. Products are taxed for two basic reasons:

1. to discourage purchases of that product
2. to generate revenue

Any tax creates a disincentive, so consumers will reduce their purchases and seek alternatives. Comparing Figures 12.2 and 12.3 we see that the disincentive effect of a tax is greatest when the demand curve is highly elastic. However, the products that society generally wants to discourage people from buying, such as cigarettes and alcohol, tend to have inelastic demand curves. As shown in Figure 12.2, a tax on a good with inelastic demand will only reduce the quantity sold a little bit. So, in order for a tax to significantly reduce the quantity sold when demand is inelastic, the tax must be substantial.

The elasticity of demand also has implications for tax revenues. If the demand curve is elastic, an excise tax significantly reduces the quantity demanded (see Figure 12.3), and the government does not collect that much tax revenue. But if the demand curve is inelastic, the tax does not reduce the quantity demanded much (see Figure 12.2), and the government collects significant revenues.

It is no surprise that excise taxes tend to be imposed on products with inelastic demand curves, such as gasoline, cigarettes, and alcohol. This suggests that the primary motivation for taxes on these products is revenue generation rather than encouraging behavioral changes. But recall that demand for these products tends to be more elastic in the long run. So we would expect tax revenues to decline gradually over time, ceteris paribus, as people have more time to adjust their behavior.

We can summarize the impact of an excise tax on products with elastic and inelastic demand curves in Table 12.1.*

Table 12.1 **Summary of Excise Tax Impacts for Products with Elastic and Inelastic Demand Curves**

	Inelastic demand	Elastic demand
Change in price	Large, nearly equal to the per-unit tax	Small, much less than the per-unit tax
Change in quantity sold	Relatively small	Relatively large
Tax revenues	Relatively large	Relatively small
Tax burden	Primarily borne by consumers	Primarily borne by producers

1.3 Welfare Analysis of Taxation

We can now apply welfare analysis, as presented in Chapter 6, to the issue of taxation. We consider what happens to consumer and producer surplus when an excise tax is applied to a product. Again, we can rely on common sense to predict what the welfare effects will be. Consumers generally do not like taxes on the products that they purchase, so we might expect that consumer surplus will decline when a product is taxed. Producers also do not favor taxes on the products that they sell, so it seems reasonable to expect producer surplus to decline.

Recall from Chapter 6 we mentioned that welfare analysis should also consider the impacts of a market on "the rest of society," meaning those not directly involved in a market transaction. Taxes represent revenue to a government entity, but these revenues can be used for any beneficial social use—building schools or roads, providing health care, protecting

*As noted, the elasticity of supply also affects distribution of the tax burden, but in general this effect is less important, so we concentrate here on demand elasticity.

the environment, scientific research, or any other use. Although the ultimate benefit of tax revenues depends on their particular use, in this chapter our analysis only goes as far as the tax collection. In other words, if a government collects \$5 million in taxes, that revenue represents a potential \$5 million benefit to society. If the government uses these tax dollars wisely, say, investing in education or infrastructure, \$5 million may generate more than \$5 million in long-run benefits. Of course, if the government squanders its tax revenues, less than \$5 million in social benefits may result.

Figure 12.5 shows the welfare effects of an excise tax on a product. Before the tax, we again have the supply curve $Supply_0$, with an equilibrium price of P_0 and quantity of Q_0. The welfare of the market without a tax is:

$$Consumer\ Surplus = A + B + E + H$$
$$Producer\ Surplus = C + D + F + G + I$$

There is no tax revenue, so total social welfare is simply the sum of consumer and producer surplus.

Instituting a tax shifts the supply curve to $Supply_{Tax}$, with a new equilibrium at E_{Tax}. With price rising to P_{Tax}, consumer surplus is only area A. Thus we can conclude that consumer surplus has decreased, as we expected.

Figuring out the producer surplus is a little tricky. First, realize that producers receive total revenues of price times quantity, or ($P_{Tax} * Q_{Tax}$). In Figure 12.5, total revenues are:

$$Total\ Producer\ Revenues = B + C + D + E + F + G + J$$

Producers have two costs: the cost of production and the tax. The cost of production is the area under their marginal cost curve, $Supply_0$, which is area J. The tax is:

$$Tax\ Revenues = B + C + E + F$$

When we subtract production costs and the tax paid from total revenues, we are left with producer surplus:

$$Producer\ Surplus = (B + C + D + E + F + G + J) - J - (B + C + E + F)$$
$$= D + G$$

Figure 12.5 **Welfare Analysis of an Excise Tax**

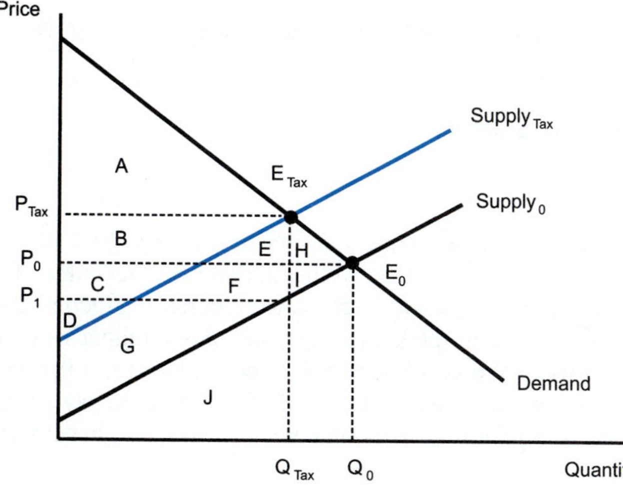

An excise tax in a market results in a deadweight loss equal to areas H and I.

Note that producer surplus has also decreased. Total social welfare with the tax is the sum of consumer and producer surplus, plus the tax revenues:

$$Social\ Welfare = A + (D + G) + (B + C + E + F)$$

How does this compare to social welfare before the tax? Before the tax, social welfare also included area (H + I). So even accounting for the benefits of the tax revenues, the tax has resulted in a deadweight loss, similar to the price controls that we discussed in Chapter 6. We can conclude that imposing a tax on a product:

- reduces consumer surplus
- reduces producer surplus
- provides social benefits in the form of tax revenues
- creates a deadweight loss

Based on this analysis, it may seem that taxing is always a bad idea. But as usual, we need to consider a broader context in order to determine whether a particular tax is justified. The potentially valid reasons for taxing include:

1. Governments obviously cannot rely on voluntary donations, thus *something* must be taxed in any society.
2. As mentioned earlier, a tax may be justified on the basis that it creates a disincentive for something. As we saw in Chapter 8, consumer behavior is not always rational and a tax can be used to encourage people to make better decisions.
3. The tax revenues may be spent wisely such that the net increase in social benefits exceeds the deadweight loss.
4. A tax may be justified on the basis of equity, in order to reduce inequality. This is generally not true of excise taxes, but may apply to other taxes, such as the income tax, which falls more heavily on higher-income individuals and families.

An excise tax is just one type of tax. In most countries, the majority of tax revenues come from other taxes, such as taxes on income or property. We now turn to a summary of the tax system of the United States. Later, we compare the U.S. tax system to that of other countries.

Discussion Questions

1. What recent news stories have you heard about taxes? How does the material in the previous section relate to these stories?
2. What goods and services do you think should be subjected to excise taxes? How would these taxes affect different groups of people?

2. THE STRUCTURE OF TAXATION IN THE UNITED STATES

2.1 TAX PROGRESSIVITY

progressive tax: a tax in which the percentage of one's income that is paid in taxes tends to increase with increasing income levels

Before we discuss the different types of taxes in the United States, we need to first define the concept of tax progressivity. By a **progressive tax**, we mean that the percentage of income an individual (or household) pays in taxes tends to increase with increasing income. Not only do those with higher incomes pay more in total taxes, but they pay a higher *rate* of taxes. For example, a person making $100,000 a year might pay 25 percent of his or her income in taxes ($25,000 in taxes), while someone with an income of $30,000 might pay a tax rate of only 10 percent ($3,000 in taxes). So the higher-income person pays a higher tax rate, and thus this tax is progressive.

regressive tax: a tax in which the percentage of one's income paid in taxes tends to decrease with increasing income levels

proportional tax: a tax in which all taxpayers pay the same tax rate, regardless of income

A tax can also be regressive or proportional. A **regressive tax** is one in which the proportion of income paid in taxes tends to decrease as one's income increases. A **proportional tax** means that everyone pays the same tax rate regardless of income. Most countries' overall tax system, including that of the United States, includes a mix of progressive and regressive taxes, as different taxes are designed with different purposes.

The overall tax system of the United States and most other countries is progressive. A progressive tax system is used for many reasons, including:

1. A progressive tax embodies the concept that those with high incomes should pay more of their income in taxes because of their greater ability to pay without a harmful sacrifice. By paying a tax, any household must forgo an equivalent amount of spending on goods, services, or investments. For a high-income household, these forgone opportunities might include a second home, an expensive vehicle, or a purchase of corporate stock. A low-income household, by comparison, might have to forgo basic medical care, postsecondary education, or vehicle safety repairs.
2. A progressive tax system can be used to address economic inequality in a society. If the benefits of programs funded by taxation primarily benefit low-income households while high-income households pay the majority of taxes, then a tax system effectively operates as a means to reduce inequality.
3. There is also an economic argument for a progressive tax system—it can yield a given level of public revenue with the least macroeconomic impact. To see why, consider how households with different levels of income respond to a $1,000 tax cut. A low-income household tends to spend the entire amount quickly on needed goods and services—injecting $1,000 of increased demand into the economy. By comparison, a high-income household might only spend a fraction of the tax cut on goods and services, choosing to save or invest a portion of the money. The money that a high-income household saves or invests does not add to the overall level of effective demand in an economy.* In economic terms, we say that the **marginal propensity to consume** (the tendency to spend, rather than save, an additional dollar of income) tends to decrease as income increases. Collecting proportionately more taxes from high-income households thus has less effect on total effective demand in the economy.

marginal propensity to consume: the number of additional dollars of consumption for every additional dollar of income (typically a fraction between zero and one)

Despite these arguments for a progressive tax, it is possible for a tax system to become too progressive. Extremely high tax rates on income create a disincentive for individuals to expend economically productive effort. Very high taxes might limit the risks taken by entrepreneurs, stifling innovation and technological advance. The desire to "soak the rich" through an extremely progressive tax system might be viewed as unfair and economically unwise and can promote "tax flight," in which wealthy individuals relocate in order to avoid high tax rates. We consider these issues in more detail later in the chapter. But next we turn to a discussion of the U.S. tax system.

2.2 FEDERAL INCOME TAXES

The federal income tax is the most visible, complicated, and debated tax in the United States. The federal income tax was established with the ratification of the Sixteenth Amendment to the U.S. Constitution in 1913. It is levied on wages and salaries as well as income from many other sources, including interest, dividends, capital gains, self-employment income, alimony, and prizes. To understand the basic workings of federal income taxes, fortunately you need to comprehend only two major issues:

*Money saved or invested can, however, provide the financial capital necessary to increase the productive capacity of the economy. "Supply-side" economics stresses the importance of investment by the wealthy as critical to macroeconomic growth.

1. Not all income is not taxable—there are important differences between "total income" and "taxable income."
2. There is also an important difference between the "effective tax rate" and the "marginal tax rate."

total income: the sum of income that an individual or couple receives from all sources

Total income is simply the sum of income that an individual or couple receives from all sources.* For most people, the largest portion of total income comes from wages or salaries. Many people also receive investment income from interest, capital gains, and dividends. Self-employment income is also included in total income, along with other types of income such as alimony, farm income, and winnings from gambling.

The amount of federal taxes that a person owes is not calculated based on total income. Instead, after total income is calculated, tax filers are allowed to subtract some expenses as nontaxable. Each filer receives an exemption as well as various deductions. For example, in 2013 a single filer with no children was allowed to deduct the first $10,000 of income as nontaxable.** Other expenses that can be deducted include individual retirement account (IRA) contributions, allowable moving expenses (e.g., for a job), student loan interest, and certain tuition expenses.

taxable income: the portion of one's income that is subject to taxation after deductions and exemptions

marginal tax rate: the tax rate applicable to an additional dollar of income

Taxable income is the income that is subject to taxation, after all deductions and exemptions. However, the amount of tax owed is not simply a multiple of taxable income and a single tax rate. The federal income tax system in the United States uses increasing **marginal tax rates** (the tax rate applicable to an additional dollar of income). This means that different tax rates apply to different portions of a person's income. The marginal tax rates in effect for 2013 are listed in Table 12.2. For a single filer, the first $8,925 of taxable income is taxed at a rate of 10 percent. Taxable income above $8,925 but less than $36,250 is taxed at a rate of 15 percent, and so on up to a maximum marginal tax rate of 39.6 percent. The income levels that are taxed at each rate are higher for married filers, filing jointly.

The way that one's income tax bill is determined is best illustrated with an example. Suppose that we want to calculate the taxes owed by a single person (let's call her Susan) with no children and a total income of $49,000. As mentioned above, in 2013 she would be allowed to claim the first $10,000 of income as nontaxable. Assume that Susan contributed $2,000 to an IRA, so this contribution can also be deducted from her total income. Thus her taxable income would be $37,000, as shown in Table 12.3. On the first $8,925 of taxable income, she owes 10 percent in taxes, or $892.50. The tax rate on her taxable income above $8,925 but below $36,250 is 15 percent, for a tax of (($36,250 – $8,925) × 0.15), or $4,098.75. Finally, her tax rate is 25 percent for her taxable income above $36,250, for a tax of (($37,000 – $36,250) × 0.25), or $187.50. So, we see in Table 12.3 that her total federal income tax bill is $5,178.75.

Table 12.2 **U.S. Federal Marginal Tax Rates, 2013**

Marginal tax rate	Income range for single filers	Income range for married couples
10%	Up to $8,925	Up to $12,750
15%	$8,925 to $36,250	$12,750 to $48,600
25%	$36,250 to $87,850	$48,600 to $125,450
28%	$87,850 to $183,250	$125,450 to $203,150
33%	$183,250 to $398,350	$203,150 to $398,350
35%	$398,350 to $400,00	$398,350 to $425,000
39.6%	Above $400,000	Above $425,000

*Married couples have the option of filing their federal taxes either jointly or separately.

**Couples, and those with children, can deduct higher amounts of income as nontaxable. Filers have the option of "itemizing" their deductions rather than taking the "standard" deduction, depending on which deduction is larger. Deductions that can be itemized include mortgage interest, state and local taxes, major health-care expenses, real estate taxes, and gifts to charity.

Table 12.3 **Susan's Federal Income Tax Calculations**

Variable	Amount	Taxes owed
Total income	$49,000	
Nontaxable deduction	–$10,000	
Retirement contribution	–$2,000	
Taxable income	$37,000	
Income taxed at 10% rate	$8,925	$892.50
Income taxed at 15% rate	$27,325	$4,098.75
Income taxed at 25% rate	$750	$187.50
Total income tax owed		$5,178.75

effective tax rate: one's taxes expressed as a percentage of total income

Note that Susan paid a maximum *marginal* tax rate of 25 percent but *only* on her last $750 of income. Someone's **effective tax rate** is their total taxes divided by total income, expressed as a percentage. Thus Susan's effective tax rate is:

$$\frac{\$5{,}178.75}{\$49{,}000} = 0.1057 \times 100 = 10.57 \textit{ percent}$$

As we see later in the chapter, which tax rate is most relevant—marginal or effective—depends on the policy situation. But the distinction can help us dispel one common myth about federal income taxes. Many people mistakenly worry that if they move into a higher tax bracket, their remaining income after taxes will decline. But if one moves, for example, from the 15 percent tax bracket to the 25 percent tax bracket, it is only the *additional* income that is taxed at 25 percent, not total income. Thus if Susan had recently received a raise of $750 that increased her total income to $49,000, she paid $187.50 in taxes on her additional income, but all her other income was taxed at the same rates as before her raise. The only way one's total after-tax income could decline with an increase in income would be if the marginal tax rate exceeded 100 percent.*

2.3 FEDERAL SOCIAL INSURANCE TAXES

social insurance taxes: taxes used to fund social insurance programs such as Social Security, Medicare, and Medicaid

Taxes for federal social insurance programs, including Social Security, Medicaid, and Medicare, are collected in addition to federal income taxes. **Social insurance taxes** are levied on salaries and wages, as well as income from self-employment. For those employed by others, these taxes are generally withheld directly from their pay—that is, deducted from their pay before they receive it. These deductions commonly appear as FICA taxes—a reference to the Federal Insurance Contributions Act.

Federal social insurance taxes are actually two separate taxes. The first is a tax of 12.4 percent of pay, which is used primarily to fund Social Security. Half this tax is deducted from an employee's pay, and the employer is responsible for matching this contribution. The other is a tax of 2.9 percent for Medicare and Medicaid, for which the employee and employer again each pay half. Thus social insurance taxes normally amount to a 7.65 percent deduction from an employee's pay (6.2 percent + 1.45 percent). Self-employed individuals are responsible for paying the entire share, 15.3 percent, themselves.

These two taxes have a very important difference. The Social Security tax is due *only* on the first $113,700 of income, as of 2013. On income above $113,700, *no* additional Social

*Some low-income workers in the United States are subjected to marginal income tax rates that approach and even exceed 100 percent. Low-income workers are eligible for the Earned Income Tax Credit (EITC), which provides a tax rebate as an incentive to work, but the EITC is phased out as income increases. At some income levels, increases in income can be fully offset by a reduction in the EITC rebate.

Security tax is paid. In other words, the maximum Social Security tax that could be deducted from total pay in 2013 was $7,049.40 ($113,700 × 0.062). The Medicare tax, however, is paid on *all* wages and salaries. Thus, the Medicare tax is truly a proportional tax while the Social Security tax is a proportional tax on the first $113,700 of income but then becomes a regressive tax when we consider income above this limit.

Consider the impact of social insurance taxes on two individuals, Susan with her $49,000 annual salary and Leah, who makes $300,000. Susan would pay a social insurance tax of 7.65 percent on all her income, or $3,748.50. Leah would pay the maximum Social Security contribution of $7,049.40 plus $4,350 for Medicare/Medicaid (1.45 percent of $300,000) for a total social insurance tax bill of $11,399.40. This works out to an effective tax rate of 3.8 percent, or less than half the tax rate paid by Susan. Thus we see that overall social insurance taxes are regressive, with higher-income individuals paying a significantly lower effective rate.

2.4 Federal Corporate Taxes

Corporations must file federal tax forms that are in many ways similar to the forms that individuals complete. Corporate taxable income is defined as total revenue minus the cost of goods sold, wages and salaries, depreciation, repairs, interest paid, and other deductions. Thus corporations, like individuals, can take advantage of many deductions to reduce their taxable income. In fact, a corporation may have so many deductions that it actually ends up paying no tax at all or even receives a rebate check from the federal government.

Corporate tax rates, like personal income tax rates, are progressive and calculated on a marginal basis. In 2013, the lowest corporate tax rate, applied to profits of less than $50,000, was 15 percent. The highest marginal corporate tax rate, applied to profits of between $100,000 and $335,000, was 39 percent.* As for individuals, the effective tax rate that corporations pay is lower than their marginal tax rate. For more on federal corporate taxes, see Box 12.1.

2.5 Other Federal Taxes

The U.S. federal government collects excise taxes on numerous commodities and services, including tires, telephone services, air travel, transportation fuels, alcohol, tobacco, and firearms. Consumers may be unaware that they are paying federal excise taxes, as the tax amounts are normally incorporated into the prices of products. For example, the federal excise tax on gasoline is about 18 cents per gallon.

estate taxes: taxes on the transfers of large estates to beneficiaries

The final federal taxes that we consider are federal estate and gift taxes. The **estate tax** is applied to transfers of large estates to beneficiaries. Like the federal income tax, the estate tax has an exemption amount that is not taxed—in 2013 it was $5.25 million. Only estates valued above the exemption amount are subject to the estate tax, and the tax applies only to the value of the estate above the exemption. The maximum marginal tax rate on estates in 2013 was 40 percent.

gift taxes: taxes on the transfer of large gifts to beneficiaries

The transfer of large gifts is also subject to federal taxation. The estate tax and **gift tax** (taxes on the transfer of large gifts to beneficiaries) are complementary because the gift tax essentially prevents people from giving away their estate to beneficiaries tax-free while they are still alive. In 2013, gifts under $11,000 per year per recipient were excluded from taxation. Like federal income tax rates, the gift tax rates are marginal and progressive, with a maximum tax rate of 40 percent.

The estate and gift taxes are the most progressive element of federal taxation. The estate tax is paid exclusively by those with considerable assets. Moreover, the majority of estate taxes are paid by a very small number of wealthy taxpayers. According to the Tax Policy Center, in 2011 the richest 0.1 percent of those subject to the estate tax paid 51 percent of the total estate tax revenue.[1]

*For the highest profit bracket—profits above $18,333,333—the marginal rate was 35 percent.

BOX 12.1 CORPORATE TAXES: THE USE AND MISUSE OF INFORMATION

You may have heard politicians and media commentators mention that the United States has the highest corporate taxes in the world, normally when arguing in favor of lower tax rates. For example, a 2012 article noted:

> Our high corporate tax rate has long made the United States an uncompetitive place for new investment. . . . The U.S. rate [of 39 percent] is well above the 25 percent average of other developed nations in the Organization for Economic Cooperation and Development (OECD). In fact, the U.S. rate is almost 15 percentage points higher than the OECD average. (Dubay 2012)

Looking only at top marginal rates, it is true that the United States does have the highest corporate tax rate among OECD member countries. But as we discussed in Chapter 1, this is an example of a positive statement with normative policy implications that needs to be scrutinized in order to get a more complete picture. In particular, the article mentions nothing about effective tax rates, which as we saw with federal income taxes, can differ significantly from marginal tax rates.

A different 2012 article presents a more balanced approach, indicating that the top marginal rate

> only tells part of the story. Loopholes and other special treatment for different kinds of businesses mean that businesses pay an effective rate of only 29.2 percent of their income, which puts the United States below the average of 31.9 percent among other major economies, according to analysis by the Treasury Department. (Isidore 2012)

Providing yet another way of viewing corporate taxes in an international perspective, the same article mentions that

> the Organization for Economic Cooperation and Development, the multinational group that tracks global economic growth, estimates the United States collects less corporate tax relative to the overall economy than almost any other country in the world. Some economists argue that tax collection relative to gross domestic product is the more relevant measure. That's because different accounting rules around the world mean what's counted as income in one country isn't counted in another, making comparisons of tax rates misleading.

So depending on one's perspective, the United States either has the highest corporate taxes in the world or one of the lowest! Marginal tax rates are relevant when making decisions about *additional* income. But effective tax rates are generally more relevant when a company decides where to locate in the first place. As with many economic policy applications, what information we focus on depends on the details of the situation.

Sources: Curtis Dubay, "No Fooling: U.S. Now Has Highest Corporate Tax Rate in the World," *The Foundry*, Heritage Foundation, March 30, 2012; Chris Isidore, "U.S. Corporate Tax Rate: No. 1 in the World," CNN Money, March 27, 2012.

2.6 STATE AND LOCAL TAXES

Like the federal government, state and local governments rely on several different tax mechanisms, including income taxes, excise taxes, and corporate taxes. Thus much of the above discussion applies to the tax structures in place in most states. However, some important differences deserve mention.

First, nearly all states (45 as of 2013) have instituted some type of general sales tax. State sales tax rates range from 2.9 percent (Colorado) to 7.25 percent (California). A few states reduce the tax rate on certain goods considered necessities, such as food and prescription drugs. For example, the general sales tax in Illinois is 6.25 percent, but most food and drug sales are taxed at only 1 percent. Many states with sales taxes exempt some necessities from taxation entirely. In most states, municipal localities can charge an additional sales tax. Although local sales taxes are generally lower than state sales taxes, there are exceptions. In New York the state sales tax is 4 percent, but local sales taxes are often higher than 4 percent. The combined state and local sales tax can be higher than 11 percent in Arizona, Arkansas, and Illinois.

Unlike income taxes, sales taxes tend to be quite regressive. The reason is that low-income households tend to spend a larger share of their income on taxable items than do high-income households. Consider gasoline—a product that tends to comprise a smaller share of total expenditures as income rises. An increase in state taxes on gasoline affects low-income households more than high-income households, measured as a percentage of income. Some states, such as Idaho and Kansas, offer low-income households a tax credit to compensate for the regressive nature of state sales taxes.

Forty-one states levy an income tax.* Most of these states have several progressive tax brackets (as many as 12 rates), like the federal income tax. However, state income taxes tend to be less progressive than the federal income tax. Six states have only one income tax rate, meaning that their income tax approaches a proportional tax. Several additional states approach a proportional tax because the top rate applies at a low income or the rates are relatively constant. For example, North Carolina's tax rates only range from 6.0 percent to 7.75 percent.

Another important distinction between the federal system of taxation and the taxes levied at state and local levels is the use of property taxes. Property taxes tend to be the largest revenue source for state and local governments. The primary property tax levied in the United States is a tax on real estate, including land, private residences, and commercial properties. Generally, the tax is calculated as a proportion of the value of the property, although the formulas used by localities differ significantly.

Property taxes tend to be regressive, although less regressive than excise and sales taxes. The reason is that high-income households tend to have a lower proportion of their assets subjected to property taxes. Although renters do not pay property taxes directly, economic analysis indicates that the costs of property taxes are largely passed on to renters as part of their rent, as we discuss later in the chapter.

Discussion Questions

1. Do you think it is necessary for the United States to have so many different types of taxes? What would you change about the structure of taxation in the United States?
2. Compare the tax policies of the area in which you live to a neighboring state or country? What factors do you think explain the differences in tax policies?

3. TAX ANALYSIS AND POLICY ISSUES

3.1 TAX DATA FOR THE UNITED STATES

One of the main debates about tax policy in the United States, which we discuss later in this section, concerns the overall level of taxation. Although tax receipts have grown dramatically in recent decades, to provide the proper context, economists normally measure taxes as a percentage of GDP. Figure 12.6 presents data on overall U.S. tax receipts, as a percentage of GDP, from 1950 to 2012.

We see that the overall level of taxation tended to rise from 1950 to 2000, from about 23 percent to 34 percent. Although critics of "big government" often focus on the growth of the federal government, most of the growth in total tax receipts was due to an increase in state and local taxation from 1950 to the early 1970s. Federal tax revenues have remained at about the same level over most of this period and have declined as a percentage of GDP since 2000.

Note that the fluctuations in total tax receipts closely follow the fluctuations in federal tax receipts. The reason for this is that state and local tax revenues remain relatively constant whether the economy is expanding or in a recession. State and local governments rely heavily on property and sales taxes, which fluctuate relatively less than income and corporate taxes as economic activity varies.

We see in Figure 12.6 that federal tax receipts did increase during the 1990s. Although federal income tax *rates* increased slightly in the early 1990s, the primary reason that federal tax *receipts* grew was an economic expansion that raised incomes. As incomes rise, people

*Two additional states, Tennessee and New Hampshire, levy no state income tax but do tax dividends and interest.

Figure 12.6 **Tax Receipts in the United States, as a Percent of GDP, 1950–2012**

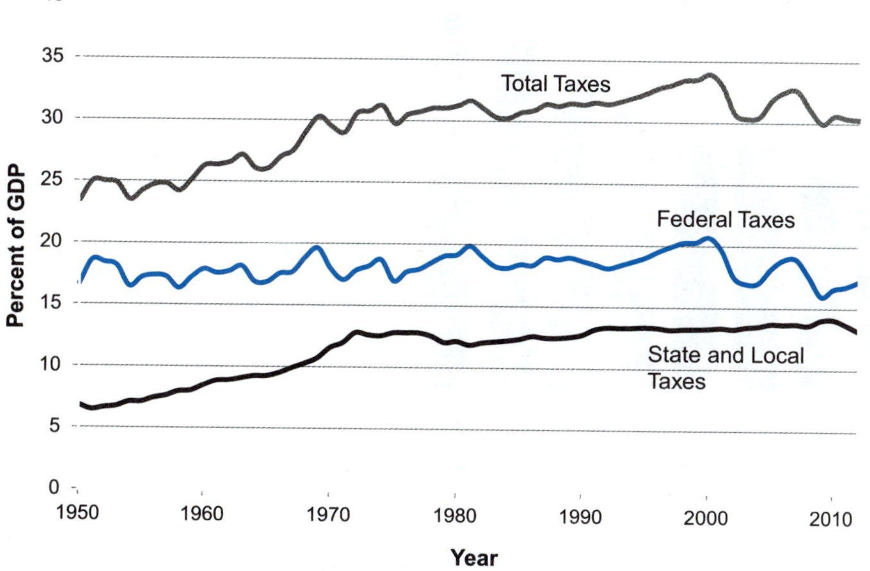

Total tax receipts in the U.S. as a share of GDP have generally increased since the 1950s, but have declined in recent years.

Source: U.S. Bureau of Economic Analysis, online database.

tend to move into higher marginal tax brackets, and thus their effective tax rate increases. In addition, corporate profits rose during this period. Another reason that federal tax receipts rose was an increase in capital gains taxes, which are paid on the profitable sale of investments such as stocks and mutual funds.

When the economy fell into a recession in 2001, federal tax receipts declined along with falling income and profits. In addition, significant tax cuts were implemented under the George W. Bush administration. As the economy recovered in the mid-2000s, federal tax receipts began to rise. But with the Great Recession (2007–9), federal tax receipts declined further and then began to rise starting in 2010.

As we discuss later, some of the variations in tax receipts are related to tax policy changes. But we can draw three important lessons from Figure 12.6—lessons that are not necessarily consistent with discussions of tax issues in the media:

1. The primary reason that tax receipts have fluctuated in the past couple of decades is due not to major changes in tax policy but to macroeconomic fluctuations.
2. Federal tax receipts are relatively low by historical standards. In fact, in 2009 federal tax receipts reached their lowest level, as a percentage of GDP, since before 1950.
3. Total tax receipts, as of 2012, are also relatively low, considering the period since 1970. Total tax receipts as a percentage of GDP were at the same level in 2012 as in the early 1970s and early 1980s.

3.2 International Data on Taxes

In addition to looking at historical data, we can also gain some context for tax policy discussions by comparing the United States to other countries. Figure 12.7 shows the overall rate of taxation in various member countries of the Organisation for Economic Co-operation and Development (OECD).* We see that the overall rate of taxation in the United States is relatively low—with a rate similar to that in Turkey but lower than that in all other industrialized countries.

*The OECD's mission is "to promote policies that will improve the economic and social well-being of people around the world." It has 34 member countries, most of them advanced industrialized countries with high income.

Figure 12.7 **International Comparisons of Overall Tax Receipts, 2011**

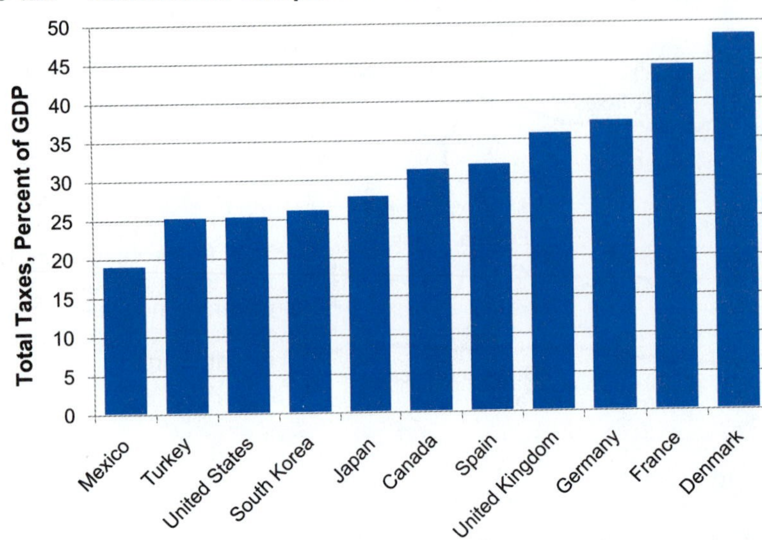

The United States has a relatively low overall rate of taxation compared to other industrialized countries.

Source: Organisation for Economic Co-operation and Development, online tax statistics database.

In addition to the overall level of taxation, another difference in tax policy across countries is the relative reliance upon different types of taxes. For example, the United States tends to rely on individual income taxes more than most countries do. Income taxes comprised 33 percent of all tax revenue in the United States in 2010, compared to an OECD average of 24 percent. Several other types of taxes are relied on more in other countries than in the United States. For more on these other types of taxes, see Box 12.2.

3.3 Current Tax Policy Issues

Taxation and Economic Growth

Although this book is concerned primarily with microeconomics, any discussion of tax policy should consider the debate over the relationship between taxation and macroeconomic growth. In addition to raising revenues, taxes generally create a disincentive to engage in certain activities. For example, high taxes on investment are expected to reduce overall investment.

supply-side economics: the macroeconomic theory that low marginal tax rates lead to higher rates of economic growth by encouraging entrepreneurship and investment

One theory is that a high overall rate of taxation creates a disincentive for people to work hard and invest, because they will keep less of their money after taxes. This theory implies that rates of macroeconomic growth will be higher when tax rates are low. Many proponents of this theory focus in particular on the marginal tax rates of high-income earners. According to **supply-side economics**, low marginal tax rates encourage entrepreneurs and investors to increase their economic efforts, leading to more employment and, ultimately, benefits that "trickle down" to workers and the broader economy.

Does the evidence support the view that taxes represent a drag on economic growth? We can analyze the relationship between economic growth and taxes by comparing data across countries and by looking at data over time within a single country. When we analyze a broad range of developing and developed countries, the evidence does not support the view that low taxes lead to high growth rates.

> If you look at the relationship between the tax ratio and the level of prosperity, measured by GDP per capita, there is no supportive evidence for the claim that low taxes guarantee

Box 12.2 International Tax Alternatives

Several tax types are heavily used in other countries but are relatively insignificant in the United States. Some of these tax types are central to different tax policy reforms proposed in the United States. We summarize five tax types here:

- *National sales tax:* This would function similar to a state sales tax—as an addition to the retail price of certain products. A national sales tax would clearly be simpler and cheaper to administer than the current U.S. federal income tax. It would also encourage savings because, under most proposals, income that is not spent on taxable goods and services is not taxed. However, a national sales tax has two significant disadvantages. First, it would create a strong incentive for the emergence of black market exchanges to evade the tax. Second, it can be highly regressive. A national sales tax could be made less regressive, or even progressive, by providing rebates for low-income households. Eligible households could complete a form at the end of the year to determine their rebate amount.
- *National consumption tax:* This is slightly different from a national sales tax. A household would pay the tax at the end of the year, or through estimated monthly payments, based on the value of its annual consumption of goods and services. Rather than having a household keep track of everything purchased, consumption can be calculated as total income less money not spent on goods and services (i.e., invested or saved). Again, a consumption tax would promote savings by exempting it from taxation. A consumption tax could also be designed to be progressive by taxing different levels of consumption at different marginal rates.
- *Value-added tax:* Most developed countries levy some form of value-added tax (VAT). A VAT is levied at each stage in the production process of a product, collected from manufacturers according to the value added at each stage. Thus the tax is not added to the retail price but incorporated into the price of the product, similar to the way excise taxes become embedded in the price of products.
- *Wealth taxes:* Although the U.S. tax system includes local property taxes and estate taxes, it does not have a tax on holdings of other assets such as corporate stocks, bonds, and personal property. Several European countries, including Sweden, Spain, and Switzerland, have instituted an annual wealth tax. A wealth tax could be very progressive by applying only to very high wealth levels.
- *Environmental taxes:* Such a tax is levied on goods and services in proportion to their environmental impact. One example is a carbon tax, which taxes products based on the carbon emissions attributable to their production or consumption. The rationale of environmental taxation is that it encourages the use and development of goods and services with reduced environmental impacts. Like other taxes on goods and services, environmental taxes can be regressive—suggesting that environmental taxes need to be combined with other progressive taxes or rebates for low-income households. Among developed countries, the United States collects the smallest share of tax revenues from environmental taxes, both as a share of GDP and as a share of total tax revenues.

> prosperity. In fact, if you just plot out the points, you will find a clear, positive correlation between high tax rates and prosperity, and that is because developed countries are the ones with the high tax ratios . . . that evidence [does not] necessarily mean that high taxes (and high government spending) cause prosperity, but it is a troubling fact that the people who say low taxes are the key to prosperity must confront.[2]

If we look instead at a smaller group of countries, some studies have found that low tax levels are associated with higher growth rates. For example, a 2010 study found that OECD member countries with higher tax levels as a percentage of GDP had lower rates of economic growth from 1991 to 2006, but that the net effect was "very small."[3] Another study that looked at tax levels across different U.S. states found that property and sales taxes did have a negative effect on economic growth rates but that income taxes did not.[4]

Data over time within a single country do not offer support for supply-side economics. As shown in Figure 12.8, the top marginal federal income tax rate in the United States has varied considerably over time, from above 90 percent to as low as 28 percent. Figure 12.8 also shows the average annual rate of economic growth in each decade since 1950. We see that the periods with the highest average growth rates, the 1950s and 1960s, were associated with the highest marginal tax rates. When the top marginal rate fell significantly in the 1980s, growth rates stayed about the same as they were in the 1970s. The top rate increased in the early 1990s, without a noticeable effect on average growth rates. It fell in the early 2000s, but that decade experienced the lowest overall growth rates.

Figure 12.8 **The Top Marginal Federal Tax Rate and Average Economic Growth, 1950–2010**
(Average Economic Growth Shown by Decade as a Percentage)

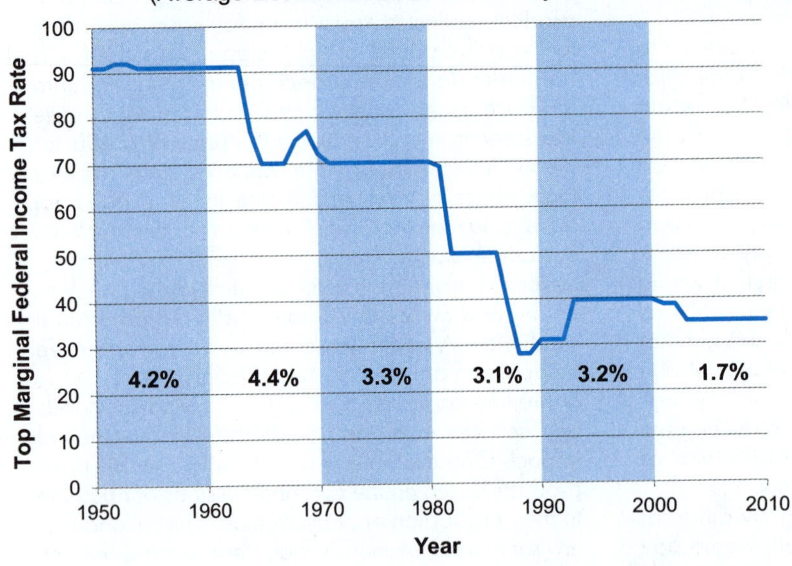

The graph indicates that lowering the top marginal federal income tax rate does not seem to be correlated with higher economic growth.

Source: Sarah Anderson, "Full Testimony to the Senate Budget Committee on Inequality, Mobility, and Opportunity," Institute for Policy Studies, February 8, 2012.

The Distribution of Taxes

An often-quoted fact is that nearly half of Americans do not pay any federal income tax. Some people conclude that this implies that nearly half of Americans are not paying *any* taxes and thus are a drain on government resources who are not paying their fair share. But this represents an incomplete picture of who pays taxes. Of course, we have learned that the federal income tax is just one of the many taxes paid by Americans. In order to analyze the distribution of the tax burden accurately, we need to consider all taxes, not just focus on one specific tax.

Another important point is that we need to understand the difference between who actually pays a tax and who feels the burden of the tax. Let's take the Social Security tax as an example. On paper, both an employee and an employer pay half the tax. But are employers able to essentially pass on the burden of their share of the tax to employees by offering them lower wages? Another example is property taxes paid by landlords. Do landlords bear the burden of these taxes or are they able to pass them on to renters by charging higher rents than they would otherwise?

tax incidence analysis: the study of who bears the ultimate burden of a tax

Economists rely upon **tax incidence analysis** to determine who bears the ultimate burden of a tax. Tax incidence analysis is:

> the study of who bears the economic burden of a tax. More generally, it is the positive analysis of the impact of taxes on the distribution of welfare within a society. It begins with the very basic insight that the person who has the legal obligation to make a tax payment may not be the person whose welfare is reduced by the existence of the tax.[5]

Tax incidence analysis has produced some generally accepted conclusions regarding the burden of different taxes.

- Social insurance taxes, even though they are split evenly on paper, are borne almost entirely by employees. The reason is that an employer will pay a worker only the value of his or her marginal contribution to profits (recall our discussion from Chapter 10). As an employer's share of social insurance taxes reduces their profits, employers will accordingly reduce the amount of pay offered to employees.
- The burden of corporate taxes ultimately falls on real people. The general consensus is that the burden of corporate taxes falls primarily on owners of capital investments such as stocks and mutual funds.
- Excise taxes, though paid by manufacturers and retailers, are actually mostly paid by consumers based on their consumption patterns. In other words, businesses are generally able to pass on excise taxes to consumers. The reason is that most excises taxes are placed on goods with relatively inelastic demand curves.
- Property taxes paid by landlords are passed on to renters.

Based on research using tax incidence analysis, we can gain a complete picture of how taxes are distributed within a society. Table 12.4 provides an estimate of the U.S. tax burden in 2013 at different income levels.

We see that the overall U.S. tax system is progressive—meaning that tax rates tend to increase with increases in income. But, far from paying nothing in taxes, even those in the lowest income group pay nearly 20 percent of their income in taxes (even if they do not pay federal income tax) when we consider all taxes. Those in the middle-income group pay about 27 percent of their total income in taxes. After the middle-income group, average tax rates continue to rise, though rather modestly, especially for the top 20 percent.

Table 12.4 **The Distribution of Taxes in the United States, 2013**

Income group	Average income	Average total tax rate	Share of all taxes	Share of all income
Lowest 20%	$13,500	18.8%	2.1%	3.3%
Second 20%	$27,200	22.5%	5.1%	6.9%
Middle 20%	$43,600	26.6%	9.9%	11.2%
Fourth 20%	$71,600	29.8%	18.2%	18.4%
Next 10%	$109,000	31.4%	14.6%	14.0%
Next 5%	$154,000	32.0%	10.7%	10.1%
Next 4%	$268,000	32.2%	15.3%	14.3%
Top 1%	$1,462,000	33.0%	24.0%	21.9%

Source: Citizens for Tax Justice, "New Tax Laws in Effect in 2013 Have Modest Progressive Impact," April 2, 2013.

It is true that high-income earners bear a large share of the tax burden, but this must be assessed relative to their income. For example, those in the top 1 percent pay 24 percent of all taxes, but they also receive about 22 percent of all income. Combined, the top 20 percent pay 65 percent of all taxes and receive about 60 percent of all income. These figures indicate that the overall tax system is slightly, but not heavily, progressive.

Whether the current progressivity of the overall tax system in the United States is appropriate is, of course, a normative issue. According to a 2012 survey, 58 percent of Americans think that the "rich" pay too little in taxes, 26 percent say that the rich pay their fair share, and only 8 percent say that the rich pay too much.[6] Changes in tax policies can be used to change the overall progressivity of the tax system. Most tax policy debates emphasize the federal income tax. But considering that nearly half of Americans do not pay federal income taxes, reducing those rates would benefit only the richer half. Similarly, raising federal income tax rates tends to affect higher-income taxpayers. Again, we should assess any change in tax policy by considering its impact on the overall progressivity of taxes, rather than focusing on a single tax.

Discussion Questions

1. Do you think the current tax system in the United States is too progressive, about right, or not progressive enough? How much do you think different income groups should pay in taxes?
2. Suppose that a relative of yours is complaining that taxes are always going up on average people while the rich can always avoid taxes because of exemptions, deductions, and other loopholes. How would you respond to him or her based on what you learned in this chapter?

REVIEW QUESTIONS

1. How is an excise tax represented in a supply-and-demand graph?
2. How does the elasticity of demand affect a price increase as a result of an excise tax?
3. What are the two motivations for taxing a product?
4. How are tax revenues represented in a supply-and-demand graph?
5. How does the elasticity of demand affect the amount of tax revenues from an excise tax? How does it affect the distribution of the tax burden?
6. How does an excise tax affect the amount of consumer and producer surplus in a market?
7. How does an excise tax affect overall social welfare?
8. What are the four justifications for taxation?
9. What is a progressive tax? A regressive tax? A proportional tax?
10. What are three reasons in support of progressive taxation?
11. What is the difference between total income and taxable income, with respect to federal income taxes?
12. How do marginal tax rates work in calculating one's income taxes?
13. How is an effective tax rate calculated?
14. What are federal social insurance taxes?
15. How have tax revenues changed in the United States over time?
16. How do overall tax rates in the United States compare with those in other countries?
17. What is supply-side economics?
18. What does the research on the relationship between taxes and economic growth indicate?
19. What is tax incidence analysis? What are some of the findings of this research?
20. How progressive is the overall tax system in the United States?

EXERCISES

1. Suppose that your town decides to impose a tax on 2-liter bottles of soda to encourage healthier dietary habits. Before the tax, the supply and demand schedules for bottles of soda are given in the table below.

Price per bottle	Quantity supplied per month	Quantity demanded per month
$1.00	16,000	20,000
$1.10	17,000	19,000
$1.20	18,000	18,000
$1.30	19,000	17,000
$1.40	20,000	16,000
$1.50	21,000	15,000

   a. Draw a supply-and-demand graph illustrating the market before the tax. What is the equilibrium price and quantity for bottles of soda?
   b. The town then imposes a tax of $0.20 per bottle. Illustrate this on your graph. What is the new equilibrium price and quantity for bottles of soda?
   c. How much in taxes will the local government collect?

2. For each of the taxes below, indicate whether you think the tax burden will be borne primarily by consumers or producers. Also, how successful do you think each tax will be in raising revenues?
   a. A city tax on the use of paper bags in supermarkets. Consumers have the option of asking for plastic bags or bringing their own bags.
   b. An increase in the national gasoline tax.

c. A tax on paper copies of textbooks when online versions of the books are available. Discuss why students' preferences (i.e., whether they are willing to use online texts) are important in determining the effect of the tax.

3. Suppose that gasoline is not taxed in the country of Autopia, and the price of gasoline is $3.00 a gallon. In order to alleviate problems with air pollution and traffic, the government of Autopia decides to institute a $0.50 a gallon tax on gasoline. After the tax, the price of gasoline rises to $3.45 a gallon.
   a. Assuming no other significant changes in the gasoline market, what can we conclude about the elasticity of demand for gasoline in Autopia?
   b. Draw a supply-and-demand graph illustrating the effects of the gasoline tax. Assume that the supply of gasoline is not particularly elastic or inelastic.
   c. Who has borne most of the burden of this tax, consumers or producers?
   d. Do you think that the tax will be effective in reducing Autopia's problems with air pollution and traffic? Why or why not? Support your answer with reference to your graph.

4. Consider the following table, which shows the total amount of taxes paid at different total income levels in a society. For each income level, calculate the effective tax rate. Is this tax system progressive or regressive? Explain.

Total income	Total taxes paid
$200,000	$50,000
$100,000	$22,000
$80,000	$16,000
$50,000	$8,000
$40,000	$4,000
$20,000	$1,000

5. Suppose that Shafik is a single person in the United States with a total income of $52,000. He is allowed to claim $10,000 of his income as nontaxable. He also contributes $1,000 to his retirement account. Based on the data in Table 12.2, how much would Shafik owe in federal income taxes?

6. As mentioned in the text, social insurance taxes in the United States are currently split equally between employers and employees. If Congress were considering a law in which employers would pay the entire amount for social insurance taxes, in order to reduce the burden on employees, would you support such a law? If the law passed, would you expect average wages to increase, decrease, or stay the same?

7. Match each concept in Column A with an example in Column B.

Column A	Column B
a. An example of a progressive tax	1. The tax burden falls primarily on producers
b. An example of a regressive tax	2. A tax on each unit of a product
c. A proportional tax	3. Total taxes divided by total income
d. An excise tax	4. Estate taxes
e. Inelastic demand	5. The study of how tax burdens are distributed
f. Elastic demand	6. Social insurance taxes
g. Effective tax rate	7. The tax burden falls primarily on consumers
h. Supply-side economics	8. A tax that is the same rate regardless of income levels
i. Tax incidence analysis	9. The theory that economic growth depends on low marginal tax rates

NOTES

1. Tax Policy Center, "The Tax Policy Briefing Book." www.taxpolicycenter.org/briefing-book/TPC_briefingbook_full.pdf. 2012.

2. "The Truth About Taxes and Economic Growth: Interview with Joel Slemrod," *Challenge* 46(1) (2003): 5–11.

3. Keshab Bhattarai, "Taxes, Public Spending and Economic Growth in OECD Countries," *Problems and Perspectives in Management* 8(1) (2010): 11–30.

4. Andrew Ojede and Steven Yamarik, "Tax Policy and State Economic Growth: The Long-Run and Short-Run of It," *Economics Letters* 116(2) (2012): 161–165.

5. Gilbert Metcalf and Don Fullerton, "The Distribution of Tax Burdens: An Introduction," National Bureau of Economic Research Working Paper 8978, Cambridge, MA, 2002, p. 1.

6. Kim Parker, "Yes, the Rich Are Different," Pew Research, Social and Demographic Trends, August 27, 2012.

13 The Economics of the Environment

A 2012 opinion poll asked Americans which should be given the higher priority: economic growth or protecting the environment.[1] By 49 percent to 41 percent, more people thought that economic growth was the higher priority. This result is a reversal of similar polls conducted between 1985 and 2007, in which large majorities were more concerned about protecting the environment. The way that this survey was formulated reflects a common perspective that a tradeoff frequently exists between economic goals and environmental goals. For example, we often hear from politicians and media pundits that environmental regulations lead to job losses and hamper economic growth. But is this perspective factually accurate?

Environmental issues are certainly not separate from economics. Deteriorating environmental conditions can create serious health problems as well as reduce the quantity and quality of natural resources that contribute to productivity and other important aspects of quality of life. Climate change is an example of environmental deterioration that is also imposing costs on people in many countries. Although no individual weather event can be linked conclusively to global climate change, more "extreme weather events" are likely to result from a global buildup of carbon dioxide (CO_2) and other greenhouse gases that contribute to planetary warming.

Because improvements in environmental quality enhance most people's well-being, economists would not be expected to oppose protecting the environment. In fact, economics has subdisciplines known as environmental economics, natural resource economics, and ecological economics. The Nobel prize–winning economist Paul Krugman has written that:

> my unscientific impression is that economists are on average more pro-environment than other people of similar incomes and backgrounds. Why? Because standard economic theory automatically predisposes those who believe in it to favor strong environmental protection.[2]

In this chapter and Chapter 14, we summarize how to use insights from economics to better manage our shared environment. Among other things, we find that environmental concerns often present a valid justification for government intervention in markets. Recall from our study of welfare analysis in Chapter 6 that government intervention is often expected to decrease economic efficiency. In this chapter, we see important examples of where, even by the most standard definitions of efficiency, this is not always the case. When economic production and consumption cause negative environmental impacts, government intervention can actually *increase* economic efficiency.

We also discuss the environmental policy tools that economists have developed to address environmental problems, and the ways in which economists express the value of the environment in monetary terms. By the end of the next chapter, we will have developed the rationale behind the following quotation:

> If you want to fight for the environment, don't hug a tree, hug an economist. Hug the economist who tells you that fossil fuels are not only the third most heavily subsidized economic sector after road transportation and agriculture but that they also promote vast inefficiencies. Hug the economist who tells you that the most efficient investment of a dollar is not in fossil fuels but in renewable energy sources that not only provide new jobs but cost less over time. Hug the economist who tells you that the price system matters; it's potentially the most potent tool of all for creating social change.[3]

1. THE THEORY OF EXTERNALITIES

In Chapter 1 we introduced the concept of **externalities**. Recall that externalities are side effects, positive or negative, of an economic transaction that affect those not directly involved in the transaction. Pollution is the classic example of a negative externality. When a consumer buys a product, such as a t-shirt, he or she rarely considers the negative environmental impacts associated with its production. T-shirt producers generally do not consider these environmental impacts either. But these impacts clearly do occur, and society as a whole suffers some damages from them.

1.1 NEGATIVE EXTERNALITIES IN THE SUPPLY-AND-DEMAND MODEL

externalities: side effects or unintended consequences, either positive or negative, that affect persons or entities such as the environment that are not among the economic actors directly involved in the economic activity that caused the effect

We can analyze externalities using our standard supply-and-demand graph. As discussed in Chapter 6, a demand curve represents the marginal benefits to consumers while a supply curve represents the marginal costs to producers. How can we incorporate the concept of externalities into this framework?

Remember that our welfare analysis in Chapter 6 excluded "the rest of society." We considered only the welfare of consumers and producers in the market. But a complete welfare analysis of a market must consider the impacts to all of society, even those outside the particular market. The key point to understand if we are to incorporate negative externalities into our supply-and-demand graph is that *negative externalities represent an additional cost of production,* over and above actual production costs. The producers do not pay this cost, but the rest of society does. So if we want to determine the total cost of providing a good or service, we must add the externality costs to the regular production costs.

Therefore, we can incorporate it into our supply-and-demand model by *adding it to the supply curve.* We do this in Figure 13.1, which represents a market for t-shirts. The normal supply curve represents the private marginal costs of producing t-shirts—the actual manufacturing costs. But to obtain the marginal cost of providing t-shirts from the broader social perspective, we need to add the negative externality costs. The externalities associated with producing t-shirts include the pesticides used to grow the cotton, the chemicals used to dye the shirts, the fuels burned to transport the shirts to stores, and other costs.

Supply–and-demand curves are expressed in monetary units. So in order to incorporate externalities into this model, they also need to be measured in dollars. Assume for now that the negative externalities associated with the production of each t-shirt total $3.00 in damages. We consider the issue of how these damages are actually measured later in the chapter.

The social marginal cost curve in Figure 13.1 equals the private production costs plus the $3.00 externality cost. But for the market participants—the consumers and producers—the externalities costs are irrelevant. The equilibrium outcome will be determined through the normal interaction of demand and (private) supply. Thus market equilibrium is at point E_M, at a price of $8.00 per shirt and a quantity of 25,000 shirts.

Our welfare analysis from Chapter 6 found E_M to be the economically efficient outcome. But now we consider the impact of the negative externalities. The vertical distance between

Figure 13.1 **The Negative Externalities of T-Shirt Production**

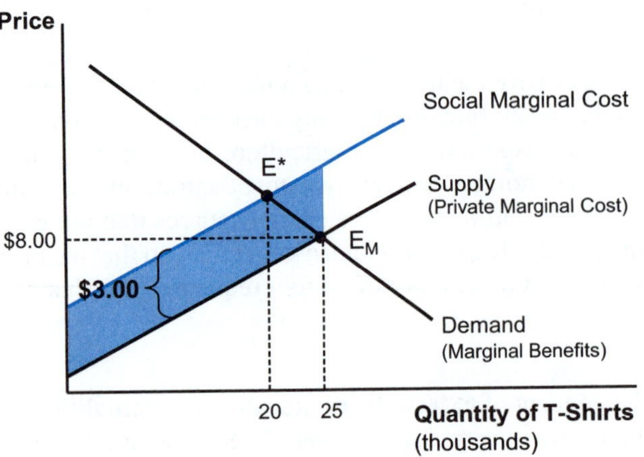

A negative externality can be represented in a supply-and-demand graph as an additional marginal cost. The socially efficient level of production occurs at E^*, but the unregulated market outcome is E_M.

the two marginal cost curves represents the $3.00 externality damage per shirt. This damage occurs for every shirt up to the quantity sold of 25,000. Thus the total externality damage is the shaded area in Figure 13.1. With 25,000 shirts and damage of $3.00 per shirt, the externality damage thus totals $75,000.

1.2 Internalizing Negative Externalities

In a market without externalities, we learned in Chapter 6 that the market outcome was economically efficient. Any government intervention, such as price floors or price ceilings, reduced total welfare. But when we introduce negative externalities, is the market outcome still efficient?

We can answer this question by looking at Figure 13.1. The marginal benefits of t-shirts exceed the social marginal costs up to point E^*, at 20,000 t-shirts. So up to 20,000 t-shirts, net social benefits are positive, and even with the externality damage, it makes sense to produce each of these t-shirts.

But notice that, beyond point E^*, the social marginal costs exceed the marginal benefits. For every t-shirt above 20,000, society is actually becoming worse off when we consider the externality damage as well as the production costs. Thus the market equilibrium quantity of 25,000 is too high. The economically efficient outcome is E^*, at 20,000 shirts. The market outcome is inefficient.

Pigovian tax: a tax levied on a product to reduce or eliminate the negative externality associated with its production

Given that the unregulated market outcome is inefficient when externalities are present, can economic efficiency be increased through government intervention? The most common policy response to a market with externalities is to tax the product. When a product causes a negative externality, a tax that is levied specifically to lower or eliminate that externality is called a **Pigovian tax**, after British economist Arthur Pigou, who proposed the idea in the 1920s.

internalizing negative externalities: bringing external costs into the market (for example, by instituting a Pigovian tax at a level equal to the externality damage), thus making market participants pay the true social cost of their actions

A Pigovian tax operates in the same way as an excise tax. As you will remember from Chapter 12, instituting a tax increases production costs, effectively shifting the supply curve upward. By setting the Pigovian tax at the "right" level, we obtain a new supply curve, $Supply_{Tax}$, illustrated in Figure 13.2. Note that this supply curve is the same as the social marginal cost curve from Figure 13.1. With this tax in place, the new market outcome will be E_{Tax}, which is the efficient outcome, corresponding to E^* in Figure 13.1.

We say that the Pigovian tax has "**internalized the negative externality**" because the external costs of $3.00 per t-shirt are now integrated into the market. Setting the tax equal to the externality damage, $3.00 per shirt, now means that the market participants pay the true social cost of producing t-shirts. Note that the price of t-shirts has increased from $8 to $10. So some of the burden of the tax has been passed on to consumers as higher prices, but

Figure 13.2 **Internalizing a Negative Externality with a Pigovian Tax**

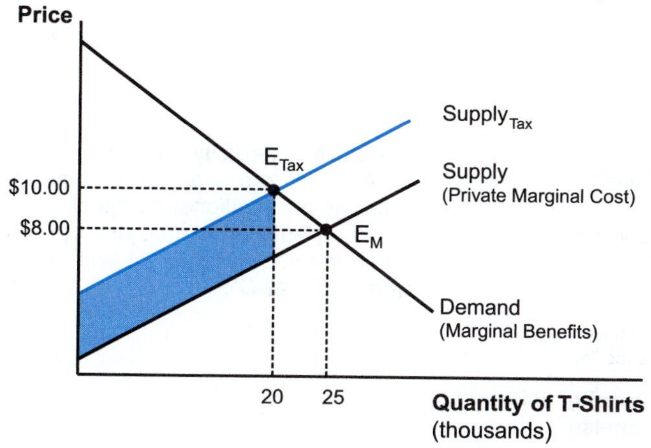

A Pigovian tax reduces the magnitude of a negative externality. If set at the correct level, the tax results in the socially efficient level of production.

producers also bear some of the tax burden in terms of lower profits (again, similar to our discussion of taxes from last chapter).

A detailed welfare analysis of a Pigovian tax with a negative externality is presented in the appendix to this chapter. That analysis proves that total social welfare increases when the negative externality is internalized. So unlike our welfare analysis of a tax in Chapter 12, in the case of a negative externality a Pigovian tax is economically efficient and increases social welfare.

Even with a Pigovian tax, we still have some externality damage, represented by the shaded area in Figure 13.2. Externality damages are still $3.00 per shirt, but the quantity sold is now only 20,000 shirts, for a total damage of $60,000. But note that the revenue from the tax is also $60,000 (a $3.00 tax per shirt, collected on 20,000 shirts). Thus the government collects exactly enough in tax revenue to compensate society for the damage done by producing t-shirts! If conditions change in such a way that the same kind of pollution caused greater harm—suppose, for example, that more people develop allergic reactions to the chemicals used to dye the shirts—then it would be appropriate to raise the tax accordingly.

Although the use of a Pigovian tax corrects the inefficiency caused by the negative externality, it does not provide a mechanism for compensating those who continue to suffer pollution damage. Nor does it indicate how the government revenues from the tax should be used. Some economists suggest that the tax revenues should be used simply to lower other taxes (discussed further below). It is also possible to use the revenues for direct compensation of those affected or environmental improvement. Given that environmental taxes tend to be regressive (because, e.g., purchases of t-shirts would be a higher proportion of income for a poor person than for a rich one), it may make sense to devote at least part of the revenues to rebates to compensate lower-income people for the impact of the tax.

1.3 Positive Externalities

Externalities can also be positive, meaning that an economic transaction positively affects those outside the market. One example is a homeowner who installs solar panels on his or her house. Society as a whole benefits because the solar panels reduce the need for generating electricity from fossil fuels, thus improving air quality and reducing other ecological damages.

We present a basic analysis of a positive externality in Figure 13.3. The normal demand curve represents the marginal benefits of the product, solar panels in this example, to consumers—or the "private" marginal benefits. The market equilibrium is E_M, which is the normal intersection of supply and demand. The market price of solar panels would be P_M and the quantity sold would be Q_M.

Figure 13.3 **Analysis of a Positive Externality**

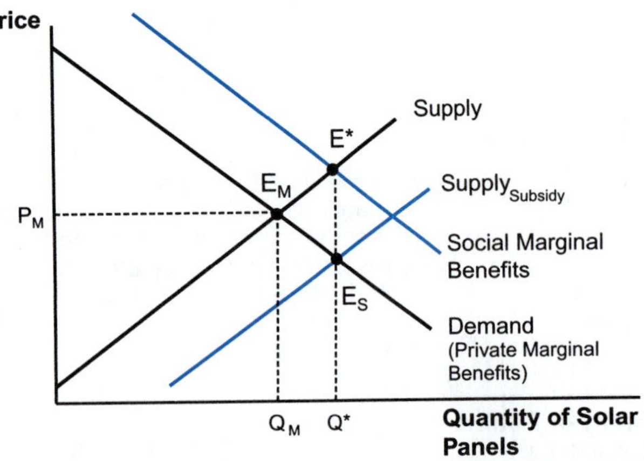

A positive externality can be represented in a supply-and-demand graph as an additional marginal benefit. A subsidy can be used to obtain the socially efficient level of production, at Q^*.

We can incorporate a positive externality into our supply-and-demand model by realizing that a positive externality is *an additional benefit obtained by society,* over and above the private benefits of consumers. Thus we can add the positive externality benefits to the demand curve to obtain the social marginal benefits of the product. This is shown in Figure 13.3. Note that for every solar panel between Q_M and Q^*, the social marginal benefits exceed the marginal costs (i.e., the supply curve). The economically efficient level of solar panel production is E^*, not E_M. The unregulated market produces too few solar panels, from the broader perspective of social welfare.

subsidy: a per-unit payment to producers to lower production costs and encourage greater production

In the case of a positive externality, a common policy recommendation is to subsidize the product to encourage greater production. A **subsidy** is a per-unit payment to producers to offset, and thus lower, their production costs. This effectively encourages greater production. We model a subsidy by shifting the supply curve downward. With the subsidy in place, the new supply curve is $Supply_{Subsidy}$, and the new equilibrium point is E_S. The resulting level of solar panels sales, Q^*, is the "right" level from the broader social perspective.

The complete welfare analysis of a positive externality is slightly complex, so we do not present it here. But the conclusion of a formal welfare analysis is that a subsidy in the case of a product with a positive externality increases overall social welfare. As in the case of a negative externality, the unregulated market is inefficient and government intervention is necessary to obtain the efficient outcome.

1.4 Policy Implications of Externalities

The existence of externalities presents one of the strongest justifications for government intervention in markets. Externalities are an example of market failure, as discussed in Chapter 6. When externalities exist, the unregulated market does not produce the socially efficient outcome.

Our analysis of externalities has profound policy implications, particularly for negative environmental externalities. Virtually every product produced in modern markets results in *some* pollution and polluting waste. Given that a Pigovian tax increases economic efficiency, is it then reasonable to ask whether we should tax *every* product based on its environmental impacts?

Few economists would support trying to place an environmental tax on every product. The first reason is that we must consider the administrative costs of collecting Pigovian taxes. For some products with relatively minor environmental impacts, the social benefits probably are not worth the administrative costs. Second, the task of estimating the environmental damage of every product, in dollars, is clearly excessive. Again, for many products the cost of obtaining a monetary estimate probably is not worth the effort.

upstream taxes: taxes instituted as close as possible in a production process to the extraction of raw materials

But some economists have suggested a broad system of **upstream taxes** on the most environmentally damaging products, particularly on fossil fuels (coal, oil, and natural gas) and important minerals. An upstream tax is placed as close as possible to the point where raw materials are extracted. In the case of coal, for example, an upstream tax might be instituted on each ton of coal extracted from coal mines. In addition to administrative simplicity, another advantage of upstream taxes is that the environmental damages of final consumer products do not need to be estimated. Instead, after we have estimated the damages associated with coal extraction and burning, the costs of the upstream tax would carry through numerous production processes and eventually increase the price of goods and services that are dependent on coal as an input, such as electricity.

Although various countries have some negative externality taxes, such as excise taxes on gasoline, no country has such a broad system of upstream Pigovian taxes. Figure 13.4 shows the magnitude of environmental taxation, as a percentage of total tax revenues, in various developed countries. Few countries collect more than 10 percent of their total tax revenue from environmental taxes. Among developed countries, the United States collects the lowest percentage.

revenue-neutral (taxes): offsetting any tax increases with decreases in other taxes such that overall tax collections remain constant

The main barrier to increasing environmental taxes is that few politicians are willing to support higher taxes. However, environmental taxes can be **revenue-neutral** if any tax increases are offset by lowering other taxes so that the total taxes on an average household remain unchanged. Given that environmental taxes tend to be regressive, revenue neutrality could be achieved by reducing a regressive tax, such as social insurance taxes. In addition to economic efficiency, a broad shift away from taxes on income and toward taxes on negative externalities also provides people with more options to reduce their tax burden.

If environmental taxes constituted a large portion of someone's total tax burden, he or she could reduce this burden by using more efficient vehicles and appliances, relying more on public transportation, reducing energy use, and numerous other options. Of course, that is not always easy to do; one example is someone whose job requires a long commute in a location in which public transportation is not available. In such a case, it becomes necessary

Figure 13.4 **Environmental Taxes in Select Developed Countries, as a Percent of Total Tax Revenue, 2010**

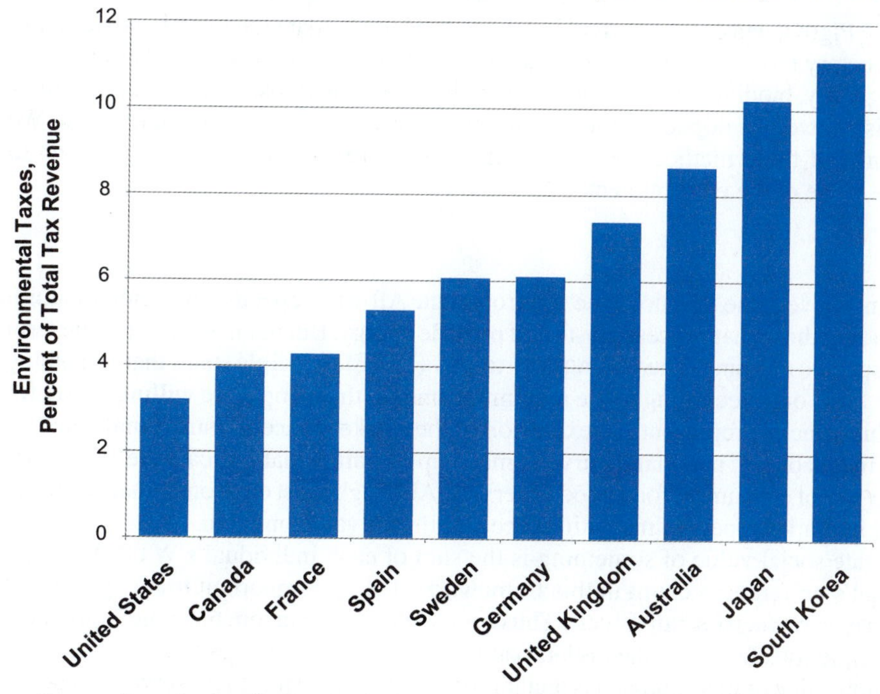

Environmental taxes generally comprise less than 10 percent of a country's total tax revenue. Among developed countries, the United States receives the lowest portion of its total tax revenues from environmental taxes.

Source: Organisation for Economic Co-operation and Development, OECD/EEA database on instruments used for environmental policy and natural resources management. Updated April 13, 2012.

for government involvement to go beyond taxes and subsidies, to take into account the social infrastructure and institutions that will allow people—especially those whose financial resources limit their individual options—to respond without undue pain to the signals given by a market that has been shifted toward greater environmental responsibility.

Despite the economic logic supporting taxes on negative externalities, many environmentally damaging activities, including fossil-fuel production, mining minerals, and harvesting timber, are actually subsidized instead of taxed (see Box 13.1). Obviously, this results in pollution levels that are not optimal. From an economic point of view, these subsidies are perverse—that is, they encourage exactly those activities that we should be seeking to discourage.

Box 13.1 Fossil-Fuel Subsidies

According to analysis by Bloomberg New Energy Finance, global subsidies for fossil fuels are about twelve times higher than those allocated for renewable energy. In 2009 global subsidies for renewable energy totaled $43 million to $46 billion, mainly in the form of tax credits and price guarantees. Meanwhile, the International Energy Agency estimated that governments spent about $550 billion to subsidize fossil fuels.

The Group of 20, a group of major countries including the United States, China, Germany, and Russia, have agreed to phase out fossil-fuel subsidies over "the medium term," but progress has been slow and no specific target date has been set. Meanwhile, many countries are ramping up their commitment to renewable energy. The most expensive renewable energy subsidy in 2009 was about $10 billion for Germany's feed-in tariff, a policy that guarantees long-term prices for suppliers of renewable energy. Other feed-in tariffs in Europe totaled another $10 billion.

The United States spent more than any other country in renewable-energy subsidies in 2009, around $18 billion. China provided about $2 billion, although this figure is likely too low as it does not include the value of low-interest loans offered for renewable energy projects by state-owned banks.

Source: Alex Morales,"Fossil Fuel Subsidies Are Twelve Times Renewables Support," Bloomberg, July 29, 2010.

2. Valuing the Environment

In order to set a Pigovian tax at the correct level, we need to estimate the negative externality damage in monetary terms. Environmental damage includes such diverse effects as reduced air and water quality, biodiversity loss, human health impacts, and lost recreation opportunities. Economists have developed various techniques to estimate environmental values. We summarize some of these methods below, but first we address the conceptual approach to measuring the value of the environment.

2.1 Total Economic Value

willingness-to-pay (WTP) principle: the economic value of something, such as an environmental benefit, is equal to the maximum amount people are willing to pay for it

In a broad sense, everyone "values" the environment. All life depends on various natural systems, including those that process waste and provide energy. But to an economist, the term "value" has a specific meaning. The **willingness-to-pay (WTP) principle** states that something has economic value only according to the maximum amount that people are willing to pay for it. Note that this principle represents an extension of the market concept of marginal benefits. As discussed in Chapter 4, a demand curve is made up of points that indicate the maximum willingness-to-pay of consumers for a good or service. Although most environmental attributes are not traded in markets, people may still place significant value on them.

The aggregate social value of something is the sum of each individual's WTP. Although each individual's preferences count in this framework, it is also important to recognize that the ability to pay varies across individuals. Thus instead of a "one person, one vote" approach, the WTP principle translates to "one dollar, one vote."

Another implication of this approach is that if no one is willing to pay to preserve something, then it does not have economic value. So the economic value of an endangered insect species in a remote forest, which has no obvious human uses, may well be zero. However, some economists believe that nature has certain inherent rights apart from any human economic values. In particular, even if the WTP to preserve a species is zero, the species could still be said to have **intrinsic value**, or value in a broader ecological or ethical sense, and thus have a right to exist.* Intrinsic value is especially difficult to express in monetary terms.

intrinsic value: the value of something in an ecological or ethical sense, apart from any economic value based on willingness to pay

People's willingness to pay for environmental attributes may derive from a variety of motivations. Potential reasons for valuing the environment include:

1. *Profit-making enterprises:* activities such as harvesting timber, fishing, grazing, and agriculture depend on natural systems.
2. *Recreation:* natural sites provide places for outdoor recreation, including camping, hiking, fishing, hunting, and viewing wildlife.
3. **Ecosystem services**: tangible benefits obtained freely from nature, simply as a result of natural processes. Ecosystem services include nutrient recycling, flood protection from wetlands and vegetation, waste assimilation, carbon storage in trees and other plants, water purification, and pollination by bees.
4. **Nonuse benefits**: nontangible welfare benefits that we obtain from nature. Nonuse benefits include the psychological benefits that people gain just from knowing that natural places exist, even if they will never visit them. The value that people gain from knowing that ecosystems will be available to future generations is another type of nonuse benefit.

ecosystem services: tangible benefits that humans obtain from natural processes, such as nutrient recycling, flood control, and pollination

nonuse benefits: nontangible welfare benefits that people derive from ecosystems without physical interaction (i.e., psychological benefits)

The **total economic value** of a natural system is the sum of all the benefits for which people are willing to pay. Thus the total economic value of, for eample, a national forest is the sum of any profits obtained from harvesting timber, the WTP of all those who engage in recreation in the forest, the value of the ecosystem services such as soil erosion prevention and carbon storage, and the nonuse benefits that people obtain from knowing that the forest exists. It is important to realize that in calculating total economic value, priority is not given to any particular use of the forest. When uses are incompatible, such as deciding whether a particular tract of forest should be clear cut or preserved for recreation and wildlife habitat, economic analysis can help to determine which use provides the highest overall economic value to society.

total economic value: the sum of all the benefits for which people are willing to pay, with respect to an ecosystem or natural place

2.2 NONMARKET VALUATION METHODOLOGIES

We have already seen how we can determine the economic benefits of a market good or service—it is equal to the sum of consumer and producer surplus. But many of the benefits that we obtain from the environment are not traded in markets. If we are to estimate total economic value, we need techniques to estimate such values as recreation benefits, ecosystem services, and nonuse values. These techniques are referred to as **nonmarket valuation**, because they produce benefit estimates for goods and services that are not directly traded in markets.

nonmarket valuation techniques: economic valuation methods that obtain estimates for goods and services not directly traded in markets

Nonmarket valuation techniques come in four main types:

1. the cost of illness method
2. replacement cost methods
3. revealed preference methods
4. stated preference methods

We summarize each of these methods, including the advantages and disadvantages of each.

*There is a disciplinary distinction between economists who study environmental issues. Traditional environmental economics generally recognizes only values backed by WTP. The notion that nature has certain inherent rights is a principle of ecological economics, a more recent subdiscipline that emphasizes the need to preserve ecosystem functions.

Cost of Illness Method

cost of illness method: a nonmarket valuation technique that estimates the direct and indirect costs associated with illnesses with environmental causes

The **cost of illness method** is used to estimate the damage of reductions in environmental quality that have human health consequences. Conversely, it can be used to estimate the benefits of improvements in environmental quality (i.e., the avoided damages). This method estimates the direct and indirect costs related to illnesses with environmental causes. The direct costs include medical costs such as office visits and medication paid by individuals and insurers and lost wages due to illness. Indirect costs can include decreases in human capital (e.g., if a child misses a significant number of school days due to illness), welfare losses from pain and suffering, and decreases in economic productivity due to work absences.

lower-bound estimate: an estimate that represents the minimum potential value of something. The actual value is thus greater than or equal to the lower-bound estimate.

The cost of illness method generally provides us with only a **lower-bound estimate** of the WTP to avoid illnesses. The true WTP could be higher because the actual expenses may not capture the full losses to individuals from illness. But even a lower-bound estimate could provide policy guidance. For example, in 2007 the cost of asthma in the United States was estimated to be $56 billion, based on direct medical costs and productivity losses from missed days of school and work.[4] The costs for a typical affected worker totaled about $3,500. These estimates provide a starting point for determining whether efforts to reduce asthma cases are economically efficient.

Replacement Cost Methods

replacement cost methods: nonmarket valuation techniques that estimate the value of ecosystem services based on the cost of actions that provide substitute services

Replacement cost methods can be used to estimate the value of ecosystem services. These approaches consider the costs of human actions that substitute for lost ecosystem services. For example, a community could construct a water treatment plant to make up for the lost water purification benefits from a forest habitat. The natural pollination of plants by bees could, to some extent, be done by hand or machine. If we can estimate the costs of these substitute actions, in terms of construction and labor costs, these can be considered an approximation of society's WTP for these ecosystem services.

Although replacement cost methods are often used to estimate ecosystem service values, they are not necessarily measures of WTP. Suppose that a community could construct a water treatment plant for $50 million to offset the water purification services of a nearby forest. This estimate does not tell us whether the community would actually be willing to pay the $50 million should the forest be damaged. Actual WTP could be more or less than $50 million and is fundamentally unrelated to the cost of the water purification plant. So, in this sense, replacement cost estimates should be used with caution. However, if we know that the community would be willing to pay $50 million for a water treatment plant if the ecosystem services of the forest are lost, then we could conclude that $50 million represents a lower bound of the value of the water purification benefits of the forest.

revealed preference methods: valuation techniques that infer the value of nonmarket goods and services based on people's decisions in related markets

Revealed Preference Methods

Although markets do not exist for many environmental goods and services, we can sometimes infer the values that people place on them through their behavior in other markets. **Revealed preference methods** are techniques that obtain nonmarket values based on people's decisions in related markets. Economists generally prefer deriving nonmarket values based on actual market behavior. Thus revealed preference methods are generally considered the most valid approach to nonmarket valuation. However, the environmental benefits for which revealed preference methods can be used to provide nonmarket values are limited.

travel cost models: a revealed preference method used to obtain estimates of the recreation benefits of natural sites based on variations in the travel costs paid by visitors from different regions

One common type of revealed preference method is represented by **travel cost models**. These models are used to estimate the economic benefits that people obtain by engaging in recreation at natural sites such as national parks or lakes. Even if the recreation site does not charge an entry fee, all visitors must pay a "price" equal to their costs to travel to the site, such as gas, plane tickets, accommodations, and even the time required to travel to the site. As visitors to a recreation site from different regions effectively pay a different price, economists can use this information to derive a demand curve for the site using statistical models, and thus estimate consumer surplus. Travel cost models are most applicable for recreation sites that attract visitors from distant places, in order to provide enough variation in travel costs to estimate a demand curve.

Numerous travel cost models have estimated the recreational benefits of natural sites. For example, a 2010 study of recreational visitors to the Murray River in Australia found that the average visitor received a consumer surplus of US$155 per day.[5] Travel cost models have been used to explore how changes in the fish catch rate affect the consumer surplus of anglers visiting sites in Wisconsin[6] and how a drought affects the benefits of visitors to reservoirs in California.[7]

defensive expenditures approach: a nonmarket valuation technique that obtains benefit estimates based on the cost of actions that people take to avoid environmental harm

Another type of revealed preference method is the **defensive expenditures approach.** This approach is applicable in situations where people are able to take actions to reduce their exposure to environmental harm. For example, people with concerns about their drinking water quality may choose to purchase bottled water or install a water filtration system. These expenditures may reflect their WTP for water quality. For example, a 2006 study in Brazil found that households were paying US$16–$19 per month on defensive expenditures to improve drinking water quality.[8]

A limitation of the defensive expenditures approach is that people may be taking defensive actions for a variety of reasons, some unrelated to environmental quality. For example, other reasons for buying bottled water may include convenience or status. Thus attributing the entire cost of bottled water as a measure of concern about drinking water quality would not be appropriate in such cases. It also suffers from the inherent problem of any market valuation: The preferences of the rich weigh much more heavily than the preferences of the poor. Plenty of people around the world who are actually suffering from the health effects of impure water may not be able to afford to buy bottled water; thus their abstract WTP is made invisible by inability to pay.

In addition to the serious problem of unequal ability to pay, the approaches just described—the defensive expenditures approach and travel cost models—cannot be used to obtain benefit estimates for ecosystem services and nonuse values. Thus in order to obtain estimates of total economic value for many environmental goods and services, we need a technique that can provide us some estimate of these values.

Stated Preference Methods

stated preference methods: nonmarket valuation techniques that directly ask survey respondents about their preferences in a hypothetical scenario

contingent valuation: a stated preference method where survey respondents are asked about their willingness to pay for a hypothetical outcome

The final nonmarket valuation technique that we consider is the most used, as well as the most controversial. **Stated preference methods** directly obtain information on people's preferences in a hypothetical scenario simply by asking them. The most common stated preference method is **contingent valuation**, in which survey respondents are asked questions about their WTP for a specific hypothetical outcome.

The main advantage of contingent valuation is that surveys can be designed to ask respondents about *any* type of environmental benefit. For example, a 2012 study found that households in Spain were willing to pay an average of $22 per year for a hypothetical reduction in highway noise and air pollution.[9] A 2011 paper determined that the WTP for preserving marine biodiversity in the Azores Islands was $121 to $837 (as a one-time payment).[10]

Although hundreds of contingent valuation studies have been conducted in the past several decades, the validity of the results remains highly controversial. Given that respondents' preferences are based on a hypothetical scenario, and they do not actually have to pay anything, some economists consider the results flawed because of various biases. For example, a respondent who generally favors biodiversity preservation may have an incentive to overstate his or her actual WTP in order to influence the policy process. Some respondents may not accurately consider their income limitations when stating WTP values; this gets around the "ability to pay" problem, but does not produce the kind of WTP estimates that many economists seek as "realistic."

Yet contingent valuation remains the only way to estimate some environmental benefits, particularly nonuse values. So, the debate over the method often centers on whether some estimate is better than no estimate. The debate over contingent valuation occurs mostly among academics, but the issue became relevant to businesses and policymakers in the wake of the 1989 *Exxon Valdez* oil spill in Alaska. The lawsuit against Exxon sought compensation for billions of dollars in lost nonuse values, as a result of the damage done to a relatively pristine marine environment. The federal government convened a panel of top economists, including two Nobel Prize winners, to review the contingent valuation method. Their report concluded that contingent valuation studies "can produce estimates reliable enough to be the starting point of a judicial process," but it also recognized the method's "likely tendency to exaggerate willingness to pay" and provided a list of demanding guidelines for future studies.[11]

contingent ranking: a stated preference method in which respondents are asked to rank various hypothetical scenarios

Some of the problems associated with contingent valuation can be avoided by using **contingent ranking**, another stated preference method. In contingent ranking, respondents are asked to rank various hypothetical scenarios according to their preferences. Thus there is no potential for respondents to exaggerate their WTP.

2.3 Cost-Benefit Analysis

cost-benefit analysis: a technique to analyze a policy or project proposal in which all costs and benefits are converted to monetary estimates, if possible, to determine the net social value

The nonmarket valuation methods discussed above can be used to estimate the negative externalities associated with various goods and services. These methods can also be used to determine whether a particular policy or public project should be undertaken. For example, consider a proposal to build a large dam or a new law to increase air quality standards. One of the approaches used to evaluate these proposals is to ask whether its economic benefits exceed its costs. **Cost-benefit analysis** (CBA) seeks to convert all costs and benefits to a common metric.

In theory, measuring all impacts in dollars (or another monetary unit) produces a "bottom-line" result (i.e., a single number) so that we can choose which alternative results in the highest net social value. In practice, however, CBA is often incomplete, with some impacts unable to be estimated in monetary terms. The results may be dependent on specific assumptions. Sometimes, one side of the analysis—the costs or the benefits—are more fully fleshed out than the other, making it difficult to arrive at an objective recommendation.

The basic steps of a CBA are relatively straightforward:

1. List all costs and benefits of the project or policy proposal. Typically, this involves developing several scenarios.
2. Convert all costs and benefits to monetary values. Some values can be obtained based on market analysis, while other values will require nonmarket valuation.
3. Add up all the costs and benefits to determine the net benefits of each scenario. Sometimes, the results are expressed as a ratio (i.e., benefits divided by costs).
4. Choose the scenario that is the most economically efficient.

The most appealing feature of CBA may be its seeming objectivity. It also presents a way to argue for environmental protection in economic terms, rather than on ethical or ecological terms. Many CBAs have shown that the WTP for environmental protection can be quite high.

Of course, all the problems with the nonmarket valuation techniques discussed above can complicate CBA. Two additional issues often arise in environmental CBAs: how to value costs and benefits that occur in the future, and how to value human lives.

Discounting the Future

Many environmental policies involve paying costs in the short term, while the benefits will be obtained further in the future. For example, installing pollution control equipment has an upfront cost, while the health benefits of reduced cancer rates will only be realized decades in the future. Thus we need a way to compare impacts that occur at different times.

There is a natural human tendency to focus on the present more than the future. Most people would prefer to receive a benefit now over a similar benefit in the future. There may also be practical reasons to prefer monetary benefits now, if they can be invested to provide increased returns in the future. Economists incorporate this concept into CBA through **discounting**. Discounting effectively reduces the weight placed on any cost or benefit that occurs in the future. The further in the future the cost or benefit occurs, the less weight is given to that impact. In order to compare an impact that occurs in the present to an impact that occurs in the future, the future impact must be converted to an equivalent **present value** using the following formula:

discounting: an approach in which costs and benefits that occur in the future are assigned less weight (i.e., discounted) relative to current costs and benefits

present value: the current value of a future cost or benefit, obtained by discounting

discount rate: the annual percentage rate at which future costs and benefits are discounted relative to current costs and benefits

$$PV(X_n) = X_n / (1 + r)^n$$

where X_n is the monetary value of the cost or benefit, n is the number of years in the future the impact occurs, and r is the **discount rate**—the annual percentage rate by which future impacts are reduced, expressed as a proportion. For example, if the discount rate was 3 percent, r would be 0.03.

A simple example illustrates how discounting works. Suppose that we are analyzing a proposal to improve air quality. Assume that the cost of this proposal, including the installation of new pollution control equipment, is $10 million, to be paid right now. The benefits of cleaner air are estimated at $20 million, but these benefits will occur 25 years in the future.* Should we approve this law?

In order to obtain the present value of the $20 million benefit, we need to choose a discount rate. Suppose that we apply a discount rate of 5 percent. The present value of the benefits would be:

$$PV = \$20\ million / (1.05)^{25} = \$5{,}906{,}055$$

As the present value of the $20 million benefit in 25 years is only about $6 million, it does not make economic sense to pay $10 million now to obtain this benefit. But suppose instead that we apply a discount rate of 2 percent. In this case, the present value of the benefits is:

$$PV = \$20\ million / (1.02)^{25} = \$12{,}190{,}617$$

In this case, the net benefits of the proposal are positive (i.e., the present value of the benefits exceeds the costs by about $2 million). At the lower discount rate, the proposal makes economic sense. This example illustrates the importance of the choice of a discount rate. We will see that this is particularly true in Chapter 14, when we discuss analyses of global climate change.

One approach for choosing a discount rate is to set it equal to the rate of return on low-risk investments such as government bonds. The rationale for this is that any funds used for a beneficial public project could otherwise be invested to provide society with greater resources in the future. In early 2013, the nominal rate of return on a 30-year U.S. Treasury bond was 3 percent.[12] However, this rate has varied considerably over time. Thus some economists question whether we should base the valuation of long-term environmental impacts on an interest rate that is subject to changeable financial market conditions.

Other approaches to choosing a discount rate consider the ethical dimension of valuing future impacts. In some sense, a positive discount rate implies that future generations count less than the current generation. Although nearly all economists believe in the principle of

*In reality, the benefits would occur over the course of several years in the future. Here, for the sake of simplicity, we assume that all the benefits occur in a single year, 25 years from now.

discounting, economists who are more concerned about long-term environmental damages tend to prefer lower discount rates.*

Valuing Human Lives

Another controversial aspect of CBA is analyzing policies that affect human mortality rates. The benefits of many environmental policies, such as those addressing air and water quality, are often expressed in terms of the number of avoided deaths. In a CBA framework, we seek to convert all benefits to monetary values to make them directly comparable to the costs. Suppose that we are analyzing a policy that will improve air quality at a cost of $500 million to society, but reduce the number of deaths associated with air pollution by 50. Is such a policy "worth it" to society?

Although economists are not in the business of placing a value on the life of any particular person, their goal is to estimate how people value relatively minor changes in mortality risk and use this information to infer the **value of a statistical life (VSL)**. A VSL estimate, in theory, indicates how much society is willing to pay to reduce the number of deaths from environmental pollution by one, without any reference to whose death will be avoided.

value of a statistical life (VSL): society's willingness to pay to avoid one death, based on the valuation of relatively small changes in mortality risks

An example illustrates how a VSL is estimated. Let's assume that we conduct a contingent valuation survey to ask people how much they would be willing to pay to improve air quality such that the number of deaths from air pollution would decline by 50. Each respondent's risk of dying from air pollution would decline slightly as a result of the policy. Suppose that the survey results indicate that the average household is willing to pay $10 per year for this policy. If society comprises 100 million households, then the total WTP for the policy would be:

$$100\ \textit{million} * \$10 = \$1\ \textit{billion}$$

Because this is the aggregate WTP to reduce deaths by 50, the VSL would be:

$$\$1\ \textit{billion} / \textit{50} = \$20\ \textit{million}$$

Some people object to valuing human lives on ethical grounds. Others counter that we must explicitly or implicitly analyze the tradeoffs between public expenditures and health benefits, and the VSL methodology provides a transparent approach. Major environmental policy proposals in the United States must be reviewed using CBA, and thus government agencies must often apply a VSL. The VSLs used by government agencies have varied but generally increased over time, from around $2 million in the 1980s to nearly $10 million more recently. In other words, regulations that can reduce environmental deaths at a cost of less than $10 million per avoided death would be considered economically efficient. (For more on the economic, and political, debate about the VSL in the United States, see Box 13.2.)

Other Difficulties with Cost Benefit Analysis

Most environmental cost-benefit analyses are further complicated by several other issues. These include:

1. analysis of uncertainty
2. missing monetary values
3. sensitivity to assumptions

Consider a proposal to build a large dam for flood protection. The benefits of flood protection depend somewhat on future climate conditions, which are difficult to predict with

*A 0 percent discount rate implies that any impact that occurs in the future, even those in the distant future, count the same as a current impact. Economists have tended to justify some discounting on the assumption that future generations will have higher incomes and better technology and will thus be better equipped to deal with problems created in the present. However, some economists note that environmental damages and resource constraints could lead to lower standards of living in the future.

Box 13.2 The Politics of Valuing Life

The valuation of human lives is not merely an economic issue but a political one, as demonstrated by changes in the VSLs used by U.S. federal agencies in recent years. During the administration of George W. Bush, the VSL used by the Environmental Protection Agency (EPA) was as low as $6.8 million. But in 2010, the EPA increased its VSL to $9.1 million in a cost-benefit analysis of air pollution standards. Under the administration of Barack Obama, the Food and Drug Administration also increased its VSL, from $5 million in 2008 to $7.9 million in 2010. Based on higher VSLs, the Transportation Department now requires stronger car roofs—a regulation that was rejected under the Bush administration as too expensive.

Under the Obama administration, federal regulators are also considering adjusting the VSL based on the type of risk. For example, the EPA is considering the application of a "cancer differential" that would increase the VSL for cancer risks, based on surveys that show that people are willing to pay more to avoid cancer, as opposed to other health risks. The Department of Homeland Security has suggested that the willingness to pay to avoid terrorism deaths is about double that of other risks.

Manufacturers and power companies have traditionally advocated the use of cost-benefit analysis for environmental policies, essentially forcing regulators to prove the economic efficiency of environmental improvements. But the recent VSL increases have led them to reconsider their approach. For example, the U.S. Chamber of Commerce (a group that represents businesses) is now lobbying for Congress to have greater oversight of federal regulators. On the other hand, environmental groups, which remain critical of the VSL methodology, have praised the Obama administration for increasing these values.

Source: Binyamin Appelbaum, "As U.S. Agencies Put More Value on a Life, Businesses Fret," *New York Times*, February 16, 2011.

precautionary principle: the notion that policies should err on the side of caution when there is a low-probability risk of a catastrophic outcome

a high degree of certainty. There may also be a small chance that the dam will fail, perhaps causing catastrophic damage. Another example is analyzing the risk of a major oil spill, which requires one to estimate the probability that such a spill will occur. Incorporating such uncertainty into a CBA is possible if we have some idea of the probability of various outcomes, but some risks are fundamentally difficult to predict. In these cases, some economists advocate the **precautionary principle**: that policies should err on the side of caution when there is a low-probability risk of a catastrophic outcome.

In almost any real-world environmental CBA, we will be unable to estimate all impacts in monetary terms. For example, how can we estimate the benefits of a recreation site that is not yet available? We may be able to "transfer" an estimate from an existing similar recreation site, but we cannot be sure that the transferred estimate is valid for the new site. Also, government agencies frequently do not have the resources to fund original studies to estimate all needed values. We may be able to make an educated guess about certain missing values, but this obviously reduces the objectivity of a CBA.

Finally, the recommendations of many CBAs are highly dependent on various assumptions. As we saw earlier, the choice of a discount rate may determine whether a particular policy is recommended. Other assumptions may relate to how risk is analyzed or how contingent valuation results are interpreted. Ideally, a CBA should consider a broad range of assumptions. Of course, if different assumptions produce different results, then we must make a subjective decision about which result we should rely upon. These considerations suggest that CBA is often not as objective as it may seem at first.

3. Environmental Policies in Practice

3.1 Policy Options

A Pigovian tax is just one type of environmental policy. Policymakers generally have other policy options, and which one is appropriate depends on the particular context. The four basic environmental policy options are:

1. pollution standards
2. technology-based regulation
3. Pigovian (or pollution) taxes
4. tradable pollution permits

Pollution Standards

pollution standards: policies that control pollution by setting allowable pollution standards or controlling the uses of a product or process

Pollution standards control environmental impacts by setting allowable pollution levels or controlling the uses of a product or process. Many people are faced with such standards at an automobile inspection. Cars must meet certain standards for tailpipe emissions; if your car fails to meet them, you must correct the problem before you can receive an inspection sticker.

The clear advantage of standards is that they can specify a definite result. This is particularly important in the case of substances that pose a clear hazard to public health. By imposing a uniform rule on all producers, we can be sure that no factory or product will produce hazardous levels of pollutants. In extreme cases, a regulation can simply ban a particular pollutant, as has been the case with DDT (a toxic pesticide) in most countries.

However, requiring all firms or products to meet the same standard is normally not cost effective. The overall use of society's resources is reduced if firms that can reduce pollution at low marginal costs reduce pollution more than firms that have high marginal reduction costs. Thus requiring all firms to reduce pollution by the same amount or to meet the same standards is not the least-cost way to achieve a given level of pollution reduction. Another problem with standards is that after firms meet the standard, they have little incentive to reduce pollution further.

Technology-Based Regulation

A second approach to environmental regulation is requiring firms or products to incorporate a particular pollution-control technology. For example, in 1975 the United States required that all new automobiles include a catalytic converter to reduce tailpipe emissions. Although auto manufacturers are free to design their own catalytic converters, each must meet certain emissions specifications.

Perhaps the main advantage of technology-based regulation is that enforcement and monitoring costs are relatively low. Unlike a pollution standard, which requires that firms' pollution levels be monitored to ensure compliance, a technology-based approach might require only an occasional check to ensure that the equipment is installed and functioning properly.

Technology-based approaches are also unlikely to be cost effective, however, because they do not provide firms with the flexibility to pursue a wide range of options. Like meeting pollution standards, the cost of implementing specific technologies varies among firms. Technology-based approaches may, however, offer a cost advantage due to standardization. If all firms must adopt a specific technology, then widespread production of that technology may drive down its production cost down over time.

Pigovian (or Pollution) Taxes

market-based approaches (to pollution regulation): policies that create an economic incentive for firms to reduce pollution without mandating that firms take any specific actions

Pollution taxes, along with tradable pollution permits, are considered **market-based approaches** to pollution regulation because they send information to polluters about the costs of pollution without mandating that firms take specific actions. Individual firms are not required to reduce pollution under a market-based approach, but the regulation creates a strong incentive for action.

As we saw earlier in the chapter, a pollution tax reflects the principle of internalizing externalities. If producers must bear the costs associated with pollution by paying a tax, they will find it in their interest to reduce pollution so long as the marginal costs of reducing pollution are lower than the tax.

Figure 13.5 **A Firm's Response to a Pollution Tax**

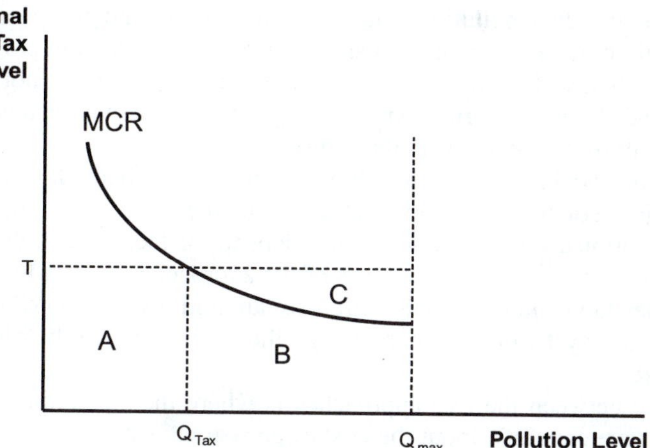

When faced with a pollution tax, a firm will reduce its pollution level as long as the marginal cost of reducing pollution is lower than the tax.

Figure 13.5 illustrates how an individual firm will respond in the presence of a pollution tax. Q_{max} is the level of pollution emitted without any regulation. The MCR curve shows the marginal cost of pollution reduction for the firm. If a pollution tax of *T* is imposed, the firm will be motivated to reduce pollution to level Q_{Tax}, at a total cost of B, equal to the area under its MCR curve between Q_{Tax} and Q_{max}. If the firm maintained pollution at Q_{max} it would have to pay a tax of (B + C) on these units of pollution. Thus the firm saves area C by reducing pollution to Q_{Tax}.

After reducing pollution to Q_{Tax}, the firm will still need to pay a tax on its remaining units of pollution, equal to area A. The total cost to the firm from the pollution tax is the sum of its pollution reduction costs and tax payments, or areas (A + B). This is smaller than areas (A + B + C), which is what it would have to pay in taxes if it undertook no pollution reduction. The firm's response to the tax is cost effective, as any other level of pollution different from Q_{Tax} would impose higher costs.

All other firms in the industry will determine how much to reduce their pollution based on their own MCR curve. Assuming that each firm is acting in a cost-effective manner, the total cost of pollution reduction is minimized. Firms that can reduce pollution at low cost will reduce pollution more than firms that face a higher cost. This is the main advantage of market-based approaches to pollution regulation—they achieve a given level of pollution reduction at the lowest overall cost. In other words, they are more economically efficient than pollution standards or technology-based approaches.

Tradable Pollution Permits

Economic efficiency in pollution control is clearly an advantage. One disadvantage of pollution taxes, however, is that it is very difficult to predict the total amount of pollution reduction a given tax will achieve. It depends on the shape of each firm's MCR curve, which is usually not known to policymakers.

tradable pollution permits: a system of pollution regulation in which a government allocates permits that are required in order to produce pollution. After they are allocated, these permits may be traded among firms or other interested parties.

An alternative is to set up a system of **tradable pollution permits**. The total number of permits issued equals the desired target level of pollution. These permits can then be allocated freely to existing firms or sold at auction. After they are allocated, they are fully tradable, or transferable, among firms or other interested parties. Firms can choose for themselves whether to reduce pollution or to purchase permits for the pollution that they produce—but the total volume of pollution produced by all firms cannot exceed a maximum amount equal to the total number of permits.

Firms with higher MCR curves will generally seek to purchase permits so that they do not have to pay high pollution reduction costs. Firms that can reduce pollution at a lower cost may be willing to sell permits, as long as they can receive more money for the permits than it would cost them to reduce pollution. Under this system, private groups interested in reducing pollution could purchase permits and simply not use them to emit pollution, thus reducing total emissions below the original target level. Pollution permits are normally valid only for a specific period. After this period expires, the government can issue fewer permits, resulting in lower overall pollution levels in the future.

A detailed analysis of tradable permits, which we do not present here, demonstrates that a given level of pollution reduction is achieved at the same total cost as levying a tax. Thus whether one prefers pollution taxes or tradable permits depends on factors other than pollution reduction costs (however, the administrative costs of the approaches may differ). Taxes are generally easier to understand and implement. But taxes are politically unpopular, and firms may prefer to use a permit system if they believe that they can successfully lobby in order to obtain permits for free.

The main difference between the two approaches is where the uncertainty lies. Using pollution taxes, firms have certainty about the cost of emissions, which makes it easier for them to make decisions about long-term investments. But the resulting level of total pollution with a tax is unknown in advance. If pollution levels turn out to be higher than expected, then the government might have to take the unpopular step of raising taxes further.

Under a permit system, the level of pollution is known because the government sets the number of available permits. But the price of permits is unknown, and permit prices can vary significantly over time. This has been the case with the European permit system for carbon emissions. The price of permits initially rose to around €30/ton in 2006, shortly after the system was instituted. But then prices plummeted to €0.10/ton in 2007, when it became evident that too many permits had been allocated. After some changes to the system, prices rose to exceed €20/ton in 2008 but then fell again to less than €3/ton in 2013. Such price volatility makes it difficult for firms to decide whether they should make investments in technologies to reduce emissions.

3.2 Design and Performance of Environmental Policies

Summary of Major Environmental Policies

Early pollution regulations enacted in the 1960s and 1970s relied primarily on standards and technology-based approaches. For example, the Clean Air Act, enacted by Congress in 1970, set maximum allowable levels of emissions for several key pollutants. The Clean Air Act specifies that pollution standards are to be set based on the best scientific evidence to protect human health with an "adequate margin of safety" and adjusted over time as new evidence becomes available. The Act specifically rules out CBA as a factor in setting standards.

The Clean Air Act has been very successful at reducing pollution levels in the United States. The aggregate concentration of the six major air pollutants* has declined 68 percent between 1970 and 2011.[13] The decline in lead pollution has been particularly dramatic—lead concentrations have declined 97 percent over this period, primarily as a result of banning lead in gasoline. A comprehensive CBA of the Clean Air Act found that in 2010 the annual compliance costs of the Act were $53 billion but estimates of the benefits ranged from $160 billion to $3.8 *trillion.*[14] In other words, for every dollar spent to meet the requirements of the Clean Air Act, society receives between $3 to $72 in economic benefits.

Technology-based approaches are often used to regulate other air pollutants as well as surface water quality. The Clean Water Act of 1972, for example, requires the U.S. Environmental Protection Agency to specify the "best available technology" for various

*The six major, or criteria, pollutants are particulate matter, ground-level ozone, carbon monoxide, sulfur oxides, nitrogen oxides, and lead.

types of facilities. The Act initially focused on reducing surface water pollution from clearly-identified sources, such as industrial plants. More recently, legislation has shifted toward the reduction of water pollution from stormwater and agricultural runoff.

As discussed above, the extent of environmental taxation varies across countries. One indication of this is the difference in national gas taxes. Gas prices vary across countries, even though the wholesale price of gasoline on the global market is fairly even around the world. The main reason for varying gasoline prices to consumers in different countries is that the level of taxation differs, sometimes significantly. In the United States, federal gasoline taxes are 18 cents per gallon, combined with state and local taxes that range from 8 to 51 cents per gallon, for a total average tax of 49 cents per gallon. In European countries, gasoline taxes are typically about 10 times higher, equivalent to around \$4 or \$5 per gallon. At the same time, some countries actually subsidize gasoline prices. In 2010 the cheapest gasoline prices were found in Venezuela (\$0.09/gallon), Iran (\$0.37/gallon), and Saudi Arabia (\$0.61/gallon).

We can see the effect of differences in gas taxes in Figure 13.6, which shows gasoline prices in various countries plotted against average annual consumption per person. We observe a general inverse relationship, similar to a demand curve—higher gasoline prices tend to be associated with lower consumption. The relationship shown here, however, is not exactly the same as a demand curve. As we are looking at data from different countries, the assumption of "other things equal," which is needed to construct a demand curve, does not hold. Differences in consumption may be partly a function of differences in factors other than prices, such as income levels. For example, while Saudi Arabia has very low gasoline prices, income levels are only about half those in the United States. Other reasons that gasoline consumption is so high in the United States may be that people need to drive longer distances for work (especially in the Western United States) and that public transportation options are less prevalent than in European countries. But the overall negative relationship suggests that higher gasoline taxes can be effective at reducing gasoline consumption, and thus emissions of various air pollutants.

The first major attempt to use a tradable pollution system to control pollution was the U.S. program to regulate sulfur dioxide, enacted with the 1990 Amendments to the Clean Air Act. The goal of the program was to reduce sulfur dioxide emissions to 50 percent of 1980 levels by 2010. The program is widely considered a success, with a decline in emissions of 83 percent by 2010 and costs significantly lower than expected. (For more on this program, see Box 13.3.)

Figure 13.6 **Gasoline Prices and Consumption, Select Countries, 2010**

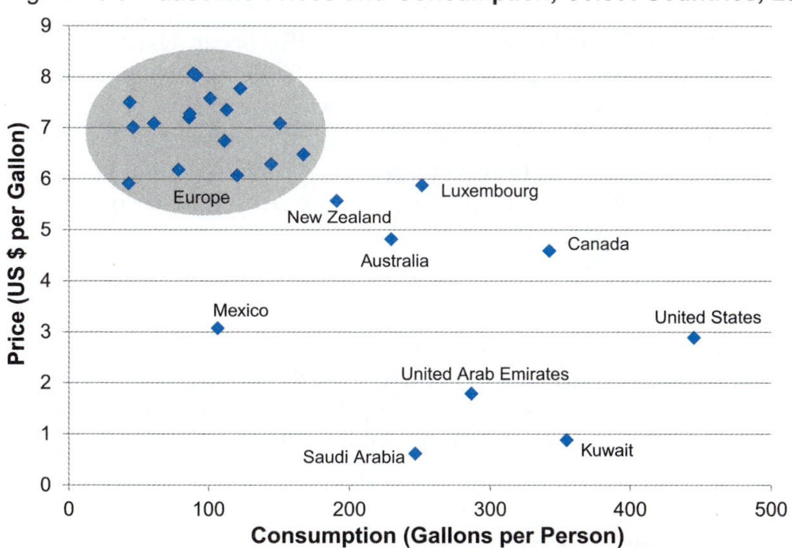

Higher gas prices, typically as a result of higher gas taxes, generally result in lower average consumption.

Sources: GIZ, *International Fuel Prices 2010/2011,* 7th ed. Federal Ministry for Economic Cooperation and Development (Germany), 2011; U.S. Energy Information Administration online database.

Box 13.3 Sulfur Dioxide Emissions Trading

The 1990 Clean Air Act Amendments in the United States created a national program to allow trading and banking of sulfur dioxide (SO_2) emissions, the primary cause of acid rain. The program applies to more than 2,000 large electricity plants, which must hold permits in order to emit SO_2. Most permits are freely allocated to plants based on their capacity to generate electricity. About 3 percent of the permits are auctioned off every year. Permits may then be traded, normally with brokers facilitating trades. Although most trades occur between two electricity-generating plants, some permits are purchased by environmental groups or individuals (and even economics classes!) and then "retired" to reduce the overall quantity of SO_2 emissions.

Economic theory suggests that a system of tradable permits can reduce pollution at a lower overall cost than a uniform standard. Dallas Burtraw, an economist with Resources for the Future, notes that the "SO_2 allowance market presents the first real test of economists' advice, and therefore merits careful evaluation." After about twenty years in operation, how has the program performed?

To evaluate the policy, the effects of emissions trading must be isolated from other factors. Even without a trading system, declining prices for low-sulfur coal in the 1990s, along with technological advances, would have reduced the cost of lowering emissions. Economic simulation models comparing the SO_2 program to an emissions standard suggest that the cost savings from trading were about 50 percent. The savings are even greater than in a technology-based approach.

The emissions targets of the SO_2 program have been met at a lower cost than originally anticipated. Acidification problems in the Northeastern states, widespread in the past, have declined. However, aquatic systems in the Southeastern states are expected to continue to decline without further emissions reductions. And although the program has been effective, analysis of the marginal benefits and marginal costs of emissions suggests that further emissions reductions would produce even larger net benefits.

Burtraw, along with colleague Sarah Jo Szambelan, concludes that the SO_2 market has

> been liquid and active, and according to most observers [has] worked well in achieving the emissions caps at less cost than would have been achieved with traditional approaches to regulation. There is evidence that both process and patentable types of innovation are attributable to the [SO_2 program]. At the same time, there is evidence that some cost savings have been not been realized. Moreover, despite substantial emissions reductions, ultimate environmental goals have not been achieved.

Sources: Dallas Burtraw, "Innovation Under the Tradable Sulfur Dioxide Emission Permits Program in the U.S. Electricity Sector," Resources for the Future Discussion Paper 00-38, Washington, DC, 2000; Dallas Burtraw and Sarah Jo Szambelan, "U.S. Emissions Trading Markets for SO_2 and NO_x," Resources for the Future Discussion Paper 09-40, Washington, DC, 2009.

The other major attempt at emissions trading has been the European Union's carbon trading system, enacted in 2005. The initial phase covered major facilities such as electricity plants, cement plants, and paper mills. In 2012 the program was extended to cover airline transportation. As mentioned earlier, the main problem with the program has been price volatility, generally attributed to an over-allocation of permits during the initial phases. In the current phase (2013–20) the European Union is moving toward setting an overall EU emission limit rather than individual national limits.

The Economic Impact of Environmental Regulation

Finally, we briefly consider the economic impact of environmental regulations. Environmental laws are often accused of slowing economic growth and causing job losses. However, most of the evidence suggests that the notion of a tradeoff between environmental quality and economic vitality is a myth. For example, a 2008 analysis of the U.S. economy found that

> contrary to conventional wisdom, [environmental protection (EP)], economic growth, and jobs creation are complementary and compatible: Investments in EP create jobs and displace jobs, but the net effect on employment is positive.[15]

A 2007 study in the United Kingdom also studied the effect of environmental regulation on employment. The results found that regulations had a slightly negative impact on employment, although the results were not statistically significant. They concluded that their analysis found "no evidence of a trade-off between jobs and the environment."[16]

Under various executive orders in the United States, starting with Ronald Reagan and more recently by Barack Obama, all major federal regulations, including environmental laws, must be reviewed using CBA. This process is designed to screen out inefficient policy proposals. A 2011 study by the U.S. Office of Management and Budget found that the aggregate cost of all federal environmental regulations enacted from 2000 to 2010 was $24 billion to $29 billion, but benefits were estimated to be $82 billion to $550 billion.[17] During this period, environmental laws were responsible for about 60 percent to 85 percent of the benefits of all federal regulations.

Analysis by the United Nations concludes that a significant increase in global investment in renewable energy and energy efficiency—an amount equal to 2 percent of global GDP—would result in higher rates of long-term economic growth than a "business-as-usual" scenario.[18] The report finds that "green" investments benefit the world's poorest in particular. The poor disproportionately depend on natural resources for their livelihood. So investment in natural capital, including water resources, sustainable agriculture, and forests, increases incomes while also improving the natural environment. Investment in natural capital also fosters ecotourism, which offers another way to increase incomes in developing countries.

We have seen in this chapter that a strong *economic* case can be made for protecting the natural environment. Given existing market failures, especially those arising from externalities, government intervention is not only justified; it is necessary to achieve an efficient outcome. Nature has significant economic value, and techniques have been devised to measure these values. Despite common perceptions, environmental regulations are generally effective and do not harm economic vitality. Economic research suggests that we need more, not less, environmental regulation.

In Chapter 14, we turn to additional theoretical insights from economics on environmental management. We also focus on the issue of global climate change, one of the major challenges of the twenty-first century.

REVIEW QUESTIONS

1. How are negative externalities represented in a supply-and-demand graph?
2. What is a Pigovian tax? How is it represented in a supply-and-demand graph?
3. How are positive externalities represented in a supply-and-demand graph?
4. How does a subsidy result in the efficient quantity in a market with a positive externality?
5. What is an upstream tax? What is a revenue-neutral tax?
6. What is the willingness-to-pay principle?
7. What is intrinsic value?
8. What are ecosystem services?
9. What are nonuse benefits? What is total economic value?
10. What is nonmarket valuation? What are the four main nonmarket valuation techniques?
11. What is the cost of illness method? Why is it considered a lower-bound estimate?
12. What are replacement cost methods?
13. What are revealed preference methods? What are stated preference methods?
14. What is cost-benefit analysis?
15. What is discounting? How do we calculate a present value using discounting?
16. How can human lives be valued?
17. What is the precautionary principle?
18. What are the four main approaches for regulating pollution levels?
19. Demonstrate how a firm would respond to a pollution tax, using a graph.
20. How does a system of tradable pollution permits operate?

EXERCISES

1. Suppose that a friend of yours states: "The optimal pollution level is clearly zero. Any level of pollution is obviously undesirable." How would you respond to your friend? Use a graph to support your answer.
2. Burning gasoline generates negative externalities. Assume the current tax on gas in the country of Optiland fully internalizes these externalities. But suppose that gas prices in Optiland have risen lately due to increased demand. A politician gives a speech in which he says that the best response to rising gas prices is to eliminate the gas tax temporarily. Do you agree with his position? Use a graph to support your answer.
3. The supply and demand schedules for gasoline in the country of Drivia are given in the table below. Initially, there are no taxes on gasoline. Assume that the externality damage from consuming gasoline in Drivia is 60 cents per gallon.

Price per gallon	Quantity supplied (gallons per day)	Quantity demanded (gallons per day)
$3.00	60,000	90,000
$3.20	70,000	85,000
$3.40	80,000	80,000
$3.60	90,000	75,000
$3.80	100,000	70,000
$4.00	110,000	65,000
$4.20	120,000	60,000

   a. Draw a supply-and-demand graph for gasoline in Drivia. What are the equilibrium price and quantity?
   b. Illustrate the externality damage in your graph. How much is externality damage (in dollars per day)?
   c. What is the optimal Pigovian tax on gas in Drivia?
   d. If Drivia instituted an optimal Pigovian tax on gasoline, what would the new equilibrium price and quantity be? Create a new graph illustrating the impacts of the tax.
   e. How much would Drivia collect in taxes with an optimal Pigovian tax? Illustrate this on your graph.
4. Suppose that the World Bank is considering funding a dam project in the developing country of Hydroland which will generate hydroelectricity and reduce flooding. The reservoir will be used for recreation but will require relocation of several villages. You have been hired by the Bank to determine the economic costs and benefits of the dam. Develop a list of potential costs and benefits. Be sure to include at least two potential ecosystem service impacts and one nonuse cost or benefit. For each of these impacts, what nonmarket valuation techniques do you think are appropriate for estimating the economic value?
5. Suppose that the government of Aqualand is considering a new law that would improve drinking water quality. The cost of complying with the new regulation is $100 million. The benefits of improved drinking water are estimated to be $250 million, but these benefits will occur 25 years from now.
   a. At a discount rate of 5 percent, do you recommend that Aqualand institute this new regulation?
   b. Would your recommendation change if the discount rate were 3 percent?
6. For each of the four main approaches for regulating pollution, list at least one advantage and one disadvantage of the approach.
7. Match each concept in Column A with an example in Column B.

Column A	Column B
a. A negative externality	1. A policy to increase production when a good generates a positive externality
b. A Pigovian tax	2. Represented by the difference between the private marginal benefits and the social marginal benefits
c. A positive externality	3. A tax on raw materials
d. A subsidy	4. Converting future costs and benefits to present value
e. An upstream tax	5. Represented by the difference between the private marginal costs and the social marginal costs
f. An ecosystem service benefit	6. Using the costs of building a water treatment plant to estimate the value of natural water purification
g. A nonuse benefit	7. Using surveys to elicit willingness to pay information
h. Replacement cost method	8. Internalizes a negative externality
i. Revealed preference method	9. Flood protection from a wetlands
j. Contingent valuation	10. Estimating the recreation benefits of a lake using data on visitation patterns
k. Discounting	11. The value of just knowing a national park exists

Notes

1. Dennis Jacobe, "Americans Still Prioritize Economic Growth Over Environment," Gallup Economy, March 29, 2012.

2. Paul Krugman, "Earth in the Balance Sheet: Economists Go for the Green," *Slate,* April 18, 1997.

3. Bill Moyers, Keynote address to the Environmental Grantmakers Association, Brainerd, Minnesota, October 16, 2001.

4. Sarah Beth L. Barnett and Tursynbek A. Nurmagambetov, "Costs of Asthma in the United States, 2002–2007," *Journal of Allergy and Clinical Immunology* 127(1) (2011): 142–152.

5. John Rolfe and Brenda Dyack, "Testing for Convergent Validity between Travel Cost and Contingent Valuation Estimates of Recreation Values in the Coorong, Australia," *Australian Journal of Agricultural and Resource Economics* 54 (2010): 583–599.

6. Jennifer Murdock, "Handling Unobserved Site Characteristics in Random Utility Models of Recreation Demand," *Journal of Environmental Economics and Management* 51(1) (2006): 1–25.

7. Frank Ward, Brian Roach, and Jim Henderson, "The Economic Value of Water in Recreation: Evidence from the California Drought," *Water Resources Research* 32(4) (1996): 1075–1081.

8. Marcia A. Rosado, Maria A. Cunha-e-Sa, Maria M. Dulca-Soares, and Luis C. Nunes, "Combining Averting Behavior and Contingent Valuation Data: An Application to Drinking Water Treatment in Brazil," *Environment and Development Economics* 11(6) (2006): 729–746.

9. Fernando Lera-Lopez, Javier Faulin, and Mercedes Sanchez, "Determinants of the Willingness-to-Pay for Reducing the Environmental Impacts of Road Transportation," *Transportation Research: Part D: Transport and Environment* 17(3) (2012): 215–220.

10. Adriana Ressurreição, James Gibbons, Tomaz Ponce Dentinho, Michel Kaiser, Ricardo S. Santos, and Gareth Edwards-Jones, "Economic Valuation of Species Loss in the Open Sea," *Ecological Economics* 70(4) (2011): 729–739.

11. Kenneth Arrow, Robert Solow, Paul R. Portney, Edward E. Leamer, Roy Radner, and Howard Schuman, "Report of the NOAA Panel on Contingent Valuation," *Federal Register* 58(10) (1993): 4601–4614.

12. U.S. Office of Management and Budget, "Memorandum for the Heads of Departments and Agencies," OMB Circular No. A-94, January 24, 2013.

13. http://epa.gov/airtrends/images/comparison70.jpg.

14. U.S. Environmental Protection Agency, "Benefits and Costs of the Clean Air Act, Second Prospective Study—1990 to 2020," 2011.

15. Roger H. Bezdek, Robert M. Wendling, and Paula DiPerna, "Environmental Protection, the Economy, and Jobs: National and Regional Analyses," *Journal of Environmental Management* 86 (2008): 63–79.

16. Matthew A. Cole and Rob J. Elliott, "Do Environmental Regulations Cost Jobs? An Industry-Level Analysis of the UK," *Journal of Economic Analysis and Policy: Topics in Economic Analysis and Policy* 7(1) (2007): 1–25.

17. U.S. Office of Management and Budget, "Draft 2011 Report to Congress on the Benefits and Costs of Federal Regulations and Unfunded Mandates on State, Local, and Tribal Entities," Washington, DC, 2011.

18. United Nations Environment Programme, "Towards a Green Economy: Pathways to Sustainable Development and Poverty Eradication, A Synthesis for Policymakers," 2011.

Appendix: Formal Analysis of Negative Externalities

In this Appendix, we present a more formal analysis of negative externalities. The objective is to demonstrate that internalizing a negative externality using a Pigovian tax clearly makes society "better off," based on an application of welfare analysis. Prior to the imposition of any tax on a product that generates a negative externality, social welfare includes three components:

1. consumer surplus
2. producer surplus
3. externality damages

Consumer and producer surplus are both positive contributions to social welfare, while the externality damages decrease welfare.

We refer to Figure 13.7 to determine each of these three effects. Figure 13.7 is essentially the same as Figure 13.1, with the addition of labels for various areas. You might also note that Figure 13.7 is very similar to Figure 12.5, which presented the welfare analysis of a tax. As some of the same concepts we learned in Chapter 12 are applicable here, the labels for various areas are the same in both figures.

Without any regulation, the market equilibrium is E_M. Consumer surplus is the area above price but below the demand curve:

$$Consumer\ Surplus = A + B + E + H$$

Producer surplus at the market equilibrium Q_M is the area below price but above the supply curve:

$$Producer\ Surplus = C + D + F + G + I$$

As in Figure 13.1, the externality damages are represented by the shaded area between the private marginal costs and the social marginal costs, equal to:

$$Externality = E + F + G + H + I + K$$

Figure 13.7 **Welfare Analysis of a Negative Externality, without a Pigovian Tax**

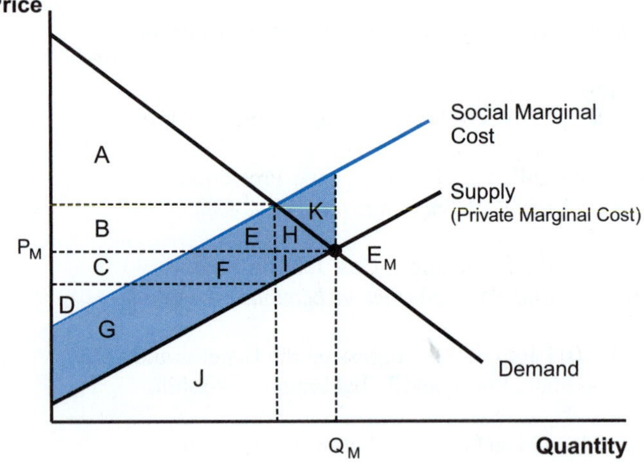

Without a Pigovian tax, quantity will be Q_M and price will be P_M, with the externality damage equal to the shaded region.

Because the externality represents a cost, to determine the net social welfare we need to subtract these costs from the market benefits. Thus the net social welfare of the unregulated market is:

$$Net\ Benefits = (A + B + E + H) + (C + D + F + G + I) - (E + F + G + H + I + K)$$

Canceling out the positive and negative terms, we are left with:

$$Net\ Benefits = A + B + C + D - K$$

Now, we impose a Pigovian tax that fully internalizes the externality. This is shown in Figure 13.8, which is similar to Figure 13.2. We again need to determine the areas that represent consumer surplus, producer surplus, and the externality damage. But we also need to consider that tax revenues represent a benefit to society, as we did in Chapter 12.

With the Pigovian tax, the new equilibrium is E_{Tax}, with a higher price of P_{Tax} and a lower quantity of Q_{Tax}. At the higher price, consumer surplus is:

$$CS = A$$

As in Chapter 12, we can figure out producer surplus by first realizing that total revenues equal price times quantity, or (P_{Tax} * Q_{Tax}). In Figure 13.8, total revenues are:

$$\textit{Total Producer Revenues} = B + C + D + E + F + G + J$$

Producers have two costs: the cost of production and the tax. The cost of production is the area under their marginal cost curve, which is area J. The tax per unit is equal to the difference between P_{Tax} and P_0, which must be paid for every unit produced. Total taxes paid equal the shaded area in Figure 13.8, or*

$$\textit{Taxes} = E + F + G$$

Figure 13.8 **Welfare Analysis of a Negative Externality, with a Pigovian Tax**

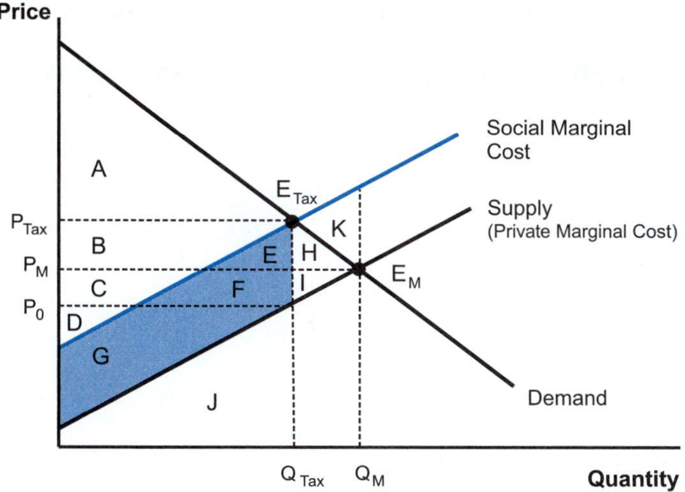

With a Pigovian tax, quantity falls to Q_{Tax} and price rises to P_{Tax}, with the externality damage reduced to the shaded region.

When we subtract production costs and the tax paid from total revenues, we are left with producer surplus:

$$\textit{Producer Surplus} = (B + C + D + E + F + G + J) - J - (E + F + G)$$
$$= B + C + D$$

Note that both consumer and producer surplus have decreased as a result of the Pigovian tax. If both consumer and producer surplus have gone down, how can it be that the tax increases

*Note that in Figure 12.5 tax revenues equaled area (*B* + *C* + *E* + *F*). However, this is exactly the same as area (*E* + *F* + *G*). We represent tax revenues differently here because we wish to demonstrate that the tax revenues are equal to the externality damages.

social welfare? First, we need to account for the reduced pollution. With quantity reduced to Q_{Tax}, the total externality damage is now the shaded area in Figure 13.8:

$$Externality = E + F + G$$

The externality damage associated with production between Q_{Tax} and Q_M, or area $(H + I + K)$, has been avoided. Note that the tax revenues exactly equal the externality damages—both are equal to $(E + F + G)$.

Considering all welfare impacts, net social benefits are now:

$$Net\ Benefits = (A) + (B + C + D) + (E + F + G) - (E + F + G)$$

Canceling out the positive and negative terms we get:

$$Net\ Benefits = A + B + C + D$$

How does this compare to net benefits before the tax? Recall that benefits were $(A + B + C + D - K)$. So benefits have increased by area K as a result of the tax. Another way of looking at this is that we have avoided the negative impacts of "too much" production, represented by area K, which shows the excess of marginal costs (including external costs) over marginal benefits. The level of production that maximizes social welfare is Q_{Tax}.

Unlike our welfare analysis in Chapters 6 and 12, in the case of negative externality the unregulated market is inefficient. Market intervention, in the form of a Pigovian tax, increases social welfare.

14 Common Property Resources and Public Goods

The theory of negative externalities, presented in Chapter 13, provides us with one important way of thinking about environmental issues. In that approach, we start with the market equilibrium and examine ways of modifying it to take into account environmental costs and benefits. But what if there is no market equilibrium, or even no market? This might be the case when social or environmental resources are not owned or ownership rights are not clear. In other cases, there may be a market equilibrium, but one that is highly distorted by failure to reflect crucial costs or benefits of the resource in question. Some important examples are:

- The oceans, which generally are not subject to private property rights and for the most part are not controlled by individual countries, except in coastal zones. The world's oceans contain some of the most important planetary ecosystems. Healthy fisheries are a critical source of food for the world's population, supplying an important source of protein for many lower-income people.
- Many forested areas and wetlands are not privately owned. They may be considered national assets or may be managed by local communities, but in many cases there may be no clear management rules.
- The earth's atmosphere is crucial to all of us but is owned by nobody. Atmospheric functions include the carbon cycle that supports both plant and animal life, climate stabilization, and parts of the water cycle—all crucial to planetary ecology. The issue of climate change has become particularly important in recent years, and is one that we will focus on later in this chapter.
- At the national level, public parks, public beaches, river and lake fisheries, and many recreational areas are important aspects of social and economic life for which there is generally no established market.
- A slightly different kind of example is public airwaves, which are often available for use by private companies under rules set by government.

This chapter provides further insights into economic policies concerning issues such as the public airwaves, ocean fisheries, and climate change as well as other policy issues in related areas. We consider several new instances of market failure—where private markets fail to maximize social welfare. In each of these cases, we also suggest policy responses that can increase the well-being of society.

1. Goods Other Than Private Goods

In the previous chapters, we discussed economic activities related to **private goods**. A private good can be defined as having two distinguishing characteristics:

private good: a good that is excludable and rival

excludable good: a good whose consumption by others can be prevented by its owner(s)

rival good: a good that can only be consumed by only one person at a time

public good: a good that is nonexcludable and nonrival

nonexcludable good: a good whose benefits are freely available to all users

nonrival good: a good that can be consumed by more than one person at a time. The marginal cost of providing a nonrival good to an additional person is zero.

common property resource: a resource that is nonexcludable and rival

artificially scarce good: a good that is excludable but nonrival

congestion: the point at which the demand for a nonrival good results in a diminished benefit to each user, and thus it becomes rival

1. A private good is **excludable**. This means that owners of the good can prevent others from consuming it or enjoying its benefits. For example, the textbooks that you own are excludable goods because, if you wish, you can prevent anyone else from using them. Generally, purchasing a private good establishes an owner's legal right to exclude others from accessing the good.
2. A private good is **rival**. This means that a unit of the good can be consumed by only one person at a time. So, if you are wearing a shirt, no one else can wear that shirt at the same time.

It will help us understand the concept of a private good if we contrast it with three other types of goods.

First, we can define a **public good** as one that is **nonexcludable** and **nonrival**. This means that no one can be excluded from consuming it because they did not pay for it and that more than one person at a time can enjoy its benefits. An important economic result is that, because many people can simultaneously enjoy a nonrival good at the same time, the marginal cost of providing it to one more person is zero.

A common example of a public good is national defense—everyone in a country can simultaneously enjoy its benefits, and none can be excluded. Another example is a national park, because it is freely available to everyone, and many people can enjoy it at the same time.*

Some people mistakenly consider any good "owned" or managed by a government a public good. But a natural reserve managed by an environmental group may also meet the qualifications of a public good, while some public resources may be managed by governments as private goods. An example would be a plot of public grazing land that is leased exclusively to the highest-bidding rancher.

Some goods, known as **common property resources,** are nonexcludable but rival. In other words, common property resources can be freely consumed or enjoyed by anyone, but their use by one person diminishes their availability to others. A classic example of a common property resource is the stock of fish in an open ocean fishery. Anyone with a boat can catch as much fish as he or she is able to. However, a fish caught by one fisher is not available to be caught by anyone else.

The concepts of common property resource and public good may overlap. We mentioned above that a national park can be considered a public good. But if the park becomes so crowded that the benefits of each visitor start to decline, then we can say that the park no longer meets the strict definition of a nonrival good. In general, the availability or quality of a common property resource eventually declines when demands on it increase. But a public good remains available in undiminished quality despite increasing demands.

Finally, we have **artificially scarce goods,** which are excludable but nonrival.** In other words, artificially scarce goods can be simultaneously consumed by many people at a time, but those who do not pay can be excluded from enjoying the good. An example of an artificially scarce good is a toll road. Those who do not pay the toll can be excluded from using the road, but (at least up to a point) many people can simultaneously use the road.

So we can classify different goods into four basic categories as shown in Table 14.1, with examples for each type of good. These categories are not absolutely distinct; particular goods often display characteristics along a spectrum from rival to nonrival and from excludable to nonexcludable. Many goods are subject to **congestion**, meaning that they are nonrival if relatively few people use them at once, but when demand reaches a certain level each user's benefit begins to decrease due to crowding or scarcity. For example, a health club is

*Some national parks do charge a small entry fee, but these fees rarely present a significant barrier for visitors. So, for practical purposes they are available for everyone's enjoyment.

**Artificially scarce goods are also called club goods.

Table 14.1 **Classification of Different Types of Goods**

	Excludable	Nonexcludable
Rival	**Private goods** t-shirts, groceries, cars, cell phones, haircuts	**Common property resources** ocean fisheries, groundwater, a community basketball court
Nonrival	**Artificially scarce goods** cable television, health clubs, toll roads	**Public goods** national defense, free radio, public education, national parks

a nonrival good if only a few people are using it. But if the club becomes too crowded, it becomes more like a rival good.

Private goods are most often distributed through markets. This is also the case with artificially scarce goods—those who do not pay can be excluded from obtaining the good's benefits, so suppliers can charge a price to those who wish to consume or enjoy the good. But some artificially scarce goods, such as toll roads, are provided by governments without necessarily yielding a profit.

Common property resources and public goods tend to be supplied or managed by governments. But other organizations can also provide goods or services that benefit everyone, such as land conservation by environmental groups. Also, some resources may not be managed at all, such as a river with unregulated water withdrawals.

We have seen in other chapters that markets that provide private goods can suffer from market failure. For the other three types of goods in Table 14.1, distribution via private markets *almost always results in market failure*. In other words, private markets are generally inefficient in the provision of artificially scarce goods, common property resources, and public goods. Thus market intervention is generally justified for these goods solely on the basis of economic efficiency. Intervention may also be justified on the basis of equity and other final goals. We now turn to the economic theory and policy implications for each of these three types of goods.

Discussion Questions

1. In addition to the examples listed in Table 14.1, try to think of other instances of artificially scarce goods, common property resources, and public goods. Discuss how these goods are supplied—whether through markets, through government provision, or through other approaches.
2. Do you think that the current balance in your society among the four different types of goods is appropriate? Should policies be enacted to shift production so that, in general, society has more public goods and common property resources? Or should more goods be made available instead through private markets? Can you think of specific policies that could achieve the kinds of shifts that you would favor?

2. Artificially Scarce Goods

In a market for a private good, the efficient level of provision occurs when the marginal benefits just equal the marginal costs, assuming no other market failures. But for an artificially scarce good, the marginal cost of providing it is zero, at least within a specific quantity range. For example, for homes equipped with cable television, the cost to the provider of sending the broadcast signal to one more household is essentially zero. Note that this does not mean that total production costs are zero. The start-up cost of a cable television company is quite high. Instead, what distinguishes an artificially scarce good from a private good is that its *marginal* supply costs are zero.

Figure 14.1 **The Market for an Artificially Scarce Good** (Cable Television)

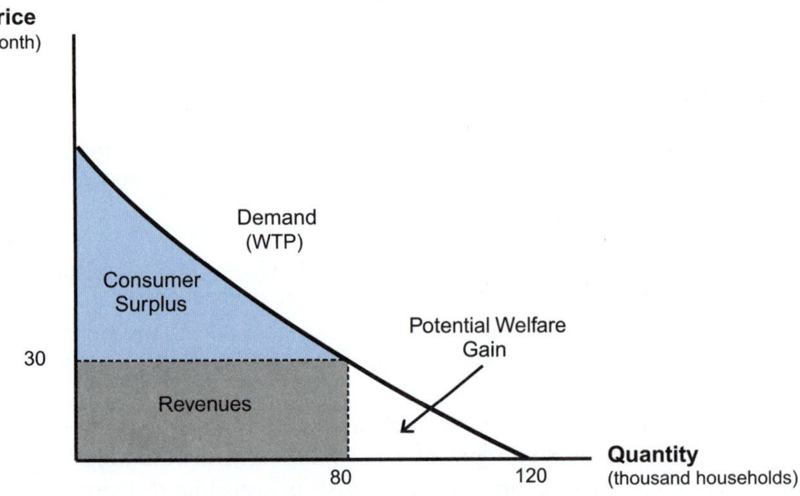

The socially efficient level of provision is to supply cable television to 120,000 households, but at the market price of $30/ month, only 80,000 households are willing to pay for a subscription.

Figure 14.1 illustrates the market for an artificially scarce good, cable television. The demand curve shows the maximum willingness to pay for different households in the region. Assume the cable television company charges $30 per month for a basic cable subscription. At this price, 80,000 households sign up for the service, as shown in the graph. The revenues of the cable company are $2.4 million per month ($30 × 80,000 households). The consumer surplus in the market is represented by the shaded region above the price but below the demand curve.

But you might note that something is missing from Figure 14.1—*there is no supply curve!* As the supply curve represents the marginal costs of providing the good, for an artificially scarce good, there is no supply curve. Or more precisely, the supply curve is a horizontal line at a price of zero.

So if we apply our rule that social welfare is maximized when the marginal benefits are equal to the marginal costs, then the efficient quantity of cable television is to provide it to all 120,000 households that are willing to pay something for it. Note that if the cable company provided services at no cost to the 40,000 additional households that value it (but are not willing to pay $30/month), then total social welfare would increase by the triangle on the right-hand side of the graph.

price discrimination: a seller's charging different prices to different buyers, depending on their ability and willingness to pay

Of course, the cable company will not do this. Profit-making companies are rarely inclined to provide their goods and services for free. Note that the company could theoretically attract additional customers by charging them a monthly fee of less than $30/month. However, this requires that the company engage in **price discrimination**—a seller's charging different prices to different buyers, depending on their ability and willingness to pay. So, while it would keep charging $30/month to most of its customers, the company might charge $10/month to other customers who have a lower willingness-to-pay. As the marginal cost of providing cable services is zero, the company's profits would increase nonetheless and those additional customers would obtain some consumer surplus.

This outcome is unlikely, because price discrimination is often illegal, and even where it is legal it is difficult to implement. One common exception is college tuition. Students from households that are unable to pay the full tuition commonly receive financial aid, so these students can obtain the same education at a lower cost. (Note that this is not a case in which the marginal cost of supply is zero—the reason for price discrimination in education is a matter of society's ethical standards more than profit-maximizing.)

The cable TV company in Figure 14.1 will seek to set its price to maximize its profits, based on the elasticity of demand. However, this price will not result in a level of provision that maximizes social welfare. For this reason, government intervention sometimes occurs in markets for artificially scarce goods, which are often supplied by monopolies. Government regulation could require, for example, that a lower price be set or that special rates be made available to lower-income consumers. We discuss markets with monopoly suppliers and the role of government regulation in more detail in Chapter 18.

Discussion Questions

1. Do you think that price discrimination should be illegal? Does it make economic sense for everyone to pay the same price for something? Do you think that it is fair for everyone to pay the same price for something?
2. Do you think that the profits of a company that provides cable television should be regulated by the government? Is competition in the cable industry sufficient to keep prices reasonable? How is technology changing the nature of competition for video programming?

3. COMMON PROPERTY RESOURCES

A common property resource is available to essentially anyone, but it cannot be used or enjoyed by multiple people at the same time, at least with the same level of quality. Overuse is often a problem with a common property resource, as when too many people fish the same fishery, want to play ball games in the same recreation area, or withdraw groundwater from the same aquifer. We can use tools of economic analysis to examine how this problems arises and what policy solutions may be available.

3.1 MODELING A COMMON PROPERTY RESOURCE

One way to model a common property resource is to realize that every user of the resource essentially imposes a cost on other users. In the example of a fishery, if the number of fishing trips is relatively low, adding one more trip is unlikely to affect the catch of other fishers. But above a critical level, each additional fishing trip begins to harm the overall health of the fishery and thus reduce the catch of everyone in the fishery. Each individual fisher will consider only whether he or she is making a profit. So, the fact that others' profits have declined will not be taken into account by additional fishers. This is similar to the idea of a negative externality, but in this case market participants are harming other market participants.

Figure 14.2 models a fishery as an example of a common property resource. The horizontal axis indicates the number of fishing trips taken in the fishery. Assume that it costs $15,000 to operate a fishing trip, considering labor costs, boat payments, fuel, and other costs. This is the private cost of each fishing trip, as shown by the PC line in the graph. Note that the cost to operate a fishing trip is constant, regardless of the number of trips taken.

Next, we need to consider the revenue obtained from each fishing trip. Obviously, this depends on the number of fish caught. For the first few trips, we assume that each fishing trip yields $25,000 in revenues per trip (see curve RT in the graph). When we subtract operating costs, each fishing trip results in $10,000 in profits.

Initially, plenty of fish are available for all fishers, so each additional trip does not affect the catch of anyone else. Until T_0, each fisher is able to obtain revenues of $25,000 per trip. But after the number of trips exceeds T_0, the revenue per trip begins to decline. The fishery is becoming crowded, and because more fishers are competing for limited fish stocks, it becomes more difficult to catch fish. Each fishing trip will still result in a profit but, instead of making a $10,000 profit, each trip will result in a lower profit.

Each fisher will obviously be disappointed to have lower profits. But as long as profits are still positive (RT > PC), there is an incentive for more fishers to take trips to the area. In fact, as fishers begin to realize declining catches, they may be motivated to increase their fishing efforts further in order to catch fish while they still have the opportunity.

Figure 14.2 **Common Property Model of a Fishery**

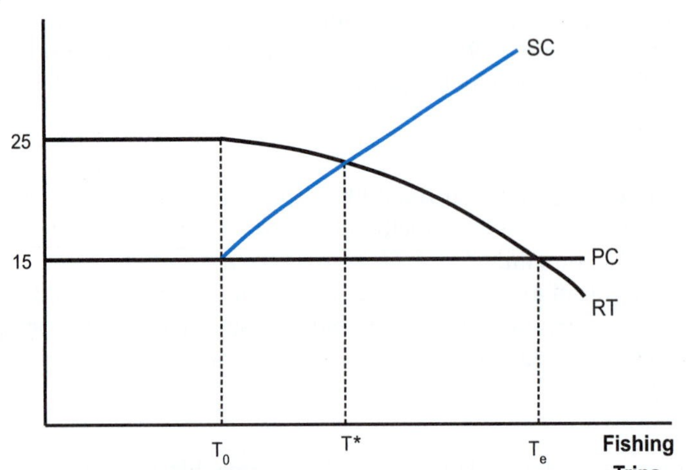

The unregulated outcome will result in T_e fishing trips. But above T_0 trips, each additional trip imposes a cost on other fishers. The socially efficient level of fishing trips is *T**.

We can model the cost that additional fishers impose on others much as we modeled a negative externality. It represents an additional cost above the private cost of operating a boat trip. Above T_0, each additional trip imposes a social cost as shown by curve SC, equal to the reduction in the profits of *all other fishers*. In other words, SC represents the total social cost of operating a boat trip above T_0, considering the out-of-pocket costs of $10,000 plus the external cost equal to the reduction in others' profits.

The socially efficient level of fishing trips is equal to *T**. This is the level at which the profits from a new fishing trip are just enough to compensate the loss of others' profits.

But in an unregulated fishery, there is no reason for fishers to stop at *T**. So long as individual fishers can make profit, the number of fishing trips will continue to increase until we reach T_e. At this point, profit for each fishing boat falls to 0. There will then be no further incentive for additional fishing trips. But at such a high level of fishing effort, the health of the fishery may begin to decline. Over time, the stock of fish may become so depleted that the fishery crashes, leading to the collapse of the local fishing industry.

3.2 Policies for Common Property Resource Management

One solution to the problem of the overuse of a common property resource is much like the implementation of a Pigovian tax. We could charge a fee for each fishing trip equal to the external cost imposed on others. If fishers had to pay this fee in addition to their out-of-pocket costs of $15,000, we could adjust the fee until we reached the efficient level of fishing trips, *T**.

individual transferable quota (ITQ): tradable rights to access or harvest a common property resource, such as the right to harvest a particular quantity of fish

Another solution is to institute **individual transferable quotas (ITQs)**. These operate much like tradable pollution permits, discussed in Chapter 13. With this approach, an organization managing the resource (such as a government agency) sets the total allowable fishing level, such as the number of fishing trips or the total harvest per season. This level of effort is set low enough to maintain the ecological integrity of the resource. The ITQs can be distributed for free or auctioned off to the highest bidders. If they are auctioned, the proceeds can be used by the government to maintain the quality of the resource or as compensation for those who are forced out of the industry. Holders of ITQs may then use them to fish or offer them for sale to interested parties. The price of an ITQ is not set by the government but allowed to vary depending on supply and demand. ITQ programs for ocean fisheries have been established in several countries, including Australia, Canada, Iceland, and the United States. (For a real-world example of ITQs, see Box 14.1.)

Box 14.1 Fisheries Management in Practice: Individual Transferable Quotas

One real-world example of regulating a fishery through individual transferable quotas is the Long Island clam fishery. This example shows that the details of the quota system can significantly influence the efficiency of the industry.

The New York Department of Environmental Conservation allocates only 22 clam permits, which limit the total annual harvest to 300,000 bushels (about 13,600 bushels per permit). Based on 2011 clam prices, the gross revenue potential of each permit was about $135,000.

However, clam fishers claimed that after deducting operating costs, a single permit was insufficient to make a living. The permits are transferrable, meaning that a single fisher could purchase multiple permits. But the permit system initially required each permit to be associated with one boat. If you purchased a second permit then you would have to also operate a second boat, effectively doubling your operating costs. This requirement meant that efficiency gains from applying multiple permits to the same boat could not be realized.

In 2011 the state changed the law to allow "cooperative harvesting"—meaning that a fisher could buy additional permits without having to operate more boats. Given that the total quota allocation remained at 300,000 bushels, the law change shouldn't affect the health of the fishery, but it offers the potential to increase the economic efficiency of the industry.

Source: "Ensure that Permits Protect Long Island's Surf Clam Fishery," *Newsday* (New York), July 6, 2012, p. A28.

Although ITQs or other regulations of a common property resource may not be popular with those who are used to accessing the resource for free, these policies are required to prevent the unsustainable use of the resource.

tragedy of the commons: a situation in which an unregulated common property resource is seriously degraded due to overuse

The overuse of a common property resource has famously been described as the "**tragedy of the commons**" (see Box 14.2), and it also can be viewed as a type of negative externality. Each user of the resource imposes a negative cost on others, yet makes decisions based solely on his or her own profits. Just as in our externality analysis, the unregulated market outcome with a common property resource will be inefficient.

Discussion Questions

1. Suppose that you and three roommates are living in an apartment or dorm suite with a common area for living, dining, and cooking. Do you think that a "tragedy of the commons" outcome is a likely result without some rules regarding cleaning? What rules would you propose instituting?
2. Suppose that a small fishing community in a developing country has been operating successfully for centuries without any regulations. Each fishing family owns a boat and makes a small profit. However, suppose that climate change reduces the health of the fish stock, and the community is forced to reduce its overall fishing activities. Should the community institute an auction system to allocate fishing rights or begin charging a license fee? Can you think of a fair way to reduce the community's fishing activities?

4. Public Goods

Public goods are at the opposite end of the spectrum from private goods. Public goods are both nonexcludable and nonrival. We saw examples of market failure with artificially scarce goods and common property resources. As you might expect, private markets fail to provide the efficient level of public goods. In fact, even though many people value the benefits of public goods, private markets often fail to provide any public goods at all.

In private market goods, the ability to charge a price acts as a way to exclude nonbuyers and thus make a profit. Anyone can enjoy the benefits of a public good without paying, and each additional user does not affect the amount or quality of the good available to others. Consider national defense as an example of a public good. Could we rely on a megacorporation

BOX 14.2 THE "TRAGEDY OF THE COMMONS" DEBATE

The term "tragedy of the commons" comes from an influential paper written by ecologist Garrett Hardin in 1968. Discussing the degradation of common grazing properties in England, Hardin wrote:

> Picture a pasture open to all. It is to be expected that each herdsman will try to keep as many cattle as possible on the commons. Such an arrangement may work reasonably satisfactorily for centuries because tribal wars, poaching, and disease keep the numbers of both man and beast well below the carrying capacity of the land. Finally, however, comes the day of reckoning, that is, the day when the long-desired goal of social stability becomes a reality. At this point, the inherent logic of the commons remorselessly generates tragedy.
>
> As a rational being, each herdsman seeks to maximize his gain. Explicitly or implicitly, more or less consciously, he asks, "What is the utility to me of adding one more animal to my herd?" This utility has one negative and one positive component.
>
> 1. The positive component is a function of the increment of one animal. Since the herdsman receives all the proceeds from the sale of the additional animal, the positive utility is nearly +1.
> 2. The negative component is a function of the additional overgrazing created by one more animal. Since, however, the effects of overgrazing are shared by all the herdsmen, the negative utility for any particular decision-making herdsman is only a fraction of [the shared negatives].
>
> Adding together the component partial utilities, the rational herdsman concludes that the only sensible course for him to pursue is to add another animal to his herd. And another; and another. . . . But this is the conclusion reached by each and every rational herdsman sharing a commons. Therein is the tragedy. Each man is locked into a system that compels him to increase his herd without limit—in a world that is limited. (Hardin, 1968, p. 1244)

The "tragedy of the commons" essentially describes the fate of an "open-access resource"—one to which everyone has access without limitation or regulation. But there has often been confusion between the concepts of common property and open access. Common property resources are not necessarily open-access resources; their use may be regulated, for example, by customs and traditional rules.

The story told by Hardin was significantly modified by the political scientist Elinor Ostrom, who won the Nobel Memorial Prize in economic science for work "showing how common resources—forests, fisheries, oil fields or grazing lands—can be managed successfully by the people who use them, rather than by governments or private companies." Ostrom's point was that it was not just "tribal wars, poaching, and disease" that kept the system in balance. Instead, many societies have worked out institutional arrangements that operate with the same result as government regulations but that depend on social norms and customs instead of laws. In many parts of the world, such systems have endured for generations, sometimes centuries.

It is often the encroachment of market institutions on situations in which community management of common property has been successful that leads to degradation. As Hardin pointed out, when a common property resource exists within a market context, without any regulation by institutions of government or of society, there is an incentive at the individual level to keep using the resource as long as profits can be made. But each individual fails to consider the cost he or she imposes on other users, and the likely outcome is the destruction of the resource. Thus in the case of an open-access resource, the unregulated market outcome is both inefficient and ecologically unsustainable.

Sources: Garrett Hardin, "The Tragedy of the Commons," *Science* 162 (3859): 1243-1248, 1968; Elinor Ostrom, *Governing the Commons: The Evolution of Institutions for Collective Action* (Cambridge, UK: Cambridge University Press, 1990).

to provide national defense in a market setting? Obviously not. No individual would have an incentive to pay because he or she could receive essentially the same level of benefits without paying. Thus the "equilibrium" quantity of public goods in a market setting is normally zero, as no company would want to produce something for which no one is willing to pay. Clearly, this is an example of market failure.

Perhaps, we could rely on donations to supply public goods. This is done with some public goods, such as public radio and public television. Also, some environmental groups conserve habitats that, while privately owned, can be considered public goods because they are open for

free riders: those who obtain the benefits of a public good without paying anything for it

public enjoyment. Donations, however, generally are not sufficient for an efficient provision of public goods. Because public goods are nonexclusive, each person can receive the benefits of public goods regardless of whether he or she pays. So although some people may be willing to donate money to public radio, many others simply listen to it without paying anything. Those who do not pay are called **free riders**.

It is obvious that a voluntary donation system would not work for the provision of many public goods, including national defense. Although we cannot rely on private markets or voluntary donations to supply public goods, their adequate supply is of crucial interest to the entire society. In democracies, decisions regarding the provision of public goods are commonly decided in the political arena. This is generally true of national defense. A political decision must be made, taking into account that some citizens may favor more defense spending and others less. After the decision is made, we all pay a share of the cost through taxes.

Similarly, decisions on the provision of environmental public goods may be made through the political system. Congress, for example, must decide on funding for the national park system. Will more land be acquired for parks? Might some existing park areas be sold or leased for development? In making decisions like this, we need some indication of the level of citizen demand for public goods. What insights can we gain from economic theory?

Recall that in Chapter 4 we referred to a demand curve as both a marginal benefit curve and a willingness-to-pay curve. A consumer is willing to pay, say, as much as \$30 for a t-shirt because that is his or her perceived benefit from owning the shirt. But in the case of a public good, the marginal benefits that someone obtains from a public good are *not* the same as his or her willingness to pay for it. In particular, the person's willingness to pay is likely to be significantly lower than his or her marginal benefits.

A simple example illustrates this point. Consider a society with just two individuals: Doug and Sasha. Both individuals value forest preservation—a public good. Figure 14.3 shows the marginal benefits that each person receives from the preservation of forest land. As in a regular demand curve, the marginal benefits of each acre preserved decline with more preservation. We see that Doug receives greater marginal benefits than Sasha does. This may be because Doug obtains more recreational use of forests, or it may simply reflect different preferences.

The social marginal benefits from preserved forest land are obtained by the vertical addition of the two marginal benefit curves. In the top graph in Figure 14.3, we see that Doug receives a marginal benefit of \$5 for an additional acre of forest preservation if 10 acres are already preserved. Sasha receives a marginal benefit of only \$2. The social, or aggregate, benefits of an additional acre of preserved forest are \$7, as shown in the bottom graph. The "social benefits" graph represents the addition of the marginal benefits to both Doug and Sasha. In this case, the aggregate curve is kinked (i.e., not straight) because to the right of the kink Sasha's marginal benefits are zero, and the curve showing the value of preserving additional acres reflects only Doug's marginal benefits.

Suppose for simplicity that forest preservation costs society a constant \$7/acre for administrative and management costs. This is shown in the bottom graph in Figure 14.3. In this example, the optimal level of forest preservation is 10 acres—the point where the marginal social benefits just equal the marginal costs.

But we have not addressed the question of how much Doug and Sasha are actually willing to pay for forest preservation. In the case of a public good, a person's marginal benefit curve is not the same as his or her willingness-to-pay curve. For example, although Doug receives a marginal benefit of \$5 for an acre of forest preservation, he has an incentive to be a free rider and he may be willing to pay only \$3 or even nothing at all.

The problem is that we do not have a market in which people accurately indicate their preferences for public goods. Perhaps we could conduct a survey to collect information on how much people value certain public goods, but sometimes people do not provide accurate responses (recall our discussion of contingent valuation surveys in Chapter 13). Ultimately,

Figure 14.3 **The Benefits of Public Goods**

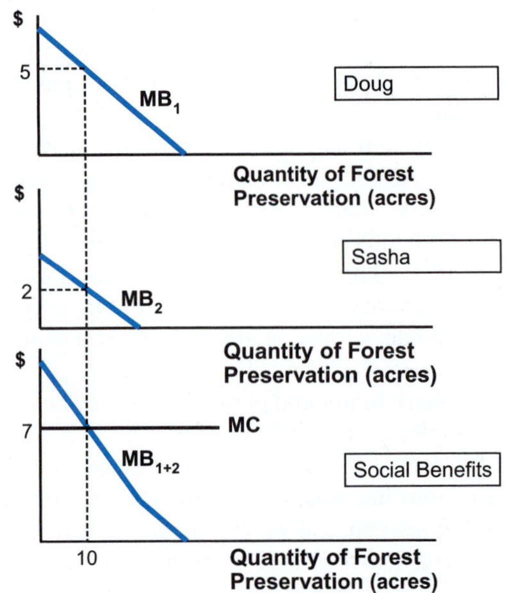

The aggregate social marginal benefits of supplying public goods can be obtained by vertically adding each individual's marginal benefit curve.

decisions regarding public goods require some kind of social deliberation. One option is to rely on elected officials to make public goods decisions for their constituents. Another is to rely on a democratic process such as direct voting or local town meetings.

Suppose that we correctly determine that the appropriate level of forest preservation in Figure 14.3 is 10 acres. At a marginal cost of $7/acre, we need to raise $70 in revenues to pay for preservation. We could tax Doug and Sasha $35 each to cover these costs. Doug receives at least $5 in benefits for every acre preserved, or a total of at least $50 in benefits, so he may not object to the $35 tax. However, Sasha receives significantly lower benefits, and she may view the tax as excessive.

Now, let us extend our two-person example to the entire population of the United States—about 115 million households. If preferences in the general population are similar to Doug and Sasha's, we will need to raise $35 multiplied by 115 million, or about $4 billion, for forest preservation in order to reflect its true social benefits. This could be done with a tax of $35 per household. But, of course, marginal benefits vary across households. It is clearly impractical to assess the actual marginal benefit of each household. A society-wide decision must be made.

After this decision has been made, some people might think that they have to pay too much and others that the allocation of money for forest preservation is inadequate. But assessing a broad tax is essential for achieving the goal of forest preservation. Debates regarding efficiency and fairness in the case of public goods are thus inevitably both political and economic in nature.

Discussion Questions

1. Some people have suggested that certain public lands would be managed more efficiently if they were auctioned off to the highest bidders. In theory, the highest bidder would put the land to its highest-valued use. Employing a market valuation, that use might be logging or developing the land for vacation homes. Such an auction would provide the government with revenue, which could be used for socially beneficial purposes or for lowering taxes. Do you think that some public lands should be sold to private interests?
2. Consider the provision levels of the following public goods in society: national defense, public education, environmental quality, and highways. Do you think that the current

"supply" of each of these goods is too high, too low, or about right? What factors do you think determine the amount of resources that are allocated toward each of these goods? Do policies need to be changed to adjust the allocation?

5. Climate Change

climate change: long-term changes in global climate, including warmer temperatures, changing precipitation patterns, more extreme weather events, and rising sea levels

Global warming, sometimes more accurately described as **climate change**, has become a major issue in recent decades. The vast majority of scientists concur that global climate change is largely caused by human activity, in particular, the emission of atmospheric pollutants.* See Box 14.3 for more on the scientific opinion on climate change.

According to the National Oceanic and Atmospheric Administration (NOAA), a U.S. government agency, 2012 was the tenth-warmest year on record. More importantly, it marked the thirty-sixth consecutive year of above-average global temperatures.**

Climate change has significant economic costs. According to NOAA's National Climate Data Center, 11 severe weather events in 2012 in the United States cost the country $110 billion. The two costliest events that year were Hurricane Sandy ($65 billion) and the yearlong drought across the country ($30 billion).[1]

Numerous projections conclude that these impacts will become more severe over time unless significant steps are taken. In 2013 the managing director of the International Monetary

Box 14.3 The Scientific Consensus on Climate Change

Although few dispute the finding that the world is becoming warmer, media reports commonly refer to the debate over the causes of this warming as ongoing. The global climate has varied considerably over time due to natural factors. Some people think the current warming represents just another natural variation, while others attribute the warming primarily to human factors, mainly the burning of fossil fuels. What is the unbiased scientific opinion on the causes of climate change?

Several articles have been published based on surveys of either the scientific literature on climate change or climate scientists themselves. In a 2004 paper published in the highly respected journal *Science,* the abstracts of 928 articles on the topic of climate change were reviewed. Of these, 75 percent agreed with the "consensus position" that humans are causing climate change, and 25 percent dealt with methods or past climate change and thus took no position on current warming. But the author writes, "Remarkably, none of the papers disagreed with the consensus position."

In a 2013 study climate researchers were directly asked whether their research supported or refuted the view that humans are affecting the climate. Of those who expressed an opinion, 97 percent supported the consensus position. The paper concludes that the "number of papers rejecting [the view that humans are impacting the climate] is a minuscule proportion of the published research." The results of a larger survey of earth scientists, published in 2009, concluded:

> It seems that the debate on the authenticity of global warming and the role played by human activity is largely nonexistent among those who understand the nuances and scientific basis of long-term climate processes. The challenge, rather, appears to be how to effectively communicate this fact to policy makers and to a public that continues to mistakenly perceive debate among scientists.

Sources: William R.L. Anderegg, James W. Prall, Jacob Harold, and Stephen H. Schneider, "Expert Credibility in Climate Change," *Proceedings of the National Academies of Science* 107(27) (2010): 12107–12109; J. Cook, D. Nuccitelli, S.A. Green, M. Richardson, B. Winkler, R. Painting, R. Way, P. Jacobs, and A. Skuc, "Quantifying the Consensus on Anthropogenic Global Warming the Scientific Literature," *Environmental Research Letters* 8(2) (2013): 1–7; Peter T. Doran and Maggie Kendall Zimmerman, "Examining the Scientific Consensus on Climate Change," *EOS* 90(3) (2009): 22–23; Naomi Oreskes, "Beyond the Ivory Tower: The Scientific Consensus on Climate Change," *Science* 306 (5702) (2004): 1686.

*We use the term "climate change" instead of "global warming" because, in addition to warmer average temperatures, this hugely complex system change has numerous other effects—sometimes even including colder than normal temperatures in certain locations.

**Relative to the twentieth-century average of 57 degrees Fahrenheit (about 13.9 degrees Celsius).

Fund, Christine Lagarde, called climate change "the greatest economic challenge of the twenty-first century." She went on to say:

> Make no mistake: without concerted action, the very future of our planet is in peril. So we need growth, but we also need green growth that respects environmental sustainability. Good ecology is good economics.[2]

A well-known 2006 report on climate change sponsored by the British government concluded:

> Climate change presents a unique challenge for economics: it is the greatest and widest-ranging market failure ever seen. . . . Our actions over the coming few decades could create risks of major disruption to economic and social activity, later in this century and in the next, on a scale similar to those associated with the great wars and the economic depression of the first half of the twentieth century.[3]

Many of the principles discussed in this chapter and Chapter 13 are applicable to solving the challenge of climate change. But an adequate response to climate change is not simply a matter of instituting economic policies. It will also involve questions about fairness concerning rich and poor countries as well as different groups within countries. Other relevant issues concern how to act under uncertainty and how to define well-being, both now and in the future.

5.1 Climate Change Data and Projections

greenhouse gases: gases such as carbon dioxide and methane whose atmospheric concentrations influence global climate by trapping solar radiation

Humans can influence the global climate by the emissions of various **greenhouse gases**. These gases act much like the glass in a greenhouse—allowing solar radiation to penetrate but then trapping it and increasing temperatures. Although various greenhouse gases exist naturally in the earth's atmosphere and make life possible on earth, human activities have increased the concentration of many of these gases and introduced greenhouse gases into the atmosphere that do not occur naturally. The most relevant greenhouse gas emitted by humans is carbon dioxide (CO_2), which is formed when fossil fuels (coal, oil, and natural gas) are burned. Other important greenhouse gases include methane, nitrous oxide, and chlorofluorocarbons (CFCs).*

As shown in Figure 14.4, global emissions of CO_2 have increased significantly over the past couple of decades and are projected to increase a further 30 percent between 2015 and 2035. We see that virtually all the increase in emissions in the coming decades will be a result of higher emissions in developing countries (i.e., those that are not members of the OECD). Most of the carbon emitted from human activities to date, however, has come from developed countries.

Further, CO_2 emissions *per capita* are much higher in developed countries and will continue to be so for the foreseeable future. For example, annual emissions per capita are currently about 18 tons in the United States, 9 tons in Germany, 7 tons in China, 1.4 tons in India, and 0.3 tons in Kenya. This disparity in emissions per capita roughly reflects the global disparity in income. Any climate proposal that seeks broad international participation will need to allow the world's poorest to increase their material living standards. Thus simply requiring all countries, say, to reduce emissions by 50 percent would reinforce current inequality.

CO_2 and other greenhouse gas emissions remain in the atmosphere for a long time, decades or even centuries. This means that even if we reduce annual emissions by 50 percent or more, total concentrations will continue to rise. The atmosphere can be viewed as a bathtub with a

*CFCs have also been implicated in depletion of the ozone layer, a critical layer of the atmosphere. It is important to note that degradation of the ozone layer, while serious, is an issue almost entirely unrelated to global climate change.

Figure 14.4 **Past and Projected Global Emissions of Carbon Dioxide, 1990–2035**

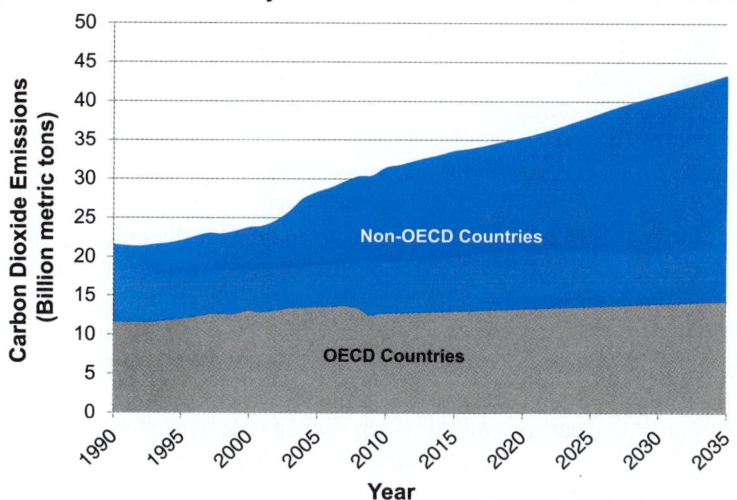

Global emissions of carbon dioxide are projected to increase 30 percent between 2015 and 2035, with most of the increase a result of higher emissions in developing countries.

Source: United States Energy Information Administration database.
Note: OECD is the Organisation for Economic Co-Operation and Development, comprised mostly of developed nations.

very, very slow leak. As long as we keep adding more water (i.e., greenhouse gases) beyond a slight trickle to the bathtub, its level will continue to rise.

As atmospheric concentrations of greenhouse gases increase, the world is expected to become warmer, on average. Not all regions will warm equally, and some regions may actually become cooler. Warmer average temperatures increase evaporation, which in turn leads to more frequent precipitation, but again all regions will not be affected equally. In general, areas that are already wet will become wetter and dry areas will become drier. Climate change is also expected to result in more frequent and more intense tropical storms. The melting of polar ice caps and glaciers will contribute to rising sea levels. Sea levels are also rising because the volume of ocean water expands when it is heated.

Global average temperatures have already increased by about 1 degree Celsius (1.8 degrees Fahrenheit) over the past several decades. At a 2009 international meeting on climate change in Copenhagen, Denmark, more than 130 countries agreed that it was necessary to limit the eventual warming to no more than 2 degrees Celsius, based on the scientific consensus that warming above this level is likely to cause dangerous impacts.

Climate scientists have developed complex models to predict how much average temperatures will increase as CO_2 concentrations increase. Because predicting long-term climate trends involves considerable uncertainty, these models have produced a range of potential outcomes. Adding to the uncertainty in models is the extent to which warming will be influenced by the policy decisions made in the next couple of decades.

The Intergovernmental Panel on Climate Change (IPCC) was established in 1988 by the United Nations Environment Programme (UNEP) and the World Meteorological Organization (WMO) under the United Nations to assess the science of climate change. A 2007 IPCC report estimated that temperatures will rise between 1.1 and 6.4 degrees Celsius in the twenty-first century, with the most likely range between 1.8 and 4.0 degrees.[4] A 2009 analysis by researchers at MIT, however, predicted that, without significant policy changes, warming would be much greater—in the range of 3.5 to 7.4 degrees Celsius.[5] Warming above 5 degrees is considered particularly dangerous, as 5 degrees represents the difference in global average temperatures between now and the last ice age. Such a large temperature change in a short period (although in the opposite directions) would cause significant ecological impacts, such as the extinction of as much as 50 percent of the earth's species according to one estimate.

5.2 Economic Analysis of Climate Change

Strong policy action to reduce emissions of greenhouse gases could avoid the most damaging effects of climate change. Scientists at the IPCC estimate that, rather than increasing as projected in Figure 14.4, global CO_2 emissions must be reduced 50–80 percent by 2050. Of course, most countries are highly dependent on fossil fuels as an energy source. Transitioning to a low-carbon economy will require investment in energy efficiency and renewable energy technologies.

Various economic studies have analyzed climate change using the techniques of cost-benefit analysis, which was discussed in Chapter 13. Cost-benefit analysis of climate change is particularly difficult for two main reasons: the high degree of uncertainty about future impacts and the long period of the analysis. Most of the costs of responding to climate change are borne in the short term, while most of the benefits (in terms of avoided damages) occur in the long term. Thus the choice of a discount rate is critical.

Virtually all economists agree that carbon emissions represent a negative externality and that a market-based policy such as a Pigovian tax or a tradable permit system should internalize this externality. However, there is a lively debate among economists about how aggressive such policies should be. Until recently, most economic studies of climate change suggested a relatively modest carbon tax, perhaps around \$20–\$40 per ton of carbon emitted (a \$30 per ton tax on carbon would increase the price of gasoline by about 8 cents per gallon).

The economic debate over climate change changed significantly in 2006 when Nicholas Stern, a former chief economist at the World Bank, released a 700-page report, sponsored by the British government, titled *The Economics of Climate Change: The Stern Review.* Publication of the "Stern Review" generated significant media attention and has intensified the debate over climate change in policy and academic circles. Unlike previous studies, the Executive Summary of the "Stern Review" strongly recommends immediate and substantial policy action:

> The scientific evidence is now overwhelming: climate change is a serious global threat, and it demands an urgent global response. This Review has assessed a wide range of evidence on the impacts of climate change and on the economic costs, and has used a number of different techniques to assess costs and risks. From all these perspectives, the evidence gathered by the Review leads to a simple conclusion: the benefits of strong and early action far outweigh the economic costs of not acting.

The "Stern Review" estimated that if humanity continues "business as usual," the costs of climate change in the twenty-first century would reach at least 5 percent of global GDP and could be as high as 20 percent. It also suggested the need for a much higher carbon tax—over \$300 per ton of carbon.

What accounts for the difference between the "Stern Review" and most earlier analyses? The primary difference was that Stern applied a lower discount rate, 1.4 percent, compared to 4–5 percent in most other studies. Stern argued that his discount rate reflected the view that each generation should have approximately the same inherent value. Stern's analysis also incorporated the precautionary principle (discussed in Chapter 13), in that he placed greater weight on the possibility of catastrophic damages.

5.3 Climate Change Policy

Because climate change can be considered a very large environmental externality associated with carbon emissions, economic theory suggests a carbon tax as an economic policy response. Alternatively, a tradable permit system (also known as cap-and-trade) could be applied to carbon emissions.

As discussed in Chapter 13, a tax offers price certainty, while a tradable permit system offers emissions certainty. If you take the perspective that price certainty is important because it allows for better long-term planning, then a carbon tax is preferable. If you believe that the relevant policy goal is to reduce carbon emissions by a specified amount with certainty, then a cap-and-trade approach is preferable, although it may lead to some price volatility.

Both approaches have been used. Carbon taxes have been instituted in several countries, including a nationwide tax on coal in India (about $1/ton, enacted in 2010), a tax on new vehicles based on their carbon emissions in South Africa (also enacted in 2010), a carbon tax on fuels in Costa Rica (enacted in 1997), and local carbon taxes in the Canadian provinces of Quebec, British Columbia, and Alberta that apply to large carbon emitters and motor fuels.

The European Union instituted a cap-and-trade system for carbon emissions in 2005. The system covers more than 11,000 facilities that collectively are responsible for nearly half the EU's carbon emissions. In 2012 the system was expanded to cover the aviation sector, including incoming flights from outside the EU. The state of California instituted a cap-and-trade system in 2013 for electrical utilities and large industrial facilities, with a goal of an annual decline in carbon emissions of 3 percent.

Regardless of which policy approach is taken, it must ultimately be applied at the international level. Each individual country has very little incentive for reducing its emissions if other countries do not agree to similar reductions. Action to reduce climate change can be regarded as a public good that also generates a positive externality. As we have noted, in the case of public goods, the problem of free riders means that they will not be provided effectively without collective action. In the case of stabilizing the health of a **global public good** such as the climate, international agreement is required.

global public good: a public good available to the entire population of the planet

The most comprehensive international agreement on climate change was the Kyoto Protocol, which was drafted in 1997. Under that treaty, industrialized countries agreed to emission reduction targets by 2012 compared to their baseline emissions, normally set to 1990 levels. For example, the United States agreed to a 7 percent reduction, France to an 8 percent reduction, and Japan to a 6 percent reduction. Developing countries such as China and India were not bound to emissions targets under the treaty (an omission that drew objections from the United States and some other countries).

By 2012, 191 countries had signed and ratified the Kyoto Protocol. The United States was the only country that signed the treaty but never ratified it. In 2001, the George W. Bush administration rejected the Kyoto Protocol, arguing that negotiations had failed and that a new approach was necessary. Despite the U.S. withdrawal, the Kyoto Protocol entered into force in early 2005 after Russia ratified the treaty in November 2004.

Countries that have met their targets under the Kyoto Protocol include France, Germany, Russia, and the United Kingdom. Countries that have apparently failed to meet their targets include Canada, Australia, Spain, and Sweden. The overall Kyoto program target of a 5 percent reduction in industrialized country emissions was likely to be met based on preliminary data, but only because of very large reductions in Russia due largely to its economic collapse after the demise of the Soviet Union in 1991 rather than any deliberate policy.

Countries that failed to meet their targets are supposed to make up for it in the future, but attempts to create a successor to the Kyoto Protocol have so far been unsuccessful. Perhaps, the most contentious point of disagreement is still whether developing countries should be bound by mandatory cuts in emissions. Although some countries, particularly the United States, argue that all participants must agree to reductions in order to address the problem, developing countries contend that mandatory cuts would limit their economic development and reinforce existing global inequities.

A more radical approach, which treats the entire atmosphere as a common property resource, is described in Box 14.4. Although such a solution is politically highly unlikely, it indicates that the application of standard economic principles to dealing with common property resources and public goods could respond effectively to the problem of climate change as well as promote greater global equity.

BOX 14.4 AN EARTH ATMOSPHERIC TRUST

The global atmosphere is a common property resource with respect to carbon emissions. For the most part, anyone can emit carbon into the atmosphere without cost. The apparent outcome is the largest example of the tragedy of the commons that the world has ever seen.

A common property resource is essentially equally "owned" by all with access to it. As a global resource, the atmosphere can be viewed as something to which all people on earth have an equal right. This principle forms the basis for perhaps the most innovative and comprehensive policy approach to reducing carbon emissions, called an Earth Atmospheric Trust.

The program would establish a global cap-and-trade system for carbon emissions. The cap would be established to prevent damaging climate change, based on the best available scientific evidence. All permits would be auctioned off to the highest bidders, such as electricity plants, industrial facilities, and transportation companies. The cost of permits would ultimately be reflected as higher prices to consumers.

A global auction system would yield significant revenues, about $1 trillion–$4 trillion annually depending on the price of permits. Some of this money (the Earth Atmospheric Trust) would be used to invest in low-carbon technologies, fund adaption measures, and restore ecological damage. The remainder, perhaps half or more, would be distributed to all people on earth as an equal per-capita annual payment. This reflects the concept of equal "ownership" of the atmosphere, such that everyone is equally compensated for the damage done to the resource.

Of course, the logistics of distributing an annual payment to all people on the planet are currently daunting, but the principle is supported by standard economic theory. The annual payment would amount to about $300 per person per year. In rich countries, the payment would partially, but not totally, offset higher prices for goods such as electricity and gasoline. In poor countries, the payment would reflect a substantial increase in annual incomes. Consider that about a billion people currently live on $1 or less per day. Thus in addition to limiting carbon emissions, the Trust would significantly reduce abject poverty in the world.

Source: Peter Barnes, Robert Costanza, Paul Hawken, David Orr, Elinor Ostrom, Alvaro Umana, and Oran Young, "Creating an Earth Atmospheric Trust," *Science* 319 (2008): 724.

Discussion Questions

1. How serious a problem do you think climate change is? Compare your judgment of this based on news reports and the economic studies that have tried to evaluate the costs and benefits of climate change. How effective do you think economic analysis has been in approaching the problem?
2. Which policies do you think are most likely to be effective in responding to climate change? Given the political resistance to taxes, what do you think would be the best strategy for achieving reduction of greenhouse gas emissions?

REVIEW QUESTIONS

1. What are the two characteristics of private goods? Provide some examples.
2. What are the two characteristics of public goods? Provide some examples.
3. What are the two characteristics of common property goods? Provide some examples.
4. What are the two characteristics of artificially scarce goods? Provide some examples.
5. How do economists define congestion?
6. What is the supply curve for an artificially scarce good?
7. Why does the private provision of an artificially scarce good result in economic inefficiency?
8. What is price discrimination?
9. How can we model the market for a common property resource?
10. How can we determine the utilization or harvest for a common property resource without any regulation?
11. How do we determine the efficient outcome for a common property resource?
12. What policies can be implemented in the case of a common property resource?
13. What is the tragedy of the commons?
14. What is the likely equilibrium outcome for a public good in a private market?

15. Can voluntary donations result in the efficient provision of public goods?
16. What are free riders?
17. How can we model the demand for a public good in a simple society with two individuals?
18. Why do someone's marginal benefits differ from his willingness to pay in the case of a public good?
19. What policies are needed to provide for the efficient provision of public goods?
20. What is climate change?
21. What are the projections for future greenhouse gas emissions, considering both developed and developing countries?
22. What do most economic analyses of climate change conclude? What are some major differences?
23. What are some economic policies to address climate change?

EXERCISES

1. For each of the following examples, discuss whether it is a private good, a public good, a common property resource, or an artificially scarce good. Note that some examples may be considered more than one type of good.
   a. Seats in a movie theater
   b. Traffic lights
   c. A lake on private land
   d. A lake on public land
   e. Cars owned by a car rental company
   f. The water in a currently pure river, which can be used for drinking water as well as waste disposal
   g. A hospital that provides free health care to low-income households
2. An underground aquifer in a developing country is available to all farms in a small community. Assume that it costs 50 pesos per day to operate a pump that can extract groundwater from the aquifer. The value that a farm can obtain by using or selling the water depends on how many farms extract water, as given in the table below.

Number of farms extracting water	Revenue per day per farm (pesos)	Profit per day per farm (pesos)	Total profit (pesos)
1	100		
2	100		
3	100		
4	90		
5	80		
6	65		
7	55		
8	40		
9	20		

   a. Assuming that there is no regulation of the aquifer, how many farms will extract groundwater? Assume that as long as each farm is making a profit, there is an incentive for more farms to extract water. Fill in the third column of the table to help you answer this question.
   b. Is this unregulated outcome economically efficient? Explain.
   c. What would be the economically efficient level of groundwater extraction (number of farms extracting water)? Hint: calculate total profit by multiplying number of farms by profit per farm and see where total profit reaches a maximum. At this point, the extra profit made by adding one more farm is just balanced by the losses to other farms.
3. The marginal benefits of wildlife habitat preservation in a society with just two individuals, Katya and Miguel, are given in the table below.

Acres of wildlife habitat	Katya's marginal benefits (dollars)	Miguel's marginal benefits (dollars)
1	50	30
2	40	25
3	30	20
4	20	15
5	10	10
6	0	5

   a. Draw a graph showing the social marginal benefits of wildlife preservation.
   b. Suppose that wildlife preservation costs $40 per acre. How many acres of wildlife habitat should be preserved in this society?
   c. What policy would you propose to achieve the efficient provision of wildlife habitat?
   d. Which individual do you think would be less willing to support your policy proposal? Explain.

4. Match each concept in Column A with an example in Column B.

Column A	Column B
a. A private good	1. A policy solution to the tragedy of the commons
b. A free rider	2. National defense
c. Price discrimination	3. The primary factor on which some economists disagree regarding climate policy
d. A public good	4. Your shoes
e. An artificially scarce good	5. Someone who listens to public radio without contributing to it
f. Individual transferable quotas	6. Charging airline passengers different fares
g. The discount rate	7. The wifi signal at a hotel that charges for Internet access

NOTES

1. NOAA press release, "2012 Was the Tenth Warmest Year on Record," June 13, 2013.

2. Jeremy Hance, "Head of IMF: Climate Change Is the 'Greatest Economic Challenge of the Twenty-First Century,'" REGATTA, United Nations Environment Programme, February 6, 2013.

3. Nicholas Stern, *The Economics of Climate Change: The Stern Review* (Cambridge: Cambridge University Press, 2007).

4. Intergovernmental Panel on Climate Change, *Climate Change 2007: The Physical Science Basis* (Cambridge: Cambridge University Press, 2007).

5. David Chandler, "Climate Change Odds Much Worse Than Thought," *MIT News,* May 19, 2009.

PART V
Resources, Production, and Market Organization

15 Capital Stocks and Resource Maintenance

Economics is about how people manage their resources. All economic actors—businesses, governments, nonprofit organizations, and each of us as individuals—have to make decisions every day about how to use (or not use) our resources. In managing your financial resources, you choose how to allocate your money between food, entertainment, books, and many other things. Companies decide how to use their workers and physical resources to produce efficiently. Governments must allocate tax revenues among many competing needs. As a society, we are faced with choices about how to use our natural resources and how much to save for the future.

In this final section of the book, we focus on how we manage our resources and use them to produce goods and services, generally for sale in markets. We saw in Chapter 1 that production decisions always involve tradeoffs—recall our discussion of the production-possibilities frontier. Producing more of one thing requires us to give up something in return. We can also think of tradeoffs over time. Using up a critical natural resource now may increase current production, but lead to reduced opportunities in the future. Thus the activity of resource maintenance goes hand-in-hand with production decisions.

In this chapter, we focus on the different types of resources available to society, from manufacturing equipment to credit worthiness, from oil reserves to human knowledge. We see how we can track the availability of resources over time. The importance of each type of resource is discussed. We end with a discussion about the sustainable management of resources.

1. Capital Stocks

As you have probably learned by now, sometimes economists speak a slightly different language from most people. Let's consider how most people define the following words:

- *Capital:* This commonly refers to something to do with finance, such as "capital markets" or "venture capital."
- *Stocks:* This commonly refers to ownership shares in companies, which are traded in "stock markets."
- *Investment:* This commonly refers to activity such as buying stocks or "investing" in a retirement account.

capital: any resource that is valued for its potential economic contributions

To an economist, these terms mean slightly different things. The economist's definition of **capital** includes not only financial resources, but any resource that is valued for its potential economic contributions. Money is one type of capital, but other types of capital include a factory, a highway, a natural gas field, or a farm. Capital does not even need to be something physical. The knowledge that you are gaining from your education is a form of capital. So, too, are systems of laws and customs that facilitate economic activities. Below we will define the main different types of capital.

stock: something whose quantity can be measured at a point in time

To an economist, a **stock** refers to the quantity of something at a particular point in time. For example, the amount of water currently in a bathtub is a stock, as is the amount of money in your checking account on January 1. The number of hairs on your head right now is a stock. In this chapter, we often focus on the stock of a particular capital resource, such as the stock of oil reserves or the stock of a species of fish in a lake. Stocks of capital may increase or decrease as a consequence of natural forces, as in the case of a natural forest, or they may be deliberately managed by humans to provide the inputs for production.

investment: any activity intended to increase the quantity or quality of a resource over time

Finally, economists view **investment** as any activity intended to increase the quantity or quality of a resource over time. In other words, investment is designed to result in the growth of capital stocks. An employee who puts funds into her individual retirement account (IRA) is investing in the stock of financial assets that she will draw on in the future. So is the business that trains its workers, the subsistence farmer who sets aside seeds for his next planting season, and the community that works to clean up its air and water. The economic activity of resource maintenance can be viewed as investment, leading to greater production possibilities in the future.

1.1 Stocks Versus Flows

flow: something whose quantity can be measured over a period of time

Capital stocks can increase over time, with proper investment, or decrease if they are simply used up. While the stock of something is measured at a single point in time, a **flow** is measured *over a period of time.* An obvious example is the amount of water flowing into a bathtub. We could speak of the amount of water flowing into the tub per minute, per hour, or another time interval. The flow of new tools into a warehouse, and the flow of tools out of it as they are sold, can be measured over the day or week. The number of haircuts that you had in the previous year is a flow of services. (Note that it is impossible to keep a stock of haircuts in a warehouse. Flows can be of either goods or services, but stocks can only be goods.)

stock-flow diagram: a diagram that shows how a stock changes over time, as flows add to it or subtract from it

Flows can either add to capital stocks or decrease them. Figure 15.1 presents a **stock-flow diagram,** which shows how flows change the level of a stock over time, by either adding to it or subtracting from it. Some of the stocks in Figure 15.1 carry over, meaning that they are still there in the next period. In this figure, the new stock is larger than the initial stock, because the additions are greater than the subtractions (represented by the thickness of arrows).

Figure 15.2 provides a specific example of a stock-flow diagram using a bank account as an example. Suppose that you start the month with exactly $1,400 in your checking account. This is your initial stock. During the month, the flows into your checking account include $700 from your job, $50 from someone who owed you money, and $5 in interest on the account, for a total of $755. Note that this is a flow that represents an addition to your stock over time.

Figure 15.1 **A Stock-Flow Diagram**

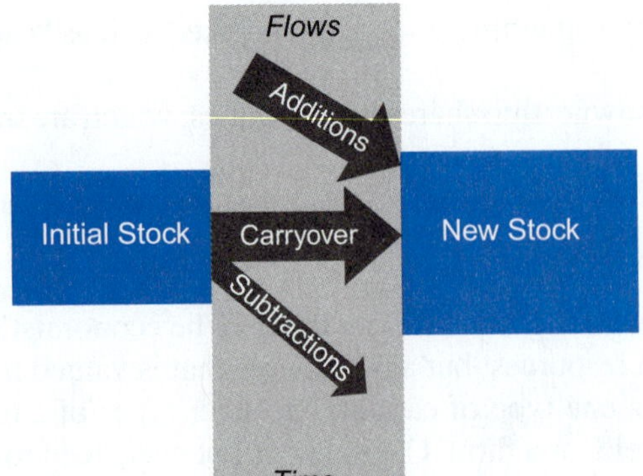

A stock-flow diagram shows how flows change the quantity of a stock over time. In this case, additions exceed subtractions, so the stock increases over time.

Figure 15.2 **A Stock-Flow Diagram for a Checking Account**

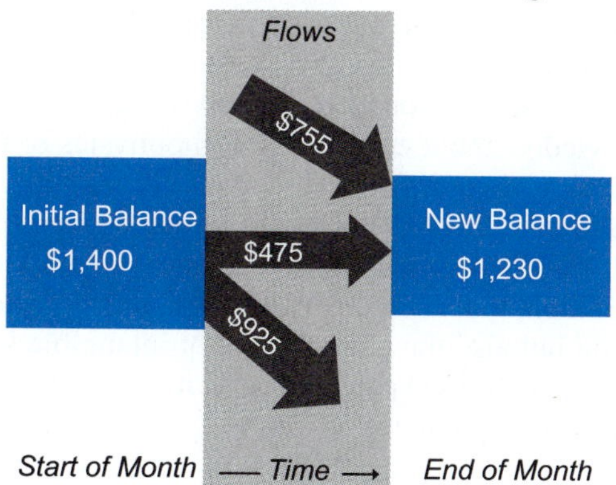

In this example, flows out of the checking account exceed the flows into the account, so the checking account balance declines over time.

The flows out of your account over the month include $600 for rent and $325 in other expenses, for a total of $925. Thus your new bank account balance at the end of the month (i.e., your stock of money on that day) is $1,230. Your balance has declined over the month because the flows out of your account were greater than the flows into it.

1.2 The Five Types of Capital

Capital can be classified into five basic categories:

1. natural capital
2. manufactured (or produced) capital
3. human capital
4. social capital
5. financial capital

natural capital: physical assets provided by nature

manufactured (or produced) capital: physical assets generated by applying human productive activities to natural capital

human capital: people's capacity for engaging in productive activities

social capital: the stock of relationships, including trust and shared values, that facilitates economic activities

financial capital: funds of purchasing power available to purchase goods and services or facilitate economic activity

physical capital: resources that are tangible (i.e., can be touched or seen)

Natural capital consists of physical assets provided by nature, such as land that is suitable for agriculture or other human uses, sources of fresh water, and stocks of minerals and fossil fuels (such as crude oil or coal) that are still in the ground. **Manufactured capital** is physical assets that are produced by humans using natural capital. These include such things as buildings, machinery, stocks of refined oil, and inventories of produced goods that are waiting to be sold.

Human capital is the capacity of people to engage in productive activities. Specifically, it includes the knowledge and skills that each person can bring to his or her work as well as the physical and mental health that allows people to make use of their knowledge and skills. **Social capital** is the stock of relationships among people that facilitates economic activities, including shared norms, values, and trust. For example, when you buy something on eBay, you trust that the seller will actually send you the item that you purchased after you pay for it, based on a mutual understanding of how an eBay transaction works.

Financial capital consists of resources that can be used to purchase goods and services. Money, either cash or bank accounts, is probably the most common form of financial capital, but it can also include assets such as stocks and bonds and one's ability to borrow in the form of loans or credit cards. Although financial capital does not directly produce anything, it contributes to production by making it possible for people to produce goods and services in advance of getting paid for them.

Capital can be classified as being either in physical or intangible forms (some capital can be both). Capital takes the form of **physical capital** when it can be touched or seen. Natural capital is primarily physical in form. Anything that we produce or use in the physical world either comes directly from a natural capital stock—as a fruit is picked from a wild tree—or has been transformed from its original, natural form. Even such human inventions as plastics, microchips, and advanced medicines are all made out of something physical that was at one time a part of the stock of natural capital.

intangible capital: resources that cannot be seen or touched

Intangible capital, which cannot be seen or touched, is less visible but no less important. Some human capital, such as knowledge about economics or biophysics or Chinese art, is a purely intangible type of capital. Social capital is also commonly intangible, such as the trust between a buyer and seller. But many forms of physical capital can also be viewed as a representation of intangible capital. A DVD, for example, is a physical object, but its true value lies in the information and entertainment that it can provide. Even a machine can be viewed as not only a hunk of physical metal but also the embodiment of intangible knowledge and software. Paper money is more than just physical paper because it also represents intangible, socially created trust that it can be used in payment.

Discussion Questions

1. Linda thinks that a rich person is someone who earns a lot of money. Meng thinks that a rich person is someone who has a big house and owns lots of stocks and bonds. How would the distinction between stocks and flows lend clarity to their discussion?
2. Think of a common activity that you enjoy. For example, perhaps you like to get together with friends and listen to music while making popcorn in the microwave. List the stocks of natural, manufactured, human, financial, and social capital on which you draw when engaging in this activity.

2. NATURAL CAPITAL

Natural capital forms the basis for all life on earth. Yet it is less obvious that natural capital is crucial to all economic activity. Sometimes, it is easy to forget that everything we see around us—computers, books, cars, buildings—can all be traced back to a natural capital origin. As human economic activity has increased, our demands on natural capital have also increased. Whether natural resources will be sufficient to meet human demands in the future has become a question of considerable debate. Moreover, some forms of natural capital are becoming degraded or fundamentally changed due to human activities, such as the changes in the global climate that we discussed in Chapter 14.

2.1 RENEWABLE AND NONRENEWABLE NATURAL CAPITAL

renewable resource: a resource that regenerates through short-term natural processes

nonrenewable resource: a resource whose stock diminishes with use over time

Different kinds of natural capital can be classified according to whether they are renewable. A **renewable resource** regenerates through biological or other short-term processes, which may be helped by human activity. The quantity and quality of its stock depend simultaneously on the rate at which the stock regenerates or renews and on the rate at which it is harvested or polluted. A healthy forest will go on indefinitely producing trees that may be harvested, yielding a flow of lumber that will be used up in production processes such as papermaking. (For more on the management of renewable natural capital stocks, see Box 15.1.)

Other kinds of natural capital are **nonrenewable resources**. Their supply is fixed, although new discoveries can increase the stock that is known to be available. For example, there is a finite amount of oil reserves, and a finite amount of each kind of mineral, available on earth. Although these resources were created over a very long period spanning millions of years, they are considered nonrenewable on a human time scale. Nonrenewable resources do not have self-regenerating flows, and the stock can only diminish over time as a result of human use or natural deterioration, as illustrated in Figure 15.3.

How much of its stock of natural resources a society chooses to use as inputs into current production, rather than to preserve for the future, is clearly a very important economic question. In addition to any carryover, the initial stock of a renewable resource is able

Box 15.1 Renewable Resource Management: Fishery Stocks

Since 1971 the Food and Agriculture Organization (FAO) of the United Nations (UN) has published reports on the status of the world's ocean fisheries. The FAO classifies fishery stocks into three categories, based on the relationship between actual harvest levels and the "maximum sustainable yield," which is the harvest level that equals the rate of natural regeneration of the stock. The three FAO fishery stock categories are:

1. *Non–fully exploited:* stocks with harvest levels below the maximum sustainable yield; harvest levels can be potentially increased without harming the fishing stock
2. *Fully exploited:* stocks with harvest levels at or near the maximum sustainable yield; harvest levels cannot be increased any further without harming the fishing stock
3. *Overexploited:* stocks with harvest levels already above the maximum sustainable yield; harvest levels need to be reduced in order to preserve the health of the fishing stock

According to the FAO, in 2009 57 percent of the world's fishery stocks were considered fully exploited, a percentage that has not significantly changed since the 1970s. About 30 percent of fishery stocks in 2009 were classified as overexploited, compared to only about 10 percent in the 1970s. Meanwhile, the percentage of stocks classified as non–fully exploited decreased from about 40 percent in the 1970s to only 13 percent in 2009.

These results suggest that about 87 percent of the world's fishery stocks are already being fished at or above their natural limits. For the 13 percent of stocks that are not being fully exploited, the FAO notes that these stocks generally have a low production potential and that the "potential for increase in catch may be generally limited." The FAO also mentions that the increase in overfished stocks is a cause for concern. It indicates that, at the global level, the UN targets for rebuilding the overfished stocks and implementing an ecosystem approach are not being met.

The FAO concludes that careful fisheries management is needed to restore overexploited stocks to ecological health and to ensure that fully exploited stocks are not overfished.

Source: Food and Agriculture Organization of the United Nations, "Review of the State of the World Marine Fishery Resources," FAO Fisheries and Aquaculture Technical Paper 569, Rome, 2011.

Figure 15.3 **Depletion of Nonrenewable Natural Capital Over Time**

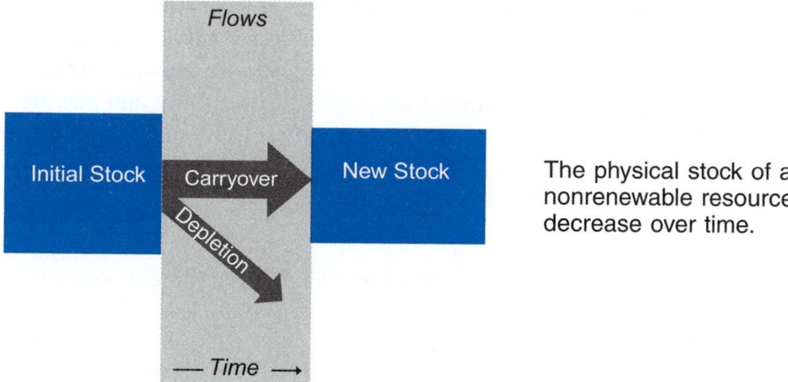

to regenerate and thus contribute to greater stocks in the future, as illustrated in Figure 15.4. But natural inputs that are renewable—such as lumber from forests and fish from the seas—can be exhausted if so much of them are destroyed or extracted that they can no longer renew themselves.

In addition, nature's ability to absorb pollution and break down waste is limited, and there are tipping points beyond which degraded natural capital may be dramatically altered in some essential respect. As we saw with climate change, dramatic ecological change may occur over the next several decades, including the extinction of numerous species. It is very difficult to predict whether ecosystems will be sustainable in the face of such dramatic changes. Rising

Figure 15.4 **Stock Changes for a Renewable Natural Resource**

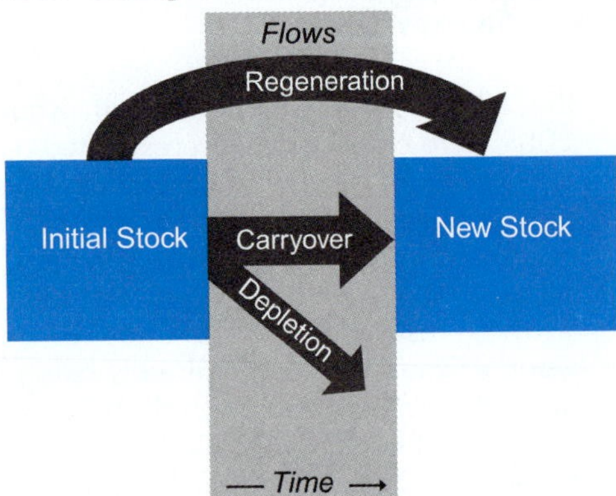

The stock of a renewable resource can remain stable, or even increase, over time due to natural regeneration. But if managed poorly or exploited, the stock of a renewable resource can also decrease over time.

sea levels could cause the flooding of many low-lying areas; New Orleans and southern Florida, in the United States, and Bangladesh are examples, but many cities worldwide are in low-lying areas close to oceans. Some island countries are already losing significant land mass. Resource maintenance for natural capital means tracking the size, quality, and changes in natural resources and making wise decisions about their management.

2.2 Natural Capital and Sustainability

substitutability: the possibility of using one resource instead of another

sustainable socioeconomic system: one that maintains its resources such that at least the same level of social well-being can be maintained over time

Production and consumption levels in modern societies, particularly in industrialized countries, may be leading to the depletion of important natural capital stocks. Thus it becomes important to determine the extent of possible **substitutability** of resources. That is, the depletion of any one resource (e.g., fossil fuels) is a less serious problem for future generations if other resources (such as nuclear or solar energy) can be cheaply and safely substituted for it. The extent of substitutability that can be achieved depends both on the characteristics of the resources and on the speed of technological advance.

A **sustainable socioeconomic system** is one that maintains its resources such that at least the same level of social well-being can be maintained over time. For renewable resources, this generally means that rates of depletion and use do not exceed natural regeneration rates. Ecological impacts are kept safely below critical levels to ensure ecosystem stability. For nonrenewable resources, depletion rates are kept to a minimum and adequate investment is made to develop renewable substitutes. It is important to identify critical natural resources, for which substitution may be difficult if not impossible.

Discussion Questions

1. Give three examples of renewable natural capital. Give three examples of nonrenewable natural capital. (Do not duplicate examples given in the text.)
2. Do you think that a cheap and safe substitute for the use of fossil fuels in cars will ever be found? Discuss. (Note that the electricity for electric cars is currently generated primarily by fossil fuels.)

3. Manufactured Capital

The stock of manufactured capital is the stock of physical things produced by human beings, which in turn are used to produce other goods. In modern societies, manufactured capital includes such things as roads, factories, communication systems, buildings, machinery, and computers. The major form of manufactured capital is fixed manufactured capital. Inventories are another form of manufactured capital. We turn now to a discussion of these two types of manufactured capital.

3.1 FIXED MANUFACTURED CAPITAL

fixed manufactured capital: manufactured goods that yield a flow of productive services over an extended period

Most of what we consider manufactured capital is in the form of **fixed manufactured capital**, which is designed to supply a flow of productive services over an extended period. When economists speak of "capital" as an input to production, what they usually mean is that *stocks of manufactured capital,* such as tools, machines, buildings, and infrastructure, yield *flows of services,* such as making it possible to dig or drill more rapidly, expediting communications and transportation or giving shelter. The fixed manufactured capital stocks themselves are not used up during the production process (aside from normal wear and tear), nor do they become part of the product itself.

If you find the distinction between stocks and flows confusing, consider the example of a tax accountant renting an office from a real estate firm. The stock of manufactured capital here—the physical office itself—belongs to the real estate firm, but the service arising from the use of the office space is an input flow into the production of services to the tax account's clients. Similarly, when truckers drive along a highway, they are using the services of the government-provided physical road. The actual physical office and the road are not in themselves inputs into production—they do not get used up or converted into something else on the way to creating new goods and services. Only the *flow of services* yielded by these capital goods can properly be referred to as inputs.

The stock of fixed manufactured capital is increased when people decide to make physical investments—that is, to build or improve productive assets. Although fixed manufactured capital is not directly used up in the process of production, physical assets commonly lose their usefulness over time, as computers become obsolete, roads develop potholes, and equipment breaks. Commonly, these losses are referred to as **depreciation** of the manufactured capital stock. Resource maintenance activities for fixed manufactured capital include all the checking, cleaning, protection, and repair activities needed to keep buildings, machines, and other manufactured capital in good working order.

depreciation: decrease in the usefulness of a stock of capital due to wear and tear or obsolescence

A society's stock of manufactured capital is dependent upon its technology. For example, a plow pulled by an ox and a modern tractor are both manufactured capital, but they incorporate very different technologies. In a way, manufactured capital can be viewed as an embodied form of human capital, representing accumulated human knowledge and innovation. Thus investment in human capital tends to yield benefits in terms of improved manufactured capital stocks.

3.2 INVENTORIES

inventories: stocks of raw materials or manufactured goods being stored until they can be used or sold

A smaller amount of manufactured capital exists in the form of **inventories**. Inventories are stocks of raw materials or produced goods that are not currently being used or sold but are expected to be used or sold in the foreseeable future.

Like other forms of capital, inventories contribute to production. For example, you cannot start baking bread until you have accumulated a stock of flour, nor can you provide retail services selling shoes until you have an inventory of shoes. Also like other forms of capital, inventories are valuable assets. If you were to sell your shoe store, the value of your stock of salable shoes would be figured into the sale price of the business. But unlike fixed manufactured capital, inventories are generally meant to be used up relatively quickly or to become part of another product, rather than to provide a flow of services over an extended period.

Recall the definition of a stock as something measured at a point in time. Imagine that at one single moment we could freeze all useful manufactured goods where they are—including those in warehouses and on shelves—and make a long list. Everything on the list that is not fixed manufactured capital would be counted, *at that moment,* as inventory manufactured capital. (If we unfreeze those goods, however, we see that inventories are constantly being added to and drawn down, as stocks of materials are used up and goods are sold.)

3.3 Manufactured Capital in the Core and Public Purpose Spheres

When we think of manufactured capital as the stock of physical assets that provide inputs to productive activities, it is important to remember that productive activities take place in all spheres. Sometimes, economists discuss manufactured capital largely in terms of business investment, ignoring the manufactured capital stocks that have accumulated in the core and public purpose spheres. For example, economists have traditionally viewed a stove purchased by a restaurant as an investment in manufactured capital. But exactly the same stove purchased by a household would normally be classified as "consumption" rather than a productive investment (unless the household used the stove to cook meals for sale).

To account fully for the productive capacity of an economy, some economists suggest that manufactured capital should be accounted for in similar ways, no matter who holds it. Production by households, neighborhoods, nonprofits, and governments depends on stocks of manufactured capital, just as much as production by businesses does.

Discussion Questions

1. Come up with one new example of each of the following: fixed manufactured capital, inventory, investment, depreciation.
2. In the early twentieth century, photos or drawings of big factories with tall stacks belching smoke were popularly used to represent the productivity of the contemporary economy. What images come to mind now, when you think of economic activity in the early twenty-first century?

4. Human Capital

Human bodies are amazing machines that have evolved to survive in a wide variety of conditions, from arctic cold to tropical heat. We are extremely adept at endurance activities. For example, over long distances human runners can outpace almost any other animal, including dogs, horses, and cheetahs.* But the most remarkable evolutionary achievement of humans is our large and complex brain. No one can claim to have yet explored the full potential for human creativity and innovation.

Our human capital includes both our physical capacity for exertion and our mental capacity for productive application of our knowledge and skills. Such individual productive capabilities must be created and enhanced through nurturance, nutrition, education, training, and other aspects of life experience.

The raw quantity of human capital in an economy might be crudely measured in terms of the number of people in its population who are of normal working age. To attempt to measure its quality, measures of health status or of years of schooling achieved might also be considered. As with the various kinds of physical capital, we can think of human capital as a stock of capabilities, which can yield a flow of services. Economists often view "labor" as the flow of effort, skill, and knowledge that humans directly provide as inputs into productive activities. Because it is a flow, labor is usually measured over a period of time, such as by the number of person-hours of work of a particular skill that has been used in the course of a week or month.

4.1 Physical Human Capital

Human capital can take physical and intangible forms. In physical form, humans operate much like a manufactured machine—requiring energy inputs to produce physical work. Manual

*Since 1980 an annual "horse versus human" marathon race has been held in Wales, UK. Although a horse with a rider is normally the winner, a couple of times the winner was human.

labor, for example, taps human physical energy, just as another productive process might tap a stock of fossil fuel. Thus the term "human capital" is based on an analogy between a human being and a manufactured machine. Although some people find this analogy offensive, others find it a useful way of analyzing an important input to production—as long as it does not lead to treating human beings as though they really were machines!

Health, strength, and fitness are important forms of physical human capital. In circumstances of deprivation, in which some workers perform below their potential because they are weakened by hunger or illness, basic nutrition and medical care can be seen as important ways of investing in human capital as well as direct contributions to well-being. This is particularly true in the case of children, whose future capabilities can be permanently stunted by deprivation at critical times. (See Box 15.2 for more on this issue.)

BOX 15.2 NUTRITION AND SCHOOL PERFORMANCE

A growing body of scientific evidence demonstrates the importance of good nutrition for children's development and school performance. A 1998 research project at Tufts University found that:

> Recent research provides compelling evidence that undernutrition during any period of childhood can have detrimental effects on the cognitive development of children and their later productivity as adults. In ways not previously known, undernutrition impacts the behavior of children, their school performance, and their overall cognitive development. These findings are extremely sobering in light of the existence of hunger among millions of American children.

Research on nutrition and education has especially focused on breakfast. According to Leia Kedem, a University of Illinois Extension nutrition and wellness educator:

> Although any breakfast is better than no breakfast, making the extra effort to make it healthy might help your kids do better in school. Studies show that kids who eat a balanced breakfast have higher test scores and can concentrate better and solve problems more easily in class. The nutritional value of meals can also make a difference. A breakfast low in fiber and protein, like sugary toaster pastries, can lead to a midmorning energy crash. This is because the carbohydrates are digested and absorbed quickly, causing blood sugar levels to dive after an initial spike. Other than sudden fatigue, kids may also experience headaches and irritability.

Beyond just breakfast, overall diet sufficiency and quality are also related to academic performance. A 2008 study in Canada concluded that intake of fruit and vegetables were positively correlated with school performance, while fat intake was negatively correlated. The research validates the "importance of children's nutrition not only at breakfast but also throughout the day," with a recommendation for greater investment in school nutrition programs.

Sources: Center on Hunger, Poverty, and Nutrition, "The Link Between Nutrition and Cognitive Development in Children," Tufts University, School of Nutrition, Medford, MA, 1998; Michelle D. Florence, Mark Asbridge, and Paul J. V. Eugelers, "Diet Quality and Academic Performance," *Journal of School Health* 78(4) (2008): 209–215; "Good Nutrition Means Better School Performance," *Journal Gazette and Times Courier* (Illinois), August 6, 2013.

4.2 INTANGIBLE HUMAN CAPITAL

The dramatic rise in living standards since the Industrial Revolution started in the eighteenth century rests more than anything else on the remarkable rise in output of the average worker. This increase in productivity is based not on an increase in the human capacity for physical labor but on how technological innovations have been applied to productive processes. Sometimes, these innovations involved new ways of using the energy stored in natural resources, such as the use of coal to move trains and generate electricity. At other times, these innovations involved creating machines to perform tasks much more efficiently than was possible solely through human physical or mental effort. For example, computers are able to perform tasks in nanoseconds that would take a human a lifetime of work.

The development of such technologies makes it evident that the continuing increase in human productivity does not depend only on physical capital and sheer human effort. It also depends on intangible kinds of capital, including the knowledge, skills, and habits embodied in individuals.

Formal education, along with less formal ways of acquiring skills (e.g., early childhood education in homes and knowledge gained from on-the-job experience) are important contributors to human capital. As you read this paragraph, you are investing in your own human capital, in the form of an economics education.

Clearly, human capital has a way of accumulating over time. Scientific research is one good example of this. Scientists generally build upon the knowledge produced by previous scientists. Again, this accumulation of knowledge can be embodied in manufactured capital, indicating technological progress. For example, a worker at an automobile company may start with an existing engine design, and develop a new technique to make that engine more fuel efficient.

Discussion Questions

1. In what ways is it useful to think of human bodies and brains as if they were like productive machinery? What might be some drawbacks of this way of thinking?
2. One obvious way that you are increasing your human capital by going to school is that you can be more productive in a career. In what other ways do you believe that you are increasing your human capital through your education?

5. SOCIAL CAPITAL

The English poet John Donne penned the famous line that "no man is an island." Although the development of individual human capital is important for increasing productivity, nearly all economic activity involves the coordination of actions among numerous actors. Social capital consists of shared knowledge, ideas, and values, along with social organization and workplace relationships. These relationships and common understandings provide the social context for economic activity.

social organization: the ways in which human productive activities are structured and coordinated

Production possibilities depend on the ability to coordinate production among different people. Even with no change in machinery or technology, productivity can increase if coordination among workers improves or if workers become more motivated because of good management techniques. **Social organization** refers to the ways in which human productive activities are structured and coordinated.

Social capital also includes the cultural beliefs and goals that determine which knowledge is applied, which scientific questions are researched, and which technological possibilities are explored. A growing public awareness and acceptance of the hazards posed by global climate change, for example, could be considered a form of social capital, because it increases the ability of society to respond to a significant threat to its future well-being.

In contemporary industrialized economies, the term "social capital" is most often used to refer to characteristics of a society that encourage cooperation among groups of people (e.g., workers and managers) whose joint efforts are needed to achieve a common goal. This kind of capital is built up to the extent that a society is characterized by strong norms of reciprocity, which lead people to trust and help one another, and dense networks of civic participation, which encourage people to engage in mutually beneficial efforts rather than seeking only to gain individual advantage. Business accountants have led the way in recognizing one kind of social capital—good will—which they view as a significant business asset that makes a firm more valuable than one might think from looking at its physical assets alone. Good will includes a number of intangible factors, such as a firm's good reputation among its customers and creditors, good management, and good labor relations. It has become common practice to list good will among the assets of a firm that is for sale.

Social capital resembles other forms of capital in that it generates a service that enhances the output obtainable from other inputs, without being used up in the process of production.

Recognition of this concept by economists is fairly recent and has been strengthened by the observation that variation in social capital across societies can help to explain some of the differences in their economic development.

Discussion Questions

1. In what ways is it useful to think of knowledge, trust, motivation, and the like as though they were similar to productive machinery? What might be some drawbacks of this way of thinking?
2. Economic issues are often discussed in terms of money and prices, but it is difficult to quantify social capital in such terms. Can you think of topics, both within the category of social capital and in other categories, that have economic importance but are hard to express in terms of money?

6. FINANCIAL CAPITAL

For most production processes, you have to acquire inputs before you can create outputs. Before it can make its first sale, a start-up business needs to buy or rent a building and equipment, hire staff, and amass inventories of materials and supplies. You, as a student, must pay for tuition and textbooks either by using your savings or borrowing, in order to increase your human capital and eventually obtain a job. In a money economy financial capital is what allows all these productive activities to get going in advance of the returns that will flow from them.

Financial capital is a largely intangible form of capital. Its importance in the economy relies on the social beliefs that sustain the financial system, much more than on the physical paper or the electronic documents that record its existence. Economists distinguish between two different forms of financial capital: equity finance and debt finance.

6.1 EQUITY FINANCE

equity finance: an economic actor's use of its own funds to make productive investments

Suppose that you pay for a car completely in cash, as opposed to taking out a loan. This represents a form of **equity finance**, which means using your own money (i.e., wealth) to make a purchase. A business that uses its accumulated profits to purchase new computers or machinery is also undertaking equity finance. "Equity" means having an ownership right. Thus equity finance means using resources that an individual or business currently owns. (This use of the term "equity" should not be confused with another meaning of the same word, "justice or fairness.")

Like other forms of capital, financial capital can be thought of in terms of stocks that increase or decrease over time and that provide a flow of services. A farmer increases her financial capital stock by laying aside the proceeds from her last harvest. She will use (and, very often, use up) her equity financial capital as she spends it on supplies for the next productive season.

debt finance: borrowing others' funds to make productive investments

What are the commonest sources of equity finance? Individuals can finance their productive activities out of money that they have inherited or saved. Governments finance some programs out of accumulated past taxes. Businesses can accumulate funds by retaining some of their profits or by selling shares of the business in the form of stocks. People add to their stock of equity financial capital by saving, and they diminish their stock of equity financial capital by spending.

6.2 DEBT FINANCE

loan: money borrowed for temporary use, on the condition that it be repaid, usually with interest

Suppose instead that you need to take out a car loan, instead of paying all cash. As you do not have the ability to use equity finance to buy a car, you must rely upon **debt finance.** Debt finance means that you are able to gain access, temporarily, to the purchasing power of *other* actors' wealth.

One can think of taking out a **loan** as "renting" financial capital—renting the use of money. Just as an office can be rented and *used* productively by one enterprise while it is *owned* by another, the services of the financial capital are *used* by someone taking out a car loan while

principal: the original amount of money borrowed

interest: the charge for borrowing money

the financial capital is technically owned by a bank. Borrowers agree not only to repay the **principal** (the original amount) of the loan but also to give the lender **interest**, a charge for borrowing the funds, usually calculated as a percentage of the principal. (If the person taking out the car loan is not able to pay back the loan, the bank can usually take over ownership of the car in exchange for its lost funds.)

Banks and nonbank financial institutions, such as credit unions, are not the only providers of debt finance. Governments and large companies often raise financial capital directly by selling bonds, which are financial instruments that promise repayment of funds with interest.

Discussion Questions

1. Financial capital is important not only in the business and government spheres but also in the core sphere. What major purchases do families often finance through taking out a loan (i.e., debt finance)?
2. Explain how the concept of opportunity cost can influence the way in which you think about your use of financial capital.

7. SUSTAINING CAPITAL STOCKS

Only recently has the field of economics formally recognized that natural capital, human capital, and social capital are at least as critical to production as manufactured and financial capital—and sometimes more so. Along with this realization has come the recognition that all these forms of capital are subject to erosion as well as growth. Because all production begins with, and depends on, the availability of the necessary capital stocks—including, in most cases, all five kinds that we have discussed—it is important to consider how these capital stocks are produced and maintained, and what circumstances might endanger their quantity or quality. The necessity of attending to the basic economic activity of resource maintenance has become more evident in recent years.

For example, what happens if stocks of manufactured capital are not maintained? If our stocks of housing, roads, communication systems, factories, and equipment are wearing out without being replaced, our standard of living can decline. What about social and human capital? If formal education systems, norms of raising children, or patterns of behavior change in ways that cause a deterioration in the education and health of a population or in prevailing standards of honesty, reliability, and originality, then it is likely, again, that standards of living will decline in the future.

At this moment in history, the deterioration of natural capital stocks is an especially widely recognized problem. Only in recent decades have we encountered global limits on the capacity of nature to absorb the intended and unintended effects of our economic activity. Increasingly, humans have gone beyond harvesting the annual produce of seas and soils and have begun to deplete the natural capacity for regeneration.

It is possible for economic activity to augment stocks of manufactured and human capital continually, more than offsetting any decline associated with the depreciation of manufactured capital and the retirement of existing workers. In contrast, the impact of economic activity on the stock of natural capital is most often negative; either the existing stock is drawn down (when natural resource inputs are used) or the quality of the stock is diminished (as by the introduction of waste products).

The stock of renewable natural capital can be maintained or augmented using wise resource management, and the (apparent) stock of nonrenewable resources can be increased through new discoveries. Moreover, the problem of a deteriorating natural resource stock can be allayed or postponed by technological and production method changes that reduce the amount of natural resource depletion or waste product generation associated with a given amount of production. Yet the fact that the earth and its resources are finite suggests that sooner or later the limit to the size of the physical flow of production that can be maintained over time will be reached.

Many types of decline can be reversed, so these observations should not be taken as cause for despair. They do, however, point to the fact that economic policy and analysis are not simple matters. The economic health of a contemporary society depends on schools and family support systems as much as on factories and roads; it depends on workplace morale as well as on protection of air, soil, water, and species. And whether we are thinking about the long-term or the short-term health of the economy and the individuals in it, we must judge economic activities not only in relation to their intended effects but also in terms of their unplanned effects on the physical and social environments.

REVIEW QUESTIONS

1. What distinguishes a stock from a flow?
2. How can we distinguish a stock from a flow using a diagram?
3. What are the five major types of capital?
4. What are the two main types of natural capital?
5. What is a sustainable socioeconomic system?
6. What are the two main types of manufactured capital?
7. What are the two main types of human capital?
8. What is social capital?
9. What are the two main types of financial capital?

EXERCISES

1. Which of the following are flows? Which are stocks? If a flow, which of the five major kind(s) of capital does it increase or decrease? If a stock, what kind of capital is it?
   a. The fish in a lake
   b. The output of a factory during a year
   c. The income that you receive in a month
   d. The reputation of a business among its customers
   e. The assets of a bank
   f. The equipment in a factory
   g. A process of diplomatic negotiations
   h. The discussion in an economics class
2. Consider the case of a new computer antivirus software package.
   a. In a paragraph, briefly describe the capital stocks that provided the resource base for its creation.
   b. Which of the four economic activities is antivirus software designed to address? (Note: It may address more than one economic activity.)
3. A forest originally has 10,000 trees. Suppose that the forest naturally replenishes itself by 10 percent per year. That is, at the end of one year, if nothing else happened, it would have $10{,}000 + (0.10 \times 10{,}000) = 11{,}000$ trees. (This assumption is not biologically accurate, but it keeps the math simple.) Suppose that 1,500 trees are harvested at the end of each year.
   a. How many trees will the forest have at the end of one year, after accounting for both natural replenishment and the effects of harvesting?
   b. Draw a stock–flow diagram illustrating the change in the forest stock from year 1 to year 2.
   c. How many trees will there be at the end of two years? (*Note:* Base the 10 percent replenishment amount on the number of trees that exist at the *beginning of the second year.*)
   d. How many trees will there be at the end of three years?
   e. For the harvest of trees to be sustainable, what is the largest number of trees that could be harvested each year (starting with the original stock of 10,000 trees)?
4. Match each concept in Column A with an example in Column B.

Column A	Column B
a. Equity finance	1. Fish in the ocean
b. Social capital	2. Starting a business by using money that you have saved
c. A renewable natural resource	3. Iron ore
d. Fixed manufactured capital	4. Spare parts at an auto repair shop
e. Human capital	5. A factory building
f. Inventories	6. A shared language within a community
g. A nonrenewable natural resource	7. Your own health

16 Production Costs

The United States is home to more than 30,000 businesses, ranging in size from the largest corporation in the world (in 2012, this was Walmart, which had revenues of nearly half a *trillion* dollars) to numerous businesses consisting of a single individual. Every day, many of these businesses are faced with decisions about what to produce, how to produce it, how to market it, and how much to sell it for. In this chapter, we focus on the economic activity of production: the conversion of resources into goods and services.

Although we focus on the production process of for-profit businesses, economic production takes places in all three spheres. According to published statistics, about 12 percent of economic production in the United States in 2012 was attributed to government, including federal, state, and local governments. Another 12 percent of economic production took place in households and institutions. However, these statistics understate the amount of production that occurs in the public purpose and core spheres, because it fails to include production that is not distributed through markets. We develop a model of production costs based on a for-profit firm, but many of the lessons of this model are applicable to public purpose and core production as well.

1. An Overview of Production

Before we begin our analysis of production costs, we first consider the goals of production and define some important concepts.

1.1 The Goals of Production

In the business sphere, it is normally essential that one of the goals of production be to make a profit. This is not to say that the generation of profit is the only goal pursued by businesses. Many companies balance social and environmental objectives with profit-making. As one remarkable example, in 2011 the outdoor clothing and gear company Patagonia took out an ad in the *New York Times* advising readers: "Don't buy what you don't need. Think twice before buying anything," based on concern about the environmental impacts of all production.[1]

At the same time, every period of history provides examples of businesses that have behaved unethically in the pursuit of profits, including violence against workers. However, norms of what is generally acceptable change over time, sometimes swinging toward more social disapproval of harsh business practices, and at other times accepting—even celebrating—a "culture of greed," as seemed to be the case in the last quarter of the twentieth century and into the twenty-first century.

Economic analysis of production has tended to emphasize the objective of profit-making. Starting in the 1960s, some economists began to argue that business managers should *only* seek to maximize profits, without concern for any broader social or environmental objectives. The Nobel Prize–winning economist Milton Friedman once wrote:

> [T]here is one and only one social responsibility of business—to use its resources and engage in activities designed to increase its profits so long as it stays within the rules of the game.[2]

triple bottom line: an assessment of the performance of a business according to social and environmental goals, as well as making profits

But businesses are increasingly operating with a broader set of objectives, often referred to as the **triple bottom line.** This perspective reflects a commitment to social and environmental goals, as well as making profits.

Looking farther back in history, before the Civil War in the United States, corporations were fully accountable to the public to ensure that they acted in a manner that served the public good. Corporate charters could be revoked for failing to serve the public interest and were valid for only a certain period of time. For example, in 1831 a Delaware constitutional amendment specified that all corporations were limited to a twenty-year life span.

More recently, an emphasis on externalities is giving renewed attention to the question of whether particular productive activities are consistent with social and environmental well-being. This question requires considering *all* costs and benefits of the production process. In Chapter 13 we focused on environmental externalities, but negative social externalities should also be considered. For example, a business that increases its profits by making its employees work overtime without pay is creating a negative social externality, not reflected in the prices of the products that it sells. Lawsuits have been brought against Walmart in several U.S. states that found the corporation guilty of forcing some employees to work without pay.[3] The negative social externality resulting from Walmart's minimizing what it pays workers extends to policies of hiring employees to work just below the number of hours that would qualify them for full-time benefits, including health insurance coverage. Lacking health-care benefits, and with salaries that leave them little spare money for regular doctor visits, such workers often use emergency rooms as their only venue for medical care. These costs are generally externalized onto states, which have to pay for emergency room visits that could easily have been avoided, at much less cost to society, if the workers had access to health insurance.

We can use the technique of cost-benefit analysis, also discussed in Chapter 13, to estimate the net social impacts of production decisions. One problem with implementing such an analysis, however, arises from the fact that some costs and benefits are easier to measure than others. It is relatively easy, for example, to determine how many jobs will be created if a large retailer builds a new store in an area. It may even be relatively easy to convert the number of jobs gained into a benefit that can be expressed in dollars. It is harder to quantify the costs to social well-being from any environmental damages associated with the store or the loss of community as people become less likely to shop at "mom and pop" competitors.

So, although much of our discussion about production costs and decisions is in the context of making profits, we also keep in mind the broader environmental and social context in which all production occurs.

1.2 An Economic Perspective on Production

inputs: resources that go into production

outputs: the goods and services that result from production

As we have stated before, production involves the conversion of resources into goods and services. We define **inputs** as the resources that go into production, and **outputs** as the goods and services that result from production. In addition to desired goods and services, all production processes also generate waste, including pollution, waste materials, and waste heat.

We tend to think of production in terms of physical goods. For example, cotton goes into a textile mill as fiber and comes out as fabric. This fabric is then shipped to another location, printed with small red hearts, cut into pieces, sewn into boxer shorts, distributed through wholesalers, and eventually marketed by retailers. Or households may purchase cotton fabric and use it to produce homemade curtains or Halloween costumes. To most people, the various stages of manufacturing would be regarded as production, but the transport, distribution, and sale that are involved would not.

Economists think of production more broadly, including any activity involved in the conversion of resources into final goods and services. For example, Texas oil "producers" do not actually make oil; they merely transport it from its natural state under the ground to the nearest refinery. Yet this activity is still considered production in a broad economic sense. Similarly, such activities as storage, packaging, and retailing all can be interpreted as forms of production.

Nor is production confined to processes that involve tangible goods. Production also includes providing services. Accordingly, from an economist's point of view, physicians, child-care providers, mechanics, musicians, park rangers, lawyers, professors, house cleaners, tax auditors, and massage therapists are all engaged in production, even though they don't produce a physical product.

marginal analysis: analysis based on incremental changes, comparing marginal benefits to marginal costs

Another important concept in thinking about production from an economic perspective is **marginal analysis**, which involves thinking about incremental changes. We have already seen the importance of marginal thinking in Chapter 6. When we apply marginal analysis to production decisions, we ask whether it makes economic sense to produce one more unit of a good or service. In other words, we should compare the marginal benefits of a decision to its marginal costs.

As long as marginal benefits exceed marginal costs, it makes sense for a business to expand production. But after the marginal costs rise to the level of marginal benefits, the firm should stop increasing production. We spend much of the remainder of the chapter introducing an economic model of marginal production costs. We will then use this model in the next chapter to illustrate how a hypothetical firm can maximize its profits. But as we have discussed previously, a model is a simplification of the real world that focuses on some issues while ignoring others. So although this model is considered applicable to many production decisions, it is not intended to apply to every production situation.

Discussion Questions

1. What distinguishes the economic activity of production from the activity of resource maintenance? Of consumption? Of distribution?
2. Think about the processes involved in producing this textbook. Describe these processes, considering all the steps of production from an economic perspective. What inputs were required? What waste was generated?

2. Types of Production Costs

We begin our analysis by differentiating between different types of costs. As with several other topics explored here, economists view production costs from a perspective that differs somewhat from that of noneconomists.

2.1 Fixed Versus Variable Costs

Consider the production costs of farming. A farmer who grows corn, let's call her Gail, needs to purchase various inputs, such as seed, fertilizer, and fuel for machinery. To some extent, Gail can vary the amount of these inputs that she purchases. For example, she can use a little fertilizer or a lot. The amount that she spends on fertilizer will also depend on the type of fertilizer that she applies. Her options may include purchasing a chemical fertilizer, purchasing compost, or obtaining compost from her own farm residues.

variable costs: production costs that can be adjusted relatively quickly and that do not need to be paid if no production occurs

The production costs that Gail can easily adjust are called **variable costs**. Variable costs can be adjusted relatively quickly in response to changes in market conditions, production targets, or other circumstances. Another way to define variable costs is that these costs do not need to be paid if, for some reason, Gail decides not to produce corn.

fixed costs (or sunk costs): production costs that cannot be adjusted quickly and that must be paid even if no production occurs

Gail has other costs to pay regardless of whether she decides to produce corn. These are called **fixed costs**, which include such expenses as a mortgage and monthly payments on machinery. Another term economists use for fixed costs is "sunk costs." Regardless of how much corn Gail produces, she cannot avoid paying these costs. The distinction between fixed and variable costs is not always clear. Gail could decide to sell all her farm machinery, so in this sense machinery becomes a variable cost, but it may take some time for her to find buyers. Given enough time, *all* production costs become variable as a business could decide to shut down entirely and sell off all its resources.

Differentiating between fixed and variable costs is important in order to analyze how producers will respond to changes in market conditions. By changing its variable costs, a business can normally change its output level. So, if corn prices rise, Gail may bring some new land into corn production, which will require greater expenses for seed, fertilizer, and fuel. But Gail cannot adjust her fixed costs in a relatively short period. If corn prices go down, she has the option of spending less on corn seed, but she still must pay the mortgage on her farm and other fixed costs. If corn prices stay down for an extended period, say several years, she may be forced to sell her farm and pursue a different career.

2.2 Accounting Versus Economic Costs

accounting costs: actual monetary costs paid by a producer as well as estimated reduction in the value of the producer's capital stock

The costs just discussed are all actual monetary costs paid by a producer. When Gail completes her tax return and calculates her farming profits, she (or her accountant) can list all these costs—both fixed and variable—as valid business expenses. **Accounting costs** can also include some items that are not actual out-of-pocket expenditures but that are understood to reduce the value of the stock of capital owned by the business; the most common example is depreciation of buildings or equipment. Table 16.1 presents an example of Gail's accounting costs.

We can take a broader perspective on Gail's costs of farming by considering other costs that, like depreciation, do not appear as monetary outflows. Perhaps the most obvious example is the value of Gail's time. If Gail is a full-time farmer, she is thus giving up the opportunity to work at a different job, say as an engineer or a teacher. The salary that she could obtain at her next-best option is the opportunity cost of Gail's decision to be a farmer. So if Gail's best alternative to farming is to be a teacher and earn $30,000 per year, this forgone salary also represents a production cost, as shown in Table 16.1.

Table 16.1 **Gail's Costs of Farming**

Accounting Costs		
Seeds	$20,000	
Fertilizer	$3,000	
Fuel	$5,000	
Interest on bank loan	$15,000	
Depreciation of equipment	$5,000	
Total accounting costs		$48,000
Opportunity Costs		
Forgone salary	$30,000	
Forgone return on equity capital	$12,000	
Total opportunity costs		$42,000
Total economic costs		$90,000
Externality Costs		
Pollution damage	$5,000	
Total social costs		$95,000

economic cost: the total cost of production, including both accounting and opportunity costs

Economic costs include accounting costs but also add in the value of forgone opportunities. In addition to a forgone salary, another economic cost would be the value of forgone investments. Suppose that, in addition to taking out a bank loan, Gail also uses her own equity capital to finance some of the costs of farming (recall our discussion of equity finance from Chapter 15). Her next-best alternative may have been to invest that money in the stock market and make a return on her investment. Her forgone investment returns are another economic cost, as shown in Table 16.1.

If Gail looks at the full economic costs of farming over this season—rather than just at the accounting costs—she will find that farming is more costly than she may have initially thought. Whereas her account books show costs of $48,000, it is really costing her $90,000 to farm for the season when we consider her opportunity costs.

The same concept applies to the costs of production in other spheres of the economy. For example, think about the government of an economically depressed county, which is considering whether to invest in building a new highway. The project will hire people and pay them a salary. The *accounting* costs for this labor, included in the project's budget, will be the actual salary paid. To calculate the *economic* costs of this labor, however, from the perspective of society's production possibilities, you have to think about how much this highway project pulls out of other productive activities that would otherwise have been undertaken. If the workers would otherwise have been unemployed and not productively engaged at home or in their communities, the answer might be that not very much is lost elsewhere. But if the workers could have otherwise been building needed new schools or hospitals, it may be that the economic costs are much higher than the accounting costs.

The advantage of considering economic costs, rather than just accounting costs, is that we have a more complete framework for making production decisions. Producers should always weigh the benefits of a decision against its costs, both its financial costs and the costs of what must be given up.

2.3 Private Versus External Costs

Suppose that Gail's farming practices result in fertilizer runoff that pollutes a river, reducing downstream fishing and swimming opportunities and harming the ecosystem. As we saw in Chapter 13, this represents a negative externality. Gail is unlikely to take such costs into account when making production decisions. She will consider only her private costs—her accounting costs and perhaps her economic costs as well.

But the pollution represents a real cost imposed on society. Suppose that, using the techniques discussed in Chapter 13, we estimate the negative externality costs of Gail's farming at $5,000 per year. From the perspective of social welfare, this is an additional cost of farming, as shown in Table 16.1. The true social cost of farming would be the sum of the economic and externality costs. In an ideal world, there would be ways of ensuring that externality costs are internalized. For example, if Gail had to pay a "farming tax" of $5,000 per year to compensate society for the pollution damage, then the tax would be an accounting cost and thus enter directly into Gail's production decisions.

The distinction between private and external costs is important because a production process chosen by a producer that may appear to be the least expensive based on accounting, and perhaps economic, costs, may not be the least-cost option when externalities are considered. In the absence of any motivation to consider the social or environmental externalities, Gail may conclude that her optimal production decision is to rely on chemical fertilizers to grow corn. But the optimal production decision from the perspective of society may be that she should replace some chemical fertilizer with organic farming techniques. This exemplifies the fact that private production decisions may not always align with the best choice in terms of social well-being.

Discussion Questions

1. In order to take this course, you have paid tuition and bought this book. What other costs should be added in to calculate the *economic* costs of this course to you personally? (*Hint:* What is your best alternative to spending time taking this course? How are you financing your education?) Does your taking this course entail any externality costs, in addition to your private economic costs?
2. What fairness issues arise when producers are required to take social or environmental costs into account in their decision-making? For example, suppose that Gail is just barely making ends meet, using proceeds from the sale of her farm's output to feed and house her family—while the neighbors who are suffering the consequences of runoff from her fertilizer applications are mostly better off than she is. Should government policies take this into consideration? Who should make such a decision?

3. THE PRODUCTION FUNCTION

production function: an equation or graph that represents a relationship between types and quantities of inputs and the quantity of output

Actual production decisions are often a matter of trial and error. Firms might experiment with different levels of various inputs to determine which production processes are the least costly. Often the results will be difficult to predict in advance, and firms can make costly mistakes. But with our model of production, we assume for now that firms have accurate information about the relationship between the levels of various inputs and output. This enables us to define a **production function**, an equation or graph that represents the relationship between a set of inputs and the amount of output that a firm (or other economic actor) can produce over a given period. Production functions typically do not exist "out there" in the real-world economy, but this model can help us think about certain aspects of production in a very simple, and sometimes useful, way.

3.1 THINKING ABOUT INPUTS AND OUTPUTS

Many inputs go into real-world production processes. We continue to use the example of farming because it is relatively easy to produce fairly realistic, easy to comprehend, production functions for farms—and because there have been many studies of farming production functions. The normal inputs include land (a type of natural capital), machinery (manufactured capital), and labor (human capital). Human capital, as we have seen in earlier chapters, is more than just hours of labor; it also includes a component of formal education that has become increasingly important for modern farmers. Social capital can also be considered a farming input in terms of the strength and quality of relations among farm workers and managers. Financial capital is also needed by most farmers in terms of loans to finance the purchase of land, equipment, and other inputs.

In a very general sense, we can define a production function using the following mathematical equation:

$$Y = f(\textit{natural capital, manufactured capital, human capital, social capital, financial capital})$$

where Y represents a quantity of output, $f()$ is read "is a function of," and the inputs include the levels of different types of capital discussed in Chapter 15. In the case of corn production, we can define a more specific production function as:

$$Y = f(\textit{seeds, fertilizer, pesticides, labor, land, equipment}\ldots)$$

This means that the quantity of output (say bushels of corn) is a function of the number of seeds planted, the amount of fertilizer applied, the amount of pesticides applied, the amount of labor allocated to corn production, the amount of land used for corn production, the type of equipment used, and so on.

fixed input: a production input that is fixed in quantity, regardless of the level of production

variable input: a production input whose quantity can be changed relatively quickly, resulting in changes in the level of production

short run (in terms of production processes): a period in which at least one production input has a fixed quantity

limiting factor: a fixed input that creates a constraint to increasing production

Extending our discussion about fixed and variable costs, we can correspondingly define various inputs as fixed or variable. **Fixed inputs** by definition are those for which the quantities do not change, regardless of the level of production. An example of a fixed input is a farmer who has leased a field for the growing season. If the farmer already signed a lease for the use of the field, she is not able *right now* to avoid paying for this input. By contrast, **variable inputs** are those for which the quantities can be changed quickly, resulting in changes in the level of production. In our farming example, fertilizers and pesticides are variable inputs because a farmer can change her use of these inputs relatively quickly.

As mentioned earlier, over a very long period all inputs might be considered variable. So economists try to make the distinction more specific by defining the **short run** as a period in which at least one production input is fixed in quantity. A farmer, for example, may be temporarily constrained by the size of her land holdings and by the amount of equipment she owns, but can vary many other inputs, such as seeds, fertilizers, and labor. In other production processes, an organization may be constrained by a lack of space, a shortage of materials, a dearth of suitably talented workers, or any other production input. The key aspect is that a **limiting factor** creates a constraint to increasing production. Even with access to unlimited amounts of all the *variable* inputs, production can go only so far, because of this one limiting factor.

In the **long run,** the quantities of all production inputs may be varied. In the case of farming, this means the amount of time (perhaps several months) in which more land can be purchased, more machinery purchased, and more labor hired. In other situations, it might take years for a business to increase or decrease (or eliminate) the quantities of all inputs.

3.2 GRAPHING PRODUCTION FUNCTIONS

long run: (in terms of production processes) a period in which all production inputs can be varied in quantity

As with supply and demand in Chapter 4, we can represent a production function using either a table or a graph. We keep our model simple by focusing on just one input at a time. One production relationship that has been studied by numerous researchers is the impact of different fertilizer levels on crop yields. Table 16.2 presents the results of one such study, showing the effect of applying various amounts of nitrogen fertilizer on corn yields over a season. The study was performed in Missouri in the late 1990s.[4] The researchers varied the amount of fertilizer used on different fields in increments of 20 pounds per acre. At harvest time, the corn yield was recorded in bushels per acre. For mathematical simplicity, we call each 20-pound increment a "bag" of fertilizer and express all values in per-acre terms. Nitrogen can be obtained from renewable, organic sources such as manure or alfalfa or from chemical fertilizer produced using nonrenewable natural gas. This study looked at nitrogen from chemical sources.

In this case, nitrogen fertilizer is a variable input, and corn is the output. Corn yields increase as more fertilizer is added. We can take the data in Table 16.2 and convert it to a

Table 16.2 **Corn Production Function**

Quantity of nitrogen fertilizer (bags per acre)	Corn yield (bushels per acre)
0	100
1	115
2	127
3	137
4	145
5	150
6	154
7	157
8	159

Figure 16.1 **Corn Production Function**

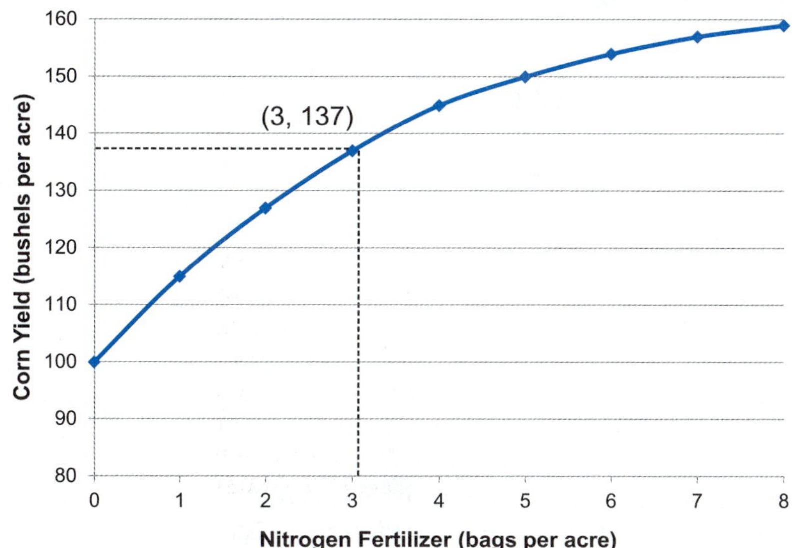

Corn yields per acre increase as more nitrogen fertilizer is applied, but at a decreasing rate.

graph, as shown in Figure 16.1. So, we can see, for example, that when 3 bags of fertilizer are applied per acre, corn yields are 137 bushels per acre. Note that we have started the vertical axes at 80 bushels per acre for graphical convenience, to focus on the range where corn yields occur in the study.

For this production function, we are only measuring the impact of one variable input—nitrogen fertilizer. The researchers in this case tried to keep all other variable inputs, such as the amount of seed applied, the amount of water, soil quality, and so on, unchanging across the various corn fields, to isolate the impact of one variable input. Recall that in economics, when we want to isolate the effect of one particular variable on another, we hope to study the particular relationship *ceteris paribus,* or "with all else constant." Remember, also, that a relationship in which an increase in one variable is accompanied by an increase in the other is called a "positive" or "direct" relationship. You can see in Figure 16.1 that nitrogen and crop yields have a positive relationship, though the curve goes upward less steeply as one moves to the right.

3.3 Production in the Short Run

total product curve: a curve showing the total amount of output produced with different levels of one variable input, holding all other inputs constant

marginal product: the additional quantity of output produced by increasing the level of a variable input by one, holding all other inputs constant

Another term that economists use to describe the production function in Figure 16.1 is a **total product curve**. A total product curve shows the total amount of product (i.e., output) as a function of one variable input, holding all other inputs constant. But as we mentioned earlier in the chapter, production decisions are based on marginal analysis. So, we focus on how much corn output changes with each additional bag of fertilizer. We call the additional corn output with each additional bag of fertilizer (holding all other inputs constant) the **marginal product**. We can take the data in Table 16.2 and calculate the marginal product for each additional bag of fertilizer, as shown in Table 16.3.

Table 16.3 shows that adding the first bag of fertilizer increases corn yields from 100 bushels per acre to 115 bushels per acre, for a marginal product of 15 bushels. The marginal product going from 1 to 2 bags of fertilizer is 12 bushels, as shown in the table as the difference between 127 and 115 bushels. You can calculate the marginal product for the fourth bag of fertilizer yourself for practice.

Table 16.3 indicates that the marginal product of additional fertilizer is constantly declining, referred to by economists as **diminishing marginal returns**. For each additional unit of an input, the marginal product (or return) increases by a smaller amount.

Table 16.3 **Calculating Marginal Product**

Quantity of nitrogen fertilizer (bags per acre)	Corn yield (bushels per acre)	Marginal product
0	100	—
1	115	= 115 – 110 = 15
2	127	= 127 – 115 = 12
3	137	10
4	145	??
5	150	5
6	154	4
7	157	3
8	159	2

diminishing marginal returns: a situation in which each successive unit of a variable input produces a smaller marginal product

We should not be surprised that the production function for corn displays diminishing marginal returns. If there were *not* diminishing marginal returns, you could feed the whole world from one farmer's field just by adding more and more nitrogen fertilizer forever. But, in reality, as more and more nitrogen is added to the same amount of land, eventually the corn plants become unable to make use of the extra amounts. Eventually, if excessive fertilizer were added, the graph would turn *downward,* with a negative slope, as the crop would suffer from fertilizer "burn."

In a case of diminishing marginal returns, as we have seen for corn production, the total product curve gets flatter as you move out to the right. Not all production functions display diminishing marginal returns, at least not throughout the entire production range. Suppose that we consider a production function for handmade shoes. Let's assume that one worker can make two shoes a day. So if we have only one worker (our variable input), two shoes per day can be produced. If we have two workers, then four shoes can be produced per day. Three workers means that six shoes can be produced. In this case, each additional unit of our variable input (workers) results in the same marginal product—two additional shoes per day. Economists refer to this as a case of **constant marginal returns**.

constant marginal returns: a situation in which each successive unit of a variable input produces the same marginal product

increasing marginal returns: a situation in which each successive unit of a variable input produces a larger marginal product

Finally, a production function can display **increasing marginal returns**. This can occur in our shoemaking example if adding workers allows for specialization and an overall increase in efficiency. For example, one worker might specialize in cutting leather, another might make only soles, and a third could focus on stitching. In this case, the total product curve would increase at an increasing rate, at least up to a certain number of workers.

Figure 16.2 illustrates production functions with constant and increasing marginal returns. For constant marginal returns, the total product curve is a straight line sloping upward. For increasing marginal returns, the total product curve becomes steeper as we move to the right.

Figure 16.2 **Total Product Curves with Constant and Increasing Marginal Returns**

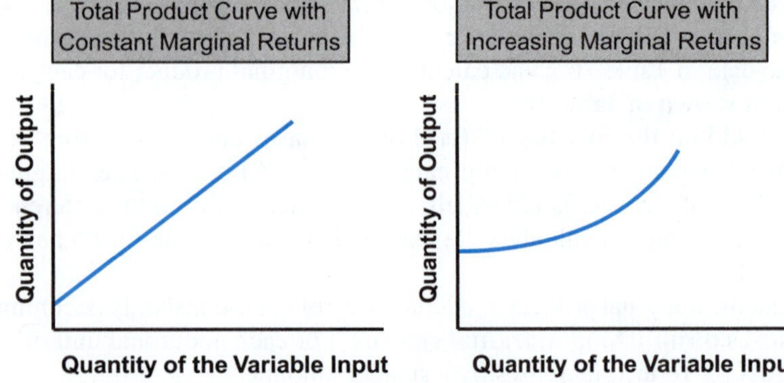

A total product curve with constant marginal returns is a straight line sloping upward. In the case of increasing marginal returns, the total product curve becomes steeper as we move to the right.

It is possible for a production process to exhibit *all* three patterns of marginal returns when we consider the entire range of production levels. Figure 16.3 shows increasing marginal returns at very low levels of the input, constant marginal returns for moderate levels of the input, and then decreasing marginal returns for high levels of the input. Such a production function may be common in the real world. Consider a restaurant. If there is only one worker to take orders, cook the food, and wash dishes, production is likely to be very inefficient. Adding more workers allows for specialization and increasing marginal returns. Once a restaurant has enough workers for each separate task, then perhaps doubling the number of workers (e.g., increasing from one cook to two cooks) might exactly double total production. However, eventually hiring more workers leads to decreasing marginal returns as the kitchen become too crowded to allow for effective production. As the old saying goes, too many cooks spoil the broth.

Figure 16.3 **A Total Product Curve with Increasing, Constant, and Decreasing Marginal Returns**

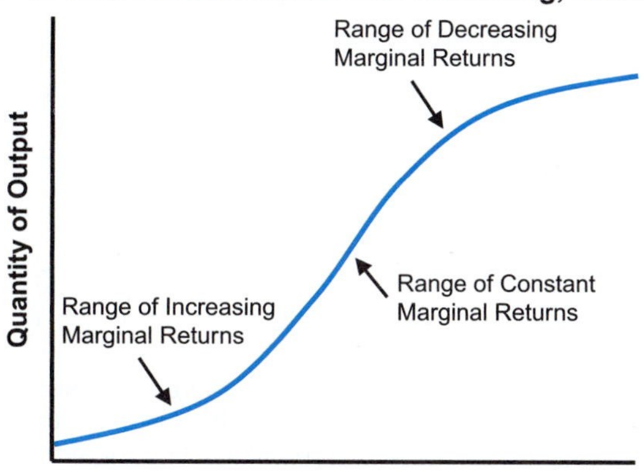

Many real-world production functions display increasing, constant, and decreasing marginal returns when we consider the full range of production levels.

4. PRODUCTION COSTS

In this last section, we combine information about production costs with a production function to determine the costs of different levels of production. We will differentiate between production in the short run and in the long run.

4.1 PRODUCTION COSTS IN THE SHORT RUN

Now that we understand the physical side of production, we can turn back to the topic of production costs. Our distinction between fixed and variable costs can be related to our discussion of fixed and variable inputs. Specifically, variable costs are costs that vary by changing the level of a variable input. So in order to apply more fertilizer, a farmer must increase her variable costs. Fixed costs are those that arise from fixed inputs. Gail's mortgage payments on her farm are fixed as she cannot vary the amount of land that she owns in the short run.

total cost: the sum of fixed and variable costs

Total cost is simply the sum of fixed and variable costs. We can apply this concept to our example of nitrogen fertilizer. Let's suppose that the cost of nitrogen fertilizer is $15 per bag. For simplicity, for now we assume that this is our only variable cost. All other costs of producing corn are considered fixed in the short run and total $500 per acre. Table 16.4 calculates the fixed and variable cost of applying different amounts of nitrogen fertilizer. For each additional bag of fertilizer, total costs increase by $15. In other words, the marginal cost of each additional bag of fertilizer is $15.

total cost curve: a graph showing the relationship between the total cost of production and the level of output

We can take the data in Table 16.4 and graph a **total cost curve**, which relates the total cost of production to the level of output, as shown in Figure 16.4. We see that the slope becomes steeper as we move to the right. This makes sense, as it becomes increasingly

Table 16.4 **Fixed, Variable, and Marginal Costs**

Quantity of nitrogen fertilizer (bags per acre)	Corn yield (bushels per acre)	Fixed costs ($)	Variable costs ($15 per bag of fertilizer)	Total costs ($)
0	100	500	0	500
1	115	500	15	515
2	127	500	30	530
3	137	500	45	545
4	145	500	60	560
5	150	500	75	575
6	154	500	90	590
7	157	500	105	605
8	159	500	120	620

Figure 16.4 **The Total Cost Curve for Corn**

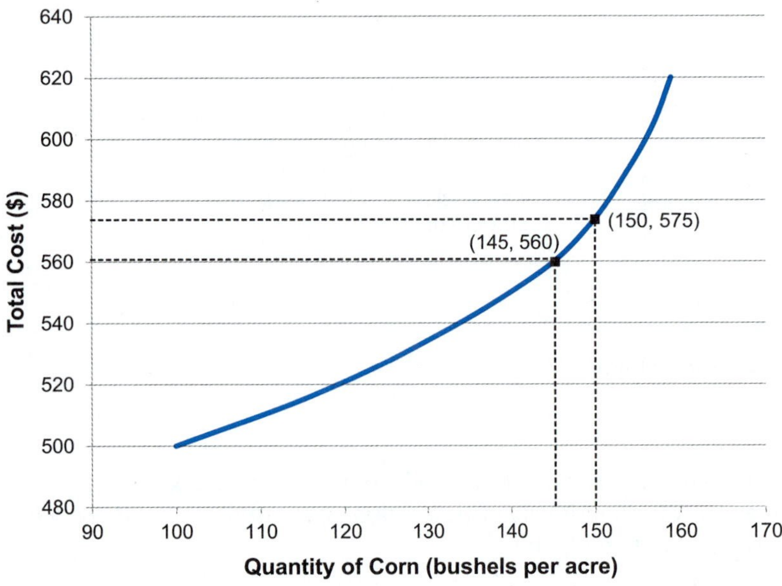

A total cost curve shows the relationship between the total cost of production and the level of output.

expensive to produce an additional bushel of corn per acre. In other words, the higher the level of corn production, the more fertilizer needs to be added to produce one more bushel per acre. This is consistent with a total product curve with diminishing marginal returns.

We can examine the total cost curve in more detail to determine the marginal cost of producing corn. Specifically, we can use the total cost curve, and the data in Table 16.4, to determine the marginal cost of producing one more bushel of corn. This will vary depending on the level of corn production. Note that this is fundamentally different from the marginal cost of a bag of nitrogen fertilizer, which is always $15 per bag.

Let's determine what the marginal cost of corn production is as we go from producing 145 bushels per acre to 150 bushels. We see in Table 16.4 that total costs increase from $560 to $575 as we go from adding 4 bags of fertilizer to 5 bags. As it costs an additional $15 to produce 5 more bushels of corn, the marginal cost *per bushel* is $3, obtained by dividing the additional cost of $15 by five bushels, as shown in Figure 16.5.

We can calculate the marginal cost of corn production for other levels of corn production, as shown in the last column of Table 16.5. You can test yourself by calculating the marginal cost of corn production going from 154 to 157 bushels per acre.

Table 16.5 **Marginal Cost of Corn Production**

Quantity of nitrogen fertilizer (bags per acre)	Corn yield (bushels per acre)	Marginal return of additional nitrogen (bushels of corn)	Cost of additional nitrogen ($ per bag)	Marginal cost (dollars per bushel of corn)
0	100	—	—	—
1	115	15	15	15 ÷ 15 = 1.00
2	127	12	15	15 ÷ 12 = 1.25
3	137	10	15	15 ÷ 10 = 1.33
4	145	8	15	15 ÷ 8 = 1.88
5	150	5	15	15 ÷ 5 = 3.00
6	154	4	15	15 ÷ 4 = 3.75
7	157	3	15	??
8	159	2	15	15 ÷ 2 = 7.50

increasing marginal costs: the situation in which the cost of producing one additional unit of output rises as more output is produced

We can see that the marginal cost of producing corn increases as production levels increase. Diminishing marginal returns to fertilizer application have resulted in **increasing marginal costs** for corn production. In other words, the cost of producing one more bushel of corn rises as more output is produced.

In computing the marginal costs, we ignored the fixed costs. This is correct, because we assumed that fixed costs would be paid regardless of whether any nitrogen fertilizer was used, and we were interested only in the cost of the "additional" or "marginal" bushel of corn production.

The important part of this discussion of diminishing marginal returns and increasing marginal costs is not so much the algebra involved, or even the graphs, though both can be helpful. The significant implication for producer behavior is that diminishing marginal returns and increasing marginal costs mean that, in the short run, the quantity of production will tend to be naturally limited.

Diminishing returns mean that it does not make sense for the farmer to try to feed the whole world from one plot. Increasing costs mean that at some point production will become too expensive relative to benefits received (e.g., revenue from sales of the harvest) to be worthwhile. In Chapter 17 we will see that diminishing returns are assumed in the case of the profit-maximizing competitive firm. Because marginal costs are increasing, whereas the price that the firm receives for its output is constant, the traditional microeconomic model gives a neat diagrammatic explanation of how a firm will choose a unique, profit-maximizing level of output.

constant marginal costs: the situation in which the cost of producing one additional unit of output stays the same as more output is produced

decreasing marginal costs: the situation in which the cost of producing one additional unit of output falls as more output is produced

What if marginal returns are constant, as illustrated in the left-hand graph in Figure 16.2? Then we will have **constant marginal costs**. In this case, each unit of the variable input (which has a constant price) adds exactly the same amount to output, so the cost for each additional unit of output is the same. The total cost curve will be a straight line.

What if marginal returns are increasing, as illustrated in the right-hand graph in Figure 16.2? Then we will have **decreasing marginal costs**. To portray a total cost curve with increasing marginal returns, you would draw a line that rises but also *flattens out* or curves toward the horizontal axis as you move to the right. Increasing marginal returns mean decreasing marginal costs, because additional production is getting *cheaper* as output increases.

Sometimes all these cost patterns are combined in one graph, such as Figure 16.5. Figure 16.5 shows the pattern of costs that corresponds to the pattern of returns that we saw in Figure 16.3, with decreasing marginal costs, followed by constant and then increasing marginal costs, as the quantity of output increases. In the lower part of the graph, the pattern of marginal costs is graphed explicitly.

For certain production processes, such as the application of fertilizer to corn, curves like these can actually be quite accurately graphed on the basis of real-world studies done by

Figure 16.5 **A Possible Pattern of Costs**

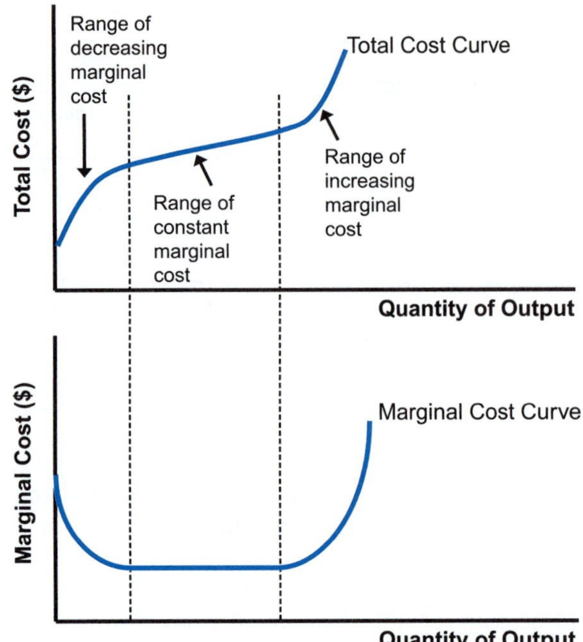

The graphs show the relationship between total and marginal cost curves. For many real-world enterprises, their marginal cost curve is U-shaped.

researchers. In most cases, however, these curves are only hypothetical. Rarely would lone producers, concerned with providing for a family or staying in business, have the luxury of being able to conduct such a study. While they were holding some inputs constant, and varying others from zero up to high amounts in order to find out what exactly their total product curve and total cost curve were, they could easily go out of business!

These graphs do, however, give us a visual image that can help us think about the many ways in which production and cost may be related, for many producers. We see that the concepts of diminishing returns and increasing returns, in particular, are important throughout the study of microeconomics.

4.2 Production Costs in the Long Run

In the long run, as we noted earlier, all inputs are variable. A farmer can buy or rent more land or equipment. A factory owner can build a new factory. More engineers can be trained in software development, if skilled engineers are a short-run fixed input. A business owner may be able to expand by hiring an assistant, if his or her own time for decision making is the limiting factor. A child-care enterprise can expand from a private home to a larger center, if space is the capacity constraint.

Given sufficient time to acquire the needed machines or other resources, or to make other necessary adjustments, a producer should be able to remove all obstacles to getting the highest net benefits (profits) from production. Although in the short run space, equipment, skills, or time present a constraint on capacity, in the long run these constraints can be loosened. Then a question arises: How big should an enterprise get?

Why do we observe, for example, small neighborhood child-care centers and single-worker locksmith businesses, but not small neighborhood steel foundries or hospitals? Many factors can contribute to the explanation of enterprise size, including factors related to history, culture, and the level of demand for a producer's output. Here we focus on technological and cost-related reasons that one size, or scale, may be more advantageous than another.

average cost (or average total cost): cost per unit of output, computed as total cost divided by the quantity of output produced

Because we are now looking at these issues with a long-term perspective, marginal cost—discussed above for the case of the short run, in which one input is fixed—is no longer the relevant concept, because now *all* inputs can be varied. It is, however, relevant to calculate the **average cost** (or **average total cost**) per unit of production. This can be done simply by dividing total cost by the quantity of output produced, at any production level. For example, if it costs \$500 to produce 100 bushels of corn, the average cost per bushel at this level of production is simply \$500/100 bushels = \$5 per bushel.

long-run average cost: the cost of production per unit of output when all inputs can be varied in quantity

The relevant type of cost when the entire scale of production can be varied is the **long-run average cost**, which is the cost per unit of output when all inputs are variable. It is logical to think that, to whatever extent possible, enterprises will tend to grow to the size where the long-run average costs are lowest. Enterprises that are bigger or smaller than this optimal size would be unnecessarily expensive to run.

For example, to go into business, a locksmith needs primarily a set of tools and a van. To double the output of a single-locksmith enterprise would require a second locksmith, another set of tools, and another van. Except for perhaps some small savings in costs, such as advertising or billing, there is no reason to believe that the new, larger firm would be any cheaper to run, per unit of output, than the old, smaller one. In fact, if the new locksmith has to service customers who are farther away from the head office, it may be more expensive per unit of output. It may therefore make more sense for each neighborhood to have its own local locksmith (though perhaps a group of locksmiths might jointly hire advertising and billing services). Bigger is not necessarily better in this case.

economies of scale: situations in which the long-run average cost of production falls as the size of the enterprise increases

constant returns to scale: situations in which the long-run average cost of production stays the same as the size of the enterprise increases

By contrast, a steel foundry requires a sizable investment in plant and equipment, and a hospital that has only a few beds would be either exceedingly expensive to run (as a consequence of underutilization of skilled labor and laboratory facilities) or exceedingly limited in its services. Enterprises in such industries tend to be big because of what economists call **economies of scale**. A process exhibits economies of scale when, in the long run, average production costs decline as the size of the enterprise increases. You could build a single foundry furnace to turn out a few pounds of iron a year—but it might cost its weight in gold to produce each pound of iron. A foundry reaches a stage of low costs per unit only when it is producing steel in much larger quantities.

diseconomies of scale: situations in which the long-run average cost of production rises as the size of the enterprise increases

A production process exhibits **constant returns to scale** over the range where the long-run average cost is constant as the size of the enterprise changes. Finally, a process exhibits **diseconomies of scale** if the long-run average cost rises with the size of an enterprise. Similar to our previous discussion, a production process can display all three types of returns to scale. This is illustrated as a U-shaped long-run average cost curve in Figure 16.6.

What might cause diseconomies of scale? It is generally thought that no matter how many technical economies of scale there may be, for most enterprises there is a point at which

Figure 16.6 **A Possible Pattern of Long-Run Average Costs**

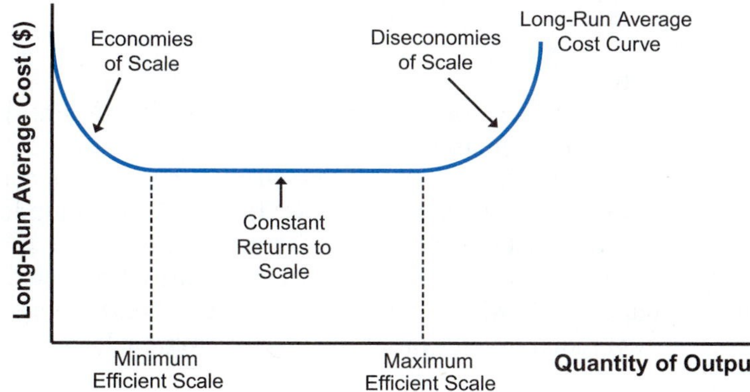

Long-run average cost curves tend to be U-shaped, with a minimum and maximum efficient scale.

they are just too big for all the human beings and all the functions involved to be managed effectively. Some of the big business mergers in recent decades were inspired by hopes of reaping economies of scale (as well as market power or simply in the belief that bigger would be better). Such hopes were sometimes dashed, with the failure of such megamergers as AOL and Time Warner in 2001 and Sprint and Nextel in 2005.

minimum efficient scale: the lowest quantity of output at which a firm achieves its minimum per-unit production costs

maximum efficient scale: the highest quantity of output at which a firm achieves its minimum per-unit production costs

Many production processes appear to have a **minimum efficient scale**. This is the point at which the long-run average cost curve begins to bottom out, as shown in Figure 16.6. For locksmiths, the minimum efficient scale might be the output level corresponding to a one-person shop; for an automobile company, it may be several thousand vehicles per year. Levels of output *less* than these may leave some resources underemployed, thus creating the downward-sloping portion of the long-run average cost curve. Given the problems of managing very large organizations, one can also posit the existence of a **maximum efficient scale**—which is the largest an enterprise can be and still benefit from low long-run average costs.

4.3 Production Process Choice

Another important issue in the economics of production is the choice of production process. If two or more processes exist that can make the same output, which should be chosen? Producers, to be economically efficient, should choose the process that entails the lowest cost.

input substitution: increasing the use of some inputs, and decreasing that of others, while producing the same good or service

Because various technologies are available, producers can engage in **input substitution**, using less of one input and more of another while producing the same good or service, as costs and availability change. As we mentioned earlier, in the case of corn farming, nitrogen can be obtained from renewable, organic sources such as manure and alfalfa or from chemical fertilizer produced using nonrenewable natural gas. Generally, whenever prices change, producers will want to substitute cheaper inputs for inputs that have become more expensive. From a public welfare perspective, input substitution will enhance well-being when the choices that are made take into account external as well as internal costs.

Of particular importance, historically, has been the process of substituting the use of machinery for human labor. This is dramatically exemplified in the American folk hero John Henry, the railway worker who pitted himself against the new steam drill that threatened to take jobs away from him and his fellows. In his heroic effort, John Henry fulfilled his promise to "die with a hammer in my hand."

Yet even with modern production methods that rely heavily on machines, labor remains an important input cost. Because of globalization and the possibility of moving production to any part of the world, an increasingly important question has been *where* to produce. Low wages in countries such as China, Vietnam, and Bangladesh have motivated many companies to locate production facilities in those countries. In general, the cost savings associated with production in a low-wage country outweigh the increased costs of transporting goods long distances to market. However, wage trends are beginning to reverse in some cases, and manufacturing in the United States may be making a comeback, as discussed in Box 16.1.

Discussion Questions

1. Explain in your own words why a firm's marginal cost curve may initially decline, but then increase, as the quantity of output increases.
2. Diminishing marginal returns is a valuable concept, not only in economics, but in many other areas of life: an obvious example (which we saw in Chapter 9, on consumption) was the diminishing pleasure received by eating successive units of the same food. Suggest two other areas in life that exhibit diminishing marginal returns. Can you also think of some examples in your own life where there are constant or increasing returns to scale (i.e., you get the same, or more, psychic or other "returns" from each additional increment of something)?

BOX 16.1 MADE IN THE USA AGAIN?

The production cost savings from low wages are a primary reason manufacturing has shifted from the United States and other developed countries to emerging countries such as China. But with rapid economic growth in China, the choice between "Made in China" and "Made in the USA" has become more difficult. Between 2005 and 2010 the average wage for factory workers in China increased by 69 percent. Meanwhile, wage growth in the United States has stagnated (recall our discussion of median wages in the United States in Chapter 10). Thus the relative wage advantage of producing in China is decreasing.

According to a study by Boston Consulting Group (BCG), the change in relative wage growth suggests the potential for an "American renaissance" in manufacturing. Hal Sirkin of BCG states, "Sometime around 2015, manufacturers will be indifferent between locating in America or China for production for consumption in America." He bases this prediction on the assumption that annual wage growth will continue to be a robust 17 percent per year in China but rather slow in the United States.

Firms are also finding that there are advantages to reducing the complexity of supply chains. When production occurs across several countries, an unexpected event in only one of those countries, such as an earthquake or a disease outbreak, can cause a costly supply disruption. Thus, keeping production domestic reduces overall risk.

BCG indicates that several companies have already brought overseas production back to the United States. The heavy equipment manufacturer Caterpillar has shifted some production from overseas to a factory in Texas. In 2010 Wham-O moved half its Frisbee and Hula Hoop production to the United States from China and Mexico.

But even if China's production cost advantage vanishes, other countries with even lower wages provide companies with viable options. For example, the manufacturing cost advantage of producing in India and Bangladesh is likely to persist for some time. Also, with rapid demand growth in emerging markets, production in China still makes economic sense for goods sold there.

Finally, shifting production back to the United States may not be feasible in some cases, at least in the short run. For example, the United States no longer has the supply base or the infrastructure to support consumer electronics manufacturing. While firms may not have realized it at the time, some production shifts will be very difficult to reverse.

Source: "Moving Back to America," *Economist,* May 12, 2011.

REVIEW QUESTIONS

1. What is the "triple bottom line" and how does it differ from the traditional economic assumption about the goal of production?
2. What is the difference between fixed costs and variable costs?
3. What is the difference between accounting costs and economic costs?
4. Name all the categories that comprise economic costs.
5. What is the difference between private costs and external costs?
6. What is a production function?
7. What is a limiting factor in production?
8. What distinguishes the short run from the long run?
9. How can we express a production function graphically?
10. What is marginal product?
11. Describe the meaning of diminishing returns, constant returns, and increasing marginal returns, and explain how each might come about.
12. Sketch a total product curve illustrating increasing returns, constant returns, and diminishing returns.
13. Distinguish among fixed cost, variable cost, total cost, and marginal cost.
14. Sketch a total cost curve illustrating fixed cost and decreasing, constant, and increasing marginal costs.
15. What are average costs?
16. What are economies of scale?
17. Sketch a long-run average cost curve illustrating economies of scale, constant returns to scale, and diseconomies of scale.
18. How do we define the efficient scale of production?

EXERCISES

1. Kai's records show that last month he spent $5,000 on rent for his shop, $3,000 on materials, $3,000 on wages and benefits for an employee, and $500 in interest on the loan that he used to start his business. He quit a job that had paid him $3,000 a month to devote himself full time to this business. Suppose that he has to pay the lease on his shop and the interest on the loan regardless of whether he produces. However, suppose that at any time he can change the amount of materials that he buys and the hours that his employee works and that he can also go back to his old job (perhaps part time).
   a. What are the accounting costs of operating his shop for the month?
   b. What are the economic costs?
   c. Which types of costs of running his business for a month are fixed? Which are variable?
2. A nonprofit organization dedicated to health care wants to open a new hospital near a residential neighborhood. A group of residents of that neighborhood protests this decision, claiming that traffic caused by the hospital will increase noise and auto emissions. The hospital rejects the idea of building a wall to contain the noise and fumes, claiming that this would be too expensive. Describe in a few sentences, using at least two terms introduced in this chapter, how an economist might describe this situation.
3. The production relationship between the number of chapters that Tiffany studies in her history book (the variable input) and the number of points that she will earn on a history exam (the output) is as follows:

Input: number of chapters studied	0	1	2	3
Output: test score	15	35	60	95

   a. Using graph paper or a computer spreadsheet or presentation program, graph the total product curve for exam points. Label clearly.
   b. What is the marginal return of the first chapter that Tiffany reads? And what is the marginal return of the third chapter that she reads?
   c. How would you describe, in words, this pattern of returns?
4. Match each concept in Column A with an example in Column B.

Column A	Column B
a. Fixed input	1. The more months that you work at consulting, the better you become at it
b. Variable input	2. The way that you irritate your roommate by working late at night
c. Opportunity cost	3. The lost salary that you could have had as an employee elsewhere
d. External cost	4. The more hours you work without a break, the less effectively you work
e. Increasing returns	5. The time that you spend consulting
f. Diminishing returns	6. The computer that you initially purchased when you started the business

5. Ramona designs Web pages and needs the jolt that she gets from the caffeine in cola drinks to keep herself awake and alert. The total product curve for the relationship between her cola consumption per day and the number of pages that she can design in one day is given in the following figure.

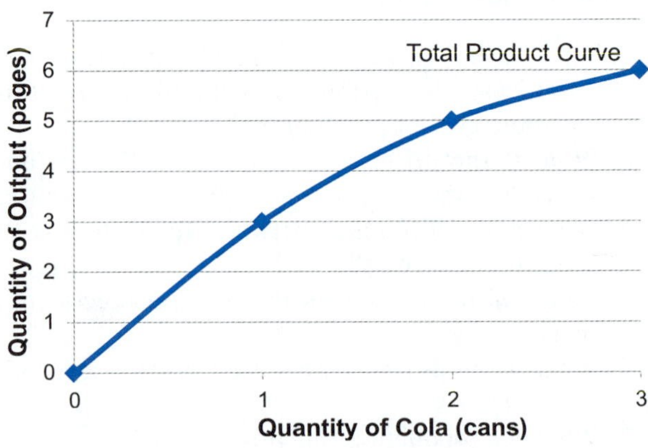

   a. Fill out Columns (2) and (3) of the table that follows, referring to the graph above.

Quantity of variable input (cans of cola)	(2) Quantity of output (pages)	(3) Marginal product (pages)	Fixed cost ($)	Variable cost ($)	Total cost ($)
0					
1					
2					
3					

b. Ramona's employer pays her $50 per day regardless of whether she is productive and provides her with all the cola that she wants to drink. Cola costs her employer $2 per can. Add to your table information on the fixed, variable, and total costs of Ramona's producing from 0 to 3 web pages.

c. Using graph paper or a spreadsheet or presentation program, graph the total cost curve. (What is measured on the horizontal axis? The vertical axis?)

d. Using information on the marginal product from your table above, calculate the marginal cost per page of output at each level of soda consumption.

6. Suppose that in her first hour of work, Lynn can hand-knit four pairs of mittens. During her second consecutive hour, Lynn can hand-knit three additional pairs of mittens, and during her third hour of work, as a consequence of fatigue, she can hand-knit only one additional pair. Suppose that she works for up to three hours and makes a wage of $15 per hour.

a. Create a table relating the number of hours worked to the *total* number of pairs of mittens produced, and graph the *total* product curve for the production of pairs of mittens. Label clearly.

b. Looking at labor costs only (ignoring, for the purposes of this exercise, the cost of the yarn that she uses and any fixed costs), make a table relating costs to the number of pairs of mittens produced. Graph the total (labor) cost curve for the production of mittens. Label clearly.

c. How would you describe in words the pattern of marginal returns? The pattern of marginal costs?

d. What is the marginal product, in pairs of mittens per hour, of her second hour of work? Of her third hour of work?

e. What is the marginal cost, in dollars per pairs of mittens, as she goes from an output of four pairs of mittens to an output of seven pairs of mittens? What is the marginal cost of the eighth pair of mittens?

NOTES

1. Patagonia, "Don't Buy This Jacket, Black Friday and the New York Times," www.thecleanestline.com/2011/11/dont-buy-this-jacket-black-friday-and-the-new-york-times.html.

2. Milton Friedman, "The Social Responsibility of Business Is to Increase Its Profits," *New York Times Magazine,* September 13, 1970.

3. See, for example, Amy Joyce, "Wal-Mart Workers Win Wage Suit," *Washington Post,* October 13, 2006.

4. Peter Scharf and Bill Wiebold, "Nitrogen Prices—How Do They Affect Optimum N Management?" *Integrated Pest & Crop Management Newsletter* 11(2) (2001).

17 Markets Without Power

Chances are that you have heard politicians or media commentators expound on the benefits of "free markets." One of the benefits claimed for free markets is that they result in economic efficiency—resources are allocated to their highest-valued uses, measured using welfare analysis. Behind this political argument is an economic model—a model of markets in which no one individual, company, or institution has power over the market. Economists call such markets "perfectly competitive." In this chapter, we discuss perfectly competitive markets and the implications of these markets for economic efficiency and equity.

1. Understanding Market Power and Competition

market power: the ability to control, or at least affect, the terms and conditions of a market exchange

Having power means having the ability to influence something. **Market power** is the ability to control, or at least affect, the terms and conditions of a market exchange. In this chapter and Chapter 18, we consider different types of markets based on the degree of market power held by sellers. In this chapter, we consider markets in which sellers, as well as buyers, possess *no market power*. In Chapter 18, we consider three types of markets in which sellers do possess a degree of market power.

Market power is related to the degree of competition in a market. In most markets, sellers compete with other sellers. A very general rule of thumb is that the more competitive a market is, the less market power is held by individual sellers. But what exactly do we mean by "competition"? As we have seen with other topics, economists' definition of competition differs from how people commonly use the term. So we briefly discuss four potential definitions of competition and how they relate to market power:

1. competition from the perspective of businesses
2. competition from the perspective of consumers
3. competition from the perspective of citizens
4. competition from the perspective of economists

1.1 The Business Perspective on Competition and Market Power

From the point of view of an individual business, competition is generally a bad thing—something to be reduced or eliminated. Competition means that other businesses are working to reduce your sales and profits. It also means that you have to be very aware of what your competitors are charging for their goods and services, and you may have to adjust your prices to reflect what your competitors are doing.

From the perspective of a business, market power is a good thing. You want to be able to influence people to buy what you are selling. You want to be able to command a high price for what you sell. You want to have the power to bargain for low prices for the resources that you buy. You want your business to grow, capturing a large share of the market in which you sell.

1.2 The Consumer Perspective on Competition and Market Power

To consumers, competition is generally a good thing. Competition among businesses tends to drive prices down, making goods and services more affordable to consumers. Many consumers like to "shop around" for the lowest prices. Having several competing stores (or Internet shopping sites) to choose from means that consumers are more likely to find bargains. (For more on competition from the perspective of both businesses and consumers, see Box 17.1.)

Consumers generally do not benefit when sellers possess market power. People who live in rural areas with just a single local gas station or grocery store will generally pay higher prices than people living in urban areas. While the higher prices may partly reflect higher wholesale costs to sellers, a seller that possesses market power can use that power to charge relatively high prices just because the seller knows that consumers must otherwise travel long distances to shop elsewhere.

1.3 The Citizen Perspective on Competition and Market Power

People are both consumers and citizens. Sometimes their goals as consumers may not align with their views as concerned citizens. Competition and market power is one such issue.

Box 17.1 Amazon and Market Competition

Amazon is the world's top online retailer, with 2012 global revenues of more than $60 billion. In the United States, Amazon accounted for 15 percent of all e-commerce in 2012. Amazon's founder, Jeff Bezos, has become one of the twenty richest people in the world, with a net worth of about $25 billion.

Amazon's success is based largely on its ability to offer a lower price than its competitors, especially "brick-and-mortar" competitors that must pay the cost of operating physical stores. Consumers benefit from Amazon's low prices, free shipping on many orders, and avoiding having to drive to stores.

But Amazon's price-based competitive advantage appears to be slipping. Amazon's competitors are increasingly willing to match, or even beat, Amazon's prices. For example, in July 2013 the online retailer Overstock announced that it would undercut Amazon's book prices by 10 percent. Amazon had no choice but to match the price discount. Best Buy has a policy of matching Amazon's price on similar items. Moreover, customers can pick up items at local Best Buy stores, so they do not have to wait days for delivery. In addition, Walmart is increasing its online shopping presence, looking to grab market share from Amazon.

Bed Bath & Beyond is another competitor that may be chipping away at Amazon's sales. A 2013 price survey found that the total cost of a basket of thirty items was 6.5 percent cheaper at Bed Bath & Beyond than at Amazon. For example, a shower curtain that sold for $32.39 at Amazon was priced at $24.99 at Bed Bath & Beyond. In addition, Bed Bath & Beyond frequently sends its customers coupons for a 20 percent discount, which makes their prices even lower.

Another factor that may hurt Amazon's ability to offer lower prices than its brick-and-mortar competitors is that Internet retailers may soon be required to collect state sales tax. Previously, Amazon did not charge its customers state sales taxes, even for orders delivered to states that levy them, giving Amazon a 5–10 percent price advantage in those states. However, Amazon began to collect state sales tax as early as 2008 for orders to New York, and now collects such taxes for orders delivered to sixteen states. The Marketplace Fairness Act, which would require all Internet retailers to collect state sales taxes, has passed the U.S. Senate, but has not yet been voted on by the full Congress as of this book's publication. Because of changing laws and increasing competition, Amazon may no longer be the dominant retailing force that it has been in the past.

Source: Tom Gara, "Problem for Bezos: Mall Becoming Cheaper Than Amazon," *Wall Street Journal,* August 20, 2013; Greg Bensinger, "Amazon Passes Tax Milestone," *Wall Street Journal,* November 1, 2013; Amazon.com, "About Sales Tax on Items sold by Amazon.com," www.amazon.com/gp/help/customer/display.html?nodeId=468512; GovTrack.us, "S. 743: Marketplace Fairness Act of 2013," www.govtrack.us/congress/bills/113/s743#overview.

While consumers generally approve of competition because it tends to lead to lower prices, as concerned citizens they may perceive competition as the cause of undesirable social and environmental impacts. For example, consumers may support the construction of a new suburban "big box" store in their town because it will increase consumer choice and offer low prices. But others may oppose the store, on the basis that it will harm the environment, hurt "mom-and-pop" stores, and reduce the vitality of a downtown area.

Concerned citizens may also worry about businesses that cite the "need to stay competitive" as their reason for eliminating jobs, taking over smaller companies, refusing to implement voluntary pollution controls, or moving their production overseas, all of which are perceived as harmful. From the point of view of a concerned citizen, neither market power nor tooth-and-nail competition serves the interests of a peaceful and humane society. Many concerned citizens would prefer to see markets based on decentralized power, along with ethical and cooperative behavior that serves the common good.

Many citizens view market power primarily in terms of the size and financial clout of large corporations. They believe that "big business" disproportionately influences public policy to obtain tax breaks, subsidies, or exemption from environmental regulations. They cite examples of big businesses acting callously or unethically, raising prices on goods that people need, forcing workers to accept low wages, or intimidating people with lawsuits.

1.4 The Economists' Perspective on Competition and Market Power

Some economists view competition and market power through the lens of traditional welfare analysis. From this perspective, competition is generally a good thing (and market power can be a bad thing) because competition tends to increase the social welfare of a market. To an economist, the term "competitive market" does not imply the use of cutthroat or illegal policies. Instead, it is shorthand for the case in which so many buyers and sellers interact in a market that none are able to exercise significant market power. The fact that a competitor is always trying to take away your customers or your workers is what keeps you on your toes and makes you run your organization efficiently. Competition, to an economist, *means* decentralized power. The image of a self-regulating, "free" competitive market is at the core of traditional neoclassical economics.

As a social science, economics tends to make normative judgments from the point of view of social efficiency, not just from the perspective of one particular actor. The traditional neoclassical view, focused almost entirely on efficiency goals, notes that market power can create inefficiency. (We demonstrate this in Chapter 18.) Hence it considers market power largely harmful, except in certain unavoidable cases.

But as we have learned in other chapters, a complete economic analysis needs to consider all costs and benefits, not just those that accrue to market participants. In particular, we should consider social and environmental externalities. If competition drives businesses to treat their workers poorly or ignore environmental and safety regulations, these costs must be considered when we evaluate the extent to which an unregulated market leads to an efficient outcome. As economists, we may also be concerned about whether competitive markets lead to just outcomes, based on normative views of fairness.

Discussion Questions

1. To which of the four views of market power and competition do you most relate? Do you think all four views are valid, or is one particular view more worthwhile or "correct" than the others?
2. Can you think of an example of an economic actor that is *not* a business firm but that has "market power" in the sense defined in the text?

2. PERFECT COMPETITION

The economic model of perfect competition relies on particular assumptions and leads to certain conclusions about how firms will behave and what profits they can make.

2.1 THE CONDITIONS OF PERFECT COMPETITION

perfect competition: a market for the exchange of identical units of a good or service, in which there are numerous small sellers and buyers, all of whom have perfect information

The model of **perfect competition** is based on four key assumptions about a market:

1. There are *numerous small sellers and buyers.* Each buyer and seller is so small relative to the size of the relevant market that none can affect the market price.
2. Within any particular market, only one kind of good or service is traded and all units of the good or service offered for sale *are identical.* Therefore, buyers will not care which firm they buy from and will make purchasing decisions based solely on price.
3. Producers of the good or service can *freely enter or exit* the industry. There are no barriers preventing a new firm from joining the market or preventing an existing one from leaving the market.
4. Buyers and sellers all have *perfect information.* They all know where the good is available, at what prices it is offered, and whether profits are being made.

Another assumption is that the long-run minimum efficient scale (which we discussed in Chapter 16) of a producer in this industry is fairly small, relative to total demand in the market. In other words, production is characterized by constant returns to scale, not by economies of scale. This is important because, if it were *not* the case, the market might not be large enough for the many efficient firms assumed by the theory.

price taker: a seller that has no market power to set price. Price is determined solely by the interaction of market supply and market demand.

In a perfectly competitive market, every individual seller is a **price taker**, which means that each seller has no market power and price is determined by the interaction of market supply and demand. As each seller is relatively small, each can basically sell all they want to at the going price. But if they raise their price even just a little above the market-determined price, *no one* will buy from them because consumers can purchase identical items for a lower price from their competitors.

Being a price taker means that you face a perfectly elastic demand curve, as we discussed in Chapter 5. This is shown in Figure 17.1. A seller can sell all it wants at the market price of P^*. At any price above P^*, however, it will sell nothing. There is also no reason to sell at any price below P^* because it can sell as much as it wants at P^*.

Note that the *market* demand curve in a perfectly competitive market has the normal downward slope. Each individual seller faces a perfectly elastic demand curve, but the demand curve for the market as a whole will be less elastic, or perhaps inelastic.

Figure 17.1 **The Demand Curve for a Perfectly Competitive Seller**

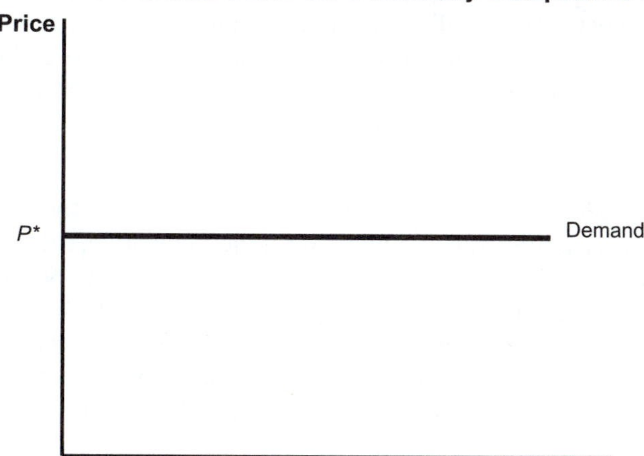

In a perfectly competitive market, each seller is able to sell all they want at the market equilibrium price. But at any price higher than the equilibrium price, a seller is not able to sell anything at all as buyers can simply obtain the same good or service elsewhere for a lower price.

2.2 Examples of Perfect Competition?

Examples of perfectly competitive markets in the real world are hard to come by. In older textbooks, agricultural commodities such as wheat were often given as examples of goods traded in perfectly competitive markets. It was argued that one farmer's wheat, of a given type, was nearly identical to the wheat of the same type sold by other farmers. Further, no individual farmer had any perceptible influence on the market price. However, in industrialized countries, agricultural markets today tend to be highly organized and regulated, with farmer-supported marketing boards, government-guaranteed minimum prices, long-term contracts, and the like deliberately influencing the terms and conditions of the market. Further (as discussed in Chapter 18), some large agricultural corporations, such as Monsanto and Cargill, possess significant market power.

Perhaps the markets that most closely approach perfect competition today are not markets for goods but certain financial resale markets. For example, the conditions that prevail in the stock market often approximate those of perfect competition. The shares of stock of a particular company are all identical. Because this is a financial resale market, the cost of "production" is irrelevant, so there are no barriers to entry. Well-defined stock exchanges set up a structure under which the going price becomes common knowledge. When many shares of stock are outstanding, the trading of a few shares does not perceptibly affect the share price. If you own a few shares of stock and think about selling them, your broker will quote you a price—take it or leave it. The demand curve that you face, as an individual seller, is horizontal.

In some labor markets as well, conditions may approximate perfect competition. Workers with general skills, such as flipping burgers or sweeping floors, may provide nearly identical services from an employer's point of view. When there are many such "sellers," they may find that they have a choice of a job at "the going wage" or no job at all.

Discussion Questions

1. Suppose that you are thinking of starting your own business. Would you want to start a business in a perfectly competitive market? What do you think are the advantages and disadvantages of selling in a perfectly competitive market?
2. In addition to the markets mentioned in this section, can you think of any other markets that meet the assumptions of perfect competition?

3. Profit Maximization Under Perfect Competition

We now consider the production decisions of perfectly competitive sellers. Although a perfectly competitive seller can *theoretically* sell all he wants, in practice a seller will limit production to maximize his profits. We illustrate profit maximization by building on the corn farming example that we developed in Chapter 16. We assume that corn farming occurs in a perfectly competitive market. Even though this may not be a totally realistic assumption, it allows us to illustrate the production decisions of a perfectly competitive seller. We present a more formal model of production decisions in a perfectly competitive market in the appendix to this chapter.

3.1 Revenues

total revenues: the total amount of money received by a seller, equal to price times quantity

In Chapter 16, we discussed production costs. We now consider revenues—the money that sellers receive from their sales. Assuming that all units sell for the same price, **total revenues** are simply equal to price multiplied by quantity. So if the price of corn were $4 per bushel and a farmer sold 1,000 bushels of corn, her total revenues would be $4,000.*

We can now define profits as the difference between total revenues and total costs. But recall from Chapter 16 that we have two different definitions of costs—accounting costs and economic costs. The difference is that economic costs include all opportunity costs,

*This was approximately the actual price of corn at the time that this book was written.

accounting profits: the difference between total revenues and accounting costs

economic profits: the difference between total revenues and economic costs

marginal revenue: the additional revenue obtained by selling one more unit. In a perfectly competitive market, marginal revenue equals price.

such as the wages that one could potentially earn doing something else. Comparably, we also have two definitions of profits. **Accounting profits** are calculated as the difference between total revenues and accounting costs. **Economic profits** are the difference between total revenues and economic costs. Accounting profits are higher than economic profits, because economic costs are higher than accounting costs. Note that it is entirely possible for a seller to make a positive accounting profit, but no economic profit, or even a negative profit (i.e., a loss).

The standard neoclassical model of perfect competition assumes that each seller seeks to maximize his or her profits. In the numerical model that we present here, we assume that costs mean economic costs, and thus profits are economic profits. We will see that economic profits are an important concept in the traditional model of perfect competition.

We also need to define **marginal revenue**, which is the *additional* revenue obtained by selling one more unit. In a perfectly competitive market, marginal revenue is simply the market price. So if the price of corn is $4 per bushel, the marginal revenue from selling one more bushel is simply $4. In Chapter 18, we consider markets in which the marginal revenue is not equal to price.

We can represent total revenues graphically, as shown in Figure 17.2. The total revenue curve is a straight line because marginal revenue is constant at $4 per bushel. So if a farmer sells 100 bushels of corn, for example, total revenues will be $400; if she sells 140 bushels of corn, total revenues will be $560.

Figure 17.2 **Total Revenues**

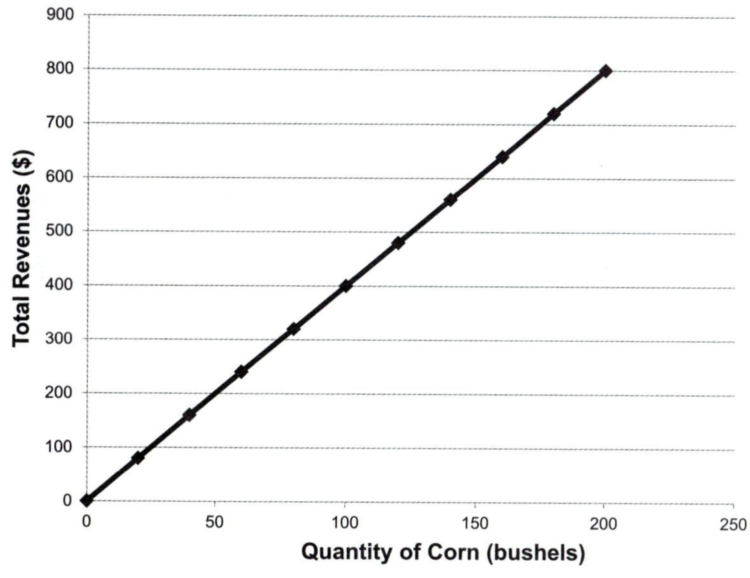

Total revenues increase linearly with the quantity sold given that the price for each unit (in this case, bushels of corn) is constant in a perfectly competitive market.

3.2 Profit Maximization Example

Continuing with our corn farming example, we need to determine the level of corn production that will result in the maximum profit. To compile Table 17.1, we can combine our information from Chapter 15 about production costs with the fact that corn sells for $4 per bushel. We have calculated the profit (or loss) of each level of corn production, based on different levels of fertilizer application. Note that Table 17.1 repeats the information from Table 16.4, but adds a total revenue and profit column. As discussed above, we assume that the fixed cost of $500 per acre is an economic cost, including both accounting and opportunity costs.

We see that the farmer's profits are maximized at a production level of 154 bushels per acre, applying 6 bags of fertilizer per acre. At this point, economic profits are $26 per acre. Any other level of production results in lower (or negative) profits.

Table 17.1 **Profit Maximization, Based on Analysis of Total Costs and Total Revenues**

Quantity of nitrogen fertilizer (bags/acre)	Corn yield (bushels per acre)	Fixed costs ($)	Variable costs ($15 per bag of fertilizer)	Total costs ($)	Total revenues ($)	Economic profit/loss ($)
0	100	500	0	500	400	–100
1	115	500	15	515	460	–55
2	127	500	30	530	508	–22
3	137	500	45	545	548	3
4	145	500	60	560	580	20
5	150	500	75	575	600	25
6	154	500	90	590	616	26
7	157	500	105	605	628	23
8	159	500	120	620	636	16

Profit maximization can be shown graphically as the difference between total revenues and total costs, as shown in Figure 17.3. In this figure we have combined Figure 17.2, showing total revenues, with our total cost curve from Figure 16.4. The vertical distance between the total revenue curve and the total cost curve represents profits. This vertical distance is greatest, and profits are maximized, at 154 bushels per acre.

In addition to determining the profit-maximizing level of production using a table or a graph of total revenues and total costs, we can also use marginal analysis. Recall that in Chapter 16 we calculated the marginal cost of producing one more bushel of corn at each level of fertilizer application (Table 16.5). We repeat this table here as Table 17.2, with the addition of one more column to the right indicating the marginal revenue from selling corn, which is constant at $4 per bushel.

Marginal analysis tells us that it makes economic sense to do something as long as the marginal benefits are greater than the marginal costs. So the farmer's question is whether it makes economic sense to add each bag of fertilizer. As long as the marginal revenues exceed

Figure 17.3 **Profit Maximization, Based on Analysis of Total Costs and Total Revenues**

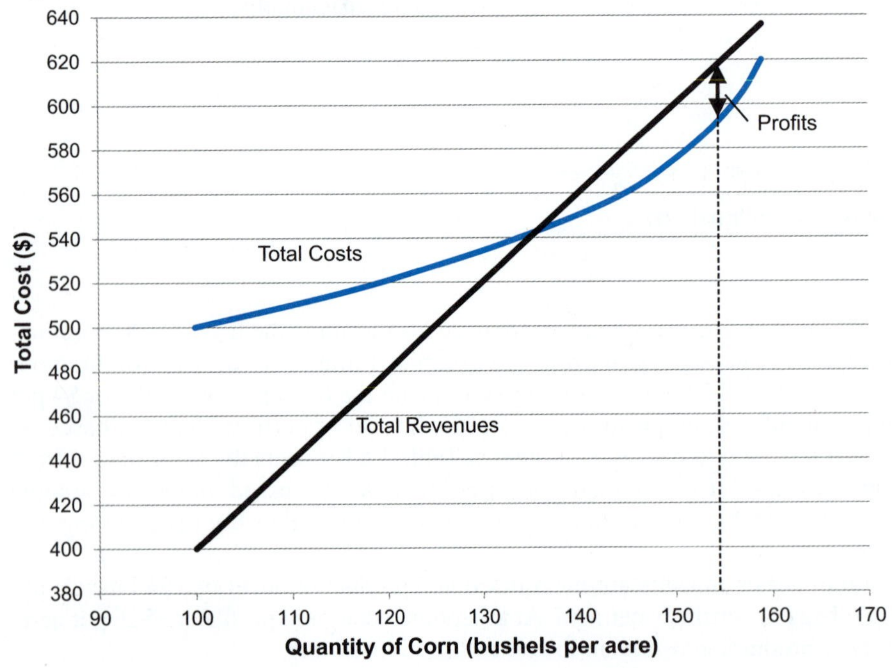

Profit maximization occurs at the level of production where the difference between total revenues and total costs is greatest.

Table 17.2 **The Marginal Cost and Marginal Revenue of Corn Production**

Quantity of nitrogen fertilizer (bags per acre)	Corn yield (bushels per acre)	Marginal return to additional nitrogen (bushels of corn)	Cost of additional nitrogen ($ per bag)	Marginal cost in dollars per bushel of corn	Marginal revenue in dollars per bushel of corn
0	100	—	—	—	4
1	115	15	15	15 ÷ 15 = 1.00	4
2	127	12	15	15 ÷ 12 = 1.25	4
3	137	10	15	15 ÷ 10 = 1.33	4
4	145	8	15	15 ÷ 8 = 1.88	4
5	150	5	15	15 ÷ 5 = 3.00	4
6	154	4	15	15 ÷ 4 = 3.75	4
7	157	3	15	15 ÷ 3 = 5.00	4
8	159	2	15	15 ÷ 2 = 7.50	4

the marginal costs the farmer should keeping adding fertilizer, because profits are increasing. So, for example, we can see that adding the third bag of fertilizer increases profits because the marginal cost, measured in dollars per bushel of corn, is $1.33 while the marginal revenues per bushel are $4.00.

Marginal revenues exceed marginal cost for every production level up to six bags of fertilizer. For the seventh bag of fertilizer, the marginal cost of $5 exceeds the marginal revenue of $4. By adding the seventh bag of fertilizer, the farmer loses money. So the profit-maximizing level of fertilizer application is six bags, at which the farmer produces 154 bushels of corn per acre. This is the same answer that we obtained previously based on tabular and graphical analysis of total costs and revenues.

We can also illustrate profit maximization using a graph of marginal costs and marginal revenues, shown in Figure 17.4. We see that marginal revenue is constant at $4 per bushel. The marginal cost of corn production is increasing, as we discussed in Chapter 16. The

Figure 17.4 **Profit Maximization, Based on Marginal Analysis**

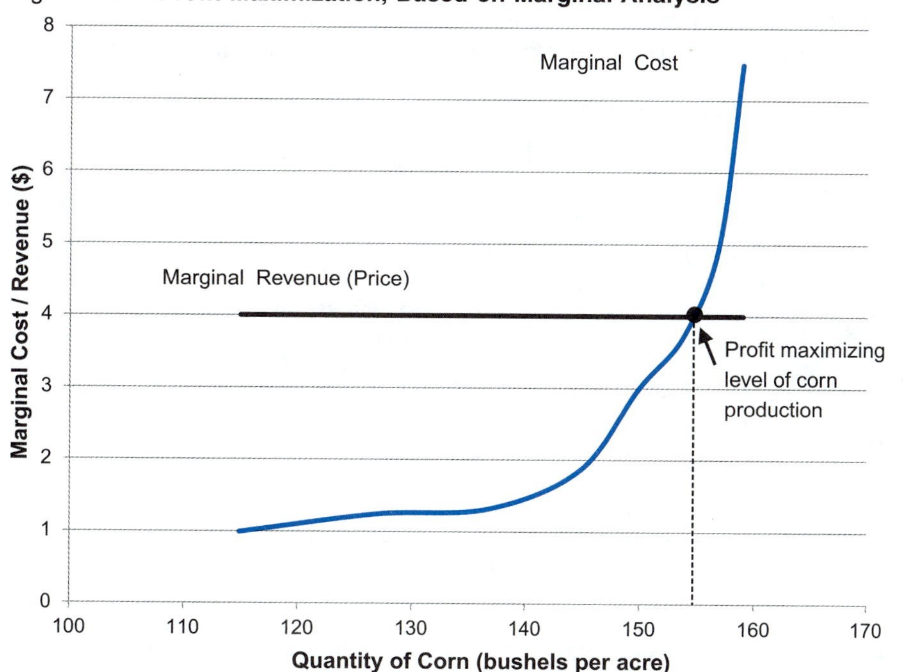

Profit maximization occurs at the level of production where the marginal cost rises to the level of marginal revenues (equal to price in a perfectly competitive market).

profit-maximizing level of corn production is 154 bushels, again up to the point where the marginal revenue equals marginal cost.

We can now state the general rule for **profit maximization under perfect competition**: A seller should increase production up to the point where marginal revenues equal marginal costs, commonly expressed as $MR = MC$. Given that marginal revenue is always equal to price under perfect competition, we can also state that profit maximizing means setting $P = MC$.

3.3 PROFITS UNDER PERFECT COMPETITION

profit maximization (under perfect competition): a seller should increase production up to the point where $MR = MC$. As $MR = P$ under perfect competition, we can also define the profit maximizing solution by setting $P = MC$.

In Table 17.1 we found that at the profit-maximizing level of production (154 bushels of corn per acre), the farmer is making $26 per acre in profits. Recall that this is an economic profit. Although this may not sound like much, a farmer may have many acres, perhaps hundreds, in corn production. Also, as an *economic* profit, this means that farming is providing a better income than *any other opportunity,* such as working as a police officer or an administrative assistant.

We now ask an important question: Can economic profits persist under perfect competition? The answer is no, based on the assumptions of perfect competition. Specifically:

- With free entry and exit, anyone can easily become a farmer, switching from any other profession.*
- With perfect information, everyone is aware that farming is providing higher profits than other opportunities.
- Another implication of perfect information is that everyone has access to information that will allow him or her to produce corn as efficiently as possible (i.e., at the lowest cost).
- All bushels of corn are identical, so anyone producing corn can sell as much as he or she wants at the market price.

Thus the existence of economic profits in our idealized picture of corn production will attract some people to switch what they are doing and take up corn farming. We assume that this will not affect the costs of corn farming—the costs remain the same as in Tables 17.1 and 17.2. However, the influx of new farmers increases the *market supply* of corn. In other words, at any given corn price, more corn will be supplied because more farmers are growing corn, as illustrated in Figure 17.5. The original market equilibrium, with a corn price of $4.00 per bushel, is E_0. As more farmers enter the market, the supply curve shifts to the right, moving from $Supply_0$ to $Supply_1$. With the increase in supply, the market price falls from $4.00 per bushel to a lower price, P_1.

Figure 17.5 **The Impact of an Increase in Supply as Farmers Enter the Corn Market**

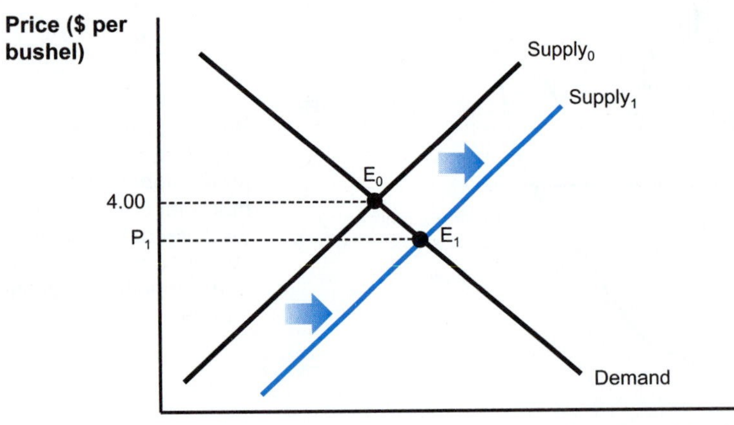

An increase in supply, as more farmers enter the market, will lower the equilibrium price (from $4.00 per bushel to P_1) and increase the quantity sold.

*Of course, becoming a corn farmer is not "free"—it normally requires training and significant investment in land and equipment. But, as in any economic model, we are abstracting from reality to illustrate a point.

Our next question becomes: How much will supply increase? Or, given that the equilibrium price will vary depending on how much supply shifts, what will P_1 eventually be?

Note that as the price of corn falls below $4.00 per bushel, each farmer's profits will fall. Thus the increase in supply reduces the amount of economic profits made by each farmer. But as long as economic profits exist, even if they are small, farming is still more attractive than all other opportunities. *Thus as long as economic profits exist, entry of new farmers into the market will continue.*

As each new farmer enters the market, three things will happen simultaneously:

1. The market supply curve shifts a little further to the right.
2. The market price falls a little further.
3. Economic profits for each farmer become a little lower.

We can illustrate what is happening in the market as a whole and for each individual farmer by putting the market supply and demand graph next to our graph of marginal costs and revenues for an individual farmer, as shown in Figure 17.6. Each farmer's marginal revenue curve is equal to price (a horizontal line), which is determined by market conditions (i.e., market supply and demand). When more farmers enter the market, shifting the supply curve from $Supply_0$ to $Supply_1$, each farmer's marginal revenue curve falls from MR_0 to MR_1. Each farmer's profit-maximizing level of production is still where $MR = MC$. So each farmer will respond to the decrease in price by shifting production from point A to point B. At the lower price, each farmer is making a smaller profit.

Figure 17.6 **The Relationship between Market Conditions and Individual Production Decisions**

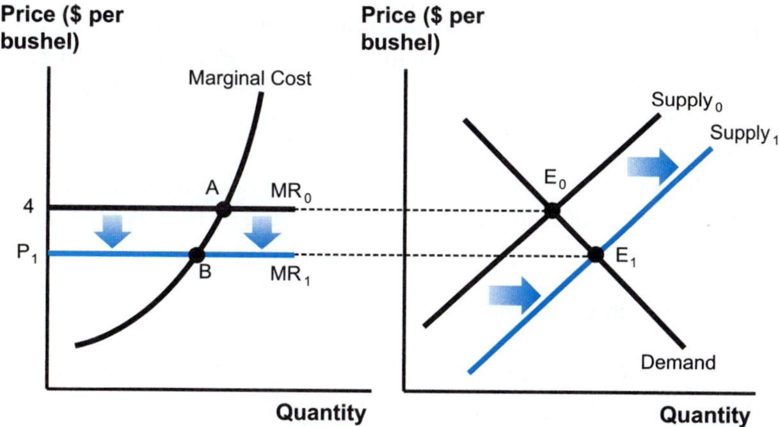

As more farmers enter the market, the equilibrium price will fall, and the economic profits of each individual farmer will decrease.

Eventually, we will reach a point where price falls enough that economic profits fall to zero. At this point, farming is equally attractive to the next best alternative, and there is no incentive for further entry to the market. In other words, under the assumptions of perfect competition, *economic profits will eventually fall to zero.* We call this the **perfectly competitive market equilibrium**. At this market equilibrium, there is no further incentive for entry or exit.

perfectly competitive market equilibrium: the market equilibrium in a perfectly competitive market in which the economic profits of each individual seller are zero, and there is no incentive for entry or exit

It is important to remember that even though economic profits are zero at the perfectly competitive market equilibrium, each farmer is still making an *accounting* profit. For every bushel of corn up to point B in Figure 17.6, marginal revenue is greater than marginal cost. So each farmer is making an accounting profit on every bushel of corn up to point B. Perfect competition drives economic profits to zero, but not accounting profits.

We can ask one final question based on our corn farming example: What is P_1, the price that will eventually drive economic profits to zero? Algebraically solving for P_1 requires more math than we cover in this book, but you can solve for P_1 with some trial and error. You would calculate total revenues in Table 17.1 based on successively lower corn prices until the maximum attainable profit equals zero. For example, if the corn price were $3.90 per bushel instead of $4.00, 154 bushels of corn would sell for $600.60 (instead of $616.00). This is still higher than the total cost of $590, so an economic profit is still being made. Thus price at the perfectly competitive market equilibrium must be lower than $3.90. The solution for the perfectly competitive equilibrium price is slightly more than $3.83 per bushel. At this price, 154 bushels would sell for exactly $590, total revenues would equal total costs, and economic profits would be zero.*

Discussion Questions

1. Explain, in your words without a table or a graph, why economic profits fall to zero in a perfectly competitive market.
2. How useful do you think the model of a perfectly competitive market presented in this section is in explaining economic behavior in the real world? What do you think is the most relevant insight from the model?

4. LOSSES AND EXIT

In our corn example, each farmer is always making an accounting profit, even at the perfectly competitive market equilibrium. But in the real world, sometimes businesses do lose money and may even decide to shut down production and exit a market. In this section, we consider how a seller will behave when it is accruing losses rather than making a profit.**

4.1. LOSSES IN THE SHORT RUN

Let's suppose that the price of corn decreased to $3.60 per bushel, perhaps due to a decrease in the demand for corn. We can see how this affects an individual farmer by looking at Table 17.3. This is the same as Table 17.1 except that total revenues are now calculated based on a corn price of $3.60 per bushel instead of $4.00 per bushel. The fixed and variable costs of corn production have stayed the same.

We see that at the lower corn price, the "profit-maximizing" level of corn production, now at 150 bushels per acre with five bags of fertilizer, is actually a loss. The best that the farmer can do is to lose $35 per acre!

Table 17.3 **Impact of a Decrease in Corn Prices**

Quantity of nitrogen fertilizer (bags/acre)	Corn yield (bushels per acre)	Fixed costs ($)	Variable costs ($15 per bag of fertilizer)	Total costs ($)	Total revenues ($)	Economic profit/loss ($)
0	100	500	0	500	360	–140
1	115	500	15	515	414	–101
2	127	500	30	530	457	–73
3	137	500	45	545	493	–52
4	145	500	60	560	522	–38
5	150	500	75	575	540	–35
6	154	500	90	590	554	–36
7	157	500	105	605	565	–40
8	159	500	120	620	572	–48

*Note that in this particular example, the profit-maximizing level of production under the perfectly competitive market equilibrium remains 154 bushels of corn. However, as shown in Figure 17.6, the movement from point A to point B will generally result in a decrease in the optimal production level for each farmer. If we conducted this analysis such that farmers could add partial bags of fertilizer, then movement from point A to point B would result in a slight decrease in fertilizer application and thus a slight decrease in corn production per acre.

**In this section, we are still referring to economic, rather than accounting, losses.

Would it ever make sense for a farmer to stay in business when she is losing money? We know in the real world that businesses frequently lose money temporarily, only to make profits later. During the Great Recession in 2007–9, many businesses lost money, including banks and auto manufacturers. While some did go out of business, others survived and eventually returned to profitability.

Thus a farmer's decision comes down to whether she is willing and able to accept temporary losses, with the hope of making profits in the future, or quit farming. To understand how a rational farmer will behave, we have to recall, from Chapter 16, the distinction between the short run and the long run. In the short run, at least one input is fixed in quantity, and thus the cost of paying for any fixed inputs must be paid regardless of production levels. In the long run, all inputs are variable, and thus a seller can avoid paying all costs simply by leaving the market.

In our corn example, the fixed cost of $500 must be paid in the short term, regardless of the level of corn production. Even if the farmer decides to produce no corn, she must still pay this fixed cost. So the farmer's short-term production decision comes down to two options:

1. continue to produce some corn, even at a loss
2. produce no corn at all, and just pay the fixed costs

Table 17.3 shows that at 150 bushels of corn (the best the farmer can do), the farmer loses $35 per acre—total costs are $575, and total revenues are $540. Her other option is to not produce any corn. In this case, she will still have to pay her fixed cost of $500 per acre. She avoids having to pay any variable costs, but she also receives no revenues. So her losses will be $500 per acre if she produces no corn.

Obviously, it is better to lose only $35 per acre than to lose $500 per acre. By producing some corn, rather than none, she is able to more than cover her variable costs, recovering a large portion of her fixed costs as well. In other words, as long as she is able to cover her variable costs, in the short term it makes economic sense to continue production, even if losses are occurring.

A surprising implication of this conclusion is that *it does not matter how big the fixed costs are.* As long as there is something left over, after variable costs are paid, to go toward paying the fixed costs—*whatever they may be*—the farmer should continue to produce corn. Whether the fixed costs are $500 per acre or $5,000 per acre does not matter. You can prove this to yourself by calculating that the farmer does better by producing 150 bushels of corn and losing $4,535 per acre than by not producing and losing $5,000 per acre. The same would be true even if fixed costs were $1 million per acre!

sunk cost: an expenditure that was incurred or committed to in the past and is irreversible in the short run

This is a specific example of a more general economic principle concerning production decisions. *Sunk costs should not affect short-run production decisions.* A **sunk cost** is a cost that, in the short run, is the proverbial "water over the dam." The expense has already been incurred (or committed to) and cannot be reversed.

This principle often seems to contradict common sense. Humans seem to have an illogical but psychologically strong tendency to want to make past investments "pay off." And the larger the past investment, the more likely people are to be influenced by sunk costs. This is true not only of production decisions but of economic behavior in general. This is yet another example of seemingly irrational economic behavior, as we discussed in Chapter 8. Economics teaches us that when making decisions, we should focus on what is the best decision for us now and that past investment is irrelevant. (For some examples of how sunk costs can influence economic behavior, see Box 17.2.)

4.2 Losses in the Long Run

In the long run, all costs are variable. So in the long run the farmer can avoid having to pay the short-run fixed cost of $500 per acre simply by exiting the corn market. The farmer can

Box 17.2 Sunk Costs and Decision Making

Suppose that you have paid $50 in advance for a ticket to a concert. Assume that the ticket is nonrefundable and nontransferable. In other words, it is a sunk cost. But suppose that there is a blizzard the night of the concert, and traveling there would be miserable. Faced with a simple choice between relaxing at home and heading out into the blizzard to go to the concert, assume that you would prefer to stay home. But you have already paid $50 for the concert ticket. What do you do?

According to economic logic, the sunk cost of $50 should be irrelevant to your decision. What should matter is which option is the best choice for you now. But surveys show that many people are swayed by sunk costs and that the amount of the sunk cost matters. Now, suppose instead that you had won the concert ticket in a contest rather than paying $50 for it. Would that affect your decision? According to economic logic, it shouldn't.

It seems that people create "psychological accounts" in their heads about different expenditures, which can influence their decisions. Consider the following example from a paper published by Daniel Kahneman and his colleague Amos Tversky (recall that we discussed them in Chapter 8). First, suppose that you are going to see a play and the tickets cost $10. As you enter the theater, you discover that you have lost a $10 bill. Do you still pay $10 for a ticket? Their survey results indicate that 82 percent of respondents would still buy a ticket. Most people viewed the loss of $10 as belonging to a different "account" than the one used to pay for the ticket.

However, imagine that you have already paid $10 for a ticket and you discover as you enter the theater that you have lost the ticket. Do you pay $10 for another ticket? In this case, only about half of respondents would buy another ticket. In this case, many people consider buying another ticket equivalent to paying $20 for a ticket, and thus overpaying.

In either case, $10 is a sunk cost—you either lost a $10 bill or you already paid $10 for a ticket. So the decision in either case as you enter the theater is whether you should pay a marginal $10 to see the play. But how the sunk cost is presented to people does have a significant influence on their answer. As usual, human behavior is complicated and context does matter.

Sources: Hal R. Arkes and Catherine Blumer, "The Psychology of Sunk Cost," *Organizational Behavior and Human Decision Processes* 35 (1985): 124–140; Amos Tversky and Daniel Kahneman, "The Framing of Decisions and the Psychology of Choice," *Science* 211 (4481) (1981): 453–458.

sell her land and machinery and take up a different profession. In a perfectly competitive market, or any market, short-term losses may be rational, but in the long run exit becomes preferable to losing money.

Again, human behavior may be more complicated than this, and exiting a market may be a difficult decision. For example, the decision to sell a farm that has been in a family for generations may involve more than financial factors. Selling the farm, say to a developer, may also create negative externalities, such as the loss of wildlife habitat. What is optimal for an individual seller may not be optimal for social welfare. In some cases where farms are losing money, it may be better from a social welfare perspective to subsidize the farmer so that she does not feel compelled to sell to a developer.

Discussion Questions

1. "Why would anyone run a business if he couldn't make a profit?" This is a frequent response to economists' idea that all firms in a particular market make zero "economic profits."
   a. In your own words, explain what economists mean by zero economic profits and why an entrepreneur would choose to operate a perfectly competitive business.
   b. Explain why perfectly competitive firms are assumed to make zero economic profits in the long run.
2. Suppose that you are halfway through a particular course and you decide that you are not learning anything useful and the rest of the course is not worth your effort (obviously we are not describing this course!). It is too late to drop the course and sign up for another one. Is this an example of a sunk cost? How does economics suggest that you decide whether to complete the course?

5. PRODUCTION, EFFICIENCY, AND EQUITY

One of the implications of the perfectly competitive market model is that each firm *must* act in an economically efficient manner. As economic profits are assumed to be zero in the long run, any firm that operates in an inefficient manner will make negative economic profits. In the long run, inefficient firms will thus be forced out of the market.

But in the real world, inefficiencies may be quite common, even in markets that approach the conditions of perfect competition. We next consider two types of inefficiencies that may exist in any market. Then we end this chapter with a discussion of efficiency and equity in perfectly competitive markets.

5.1 PATH DEPENDENCE

path dependence: a condition that exists when economic developments depend on initial conditions and past events—that is, when "history matters"

Path dependence, a term borrowed from mathematics, basically means that "history matters" in determining how production technologies—and even entire economies—develop. When a process is path dependent, the way in which it develops may depend crucially on "initial conditions" and past events. The present state of manufactured capital or human capital, for example, can be thought of as making up part of the initial conditions for current production decisions.

Agriculture offers a good example of path dependence. For example, in the western part of Germany farms tend to be relatively small, but in the eastern part of Germany farms tend to be much larger. The explanation has nothing to do with a difference in the minimum efficient scale in the two regions. Instead, it is a result of history—until 1990 Germany was split into two countries, and in East Germany farms were organized by the government as large collectives.[1]

Another agricultural example of path dependence concerns the allocation of water rights in the western United States.[2] To promote agricultural development in the West, water rights were allocated under the "prior appropriation doctrine," which states that the first person to establish any beneficial use of a given quantity of water obtains the right to that quantity of water in the future. Other water users who come later may also obtain water rights by establishing beneficial uses, but they are able to access water only after the demands of all "senior" water rights holders, who established rights before them, have been met.

The allocation of water under the prior appropriation doctrine is based on history, not economic efficiency. As water demands have increased in the West, economists have advocated for the establishment of water markets that would allow water rights holders to trade water, theoretically allocating water to more efficient uses. However, the efficiency gains from water trading have been much smaller than predicted, as many water rights holders have been concerned that if they do not put their water to beneficial uses, but trade it instead, they may lose their rights. Even worse, prior appropriation encourages inefficient water use because it basically means "use it or lose it." So, rather than adopt efficient irrigation techniques and risk losing some of their water rights, farmers may continue to rely on inefficient practices.

Historical evidence suggests that health care in the United States also developed in a path-dependent fashion, rather than an economically efficient manner.[3] As part of the New Deal legislation in the 1930s, President Franklin Roosevelt supported universal public health-insurance coverage, but it was defeated in Congress. Then during World War II wage controls were implemented that prevented businesses from increasing wages. To attract workers while being unable to offer higher wages, some firms began to offer health-insurance coverage as a fringe benefit. Labor unions then began to demand health-insurance coverage from employers. As employer-provided health insurance became more common, interest in universal health care faded. The United States now spends more than any other country on health care, as a percentage of GDP, yet many of its health outcomes are rather mediocre. We discuss health care in the United States in more detail in Chapter 18.

5.2 NETWORK EXTERNALITIES

network externality (in production): a situation in which a particular technology or production process is more likely to be adopted because other economic actors have already adopted it

In addition to taking place in a historical context, production decisions also take place within a rich social context. Many technologies, such as standards for computers, automobiles, and kitchen appliance sizes, are widely shared. A production technology is characterized by a **network eternality** if people are more likely to adopt it, the more *other* people have adopted it.

A common example of a network externality is the widespread use of Microsoft Windows operating systems on personal computers (PCs). Although other operating systems, such as Linux and Macintosh, exist and offer some advantages, the vast majority of users have a computer with a Windows operating system mainly because that is what other users have adopted. The dominance of Windows is also an example of path dependence, because of the history in which Microsoft was able to gain a strong initial position in the PC market after it established a partnership with IBM in the 1980s. (Another interesting question, likely explained in part due to network externalities, is why students are much more likely than professors to use Macs.)

A network externality is a type of "positive feedback" loop—the more that people adopt a given technology, the more likely it is that additional people will adopt that technology. In the case of Microsoft Windows, as it became more common, more software and computers were designed for Windows. This makes it even more difficult for a new operating system to gain market share, even if it is more efficient.

Suppose that you develop an alternative to Windows that is superior in many respects. Most users will not adopt your operating system until they believe that a lot of software that they need will be written for it, that upgrades will be available in the future, and that they will be able to communicate easily with others. But none of this can be assured until your invention has been widely adopted across a whole network of users. Your problem is that in order to *gain* widespread adoption, you must already *have* it! Unless you are in a position to create a widespread network out of nothing—perhaps, for example, by blanketing the country with free software and training—your technically superior invention will not be adopted broadly.

A similar problem exists for a city that is trying to increase the use of public transportation in order to decrease road congestion and pollution. If most of the people in the city use the public transportation system, as in New York City and many European cities, it will seem like a normal thing to do, residential and workplace location patterns will reflect the availability of public transportation, the buses and subways will run frequently, and service may be so good that people freely choose it over using a private car. By contrast, if few people use public transportation, it may be stigmatized, routes and services will (in the absence of massive subsidies) tend to be very limited and inconvenient, residences and workplaces will tend to sprawl, and thus ridership will be further discouraged.

Network externalities create another way in which rational decision making by individuals can lead to inefficient production processes and a failure to maximize long-run social welfare. (See Box 17.3 for another example of path dependence and network externalities.)

5.3 MARKETS, EFFICIENCY, AND EQUITY

A perfectly competitive market is, under certain assumptions, economically efficient according to welfare analysis (as discussed in Chapter 6). In theory, if nothing prevents a perfectly competitive market from reaching equilibrium then the sum of consumer and producer surplus is maximized. However, this equilibrium is economically efficient only if:

1. There are no positive or negative externalities associated with the production and consumption of the good or service, including externalities that might occur in the future. As we discussed in Chapter 13, externalities may be pervasive, in terms of environmental or social effects.
2. All buyers and sellers have perfect information, or at least the ability to correctly determine when the marginal benefits of acquiring additional information become smaller than the

Box 17.3 The QWERTY Keyboard

A classic example of path dependency is the layout of typewriters and computer keyboards. The conventional QWERTY layout, named for the first several letters in the top left row, was developed in the nineteenth century and rapidly became the norm throughout the English-speaking world. The QWERTY layout was actually designed to *slow down* typing in order to prevent the keys from jamming on old-fashioned typewriters!

Studies with modern typewriters and computer keyboards have shown that the QWERTY layout is far from the most efficient. Alternative keyboard designs have been developed that, with sufficient practice, increase typing speeds and reduce errors. For example, the "Dvorak Simplified Keyboard," patented in the 1930s, groups common letter combinations together to reduce awkward finger movements. Also, based on the usage rates of different letters, about 70 percent of key strokes occur on the row of letters where people commonly rest their fingers, making it more ergonomic. However, efforts to market an alternative keyboard layout have consistently failed.

The major reason for the failure of alternatives to the QWERTY layout is that it has historically been built into an interlinked, economy-wide structure of equipment and training. Office equipment manufacturers are all set up to produce it. Keyboarding classes all teach it. A shift to a more efficient layout would entail substantial costs in time and money, even though long-run efficiency gains could be achieved.

In sum, you type on a QWERTY keyboard not because it is the most efficient layout but because of a historical quirk and the fact that everyone else is using it.

Source: Paul A. David, "Clio and the Economics of QWERTY," *American Economic Review* 75(2) (1985): 332–337.

marginal costs. As we discussed in Chapter 8, information is often lacking, even intentionally distorted to serve other economic interests, and economic actors often behave in ways that are inconsistent with the assumption of perfect information.

3. Consumer demand curves, based on willingness to pay, accurately reflect the benefits consumers obtain from their purchases. As we saw in Chapter 9, consumers often fail to accurately predict the benefits of goods and services.

So a market that meets all the conditions of perfect competition may still fail to maximize social and individual welfare if these additional conditions are not satisfied. Further, our analysis of perfect competition says nothing about whether the market outcome is considered equitable. An appealing feature of perfectly competitive markets to most economists is that they force firms to be efficient in their production decisions. As we mentioned at the start of this section, all perfectly competitive firms must be efficient or face going out of business. This production efficiency also ensures that consumers are offered the lowest possible prices. But the constant competitive pressure on firms can lead to job cuts and other cost-minimizing decisions that create social disruptions and externalities. For example, a perfectly competitive firm may try to temporarily capture positive economic profits by ignoring pollution regulations, increasing the negative externalities they impose on society.

Moving beyond a single perfectly competitive market, economists have proven that an entire economy that consists *only* of perfectly competitive markets will have an efficient allocation of all resources, without any government regulation.* This conclusion, which requires a complex mathematical proof, has been used by some economists to support limiting government involvement in markets.

Although no economy consists entirely of perfectly competitive markets, any movement toward the perfectly competitive ideal would seem to generally increase economic efficiency. However, this is not necessarily the case. In the 1950s the economists R.G. Lipsey and Kelvin

*This finding is known as the first fundamental theorem of welfare economics.

Lancaster demonstrated that *any* deviation from the perfectly competitive economy-wide ideal—even a slight deviation in a single market—may require government intervention in many markets to achieve the best possible outcome from the standpoint of economic efficiency.*

In the real world, the vast majority of markets in any economy are not perfectly competitive. Thus basing economic policy suggestions on an assumption of perfectly competitive markets is questionable, to say the least. Further, policy suggestions that focus exclusively on economic efficiency as a final goal, while ignoring other final goals such as environmental sustainability, fairness, and good social relations, are unlikely to be in the best interest of overall well-being.

So while our analysis of perfectly competitive markets is a useful tool in our economic toolbox, it does not say much about how the real world operates or what types of policies we should institute. More interesting and useful analyses concern what happens to markets when the conditions of perfect competition are not satisfied. But to understand these analyses, we first need to understand the perfectly competitive model presented in this chapter. In Chapter 18, we consider markets that are not perfectly competitive, including the implications of these markets for efficiency, fairness, and public policies.

Discussion Questions

1. Try to think of other examples, not mentioned in the text, of path dependence or network externalities. Do you think that these situations are inefficient? Do you think that government policy should play a role in eliminating path dependence and network externalities?
2. An interesting book published in the 1990s, titled *No Contest*, argues for the restructuring of society to promote cooperation rather than competition. The book contends that the pervasive existence of competition in society actually destroys social capital, creates anxiety, and lowers productivity. Do you think that there could be a viable alternative to an economy based on competitive pressures? Should government policies promote competition, cooperation, neither, or both?

REVIEW QUESTIONS

1. What is market power?
2. What is the business perspective on competition and market power?
3. What is the consumer perspective on competition and market power?
4. What is the citizen perspective on competition and market power?
5. What is the economists' perspective on competition and market power?
6. What are the four conditions of perfect competition?
7. What does the demand curve for a perfectly competitive seller look like?
8. What is the difference between accounting and economic profits?
9. How do we determine the profit-maximizing level of production using analysis of total costs and total revenues?
10. What is the rule for profit maximization using marginal analysis?
11. What happens to economic profits in a perfectly competitive market in the long run?
12. What is the graphical relationship between market conditions and an individual perfectly competitive seller's production decision?
13. What is the perfectly competitive market equilibrium?
14. What is a sunk cost? How does it influence production decisions, according to economic theory?
15. How should a producer decide whether to operate at a loss or shut down production in the short run?
16. Would a seller be expected to operate at a loss in the long run?
17. What is path dependence?
18. What are network externalities?
19. Under what conditions are perfectly competitive markets economically efficient?

*This finding is known as the theory of the second best.

EXERCISES

1. The Top Notch Grill's marginal costs of producing take-out meals are described below.

Quantity of meals	Marginal cost ($)
0	—
1	6
2	5
3	7
4	10
5	12
6	17

a. Assuming that the Grill has fixed costs of $7, what is its total cost at each level of production? (Add a column to the table.)
b. Assume that meals sell for $10 each and the Grill is a perfectly competitive firm. What are the Grill's total revenue (price × quantity), marginal revenue, and total profit (total revenue – total cost), at each level of production? (Add three more columns to the table.)
c. How many meals should the Grill produce, to maximize profits? Explain in a sentence or two how you arrived at your answer.

2. Suppose a firm that manufactures bicycles has the following cost structure:

Quantity of bicycles	Total cost ($)
0	50
1	100
2	200
3	400
4	800

a. How much does this firm have in fixed costs?
b. Using graph paper or a computer program, graph the total cost curve for this firm.
c. Suppose that bicycles sell for $200 each, and the firm is a price taker. Create a table showing the marginal cost, total cost, marginal revenue, total revenue (price × quantity), and total profit (total revenue – total cost) at each level of production.
d. Add a total revenue curve to the graph that you created in (b). Indicate with arrows the approximate quantity at which the vertical distance between the two curves is the greatest.
e. Would the firm make a profit by producing and selling only one bicycle? Would one bicycle be the best output level for the firm? What is the output level that maximizes profits?

3. Continuing with the bicycle firm described in the previous problem, consider how the firm's decision-making will change as the price of bicycles changes. For each of the following, make a new table.
a. If the price per bicycle were $100, what would the profit-maximizing level of output be? How much profit would the firm make?
b. If the price per bicycle were $20, what would the profit-maximizing level of output be? How much profit would the firm make?

4. Suppose that a perfectly competitive firm manufactures gizmos with the following cost structure (including all opportunity costs):

Quantity of gizmos	Total cost ($)
0	75
1	150
2	250
3	425
4	675

a. Calculate the marginal cost schedule for this firm in a table, and then graph the marginal cost curve.
b. If the price of gizmos on the market is $175 each, how many gizmos should the firm produce to maximize profits? What is the level of the firm's revenues at its chosen output level? How much does it make in profit?
c. Suppose that more firms start producing gizmos, and the market price drops to $125. How many gizmos should this firm now produce to maximize profits? (*Note:* In the case of discrete quantities such as these, interpret the $P = MC$ rule as "produce as long as price *is at least as great as* marginal cost.") What is this firm's new revenue level? How much does it make in profits?
d. When the price is $125, will more firms want to enter the market? Will existing firms want to exit?

5. Match each item in Column A with an example in Column B.

	Column A	Column B
a.	Condition for perfect competition	1. Accounting profits
b.	Business perspective on competition	2. I buy an iPhone because everyone else has iPhones
c.	Consumer perspective on competition	3. Competition drives prices lower, leading to bargain opportunities
d.	Type of profit equal to zero at the perfectly competitive market equilibrium	4. History matters
e.	Type of profit that is still positive at the perfectly competitive market equilibrium	5. Economic profits
f.	Network externality	6. A lack of market power can lead to efficiency
g.	Path dependence	7. The goal is to reduce or eliminate competition
h.	Economists' perspective on competition	8. Each firm is a price taker

Notes

1. Arlette Ostermeyer and Alfons Balmann, "Perception of Dairy Farming from Different Views—Results of a Stakeholder Discussion in the Region Altmark, Germany," paper presented at the EAAE 2011 Congress, Change and Uncertainty, Zurich, Switzerland, August 30–September 2, 2011.

2. Gary D. Libecap, "Institutional Path Dependence in Climate Adaptation: Coman's 'Some Unsettled Problems of Irrigation,' " *American Economic Review* 101 (2011): 1–19.

3. Scott E. Page, "Path Dependence," *Quarterly Journal of Political Science* 1 (2006): 87–115.

Appendix: A Formal Model of Perfect Competition

In this appendix, we present a formal conceptual model of perfect competition. We start by introducing new material on production costs and then combine that with the production decisions of a price-taking firm.

Recall from Chapter 16 the definition of average total cost (*ATC*) as total cost divided by the quantity produced. For example, if the total cost of producing 200 bushels of corn were \$800, the *ATC* would be \$4.00 (\$800 ÷ 200). *ATC* relates to marginal cost (*MC*) in the following manner:

- If $MC < ATC$, then *ATC* is decreasing
- If $MC > ATC$, then *ATC* is increasing
- When $ATC = MC$, *ATC* is at its lowest point

While this may seem difficult to grasp, consider the following analogy. Suppose that your current grade average in a class is a 90, and you get a new grade of 80 on a quiz. As your marginal grade (the quiz grade of 80) is lower than your average grade, your average grade will go down. However, if you instead score a 95 on the quiz, your marginal grade is higher than your average and your average will go up.

The relationship between *ATC* and *MC* is shown in Figure 17.7. We see that *ATC* starts out relatively high because fixed costs (which are often relatively large) are divided by a relative small quantity. As quantity increases, the average cost of production declines, even as marginal costs begin to rise (i.e., the reduction of *ATC* that is due to dividing by a larger

Figure 17.7 **The Relationship Between Average Total Costs and Marginal Costs**

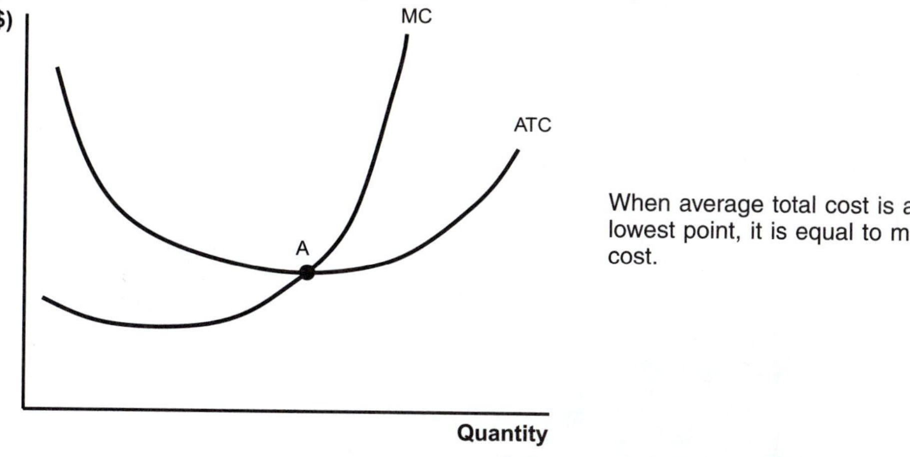

When average total cost is at its lowest point, it is equal to marginal cost.

average variable cost (*AVC*): total variable cost divided by the quantity produced

quantity more than offsets the rising marginal production costs). Eventually, the marginal cost rises above *ATC*, and then *ATC* rises. The minimum *ATC* is at point A.

Next we introduce a new cost variable, **average variable cost (*AVC*).** *AVC* is equal to total variable cost divided by quantity. As *AVC* excludes fixed costs, it will always be less than *ATC*. Like *ATC*, the minimum *AVC* will occur where it intercepts the *MC* curve. Realize that all marginal costs are variable costs. So whenever $MC < AVC$, *AVC* is declining, and whenever $MC > AVC$, *AVC* will rise.

In Figure 17.8 we have added an *AVC* curve to the graph shown in Figure 17.7. Note that the distance between *ATC* and *AVC* is initially large because fixed costs are divided by a relatively small quantity. As quantity increases, fixed costs become less dominant in determining *ATC*, and *AVC* moves closer to *ATC*.

We can refer to this graph to determine the total costs of producing a given quantity and divide total costs into fixed and variable costs, as shown in Figure 17.9. Production is at Q_0. Total cost is the average per-unit cost (*ATC*) multiplied by Q_0, or the entire shaded area in the graph. The total variable costs are obtained by multiplying Q_0 by the average variable cost, which is the blue-shaded area in the graph. The difference is fixed costs, the gray-shaded area. Note that the area of fixed costs must be the same for any level of production, as it does not vary according to production levels.

Suppose that price is initially at P_0. A perfectly competitive firm would produce where $P = MC$, or at point X in Figure 17.10. Assuming the firm's costs include opportunity costs,

Figure 17.8 **The Relationship Between Average Total Costs, Marginal Costs, and Average Variable Costs**

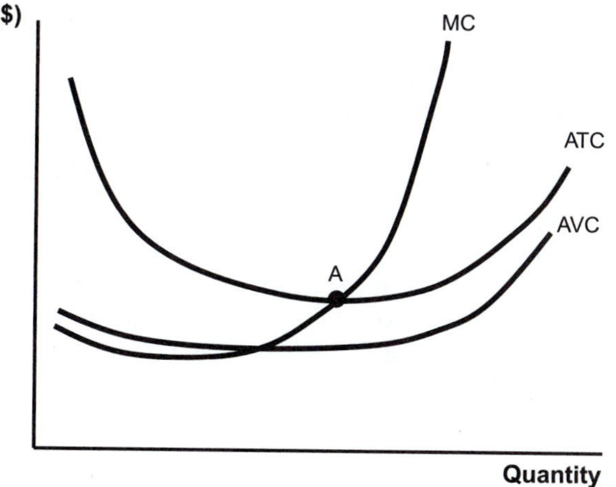

When average variable cost is at its lowest point, it is also equal to marginal cost.

Figure 17.9 **The Relationship Between Cost Curves and Areas of Total Costs, Fixed Costs, and Total Variable Costs**

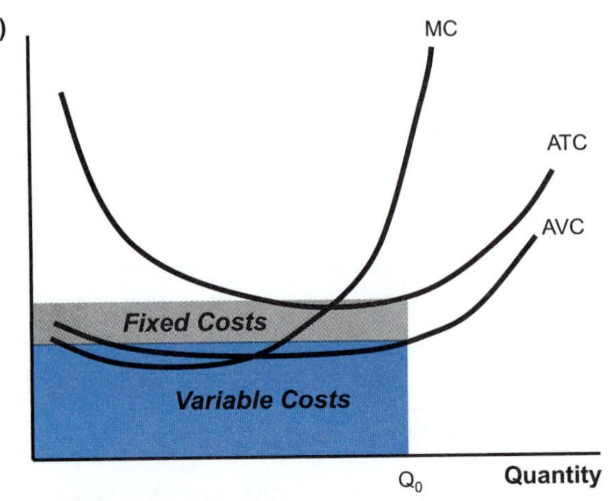

We can use the *ATC* and *AVC* curves to determine the areas of total costs, fixed costs, and variable costs for any level of production.

Figure 17.10 **Positive Economic Profits**

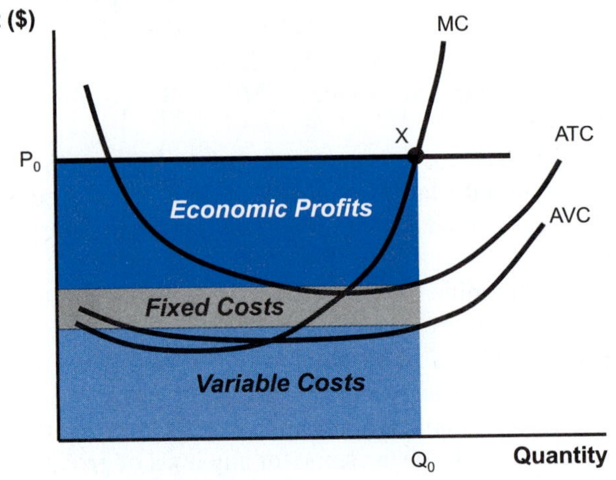

When price is greater than average total costs, a firm is making economic profits.

in this case the firm is making an economic profit, as shown in the graph as the blue-shaded area above the firm's total costs. Note that total revenues would be P_0 multiplied by Q_0, or the sum of all shaded areas.

As discussed in the chapter, the existence of economic profits creates an incentive for entry into the market. Assuming no barriers to entry, new firms will enter the market until economic profits are eliminated. This occurs when total revenues are just equal to total costs. As price falls, each perfectly competitive firm will reduce its production as the point where $P = MC$ moves to the left. The perfectly competitive market equilibrium is shown in Figure 17.11, with each firm producing at point Y (a quantity of Q_1 at a price of P_1). At this point, each firm is earning a zero economic profit—a profit just equal to what they could be making with their next-best alternative.

Finally, we consider the decision whether a firm should continue to produce in the short run while experiencing losses. As discussed in the chapter, perfectly competitive firms will continue to produce as long as they can recover their variable costs. So if price falls a little below P_1 in Figure 17.11, the firm will be making negative economic profits, but it will still be making enough revenues to cover its variable costs as well as pay some fixed costs—which is still better than shutting down production, earning no revenues, and having to pay all its fixed costs.

Figure 17.11 **Zero Economic Profits—The Perfectly Competitive Market Equilibrium**

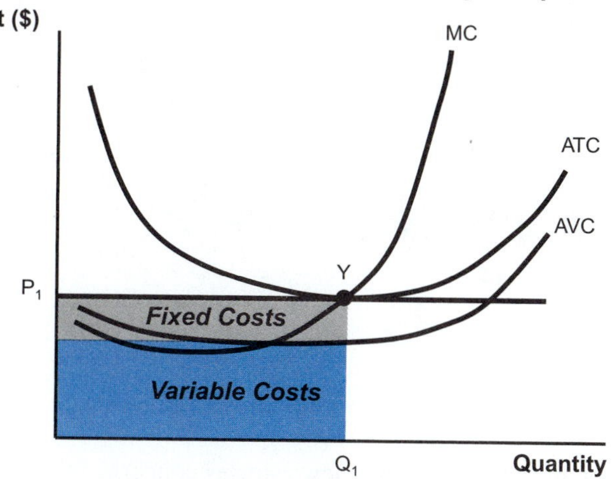

At the perfectly competitive market equilibrium, price equals *ATC* and each firm is making zero economic profits.

Eventually, the price will fall enough that the firm will not be able to cover its variable costs, and it is better off shutting down production and just paying its fixed costs, as illustrated in Figure 17.12. At a price of P_2 the firm produces at point Z (where $P = MC$) and makes just enough in revenues to cover its variable costs. However, if price falls below P_2, the firm will not be able to cover its variable costs and it is better off shutting down production and just paying its fixed costs.

Figure 17.12 **The Decision to Produce with Losses**

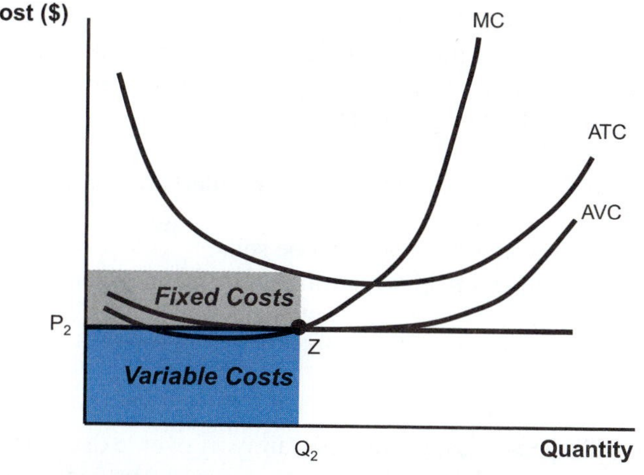

In the short run, a firm will continue to produce as long as revenues are sufficient to cover its variable costs.

18 Markets with Market Power

At the turn of the century, one of the ongoing big news stories concerned the lawsuits being brought against Microsoft—a company that had made its founder, Bill Gates, the richest person on the planet. At issue was the question of whether Microsoft had too much control over its market—in other words, whether its "market power" was excessive. As we will see, markets are rarely as competitive as described under the conditions of perfect competition from the last chapter. Indeed, many industries—from transportation and utilities to agriculture and health care—are characterized by a considerable degree of market power.

1. The Traditional Models

Traditional neoclassical economics asks the question: "How do the number of firms in a product market and the characteristics of the good being sold affect the profit-maximizing decisions of the firm?" The four traditional types of market structure are perfect competition, pure monopoly, monopolistic competition, and oligopoly.

- perfect competition: the situation in which there are many sellers, selling identical goods (see Chapter 17)
- **pure monopoly**: the situation in which there is only one seller
- **monopolistic competition**: the situation in which there are many sellers, but they sell slightly different things
- **oligopoly**: the situation in which there are so few sellers that each needs to watch what the others are doing

pure monopoly: the situation in which there is only one seller

monopolistic competition: the situation in which there are many sellers, but they sell slightly different things

oligopoly: the situation in which there are so few sellers that each needs to watch what the others are doing

The first two are "idealized" types because they do rarely, if ever, exist in their "pure" form. In other words, although competition may exist to a significant degree, it is never "perfect"; and absolute monopolies also do not exist in the United States because they are prohibited by laws meant to encourage competitive behavior. These two "idealized types" are at opposite ends of a "competitiveness continuum," along which we find the other two types, monopolistic competition and oligopoly. Basically, the degree of competitiveness within an industry will inform whether the market more closely resembles monopolistic competition or oligopoly. In the latter case, markets are found to be truly complex, evolving social *organizations*. Arguably, oligopoly is the most important and prevalent type of market in contemporary industrialized economies.

Why model the first two types if they do not occur in the real world? As we have seen in earlier chapters, economists often sacrifice some realism in their analytical models in order to present simplified cases that can provide useful insights into economic behavior and decisions. The perfect competition and monopoly outcomes represent baseline cases to which we can then compare our conclusions about monopolistic competition and oligopoly.

2. Pure Monopoly: One Seller

The case that is diametrically opposed to perfect competition is pure monopoly, in which there is only one seller. As in the case of perfect competition, the traditional model of profit maximization for monopoly leads to clear and definite predictions. But the predicted outcomes are, perhaps not surprisingly, very different from those of the perfect competition model.

2.1 The Conditions of Monopoly

Monopoly is characterized by the following conditions:

1. There is only *one seller.*
2. The good being sold has *no close substitutes.* This means that buyers must buy from the monopolist or not at all.
3. *Barriers to entry* prevent other firms from starting to produce the good.

barriers to entry: economic, legal, or deliberate obstacles that keep new sellers from entering a market

Because the monopolist is the only seller in the market, it faces no competition from other firms. The condition of "no close substitutes" means that the good that the monopolist sells must be substantially different from anything else, so the monopolist does not have to worry about losing buyers to markets for similar, even if not identical, goods. If the monopolist made economic profits, other firms would, of course, want to enter the market. **Barriers to entry** are necessary to keep those other firms out. They come in three major kinds: economic barriers, legal barriers, and deliberate barriers.

Economic Barriers

Economic barriers derive primarily from the nature of the production technology. For example, the production technology may be characterized by high fixed costs, economies of scale, or network externalities.

High fixed costs prevent potential competitors from entering the industry on a small scale and expanding, because while they are small they cannot generate enough revenue to recover the sizable fixed costs. Competitors must therefore enter as very large-scale operations, which may be a difficult and risky thing to do. For example, the large initial investment required to build facilities that can produce specialized military aircraft make it difficult for any potential entrant to challenge existing firms.

natural monopoly: a monopoly that arises because the minimum efficient scale of the producing unit is large relative to the total market demand

The size of the market relative to the minimum efficient scale of a firm is also important (recall our discussion in Chapter 16). A monopoly will likely arise if the minimum efficient scale is large enough to correspond to the majority of a particular market. In such situations, any firm with less than the majority of the market will be producing at higher per-unit costs than a firm that is producing above the minimum efficient scale. Ultimately, these smaller competitors will be uncompetitive compared to a firm with monopoly power. A monopoly that emerges because of economies of scale is called a **natural monopoly**.

Network externalities (see Chapter 17) can also lead to monopolization. The fact that most PC users have come to use Windows operating systems and software written for those systems gives Microsoft an advantage that a competitor would find extremely hard to challenge.

Legal Barriers

Legal barriers include copyrights (which protect creative works), franchises and concessions (which directly prohibit entry), patents (which prevent other firms from using innovations), and trademarks (which protect brand names). Legal barriers provide the oldest and most secure foundations for monopoly. In times past, kings frequently granted monopoly rights as a reward for services rendered to them. In the United States, patent protection allows a firm exclusive use of an invention for an extended period of time, usually 17 to 20 years. If the invention produces a new and unique good or facilitates production at much lower costs than competitors incur, a monopoly can result.

How can one determine which type of enterprise, brand, or type of work deserves such legal protection? Critics often argue that the government is excessively generous in providing patents or trademarks, which can stifle market competition, noting that a well-endowed firm with market power has resources available to lobby the government to grant such concessions. When this occurs, it is another example of the rent-seeking behavior described in earlier chapters.

Deliberate Barriers

exclusionary practices: when a firm gets its suppliers or distributors to agree not to provide goods or services to potential competitors

A deliberate barrier involves the physical, financial, or political intimidation of potential competitors. Not surprisingly, many such "barriers" are illegal. For example, a monopolist might induce the supplier of an essential raw material not to supply potential competitors, or it might get a distributor to agree not to distribute products produced by a rival. Such deals, designed to exclude competitors from access to necessary goods and services, are called **exclusionary practices**.

predatory pricing: a powerful seller's temporary pricing of its goods or services below cost, in order to drive weaker competitors out of business

dumping: selling in foreign countries at prices that are below the firm's costs of production

A powerful monopolist might also discourage potential competitors by engaging in **predatory pricing**. Whenever small competitors enter the market, the monopolist may temporarily lower the price of its product to a level so low that it does not cover costs, in order to drive its new rivals out of business. In international markets, selling output in another country at prices below the cost of domestic production is called **dumping**.

A powerful monopolist might also threaten smaller potential competitors with unfounded (but very expensive) lawsuits, in attempts to intimidate or bankrupt them. In such cases, the size of the monopolist relative to potential competitors is clearly important: These strategies are possible only for relatively large, established firms with "deep pockets." Acts of violence are not unheard of as barriers to entry, most notably in monopolies run by organized crime.

2.2 EXAMPLES OF MONOPOLY

local monopoly: a monopoly limited to a specific geographic area

Although earlier we described monopoly as an "idealized" case, rarely if ever found in reality, examples of *near*-monopolies are fairly easy to find. For example, we have already mentioned Microsoft's dominance in PC operating systems. If a firm is the only supplier in a given geographic area, it is called a **local monopoly**. For example, a small, isolated town may have only one hardware store, which has a local monopoly for the sale of certain products. A university bookstore is another example of a local monopoly, in the provision of textbooks (although the store may face competition from online retailers).

regulated monopoly: a monopoly run under government supervision

Older textbooks often cited industries in transportation, communications, and public utilities as examples of natural monopolies. Until relatively recently, for example, the U.S. Postal Service had a monopoly on the delivery of letters and packages. Railroads, phone companies, and electric companies were traditionally operated either directly by the government or as **regulated monopolies**—that is, private companies run under government supervision. It would obviously have been inefficient, it was often argued, to have two mail carriers delivering to the same house, or two lines of railroad tracks, or multiple separate grids of electrical transmission wires.

In recent years, however, competition, deregulation, and privatization have complicated this picture. Nowadays, the U.S. Postal Service has competition in many markets from FedEx, UPS, and other firms, and it is not rare to see trucks with each of the three insignias delivering to the same business district or neighborhood on the same day. Market structure in communications and utilities has become more sophisticated; the aspects with large economies of scale (such as maintenance of the electrical grid) are separated from parts of the business where economies of scale are not so great (such as generation of electricity). What might once have seemed obvious (i.e., that utilities should be run as natural monopolies) may therefore no longer be so.

2.3 PROFIT MAXIMIZATION FOR A MONOPOLIST

In choosing what level of output to produce, a monopolistic firm follows the general pattern of behavior of a profit-maximizing firm as described in Chapter 17, seeking the level at which its marginal cost is equal to its marginal revenue ($MC = MR$). But although its costs are determined in the same way as those of a perfectly competitive firm, its revenues are significantly different.

A price-taking firm has such a small market share that it can sell however much of its product it chooses to at the going price. Because it is "small," no amount sold would, in theory, have any impact on the price determined by market conditions of supply and demand. In contrast, because a monopolistic firm is the sole supplier of a given product, it possesses enormous influence over the price of its product. Whereas the demand curve for the price-taking firm is horizontal, reflecting the firm's powerlessness over price, the demand curve for the monopolist's output is identical to the overall market demand curve for that product. In other words, it slopes downward.

The monopolistic firm is able to sell more only by inducing consumers as a group to buy more. That is, to sell more it must either mount an effective advertising campaign (to shift out the demand curve that it faces) or offer its product at a lower price. Another way to look at the difference is to note that the monopolist can raise its price, losing some sales but obtaining more revenue per unit for those remaining. In contrast, the price-taking firm will sell absolutely nothing if it raises its price above the existing market level. In short, a monopolist is a **price maker**, not a price taker. It can set both price and quantity, although the price-quantity combinations that it can choose are constrained by market demand.

price maker: a seller that can set the selling price, constrained only by demand conditions

Consider how a producer would behave if, instead of receiving a flat amount for each unit of output sold, it were a monopolist and faced the full schedule of market demand. Table 18.1 shows how the firm must, in order to sell more of its output, drop its selling price. It can sell 1 unit if it sets the price at $44, for example. But if it wants to sell 2 units, it must drop the price to $40 each in order to find another buyer. The first two columns of Table 18.1 thus describe the demand curve for this good.

The fourth column in Table 18.1 indicates how much *extra* revenue the monopolist would gain for producing and selling an additional unit. Although initial revenue for selling 1 unit is $44, if the monopolist wants instead to sell 2 units it must sell *both* units at the lower price of $40, receiving total revenue of $80. It thus gains $40 from selling the second unit but also loses the $4 (from the original $44) that it would have gotten from selling the first unit alone. Marginal revenue from the second unit, then, is only $36 (40 minus 4 or, what amounts to the same thing, 80 minus 44).

The remainder of Table 18.1 is calculated in the same fashion. Note that after the monopolist sells 6 units, total revenue starts to go *down* (from its peak at $144), and marginal revenue becomes negative. Recall from Chapter 5 that the upper regions of demand curves (where

Table 18.1 **Marginal Revenue for a Monopolist**

Quantity of output	Selling price ($)	Total revenue ($)	Marginal revenue ($)
1	44	44	44
2	40	80	36
3	36	108	28
4	32	128	20
5	28	140	12
6	24	144	4
7	20	140	–4
8	16	128	–12
9	12	108	–20

quantities are low and prices are high) tend to be elastic, meaning that reductions in price increase revenue. The lower regions tend to be inelastic, such that reductions in price *decrease* revenue. This is exactly what is illustrated numerically in Table 18.1.

We can use the data from Table 18.1 to construct a demand curve for the good, as well as a marginal revenue curve. These are shown in Figure 18.1. The marginal revenue curve lies below the demand curve (after the first unit) and falls off more steeply, entering the negative part of the graph after 6 units.

Figure 18.1 also shows the marginal cost curve for the good, which is similar to the cost curves we derived in Chapter 16. (The cost curves are independent of whether a producer is competitive or a monopolist; only the demand side of the market is different.) The monopolist will maximize profits by producing the quantity at which $MR = MC$, which occurs at point A in Figure 18.1. This is an output level of 5 units. Reading horizontally from the *MC* curve, you see that the marginal cost of producing the fifth unit is $12. The graph and table show that the marginal revenue from the fifth unit is also $12.

Figure 18.1 **Monopoly Profit Maximization**

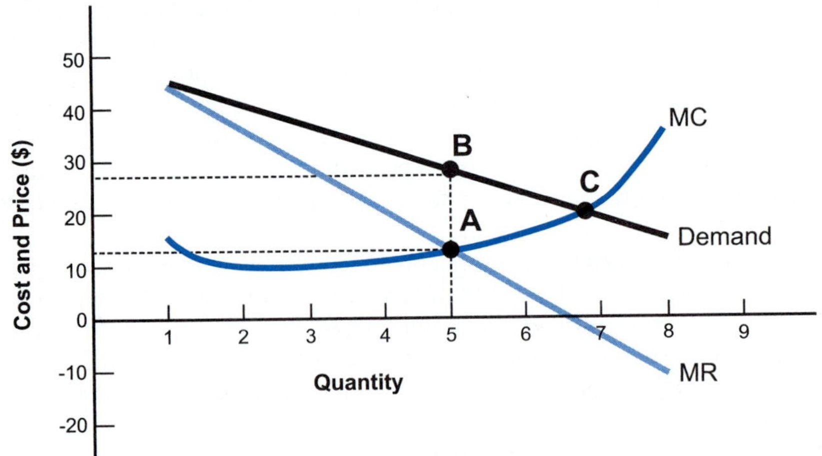

A monopolist decides how much to produce by setting marginal cost equal to marginal revenue (point A). The price that buyers are willing to pay for this quantity is read off the demand curve (point B). The monopolist produces less, and charges more, than would firms in a competitive equilibrium (point C).

The monopolist, however, will not charge its customers $12 per unit. Reading up from a quantity of 5 to the demand curve, we see that customers are willing to pay up to $28 each for the 5 units produced, as shown by point B on the demand curve in Figure 18.1 (see also the "Selling price" column in Table 18.1). The monopolist will produce at a marginal cost to itself of $12 per unit but will charge customers $28 per unit to maximize profits.

What level of profits will the monopolist make in the long run? Unlike in the competitive case, in which we assume that economic profits are driven to zero by the entrance of new producers, monopolists *can* make sustained positive economic profits, as long as barriers to entry keep potential competitors out. To determine the actual level of profits, you need to know more about the cost structure of the firm. This is investigated in the appendix to this chapter. If the monopolist's cost structure is such that it makes economic *losses,* presumably in the long run it will choose to exit the industry.

2.4 Monopoly and Inefficiency

Monopoly power generally leads to inefficiencies in the form of deadweight loss (discussed in Chapter 6), when compared to a competitive outcome. Because the monopolist produces at an output level at which the marginal willingness to pay (price) exceeds marginal cost, society could gain from increased output of the product. From the point of view of society, in other words, the cost of additional production is lower than the marginal benefits.

In the above example, buyers value the sixth unit at $24, whereas the cost of producing the sixth unit is less than $24 (as seen in Figure 18.1). The social benefit of producing the sixth unit is greater than the social marginal cost, and society would be better off if it were produced. The "curving triangle" ABC in Figure 18.1 represents the deadweight loss from the monopolist's decision, compared to a competitive situation in which marginal willingness to pay and marginal cost would be equal (at point C, where 7 units are produced).

Another way to examine the efficiency and distributional effects is to analyze producer surplus and consumer surplus. In Figure 18.2 the competitive equilibrium (price-taking) situation is portrayed by thinking of the *MC* curve as the sum of the *MC* curves of numerous competitive firms. The resulting competitive price and quantity are P_E and Q_E. The contrasting monopoly price and quantity are P_M and Q_M. As we have just noted, the fact that the monopolist will supply a lower quantity and charge a higher price creates deadweight loss. It also causes a distributional shift away from the buyers of the good and toward the monopolist. The rectangle labeled "transfer" would be part of consumer surplus in a competitive market, but the monopolist extracts the value represented by the rectangle from the consumer, thus *reducing overall consumer surplus.* Market power creates more benefit for the seller—which is why businesses like to get it—but at the expense of buyers of the good (lost consumer surplus) and of efficiency for society as a whole as it creates a deadweight loss relative to the competitive outcome.

Figure 18.2 **The Welfare Costs of Monopoly Power**

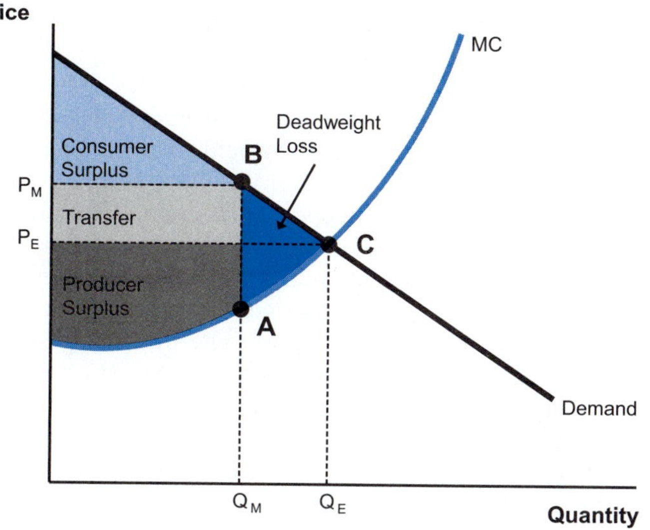

A monopolist imposes a deadweight loss on society relative to a situation of perfect competition and transfers surplus from consumers to itself.

Sometimes, people justify monopolies on the grounds that they create situations that foster innovation. Other justifications note that, in the 1950s and 1960s, the large U.S. firms in the steel and automotive industries shared some of their monopoly profits with their workers, providing levels of wages and benefits (especially pensions) that helped cast large firms with such market power in a positive light. Such benefits could not, however, be maintained when foreign competition forced them to cut such costs in order to remain profitable. But there are other economic objections to monopoly power. One of the most common is the claim that a lack of competition makes a monopolist lazy. A secure monopolist has less incentive to please customers, manage costs efficiently, and adopt new ideas than a firm that has its survival on the line. We should, moreover, consider what monopolists do with their positive economic profits. A monopolist may, in fact, need to spend most or all of the profits merely keeping entry barriers up. For instance, when monopolies are generated by exclusive concessions or licenses given out by governments, producers might spend much or all of their economic profits on rent-seeking activities of lobbying and bribing government officials in order to maintain their exclusive right to produce a good.

2.5 Can Monopoly Be Efficient?

However, in some situations the efficiency cost of monopoly may not be as negative as the foregoing analysis suggests. In some cases, monopoly may even be preferable to a competitive market.

Natural Monopoly

We have already mentioned one case in which a single big firm may be socially preferable to many small ones: natural monopoly. Competitive firms would face per-unit costs that were unnecessarily high, but a monopolist could exploit its economies of scale. Often, natural monopolies are regulated. The government allows only one firm to produce the good but mandates that it produce at higher levels, and sell at lower prices, than the firm would choose on its own. One prominent example is the Metropolitan Transportation Authority in greater New York. A private company that provides a variety of public transportation services, it is fundamentally a monopoly, but the local government regulates its pricing policy.

Regulated monopolies can, nonetheless, present the government with a dilemma, especially when substantial economies of scale are present. Often the marginal cost of production is very low. For example, on a passenger railroad line the marginal cost of transporting one more rider, assuming some seats are empty, is very low after the rails, engines, and schedules are all in place. Efficiently setting the price of a ticket equal to the marginal cost of providing a ride, however, would mean that the monopolist's revenues would not cover its costs, making its business untenable.

In some cases, the government subsidizes the monopolist to encourage socially beneficial price setting and levels of production. But although subsidies are a commonsense manner of persuading natural monopolists to increase production, they are politically very unpopular: Many taxpayers resent having their tax dollars go to private companies. Rather than regulating price, government might also regulate the company's profit rate or its output level. Alas, each comes with its own problem. Compelling companies not to exceed a specified profit rate creates an incentive to engage in wasteful spending (on, e.g., excess administration or perks for company executives), because higher costs permit the generation of greater absolute profits, whatever the maximum profit *rate*. And requiring companies to provide a minimum level of output to meet the needs of society creates an incentive to skimp on quality of service and materials used, in order to cut costs and thereby earn a higher profit. So although it is certainly true that natural monopolies make sense in certain industries and that such monopolies must be regulated, there is no single optimal method of regulation. It is likely to depend on the individual case.

Despite the economic case in favor of natural monopolies in some instances, many economists argue that *all* monopolies should be discouraged, if not abolished, because of their belief that competition always leads to a more efficient distribution and, invariably, lower prices. In recent decades, a significant deregulation of natural monopolies has taken place and not only in the United States. One well-publicized case was the privatization of municipal water supplies in Bolivia in the late 1990s. Such a move does not always deliver the expected benefits, namely, lower prices and greater availability of the commodity for consumers (see Box 18.1).

Box 18.1 Privatization of Municipal Water Supplies

Municipal water supply is a common example of a natural monopoly. The significant fixed cost of water treatment facilities and supply pipes means that the minimum efficient scale is normally so large that it forms an effective barrier to entry for potential competitors. Municipal water has been traditionally supplied either by nonprofit public utilities or by highly regulated private companies that are limited in the prices that they can charge their customers.

In recent decades, some economists have proposed moving toward a greater degree of privatization of municipal water supplies, with fewer regulations on the prices that companies can charge. With water privatization, different companies bid for the right to become the monopoly provider. Under most privatization contracts, which commonly last for four to ten years, the water supply infrastructure remains publicly owned. However, proponents of privatization contend that for-profit companies will be motivated to operate water supply systems in a more efficient manner than public utilities.

Privatization of water supplies has been most controversial in developing countries. In the late 1990s, the World Bank pushed scores of poor countries to privatize their water supplies as a condition for receiving much-needed economic assistance. In several cases, most infamously Bolivia, private companies raised the price of water so much that poor families could not afford enough to meet basic needs.

The need for better water management is especially acute in China. With contracts to supply water becoming more lucrative, the number of private water utilities in China has skyrocketed. As water demands increase in Beijing, wells dug around the city must reach ever-greater depths to hit fresh water. But in China private water suppliers must pay the cost of constructing new wells. In order to recover investment costs, companies have dramatically raised the price of water. "It's more than most families can afford to pay," says Ge Yun, an economist with the Xinjiang Conservation Fund. "So as more water goes private, fewer people have access to it."

The World Bank continues to promote privatization, noting that higher water prices are necessary to induce conservation. Public utilities rarely charge enough to reflect the true economic and social costs of water; privatization advocates argue that this is the root cause of unsustainable water use. From the perspective of social welfare, market prices are too low if they fail to account for externalities. But economic efficiency may conflict with the goal of equity. Privatization may work best when combined with policies ensuring that the poorest can afford enough water to meet their basic needs, as in the South African system, which provides a minimum supply of water to all households free to ensure that basic needs can be met. Only water usage above this minimum amount is billed to households.

Source: Jennen Interlandi, "The New Oil: Should Private Companies Control Our Most Precious Natural Resource?" *Newsweek*, October 18, 2010.

Intellectual Property

The problem of covering costs arises again in the case of research costs for the development of new technologies. Patents, copyrights, and other protections of intellectual property are not granted simply to enrich inventors. The rationale for these forms of government-granted monopoly power is to *encourage* research and innovation. Development of new computer technologies, medical technologies, and drugs can be very expensive. Firms argue that they need a period of exclusive, high profits to finance their research and development. Without the ability to patent an innovation, it is argued, firms might find research unprofitable and so do less of it, to the detriment of all.

Of course, patents also have a social cost in that they restrict the production of some important and valuable goods while raising their price. The cost can be extremely high: In many cases, restricted access to certain indispensable medications results in unnecessary human suffering and premature death. Also, as societies become more concerned about climate change, there is concern that allowing new low-emission energy technologies to be patented could slow their rates of adoption, as the owner of the patent would produce such technologies based on maximum profit, not social need. Other forms of government action have been suggested as ways of encouraging invention that would not carry the patent system's harmful effect of restricting production and use. These include direct funding of research, offering research prizes, and buying patents from companies for a one-time fee.

Pressure to Appear Competitive

In the idealized case of pure monopoly, the seller is free to maximize profits. But do unregulated monopolists in the real world always maximize profits? Even if a monopolist faces neither a serious rival nor any meaningful government restriction, it may fear *potential* competitors or government action. If so, the monopolist might produce and price in a way that more closely resembles a competitive firm, out of fear that excessive monopoly profits would attract too much attention.

Often the barriers protecting a monopoly can be bypassed by producing a similar, though not identical, product. Monopolies held by American railroads in the early twentieth century, for example, were weakened not by competing railroads but by truck and airline competition that increased the elasticity of demand for railroad transportation. Textbooks written as recently as the 1970s sometimes asserted that competition between telephone companies and postal systems was impossible, because there was no way of sending documents by telephone—an idea that seems quaintly old-fashioned in an era of fax machines and e-mail. Microsoft has argued that even though it currently enjoys a near-monopoly, it is "competitive" in a dynamic sense because new technologies could arise at any time to upset its dominance in the market for PC operating systems.

Firms with market power might also be cautious out of fear of government action. Since the 1930s, most industrialized countries have created government agencies charged with investigating cases of monopoly power. Governments may take over monopolies, regulate them, or break them up into smaller companies if their existence is found to be socially harmful. The first ruling in the *United States vs. Microsoft* case (in which Microsoft was charged with violating antitrust statutes and engaging in abusive practices in its operating system and Web browser sales) mandated a breakup, although a federal appeals court ruling focused instead on changing its business practices. Some monopolists may refrain from fully exploiting their power in order to be less visibly irksome—hence less likely to be targeted for the sort of attention that Microsoft repeatedly receives.

Perfect Price Discrimination

Although we usually think of firms as charging the same price to all buyers, this need not be the case. An interesting—if rare—welfare result occurs in the case of what is called a "perfectly price-discriminating" monopolist.

price discrimination: a seller's charging different prices to different buyers, depending on their ability and willingness to pay

A **price-discriminating** seller is one that charges different prices to different buyers, depending on their ability and willingness to pay. How can a seller do this? One way is to keep its prices a secret. In the real world, car salespeople often carry out a version of price discrimination, offering a price that is closer to the list price and pressing more options on a buyer who comes into the showroom dressed in expensive clothing, while more rapidly offering discounts to a less–affluent-looking client. Airline companies characteristically do something similar, charging business travelers—who are generally quite inflexible about when they must fly—a higher price, on average, than vacationers. A clever way of doing this is by offering discounts for flights that require a weekend stay away (because doing so generally excludes business travelers).

Another way is to offer discounts structured so that some people, but—importantly—not others, will pass them up. Why do stores sometimes offer bulk discounts or "two for the price of one" sales or offer discounts only if you come on particular "sale days" or go to the trouble of bringing in a coupon? They are also trying to separate out the price-unresponsive

Figure 18.3 **Price Discrimination**

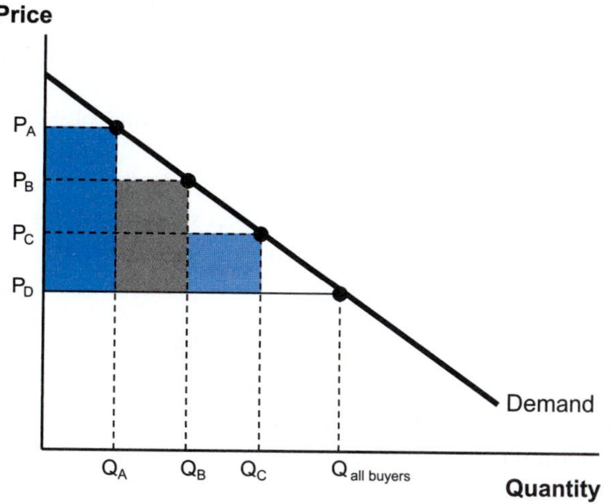

A price-discriminating seller can charge different prices to different people, thereby capturing what would otherwise be consumer surplus.

customers (who will buy anyway) from the price-responsive ones, who will take the time and trouble to find sales, mail in coupons for rebates, and so on.

This possibility is illustrated in the demand curve in Figure 18.3. Customer A does not care about getting a low price and would be willing to pay price P_A for the first few units (Q_A) of the good. The seller would like to be able to charge Customer A this high price and then drop the price a little for Customer B, who would not buy any of the good at price P_A but is happy to buy at price P_B, increasing the total quantity sold to Q_B. And so on. In this case, consumer surplus is whittled away—each customer is paying close to the maximum that he or she is willing to pay. The seller is reaping the benefits—extra revenue, represented by shaded rectangles on the graph, for each sale made above the price charged to the last buyer (P_D). Compare this to the "baseline" monopoly case discussed earlier. Remember that the monopolist faced the dilemma of undercutting itself by lowering the price on all goods sold by offering more to consumers; in the case of price discrimination, this problem is at least partially overcome.

If a monopolist could vary the price continuously—that is, not in discrete steps but over the entire demand curve, as shown in Figure 18.4—it would be engaging in "perfect" price discrimination. In such a hypothetical case, the monopolist captures the entire consumer surplus. Consumers therefore "gain" nothing from their purchases, because everyone spends exactly how much he or she is willing to pay—not a penny less. From a social point of view, a large transfer of benefit takes place from buyers to the monopolist. But the earlier deadweight efficiency

Figure 18.4 **Perfectly Price-Discriminating Monopolist**

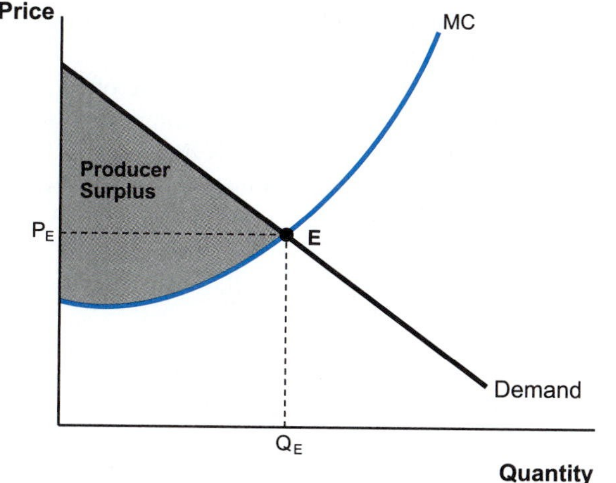

With perfect price discrimination, a monopolist has no reason to restrict output and will therefore create no deadweight loss.

loss would also be eliminated, in contrast to the case of a monopolist that is *not* perfectly price discriminating. This is because the seller in this case has no reason to restrict output and would produce until $P = MC$, which is no different from the outcome under perfect competition.

The equity consequences of price discrimination are interesting. In a case in which the monopolist reaps large profits at consumers' expense, price discrimination seems unfair to consumers. However, price discrimination may sometimes just allow a producer to break even. The only nonprofit mental health clinic in town, for example, may offer its services on a "sliding scale," in which the price charged to a client rises with his or her income. The care given to lower-income clients is thus subsidized by the higher prices paid by those with a higher ability to pay. If it were forced to charge only a single price, the clinic might have to close or turn away its poorest clients.

We can summarize the discussion of monopolies and efficiency in a few points:

- In cases in which a monopolist could be broken up into many cost-efficient, more competitive firms, the competitive option would generally be more socially beneficial.
- In cases of natural monopolies, in which competitive firms would not be cost efficient, the question is not one of "monopoly versus competition" but, rather, one of how best to structure and regulate a monopoly.
- When it comes to fostering innovation, a system of government-granted exclusive monopoly rights may bring about benefits. However, alternative methods of encouraging research and development might bring about even higher benefits.
- Monopolists that fear potential competition or government regulatory action might behave in a more socially efficient manner than otherwise (something not considered by the baseline monopoly model).
- Perfectly price-discriminating monopolists do not restrict output, and therefore cause no efficiency loss, but their actions may lead to concerns about negative distributional consequences.

As noted earlier, however, cases of *pure* monopoly happen extremely rarely—if at all—in the real world. Most goods have *some* reasonable substitutes. If railroads were monopolized, people might turn to trucks or cars, for example. Even if only one drug company produced the most effective drug for a medical condition, drugs produced by other companies can normally at least help. This brings us to a discussion of cases that are neither perfect competition nor pure monopoly.

Discussion Questions

1. On many campuses, the official college or university bookstores used to have monopoly power in selling textbooks to students. What would you call this kind of monopoly? Is it still the case at your institution? Why or why not?
2. Does it sometimes make sense to have just one company in charge of providing something? Some users of electronics are frustrated by the lack of compatibility among their gadgets and between their gadgets and those of their friends. Might it be better to have just one company manufacture computers, gaming machines, music players, cell phones, and the like in such a way that they all work smoothly with one another? What would be the advantages and disadvantages of such a situation?

3. MONOPOLISTIC COMPETITION

Monopolistic competition shares characteristics with both perfect competition and monopoly. Because of its name, however, many students confuse monopolistic competition with monopoly. It is important not to, because monopolistic competition is generally closer to the competitive end of the spectrum.

3.1 THE CONDITIONS OF MONOPOLISTIC COMPETITION

Monopolistic competition is generally characterized by the following conditions:

1. There are numerous small buyers and sellers.
2. The sellers produce goods that are close substitutes but are not identical. Products are often *differentiated,* which means that each seller's product is somewhat different from that offered by the other sellers.
3. Producers of the good or service can freely enter or exit the industry.
4. Buyers and sellers have perfect information.

The above conditions are identical to those of perfect competition, except that products are differentiated instead of identical. In this case, buyers care which producer they buy from.

3.2 EXAMPLES OF MONOPOLISTIC COMPETITION

How many different brands of blue jeans can you name? How many fast-food restaurants might you find in a large town or a city? Why might there be three different brands of gasoline offered at stations at the same busy intersection? These are all examples of differentiated products. McDonald's, Burger King, and Wendy's franchises all sell hamburgers, but they prepare them a little differently, and each franchise is located in a different spot. Different gas stations may offer slightly different products, different levels of service, or different complementary products or services (e.g., a convenience store or a car wash). Such differences in product offerings, however slight, often are sufficient to elicit a degree of brand loyalty on the part of the consumer, although its strength varies considerably across the population.

Situations of monopolistic competition seem to be ubiquitous in contemporary industrialized societies. In everyday life, we see many firms competing to sell us slightly different varieties of the same goods and services.

3.3 PROFIT MAXIMIZATION WITH MONOPOLISTIC COMPETITION

Product differentiation means that each seller is a miniature monopoly, the only producer of its particular good. Indeed, it is this fact that makes the firms *monopolistically* competitive. Starbucks coffee is a classic example. Although many argue that it produces superior coffee (and many others argue the contrary), it once had a virtual "monopoly" on the "amenities" that it offered along with its coffee—comfortable couches and Wi-Fi access, for example—as part of its "product line." These produced legions of loyal customers, and while many other smaller coffee outlets have mimicked Starbucks in this regard, Starbucks obtained an early enough start on the competition to secure for itself a sizable share of the coffee-drinking population.

We see similar brand loyalty in the fast-food industry. Some people, for example, might claim that McDonald's hamburgers are far superior to Wendy's and might be willing to continue to buy from McDonald's even if it raises its prices. You might be willing to pay a higher price for milk at a local convenience store, even though you know that the price is lower at the big supermarket miles away. Whereas perfectly competitive sellers will lose *all* their customers if they raise their prices above the prevailing market price, a firm that sells a differentiated product may have a little leeway. Firms in a situation of monopolistic competition face a downward-sloping demand curve for their particular product.

The fact that such firms face a downward-sloping demand curve means that their profit-maximization problem more closely resembles that of a monopolist (illustrated in Figure 18.1). They also face marginal revenue curves that lie below the demand curve. A sophisticated monopolistic competitor, with good information, or at least a good "feel" for market circumstances, will choose an output level by setting $MR = MC$ at point A in Figure 18.1 and will charge customers the price set by the demand curve, at point B.

Unlike what occurs in the case of monopoly, however, the demand for such a firm's good is affected by the availability of close substitutes. If a Wendy's restaurant shuts down, demand at McDonald's, Burger King, and other restaurants and franchises nearby is likely to rise. If a new Burger King opens up, demand for food provided by many existing nearby restaurants may fall. Even though no other firm produces an *identical* good, substitutes often are close enough to induce meaningful changes in the market.

The fact that entry and exit are easy means that if any monopolistically competitive firm is making positive economic profits, new producers will be attracted to the market and will begin to sell similar goods (e.g., other hamburgers). As new firms enter the market, the demand for the specific product in question (e.g., a McDonald's hamburger) will fall, as illustrated in Figure 18.5. Suppose the demand for a particular firm's products is D_1, and it is making positive economic profits. Other firms will enter the market, selling similar products, reducing the firm's demand to D_2. This will cut into the firm's revenues and profits. How many new firms will enter, and how much will demand fall for any one firm? In economists' approximation, it happens just up to the point where every firm is making zero economic profits. (See the appendix to this chapter for a graphical explanation.)

Figure 18.5 **The Effect of the Entry of New Firms on a Monopolistically Competitive Firm**

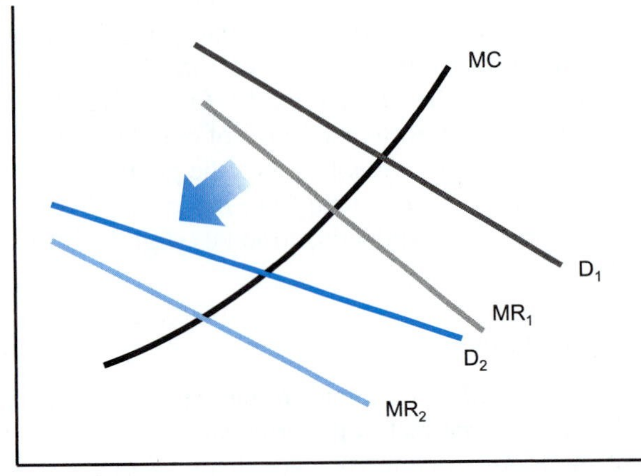

A condition of easy entry and exit means that new firms can enter, driving down the demand experienced by any one monopolistically competitive firm.

Like the monopolist, the monopolistically competitive firm faces a downward-sloping demand curve and so produces less, and charges a higher price, than a perfectly competitive firm. As in the case of a perfectly competitive firm, however, free entry and exit in monopolistically competitive markets means that any positive economic profits to be gained should only be temporary, as new competitors move in to exploit new opportunities to earn money.

3.4 MONOPOLISTIC COMPETITION AND LONG-RUN EFFICIENCY

Compared to perfectly competitive firms, monopolistically competitive firms produce lower levels of output and charge higher prices. Like monopolies, they stop short of producing at levels where the social marginal benefit of production is just equal to the social marginal cost. It can also be shown (and *is* shown in the appendix to this chapter) that such firms have higher unit costs than would occur in a perfectly competitive market. In short, they operate inefficiently.

Monopolistically competitive firms may, like monopolists, expend considerable resources to protect their miniature monopoly. While perhaps unable to keep competitors from entering their general industry, they can try, increasingly, to differentiate their product. Firms in this

nonprice competition: competition through activities other than setting prices, such as advertising and location

kind of market structure are observed to engage in a great deal of **nonprice competition**. That is, they compete with other producers by advertising heavily in order to make buyers want *their* particular product (e.g., Gap jeans) and by using attractive signs and packaging, selecting better locations, varying their hours of operation, and so on.

In terms of social benefit, it seems evident that resources would be better spent producing fewer varieties of goods and services, at lower costs, and with less advertising. Yet some cast a more positive light on the problem, focusing instead on consumer preferences. They argue that inefficiencies in production are merely the price that must be paid to satisfy consumers' *desire* for variety (and, presumably, also for massive advertising and flashy packaging). Although probably not the whole story, it may very well be that the highest social benefit lies somewhere between dull, completely standardized products and the extreme proliferation of consumer goods that we currently observe.

Discussion Questions

1. Think of a somewhat differentiated good or service that you can buy locally in any number of different places—for example, a gallon of gasoline or a cup of coffee. Do you observe differences in prices? What differences might lead to these variations in prices? (Or is the assumption of perfect information violated? Does everyone know where the cheapest version can be found?) What examples of nonprice competition can you identify among the various sellers?
2. Do you think that the amount of variety in the goods and services that you are offered as a consumer is excessive? Just about right? Too limited? Do some forms of nonprice competition have consequences for long-term well-being and sustainability?

4. OLIGOPOLY

While oligopoly shares some characteristics of competitive markets, it is closer to monopoly in that a small number of firms possess a sizable share of the market. Oligopoly is similar to monopoly (and monopolistic competition) in that output is lower, and prices are higher, than would be the case under perfect competition. Oligopolists, like monopolists, may also possess significant political and economic clout on local or national levels.

4.1 MARKET STRUCTURE OF AN OLIGOPOLISTIC INDUSTRY

The oligopolistic market structure is characterized by the following conditions:

1. The market is dominated by *only a few* sellers, at least some of which control enough of the market to be able to influence the market price.
2. Entry is difficult.

The products produced by oligopolists may be either standardized or differentiated. Various assumptions may be made about how much information is available to producers and their customers in markets with oligopolies.

The most important implication of the condition that there are few firms is that the actions of each firm have effects on the market that rival firms cannot ignore. It means, among other things, that the rivals may respond in ways that, in turn, require a response from the original firm(s). In short, oligopoly exists if each firm must include, among the factors that it considers in deciding on its own actions, the possible reactions of rival firms.

Remember that in perfect competition the seller need not be concerned with the actions of others. All that such a seller needs to know is the market price. In the case of monopoly, of course, there are no other sellers to worry about. In the case of monopolistic competition, with many sellers, the effect of the action of any one seller is spread out over many other sellers. But in an oligopolistic situation, each firm needs to be keenly aware of what each of the (few) other firms is doing.

4.2 Examples of Oligopoly

industrial concentration ratio: the share of production, sales, or revenues attributable to the largest firms in an industry

An **industrial concentration ratio** is the share of total *production, sales,* or *revenues* attributable to the largest producers in an industry. The share of domestic *production* accounted for by the four largest firms is a traditional indicator of how oligopolistic an industry has become. Despite the absence of a precise definition, we say that an oligopoly exists wherever a "small" number of firms (perhaps between four and ten) possess something more than a majority of the market share (e.g., about two-thirds of the market share or more).

We presented some data on industrial concentration ratios in Chapter 0. In addition, according to the U.S. government's 2007 Economic Census (the most recent data available), the concentration ratio for credit card companies is 79 percent, for breakfast cereal manufacturing, 85 percent, and for glass container manufacturing, 86 percent. All three appear to satisfy even stringent criteria for oligopoly. The market for wireless telecommunications services is also dominated by just a few sellers. (See Box 18.2 for another example of oligopoly.)

4.3 Oligopoly and the Behavior of Firms

The behavior of oligopolistic firms is truly *social* in the sense of being interdependent with the behavior of other actors; hence it appears more complex than other market structures. Instead of one theory for oligopolies, economists have many, any of which might be helpful but none of which is definitive. We briefly describe two of them here: first, the theory of strategic interaction and game theory and, second, models of collusion, cartels, and price leadership.

Box 18.2 Oligopoly and Airline Mergers

In February 2013, US Airways and American Airlines announced their intention to merge, an $11 billion deal that would create the world's largest airline. The proposed merger follows a trend of consolidation in the airline industry in the United States. Between 2001 and 2013, the top ten airline companies in the country had already combined to form five major carriers, including mergers of Northwest and Delta in 2008 and United and Continental in 2010. If approved by federal regulators, the US Airways and American Airlines merger would create four "megacarriers" that would control 83 percent of the U.S. air passenger market.

Initially it seemed that the merger would easily receive approval, as had been the case with previous airline mergers. But in August 2013, the U.S. Justice Department, joined by the attorneys general of seven states, filed a lawsuit to block the merger, arguing that it would cause "substantial harm" to passengers by raising fares and reducing competition. The government noted that the merger would eliminate competition on more than 1,000 routes. Assistant Attorney General Bill Baer said, "As we look at the market today, it's not functioning as competitively as it ought to be, and if this deal goes through, it's going to be much worse."

"This is the best news that consumers could have possible gotten," said Charlie Leocha, director of the Consumer Travel Alliance. Leocha indicated that previous mergers have led to higher fares and reduced choices for travelers and that the proposed merger would have the same result.

One possible outcome is that the merger will still be approved, but only with some concessions by the two airlines. For example, they may be forced to give up some landing and take-off slots at busy Reagan National Airport outside Washington, DC, thus allowing for increased competition from other airlines. Meanwhile, the airlines contend that allowing them to merge will improve their ability to compete with other large carriers, such as United and Delta.

Sources: Chris Isidore, "American-US Air Deal Would Cut Passenger Choices," CNN Money, February 8, 2013; Pete Yost and David Koenig, "Government, States Challenge Proposed Airline Merger," Associated Press, August 13, 2013.

Strategic Interaction and Game Theory

One theory is that oligopolistic firms will act strategically against one another, plotting their moves as though they were generals planning a war or opponents in a game of chess. Oligopolistic sellers are often seen as engaging in "competition" in the active, aggressive sense in which business managers use this term. That is, oligopolistic firms choose prices, marketing strategies, and the like, with an eye to "beating out" specific rivals and gaining greater market share at their expense. A classic example is the rivalry between Coke and Pepsi.

duopoly: a market with only two sellers

payoff matrix: a table used in game theory to illustrate possible outcomes for each of two players, depending on the strategy that each chooses

Game theory, which has its origin in the work of mathematician John von Neumann (1903–1957) and economist Oskar Morgenstern (1902–1977), provides a framework for the formal analysis of some types of strategic behavior. For example, consider a market with two sellers, also known as a **duopoly**. Suppose that each is trying to decide whether to set a low or a high price for the good that they both sell. They need to pay attention to what the other one does, because if Firm 1 sets a high price, Firm 2 might set a low price and end up with all the customers (or vice versa). Using game theory, we can describe a **payoff matrix**, as shown in Figure 18.6.

Figure 18.6 **A Payoff Matrix**

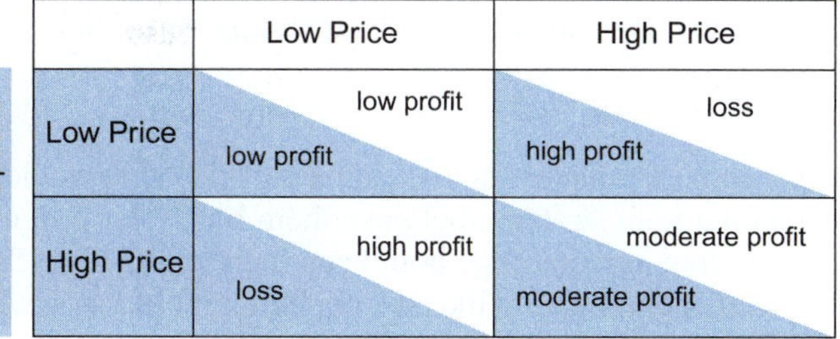

A payoff matrix shows what the profit outcomes will be for each of two oligopolistic firms, given their decisions about what price to charge.

The entries in the payoff matrix show the profit level that each firm can expect, given its choice and the choice of its rival. The combination "loss, high profit" in the bottom-left cell, for example, shows that if Firm 1 sets a high price while Firm 2 sets a low price, Firm 1 will make a loss, while Firm 2—which now has all the customers—will make high profits. (Test yourself: What does the upper-right-hand cell represent?) Clearly, each firm would find it to its own advantage to be the only low-price seller in the market. Recognition of this fact could lead to a **price war**, in which each firm progressively cuts its prices in order to try to be the low-price seller. Although a price war could, in some real-world cases, last until one party went out of business, in Figure 18.6 we have illustrated a case in which, when both firms set low prices, both keep a share of customers and make low profits. This is shown in the cell at the upper left. However, if both set high prices, as shown in the bottom-right cell, they could both make moderate profits while keeping a share of customers.

price war: a situation in which a firm cuts prices in order to try to undercut its rivals, and the rivals react by cutting prices even more

In this model, we assume that the firms are "noncooperative"—that is, that they are archrivals and do not communicate or cooperate with each other. Noncooperative game theory suggests that a rational firm will choose the option that will leave it best off (or least damaged) regardless of what its rival does. Looking at the payoff matrix in Figure 18.6, we can see that Firm 1 will choose to set a low price rather than a high price. If Firm 1 sets a low price and Firm 2 chooses "low," Firm 1 gets low, but positive, profits. If Firm 1 sets a low price and Firm 2 chooses "high," Firm 1 gets high profits. Regardless of what Firm 2 does, then, Firm 1 gets better outcomes than the corresponding loss or moderate profits than it would get by setting a high price. A similar analysis for Firm 2 shows that it also will choose to set its prices *low*. The "solution" to the game is the (low profit, low profit) cell. Yet in a certain sense it is not a solution at all, since what appears *individually* rational for each firm actually produces a perverse outcome that is suboptimal for both.

Scenarios such as this are often referred to as "prisoner's dilemmas" because of the well-known formulation in terms of prisoners who are held separately and asked to confess to a crime that they committed together. If neither confesses, they both go free after one year (call this situation a "plea bargain"). However, if only one confesses (ratting on the other), he goes free while the other goes to jail for 10 years. If both confess, they each are sentenced to jail for three years. The best strategy, for a prisoner who does not know what his partner in crime will do, is to confess. That way, he is assured of not having to go to jail for more than three years. (What outcome would be *best* for both? What would be necessary for them to achieve it?)

Strategic thinking can also be applied to nonprice competition, which oligopolists also frequently employ. For example, sellers may need to decide whether to spend a lot or a little on advertising, packaging, and booths at sales conventions. What they decide to do will, at least in part, depend on what their rivals do. Nonprice competition is most likely when each firm is selling a somewhat differentiated product.

Another form of game theory imagines that the parties do not make their decisions simultaneously, as in our example, but one after the other. The theory of "sequential games" covers situations in which one firm moves first and then the second chooses its strategy. Each firm's expectations about the reaction of the other are key to describing the probable outcomes of such a game. More recently, formal game theory has also been applied to "cooperative" games in which, for example, actors may bargain toward a mutually beneficial outcome.

Collusion, Cartels, and Price Leadership

Clearly, Firm 1 and Firm 2 in the above example (not to mention the prisoners) would do better if they got together and agreed on a joint strategy that gave them both their best outcomes. If the two firms could make a binding agreement to both keep their prices high, they could both make moderate profits instead of ending up at the noncooperative solution in which each makes low profits. Firms that cooperate in this way are said to engage in **collusion**. They get together and form a monopoly (at least a local one) for pricing purposes, even though they keep their production activities separate.

collusion: cooperation among potential rivals to gain market power as a group

Cartels such as the Organization of Petroleum Exporting Countries (OPEC) are examples of explicit collusion. OPEC did not try to keep its collusion a secret but instead announced its formation and its high prices.

Tacit collusion takes place when sellers collude more subtly, without creation of a cartel. Because cartels are by and large illegal in many industrialized countries, sellers must often pass information around on the sly. An industry association may collect information and post it on the Web so that all members will know what price the others are charging. Such flows of information make it easier to cooperate and to monitor compliance with tacit **price fixing**, in which all sellers implicitly agree to maintain a common price. One form of implicit collusion is **price leadership**, in which everyone in the industry looks to one firm, raising their prices when it does and lowering them likewise. Such price leadership, many believe, characterized the U.S. steel and airlines industries for years. Price leadership tends to be more common when the firms all sell identical, standardized products.

tacit collusion: collusion that takes place without creation of a cartel

price fixing: a form of collusion in which a group of sellers implicitly agrees to maintain a common price

price leadership: a form of collusion in which many sellers follow the price changes instituted by one particular seller

However, as members of OPEC discovered, collusion can be hard to sustain. Each seller has an incentive to undercut the set price privately, in order to sell a little more. Nevertheless, collusion has sometimes been persistent. Members may realize that it is in their greater long-term interest to stick with the collusive price rather than to risk losing everything by starting a price war.

4.4 How Common Is Oligopoly?

Oligopolistic industries tend to be inefficient, for the same reasons that monopoly often is. In fact, oligopoly is often even less efficient. Because production decisions remain separate, there is less possibility of even reaping advantages of economies of scale.

Although oligopoly has traditionally been defined in terms of few sellers and difficult entry, the key feature that distinguishes the *behavior* of sellers is not so much the number of them as the existence of interdependence among them. A market can, in fact, display oligopolistic characteristics even with easy entry and hence many possible sellers. When four firms control 80 percent of the market, for example, it has little effect on their behavior whether the remaining 20 percent of the market is divided among 10 sellers or 1,000.

Oligopolies can also be local. Not all industries experience high concentration ratios at the national level. For example, the U.S. Census indicates that in 2007 the top four retail florists shared 2.1 percent of the total national market, and the top four credit unions shared 10.1 percent. Even when industries are not so concentrated at the national level, however, firms may behave in somewhat oligopolistic ways more locally. If there are two florists in a town, for example, you can bet that each keeps track of what the other is charging, where it is advertising, and how it adjusts its prices on Valentine's Day and Mother's Day!

Market structures in which sellers need to take into account the actions of other sellers, and then respond effectively and creatively, are possibly more prevalent in the real world than monopolistic competition (although certainty on this question would require precise definitions of each in terms of the respective concentration ratios). And even apparent monopolies are normally oligopolistic when one takes a closer look.

Take Microsoft, which is a good real-world example of a near-monopoly. Because computer users can still choose Macintosh or Linux operating systems, and because Microsoft can reasonably fear that the creation of a new technology could destroy its monopoly powers, it is not quite a pure monopoly. And we had mentioned McDonald's and Wendy's as monopolistic competitors, but you can be sure that they keep a watchful eye on each other's locations, pricing, and promotional strategies.

The need to take into account others' actions is important in traditional economics' narrowly defined (i.e., "few sellers") idea of oligopoly. But it is also of broader importance because rarely can *any* real-world company, of any size or in any industry, safely ignore the actions taken by others. Studies of economics, business, sociology, and politics share many common concerns when the prevalence of truly interdependent economic decision-making is taken into account.

Discussion Questions

1. What would it mean for two sellers to act noncooperatively, in a "prisoner's dilemma" manner? What real world examples can you think of? What, instead, would it mean for two sellers to collude? Which of the two outcomes is more common in the real world? Why?
2. Suppose that a seller in a duopoly needs to decide whether to spend a lot or a little on advertising. Assume that the consumers are already reasonably well informed about the product, so the purpose of a lot of advertising is to draw customers away from the rival. How could the payoffs from this situation resemble those in Figure 18.6? Draw a payoff matrix illustrating this case (with options "spend a lot" or "spend a little" and outcomes of low, moderate, or high profits) and describe the noncooperative solution. What if the government decided to ban advertising in this industry (as it has, in the past, banned advertising of cigarettes and alcohol in various media)? Would that help or hurt the companies' profits?

5. IMPERFECT COMPETITION IN AGRICULTURE AND HEALTH CARE

We now turn to a more in-depth discussion of two markets: agriculture and health care. These two markets are illustrative of many of the concepts we have been discussing in this chapter, as well as throughout the book, including economic efficiency, market failure, externalities, equity, and the role of government.

5.1 AGRICULTURE

On the face of it, markets for agricultural products should be a textbook case of perfect competition or at least something approaching it. Products are mostly undifferentiated—although this has changed in recent years, with growing attention to organic and locally produced food—and there exist a multitude of producers, many small and without market power. Yet U.S. agriculture has not been "competitive" for many years. Indeed, many economists find ironic the fact that, when they teach introductory economics, they often cite this market as a classic example of market *distortion.*

What types of distortion are present in agriculture, and how did the market get to be this way? Without going into great detail about the history, U.S. farmers struggled immensely during the Great Depression, when food prices dropped precipitously, because of both the forces of demand (a drop in demand from European countries) and supply (overproduction in response to price spikes during the 1920s). In order to keep many thousands of farmers from going bankrupt, the U.S. government embarked on an ambitious farm policy that, in many ways, continues to this day. What it entailed was basically the creation of a price floor in the agricultural markets (recall the discussion of price floors and price ceilings in Chapter 6), in which the government subsidized farmers for any difference between the food market price and what was deemed to be a "fair" price.

The problem with such a policy—and in 80 years it has never encountered a shortage of critics—is that it tends to "distort" markets for food. By setting a minimum price above the market price, the effect has been to stimulate overproduction—that is, production of food in an amount far greater than the quantity demanded at the market (i.e., unsubsidized) price.

We can see this in Figure 18.7. In the absence of any distortion, the market achieves equilibrium (point E) where the market price is P_m and the quantity produced, Q_m. When the government agrees to pay the subsidy to the farmer, the farmer now receives $P_m + s$. The "distortion" is the artificially produced surplus that, you will note, does not look the same as in the example from Chapter 6. The reason is that in this case the consumer *still pays* P_m (the whole purpose of the subsidy) and is therefore still motivated to buy Q_m. The surplus, or amount overproduced, is shown as $Q_P - Q_m$.

Figure 18.7 **Impact of Agricultural Subsidies**

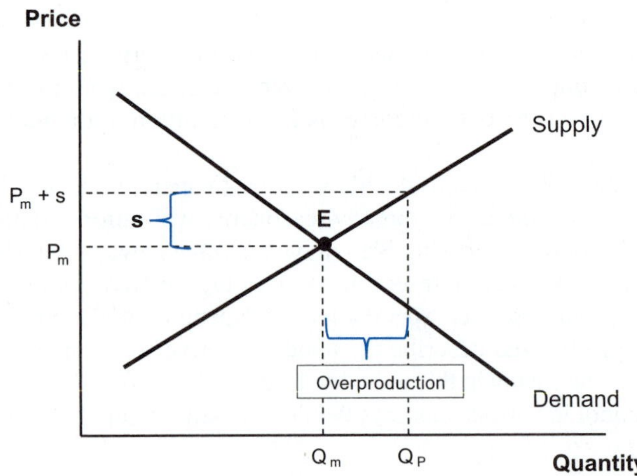

When the government provides a subsidy, it distorts the market. With the subsidy, farmers overproduce, and inefficiency results.

The manner in which the United States disposes of its surplus has varied over the years, and depending on crop type, but it usually has involved either selling it to other countries—as when the United States shipped vast amounts of surplus wheat to the Soviet Union in the early 1970s—providing it at low or no cost to very poor countries, or simply destroying it. The critics of the overall policy make the following points:

- U.S. farmland is being degraded faster than it would be with less incentive to overproduce.
- Rich farmers with large landholdings have received a disproportionately large share of the subsidies, making it all the harder for small farms to survive against this competition.
- Although in the short run the cheap or free food that poor countries receive from the United States may be essential to relieve a famine, in the long run it often drives farmers in those countries out of business, as they have to lower their prices to compete and often are unable to cover their production costs.

Taking another approach, the government has sometimes subsidized (i.e., paid) farmers to keep their land fallow (i.e., unplanted). In any case, what seems clear is that allocative efficiency was not the primary goal of U.S. agricultural policy. Instead, since the 1930s, the government has placed a great priority on protecting the U.S. farmer's livelihood.

In itself, this is a laudable objective. But aside from inefficiency, there is another consequence not visible in the above diagram. Figure 18.7, like many others in the book, presents a static interpretation of the problem—that is, viewed at a particular point in time. It does not provide any *dynamic* analysis or explanation of the likely response to the distortion in the market. That omission is critical, because herein lies one of the principal causes of the transformation of U.S. agriculture into an oligopolistic market. Whereas small family farms once dominated U.S. farming, today the majority of agricultural products are grown on a small number of (increasingly large) farms controlled by agribusiness giants like Cargill or Archer-Daniels Midland. As of 2010, the United States had 2.2 million farms, compared with 5.7 million in 1950, and the average farm size in 2010 was 418 acres, more than twice the average 60 years earlier (208 acres).

The growth in U.S average farm size since the 1930s has two main causes. The first, indeed, is a response to the original farm support policies, which both provoked new farming ventures and motivated consolidation of landholding, because the amount of the government subsidy was often tied to the size of the farm. The second was the self-perpetuating nature of scale economies. As farms became larger, they, like other industries, profited from economies of scale and were better able to shoulder rapidly increasing costs—especially after 1970—associated with the increasing mechanization of agriculture, increased price of petroleum, and higher interest rates on loans. A not-uncommon story, consequently, was the failure of smaller farms to compete and their sale to larger farms. The process, repeated many times across the country, only contributed to the concentration of land ownership.

Politics also played a role. Although the United States had been moving to limit overproduction in agriculture in earlier decades, in the early 1970s, U.S. Secretary of Agriculture Earl Butz took a very strident pro–big business approach. He is often credited with (or blamed for, depending on one's point of view) subsidizing the development of large commercial corn production and the growing use of inexpensive corn in prepared foods. It was not until 1996 that U.S. farm policy took a turn in the direction of a greater exposure to the market (with the Federal Agriculture Improvement and Reform Act), but stern opposition from politicians representing farming states in Congress led to a reversion to the earlier support policies.

As mentioned earlier in the section on monopoly, large companies with economies of scale have the potential to be very efficient if they produce large volumes at lower prices. This was Secretary Butz's argument in the early 1970s: Farms should be *big* in order to justify and support the mechanization and investment in new technology that would make farms much more efficient. Although the debate continues on whether large farms are more efficient than small ones, there are certainly disadvantages to excess market power in agriculture. As also noted earlier, lack of sufficient competition potentially makes oligopolistic firms complacent and less innovative. For those who believe that economics is not just about efficiency and production growth but also about people, output and price controls seemed to be the best way of dealing with the problem at the time.

The Great Depression was admittedly an exceptional period in our history, and the argument that farm policy has outlived its usefulness has its merits. Certainly, it has produced some unintended consequences, most of all the reduced number and viability of small farms. But many maintain that because food is a basic necessity, and because food prices are sometimes quite volatile, agricultural markets should continue to be regulated. Indeed, the main issue today might be not *whether* to regulate agriculture but the extent to which agricultural subsidies should favor the giant agricultural middlemen and the large producers who appear least to need them.

5.2 Health Care

The market for health care is remarkable in its complexity. It is, in fact, composed of numerous interrelated markets. For example, a variety of markets exist for different types of care—traditional medicine, allopathic medicine, homeopathy, herbal healers, and so forth—and markets for drugs and other pharmaceuticals. Moreover, there are markets for the insurance that in many cases pay for a variety of health-care services.

Classification of health care in terms of market structure depends on the specific market. The health insurance industry is oligopolistic because insurance premiums are more or less "set" by the relatively few insurers that control most of the market. Likewise, the relatively few pharmaceutical companies—or to be more precise, few *large* ones—have considerable market power, enhanced by generous patents granted by the government. Hospitals might also be reasonably considered regional oligopolies—or even monopolies, in more sparsely populated areas. Many attribute rapidly rising health-care costs in recent years to the substantial market power present in the industry (see Box 18.3).

The markets that connect individual health-care providers and "consumers" are, however, more difficult to classify. They would appear to have more of the attributes of competitive

Box 18.3 Rising Health-Care Costs and Market Power

A 2010 analysis by the Massachusetts Attorney General's office analyzed possible causes of rising health-care costs in the state. The report's conclusion is that higher costs can be attributed primarily to the exercise of market power by hospitals and physicians groups, rather than by improvements in the quality of care or the cost of providing care.

The analysis looked at the compensation that different health-care providers received from insurance companies. It found that the amount of compensation received by hospitals can vary by a factor of two for the same health-care services. In other words, some hospitals appear to be able to negotiate higher rates from insurance companies, not on the basis of providing better care but due to an ability to leverage their market power. Insurance companies, in turn, charge higher premiums to their customers.

The report found that "serious systemwide failings in the commercial health insurance marketplace" exist in the state. Massachusetts Attorney General Martha Coakley said, "Our review shows that the current system of health care payment is not always value-based, and health care providers throughout the state are compensated at widely different rates for providing similar quality and complexity of services."

Based on the report, the state is looking at evaluating ways to rein in rising health-care costs. One proposal is to move away from a "fee-for-service" system, in which hospitals and physicians are paid for each procedure that they perform, thus creating an incentive for unnecessary tests and operations. An alternative is a "capitated" system, in which hospitals and physicians receive a set payment from insurers for each patient they serve. Another cost-control option, favored by Governor Deval Patrick, is to give the state the authority to regulate "excessive or unreasonable" insurance premium rate increases. But Jim Klocke, executive vice president of the Greater Boston Chamber of Commerce, said that giving the state the power "to play a formal role in the price-setting process is not the right approach."

Source: Doug Trapp, "Cost Increases Tied to Market Power's Impact on Payment: Mass. Study," *American Medical News*, amednews.com, February 22, 2010.

markets, and it is certainly true that no providers control a substantial share of any mass market. Yet none of the individual markets are highly competitive either, for a number of reasons. Here we discuss four.

Heterogeneous Product

To begin with, recall that an important feature of perfect competition is that the product sold be identical or homogenous. This is clearly not the case in some markets in the health-care industry. One example is the quality of medical treatment. As countless online "reviews" attest, there is a great variety in quality, both of individual physicians and specialists and of hospitals. To the extent that the reviews accurately reflect reality, a doctor or a hospital judged "superior" might be justified in charging a higher price than other providers.

Even the "product" sold by the health insurance companies is highly variable. In contrast to the "single payer" insurance found in Canada and most European countries, for which coverage is more or less the same for all residents, there are numerous "tiers" of insurance in the United States. And each tier differs in the details, depending on the specific company offering the coverage. For example, most insurance companies today require a copayment, a way of ensuring that the consumer has some "skin in the game" so as to discourage overuse of health-care services. The size of this payment varies greatly as do the conditions under which it is paid—for example, for specialists only or for emergency care—and the restrictions on services covered (based on, e.g., if a provider is "signed up" with the insurance company). So we might almost consider meaningless the question of the "market price" of a particular health-care service.

Barriers to Entry

Another way in which health care differs from the idealized model of perfect competition is in the presence of barriers to entry. In the case of U.S. health insurance, the industry is oligopolistic, dominated by several fairly large companies that cover most of the market. As discussed earlier, it is exceedingly difficult to break into such a market as a small upstart. Providers of medical care face licensing requirements—medical school, licensing exams, and so on—that keep all but the most qualified from becoming doctors.

There certainly are good reasons for keeping unqualified individuals from practicing medicine. Yet the problem with such an entry barrier, many have argued, is that it grants undue protection to *existing* practitioners, potentially providing insufficient incentive to deliver the best possible quality. It is not our place to say whether these restrictions and protections are, on balance, for good or ill; certainly, both sides have valid arguments. But it is sufficient here to emphasize that entry barriers in health care can be substantial.

Information Asymmetry

Another basic attribute of a perfectly competitive market is the presence of "perfect information." In other words, classical economic theory presumes that both sides of the market—suppliers and "demanders"—have access to all the relevant information necessary to make an informed decision. This is decidedly not the case with health care.

What some economists call "information asymmetry"—a situation in which some market participants are more informed than others—is present, for example, when a doctor sees a patient. The patient is, in most cases, inadequately informed to make a proper judgment about whether a particular test or procedure that the doctor recommends is really necessary, so generally the doctor is simply trusted. Although the patient in many cases does not directly pay for most of what might be unnecessary procedures, the ultimate consequence—since the insurance companies end up financing an inefficiently high number of them—is that everyone's health insurance premiums go up.

Such asymmetry of information is also present between the patient and the insurance company. Most Americans have their health insurance company pay directly for a majority of their health-care expenses (in exchange for payment—usually monthly—of a fixed premium, privately or through an employer), and one can easily imagine how such a system could encourage overuse of medical services. As the marginal cost of many health-care services for insured individuals is zero, or very low, people have an incentive to demand services that may be unnecessary or very expensive. Further contributing to rising health-care costs, doctors are typically paid by insurance companies on the basis of each service performed, rather than actual health care outcomes.

Another issue is that individuals in poor health have a greater incentive to purchase insurance in the first place than those in relatively good health. This requires insurance companies to make more payments than they would expect if they were covering a random mix of sick and well, causing them to raise premiums to avoid losing money. This is a problem of **adverse selection**, in which the higher premiums further discourage healthy members of the population from signing up, and so on in a vicious cycle, eventually making the premiums so high as to jeopardize the system itself. While it is not actually as simple as this—to be sure, millions of healthy Americans have insurance, most because their employer helps pay for it—there is no question that premiums are inefficiently high due to disproportionate use of health-care services by the unhealthy.

adverse selection: a system that favors the weaker members of a given population, generally to the detriment of the system itself

The problem would easily be avoided by charging lower premiums to healthier people, not unlike what is done by life insurance companies. But this is, in practice, extremely difficult to do, because information asymmetry is much greater when it comes to determining the overall "healthiness" of an individual (e.g., one person might have a chronically bad back but be otherwise healthy, another might suffer from allergies, etc.) than for statistically assessing mortality based on a few critical health indicators. Also, even if feasible, it would imply that those who are already chronically ill would face prohibitively high premiums, an outcome that few people desire. Some insurance companies retain provisions for "pre-existing conditions" as a pretext for excluding new participants who are already sick, and these are precisely the people that the Affordable Care Act, or "Obamacare," is in part designed to protect.

Market Price

A final feature of a perfectly competitive market that is absent from health care is the presence of a clear and unambiguous market price. This is lacking even for basic medicines. Anyone who purchases pharmaceuticals has no doubt observed the significantly higher price charged for, say, the branded aspirin than for the generic (or "store brand") version—even though the two products are identical in their formulation. For another example, Walmart can sell some over-the-counter medicines (such as eye drops) at half the price set by other pharmacies due to a number of the store's outstanding characteristics: low costs due to efficiency, economies of scale, and low wages as well as enormous price-setting power, which allows it to negotiate prices with pharmaceutical companies. It is even harder to imagine a single, clear price for other health-care services, such as visits to doctor's offices or to hospitals, because there is so much variability among them.

Entry barriers, mentioned earlier, confound matters further. Lack of severe competition permits doctors, for instance, to discriminate based on price—familiar to most as having a "sliding scale." It is difficult to imagine the higher prices being sustained in the presence of greater competition. And information asymmetry plays perhaps the greatest role in failure to achieve a clear market price. Because insurance companies, health-care providers, and ordinary people all "trade" using different amounts—and quality—of information (about how necessary a procedure might be, its likelihood of success, its affordability, etc.), it might be surprising that prices are *ever* consistent.

Regarding price, another important consideration is that health care has an important "public good" dimension. The benefit of a vaccine, for example, is not only obtained by individuals, but also by everyone else living in a population of (mostly) vaccinated individuals (namely, a much lower chance of contracting the disease in question). Likewise, the benefits of psychiatric medications include the diminished likelihood, for everyone, of confronting an overabundance of mentally ill individuals. Because such indirect or residual benefits are "public"—that is, they do not enter into the private benefit-cost calculation of buyer and seller—they cannot be reflected in the market price.

Many have raised arguments about ways in which this sector of the economy could be made more competitive, with the goal of allocating resources more efficiently. Laudable as the goal no doubt is, there is something unique about health care—the fact that it is a fundamental human necessity *and* its provision is often plagued by market failure—that forces us to reconsider whether market-based approaches work best.

Another element to the problem is perhaps the most critical. Health insurance companies ultimately decide which claims they will pay. In most cases, then, they effectively decide whether a prescribed medical treatment will be undertaken, because most people would be unwilling (or, often, unable) to pay for it out of pocket. If the decisions of the insurers were based on their expertise in the area of medicine and their concern for the well-being of the insured, the present system would make a lot more sense. But the insurance company is fundamentally pursuing *profit,* which, of course, is not in itself a bad thing. The problem is when the pursuit of profit conflicts with the objective of ensuring patient health.

When compared to other countries, the United States does not perform well in terms of national health indicators. Although average life expectancy certainly is much higher in the country than in the far poorer countries of sub-Saharan Africa and South Asia, it is not as high as in most industrialized countries—that is, Western European countries, Canada, Japan, Australia, and New Zealand. And the United States also compares unfavorably, in terms of life expectancy and infant mortality, with a growing number of "middle-income" countries (e.g., Costa Rica, Cuba). None of this proves that other health-care systems—such as, most notably, a "single payer" system—are superior to one based on private profits and markets. But the evidence does call for research into the question of whether better systems might exist for delivering health care.

Discussion Questions

1. Select the topic of either agriculture or health, and answer the following questions:
   a. What do you think is the single biggest problem in this area of the economy?
   b. What kind of policy do you favor to help to overcome that problem?
   c. What makes it difficult to implement the policy that you favor?
2. Should the health-care industry become more like a competitive free market? Do you think that it would help bring costs down? How might such a change come about? What might be some potentially undesirable consequences?

6. Summary and a Final Note

The traditional four-way categorization of markets, summarized in Table 18.2, can be helpful in thinking about how market structure can affect the incentives facing firms. It is important to remember that the differences between these classifications are not always clear. In particular, in many real-world markets, sellers need to keep track of what others in their industry are doing and to plan strategically, whether there are few sellers or many. Such interdependent activity requires analysis that is beyond the scope of simple models of marginal thinking. Moreover, as we think about market power, we need to recognize that globalization, which has intensified in recent decades, has made dramatic changes in market conditions. Traditional categories may therefore no longer cover all of the most important situations.

Table 18.2 **Summary of Traditional Market Structures**

	Perfect competition	Pure monopoly	Monopolistic competition	Oligopoly
Number of sellers in the market	many	one	many	few
Type of item(s) sold	identical	unique	differentiated	varies
Market power of an individual seller	none	very high	some	substantial
Entry barriers	none	very high	none	some
Long-run economic profit	zero	positive	zero	varies
Profit-maximizing condition	MC = P	MC = MR	MC = MR	varies

The classical economic discussion of markets tends to focus on the benefits of "free" markets and competition. When the discussion turns to market power, economists mostly focus largely on *firms* that may have the power to affect *prices* in the markets where they *sell* goods that they have *produced.*

Market power, however, is much more widespread. For example,

- Governments, nonprofit organizations, and individuals can have market power. In some states and counties, for example, governments have a monopoly on liquor sales. An individual selling a unique work of art has market power.
- Nonprice terms and conditions of exchange such as delivery dates, quality standards, and length of contracts can be manipulated by economic actors with market power.
- Market power can exist in nonproduct markets, such as markets for resale of goods, markets for resources, and financial markets.
- Market power can occur on the buyers' side. That is, market power can be used to affect the prices paid by firms to their suppliers for *inputs,* including human labor. The cases of monopsony (one buyer) and oligopsony (few buyers) were discussed in Chapter 10 on labor markets.

Market power, therefore, refers to much more than the ability of firms to set prices above marginal cost. Although the classical analysis of market power tends to stress its detrimental consequences in terms of lost efficiency—an issue of concern from the point of view of the consumer—the consequences of market power in terms of fairness and distributional effects are often at least as important, if not more so, to human well-being. If, for example, market power allows a few large companies to force consumers to pay more for food while at the same time making earning a living increasingly difficult for small farmers, this could be at least as damaging to human well-being as the market power that allows a firm to set prices above marginal cost. A similar argument is easily made regarding the market power enjoyed by the pharmaceutical and the health insurance giants.

Market power is frequently used to impose externalities upon society. For example, a large manufacturer may lobby to gain an exemption from a pollution regulation. Thus instead of having the manufacturer pay the costs of pollution control, society pays costs in terms of poorer health and ecosystem damages.

The most important lesson here is to remember both the usefulness and limitations of textbook models. Abstract and admittedly simplified models of perfect competition and monopoly help us to understand the basics of how certain key ingredients of a market economy function. It is critically important to be able to generalize across many examples across the world, and over time, in order to gain general insight into how the economy works. But it is equally important—if not more so—not to idealize the models to the point that they come to be seen as reality itself.

Neither free markets nor monopolies exist in their purest sense; the world is far more complicated than this. The challenge is to learn to properly utilize the insights gained from economic models in the analysis of complex real-world problems. As should be clear from the examples in this book, it is often difficult to separate economic concepts of efficiency from issues of ethics, fairness, sustainability, and distribution. As the present chapter illustrates, market power often implies other forms of political power. The proper use of economic modeling and analysis recognizes both its usefulness and its limitations, in guiding us to a better understanding, and better policies, on agriculture, health, and many other issues that are critical for human well-being.

REVIEW QUESTIONS

1. List and briefly define the three market structure types in addition to perfect competition.
2. What market conditions characterize pure monopoly?
3. Describe three types of barriers to entry, giving examples of each.
4. How does a pure monopolist maximize profits?
5. In what ways are monopolies inefficient?
6. Explain, with a graph, how monopoly market power generally leads to inefficiency.
7. List and describe four cases in which monopolies might be efficient.
8. Explain, with a graph, how a price-discriminating seller behaves.
9. What market conditions characterize monopolistic competition?
10. How is a monopolistically competitive firm imagined to maximize profits?
11. Are monopolistically competitive markets efficient? Explain.
12. What market conditions characterize oligopoly?
13. Describe two theories used to describe the behavior of oligopolists.
14. Explain why the U.S. government would pay farmers to leave their land fallow.
15. Does present-day U.S. farm policy "protect" the farmer? Explain.
16. Is the health-care industry competitive? Explain.
17. What is "information asymmetry," and how does it lead to inefficiently high insurance premiums?

EXERCISES

1. When Braeburn Publishing priced its poetry book at \$5, it sold 5 books, and when it priced the volume at \$8, it sold 4 books. You can calculate that its revenues were higher with the higher price. Suppose that, from further test marketing, this firm determines that it faces the demand curve described by the following schedule.

Quantity of output (demanded)	Selling price (\$)	Total revenue (\$)	Marginal revenue (\$)
1	17		—
2	14		
3	11		
4	8		
5	5		

a. Graph the demand curve for the poetry book, labeling carefully. (Compare your graph to Figure 5.1.)
b. Calculate total revenue and marginal revenue at each output level, and add a marginal revenue curve to your graph.
c. Can the \$8 price be Braeburn's profit-maximizing choice? Why or why not?
d. Suppose that, thanks to computerized, on-demand publishing technology, Braeburn can produce any number of books at a constant cost of \$5 each. (That is, average cost and marginal cost are both \$5 for any quantity of books, and total costs are simply the number of books times \$5.) Add a marginal cost curve to your graph. (It will *not* look like the "usual" *MC* curve—it will be horizontal.)

e. What are Braeburn's profit-maximizing price and output levels for the poetry book? State these, and label them on the graph.
f. What level of profit would Braeburn earn with the $8 price? (Recall that profits equal total revenue minus total cost.) What is the level of profit with the price you just found that maximizes profit?

2. Suppose that two oligopolistic retail chains are considering opening a new sales outlet in a particular town. The changes to each firm's profits, depending on the actions taken, are given in the following payoff matrix. If a chain does not open a new outlet, it earns no addition to profits. If one of the chains is the only one to open an outlet, it makes high additional profits. If they both open outlets, they have to split the available market, and they make only more moderate additional profits.

Firm 2's Options

Firm 1's Options	New Outlet	No New Outlet
New Outlet	moderate profit (upper right); moderate profit (lower left)	no profit (upper right); high profit (lower left)
No New Outlet	high profit (upper right); no profit (lower left)	no profit (upper right); no profit (lower left)

a. If Firm 1 decides to open a new outlet, but Firm 2 does *not* open a new outlet, how much additional profit does each firm make?
b. If Firm 1 decides to open a new outlet, what is the worst that can happen to it? If Firm 1 decides *not* to open a new outlet, what is the worst that can happen to it? Which option, then, should Firm 1 choose, if it wants to make the choice that leaves it best off, regardless of what the other firm does?
c. If the firms are noncooperative and each firm makes the choice that will leave it best off regardless of the other's choice, what will the outcome be?
d. Is this like the "prisoner's dilemma," in which both parties could get a better outcome by communicating and cooperating?
e. Now suppose that each firm is thinking of opening new outlets in a *number* of towns, and each town has a payoff matrix similar to this one. Would there be advantages in having the two chains communicate and cooperate in this case? If they decide to collude, what form do you think their collusion might take?

3. Match each concept in Column A with an example in Column B.

Column A	Column B
a. A legal barrier to entry	1. Lobbying to get a concession
b. Predatory pricing	2. Patent rights
c. Rent-seeking behavior	3. Electricity distribution
d. Nonprice competition	4. Cornflakes in different-colored boxes
e. Product differentiation	5. Cutting prices to below cost to drive out a rival
f. Price fixing	6. Cooperating with a rival to charge the same price
g. Natural monopoly	7. Advertising

APPENDIX: FORMAL ANALYSIS OF MONOPOLY AND MONOPOLISTIC COMPETITION

A1. THE ASSUMPTIONS

This appendix shows how monopoly and monopolistic competition market structures can be formally treated within a model of profit-maximizing firms.

A2. MONOPOLY

Suppose that our firm is a monopolist, with the marginal revenue schedule shown in Table 18.1 and Figure 18.1 and with the marginal cost curve shown in Figure 18.1. As described in this chapter, the monopolist maximizes profits by setting $MR = MC$. It produces 5 units, at a marginal cost of about $12, and sells them for a price of $28. Adding in the average total cost curve of the firm enables us to identify the area of economic profit, as shown in Figure

Figure 18.8 **Monopoly Profits**

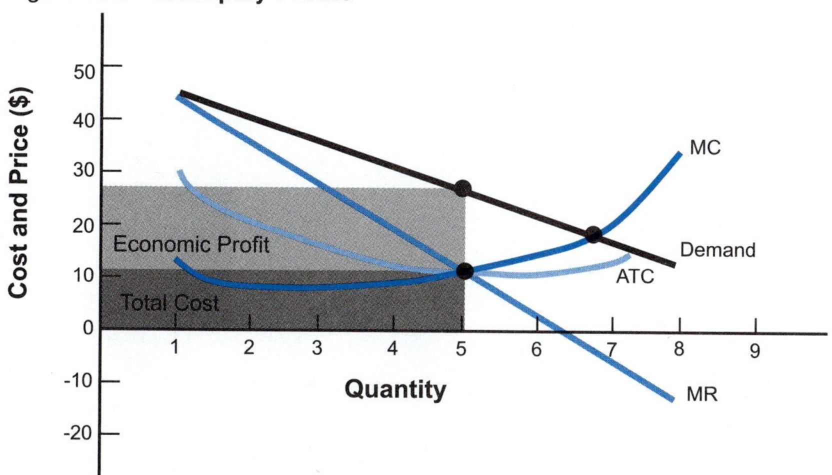

The monopolist sells its product at a per-unit price that is higher than its per-unit cost of production, thus reaping positive economic profits. Revenues are represented by the total shaded area. The part of revenues that goes to paying costs is represented by the darker shaded area. Thus the lighter area represents an excess of revenues over costs—the economic profit.

18.8. The firm's revenues include both shaded areas, whereas its costs are represented by the darker-shaded rectangle. The monopolist makes positive economic profit equal to the area of the ligher-shaded rectangle.

A3. Monopolistic Competition

A monopolistically competitive firm faces a downward-sloping demand curve. Yet, like a perfectly competitive firm, it also makes zero economic profits in the long run.

This case is illustrated in Figure 18.9. Like a monopolist, the monopolistically competitive firm will choose to produce the quantity corresponding to point A, where $MR = MC$. It will charge a price corresponding to point B on the demand curve. Point B is also on the *ATC* curve in the long run. Thus the shaded rectangle represents both total revenue (price × quantity) and total cost (average total cost × quantity). The firm makes zero economic profits.

How does this come about? Look back at Figure 18.5. If the price were above the *ATC* curve, the firm would make positive economic profits, and (because there is free entry) new firms would enter the industry. This causes the demand curve for this firm's differentiated product to shift downward. The demand curve is imagined to shift downward until it just touches the *ATC* curve, as shown in Figure 18.9.

Figure 18.9 **Zero Economic Profits for a Monopolistically Competitive Firm**

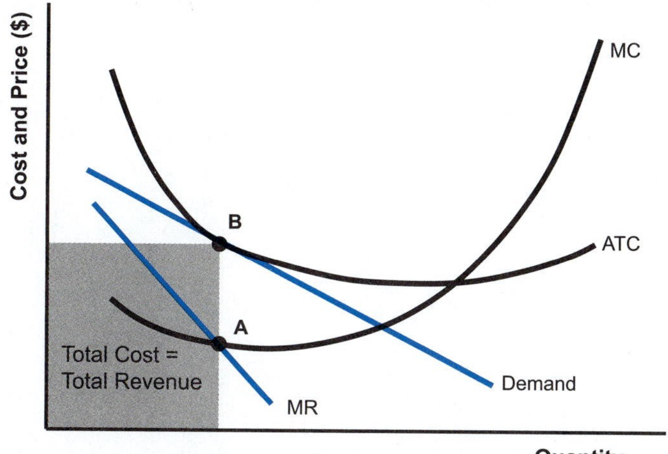

A monopolistically competitive firm sets $MC = MR$, but economic profits are kept at zero by the free entry and exit of firms.

Macroeconomic Basics

19 Introduction to Macroeconomics

1. What Is Macroeconomics About?

macroeconomics: the subfield of economics that focuses on the economy as a whole

recession: a downturn in economic activity, usually defined as lasting for two consecutive calendar quarters or more

unemployment: a situation in which people seek a paying job, but cannot obtain one

inflation: a rise in the general level of prices

As we noted in Chapter 1, while microeconomics emphasizes the economic activities and interactions of individuals, firms, and other specific organizations, **macroeconomics** looks at the workings of the economy as a whole, at the national—and often the global—level. There is continuous interaction between the microeconomic and macroeconomic levels of the economy. The macroeconomic situation is based on the behavior of millions of individual economic actors, and at the same time economic conditions at the aggregate level create the environment in which individual economic actors make their decisions. These conditions include rates of unemployment and inflation, ecological limits and constraints, degrees of economic inequality, and social/cultural assumptions about trust and responsibility.

For example, when you seek paid work in your chosen field, your success will depend in part on both micro- and macroeconomic factors. On the microeconomic side, you will need to have prepared yourself for the work—invested in your own "human capital," an economist would say. You will need to find a particular business or other agency that can use your skills—or find direct buyers for your services, if you decide to strike out on your own. You will want to find work that gives you a combination of job satisfaction, income, and benefits that you like.

But will employers in general be hiring? Some graduating classes are unlucky and flood the job market just as the national economy is "going sour"—that is, entering a **recession**. No matter how well-prepared you are, finding a job can be tough during a period of high **unemployment**, when many people who seek jobs are not successful in finding one. And if you do find a job, how far will your paycheck go toward meeting your standard-of-living desires? If you start working during a period of high **inflation**, when the overall level of prices is increasing, the purchasing power of a fixed paycheck will be quickly eroded.

Macroeconomic conditions also affect personal debt. If you are like most students these days, you will be paying back loans for a number of years. The higher the prevailing real interest rates in the economy, the more costly this borrowing will be. Your own economic well-being will also be tied to global issues such as trade flows and currency exchange rates—especially if you go to work for a business that does a lot of importing or exporting or you send money back to relatives in a home country. If you are lucky, all these factors will fall in your favor. If you are not . . . well, then you can join the chorus blaming "the economy" for your troubles.

Such macroeconomic issues are considered "short run"—economists refer to them as having to do with macroeconomic "fluctuations." Sometimes unemployment is high, and sometimes it is low, and the same goes for inflation, interest rates, trade deficits, and exchange rates.

Other macroeconomic issues have to do with the long run. Can you expect your standard of living twenty years from now, or the standard of living of your children, to be higher or lower than what you enjoy now? Are you living in a society where all people have a chance to develop themselves, or are extremes of wealth and poverty becoming more pronounced over time? What is the supply of natural resources used in production processes, and what is the quality of those resources? What other social and environmental factors affect the ability of the economy to prosper, or threaten its success?

Macroeconomics seeks to explain an especially interesting phenomenon: the fact that bad things can often happen on a national or global level even though virtually no individual or microeconomic-level organization *wants* or *intends* them to happen. People generally agree that high unemployment, persistent high inflation, and destruction of the natural environment, for example, are bad things, yet they occur nonetheless.

macroeconomy: an economic system whose boundaries are normally understood to be the boundaries of a country

global economy: the system of economic rules, norms, and interactions by which economic actors and actions in different parts of the world are connected to one another

economic actor (economic agent): an individual, group, or organization that is involved in economic activities

Microeconomics and macroeconomics are terms that are applied rather loosely, covering or emphasizing different topics as times and circumstances change. Many issues have both macroeconomic and microeconomic aspects. For example, imposition of a sales tax will affect microeconomic behavior—people may consume less or shift their patterns of consumption toward untaxed items—but it also affects government revenues, which, as we will see, are an important element of macroeconomic analysis. No one speaks of "the microeconomy" because there are too many subnational economic systems of varied sizes that are studied in the field of microeconomics. However, the term **macroeconomy** is used to refer to a national economic system.

People also speak of the **global economy**, meaning the system of economic rules, norms, and interactions by which economic actors and actions in different parts of the world are connected to one another. **Economic actors (or economic agents)** include all individuals, groups, and organizations that engage in or influence economic activity. As the global economy has become an increasingly important part of the experience of more and more people, it has become more essential to include its study in introductory macroeconomics courses. You can expect to find global as well as macroeconomic issues extensively covered in this book.

Discussion Questions

1. You have evidently made a decision to dedicate some of your personal resources of time and money in college to studying economics. Why? What do you hope to learn in this course that will be helpful for you in reaching your goals?
2. Are you familiar with the following terms? While you will study them in detail in this course, see how well you can come up with a definition for them just from your previous knowledge. (It does not matter at this point if you are not familiar with them.)

unemployment	recession
inflation	economic boom
economic growth	money
development	fiscal policy
GDP	monetary policy
investment	sustainability

2. MACROECONOMICS AND THE DYNAMICS OF REAL-WORLD MARKETS

Much of microeconomics, as we have seen, is based on supply and demand analysis, in which price adjustments lead to economic equilibrium. If this same logic applied to the economy as a whole, there would be little need for a separate theory of macroeconomics. But, as described in earlier chapters, few if any markets truly approach perfect competition. Markets may be characterized by market power (as discussed in Chapter 18). Buyers and sellers may have imperfect information, or be bound by long-term contracts. The role of assumptions and expectations can be significant. For example, if people were used to paying more for the services of lawyers than for the services of teachers, lawyers would be very resistant to changes in the relative prices. In general, wages, which are a special kind of price, can be affected by a variety of things aside from simple supply and demand. For these and other reasons, the mechanism of price adjustment may not work as smoothly as a simple supply-and-demand model might suggest.

2.1 WHEN PRICE ADJUSTMENTS ARE SLOW

An issue of particular importance to macroeconomics is the question of the speed at which real-world price adjustments take place. How long will it take markets to reach equilibrium? Minutes? An hour? A day? The theory of supply and demand does not tell us. As discussed in Chapter 3, basic market analysis represents a static model, which does not take into account the passage of time.

Some markets, such as stock markets, tend to clear quickly. But other markets involve significant time delays. For example, consider the market for shirts. When you go into a clothing store, you see a rack of shirts and, on their tags, a given price. The price probably reflects a markup by the retailer over what he or she paid to a distributor to get the shirts. The distributor in turn probably charged a markup over the price charged by the manufacturer. Now, if the shirts were overpriced, they would not sell very well. In terms of market analysis, there will be a surplus. If the market adjusted instantaneously, the supplier and demander would quickly be able to fine tune the price and quantity to get it just right. The price would fall, the surplus of shirts would disappear immediately, and equilibrium would be restored.

In a realistic, complicated case such as this one, however, there is actually a *chain* of markets involved—the manufacturer sells to the distributor, the distributor to the retailer, and the retailer to the final buyer. A quick adjustment of prices is unlikely. More commonly, when retailers mark down the prices on the shirts they have in stock in order to clear them out, the drop in the price will not immediately travel back up the supply chain. In the next order that the retailers place with their distributors, the retailers might just ask for a smaller quantity of shirts, at the price at which the distributor is offering them—especially if the retailer were small relative to the distributor and had little power to bargain over prices. Any changes in prices or quantities at the manufacturing level would only develop over time, as the manufacturers saw the level of their inventories either rise (because the shirts are not selling) or fall (because the distributors order more).

quantity adjustments: a response by suppliers in which they react to unexpectedly low sales of their good primarily by reducing production levels rather than by reducing the price and to unexpectedly high sales by increasing production rather than raising the price

Because of the time it takes for all these things to happen, some economists believe that the most likely first response to a surplus is that manufacturers would cut *production*—perhaps laying off workers—rather than reducing their price. In such a case, the *quantity* produced adjusts to meet the quantity demanded at a given price, rather than the price adjusting to clear the market. If such **quantity adjustments** happened throughout the economy, unemployment could rise.

menu costs: the costs to a supplier of changing prices listed on order forms, brochures, menus, and the like

Suppliers may also be reluctant to change the prices that they offer because of **menu costs**—literally, the costs of changing the prices listed on such things as order forms and restaurant menus. Other factors that could slow the process of price adjustment include union contracts, lengthy production processes, and information problems.

2.2 WHEN PRICES SWING TOO MUCH: MARKET INSTABILITY

speculation: buying and selling assets with the expectation of profiting from appreciation or depreciation in their value

speculative bubble: the situation that occurs when mutually reinforcing investor optimism raises the value of an asset far above what can be justified by fundamental value

Other markets have adjustment processes in which prices may change rapidly. In electronic stock markets, for example, thousands of trades may take place every minute, as buyers and sellers find each other and quickly negotiate a price. Such a market can probably be thought of as in equilibrium, or moving quickly toward one, nearly all the time.

Very rapid adjustments of prices, however, create their own set of problems. They can encourage **speculation**—the buying and selling of assets with the expectation of profiting from appreciation or depreciation in their values, usually over a relatively short period of time. Speculators buy items such as stocks in companies, commodities futures (e.g., contracts to buy or sell items such as pork bellies or copper at a specific price on a future date), foreign exchange, real estate, or other investment vehicles, purely in the hopes that they will be able to sell them in the future for more than they have paid.

When many people come to believe that the price of something will rise, a **speculative bubble** can occur, in which people buy the asset because so many other people also believe that its price will continue to rise. In a mass phenomenon often referred to using terms such as "herd mentality" or "bandwagon effect," speculators' mutually reinforcing optimism causes asset values to rise far above any price that could be rationalized in terms of "economic fundamentals."

In the case of a stock price, for example, the rational economic basis for valuation should be the returns that an investor can expect from the firm of which the stock represents an ownership share, while in the case of real estate the value should be determined by the stream of likely rents, from the present into the future. Someone who buys a home to live in should rationally select one whose costs (mortgage payments plus lost income on the money used for down payment) are similar to the rent that would be demanded for a comparable property.

During a bubble, however, people pay less attention to (or take a biased view of) such fundamental factors. Instead, demand for an asset is determined largely by purchasers' perception that they will be able to find someone to whom they can sell the asset at a higher price. Eventually, however, people begin to figure out that prices have become unrealistically high. Then demand drops, the bubble bursts, and prices fall. This happened during the "dot-com" bubble of the late 1990s (see Figure 19.1).

Figure 19.1 **The Stock Market Bubble of 1999–2000**

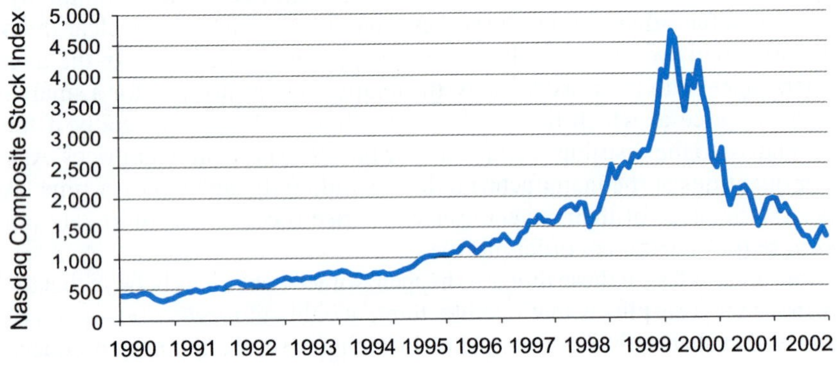

Enthusiasm about new technologies, and Internet e-commerce in particular, temporarily drove the prices of many companies' stocks very high. During the bubble, the prices of stocks as determined by supply and demand rose far above the prices that would occur if valuation had been based on the companies' actual performances.

Source: Yahoo! Finance, Monthly data.

It is fairly easy, of course, to recognize a bubble after the fact. However, during the spectacular rise in stock prices that took place in the late 1990s, many otherwise rational and intelligent people convinced one another—and themselves—that the stock market boom reflected an immense jump in productivity, not a speculative bubble. This led to a major crash in stock prices during 2000–2.

subprime mortgage: a mortgage given to someone with poor credit

In spite of the painful lesson of this crash, soon afterward the buildup began for another boom and bust, this time originating in the U.S. market for **subprime mortgages**. Such mortgages are housing loans given to people whose income or credit history is not good enough to qualify them for regular mortgages.

Many banks aggressively marketed subprime housing loans to prospective homeowners from early 2004 to 2007, sometimes using fraudulent techniques and making profits by collecting fees on each loan made. Some of the world's largest banks moved aggressively into this area, bundling and repackaging the mortgages in such a way that their riskiness was not immediately apparent. Eventually, however, softening of housing prices and rising adjustable interest rates caused a steep increase in the number of U.S. homeowners who were defaulting on their loans. Securities based on "bundled" subprime mortgages rapidly lost market value as questions were finally raised about the actual worth of the assets on which they were based. During the subprime crisis, many people lost their homes, and many of the largest commercial banks lost billions of dollars. We will examine this financial crisis in Chapter 30. (See Box 19.1 for a presentation of recent developments in the housing market).

BOX 19.1 RECOVERY IN THE HOUSING MARKET

The housing market is considered an important indicator of the overall economy. In the wake of the Great Recession, the average house price in the United States fell by about one-third between 2006 and 2011. Finally, in 2012 the housing market began to show signs of recovery. By the end of 2012 prices were rising at an annual rate of over 7percent.

The rising prices are a function of both supply and demand factors. The number of homes sold nationally in 2012 was up by about 30 percent compared to the previous year. At the same time, the supply of homes for sale reached its lowest level since 2005.

The increase in house prices varied significantly across regions of the country. The biggest gains were found in areas hit the hardest when the housing bubble burst in 2007. Prices increased by 23 percent in Phoenix, 14 percent in Detroit, 13 percent in Las Vegas, and 10 percent in Miami. Of the 20 major metropolitan markets, only New York City saw further declines in house prices in 2012.

The reasons housing prices have increased include an improvement in the overall economy, lower unemployment rates, very low mortgage rates, and the tight supply. Richard Green of the USC Lusk Center for Real Estate, said the recovery in housing prices has not been even across all the different price segments. He said the upper end of the market has done well as the wealthier families' earnings have recovered and foreign buyers have come into the market. The lower end of the market has recovered due to purchases by investors looking for bargains. "It's the middle market that needs help—particularly in the form of higher income—if it is going to have a sustained recovery," Green said.

Source: Chris Isidore, "Housing Recovery Gains Strength," CNN Money, February 26, 2013.

Situations of speculative bubbles and volatile (that is, rapidly changing) prices have important implications for macroeconomics, even though there is some disagreement among economists about the importance of market volatility. Issues such as quantity adjustment and market volatility suggest that markets in the real world may not be as well-behaved as those in a basic supply and demand model. Things may look different when we consider them from the perspective of the economy as a whole. For this reason, explaining national-level economic phenomena may require different theoretical tools.

3. MACROECONOMIC GOALS

We have introduced the idea of an economy working "well" or "badly" and have referred to high unemployment, persistent high inflation, and destruction of the natural environment as bad things that virtually no one wants. "Bad" and "good" are value-laden terms. Do they belong in an economics textbook?

As noted in Chapter 1, social scientists often make a distinction between positive questions, which concern issues of fact, or "what is," and normative questions, which have to do with goals and values, or "what should be." For example, "What is the level of poverty in our country?" is a positive question, requiring descriptive facts as an answer. "How much effort should be given to poverty reduction?" is a normative question, requiring analysis of our values and goals. In our study of economics, we often find that positive and normative questions are inevitably intertwined. For example, consider the definition of poverty. To construct a definition of poverty, we need to combine facts about income distribution with a normative assessment of where to draw the poverty line. We also need to consider whether the definition of poverty should be based solely on income, or whether it should include information about people's **assets** or opportunities. Life rarely offers us a neat distinction between " what is" and "what ought to be"; more often, we have to deal with a mixture of the two.

assets: property owned by an individual or company

Much of macroeconomic analysis is concerned with positive issues. Using both empirical evidence and various theories, we describe—using the best available economic research—how an economy functions at the macro level. Yet, although a few people perhaps enjoy studying economic principles for their own sake, the main reason that anyone would study macroeconomics is to try to understand how we—as a society, country, and world—can reach our desired goals. Thus we cannot avoid the normative question of what goals the macroeconomy *should* achieve.

Three major macroeconomic goals are the achievement of **good living standards, stability and security,** and **sustainability**

Not everyone has the same goals, either at a personal level or as part of their idea of a "good" society. However, agreement becomes easier at a more general level. In the context of macroeconomics, we can say that three especially important components of well-being are **good living standards, stability and security,** and **sustainability**.

3.1 LIVING STANDARDS

One macroeconomic goal is to achieve and maintain people's living standards at a high enough level that their lives can be long, healthy, and enjoyable and offer them the opportunity to accomplish the things that they believe give their lives meaning.

The most basic living standard issues relate to the quality of people's diets and housing, their access to means of transportation and communication, and the quality of medical attention that they receive. Taking a somewhat broader view, we might also include less tangible aspects of life, such as the quality of education that people receive and the variety of entertainment and other non-work-related activities that they can enjoy.

living standards growth: improvements in people's diet, housing, medical care, education, working conditions, and access to transportation, communication, entertainment, and other amenities

In addition, the way in which people participate in producing goods and services—as well as their consumption of them—has important implications for their health and happiness. So, for working-age people, the quality of their working lives is part of their standard of living. And for people who cannot do much work because they are too young, old, ill, or handicapped, the quality of the hands-on care that they receive is a major component of their living standard.

As we will see in Chapter 21, we could add even more categories to broaden our notion of well-being, going beyond economic issues to include things like political freedom and social inclusion (see Box 19.2). Traditionally, however, economics has regarded **living standards growth** as the top concern.

economic growth: increases in the level of marketed production in a country or region

How can living standards be maintained or improved? For a long time, "raising living standards" was considered nearly synonymous with "achieving economic growth." By **economic growth**, we mean growth in the level of marketed production or output. Traditionally, this has been measured within a country by the growth of its gross domestic product (GDP)—a measure that you will hear much more about in later chapters.

BOX 19.2 ELEMENTS OF WELL-BEING

The following are some elements that might go into a broad concept of well-being. When you think about a good life for yourself, are there elements that you would wish to add to or subtract from this list?

- Satisfaction of basic physical needs, such as adequate nutrition, health care, and a comfortable living environment.
- Security that one's basic needs will continue to be met, as well as security against aggression or unjust persecution.
- Happiness, expressed though feelings of joy, contentment, pleasure, etc.
- The ability to realize one's potential, including physical, intellectual, moral, social, and spiritual development.
- A sense of meaning in one's life; a reason or purpose for one's efforts.
- Fairness, including appropriate rewards for one's efforts and fair and equal treatment by social institutions.
- Freedom to make personal decisions within the limits of responsible relations with others (and the limits of their decision-making capacity, as in the case of children).
- Participation in social decision-making processes.
- Good social relations, including those with friends, family, business associates, and fellow citizens, as well as peaceful relations among countries.
- Ecological balance, meaning that natural resources are preserved and, where necessary, restored to a healthy and resilient state.

Global economic growth has been impressive in recent decades. Figure 19.2 plots the sum of GDP for all countries from 1960 to 2006. The data from which this chart has been plotted are far from perfect—different countries have at different times used a variety of methods to calculate their GDP. The definition of GDP can also be controversial, as we explore in Chapters 20 and 21. Nevertheless, we can reasonably conclude from this picture that global production of goods and services has increased greatly over the past few decades. By this measure, the value of global production in 2010 was about 5.7 times the value in 1960.

The growth in economic production has not been equal in all countries, and material living standards are still very low in much of the world. This fact is important for people's options and their enjoyment of life. Poverty can mean that people are crowded together in unsanitary urban slums or isolated in rural huts, have barely enough to eat, receive little or no education, and never see a doctor.

Worldwide, extreme poverty is still a major concern; according to a 2008 World Bank study, 1.4 billion people—about a quarter of the population of the developing world—had less than $1.25 to spend per day. The production of more and better housing, better roads, more grain, more schooling, and more medical care—*more goods and services*—is necessary to raise living standards in such situations.

economic development: the process of moving from a situation of poverty and deprivation to a situation of increased production and plenty, through investments and changes in the organization of work

Because of this underlying concern with living standards, for many decades economists focused very strongly on measures of economic growth and the question of how it could be maintained and increased. The process of moving from a general situation of poverty and deprivation to one of increased production and plenty is what has traditionally been referred to as **economic development**. (This topic is discussed at greater length in Chapter 32.)

labor productivity: the level of output that can be produced per worker per hour

Generally, economic development has been thought of as a process of increasing agricultural productivity, investing in machinery and technology, and making changes in the organization of work (from home-based shops to factories, for example), so that **labor productivity** rises—meaning that people can produce more in each hour that they work.

Of course, while increased production is *necessary* in such a situation, it is not *sufficient* on its own to improve living standards for the people living in a poor country. For one thing, the increase in production may not be enough to keep pace with a growing population. Improvement in general living standards can result only if production *per person* (GDP *per capita*) on average rises.

Some of the increase in global production shown in Figure 19.2 is simply a result of more people producing goods and services. When we adjust for the growth in the world's population, we see that production per capita, measured by dividing global production by

Figure 19.2 **Global Production, 1960–2010**

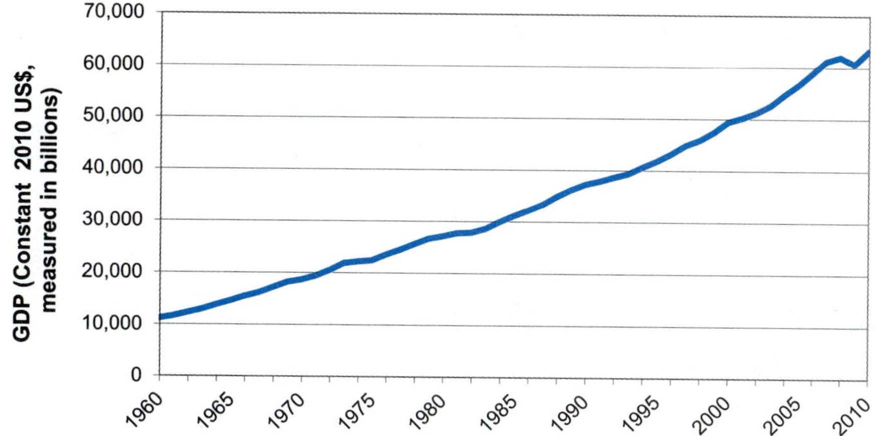

As measured by summing up the GDP of all countries, global production has more than quintupled in the last five decades.

Source: The World Bank Group, World Development Indicators Online.

global population, has also grown over the past several decades, but not by as much. Figure 19.3 shows that global production per capita increased by about a factor of 2.5 between 1960 and 2010, according to this measure.*

If we were to disaggregate from the global figures, we would see that increases in economic production over these years vary significantly across different regions and countries. In East Asian countries, GDP per capita increased more than sevenfold. In sub-Saharan Africa, however, GDP per capita increased only about 15 percent between 1960 and 2010.

Even if GDP *per capita* is rising, other factors are still important in ensuring that economic growth benefits the world's and each country's population as a whole. Recall from Chapter 1 the three basic economic questions: *what*, *how*, and *for whom*.

- First, it matters *what* is produced. An economy may experience "economic growth" by increasing its production of military hardware or large public monuments, for example, but these kinds of production raise living standards less than growth in production of nutritious food, widely available health care, or the quality of basic education.
- Second, it matters *how* it is produced. In some poorer countries today, many workers—including young children—work 14- to 16-hour days in unsafe, badly ventilated mines and factories; many suffer severe illnesses and early death. And in both rich and poor countries, production is often carried out in ways that deplete or degrade essential natural resources.
- Third, it matters *for whom* economic growth occurs. How are the increases in production, or in incomes arising from production, distributed among the population? Do some regions, or some groups of people as defined by income class, race, ethnicity, gender, or other factors, receive more of the gains from growth than others? If the benefits of economic growth go only to a tiny global or national elite, the bulk of the population may remain very poor.

Even given the qualifications raised by these questions, it is generally true that in regions that are very poor economic growth, as measured by an increase in GDP, is necessary and important to increase well-being.

In richer regions, the situation may be different. In a country that is already rich, is economic growth still the key to improving living standards and increasing overall well-being? In most highly industrialized countries, populations are growing very slowly—in many countries they

Figure 19.3 **Global Production Per Capita, 1960–2010**

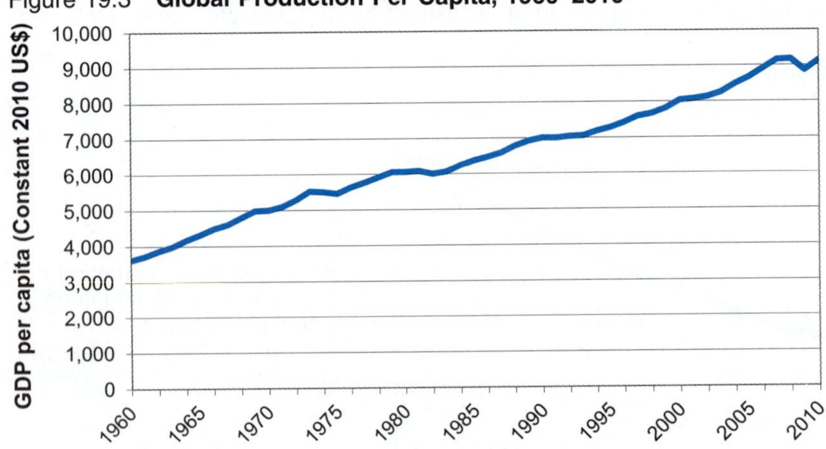

Global production per person has more than doubled in the last five decades.

Source: The World Bank Group, World Development Indicators Online.

*These figures are corrected for inflation. We examine the process by which economists correct GDP figures for inflation in Chapter 20.

are declining or on a trajectory that will soon bring about population decline.* When the population is not growing, and when the majority of families already enjoy decent housing, safe water, plenty of food, readily available heating and refrigeration, a car or two (or more), airline travel, TVs and the like, do we really need *more* in general?

Some people would say that we do, but others believe that we should instead switch our national priorities into making sure that production is designed to increase well-being. In countries that already have a high level of production, *living standards growth* may be achievable even in the absence of *economic growth,* by improving cultural, educational, and environmental conditions, raising the quality of work-life and the quantity and quality of leisure, and by promoting an equitable allocation of economic rewards.

We will return to these questions—and to the critical issue of the relationships among economic growth, job creation, and well-being—in later chapters.

3.2 Stability and Security

While closely linked to goals for living standards, the goal of stability and security brings in a dimension that we have not yet discussed. Imagine that you are elderly, and looking back over your life you can say that *on average,* you enjoyed a good standard of living. This might arise from two quite different scenarios. In one scenario, you enjoy a fairly steady, or gently rising, living standard and are always able to plan confidently for your financial future.

In the other scenario, you are quite successful at some points in your life but also periodically have to face the real possibility of "losing it all." You do well and buy a very nice house, but then you become unemployed and your house is foreclosed on because you are not able to make the payments. Then you start to do well again and believe you are on a solid path to a pleasant retirement, but steeply rising price levels or a jumpy stock market reduces the value of your savings and pension. Even if, after the fact and "over the long run," you can say that *on average* you have done OK in terms of your living standards, the uncertainty and anxiety of living with economic fluctuations in the second scenario would take a toll on your overall well-being, relative to the more stable case.

High rates of unemployment are associated with many indicators of individual and social stress, such as suicide, domestic violence, and stress-related illnesses among those affected, and crime. Unpredictable fluctuations in employment levels and rates of inflation, interest rates, and foreign exchange rates make it difficult—and, in the worst cases, impossible—for individuals and organizations to make productive and economically sensible plans for the future. This has been a major concern for many young people who entered the work force during or after the major recession of 2007–9.

One common pattern is for fluctuations in the level of production to occur as a cycle in which recessions (or "contractions" or "slumps") and their attendant problem of high unemployment alternate with booms (also called "expansions" or "recoveries"), which often bring with them the problem of more rapidly rising prices. This is called the **business cycle** or **trade cycle**. Even if these problems are "short run" and do not last long—people eventually find jobs or inflation slows down—fluctuations cause considerable "ill-being" while they last. So creating a stable, secure economic environment is a separate important macroeconomic goal.

business (trade) cycle: recurrent fluctuations in the level of national production, with alternating periods of recession and boom

In this chapter, we follow the common convention of using GDP as an indicator of prosperity. In Chapters 20 and 21, as well as later, we discuss with more precision exactly what it is that GDP does—and does not—measure. For now, we will use GDP as an overall measure of economic activity. For example, consider Figure 19.4, which shows GDP for the United States since 1800. You can see that while the general trend is upward, the curve on the graph does not indicate *steady* growth. The curve is somewhat wavy. During some periods GDP fell as the country experienced economic contractions, and during other periods GDP

*For more on this subject see the Appendix to Chapter 33.

Figure 19.4 **GDP in the United States, 1800–2010**

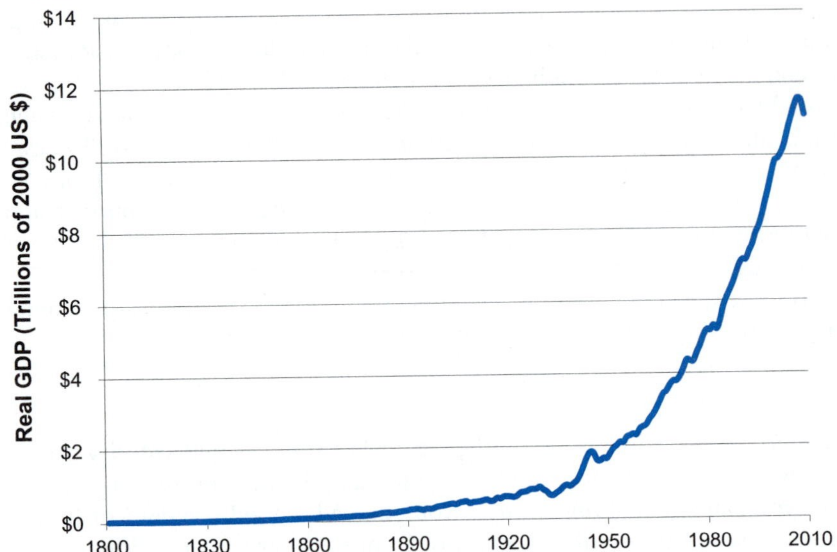

GDP in the United States has grown over time, but it has not grown steadily. The economy has experienced alternating periods of expansion and contraction.

Source: Louis D. Johnston and Samuel H. Williamson, "The Annual Real and Nominal GDP for the United States, 1790–Present." Economic History Services, http://www.eh.net/hmit/gdp/.
Updated with data from the World Bank Development Indicators. http://data.worldbank.org/indicator

rose very steeply due to rapid economic expansion. (As in all other graphs of production in this chapter, GDP numbers in Figure 19.4 are expressed in "real," or inflation-adjusted, terms.)

One widely accepted macroeconomic goal is the achievement of sufficient economic stability to enable individuals and families to enjoy economic security and to be able to make reasonable predictions about their future. In the light of new knowledge about our dependence on the natural world, which is undergoing radical alterations due to human economic activity, the goal of security now must also include a much longer time horizon, recognizing a serious responsibility to future generations. This leads us to our third goal: sustainability.

3.3 SUSTAINABILITY

We want good living standards and stability not only for ourselves right now but also for ourselves later in our lives and for our children, grandchildren, and other generations to come.

In order to understand how well we are achieving the goal of sustainability, we must address the questions:

- Are economic activities *financially* sustainable into the future? Or is a country incurring a high amount of debt that may create a heavy burden on its future inhabitants?
- Are economic activities *socially* sustainable into the future? Are disparities between the "haves" and the "have-nots" accelerating or diminishing? Are they based on justifiable causes or on unequal power relations? Are young people receiving the upbringing and education required to enable them to contribute to a healthy economy and society? Or is the current structure of economic activity setting the stage for future social disruption and political strife?
- Are economic activities *ecologically* sustainable into the future? Is the natural environment that supports life being treated in a way that will sustain its quality into the future? Or is it becoming depleted or degraded?

For many generations, it seemed that technological progress and economic growth were magical keys that unlocked the door to unlimited improvements in the standard of living. For example, real output per person in the United States in 2010 was about sixteen times what it had been in 1840. "Developed" countries in North America, Western Europe, and elsewhere experienced long-run rising standards of living through industrialization, improvements in agricultural technology, and the development of service industries.

Can this process continue indefinitely? Some have argued that sustainability problems can be remedied by *more* GDP growth. For example, the issue of financial sustainability includes both concerns about the level of government debt (which accumulates whenever governments spend more than they take in) and external debt (what all people and organizations in a country owe to foreigners). Too much debt is a problem since it means that a large proportion of a country's income in the future may need to be directed toward paying back the debt rather than to other, more socially beneficial, uses. Indebtedness, however, is usually considered manageable as long as the growth of GDP is at least keeping pace with the level of debt, so that debt does not increase as a percent of GDP.

Regarding social sustainability, some people believe that economic growth is also the way to relieve social ills and political strife. They reason that the bigger the pie, the bigger everyone's share can be, and that rising personal incomes will naturally lead to a peaceful and productive population. Concerning ecological issues, some economists think that any current negative effects of economic growth on the environment can be remedied by additional economic growth, since higher incomes give countries the wherewithal to invest in new exploration for resources and new pollution-controlling technologies. So, to the most growth-oriented economists, "sustainable growth" simply means making sure that the growth rate of GDP stays high well into the future.

In contrast to those who believe that economic growth, as traditionally defined, holds the best answers to financial, social, and environmental problems, by the end of the twentieth century some economists had started asking whether these might instead *contribute to* these problems.

To the extent that a country's economic prosperity depends on short-sighted or unrealistic financial planning, prosperity may be unsustainable. For decades, for example, many poorer countries were encouraged to borrow heavily from richer countries in order to make progress in economic development. However, many of them did not achieve the high rate of economic growth that was supposed to result from the borrowing, and a severe "debt crisis" resulted. Some very poor countries currently spend more funds simply to pay the interest on their debt than they pay for health care for their own population; many also pay more in principal and interest than they currently receive in grants and loans.

Some industrialized countries, including the United States, also borrow heavily to fund their activities. Many fear that such borrowing may become so excessive that dramatically higher taxes will be required in the future in order to pay interest on the debt. Those called on to pay these higher taxes—and, hence, suffer lower living standards—would be future workers like you. Setting good priorities about how we borrow—and what we borrow for—is important for long-run sustainability. This issue will be discussed in detail in Chapter 31.

Turning to social sustainability, many economists and other observers have come to question whether "development" as traditionally defined will solve the problem of global disparities in living standards. Some economists suggest that historical factors such as the legacy of colonization, and political factors such as rich countries' protection of their own industries within the system of global trade, mean that it is impossible to expect poorer countries to "develop" in the same way as countries that industrialized earlier. Analysts have also estimated that giving everyone in the world an American lifestyle, including a meat-rich diet and multiple cars per family, would require an extra two to four planets to supply resources and absorb waste!

Traditional goals of unlimited material affluence have also been called into question within richer countries, and some social scientists have suggested that consumerist and "more-is-better" values may actually contribute to personal and social discontent and the weakening of social norms of trust and reciprocity. Societies that suffer wide divisions between "haves" and "have-nots," or a general sense that everybody is just out for him- or herself, are more likely to suffer social and political breakdown—perhaps to the point of violence—than societies where people enjoy a greater sense of social cohesion.

Regarding environmental issues, land development and certain agricultural practices have caused extinction of some species and notable decreases in genetic diversity in others. Contemporary "developed" economies are presently heavily dependent on the consumption of fossil fuels; but scientists warn that carbon dioxide emissions from the burning of fossil fuels are rapidly exacerbating global climate change.

restorative development: economic progress that restores economic, financial, social, or ecological systems that have been degraded and are no longer adequately supportive of human well-being in the present and the future

This raises the question of whether it is sufficient to sustain the financial, economic, and ecological systems *as they are now.* Some of the ecological systems that support economic activity may already be severely degraded. In such cases, it is not enough to sustain what exists now—rather, we need to take on a goal of **restorative development**, to rebuild systems that are no longer supporting well-being in the present and the future.

precautionary principle: the principle that we should err on the side of caution when dealing with natural systems or human health, especially when major health or environmental damage could result

Some ecologically-oriented economists have suggested that that, instead of placing blind faith in technological progress and economic growth, society should adopt a **precautionary principle**. This principle says that we should err on the side of caution, or, as stated by one group of experts, "When an activity raises threats of harm to the environment or human health, precautionary measures should be taken even if some cause and effect relationships are not fully established scientifically."[1] Such attention to environmental sustainability need not preclude also giving attention to the goals of living standards improvement and stability, but it does clearly call into question the idea that economic growth, in itself, is always the only or the best goal.

Many economists in the twentieth century did not explicitly address the question of macroeconomic goals, content in the belief that economic growth would naturally contribute to the achievement of any other goals that we might choose. This textbook attempts to balance ideas on how to achieve economic growth with questions about what kinds of growth actually contribute to well-being and ideas on how present and future well-being can be enhanced by restorative development.

Discussion Questions

1. Which of the macroeconomic goals discussed above do you think should have the highest priority? Why? Are there other major goals that you think are missing from the preceding discussion?
2. No one would argue that the goal of macroeconomics is to make people *worse* off! Yet the above outline of macroeconomic goals suggests that trying too hard to achieve some narrowly defined goals may lead to such a result. Why do you think that some economists would view economic growth as the major goal, while others view it as potentially in conflict with other goals such as sustainability or restorative development?

4. MACROECONOMICS IN CONTEXT

Macroeconomics, as a field of study, is not a set of principles that is set in stone. Rather, the field has developed and changed over time as new empirical and theoretical techniques have been invented and as historical events have raised new questions for which people have urgently sought answers. To give you an idea of how the various principles in this book fit into social and historical contexts, we end this chapter with a short overview of the major historical developments in macroeconomics. This is not just dusty history; you will see as you progress through this textbook that many themes keep arising in slightly new forms, while other challenges are unique to our twenty-first-century world.

4.1 THE CLASSICAL PERIOD

Centuries ago, most people in the world were involved in agriculture or in home production, such as when a family would work together to turn raw wool into cloth. Merchants were a minority, and industrial production and large-scale trade were unknown. All this changed with the coming of the Industrial Revolution, which began in England in the mid-eighteenth century. In many countries, technological progress led to new methods of production, and more productive economies both increased and diversified their output. Necessities like food and clothing used up a decreasing proportion of the average family income, while a growing fraction of the population was able to acquire more comforts and luxuries—better bedding, plumbing, housing, and transportation, to name just a few of the improvements in living standards. Academic thinkers started to try to understand and explain how these changes came about—and **classical economics** was born.

classical economics: the school of economics, originating in the eighteenth century, that stressed issues of growth and distribution, based on an image of smoothly functioning markets

division of labor: an approach to production in which a process is broken down into smaller tasks, with each worker assigned only one or a few tasks

specialization: in production, a system of organization in which each worker performs only one type of task

During this period, macroeconomic study focused on economic growth and distribution. The most famous classical economist was the Scottish philosopher Adam Smith (1723–1790), whose 1776 book *An Inquiry into the Nature and Causes of the Wealth of Nations* set the terms of discussion for centuries to come. Smith attributed the growing "wealth of nations" to various factors. One was changes in the organization of work, particularly the **division of labor** that assigned workers to **specialized**, narrowly defined tasks. Whereas in family-based production each individual had usually performed a variety of tasks, in industrial production a person would repeat one specific task over and over, presumably becoming more proficient with increased practice. Another factor was technological progress, such as the invention of new machines powered by burning coal. The third was the accumulation of funds to invest in plants and machinery ("capital accumulation"). Classical economists were also particularly concerned with theorizing about how the funds generated by selling output would come to be distributed between the people who worked in factories and the capitalists who owned the factories.

Classical economists, including Smith, David Ricardo, Thomas Malthus, John Stuart Mill, and Karl Marx, were interested in several questions that are still among the most important issues for macroeconomics: How is the total wealth generated by a society divided between those who own the means of production and those who work for them? Is the existing division optimal? What are the forces that determine how society's wealth will be divided?

Smith is known in particular for promulgating the idea that market systems could coordinate the self-interested actions of individuals so that they would ultimately serve the social good. While Smith himself supported a number of government interventions and discussed the moral basis of social and economic behavior at length in other works, the school of classical economics has been popularly identified with the idea that individual self-interest is a positive force and that governments should let markets function without interference—that economies should be **laissez-faire**.*

laissez-faire economy: an economy with little government regulation

Say's Law: the classical belief that "supply creates its own demand"

The classical economists, with the exception of Malthus and Marx, did not much address the problem of economic fluctuations. Most of them thought that a smoothly functioning market system should be entirely self-regulating, and full employment should generally prevail. This view was summarized in **Say's Law**, named after the French classical economist Jean-Baptiste Say (1767–1832), which was said to prove that "supply creates its own demand." The example Say gave was of a tradesman, for example, a shoemaker, who sold $100 worth of shoes. Say argued that the shoemaker would naturally want to spend the $100 on other goods, thereby creating a level of demand that was exactly equal in monetary value to the supply of shoes that he had provided. If this example is extended to the whole economy, it suggests that the quantities demanded and quantities supplied of goods will exactly balance. From this, Say also deduced that the system would always generate the right number of jobs for those needing work. Classical economists discussed issues related to a country's monetary system, but tended to assume that monetary issues affected only the price levels, and not the level of production, in a country.

4.2 The Great Depression, Keynes, and Monetarism

In practice, however, economies do not always work so smoothly. Some periods, like 1904–6 and the 1920s in the United States, were boom years in which everyone seemed eager to invest and spend. People with extra funds would buy stocks (ownership shares in companies) or deposit their funds in banks (to be lent to others) with great confidence and optimism. But it appeared

*"Laissez-faire," a French term, means "leave alone" and is pronounced "lez-say fair."

that these booms frequently ended in painful recessions. Suddenly, the tide would turn, and everyone would want to sell—not buy—and stock prices would plummet. A lack of confidence in banks would lead to "bank runs" or "banking panics," such as occurred in 1907 and 1930–33 in the United States, when many people tried to withdraw their deposits all at once. With financial markets in tatters, businesses and individuals would be unable or unwilling to maintain or expand their activities. Because people were cutting back on spending, produced goods would go unsold. Industries would cut back on production. People would become unemployed.

A great many people in the United States (and much of the rest of the industrialized world) suffered considerable hardship during the Great Depression that followed the 1929 stock market crash. Production dropped by about 30 percent between 1929 and 1933. At its worst, the unemployment rate during the Great Depression topped 25 percent—one in four workers in the United States could not find a job. High unemployment persisted throughout the 1930s, and classical economic theory did not seem to be of much help in either explaining or correcting the situation.

The publication of the British economist John Maynard Keynes's *The General Theory of Employment, Interest, and Money* in 1936 was a watershed event. In this book, Keynes (pronounced "canes") argued that Say's Law was wrong. It *is* possible for an economy to have a level of demand for goods that is insufficient to meet the supply from production, he said. In such a case, producers, unable to sell their goods, will cut back on production, laying off workers and thus creating economic slumps. The key to getting out of such a slump, Keynes argued, is to increase **aggregate demand**—the total demand for goods and services in the national economy as a whole.

aggregate demand: the total demand for all goods and services in a national economy

Keynesian economics: the school of thought, named after John Maynard Keynes, that argued for the active use of fiscal policy to keep aggregate demand high and employment rates up

fiscal policy: the manipulation of levels of government spending and taxation to raise or lower the level of aggregate demand

monetarist economics: the school of economic thought that focused on the effects of monetary policy and argued that governments should aim for steadiness in the money supply rather than play an active role

monetary policy: the use of tools controlled by the government, such as banking regulations and the issuance of currency, to try to affect the levels of money supply, interest rates, and credit

Keynes suggested a number of ways to achieve this. People could be encouraged to consume more, the government could buy more goods and services, or businesses could be encouraged to spend more. Some economists thought that the best way to encourage business spending was to keep interest rates low, so that businesses could borrow easily to invest in their enterprises. But, while Keynes believed that increasing investment spending would be the key to getting out of a depression, he thought that low interest rates alone would be insufficient to tempt discouraged and uncertain business leaders to start investing again. He wrote in *The General Theory* that the solution to business cycles lay in having the government take more direct control of the level of national investment. In his view, capitalist economies were inherently unstable, and only a more socially oriented direction of investment could cure this instability. This policy, however, was not generally adopted, and the Great Depression continued for the remainder of the 1930s.

It was the high government spending associated with national mobilization for World War II that finally brought the Great Depression to an end. Perhaps this is one reason that the followers of what came to be known as **Keynesian economics** did not follow Keynes on all points. While they retained his emphasis on deficiencies in aggregate demand, they tended to emphasize the use of **fiscal policy** to keep employment rates up. Fiscal policy is the manipulation of levels of government spending and taxation to raise or lower the level of aggregate demand.

Other economists in the years after the conclusion of World War II—most notably University of Chicago economist Milton Friedman—took a different tack. While the Keynesians argued that active government fiscal policies were the way to get *out* of a recession, the **monetarists** argued that bad government **monetary policies** were how economies tend to get *into* bad situations in the first place. In this view, it was primarily the U.S. government's poor use of its monetary policy tools, such as banking regulations and the issuance of currency (most often understood as "printing money"), that led to the Great Depression. They blamed government policies that encouraged overly "loose" money (i.e., easy credit, low interest rates, and high levels of money supply) for the overspending of the late 1920s. Then, they claimed, "tight" money policies (tight credit, higher-than-optimal interest rates, and low money supply) during the early 1930s turned what could have been a more minor slump into a major depression. They argued that governments should focus on keeping the money supply steady and not try to take an active role in directing the economy, even when unemployment is high. Like the classical economists, they believed that the economy would best be left to adjust on its own.

The Keynesian approach to monetary policy, in contrast, favors an active use of monetary policy together with fiscal policy to try to maintain full employment. This approach strongly influenced macroeconomic policy-making in the United States and many other countries after the Second World War. The idea became popular that the government might even be able to "fine tune" the economy, counteracting any tendencies to slump with expansionary (high spending or loose money) policies, and any excessive expansion with contractionary (low spending or tight money) policies, thereby largely eliminating business cycles. A related idea was that the government could choose to "trade off" unemployment and inflation—letting the economy suffer a little more inflation to get the unemployment rate down, or vice versa.

4.3 Synthesizing Classical and Keynesian Economics

In the early 1970s, this rosy picture was shattered, however, as many industrialized countries began to experience rising unemployment *combined with* increased inflation. To explain this, many macroeconomists attempted to merge elements of both classical and Keynesian economics, making a distinction between the long run and the short run as follows:

- Classical theories assert, first, that economies should naturally settle at full-employment levels of output and, second, that the primary outcome of changes in the money supply are changes in the price level or rate of inflation. In an idealized smoothly functioning market system—as we see in detail in a later chapter—any unemployment (i.e., surplus labor) should be corrected by a drop in the (equilibrium) wage. In the emerging synthesis, full employment and purely inflationary effects came to be thought of as *long-run* outcomes, which occur only after all markets have had sufficient time to adjust.
- Keynesian economists after World War II had come to accept the idea that their theories should be explainable in terms of market models, but explained unemployment as being due to the fact that markets for labor do not adjust as quickly as classical theory implies. Some Keynesian economists argued that wages are "sticky" in real-world markets and will not fall fast enough during a slump for full employment to be quickly restored. Fiscal and monetary policies were thought, in this emerging synthesis, to be effective mechanisms for coping with this *short-run* phenomenon.

Thus the dominant macroeconomic theory that emerged argued that in the short run—a period of some months or years—we are in a primarily Keynesian world where fiscal and monetary policies can be effective. In the long run, however—after such a period of time that even "sticky" markets are able to adjust—we are in a classical world, where market adjustments ensure full employment and money only affects prices.

Economists thus explained the inflation that occurred in the first few years of the 1970s (in spite of the simultaneous presence of unemployment) as the long-run outcome of expansionary monetary policies of the previous years. It appeared that short-run active (Keynesian) government policies could have unintended negative long-term (classical) consequences.

While many economists came to agree on this general theoretical picture, debates have continued, now centered on the value of active government policies. Macroeconomists at the classical end of the spectrum tend to emphasize market efficiency and a small role for government. They are suspicious about the use of monetary policy because of the possible negative effects of inflation. They also reject active fiscal policy, arguing that increases in government spending or taxation primarily lead to a larger government. Large governments, they believe, discourage private sector activities and economic growth.

Economists on the Keynesian end of the spectrum, meanwhile, tend to emphasize the way in which unemployment can cause severe human suffering and may persist for a long time. They argue for a more active role for government. Waiting for markets to adjust on their own, they believe, may mean waiting too long. And, as Keynes himself put it, "In the long run, we are all dead."

This argument between classical and Keynesian economists is very much alive today. New developments in recent years—in particular the severe recession of 2007–9 and its aftermath—have revived many of these long-running debates about the appropriate role of government fiscal and monetary policy.

4.4 MACROECONOMICS FOR THE TWENTY-FIRST CENTURY

While issues of economic growth and the business cycle preoccupied macroeconomic thinking for generations, once again, in the twenty-first century, new developments are demanding new ways of looking at the economic world.

Most recently, great suffering, including loss of homes and income, resulted from the 2007–8 financial crisis and the ensuing recession and slow recovery. Concerns have arisen over levels of national debt, and there has been intense debate about appropriate policy responses. These issues are discussed in Part VIII of this book.

In a broader perspective, the persistence of substantial global poverty, as mentioned in the earlier discussion of social sustainability, has called into question the appropriateness of traditional ideas about economic development. Questions of *what, how,* and *for whom*—rather than just "how much"—are becoming ever more important in evaluating the effects of economic activity on human well-being. Increasingly unequal distributions of resources and disparities in power, on local, national, and global scales, are rising to the fore as critical issues for human well-being. Inequality and resource constraints have cascading effects in political instability as well as armed conflicts.

The environmental impact of fossil fuel–based economic growth has become a major focus of economic, social, and political concern, along with other environmental issues. Most previous economic theories assumed that resources and the capacity of the environment to absorb the by-products of economic growth were essentially unlimited—or at least that continued developments in technology would keep problems of depletion and pollution at bay. This has been increasingly questioned as the scale of human economic activity grows larger.

The graphs of economic growth, seen earlier in this chapter, illustrate an impressive human ability to increase production. The growth in global atmospheric carbon dioxide (CO_2, the principal gas associated with climate change) illustrated in Figure 19.5 is equally impressive but more sobering, as it shows the human ability to affect our environment significantly—sometimes in dangerous ways. CO_2 is released in fossil fuel–burning industrial production, transportation, and heating, and the more such production takes place, the more is released. Deforestation also contributes to increases in atmospheric CO_2.

Figure 19.5 **Growth in Atmospheric Carbon Dioxide, 1815–2010**

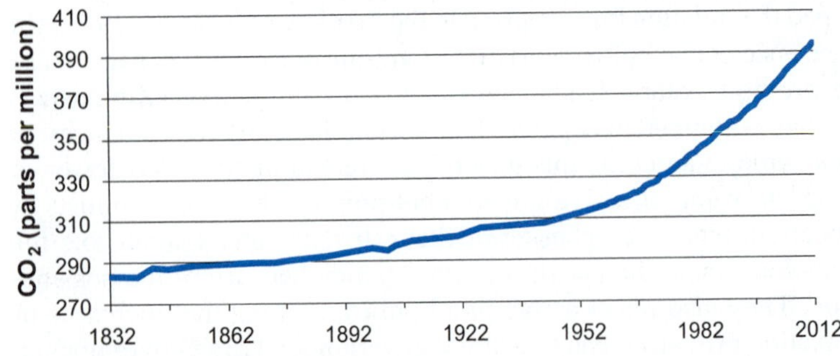

As fossil-fuel based industrialization and deforestation have increased, so has the atmospheric concentration of the gases involved in global warming.

Source: Carbon Dioxide Information Analysis Center, http://cdiac.ornl.gov/ftp/trends/co2/siple2.013 and http://cdiac.ornl.gov/trends/co2/sio-mlo.htm.

Updated using NOAA ESRL data. ftp://ftp.cmdl.noaa.gov/ccg/co2/trends/co2_mm_mlo.txt

Unless emissions of greenhouse gases are reduced dramatically, we can expect to see a number of dangerous results from climate change, including increasingly severe disturbances to agriculture, disruptions in water supply, an expansion of the reach of tropical diseases, and threats from increasingly severe weather including hurricanes, floods, and droughts. Reconciling ecological sustainability and restoration with full employment and growth in living standards is rising in prominence as a macroeconomic issue. Related environmental issues concerning the depletion or degradation of a wide variety of critical natural resources will require new thinking about the relationship between production and living standards.

This is an exciting moment in the study of macroeconomics, when so much is at stake—and when there is both need and opportunity for creative new ideas. If you had embarked on this course 20 years ago, you would likely have read a textbook that implied that "everything we need to know about the macroeconomy is here—just learn it." Given recent developments, it is more appropriate to invite you to contemplate and discuss how the economy works, how it doesn't, and how it should.

Discussion Questions

1. Which major historical events influenced the development of macroeconomics as a field of study? In addition to the problems listed in the text, do you think there are other current problems that macroeconomics should be addressing?
2. The fact that economists do not always agree, and that there are alternative "schools" of macroeconomic thought, can sometimes seem confusing. It may help to think about, or discuss in a group, how economics compares to other subjects that you or your classmates have studied. What kinds of changes in the fields of physics or biology have occurred in the past hundred years? Are there major debates, disagreements, and unsettled issues in other fields such as psychology, sociology, or political science?

REVIEW QUESTIONS

1. How does macroeconomics differ from microeconomics?
2. Describe how and why sellers of a good might adjust the quantity of what they produce, rather than the price.
3. What are some of the problems that can be created by large price swings?
4. What is meant by "living standards growth"? Is this the same as "economic growth"?
5. What is economic development? What factors are important in ensuring that economic growth benefits a country's population as a whole?
6. Why are macroeconomic fluctuations a cause for concern?
7. What global developments have caused financial, social, and ecological sustainability or restoration to become increasingly prominent as macroeconomic concerns?
8. What is the "precautionary principle"?
9. What historical developments and concerns motivated—and what beliefs characterized—the classical economists? The school of Keynesian economics? The work of the monetarists? The synthesis of Keynesian and classical thought?
10. Name two or more global issues that will likely shape the development of macroeconomics in the twenty-first century.

EXERCISES

1. The more you pay attention to what is going on in the macroeconomy around you, the more meaningful this class will be to you. Find an article in a newspaper or newsmagazine (hard copy or on-line) that deals with a macroeconomic topic. Make a list of terms, concepts, people, organizations, or historical events mentioned in the article that are also mentioned in this chapter.
2. Classify each of the following as to whether it is an example of a positive question or a normative question (some may have elements of both).
   a. "What is the level of the U.S. national debt?"

b. "Is the national debt too high?"
c. "How low should the unemployment rate be?"
d. "What policies can lower the unemployment rate?"
e. "What kinds of production should be counted in measuring gross domestic product?"
f. "Is it better to have low unemployment or low inflation?"

3. State whether the following statements are true or false. If false, also write a corrected statement.
   a. Macroeconomics is about the activities of government agencies.
   b. Economic growth always leads to improvements in living standards.
   c. The three aspects to consider in thinking about sustainability are financial, monetary, and ecological.
   d. Over a billion people live in absolute poverty, defined as $1.25 or less per day.
   e. Poor countries have had little problem paying back economic development loans.
4. State whether the following statements are true or false. If false, also write a corrected statement.
   a. Fiscal policy refers to government influences on credit and interest rates.
   b. Specialization and the division of labor are characteristics of industrial production.
   c. Classical economists believe that the Great Depression was caused by aggregate demand that was too low.
   d. During "bank runs" and stock market crashes, people lose confidence in the financial system and tend to cut back on their spending.
   e. Keynesian economists believe that an economy that experiences a high rate of unemployment will quickly self-correct.
5. Match each concept in Column A with a definition or example in Column B:

Column A	Column B
a. Keynesian economics	1. Lowering the income tax rate
b. Classical economics	2. Studies how economics applies at the national and global level
c. Monetary policy	3. Supply creates its own demand
d. Fiscal policy	4. Expansion in GDP as a result of new production
e. Living standards growth	5. A school that focuses on aggregate demand and encourages government action
f. Business cycle	6. Government expansion of credit availability
g. Monetarism	7. The short-run fluctuations of a national economy
h. Macroeconomics	8. The school of economic thought originally associated with the idea of laissez-faire economics
i. Say's law	9. More of the population gets access to basic health care
j. Microeconomics	10. Studies how economics applies at the level of households, businesses, and other organizations
k. Economic growth	11. A school of economic thought that argues that active government monetary policies usually make economic fluctuations worse

NOTE

1. This well-known formulation of the precautionary principle was spelled out in a 1998 meeting of scientists, lawyers, policymakers, and environmentalists at Wingspread, the headquarters of the Johnson Foundation in Racine, Wisconsin.

20 Macroeconomic Measurement: The Current Approach

In order to make good macroeconomic policy choices, we need to have reliable information on how the economy is performing. Gross domestic product (GDP) is the metric that is most often cited to assess overall economic performance.* For example, a common definition of a recession is when an economy's GDP decreases for two consecutive quarters. Of course, other variables, such as unemployment, inflation, and interest rates, are of great interest to economists and policymakers, but they tend to rely most heavily on GDP data to guide their policy recommendations.

In this chapter, we take a detailed look at GDP and related national economic data. But before we begin, a note of caution is in order. Although it is true that GDP growth improves average material living standards, which in turn contributes to well-being, it is not true that GDP growth always increases well-being. For example, if GDP grows simply because people are working longer hours, we would need to evaluate the increase in GDP against the loss in leisure time to determine whether well-being has actually increased. In Chapter 21, we look at the limitations of, and alternatives to, GDP as a measure of well-being, in order to place our discussion of GDP "in context" with our broader discussion of well-being.

1. An Overview of National Accounting

National Income and Product Accounts (NIPA): a set of statistics compiled by the BEA concerning production, income, spending, prices, and employment

Bureau of Economic Analysis (BEA): the agency in the United States in charge of compiling and publishing the national accounts

The idea of creating a system of national accounting to guide U.S. economic policies first took hold during the Great Depression in the 1930s. Presidents Herbert Hoover and Franklin Roosevelt knew that national production was down, but other than a few numbers representing the volumes of railroad shipments and steel production, they had no information on *how much* it was down. Likewise, they had little way of knowing whether the policies that they were trying to implement were actually helping the economy to rebound.

The Department of Commerce commissioned economist Simon Kuznets to begin to develop national accounts. The first set of accounts was presented to Congress in 1937. Interest in keeping national accounts increased in the 1940s because of the need for national economic mobilization during World War II. Now, every functioning country compiles national accounts using standardized approaches.

National accounting involves more than just measuring GDP. Thus we refer to a system of **National Income and Product Accounts (NIPA)** that collects data on production, income, spending, prices, and employment. In the United States, the national accounts are maintained by a federal agency, the **Bureau of Economic Analysis (BEA).**

*A closely related measure is gross national product (GNP). The difference between GNP and GDP concerns whether foreign earnings are included. GNP includes the earnings of a country's citizens and corporations regardless of where they are located in the world. GDP includes all earnings within a country's borders, even the earnings of foreign citizens and corporations. GDP is the more common measure used when comparing international statistics.

1.1 CONVENTIONS ABOUT NATIONAL ACCOUNTING SECTORS

national accounting conventions: habits or agreements, adopted by government agencies in order to make national accounts as standardized and comparable across different countries and periods as possible

Before we focus on how GDP is measured, we first need to discuss some of the "conventions," or assumptions, used in the NIPA. **National accounting conventions** are simply habits or agreements, adopted by agencies in order to try to make the accounts as standardized and comparable across different countries and periods as possible. Some of these conventions concern how data are categorized. For example, there are conventions concerning what is classified as investment versus consumption or a durable versus a nondurable good. Other conventions address how estimates are made for some components of the NIPA for which readily available data are lacking. Of course, there are alternatives to the common conventions, but the emphasis is on standardization rather than always choosing the "best" approach.

One of the common national accounting conventions concerns how the entire economy is broken down into four national accounting sectors.* These sectors, as defined by the BEA, are:

1. *Households and institutions sector:* This includes both households and nonprofit institutions that serve households, such as nonprofit hospitals, universities, museums, trade unions, and charities. The BEA also refers to the households and institutions sector as the "personal" sector. (Note how this overlaps with, but is not identical to, the "core sphere" described in Chapter 2.)
2. *Business sector:* The BEA business sector is somewhat broader than just for-profit businesses. Certain business-serving nonprofit organizations, such as trade associations and chambers of commerce, are included in this category. In addition, government agencies that produce goods and services for sale—such as the U.S. Postal Service, municipal gas and electric companies, and airports—are also classified as being in the business sector.
3. *Government sector:* The government sector includes all federal, state, and local government entities, except for the "business-like" government enterprises mentioned above.
4. *Foreign sector:* The entities in the first three sectors include, for the national accounts, only those located within the physical borders of the United States. The foreign sector (or "rest of the world") includes all entities—household, nonprofit, business, or government—located outside the borders of the United States. An individual in another country who buys imported U.S. products, for example, or a company located abroad that sells goods or services to the United States, figures into U.S. accounts as part of the foreign sector.

1.2 CONVENTIONS ABOUT CAPITAL STOCKS

Although natural, manufactured, human, and social capital are all crucial resources for economic activity, it is largely only *manufactured* capital that is currently included in the accounting of national nonfinancial assets. This might be because the national accounts were originally devised at a time when the rise of manufacturing made the accumulation of machinery and factory buildings appear to be the main road to prosperity. In the twenty-first century, the rise in importance of knowledge, along with concerns for ecological issues, suggests that additional accounts should be added—a topic we take up in Chapter 21.

fixed assets: equipment owned by businesses and governments; structures; residences; and software

inventories: stocks of raw materials or manufactured goods being stored until they can be used or sold

The first category of manufactured capital in the national accounts is **fixed assets**. Fixed assets include equipment owned by businesses and governments, structures such as factories and office buildings, and residences (i.e., houses and apartment buildings). In 1999, in partial recognition of the increasingly important role of knowledge and technology in production, computer software was added as an additional type of fixed asset.

A second—and much smaller—component of the manufactured capital stock is **inventories**. Inventories are stocks of raw materials, such as crude oil awaiting refining, or manufactured

*We call them "national accounting sectors" to differentiate them from the classification of the economy into sectors discussed in Chapter 22, where we refer to "production" sectors.

Table 20.1 **The Estimated Size of U.S. Manufactured Capital Stock, 2011**

Type of capital	Value in trillions of dollars at the end of the year
Equipment and software (businesses and government)	7.0
Structures (businesses and government)	21.5
Residences	17.6
Inventories	2.2
Consumer durable goods	4.7
Total value of manufactured capital	53.0

Sources: BEA, Fixed Asset Accounts, table 1.1; NIPA, table 5.9; and authors' calculations.

consumer durable goods: consumer purchases that are expected to last longer than three years. These are generally items of equipment, such as vehicles and appliances, used by households to produce goods and services for their own use.

goods, such as the shoe inventory of a retail shoe store, that are held until they can be used or sold. The BEA only counts inventories held by the business sector.

Equipment used by governments and businesses is included in "fixed assets." But what about equipment owned by households, such as cars and stoves, that are used in household production of goods and services? The BEA calls all goods bought by households that are expected to last longer than three years **consumer durable goods**. In 2003, the BEA began including consumer durables in its accounts of assets.

The BEA estimates of the dollar value of the country's stock of manufactured assets at the end of 2011 are given in Table 20.1.

1.3 Conventions About Investment

The way that the national accounts measure investment spending may seem confusing if one does not keep in mind some basic facts. First, recall from Chapter 3 that economists generally use the term "investment" to mean additions to stocks of *non*financial assets. This contrasts with the common use of the term "investment" to refer to financial investment, such as the purchase of stocks and bonds. Second, it is important to remember that investment represents a *flow*. A machine added to a factory in 2013, for example, is considered part of the national *stock* of nonresidential assets for every year from the time it is installed until the time it is junked. However, the machine was an *addition* to assets only in 2013, and hence its value would be counted as an *investment* only in that one year. Lastly, as was also discussed in Chapter 3, *gross* investment includes all measured flows into the capital stock over a period while *net* investment adjusts this measure for the fact that some portion of the capital stock wears out, becomes obsolete, or is destroyed—that is, depreciates—over the period.

gross investment: all flows into the capital stock over a period of time

net investment: gross investment minus an adjustment for depreciation

For example, suppose that an office complex built in 1980 is torn down this year and replaced by a new, larger office complex. Measured **gross investment** for this year would include the full value of the new office complex. **Net investment** for this year would be calculated as the value of the new office complex *minus* the value of the depreciated building that was torn down. If the new building has 100,000 square feet of space, while the old one had 60,000 square feet, for example, the economy has a net gain of only 40,000 square feet of office space. Net investment, which measures only the value of the *new* space and any improvements in quality, gives a better idea of the actual addition to productive capacity.

depreciation: a decrease in the quantity or quality of a stock of capital

Gross investment in fixed assets is always zero or positive. However, if, over a period of time, the capital stock depreciates faster than it is being replaced, net investment can be negative. This can sometimes happen to manufactured capital stocks when a country is hit by major disasters such as wars or floods, or during a period when new investment is very low, meaning that gross investment is less than **depreciation**.

Ideally, productive investments by all sectors would be recognized in the national accounts. But it was not until 1996 that government investment in fixed assets was recognized, and household investment in consumer durables is still, by convention, not considered part of investment in the national accounts.

Discussion Questions

1. The BEA definitions of sectors use some conventions that are not obvious. To which sector might the BEA assign each of the following entities? Why?
   a. A local city government–owned golf course that charges fees similar to those at local private courses
   b. A large nonprofit hospital
   c. A U.S.-owned movie company whose offices and studio are in Japan
   d. A nonprofit trade association, such as the Chocolate Manufacturers Association
2. Under the BEA definitions, would spending on education be counted as investment? Would buying shares in a company be considered investment? Why?

2. DEFINING GROSS DOMESTIC PRODUCT

gross domestic product (GDP) (BEA definition)**:** a measure of the total market value of final goods and services newly produced within a country's borders over a period of time (usually one year)

As we mentioned earlier, the most referenced single number that comes out of the national accounts is GDP. A wide range of policymakers and media outlets await the announcement of newly published figures on GDP with great anticipation (see Box 20.1). The figures on the growth rate of GDP are often taken to signal the success or failure of macroeconomic policy-making.

According to the BEA, GDP is supposed to measure the total market value of final goods and services newly produced within a country's borders over a period of time (usually one year).

This definition contains several key phrases. Let us consider each of them.

"Market value": For most components of GDP, we can simply refer to the market prices of goods and services to determine their contribution to GDP. However, in some cases (as we discuss later in the chapter), we do not have market prices for certain goods and services and thus need to estimate their value using another approach.

final good: a good that is ready for use, needing no further processing

intermediate good: a good that will undergo further processing

"Final goods and services": A **final good** is one that is ready for use. That is, no further productive activity needs to occur before the good can be consumed (if it is a good that is used up as it is put to use) or put to work producing other goods and services (e.g., if it is a piece of equipment). The reason for limiting measurement to *final* goods and services is to avoid double counting. For example, suppose that over the course of a year, paper is produced by one company and sold to another company that uses it to make books. The books are then sold to their final buyers. Books in this case are the final goods, while the paper used in them is an **intermediate good**. By limiting the accounting to final goods, production is only counted once—the paper is only counted as part of the books.

"Over a period of time": Since GDP measures a flow, it of course must be measured over a time period. Macroeconomists usually work with GDP measured on a yearly basis. Estimates of GDP are released more often than once a year—generally on a quarterly basis (the first quarter covering January through March, the second April through June, and so on). However, even when only a part of the year is being covered, GDP and its growth rates are usually expressed in annual terms.

"Newly produced": Only new goods and services are counted. For example, if you buy a book published in 2010 at a used bookshop, the value of the book itself is not included in this year's GDP. Only the retail services provided by the used bookshop are "newly produced," and are part of this year's GDP.

"Within a country's borders": This means that the goods and services are produced within the physical borders of the country. If a U.S. citizen goes abroad to work, for example, what he or she produces while away is *not* part of U.S. GDP. On the other hand, the work of a Japanese citizen at a Japanese-owned factory *is* part of U.S. GDP if that factory is located inside the borders of the United States.

Box 20.1 U.S. Economy Contracts for the First Time Since the Great Recession

The U.S. Bureau of Economic Analysis reported in January 2013 that the U.S. economy contracted for the first time since the Great Recession officially ended in 2009. Real gross domestic product (GDP) for the last quarter of 2012 shrank at an annual rate of 0.1 percent. The decline in GDP was attributed to decreases in private inventory investment, government spending, and exports. The decline in federal defense spending was particularly large, at 22 percent. The BEA also noted that personal consumption expenditures increased by 2.2 percent, with a significant increase in durable goods expenditures of 13.9 percent.

Did the decline in GDP suggest the United States in early 2013 was on the brink of another recession? Most economists rejected this idea. The negative influences on GDP were viewed as temporary factors, rather than indicative of a trend. And indeed, GDP growth resumed, though at only moderate rates, later in 2013.

It's "the best-looking contraction in U.S. GDP you'll ever see," Paul Ashworth, chief U.S. economist for Capital Economics said in a research note. "The drag from defense spending and inventories is a one-off. The rest of the report is all encouraging."

Also, the decline in private inventories was viewed as a sign that businesses would need to increase purchases to restore depleted inventories. In the wake of this report, most economists projected that the economic recovery in the United States would continue, with projections for annual GDP growth of 2.0 percent to 2.5 percent GDP in 2013.

Sources: "National Income and Product Accounts Gross Domestic Product, 4th quarter and annual 2012 (advance estimate)," BEA News Release, January 30, 2013; "U.S. Economy Contracts for First Time Since Recession," CNN Money, January 30, 2013.

3. Measuring Gross Domestic Product

The BEA publishes tables showing the components of GDP, as well as many other tables dealing with assets, employment, prices, and other topics in the NIPA. (These are easily accessed at www.bea.gov.) To understand these tabulations, however, you need to understand how aggregate *production, spending,* and *income* are related in an economic system.

Imagine a simple economy with no foreign sector, no depreciation, no inventories, and in which all the profits that companies earn end up in the bank accounts of households. In this case, three quite different measures of counting GDP would in theory all add up to the same number:

Value of Production = Value of Spending = Value of Income

Using a *production approach,* which might seem to be the most natural and direct method, we could sum up the dollar value of all final goods and services produced in each national accounting sector—by the household and institutions sector, the business sector, and the government sector.

Using the *spending approach,* we could look at who *buys* the final goods and services that have been produced. Since we assumed that no goods are carried as inventory in this very simple economy, everything produced must be bought. Totaling the dollar value of spending on all various kinds of goods and services by all sectors in this imaginary simple economy will indicate a second way of arriving at the figure for a country's aggregate production.

Lastly, because in this simple economy everyone who is involved in production also receives monetary payment for their contribution to it, we could, alternatively, take an *income approach.* In this approach, we total the compensation received by everyone involved in production, including workers, investors, creditors, and owners of land or equipment rented for productive use.

In this very simple economy if, say, \$10 billion worth of goods and services is produced, then the amount spent on goods and services must also be \$10 billion and the amount of payment received as income must also be \$10 billion. Sometimes in dealing with national accounts economists hence use the terms "production," "income," and "expenditure" interchangeably.

While there is a rough equivalence in theory among the product, spending, and income approaches to calculating GDP, making estimates for an actual economy requires a number of conventions and adjustments. We now consider each approach in more detail.

3.1 THE PRODUCT APPROACH

The BEA measures the "value" of final goods and services primarily by their *dollar market value.* For example, if the business sector produces 1,000 automobiles of a certain type this year, which are which are then sold to final users for $20,000 each, this production contributes $20 million to GDP.

Rather than looking at the final sale, however, it is sometimes useful for accounting and analytical purposes to follow an alternative approach. This is to think about how much each industry contributes to the value of the final good or service. In the **value-added** approach to GDP accounting, you start with the raw materials—say, iron ore—used in producing a good or service—say, an automobile—and then see how much market value is added at each stage in the production process.

value-added: the value of what a producer sells, less the value of the intermediate inputs it uses, except labor. This is equal to the wages paid out by the producer plus its profits

For example, suppose a steel manufacturer buys $500 worth of iron ore from a mining company and uses this ore to produce steel automobile frames, which it then sells to Ford Motor Company for $1,800 each. The difference between the price of the iron ore and the cost of any other materials needed to convert iron ore into automobile frames, including energy and equipment costs, represents value added. So if the steel manufacturer requires another $200 in additional materials and other costs to produce an automobile frame, then the difference between their total costs ($700) and the selling price ($1,800) is the value added at this stage in production ($1,100). This $1,100 is the amount that is left over after paying for inputs, and it becomes either wages to steel workers or profits to the steel manufacturing company. Similarly, we can determine the value added by Ford Motor Company as the difference between all its input costs (except labor) and the final selling price of the car. If the car sells for $20,000, Ford's value added can be calculated by subtracting the price of the steel, rubber, glass, energy, and all other purchased inputs. Supposing that these added up to $12,000, Ford's value added would be $8,000.

The BEA maintains an extensive set of tables, called Input-Output Accounts, to keep track of the contributions to GDP by various industries. These tables show that outputs of each industrial sector (e.g., agriculture, manufacturing, or services) can become inputs (intermediate goods) to production in other sectors.

If we add up the value-added contribution of each step in the production process, we should end up with the final market price of the good. The fact that these numbers should be the same serves as a "check" on the validity of data that the BEA collects from different sources.

While finding the market value of goods may seem fairly straightforward for manufacturing industries, in practice the idea of "market value" is often much harder to determine. In many cases the BEA uses **imputation** to estimate the value of components of GDP. An imputation is a sort of educated guess, usually based on the value of similar outputs or on the value of inputs used in production.

imputation: a procedure in which values are assigned for a category of products, usually using values of related products or inputs

For example, the housing stock of a country produces a flow of services—the services of shelter. For housing units that are rented, the rent paid is the market value of the housing services. But how can we find out the value of the services generated by houses occupied by their owners? For these, the BEA must impute a value. They use data from the rental housing market to impute what owner-occupiers might be said to be "paying in rent" to themselves.

In cases where no similar marketed product exists, the BEA often falls back on using a value-added approach, looking exclusively at the value of inputs. We know, for example, that governments purchase many intermediate goods, and then produce goods and services.

But rarely are government outputs—new highways, the services of parks, the services of public education, national defense, and so on—actually sold on markets. How, then, can the production of the government be valued?

In the actual GDP accounts, the value of government production is imputed by adding up the amount that governments pay their workers, the amount that they pay for intermediate goods and services, and an allowance for depreciation of fixed assets. Likewise, the production of nonprofit institutions is measured in large part by looking at their inputs. For example, data on payroll expenses form an important part of the information used in estimating the value of the services produced by nonprofit agencies.

Imputations are also used when data are difficult or impossible to obtain. Although it might be tempting to imagine the BEA as an all-knowing agency that can directly observe all market transactions, gathering data is a laborious (and often expensive) process. The BEA relies on a variety of censuses and surveys to obtain information, as well as on data such as government budgets and tax records. Market transactions that people take pains *not* to have observed by the government—such as illegal drug deals or work performed "off the books" to avoid taxes—hence are usually not represented in the national statistics. The BEA updates all its estimates periodically, as it receives better data or improves its statistical techniques—hence you may see many slightly varying numbers quoted for, say "U.S. GDP, 2013" depending on when the data were published.

In one significant case, however, the designers of the national accounts decided not even to attempt to impute a value for production: the production of goods and services within households for their own use. The official measure of production by households includes the value of services produced by the *house itself* (i.e., the rent or imputed rent) and production within the households to the extent that work is paid (i.e., done by hired housekeepers, babysitters, or private gardeners). But activities such as unpaid child care, cooking, or the cleaning or landscaping of a home done without pay by household members—traditionally, mostly by women—are not counted in GDP. This creates an anomaly in the accounts. For many years, textbooks noted that "if a man marries his housekeeper, GDP falls." That is, marriage would convert the woman's housekeeping work from being paid and counted to being unpaid and uncounted.

We can summarize the product approach to measuring GDP using the equation:

$$GDP = Business\ production + Household\ and\ institutions\ production \\ + Government\ production$$

identity (accounting identity): an equation in which the two sides are equal by definition

This sort of equation is called an **identity** or an **accounting identity**. It holds simply because of the way in which the various terms have been defined. Once we agree on the definitions of terms, then there remains nothing controversial about an identity. (When we begin to deal with macroeconomic modeling in Chapter 24 we introduce another kind of equation, called a behavioral equation. A behavioral equation represents an economist's supposition about how an economic actor behaves—and because it may or may not hold well in practice, it can be more controversial.)

Note that the foreign sector does not contribute to the production of GDP in the above equation. Can you explain why? (Hint: Look back at the definition of GDP.)

Table 20.2 presents the BEA estimate of GDP in 2012 using the product approach, divided into national accounting sectors and subsectors. Not surprisingly, given the conventions and accounting procedures, the BEA attributes a very large share of productive activity to the business sector. In 2012, the business sector was estimated to have produced goods and services worth about $12 trillion, or about 76 percent of the total GDP of $15.68 trillion. The household and institutions sector and the government sector were each estimated to have contributed about 12 percent. (In Table 20.2, as in later tables, the totals for sectors are often divided into values for subsectors.)

Table 20.2 **Gross Domestic Product, Product Approach, 2012**

Sector and subsector	Production by sector (trillions of dollars)	Production by subsector (trillions of dollars)
Households and institutions production	1.93	
Private households		1.07
Nonprofit institutions		0.86
Business production	11.87	
Government production	1.87	
Federal government		0.62
State and local governments		1.26
Total: Gross domestic product	15.68	

Source: BEA, NIPA, Table 1.3.5, January 30, 2013.
Note: Totals may not add up exactly due to rounding.

3.2 The Spending Approach

The spending approach adds up the value of newly produced goods and services bought by the household and institution, business, foreign, and government sectors. The estimated values for these expenditures for 2012 are listed in Table 20.3.

Purchases of goods and services by households and nonprofit institutions serving households are called "personal consumption expenditures" by the BEA. By convention, they are all considered "final" goods and services (even though, as discussed earlier, many of these are used in household and nonprofit production processes).

Table 20.3 **Gross Domestic Product, Spending Approach, 2012**

Sector and type of spending	Spending by sector (trillions of dollars)	Spending by type (trillions of dollars)
Household and institutions spending *(personal consumption expenditures)*	11.12	
Durable goods		1.22
Nondurable goods		2.56
Services		7.34
Business spending *(gross private domestic investment)*	2.06	
Fixed investment		2.00
Change in private inventories		0.06
Net foreign sector spending *(net exports of goods and services)*	*–0.57*	
Exports		2.18
Less: Imports		*2.75*
Government spending *(government consumption expenditures and gross investment)*	3.07	
Federal		1.21
State and local		1.85
Total: Gross domestic product	15.68	

Source: BEA, NIPA, Table 1.1.5, January 30, 2013.
Note: Totals may not add up exactly due to rounding.

Business spending on final goods and services is called "gross private domestic investment" by the BEA. This includes business spending on fixed assets including structures, equipment, and software, as well as the value of changes in inventories within that sector. Why isn't business spending on wages or on materials such as energy and

Box 20.2 With the Stroke of a Pen, GDP Increases by $560 Billion

In July 2013, U.S. GDP increased by $560 billion—overnight. No change took place in actual production. What happened was that the Bureau of Economic Analysis (BEA), which is responsible for calculating GDP, decided to change the way it counts business spending.

The BEA established a new category called "intellectual property products," which includes "entertainment originals" such as TV shows that generate long-term streams of income. Production costs for such items are counted as investment, which is a part of GDP, rather than as business expenses, which are excluded from GDP as "intermediate goods." Similarly, research and development expenditures, previously considered to be a business expense like paper clips or electricity, will now also be treated as investment with the possibility to generate future income.

This change increased GDP by 3.6 percent in a single month. This won't be added to figures for economic growth, though. Economic growth will now be calculated using the adjusted method, so that while the overall level of GDP will rise, its trend over time will not change. The Commerce Department reported that rate as an annual 1.7 percent during the second quarter of 2013—unaffected by the BEA's new method for calculation. It will, however, affect the debt-to-GDP ratio, making the national debt look a little smaller relative to current GDP.

Source: Jared Bernstein and Dean Baker, "What is 'Seinfeld' Worth?" *New York Times*, August 1, 2013.

raw materials counted here? Recall that GDP only accounts for *final* goods and services. Including the value of intermediate inputs with business spending as well would result in double counting.

Sometimes it is not so easy to say what is an intermediate good and what is a final good. Recently, the BEA changed its definitions to include business spending on intellectual property, as well as research and development, as investments (final goods) rather than intermediate goods. Making this change raised the value of GDP by $560 billion—not reflecting any actual increase in production, just a change in the way production is defined (see Box 20.2).

closed economy: an economy with no foreign sector

open economy: an economy with a foreign sector

The simple economy that we discussed when noting how, in concept, "production = spending = income" was a **closed economy**, with no foreign sector. Although sometimes countries isolate themselves from world trade (China during the 1960s being a prime example), for the most part global economic relations have become increasingly important as advances in transportation and communication have accelerated. Because the United States is an **open economy**, we need to take into account interactions with the foreign sector.

Some of the goods and services produced inside the United States are bought by entities in the foreign sector. The value of these exported goods must be added to the value of domestic spending in calculating GDP. In addition, some of the spending by U.S. residents is for goods and services produced abroad. Such spending is, in fact, already included in the calculation of spending by the various other sectors in Table 20.3. So the value of imported goods and services must be *subtracted* to arrive at a measure of *domestic* production.

net exports: the value of exports less the value of imports

Net exports measures the overall impact of international trade on GDP. It is the difference between exports and imports:

$$\textit{Net exports} = \textit{Exports} - \textit{Imports}$$

Net exports may be either positive (if we sell more abroad than we buy) or negative (if we buy more than we sell). In 2012, for example, we can see in Table 20.3 that the United States imported goods and services worth $0.57 trillion (or $570 billion) more than the value of the goods and services exported. (In the table, the fact that the value of imports is subtracted rather than added is denoted by putting the number in italics.) Hence, that year, U.S. net exports were negative.

Lastly, we come to the expenditures made by the government sector. The BEA calls these "government consumption expenditures and gross investment" and breaks them down by whether they are made at the federal level or at the state and local level. These figures represent only spending for final goods and services, so they exclude the parts of government budgets that go for transfers (such as Social Security). In 2012, about two-thirds of federal government spending was on national defense.

Based on the spending by different sectors, we can summarize the spending approach with the identity:

GDP = *Household and institution spending*
+ *Business spending*
+ *Net foreign sector spending*
+ *Government spending*

Or, if we want to highlight the portions that are (by convention) considered consumption versus those considered investment, we can summarize this approach with the identity:

GDP = *Personal consumption*
+ *Private investment*
+ *Government consumption*
+ *Government investment*
+ *Net exports*

3.3 The Income Approach

national income (NI): a measure of all domestic incomes earned in production

The production-related incomes (such as from wages, rents, and profits) earned by all people and organizations located inside the United States can be summed up in a measure called **national income (NI)**.

If this were a simple economy with no foreign sector and no depreciation, the sum of the incomes from production (NI) would exactly equal GDP. But in our more complex economy, three adjustments are needed to reconcile figures on domestic income and domestic production.

First, we need to note that some domestic incomes reflect *foreign* production. For example, as mentioned above, the profits of a U.S. company may include earnings from overseas plants. Such incomes must be subtracted from NI order to reconcile this measure with the figure for gross *domestic product.* Conversely, the income from some domestic production is received by foreign residents, and so not counted in NI. A German-owned factory in the United States may send its profits back to its Berlin headquarters, for example. The value of these incomes must be added to NI in order to approximate GDP.

In 2011, income receipts from the rest of the world exceeded income paid out to foreign residents by more than $250 billion. These "net income receipts from the rest of the world" are shown in Table 20.4. When net income receipts from the rest of the world are added to GDP, the result is a measure called gross national product (GNP). For many years, GNP was used as the primary measure of U.S. production. It measures a country's production in terms of the output produced *by its workers and companies,* no matter where in the world they were located. The BEA switched its emphasis from GNP to GDP in 1991, believing that it is more important, for the purposes for which the accounts are used, to track economic activity *within the borders* of the United States. Most other countries, and international economic agencies that collect national income data, also use GDP as the standard measure.

Second, we need to account for the fact that not all of GDP creates income, since some domestic production simply goes into replacing structures, equipment, and software that have worn out or become obsolete. So we must *add* depreciation (what the BEA calls "consumption of fixed capital") to NI to get a number closer to GDP. This is a bit confusing—but it is in effect

Table 20.4 **Gross Domestic Product, Income Approach, 2011**

Types of income and adjustments	Income and adjustments (trillions of dollars)
National income	13.36
Less: Net income receipts from the rest of the world	0.25
Plus: Depreciation *(consumption of fixed capital)*	1.94
Plus: Statistical discrepancy	0.03
Total: Gross domestic product	15.08

Source: BEA, NIPA, Table 1.7.5, January 30, 2013, and authors' calculations.

the reverse of what we did above, when we subtracted depreciation from gross investment to get net investment. (In calculating incomes, depreciation is typically deducted from profits.)

The third adjustment in Table 20.4 is what is called the "statistical discrepancy." It reflects the fact that, no matter how diligently the BEA compiles the accounts, it cannot exactly reconcile the results from the income approach with the results from the product and spending approaches.

We can summarize the meaningful parts of the income approach by the identity:

$$\begin{aligned} GDP = {} & \textit{National income} \\ & - \textit{Net income payments from the foreign sector} \\ & + \textit{Depreciation} \end{aligned}$$

Discussion Questions

1. The previous section explained why a country's "production" and "income" can be thought of as roughly equal in a conceptual sense. Why, in practice, does the value of domestic production actually differ from the total of domestic incomes?
2. Sometimes GDP is defined as "The total *market* value of all final goods and services newly produced in a country over time." Given the above discussion, how true is this definition, really? Does GDP really count only goods and services exchanged *in markets?* Does it really account for *all* production?

4. GROWTH, PRICE CHANGES, AND REAL GDP

Economic growth (traditionally defined as increasing GDP) is a statistic that is closely followed by policymakers and the media. Inflation, or the growth rate of prices, is another of the macroeconomic statistics that is considered most significant. We now consider the measurement of these two factors and how they relate to each other.

4.1 CALCULATING GDP GROWTH RATES

So far, we have concentrated on calculating GDP in only one year. To calculate rates of economic growth, economists must look at how GDP changes over time. The percentage change in GDP from year to year can be calculated using the standard percentage-change formula. The standard formula, for something that takes one value in year 1 ($Value_1$) and another in year 2 ($Value_2$), is:

$$percentage\ change = \frac{Value_2 - Value_1}{Value_1} \times 100$$

So to compute the growth rate of GDP from, say, 2011 to 2012, we calculate:

$$growth\ rate\ of\ GDP = \frac{GDP_{2012} - GDP_{2011}}{GDP_{2011}} \times 100$$

For example, U.S. GDP in 2011 was estimated at $15.08 trillion, while in 2012 it was estimated at $15.68 trillion. Fitting these into the equation, we have

$$\begin{aligned} growth\ rate\ of\ GDP &= \frac{15.68 - 15.08}{15.08} \times 100 \\ &= .04 \times 100 \\ &= 4.0 \end{aligned}$$

indicating that GDP grew 4.0 percent between 2011 and 2012.

The BEA and newspapers commonly report the GDP growth rates for quarters, expressed in terms of an "annual growth rate." This is a measure of how much the economy would grow if it were to continue to expand for the entire year at the speed reported for the three-month period.

4.2 Nominal vs. Real GDP

nominal (current dollar) GDP: gross domestic product expressed in terms of current prices

real GDP: a measure of gross domestic product that seeks to reflect the actual value of goods and services produced, by removing the effect of changes in prices

Does the number we just calculated mean that the level of aggregate production in 2012 was 4.0 percent larger than production in 2011? Not necessarily. The measure of GDP used in the previous section is **nominal or current-dollar GDP**, or GDP expressed in terms of the prices of goods and services that were current at the time. The 2012 figure for GDP that we used, for example, is based on prices as they were in 2012, and the 2011 figure is based on prices that prevailed in 2011.

Not only does output change between two years, but generally the *prices at which output is valued* change as well. If prices rose between 2011 and 2012, part of the measured GDP growth would be an increase in prices rather than in actual production. **Real GDP** is a measure that seeks to reflect the actual value of goods and services produced, by removing the effect of changes in prices.

For example, suppose a very simple economy produces only two goods, apples and oranges, as shown in Table 20.5. Column (2) shows the price of each good in each year, while Column (3) gives the physical production, measured in pounds. Nominal GDP is just the sum of the dollar values of the goods produced in a year, evaluated at the prices in that same year:

Nominal GDP = Total production valued at current prices

As we can see in Table 20.5, in Year 1 the value of nominal GDP is $200. In Year 2, the value of nominal GDP is $300. The percentage growth of GDP from Year 1 to Year 2 can be calculated as 50 percent, applying the percentage-change formula from the previous section.

But if you look carefully, you can see that only part of the change in nominal GDP is due to an increase in production: The quantity of oranges produced rises from 50 pounds to 75 pounds from Year 1 to Year 2. The rest of the GDP increase is due to an increase in the price of apples, from $1.00 to $1.50. Note that the quantity of apples produced has not changed.

4.3 Calculating Real GDP

Until 1995, the BEA calculated real GDP using the "constant-dollar method." Because the constant-dollar method is relatively easy to understand and contains most of the information that you need to have as a beginning economics student, we cover it in some detail.

Table 20.5 **Calculation of Nominal GDP in an "Apples-and-Oranges" Economy**

(1) Description	(2) Price per pound ($)	(3) Quantity (pounds)	(4) Contribution to nominal GDP [column (2) × column (3)] ($)
Year 1			
Apples	$1.00	100	$100
Oranges	$2.00	50	$100
			$200
Year 2			
Apples	$1.50	100	$150
Oranges	$2.00	75	$150
			$300

base year (in the constant-dollar method of estimating GDP): the year whose prices are chosen for evaluating production in all years. Normally real and nominal GDP are equal only in the base year.

The constant-dollar method uses prices from one particular year, called the **base year**, to evaluate the value of production in all years.

Constant-dollar real GDP is calculated by doing the same sort of multiplying and summing exercise as shown in Table 20.5, but using the *same* prices for all years:

Constant-Dollar Real GDP = Total production valued at base year prices

Applying the constant-dollar method to our simple "apples-and-oranges" example, for instance, we might take Year 1 as the base year and express GDP in both Year 1 and Year 2 in terms of Year 1's prices. Calculations of constant-dollar real GDP for each year are shown in Table 20.6. While the quantities in Column (3) are the same as in Table 20.5, the prices in Column (2) are *all from Year 1.* GDP in Year 2 expressed in "constant (Year 1) dollars" is the sum of quantities in Year 2 multiplied by prices in Year 1. This comes out to be $250. In the base year, real and nominal GDP are the same.

Using the percentage growth rate formula from the previous section, we can see that constant-dollar *real* GDP has grown by 25 percent. Note that this is less than the 50 percent growth figure for nominal GDP. Some of the growth in nominal GDP is due to price changes, not production changes.

The convention of using "constant dollars," however, has a number of problems. One of the most bothersome is that it makes measured GDP growth calculations depend on which year is chosen as base. For example, what if we chose Year 2 as the base instead of Year 1? Applying Year 2 prices to both years would yield a measured growth rate of 20 percent, instead of the 25 percent that we calculated using Year 1 as the base. (You can check this as an exercise.) The

Table 20.6 **Calculation of Constant-Dollar Real GDP**

(1) Description	(2) Price per pound **in base year** ($)	(3) Quantity (pounds)	(4) Contribution to real GDP [column (2) × column (3)] ($)
Year 1 **(Base)**			
Apples	$1.00	100	$100
Oranges	$2.00	50	$100
			$200
Year 2			
Apples	**$1.00**	100	$100
Oranges	**$2.00**	75	$150
			$250

*Bold type indicates base year *prices*

Figure 20.1 **Real versus Nominal GDP, Chained 2005 Dollars, 1980–2012**

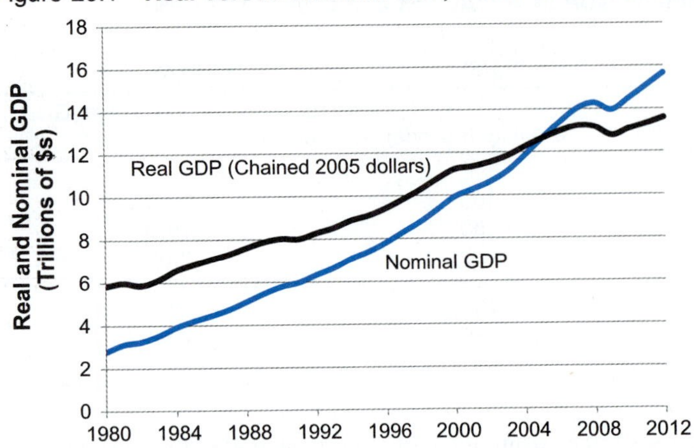

Nominal GDP grows faster than real GDP when prices are rising.

Source: BEA NIPA Tables 1.1.5 and 1.1.6, published 1/30/2013.

method also suffers from various biases, which become more important the more dissimilar relative prices and spending patterns are between the base year and a current year.

Beginning in 1996, the BEA switched to calculating real GDP using the "chained-dollar" method. The concept behind the new measure is still the same—real GDP still is an attempt to measure output changes free of the influence of changing prices. Although there is still one year for which real and nominal GDP are equal, it is now called the "reference year," and real GDP is currently expressed in BEA publications in terms of "chained (2005) dollars." An advantage of the chained-dollar method is that, unlike the constant-dollar method, it yields a unique growth rate. But the chained-dollar method requires a steep jump in computational complexity. Because these calculations are much harder than for the constant-dollar method, their explanation is in the Appendix to this chapter.

In Figure 20.1 you can see how measures of real and nominal GDP diverge. Because prices were generally rising over the period 1980–2012, nominal GDP grew faster than real GDP, as shown by the more steeply rising line. The difference between the rate of growth of nominal GDP and the rate of growth of real GDP is the inflation rate (discussed in the next section). Note that the reference year in Figure 20.1 is 2005; thus real and nominal GDP are the same in that year.

4.4 PRICE INDEXES AND INFLATION RATES

index number: a figure that measures the change in magnitude of a variable, such as a quantity or price, compared to another period

consumer price index (CPI): an index measuring changes in the prices of goods and services bought by households

Price indexes are interesting both for how they relate to calculation of real GDP and on their own because of their relevance to the policy interest in measuring (and controlling) inflation. An **index number** measures the change in magnitude, in this case the price level, compared to another period. Generally, the value of the index number in the reference or base year is set at 100, though sometimes other values (such as 1 or 10) are used.

The price index most often reported in the news is the **consumer price index (CPI)**, calculated by the U.S. Bureau of Labor Statistics (BLS). The CPI measures changes in the prices of goods and services bought by households.

Calculating price increases is not quite so straightforward as it might seem at first sight. For example, in Table 20.5 the price of apples increased from $1.00 per pound to $1.50 per pound. Using the standard percentage-change formula, we would say that the price of apples increased by 50 percent. However, we also see in Table 20.5 that the price of oranges did not change. So how do we calculate the overall price change in our two-good economy?

We would not simply average the two price changes to arrive at an overall price increase of 25 percent. Instead, we must realize that changes in some prices are more significant to consumers because they either purchase more of certain products (such as gallons of milk) or because they spend a large portion of their incomes on something (such as rent).

Thus the CPI is calculated using a *weighted average* of the prices of the various goods and services that it tracks. The mathematics of this is worth a little explaining. A "weighted average" is an average in which the different numbers being averaged together are "weighted" to indicate their relative importance in the calculation. You are probably already familiar with this, in the calculation of your own Grade Point Average. Each grade that you receive for a course is "weighted" by the number of credits (or hours) the course is worth. These weighted grade points are added up and then divided by the total number of credits or hours to yield your GPA. An "A" received for a two-credit course thus receives less emphasis in the calculation than an "A" received for a four-credit course.

Similarly, in measuring price levels in the economy, we want to give greater emphasis to prices for goods and services that affect consumers the most and less emphasis to the prices of relatively minor goods and services. The way to do this is to weight each price by the corresponding quantity that is sold at that price.

Once again, however, we face choices about which standards to use. Should we use as weights the quantities bought in Year 1, Year 2, or some combination? Until recently, the BLS used a *constant-weight method* to calculate the CPI. Quantities bought during one period are chosen as the "base." These quantities are said to represent a typical "market basket" of goods bought by households. A constant-weight price index is calculated according to the following formula:

$$\textit{Constant Weight Price Index} = \frac{\textit{sum of current prices weighted by base quantities}}{\textit{sum of base prices weighted by base quantities}} \times 100$$

The price-index problem is analogous to the calculation of "constant-dollar" GDP—only now it is a common set of *quantity weights,* rather than prices, from the base period that are applied to every calculation.

Consider, again, our "apples-and-oranges" economy. Table 20.7 shows how we would calculate the numerator and denominator for the constant-weight price index formula, considering Year 2 the current year and using the Year 1 "market basket" as the base. The sum of current (Year 2) prices weighted by base quantities is $250, while the sum of base prices weighted by base quantities is $200. The CPI for Year 2 is therefore calculated as (250 ÷ 200) × 100 = 125. The price index for the base year (here, Year 1) always equals 100.

Table 20.7 **Calculation of a Constant-Weight Price Index**

(1)	(2)	(3)	(4)
Description	Price per pound ($)	Quantity **in base year**	Sum of (prices × base quantities) [column (2) × column (3)] ($)
Year 1 **(Base)**			
Apples	$1.00	100	$100
Oranges	$2.00	50	$100
			$200
Year 2			
Apples	$1.50	**100**	$150
Oranges	$2.00	**50**	$100
			$250

*Bold type indicates base year *quantities.*

The growth rate of prices—that is, the inflation rate affecting consumers—is measured by the growth rate of this price index:

$$Inflation\ rate = \frac{CPI_2 - CPI_1}{CPI_1} \times 100$$

So, in this case, with the price index rising from 100 to 125, the inflation rate is 25 percent.

Unfortunately, when a price index is based on constant weights, it may tend to overstate inflation for periods after the base year. When the price of a good is rising particularly quickly relative to other goods, people tend to look for cheaper substitutes. But a constant-weight index assumes that people are still buying the same quantities of the expensive goods. Various innovations have recently been made in the CPI to attempt to get around this problem. Currently, the "market basket" is updated periodically using data from ongoing household expenditure surveys (see Box 20.3). The BLS now also publishes "chained" price indexes. The mathematics of these more advanced calculations will not be presented here.

The CPI is not the only price index in use. The producer price index (PPI) measures prices that domestic producers receive for their output and so tracks many intermediate goods not included in the CPI market basket. Import and export price indexes track prices of goods traded between domestic residents and the foreign sector. Because they track different goods, these indexes—and inflation rates calculated from them—may vary.

Box 20.3 How Quantity Weights Can Lose Validity Over Time

Why do economists and statisticians make a fuss about updating the quantity weights used in calculating the Consumer Price Index? Consider how household expenditure patterns have changed over time.

In 1901, nearly half the budget of a typical urban, working family went toward food, while 15 percent toward shelter and an equal proportion toward clothing. The family probably spent nothing at all on cars or gasoline—because automobiles were not yet in wide use!

By 1950, the picture had changed considerably. Now only a third of the family's spending was on food, while only 11 percent was on shelter and 12 percent on clothing. On average, families were now spending about 12 percent of their budget on expenses related to private vehicles.

In recent data on consumer expenditures, the share devoted to food has dropped even further—to 13 percent (possibly the lowest the world has ever seen). Expenditures on clothing have dropped to less than 5 percent of a household's budget, on average. Meanwhile, families are spending more on shelter (20 to 30 percent of their budget) and private vehicle expenses (16 percent of their budget), than they were in the mid-twentieth century.

Using expenditure patterns from one of these periods to "weight" the CPI in another would clearly result in biased figures. Using the 1901 expenditure pattern nowadays, for example, would mean that auto and gasoline prices would not figure into the CPI at all.

The invention of new goods and services (e.g., MP3 players) and quality improvements in existing goods (e.g., in products for home entertainment and computing) continue to create special challenges for the economists working to measure price changes.

Sources: Eva Jacobs and Stephanie Shipp, "How Family Spending Has Changed in the U.S.," *Monthly Labor Review* (March 1990), pp. 20–27; U.S. Bureau of Labor Statistics, *Consumer Expenditure Survey 2011,* data tables; and authors' calculations.

4.5 Growth and Growth Rates

rule of 72: a shorthand calculation that states that dividing 72 by an annual growth rate yields approximately the number of years it will take for an amount to double

We have calculated year-to-year growth rates for GDP and prices. But suppose that we want to ask how much GDP has grown over the past five years or twenty years? How do we calculate those numbers? The answer is rather complicated, but fortunately you can use BEA's published NIPA tables to answer such questions.

An even simpler (though less precise) way to get a grasp on the relation of annual growth rates to changes over a longer period is by using **the rule of 72**. Taking $72/x$, where x equals the annual growth rate, will give you approximately the number of years it will take for an amount to double if it grows at that constant rate (as long as the numbers you are using are not extremely high or low). For example, if real GDP grew at a constant 4 percent rate per year, it would double in about eighteen years (since 72/4 = 18).

Discussion Questions

1. The "constant-dollar" method of estimating real GDP uses prices for one year to calculate measures of GDP for all years. Why is it sometimes important to evaluate GDP in the current year using prices from some other year? Why can't we just always use current prices? Explain.
2. How is the "constant-dollar" method of estimating real GDP similar to the use of "constant weights" in the computation of the price indexes? Explain.

5. SAVINGS, INVESTMENT, AND TRADE

At a personal level, you produce goods and services, earn income, consume, save, and borrow or lend. One of the reasons that you keep personal accounts might be to try to track your inflows and outflows, so that you know whether you are depleting your personal assets or accumulating them. If you can save money out of your current income, you are improving your financial position for the future. However, if you spend down your savings or go into debt merely to finance a high level of consumption, you may find yourself in trouble later on. Spending down financial savings or going into debt can be a good choice for your future only if you use the funds to gain another valuable asset. Students often go into debt in order to finance their education, for example, with the idea that it will pay off later by enabling them to earn a higher income than they would have been able to otherwise.

There are analogous issues at the national level. Besides keeping track of economic growth and inflation, systems of national accounting serve another important purpose. They allow us to look at the savings-and-assets situation of a national economy as a whole (at least as far as *manufactured* assets and financial flows are concerned).

5.1 THE RELATIONSHIP OF SAVINGS, INVESTMENT, AND TRADE

The category at the national level that is analogous to your personal day-to-day consumption spending is the consumption spending done by the "household and institutions" and "government" sectors. This is spending on goods and services that are presumably "used up" right now—they are not expected to help the country over the long term. The analogous category to your income is—at least roughly—GDP.

Recall that the spending approach to GDP says that

$$\begin{aligned} GDP &= \textit{Personal consumption} + \textit{Private investment} + \textit{Net exports} \\ &\quad + \textit{Government consumption} + \textit{Government investment} \end{aligned}$$

Rearranging, we obtain

$$\begin{aligned} &GDP - \textit{Personal consumption} - \textit{Government consumption} \\ &= \textit{Private investment} + \textit{Government investment} + \textit{Net exports} \end{aligned}$$

Because saving is what is left over from income after spending on consumption (the left-hand side of the equation above), we can combine private and government investment on the right-hand side to get:

$$\textit{Saving} = \textit{Investment} + \textit{Net exports}.$$

Thinking about these quantities in terms of valuable goods and services, this important identity says, intuitively, that goods and services that are produced in our domestic economy in excess of what we currently use for consumption can be investment goods—additions to our stock of manufactured assets (including replacement of depreciated assets)—or can be sold to foreign countries (in excess of the value of what we import from them).

5.2 Net Domestic Product and Saving

net domestic product (NDP): a measure of national production in excess of that needed to replace worn-out manufactured capital, calculated by subtracting depreciation from GDP

The investment concept used in defining *gross* domestic product (GDP) is *gross* investment. To calculate what the level of production is during a year, above and beyond the production that simply replaces worn-out manufactured capital, we need another concept, **net domestic product (NDP)**. NDP is GDP less depreciation (just as net investment, we saw earlier, is gross investment less depreciation):

Net domestic product = GDP – Depreciation

Similarly, we can differentiate between gross saving and net saving. To really find out the extent to which we have "put something aside for the future," we would subtract depreciation from our gross measure of saving. For example, even if our savings were positive, if they did not finance enough investment to make up for the deterioration of capital stock, we would actually start the next year in a *worse* position. Net saving is thus gross saving minus depreciation.

Net saving = (Gross) Saving – Depreciation

Net saving is a better measure than gross saving of whether we are "putting something aside for the future."

How much has the United States been "putting something aside for the future" lately? According to BEA data, gross savings in the United States were $1.84 trillion in 2011. But since fixed capital depreciation in 2011 was $1.94 trillion, net savings were actually negative! Net savings in the United States were also negative in 2010 and 2009. Compared to other countries, the United States has had relatively low savings rates for many years.

Discussion Questions

1. Suppose that the country of Atlantis is investing and exporting a great deal, while it imports little. What can you say about its level of national saving? Suppose the country of Olympus invests more than it saves. How can it do this?
2. Do you think it is a problem that the United States has a relatively low savings rate? What might be done to raise this rate, by individuals, corporations, or government?

Review Questions

1. For what purpose was national accounting in the United States originally begun?
2. Who compiles the National Income and Product Accounts?
3. What are the four accounting sectors of the economy, according to the BEA? What sorts of entities are included in each sector?
4. What forms of capital assets are tracked by the BEA?
5. Explain the difference between gross and net investment.
6. Explain four key phrases that appear in the definition of GDP.
7. What are the three approaches to GDP measurement?
8. Explain why, in a simple economy, the three approaches would yield the same figure for the value of total production.

9. Explain why the following two approaches arrive at the same number for the value of a final good: (a) looking at the market price of the good and (b) counting up the value-added at each stage of its production.
10. How are "market values" determined for goods and services that are not exchanged in markets or when data is not available?
11. Describe the components of GDP according to the product approach.
12. Describe the components of GDP according to the spending approach.
13. What are the major differences between GDP and national income?
14. Describe the reasoning behind the "constant-dollar" approach to calculating real GDP.
15. What are some problems with the "constant-dollar" approach to calculating real GDP?
16. Describe the reasoning behind the "constant-weight" method traditionally used in estimating the price indexes.
17. Is there only one kind of price index? Explain.
18. Explain how savings, investment, and trade are related in the national accounts.
19. Explain how a country can finance an excess of imports over exports.

EXERCISES

1. If you look at the government-supplied statistical tables regarding the national accounts, you might find that they often go into considerable detail about "farm" vs. "nonfarm" activities, while it is much harder to dig out good information on, for example, the activities of the finance industry. Can you conjecture how this might relate to the history of the national accounts?
2. In which line (or lines) of Table 20.2 (the product approach) would the value of each of the following be counted? "Not counted in any category" is also an option.
   a. Production of fresh apples, domestically grown for profitable sale
   b. State health inspection services
   c. Education services provided by a private, nonprofit domestic college
   d. Child-care services provided by a child's parents and relatives
   e. Production by a U.S.-owned company at its factory in Singapore
3. In which line (or lines) of Table 20.4 (the income approach) would the value of each of the following be counted? If it is part of "net income flows from the rest of the world," explain whether it reflects domestic (or foreign) production and whether it reflects domestic (or foreign) income. "Not counted in any category" is also an option.
   a. Wages paid by your local supermarket to its employees
   b. Profits received by a U.S. electronics firm from its factory in Mexico
   c. Business spending to replace worn-out equipment
   d. Wages paid by a U.S. electronics firm to the employees of its factory in Mexico
   e. Profits received by a Japanese automaker from its factory in the United States
4. In which line (or lines) of Table 20.3 (the spending approach) would the value of each of the following be counted? "Not counted in any category" is also an option.
   a. A new refrigerator bought by a family
   b. A book newly produced in Indiana and bought by a store in Mexico
   c. New computers, manufactured in Asia, bought by a U.S. accounting company
   d. Meals produced and served in Virginia to military personnel
   e. New computers, produced in the United States, bought by a U.S. computer retail chain and not yet sold by the end of the year
   f. A three-year-old couch bought by a used furniture store in Arizona
   g. Cleaning services bought by a nonprofit hospital in New York
   h. The services of volunteers in an environmental action campaign
5. Using the relations among accounting categories demonstrated in the tables and identities in the text, use the information on values in the chart on the next page (measured in Neverlandian pesos) from the country of Neverland in 2010 to find values for the following categories:
   a. Private household production
   b. Business production
   c. Fixed investment spending (by business)
   d. Federal government spending
   e. National income

Household and institutions spending = 650	Business spending = 50
Household and institutions production =150	Exports = 225
Net income payments from the rest of the world = 5	Imports = 125
Nonprofit institutions production = 50	Government production = 200
State and local government spending = 30	Statistical discrepancy = 0
Change in private inventories = 2	GDP = 850
Depreciation = 60	

6. Suppose an extremely simple economy produces only two goods, pillows and rugs. In the first year, 50 pillows are produced and sold at $5 each; 11 rugs are produced and sold at $50 each. In the second year, 56 pillows are produced and sold for $5 each; 12 rugs are produced and sold at $60 each.
   a. What is nominal GDP in each of the two years?
   b. What is the growth rate of nominal GDP?
   c. What is real GDP in each year, expressed in terms of constant Year 1 dollars?
   d. What is the growth rate of real GDP (in constant Year 1 dollars)?
7. Assume the same simple economy described in the previous question.
   a. Calculate a constant-weight price index for the second year, using the first year as the base.
   b. What is the growth rate of prices (inflation rate) from the first to the second year?
8. List the key simplifying assumptions of the traditional macro model concerning:
   a. The forms of capital included in the model
   b. The sectors of the economy
   c. Who in the economy produces and invests
9. Go to the Bureau of Economic Analysis Web site (www.bea.gov). What are the latest figures for real GDP, current dollar GDP, and the growth rate of GDP? What time period do these represent? In what sort of dollars is real GDP expressed?
10. Match each concept in Column A with a definition or example in Column B:

Column A	Column B
a. A negative (subtracted) item in GDP	1. The year in which real and nominal values are equal
b. A major cause of difference between GDP and NI	2. Purchases of computer software
c. An imputed value	3. Consumption of fixed capital (depreciation)
d. An entity in the government sector	4. Unpaid household production
e. Reflects the prices of all goods and services counted in GDP	5. Implicit price deflator
f. Base year	6. National income
g. An assumption of the traditional macro model	7. Spending on imported cheese
h. Something not counted in by the BEA in calculating GDP	8. A measure that seeks to remove the effects of price changes
i. Real GDP	9. Uses a fixed “market basket”
j. A component of the “income approach” to GDP accounting	10. What homeowners “pay” themselves in rent
k. A constant-weight price index	11. “Governments do not produce”
l. Part of business investment (gross private domestic investment)	12. A state university

11. Go to the Bureau of Labor Statistics Web site (www.bls.gov) and locate its information on the Consumer Price Index for All Urban Consumers (called the “CPI-U”). What is its current value? What month is this for? How does its value in this month compare to its value for the same month a year ago? (That is, by what percentage has the index risen? Use the “seasonally adjusted” number.)
12. (If Appendix is assigned.) The “chained Year 1 dollar” estimate of real GDP in the apples-and-oranges example (see Appendix) is smaller than the “constant Year 1 dollar” estimate of real GDP. Can you explain why? (Hint: Compare the GDP growth rates derived using the two methods.)

APPENDIX: CHAINED DOLLAR REAL GDP

quantity index: an index measuring changes in levels of quantities produced

The key new concept in the "chained-dollar" method is an emphasis on estimating **quantity indexes** for GDP in the current year relative to the year before and relative to the reference year.

Chained-dollar measures of real GDP and GDP growth are based on the use of index numbers. The ratio of two values of GDP in adjacent years, measured at a common set of prices, can be used as a quantity index to measure production in one year relative to another.

Fisher quantity index: an index that measures production in one year relative to an adjacent year by using an average of the ratios that would be found by using first one year and then the other as the source of prices at which production is valued

The calculation of chained-dollar real GDP starts with the calculation of a **Fisher quantity index**, which measures production in one year relative to an adjacent year by using an *average* of the ratios that would be found by using first one year and then the other as the source of prices at which production is valued. The type of average used is a "geometric" average. Instead of adding two numbers and then dividing by two, as you would in calculating the most common type of average (the arithmetic mean), to get a geometric average you *multiply* the two numbers together and then take the *square root.* The formula for this Fisher quantity index is:

$$\textit{Fisher quantity index (for year-to-year comparison)}$$
$$= \sqrt{\left(\frac{\textit{Year 2 GDP in Year 1 prices}}{\textit{Year 1 GDP in Year 1 prices}}\right) \times \left(\frac{\textit{Year 2 GDP in Year 2 prices}}{\textit{Year 1 GDP in Year 2 prices}}\right)}$$

This index has a value of 1 in the reference year, which we take to be Year 1.

The growth rate of real GDP between the reference year and the next year can then be calculated as:

$$\textit{growth rate} = (\textit{Fisher quantity index} - 1) \times 100$$

For example, we have already made many of the necessary calculations for the "apples-and-oranges" economy in Tables 20.5 and 20.6. Plugging these in, we get

$$\textit{Fisher quantity index (for Year 2 compared to Year 1)}$$
$$= \sqrt{\left(\frac{250}{200}\right) \times \left(\frac{300}{250}\right)} = \sqrt{1.25 \times 1.20} = \sqrt{1.5} = 1.225$$

The growth rate of real GDP for the "apples-and-oranges" economy between these two years is

$$\textit{growth rate} = (1.225 - 1) \times 100 = 22.5 \textit{ percent}$$

Note that this growth rate is *between* the two growth rates (20 percent and 25 percent) we obtained by using the constant-dollar method with various base years. The Fisher quantity index method gives us a unique *average* number for estimated growth.

chain-type quantity index: an index comparing real production in the current year to the reference year, calculated using a series of year-to-year Fisher quantity indexes

A quantity index for the current year in terms of a reference year that may be several years in the past is created by "chaining together" year-to-year Fisher quantity indexes to make a **chain-type quantity index** comparing real production relative to the reference year. The chain-type quantity index has a value of 100 in the reference year. In any subsequent year, it is set equal to the chain-type quantity index from the previous year multiplied by the Fisher quantity index calculated for the current year.

Finally, estimation of real GDP in (chained) dollar terms is made by multiplying the chain-type quantity index for a year times the level of nominal GDP in the reference year and dividing by 100.

For example, suppose that we take our "apples-and-oranges" economy, making Year 1 the reference year. Year 1's chain-type quantity index is thus set equal to 100, and its nominal and real GDP are equal. These are shown in Table 20.8. The chain-type quantity index for Year 2 is the previous year's value (100) times the Fisher quantity index that we just calculated (1.225). We multiply this result, the new index number 122.5, times nominal GDP in the base year ($200) and divide by 100 to get real GDP, $245. Whew!

Table 20.8 **Deriving Real GDP in Chained (Year 1) Dollars**

Type of measure	Year 1	Year 2
Nominal GDP	$200	$300
Fisher quantity index (current to previous year)	——	1.225
Chain-type quantity index	100	100 × 1.225 = 122.5
Real GDP (chained Year 1 dollars)	= $200	(122.5 × $200)/100 = $245

This can be continued for many years into the future—or into the past. (For example, if the Fisher quantity index calculated for Year 3 were to come out to be 1.152, then the chain-type quantity index for Year 3 would be 122.5 × 1.152.) If you want to check to see that this method actually makes some sense, calculate the percentage change in real GDP from Year 1 to Year 2 using the values in the table above. You will find it does, in fact, equal 22.5 percent!

A price index can be calculated for Year 2 (using Year 1 as the reference year) as (300/245) × 100 = 122.5, showing a 22.5 percent price increase over Year 1. This kind of price index is known as a "**GDP deflator**" or "**implicit price deflator**."

GDP deflator (implicit price deflator): a price index created by dividing nominal GDP by real GDP

The new method has some other drawbacks, as well. The sum of real components of GDP in chained-dollar terms do not generally exactly add up to real GDP. Users of the data are also warned not to make comparisons of chained-dollar amounts for years far away from the reference year. The BEA tries to make the data more usable by providing tables in which, for example, year to year growth rates in components of GDP are already calculated for the user.

21 Macroeconomic Measurement: Environmental and Social Dimensions

1. A Broader View of National Income Accounting

As discussed in Chapter 20, GDP is a good (though not perfect) summary of the annual flow of goods and services through the market. In the 80-plus years since the introduction of U.S. national income accounting, GDP has become the official barometer of living standards and business cycles. It appears in newspapers and political debates as a measure of government performance and an indicator of economic, political, and social progress.

GDP is not just something that economists look at; rather, numbers on the size and growth rate of GDP affect critical national and international policies. It is a measure by which we judge presidents and a basis on which multilateral institutions determine how much money they will lend to developing countries. GDP numbers are widely used as a proxy for national success.

Yet GDP was never intended to play such a role. Economists dating back to Simon Kuznets, the originator of U.S. national accounting systems, have warned that GDP is a specialized tool for measuring market activity, which should not be confused with national well-being. As suggested in Box 21.1, GDP often rises with increases in things that most people would want to have less of, while it often fails to rise with positive contributions to individual and social well-being that are not bought and sold in markets.

As discussed in Chapter 3, marketed economic activity occurs within broader social and environmental contexts. These contexts can have an effect on national welfare that is no less important than marketed economic activity. The various alternatives to national accounting presented in this chapter represent our growing awareness of the importance of these social and environmental contexts of economic activity.

In Chapter 1, we mentioned that neglect of the questions of what, how, and for whom can mean that growth in production per capita may not lead to increased welfare. Now we can go into more detail about the problems that arise from focusing on production alone—or from focusing only on the money value of output, with too little attention to the details of what is being produced. Many economists, and others analysts, believe that if we are really to understand this more complete picture of the economy, and what it is doing for human well-being, national governments need to start gathering new kinds of data and creating new indicators.

Before we begin to discuss specific options for adjusting, replacing, or supplementing GDP, we first need to ask ourselves three important questions:

1. *What should we measure?* GDP measures only economic production. Are there some things that GDP excludes that should be included as a component of well-being, such as health outcomes or environmental quality? Should some parts of GDP be excluded because they harm well-being, in the short or long term?

BOX 21.1 THERE'S NO G-D-P IN "A BETTER ECONOMY"

The year-end numbers have been tabulated, and America is winning the race by a large margin. The nation's closest competitor, China, scores only half as high, and European nations, Japan, and Brazil lag way behind with little chance of catching up.

This statement is not about medal counts from the summer Olympics; it's not about citizens' health; and it's certainly not about student test scores in math and science. It's about GDP. The United States continues to dominate the race for the biggest economy.

Gross domestic product has become the most watched and most misinterpreted of all economic indicators. It's a measure of economic activity—of money changing hands. Despite the mundane nature of this economic indicator, politicians fiercely compete with each other to see who can promise the fastest GDP growth. Government programs and investments in technology get the green light only when they are predicted to spur GDP growth. Economists, bankers, and businesspeople pop the champagne corks when they hear "good news" about quarterly GDP numbers.

And while the United States leads in GDP, it also leads in military spending, the number of people in prison, and the percentage of people who are obese. These other first-place finishes seem at odds with America's position atop the GDP standings—that is, until you realize that spending on war, incarceration, and disease, as well as other "defensive expenditures," all count toward GDP. The arithmetic of GDP doesn't consider what the money is actually being spent on, and over time, we've been spending more and more money on remedial activities and calling this "progress."

Counting all these negatives in GDP (not to mention omitting positive activities such as raising children, volunteering, and caring for elderly people) seems like an oversight or an accounting mix-up. But it also seems like something that could be easily fixed. Many people, including Nobel laureates in economics (and even the laureate who invented national income accounting) have issued stern warnings not to confuse GDP with national progress, and many forward-thinking economists have proposed alternative indicators of progress.

Source: Rob Dietz and Dan O'Neill, "There's No G-D-P in 'A Better Economy,'" *Stanford Social Innovation Review,* January 7, 2013.

2. *What should be used as the unit of measurement?* Although GDP is measured in dollars, what units should be used to measure other variables of well-being, such as levels of violence or air quality?
3. *Should we seek to combine disparate well-being indicators into a single "bottom-line" number, or should we keep the variables disaggregated (i.e., split up into component categories)?* One tempting approach is to convert all variables to dollars to allow for comparability. But what techniques can we use to measure variables such as environmental quality or social capital in dollars, and should we even try?

satellite accounts: additional or parallel accounting systems that provide measures of social and environmental factors in physical terms, without necessarily including monetary valuation

One response to the last question has been the development of **satellite accounts,*** which are intended to supplement standard accounts by tracking data on other well-being indicators, such as health, education, and other aspects of social and environmental well-being. For example, the United Kingdom maintains environmental accounts that track data on forested area, oil and gas reserves, waste generation, greenhouse gas emissions, and expenditures on environmental protection.

The U.S. Bureau of Economic Analysis (BEA) uses dollar-denominated satellite accounts to highlight certain existing components of GDP. For example, the BEA is creating a new satellite account that highlights health-care expenditures that fall under GDP but are currently obscured by the aggregate measure.[1] Beginning in 1994 the BEA also operated a satellite account that was designed to see how GDP would be different if research and development were counted as investment rather than spending. As noted in Chapter 20, this change was

*The United Nations differentiates between "internal" satellite accounts (those that are linked to standard accounts and typically measured in monetary units) and "external" satellite accounts (not necessarily linked and measured in either physical or monetary units). See http://unstats.un.org/unsd/nationalaccount/AEG/papers/m4SatelliteAccounts.pdf.

incorporated into the core GDP account beginning in 2013.[2] Future uses of satellite accounts in the BEA may start experimenting with changes such as valuing household labor or counting environmental losses as losses.

In general, the BEA's satellite accounts rely on monetary valuation and are readily comparable to GDP. Other countries use satellite accounts in which the unit of measurement is physical units. Even where resources can be easily valued in dollars, data in physical units may be more meaningful. Consider that we could measure the economic value of oil and gas reserves by multiplying the quantity of reserves in physical units multiplied by the market price. But suppose that the market price increases considerably at the same time that reserves are drawn down. Although the economic value of reserves could increase, that information would fail to tell us that our physical reserves have declined.

Often it is very difficult to convert variables to monetary units. How can we express changes in violence or health levels in terms of dollar values? Such questions raise important methodological issues, such as whether the economic value of higher asthma rates includes only medical expenditures and lost productivity or whether other quality of life factors need to be considered. Some may raise ethical objections to attaching dollar values to variables such as traffic deaths or biodiversity.

Satellite accounts can be viewed as a "dashboard" approach to national accounting. The dashboard on a car provides not only a speedometer but also a gas gauge and an indicator of temperature and battery level—and we have in recent years come to recognize the value of adding an indicator of how many miles are being driven per gallon of fuel. The dashboard on an airplane contains even more indicators, and an economy is considerably more complex than an airplane.* Proponents of this approach agree that GDP is a very useful record of national output for historical and international comparisons, but believe that GDP tells us only one of the things that we want to know about the economy. Some of the things that it does not tell us are very important, and they deserve to have their own indicators.

As we delve into additional categories that we might wish to have reported in national accounts, we may find ourselves straying into areas where measurement becomes more difficult. Thus we can add a fourth question to our list above: Should we include only variables that can be measured objectively (whether in money or other units), or should we also consider subjective data? In particular, should one or more of our "dashboard" indicators present the results from surveys that ask people about their well-being? We consider this possibility in the next section.

Due to funding cutbacks, in the United States progress on improving macroeconomic measurement in the national accounts has slowed considerably. Nevertheless, many private groups, as well as subnational entities (such as states) in the United States and official statistical agencies in a number of other countries are making progress in developing better measures to address the social and environmental issues of the twenty-first century.

For example, the national statistical agencies of the UK, France, and Germany are currently constructing alternative measures of well-being. There has been a proliferation of new indicators, more than a dozen of which have emerged in the past decade. Some are concentrating on developing refined measures of national assets and production, keeping as close as possible to the framework of the National Income and Product Accounts (NIPA). Others are working to develop wholly new indicators, hoping either to replace GDP as the major measure of economic success or to persuade the public and policymakers that GDP is useful only for some purposes and that other measures are needed to make different assessments.

*An example of the dashboard approach is the Key National Indicators System, housed at the National Academies. Created by act of Congress but not yet funded, the proposal creates a dashboard of more than 200 indicators. For more info, see www.stateoftheusa.org.

Discussion Questions

1. GDP can be characterized as a (rough) measure of the amount of "throughput" taking place in an economy—as measuring the level of activity whose purpose it is to turn renewable and nonrenewable resources into new products. How does "throughput" relate to sustainable well-being? Is more "throughput" always a good thing?
2. In Chapter 1, we discussed how economies are based on natural, manufactured, social, and human capital. Only the value of manufactured capital (structures and equipment)—and recently, software—is estimated in the current national accounts. Can you think of ways that the stocks of natural, social, and human capital might be measured? What kind of information would be needed?

2. WHY GDP IS NOT A MEASURE OF WELL-BEING

Recognizing the limitations of GDP and the need to develop indicators that incorporate social and environmental factors, in 2008 French president Nicolas Sarkozy created the Commission on the Measurement of Economic Performance and Social Progress. The commission was chaired by Nobel Prize–winning economist Joseph Stiglitz, and the chair of the advisory board was another Nobel laureate economist, Amartya Sen. Other members of the commission included numerous prominent economists.

In September 2009, the commission produced its nearly 300-page report. It concluded that it is necessary to shift from an emphasis on measuring economic production to measuring well-being. It also distinguished between current well-being and sustainability, recognizing that whether current well-being can be sustained depends upon the levels of capital (natural, physical, human, and social) passed on to future generations.

2.1 SUBJECTIVE WELL-BEING

As mentioned above, GDP was never intended to measure welfare or well-being. Even if increases in GDP produce increases in well-being, ceteris paribus, many other factors may be equally or more important in determining well-being levels. In other words, well-being is clearly multidimensional. The Sarkozy Commission, for example, defined eight dimensions of well-being, including material living standards, health, education, political voice, social connections, and the environment.

Objective data can be collected that provide information on many of these dimensions, such as average life expectancy, literacy rates, and air pollution levels. But such data still do not tell us exactly how these factors relate to well-being. If the goal of economics is to promote well-being, you may wonder why economists do not try to measure it directly. Until recently, most economists believed that it was not possible to obtain quantitative data on something that is inherently subjective; we cannot hook up individuals to a machine and measure their well-being in unambiguous quantitative terms. But we can take a much more intuitive approach—we can simply ask people about their well-being. Although this approach may seem unscientific, a large body of scientific research has emerged in recent decades that suggests that data on **subjective well-being (SWB)** provides meaningful information regarding social welfare levels and the factors that influence well-being.

subjective well-being: a measure of welfare based on survey questions asking people about their own degree of life satisfaction

Collecting data on SWB involves surveying individuals and asking them a question such as: "All things considered, how satisfied are you with your life as a whole these days?" Respondents then answer based on a scale from 1 (dissatisfied) to 10 (satisfied). How much credence can we give to the answers to such questions?

A wide variety of efforts, such as the World Happiness Report from Columbia University's Earth Institute,[3] the Gallup World Poll, and the European Social Survey, have come up with remarkably consistent measures of "happiness" or "life satisfaction." The Sarkozy Commission concludes:

> Research has shown that it is possible to collect meaningful and reliable data on subjective as well as objective well-being. Quantitative measures of [SWB] hold the promise of delivering not just a good measure of quality of life per se, but also a better understanding of its determinants, reaching beyond people's income and material conditions. Despite the persistence of many unresolved issues, these subjective measures provide important information about quality of life.[4]

The Sarkozy Commission recommends using SWB data in conjunction with objective data on various well-being dimensions such as income levels and health outcomes to obtain a more comprehensive picture of welfare.

Most relevant for our study of macroeconomics is how SWB results correlate with standard economic measures of national welfare such as GDP. We can study the relationship in two ways:

1. Are average SWB levels higher in countries with higher GDP per capita?
2. As GDP per capita increases in a particular country over time, do SWB levels rise?

SWB data have been collected for many developed and developing countries. Figure 21.1 plots average SWB against per-capita GDP, adjusted for differences in purchasing power, for 56 countries. In general, SWB is positively correlated with higher levels of GDP, but note that the benefits of income gains decline at higher income levels, as shown by the curved trendline. However, SWB can be high in both rich and poor countries. In fact, the countries with the highest SWB levels are Mexico and Colombia, both middle-income countries.

Figure 21.1 also shows that while SWB varies among richer countries, all developed countries have relatively high SWB. There are no countries above a per-capita GDP of $20,000 per year that have an average SWB below 6.0, and many poorer countries have an average SWB below 6.0. Thus it appears from this graph that for at least some developing countries, increasing GDP could lead to higher SWB levels. But income gains in richer countries are associated with much smaller increases in SWB.

Figure 21.1 **Average Subjective Well-Being and GDP per Capita**

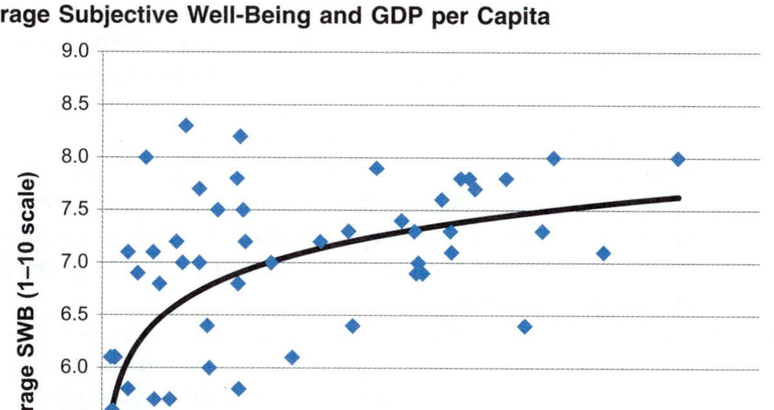

Sources: SWB from World Values Survey online data analysis, 2005–2008 survey wave; GDP from World Development Indicators online database.

The other way to analyze country-level SWB data is to consider how SWB changes as a country develops economically over time. The longest time series of SWB data comes from the United States, dating back to 1946. While real GDP per capita has increased by about a factor of three since 1946, average SWB levels have essentially remained constant. But an analysis of country trends in SWB over the period 1981–2007 found that average SWB rose in 45 of 52 countries, with economic growth leading to greater SWB gains for low-income countries. India is an example of a country that has experienced significant gains in SWB levels as its economy has grown in recent decades.[5]

Based on both approaches to evaluating SWB, the results imply that as people are able to meet their basic needs, such as adequate nutrition and basic health care, their happiness generally increases. Beyond that, further income gains are associated with smaller increases in SWB or no increase at all. At higher income levels, people seem more likely to judge their happiness relative to others. So even if everyone's income doubles, average happiness levels may be unchanged.

As the Sarkozy Commission mentions, further work is needed to understand the relationship between SWB and other well-being measures. But the results so far suggest that SWB should be one of the indicators on our "dashboard" of well-being measures.

2.2 Critiques of GDP

Many important issues are not included adequately, if at all in GDP. In addition, some things that are included in GDP can be misleading or represent actively harmful activities.

- A critical issue is *household production,* which is examined at more length later in this chapter. While standard accounting measures include the paid labor from such household activities as child care and gardening, these services are not counted when they are unpaid.
- Standard measures do not count the benefits of *volunteer work,* even though such work can contribute to social well-being as much as economic production does. Also, the free services provided by many nonprofit organizations (e.g., a homeless shelter funded by donations) go unaccounted, even if the workers in the organization are paid.
- *Leisure* is another important neglected factor. A rise in output might come about because people expend more time and effort at paid work. The resulting increase in measured output does not take into account the fact that overwork makes people more tired and stressed and takes away from time that they could use for enjoying other activities. But if people spend more time in leisure, increasing their well-being, this will not be reflected in GDP (except insofar as they spend money on leisure-related activities).
- Also inadequately reflected are issues around loss (or gain) of *human and social capital formation.* Social and political factors that may significantly affect well-being include the health and education levels of a country's citizens, as well as political participation, government effectiveness (or lack thereof), and issues of trust, corruption, or other aspects of the economic and social culture.
- Another significant criticism of GDP, when used as a general measure of economic progress or success, is that *interactions between the economy and the natural world are often ignored.* GDP generally does not account for environmental degradation and resource depletion, while treating natural resources that do not go through the market as having no monetary value.
- Some outputs merely compensate for, or defend against, harmful events that result, directly or indirectly, from the economic activity represented in GDP. Referred to as **defensive expenditures**, these show up as positive contributions to GDP but we do not account for the associated negative impacts. Consider, for example, an oil spill that results in massive clean-up efforts: The billions of dollars spent cleaning up after the 2011 Deepwater Horizon oil spill in the Gulf of Mexico turned up as positive additions to GDP, even while the environmental and human losses are mostly not reflected. When environmental issues are

defensive expenditures: money spent to counteract economic activities that have caused harm to human or environmental health

mostly invisible, there can be an appearance of economic growth even as the ecological basis for future economic health is being seriously undermined.

- *Products or production methods that reduce, rather than increase, well-being* may show up as additions to GDP. Unhealthy foods and drugs and dangerous equipment, for example, may lower, not raise, overall well-being. Even if people are willing to pay for such goods and services, either individually (perhaps influenced by advertising) or through their governments (perhaps influenced by interest group lobbyists), such decisions might reflect poor information or bad judgment when looked at from the point of view of well-being. In terms of production methods, if people are miserable at their jobs, suffering boring, degrading, unpleasant, or harmful working conditions, their well-being is compromised. The divergence between output and well-being is especially obvious in cases where workers' lives or health are threatened by their working conditions, even while their work results in a high volume of marketed goods and services.
- Another gap between GDP and well-being is *financial debt.* GDP counts consumption levels as rising even if the rise is financed by unsustainably large debt burdens, whether the debt is held by consumers or by governments. When debts are high enough to require painful changes in future consumption, not accounting for financial debt is similar to not accounting for unsustainable tolls exacted on the natural environment.
- Finally, increased economic activity in a given country is counted as an addition to GDP even if it *increases inequality.* Two countries with the same per-capita GDP may have a significantly different income distribution and, closely related, different levels of overall well-being. At an individual level, if someone making just $20,000 per year receives a raise of $1,000, this is counted as the same societal gain as it would be if that raise went to someone with an income of $100,000. Obviously, the additional income means much more for the individual well-being of the person with the lower salary. Although economists generally accept this concept (called the diminishing marginal utility of income), GDP counts income gains the same regardless of whether the person receiving the increase desperately needs the income or is already rich.

The foregoing examples all indicate the social dangers of pursuing policies geared only to raising GDP. A narrow national focus solely on increasing output may result in decreased leisure and less time for parenting, friendships, and community relations; it can increase levels of stress and mental illness, or raise economic inequality to a socially destructive level. For all these reasons, improvements are needed in the design of measures of national success and in defining and gathering the data needed for such measures. The next two sections describe three leading alternative measures.

3. Alternative Approaches to Representing Well-Being

3.1 The Genuine Progress Indicator (GPI)

In 1989, economist Herman Daly and theologian John Cobb Jr. suggested an alternative measure to GDP that they called the Index of Sustainable Economic Welfare (ISEW). This measure was later transformed into the Genuine Progress Indicator (GPI), one of the most ambitious attempts to date to design a replacement to GDP.* The GPI is a measure of economic well-being that adds many benefits and subtracts many costs that are not included in GDP. It is designed to differentiate

> between economic activity that diminishes both natural and social capital and activity that enhances such capital. . . . In particular, if GPI is stable or increasing in a given

*Another predecessor to the GPI and the ISEW was the Measure of Economic Welfare, by William Nordhaus and James Tobin. This 1973 effort was the first serious attempt to create an alternative to GDP.

year the implication is that stocks of natural and social capital on which all goods and services flows depend will be at least as great for the next generation, while if GPI is falling it implies that the economic system is eroding those stocks and limiting the next generation's prospects.[6]

The starting point of the GPI is personal consumption expenditures (PCE). In the United States, about 70 percent of GDP consists of personal consumption, with the remainder made up of government consumption, investment, and net exports. In calculating the GPI, the level of PCE is first adjusted for income inequality, measured by dividing PCE by a factor that reflects the change in the Gini ratio since 1968. (Recall from Chapter 11 that a higher Gini ratio indicates greater inequality; the ratio was at a low point in the United States in 1968, and has generally risen since then.)

Next, some items that increase well-being but are not measured in PCE are added, including estimates of the value of time spent on household and volunteer work and the value of higher education. A measure of the services of consumer durables is added, reflecting the well-being gained from having items such as appliances and cars. Although most government spending is excluded from the GPI because it is argued that such spending is defensive, services such as those that come from government spending on highways and streets is added.

Then cost items are subtracted, including estimates of social costs, such as the costs of crime and lost leisure time, and environmental costs, including water pollution, the loss of wetlands, and damage from CO_2 emissions. A few other adjustments are made, including an addition for the amount by which the net (manufactured) capital stock grows, on a per-worker basis, based on the rationale that constant or increasing stocks are necessary for sustainability. A measure of net foreign borrowing is subtracted, because consumption financed from foreign borrowing is offset by increased debt, and thus does not represent a net addition to national well-being. The cost of consumer-durable purchases is subtracted to avoid double counting, given that a measure of the *services* of consumer durables has already been included. The adjustments made in order to arrive at the GPI for a recent year (2004) are described in Table 21.1.

Table 21.1 **Genuine Progress Indicator, United States, 2004**

Component of GPI		Value (billions of dollars)
Personal consumption		7,589
Personal consumption after inequality adjustment		6,318
Value of household work and parenting	+	2,542
Value of higher education	+	828
Value of volunteer work	+	131
Service value of consumer durables	+	744
Service value of highways and streets	+	112
Costs of crime	–	34
Loss of leisure time	–	402
Costs of underemployment	–	177
Cost of consumer durables	–	1,090
Costs of commuting and auto accidents	–	698
Costs of environmental defensive expenditures	–	21
Costs of pollution	–	178
Value of lost wetlands, farmland, and forests	–	368
Costs of nonrenewable energy depletion	–	1,761
Damage from carbon emissions and ozone depletion	–	1,662
Adjustment for capital investment and foreign borrowing	+	135
Genuine Progress Indicator		**4,419**

Source: Talberth et al., *The Genuine Progress Indicator 2006: A Tool for Sustainable Development.* Redefining Progress, 2007, pp. 1–2. http://rprogress.org.

Figure 21.2 **Comparison of GDP and GPI per Capita, United States, 1950–2004**

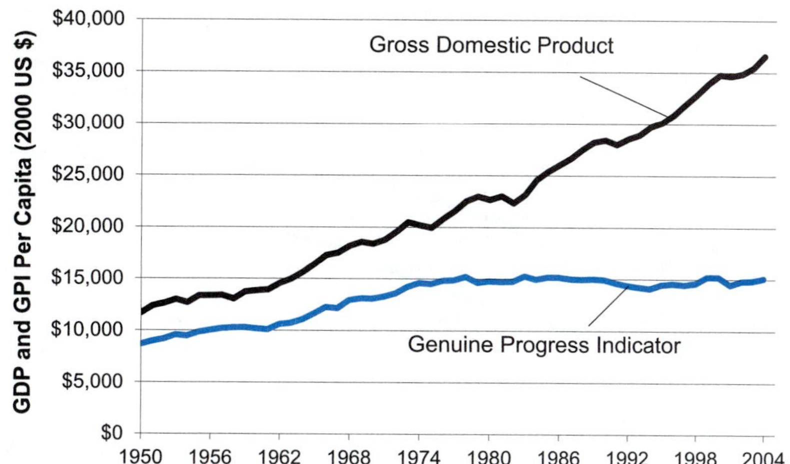

Source: Talberth et al., *The Genuine Progress Indicator 2006: A Tool for Sustainable Development.* Redefining Progress, 2007, pp. 1–2. http://rprogress.org.

As we might expect, with all the adjustments outlined above, the GPI differs significantly from GDP in magnitude and trends. The largest positive adjustments to inequality-adjusted personal consumption are the value of household work and parenting and the benefits of higher education. But the additions are more than offset by the various deductions, most importantly the deductions for nonrenewable energy depletion and CO_2 emissions. Thus the GPI is significantly less than personal consumption.

Trends in real (i.e., inflation-adjusted) GDP per capita and real GPI per capita are tracked from 1950 to 2002 in Figure 21.2. Not only is per-capita GPI lower than per-capita GDP, but its growth trajectory has diverged from GDP since 1978. Since that year, the GPI has flat-lined, while GDP continued to grow, indicating that environmental and social costs omitted from GDP have been increasing faster than the value of the omitted benefits. Relying on the GPI instead of GDP would suggest significantly different policy recommendations, focusing more on reducing environmental damage, preserving natural capital, developing renewable energy resources, and redressing rising inequality.

GPI estimates have been developed for countries other than the United States, including Australia, China, Germany, and India. The GPI has also been applied at the subnational level, not only in the United States (as discussed below) but also in other countries. For example, a 2009 analysis of the Auckland region in New Zealand showed that, unlike in the United States, in 1990–2006 the GPI grew at nearly the same rate as the region's GDP (Figure 21.3). Even in this case, environmental losses grew at a more rapid rate than the GPI—rising 27 percent during this period while the GPI rose 18 percent. But the positive contributions to the GPI, in particular growth in personal consumption, were enough to more than offset the environmental losses.

The state of Maryland, in the United States, also measures its GPI, defining each of the variables in Table 21.1 as an economic, environmental, or social component. Figure 21.4 breaks down the state's GPI into these three aggregate components, over the period 1960–2010.[7] While the economic contributions to the GPI rose steadily, the net social contributions increased only slightly, and the environmental costs (negative contributions) more than doubled.

Calculating the GPI requires converting various environmental factors into a single metric—dollars. Among the questions this raises is: Can disparate environmental and social resources and amenities be compared directly, by any metric? Other approaches to measuring national well-being have been developed that avoid the use of a monetary metric but consider different aspects of the environment or quality of life rather than using a dollar value.

Figure 21.3 **New Zealand's Auckland Regional GPI vs. GDP, 1990–2006**

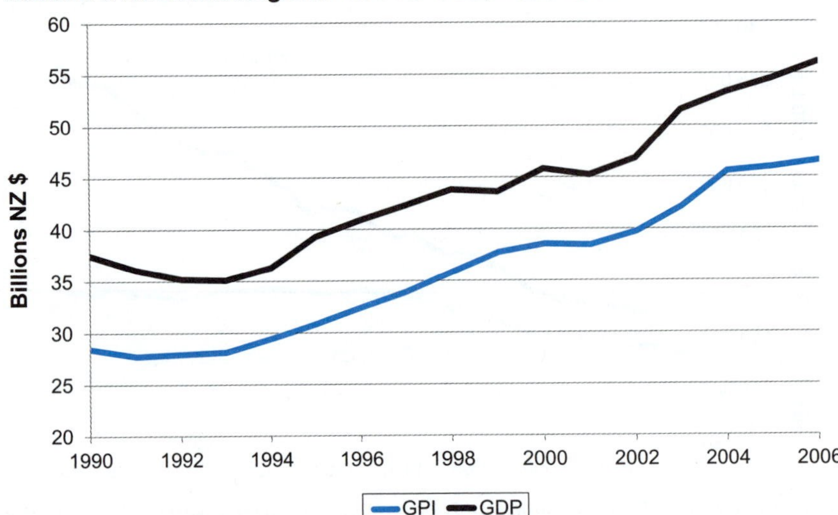

Source: McDonald, et al., *A Genuine Progress Indicator for the Auckland Region*, Auckland Regional Council and New Zealand Centre for Ecological Economists, 2009.

Figure 21.4 **Components of the GPI for Maryland, 1960–2010**

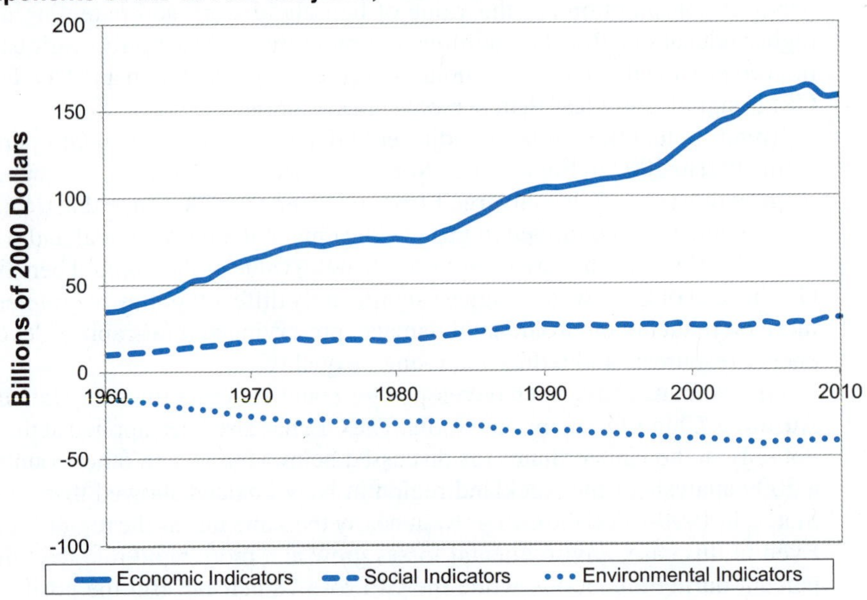

Source: http://www.green.maryland.gov/mdgpi/mdgpioverview.asp

3.2 The Better Life Index (BLI)

A major challenge to efforts to create better indicators is the difficulty of obtaining measurements of the non-monetary variables. The Better Life Index (BLI) launched by the Organization for Economic Cooperation and Development (OECD) is somewhat more ambitious than the GPI in attempting to include more variables that are not commonly included, precisely because they are hard to measure.* (We consider measurement issues at greater length below, in our discussion of environmental indicators.)

BLI considers well-being a function of the following 11 dimensions:

*The OECD is a group of the world's advanced industrialized countries, now including some developing countries, such as Mexico. The BLI was created, in part, as a response to the 2009 Sarkozy Commission report discussed above.

1. Income, Wealth, and Inequality: The main variables used for this dimension are disposable household income and net financial wealth.* The BLI also considers the degree of inequality in income and wealth.
2. Jobs and Earnings: The main variables comprising this dimension are the unemployment rate, the long-term unemployment rate, and average earnings per employee.
3. Housing Conditions: Sufficient housing is important to provide security, privacy, and stability.
4. Health Status: The BLI includes life expectancy and a subjective evaluation of one's overall health status.
5. Work and Life Balance: The BLI measures the proportion of employees who work long (50 or more) hours per week, the time available for leisure and personal care, and the employment rate for women with school-age children.
6. Education and Skills: This is measured as the percentage of the adult (25–64 year old) population that has a secondary-school degree, and students' cognitive skills based on standardized testing.
7. Social Connections: This dimension is measured by people's responses to a standardized question asking whether they have friends or relatives on whom they can count in times of need.
8. Civic Engagement and Governance: This dimension is based on voter turnout data and a composite index that measures citizen input into policy-making.
9. Environmental Quality: The main variable used to measure environmental quality is air pollution levels, specifically levels of particulate matter. Secondary environmental variables include an estimate of the degree to which diseases are caused by environmental factors, people's subjective satisfaction with their local environment, and access to green space.
10. Personal Security: This dimension focuses on threats to one's safety. It is measured using homicide and assault rates.
11. Subjective Well-Being: This dimension measures people's overall satisfaction with their lives as well as reported negative feelings.

Although the BLI includes many components, it is designed to produce an overall well-being index. The results for each dimension are standardized across countries, resulting in a score from 0 to 10. But how do we assign a weight to the various components? One approach is simply to weigh each of the 11 dimensions equally. The BLI report makes no specific recommendations for weighing the different dimensions, but its Web site allows users to select their own weights for each of the dimensions (see www.oecdbetterlifeindex.org). The OECD is collecting user input and will use this information to gain a better understanding of the factors that are most important for measuring well-being.

3.3 The Human Development Index (HDI)

In contrast to the BLI, the United Nations **Human Development Index (HDI)** is calculated based on only three components of well-being: life expectancy at birth, years of formal education, and real per-capita GDP. Although they are denominated in different units—both years and money—no attempt is made to translate one into the other. Rather, relative performance is presented in a scaled index (Figure 21.5).

Like the BLI, the HDI then faces the issue of how to assign relative weights. The standard HDI approach is to give equal weight to each of the three indicators. Inclusion of standard measures of income as one-third of the indicator makes it highly, although not perfectly, correlated with GDP; of the 30 countries with the highest HDI scores in 2011, all but one was also ranked in the top 40 by national income per capita.

*In addition to the main variables discussed here, most of the dimensions also consider secondary variables. For example, the dimension of income and wealth also includes data on household consumption and a subjective evaluation of material well-being.

Figure 21.5 **Selected countries as ranked in the Human Development Index**

Human Development Index (Scale: 1 - 100)	
95 - 100 —	Australia, Norway, Ireland
90 - 94.9 —	Canada, Netherlands, Germany, Japan, Sweden, United States, Denmark, Switzerland, Spain, France, Belgium, Italy, Finland, Austria, Greece
85 - 89.9 —	United Kingdom, Poland, Singapore
80 - 84.9 —	Argentina, Portugal, Mexico
75 - 79.9 —	Russia, Colombia
70 - 74.9 —	Brazil, China, Philippines, Thailand, Turkey
65 - 69.9 —	Indonesia
60 - 64.9 —	South Africa
55 - 59.9 —	Kenya, India, Bangladesh
50 - 54.9 —	Pakistan
45 - 49.9 —	Nigeria

Source: UNDP, Human Development Report, 2011 data.

At the same time, the results often show that countries with similar GDP levels vary dramatically in overall human welfare, as measured by the HDI. For example, Belize, Namibia, and Panama have similar levels of GDP, but their HDI scores vary significantly. Panama has the highest score in this group because of high education levels and relatively long life expectancy. Namibia's low life expectancy pulls down its HDI score. Angola, Vietnam, and Zimbabwe also have similar per-capita GDP values but widely varying HDI scores. Vietnam does well on the two nonmonetary measures while Angola scores poorly on both of them, and Zimbabwe scores well on education but not longevity.

The relative simplicity of the HDI has made it much easier to apply in countries with less money to spend on data collection; hence, it has been especially valuable for developing countries. It has been an annual feature of every UN *Human Development Report* since 1990. In a number of countries, the HDI is now an official government statistic; its annual publication inaugurates serious political discussion and renewed efforts, nationally and regionally, to improve lives and is followed by many development agencies interested in tracking progress. The HDI continues to be modified, with new versions that adjust for inequality and gender equity.

3.4 OTHER NATIONAL ACCOUNTING ALTERNATIVES

Aside from the three measures just described (GPI, BLI, and HDI), many other proposals have been made either to supplement GDP, adjust it, or replace it. To give a sense of this landscape, we briefly describe a sample of them. Except for the first one, they are all indicators that have been developed for use in specific locales.

- The **Happy Planet Index** (HPI) has been proposed by the new economics foundation of London, UK. Like the HDI, the HPI is designed to compare the success of different countries, to see how efficiently (in environmental terms) each country is able to promote the well-being of its inhabitants. The measure multiplies life expectancy by a measure of life satisfaction, then divides by ecological footprint, a measure of ecological impact.* Life expectancy is a statistic obtainable for almost all countries. Life satisfaction has been measured in a variety of ways: The HPI uses subjective well-being data from the Gallup World Poll. HPI has been calculated for 151 countries. The index tends to rise with per-capita GDP up to $5,000, after which it tends to decline, because thereafter the ecological footprint increases more rapidly than life satisfaction or life expectancy (see Box 21.2).

*A country's ecological footprint is a measure of the amount of land required to provide its inhabitants with all their natural resources and assimilate their wastes, including carbon dioxide emissions.

Box 21.2 The Happy Planet Index

The Happy Planet Index asserts that the goal of society is to create long and happy lives for its members. To do this, natural resources must be used and wastes generated. The HPI is made up of three variables that reflect these concepts:

1. *Average life expectancy:* This measures whether a society's members lead long lives.
2. *Average subjective well-being:* This measures whether a society's members lead happy lives. The data are obtained from surveys that ask people how satisfied they are with their lives. Despite the simplicity of the approach, years of research have demonstrated that the results provide reasonably accurate estimates of an individual's welfare.
3. *Ecological footprint:* This measures a society's overall ecological impact. It is defined as the amount of land required to provide a society with the resources that it consumes and assimilate the waste that it generates. While it has been subject to methodological critiques, by converting all ecological impacts into a single value, it provides an overall assessment of sustainability.

Average subjective well-being, scaled between 0 and 1, is multiplied by life expectancy to obtain the "happy life years" of a society. Then the HPI is calculated as:

HPI = Happy Life Years/Ecological Footprint

The HPI has been calculated for 143 countries. The countries with the highest HPI scores are those whose citizens tend to be rather happy and long-lived but have relatively modest ecological footprints, including Costa Rica, the Dominican Republic, Jamaica, Guatemala, and Vietnam. One interesting aspect of the HPI is that a country's HPI ranking tends to be unrelated to its GDP. The United States ranks 114, just above Nigeria.

The interpretation and policy implications of the HPI are unclear. For example, India and Haiti have a higher HPI score than Germany or France. Does this imply that India and Haiti are more desirable to live in, or more ecologically sustainable, than Germany or France? Probably not. Another issue is whether a country's policies can affect happiness levels, which may be more a construction of inherent social and cultural factors rather than policy choices.

But despite its limitations, the HPI has received attention as an alternative or supplement to GDP, especially in Europe. A 2007 report to the European Parliament cites several strengths of the HPI, including:

- It considers the ends of economic activity, namely, happiness and life expectancy.
- The innovative way it combines well-being and environmental factors.
- Its calculations are easy to understand.
- Data can be easily compared across countries.

So while the HPI is unlikely to become a widespread alternative to GDP, it does provide information that is not currently captured in any other national accounting metric.

Sources: Y. Goossens et al. (2007), *Alternative Progress Indicators to Gross Domestic Product (GDP)*. London: new economics foundation, www.neweconomics.org.

- **The Measure of America** presents an HDI modified for application in the United States. For example, although the standard HDI measures access to knowledge using the average number of years that students spend in school, Measure of America uses average achievement scores at various grade levels. The results, calculated down to the level of congressional districts, are available at www.measureofamerica.org.
- Another indicator that has been developed for national or regional use in this country is the **Index of Social Health of the United States**. Created by the public policy organization Demos, this index is a composite indicator combining data on infant mortality, child abuse, child poverty, teenage suicide, teenage drug abuse, the high school dropout rate, unemployment, weekly wages, health insurance coverage, poverty among the elderly, food insecurity, affordable housing, and several other categories of social concern. (See www.demos.org/data-byte/index-social-health-united-states-1970-2008/.)
- **Indicators of Well-Being in Canada** are listed on the Web site of the Canadian Department of Human Resources and Skills Development. Data collected by Statistics Canada are used to develop indicators of well-being in the domains of work, education,

financial security, family life, housing, social participation, leisure, health, security, and environment.

- Other national examples include Italy, which has a **Regional Quality of Development Index,** a composite index of 45 variables pertaining to environment, economy, rights, gender equality, education, culture, working conditions, health, and political participation. France has the **Fleurbaey/Gaulier Indicator,** which is similar to GPI but tries to incorporate even more monetary values of nonmonetary factors (job security, healthy life expectancy, environmental sustainability), using subjective valuations of these factors to create adjusted "equivalent incomes." They are aggregated and then reduced by the degree of inequality in the equivalent incomes.
- The **Gross National Happiness (GNH)** concept was proposed in Bhutan in 1972 as a guiding principle for economic development that takes a holistic approach to improving the quality of people's lives. Although the concept of GNH has been used for decades, the attempt to quantify it is recent.[8] In 2010 it was formally defined along nine different dimensions of welfare, including 33 distinct indicators. For example, the education dimension includes literacy and education rates; the psychological well-being dimension includes subjective well-being and an indicator of spirituality; and the governance dimension includes data on political participation and government performance. The index is made up of both objective and subjective data.

One lesson from all these alternatives is that there is not necessarily a positive correlation between the total of final purchases in an economy (one of the things that GDP is designed to measure) and other measures of well-being in the present or of economic possibility (even as measured by GDP) in the future. In many instances, GDP is rising while other measures stay flat or fall.

The next two sections focus on the issues surrounding two particular elements that have been seriously underrepresented in GDP. Section 4 discusses issues of accounting for household production. Section 5 takes up environmental accounting, including subsections on the methodological problems of how to assign values to things that are not sold through markets.

Discussion Questions

1. Does the Genuine Progress Indicator include anything that you think should be left out or fail to account for something that you think should be included? Think hard about what you really think human well-being is about.
2. Give examples of each of the following:

   - Efforts to supplement GDP
   - Efforts to adjust GDP
   - Efforts to replace GDP

   Are there some alternatives discussed above that would fit into more than one of these categories? Are there some that are difficult to fit into any of them? Would you suggest any other ways of categorizing efforts that are being made to improve how we measure the success of an economy in achieving well-being for present and future people?

4. MEASURING HOUSEHOLD PRODUCTION

The preceding section described efforts around the world to improve the statistics that are used to assess a country's economic performance. Part of this movement includes interest in gathering data on household production. Many countries, including Australia, Canada, India, Japan, Mexico, Thailand, and the UK, have conducted or are conducting national time-use surveys to aid their understanding of unpaid productive activities. The United Nations Statistical Commission and Eurostat (the statistical office of the European Union) are encouraging countries to develop satellite accounts that provide the necessary information to adjust measures of GDP so that they take into account both household production and interactions between the economy and the environment, while not changing the official definition of GDP.

Efforts to calculate household labor actually predate standard GDP accounts. In 1921 a group of economists at the National Bureau of Economic Research calculated that the value of household services would be about 25 to 30 percent of marketed production. Decades later, in 1988, economist Robert Eisner reviewed six major proposed redesigns of the National Income and Product Accounts (NIPA), all of which included substantial estimated values for household production.[9] Despite numerous demonstrations of its practicality dating back more than 85 years, however, household production has never been included in the U.S. GDP accounts.

There are strong arguments to suggest that current GDP figures are less accurate for having neglected household production. Most obviously, GDP is understated—a substantial area of valuable productive activity has been overlooked (see Box 21.3). This was stressed by Simon Kuznets, the architect of national income accounting, when he presented his original set of estimates to Congress in 1937. With his typical candor, he noted what was missing, pointing in particular to "services of housewives and other members of the family."

Even the most conservative estimates of the total value of household production arrive at numbers equal to about 25–30 percent of standard GDP in the United States, and less conservative estimates put the value as equal to or greater than the value of marketed production.

One of the major economic shifts during the twentieth century was the movement of a large proportion of women from unpaid employment as full-time homemakers to paid employment outside the home. In 1870, 40 percent of all U.S. workers were women working as full-time homemakers; by 2000, the proportion had dropped to 16 percent. This increase in work outside the home, as well as the increase in purchases of substitutes for home production, such as paid child care and prepared foods, was counted as an increase in GDP. The value of *lost* household production, however, was not subtracted. This failure to account for reductions

Box 21.3 What Are Stay-at-Home Moms Really Worth?

What is the fair market value of all the work a typical stay-at-home mom does in a year? To answer this question we can multiply the hours spent at different tasks by the typical wage paid to workers who perform those tasks. For example, according to 2012 research by insure.com, the typical mom spends 14 hours per week cooking. The U.S. Bureau of Labor Statistics estimates the average wage for cooks at about $9 per hour. This implies that the annual value of a mom's cooking labor is over $6,000. Applying the same approach to other household tasks, including child care, cleaning, shopping, yard work, and driving, the annual value of a full-time stay-at-home mom is over $60,000. Similar research by salary.com comes up with an even larger market value—about $113,000 annually!

While there are some stay-at-home dads in the United States, about 150,000, they are far outnumbered by the 5 million stay-at-home moms. But the number of stay-at-home moms has been declining in recent decades as more women have entered the workforce. While this brings additional income to households, the income is partially offset by additional expenses. In many states, the cost of full-time child care exceeds the typical annual cost of college tuition. For example, in Massachusetts the average cost of child care is $19,000 per year.

While the additional household income and market expenditures are counted as increases to GDP, the median salary in the United States for a woman working full-time is only about $37,000. So based on the values presented above, it isn't clear whether total social welfare increases or decreases when many women are compelled to enter the workforce.

Source: "What Are Stay-at-Home Moms Really Worth?" *Fiscal Times*, May 4, 2012, www.thefiscaltimes.com/Articles/2012/05/04/What-Are-Stay-at-Home-Moms-Really-Worth.aspx.

in some home-produced goods and services means that GDP growth during the period was *overstated.* For example, an article in the May 2012 *Survey of Current Business* found that

> if "home production"—the value of the time spent cooking, cleaning, watching the kids, and so forth—were counted, it would raise the level of nominal GDP nearly 26 percent in 2010. Back in 1965, when fewer women were in the formal labor force and more were working in the nonmarket sector, GDP would have been raised by 39 percent. Because the inclusion of "home production" would add more to the level of GDP in 1965 than in 2010, factoring in the value of these nonmarket activities was found to reduce the average annual growth rate of GDP over this period. [10]

Comparisons between countries are also made more difficult by the lack of accounting for household production in GDP. In countries of the global South, where such activities make up a much higher proportion of total production than they do in the developed countries of the global North, GDP is even more inadequate as an indicator of national production. When we focus on well-being—rather than money flows—as the goal of an economy, it becomes especially evident that there is important economic activity in households that is going unreported in national income accounts.

Why does this matter? One important reason is that the omission of most household production from the national accounts may contribute to a subtle bias in the perceptions of policymakers who base their economic decisions on them. Because household work is not measured, it may be easy to think that it is not important or not even part of the economy.

The U.S. Social Security retirement system, for example, makes payments to people based only on their market wages and years in paid work. Some advocates suggest that people should also get credit for time spent raising children—for example, a year of Social Security credit for time taken off with each child, in recognition of the contribution that such unpaid work makes to social and economic life. Having home production counted in GDP might help make policymakers more aware of its productive contributions.[11] Interestingly, critiques of GDP for its failure to count household labor arise out of both conservative principles, which emphasize family values, and progressive ones, which seek to recognize the value of labor that has been historically and disproportionately performed by women.

4.1 Time-Use Surveys

A first step in determining a value for household production is to find out how much time people spend in unpaid productive activities. In the past, estimates of time use in the United States came from small and sporadic surveys. However, in 2003, following the lead of many other industrialized countries, the U.S. Bureau of Labor Statistics (BLS) began to collect data for the first national ongoing survey of time use. The American Time Use Study (ATUS), conducted by the BLS, asks people age sixteen or over in a nationally representative sample to report in detail how they used their time on one particular day.[12]

The results of the survey for 2011 indicate that, on average on any given day, 83 percent of women and 65 percent of men spend some time engaging in household activities, including housework, food preparation and cleanup, lawn and garden care, or household management (such as paying bills). When averaged over all responses (including those who had not spent any time on household activities), women spent an average of 2.2 hours per day on these activities, while men spent 1.4 hours. On an average day, 19 percent of men reported doing housework, such as cleaning or doing laundry, compared with 53 percent of women.

4.2 Methods of Valuing Household Production

After time use has been measured in terms of hours spent on various activities, standard national accounting procedures require that these hours be assigned a monetary value using market or quasi-market prices. Economists have developed two main methods of assigning a monetary value to household time use: the replacement-cost method and the opportunity-cost method.

replacement-cost method (for estimating the value of household production): valuing hours at the amount it would be necessary to pay someone to do the work

In the **replacement-cost method**, hours spent on household labor are valued at what it would cost to pay someone else to do the same job. In the most popular approach—and the one used to generate the most conservative estimates—economists use the wages paid in a general category such as "domestic worker" or "housekeeper" to impute a wage. A variant of this method, which usually results in higher estimates, is to value each type of task separately: child-care time is valued according to the wage of a professional child-care worker, housecleaning by the wages of professional housecleaners, plumbing repair by the wages of a plumber, and so forth.

opportunity-cost method (for estimating the value of household production): valuing hours at the amount that the unpaid worker could have earned at a paid job

The **opportunity-cost method** starts from a different view, based on microeconomic "marginal" thinking. Presumably, if someone reduces his or her hours at paid work in order to engage in household production, he or she is assumed to value the time spent in household production (at the margin) at least at the wage rate that he or she could have been earned by doing paid work for another hour. That is, if you choose to give up $30 that you could have earned working an extra hour in order to spend an hour with your child, you must presumably think that the value of spending that hour with your child is at least $30. This leads to using the wage rate that the household producer would have earned in the market to value the time spent doing household work. In this case, estimates of the value of nonmarket production can be quite a bit higher than using the replacement-cost method, since some hours would be valued at the wage rates earned by doctors, lawyers, and other more highly-paid workers.

Neither approach to imputing a wage rate is perfect. However, it would be hard to argue that perfection has been achieved in any of the other measurements and imputations involved in creating the national accounts, and many argue that imputing any value for household labor time, even using minimal replacement costs, is more accurate than imputing a value of zero.

Similar arguments have been made concerning unpaid volunteer work in communities and nonprofit organizations—the time that people spend coaching children's sports teams, visiting nursing homes, serving on church and school committees, and so on. In the American Time Use Survey, 13 percent of the people surveyed reported participating in organizational, civic, and religious activities on their surveyed day, a figure that includes organized volunteer activities. If volunteer work as well as household work were both counted in national accounts, the proportion of production attributed to the core sphere of the economy would rise considerably.

Discussion Questions

1. Do you think that national governments should incorporate a monetary estimate of the value of household production in national accounting statistics? How do you think the inclusion of household production would affect the measurement of economic activity in developed versus developing countries?
2. Think back on at least one household activity in which you have engaged in the past couple of days that in principle would be replaceable by market or third-person services. How would that activity be valued by the replacement-cost method? By the opportunity-cost method? What sorts of manufactured capital goods were important, along with your labor, in the activity?

5. ACCOUNTING FOR THE ENVIRONMENT

The natural environment underpins all economic activities. To express this observation in accounting terms, consider the example of a developing country that depends heavily on natural resources. If its forests are cut down, its soil fertility depleted, and its water supplies polluted, surely the country has become poorer. But national income accounting will merely record the market value of the timber, agricultural produce, and industrial output as positive contributions to GDP.

The danger of omitting important environmental considerations from our measures of success is not limited to developing countries. The United States also depends in many ways on its natural resources. Soil depletion has not yet raised the cost of land-based food but is likely to do so in the future without significant changes in farming practices. The market price of fish has increased with depletion of many species. The United States shares with all other countries a reliance on weather patterns that support existing lives and lifestyles; if human activities increase the level of greenhouse gases emissions that lead to serious disruptions in climate, more severe storms, and rising sea levels, more and more money will be spent in what we have described as "defensive expenditures." Serious attention is now being paid to whether these should go into our national accounting on the plus or the minus side.

Recall Figure 2.2, which indicated that the natural environment provides resources and environmental services as inflows to economic activity and that economic activity also releases waste products into the environment. How can these environmental connections be reflected in national accounting?

Environmental economists describe the economic functions of the natural world under three headings:*

1. *Resource functions:* The natural environment provides natural resources that are inputs into human production processes. They include mineral ores, crude petroleum, fish, soil, and forests. Some of these resources, such as fish and forests, are renewable while others, such as minerals and petroleum, are not.
2. *Environmental service functions:* The natural environment provides the basic habitat of clean air, drinkable water, and suitable climate that directly support all forms of life on the planet. Water filtration provided by wetlands and erosion control provided by tree-covered hillsides are other examples of services provided by ecosystems. People enjoy the services of the natural environment directly when they enjoy pleasant scenery or outdoor recreation.
3. *Sink functions:* The natural environment also serves as a "sink" that absorbs (up to a point) the pollution and waste generated by economic activity. Car exhaust dissipates into the atmosphere, for example, while used packaging goes into landfill, and fluid industrial waste ends up in rivers and oceans. Some waste breaks down relatively quickly into harmless substances. Others are toxic or accumulate over time, eventually compromising the quality of the environment.

Although for centuries these environmental functions were treated as though they were provided "free" and in unlimited amounts, more recently the problems of depletion of resources, degradation of environmental services, and overuse of environmental sink functions have become increasingly apparent. The next section describes some efforts to account for them.

5.1 ENVIRONMENTALLY ADJUSTED NET DOMESTIC PRODUCT

The most basic approach to "green" accounting is to start with traditional measures and make adjustments that reflect environmental concerns. In current national income accounting, it is commonly recognized that some of each year's economic production is offset by the depre-

*A fourth category of environmental value stems not from use but from mere appreciation of the existence of species and environmental amenities; this is felt by some people even if they do not expect to see, for example, a blue whale or Victoria Falls. The "existence value" of a given species or resource is difficult to quantify, but it is recognized as a legitimate economic value by economists.

ciation of manufactured, or fixed, capital such as buildings and machinery.* In other words, while economic activity provides society with the benefits of new goods and services, each year the value of previously produced assets declines, and this loss of benefits should be accounted for. Thus national accounting methods produce estimates of net domestic product (NDP), which starts with GDP and then deducts the annual depreciation value of existing fixed capital. For example, in 2010 the GDP of the United States was $14.7 trillion. But the depreciation of fixed capital that year totaled $1.9 trillion.** Thus the NDP of the United States in 2010 was $12.8 trillion.

environmentally adjusted net domestic product (EDP): GDP less depreciation of both manufactured and natural capital

Extending this logic, we can see that each year the value of natural capital may also depreciate as a result of resource extraction or environmental degradation. In some cases, the value of natural capital could increase as well if environmental quality improves; that, after all, is the point of restorative development. The net annual change in the value of natural capital in a country can simply be added or subtracted from NDP to obtain what has been called **environmentally adjusted NDP (EDP)**. Thus:

$$EDP = GDP - D_m - D_n.$$

where D_m is the depreciation of manufactured capital and D_n is the depreciation of natural capital.

This measure requires estimating natural capital depreciation in monetary terms, rather than physical units such as biomass volume or habitat area. The methods discussed in Chapter 20 can theoretically be used to estimate such values, but to estimate all types of natural capital depreciation in monetary terms is a daunting task that would require many assumptions. Thus the estimates of EDP that have been produced focus on only a few categories of natural capital depreciation.

One of the earliest attempts at green accounting estimated EDP for Indonesia over a 14-year period, 1971–84.[13] This pioneering analysis deducted the value of depreciation for three categories of natural capital: oil, forests, and soil. The values of GDP and EDP over this time period are shown in Figure 21.6.***

The results suggest several important points:

- Natural capital depreciation can amount to a significant portion of GDP, in this case about 20 percent; in other words, natural capital depreciation offset about 20 percent of total economic production. Thus, GDP presents an overly positive assessment of social welfare.
- Measuring the growth of GDP to illustrate changes in social welfare may not produce accurate results. Over the time period covered in Figure 21.6, GDP grew at an annual rate of 7.1 percent. However, EDP grew at an annual rate of only 4.0 percent. So this case demonstrates that looking only at GDP to determine the trend in national welfare may lead policymakers to conclude that growth is robust. But accounting for environmental degradation shows that much of the apparent growth was at the expense of the environment.
- Monetization of natural capital needs to be approached carefully. Figure 21.6 indicates a noticeable spike in EDP in 1974. Does this indicate an appreciation of natural capital and an environmental improvement? Not necessarily; in fact, this spike is mainly a result of a dramatic increase in world oil prices resulting from the 1973–74 Arab oil

*Depreciation is simply a measure of the loss of capital value through wear and tear. For accounting purposes, it can be calculated using a "straight-line" formula according to which, for example, a new machine is estimated to lose 10 percent of its original value each year over ten-year period or using more complex valuation methods.

**Estimates of fixed capital depreciation are obtained from tax records. Businesses are not taxed on the value of their fixed capital depreciation—thus they have a strong incentive to claim this deduction.

***The analysis actually refers to EDP as "NDP*," which the study authors called "adjusted net domestic product." But to avoid confusion with the more common usage of the term "net domestic product"—only deducting for fixed capital depreciation—we call their environmentally adjusted values EDP.

Figure 21.6 **Indonesian GDP Adjusted for Resource Depreciation**

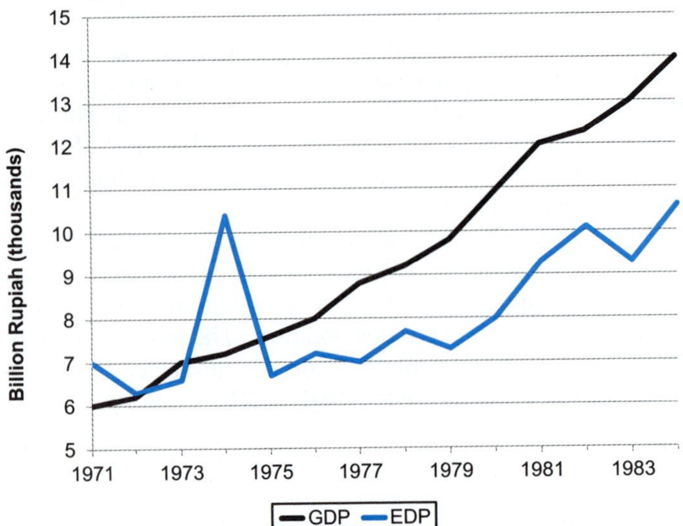

Source: Robert Repetto, et al., *Wasting Assets: Natural Resources in the National Income Accounts*. Washington, D.C.: World Resources Institute, 1989.

embargo, rather than a change in the actual oil reserves in Indonesia. Similarly, in some years the total volume of timber decreased, but the market price went up, resulting in an increase in the overall value of timber resources. This increase in value masks the physical degradation of timber resources. So if we measure the value of natural capital at market prices, we may lose important information regarding the actual physical stock of those resources.*

Since this pioneering study, many countries have attempted to arrive at a valuation of their natural resources and environment (see Box 21.4). Similarly, the World Bank has developed an indicator of adjusted net saving, which seeks to measure what a society is truly saving for its future, starting with net savings (gross savings minus manufactured capital depreciation) and making adjustments for education, pollution, and the depreciation of natural capital.[14]

5.2 Valuing Environmental Factors

If assigning a monetary value to manufactured assets that are used for only a few years is difficult, think about how much more difficult it is to determine a dollar measure for natural assets! Consider, for example, the value of uranium reserves still in the ground. Perhaps uranium will become more valuable a hundred years in the future because countries turn increasingly to nuclear power. Or the price of uranium may fall in the future as countries, concerned about safety and the disposal of nuclear wastes, explore other energy sources instead. The discovery of previously unknown mineral deposits, changes in policies, shifts in consumer demand, and new technologies are among the factors that make predicting the future over the long term very difficult and thus make it very hard to determine the value of many assets.

Other assets are difficult to value because, although we have a sense that overall ecological balance is important to human as well as other life on the planet, some forms of natural capital have no apparent *market* value. Biologists tell us, for example, that in recent decades there has been a worldwide decline in populations of amphibians (frogs, toads, and salamanders), along with a large increase in deformities in these animals. Clearly, degradation of the natural environment is occurring. But since the market value of most frog species is zero,

*Various suggestions have been made to overcome this barrier. For example, rather than using current market prices in a given year, one could use a five-year moving average to smooth out price spikes and dips.

Box 21.4 Environmental Accounting in China

In 2004 China's State Environmental Protection Agency (SEPA) announced that it would undertake a study to estimate the cost of various types of environmental damage. The initial findings released in 2006 indicated that environmental costs equaled about 3 percent of China's GDP. The report was widely criticized because it failed to include numerous categories of environmental damage such as groundwater contamination. Shortly afterward, Zhu Guangyao, the deputy chief of SEPA, released a separate report that concluded that environmental damage was closer to 10 percent of China's GDP—a value similar to what many observers were expecting.

In a 2007 report jointly produced by the World Bank and SEPA, the health and nonhealth costs of air and water pollution alone were estimated to be 5.8 percent of China's GDP.

The results indicate that much of China's recent economic growth has been partially offset by increased resource depletion and pollution. Recognizing the costs of environmental damage, the Chinese government set targets in 2006 for such variables as energy consumption per unit of GDP, releases of major air pollutants, and total forest cover. China's investment in pollution control and renewable energy is growing rapidly. However, the Chinese government's effort to develop green GDP measures have abated somewhat in recent years, and some of the targets that were set in 2006 were not met.

Further analysis of the cost of pollution and resource depletion in China can help the government implement policies that achieve true human development.

Past policies and decisions have been made in the absence of concrete knowledge of the environmental impacts and costs. [New], quantitative information based on Chinese research under Chinese conditions [can] reduce this information gap. At the same time . . . substantially more information is needed in order to understand the health and nonhealth consequences of pollution, particularly in the water sector.

Source: World Bank and SEPA, 2007, *Cost of Pollution in China,* p. xix.

there are wide disagreements about how—or even whether—a dollar value can be put on these losses.*

As an example, suppose that a hillside is stripped of its forest covering, and the wood is sold as pulp for papermaking. The lack of vegetation now means that run-off from rain increases, and "Streamside," a town at the bottom of the hill, suffers flooding and has to repair many buildings. In the national accounts as currently constructed, the logging activity contributes to GDP in this year (in the form of valuable wood products) and the activity of repairing buildings is counted as an economic activity that also adds to GDP in this year.

Or consider an alternative scenario, in which the town realizes that flooding is likely and fills sandbags to line its riverbank. It thereby avoids costly repairs. But, again, both the logging and the sandbag making are counted as adding to GDP.

What is wrong with this, of course, is that the initial environmental services of the forest in terms of water retention were not counted as part of GDP. If they had been, we would have noticed that the efforts of the town did not reflect new production so much as a *shift* in production from the "nature sector" to the human sector. Had we included the "nature sector" from the beginning, our national accounts would have shown a decrease in the production of that sector (decreased water retention) offsetting the increase in production of the human sector (that is, repairing buildings or constructing sandbag barriers).

But how should we go about evaluating the environmental services received from the trees on the hillside? Normally, economists would try to value the production of water retention services of an existing forest by looking at some places in which this value has been translated

*Going beyond the "existence value" that some people would ascribe to amphibians, others use the analogy of how canaries are used in coal mines. Given their high sensitivity to air quality, canaries in distress indicate the danger of bad air before it rises to the level that causes humans to lose consciousness. Amphibians are highly sensitive to ground and water pollutants, including chemicals that are common in consumer products; their situation may be an important warning about dangers to human beings. But this does not resolve the question of how to value them.

damage-cost approach: assigning a monetary value to an environmental service that is equal to the actual damage done when the service is withdrawn

maintenance-cost approach: assigning a monetary value to an environmental service that is equal to what it would cost to maintain the same standard of services using an alternative method

into dollar terms. Let's imagine that near Streamside there is another town, "Sandybank," which has an identical situation, with identical logging, but it has avoided damage by spending $100,000 on sandbagging. Our goal is to figure out the dollar value of a year's worth of water retention services provided by the forest near Streamside.

Suppose that the cost of repairs in Streamside, after the flooding, was $5 million. If you estimate the value of the water retention services of the hillside forest using the **damage-cost approach**, you would say that the services are worth $5 million.

However, we could also use the experience of Sandybank as the basis for our value estimate. Using the equally plausible **maintenance-cost approach**, we could say that the value of the forest's services is $100,000. (This is similar to the "replacement-cost" approach discussed earlier in the chapter.) As often happens, the two approaches do not agree—in this case the value of the forest's services could be estimated at either $5 million or $100,000.

Economists and environmental scientists face a similar choice in many other areas; for example, whether to measure the value of unpolluted air in terms of effects of pollution on human health (damage) or in terms of the cost of pollution-control devices (maintenance). So far, some national and international agencies have adopted one convention and some the other in their experimental environmental accounts.

If the withdrawal of environmental services makes people suffer or die, then we enter the even more controversial area of trying to assign dollar values to human suffering and human lives. And many environmental effects cross national lines. What is the monetary value of a global "public good" such as a stable climate? On whose account should we tally the loss of deep-sea fisheries located in international waters?

One approach to the problem of valuation is simply to use satellite accounts, as described above, which can be recorded in physical terms, without monetary valuation. So, for example, we might note that the forest cover in a country has declined by 10 percent without attempting to value all the ecological functions of forests. Many governments have already committed in principle to creating such accounts for their own country, and some, such as Norway, maintain extensive satellite accounts for many resource and environmental categories.

Discussion Questions

1. In Burgess County, current irrigation methods are leading to rising salt levels in agricultural fields. As a result, the number of bushels of corn that can be harvested per acre is declining. If you are a county agricultural economist, what two approaches might you consider using to estimate the value of the lost fertility of the soil during the current year? What sorts of economic and technological information would you need to come up with your estimates?
2. Some people have argued that the monetary valuation of environmental costs and benefits is important because "any number is better than no number"—without valuation, these factors are omitted from GDP accounts. Others say that it is impossible to express environmental factors adequately in dollar terms. What are some valid points on each side of this debate? How do you think this debate should be resolved?

6. CONCLUSION: MEASURING ECONOMIC WELL-BEING

No one—and especially not their creators—would argue that alternative macroeconomic indicators have been perfected. It is quite possible to argue about whether damage cost or replacement cost should be used in evaluating environmental services, for example, or whether more direct measures of poverty should be included in the HDI. Much is still open for discussion.

No single approach has emerged as the "best" way to adjust, replace, or supplement GDP. As we have seen, any macroeconomic indicator involves numerous assumptions. One of the strengths of some of the new measures is that they allow users to see how the results change under different assumptions. For example, the BLI allows users to adjust the weights on each of the 11 well-being dimensions according to their personal preferences. Some have suggested that the best approach is to use multiple indicators, along the lines of the "dashboard" analogy mentioned earlier. One thing is clear—reliance on a single traditional GDP measure omits or distorts many crucial variables. Thus all the alternative approaches discussed in this chapter have some value in providing broader perspectives on the measurement of well-being.

Discussion Questions

1. Of the various alternative indicators presented in this chapter, which one would you advocate as the best approach for measuring economic well-being? What do you think are the strengths and weaknesses of this indicator?
2. Suppose that your national government officially adopted your preferred indicator from the previous question. How do you think this would change specific policy debates in your country? What new policies do you think could be enacted?

REVIEW QUESTIONS

1. What are the two major contexts for economic activity?
2. What are satellite accounts?
3. What is subjective well-being (SWB), and how is it commonly measured?
4. Based on the scientific research, what is the relationship between the average level of SWB in a country and its GDP per capita?
5. Do average levels of SWB increase as a country develops economically?
6. What are some of the main critiques of GDP as a measure of well-being?
7. What is the Genuine Progress Indicator (GPI), and how is it measured?
8. What is the relationship between GDP per capita and GPI per capita in the United States over the past several decades?
9. What is the Better Life Index?
10. What is the Human Development Index?
11. What are some examples of household production?
12. What is the difference between the replacement-cost method and the opportunity-cost method for valuing household production?
13. What are the three main functions of natural systems?
14. What is environmentally adjusted net domestic product?
15. What are the potential problems with estimating environmental impacts in monetary terms?
16. What is the damage-cost approach to estimating the value of environmental services?
17. What is the maintenance-cost approach to estimating the value of environmental services?

EXERCISES

1. Describe in a short paragraph why measures of *output* do not always measure *well-being*. Include some specific examples beyond those given in the text.
2. Indicate whether each of the following actions or impacts would increase GDP.
   a. An individual purchases bottled water to avoid a contaminated municipal water supply.
   b. An individual obtains her drinking water from a water fountain at her workplace to avoid a contaminated municipal water supply.
   c. A homeowner pays a lawn-care company for landscaping services.
   d. A neighbor agrees to help a homeowner with landscaping work in exchange for assistance with plumbing work.
   e. A paper company employs workers to plant trees.
   f. An environmental organization provides volunteers to plant trees.
3. In calculating the Genuine Progress Indicator,
   a. Which factors are subtracted because they represent negative effects on well-being?
   b. Which factors are *not* included in GPI, even though they are included in GDP, because they are defensive expenditures or because of differences in accounting methods?
4. Go to the OECD's Web site for the Better Life Index (www.oecdbetterlifeindex.org). Note that you can adjust the weights applied to each of the 11 well-being dimensions using a sliding scale.

Adjust the weights based on your personal opinions. To which factors do you assign the most weight? To which factors do you assign the least weight? Briefly summarize the rationale for your weights. Also, which countries rank the highest according to your weighted BLI?

5. The UNDP *Human Development Report* is available at its Web site (www.undp.org). Consult this report, and choose a country that is not included in Figure 21.5. Write a paragraph describing this country's performance on the HDI as well as on three other indicators reported in the tables (such as inequality, HIV rates, or malnourishment).
6. Suppose that you buy a bread-making machine, flour, and other foodstuffs, take them home, and bake bread with a group of young children who are in your care (unpaid). How would these activities be accounted for in current GDP accounting? How might they be accounted for in an expanded account that includes household production?
7. Estimate how much time you spend each week doing two unpaid household production tasks (e.g., cleaning, cooking, or repairs). Then, locate data on the typical wages paid to workers who perform these tasks on the Bureau of Labor Statistics Web site (www.bls.gov/bls/blswage.htm). Based on these data, what is the monetary value of your weekly household production for these tasks?
8. Which of the following describe a resource function of the natural environment? An environmental service function? A sink function?
   a. A landfill
   b. A copper mine
   c. Carbon dioxide (a byproduct of combustion) entering the atmosphere
   d. Wild blueberries growing in a meadow
   e. A suitable temperature for growing corn
   f. A view of the Grand Canyon
9. In 2011, the Deepwater Horizon oil spill in the Gulf of Mexico caused heavy damage to the fishing and tourism industries of Louisiana and other coastal states. In addition, there were long-term ecological impacts on fish and wildlife. Describe how this might be accounted for in the 2011 national accounts of the United States, if they were environmentally adjusted:
   a. In terms of depreciation of assets
   b. In terms of flows of produced goods and services. (Describe in detail how two approaches to assigning dollar values might be applied.)
10. Consumption of oil, gas, and coal currently fuels the U.S. economy but also has other effects. How might the following be accounted for in the U.S. national accounts, if they were environmentally adjusted?
    a. Depletion of domestic oil, natural gas, and coal reserves
    b. Release of greenhouse gases into the atmosphere
    c. Smoggy air that hides scenery and makes outdoor activity unpleasant
11. Match each concept in Column A with a definition or example in Column B.

Column A	Column B
a. Depreciation of natural capital	1. Valuing time at the wage that someone gives up
b. Satellite accounts	2. Comparison with GDP supports the diminishing marginal utility of income
c. An indicator of well-being including 11 dimensions	3. Costs of cleaning up a toxic waste site
d. An example of non-market production	4. The value of fish killed by toxic waste
e. Opportunity-cost method	5. Government production
f. Subjective well-being	6. The effect on copper reserves of copper mining
g. Maintenance costs	7. Better Life Index
h. Defensive expenditures	8. The service performed by a garbage dump
i. A way of measuring well-being (not production) using dollar amounts	9. Cleanup costs following an oil spill
j. Damage costs	10. Monetary or physical measures that can be related to GDP
k. Sink function	11. Genuine Progress Indicator

NOTES

1. www.bea.gov/scb/pdf/2008/05%20May/0508_healthcare.pdf.
2. www.bea.gov/scb/pdf/2010/12%20December/1210_r-d_text.pdf.
3. www.earth.columbia.edu/sitefiles/file/Sachs%20Writing/2012/World%20Happiness%20Report.pdf.

4. Stiglitz, Joseph E., Amartya Sen, and Jean-Paul Fitoussi, 2009. *Report by the Commission on the Measurement of Economic Performance and Social Progress*, p. 16. http://www.stiglitz-sen-fitoussi.fr/en/index.htm.

5. Robert Ingelhart, Roberto Foa, Christopher Peterson, and Christian Welze, "Development, Freedom, and Rising Happiness," *Perspectives on Psychological Science* 3(4) (2008): 264–285.

6. Talberth et al. (2007), *The Genuine Progress Indicator 2006: A Tool for Sustainable Development.* Redefining Progress, pp. 1–2. http://rprogress.org/.

7. www.green.maryland.gov/mdgpi/mdgpioverview.asp. The GPI has also been applied at the state level in Vermont.

8. Karma Ura, Sabina Alkire, Tshoki Zangmo, and Karma Wangd, "A Short Guide to Gross National Happiness Index," Centre for Bhutan Studies, Thimpu, Bhutan, 2012.

9. Robert Eisner, "Extended Accounts for National Income and Product," *Journal of Economic Literature* 26(4), December 1988, 1611–1684.

10. Benjamin Bridgman, Andrew Dugan, Mikhael Lal, Matthew Osborne, and Shaunda Villones, "Accounting for Household Production in the National Accounts, 1965–2010," *Survey of Current Business* (May 2012): 23–36.

11. A prominent advocate of this view is Marilyn Waring, author of *If Women Counted* (San Francisco: Harper and Row, 1988).

12. www.bls.gov/tus/datafiles_2010.htm.

13. Repetto, Robert, et al. (1989), *Wasting Assets: Natural Resources in the National Income Accounts*. Washington, D.C.: World Resources Institute.

14. See http://data.worldbank.org/data-catalog/environmental-accounting/.

22 The Structure of the U.S. Economy

The U. S. economy is the largest in the world. In 2012 it produced over $15.5 trillion in final goods and services—almost 22 percent of total global economic production as measured by GDP of all the world's countries. In order to understand in more detail how a national economy functions, in this chapter we take a closer look at the U.S. economy. This also requires thinking beyond the country's borders, because the management of a country's natural resources or financial system can affect the welfare of other countries or the entire planet. Thus while our discussion in this chapter focuses on the United States, at times we consider this country in a broader international framework.

Although the U.S. economy has *grown* significantly over time, it has also *changed.* An elaboration of these changes also provides more historical context to our study of macroeconomics. A clear example is the role of agriculture in the U.S. economy. Early in U.S. history, most people worked as small farmers. The United States is currently one of the world's major agricultural producers, but less than 2 percent of the workforce is directly engaged in agriculture.* What is the rest of the workforce doing? You may, or may not, be surprised to know that more than three-quarters of the workforce is engaged in producing "services" of one kind or another, with about 5 percent working in government, while as of 2012 only about 17 percent of workers were employed in manufacturing and construction.[1] This chapter provides some insight into what is going on in this complex macroeconomy.

1. The Three Major Productive Sectors in an Economy

1.1 A Quick Review of Categories

Although macroeconomics often considers "the economy" as a whole, it is very far from being a homogeneous entity. We have already considered some ways to classify a macroeconomy into smaller units.

- In Chapter 1 we described *four essential economic activities*: production, distribution and consumption of goods and services, and resource maintenance.
- In Chapter 2 we defined the *three economic spheres:* core, business, and public purpose.
- In Chapter 20 we saw that the U.S. national accounts classify the economy into *four accounting sectors:* households and institutions, businesses, government, and the foreign sector.

The traditional accounting division by sector, explained in Chapter 20, was a way of defining groups according to *who* produces goods and services. In this chapter, we turn to

*The United States is the world's third-largest agricultural producer, based on agricultural value added, behind China and India.

output sectors: divisions of a macroeconomy based on what is being produced

primary sector: the sector of the economy that involves the harvesting and extraction of natural resources and simple processing of these raw materials into products that are generally sold to manufacturers as inputs

secondary sector: the sector of the economy that involves converting the outputs of the primary sector into products suitable for use or consumption. It includes manufacturing, construction, and utilities.

tertiary sector: the sector of the economy that involves the provision of services rather than of tangible goods

different classification groups, which we refer to as **output sectors**, based on *what* is being produced. This is slightly confusing, but it is important to remember that these sectors are not the same ones discussed in Chapter 20.

The three productive sectors that constitute any national economy are called primary, secondary, and tertiary. The **primary sector** involves the harvesting and extraction of natural resources and rudimentary processing of these raw materials. Industries in the primary sector include agriculture, commercial fishing, mining, and the timber industry. Generally, the products produced in the primary sector are not sold directly to households for final consumption but to manufacturers as inputs. For example, the wheat grown, harvested, sorted, and dried in the primary sector would be sold to milling and baking companies in the secondary sector, which would then process the wheat into bread.

The **secondary sector** involves converting the outputs of the primary sector into products suitable for use or consumption. The secondary sector includes manufacturing industries such as automobile production, the chemical industry, petroleum refining, the pharmaceutical industry, and electronics production. It also includes the construction of buildings and highways and utilities such as those that generate and distribute electricity.

Finally we have the **tertiary sector**, also called the service sector. This sector involves the provision of services rather than tangible goods. The tertiary sector includes such services as the transportation, marketing, and retailing of physical goods. It also includes direct services without the distribution of any physical goods, such as consulting, education, technology, finance, administration, and tourism.

There is no simple mapping from the three spheres that make up the economy (as described in Chapter 2) into the three output sectors just described. Firms in the *business sphere* of the economy are distributed among all three sectors. Entities from the *public-purpose* and *core spheres* can also be classified as working in one or more of the sectors. In the core sphere, for example, a household growing food in a garden is contributing to the primary sector. Production of home-cooked meals is a secondary-sector activity. The activities of care and maintenance in the home are best understood as services—thus in the tertiary sector. Much of the work of government and nonprofit organizations (in the public-purpose sphere) is accounted for in the tertiary sector but may also be active in each of the other two sectors.

1.2 The Relative Size of the Output Sectors in the United States

In looking at the National Income and Product Accounts (NIPA) in Chapter 20, you might have been surprised to see that less than a quarter of GDP comes from production that has to do with physical things, and less than 18 percent of workers are involved in that production—*when production is measured in terms of the money value of output.*

The italicized caveat summarizes some of what we reviewed in Chapter 21, where we noted that the percentages just cited do not include work that is done without pay, such as volunteer work, or child care by parents. Indeed, they leave out many other issues of importance to human well-being. Nevertheless, because in many instances the most available and consistent data are to be found in the National Income and Product Accounts (NIPA) from the U.S. Bureau of Economic Analysis (BEA), this chapter relies on the NIPA to classify the three output sectors in the United States.

This means that our discussion of the relative proportions of economic production is based on the market value of goods and services. In such an analysis, a financial service that is produced in a few minutes might count for more than the education produced by a primary school teacher in a year—or, to use an image cited by Adam Smith, the production of a handful of diamonds could count for more than the production of a reservoir full of water.

Based on such measures, this chapter shows that in the United States, as in most countries, the production of physical things is a relatively small, and declining, part of the measured economy. Does this mean that we are moving toward a "dematerialized" economy, more concerned with the production of services such as communication and education than manufactured goods? Is this shift toward services good news for the environment? What does it mean for our quality of life, as workers, consumers, and citizens?

Market value does not tell us everything that we need to know about the human value of different goods, services, and other economic activities. In some parts of the chapter, we go beyond NIPA figures to discuss the parts of the existing economy that do not show up there and also to consider issues of potentially great importance for the future that are not yet well represented in current accounts.

As you will remember from Chapters 20 and 21, while most government activity is included in NIPA data, with outputs valued essentially in terms of the government's cost of procuring inputs, many nonprofit as well as most core contributions to the economy are not measured in traditional national income accounting. However, we can begin to understand the relative size of the three sectors by using NIPA data.

Table 22.1 presents, based on NIPA data, the market value of the annual production of the three output sectors in the United States. We see that the private (i.e., nongovernment) tertiary sector dominates the U.S. economy, contributing 64.3 percent of total GDP (close to two-thirds). Because the majority of government activities (about 13% of GDP) also involve providing services, this implies that about three-quarters of the U.S. GDP derives from services.

Does this mean that the other sectors are relatively unimportant? Not at all. The tertiary sector relies heavily on outputs from the other two sectors. Consider, for example, that a restaurant would not be able to provide food services without meat and vegetable products, furniture made from wood, and building and equipment based on rock, metal ores, or petroleum products (plastics). Some of the money that the restaurant pays for the products derived from agriculture, wood, and metal finds its way back to workers and owners in the primary sector, but the larger portion goes to secondary industries such as construction and fabrication of equipment.

Even a partner in an investment firm will need a desk in an office building, with computer and communications media, all ultimately based on outputs from the primary and secondary sectors. In the latter case, the economic value added in the tertiary sector is a giant step beyond what had been created in the other two sectors. You might wonder whether this is a sensible assessment of "value." Has the investment manager, compared to the restaurateur, contributed much more to the real wealth and well-being of the economy as is suggested by the difference in their value added? (We discuss this issue further in section 4.2 on financialization.)

Discussion Questions

1. Think about the businesses and industries in your community. How would you classify those businesses according to each of the three sectors described above? Does your answer to this question concur with the notion that the majority of economic activity takes place in the tertiary sector?
2. Try to estimate what share of your total expenditures is spent on products from the primary, secondary, and tertiary sectors. How do you think your expenditure patterns will change in the future? For example, assuming that your income will rise after you graduate, do you think that your share of expenditures on services will increase or decrease?

2. The Primary Sector in the United States

The primary sector, as we have discussed, is concerned with the harvesting and extraction of natural resources. Countries vary widely in their natural resource endowments, and their particular resource advantages or deficits affect their economic development and future prospects. This is especially true of the United States. When Europeans arrived in North America in the fifteenth through the nineteenth centuries they found extraordinary natural resources:

Table 22.1 **Value Added by Output Sector in the United States, 2011** (billions of dollars)

Industry	Value Added	Percent of GDP
Primary Sector		
Agriculture, forestry, and fishing	173.5	1.2
Mining	289.9	1.9
Primary Sector Total	463.4	3.1
Secondary Sector		
Utilities	297.9	2.0
Construction	529.5	3.5
Durable goods manufacturing	910.1	6.0
Nondurable goods manufacturing	821.3	5.4
Secondary Sector Total	2,558.9	17.0
Tertiary Sector		
Wholesale trade	845.1	5.6
Retail trade	905.7	6.0
Transportation and warehousing	447.9	3.0
Information	646.6	4.3
Finance and insurance	1,159.3	7.7
Real estate and rental and leasing	1,898.8	12.6
Professional, scientific, and technical services	1,151.5	7.6
Management of companies and enterprises	283.6	1.9
Administrative and waste management	448.8	3.0
Educational services	174.2	1.2
Health care and social assistance	1,136.9	7.5
Arts, entertainment, and recreation	148.0	1.0
Accommodation and food services	443.1	2.9
Tertiary Sector Total	9,689.5	64.3
GDP Attributed to Government	1,993.8	13.2
Economy Total	15,075.7	100.0

Source: U.S. Bureau of Economic Analysis, Survey of Current Business, 2011.

Note: The category of "real estate" included in the tertiary sector differs from "construction" (in the secondary sector), because it refers to the services of existing structures, as well as to the services provided by those who help people buy, sell, or lease properties. Real estate appears to be the largest single industry listed in Table 22.1, accounting for 12.6 percent of GDP. This is an artifact of the way GDP is calculated. As mentioned in Chapter 2, GDP includes the non-marketed value of services that are provided by owner-occupied housing—the value of the housing services that owners "rent to themselves."

The total for GDP is greater than the sum of GDP for the three private sectors and government because the total includes additional industries not classified separately.

fresh and salt waters teeming with fish, forests full of birds and animals, and huge stocks of valuable timber and great plains that were suitable for highly productive agriculture. Europeans and later immigrants brought with them, and developed after their arrival, methods of using these resources that have changed the landscape and the human experience of living here to an extraordinary extent. A quick look at the food, water, and energy systems illustrates the evolution of the production and use of primary sector products in the United States.

2.1 THE FOOD SYSTEM

Food, or the land on which it is raised, is a renewable—though, like fish, also potentially exhaustible—resource. Throughout its early history, the United States was an agrarian economy. In the late 1700s approximately 90 percent of the labor force was composed of farmers. By 1880, farmers still made up about half the labor force. Now less than 2 percent of the U.S. workforce is employed in agriculture yet agriculture currently occupies 42 percent of the entire land area of the United States—around 1 billion acres—and thus continues to dominate the geographic landscape of the country.

During the twentieth century, agriculture in the United States underwent dramatic changes. Major trends included a decline in the total farm population, a decrease in the total number of farms, an increase in average farm size, and an increase in agricultural productivity (i.e., output per acre, as well as output per worker). There are now about 2 million farms in the United States, of which about 92 percent are classified by the U.S. Department of Agriculture as "small family farms": those with annual sales of $250,000 or less. The small farms produce less than one-third of the country's agricultural output. Meanwhile, farms with annual sales of more than $1 million (only about 1 percent of all farms) account for nearly half the value of agricultural production. The largest farms in the country tend to be owned as corporate enterprises with annual sales of millions of dollars. Farm receipts in the United States are approximately evenly divided between livestock and crops. The majority of the grain produced in the United States (about 60 percent) is not directly used for human consumption but instead is fed to livestock.

Agricultural productivity has increased as human labor has been replaced by mechanization and as the use of modern agricultural technologies has spread. For example, in the past hundred years, average corn yields in the United States have risen from around 25 to 140 bushels per acre, and wheat yields have increased from 12 to 40 bushels per acre. One American farmer now provides enough food and clothing for about 130 people.

Most of the agricultural products that people consume are not obtained directly from farmers but undergo significant processing prior to being sold to consumers. As we see in Figure 22.1, less than 12 cents of every dollar spent on food in the United States is paid to farmers. Food services—restaurants and other places serving food away from home—receive more than one-third of what Americans pay for food. The next largest portion (18.6 cents of every dollar) is spent on food processing before the point of sale to consumers or food services. Of each dollar, 13.6 cents goes to the retailer who mediates between the producers/processors and consumers. The remainder is spent for packaging, transportation, energy, finance, insurance, and "other," which includes advertising (2 cents) and legal and accounting services (1.8 cents).

Figure 22.1 suggests that the impact of agriculture extends well into the secondary and tertiary sectors. Even though few people are directly employed in agriculture, nearly 20 percent of all American jobs can be considered dependent on agriculture. Most of these jobs are in wholesaling, retailing, or food services.

2.2 WATER

Depletion of groundwater supplies in the United States is a serious threat to agriculture as well as to patterns of habitation. Agriculture is responsible for about four-fifths of our country's

Figure 22.1 **The Allocation of a Dollar Spent on Food in the United States**

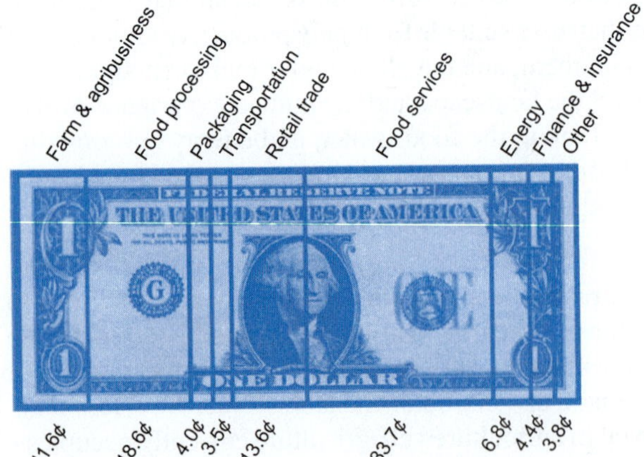

What we eat comes from the primary sector, but only about 18.4 percent of the final cost of food is directly associated with the primary sector activities of growing food and supplying energy for its production, processing, etc. 22.4 percent of the final cost is attributed to the secondary sector, for processing and packaging (though we should note that the physical inputs to packaging also derive from the primary sector). All the rest—59 percent—goes to tertiary sector activities.

Source: Patrick Canning, "A Revised and Expanded Food Dollar Series: A Better Understanding of Our Food Costs," U.S. Department of Agriculture, Economic Research Report No. (ERR-114), February 2011.

water use, much of it used to irrigate crops in Western states. More than one-third of the irrigation water used in the country comes from groundwater aquifers, which are renewable resources that recharge very slowly and can become depleted when withdrawals exceed the rate of natural recharge (somewhat analogous to catching fish at a greater rate than its populations reproduce). Currently, the United States is withdrawing groundwater approximately four times faster than it is being replenished, most obviously in Texas, Kansas, and Nebraska, which rely on water from the Ogallala Aquifer, the world's largest known aquifer. The water table for the Ogallala Aquifer is declining as much as 2 feet per year, and water supplies from the aquifer have already been exhausted in some areas. The declining water table in the aquifer has motivated increased use of efficient irrigation practices, but over time many more areas will lose access to this resource. Most likely, these areas will need to either switch to different crops that require less water or be removed from agricultural production.

Fortunately, water conservation methods have dramatically decreased both the absolute and the per-person amount of fresh water used in the United States since their peak in 1980. Per-person use is about 25 percent lower today than it was then. Reasons for what is essentially a behavioral change include higher energy costs, resulting in energy conservation, as well as federal and state laws mandating efficiency in appliances (more fresh water is used to produce electricity than for any other purpose except farming). For example, through technology and redesign the average amount of water in a standard flush toilet—the domestic appliance with the largest water use—fell from 6 gallons to 1.6. And farmers have been increasingly relying on a variety of strategies to reduce water use, including crops (some genetically modified) that require less water and drip irrigation, which applies tiny amounts of water directly to the roots of crops.

2.3 The Energy System

Modern production and consumption systems require energy—a lot of energy. The United States is the world's second-largest consumer of energy, behind China. But in per capita terms, U.S. energy consumption is about four times that of China. Although the United States has less than 5 percent of the world's population, it uses about 20 percent of the world's energy. New York State, with 19.5 million residents, uses as much energy as 800 million residents of sub-Saharan Africa (all the residents of that region, except the Republic of South Africa). The United States has one of the highest per-capita energy usage rates in the world, exceeded only by a few countries, such as the high-latitude countries of Canada, Norway, and Iceland. It is worth noting that the last two of these derive most of their electricity from renewable sources (Norway 97 percent, Iceland 100 percent), while Canada gets 63 percent of its electricity from renewables (mostly hydropower).

We can also compare countries by looking at the amount of energy used per dollar of GDP. A low number is generally indicative of an economy that is energy efficient in its production processes. The United States is about average among industrialized countries in the energy efficiency of production—more efficient than Finland or Canada, but less efficient than Switzerland, Germany, or Japan.

Figure 22.2 shows the sources used to obtain energy in the United States. We can see that the country is heavily dependent on fossil fuels; petroleum is the single most important energy source, and carbon-based fossil fuels (petroleum, coal, and natural gas) provide 82 percent of all energy used in the country. Coal, often viewed as a fuel from an earlier industrial age, is still the primary fuel for electricity generation in the United States; as of 2012 it was the source of about 40 percent of the nation's electricity. Meanwhile, petroleum provides nearly all the fuel for transportation.

Nuclear power is primarily used to generate electricity, providing about 20 percent of the country's electricity supply. Although some energy analysts predicted a "nuclear renaissance" in the early twenty-first century, cost considerations and the 2011 accident at the nuclear power

Figure 22.2 **Energy Consumption in the United States, by Energy Source, 2012**

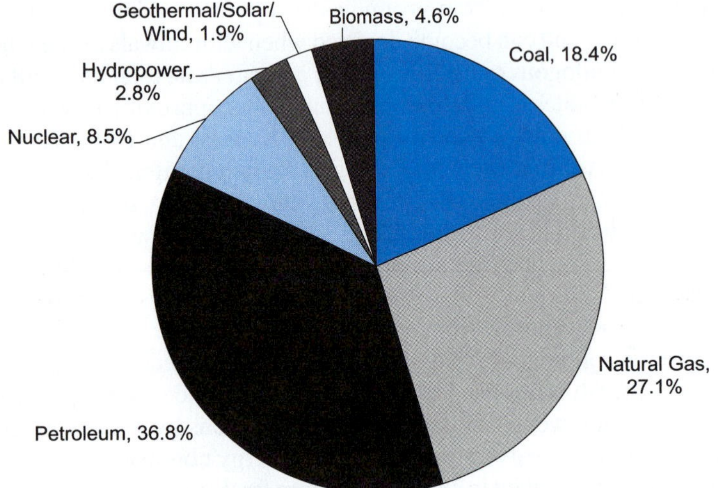

Over 80 percent of the energy consumed in the United States comes from fossil fuels. While the share of energy coming from renewables such as wind, solar, and geothermal energy is increasing, these still provide less than 2 percent of energy supplies.

Source: Monthly Energy Review, United States Energy Information Administration, February 25, 2013.

plant in Fukushima, Japan, have caused most plans to expand nuclear power in the United States to be shelved. Thus the current trend is for the national share of energy derived from nuclear power to decline in the future, as aging plants are decommissioned.

The United States currently obtains a small share of its energy from renewable resources, but the utilization of renewable energy is increasing rapidly. Wind energy is the fastest-growing energy source in the country, increasing by over 2,400 percent between 2000 and 2011. A few states, such as Iowa and South Dakota, get nearly 25 percent of their electricity from wind. Solar energy use has also grown significantly, increasing more than 200 percent between 2000 and 2011. A 2013 article in *Energy Policy* outlined how New York State could supply all its energy needs from wind, solar, and water power by 2030, creating 58,000 jobs in the process. The main author of the study commented, "You could power America with renewables, from a technical and economic standpoint. The biggest obstacles are social and political—what you need is the will to do it."[2]

The United States is not only the world's second-largest consumer of energy; it is also the world's second-largest energy producer (again, behind China). In 2010 the United States produced 15 percent of the world's energy. It has experienced an energy boom in recent years, with an increase in total energy production of about 14 percent between 2005 and 2012. The majority of this growth is due to increased production of natural gas and oil. Novel extraction technologies, particularly hydraulic fracturing, commonly known as "fracking," have made it economically viable to tap fossil fuel deposits 2 miles or more below the ground (see Box 22.1 for a discussion of the debate over fracking).

In the 1950s, the country was essentially energy independent, obtaining only about 15 percent of its oil from imports. At the onset of the first energy crisis in 1973, the United States had come to rely on imports for about 35 percent of its oil. In 2006, this dependence peaked at 60 percent but as a result of increased domestic production it has declined since then. In 2012 the United States imported 40 percent of its oil supplies.

A common fallacy is that the United States obtains most of its imported oil from the Middle East. In fact, less than 20 percent of the country's oil imports come from Persian Gulf countries. The largest exporter of oil to the United States is Canada, which supplies three times as much oil as Saudi Arabia. Other important sources of foreign oil include Mexico, Venezuela, and Russia.

Although energy *use* permeates every aspect of economic activity in the United States, the *production* of energy currently employs less than a million workers, or about 0.5 percent

BOX 22.1 FRACKING AND THE U.S. ENERGY BOOM

Fracking is the process of pumping fluids under high pressure into fossil-fuel deposits, creating numerous fractures that release the fuel from the surrounding rock and allow extraction. Combined with deep-well horizontal drilling techniques, this technology allows the development of previously uneconomic oil and gas reserves across the United States, including in Texas, North Dakota, and Pennsylvania.

Proponents of fracking in the United States argue that obtaining oil from domestic sources is better than importing it. Natural gas is the cleanest fossil fuel, thus substituting it for coal in electricity generation reduces carbon emissions and other air pollutants. Increased U.S. production of natural gas has resulted in falling prices—a decline of more than 50% between 2007 and 2012. The recent U.S. energy boom as a result of fracking has increased employment in previously impoverished areas.

Opponents of fracking point to the potential for water contamination. While the fuel deposits are normally much deeper underground than drinking water aquifers, drilling through these aquifers means that leaks in the concrete casings could threaten water supplies. Many of the chemicals used for fracking are highly toxic. The U.S. Environmental Protection Agency (EPA) has already documented several cases of drinking water contamination as a result of fracking. Another concern is that the increased availability of domestic fossil fuels distracts us from the need to develop renewable substitutes.

In December 2012, the EPA noted that "responsible development of America's oil and gas resources offers important economic, energy security, and environmental benefits. However, as the use of hydraulic fracturing has increased, so have concerns about its potential human health and environmental impacts, especially for drinking water." The EPA is currently studying the health and environmental impacts of fracking, with a draft report due out in 2014. Meanwhile, in 2011 France became the first country to ban fracking, and several other countries have prohibited the process.

Sources: U.S. Environmental Protection Agency, "Study of the Potential Impacts of Hydraulic Fracturing on Drinking Water Resources: Progress Report," December 2012; Edwin Dobb, "America Strikes New Oil," *National Geographic* (March 2013): 28–59.

of the workforce, and directly contributes a similar small share to GDP. Yet fluctuations in energy supply and prices can have significant impacts on economy-wide variables such as GDP growth, inflation, and employment. Increases in energy prices lead to downstream increases in the price of many other products and higher inflation rates. Dramatic energy price increases in recent decades, particularly in the price of oil, have precipitated recessions at both the national and international levels.

Discussion Questions

1. How do you obtain most of your food? Does it come from a supermarket, or do you get some from a farmers' market or grow your own? Are you surprised to learn that less than 12 cents of a dollar spent on food goes to the primary sector, where the food is actually produced?
2. Do you think that the heavy dependence of the United States on fossil fuels for energy is a problem? How likely is it that this might change in the future?

3. THE SECONDARY (INDUSTRIAL) SECTOR IN THE UNITED STATES

When asked what makes up an economy, many people think first of manufacturing. And although the share of GDP from manufacturing has been declining in the United States for several decades, the United States remains a major manufacturer. In fact, in 2010 the United States was the world's largest manufacturer by value added, just slightly ahead of China. The United States has about 335,000 manufacturing enterprises, which together employ about 13 million people.

The secondary sector includes construction and utilities as well as manufacturing. These industries comprise 17 percent of GDP in the United States (Table 22.1) and employ about 18 percent of the workforce, with about 10 percent in manufacturing and the rest in construction and utilities.

Figure 22.3 **Annual Number of Private Housing Starts in the United States, 1965–2012**

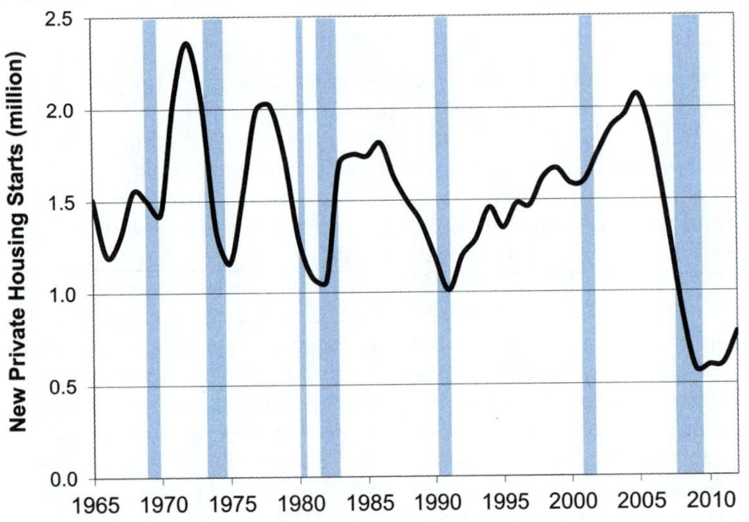

The number of private housing starts decline significantly during recessionary periods (indicated by the shaded areas) and recover once a recession is over.

Sources: Various editions of the Statistical Abstract of the United States; U.S. Census Bureau, "New Residential Construction in January 2013," press release, February 20, 2013.

3.1 Construction and Housing

The construction industry is particularly affected by macroeconomic conditions, as has been evident in the aftermath of the global financial crisis. In 2006—the peak of the housing bubble, as discussed in Chapter 30—more than $900 billion was spent on new private construction in the United States. In 2010, the value of new private construction fell by 44 percent to only $500 billion. As of 2013, it had started to rise again, but at a modest pace. Figure 22.3 shows how the number of housing starts decline during recessionary periods but then recover after a recession is over. (The data follow housing *starts* because only the flow of newly constructed housing, not the level of pre-existing housing, count in measuring the production of the secondary sector.) Note that housing starts bottomed out in 2009 at the end of the recent recession and have slowly begun to recover. But the collapse from the mid-2000s peak was so severe that as recently as 2012 starts were only about 40 percent of what they were seven years earlier. The volatility of this industry is suggested by the fact that, in 2013, some people were again starting to talk about a shortage of new housing.

3.2 Manufacturing

Even in the U.S. economy, which is dominated by services, manufacturing still employs about 10 percent of the labor force. Table 22.2 presents a summary of the production and employment in major manufacturing industries in the country. No single manufacturing industry dominates, but the top industries include transportation equipment (mostly automobiles), computers and electronics, metal products, chemicals, and food processing. Here we discuss just two: textiles and automobiles.

Textiles

In the 1800s the textile and apparel industry arose as this country's first large-scale manufacturing industry, with the majority of the mills located in the Northeast. The mills, employing mostly women and girls, were the scene of some of the nation's early labor union battles, as the women fought to limit the work day to ten hours. The textile industry expanded rapidly, increasingly using immigrant labor and becoming the largest manufacturing employer in the country by the start of the twentieth century. In 1920 nearly two million workers were

Table 22.2 **Manufacturing Industries in the United States, Production and Employment**

Industry	2011 Value Added (billions of dollars)	2012 Employment (thousands)
Durable Goods Industries		
Computers and electronics	132	1,087
Fabricated metals	122	1,424
Furniture	26	351
Machinery	132	1,101
Transportation equipment	77	1,477
Other durable goods	421	2,054
Durable Goods Total	910	8,675
Nondurable Goods Industries		
Chemical products	254	787
Food, beverages, and tobacco	215	1,466
Paper products	53	377
Petroleum and coal products	169	115
Textiles, apparel, and leather products	30	268
Other nondurable goods	100	1,444
Nondurable Goods Total	821	4,457

Sources: U.S. Bureau of Economic Analysis, Value Added by Industry database, November 13, 2012; U.S. Bureau of Labor Statistics, "Current Employment Statistics," table B-1a, March 8, 2013.

employed in the industry. Then, faced with foreign competition, particularly from Japan, the industry stopped expanding. Employment in the American textile industry remained around two million workers for the next fifty years or so.

Since the 1970s, the textile and apparel industry in the United States has been decimated—employment in the industry has declined about 90 percent, and the decline appears likely to continue into the future. Imports from China have been at the center of the debate on manufacturing job losses in the United States. In 2002 import quota restrictions were removed from 29 categories of apparel. In just two years China more than doubled its exports of textiles and apparel to the United States. Chinese imports can be produced at lower cost than domestic goods primarily because of lower wages. China currently dominates global textile manufacturing, but this may be changing. In recent years, textile manufacturing has been leaving China for countries with even lower wages, including Bangladesh, Cambodia, and India.

Textiles and clothing are outstanding examples of a category of manufactured items that (1) are labor intensive (i.e., their production requires a large number of labor hours in proportion to the cost of other inputs) and (2) can be produced with large numbers of unskilled laborers. These characteristics create conditions in which countries with large populations of poor people can compete on the international market.

Automobiles

In contrast to textiles, the automobile industry in the United States benefited from a number of factors during the twentieth century. One was the "first-mover advantage" gained by the leadership of Henry Ford and others who innovated and created strong industries before most foreign competitors. Another was the fact that the United States has a huge domestic market. Not needing to rely on exports is an advantage in an industry in which the transaction cost involved in shipping automobiles over long distances creates a cost disadvantage for foreign producers. In addition, for a long time the technology of automobile production was such that the greater productivity of more skilled workers enabled them to compete successfully against lower-wage workers who had less education, training, and skill (summarized in many economic discussions as "human capital").

The first challenge to the preeminence of the U.S. auto companies in the enormous domestic market came with the oil crises of the 1970s. This motivated a surge in imports of high-quality, fuel-efficient vehicles from Japan. By 1980 the Japanese automobile industry, virtually nonexistent twenty years earlier, had captured over 20 percent of the U.S. market. The impact of this first wave of foreign competition on the domestic motor vehicle industry was severe. Between 1977 and 1982 employment in the industry in the United States declined 30 percent.

In the 1980s and 1990s, the domestic automobile industry recovered, for several reasons. First, U.S. automobile manufacturers improved the quality of their vehicles, often either emulating Japanese production methods or forming joint ventures with foreign producers. Another factor was the decline in gasoline prices in the 1980s, which shifted demand back toward larger domestic vehicles. Sales of pickup trucks and sport utility vehicles, initially produced almost exclusively by American companies, increased dramatically during this period.

The U.S. auto industry again fell on hard times in the 2000s, first from a significant decline in sales of fuel-inefficient vehicles due to higher gas prices and then from the global financial crisis. General Motors was hit particularly hard. Between just 2006 and 2009, annual vehicle production by U.S. automakers fell more than 50 percent. In 2008 and 2009, the federal government rescued General Motors and Chrysler through loans exceeding $60 billion, made through the Troubled Asset Relief Program (TARP). The federal government also took an ownership share of each company. As the economy improved and manufacturers shifted toward more fuel-efficient vehicles, the two companies were able to repay their TARP loans. Employment in the automotive industry has begun to recover, but remains well below its peak.

3.3 Where Have All the Manufacturing Jobs Gone?

According to some measures, the size of the secondary sector has stayed fairly constant over the past half-century. For example, the value added from manufacturing, when adjusted for inflation, is about the same magnitude now as it was in the 1960s. However, as we have seen, its share of GDP has declined because the size of the service sector has grown so much.

Yet even though the value of manufacturing output has held fairly constant, *employment* in manufacturing has declined. As shown in Figure 22.4, while there were some ups and downs, total employment in manufacturing generally increased from 1950 until 1979. Since then, two periods of decline have occurred in manufacturing employment, first in the early 1980s and more recently since the late 1990s. From a peak of more than 20 million workers in 1979, the number of manufacturing jobs has declined by 30 percent.

The decline in U.S. manufacturing industries does not indicate declining demand for manufactured goods. The United States imports significantly more manufactured goods than it sells abroad, resulting in a trade deficit in goods of $736 billion in 2012. When we combine data on both foreign and domestic goods, the U.S. demand for goods increased by 226 percent between 1980 and 2012, even after adjusting for inflation. So while the U.S. economy is becoming more service oriented, as a share of GDP, this does not signify an absolute decline in the demand for manufactured goods.

These figures suggest that American manufacturing jobs have essentially shifted overseas. In 1992, American manufacturers met 73 percent of the domestic demand for goods. In 2012 they met only 51 percent. The major sources of imports in goods are (in order of the 2012 value of imports): China, Canada, Mexico, Japan, and Germany. The U.S. trade deficit with all these countries has grown, especially with China. The value of imports from China (including both goods and services) increased 290 percent between 2001 and 2012 alone.

Although imports have clearly played a role, the decline in the absolute number of U.S. manufacturing jobs predates the dramatic increase in imports from China. In fact, the decline is not unique to the United States but is a worldwide phenomenon. The absolute number

Figure 22.4 **Total U.S. Manufacturing Employment and Manufacturing Employment as a Percentage of Total Employment, 1950–2010**

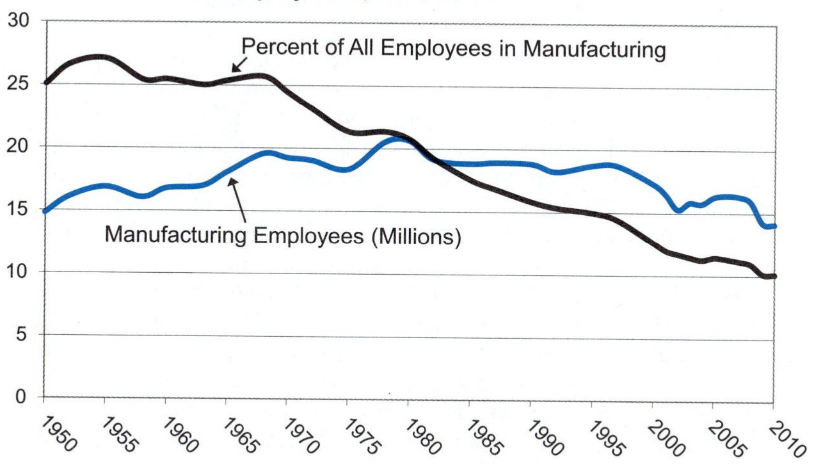

The number of manufacturing jobs in the United States has declined since 1979 while the number of manufacturing jobs as a percentage of all jobs has generally declined since the mid-1950s.

Source: Various editions of the *Statistical Abstract of the United States.*

of manufacturing jobs peaked years ago in virtually all industrial countries. The same is true, or is rapidly becoming true, in emerging markets, where rapid productivity growth allows real wages and output to rise, while the number of manufacturing jobs declines and the service sector expands relative to manufacturing. China, the trading partner that has been perceived as the greatest threat to jobs in the United States, has also generally been losing manufacturing jobs. For example, between 1995 and 2002 China lost 14.9 million manufacturing jobs—more than the entire current U.S. manufacturing workforce. This job loss happened even though value-added manufacturing in China grew by 90 percent in real terms during this period.

What is the cause of this global phenomenon? It appears that in recent decades an acceleration has taken place in the process that began with the Industrial Revolution in the mid- to late eighteenth century, in which technological change makes it possible for industries to substitute manufactured capital (i.e., machinery and automation) for human labor. **Manufacturing productivity** is commonly measured as an index of the value of the goods produced per hour of labor. Manufacturing productivity in the United States over the past few decades has been growing faster than overall business productivity, and the progress has accelerated since 1990. During the 1980s, manufacturing productivity increased by an average of 2.6 percent per year, but the rate rose to 4 percent per year during the 1990s, falling slightly to about 3.2 percent per year since then.

manufacturing productivity: an index of the value of the goods produced per hour of labor in the manufacturing sector

The increase in productivity means that more goods can be produced using fewer human labor-hours. Although global demand for manufactured goods continues to grow, it has not grown as rapidly as productivity. More goods and services are produced and sold, but fewer people are required to produce them. Hence the worldwide availability of manufacturing jobs has been a "shrinking pie." Still, changes in labor prices and the availability of productive capital mean that manufacturing does often shift across national borders. Recent wage increases in China make it less attractive to manufacturers and may even signal an opportunity for an increase in U.S. manufacturing. For more on this issue, see Box 22.2.

What does this mean for human well-being? An economist looking forward to this situation one or two hundred years ago might have said that it is exactly what progress is supposed to be about—that people can get more of what they want with less work. However, people can only purchase the output of a market economy if they have income, and for most people income comes primarily through wages, which are attached to jobs. The accelerating shift of jobs from the secondary to the tertiary sector is a topic discussed in Chapter 23.

Box 22.2 Are Manufacturing Jobs Coming Back to the United States?

At least part of the decline in American manufacturing jobs is a result of cheap labor in countries such as China and India. In the early 2000s, Chinese manufacturing wages averaged only $0.50 per hour, only about 1/25 the wages of an American worker. Even accounting for transportation costs and the lower productivity of Chinese workers, it often made economic sense to shift production from the United States to China.

However, the advantage of Chinese manufacturing has eroded in recent years. Chinese wages are growing at nearly 20 percent per year and are now close to half of U.S. wages. American workers are about three times more productive than Chinese workers. Combine that with higher transportation costs as a result of higher oil prices, and some American companies are producing goods domestically solely on cost considerations.

As opposed to "offshoring," some economists refer to "re-shoring" as the movement of manufacturing jobs from countries such as China back to the United States. For example, General Electric reversed a 2009 decision to produce refrigerators in Asia, instead opting to refurbish a factory in Indiana. The company SolarWorld decided to manufacture solar panels at a plant in Oregon rather than in China, based on comparable overall costs and higher quality.

The scale of re-shoring is currently relatively low, and China still retains a cost advantage in most manufacturing industries. But a 2011 report by Boston Consulting Group, a management consulting company, concludes that "by sometime around 2015—for many goods destined for North American consumers—manufacturing in some parts of the United States will be just as economical as manufacturing in China." The report notes that some jobs in China will shift to countries with even lower labor costs, such as Vietnam and Indonesia, but these countries currently lack the infrastructure, worker skills, and quality assurance needed for high-end manufacturing.

The potential for re-shoring can be increased through policies such as low-cost loans and subsidies. President Barack Obama proposed tax breaks for companies keeping jobs in the United States in 2012, but as of 2013 no legislation had been passed on this issue.

Sources: Jason Margolis, "Why China May Lose Manufacturing Jobs to the U.S.," The World, Public Radio International, October 20, 2011; Robert Shoenberger, "Reshoring: Are Manufacturing Jobs Coming Back to the United States?" *Plain Dealer* (Cleveland), March 9, 2013; Harold Sirkin et al., "Made in America, Again," *BCG Perspectives,* August 25, 2011.

Discussion Questions

1. One of the main impacts of the Great Recession in the United States was a significant decline in housing prices in most areas of the country. However, at the same time, the number of homes sold also declined dramatically. Shouldn't the decline in housing prices have resulted in an increase in home sales, as suggested by a basic model of supply and demand?
2. Some people cite the return from the suburbs to urban areas and the lower percentage of young people getting driver's licenses as indications that "the age of the automobile is drawing to a close." Do you think that this is true? If automobile use were to fall in half over the next 15 years, what impact would this have on the economy?

4. The Tertiary (Service) Sector

Early in this chapter, we gave an intuitive explanation for why, even though people are just as dependent as they have always been on the materials extracted from nature, the primary sector has shrunk in economic importance as societies have industrialized. It was not hard to explain how manufacturing came to claim a larger part of every household budget and therefore of the total economy; however, we are still left with questions about how "services" have more recently become so significant.

Even more than the other sectors, the tertiary sector cannot be defined as a homogeneous economic category. As we saw in Table 22.1, the service sector includes a wide variety of industries, including education, retail trade, financial services, insurance, waste management, and entertainment. The Appendix to this chapter provides one approach to putting these into categories, as a way of getting a handle on this seemingly immaterial, yet enormously important part of our economy. The remainder of this section, however, is devoted to providing some basic data on the sector, with specific attention paid to the areas of retail, financial and insurance services, and human services (including health and education).

Employment trends, wages, and other measures vary considerably across different service industries. For example, one common perception is that jobs in the service sector pay poorly. While this is true for such jobs as cashiers and child-care workers, it is clearly not true for such service jobs as doctors and lawyers. Overall, service jobs pay only slightly less on average than manufacturing jobs. In 2012 the average hourly wage in goods-producing industries was $24.91, while the average pay in the service industries was $23.46 per hour. At the same time, many jobs in finance have wages that far exceed most of those in manufacturing. From the 1940s to the early 1980s, average compensation in the financial sector stayed close to the average for all domestic private industries (including manufacturing and industries in all three sectors). Starting in the early 1980s, it began to rise rapidly. By 2012, average compensation in the financial sector was 25 percent higher than the nationwide average.

Traditionally, most international trade has involved the exchange of physical goods, but trade in services is now expanding rapidly. While it is easy to picture a physical good moving between countries, it might be harder to imagine how *services* could be internationally traded. A service is "exported" if agents in the United States provide a service used by an individual or organization based abroad. For example, if someone from Argentina stays in a U.S. hotel, this is considered an "export" of U.S.-produced accommodation services.

A service is "imported" if agents in the foreign sector provide a service used by individuals or organizations based in the United States. For example, if a U.S. manufacturer ships its goods using freighters registered in Liberia, it is said to "import" transportation services from Liberia. Between 1980 and 2011, global trade in services increased by a factor of 10.7, while trade in goods increased by a factor of 8.7. By 2011 almost 19 percent of all international trade was in services. Improvements in information technology have made services such as customer call centers, software development, and data processing more easily transferable across national boundaries in recent years. The United Nations notes that cost savings of 20–40 percent are commonly reported by companies that offshore their service needs to low-wage countries.

In 2011, the United States exported more in services than it imported, and this trade surplus has been expanding in the past several years. The principal services exported by the United States are travel, financial, and educational services, while the main service imports are travel, telecommunications, and freight services.

4.1 Retail Services

Few manufacturers sell their products directly to consumers. Instead, manufacturers typically sell their output to retailers, perhaps also using wholesalers as intermediaries. Retailers are categorized in the service sector because they normally do not manufacture any of the goods that they sell. Prominent retailers such as Walmart, Home Depot, and Target purchase virtually all their products from suppliers, in the United States and in other countries.

Retail services as a whole are not becoming a larger share of the national economy, but there is a clear trend toward the dominance of a small number of very large retailers. We can use data on concentration ratios to illustrate the ascendancy of these firms. A "four-firm concentration ratio" is calculated by dividing the domestic revenues of the four largest firms in an industry by the total domestic revenues in the industry. Figure 22.5 shows the change in the four-firm concentration ratios for several types of retailers between 1992 and 2007.

Large retailers have come to dominate their industries by offering consumers a large number of choices and low prices. In the parlance of microeconomics, the retail industry is clearly oligopolistic, meaning that it is dominated by a small number of companies. However, the

Figure 22.5 **Four-Firm Concentration Ratios in Retail Industries, 1992–2007**

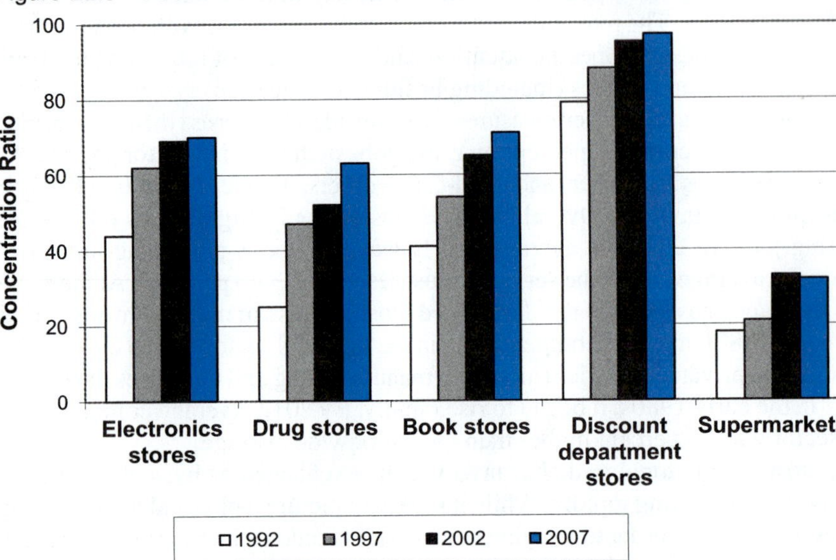

The four-firm concentration ratios in these retail industries have all increased since 1992.

Source: Economic Census publications, United States Census Bureau.

economic scale of the largest retailers has become so large that the behavior of individual firms has implications at the macroeconomic level. In 2012 Walmart was the world's largest retailer (and third-largest company) by revenue, with sales of $447 billion, and the world's largest nongovernment employer, with 2.1 million employees.

Some researchers believe that a major reason that productivity increased so much in the United States in the late 1990s is a result of Walmart's pressure on suppliers to increase their efficiency. As another example of Walmart's pervasive reach, the decline of the American textiles industry can be attributed in part to Walmart's foreign sourcing of low-priced apparel. Consider that an estimated 10 percent of Chinese imports to the United States are for Walmart. Economy-wide impacts like these blur traditional distinctions between microeconomics and macroeconomics and demand new lines of research and analysis.

4.2 Finance and Financialization

The financial, insurance, and real estate sectors are often lumped together. We give a brief overview of these sectors and then focus on the financial sector, which has had a huge impact on the U.S. economy in recent years.

The most common job categories in this group of industries are bank tellers, loan officers, real estate agents, and insurance agents. Combined, these sectors accounted for 20.3 percent of GDP in 2011 and collectively employed over seven million people (about 5 percent of the workforce). In 2009, 946 life insurance companies in the United States held almost $5 trillion in assets, but there has been a significant concentration of assets in recent years; in 1990, there were more than twice as many insurance companies as at present, but collectively they held only $1.4 trillion in assets.

financial institution: any institution that collects money and holds it as financial assets

financial assets: a variety of holdings in which wealth can be invested with an expectation of future return

From 1947 to the present, the percentage of U.S. value added from finance and insurance has more than tripled, from 2.4 percent to 7.7 percent (Figure 22.6). In contrast, the contribution of real estate has only grown from 8.1 to 12.6 percent. It is interesting to note, however, that both categories have more or less plateaued since around 2000, reflecting the two recessions that the country has experienced since then.

The area of most interest among such services today—because they are closely associated with the market dysfunctions implicated in the Great Recession—covers the **financial institutions** that manage **financial assets**. Households, nonfinancial businesses, and

Figure 22.6 **Value Added in Finance, Insurance and Real Estate, as a Percentage of GDP**

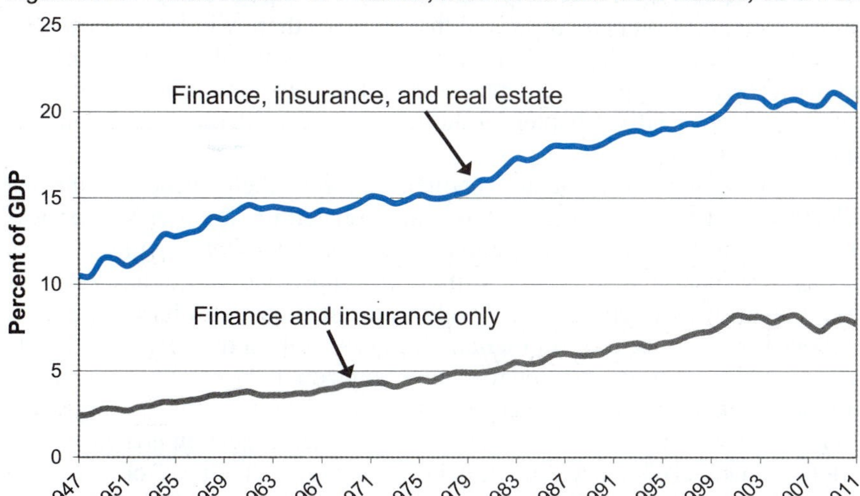

The proportion of GDP that is attributed to finance, insurance, and real estate has grown markedly over the past half century, with the strongest growth in the relative value of finance and insurance.

Source: U.S. Bureau of Economic Analysis online database, GDP-by-industry.

governments hold about half the country's financial assets. The rest are held by financial institutions, which include banks, credit unions, pension and retirement funds, mutual funds, securities brokers, and insurance companies. Financial institutions are divided into two types, according to the services that they provide (though many institutions now provide both types of services). Depository institutions, such as banks and credit unions, pay interest on deposits and then use the deposits to make loans. Nondepository institutions, such as insurance companies, pension funds, brokerage firms, and mutual fund companies, sell financial products such as insurance or money management. They then invest their profits in a variety of financial assets. Pension funds, in particular, hold extensive financial assets that they manage for the present and future benefit of retirees and workers; thus in many countries, they are the largest investors, employing the services of a variety of financial institutions.

Financial assets include stocks (shares in ownership of companies); bonds (certificates indicating that the holder has lent money to a government entity or a business, which will repay the loan over time, with interest); foreign currencies (held when the investor expects either that his own currency will depreciate or that a foreign currency will rise in relative value); certificates of deposit and money market accounts (specially designed savings accounts at banks, which pay higher interest than normal savings accounts, but generally place restrictions on withdrawals or set a minimum deposit level).

According to standard economic theory, the principal function of banks and other financial institutions is to *intermediate* the movement of funds throughout the economy. When we say that financial institutions are intermediaries, we mean that they move funds between savers and investors. For example, banks absorb savings (e.g., we deposit money in banks), and then they redirect these funds back into the economy in the form of loans that pay higher rates of interest, to cover the banks' costs of operation and give them a profit. When these loans are used to open new businesses or expand existing ones, resulting in increases in production and employment, intermediating institutions such as banks are helping the real economy to function. The "real economy" refers to the part of the economy that is concerned with actually producing goods and services, as opposed to the financial side of the economy (sometimes called "the paper economy"), whose activities focus on buying and selling on the financial markets.

Given that the primary role of the financial sector is to facilitate activities in the real economy, there is no inherent reason to expect the financial sector to grow significantly over time relative to the size of the overall economy. Yet, as we have seen, the relative size of the financial sector has increased considerably—and, indeed, is expected to continue to do so; a 2012 report by Bain and Company projected that by 2020 there will be a global total of $900 trillion in financial assets, while GDP in real economies will only total $90 trillion. How did this happen? The explanation is complex and multidimensional and is considered further in Chapter 26 and, especially, Chapter 30. At this point, consider an image that may help you to visualize the situation.

Imagine that the financial sector is a hot air balloon; the basket tethered beneath it the real economy (or at least that part of the real economy that is related to, and uses the services of, the financial sector). The relationship is essential for the financial sector: without such a relationship, it would just float up into the sky, without any substance. It also has value for the real economy: It gives the economy a "lift" by allocating savings to useful investments. However, since about 1982 a process of **financialization** has allowed the balloon to inflate more and more. Less and less of its connection to what is going on in the real economy has to do with the traditional circulation of financial capital: from production, through savings, then back to production of real-world goods and services. Instead, the connection is increasingly about the expansion of financial claims within the balloon, including "bubbles" of temporary inflation in the prices that people are willing to pay for financial assets, as well as the creation of large amounts of debt.

Financialization: a process in which the financial sector of the economy is increasingly able to generate and circulate profits that are not closely related to the real economy

This can generate huge incomes for a small group of people. Part of this income is spent in the real economy, paying for luxury cars, McMansions, and the services of personal trainers and celebrity chefs, but much of it feeds back into the expansion inside the balloon.

The simplest way of understanding the financialization that has affected the U.S. economy, as well as other advanced economies in recent decades is as a combination of two things: (1) huge increases in debt throughout the economy, along with (2) inflation in the price of assets, unconnected with any inflation in the price of real goods and services. This is what occurred in the period 1980–2007, when both asset prices and debt levels throughout the economy ballooned relative to incomes.

To give some examples on the debt side:

- In 1980 credit card debt stood at $55 billion, but by 2005 it had increased to $802 billion.
- The average American household in 2013 carries a credit card debt of about $8,500 and pays $1,000 per year in credit card interest.
- In 2009 the average college senior with a credit card had credit card debt of more than $4,000.
- Total college student loans in the United States recently passed $1 trillion for the first time.

Mortgage loans represent a large portion of consumer indebtedness; during the housing bubble that led up to the financial crisis, new mortgages were being issued at unprecedented rates. Total debt in all sectors of the economy, measured relative to GDP, increased to historic levels before the Great Recession, as shown in Figure 22.7. Particularly dramatic was the increase in debt among financial businesses, which increased from just a few percent of GDP in the 1950s to 120 percent of GDP in 2008.

Debt levels have moderated in recent years, since the financial crisis of 2008. Many households have substituted debt reduction for new spending. As discussed in Chapters 23 and 30, slow growth in wages played an important role in the credit boom, as consumers compensated for limited incomes by relying on credit cards and other loans to extend their ability to continue spending.

The financial economy, as we will see in Chapter 30, found ways to use household debt, especially mortgages, as collateral to expand its own activity, while regulatory easing and the rise of new kinds of financial institutions made it possible for money to be lent out with very little collateral. ("Collateral" is a valuable asset used as a basis for a loan.) A wide variety of

Figure 22.7 **U.S. Debt Ratios Relative to GDP, 1947–2012**

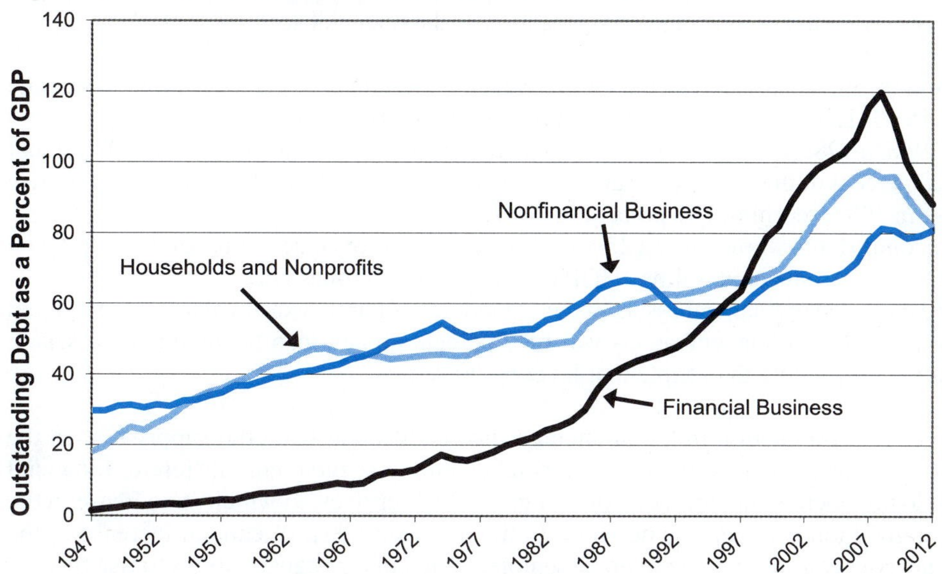

The Great Recession began in 2007, as the ratio of debt-to-GDP for all sectors of the economy reached historic levels.

Source: Federal Reserve Flow of Funds, data download program.

financial firms entered the game of taking in funds and then turning them around to invest in high-yield assets.

Financial firms may sell stock (shares in the company) to raise capital, but in recent years borrowing became a more popular way to increase the funds held by a financial firm. The higher the ratio of borrowed funds to funds contributed by stockholders, the greater a firm's financial *leverage*. Leverage essentially means using borrowed money to increase the investment power of one's own money, and it can be touted as high "return on investment" (ROI), because the return can be calculated without factoring in the borrowed funds that are involved. With a large cushion of borrowed funds, a financial institution could, for example, hold $1 million as collateral while lending out $25 million. These loans could go to other institutions, which, in turn, held back a few percent and lent out the rest. Such loans are described as "highly leveraged" ($1 million can leverage $25 million or more). This possibility made it appealing for banks and other financial institutions to keep borrowing more money in order to have a greater stake in other investments. However, it also created significant risks: If a firm is leveraged 25-fold, then a loss of just over 4 percent will be sufficient to bankrupt it.

Financialization really takes hold when the loans themselves are increasingly viewed as desirable investments. This leads to a situation in which much of the financial sector is leveraging itself to invest in financial assets that are themselves different types of loans, and increasingly these loans are bundled into other complex financial instruments. To repeat a saying that is popular in the sector, "Finance mostly finances finance."* The relative size of the financial economy increases as companies substitute this type of financial investing for "real" investment (i.e., purchasing of fixed assets like machines or computers).

As noted above, the two sources of hot air for the financialization balloon are debt and asset price inflation. In real markets, the price of a good or a service comes from an intersection of several considerations, including the cost of supplying it and how willing and able people are to pay for it. In financial markets, the cost of supply is often nothing more than the time and inventiveness of the manager who invents or promotes a financial asset that most people do not understand (and are most often not intended to understand). These assets can, at least for a while, be extremely profitable, hence the very large salaries received by the people

*This phrase originated with Jan Toporowski, a professor at the University of London.

who work on Wall Street or equivalent centers in London and other financial capitals. This is borne out by data on profits and compensation in the financial sector:

- Profits in the financial sector in the United States represented 14 percent of total corporate profits in 1981; thirty years later this figure was about 30 percent.
- From 1948 to 1982, average compensation in the financial sector ranged between 99 percent and 108 percent of the average for all domestic private industries. This figure began to rise starting in 1983, reaching 181 percent in 2007.
- In the economy as a whole, over a 25-year period the market value of financial assets, taken together, grew from about 4 times GDP to a little over 10 times GDP.
- In 1970 the value of financial assets in the United States barely exceeded the value of fixed assets. The value of financial assets was 68.7 percent greater than tangible fixed assets in 1983 and rose to more than triple that level by 2009.*

If the cost of production in the financial sector is different from the supply side in the real economy, the demand side of the financial economy is even more different. Financial markets do not operate like markets for real goods and services, in which an increase in the price of a good tends to depress demand. In financial markets, instead, an increase in the price of an asset can spur people to borrow more, which in turn causes prices to rise further. The value of an asset is what you think someone else is willing to pay for it. Whether the asset is a tulip bulb (as in the bizarre incident of tulip mania in the seventeenth century) or a piece of real estate, or some complex bundle of derivatives, as long as the balloon is inflating, the prospective buyer of an asset may pay a price that bears no relation to anything on the ground, as long as he or she believes that the price will keep going up, and the next buyer will be willing to pay still more.** When the speculative fever breaks, prices can decline even more rapidly—the financial "bubble" bursts, with bad consequences for the real economy.

The process of financialization has affected stock markets throughout the world. Average holding times for stocks has fallen as large financial institutions engage in rapid trading of stocks in search of short-term gains. Investors on the New York Stock Exchange (NYSE) held stocks for an average period of about five years in 1975, two years in 1991, but only five months in 2008.[3] This is in contrast to an approach which focuses on the ability of a business to generate revenues and generally involves holding stocks for longer periods. Short-term investing makes markets more vulnerable to "bubbles," when investors looking for a quick profit drive stock prices to excessive heights, leading to a subsequent crash.

The stock market, however, plays a relatively small role in financing investment in the real world. The majority of transactions in the stock market consist of investors transacting with other investors, while a relatively small proportion of stock purchases actually finance new investments in productive activities. Genuinely new activities, such as start-up businesses, tend to be financed through "angel" investors who have personal knowledge of the business; in the case of many small business start-ups the initial funding very often comes from family and friends. Once a new business has begun to have a track record, the next stage of financing is likely to come from venture capitalists (also outside of the public stock markets), who

*Data from Bureau of Economic Analysis, "Corporate Profits by Industry"; *Statistical Abstract of the United States*; Economic Policy Institute, Briefing Paper #331, 2011.

**Derivatives are financial instruments whose value is "derived" from the value of another, underlying asset. For example, an option to purchase a stock is a derivative whose value is based on potential changes in the value of the underlying stock.

spend their working lives scrutinizing new businesses and investing in a number of them, with the understanding that many will fail, but with the hope that a few will make it big. Finally, when a business is considered mature enough to go public, the venture capitalists and the CEO will agree on the best time to make an initial public offering (IPO). This is the main opportunity for funds invested through the stock market to make a real difference in business activity.

In contrast, established corporations do not depend on the stock market as much as is generally thought when they decide to invest in new or expanded activities. Most of the major corporations of today have accumulated large pools of retained earnings which they can invest in new activities. Indeed, since the 1980s, corporations have actually spent more on buying back their own stock than they have taken in by selling newly issued stock.

4.3 Human Services: Health

We now return to the real-world portion of the tertiary sector within the macroeconomy, with a consideration of human services. Human services include education, health care, social work, and child care. These services can be provided by private businesses, non-profit organizations, or governments. A major difference between the United States and other developed countries is that human services in the United States are less likely to be provided by the public sector. Perhaps the most vivid example of this difference is with respect to health care.

Health care is one of the fastest-growing industries in the United States. In 2013 about 13 percent of the country's workers were employed in the health-care sector. As shown in Figure 22.8, national health-care expenditures grew from about 5 percent of GDP in 1960 to 17 percent of GDP in 2011. Out-of-pocket costs (the amounts paid by individuals for health care, including payments by those without insurance and co-pays and other expenses by those with insurance) have remained relatively constant over the years, but both private insurance and public costs have risen considerably. In 2011 annual per capita spending on health care in the United States was about $8,700. Health-care costs are expected to increase further and become an even greater share of GDP, as the population ages and medical technology continues to become more sophisticated.

While the share of health expenditures by the public sector has increased in recent decades, public funding of health care in the United States is much smaller as a share of total health-care costs than in any other developed country. In 2008, public funding paid for 46 percent of health-care costs in the United States, while in other industrialized countries it ranged from 66 to 87 percent.

Figure 22.8 **Health Care Expenditures in the United States as a Percentage of GDP, 1960–2011**

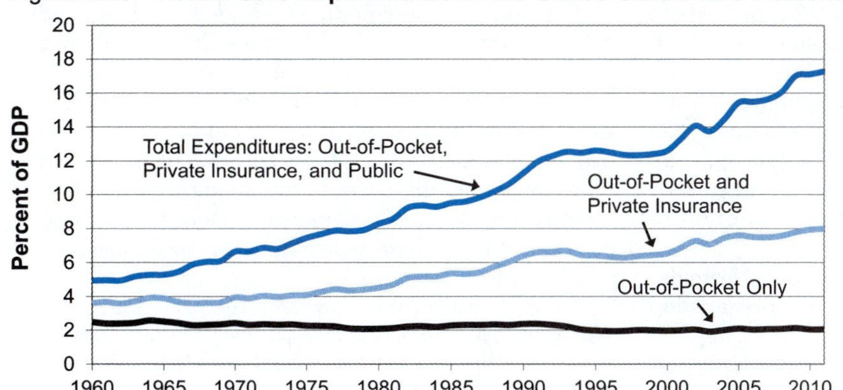

Health care expenditures in the United States have risen from about 5 percent of GDP in 1960 to 17 percent of GDP in 2011.

Source: Various editions of the *Statistical Abstract of the United States.*

The dominance of private markets for health care in the United States has not kept health-care spending or costs low. In fact, a higher share of GDP is spent on health care in the United States than in any other developed country. While in the United States health care accounts for about 17 percent of GDP, in France health care represents 11 percent, in Canada 10 percent, and in Sweden and the United Kingdom 9 percent. (See Chapter 0 for more comparisons.) Also, in the United States prices are rising much more rapidly in health care than overall: Between 2000 and 2010, the consumer price index for medical care rose 48 percent while the overall price index only rose 26 percent. The cost of health insurance premiums is rising at an even faster rate.

Given that these expenditures are so high in the United States, is the quality of health care higher than in other developed countries? Using several common measures of national health, as shown in Chapter 0, the United States actually ranks lower than most other developed countries. This country has a relatively low number of physicians per capita and a lower-than-average rate of childhood immunization. Average life spans are shorter than in most other developed countries, and infant mortality rates are slightly above the norm.

Unlike all other developed countries, the United States does not have publicly funded universal health-care coverage. For those with adequate coverage through private insurance, most often provided by employers, the United States offers some of the highest-quality medical care in the world. But about 16 percent of Americans lacked any health insurance in 2011, a proportion that has generally been increasing in recent years. In an attempt to expand health-care coverage, improve quality, and control costs, in 2010 Congress passed the Patient Protection and Affordable Care Act, commonly known as Obamacare, which could possibly reverse this trend, although this depends on its effective implementation. See Box 22.3 for more on this law.

Box 22.3 The 2010 Affordable Care Act

The passage of "Obamacare" in 2010 marked the most significant change to the American health care system in decades. The law will be phased in over the period 2010–20. Some of its main provisions include:

- An "individual mandate" that requires individuals to obtain health insurance by 2014 or pay a penalty. Individuals and families below the federal poverty line currently can receive free health care through Medicaid, and thus will not need to purchase private insurance. Individuals between 100 percent and 400 percent of the poverty line will be able to obtain subsidized coverage, based on a sliding scale.
- The law sets maximum insurance premium rates for individuals and families making up to 400 percent of the poverty line. For example, an individual making 150 percent of the poverty line cannot pay more than 4 percent of his or her income in premiums.
- The law prohibits insurance companies from denying coverage to individuals with pre-existing conditions.
- As of 2013, the law institutes a new 0.9 percent tax on individuals making more than $200,000 per year (or couples making more than $250,000). The funds from the tax will be used to subsidize health care coverage for low-income individuals and pay for other costs of the law.
- Firms with more than 50 employees will need to provide health care coverage or pay a fee if the government has to subsidize their employees' health care. Smaller firms that offer health insurance may qualify for subsidies.

The Congressional Budget Office (CBO) conducted a comprehensive analysis of the law in 2011, predicting that about 34 million more Americans will have health care coverage in 2021 as a result of it. While the CBO estimates the gross costs of the law to be $1.4 trillion over the period 2012–21, these costs will be more than offset by additional revenues and Medicare and other savings. Thus the CBO estimates that the law will actually reduce the federal deficit by about $200 billion.

Sources: "Patient Protection and Affordable Care Act," Wikipedia.com; U.S. Congressional Budget Office, "CBO's Analysis of the Major Health Care Legislation Enacted in March 2010," March 30, 2011.

4.4 Human Services: Education

The situation with respect to education in the United States in many ways mirrors that of health care. The quality of education in the United States can be excellent, which draws many foreigners to come there for higher education. About 20 percent of graduate students in the United States are foreign born. Spending per student in the United States on elementary and secondary education is significantly higher than the average among members of the Organization for Economic Cooperation and Development (OECD) (only Switzerland and Luxembourg spend more), and the United States spends more per student than any other country on postsecondary education. However, the performance of American students is only mediocre by international standards. In a standardized test given in 2009 to 15-year-old students in 74 countries with varying levels of economic development, U.S. students ranked thirty-first in math, seventeenth in reading, and twenty-third in science. (See Chapter 0 for additional comparisons.)

In section 6.2, we discussed the ballooning of debt in the U.S. economy. The cost of education has played a role in this. Between 2002 and 2012, the cost of attending a public four-year institution increased by 68 percent, much more rapidly than overall inflation, which rose 27 percent during the same period. Meanwhile, real median household income was falling.

While federal college education grants have increased, particularly since 2008, the majority of federal education assistance now comes in the form of loans. Although those who have trouble paying back federal student loans can apply for assistance programs, students who take out loans from private companies tend to face higher interest rates and less flexible conditions. According to the Pew Research Center, the debt on student loans eats up 24 percent of household incomes for the lowest-income families.

Both public and private institutions provide education in the United States. Education services employed slightly more than 2 percent of workers in 2010. About 75 million students are enrolled in American schools at all grade levels, and about 85 percent are in public schools. Among people 25 and older in the United States in 2010, 87 percent are high school graduates and 30 percent have college degrees. Educational attainment differs by race and gender. For example, while 30 percent of whites had a college degree in 2010, only 20 percent of blacks and 14 percent of those of Hispanic origin had completed college. Although males are more likely than females to have a college degree (30 percent vs. 29 percent), more females are enrolled in college than males. For the first time, in 2009 women earned more graduate degrees than men in the United States.

4.5 Concluding Thoughts

This chapter has provided a bird's-eye view of the U.S. economy. We have looked at primary sector activities that provide the raw materials on which everything else depends, noting that the importance of these activities is belied by the small percentage of GDP devoted to them. We have looked at secondary-sector activities that process physical materials, turning them into goods for sale. And we have looked at the tertiary sector, which accounts for about three-quarters of the economic activity in the United States.

The "marketed" section of the economy, on which we have concentrated here, is not the whole picture. Seemingly inherent in our economic system is a drive to find ever more ways to replace what we do for ourselves with marketed services or products. The replacement of much home cooking with fast food, take-out, and rapid meal delivery is a prime example. Still, the services that people provide as friends, neighbors, family members, and citizens continue to be a large part of the economy, though unmeasured by flows of money and therefore missing from GDP. Recall from Chapter 21 that even the most conservative estimates of the total value of household production are 25–30 percent of standard GDP in the United States. In a more fully accounted economy, covering the core as well as the business and public-purpose spheres, the tertiary sector would still loom very large—much of the (non-monetized) economic activity in the core sphere is services—but its expansion would be largely in the areas of "private social services" and "entertainment."

As we continue our analysis of the macroeconomy, we will focus primarily on the portion of the economy that is measured by standard GDP. We will be concerned primarily with aggregate figures, concentrating for example on total consumption, total investment, and total government spending. The material covered in this chapter, as well as in the preceding two, may help us to bear in mind the realities that lie behind the abstractions that are necessary to develop macroeconomic theory. Before delving into that theory, we need to review one other important area of the real economy—employment and unemployment—the topic of the next chapter.

Discussion Questions

1. Economic theory suggests that goods and services provided in competitive markets by private enterprises will result in lower prices. But we have learned that health-care costs in the United States actually are the highest in the world, although Americans do not better have health outcomes than people in countries that provide public health care. How would you explain this result? Do you think that the Affordable Care Act will improve the situation? If not, what alternative solution would you suggest?
2. Try to estimate what share of your total expenditures is on products from the primary, secondary, and tertiary sectors. How do you think your expenditure patterns will change in the future? For example, assuming that your income rises after you graduate, do you think that your share of expenditures on services will increase or decrease?

Review Questions

1. List and define the three major sectors of the U.S. economy, as discussed in this chapter.
2. Approximately what percentage of the U.S. GDP is produced in each of the three sectors? How has this allocation changed over time?
3. How do "technological optimists" view the debate about natural resource constraints?
4. What are some of the potential future natural resource constraints on economic activity?
5. Summarize how agriculture in the United States has changed over the past century. About how much of each dollar spent on food currently goes to farmers?
6. Does the declining share of the primary sector imply that it is becoming less important?
7. What is the largest source of energy in the United States?
8. Why does the number of new housing starts in the United States show a cyclical pattern?
9. Contrast the recent history of the American textile and automobile industries.
10. Are some politicians correct when they say that American manufacturing jobs have been shifted overseas?
11. Is the service sector synonymous with low-paying jobs?
12. What is meant by "financialization"? What data suggest the United States has become more financialized in recent years?
13. Summarize the state of health care in the United States.
14. What trend was emphasized in the chapter concerning retail services?

Exercises

1. Match each statement in Column A with a percentage in Column B.

Column A	Column B
a. The government percentage of U.S. GDP	1. 17 percent
b. The tertiary sector's share of GDP	2. 37 percent
c. The percentage of U.S. energy from petroleum	3. 13 percent
d. The decline in new private construction as a result of the Great Recession	4. 3 percent
e. The percentage decline in U.S. manufacturing jobs since 1979	5. 64 percent
f. The secondary sector's share of GDP	6. 44 percent
g. The percentage of U.S. health-care costs paid for with public funding	7. 46 percent
h. The primary sector's share of GDP	8. 30 percent

2. Search the Internet or other news sources for a recent article discussing the loss of U.S. jobs to other countries. Based on what you have learned in this chapter, present an analysis of the article. Can you find any statements in the article that you think may be inaccurate?
3. The *Statistical Abstract of the United States,* published annually, is the source of much of the data presented in this chapter. The *Statistical Abstract* is available online from the U.S. Census Bureau and ProQuest. It is likely that a more recent edition of the *Statistical Abstract* is now available. Go online and locate it. Then determine whether the percentage of U.S. GDP attributed to the primary, secondary, tertiary, and government sectors has increased or decreased compared to the data presented in this chapter.
4. Match each statement in Column A with an answer in Column B:

Column A	Column B
a. The largest of the three economic sectors by value added	1. Cyclical
b. The smallest of the three economic sectors by value added	2. Ford Motor Company
c. An example of a business in the primary sector	3. Primary
d. An example of a business in the secondary sector	4. Walmart
e. An example of a business in the tertiary sector	5. Declining
f. The current trend regarding the size of the secondary sector	6. Tertiary
g. The current trend regarding the size of the tertiary sector	7. A local farmer's market
h. The typical trend regarding the number of housing starts	8. Increasing

NOTES

1. Data from the *Statistical Abstract of the United States 2012,* table 620.
2. Mark Z. Jacobson et al., "Examining the Feasibility of Converting New York State's All-Purpose Energy Infrastructure to One Using Wind, Water, and Sunlight," *Energy Policy* (2013); quotation from Elisabeth Rosenthal, "Life After Oil and Gas," *New York Times,* March 23, 2013.
3. World Federation of Exchanges, "Average Holding Period for Stocks," http://world-exchanges.org/; http://topforeignstocks.com/wp-content/uploads/2012/11/Stock-Holding-Periods-1991-2010.png.

APPENDIX

A1. THE TERTIARY SECTOR IN THE OVERALL MACRO CONTEXT

Figure 22.9 is a depiction of the private (nongovernmental) U.S. economy that we have assembled to take a closer look at the tertiary sector. It starts from the value-added approach to national accounting that was used for Table 22.1. This approach, as you may remember from Chapter 20, includes intermediate inputs such as wholesale and retail trade, as well as management of companies and enterprises. The primary, secondary, and tertiary sectors of the economy are shown in Figure 22.9 at somewhat higher proportions than those given in Table 22.1 because of exclusion of the government sector.

Figure 22.9 then illustrates one potential way to further categorize the tertiary sector. These divisions are the authors' classification and do not represent any official government classification scheme. The four divisions presented in the figure are explained below.

We will identify the largest category of the tertiary activities in GDP as "Ownership Transactions," which includes 31.3 percent of private GDP. About thirteen percentage points of this category represents the imputed value, to each homeowner, of the ongoing value of being able to live in that house. The remainder—about 18 percent of private GDP—is essentially about buying and selling, covering activities that transfer ownership of goods and services from producers to buyers, or from previous owners to new owners. This includes transportation and warehousing, wholesale and retail trade, and real-estate rental and leasing (aside from the above-mentioned imputed value of homeownership).

Figure 22.9 **Classification of Private GDP in the United States, 2011**

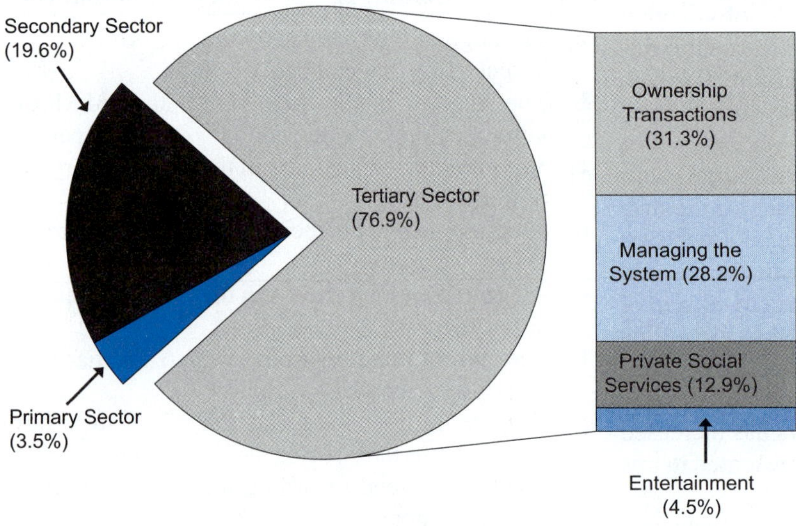

The production of services, accounting for over three-quarters of private GDP in the United States, can be best understood if broken down into several additional categories.

Transportation and transportation-related activities that allow people in a modern society to acquire items that were not produced locally are an important part of "ownership transactions." They make it possible for you to enjoy fruits and vegetables when they are out of season where you live, goods that are not produced in your area, and goods that you can purchase more cheaply because they were produced in other parts of the country—or, more often, of the world—where the cost is lower (leaving aside, for the moment, feelings that you may have about the variety of reasons that production costs for certain goods are lower in some places than in others).

Another significant portion of the value added in this category may be traced to "the middleman"—the person or organization that facilitates the transaction between the final buyer and the original producer or between the previous owner and the next one (as is often the case with stocks and bonds, real estate, fine arts, and other things that tend to have a sequence of owners). It is sometimes said that a way to lower prices without hurting producers is to "get rid of the middleman," that is, to find a way to put the end user directly in contact with the producer. Perhaps more of this will happen over time, via the Internet. In the meantime, in an advanced economy in which there is a huge amount of choice, for buyers, among objects that can come from anywhere in the world, it is not surprising that a significant portion of GDP should be devoted to making these connections.

The next largest category, "Managing the System," covers the marketed services that keep the economic system going. These include information, finance and insurance, and professional, scientific, and technical services.* This category also includes the activities that the Census Bureau calls administrative and waste management and management of companies and enterprises.

This category is about the organization and management of a hugely complex system—or, more accurately, a set of systems. Our society has come a long way from the relatively simple economies that we described early in this chapter, when discussing how the secondary sector grew relative to the primary sector. Firms are more numerous; large (and enormous) firms are

*A major part of the finance industry is the buying and selling of paper or electronic claims to ownership of productive resources, such as stocks. The financial advisers, investment companies, and other money managers whose salaries, bonuses, and so on are represented as "finance" in "Managing the System" are sometimes selling the right to own a piece of a new company; more often, they are reselling previously owned stocks and bonds. If we could readily identify these activities, perhaps it would be appropriate to move them to the category "Ownership Transactions."

more numerous; and there is much organization and management to be done in negotiating the networks of relations inside these firms and among them. Governments do some of this organization and management, and they, in turn, along with the firms, need many kinds of support. Many individuals and families, too, have resources that they can use to purchase support for the complexities of operating in an industrialized world. The kinds of support that individuals and organizations want and can pay for include insurance and advice about insurance, as well as advice and assistance with the management and operation of technologies, from automobile repair to computer hardware and software.

"Private Social Services" (within the tertiary sector) covers only those portions of education, health care, and social assistance that are not covered by government; they do not cover the cost of materials (such as medical supplies) that would show up as products of the secondary sector.

The category "Entertainment" is partially about "what we do for fun"; it covers services sold in relation to arts, entertainment and recreation, and accommodation and food services. Thus, for example, it comprises wages for musicians but not the sale price of a new painting (accounted as a secondary-sector product); it covers payments for movie tickets and wages for hotel and restaurant personnel as well as the people working in retail and wholesale who sell DVDs or food but not the materials or manufacturing cost of DVDs or of food (whose value is divided between the primary and secondary sectors). A significant portion of this category is also work related, including business lunches and accommodations for business trips.

A2: Historical Trends and Global Comparisons

The relative shares of the three output sectors in GDP have changed over time in the United States. Figure 22.10 shows the share of the U.S. private economy (excluding government) attributed to each of the three output sectors since 1800. Perhaps the most surprising conclusion from the graph is that the tertiary sector has always comprised the largest share of economic production in the United States, even in 1800. The tertiary share of GDP held steady at around 50 percent from 1800 until about 1950, then steadily climbed to its current share of about 75 percent. The secondary sector's share of GDP tended to increase from 1800 to about 1950 but has decreased since then. Finally, the primary sector's share of GDP was about 40 percent in 1800 but has since declined to its current share of about 3 percent of GDP.

The sectoral distribution of economic production in several other countries is given in Table 22.3. The classification of output sectors in the table, based on data from the World Bank, is slightly different from the definitions given above. The World Bank defines agriculture as its own output sector. The World Bank's "industrial" sector includes the secondary sector as defined above, but adds fishing, forestry, and mining output. The tertiary sector is unchanged, including all services.

As in the United States, the tertiary sector also comprises at least 70 percent of economic production in the United Kingdom, Sweden, Japan, and Germany. Norway is an example of a developed country with a relatively large share of GDP, over 40 percent, from the secondary sector. The secondary sector is the dominant share of GDP in several countries, including China, Saudi Arabia (because oil production is classified as "industrial"), Indonesia, and the Republic of the Congo (also heavily dependent on oil production). The agricultural sector is the largest sector only in a handful of lower-income countries, including Ethiopia. Even in most developing countries, the tertiary sector is the dominant output sector.

The sectoral data for different countries indicate that economic development is commonly associated with a declining share of GDP from agriculture. Economic growth in most countries is associated with a significant increase in the relative share of manufacturing, but this is not universally true. Some countries, such as Hong Kong, Bermuda, and Singapore, have achieved income growth by primarily expanding the service sector. We consider these and other issues of economic development in more detail in Chapter 32.

Figure 22.10 **Relative Shares of United States Economic Production, by Output Sector, 1800–2011**

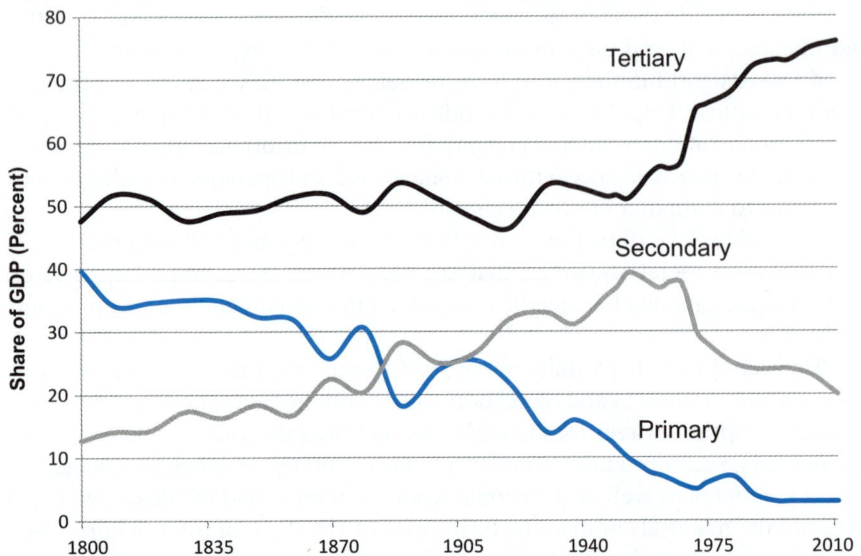

Note that this graph shows relative, not absolute, magnitudes. While the value share of the primary sector in the U.S. economy has been declining steadily since 1800, the dramatic rise of the tertiary sector only began in about 1950, about the same time as the secondary sector began its relative decline.

Sources: Historical Statistics of the United States, 1789–1945, U.S. Census Bureau, 1949 (1800–1938); Historical Statistics of the United States, Bicentennial Edition, Colonial Times to 1970, U.S. Census Bureau, 1975 (1947–1968); various annual editions of the Statistical Abstract of the United States, U.S. Census Bureau (1969–2011).

Table 22.3 **Division of GDP by Output Sector, Selected Countries**

Country	Agricultural Sector (%)	Industrial Sector (%)	Tertiary Sector (%)
Congo, Rep.	4	75	21
Indonesia	15	47	38
Saudi Arabia	2	60	38
Ethiopia	47	10	43
China	10	47	43
Bangladesh	19	28	53
India	18	27	55
Norway	2	40	58
Argentina	10	31	59
Russian Federation	4	35	61
Mexico	4	35	61
Brazil	5	28	67
South Africa	2	31	67
Germany	1	28	71
Japan	1	27	71
Sweden	2	26	72
United Kingdom	1	22	78
United States	1	20	79

Source: World Bank, World Development Indicators database.

23 Employment, Unemployment, and Wages

As discussed in Chapter 1, a primary goal of the economy is to support a good standard of living.* This normally involves making it possible for people to gain the income needed to purchase goods and services. Nonmarket factors such as household production, publicly produced goods and services, leisure time, and a healthy environment, play an important role in determining living standards, but for most people in developed economies income from work is the main factor needed to support individuals and families. In this chapter we focus on paid employment, and on levels of employment and unemployment in the economy as a whole.

The second macroeconomic goal that we cited was stability and security. Unemployment can be a major threat to people's stability and security. This chapter focuses specifically on understanding the phenomenon of unemployment. Later chapters consider the macroeconomic conditions that affect unemployment levels.

The third macroeconomic goal is to sustain and restore the various forms of capital that are essential for future as well as present well-being. This chapter discusses the ways in which the availability of natural and manufactured capital, in particular, is relevant for future employment and income.

What does all of this mean for your future? Do you, for example, feel that your future work experience will be similar to that of your parents? During some periods in history, expectations of work remained stable for decades. But expectations have changed—according to a 2012 survey in the United States, only 14 percent of respondents believe that today's children will be better off than their parents.[1]

There are many reasons for this sense of turbulence and change, including the globalization of markets, the increasing scale and concentration of many businesses, changing relations between states and corporations, the information revolution and other rapid changes in technology, and the impact of the Great Recession (the recession of 2007–9, so named because of its severity and lasting impact). This chapter and subsequent chapters will explore what macroeconomics can tell us about how these and other forces are affecting the nature of employment, the levels and impacts of unemployment, and the longer-term future of work and incomes.

1. Employment and Unemployment

We have seen in previous chapters how official data are used to draw a macro portrait of the U.S. economy—and how these data may emphasize some aspects (especially the economic

*The terms "standard of living" and "well-being" are often used interchangeably, but there is a distinction. "Standard of living" refers to the tangible aspects of one's life, while "well-being" refers to the overall state of one's life, including social and psychological aspects as well as tangible aspects.

activities that involve markets) and ignore or downplay others. We start this chapter with a similar look at the official data on work issues. These data do not cover everything that we might want to know, but it is important to know how to read the official data and what they can tell us.

1.1 Measuring Employment and Unemployment

Bureau of Labor Statistics (BLS): in the United States, the government agency that compiles and publishes employment and unemployment statistics

Every month, the U.S. **Bureau of Labor Statistics (BLS)** interviews about 60,000 households, asking whether individual household members have jobs or are looking for work. In addition to conducting this household survey, it collects data every month from nearly 400,000 employers. Based on these two surveys, the BLS publishes monthly data on work issues, including the official unemployment rate.

If you live in a U.S. household, someday you may get a telephone call from a BLS interviewer. After a few preliminaries he or she will ask you the questions shown in Box A of Figure 23.1. If you can answer "no" to *all* these questions, you are part of the *civilian, noninstitutionalized, age sixteen and over population* about which this survey gathers data, and the interviewer will ask you questions about employment. If you answer "yes" to any question in Box A, the interviewer will not ask you about employment. Official employment and unemployment statistics do not include you. Trends in employment statistics over time, then, need to be analyzed in the light of considerations such as changes in age demographics, military policy, and rates of disability and incarceration. (See Box 23.1, for more on incarceration in the United States.)

employed person (BLS household survey definition): a person who did any work for pay or profit during the week before he or she is surveyed by the BLS or who worked for fifteen hours or more in a family business

If you are part of the surveyed population, then you will be asked the questions in Box B of Figure 23.1, starting with: "Last week, did you do any work for pay or profit?" Anyone who answers "yes" will be classified as **employed**. If you did *any* paid work last week—even if you worked for only an hour or two at a casual job—the interviewer will code you as "employed." If you answer "no," then you will be asked more questions. For example, if you have a paid job but just did not happen to put in any hours last week because you were sick, on vacation, or on certain kinds of leave, you will be coded as working and "employed." Also, if you did *unpaid* work in a family-run business, such as a retail store or farm, you will be classified as "employed" as long as you worked for more than fifteen hours a week.

Figure 23.1 **Who Is In the Labor Force?** (February 2013 data)

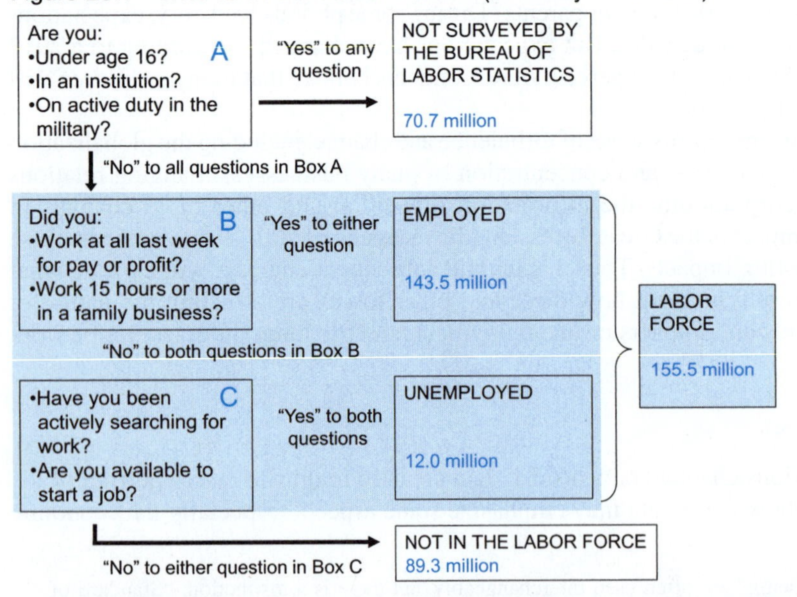

The BLS household survey asks people a series of questions to determine if they are employed, unemployed, or not in the labor force.

Source: BLS News Release, "The Employment Situation—February 2013," March 8, 2013; U.S. Census Bureau Current Population Clock.

BOX 23.1 INCARCERATION IN THE UNITED STATES

Not only does the United States incarcerate more individuals than any other country in the world but it also has the world's highest incarceration rate. In 2011 the United States prison population was about 2.2 million people, or one in every 140 people in the country. This is about seven times the incarceration rate of most other developed countries.

The U.S. prison population has increased dramatically in the past few decades. In 1980 only about 500,000 people were incarcerated in the United States. Given that violent and property crimes actually decreased between 1980 and 2011, why has the prison population risen so much?

Much of the increase is a result of the "war on drugs," which mandated long prison sentences for drug offenses, including nonviolent crimes such as drug possession. A 2010 report looks at the cost of incarcerating so many people:

> The financial costs of our corrections policies are staggering. In 2008, federal, state, and local governments spent about $75 billion on corrections. . . . Reducing the number of non-violent offenders in our prisons and jails by half would lower this bill by $16.9 billion per year, with the largest share of these savings accruing to financially squeezed state and local governments. Every indication is that these savings could be achieved without any appreciable deterioration in public safety. (Schmitt, 2010, p. 2)

The high U.S. prison population has implications for the unemployment rate. Many people currently in prison would otherwise be unemployed. According to one estimate, the U.S. unemployment rate would be about two percentage points higher if prisoners were counted. In 2013, a number of bills were introduced in the U.S. Congress proposing sentencing reform, which if passed might reduce the prison population.

Sources: International Centre for Prison Studies, World Prison Brief, www.prisonstudies.org/info/worldbrief/online; U.S. Census Bureau, *Statistical Abstract of the United States—2012*, Table 347, "Prisoners Under Jurisdiction of Federal or State Correctional Authorities"; Federal Bureau of Investigation, Crime in the United States—2012 (Lanham, MD: Rowman and Littlefield Publishing); John Schmitt et al., "The High Budgetary Cost of Incarceration," Center for Economic and Policy Research, June 2010, www.cepr.net; Justice Policy Institute, "The Punishing Decade: Prison and Jail Estimates at the Millennium," May 2000, www.justicepolicy.org.

Note that the "family business" situation is the only case in which unpaid work currently counts as being employed in the official statistics. If you work fewer than 15 hours in your family business, or are, for example, occupied with caring for your children or other family members or doing community volunteer work, you will *not* be considered "employed." Terms such as "labor," "work," and "employment" in official statistics generally refer only to *paid* work.

unemployed person (BLS definition): a person who is not employed but who is actively seeking a job and is immediately available for work

labor force (BLS definition): people who are employed or unemployed

"not in the labor force" (BLS definition): the classification given to people who are neither "employed" nor "unemployed"

If your answers to the household survey do *not* result in your being classified as "employed," you will be asked the questions about job search and availability shown in Box C of Figure 23.1. Activities such as contacting employers and sending out résumés count as an "active" job search. Merely participating in a job-training program or reading employment ads do not. The question about whether you could start a job concerns whether, in fact, you are *available* for work. If, for example, you are a college student searching during spring break for a summer job, but you are not available to start the job until June, you would answer "no" to the availability question. If you can answer "yes" to *both* these questions you are classified as **unemployed**.

If you are either employed or unemployed, the BLS classifies you as part of the **labor force**. But what if you are neither "employed" nor "unemployed"—if you do not have a job but are not actively seeking one? Then you are classified as "**not in the labor force**." People in this category are often taking care of a home and family, in school, disabled, or retired.

Notice, in Figure 23.1, that the vast majority of U.S. residents who are not "employed" either are "not in the labor force" (about 89.3 million) or are not part of the surveyed population (about 70.7 million). The latter group includes children under 16, and person who are institutionalized. In comparison, about 12.0 million people in February 2013 were formally counted as "unemployed." (Figures are updated monthly at www.bls.gov.)

1.2 The Unemployment Rate

unemployment rate: the percentage of the labor force made up of people who do not have paid jobs but are immediately available and actively looking for paid jobs

Every month, having made estimates, based on the survey responses, of the total number of employed and unemployed people in the country, the BLS calculates the official **unemployment rate**. This follows the formula:

$$\textit{unemployment rate} = \frac{\textit{number of people unemployed}}{\textit{number of people in the labor force}} \times 100$$

For example, in February 2013, looking at Figure 23.1 you can see that the BLS estimated that 143.5 million people were employed and 12.0 million people were unemployed. The unemployment rate was thus calculated as 7.7 percent:

$$\textit{unemployment rate} = \frac{12.0 \textit{ million}}{155.5 \textit{ million}} \times 100 = 7.7$$

The unemployment rate represents the fraction of the officially defined labor force that is made up of people who are not currently working at paid jobs but are currently looking for and available for paid work.

The unemployment rate reported in the media is often "seasonally adjusted." Over the course of a year, some swings in unemployment are fairly predictable. For example, agriculture and construction tend to employ fewer people in the cold winter months, and each year many students enter the labor force in May and June after graduation. The BLS releases "seasonally adjusted" figures that attempt to reflect only shifts in unemployment that are due to factors *other than* such seasonal patterns.

The BLS also estimates unemployment rates for various demographic groups, occupations, industries, and geographical areas. Historically, unemployment rates have generally been substantially higher for minority populations than for whites, for teenagers than for older people, and for less educated people than for the more educated. Unemployment rates often have differed somewhat by gender, though not with any consistent pattern. Some representative unemployment rates are given in Table 23.1.

Table 23.1 **Unemployment Rates for Different Groups**

Group	Unemployment rate
All Workers	7.7
*Race and ethnicity**	
White	6.8
Black/African American	13.8
Hispanic or Latino	9.6
Age	
Teenage (age 16–19)	25.1
Age 65 and older	5.7
Education	
Less than a high school diploma	11.2
Bachelor's degree and higher	3.8
Gender	
Adult male	7.8
Adult female	7.7

Source: BLS News Release, "The Employment Situation—February 2013," March 8, 2013.

*People are allowed to indicate more than one racial group. However, data from people who indicated more than one race are not included in these statistics.

Discouraged Workers and Underemployment

The fact that some people "not in the labor force" might want jobs but have given up looking for them has long troubled employment analysts. To the extent that people give up looking, the official unemployment rate *underestimates* people's need and desire for paid jobs.

In recent years, the BLS has added questions to the survey to try to determine how many people in the "not in the labor force" population may want employment, even if they are not currently searching for work. If someone says that he or she is available for work, wants to work, and has looked for work in the past 12 months but not in the past 4 weeks, the BLS calls them "**marginally attached workers**." In February 2013 marginally attached workers numbered 2.6 million.

marginally attached workers: people who want employment and have looked for work in the past twelve months but not in the past four weeks

If these marginally attached workers also say that the reason they are no longer looking is that they believe there are no jobs out there for them, they are called **discouraged workers**. They may have become discouraged because their skills do not match available openings, because they have experienced discrimination, or because they have been turned away time after time. In February 2013 the number of discouraged workers in the United States was estimated at about 900,000. Marginally attached workers who are not discouraged workers typically have not looked for work recently because of school attendance or family responsibilities.

discouraged workers: people who want employment but have given up looking because they believe that there are no jobs available for them

Let's also take a closer look at the people classified as "employed." In the BLS statistics, people are counted as "employed" if they do any paid work *at all* during the reference week, even if only for an hour or two. Some people prefer part-time work, of course, because of the time it leaves them for other activities, such as schooling or family care. Some are limited to part-time work for health reasons. But others want and need full-time work and are only settling for part-time work until they can find something better. The household survey asks people who work part time about their reasons for doing so.

In February 2013, 18.9 million people reported working less than 35 hours per week for "noneconomic" reasons such as health or family responsibilities. In the same month, an additional 8.0 million people reported working part time for what the BLS calls "economic reasons"—that is, slack business conditions or because part-time work was all they could find (see Box 23.2).

What indicator, then, should we look at to see whether the national employment situation is "bad" or "good"? The BLS now publishes various measures of labor underutilization that allow you to see the situation from a variety of different perspectives. For example, if the marginally attached workers and people who work part time involuntarily are added to the

BOX 23.2 MANY PART-TIME WORKERS WANT FULL-TIME WORK

By March 2013, the U.S. economy had generated thirty straight months of job growth. "But for millions of people looking for more work and greater income, that improvement provided little solace. 7.6 million Americans were stuck in part-time jobs, about the same as a year earlier." These underemployed workers did not count towards the official jobless rate of 7.6 percent in March.

"There's nothing inherently wrong with people taking part-time jobs if they want them," said Diane Swonk, chief economist at Mesirow Financial. "The problem is that people are accepting part-time pay because they have no other choice."

The rise in part-time work has been characteristic of the recession of 2007–9 and its aftermath. Part-timers usually earn less per hour than their full-time counterparts. It is often easier for companies to manage schedules with part-time workers, and they may not have to pay the same benefits as full-time workers typically get. Some of the strongest job growth has been in areas such as food services and retailing, industries that are particularly likely to use part-timers.

Source: Catherine Rampell, "Part-Time Workers in Full-Time Wait for Better Job," *New York Times*, April 20, 2013.

number of unemployed, the rate of labor underutilization in February 2013 comes to 14.3 percent, compared to the official unemployment rate of 7.7 percent.

The BLS also counts people as employed even if the kind of work that they did does not match their skills. Suppose that you paint your aunt's living room for cash while you are waiting to hear back on job applications for management or computer positions. The BLS counts you as already employed. People who are working at jobs that underutilize their abilities, as well as those who work fewer hours than they wish to, are said to be **underemployed**.

underemployment: working fewer hours than desired or at a job that does not match one's skills

If we are concerned about human well-being, underemployment as well as unemployment should be of concern. While underemployment due to an underutilization of skills is certainly of considerable concern for both efficiency and quality-of-life reasons, BLS official surveys do not currently attempt to measure this sort of underemployment.

Discussion Questions

1. How would the BLS classify you, personally, on the basis of your activities last week? Can you think of an example where someone you think of as *working* would not be considered by the BLS to be officially "employed"? Is it true that people who are *not working* are generally counted as "unemployed"?
2. Do you know anyone who is a "discouraged worker"? How about someone working part time "for economic reasons"?

1.3 LABOR FORCE PARTICIPATION

labor force participation (LFP) rate: the percentage of potential workers either with a job or actively seeking a job or the labor force as a percentage of the civilian noninstitutional population

In the first half of the twentieth century, it was common in the United States for men to be the "breadwinners" of a family while most women stayed home to care for children and engage in other household production. Thus men were much more likely to be part of the labor force, using the definition presented in Figure 23.1. We can calculate the **labor force participation (LFP) rate** by dividing the number of people officially in the labor force by the number of people age 16 or over who are not institutionalized or in the military:

$$LFP\ Rate = \frac{number\ of\ people\ in\ the\ labor\ force}{number\ of\ people\ age\ 16+,\ not\ institutionalized\ or\ in\ the\ military} \times 100$$

The LFP rate indicates the fraction of potential paid workers who either are in paid jobs or are seeking and available for paid work. In 2013 the LFP rate in the United States was about 64 percent.

In the mid-twentieth century, the labor force participation rates for men and women were very different: In 1948 the LFP rate for men age 25 to 54 was 97 percent, while for women it was only 35 percent. Since then, men's LFP rate has declined slightly while the rate for women increased dramatically until about 2000, when it began to stabilize at around 75 percent (see Figure 23.2). The women's rights movement during the 1960s and 1970s contributed to this expansion in women's labor market activities. Other factors include the expansion of the service sector (discussed in Chapter 22) and reductions in the average number of children per family.

The decline in men's LFP rate is likely a result of men's staying in school longer and being more likely to assist with raising children and other household production. Young males (age 20–24) are much less likely to be in the labor force now compared to several decades ago, primarily due to staying in school longer. As a result of higher college attendance, the percentage of the labor force with a college degree has increased in recent decades—it is currently about 35 percent.

The labor force has changed in other ways as well, reflecting broader demographic changes. In 1975 the labor force was 89 percent Caucasian, but currently whites comprise 79 percent

Figure 23.2 **Male and Female Labor Force Participation Rates, Aged 24 to 54, 1948–2012**

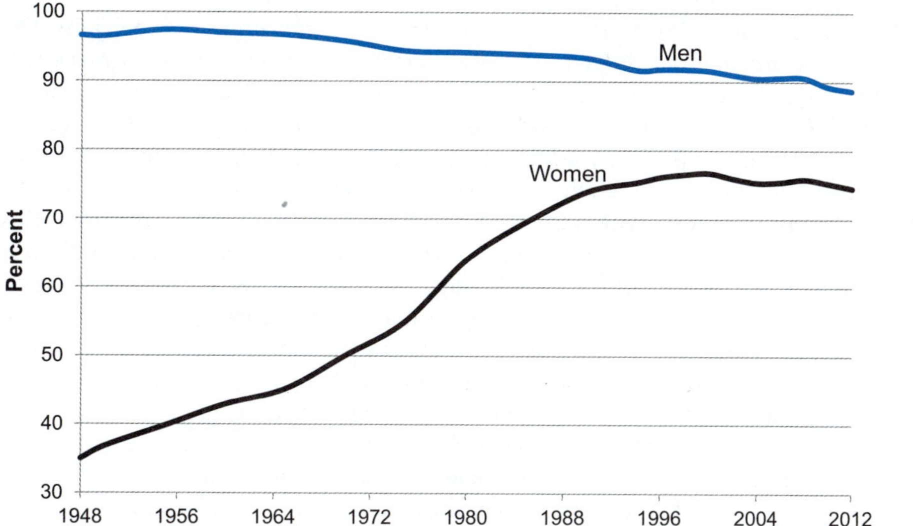

While the labor force participation rate for men has declined slightly over the last several decades, significantly more women have entered the labor force.

Sources: Abraham Mosisa and Steven Hipple, "Trends in Labor Force Participation in the United States," BLS Monthly Labor Review, pp. 35–57, October 2006; BLS 2013 Employment and Earnings Online, Household Survey Data, Table 3; various editions of the Statistical Abstract of the United States.

of the labor force. The number of Hispanics in the labor force increased from 4 percent in 1975 to 16 percent in 2013.

Discussion Questions

1. What was the labor force experience of your grandparents (or others whom you know in that generation? Of your parents (or their generation)? What do you expect your own labor force participation to be like? Do the patterns in your family reflect the national pattern of changes discussed in the text?
2. What evidence have you seen—in your own family or in the media—of increasing "flexibility" in labor markets? Do you think that these changes have been beneficial, harmful, or both?

2. A CLOSER LOOK AT UNEMPLOYMENT

The unemployment rate is one of the most important indicators that economists use to judge the state of a country's economy. As we see below, a degree of unemployment is expected and even considered healthy in an economy. But being unemployed for a long time, against one's wishes, has a significant negative impact on people's well-being, including their mental and physical health.[2]

A recession has a major impact on increasing unemployment. Why do recessions occur? We briefly address this question, which is so central to our understanding of employment and unemployment, leaving a more detailed study of the phenomenon to Part VII of this book.

2.1 TYPES OF UNEMPLOYMENT

Although BLS statisticians are concerned mainly with calculating the number of the unemployed, economists are more concerned with the causes of unemployment. Economists often apply a three-way categorization of types of unemployment, which—while not closely related to BLS categories—can be helpful in thinking about some of the major causes of unemployment.

Frictional Unemployment

frictional unemployment: unemployment that arises as people are in transition between jobs

Frictional (or search) unemployment merely reflects people's transitions between jobs. The fact that some people are unemployed does not necessarily mean that there are no jobs available. In January 2013, for example, while there were 12 million people unemployed, there were also about 3.7 million job vacancies—that is, jobs looking for people! Even in a well-functioning economy, it may take many weeks for people and suitable jobs to find each other. An unemployment rate of 0 percent could only happen if everyone who wants a job always takes one immediately, or at least within the BLS's monthly survey periods. Not only is this unlikely but it is also in some ways undesirable. Everyone benefits if people take the time to find good job matches—work that puts their skills and talents to good use. Because information about job openings takes time to find, and employers may want to spend time interviewing and testing applicants, making a good job match is not an instantaneous process.

For the most part, economists do not worry too much about frictional unemployment because some frictional unemployment—about 2 to 3 percent—is inevitable, and much of it tends to be short term. Things such as innovative Web technologies for matching job offers to job seekers may reduce frictional unemployment by reducing search time.

Many job seekers rely on state unemployment insurance programs to ease their income needs while they spend time searching for work. Unemployment compensation benefits are, in many states, set at half a worker's earnings or a state-set maximum (whichever is less). Until recently, people who qualified for unemployment programs usually received up to twenty-six weeks' worth of benefits. But in the wake of the Great Recession, unemployment benefits were extended, at one time to as long as 99 weeks. Part of the justification for these programs is to allow people the time to find job opportunities—more difficult in a time of high unemployment—and make good matches.

Structural Unemployment

structural unemployment: unemployment that arises because people's skills, experience, education, or location do not match what employers need

Structural unemployment arises when a widespread mismatch occurs between, on the one hand, the kinds of jobs being offered by employers and, on the other, the skills, experience, education, or geographic location of potential employees. One important cause of structural unemployment is sectoral shifts, such as those described in Chapter 22, where employment has been falling (relative to total population size) in the primary and secondary sectors, with the largest number of new jobs opening up in the tertiary (service) sector. The U.S. economy may have a lot of new openings for financial analysts and nurses' aides in the Southwest, for example. But these will not do you much good if you live in the Northeast and your skills are in engine assembly or Web design.

Major transitions in the kinds of work that are available—whether caused by new technologies or by sectoral shifts—are inevitably painful. Many manufacturing jobs have traditionally enjoyed institutional arrangements—including unionization and job characteristics negotiated with the help of unions—that increased the compensation and the quality of those jobs. People who had developed valuable skills in one job may find that their labor commands a lower price in other types of work. Many displaced workers, particularly older ones, may never find the kind of pay and satisfaction that they had at their earlier occupations. Older displaced workers are more likely than younger ones to stay unemployed for long periods or to exit the labor force.

Governments at all levels have tried various policies to prevent or alleviate structural unemployment. The governments of some countries, notably Germany and Japan in the 1980s and 1990s, have enacted industrial policies that directly encourage the development and retention of certain key industries through loans, subsidies, and tax credits. During negotiations on international trade (see Chapter 29), one sensitive issue is always the impact that increased trade might have on the employment levels in various industries in each country.

Government policies in the United States that target structural unemployment often focus on helping displaced workers find new employment. For example, the Trade Adjustment Assistance Reform Act of 2002 provides benefits for certain workers displaced as a result of increased imports or the shifting of production to other countries. Workers who qualify for the program can receive retraining along with temporary income support payments and assistance with health insurance. The key feature of these programs is that they are targeted to particular workers in particular sectors of the economy. There has been some question, however, as to whether they have actually been successful in getting displaced workers into good new jobs. Business policies at the firm level are also relevant: Firms can help prevent structural unemployment if they make retaining or retraining their loyal employees a priority, even while responding to changes in technology and trade.

Cyclical Unemployment

cyclical unemployment: unemployment caused by a drop in aggregate demand

Cyclical unemployment is unemployment due to macroeconomic fluctuations—specifically, unemployment that occurs due to a recession. During recessions, unemployment rises as demand for the products of business falls off. During recoveries, this kind of unemployment should decrease.

recession: traditionally defined as occurring when GDP falls for two consecutive calendar quarters, now "officially" determined by the National Bureau of Economic Research

Traditionally, a **recession** has been defined as a situation in which GDP falls for at least two consecutive calendar quarters. Most economists look to the National Bureau of Economic Research (NBER), a nonprofit and nongovernmental economic research organization, to "officially" mark the beginning and end of recessions. The NBER determinations are strongly based on GDP data, though they also consider other indicators, such as the levels of industrial production and wholesale-retail sales.

Whereas frictional unemployment and a degree of structural unemployment are almost always present in an economy, cyclical unemployment is variable and is the kind of unemployment that can be most harmful both to the individuals and families that it affects and to the economy as a whole. This is why a great deal of macroeconomic theorizing has to do with the causes of cyclical unemployment and the appropriate policy responses. In severe recessions, such as what has come to be called the Great Recession of 2007–8, cyclical unemployment becomes unacceptably high and may remain high even after the economy is no longer formally in recession. This is what has been called a "jobless recovery": Even after GDP starts to recover, job growth is very slow.

As we see later in this and the following chapters, economists have different theories about what to do in response to high unemployment. As discussed in Chapter 19, these debates trace back to the Great Depression of the 1930s and the differences between classical economics and the theories of John Maynard Keynes. We pursue these issues in greater detail starting in Chapter 24. First, we delve into patterns of unemployment and the workings of the labor market.

2.2 Patterns of Unemployment

Figure 23.3 shows the monthly unemployment rate in the United States from January 1969 to February 2013. Unemployment was at a low of 3.4 percent in 1969 and at a high of 10.8 percent in 1982. Notice in the figure that, the U.S. economy experienced four recessions between 1969 and 1982 but only two relatively short recessions between 1983 and 2006.

During the Great Recession, the unemployment rate rose dramatically from less than 5 percent in late 2007 to its peak of 10.0 percent in October 2009. Although by July 2013 the unemployment rate was down to 7.4 percent, it remained high by historical standards. In addition to persistent high unemployment, a particular feature of the Great Recession was a dramatic increase in the average duration of unemployment, shown in Figure 23.4, which plots the average duration of unemployment in addition to the unemployment rate. The figure shows that when the unemployment rate goes up, the average duration of unemployment also rises. When job opportunities are scarcer, it takes longer for workers who lose their jobs to find new ones.

Figure 23.3 **The Monthly Unemployment Rate in the United States, 1969–2013**
(Recessionary periods shaded)

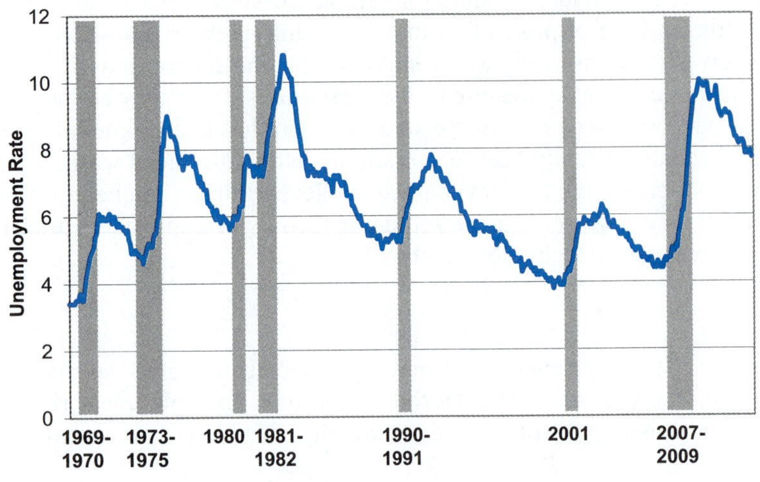

Unemployment rises during recessions (shown in grey), and decreases during economic recoveries.

Source: U.S. Bureau of Labor Statistics online database.

Figure 23.4 **Average Duration of Unemployment and Unemployment Rate, 1969–2013**

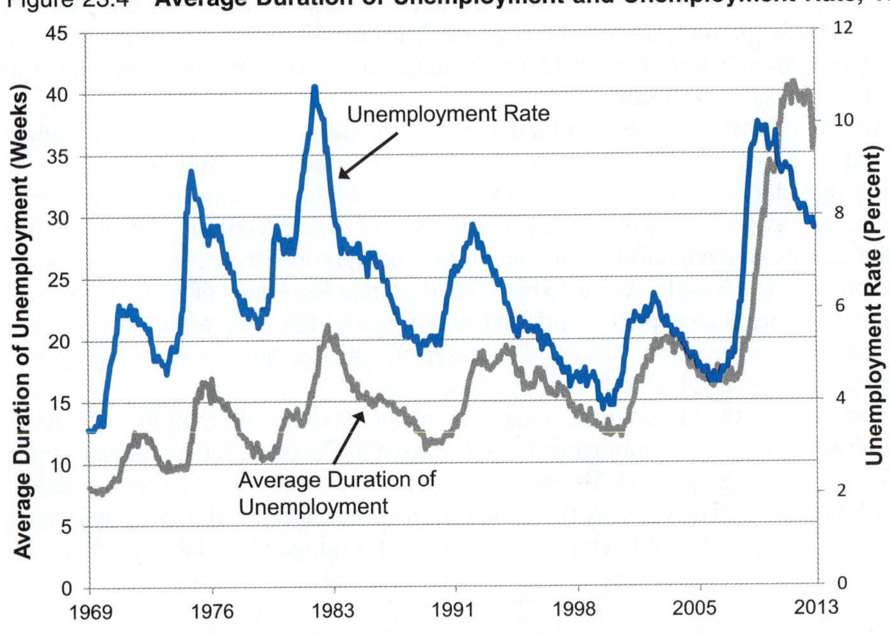

The average duration of unemployment rises along with the unemployment rate. The average duration of unemployment has been particularly long as a result of the Great Recession.

Source: U.S. Bureau of Labor Statistics online database.

We see in Figure 23.4 that even when the unemployment rate exceeded 10 percent in the early 1980s, the average duration of unemployment reached only about 20 weeks. As a result of the recession in the early 2000s, the unemployment rate peaked at around 6 percent and the average duration of unemployment again hit 20 weeks. But as the unemployment rate rose during the Great Recession, the average duration of unemployment shot up dramatically. Even as the unemployment rate began to fall in 2010, the average duration of unemployment continued to rise, eventually reaching a peak of about 41 weeks in late 2011. As mentioned above, the duration of unemployment benefits was temporarily extended to up to 99 weeks in the wake of the Great Recession. (For more on the issue of unemployment duration and benefits, see Box 23.3.)

Box 23.3 Unemployment Benefits and the Great Recession

Before the Great Recession, unemployed workers were eligible to receive up to 26 weeks' worth of unemployment benefits through state-funded programs. An individual's benefits are calculated using state-specific formulas based on his or her earnings while in employment, subject to maximum amounts that also vary by state. The weekly maximum benefit ranges from as much as about $900 in Massachusetts to as little as $250 in Mississippi, Arizona, and Louisiana.

As the economy headed into recession in 2008, Congress passed legislation that provided federal unemployment benefits after state benefits expired. Initially, the federal extension was 13 weeks, but several acts of Congress eventually increased this to as much as 73 weeks. Thus some workers became eligible for unemployment benefits for a total of 99 weeks. The previous record for total unemployment benefits was 65 weeks' worth during a recession in the mid-1970s.

More recently, the federal extension of unemployment benefits has been scaled back—a result of both an improving economy and federal budget cuts. As of August 2013 the availability of federal unemployment benefits varied by state from 14 to 47 weeks, depending on the unemployment rate in each state. Workers in states with the highest unemployment rates are eligible to receive federal benefits for the longest duration.

However, the availability of unemployment benefits in each state is not always directly related to the economic conditions in that state, due to variations in state policies and other complexities. For example, while Alaska has a relative low unemployment rate (6.8 percent in March 2013), it offers benefits for one of the longest periods. Meanwhile, South Carolina has an above-average unemployment rate but provides benefits for a relatively short maximum of 48 weeks.

> The disparity is partly the result of the nation's complex unemployment-insurance system, a web of state and federal programs that wasn't designed for such a long period of high unemployment. . . . The most dramatic recent cuts have been in North Carolina, which recently overhauled its unemployment-insurance system, reducing both the duration and the dollar amount of benefits starting in July. . . . Doug Damato will likely be one of those getting cut off. The 40-year-old Asheville resident was laid off from his job at a local utility in February 2012, and he enrolled in a program to earn an associate's degree in mechanical engineering while receiving jobless benefits. But Mr. Damato is now slated to lose his benefits before he finishes his degree. "I don't know what I'm going to do," Mr. Damato said. "I'd like to be able to finish what I started." (Casselman, 2013)

Sources: Ben Casselman, "Jobless Aid Shrinks Unevenly," *Wall Street Journal,* August 5, 2013; Center on Budget and Policy Priorities, "Policy Basics: How Many Weeks of Unemployment Compensation Are Available?" www.cbpp.org; Tami Luhby, "How Long Should We Help the Unemployed?" CNN Money, December 13, 2011, http://money.cnn.com/2011/12/13/news/economy/unemployment_benefits_extension/index.htm

While structural unemployment affects only some sectors of the economy and some amount of frictional unemployment seems inevitable, cyclical unemployment is spread broadly through the economy and can cause considerable economic hardship. In the wake of the Great Recession, cyclical unemployment persisted at high levels for many years (see Box 23.4). For this reason, it seems that avoiding or minimizing cyclical unemployment should be an important goal of economic policy. Explanations of why macroeconomic fluctuations occur and what kind of policies might be used to dampen them (and thus reduce cyclical unemployment) are discussed in Part VII of this book.

Discussion Questions

1. Reflecting on your experience or that of someone you know, how long might it normally take for someone to find a job in your area? Comparing your answers in a group, do you find different opinions? What might be some of the factors that make frictional unemployment last a longer or shorter period of time?
2. Do you know of places in your city or region (or country) that have been hit particularly hard by unemployment and underemployment, recently or in past decades? Do you know why this hardship occurred? Would you characterize this unemployment as frictional, structural, or cyclical?

BOX 23.4 HIGH UNEMPLOYMENT PROVES PERSISTENT

Employers in the United States added 162,00 jobs in July 2013, fewer than expected, with the previous two months' estimates of job growth revised downward as well. The unemployment rate ticked down from 7.6 to 7.4 percent as people got jobs or dropped out of the labor force.

According to a report by the Economic Policy Institute,

> The labor market began the second half of 2013 with a fizzle. The jobs report released by the Bureau of Labor Statistics shows the addition of 162,000 jobs in July and a 26,000 downward revision to earlier months' data, bringing the average monthly growth rate of the last three months to 175,000 jobs. At this rate, it would take six years to fill the gap of 8.3 million jobs needed to return to a healthy job market.
>
> The unemployment rate dropped from 7.6 to 7.4 percent, but this was largely due to workers dropping out of, or not entering, the labor force because of weak job opportunities. The labor force participation rate dropped to 63.4 percent, near its low of the downturn. The share of the working-age (16+) population with a job did not budge, holding steady at 58.7 percent.

The Economic Policy Institute report noted that unemployment was elevated across all categories of education, age, gender, race/ethnicity, and occupation—a pattern characteristic of cyclical unemployment. The number of people working part-time who wanted full-time jobs increased by 19,000, to 8.2 million, indicating an underemployment rate at a level about double that prior to the downturn. Long-term unemployment was also elevated, with 36.7 percent of unemployed workers having been unemployed for more than six months.

Sources: Catherine Rampell, "U.S. Adds 162,000 Jobs as Growth Remains Sluggish," *New York Times,* August 2, 2013; Heidi Sherholz, "Six Trends in the Jobs Numbers that are Due to Weak Hiring," Economic Policy Institute report, August 2, 2013, www.epi/org.

3. THEORIES OF EMPLOYMENT, UNEMPLOYMENT, AND WAGES

Employment and wages are fundamental components of macroeconomic analysis. As of 2012 income from wages and salaries accounted for 69 percent of national income in the United States. Labor income is what makes it possible for most households to purchase many of the things that they need and want. (The other sources of income mostly derive from various kinds and degrees of ownership of productive assets—such as buildings, land, or other resources or stocks, which are ownership "shares" in companies.) We now take a look at the different explanations for how wages are set and how overall employment and unemployment levels are determined.

3.1 THE CLASSICAL THEORY

You will recall from Chapter 19 that "classical" approaches to economics favor the workings of free markets, without government intervention. The classical approach to understanding wages and employment assumes that markets behave as described by the idealized supply-and-demand model presented in Chapter 4, characterized by perfect competition.

This model, as applied to the labor market, is shown as Figure 23.5a. "Quantity," on the horizontal axis, can be understood to mean either quantity of labor *services* or the amount of labor hours supplied and demanded. We can think of this quantity as being measured, for example, by the number of full-time equivalent days worked over a given time period. The "price" of labor is the wage, in this case, per day (we assume that this is a "real" wage, i.e., adjusted for inflation.) Workers supply labor, while employers demand it. This very simple model assumes that every unit of labor services is the same and every worker in this market will receive exactly the same wage. The equilibrium wage in this example is W_E and the equilibrium quantity of labor supplied is at L_E.

Because the market pictured in Figure 23.5a is free to adjust, there is no involuntary unemployment. Everyone who wants a job at the going wage gets one. There may be many

Figure 23.5a **The Classical Labor Market Model**

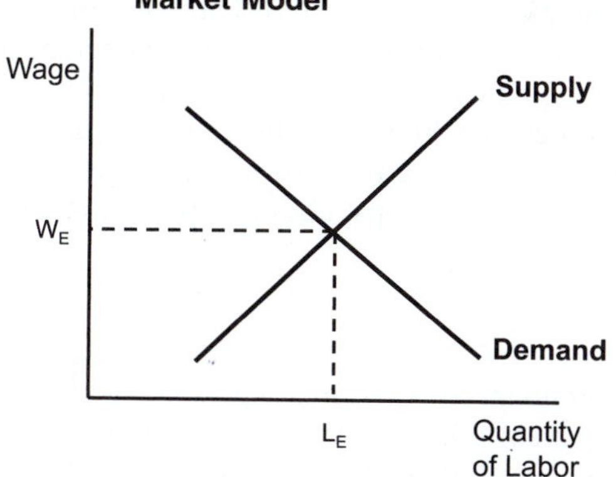

Figure 23.5b **Unemployment in the Classical Labor Market Model**

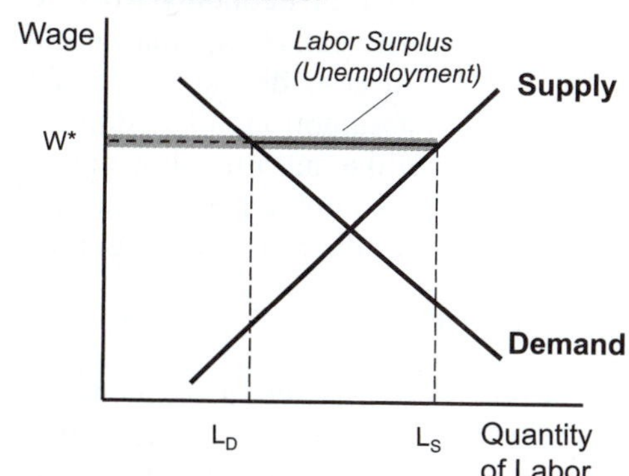

people who would offer their services on this market *if* the wage were higher—as the portion of the supply curve to the right of L_E demonstrates. But, given the currently offered wage rate, these people have made a rational choice not to participate in this labor market.

Within this model, the only way that involuntary unemployment can exist is if something gets in the way of market forces. The presence of a legal minimum wage is commonly pointed to as one such factor. As illustrated in Figure 23.5b, if employers are required to pay a minimum wage of W* ("W-star"), which is above the equilibrium wage, this model predicts that they will hire fewer workers. At an artificially high wage W*, employers want to hire only L_D workers. But at that wage more people (L_S) want jobs. There is a situation of surplus, as we discussed in Chapter 4. In this case, the market is prevented from adjusting to equilibrium by legal restrictions on employers. Now there are people who want a job at the going wage, but cannot find one—that is, they are unemployed.

In the real world, where issues of motivation, labor relations, and power are also important, the classical idea that minimum wages cause substantial unemployment can be called into question. In a well-known study, economists David Card and Alan Krueger found that a moderate increase in the minimum wage in New Jersey did not cause low-wage employment to decline and may have even increased it.[3] The study came under fire from economists who believed (given the analysis shown in Figure 23.5a) that such a result simply could not be true. But the classical world assumes perfect competition, whereas real-world employers may have enough power in the labor market to be able to pay workers less than they are worth. Labor markets seem to be more complicated than a simple supply-and-demand model suggests.

In any case, the minimum wage affects only a portion of the workforce—people who are relatively unskilled, including many teenagers—but unemployment tends to affect people at all wage levels. Classical economists suggest other "market interference" reasons for unemployment, as well. The economy might provide less than the optimal number of jobs, they believe, because:

- Regulations on businesses reduce their growth, restricting growth in the demand for labor
- Labor union activities and labor-related regulations (such as safety regulations, mandated benefits, or restrictions on layoffs and dismissals) increase the cost of labor to businesses, causing them to turn toward labor-saving technologies and thus reducing job growth
- Public "safety net" policies, such as disability insurance and unemployment insurance, reduces employment by causing people to become less willing to seek work.

Labor-market recommendations derived from a classical point of view tend to focus on getting rid of regulations and social programs that are seen as obstructing proper market behavior. Like other classical proposals, such labor market proposals assume that the economy works best under the principle of laissez-faire ("leave it alone"). But alternative explanations of the workings of labor markets suggest a different perspective. In considering some of these alternative explanations, we will step away from the assumptions of a single, homogeneous market in which all jobs and all workers are alike and the labor market is characterized by perfect competition. Labor markets are also influenced by many other factors, including history, psychology, power, resources, productivity, and technology.

3.2 ALTERNATIVE PERSPECTIVES ON LABOR MARKETS

In Chapter 19, we identified the Keynesian (pronounced "Canesian") perspective as a major alternative to the classical view. Keynes, among many other economists, pointed out aspects of real-world human psychology, history, and institutions that make it unlikely (as well as often undesirable) that wages will fall quickly in response to a labor surplus. Wages may eventually adjust in the way shown in the classical model but too slowly to keep the labor market in equilibrium. And even if wages do fall, this will not necessarily result in full employment, for reasons we will discuss.

"sticky wage" theories: theories about why wages stay at above-equilibrium levels, despite the existence of a labor surplus

efficiency wage theory: the theory that an employer can motivate workers to put forth more effort by paying them somewhat more than they could get elsewhere

The incidence of unemployment, as well as the different rates of pay going to different groups, has much to do with people's memory of recent history. When one category of work is paid more highly than another, people who were receiving those higher wages are often able to hold out for a long time against other forces (including supply and demand) that would tend to reverse the relationship. Employers may be slow to reduce wages because they fear that workers will strongly resist such a move—perhaps with strikes or other labor actions. The observed failure of wages to adjust as quickly or completely as predicted has inspired a number of theoretical explanations. Some of these fall into the category of **"sticky wage" theories.** In addition to psychological resistance to wage cuts, a minimum wage might also make wages "sticky," or wages may also become set at particular levels by long-term contracts, such as many large employers negotiate with labor unions.

A fairly recent attempt to explain wages that differ from the equilibrium point is efficiency wage theory, which points out that managers must attract, train, and motivate workers if their enterprise is to be productive. Employers may therefore find it to their advantage to pay employees more than would be strictly necessary to get them to work. This theory can be illustrated by looking back at Figure 23.5a, where W* could be read as the **efficiency wage**.

Efficiency wage theory is a good fit with many observations. When workers are better paid they may be healthier and better nourished and therefore more able to do quality work. (This is especially true when talking about wage rates at the low end of the scale.) Also, workers may be more highly motivated and may have a lower propensity to quit if they know they are getting "a really good deal" from their employer than they would be if they are getting barely enough to motivate them to take the job or just the same as they could get anywhere else. Workers with a lower likelihood of quitting are more valuable to an employer because the employer saves on the costs of training new workers. Workers may also work more efficiently if they believe that they could lose their "really good deal" if they are caught shirking. If a pool of unemployed people results from the higher-than-necessary efficiency wages, those who are employed might have greater incentives to work hard out of fear of losing their good jobs.

Legally or contractually set wages, fear of worker unrest, and efficiency wages are all possible explanations for "sticky wages." What sort of policies result from such theories? More government activity to relieve unemployment-related hardship may be proposed, such as the policies we discuss in Part VII of this book, or programs of unemployment benefits or job creation.

Some economists also argue that a moderate level of economy-wide price inflation tends to relieve some "sticky wage" unemployment. How could this be so? Suppose that you are working for $12 per hour now, and your employer wants to cut your wage to $10 per hour. You would probably resist if asked to accept this wage cut—especially if you see that other people are not suffering such wage cuts. But suppose, instead, that your wage stays at $12 per hour, and, over time, inflation reduces the purchasing power of your wage to $10 per hour (in terms of prices of the base year). Your nominal wage has stayed the same, but your real wage (and thus your real cost to your employer) has fallen. Because this has happened more subtly—and is felt more economy-wide—than a cut in your personal nominal wage, you may not feel as compelled to resist. According to some theories, such a drop in the wage (in real terms) should cause employment to increase.

While some Keynesian theorists emphasize sticky wages, Keynes's critique of classical views actually went much further. In more general terms, the Keynesian perspective challenges the entire classical assertion that unemployment results mainly from wage levels that are too high. Rather than blaming unemployment on "the wage being too high," Keynes and his followers focus on the issue of insufficient demand for labor—which they perceive as the direct result of *insufficient demand for goods and services.* (It is often said that "the demand for labor is a derived demand"—meaning that it is derived from the demand for the output produced by labor.)

aggregate demand: the total demand for all goods and services in a national economy

Thus, to Keynes and his followers, fixing the problem of unemployment in a recession or depression is not just a matter of making labor markets work more smoothly. Rather, total demand—what economists refer to as **aggregate demand**—for goods and services in the economy has to increase in order to stimulate hiring. In this analysis, falling wages would not improve labor market conditions but would make things worse, because workers would have less money to buy goods and services, leading to lower levels of business sales and further layoffs. Unlike the classical economists, Keynes believed that government policies could be effective in response to an economic downturn. We consider these theories and policies in Part VII of this book.

3.3 Longer Term Issues: Productivity, Resources, and Technology

An important macroeconomic issue is the share of total income received by labor. Data that track the share of national income received as wages indicate that this share has declined in recent years. In the nonfarm business sector (which accounts for roughly 74 percent of the output produced in the U.S. economy), labor's share of total income tended, before 1980, to fluctuate around a long-run value of approximately 65 percent. By 2012 it had decreased to 57.6 percent.

labor productivity: the market value of the output that results from a given amount of labor

One explanation for this could be that workers have become less productive—but statistics on average output per hour worked indicate that wages have in fact not been keeping up with growing labor productivity. The formal definition of **labor productivity** is the market value of the output of a given amount of labor, normally one hour. Productivity growth in the nonfarm business sector averaged 2.7 percent annually before 1973, then 1.4 percent during a slowdown in productivity growth over 1974–1995, and 2.3 percent from 1996 to 2012.

wage-productivity gap: the gap between the growth of labor productivity and the growth of hourly labor compensation

As labor becomes more productive, one would expect that wages would rise accordingly. As shown in Figure 23.6, which presents the growth of nonfarm labor productivity and nonfarm real median hourly wages since 1947, this was approximately true from 1947 up to until about 1970. Over this period, wages and productivity both increased by a real factor of about two. But since then, a gap between productivity growth and real wage growth became evident. This **wage-productivity gap** has increased over time.

As suggested in Chapter 10, the decline in the bargaining power of unions in the United States is one obvious explanation for the widening wage-productivity gap. Workers have not

Figure 23.6 **Real Nonfarm Median Wages and Labor Productivity, 1947–2012**

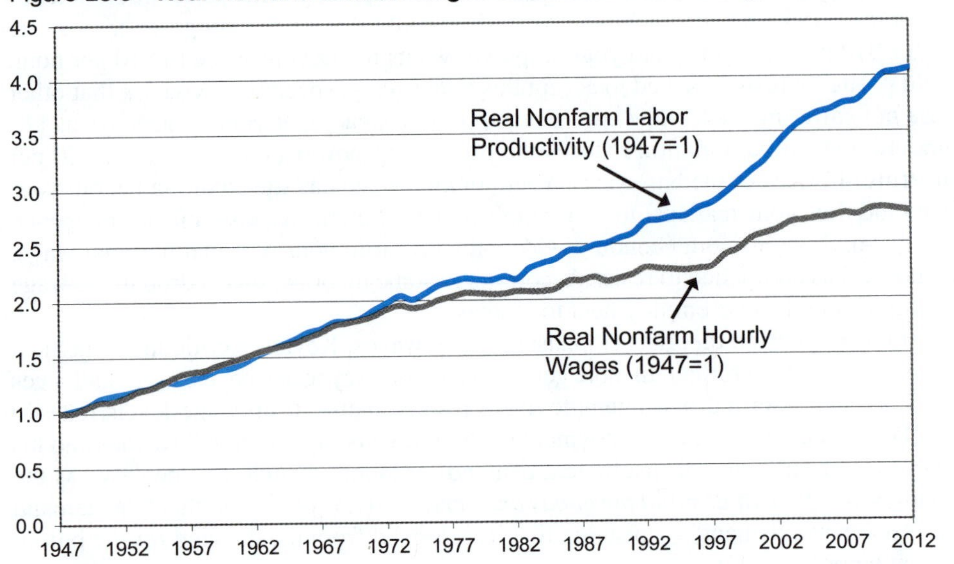

Median wages increased along with labor productivity from 1947 up to about 1970. Since then, wage growth has not kept pace with productivity gains.

Source: U.S. Bureau of Labor Statistics, Labor Productivity and Costs online database.

had the power to insist that their wages keep up with the increasing value of their output. At the same time, when we consider the share of income going to labor, we also must realize that the productivity of labor depends in part on other aspects of production.

There are a number of important determinants of labor productivity, including health and education (as aspects of human capital), work organization, and levels of cooperation in the workplace (which are aspects of social capital). This section focuses on two other determinants of labor productivity: technology, which can expand the stocks of manufactured, human, and social capital; and natural resources.

Technology and Wages

Obviously, a main reason for the upward trend in labor productivity shown in Figure 23.6 is an improvement in technology. But can technology also be part of the reason that median wages have not kept pace with productivity gains?

technological unemployment: unemployment caused by reduced demand for workers because technology has increased the productivity of those who have jobs, effectively reducing the demand for workers

Ever since the beginning of the Industrial Revolution, technology has been recognized by workers as a double-edged sword. On the one hand, it has created circumstances wherein each worker has more natural and manufactured capital to work with, raising workers' productivity and hence their earnings. On the other hand, technology can effectively replace workers, leading to **technological unemployment**; ever fewer workers are needed to produce a given quantity of output.

Fears of technological unemployment have been raised repeatedly during the last two and a half centuries. While these fears have been valid in specific areas—for example, computers have made many secretarial jobs obsolete—the total quantity of jobs has not declined as a proportion of the population. Indeed, in the twentieth century, the number of jobs in the United States increased significantly, as women successfully entered the labor force and increased the LFP rate, as mentioned above. Technological unemployment, to those who experience it, is as painful as any other type of unemployment; however, it does not become a society-wide issue if the total number of jobs keeps pace with the size of the population, and education or retraining provides workers who can adapt to the new circumstances.

skill-biased technical change: the theory that relative wage gains will be the greatest for those workers who possess the education and skills to use modern technologies

Technology can also affect wages and the distribution of wages across different types of workers. One theory, referred to as **skill-biased technical change**, proposes that workers who possess the education and skills needed to use modern technologies will see relative increases in employment and wages. For example, workers who are able to use computers and other digital technologies may gain an advantage over workers who lack such skills. If these skilled workers are a minority of the work force, they could obtain wage gains while most workers' wages stagnate. Note that *average* wages may increase while the *median* wage stays relatively constant if all the gains accrue to those at the top.* Skill-biased technical change has been hypothesized to be one of the reasons for an overall increase in inequality in the United States.

Evidence suggests that skill-biased technical change may be part of the explanation for rising wage inequality, but it may be a less important factor particularly in recent years. A 2012 paper notes:

> It is hard, however, to find the winners from technical change in the last ten years, as the wages of the bottom 70 per cent of college graduates have been flat or in decline. That would leave just 30 per cent of college graduates (6.6 per cent of the workforce) and the 11 per cent of workers with advanced degrees as the winners of technical change. It also seems unlikely that technical change has generated the upward trajectory of the top 1 per cent of wage earners.[4]

Natural Resources and Wages

The availability and prices of natural resources can also affect wages. Labor and natural resources represent two inputs in production processes, along with other types of capital, so productivity depends on a combination of inputs.

First, consider the possibility that natural resources are becoming scarcer and/or more expensive to extract, as discussed in Chapter 19. If natural resources, as one input into production processes, become more expensive, producers will seek to substitute other inputs that have become relatively less expensive. Thus the demand for labor would be expected to increase, and wages should rise. But we also have to consider the macroeconomic impact of a rise in natural resource prices. In recent years, higher prices for oil and other natural resources have had a negative impact on economic activity, contributing to higher unemployment.

As mentioned above, technology also represents an input into production processes. If natural resources become more expensive, that creates an incentive for research into ways to use these resources more efficiently, or to seek substitutes. Technological improvements or resource substitution could offset the negative impacts of natural resource scarcity on wages and the overall economy.

Productivity gains could also be the basis for reducing work hours. Figure 23.6 shows that labor productivity doubled between the mid-1970s and 2012. One interpretation of this result is that the United States can now produce twice the quantity of goods and services with the same amount of labor used in the 1970s. But an alternative possibility is that we can now produce the same quantity of goods and services produced in the 1970s, but with *half the amount of labor.*

Consider this statement in light of the notion of labor flexibility discussed earlier in the chapter. Suppose that workers had the choice between taking productivity gains as either wage increases or labor time decreases. Theoretically, American workers could be living at the same material living standards of the 1970s, but working only six months of every year! Of course, some workers may always choose more pay over shorter hours,

*The median wage is the wage received by workers at the exact middle of the wage distribution. Thus the median wage can remain constant or decline while wages in the top half of the distribution increase.

but allowing for more work choice accords with standard economic theory, stated as follows:

> According to economic theory, we should let each worker choose how many hours to work. If workers choose shorter hours, it is because they get greater satisfaction from more free time than they would get from more income. According to the basic principle of market economics, interfering with individuals' choices between more free time and more income reduces total well being, just as interfering with individuals' choices between two products would reduce total well being by forcing some people to buy the product that gives them less.[5]

Assuming that many workers are willing to work shorter hours for an equivalent reduction in pay, as mentioned in Section 2.2, this would reduce their overall consumption and thus rates of natural resource degradation and extraction.

Currently in the United States, part-time jobs are much less attractive than full-time jobs because hourly wages are often low and few benefits are provided. Some countries have enacted policies to promote higher-quality part-time jobs. One example is the Netherlands where discrimination against part-time workers is illegal and employers must offer the option of shorter work hours unless they can prove that it would impose an economic hardship on their business.

Box 23.5 What Is the Future of Work?

Discussions about the future of work tempt us to try to imagine what a better world would be like and to ask ourselves whether the economy of the future is trending in such a direction. Questions along these lines were posed to Andres McAfee, an MIT business school researcher who coauthored the book *Race Against the Machine*. Asked for an optimistic view of the future, McAfee described a "digital Athens" in which a highly automated and productive economy would greatly reduce the need for human labor—"So the optimistic version is that we finally have more hours in our week freed up from toil and drudgery." When asked if he saw a digital Athens on the horizon, he responded that, instead, "the people at the top of the skill, wage, and income distribution are working more hours," while added leisure is going to those who don't want it—the unemployed.

McAfee was also asked: "What is your advice to the individual, or to the parent educating a child?" His response: "To the parent, make sure your kid's education is geared toward things at which machines appear not to be very good. Computers are still lousy at programming computers. Computers are still bad at figuring out what questions need to be asked. I would encourage every kid these days to buckle down and do a double major, one in the liberal arts and one in the college of sciences."

Source: "When Machines Do Your Job," interview with Andres McAfee, *Technology Review* (September/October 2012): 71.

Some analysts have proposed that giving people more flexibility to set their work hours is an important way to achieve a more sustainable society (see Box 23.5). We will discuss the issue of policies needed for sustainability in more detail in Chapter 33.

Discussion Questions

1. Which arguments seem most convincing to you, those of classical labor market theorists, "sticky wage" theorists, or economists concerned with aggregate demand? What are some strengths and weaknesses of each argument?
2. Can you think of other impacts, positive and negative, of allowing workers more flexibility in setting their work hours? Would you support any specific policies to promote more choice of work hours?

REVIEW QUESTIONS

1. What population is included in the official household survey that measures employment and unemployment?
2. What questions are asked to determine whether someone is "employed"?
3. What makes a person count as "unemployed"?
4. How is the unemployment rate calculated?
5. What are marginally attached workers? Discouraged workers?
6. What does employment flexibility mean from the perspective of workers? From the perspective of employers?
7. What is the labor force participation rate and how is it calculated? How has it changed in recent decades for men and women in the United States?
8. How can high levels of unemployment be explained in the Keynesian model?
9. List and describe the three types of unemployment.
10. What policies may be used to combat frictional and structural unemployment?
11. What is the relationship between the average duration of unemployment and the unemployment rate?
12. Describe the classical theory of unemployment.
13. What are some of the reasons that an economy might offer less than the optimal number of jobs, according to classical theory?
14. Describe how "sticky wages" could lead to unemployment.
15. What are some reasons that wages might be "sticky"?
16. What are "efficiency wages," and why might payment of them lead to unemployment?
17. What has been the relationship between labor productivity and median wages in the United States since World War II?
18. How can changes in technology affect prevailing wage rates?
19. What is skill-biased technical change?
20. How can the price and availability of natural resources affect prevailing wage rates?

EXERCISES

1. The small country of Nederland counts its unemployed using the same methods as the United States. Of the population of 350 people, 70 are under age 16, 190 are employed in paid work, and 80 are adults who are not doing paid work or looking for work because they are doing full-time family care, are retired or disabled, or are in school. The rest are unemployed. (No one is institutionalized, and the country has no military.) Calculate the following:
   a. The number of unemployed
   b. The size of the labor force
   c. The unemployment rate
   d. The labor force participation rate (overall, for both sexes)
2. The population of Tatoonia is very small. Luis works full-time for pay. Robin works one shift a week as counter help at a fast-food restaurant. Sheila is retired. Shawna does not work for pay, but is thinking about getting a job and has been looking through employment postings to see what is available. Bob has given up looking for work, after months of not finding anything. Ana, the only child in the country, is 12 years old.
   a. How would a household survey, following U.S. methods, classify each person?
   b. What is the labor force participation rate in Tatoonia?
   c. What is the unemployment rate in Tatoonia?
3. Suppose an economy is suffering unemployment due to wages that are "too high," as theorized by classical economists.
   a. Draw and label a graph illustrating this case, in which the going wage is $20, the equilibrium wage is $15, 50 million people want to work, but only 30 million are employed.
   b. Describe some of the assumptions about labor markets that underlie this graph.
4. A computer software company advertises for employees, saying "We offer the best-paid jobs in the industry!" But why would any company want to pay more than it absolutely *has to* in order to attract workers? Can this phenomenon help to explain the existence of unemployment? Explain in a paragraph.
5. Locate the most recent news release on employment and unemployment statistics at the Bureau of Labor Statistics Web site (www.bls.gov). In a paragraph, describe how the labor force, overall unemployment rate, and unemployment rates by race and ethnicity, age, and education differ from the numbers (for February 2013) given in the text.

(continued)

6. Match each concept in Column A with a definition or example in Column B.

Column A	Column B
a. "Not in the labor force"	1. The theory that unemployment is caused by insufficient aggregate demand
b. Classical labor market theory	2. Occurs during a recession
c. Marginally attached workers	3. An example of an employment flexibility policy
d. Frictional unemployment	4. Occurs when the skills, experience, and education of workers do not match job openings
e. Employed	5. Wages and employment levels are determined by supply and demand, with no involuntary unemployment
f. Trade Adjustment Assistance Reform Act	6. Immediately available for and currently looking for paid work
g. Unemployed	7. Military personnel
h. "Sticky wages"	8. A policy response to structural unemployment
i. Structural unemployment	9. Worked 15 hours or more in a family business
j. Keynesian theory	10. Occurs as people move between jobs
k. Cyclical unemployment	11. Want to work and have looked in the past year but not the past month
l. Not included in the household survey covering employment	12. Unemployment may occur because wages are slow to fall
m. Technological unemployment	13. Occurs when technology reduces the overall need for workers
n. Paid parental leave	14. A retired person

Notes

1. Rasmussen Reports, "New Low: Just 14% Think Today's Children Will Be Better Off Than Their Parents," July 29, 2012. http://www.rasmussenreports.com/.

2. Rainer Winkelmann, "Unemployment, Social Capital, and Subjective Well-Being," IZA Discussion Paper No. 2346, Bonn, Germany, September 2006.

3. David Card and Alan B. Krueger, "Minimum Wages and Employment: A Case Study of the Fast-Food Industry in New Jersey and Pennsylvania," *American Economic Review,* 84(4) (1994): 774–775.

4. Lawrence Mishel and Kar-Fai Gee, "Why Aren't Workers Benefiting from Labour Productivity Growth in the United States?" *International Productivity Monitor,* 23 (2012): 31–43.

5. Charles Siegel, *The End of Economic Growth* (Berkeley, CA: Preservation Institute, Berkeley, CA 2006), p. 29.

Macroeconomic Theory and Policy

24 Aggregate Demand and Economic Fluctuations

What makes an economy experience GDP expansion or contraction, high or low employment, and good or bad business conditions? These questions have been very much in the forefront of discussion in the United States and many other countries since the financial crisis of 2007–8, the ensuing recession, widely known as the Great Recession, and the slow recovery that followed. In a sophisticated contemporary economy such as that in the United States, a decline in demand for goods and services by consumers and businesses generally leads to recessionary conditions and higher unemployment. In Chapter 30 we discuss the events of the financial crisis and its aftermath in more detail. But before getting into these specifics, we need to develop a general theory of how the demand for goods and services varies over time and how this affects economic conditions.

1. The Business Cycle

Part VII of this textbook focuses in particular on the goal of economic stabilization—that is, keeping unemployment and inflation at acceptable levels over the business cycle. For the moment, we set aside consideration of our two other goals—the goal of improvement in true living standards and the goal of maintaining the ecological, social, and financial sustainability of a national economy—to focus on stabilization. As we see, one crucial key to understanding macroeconomics is how the amount that individuals and businesses want to spend overall (or "aggregate demand," as we called it in Chapter 19) influences, and is influenced by, other macroeconomic variables. One of the key debates in macroeconomic policy is between Keynesians, who believe that aggregate demand needs active guidance if the economy is to be stable, and more classically-oriented economists, who believe that aggregate demand can take care of itself.

In Chapter 19 we introduced the notion of the "business cycle," while in Chapter 23 we considered in detail how employment and unemployment vary over the cycle. Now we look in more detail at business cycles, or recurrent fluctuations in the level of national production, with alternating periods of recession and boom.

1.1 What Happens During the Business Cycle

Figure 24.1 shows the pattern of real GDP growth over the period 1985–2012. In most years, as you can see, GDP grew. But during three periods—1990–91, and 2001, and 2007–9—GDP shrank. The level of real GDP actually went *down* from one calendar quarter to the next. As noted in Chapter 23, the National Bureau of Economic Research (NBER) declares a "recession" when economic activity declines for two consecutive quarters, relying on GDP statistics to make this judgment.

In other periods, you can see that GDP grew quite steadily. The positive GDP growth beginning in 2002 shown in Figure 24.1 continued well into 2007, but in 2007–8 the financial

Figure 24.1 **U.S. Real GDP and Recessions**

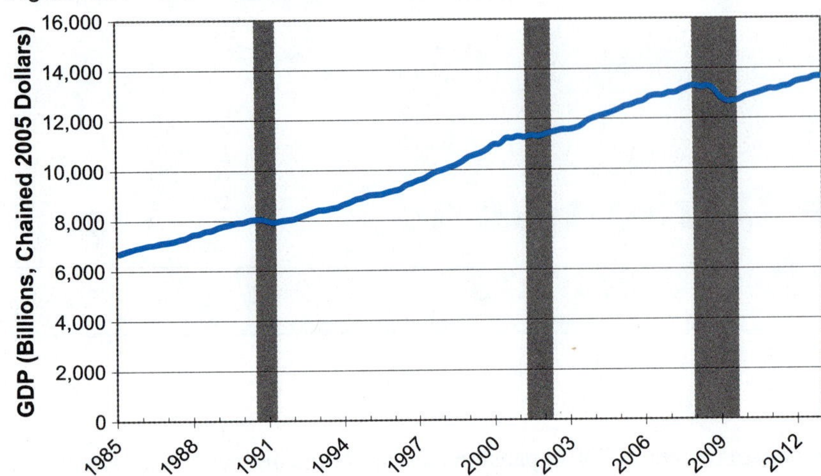

During 1985–2012, the United States experienced three recessions, as defined by the National Bureau of Economics Research. During these periods, real GDP fell.

Source: BEA quarterly data 1985–2012, and NBER.

crisis hit, and the economy plunged into a severe recession, lasting from December 2007 to June 2009. After the recession technically ended, it took several years for GDP to recover to its previous level, and as discussed in the last chapter, high unemployment lingered much longer. The goal of macroeconomic stabilization policy is to smooth out such variations.

As we discuss the ins and outs of stabilization policy, you need to keep in mind two "stylized facts." Economists call these "stylized facts" because, while they form a very important base for the way we think about the economy, they are not always literally true. Just as we use simplifying assumptions in microeconomics to draw supply and demand curves, we start from a simplified version of reality in constructing our macroeconomic theory.

Stylized Fact #1: During an economic downturn or contraction, unemployment rises, while in a recovery or expansion, unemployment falls. This is fairly easy to understand, since, when production in an economy is falling, it would seem natural to assume that producers need fewer workers—because they are producing fewer goods. Similarly, in an expansion, unemployment falls.* This relationship is sometimes expressed by an equation called **Okun's law**. In the early 1960s, economist Arthur M. Okun estimated that a one-percentage point drop in the unemployment rate was associated with an approximately 3-percentage point boost to real GDP. The equation for Okun's "law" has been estimated many times since then, and in many different variations, and is best regarded as a rule of thumb rather than a "law."

Okun's "law": an empirical inverse relationship between the unemployment rate and real GDP growth

We can see some strong evidence of this inverse relationship between output growth and employment by comparing Figure 24.1 with Figure 24.2, which shows the unemployment rate from 1985 to 2012, including the three recessions that occurred during this period, as identified by the NBER. As output turns downward in Figure 24.1, unemployment shoots dramatically upward in Figure 24.2. The inverse relation, however, is not perfect. In all three recessions, the unemployment rate continued to increase even after GDP started to rise again. But with the exception of the periods immediately following a recession, rising GDP is generally associated with increased employment.

Stylized Fact #2: An economic recovery or expansion, if it is very strong, tends to lead to an increase in the inflation rate. During a downturn or contraction, pressure on inflation eases off (and inflation may fall or even become negative). The reasoning behind this result is that, as an economy "heats up," producers increasingly compete with one another over a

*In a "jobless recovery," real GDP growth is slow (below average), so it does not create jobs fast enough to counteract the normal increase in the labor force due to population growth and decrease in labor demand due to increased output per worker.

Figure 24.2 **U.S. Unemployment Rate and Recessions**

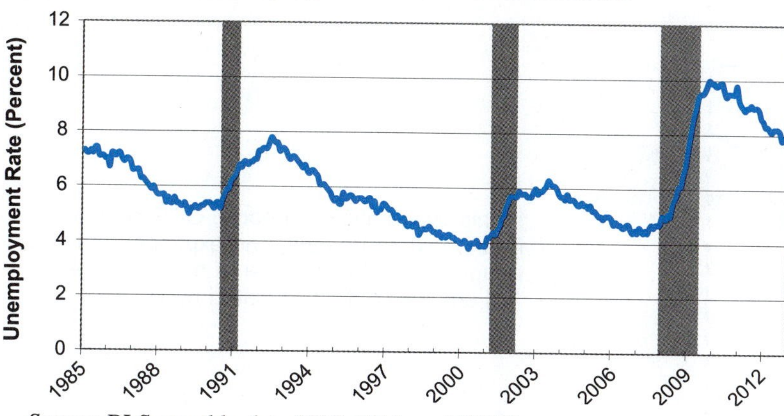

Source: BLS monthly data 1985–2012, and NBER.

During the 1990–1991, 2001, and 2007–9 recessions, unemployment shot up sharply and continued to increase after the recession formally ended, reaching a peak of 10 percent in 2010.

Figure 24.3 **U.S. Inflation Rate and Recessions**

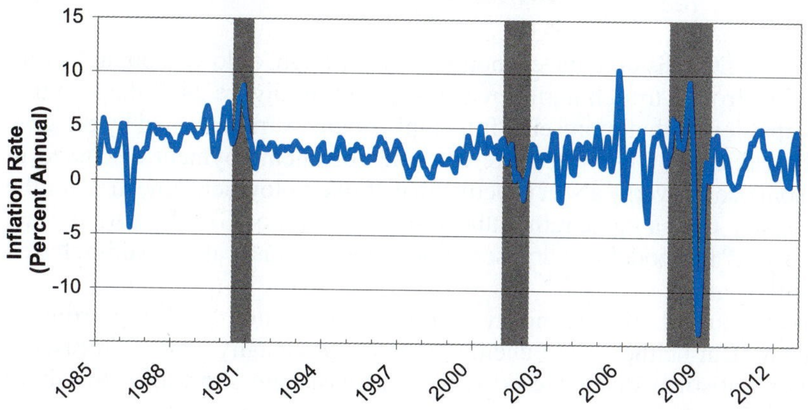

Source: "Economic Report of the President" 1985–2005; rate is calculated as a three-month moving average of the CPI; NBER.

During the 1990–91, 2001, and 2007–9 recessions, inflation fell sharply. Inflation generally reflects the business cycle, along with other factors.

limited supply of raw materials, labor, and so on. Prices and wages tend to be bid up, and inflation results or intensifies. In a slump, this upward pressure on prices slackens, or even reverses, so inflation may be lower or even, in some cases, negative (deflation). Figure 24.3 shows the inflation rate over the period 1985–2012, including the same three recessions highlighted in Figures 24.1 and 24.2.

As you can see, the "stylized fact" that inflation tends to fall during a recession seems to be borne out by the actual data for this period. The three recessions shown in Figure 24.3 were accompanied by distinct downturns in the inflation rate. But wide fluctuations in the inflation rate also occurred during other periods, with both increases and downturns occurring during economic upswings. Business cycle–led variations in the degree of competition for workers and resources are only *one* cause—and, in recent decades, not always the most important cause—of variations in inflation. We look at this issue more closely in Chapters 27 and 28. But for the discussion of business cycles in this and the following two chapters, we assume that booms lead to at least a threat of rising inflation.

1.2 A Stylized Business Cycle

When analyzing business cycles, it is often convenient to separate the issue of economic fluctuations from the issue of economic growth. In Figure 24.1 the most striking pattern is the overall growth trend in GDP. For the analysis in Part VII of this book, it will be more helpful to mentally remove the upward trend and to think of business cycles in terms of the stylized picture shown in Figure 24.4. (We return to the subjects of growth and development in Part VIII.)

Figure 24.4 **A Stylized Business Cycle**

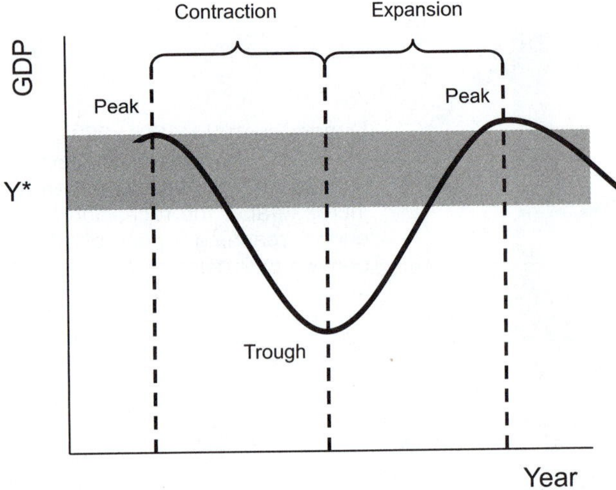

In this hypothetical economy, GDP contracts from peaks to troughs, and expands from troughs to peaks. A range of output indicating "full employment" is indicated by Y*.

"full-employment output" (Y*): for modeling purposes, a level of output that is assumed to correspond to a case of no excessive or burdensome unemployment, but the likely existence of at least some transitory unemployment

During a contraction, GDP falls until the economy hits the trough, or lowest point. During an expansion, GDP rises from a trough until it reaches a peak. In Figure 24.4, the idea that there is a range of output levels that represent "full employment" is represented by the gray area labeled with the value Y^*. Given the different kinds of unemployment discussed in Chapter 23, there is some controversy about exactly what "full employment" means over the business cycle, so we have used a range rather than a specific level of GDP here to indicate **"full-employment output"** for modeling purposes. (Sometimes you may also see this referred to as "potential output.")

At full-employment output, the economy is, presumably, not suffering from an unemployment problem. But neither is the unemployment rate actually zero (as measured by the Bureau of Labor Statistics), due to the existence of at least some short-term, transitory or "frictional," unemployment.

What economists generally do agree on is that there have been—historically, at least—episodes when economies have "overheated" and output has gone above this range—giving rise (by Stylized Fact #2) to inflationary pressures. Thus Figure 24.4 shows employment at the peak levels at the top of, or possibly slightly exceeding, the "full employment" band. And there have also been times when economies have fallen into troughs, with (due to Stylized Fact #1) unacceptable levels of unemployment. In terms of the business cycle model shown in Figure 24.4, the goal of stabilization policy is to keep an economy in the gray area, avoiding the threats of inflation and unemployment.

1.3 The Downturn Side of the Story

It will take this entire chapter and the next four to build up a workable theory of the business cycle! Because this is a large and complex topic, we need to take things one step at a time. We start by looking at the case of economic downturns.

The biggest downturn in U.S. history was, of course, the Great Depression. Production dropped dramatically from 1929 to 1930 and officially measured national unemployment soared, topping out at 25 percent. Some regions were especially hard-hit, with unemployment rates above the national average, and severe underemployment as well. Not only were times bad—they stayed bad. Unemployment stayed in the double digits all through the 1930s.

Nor was the Great Depression just a U.S. phenomenon. Most of this country's major trading partners were also hard-hit. Table 24.1 presents some additional descriptive data about the falloff in economic activity in the United States, and resulting hardships, during the Great Depression.

Table 24.1 **The Early Years of the Great Depression in the United States**

	1929	1933
a. Real Standard and Poor's Stock Index	100.0	45.7
b. Unemployment rate (official)	3.2%	24.9%
c. Price level (CPI)	100.0	75.4
d. Real gross domestic product	$865.2 billion	$635.5 billion
e. Real personal consumption expenditures	$661.4 billion	$541.0 billion
f. Real gross private domestic investment	$91.3 billion	$17 billion
g. Real private debt	$88.9 billion	$102.0 billion
h. Bankruptcy cases	56,867	67,031
i. Nonfarm real estate foreclosures	134,900	252,400
j. Food energy per capita per day (calories)	3,460	3,280

Sources: a. *Historical Statistics of the United States,* p. 1004, series X495; b–c. Rudiger Dornbusch, Stanley Fischer, and Richard Startz, *Macroeconomics.* New York: McGraw Hill, 2011; d–f. www.bea.doc.gov/bea/dn/nipaweb/TableView.asp#Mid/; g. *Historical Statistics of the United States,* p. 989, series X399; h. Bradley Hansen and Mary Eschenbach Hansen, *The Transformation of Bankruptcy in the United States* (http://academic2.american.edu/~mhansen/transform.pdf); i. *Historical Statistics of the United States,* p. 651, series N301; j. ibid., p. 328, series 851; d and e are inflation-corrected using b.

Another severe economic downturn hit the United States beginning in 2007. While not as serious as the Great Depression, this "Great Recession" resembled it in that, unlike most recessions of the past, it persisted for more than a few quarters. Even after the economy formally left recession and entered recovery, employment growth was very slow. This severe recession was caused in large part by the financial crisis of 2007 and illustrates the vulnerability of the U.S. economy to excess "financialization," a topic that we discussed in Chapter 22, and to which we return in Chapter 30.

Notice that in our stylized business cycle in Figure 24.4 there is no scale on the "year" axis. The timing of the cycle is not regular or predictable, so economists in the early years of the Great Depression differed on how to interpret it. Most economists in the 1930s, trained in the classical school, reassured public leaders that this sort of cycle was merely to be expected. They believed that the economy was in the "trough" stage but that it would soon start to expand again. In the long run, they assured officials, the economy would recover by itself, as it had recovered from other downturns in the past.

In response, British economist John Maynard Keynes quipped that "in the long run, we are all dead." He meant that simply waiting for the economy to recover would lead to an unacceptably long period of severe economic damage—which indeed is what happened during the Great Depression. In 1936 Keynes presented a theory on how economies can fall into recessions and stay there for a long time—and some ideas about how public policy might help economies get out of the trough more quickly. We start our detailed study of business cycle theory with models that illustrate classical and Keynesian theories concerning recession and depressions.

Discussion Questions

1. What impressions do you have of the Great Recession that began in 2007? What were its impacts on people whom you know or have heard about? How do you think it compares to the Great Depression of the 1930s?
2. Do you know in what phase of the business cycle we are at present? Is the U.S. economy currently in a recession or an expansion? What does this mean for employment, inflation, and GDP growth?

2. MACROECONOMIC MODELING AND AGGREGATE DEMAND

For economists, explanations often take the form of theoretical mathematical models. A theoretical model (as we saw in Chapter 2) is a "thought experiment" to help us see the world, which necessarily highlights some aspects of a situation. At the same time, due to simplifying assumptions, it neglects others. A mathematical model expresses the theory in terms of equations, graphs, or schedules. Models contain variables. These are abstract (simplified) representations of important macroeconomic measures—usually related to ones that we can observe empirically, such as GDP or the unemployment rate. Macroeconomists make simplifying assumptions about variables, for example, assuming that all the various interest rates that might coexist in the economy can be summarized as if they were a single one, referred to as "the interest rate." Mathematical models relate these variables together using algebraic formulas, graphs, or tables in such a way as to make clear how these variables affect one another, according to the theorist's understanding.

2.1 SIMPLIFYING ASSUMPTIONS

In Chapter 20, we saw that the economy could be described in terms of four sectors: household, business, government, and foreign. Household expenditures on consumption, business expenditures on investment, government spending, and exchange with the foreign sector expressed as net exports were summed up to obtain total GDP.

This approach simplifies the economy—for example, by assuming that only businesses carry out investment—and the models of aggregate demand we now develop simplify even further:*

- For the models in Part VII of this book, we assume that the full-employment output level *does not grow.* In designing models, it is often useful to separate out different issues into different models. Chapter 32 of this text examines economic growth and ignores business cycles. In Part VII, we take an opposite but complementary approach, concentrating on cycles and abstracting from growth.
- For the initial analysis in this chapter, we assume that the only actors in the economy are *households* and *businesses.* We also assume that all income in the economy goes to households, in return for the labor or capital services that they provide. (In the real world, businesses often hold onto some of their profits as "retained earnings," rather than paying them all out to households, but we ignore that here.) We reintroduce the government in Chapter 25 and discuss the foreign sector in Chapter 29.
- For the remainder of the present chapter, we concentrate on the difference between the classical and Keynesian theories about the behavior of economies that face a threat of *recession* and rising unemployment due to (potentially) insufficient aggregate demand. Booms and inflationary pressures are discussed in later chapters.

These simplifications allow us to make some important points while still keeping the stories, with their accompanying math and graphs, reasonably simple.

2.2 OUTPUT, INCOME, AND AGGREGATE DEMAND

Recall from Chapter 20 that whether GDP is measured by the product approach, the spending approach, or the income approach, the number will be the same (in theory). For the macroeconomic models that we now develop, we will assume that a single variable, which we will denote as "Y," represents GDP expressed as "output," "product," or "income" interchangeably. The top arrow in Figure 24.5 illustrates that, in our simplified macroeconomy, production by firms generates labor and capital incomes to households.

But things get more interesting when we examine the flows from income into spending and from spending (aggregate demand) to supporting a given level of output in the economy.

*As noted in Chapter 20, household investment in consumer durables and government investment in fixed assets are not specifically accounted for in national income calculations.

Figure 24.5 **The Output-Income-Spending Flow of an Economy in Equilibrium**

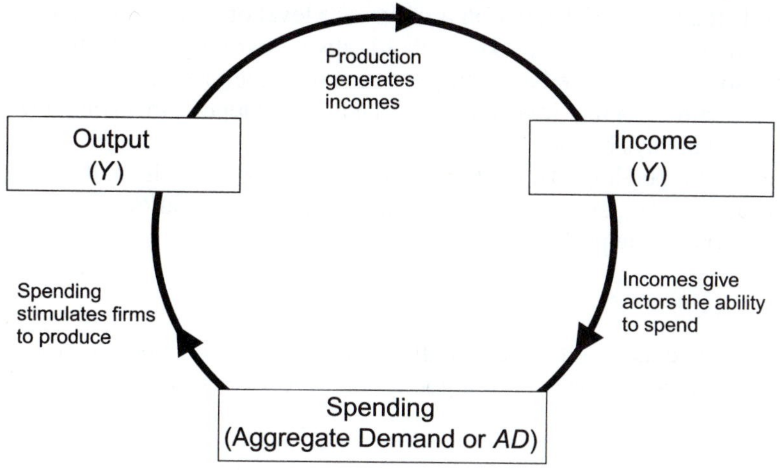

A macroeconomy is said to be in equilibrium when the incomes that arise from production give rise to a level of spending that, in turn, stimulates producers to produce the original level of output.

A macroeconomy is in an *equilibrium* situation when output, income, and spending are all in balance—when they are linked in an unbroken chain, each supported by the other at the equilibrium level, as illustrated in Figure 24.5.

aggregate demand (AD) (in a simple model without government or foreign trade): what households and firms *intend* to spend on consumption and investment: $AD = C + I_I$

The Keynesian model is based on the idea that spending or **aggregate demand**, which we denote as *AD,* may (at least temporarily) fall out of balance with the other flows. Aggregate demand in the economy depends on the spending behavior of the economic actors in the economy. Households make consumption spending decisions, and together the household sector generates an aggregate level of consumption, *C.* We assume that households always consume at the level that they plan to, given their incomes—that what they end up spending is always exactly equal to what they *intended* to spend.

But for firms, the situation can be more complicated, as we will see as this chapter progresses. Purchases of final goods by business firms are considered investment, as discussed in Chapter 20. We will denote total investment for a given year as *I.* But, as we will see, total actual investment is not always the same as what business firms *plan* to invest. We call the amount they *plan* to invest over the course of a year *intended investment,* I_I.

Because the only actors we are looking at right now are households and businesses, we begin our modeling of aggregate demand with the equation:

$$\textit{Aggregate Demand} = \textit{Consumption} + \textit{Intended Investment}$$
$$AD = C + I_I$$

AD is the level of spending that results if people are able to follow their plans.

Remembering that if "output," "income," and "spending" are all just different ways of looking at GDP, it must also be true in this simple economy that GDP is equal to consumption plus total (actual) investment:

$$Y = C + I$$

behavioral equation: in contrast to an accounting identity, a behavioral equation reflects a theory about the behavior of one or more economic agents or sectors. The variables in the equation may or may not be observable

$Y = C + I$ is an *accounting identity.* At the end of any year, when *actual* flows of output, income, and spending are tallied up in the national accounts, the spending by households and businesses *must* (in an economy with no government or foreign sector) be equal to GDP. This equation is true in the same way that, in business accounting, net worth is defined as equal to assets minus liabilities.

The equation $AD = C + I_I$, in contrast, represents something different. It is what is called a **behavioral equation**, used by economists for modeling purposes—we do not have a national agency that looks into business leaders' minds and measures their *intentions!* We work with *both* of these equations later in this chapter. The accounting identity involves the *actual* level of investment, while the behavioral equation involves the level of *planned, desired, or intended* investment. While in this simple world households always *actually* spend what they have *intended* to spend (so we do not need a separate symbol for "intended consumption"), Y and AD will only be the same if actual investment (I) is equal to intended investment (I_I). As we will see, this will not always be the case.

The link from income (Y) to spending (AD) is the potential weak link in the chain illustrated in Figure 24.5. This is because the people who get the income do not just automatically go out and spend it all. This creates the problem of *leakages*.

2.3 The Problem of Leakages

The household sector, we have assumed, receives all the income in the economy. Households spend some of this income on consumption goods and save the rest, according to the equation:

$$S = Y - C$$

where S is the aggregate level of saving. Saving is considered a "leakage" from the output-income-spending cycle, because it represents income that is *not* spent on currently produced goods and services. This is illustrated in Figure 24.6, which shows that some funds are *diverted* from the income-spending part of the cycle into savings.

The other side of the coin, however, is that businesses need funds if they are going to be able to buy investment goods. (Remember, we have assumed that they do not hold onto any of the income they receive, but pass it all along to households as wages, profits, interest, or rents.) In our simple model we assume that firms must borrow from the savings put away by households in order to be able to finance investment projects.

You can think of households depositing their savings in banks, with firms taking out loans from the banks to buy structures or equipment. In this way, firms can reinject funds to the spending stream in the form of investment. This "injection" of spending through investment is also illustrated in Figure 24.6.

If the amount that households want to save is equal to the amount that firms want to invest, then these two flows will balance each other out:

Figure 24.6 **The Output-Income-Spending Flow with Leakages and Injections**

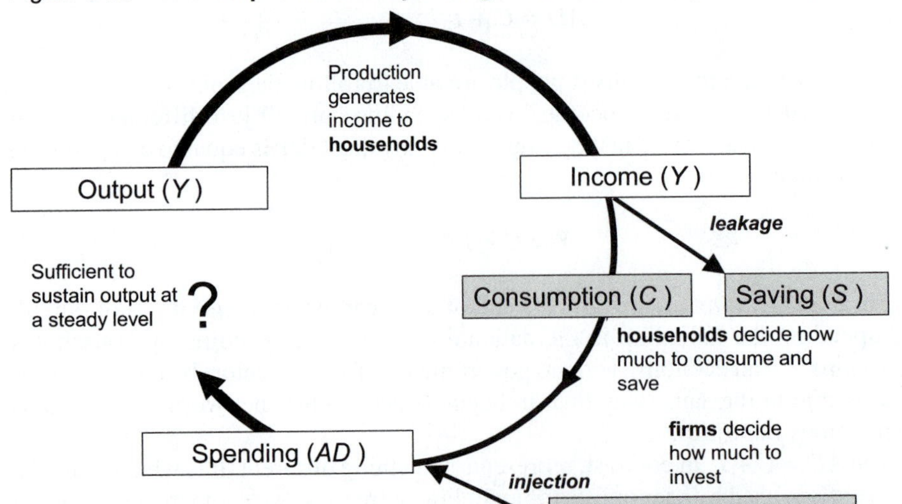

When households save rather than spend part of their incomes, funds are diverted from the income-spending flow. When firms spend on investment goods, this creates a flow into the spending stream.

In equilibrium:
leakages = injections
$$S = I_I$$

If the flows are in balance, then Figure 24.6 is just a more complicated version of the equilibrium situation portrayed in Figure 24.5. The income-spending flow is more complex, but all income still ends up feeding into *AD*, thus supporting the initial level of output (you can mentally fill in the missing part of the circle). This is the kind of equilibrium you might encounter while pumping air into an inner tube that has a leak: The inner tube stays the same size because you put in more air just as quickly as it is leaking out.

This can be seen mathematically as well. If we add *C* to each side of the equilibrium condition above, we get $C + S = C + I_I$. But from the equation that defines saving (*S*) above, we know that the left side equals *Y*, while from the definition of aggregate demand above we know that the right side equals *AD*. Therefore, when leakages equal injections:

In equilibrium:
$$Y = AD$$

This equation says that spending is exactly sufficient to buy the output produced—the economy is in a macroeconomic equilibrium. But households and firms are two different sectors—what happens if their plans *do not* mesh?

Suppose that businesses suddenly lose confidence about the future and cut back on their plans for expansion (that is, they reduce I_I). Or suppose that intended investment is unchanged, but households suddenly decide to consume less and save more, so that the flow into savings is larger than what firms want to use for investment. In either case, leakages will exceed injections. If the savings leakage in Figure 24.6 is larger than the investment injection, the result is that *AD* will be smaller than income and output:

In the case of insufficient aggregate demand:
leakages > injections
$$S > I_I$$
$$Y > AD$$

The question mark in Figure 24.6 indicates that planned spending may or may not be sufficient to support the existing level of output. If the economy is not in macroeconomic equilibrium, something will have to adjust.

Here we reach the dividing point between classical and Keynesian economists. These two theories tell very different stories about how this adjustment comes about. We start with the classical story.

2.4 The Classical Solution to Leakages

In the classical model, we are essentially in a perfectly balanced world, where output is always at its full-employment level. We saw in Chapter 23, looking at business cycles from an employment perspective, that classical economists believed that falling wages in flexible labor markets would bring the economy back to full employment.

For the moment, we put this labor market story into the background and ask our business cycle question in another way: How does an economy (which we assume to be running at a full-employment level of production) keep leakages into saving *exactly equal to* injections coming from investment spending? Or, to express this another way, how can the economy respond to a sudden shift in saving or intended investment that might cause insufficient (or excessive) aggregate demand? The classical argument is again, not surprisingly, that flexible markets will keep the economy at a full-employment level of spending and output.

In this case, the relevant market is what economists call the market for *loanable funds.* In our very simple model, households save out of income from current production. Because they can earn interest on any savings they deposit in a bank rather than stuff under a mattress, they will prefer the bank. In this market, households are the *suppliers* of loanable funds and firms are the *demanders* of loanable funds. The classical theory about the market for loanable funds is illustrated in Figure 24.7. The vertical axis is the interest rate paid from firms to households, which acts as the "price" of loanable funds.

Classical economists assume that households make their decisions about how much to save by looking at the going rate of interest in this market. The higher the interest rate, the more worthwhile it is to save, because their savings earn more. The lower the interest rate, the less appealing it is to save. So the supply of loanable funds (saving) curve in Figure 24.7 slopes upward.

To firms, however, the payment of interest is a cost. So when interest rates are low, this model assumes, firms will want to borrow more for investment projects because borrowing is inexpensive. High interest rates, in contrast, will discourage firms from borrowing. The demand curve in Figure 24.7 thus slopes downward. Where the curves cross determines the equilibrium "price" of funds—here, the interest rate of 5 percent—and the equilibrium quantity of funds borrowed and lent.

In Figure 24.7, the amount saved by households and lent out is 140—which is also the amount borrowed and invested by firms.* (All numbers in our simple models are made up and set to be easy numbers to handle. You could think of the unit for our numbers for *Y, AD, C, I,* and *S* as billions of real dollars in a fictional economy.)

In Figure 24.8 we illustrate what happens in the classical model if, after starting from a position at point E_0 (which we assume corresponds to a full-employment balance of *S* and *I*), firms suddenly change their plans, deciding to spend less on investment. The demand for loanable funds curve shifts leftward. If the interest rate remained at 5 percent, we would see a big drop in investment. But because the interest rate falls to 3 percent, part of the drop in investment will be reversed as firms take advantage of the cheaper loans. And because the interest rate is now lower, some households will choose to save less and consume more (indicated by the movement downward along the supply curve).

In the end, saving and (both intended and actual) investment will still be equal, though at a lower level—in Figure 24.8, the level drops to 60. Aggregate demand will still be equal to the full-employment level—though now it is made up of somewhat less investment, and somewhat more consumption, than before the shift in investment plans. In short, the fall

Figure 24.7 **The Classical Model of the Market for Loanable Funds**

In the classical version of the macroeconomic model, household saving creates the supply of loanable funds and firms' borrowing for investment creates the demand for loanable funds. At the equilibrium interest rate, the amount households save and the amount businesses invest are equated.

*In the real world, households and institutions, firms, governments, and the foreign sector all borrow and lend for various reasons, and much of the supply and demand for loanable funds reflects transactions in existing assets that have little to do with current flows of production and income. This model abstracts from these complications to focus on flows of savings and investment.

Figure 24.8 **Adjustment to a Reduction in Intended Investment in the Classical Model**

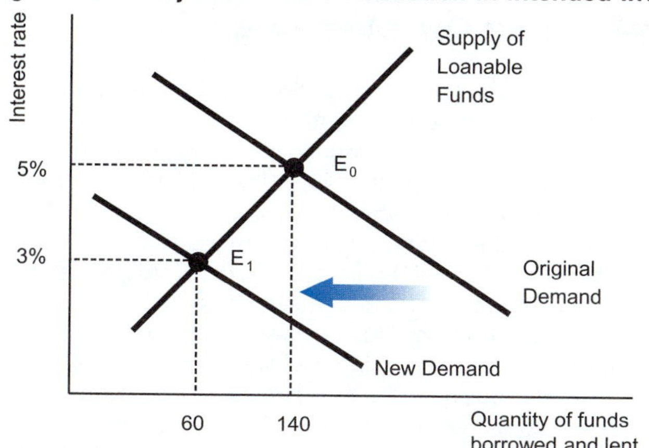

In the classical model, smooth adjustments in the market for loanable funds keep saving equal to investment, even if firms or households change their behavior.

Figure 24.9 **Macroeconomic Equilibrium at Full Employment in the Classical Model**

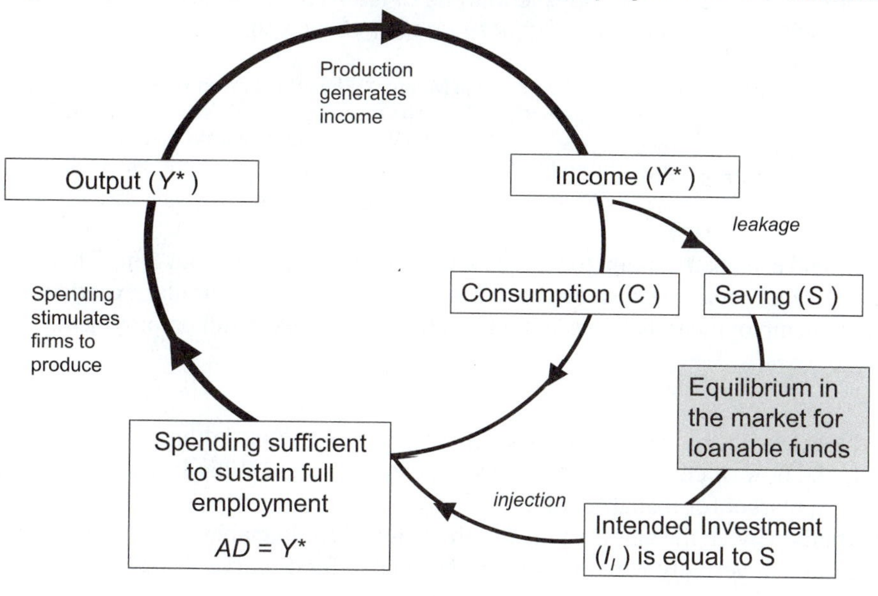

Leakages always equal injections in the classical model, because of smooth adjustments in the market for loanable funds. The economy is always in equilibrium at a full employment level of output (Y*).

in intended investment was balanced by an increase in consumer spending (a decrease in saving).

In the classical model, both households' saving activity and firms' investment spending are assumed to be quite sensitive to changes in the interest rate, which serves as the "price of loanable funds." An adjustment in the interest rate, according to this theory, will quickly correct any threat of imbalances between the leakage of savings and the injection of investment. The interest rate is assumed to adjust smoothly in a free-market economy.

With saving and intended investment always in balance, there is no reason to think that the economy would ever diverge from full employment. The economy is thus self-sustaining at full employment due to the smooth working of the market for loanable funds (see Figure 24.9). We assume (for now) that the level of output that corresponds to full employment is clearly known. As we did in Figure 24.4, we use the symbol Y^* to denote this full-employment level (or range) of output and income.

In the real world, things do not always work out so smoothly (see Box 24.1). This became evident in the Great Depression, when the economy clearly did fall into a situation of severe and prolonged unemployment. People came to be dissatisfied with the classical theory. Could there be something wrong with this story? Could another theory do a better job of explaining

Box 24.1 Small Business Loans in the Wake of the Great Recession

In the market for loanable funds, banks act as intermediaries between the savings of households and the borrowing of businesses. Banks have to determine the creditworthiness of businesses seeking loans, based on expectations about the overall economy and the profit potential of each business applicant.

As you might expect, business lending decreased during the global financial crisis in 2007–9. In part, this was a response to poor macroeconomic conditions and a decline in the demand for loans, but another factor was that banks increased the stringency of their loan requirements. Thus in the aftermath of the crisis, banks are generally less willing to provide loans to businesses perceived to be credit risks.

Business lending has rebounded more recently as macroeconomic conditions improve, but a lingering effect of the crisis is that banks remain particularly reluctant to lend to small businesses. Kenneth Walsleben, who teaches at the Whitman School of Management at Syracuse University notes: "The days of yesteryear when you could go to your corner bank are over. Small, emerging, growing businesses have few traditional sources to turn to."

This has produced essentially two separate markets for loanable funds. Bill Dunkelberg of the National Federation of Independent Business refers to it as a "bifurcated economy." Larger businesses are able to obtain traditional loans from banks at favorable interest rates, generally around 5–7 percent. Small businesses are frequently forced to seek funds from nontraditional sources, which tend to impose higher interest rates. For example, business "cash advance" loans commonly provided to restaurants and other retailers allow the lender to receive a percentage of each credit card transaction directly. The interest rates on nontraditional loans tend to be at least 15 percent, and rates of 30 percent or more are not uncommon.

Sources: Ian Mount, "When Banks Won't Lend, There Are Alternatives, Though Often Expensive," *New York Times*, August 1, 2012; Heesun Wee, "Small Business Owners to Banks: Can I Get a Loan, Please?" CNBC.com, April 24, 2013.

the depression—and even better, point toward how the economy might get out of it? This issue has particular relevance today, because we have recently been through a similar experience—stubbornly high unemployment that does not automatically readjust to full employment.

Discussion Questions

1. Who are the actors in this simple macroeconomic model? What is the role of each in determining the flow of currently produced goods and services? What is the role of each in the classical market for loanable funds?
2. Explain verbally why, in the classical model, the demand for loanable funds curve slopes downward. Explain verbally why the supply of loanable funds curve slopes upward.

3. The Keynesian Model

Keynes' major contribution was to develop a theory to explain why aggregate demand could stay persistently low. He called it *The General Theory,* because he believed that the case of full employment (Y^*) represents only a special case, one that may not often be achieved. In this section we present the basics of his theory using (for the moment) the very simple closed-economy, no-government, no-growth model introduced above.

3.1 Consumption

Many things may affect the level of aggregate consumption in an economy, but one thing that very clearly affects it is the level of current aggregate income. Households are able to spend more on consumption goods and services when the economy is generating a lot of income than they can when it is not (see Box 24.2). So Keynes used in his model a very simple *consumption function* that expresses aggregate consumption as the sum of two components: an "autonomous" part and a part that depends on the level of aggregate income. In algebraic form, the Keynesian consumption function is expressed as:

$$C = \bar{C} + mpc\ Y$$

where $\bar{C}$ is "autonomous" consumption and *mpc* is called the "marginal propensity to consume" (explained below). We first discuss the economic significance of these two parts of the function and then put the function to work.

Autonomous consumption is the part of consumption that is not related to income. It can be thought of as a minimum level of income that people feel required to spend for basic needs. It can also be seen as reflecting the amount of consumption spending that people will undertake no matter what their current incomes are, reflecting their long-term plans, their commitments and habits, and their place in the community.

marginal propensity to consume: the number of additional dollars of consumption for every additional dollar of income (typically a fraction between zero and one)

But, of course, much of consumption does reflect current income and its changes. The term "**marginal propensity to consume**" (*mpc*) reflects the number of *additional* dollars of consumption spending that occur for every *additional* dollar of aggregate income. Using the notation Δ (the Greek letter delta) to mean "change in," *mpc* can be expressed as:

$$mpc = \Delta C / \Delta Y = (\textit{the change of C resulting from a change in Y}) \div (\textit{the change in Y}).$$

In the following example, we use an *mpc* of 8/10 or 0.8. This means that for every additional \$10 in aggregate income, households will spend an additional \$8 on consumption. Logically, the *mpc* should be no greater than 1. An *mpc* greater than 1 would mean that people increase their consumption by *more* than the addition to their income. An *mpc* of about 0.8 has been the standard, historically, in Keynesian modeling exercises—though such a value may not correspond well to actual data on consumption in every time period.

Recall that any income not spent by the household sector is saved. Based on the consumption function, a savings function can be derived using the equation for savings and substituting in the equation for consumption:

marginal propensity to save: the number of additional dollars saved for each additional dollar of income (typically a fraction between zero and one)

$$S = Y - C = Y - (\bar{C} + mpc\ Y) = -\bar{C} + (1 - mpc)\ Y$$

The term $(1 - mpc)$ is called the "**marginal propensity to save**":

$$mps = 1 - mpc = \Delta S / \Delta Y$$

Box 24.2 Consumer Spending Rises with Increased Income

In June 2013, the Associated Press reported that:

> Americans spent more in May as their income rose, encouraging signs after a slow start to the year. The Commerce department said on Thursday that consumer spending rose 0.3 percent last month, nearly erasing a decline of similar size in April. Income rose 0.5 percent. Consumers, benefiting from low inflation, spent more at retail businesses in May, notably for cars, home improvements and sporting goods. The number of people who signed contracts to buy homes in the United States jumped in May to the highest level in more than six years, a sign home sales will probably rise in the months ahead.

Economists pay careful attention to trends in consumer spending, which represents about 70% of aggregate demand in the economy. When income rises, consumers tend to spend more. In turn, higher consumer spending tends to stimulate further growth in the economy. Thus this news in mid-2013 indicated a continuing, though slow, economic recovery following the recession of 2007–9.

Source: "Consumer Spending Rises, and Home Sales Are Up," *Associated Press*, June 17, 2013.

For example, if households spend 80 percent of additional income, or $8 out of an additional $10 in income, then they must save 20 percent (= 100 percent – 80 percent), or $2 out of $10. So if the *mpc* is 0.8, the *mps* must be 0.2.

If we assign number values to the parameters $\bar{C}$ and *mpc,* we can express the relation between income and consumption stated in the consumption function by a schedule, as in Table 24.2. Various income levels are shown in Column (1). For now, we set autonomous consumption at 20 (as shown in Column [2]). With an *mpc* set equal to 0.8, Column (3) shows how to calculate the second component of the consumption function. Adding together the autonomous and income-related components yields total consumption, shown in Column (4). We also show in Column (5), for later reference, the implied level of saving. For example, the shaded row indicates that when income is 400, $C = 20 + 0.8\ (400) = 20 + 320 = 340$. Saving is calculated as 400 – = 340 = 60. Consumption and saving both rise steadily as income rises.

Table 24.2 **The Consumption Schedule (and Saving)**

(1)	(2)	(3)	(4)	(5)
Income (Y)	Autonomous Consumption $\bar{C}$	The part of consumption that depends on income, with mpc = 0.8	Consumption $C = 20 + 0.8\ Y$	Saving $S = Y - C$
		= 0.8 × column(1)	= column(2) + column(3)	= column(1) – column(4)
0	20	0	20	–20
100	20	80	100	0
200	20	160	180	20
300	20	240	260	40
400	20	320	340	60
500	20	400	420	80
600	20	480	500	100
700	20	560	580	120
800	20	640	660	140

We can also see the relationships among consumption, income, and saving in this model in the graph in Figure 24.10. (For a review of graphing techniques, see Box 24.3.) The horizontal axis measures income (Y) while the vertical axis measures consumption (C). The consumption function crosses the vertical axis at the level of autonomous consumption ($\bar{C}$) of 20. The line has a slope equal to the *mpc* of 0.8. Figure 24.10 also includes a 45° line, which tells us what consumption would be if people consumed all their income instead of saving part of it. So the vertical distance between the 45° "consumption = income" line and the consumption function tells us how much people save. We can see, for example, that at an income of 100, households, in this model, consume all their income. At levels of income lower than 100, consumption is higher than income, and they "dissave."* At an income of 400, how much do people save? Check for yourself that the information given in Table 24.2 and Figure 24.10 for income levels of 0, 100, and 400 are in agreement.

A number of factors can cause the consumption schedule for a macroeconomy to change. Among the significant ones are:

*When the household sector "dissaves," it depletes assets (or increases debts) in order to pay for consumption. In this case, consumption exceeds income, and savings are *negative.* This has happened, at a national level, in only two periods in U.S. history: first during the Great Depression, and then again in 2005, when people were feeling wealthy because of large increases in the value of their homes. In 1984, U.S. households saved 10.8 percent of their after-tax income; in 2005 the figure was –0.5 percent; in 2007 the figure was positive but less than 1 percent. After 2008, households started to save more in an effort to reduce debt.

Figure 24.10 **The Keynesian Consumption Function**

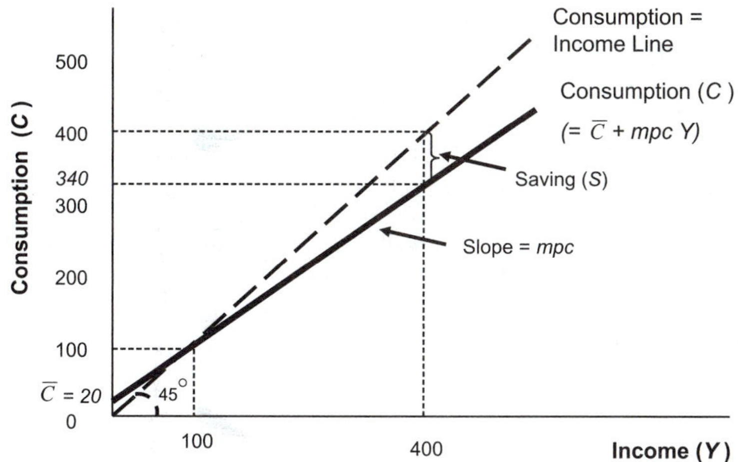

In the Keynesian model, consumption rises with income according to the equation $C = \bar{C} + mpc\,Y$.

- *Wealth.* When many people in a country feel wealthier—perhaps because the stock market or housing prices are high—the household sector as a whole may tend to spend more, even if households' actual annual incomes do not change.
- *Consumer confidence.* When people feel less confident about the future—perhaps due to political turmoil or the fear of a coming recession—they may tend to hunker down and spend less on consumption goods.
- *Attitudes toward spending and saving.* If many people decided to consume less for reasons of health, cultural shifts, or the environment, consumption would also be depressed.
- *Consumption-related government policies.* High levels of saving can be a source of capital for economic growth. Sometimes, a country's leaders will urge people to lower their consumption levels and raise their saving levels, in order to provide funds for investing in the future. (An exercise at the end of this chapter asks you to look at some implications of such a policy.) At other times, leaders urge people (especially in the United States) to consume, in order to boost the economy. Tax systems may be designed to encourage saving, or to encourage certain types of consumption.
- *The distribution of income.* Poorer people tend to spend more of their income than richer people, because just covering necessities can take most or all of their income (or more, forcing them into debt). So a redistribution of income from richer people to poorer people tends to raise consumption and depress saving.

Some of these factors may be best thought of as changing $\bar{C}$ in the Keynesian consumption function, causing the consumption schedule to shift up or down, while others may change the *mpc,* causing the schedule to become steeper or flatter.

BOX 24.3 GRAPHING WITH A SLOPE-INTERCEPT EQUATION

Linear equations are of the form $Y = a + b\,X$. On a graph the variable Y is measured on the vertical axis and the variable X is measured on the horizontal axis. X and Y are called "variables" and *a* and *b* are called "parameters." The parameter *a* is called "the intercept" and shows where the line representing the linear relationship between X and Y crosses the vertical axis. The parameter *b* is "the slope," and determines the steepness of the line. It reflects "rise over run": that is, starting from any point on the line and moving to any other point off to the right on the same line, the slope is the ratio of the number of units the line moves *upwards (rises)* to the number of units the line moves *sideways (runs)*.

The consumption function, $C = \bar{C} + mpc\,Y$, is of this same form, only with different variable and parameter names. The consumption function relates the variable C to the variable Y. It has an intercept of $\bar{C}$ and a slope of *mpc*.

Note that the classical model assumes that people make their decisions about how much income to consume and how much to save based largely on the interest rate, but the Keynesian model does not mention the interest rate because the effects of interest rates on saving are, in fact, ambiguous. If you saw that a very high interest rate is prevailing in the loanable funds market, you might want to take advantage of it and increase your rate of saving, at least for a while. In this case, you would be acting as classical economists assume: A higher interest rate causes you to save more and consume less.

But what if you are saving primarily to finance your college education or your retirement, so you have a certain target level of accumulated wealth in mind? A higher interest rate also means that you can reach this target *faster* (and so revert to higher consumption sooner) or that you can reach the target in the same amount of time while saving *less*. Common sense suggests that the amount that people save depends mainly on their ability to save, based on their income as well as their needs and plans, rather than primarily on the current interest rate.

In fact, a more significant impact of changes in interest rates on household behavior comes from their effect on what households may *pay* in interest, rather than on what households earn. While the simple classical model assumes that households are only on the saving and lending side of the market, in reality households frequently borrow to spend on capital goods for household production. When interest rates are high, households may postpone buying houses, cars, major appliances, and other consumer durables.

In any case, the simple Keynesian function that we are working with leaves out the interest rate entirely. The most important thing to remember about the Keynesian consumption function is that some income generally "leaks" into saving (and so does not create aggregate demand) and that, unlike in the classical model, the interest rate is *not* considered an important factor in determining the size of this leakage.

3.2 INVESTMENT

In the real world, firms may take into account a number of things when thinking about how much to invest. The cost of borrowing (the interest rate) is certainly one factor, as are other things, such as the prices of investment goods, their own accumulated assets and debt, and the willingness of people to lend to them. (Not everyone can qualify for a loan.) Keynes thought that, in general, interest rates were somewhat important in explaining the level of investment. But he argued that, in the case of a severe slowdown of economic activity such as the Great Depression, a low interest rate would not be enough to motivate business firms to invest in building up new capacity.

The most important factor in explaining aggregate investment spending, Keynes thought, is the general level of optimism or pessimism that investors feel about the future, or what he called "animal spirits." If firms' managers believe that they will be able to sell more of the goods or services that they produce in the future, and at a good price, they will want to invest in equipment and structures to maintain and expand their capacity. If they do not see such a rosy future ahead, then why would even a very low interest rate persuade them to invest? The borrowed funds will have to be repaid; the major question for the borrower is "are my prospects for success good enough to allow me to repay this loan?" The interest rate will marginally change the amount to be repaid but is not the major determinant of the answer to this question.

Because Keynes saw investment as future directed, rather than related to any current, observable economic variables, the "function" for intended investment in the simple Keynesian model just says that investors intend to invest whatever investors intend to invest. All of intended investment is considered "autonomous" in this model. We can denote this as:

$$I_I = \bar{I}_I$$

where $\bar{I}_I$ is "autonomous intended investment." Don't worry too much about whether to put a bar over the symbol—we have introduced it here just to show you that it is similar in concept

Figure 24.11 **The Keynesian Investment Function**

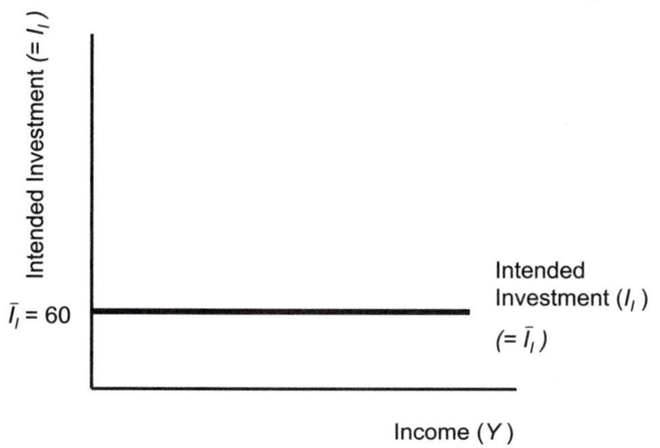

In the simplest Keynesian model, intended investment is a constant, no matter what the level of national income, being determined instead by long-term profit expectations.

to the $\bar{C}$ in the consumption function. Just as $\bar{C}$ can go up or down depending on consumer confidence, $\bar{I}_I$ can go up or down depending on investor confidence.

Figure 24.11 graphs investment against income, for the case where $\bar{I}_I = 60$. Because investment does not depend on income, the graph is horizontal. The lack of attention to interest rates is a limitation of the simple Keynesian model. In later chapters, we depart from this simplification and consider the effects of interest rates on investment.

3.3 The Aggregate Demand Schedule

Earlier we defined *AD* as the sum of consumption and intended investment. We can now add intended investment to the consumption schedule and curve to get a schedule and graph for aggregate demand. In Table 24.3, Columns (1) and (2) just repeat Table 24.2. In Column (3) we have set intended investment at 60, for any level of income, in line with the notion that it is all "autonomous." Column (4) calculates the level of aggregate intended spending in the economy. We can see that when, for example, $Y = 400$, households and businesses together plan to spend 400 on consumption and investment.

Figure 24.12 shows the relationship between income and aggregate demand. The *AD* line lies exactly 60 units vertically above the *C* line, at every level of income. Its intercept is the sum of autonomous consumption and intended investment. Its slope is the same as that of the consumption function. We can see that when, for example, $Y = 400$, then $C = 340$ and $AD = 400$.

The *AD* curve shifts up or down as autonomous consumption or autonomous investment changes. Suppose that intended investment is 140, instead of 60. Table 24.4 calculates *AD* for

Table 24.3 **Deriving Aggregate Demand from the Consumption Function and Investment**

(1)	(2)	(3)	(4)
Income (Y)	Consumption (C)	Intended Investment (I_I)	Aggregate Demand $AD = C + I_I$ = *column (2) + column (3)*
0	20	60	80
300	260	60	320
400	340	60	400
500	420	60	480
600	500	60	560
700	580	60	640
800	660	60	720

Table 24.4 **Aggregate Demand with Higher Intended Investment**

(1) Income (Y)	(2) Consumption (C)	(3) Intended Investment (I_I)	(4) Aggregate Demand (AD)
0	20	*140*	160
300	260	*140*	400
400	340	*140*	480
500	420	*140*	560
600	500	*140*	640
700	580	*140*	720
800	660	*140*	800

selected levels of income like those that we used before, but at this higher level of I_I. Because neither $\bar{C}$ nor the *mpc* has changed, Column (2) is the same as in earlier tables.

This aggregate demand schedule is graphed in Figure 24.13. The intercept is now 160, which is equal to $\bar{C}$ of 20 plus $\bar{I}_I$ of 140, while the slope is still equal to the *mpc*. Notice that now, at an income level of 400, aggregate demand is 480 instead of 400. With investment increased by 80, aggregate demand at any income level increases by 80 as well.

Figure 24.13 could also be used to illustrate an increase in $\bar{C}$ from 20 to 100 (an increase of 80) while intended investment remains at 60. Any combination of $\bar{C}$ and $\bar{I}_I$ that sums to 160 would yield this graph. In economic terms, any increase in autonomous consumer and investor desired spending increases aggregate demand.

Figure 24.12 **Aggregate Demand**

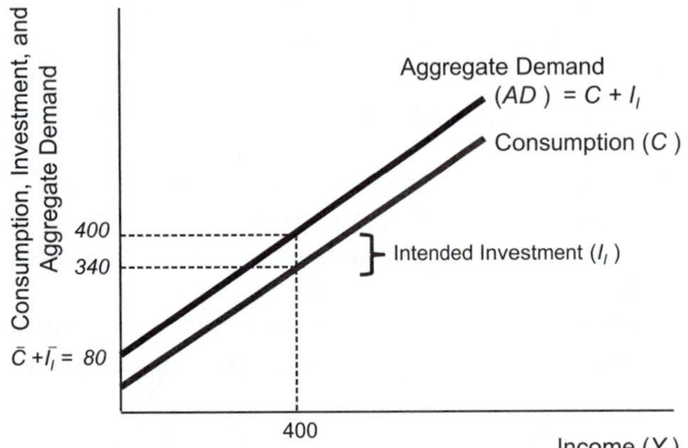

The AD curve is derived by adding the autonomous intended investment to consumption, at each income level. So at each level of Y, AD is the vertical sum of C and II.

Figure 24.13 **Aggregate Demand with Higher Intended Investment**

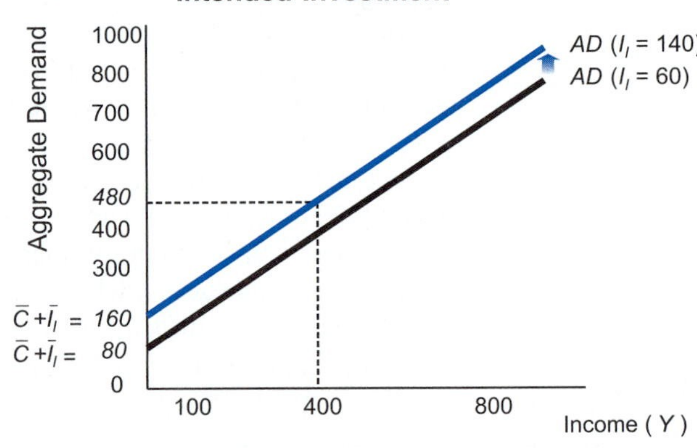

If intended investment increases (or autonomous consumption increases), the aggregate demand curve shifts upward.

3.4 The Possibility of Unintended Investment

The key to the Keynesian model is understanding why and how *unintended* investment can occur and how firms respond when they see it happening. Unintended investment occurs when aggregate demand is insufficient, because firms will not be able to sell all the goods that they produce.

Recall (from Chapter 20) that a country's manufactured capital stock includes structures, equipment, *and inventories*. Many firms normally plan to keep as inventory a level of supplies that they expect to use soon and products that they have not yet shipped. *Unintended* inventory investment occurs when these inventories build up unexpectedly. A manufacturing firm, for example, experiences *excess inventory accumulation* when it cannot sell its goods as quickly as expected and the goods pile up in warehouses. Conversely, a firm that sells its goods faster than expected experiences *excess inventory depletion,* as the goods "fly off the shelves" and the warehouse empties out.

Actual investment (*I*, as measured in the national accounts) is the sum of what businesses plan to invest, plus what they inadvertently end up investing if *AD* and *Y* do not match up exactly:

$$I = \textit{intended investment } (I_I) + \textit{excess inventory accumulation or depletion}$$

In Table 24.5, Columns (1) and (2) repeat information from Table 24.3, for intended investment of 60 and selected levels of income. Column (3) calculates levels of *un*intended investment. If, for example, income and output are 600, but aggregate demand is only 560, excess inventory accumulation of 40 will occur. Or, if income and output are 300, but firms and households want to buy 320, inventories will be depleted by 20 to meet the demand. Only at an income level of 400 is there a balance between income and spending.

Columns (4) to (6) are included in Table 24.5 to show that both the equation $AD = C + I_I$ and the identity $Y = C + I$ hold at all times in this model. Column (5) of Table 24.5 calculates actual investment (*I*) as the sum of intended and unintended investment. Notice that the figures in Column (6) match those in Column (1)—when we include *unintended,* excess inventory accumulation or depletion, the basic macroeconomic identity $Y = C + I$ is still true.

Figure 24.14—often called the "Keynesian cross" diagram—illustrates this case for two income levels. The *AD* curve, as we know, represents the sum of consumption and investment at

Table 24.5 **The Possibility of Excess Inventory Accumulation or Depletion**

(1)	(2)	(3)	(4)	(5)	(6)
Income (*Y*)	Aggregate Demand (*AD*)	Excess Inventory Accumulation (+) or Depletion (–) = *column(1) – column(2)*	Intended Investment (I_I)	Investment (*I*) = *column(3)* + *column(4)*	Check that the macroeconomic identity still holds: *Y = C+I*
300	320	–20	60	40	300
400	400	0	60	60	400
500	480	20	60	80	500
600	560	40	60	100	600
700	640	60	60	120	700
800	720	80	60	140	800

Figure 24.14 **Unintended Investment in the Keynesian Model**

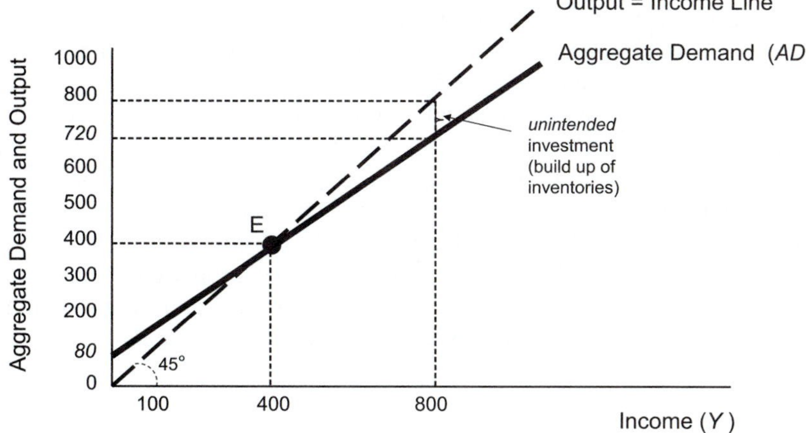

If income and output in an economy are above the level of aggregate demand, excessive inventories accumulate. This is illustrated for the income level of 800.

any income level. The dashed line is a 45° line that (as in our earlier diagram about consumption, income, and saving) illustrates equality between the values on the two axes. With income on the horizontal axis and output on the vertical axis, all points on this 45° line represent situations where output equals income. At an income level of 800, the *AD* curve indicates that aggregate demand is 720. But the "output = income" line indicates that output is 800 and so exceeds spending. There is unintended inventory build-up of 80, as indicated by the vertical distance between the *AD* curve and the 45° line, at this income level. (Check to see that this is consistent with Table 24.5.)

At an income level of 400, where the *AD* line crosses the 45° line, there is full macroeconomic equilibrium, because output, income, and spending are all at the same level. Unintended investment is 0.

At levels of income and output above 400 in Table 24.5 and Figure 24.14, business firms' managers are unhappy because more and more of their goods are gathering dust. For levels of income and output below 400, their inventories are being depleted below intended levels. These are *not* equilibrium levels of income, and the economy will not stay at any of those income levels—things will change.

3.5 Movement to Equilibrium in the Keynesian Model

If firms are unhappy about unsold goods, they will do something to correct the situation. If inventories are building up more than intended, they will cut back on production. Their cutbacks in production will continue until they are no longer seeing inventories build up excessively—that is, until the level of what is actually produced matches what they can sell. Reductions in *Y* will continue until $Y = AD$. This is a little more complicated than it may at first seem, though, since any reduction in output leads to reduced income, which leads to reduced consumption, so that *AD* is a moving target. We look at this complication below in Section 3.7, but for now we continue with the main story.

In Figure 24.14, above, suppose that the economy were (for reasons explored later) initially at an income and output level of 800. From the figure and Table 24.5, we can see that this is not an equilibrium—producers are seeing excess inventory accumulation of 80 because *AD* is only 720. Producers will cut back on production. The equilibrium point *E* is obtained when aggregate output has fallen to 400 and *AD* has also fallen to 400.

So, what has happened here? If you look back at Table 24.2, you can see that at the initial income level of 800, there was a "leakage" into saving of 140. But firms, we have assumed, only want to spend 60 on investment. Leakages exceeded injections by 80, aggregate demand was insufficient, and inventories of 80 built up. Firms cut back on production. They continued to cut back until inventories were back where they wanted them.

Yet when the economy arrives at an equilibrium, the balance between saving and investing has been restored! Why is this so? Intended investment has not changed—it has been at 60 all along. But now that income has dropped, households have less income to use for consumption and saving, and so saving has dropped from its initial level of 140 to only 60. (See Table 24.2 to check that this is the level of saving at an income level of 400.) It is changes in aggregate income, and the resulting changes in consumption and saving, that have caused leakages and injections to become equal again.

We can also see in the schedules and graphs what would happen if *AD* were for some reason to be *above* the current level of output. If output were to start out at 300, for example, desired spending of 320 (see Table 24.5) would cause produced goods to "fly off the shelves" and deplete inventories. According to this model, this situation would motivate firms to increase production. As production rises, income, consumption, and saving would also all rise. Again, equilibrium would be reached when *Y* and *AD* both equal 400, and *S* and *I* both equal 60.

3.6 THE PROBLEM OF PERSISTENT UNEMPLOYMENT

Now that the pieces of the model have been explained, the model can be put together to illustrate what Keynes taught about the Great Depression. Assume that 800 represents the full-employment level of output for this economy, as illustrated by the vertical "full-employment range" Y^* in Figure 24.15. If intended investment is 140 (the higher *AD* line in Figure 24.15), the economy is at an initial full-employment equilibrium at E_0. (Refer back to Table 24.4 and Figure 24.13 to confirm that at this level of income $Y = AD$.)

Figure 24.15 **Full Employment Equilibrium with High Intended Investment**

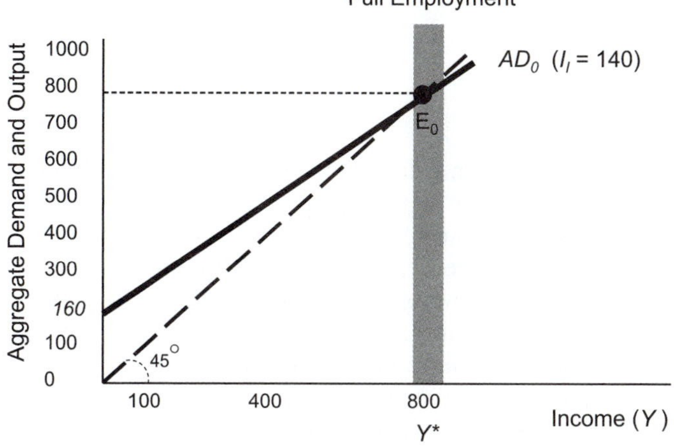

Supposing that Y = 800 represents full employment, an intended investment level of 140 generates spending sufficient to maintain this as an equilibrium.

Figure 24.16 **A Keynesian Unemployment Equilibrium**

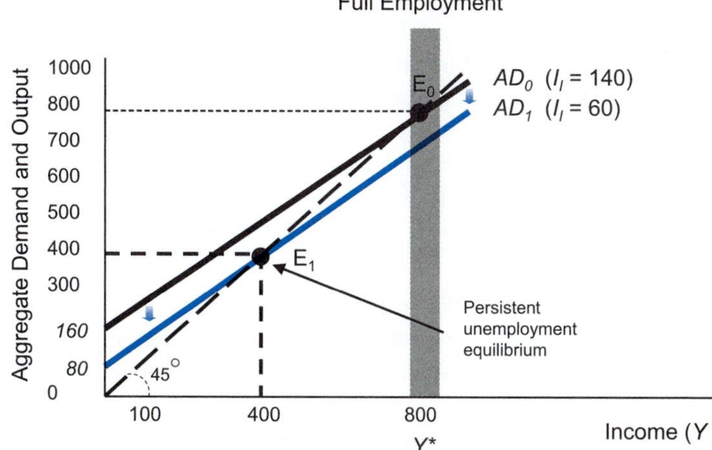

A fall in investor confidence causes the equilibrium level of output to fall. The initial excess of leakages over injections caused by low investment spending is corrected by a contraction in output, income, and saving. At E1, leakages and injections are again equal.

But at the start of the Great Depression, the 1929 stock market crash and other events caused business and investor confidence to plummet. (Consumer confidence and financial wealth also plummeted, but we are simplifying the story by concentrating on firms.) Producers became very uncertain about whether they would be able to sell what they produced, so they cut back radically on their investment spending. This is modeled in Figure 24.16 as a drop in aggregate demand caused by a drop in intended investment from 140 to 60. (Note that 60 is the number used in Table 24.3, so that AD_1 in Figure 24.16 is identical to the *AD* curve in Figure 24.12.) With the drop in *AD*, income of 800 is no longer an equilibrium. Consistent with the adjustments toward equilibrium that we just discussed, output, income, and spending contract until a new equilibrium (E_1) is reached at a level of 400.

Figure 24.17 **Movement to an Unemployment Equilibrium**

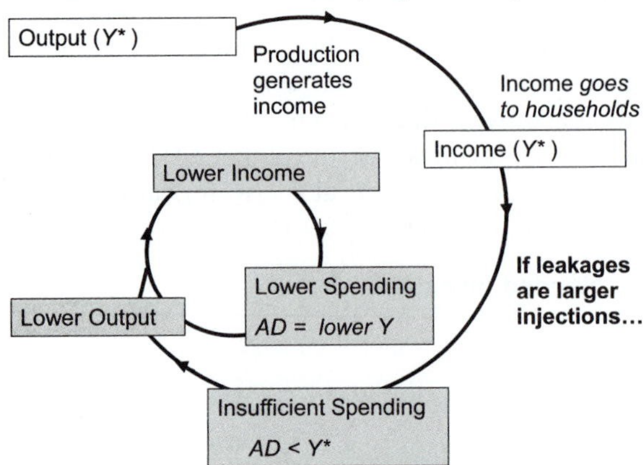

An excess of leakages over injections causes aggregate demand to be insufficient for a full employment level of output. Output and income fall until equilibrium is restored.

An income and output level of 400, however, is far below the level of production required to provide full employment for workers. Massive unemployment results. And in the Keynesian model, there is no automatic mechanism (as there was in the classical model) that rescues the economy from this situation. The economy experiences a contraction, settling at a new, persistent, self-reinforcing, low-income, and high-unemployment equilibrium, as shown in Figure 24.17.

To say that a macroeconomy is "in equilibrium" just means that output, income, and spending are in balance. The basic idea about an equilibrium is that there tend to be forces (such as, in this model, firms' desire to avoid unintended inventories) that are likely to push an economy toward equilibrium and tend to keep it there after it is achieved. But achievement of an equilibrium is not the same thing as full employment—the equilibrium level at which output, income, and spending balance may or may not be at full employment.

In Keynes's view, there was nothing that would "naturally" or "automatically" happen to pull an economy out of such a low-employment situation. A full-employment equilibrium such as E_0 in Figure 24.15 is possible, but it is merely one of a large number of possible equilibria (seen in the model as different points along the 45° line). Equally possible is a persistent unemployment equilibrium such as E_1 in Figure 24.16. Because Keynes, unlike classical economists, did not equate equilibrium with full employment, he believed that there is often a need for action to stimulate aggregate demand. Such policies are the topics of Chapters 25 and 27.

3.7 THE MULTIPLIER

In the example above, intended investment dropped from 140 to 60 because of a fall in investor confidence—a decline of 80 units. But output dropped from 800 to 400—a decline of *400* units. Why is the decline in output so much bigger than the decline in investment spending that caused it?

The intuition behind this result is that, while the drop in investment spending leads to a drop in aggregate demand, which leads directly to a contraction in output, there are also feedback effects through consumption. Because consumption depends on income, and income depends on *AD,* which depends on consumption, additional effects "echo" back and forth. For example, reducing production in a factory does not merely involve laying off assembly-line workers. The laid-off factory workers now have less income to spend at stores. This means that the stores will also need to lay off some of their employees, who then also have less income. And so on. This process is illustrated in more detail in Table 24.6.

In the first row of Table 24.6, for example, the drop in intended investment (step 1) leads to an immediate drop in *AD* of 80 (step 2). Firms see inventories piling up and cut back production by 80. But this decreases the income going to households, because firms are now paying less in wages, interest, dividends, and rents. Consumers react (in step 3) to a change in income according to the relationship $\Delta C = mpc\ \Delta Y$. With 80 less in income, they reduce their spending

Table 24.6 **The Multiplier at Work**

Change in Intended Investment	**Change in Aggregate Demand and in Output and Income**	**Change in Consumption** $\Delta C = mpc\, \Delta Y = .8 \times$ **Column (2)**
1. Investors lose confidence. $\Delta I_I = -80$	2. Reduced investment spending leads directly to $\Delta AD = -80$. Producers respond to reduced demand for their goods by cutting back on production. $\Delta Y = -80$	3. Less production means less income. With income reduced by 80, households cut consumption by $mpc\, \Delta Y = .8 \times -80$ $\Delta C = -64$
	4. Lowered consumption spending means lowered AD $\Delta AD = -64$ Producers respond. $\Delta Y = -64$	5. Households cut consumption by mpc ΔY $= .8 \times -4$ $\Delta C = -51.2$
	6. $\Delta Y = -51.2$	7. mpc $\Delta Y = .8 \times -51.2$ $\Delta C = -40.96$
	8. $\Delta Y = -40.96$	9. $\Delta C = -32.77$
	10. $\Delta Y = -32.77$	11. $\Delta C = -26.21$
	etc.	etc.
	Sum of changes in Y $= -80 + -64 + -51.2 + -40.96 + -32.77 + \ldots = -400$	

by 64. How do they manage to keep their budget in line, when they have only reduced their spending by 64 but their income went down by 80? See if you can think of the answer before you check the footnote.*

The second and later rows show how decreases in consumption decrease aggregate demand, output, and income, and thus depress consumption even further. Note that in each round, the decrease in *Y* gets a little smaller. Fortunately, a convenient result from mathematics means that we do not need to calculate the sum of all these changes in *Y* by continuing to extend the table, row after row (in theory, forever—although the numbers get very tiny after a while).** A result from the mathematics of infinite series implies that, in the end, the total change in *Y* is related in the following way to the original change in I_I:

$$\Delta Y = \frac{1}{1 - mpc} \Delta \bar{I}_I$$

which means, in this case,

$$\Delta Y = \frac{1}{1 - .08} (-80) = \frac{1}{0.2} (-80) = 5(-80) = -400$$

The expression $1/(1 - mpc)$ is called "the income/spending multiplier"—or, for short, the multiplier—and is abbreviated *mult:*

*They economize by reducing both consumption and saving. They reduce their saving by 16 (which corresponds to the remaining 20 percent of the income change).

**Column 2 of the table can be summarized as:

$$\Delta Y = 1 + mpc\, \Delta \bar{I}_I + mpc\, (mpc\, \Delta \bar{I}_I) + mpc\, (mpc\, (mpc\, \Delta \bar{I}_I)) + \ldots$$
$$= (1 + mpc + mpc^2 + mpc^3 + \ldots)\, \Delta \bar{I}_I$$

But the infinite series $(1 + x + x^2 + x^3 + x^4 + \ldots + x^\infty)$ where $x < 1$ can be simplified to $1/(1 - x)$

$$mult = \frac{1}{1 - mpc}$$

In this case, with $mpc = 0.8$, the multiplier is 5. The initial decrease in intended investment causes, in the end, a decrease in income that is five times its size. We can express this mathematically as $\Delta Y = mult\ \Delta \bar{I}$

The value of the multiplier would be the same if it had been a decrease in consumer confidence, acting through a change in $\bar{C}$ that started this cascade in incomes, instead of a decrease in investor confidence. Mathematically, this means $\Delta Y = mult\ \Delta \bar{C}$ as well. In Chapter 25, we add consideration of other factors that change aggregate demand, other than investor and consumer confidence.

Discussion Questions

1. If you received a raise of $100 per month, how would you increase your spending per month? How much would you change your saving? What is your *mpc*? What is your *mps*?
2. Describe verbally how, in the Keynesian model, an economy can end up in an equilibrium of persistent unemployment.

4. Concluding Thoughts

In classical economic theory, an economy should never go into a slump—or at least it should not stay in one very long. Any deficiency in aggregate demand would be quickly counteracted by smooth adjustments in the market for loanable funds. Keynes, by contrast, theorized that deficiencies in aggregate demand, due to drops in investor (or consumer) confidence, could explain the deep, long-term slumps that many countries experienced during the Great Depression (as well as some of the other economic depressions that various economies have experienced throughout history). Modern Keynesians argue that this theory also explains the Great Recession that began in 2007.

Any excess of "leakages" over "injections" into the aggregate demand stream would, Keynes theorized, lead to progressive rounds of declines in consumption and income, until savings are so low that a new, lower-output-level equilibrium is established. He believed that some kind of government action was required to get the economy out of its slump and to achieve a higher equilibrium level. In Chapter 25, we explore how the U.S. economy did, in fact, get out of the Great Depression, as well as some of the policies that were instituted in response to the Great Recession.

It is also worth taking a moment to consider the implications of this model as it relates to contemporary controversies over consumerism and the environment. In the Keynesian model, it does, indeed, appear that keeping consumption and spending at high levels is necessary to keep the economy humming. The idea that cutting back on consumption spending would be "bad for the economy" is based on the Keynesian notion that reductions in aggregate spending lead to recessions or depressions and that these could potentially be deep and persistent. Would our cutting back on the kinds of consumption that are environmentally damaging lead to recession and job losses? Or could we perhaps substitute other kinds of economic activity and job creation? We revisit this assumption in later chapters to see whether it really is the case that what is good for the environment (and for future generations) has to be "bad for the economy."

Discussion Questions

1. Which theory—classical or Keynesian—seems more realistic in describing today's economy? Explain why.
2. Have you ever read articles or editorials that claim that high consumption is essential for a healthy economy? Does the Keynesian model seem to confirm or challenge this idea? What are some arguments for the opposite point of view?

REVIEW QUESTIONS

1. During a business-cycle recession, which of the following typically rises: the level of output, the unemployment rate, or the inflation rate?
2. During the 1930s, how did economists' opinions about the Great Depression differ?
3. In the model laid out in this chapter, who receives income? Who spends? Who saves?
4. What is the definition of aggregate demand? How does it differ from measured GDP?
5. What conditions comprise equilibrium in a macroeconomy?
6. Saving is described as a "leakage" from the circular flow. How is it a leakage?
7. How can an increase in saving (if not balanced by an increase in intended investment) cause a shrinkage of the output-income-spending flow?
8. Describe the classical market for loanable funds. Who are the actors, and what do they each do?
9. Describe how the problem of leakages is solved in the classical model.
10. How did Keynes model consumption behavior? Draw and label a graph.
11. List five factors, aside from the level of income, that can affect the level of consumption in a macroeconomy.
12. Why isn't the interest rate included in the Keynesian consumption function?
13. What did Keynes think was the most important factor in determining investment behavior?
14. What determines aggregate demand in the Keynesian model? Draw and label a graph.
15. Do firms always end up investing the amount that they intend? Why or why not?
16. Draw a "Keynesian cross" diagram, carefully labeling the curves and the equilibrium point.
17. Describe how adjustment to equilibrium occurs in the Keynesian model.
18. Does a macroeconomy's being "in equilibrium" always mean it is in a good state? Why or why not?
19. What is "the income/spending multiplier"? Explain why a drop in autonomous intended investment, or in autonomous consumption, leads to a much larger drop in equilibrium income.

EXERCISES

1. Carefully draw and label a supply-and-demand diagram for the classical loanable funds market. Assuming that the market starts and ends in equilibrium, indicate what happens if there is a sudden drop in households' desire to consume.
   a. Which curve shifts and in what direction?
   b. What happens to the equilibrium amount of loanable funds borrowed and lent? (You do not need to put numbers on the graph—just indicate the direction of the change.)
   c. What happens to the equilibrium interest rate?
   d. What happens to the equilibrium amount of investment?
2. Suppose that you see a toy store increasing its inventories in early December, right before the Christmas/Chanukah/Kwanzaa season. Is this a case of excess inventory accumulation? Why or why not?
3. Suppose that the relation between consumption and income is $C = 90 + 0.75\,Y$.
   a. For each additional dollar that households receive, how much do they save? How much do they spend?
   b. What is the level of consumption when income is equal to 0? 360? 500? 600? (You may want to make a table similar to Table 24.2 in the text.)
   c. What is the level of saving when income is equal to 0? 360? 500? 600?
   d. As income rises from 500 to 600, by how much does consumption rise? What formula would you use to derive the *mpc* from your answer to this question, if you did not know the *mpc* already?
   e. Graph this consumption function, along with a 45° "consumption = income" line. Label the slope and intercept, and show how the level of savings when income is equal to 600 can be found on this graph.
4. Draw a Keynesian cross graph and assume that the macroeconomy starts and ends in equilibrium. Label the initial aggregate demand line AD_0. Then show what happens in the diagram when a rise in consumer wealth raises $\bar{C}$ (autonomous consumption) in your diagram. (This event might happen if the stock market or the housing market enjoys large price increases. You do not need to put numbers on the graph—just indicate the direction of the change.)

a. How does the *AD* line shift? Label the new line AD_1.
b. What is the *initial* effect of this change on inventories? How will firms change production in response to this change in inventories?
c. What happens to the equilibrium level of production, income, and spending? Does each rise, fall, or stay the same?

5. What happens in the Keynesian model if households decide to be "thriftier"—that is, spend less and save more? Do the following multistep exercise to find out.
   a. Suppose that the economy starts out in a situation we already developed in the text: $\bar{C} = 20 + .8Y$ and $I_I = 60$ (see Table 24.3). Carefully graph the resulting *AD* curve, labeling the levels of aggregate demand that result when income is equal to 0, 300, 400, and 500. Label the curve AD_0, add the 45° line, and label the equilibrium point E_0.
   b. What is the equilibrium level of income in this initial case? What is the equilibrium level of saving?
   c. Now suppose that people decide they want to save more of their income and spend less of it. In fact, their new level of autonomous consumption is 0, so the new consumption function is just $C = .8Y$. Calculate the levels of consumption and aggregate demand that would result from incomes of 0, 300, 400, and 500. (You might want to set up a table similar to Table 24.3, but using this new equation for consumption. Intended investment is still 60.)
   d. If income stayed at the equilibrium level determined in step (b) of this question, would people now be saving more? How much more? Show your work.
   e. Add the *AD* curve that arises from your calculations in step (c) on the graph that you drew earlier. Label this curve AD_1 and the new equilibrium point E_1.
   f. What is the new equilibrium level of income? What is the new equilibrium level of saving? Compare your answers to your answers in step (b).
   g. Explain why this phenomenon arising from the Keynesian model is called "the paradox of thrift." Can you explain why this "paradox" arises?

6. Suppose that the behavior of households and firms in an economy is determined by the following equations:

$$C = 90 + 0.75Y$$
$$\bar{I}_I = 35$$

   a. Show in a table what the levels of *C* and *AD* would be at income levels of 0, 500, and 600.
   b. If, for some reason, income equaled 600, would there be unintended inventory investment? If so, would inventories be excessive or depleted, and by how much?
   c. If, for some reason, income equaled 500, would there be unintended inventory investment? If so, would inventories be excessive or depleted, and by how much?
   d. What is the equilibrium level of income and output?
   e. What is the income/spending multiplier equal to, in this model?
   f. If intended investment were to rise by 25, by how much would equilibrium income increase? Use the income/spending multiplier.

7. (Appendix) Suppose that the behavior of households and firms in an economy is determined by the following equations:

$$C = 50 + 0.9Y$$
$$\bar{I}_I = 50$$

Answer the following questions, using algebraic manipulations *only*.

   a. What is the equation for the *AD* curve?
   b. What is the level of equilibrium income?
   c. If intended investment increases by 10 units to 60 units, by how much will equilibrium income rise?

8. Match each concept in Column A with a definition or example in Column B.

Column A	Column B
a. mult $\bar{I}_I$	1. Peak
b. An injection	2. An inverse relationship between unemployment and rapid GDP growth
c. An assumption evident in the equation $AD = C + I_I$	3. Households save more when income rises
d. Okun's "law"	4. $I - I_I$
e. Classical assumption about saving	5. The proportion of an additional dollar that households spend on consumption
f. Unintended investment	6. $\bar{C} + \bar{I}_I$
g. The turning point from a business cycle expansion to contraction	7. The amount that equilibrium GDP rises when autonomous investment rises
h. *mpc*	8. Households save more when the interest rate rises
i. The intercept of the *AD* curve	9. No government sector
j. A Keynesian assumption about saving	10. Intended investment

APPENDIX: AN ALGEBRAIC APPROACH TO THE MULTIPLIER

The formula for the multiplier in the simplest Keynesian model can also be derived using tools of basic algebra, starting with rearranging the equation for *AD:*

$$AD = C + \bar{I}_I$$

We can substitute in the Keynesian equation for consumption, $C = \bar{C} + mpc\,Y$, and use the fact that in this model all investment is autonomous, to get

$$\begin{aligned} AD &= (\bar{C} + mpc\,Y) + \bar{I}_I \\ &= (\bar{C} + \bar{I}_I) + mpc\,Y \end{aligned}$$

The last rearrangement shows that the *AD* curve has an intercept equal to the sum of the autonomous terms and a slope equal to the *mpc*. Changes in either of the variable in parentheses, by changing the intercept, shift the curve upward or downward in a parallel manner.

By substituting this into the equation for the equilibrium condition, $Y = AD$, we can derive an expression for equilibrium income in terms of all the other variables in the model:

$$Y = (\bar{C} + \bar{I}_I) + mpc\,Y$$

$$Y - mpc\,Y = \bar{C} + \bar{I}_I$$

$$(1 - mpc)\,Y = \bar{C} + I_I$$

$$Y = \frac{1}{(1 - mpc)}(\bar{C} + \bar{I}_I)$$

If autonomous consumption or intended investment increases, these each increase equilibrium income by $mult = 1/(1 - mpc)$ times the change in autonomous consumption or investment.

To see this explicitly, consider the changes that would come about in Y if there is a change in $\bar{I}_I$ from $\bar{I}_{I0}$ to a new level, $\bar{I}_{I1}$, while autonomous consumption (and the *mpc*) stays the same. We can solve for the change in Y by subtracting the old equation from the new one:

$$Y_1 = \frac{1}{1 - mpc} (\bar{C} + \bar{I}_{I_1})$$

$$-\left[Y_0 = \frac{1}{1 - mpc} (\bar{C} + \bar{I}_{I_0}) \right]$$

$$Y_1 - Y_0 = \frac{1}{1 - mpc} (\bar{C} - \bar{C} + \bar{I}_{I_1} - \bar{I}_{I_0})$$

But $\bar{C}$ (and the *mpc*) is unchanged, so the first subtraction in parentheses comes out to be 0. We are left with:

$$Y_1 - Y_0 = \frac{1}{1 - mpc} (\bar{I}_{I_1} - \bar{I}_{I_0})$$

or

$$\Delta Y = mult \Delta \bar{I}_I$$

where $mult = 1/(1 - mpc)$. Similar analysis of $\Delta\bar{C}$ (holding intended investment constant) would show that the multiplier for that change is also *mult*.

25 Fiscal Policy

The recession that began in the United States in 2007 was the most severe and long-lasting since the Great Depression of the 1930s. Even after the economy started to recover, growth was slow and job creation weak, with unemployment remaining over 7 percent through 2013. This led to a wide-ranging, and continuing, debate over the best way for government to respond to the recession and its aftermath. An immediate response put in place by the Obama administration in 2009 was a policy of economic stimulus through expanded government spending and tax cuts. The "stimulus package" involved more than $800 billion in new government spending and reduced taxes. This was followed by further tax cuts over the next two years, including a temporary two-percentage-point payroll tax holiday in 2011 and 2012.

The commonsense idea behind these policies is that more spending, either by government or by individuals and families who receive tax cuts, will create demand for goods and thereby expand employment and output. In terms of the macroeconomic theory sketched out in Chapter 24, these policies are intended to increase aggregate demand, generating positive multiplier effects.

The stimulus policy drew immediate criticism, especially from conservative economists and politicians, who argued that these policies would increase the deficit and national debt and would not be effective in helping the economy to recover. Proponents of the stimulus responded that it was essential to prevent an already very weak economy from slipping into Great Depression–like conditions. As you can see, in terms of economic theory, this argument reflects the difference between classical and Keynesian views of how economies operate. A similar debate raged in Europe between advocates of "austerity" policies aimed at balancing budgets and reducing debt and those who argued that in a time of high unemployment the main priority should be expanding economic activity.

We return to the specifics of these debates—and an evaluation of the results of economic stimulus and of austerity policies—in future chapters. Our goal in this chapter is to develop a basic theory of government spending and taxes and their effects on the economy, using the principles of aggregate demand and the multiplier developed in Chapter 24.

1. The Role of Government Spending and Taxes

fiscal policy: government spending and tax policy

Economists often disagree about which tax and spending policies are best in different economic situations. These debates are over **fiscal policy**—what government spends, how it gets the money that it spends, and the effects of these activities on GDP levels. To understand these issues, we need to extend the simple macroeconomic model of Chapter 24 to include the role of government.

If the role of the government is added, the equation for aggregate demand used in previous chapters becomes:

$$AD = C + I_I + G$$

government spending (G): the component of GDP that represents spending on goods and services by federal, state, and local governments

Government spending on goods and services, including spending by federal, state, and local governments (G) is added to aggregate demand (AD). Taxes do not appear directly in this equation, but, as we will see, they have an impact through their effect on consumption spending.

We examine the effects of these changes to our model one at a time, starting with the impact of a change in government spending.

1.1 A Change in Government Spending

Government spending has a direct impact on the level of GDP. Government purchases of goods and services increase aggregate demand, boosting equilibrium output. In Chapter 24, we showed how a decline in intended investment (I_I) lowered the AD line, leading to equilibrium at a lower level of income. This suggests that government spending might be used as an antidote to low investment spending.

Suppose that we start with the macroeconomic equilibrium presented in Table 24.5 and Figure 24.16 in Chapter 24. Remember that this was an unemployment equilibrium. If we start at an unemployment equilibrium, additional aggregate demand will be needed to return to full employment. Our first model assumed no government role; hence initial government spending equals 0. Thus a simple policy would be to increase government spending on goods and services from 0 to 80. As you can see in Table 25.1 and Figure 25.1, the addition of 80 units of government spending causes the equilibrium to shift up by 400, to the full employment Y^* of 800. Why does this happen?

Table 25.1 **An Increase in Government Spending**

(1) Income (Y)	(2) Consumption (C)	(3) Intended Investment (I_I)	(4) Original Aggregate Demand ($AD_0 = C + I_I$)	(5) Government Spending (G)	(6) New Aggregate Demand ($AD_1 = C + I_I + G$)
300	260	60	320	80	400
400	340	60	400	80	480
500	420	60	480	80	560
600	500	60	560	80	640
700	580	60	640	80	720
800	660	60	720	80	800

Figure 25.1 **Increased Government Spending**

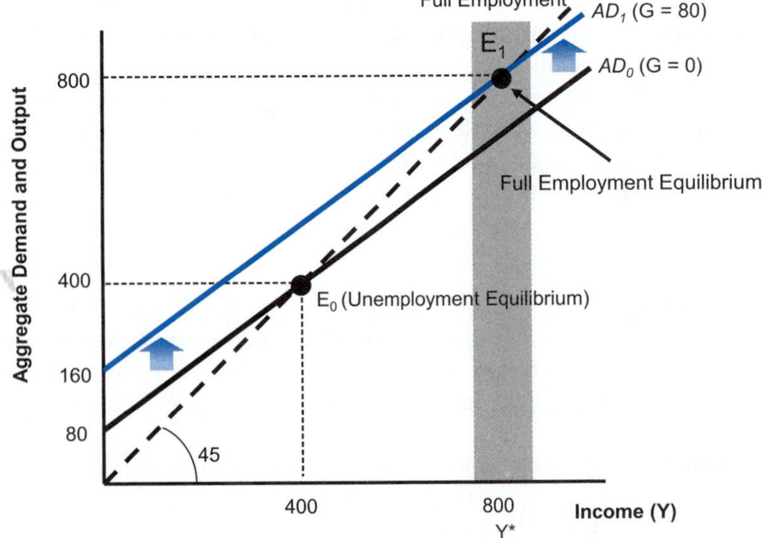

An increase in government spending has a similar effect to an increase in private fixed investment. It shifts the AD line upward, as government spending rises. This increases the equilibrium levels of income and output. The increase in Y is larger than that of G because of the multiplier effect, which occurs due to the induced consumption that occurs as the economy expands along the AD line.

Let's look at a simple example—a new building construction program. Government money is spent on goods such as concrete and steel as well as paying workers. This directly creates new aggregate demand. In addition, there are multiplier effects—construction workers will use their incomes to buy all kinds of consumer goods and services. The multiplier effects add to the original economic stimulus resulting from the government spending.

The effect is exactly the same as the multiplier for intended investment that we discussed in Chapter 24. The initial change in government spending (ΔG) becomes income to individuals (ΔY), which leads to a round of consumer spending (ΔC) equal to ($mpc*\Delta Y$), which in turn becomes income to other individuals, leading to another round of consumer spending, and so forth. The whole process can be summarized using the same formula as in Chapter 24, but now applied to government spending rather than intended investment:

$$\Delta Y = \frac{1}{1 - mpc} \Delta G$$

or:

$$\Delta Y = mult\ \Delta G$$

Using the same *mpc* and multiplier as before (we had chosen the example where $mpc = 0.8$, resulting in $mult = 5$) allows us to predict the impact of government spending on economic equilibrium. The multiplier applies to government spending in exactly the same way that it does to changes in intended investment. Therefore an increase in government spending of 80 leads to an equilibrium shift of $80 \times 5 = 400$. Looking at it the other way, if we start with the goal of an increase of 400 in *Y*, we can divide 400 by 5 to find the needed quantity of ΔG: 400/5 = 80.

Note that at the original *AD* level, there is an equilibrium at 400, where $AD = Y$, and there is significant unemployment. After the addition of 80 in government spending (*G*), the new equilibrium is at the full-employment level of 800, where $AD_1 = Y$. (You can check other levels in the table to make sure that it is the only level at which $AD_1 = Y$.) Figure 25.1 shows the same thing graphically. The aggregate demand schedule moves up by 80 at each level of income, so that the horizontal intercept of the *AD* line moves up from 80 to 160. The slope of the *AD* line remains the same, since there has been no change in the *mpc*. The change in equilibrium income is equal to the change in government spending times the multiplier.

Using the multiplier, we can easily calculate the effect of further changes in government spending. For example, suppose that government spending were reduced from 80 to 60. This negative change of 20 in *G* would lead to a change of ($5 \times -20 = -100$) in equilibrium *Y*. Income would fall from 800 to 700.

So we can see that an increase in government spending will raise the level of economic equilibrium, while a decrease in government spending will lower it. The multiplier effect, which is the same size in both directions, gives the policy extra "bang for the buck"—in this case, a change in government spending leads to five times as great a change in national income.

While we have used a multiplier of 5 to illustrate our hypothetical example, in real life the multiplier is rarely this large (as we will see later in the chapter and also in the algebraic presentation in Appendix A2), but there will usually be some multiplier effects from a change in government spending. Econometric studies of the U.S. economy generally indicate a multiplier effect of 2.0 or less.

1.2 TAXES AND TRANSFER PAYMENTS

To complete the picture of fiscal policy, we need to include the role of taxes and transfer payments. If voters and government officials do not want to raise government spending on

transfer payments: payments by government to individuals or firms, including Social Security payments, unemployment compensation, interest payments, and subsidies

goods and services, they have another option. To raise GDP, the government could cut taxes or increase **transfer payments**. Transfer payments are government grants, subsidies, or gifts to individuals or firms. Examples of transfer payments include unemployment insurance and Social Security payments, payments of interest to holders of government bonds, and subsidies to, for example, energy or agricultural corporations.

In recent decades, the fiscal tool most often chosen by policymakers has been tax reductions. (Tax reductions, of course, tend to be politically popular in addition to providing economic stimulus.) Increases in transfer payments would have the same general positive effect on aggregate demand. The opposite policies—increasing taxes or decreasing transfer payments—would have a negative effect on economic equilibrium, similar to a reduction in government spending.

Changes in taxes and transfer payments, however, do not have exactly the same effect as changes in government spending on goods and services. The mechanism by which tax and transfer changes affect output differs from the process discussed above for government spending. While government purchases *directly* affect aggregate demand and GDP, the effect of taxes and transfer payments is *indirect,* based on their effect on consumption or investment. There are many kinds of taxes and transfers, including corporate taxes, tariffs, and inheritance taxes, but we focus here on the effects of changes in personal income taxes and transfers to individuals.

For example, let's say consumers receive a tax cut of 50. If they spent it all, that would add 50 to aggregate demand. But according to the "marginal propensity to consume" (*mpc*) principle, consumers are likely to use a portion of the tax cut to increase saving or reduce debt. With the *mpc* of 0.8 that we used for our basic model in Chapter 24, the portion saved will be $0.2 \times 50 = 10$, leaving 40 for increased consumption. Thus the effect on aggregate demand would be only 40, not 50 (since saving is not part of aggregate demand).

disposable income: income remaining for consumption or saving after subtracting taxes and adding transfer payments

The same logic would hold if consumers received extra transfer income of 50. They would spend only 40, and save 10. The reverse would be true for a tax increase or a cut in transfer payments. With a tax increase or benefit cut of 50, individuals and families would have less to spend and would reduce their consumption by 40.

Economists define **disposable income** (Y_d) as the income available to consumers after paying taxes and receiving transfers:

$$Y_d = Y - T + TR$$

where T is the total of taxes paid in the economy and TR is the total of transfer payments from governments to individuals.

tax multiplier: the impact of a change in a lump sum tax on economic equilibrium, expressed mathematically as $\Delta Y / \Delta \bar{T} (mult)(mpc)$

Changes in taxes or transfer payments directly affect disposable income but only indirectly affect consumption and aggregate demand. Hence their impact on economic equilibrium is less than that of government spending, which affects aggregate demand directly.

For this reason, the multiplier effects of changes in taxes and transfer payments are smaller than the multiplier impacts of government spending. If taxes are "lump sum"—that is, set at a fixed level that does not change with income, then we can write $T = \bar{T}$. The **tax multiplier** for a lump sum tax works in two stages. In the first stage, consumption is reduced by $mpc\ (\Delta \bar{T})$, which can be expressed as:

$$\Delta C = -(mpc)\, \Delta \bar{T}$$

In the second stage, this reduction in consumption has the regular multiplier effect on equilibrium income. The combined effect can be expressed as:

$$\Delta Y = (mult)\, \Delta C = -(mult)\,(mpc)\, \Delta \bar{T}$$

The tax multiplier is equal to $\Delta Y/\Delta \bar{T} = -(mult)(mpc)$. Mathematically, $(mult)(mpc)$ always works out to exactly 1.0 less than the regular multiplier. (You can use the multiplier formula from Chapter 24 to work out why this is true.) Using the figures from our previous example, where $mpc = 0.8$ and $mult = 5$, the tax multiplier would be $-(0.8) \times 5 = -4$. (For a more detailed algebraic account of the tax multiplier for a lump sum tax, see Appendix A1.)

Just as a tax increase has a contractionary effect, a tax cut will have an expansionary effect. Historically, tax cuts played an important role in U.S. economic policy in the 1960s, 1980s, and 2000s, as well as in the response to the recession of 2007–9. In all cases, the effect on GDP was expansionary, although there is debate about the exact mechanism through which this occurred—not all economists accept the simple tax multiplier process that we have discussed.

Transfer payments, which as we noted are a kind of "negative tax," affect the level of output through a similar logic. An increase in transfer payments, like a tax cut, will give people more money that they can spend. But the expansionary effect occurs only when they actually do spend—so, according to the *mpc* logic, the impact of an increase in transfer payments is reduced by whatever portion of the extra income people decide to save. The multiplier impact of a change in transfer payments is therefore the same as that of a change in taxes, except in the opposite direction. A cut in transfer payments, like an increase in taxes, will be contractionary, tending to lower economic equilibrium.

In the real economy, income taxes are generally proportional or progressive—that is, they increase with income levels (as discussed in Chapter 12).* In our model, the effect of a proportional tax would be to *flatten* the aggregate demand curve, since it has a larger effect at higher income levels. (See Appendix A2 for a more detailed treatment of the impact of a proportional tax—we omit analysis of progressive taxes, which is a bit more complex.) This in turn will affect the multiplier, reducing it somewhat.

How can we explain the effect of a proportional tax on the multiplier? Taxes that rise with income will tend to lower the proportion consumed out of each dollar increase in income. For example, with a 15 percent tax each extra dollar of income will be reduced to 85 cents of disposable income. Applying our original *mpc* of 0.80 to the remaining 85 cents, we get $0.8 \times 0.85 = 0.68$, indicating that 68 cents will be devoted to consumption (and 17 cents to saving). The result is similar to having a lower *mpc,* which also means a lower multiplier. This will dampen the effect of income changes on aggregate demand and economic equilibrium.

balanced budget multiplier: the impact on equilibrium output of simultaneous increases of equal size in government spending and taxes

You might wonder what would be the effect of an increase in government spending that is exactly balanced by an increase in taxes? Since we have shown that the multiplier effect of taxes goes in the opposite direction from that of government spending, it might appear that the effects would cancel each other out. But this is not the case. Because the tax multiplier is smaller than the government spending multiplier, there is a net positive effect on aggregate demand and equilibrium. The difference between the two multipliers equals 1, so the net multiplier effect will also equal 1. In the example we have used, the government policy multiplier is 5, and the tax multiplier is 4, so the **balanced budget multiplier** $= +5 - 4 = 1$. Thus the impact on economic equilibrium is exactly equal to the original change in government spending (and taxes). So we can say that $\Delta Y = \Delta G$.**

For example, an increase of $50 billion in government spending, balanced by an equal increase of $50 billion in taxes, would be expected to lead to a net increase in equilibrium

*Not counting "loopholes" that sometimes allow the very wealthy to characterize some of their income in ways that allow them to pay *lower* effective tax rates than do other groups.

**Technically, simultaneous changes in government spending and taxes of equal size do not imply that the overall budget is balanced. What is required for this is that *total* spending and *total* taxes be equal.

output of \$50 billion. One way of thinking about this is to consider that the original government spending boosts GDP, but the negative multiplier effects generated by the tax increase cancel out the positive multiplier effects of the government spending. This results in a weaker net effect than government spending of \$50 billion alone, which would lead to $\Delta Y = (mult)\Delta G = 5\Delta G$, or \$250 billion in this example.

1.3 THE CIRCULAR FLOW WITH GOVERNMENT SPENDING AND TAXES

We can modify the simple circular flow model introduced in Chapter 24 (Figures 24.5 and 24.6) to add government spending and taxes. A circular flow including government spending and taxes is shown in Figure 25.2. As noted above, transfer payments are considered negative taxes, so we do not include a separate arrow for transfers. Instead, we show **net taxes**—taxes minus transfer payments—as a leakage from the circular flow and government spending as a reinjection to the circular flow.

net taxes: taxes minus transfer payments

This model thus has two leakages—savings and net taxes; and two injections—intended investment and government spending. As discussed in the previous chapter, savings and investment flow through the financial system, and may or may not balance. Similarly, taxes and government spending may or may not balance, depending on whether the government has a deficit, a surplus, or a balanced budget.

This model represents a useful, simplified way of thinking about the complex macroeconomic system. If the overall leakages and injections balance, the system should be at a full employment equilibrium. From a Keynesian perspective, the object of government policy is to achieve such a balance, by varying government spending and net taxes to offset any imbalances in savings and investment. Classical economists are more skeptical about the ability of government to achieve this and more concerned that government action will unbalance, rather than balance, the circular flow. We discuss some of these policy implications in much more detail in later chapters.

In Chapter 29 we introduce one more modification of the circular flow diagram to take into account the foreign sector, showing the effect of imports and exports. But first, we examine some of the implications of government policies aimed at balancing out the circular flow.

Figure 25.2 **A Macroeconomic Model with Government Spending and Taxes**

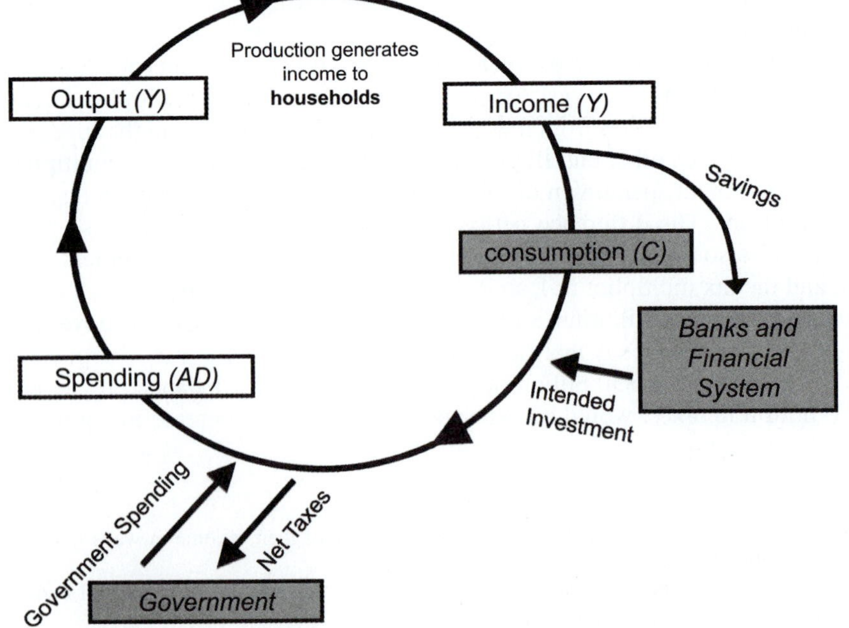

The model shows two sets of leakages and injections into the circular flow: savings (leakage) and intended investment (injection), and net taxes (leakage) and government spending (injection). These may or may not balance out at a full employment level of output.

1.4 EXPANSIONARY AND CONTRACTIONARY FISCAL POLICY

The three fiscal policy tools discussed above—changes in government spending, changes in tax levels, and changes in transfer payments—affect income and employment levels, as well as inflation rates (discussed further below and in Chapter 28). They also, of course, affect the government's budgetary position. The budget could be balanced, in surplus, or in deficit, depending on the combination of spending and tax policy that is employed.

expansionary fiscal policy: the use of government spending, transfer payments, or tax cuts to stimulate a higher level of economic activity

Increasing government spending is an example of what economists refer to as **expansionary fiscal policy**. Other expansionary fiscal policies are increasing transfer payments or lowering taxes. Whether through a direct impact on aggregate demand or through giving consumers more money to spend, these policies should increase aggregate demand and equilibrium.

If that were the whole story, macroeconomic policy would be simple—just use sufficient government spending or tax cuts to maintain the economy at full employment. But there are complications. One problem is that in order to spend more, the government has to raise taxes, borrow, or "print money." (Issues of how government finances its expenditures are discussed later in this chapter and in subsequent ones.) Raising taxes tends to counteract the expansionary effects of increased spending. Borrowing money creates deficits and raises long-term government debt that, as we will see, may or may not be a problem (these issues are discussed in depth in Chapter 31).

Another problem is that too much government spending may lead to inflation. The goal of expansionary fiscal policy is to expand the economic activity to its full-employment level. But what if fiscal policy overshoots this level? It is easy to see how this might occur. For politicians, government spending on popular programs is easy but raising taxes to pay for them is hard. This can lead to budget deficits (discussed in Section 2), but it can also cause excessive aggregate demand in the economy. Excessive demand could also, in theory, arise from high consumer or business spending, but usually government spending, alone or in combination with high consumer and business expenditures, is partly to blame when the economy "overheats." The result is likely to be inflation.

According to our basic analysis, the cure for inflation should be fairly straightforward. If the problem is too much aggregate demand, the solution is to reduce aggregate demand. We could do this by reversing the process discussed in the previous section and lowering government spending on goods and services. A similar effect can be obtained by reducing transfer payments or by increasing taxes. With lower transfer payments or higher taxes, businesses and consumers will have less spending power. Lower spending by government, businesses, and consumers will result in a lower equilibrium output level, and there will no longer be excess demand pressures to create inflation.

contractionary fiscal policy: reductions in government spending or transfer payments or increases in taxes, leading to a lower level of economic activity

Thus we have identified another important economic policy tool—**contractionary fiscal policy**. This is a weapon that can be used against inflation, though it would generally be unwise to use it at times of high unemployment. (The problem of what to do if unemployment and inflation occur at the same time—something that is not shown in our simple model—is discussed in Chapter 28.) Of course, too large a spending reduction could overshoot in a downward direction, leading to excessive unemployment and, possibly, a recession.

Although the effects of contractionary fiscal policy can be painful, it would be wrong to assume that expansionary fiscal policy is always beneficial and contractionary policy always harmful. Contractionary policy can be useful when previous policies have "overshot" the goal or when the economy is suffering from excessive inflation. We discuss this issue of policy choice extensively in this and the following chapters.

Discussion Questions

1. What recent changes in government spending or tax policy have been in the news? How would you expect these to affect GDP and employment levels?

2. In general, tax increases are politically unpopular. Would you ever be likely to favor a tax increase? Under what circumstances, if any, might a tax increase be beneficial to the economy?

2. The Federal Budget

government outlays: total government expenditures, including spending on goods and services and transfer payments

The federal government's budget includes spending on goods and services, transfer payments, and taxes. (This is also true of state and local government budgets, but our focus for purposes of fiscal policy analysis is mainly the federal budget.) Thus we can divide total government expenditures, or **government outlays**, into two categories. Total government outlays include not only government spending on goods and services (G) but also government transfer payments:

$$Government\ Outlays = G + TR$$

Recalling the earlier discussion, only government spending directly affects aggregate demand. Transfer payments do so only indirectly through their effect on consumption. As we see below, however, both types of outlay affect the federal budget, since both represent funds that the government must pay out.

government bond: an interest-bearing security constituting a promise to pay at a specified future time

On the revenue side, government income comes from taxes (T). When revenues are not sufficient to cover outlays, the government borrows to cover the difference. The actual financing of a deficit is accomplished through the sale of **government bonds** by the U.S. Treasury. Government bonds are interest-bearing securities that can be bought by firms, individuals, or foreign governments. In effect, a government bond is a promise to pay back, with interest, the amount borrowed at a specific time in the future.

off-budget expenditures: government-funded programs that are exempted from the normal budgeting process because the taxes that fund them cannot be used for budgetary items that are subject to congressional appropriations

Federal sources of revenue and outlays are shown in Figure 25.3 for fiscal year (FY) 2011*. The major sources of federal revenue are personal income and Social Security taxes. In FY 2011, the federal government also borrowed an amount equal to 36 percent of the total budget. Government borrowing varies from year to year, but deficits are more common than surpluses. The major categories of government spending are Social Security, defense spending, and social programs.

on-budget expenditures: all federal expenditures that rely on general tax revenue subject to congressional approval each year

appropriation (of federal funds): Congressional approval of funds for a particular purpose

Social Security and Medicare taxes are a special case, in that they are collected for a specific purpose—the provision of Social Security and Medicare benefits. Funds raised through such taxes are exclusively for retirement purposes and cannot be used to finance any other government programs, for example, national defense or social programs (except, as we will see, when the federal government borrows from such accounts). For this reason, they are considered to be "**off budget**." All other tax and spending categories shown are free of such restrictions and are classified as "**on budget**." Each of the on-budget spending items is subject to congressional approval, or **appropriation**, each year.

Interest payments on the existing government debt are another special case. They are "on budget," yet they are not subject to approval by Congress. To fulfill the promise made by the government when issuing bonds, interest on the debt must always be paid. Such payments amounted to 6 percent of federal spending in FY 2011.

Clearly, government borrowing and interest payments on the debt have economic impacts. What is the nature of these impacts? To answer this question, we need to look more carefully at the nature of government deficits.

*The Federal Fiscal Year runs from October 1 of the prior year through September 30 of the year being described. For example, FY 2011 runs from October 1 2010 through September 30, 2011.

Figure 25.3 **United States Government Source of Funds and Outlays, Fiscal 2011**

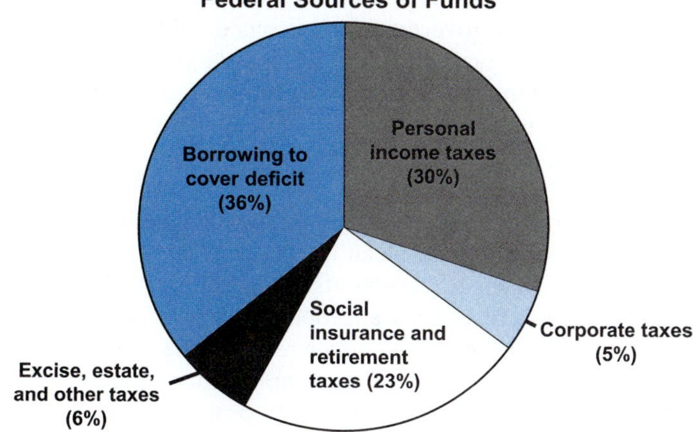

The largest sources of federal revenues are personal income and Social Security taxes. Part of the budget—36 percent in 2011—is covered by borrowing (issuing government bonds).

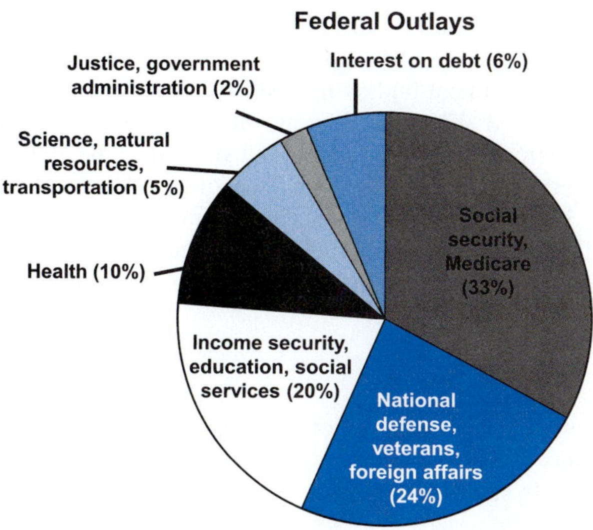

Social Security and Medicare made up 33 percent of federal outlays in 2011, and national defense 24 percent. Interest on the federal debt represented 6 percent of federal outlays.

Source: Economic Report of the President, 2013, Table B-81.

2.1 Deficits and Surpluses

budget surplus: an excess of total government tax revenues over total government outlays

budget deficit: an excess of total government outlays over total government tax revenues

First, we need to define what we mean by the **government budget surplus or deficit**. This can be calculated by subtracting total government outlays from total government tax revenues. A positive result indicates a surplus; a negative one, a deficit.

$$Budget\ Surplus\ (+)\ or\ Deficit\ (-) = T - Government\ Outlays$$
$$= T - (G + TR)$$

Showing the government's budget deficit as a percentage of nominal GDP is a simple way to correct for the effects of both inflation and the ability of the economy to handle the deficit. The larger the economy—as measured by GDP—the easier it is to manage a given deficit, since both the fiscal and budgetary impacts of the deficit will be relatively smaller compared to the size of the economy. A bigger economy means that people will have higher incomes and a larger flow of savings is likely to be available to purchase more government bonds, making it easier for the government to borrow.

State and local governments are generally required to separate their current spending and capital budgets. Current spending must be paid for out of current taxes, but money

deficit spending: government spending in excess of tax revenues collected

countercyclical policy: fiscal policy in which taxes are lowered and expenditure is raised when the economy is weak, and the opposite occurs when the economy is strong

procyclical policy: fiscal policy in which taxes are lowered and expenditure is raised when the economy is strong, and the opposite is done when the economy is weak

can be borrowed for investment ("capital") projects such as new schools, bridges, and transit systems. The federal budget, however, makes no such distinction between current and capital spending. In fact, the federal government has considerably more flexibility than state and local governments in the conduct of budget operations. A decisive factor in the difference is that the federal government is uniquely empowered to conduct **deficit spending** and to finance spending through expansion of the money supply (as we will see in Chapter 27), while the states and municipalities have no such power. We return to this point in later chapters.

Economists sometimes use the term "**countercyclical**" to describe a federal government policy of increasing spending and cutting taxes in lean times and doing the reverse when the economy strengthens. State and local governments, in contrast, tend to follow a more **procyclical policy**, in which both recessions and booms are reinforced rather than counterbalanced. This is not the intended result but simply a result of the fact that voters are more inclined to support local spending on schools, for example, when times are good. So in certain respects federal fiscal policy works against not only business-cycle fluctuations but also the unintentional reinforcement of such fluctuations by state and local governments (see Box 25.1).

Over the years, the U.S. Federal budget position has varied from deficit to surplus and back again. The U.S. federal government budget went from a large deficit in 1992 to a surplus in 2001 (Figure 25.4). Then in 2002 the government budget moved back into deficit. After moderating for a few years, deficits increased sharply following the Great Recession of 2007–9, at one point even exceeding 10 percent of GDP—a level not seen since the 1940s. This has led to an extensive debate about the impact of deficits on the economy. We focus on these issues in greater depth in Chapter 31. As we see, there is much continuing controversy, among economists and the general public, about the significance of budgetary policy and deficits and many different ideas about the best way to handle issues of government spending, taxes, and transfer payments.

2.2 Automatic Stabilizers

Deficits and surpluses are not just a result of active fiscal policy. A significant portion of the variations in government spending and tax revenues occurs "automatically," due to mechanisms built into the economic system to help stabilize it.

Box 25.1 The Effect of State and Local Government Spending on GDP

While much of the debate about government spending in the United States focuses on the federal level, changes in government spending at state and local levels can also have a significant impact on the macroeconomy. The U.S. Bureau of Economic Analysis (BEA) has developed economic models that attempt to isolate the impact of state and local government spending on GDP.

The BEA estimated, for example, that in 2009 state and local government spending provided a boost to the national economy—increasing the GDP growth rate by 0.28 percentage points. In other words, nominal GDP growth in 2009 was 0.9 percent, but would have been about 0.6 percent without the positive impact of state and local government spending. Some of this spending was money that state and local governments received from the 2009 American Recovery and Reinvestment Act (the Obama stimulus).

But when state and local governments cut spending, their impact on GDP levels can turn negative. This was the case in 2010 and 2011, as federal stimulus money dried up and states mostly looked to balance their budgets by cutting spending. The BEA estimated that state and local budget cutbacks reduced GDP growth by 0.23 percentage points in 2010 and 0.43 percentage points in 2011. Preliminary results indicate that the impact of state and local government spending on GDP in 2012 was also negative.

Source: Norton Francis, "State and Local Budget Cuts Hurt the Recovery," *Christian Science Monitor*, Tax VOX, July 30, 2012.

Figure 25.4 **Federal Surplus or Deficit as a Percent of GDP**

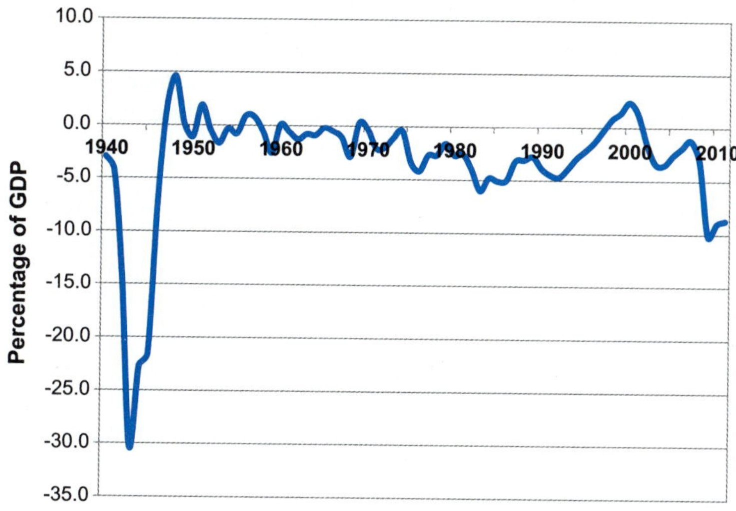

The federal deficit—as measured by government borrowing—reached 6 percent of GDP in 1983, a year of deep recession. The deficit was reduced as a percent of GDP from the early 1990s until 1998, when the budget went into surplus. From 1998 to 2001, the government had a net surplus, meaning that some debt was being retired. After 2000, a recession combined with the Bush administration tax cuts put the budget back into deficit. The recession of 2007–9 led to even larger deficits, reaching 10% of GDP before starting to decline as the economy started a slow recovery.

Source: Economic Report of the President, 2013, Table B-79.

Since the 1950s, government spending has been a major part of the U.S. economy. As we have seen, this was partly a result of the Keynesian idea that government spending was needed to prevent recession. In recent decades, the use of expansionary fiscal policy has been controversial, partly as a result of issues such as deficits and inflation. During this period, however, total government outlays (including transfers and spending on goods and services) have not declined, either in money terms or as a percentage of GDP.

automatic stabilizers: tax and spending institutions that tend to increase government revenues and lower government spending during economic expansions but lower revenues and raise government spending during economic recessions

As Figure 25.5 shows, government receipts and outlays tend to fluctuate over time. For example, beginning in 2007, when the economy stagnated as a consequence of the financial crisis, government receipts declined while outlays increased. Economists refer to the change as the **automatic stabilization** effect of government spending and taxes. It refers to the way in which the government budget moderates fluctuations of aggregate demand even without any active decision-making or legislating by the government.

Even if no specific budgetary action is taken, the government's budget will vary over the business cycle. Suppose that the economy is entering a recession. As aggregate demand falls, the government deficit generally rises. Tax revenues decline as people have less income on which to pay taxes due to the slowing economy. In addition, as more people receive unemployment

Figure 25.5 **Federal Outlays, Receipts, and Surplus/Deficit, as a Percent of GDP, 1980–2011**

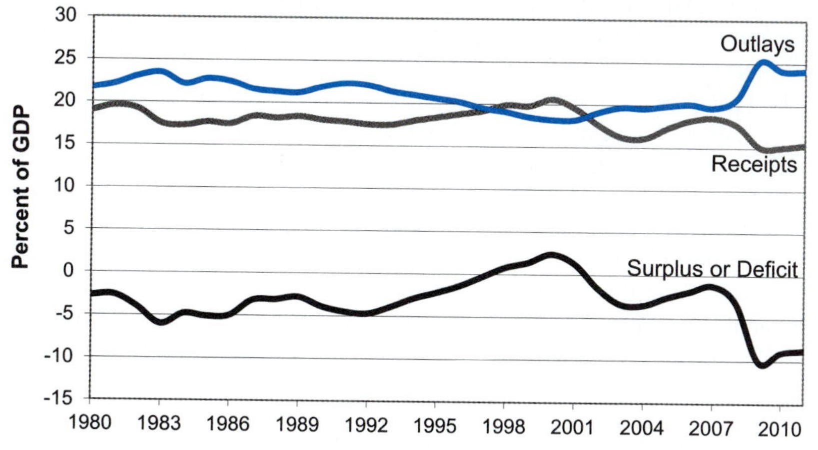

The United States federal government has operated at a deficit for most of the last few decades, with particularly high deficits in recent years.

Source: Economic Report of the President, 2013, Table B-79.

insurance, transfer payments related to programs such as food stamps increase. This cushions the fall in personal disposable income—and thus the fall in consumer spending.

If the federal government does not actively move to balance its budget, these automatic changes in spending and taxes tend to moderate the recession. In effect, the recession creates an automatic response of expansionary fiscal impacts—increased spending and lower tax revenues. It will also, of course, tend to increase the government deficit (or reduce any surplus).

Similarly, if aggregate demand is rising during an economic expansion, tax revenues rise. Fewer people receive unemployment or other transfer payments. This means that personal disposable income does not rise as quickly as national income. This, in turn, puts a damper on increases in consumer spending—and limits the inflationary overheating that can arise from increased aggregate demand.

cyclical deficit (surplus): the portion of the deficit (or surplus) that is caused by fluctuations in the business cycle

Automatic stabilizers are, therefore, inseparable from cyclical budget imbalances. Economists often say that the portion of the deficit (surplus) that is the result of automatic stabilizers is the **cyclical deficit (or surplus)**. It is, in effect, the part of the budget balance that is sensitive to fluctuations in the macroeconomy.

This phenomenon helps explain why, for example, the U.S. government was able to enjoy budgetary surpluses in the late 1990s. It is true that the policies of the Clinton administration, which included raising tax rates to try to balance the budget, contributed. But as business revenues and personal incomes soared, the resulting increase in tax revenues allowed the government's coffers to fill.

In addition to the automatic stabilizers, the federal budget has another aspect that levels the fluctuations of output. This is the steadiness of government spending. Unlike investment, consumer spending, net exports, and to some extent state and local government spending, most areas of federal spending do not change drastically from year to year. This adds an element of stability to the economy's aggregate demand.

2.3 Discretionary Policy

discretionary fiscal policy: changes in government spending and taxation resulting from deliberate policy decisions

Sometimes, the automatic stabilization effect of government spending and taxes cannot smooth economic ups and downs as much as is needed. Relatively severe problems of recession or inflation often give rise to proposals to use an active, or **discretionary fiscal policy** to remedy the situation. This issue is controversial among economists. Some economists, as we will see, believe that the government should *never* use an activist fiscal policy, believing that it is likely to do more harm than good. Other economists argue that activist fiscal policy is essential, especially to respond to severe economic problems such as deep recession. Regardless of economists' advice, the fact is that governments are making fiscal policy all the time, whether in a planned or unplanned manner. Every year, the government revises its budget, including levels of spending and taxation. These spending and tax levels have effects on the economy, and it is important to try to understand them.

Historically, the first major experience with expansionary fiscal policy was during World War II. Before the war, President Franklin D. Roosevelt's New Deal had initiated some government spending programs intended to put the unemployed to work during the Great Depression. But these programs were dwarfed by the magnitude of war spending in the 1940s. As a result, unemployment, which had been as high as 25 percent in 1933 and 19 percent in 1938, fell to about 2 percent in 1943. The fall in unemployment was a beneficial side effect of the onset of World War II and the war-induced spending.*

After the conclusion of World War II, government spending never returned to prewar levels, and the beneficial effects of the expanded government role—steady economic growth with

*Employment figures for that era covered a labor force in which a much lower proportion of women were seeking jobs than is the case today. During World War II, an unusually large number of women were employed, filling jobs left vacant by men who were serving in the armed forces.

relatively low unemployment levels—seemed to justify this. In the 1960s, economists became even more optimistic about the benefits of fiscal policy. At that time, it was suggested that it would be possible for the government to "fine-tune" the economic system using fiscal policy, to ratchet aggregate demand up or down in response to changes in the business climate.

time lags: the time that elapses between the formulation of an economic policy and its actual effects on the economy

"Fine-tuning" was largely discredited in the 1970s and 1980s, as the economy struggled with inflationary problems that were partly a result of sharp increases in oil prices, but were also seen as having been worsened by excessive government spending (we look at this in more detail in Chapter 28). In addition, many economists argued that problems of **time lags** made fiscal policy unwieldy and often counterproductive.

To understand the problems with fine-tuning and time lags, we can use a commonsense example. Imagine that when you wake up it is too cold in your apartment, so you turn up the temperature on the thermostat. It might take so much time for the apartment to warm up that you do not get the benefits before you leave for work. You might become impatient, raising the temperature again. As a result, the apartment gets too hot during the day, so when you get home you have to turn the thermostat down again. Thus delayed responses make your management of the apartment's temperature less effective. The best strategy is to set the thermostat at a single temperature (or, with a programmable thermostat, a specific daily pattern) and then to resist fiddling with it.

Similarly, time lags can make active fiscal policy less effective as a way to stabilize the economy. There are two types of lags: *inside* and *outside* lags. Inside lags refer to delays that occur within the government, while outside lags refer to the delayed effects of government policies. There are four major types of inside lags:

1. *A data lag:* It may take some time for the government to collect information about economic problems such as unemployment.
2. *A recognition lag:* Government decision-makers may not see an event as a problem right away.
3. *A legislative lag:* Discretionary fiscal policy must be instituted in the form of legal changes in the government's budget. The government's economists may want to increase spending or decrease tax rates, but they have to convince both the president and Congress to act to solve the problem.
4. *A transmission lag:* These legal changes take time to show up in actual tax forms and government budgets. One solution is that changes can be made retroactive to speed up their implementation—for instance, a tax cut legislated now may apply to income received during the previous year. However, this is not always done.

In addition, even if all these lags have been overcome, it takes time for the new policies actually to affect the economy (the "outside lag"). Suppose, for example, that the government responds to a rise in unemployment with increased government spending or a tax cut. By the time these policies are in place and create an economic stimulus, the economy may have recovered on its own. In that case, the additional aggregate demand will not be needed and is likely to create inflationary pressures.

Despite these problems with discretionary fiscal policy, governments have continued to use it, with mixed results. Government fiscal stimulus, with or without a formal economic justification, was applied during the periods 1964–68, 1975–77, 1980–87, in the early 2000s, and again in 2008–12, after the financial crisis and recession. An especially popular form of expansionary policy has been tax cuts, implemented under Presidents Kennedy, Reagan, George W. Bush, as well as by the Obama administration as part of a stimulus policy in response to recession (see Box 25.2).

structural deficit (surplus): the portion of the deficit (or surplus) that results from tax and spending policy dictated by the president and Congress at their discretion

Discretionary expenditures constitute a separate portion of the federal budget. While automatic stabilizers contribute to the cyclical deficit or surplus, we say that discretionary fiscal policy produces a **structural deficit (or surplus)**. We can (loosely) think of the

BOX 25.2 THE OBAMA STIMULUS PROGRAM

In February 2009, in response to a severe recession that had pushed the unemployment rate over 8 percent, the Obama administration proposed a $787 billion stimulus package, including $288 billion in tax cuts, $224 billion in extended unemployment benefits, education, and health care, and $275 billion for job creation through federal contracts, grants, and loans. The stimulus, formally known as the American Recovery and Reinvestment Act (ARRA), was enacted by Congress, providing for increased spending and tax reductions over a period of ten years. For the first three fiscal years, $720 billion, or 91.5 percent, was budgeted to maximize the impact in fighting the recession. Later estimates by the Congressional Budget Office (CBO) indicate that the total impact of the stimulus package over the period 2009–19 will be about $830 billion.

From the point of view of economic analysis, the stimulus amounted to a major expansionary fiscal policy, including all three fiscal policy tools: changes in government spending, changes in tax levels, and changes in transfer payments. According to the economic theories discussed in this chapter, the effects of such a program should be to expand economic activity, boost GDP, and lower unemployment (although classical economists are skeptical, especially about the effectiveness of government spending).

Was the stimulus successful? The answer was not immediately obvious, because the recession was severe (unemployment rates peaked in late 2009 at 10 percent) and the subsequent recovery slow, giving many people the impression that the stimulus failed. But there is now sufficient evidence to indicate that in fact it was very effective.

According to the CBO, the ARRA "added as many as 3.3 million jobs to the economy in the second quarter of 2010, and may have prevented the nation from lapsing back into recession." An analysis by economists Alan Blinder and Mark Zandi in 2010 found that the stimulus "probably averted what could have been called Great Depression 2.0. . . . [W]ithout the government's response, GDP in 2010 would be about 11.5 percent lower [and] payroll employment would be less by some 8½ million jobs." Blinder and Zandi's analysis takes into account negative multiplier effects. The decline in economic activity in 2009 was so steep that, without an increase in aggregate demand, a negative spiral of lower demand, lower incomes, and even lower demand would have taken place, as it did in the Great Depression in the 1930s.

The CBO report indicates that "the effects of ARRA on output peaked in the first half of 2010 and have since diminished." Even so, the stimulus continued to exert a positive impact on GDP in 2012: "ARRA raised real GDP in 2012 by between 0.1 percent and 0.8 percent, and increased the number of people employed in 2012 by between 0.2 million and 1.1 million." The CBO also estimated output multipliers for stimulus spending between 0.5 and 2.5, for middle-income tax cuts between 0.3 and 1.5, and for transfer payments between 0.4 and 2.1.

What about longer-term effects of the stimulus? The CBO estimates that ARRA will increase budget deficits by about $830 billion over the 2009–19 period; 90 percent of this impact occurred during the first three years of the program. As noted, without the stimulus the economy would have been likely to go into a much more severe decline, which would have lowered tax revenues and raised transfer payments, so it is possible that without the stimulus the deficit would have increased even more. In a survey conducted by the University of Chicago Booth School of Business in 2012, 80 percent of economists agreed that the stimulus had reduced the unemployment rate. On long-term effects, economists were more divided: 46 percent believed that "the benefits of the stimulus will end up exceeding its cost," while 27 percent were not certain, and 12 percent thought that long-term costs would outweigh benefits.

Sources: Congressional Budget Office, *Estimated Impact of the American Recovery and Reinvestment Act on Employment and Output from October 2012 through December 2012* (2012); "Congressional Budget Office Defends Stimulus," *Washington Post,* June 6, 2012; Alan S. Blinder, and Mark Zandi, "How the Great Recession Was Brought to an End," 2010, www.economy.com/mark-zandi/documents/End-of-Great-Recession.pdf.

structural deficit as the deficit that would occur if the economy were at full employment. Structural deficits represent the portion of the overall deficit that is dictated by the president and Congress, even though a significant portion of discretionary expenditures often result from decisions made years earlier. Only changes in the structural budget balance truly reflect the direction of fiscal policy—that is, whether it is stimulative or contractionary—since other changes are related to the automatic stabilizers.

supply-side economics: an economic theory that emphasizes policies to stimulate production, such as lower taxes. The theory predicts that such incentives stimulate greater economic effort, saving, and investment, thereby increasing overall economic output and tax revenues.

Changes in tax policy—tax cuts, for example—also are classified as discretionary (in contrast to changes in tax revenues resulting from business-cycle fluctuations). Proponents of tax cuts sometimes appeal to **supply-side economics** (first introduced during the Reagan administration) to support their policies. The supply-side argument for tax cuts is essentially that lower tax rates encourage more work, saving, and investment, thereby creating a more dynamic economy. According to the most enthusiastic advocates of supply-side economics, output will grow so rapidly in response to a cut in tax rates that total tax revenues will actually increase, not decrease (more on this in Chapter 31). This is different from the logic of increased aggregate demand that we have discussed, which implies that tax cuts will create an economic stimulus, but are likely to raise the government deficit.

The economic record seems to show that tax cuts do indeed create an economic stimulus—but debate continues among economists as to whether this effect is demand-led (as implied by our fiscal policy model) or based on supply-side effects. And in general, tax cuts have usually led to lower revenues and higher deficits (this was true both of the Reagan tax cuts in the 1980s and the Bush tax cuts in the 2000s).

Discussion Questions

1. Do you think that the president is mostly responsible for the persistent budget deficits? Is Congress responsible? Are budget deficits necessarily bad?
2. Why doesn't the government run surpluses every year instead of deficits? Wouldn't doing so be better for the economy?

3. Policy Issues

3.1 Crowding Out and Crowding In

A common concern of fiscal policy critics is that federal government spending gets in the way of consumption and private investment. We have already seen that while government expenditures boost aggregate demand, the tax revenues required to finance such expenditures have the opposite effect. But the expenditure effect is stronger, dollar for dollar, than the tax effect, which is why the effects do not exactly cancel each other out and why the balanced budget multiplier equals 1 instead of 0.

crowding out: a reduction in the availability of private capital resulting from federal government borrowing to finance budget deficits

That would be the end of the story if raising taxes were the only means of financing government expenditures. Yet we know that the government frequently runs deficits and, when it does so, it must borrow money. It borrows from the capital markets (i.e., the loanable funds market as discussed in Chapter 24), in theory leaving less money available for private investment. The reduced availability of loanable funds can have the effect of raising interest rates, which, by making borrowing more expensive, makes investment less likely, *ceteris paribus*. Economists therefore say that borrowing to help cover budget deficits may have the effect of "**crowding out**" private investment. Economists who favor the classical approach often claim that replacing dynamic private investment with "clumsy" government spending is wasteful and inefficient.

Figure 25.6 uses the classical model of the loanable funds market, introduced in Chapter 24 (Figure 24.7) to illustrate how government demand for loanable funds could crowd out private borrowing. The supply curve (S) represents savings or, more concretely, the supply of loanable funds. For a given supply, the interest rate will be pushed up from i_1 to i_2 when the government borrows money to pay for a budget deficit, represented by a shift in the demand curve from D_1 to D_2. The result is that private investment is now more expensive and saving becomes more attractive.

The difference between Q_2 and Q_3 represents the amount of funds borrowed by the government. Because this additional demand raises the interest rate, private investment becomes less attractive, and some is "crowded out." Q_3 now represents the quantity of loanable funds available for private investment. The amount of "crowding out" is shown on the graph

Figure 25.6 **Crowding Out in the Loanable Funds Market**

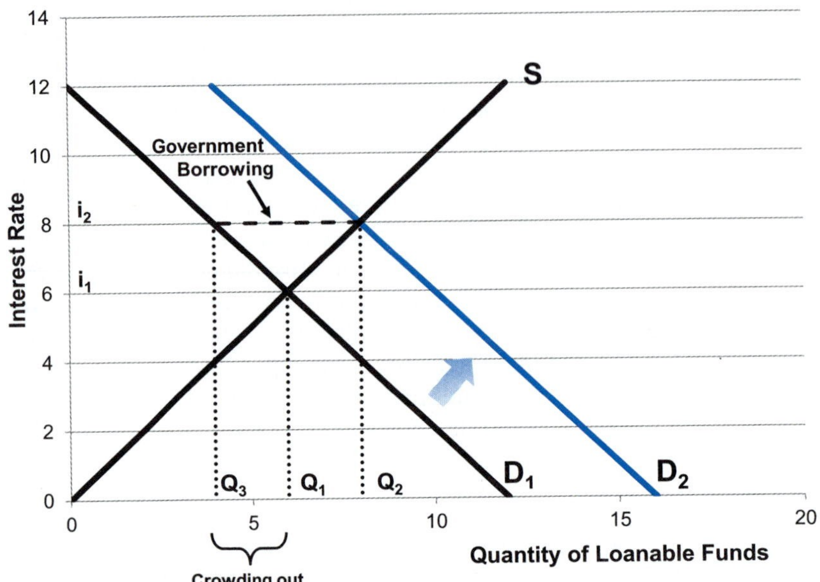

as the difference between Q_1 and Q_3. The implication of this analysis is that government deficit spending is counterproductive to the aim of promoting private investment.

John Maynard Keynes acknowledged the potential for crowding out. He did not, however, believe that deficit spending would crowd out private spending to a significant degree if, as during the Great Depression, there was considerable slack in the economy. In other words, if owners of capital are reluctant to invest anyway, there is no reason for government borrowing to drive up interest rates. Remember that in the Keynesian view, recessionary conditions are characterized by an excess of savings over investment. If there is a large excess of savings, there is no reason to worry that government borrowing will absorb too much of the available loanable funds.

Keynes also minimized the importance of crowding out for other reasons. First, recall from Chapter 24 that, according to Keynes, investment decisions are not dependent only on the rate of interest. He believed that investment decisions also are a function of expectations of future profit, what he called "animal spirits." In good economic times, investors purchase more capital goods because their growing profits reinforce an optimistic outlook about the future. And they are likely to do so despite the historical tendency for interest rates to *rise* in good economic times. The opposite might well be true in recession. Despite low interest rates, business spending will be lower due to growing pessimism. For the reasons noted above, government borrowing to finance deficits may not raise interest rates during a recession, and even if it does, this might not have any significant effect on investment, since investors will not want to invest anyway—at least until the economy starts to recover.

Second, there is significant scope for complementarity between public and private investment. According to this argument, certain government expenditures on, say, transportation, energy, or communications networks enhance the potential profits of private investment by providing critical infrastructure. Rather than being a substitute for private investment, government spending supports the productivity of private investment, and is therefore likely to encourage more of it. When such government spending generates more investment, it is called **crowding in**.

crowding in: the process in which government spending leads to more favorable expectations for the economy, thereby inducing investment

During the Great Depression, Keynes argued that the economy could be stuck in a potentially permanent low-level equilibrium (i.e., the unemployment equilibrium we saw in Chapter 24) and that the government needed to run deficits to finance the spending necessary to stimulate aggregate demand and thus attract renewed investment spending on capital goods. This argument was been reflected recently in the Obama administration's position that infrastructure spending is important to get a sluggish economy moving again.

3.2 DIFFERENT MULTIPLIER EFFECTS

Another issue of considerable policy controversy is which items in the budget deserve priority. A principal goal of government spending—especially discretionary spending—is to stimulate the economy. The multiplier ensures that every additional dollar of government spending increases aggregate demand by more than one dollar. But we have also seen that much of the effect can be offset by taxes. In addition, it is unrealistic to assume that the multiplier effect is the same regardless of the type of government expenditure.

As seen earlier, the larger the *mpc,* the greater the multiplier. Until now, we have assumed that the *mpc* is uniform—that is, that it represents the marginal propensity to consume of all individuals and groups in society. But there may be significant variations in the *mpc* depending on which income groups are involved.

The typical wealthy individual is capable of saving a significant percentage of his income, a much greater percentage than that of most poor people. Of course, what is saved is not consumed; the average poor person spends a higher percentage of each additional dollar received than would a rich person. In other words, a poor person's *mpc* tends to be higher. Because a higher *mpc* translates to a larger multiplier, Keynes argued that in general the multiplier is largest when government spending is directed toward those who have the highest *mpc*. Spending that benefits the poor or unemployed is thus likely to have larger multiplier effects.

Table 25.2 presents estimates for the multiplier effects of different fiscal policy initiatives. (The multipliers listed here are smaller than those seen in earlier examples because of offsetting effects and leakages such as those discussed in Appendix A2.) Note that unemployment benefits, food stamps, aid to state governments (which help prevent layoffs), and infrastructure spending all have relatively large multiplier effects. The smallest multiplier effects tend to be associated with tax cuts, whether for wealthy individuals or corporations. As anticipated by Keynes, cuts in this case get less "bang for the buck" due to the generally smaller *mpc* exhibited by the beneficiaries of such policies.

Table 25.2 **Different Multiplier Effects**

Tax Cuts	*Multiplier*
Nonrefundable lump-sum tax rebate	1.02
Refundable lump-sum tax rebate	1.26
Temporary Tax Cuts	
Payroll tax holiday	1.29
Across the board tax cut	1.03
Accelerated depreciation	0.27
Permanent Tax Cuts	
Extend alternative minimum tax patch	0.48
Make Bush income tax cuts permanent	0.29
Make dividend and capital gains tax cuts permanent	0.37
Cut corporate tax rate	0.30
Spending Increases	
Extend unemployment insurance benefits	1.64
Temporarily increase food stamps	1.73
Issue general aid to state governments	1.36
Increase infrastructure spending	1.59

Source: M. Zandi, "The Economic Impact of the American Recovery and Reinvestment Act," Moody's Economy.com, 2009.

3.3 APPLYING FISCAL POLICY

We have now identified a number of different fiscal policy approaches that can be used by the government to respond to various economic conditions. We have also noted some of the differences in opinion among economists as to the effectiveness and appropriate use of fiscal policy. In future chapters, we examine the application of fiscal policies to specific problems, including the financial crisis and recession that began in 2007.

Before doing this, we need to add another very important aspect of the economy to our analysis: the money supply and monetary policy. The supply of money in the economy is a very important factor affecting, among other things, interest rates and inflation. We need to understand how the money supply is created and regulated and how this relates to other macroeconomic factors. This is the topic of Chapters 26 and 27.

After we have added an analysis of money and monetary policy, we will return to a consideration of the issues of unemployment and inflation and appropriate policies to respond to them, in Chapter 28. We will then introduce the international economy in Chapter 29. In Chapter 30 we discuss the economic crisis of 2007–8 and its aftermath, in Chapter 31 we focus on issues of debt and deficits.

REVIEW QUESTIONS

1. What is the impact of a change in government spending on aggregate demand and economic equilibrium?
2. What is the impact of a lump-sum change in taxes on aggregate demand and economic equilibrium? How does it differ from a change in government spending?
3. Give some examples of expansionary and contractionary fiscal policy.
4. How is the federal budget surplus or deficit defined? How has the federal budget position varied in recent years?
5. What is meant by an automatic stabilizer? Give some examples of economic institutions that function as automatic stabilizers.
6. What are some of the advantages and disadvantages of discretionary fiscal policy? Give some examples of the use of discretionary fiscal policy.
7. What is a cyclical deficit? What is a structural deficit? How are they different?
8. What is crowding out? How specifically does crowding out happen? Explain. What is crowding in?

EXERCISES

1. Using the data in Table 25.1, determine the economic equilibrium for a government spending level of 60.
2. Using Table 25.1 and the formulas and numbers given in the text for the multiplier and tax multiplier, calculate the effect on equilibrium GDP of a government spending level of 100 combined with a tax level of 100. What does this imply about the impact of a balanced government budget on GDP, compared to government spending alone?
3. Go to the *Economic Report of the President* at www.gpoaccess.gov/eop/. Consult the most recent *Report*'s table on "Gross Domestic Product." For the last year, with final rather than preliminary figures, find the values of gross domestic product personal consumption expenditures, and gross private domestic investment. Now find the value for fixed investment. If we assume that all inventory changes are unintended, fixed investment is the same thing as what we call intended investment. You will note that the column on the right titled "Change in Private Inventories" is equal to the difference between total and fixed investment (just as we have noted that total investment equals intended investment plus change in inventories). Calculate personal consumption expenditures (C) and intended investment (I_I) as percentages of gross domestic product (Y). Calculate a simple measure of aggregate demand ($C + I_I$) without government spending.
4. Which of the following are examples of automatic stabilizers, and which are examples of discretionary policy? Could some be both? Explain.
   a. Tax revenues rise during an economic expansion
   b. Personal tax rates are reduced
   c. Government spending on highways is increased
   d. Farm support payments increase
   e. Unemployment payments rise during a recession

5. Match each concept in Column A with a definition or example in Column B.

Column A	Column B
a. Tax multiplier	1. Reduction in income tax rates
b. Disposable income	2. Unemployment compensation
c. Expansionary fiscal policy	3. $Y - T + TR$
d. Contractionary fiscal policy	4. $G + TR$
e. Government outlays	5. Reduction in government spending
f. Automatic stabilizer	6. Intended investment
g. Injection into the circular flow	7. $-(mult)\ (mpc)$

APPENDIX: MORE ALGEBRAIC APPROACHES TO THE MULTIPLIER

A1. AN ALGEBRAIC APPROACH TO THE MULTIPLIER, WITH A LUMP-SUM TAX

A lump-sum tax is a tax that is simply levied on an economy as a flat amount. This amount does not change with the level of income. Suppose that a lump-sum tax is levied in an economy with a government (but no foreign sector). Because consumption in this economy is $C = \bar{C} + mpc\, Y_d$ while disposable income is $Y_d = Y - \bar{T} + TR$, we can write the consumption function as:

$$C = \bar{C} + mpc\,(Y - \bar{T} + TR)$$

Thus aggregate demand in this economy can be expressed as:

$$\begin{aligned} AD &= C + I_I + G \\ &= \bar{C} + mpc\,(Y - \bar{T} + TR) + I_I + G \\ &= (\bar{C} - mpc\,\bar{T} + mpc\,TR + I_I + G) + mpc\,Y \end{aligned}$$

The last rearrangement shows that the *AD* curve has an intercept equal to the term in parentheses and a slope equal to the marginal propensity to consume. Changes in any of the variable in parentheses, by changing the intercept, shift the curve upward or downward in a parallel manner.

By substituting this into the equation for the equilibrium condition, $Y = AD$, we can derive an expression for equilibrium income in terms of all the other variables in the model:

$$Y = (\bar{C} - mpc\,\bar{T} + mpc\,TR + I_I + G) + mpc\,Y$$

$$Y - mpc\,Y = \bar{C} - mpc\,\bar{T} + mpc\,TR + I_I + G$$

$$(1 - mpc)Y = \bar{C} - mpc\,\bar{T} + mpcTR + I_I + G$$

$$Y = \frac{1}{1 - mpc}(\bar{C} - mpc\,\bar{T} + mpc\,TR + I_I + G)$$

If autonomous consumption, intended investment, or government spending change, these each increase equilibrium income by $mult = 1/(1 - mpc)$ times the amount of the original change. If the level of lump-sum taxes or transfers changes, these change *Y* by either negative or positive *(mult)(mpc)* times the amount of the original change.

To see this explicitly, consider the changes that would come about in *Y* if there were a change in the level of the lump sum tax from T_0 to a new level, T_1, if everything else stays the same. We can solve for the change in *Y* by subtracting the old equation from the new one:

$$Y_1 = \frac{1}{1 - mpc}(\bar{C} + I_I + G - mpc\ \bar{T}_1 + mpc\ TR)$$

$$[Y_0 = \frac{1}{1 - mpc}(\bar{C} + I_I + G - mpc\ \bar{T}_0 + mpc\ TR)]$$

$$Y_1 - Y_0 = \frac{1}{1 - mpc}(\bar{C} - \bar{C} + I_I - I_I + G - G - mpc\ \bar{T}_1 + mpc\ \bar{T}_0 + mpc\ TR - mpc\ TR)$$

But $\bar{C}$, I_I, G, TR (and the *mpc*) are all unchanged, so most of the subtractions in parentheses come out to be 0. We are left with (taking the negative sign out in front):

$$Y_1 - Y_0 = -\frac{1}{1 - mpc}\, mpc\ (\bar{T}_1 - \bar{T}_0)$$

or

$$\Delta Y = -(mult)(mpc)\Delta \bar{T}$$

As explained in the text, the multiplier for a change in taxes is smaller than the multiplier for a change in government spending, because taxation affects aggregate demand only to the extent that people *spend* their tax cut or pay their increased taxes by reducing *consumption.* Because people may also *save* part of their tax cut or pay part of their increased taxes out of their *savings,* not all the changes in taxes will carry over to changes in aggregate demand. The tax multiplier has a negative sign, since a *de*crease in taxes *in*creases consumption, aggregate demand, and income, while a tax increase decreases them.

A2. An Algebraic Approach to the Multiplier, with a Proportional Tax

With a proportional tax, total tax revenues are not set at a fixed level of revenues, as was the case with a lump sum tax but, rather, are a fixed *proportion* of total income. That is, $T = tY$ where t is the tax rate. The equation for *AD* becomes

$$\begin{aligned} AD &= \bar{C} + mpc\ (Y - tY + TR)\ I_I + G \\ &= \bar{C} + mpc\ TR + I_I + G) + mpc\ (Y - tY) \\ &= (\bar{C} + mpc\ TR + I_I + G) + mpc\ (1 - t)\ Y \end{aligned}$$

With the addition of proportional taxes, the *AD* curve now has a new slope: $mpc(1 - t)$. Because t is a fraction greater than 0 but less than 1, this slope is generally flatter than the slope we have worked with before. A *cut* in the tax rate rotates the curve *up*ward, as shown in Figure 25.7.

Substituting in the equilibrium condition, $Y = AD$, and solving yields:

$$\begin{aligned} Y &= (\bar{C} + mpc\ TR + I_I + G) + mpc\ (1 - t)\ Y \\ Y - mpc\ (1 - t)\ Y &= \bar{C} + mpc\ TR + I_I + G \\ (1 - mpc\ (1 - t))\ Y &= \bar{C} + mpc\ TR + I_I + G \end{aligned}$$

$$Y = \left[\frac{1}{1 - mpc\ (1 - t)}\right](\bar{C} + mpc\ TR + I_I + G)$$

Figure 25.7 **A Reduction in the Proportional Tax Rate**

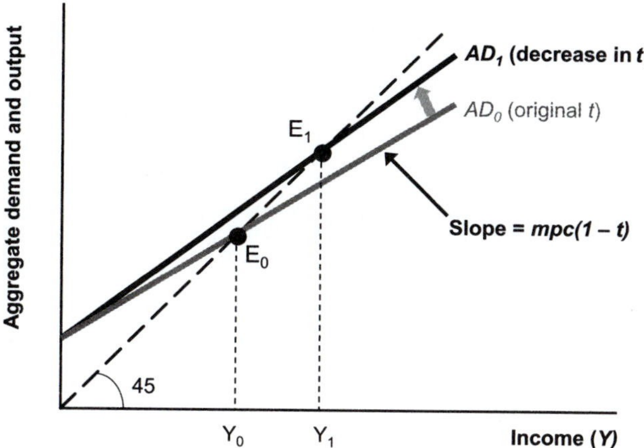

In the case of a proportional tax, a tax cut reduces the tax rate t, which increases the slope of the AD curve and raises equilibrium income from Y_0 to Y_1.

The term in brackets is a new multiplier, for the case of a proportional tax. It is smaller than the basic (no proportional taxation) multiplier, reflecting the fact that now any change in spending has smaller feedback effects through consumption. (Some of the change in income "leaks" into taxes.) For example, if $mpc = 0.8$ and $t = 0.2$, then the new multiplier is $1/(1 - 0.64)$, or approximately 2.8, compared to the simple model multiplier $1/(1 - 0.8)$, which is 5. Changes in autonomous consumption or investment (or government spending or transfers) now have less of an effect on equilibrium income—the "automatic stabilizer" effect mentioned in the text.

Is there a multiplier for the tax rate, *t?* That is, could we derive from the model a formula for how much equilibrium income should change with a change in the rate (rather than level) of taxes? For example, if the tax rate were to decrease from 0.2 to 0.15, could we calculate the size of the change from Y_0 to Y_1 illustrated in Figure 25.7? Yes, but deriving a general formula for a multiplier relating the change in Y to the change in the tax rate requires the use of calculus, which we will not pursue here. (If you are familiar with calculus, you can use the last formula above to calculate the change in Y resulting from a change in t).

26 Money, Banking, and Finance

Everyone would like to have more money, right? Well, maybe not. In 2004 it was very easy to be a millionaire in Turkey—many times over. A million Turkish lira were worth about \$0.75 in U.S. dollars. A 20 million-lira bill was worth about US\$15. People routinely just put their thumb over the last six digits when looking at a value expressed in liras. *Guinness World Records* named the Turkish lira the world's least valuable currency. But you could have lots of it!

1. Why Money?

So far, this book has said very little about money, finance, or interest rates. Economics is fundamentally about how our scarce resources—including labor—are employed in the production of goods and services that contribute to economic well-being. Money is a mere facilitator in the process. But money is essential to the functioning of modern economies, which is why money, finance, and interest rates are important macroeconomic issues.

What is the relation of money and finance to economic behavior? Before we get into the details of how money and credit work in a sophisticated contemporary economy, let's picture a few simpler—and dramatically different—scenarios, drawn from real-world situations and events, that inform how economists have come to think about money and the macroeconomy.

1.1 Money and Aggregate Demand

Let's start with a case of an economy in which inflation is low to moderate. Suppose further that this economy has a banking system that is sophisticated and in reasonably good shape. You are a businessperson who has a great idea about how to expand your business. Or, in your role as a household member, you are interested in buying a home for your family. But you do not have the cash. You go to a bank and ask for a loan. The bank will evaluate your creditworthiness, see how much it currently has available to lend, and then either deny you a loan or offer you a loan on particular terms. If you receive a loan offer and accept the terms, you will take out the loan and go out and spend. If you are denied the loan, or if you think the terms are too unfavorable, you will forgo expanding your business or buying the house.

monetary policy: the use of tools controlled by the government, such as banking regulations and the issuance of currency, to affect the levels of money supply, interest rates, and credit

To the extent the government of a country can affect the volume and terms of loans made by banks, it can thus affect the level of spending in the economy. We have seen in Chapters 24 and 25 how the level of spending (or aggregate demand) in an economy is related to levels of employment and output. **Monetary policy** that affects the behavior of banks, then, may also be a significant factor in achieving the goals of macroeconomic stabilization and low unemployment.

But not all economies enjoy low inflation rates and stable banking systems. Our next two cases illustrate these cases.

1.2 "RUNNING THE PRINTING PRESS"

Consider a country with a very simple government and banking system. The country's government is housed in a single building and pays its employees and its bills in cash. In the basement of the building is a printing press that prints paper money. The government finds it very difficult to collect enough taxes to pay its operating expenses, so it just runs the printing press every time an employee needs to be paid or a bill comes due.

How would this affect the economy? If the national economy is very large and growing, relative to the size of government expenditures, the fresh bills may just be absorbed into circulation without much impact. But if the economy was stagnant and expenditures were large, there would soon be a classic situation of inflation caused by "too much money chasing too few goods." As more and more money is put into circulation, prices will rise at an increasingly rapid rate.

If this goes on for long, a situation of hyperinflation (often defined as any annual inflation rate higher than 100 percent) can result. Germany after World War I, Hungary after World War II, Bolivia in the mid-1980s, Argentina during various periods, Ukraine in the early 1990s, and Zimbabwe in 2008–9 all experienced famous hyperinflations.

In Germany in the 1920s, for example, the economy was in tatters after the war and the government found it impossible to collect taxes in sufficient amounts to support its operations, let alone pay the reparations demanded by the victors. So it resorted to running the printing presses. Inflation reached a high of 41 percent—per *day!* In 1920 a German postage stamp cost 4 marks; in 1923 the same stamp cost *50 billion* marks.

BOX 26.1 EXPERIENCES OF HYPERINFLATION

During the period of German hyperinflation in the 1920s, a story was told of someone taking stacks of deutsche marks, the German currency, to town in a wheelbarrow in order to make a modest purchase, and—after leaving it for a moment—returning to find the wheelbarrow stolen and the bills stacked on the ground. Other stories told of people in a bar ordering their beers two at a time, because the time it took for the price of beer to rise was less than it would take for the beer to get warm.

After the fall of the Soviet Union, in the 1990s, Russia suffered from severe inflation. Many people who had saved money in cash found that it had become nearly valueless. A Russian colleague told one of the authors of this text how his mother had thought, at the beginning of the 1990s, that she had enough money saved to take care of her in old age. She watched the value of her stash of bills go down and down until finally, in desperation, rather than watch it disappear, she took it to the store and bought a bag of sugar.

barter: exchange of goods, services, or assets directly for other goods, services, or assets, without the use of money

In such a situation, it obviously becomes very difficult to keep a sophisticated economy going. People tend to resort to **barter**—exchanging goods, services, or assets directly for other goods, services, or assets—to try to avoid having to deal with a rapidly inflating currency. It becomes impossible to think about making a deposit at a bank or to work out reasonable terms for a loan, and so normal patterns of saving and lending are disrupted. If they can, people may try to acquire—or at least keep their accounts in—a "hard," noninflating currency issued by a foreign country. Hyperinflation is obviously not a good situation; production tends to be lowered and unemployment is raised by the chaos that hyperinflation causes in an economy.

Hyperinflation usually ends when the nearly valueless currency is abandoned, and people exchange very large denominations of the old currency for small denominations of a new currency. If the new currency is accompanied by a credible government promise to stop "running the printing press," the episode of hyperinflation draws to a close. This is what happened after the hyperinflation of the early 2000s in Turkey; the old lira was abandoned in favor of a new currency that removed six zeros. By 2013, the new Turkish lira had a fairly stable value of about US$0.50.

Even if inflation does not reach hyperinflation levels, high inflation can be disruptive to an economy. Over time high inflation can wipe out the value of people's savings, and it hurts people who are on fixed incomes (such as nonindexed pensions). It redistributes wealth from creditors to debtors, since people now repay debts in money that is worth less than the money that they originally borrowed. It creates "menu costs"—literally, the cost of time and effort made to update printed menus and other sorts of price lists. Rising or variable inflation rates create a great deal of uncertainty, which can make it very difficult for households and businesses to make sensible plans regarding savings, retirement, investment, and so on. For these reasons, stabilization of a country's price level is among the important goals of macroeconomic policy.

1.3 DEFLATION AND FINANCIAL CRISES

deflation: when the aggregate price level falls

Now consider an economy in the opposite situation, in which there is too *little* money in circulation. In this case, prices must be bid *down.* A situation of generally falling prices is called **deflation**. Why would deflation be a problem? While deflation makes people's savings *more* valuable and *helps* people who are on fixed incomes, it is still disruptive. In this case, wealth is redistributed from debtors to creditors. You borrow "cheap" money, but later have to pay back with money that is "expensive" It creates menu costs. It creates uncertainty. When people come to expect deflation, it may also cause them to cut back on spending. Why buy a big item such as a car or computer now, if you believe you will be able to buy the same item for less next year?

Deflation is often touched off by a financial crisis in which many people lose access to the opportunity to obtain loans and perhaps access to their own deposits at banks as well. If you cannot withdraw money from your account at a bank, and you cannot get a loan, then you cannot pay for things. If many people are in this situation, the economy grinds to a halt—or at least slows down considerably. Because less money is spent, prices fall.

The Great Depression was accompanied in the United States by just such a collapse in the banking system. The "bank runs" or "banking panics" of 1930–33, in which people rushed to try to withdraw their deposits all at once, caused many banks to fail. Because deposit insurance did not yet exist, people's accounts at those banks were wiped out. The price level dropped 25 percent in just a few years. Falling prices bankrupted business and farmers, and thus made conditions even worse.

But deflation is not merely "ancient history." Japan also experienced deflation touched off by a financial crisis in late 1989 after a speculative bubble in real estate and stocks came to a sudden end. Japanese banks had, it turned out, racked up huge amounts of bad loans—loans on which they would never be able to collect. Some banks were ordered to shut down, while others teetered. People became justifiably leery of depositing funds—or of spending, with the future so uncertain. Because deposits were shrinking, banks were unable to lend as much, and because spending was shrinking, the Japanese economy slid into recession. Over the next decade and a half, prices steadily fell at a rate of about 1 percent per year (see Box 26.2).

Many experts feared a similar deflation in the United States after the 2007–8 financial crisis. People were losing their homes and jobs all over the country. Measures aimed at bailing out failing financial institutions and providing cheaper credit pumped more money into the system, with the result that a severe collapse in economic activity was averted. While inflation remained low, the feared deflation did not materialize.

Deflation can be very damaging when looked at from the perspective of the real potential productivity of an economy. People may want to work and spend, and businesses might have great ideas for expansion, but they are constrained by the lack of spendable assets to grease the wheels of the economy. For this reason, as well as the problems discussed above with rapid inflation, stability of the monetary system is an important policy goal for governments and is closely related to both the goal of price stability and the goal of raising living standards.

BOX 26.2 DEFLATION IN JAPAN

Following a banking crisis in 1989, the Japanese economy slid into a situation of recession and deflation, which it has not been able to shake for over two decades. A very slow growth rate has been accompanied by generally falling prices, which have made it very difficult to keep the economy on track.

"As deflation became entrenched, consumers adjusted accordingly. Instead of splurging on a bottle of Chanel fragrance, they started to buy perfume by the ounce from peddlers online. Companies adjusted, and designer denims gave way to no-frill jeans that went for $10 instead of $100 . . . Consumers grew accustomed to expecting that the longer they waited, the cheaper goods would become. And they held back on spending. That led to even less demand and more years of deflation."

In 2013, the new Japanese government of Prime Minister Shinzo Abe (pronounced ah-bey) tried to revive Japan's deflated economy with economic stimulus and monetary expansion. But "for companies to feel confident enough to start raising prices, Japan's consumers have to start spending again, and data confirming that trend is mixed."

In July 2013, "prices rose in Japan last month at their fastest pace for almost five years, offering some hope for ending years of debilitating deflation that has stymied growth. The consumer price index was up 0.7 percent from a year earlier, the biggest rise since a 1.0 percent increase in November 2008. Hideo Kumano, chief economist at Dai-ichi Life Research Institute, commented: 'today's CPI data shows signs of exit from deflation, but we still need to see improvement in the job market and redistribution of wealth . . . to declare deflation is over.

"The definition of exit from deflation can be political, but the key is 'sustainable' rises in prices, which is difficult to achieve without improvement in the job market and salaries,' Kumano said."

Sources: Hiroko Tabuchi, "Getting Japan to Spend," New York Times, June 29, 2013; Miwa Suzuki, "Japan Price Rise Offers Hope for Deflation End," Yahoo News, August 30, 2013.

Discussion Questions

1. Which of the three conditions just described—low inflation, high inflation, or deflation—best characterizes the U.S. economy right now? Do you know of any country currently in one of the other conditions?
2. Unemployment and inflation are usually considered the "bads" that can come with business cycles. Compare the costs to society of unemployment to the costs to society of inflation.

2. WHAT IS MONEY?

You have no doubt that the bills and coins you have in your wallet are "money." Economists would agree with you on that. But in other ways, the manner in which economists use the term is very different from the way it is used in popular speech. Money, to an economist, is something that plays three specific roles in an economy, and the cash in your pocket is only one form of money.

2.1 THE ROLES OF MONEY

Money is a special kind of financial asset (a form of financial capital) that has three important functions.

First, it is a *medium of exchange.* When you sell something, you accept money in return. When you buy something, you hand over money to obtain the good or service that you want. Without a functional medium of exchange, an economy would have to operate as a barter system, as mentioned in the earlier example of German hyperinflation. You would have to trade tangible objects or services directly in order to get other goods or services in exchange. This could be quite inconvenient—there would have to be what is called a "double coincidence of wants." For example, if you want pizza and can offer Web design services, you would need to hunt around for pizza makers in need of Web design. Such merchants may or may not exist, but even if they did, you would certainly have to spend some considerable time finding them. With money, on the other hand, you can sell your services to anyone who wants them and use the money you receive to buy pizza from anyone who supplies it.

Second, money is also a *store of value.* That means that, even if you hold onto it for a while, it will still be good for transactions when you are ready to use it. This is obviously a necessary property, since the pizza makers are unlikely to accept your money in exchange unless they know that, a month from now, their landlord will also accept the same money when they pay their rent. In serving as a store of value, money serves as a way of holding wealth—like any other form of financial or real capital that is held because it is worth something. The thing that makes money distinct from other assets is its **liquidity**, that is, the ease with which it can be used in exchange. Money is highly liquid—you can take it to the store and use it immediately. If you own a car, shares in a business, or a valuable piece of jewelry, these are also ways of storing your wealth, but they are not liquid. You must convert the value stored in them to money before you can buy something else.

liquidity: the ease of use of an asset as a medium of exchange

The third role of money is that it is a *unit of account.* Things are often assigned money values even if they are not actually being bought and sold. When a firm estimates the value of unsold inventories in its warehouses in order to calculate its profits or losses, for example, or a town assesses the dollar value of a house even though there are no plans for it to be sold, they are using money as a unit of account.

Some ways in which we commonly use the term "money" differ from how economists use it. For example, we might say that someone "makes a lot of money" because he has a high annual *income.* Income, however, is a *flow* variable, measured (as described in Chapter 1) over a period of time. Money is a *stock* variable—a particular kind of asset. A person who makes a lot of income over a year may acquire a large stock of money—or he may not. If the income is quickly spent on goods and services, the person may have high *income* (over the year) but accumulate little *money* (measured at a point in time).

We may also say that someone "has a lot of money" if she has accumulated a lot of *wealth.* But this is also not technically correct. A wealthy person may hold a lot of her assets in the form of corporate shares, real estate, or Renaissance paintings, rather than as spendable, liquid money. Middle-class families are sometimes described as "house rich, but cash poor" exactly for this reason. If they attempt to hold a high proportion of their assets as home equity, they may end up with very little in the way of funds that they can actually spend—that is, *money.* Liquidity issues aside, holding money (a particular financial asset) is not the same as holding a tangible asset with useful physical properties. Money is thus not the same things as wealth or income. This is an important distinction, on which we will elaborate in later chapters.

2.2 Types of Money

Throughout much of history, **commodity money** was the most common type of money. Commodity money is, or is made up of, something that contains **intrinsic value** and is also used in exchange. Coins made of gold or silver are probably the most familiar example. Decorative beads, shells, fishhooks, and cattle have served the purpose in some cultures. In prisons and prisoner of war camps, cigarettes sometimes developed into a medium of exchange. "Prices" for chocolate or other goods and services were quoted in terms of numbers of cigarettes required in exchange. (Cigarettes thus had exchange value in this system even to nonsmokers, for whom they had no intrinsic value.)

commodity money: a good used as money that is also valuable in itself

intrinsic value: value related to the tangible or physical properties of the object

To be used as money, a commodity must be *generally acceptable, standardized, durable, portable, scarce,* and, preferably, easily *divisible.* Standardization is important, so that disputes do not arise about the quality and value of the money. Coins stamped by the government are a popular kind of money because the stamp is a sign that they are of equal weight and purity of mineral content. Gold and silver have historically been popular because coins made from them are durable. The scarcity of gold and silver was also an important factor. Coins made of, say, wood, in an area with many forests would rapidly lose value as everyone could just make their own. Divisibility is also important. Heavy gold ingots might be useful for buying expensive real estate, but are not very useful for buying pasta for dinner. Smaller coins, and coins made of less valuable minerals, were historically minted to provide a medium of exchange for smaller purchases.

Gold and silver coins, while fairly portable, can still be inconvenient to carry around in large quantities. Individual banks, state governments, and national governments have at various times issued paper monies that represent claims on actual commodities, usually gold or silver. For many years, starting in the late 1880s, government-issued silver certificates were the main form of domestic paper money in the United States. International transactions were, for many years, based on gold reserves. When people carried such a piece of paper, they could think of it as a certificate showing that they owned a bit of an ingot in Fort Knox.

In the 1960s, however, due to an increase in the price of silver, the government eliminated silver certificates and replaced them with what you probably have in your pocket today. What is commonly called a "dollar bill" is, if you look at it, officially called a Federal Reserve note. At about the same time, the U.S. government also removed silver coins from circulation, replacing them with look-alike coins made from cheaper nickel-clad copper. In 1971, President Richard Nixon took the U.S. economy off the international gold standard.

fiat money: a medium of exchange that is used as money because a government says it has value, and that is accepted by the people using it

exchange value: value that corresponds to the value of goods or services for which the item can be exchanged

So what is the basis of value of the coins and dollar bills we use today? The basis of value is—precisely and no more than—the expectation that the dollar bill will be acceptable in exchange. The currency and coins we use now are what are called **fiat money**. "Fiat" in Latin means "let it be done," and a legal authority does something "by fiat" when it just declares something to be so. *A dollar bill is money because the government declares it to be money.* In other words, its intrinsic value is no more than the value of the piece of paper of which it is made; but fiat money possesses **exchange value**, which is the value of the goods or services that such money can pay for in the market.

Fiat money is what some people call a "social construction"—something that works in society because of how people think and act toward it, not because of something it intrinsically "is." Fiat money works well as long as people are generally in agreement that it has value. Later, we examine some cases in which people have stopped agreeing—when people have lost confidence in the value of their money.

As economies become more and more sophisticated, however, even carrying around paper money is inconvenient for many purposes. Nowadays, you are likely to make many of your transactions by other means, such as making electronic funds transfers from your bank. Understanding what types of transactions are said to involve "money" requires understanding how various assets differ in their liquidity as well as the distinction between money and credit.

2.3 Measures of Money

Because different assets have different degrees of liquidity, it is difficult to draw distinct lines between which assets are "money," which are "near-money," and which are "not money." As a result, economists have devised various ways of defining and measuring the volume of money that is circulating in a given economy.

Coins and bills are obviously "money." In the United States today, coins are manufactured by the U.S. Mint in Philadelphia, Denver, San Francisco, and West Point, NY, while bills are created by the Bureau of Engraving and Printing in Washington, DC, and Fort Worth, Texas. When economists measure a country's "money supply," only currency that is *in circulation* is included—that is, not currency sitting in a vault at the

Mint or at a bank. In October 2012, currency in circulation in the United States totaled $1.073 trillion.

But checking accounts are also extremely liquid. People can pay for many things using paper checks and, increasingly, debit cards and electronic transfers of funds from their checking accounts. The most commonly used measure of the amount of money in an economy at a given point in time, then, includes not only currency in circulation but also the value of checkable deposits as well as the value of travelers checks, called **M1** or, less formally, "pure money." In October 2012, checkable deposits totaled $1.332 trillion, and travelers checks were $3.9 billion, so M1 totaled $2.409 trillion.

M1: a measure of the money supply that includes currency, checkable deposits, and travelers checks

Many people can now move funds from their savings accounts to their checking accounts with the click of a mouse or make electronic payments directly from their savings accounts. So shouldn't savings accounts also be considered "money"? A measure called **M2** includes everything in M1, plus savings deposits and other funds such as small certificates of deposit and retail money market funds (those owned by individuals and businesses). One can often write checks against money market accounts, so from a liquidity perspective they are in some ways almost indistinguishable from M1. M2, which totaled $10.21 trillion as of October 2012, is now more than four times the size of M1. When economists talk about "the money supply" they usually mean either M1 or M2.

M2: a measure of the money supply that includes all of M1 plus savings deposits, small certificates of deposit, and retail money market funds

While not quite as liquid as M1, M2 types of money are liquid enough to be labeled "near-money." If we include large certificates of deposit and money market funds owned or managed by large financial institutions, we arrive at M3. Specialists even use other broader categories of money. The principal reason for the different classifications is to allow for different points on the liquidity continuum that distinguish money from other kinds of assets (see Figure 26.1). While it is clear that currency is money and that real estate is not, the line separating money from nonmoney assets is not clearly defined.

What about using a credit card to make a purchase? From the user's point of view, using a credit card often seems to be like using a debit card or cash from one's pocket. In economists' terms, however, one does *not* use "money" when paying with a credit card. When paying on credit, you are, technically speaking, taking out a temporary loan from the credit card company. Only one day a month, when you send a check or electronic transfer to your credit card company from your checking account, do you make a "money" transaction.

Figure 26.1 **The Liquidity Continuum**

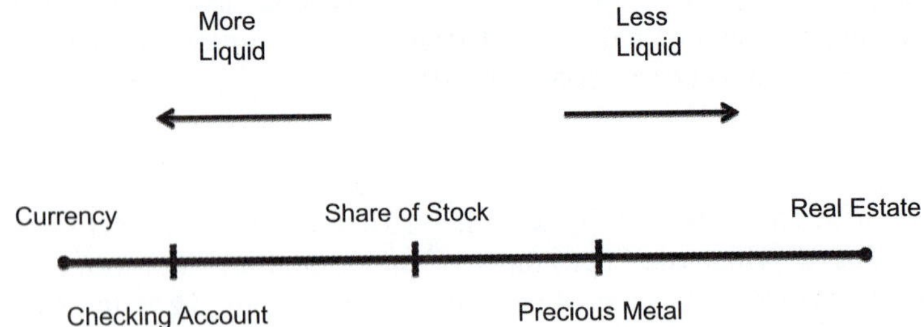

Items more to the left are more liquid or, in other words, more easily used to purchase something of value. The farther to the right on this continuum, the less liquid the item is. Currency is as liquid as it gets, and real estate is usually about the most difficult asset to convert to money (seldom taking less than a few months).

Discussion Questions

1. Suppose that you asked someone who has not taken an economics class why a dollar bill has value. What do you think he or she would say? Would he or she be correct?

2. What do you commonly use to make payments? Cash? Credit cards? Online payments? In which of these cases are you using "money"?

3. THE BANKING SYSTEM

It is easy to understand how the U.S. Mint and the Bureau of Engraving and Printing create currency, and how they could create more or less of it. But how does currency make its way into people's wallets? How are bank deposits such as checking accounts created? How can the volume of currency and deposits be increased or decreased over time, as a matter of macroeconomic policy? To understand the answer to these questions, we need to know more about how a contemporary banking system works.

The central bank of the United States, most commonly known as the Federal Reserve (or "Fed," for short) determines how much currency should be produced and puts it into circulation. In addition, the actions of the Fed together with actions of private banks create the economy's volume of checkable deposits. For much of Europe, now that many countries have joined together in using the euro as a common currency, the equivalent institution to the Fed is the European Central Bank (ECB). Most countries have combined systems of private and central banking, which work at least roughly like the system described in this chapter. The workings of this combined system are discussed in greater detail in Chapter 27. Here we start by looking at private banks.

3.1 PRIVATE BANKS

In the discussion of the market for loanable funds in Chapter 24, we assumed that some agents lend and others borrow, but we paid no attention to how borrowers and lenders would find each other. An individual might go to a relative or friend for a loan. But when the borrower is operating in a more impersonal way—perhaps because the borrower is a business, not an individual, or does not have personal contacts with individuals who can make the needed loan—an intermediary is needed to put together would-be lenders with would-be borrowers.

financial intermediary: an institution such as a bank, savings and loan association, or life insurance company that accepts funds from savers and makes loans to borrowers

A private bank is a type of institution called a **financial intermediary**. Individuals and organizations deposit funds with financial intermediaries, for safekeeping, to provide the convenience of writing checks, or to earn interest. The financial intermediaries use the funds deposited with them to make loans to individuals and organizations that seek to borrow funds.

A private bank is a for-profit business, meaning that it seeks to make earnings on its activities. It does this by charging interest (and perhaps other fees) on the loans it makes. One of its functions is to screen the parties seeking loans, in order to determine their creditworthiness. Lending is a risky business—not all loans made will be paid back in full. Demanding physical assets as collateral can alleviate some of the risk.

For example, mortgages and home-equity loans are collateralized by the value of a house; if the owner defaults on the loan the bank may take possession of the house. Many educational loans are backed up by government guarantees. Other loans are made on the basis of an evaluation of, say, the strength of a business plan and a business's record in paying back past loans. Banks may charge different interest rates depending on the riskiness of a loan or deny a loan request outright.

To understand what happens in a banking system, we start with a private bank's simplified balance sheet, shown in Table 26.1. A balance sheet is a standard double-entry accounting representation of a private bank's assets and liabilities. It must "balance" in that assets and liabilities must add up the same amount. The right-hand side of a balance sheet, as shown in Table 26.1, lists an organization's liabilities. An **economic liability** is anything that one economic actor owes to another. The funds that you deposit in a bank are listed among the bank's liabilities, because it has an obligation to repay these funds to you.

economic liability: anything that one economic actor owes to another

Except in the case of banking panics, depositors are not likely all to show up at the same time, demanding their funds in cash. Although the bank must keep some funds on hand to

Table 26.1 **A Simplified Balance Sheet of a Private Bank**

Assets		Liabilities	
Loans	$70 million	Deposits	$100 million
Government bonds	$20 million		
Reserves	$10 million		

meet depositors' withdrawal needs, normally it can use most of the deposits that it holds to obtain earnings.

bank reserves: funds not lent out or invested by a private bank but kept as vault cash or on deposit at the Federal Reserve

Assets of an organization are listed on the left-hand side of a balance sheet, as shown in Table 26.1. **Bank reserves**, shown as an asset, include vault cash that the bank keeps on hand to meet likely short-term calls, such as depositors' withdrawals. Reserves also include deposits that the private bank has made in an account at the Federal Reserve (discussed in Chapter 27). The bank owns these Federal Reserve deposits in the same way that bank customers "own" the deposits on their liability side. Banks are required to maintain a certain portion of their assets with the Federal Reserve, and these deposits do not earn interest.

One safe way for the bank to earn some interest is to lend money to the federal government (i.e., to the U.S. Treasury). Recall from Chapter 25 that the U.S. Treasury borrows from the public when it needs to finance a government deficit or refinance part of the debt. It does this by issuing government bonds, which give the buyer the right to specific payments in the future. Depending on the duration of the loan, these securities may be called "bills" (sometimes called "T-bills," i.e., Treasury bills), "bonds," or "notes." We will use the term "government bonds" to represent any type of federal government security.

Very active markets exist for trading federal bonds, and a particular bond may change hands many times before it is paid off. Banks tend to keep some of their assets—about one-quarter, on average—in government bonds, because bonds earn interest but are also relatively liquid. If it looks as if depositors will want more cash back than a bank has in its vault, the private bank can quickly sell some of its government bonds on the open bond market.

The major asset of a private bank—and the major way that it makes its earnings—is its portfolio of loans other than government bonds: funds that are owed to the bank by businesses, households, nonprofits, or nonfederal levels of government. Unlike T-bills, which can be liquidated quickly if necessary, some of these may be business loans, home mortgages, or consumer loans that will not be repaid for years.

Such assets are generally far less liquid than vault cash or T-bills. This can potentially be problematic in difficult times. The health of a private banking system depends on having depositors who are confident about the safety of the funds that they have entrusted to the banking system and are not trying to withdraw their funds more rapidly than such loans are repaid. If confidence in the banks diminished, and many customers wanted to withdraw their money, some banks might find themselves with insufficient liquidity (i.e., too many of their assets in long-term loans) to service all requests, further undermining confidence in the system.

3.2 BANK TYPES

The banks with which most people are familiar are known as retail banks, which perform the functions that we have already described: keeping money in secure deposits, providing check writing services and clearing checks, and extending loans (Table 26.2). Commercial banks are similar to—and indeed often overlap with—retail banks, the main difference being that commercial banks tend to hold more assets because their clients include businesses. Savings and loan banks are also similar to retail banks but specialize in the provision of home loans to their customers. Credit unions are also similar to retail banks, except that instead of being privately owned they are collectively owned by their customers.

Table 26.2 **Bank Types**

	Chief Functions
Retail	Safekeeping of money, checking accounts, loans
Commercial	Similar to retail bank but more diverse clients, including businesses
Savings and loan	Similar to retail bank but specializing in loans, particularly mortgages
Credit union	Same as a retail bank, but cooperatively owned by customers
Private	Caters almost exclusively to high net worth individuals; functions extend beyond traditional banking into variety of financial services
Investment	No traditional banking functions; involved in underwriting and issuing securities, assistance with company mergers and acquisitions, market making, and general advice to corporations
Central	Overseeing the monetary and interest rate stability of the national economy by directly influencing the money supply

Private banks are exclusive, catering to high net worth individuals and companies. Their functions range widely from traditional banking to many forms of investment, some of which is moderate to high risk. Investment banks mostly deal with companies instead of individuals and do not offer any traditional banking services. In other words, their principal function is to make asset values grow.

Central banks are an entirely different institution. They exist to regulate the banking system and ensure monetary and interest rate stability in the economy. Chapter 27 deals specifically with the U.S. central bank, the Federal Reserve.

The functions of banks are subject to government regulation. The Banking Act of 1933 (called the Glass-Steagall Act) required that traditional banking functions be strictly separated from the financial and investment activities of private banks and investment banks. While the most common way in which a bank was able to make money was simply to charge higher interest rates to lenders than to depositors, private banks and investment banks could engage in riskier types of investments and often enjoy much higher returns on their money. The purpose of the Glass-Steagall Act was to protect bank customers from excessively risky investment activities by their banks that might jeopardize the value of their savings accounts.

In the late 1980s, many savings and loan banks (S&Ls) went bankrupt because they had invested too many of their assets in unduly risky real estate ventures. Savings and loans had been suffering for many years because higher interest rates in the late 1970s made many customers averse to taking out loans, and the growth of money market accounts gave depositors an attractive alternative to the S&Ls. In response, the government relaxed regulations on their activity, allowing them to invest in "higher return" areas but without adequately overseeing where the money was going.

During this time and in the aftermath of the S&L crisis—for which the U.S. government had to provide sizable bailouts at taxpayer expense—many were saying that the Glass-Steagall Act survived in name only. In 1999, Congress passed the Gramm-Leach-Bliley Act, which formally overturned certain provisions in Glass-Steagall, eliminating the separation between traditional and investment banking. At the time, many hailed this as a necessary modernization of the financial system, but as we will see in later chapters, others argue that looser regulation contributed to the financial crisis of 2007–8 (see Box 26.3).

3.3 How Banks Create Money

As we saw earlier, the U.S. Mint and the Bureau of Engraving and Printing are responsible for producing the country's supply of currency. But there is another way in which money is created, and private banks play a critical role in the process.

If you have ever taken out a loan from a bank, you know that the money that you borrow is not generally delivered to you as a bundle of cash. Rather, the bank credits your bank

Box 26.3 Should We Reinstate the Glass-Steagall Act?

In response to the global financial crisis of 2007–8, various politicians and pundits have argued for the reinstatement of the Banking Act of 1933 (called the Glass-Steagall Act) provision that separated traditional banking from investment activities. Those voicing support for reinstating the Act represent a range of political views, from Representative Paul Ryan, a Republican from Wisconsin, to Elizabeth Warren, Democratic senator from Massachusetts. In 2011, Representative Marcy Kaptur, a Democrat from Ohio, introduced the Return to Prudent Banking Act, which would effectively reinstate the Glass Steagall "firewall" between ordinary banking and investment banking. Although the Act has been cosponsored by 84 other members of Congress, and supported by resolutions passed in 17 states, it has not been voted on.

Would the financial crisis have been avoided if that provision of Glass-Steagall had not been repealed in 1999? As is usually the case in economic debates, opinions differ. According to a hedge fund manager, James Rickards, who supports reinstatement:

> In 1999, Democrats led by President Bill Clinton and Republicans led by Sen. Phil Gramm joined forces to repeal Glass-Steagall at the behest of the big banks. What happened over the next eight years was an almost exact replay of the Roaring Twenties. Once again, banks originated fraudulent loans and once again they sold them to their customers in the form of securities. The bubble peaked in 2007 and collapsed in 2008. The hard-earned knowledge of 1933 had been lost in the arrogance of 1999.

But Andrew Sorkin, financial columnist for *The New York Times,* argues that while reinstatement may represent a step in the right direction, it would not have prevented the crisis. He notes that some of the most troubled banks during the crisis, including Bear Stearns, Lehman Brothers, and Merrill Lynch, were all solely investment banks and thus would not have been limited by the provisions of Glass-Steagall. Those banks that did perform both traditional banking and investment activities generally would have still encountered problems with Glass-Steagall provisions in place. For example, Bank of America's difficulties were attributed to its acquisition of Countrywide Financial, which had made many bad subprime loans that would not have been covered under Glass-Steagall. Sorkin suggests that the main cause of the crisis was simply that too many banks provided loans to businesses and individuals who could not pay them back. We discuss the causes of the financial crisis in more detail in Chapter 30.

Sources: Marcy Kaptur, "Rep. Marcy Kaptur: Reinstate the Glass-Steagall Act," *U.S. News and World Report,* September 17, 2012; James Rickards, "Repeal of Glass-Steagall Caused the Financial Crisis," *U.S. News and World Report,* August 27, 2012; Andrew Ross Sorkin, "Reinstating an Old Rule Is Not a Cure for Crisis," *New York Times,* Dealbook Column, May 21, 2012.

account—if you have one—for the amount of the loan, or it creates a new transactions account in your name. Consequently, when banks make loans they increase the money supply, because transactions accounts make up part of M1 and the broader money supply.

You might think that depositing money in the bank would similarly increase the money supply, because doing so also leads to an increase in deposits at the bank. But merely making a deposit does not, in fact, increase the money supply. While your act does increase total deposits, it also takes the same amount of currency out of circulation (i.e., into the bank's vault), thereby *reducing* the money supply. In this instance, the composition of the money supply is altered—less currency, more transactions deposits—but its total remains unchanged.

fractional reserve system: a banking system in which banks are required to keep only a fraction of the total value of their deposits on reserve

required reserves: the portion of bank reserves that banks *must* keep on reserve

Yet your deposit does enable a bank to increase the money supply because the bank can now make new loans—hence, create new money—based on your deposit. To see how this works, it is important to keep in mind that banks are not required to hold in their vaults or on reserve all the money that they receive for a deposit. Far from it. As noted earlier, banks can use most of their assets to obtain earnings.

The banking system is a **fractional reserve system** in which only a small percentage of the total value of deposits, usually around 10 percent, must be kept on reserve. The portion of bank reserves that are kept to satisfy the minimum requirement is known as **required reserves**. If banks must hold 10 percent of every new deposit on reserve, it means that banks can lend out the other 90 percent. So when you make a deposit at your local bank, at least

excess reserves: the portion of bank reserves that banks are permitted to lend to their customers

90 percent of its value is classified as **excess reserves**, which a bank is free to lend to other customers.*

So even though your deposit does not *directly* increase the money supply, it does help increase it to the extent that banks are willing to lend out their excess reserves. Banks are usually eager to lend out excess reserves, because this is how they can make money on them. But sometimes, in periods of financial crisis, banks prefer to hold onto excess reserves. In Chapter 27, we explore in greater detail how the Federal Reserve influences the banking system's process of money creation.

Discussion Questions

1. How do banks lend money that they do not physically possess to their customers? Are they *really* creating money in the process?
2. Does it bother you that banks hold only a small fraction of the value of their deposits on reserve? Why or why not?

4. MONEY AND FINANCE

In the past, the average person with a little extra money had few options for what to do with it other than putting it in the bank. Today, however, people have numerous financial investment alternatives available. Many people, including those classified as "small investors," find themselves with funds that they do not need at the moment and would like to accumulate a nest egg. But how can they choose among the many different options, including mutual funds, individual stocks, bonds, or other assets? This book does *not* attempt to offer specific advice on this question. However, a better understanding of the economy as a whole, and of finance in particular, will help you to make informed economic decisions. In this section, we begin to look at the relationship between investment decisions that are good for the investor and those that make the economy as a whole more productive—and how these may sometimes diverge.

4.1 FUNCTIONS OF FINANCE

The primary and most long-standing function of our financial system is the provision of money to support direct investment. Such "direct" investment is the same as the "intended investment" that we saw in Chapter 24, which is an important reinjection into the circular flow that comes from the market for loanable funds (i.e., the financial system). The banking system is involved in this key function, but here we are interested in the broader financial system, of which banks form only a part.

portfolio investment: the purchase of financial assets such as stocks and bonds

In recent years, finance for other purposes has grown in importance. **Portfolio investment**, once available only to rich individuals, is much more widespread today. This refers mostly to investing funds in securities such as stocks or bonds. To an economist, portfolio investment is merely another form of saving, a means of postponing consumption while hoping to earn a greater return than in a traditional bank. It is not "true" investment in that when one buys a stock or a bond, ownership of an existing security is transferred from one person to another—there is no addition to the economy's stock of capital.

A century ago, only the wealthy partook of this form of financial planning. Indeed, only a minority of the population earned enough to save significantly. As this changed, most people saved money in traditional banks instead of securities. Only more recently, over the past three or four decades, have stocks and bonds been "democratized" in the sense that a sizable percentage of the population now owns such assets. The change is largely due to the

*We say "at least" because if the bank held some excess reserves before the new deposit, then more than 90 percent of the new deposit would be available to be lent.

introduction of collective (also called "pooled" or "commingled") investment vehicles, such as mutual funds, and their association with defined contribution pension plans.

Finance now provides not only a variety of ways to invest but also more choices for long-term saving. It also supports speculation, that is, buying securities in the hopes of short-term gain. Individuals who speculate are not truly saving—they hope to exploit changes in prices to achieve short-term profit. The financial system offers them a vast, and growing, array of possible securities, each with its own market. The opportunities for speculation are therefore substantial. Speculators, unlike "true" investors, entrepreneurs, or businesspeople, do not directly contribute to economic well-being. As we will see, however, at a large enough scale, speculative activity has the potential to influence the economy through its impact on income, wealth, and spending.

leverage: the use of debt to increase the potential rate of return of one's investment (at greater risk)

As long as speculators are risking their own funds, the economic impact of their activity is limited. Most potential problems emerge when they borrow funds for the purpose. Speculators may borrow money in order to exploit what they see as market opportunities based on short-term price movements. This can create problems when speculators use excessive **leverage**—investments based on borrowed funds. As we see in greater detail in Chapter 30, borrowing excessively to finance risky speculative ventures carries the potential to destabilize the entire financial system and, with it, the economy. Another possible problem, not unrelated, is when lenders extend large lines of credit to borrowers who would not ordinarily satisfy minimum loan criteria. Both were recurrent problems during the most recent financial crisis.

Finally, public finance relates to how governments finance their activities. We say relatively little about this in the present chapter. Chapter 25 has already covered government finance with particular attention to taxes and spending, and Chapter 31 elaborates on the subject of government deficits and debt.

4.2 NONBANK FINANCIAL INSTITUTIONS

nonbank financial institution: a financial institution that performs a number of services similar to those offered by banks but that is not a licensed bank and is not subject to banking regulations

collective investment vehicle or **pooled fund:** an investment vehicle that pools investments from many different sources, making investment decisions for them all as a group

hedge fund: a type of pooled fund that often engages in highly speculative investments and to which access is generally restricted to wealthy clients

There was a time when banks were responsible for most, if not all, economic matters relating to money. Today, many other types of financial intermediaries exist; indeed, over the past few decades, banks have been declining in importance relative to these **nonbank financial institutions**. Most savings today go through such institutions, which invest in stocks, bonds, and other assets.

For instance, many people have their money in what are known as **collective investment vehicles** (CIVs), which basically offer people alternatives to saving money in a bank. Many types of CIVs fall into the category of **pooled funds**, which accept investments from many different investors and reduce the cost of making decisions about investing by managing them all together.

The best-known example of a CIV is a mutual fund.* Many individuals place their savings in such funds, which offer customers a variety of "baskets" or "pools" of investments. They purchase "shares" of a given fund, instead of individual stock shares or bonds. Some funds are invested in high-growth stocks with moderate to high risk, for example, while others are mostly in government bonds. The number of possibilities is large, as thousands of pooled funds exist, invested not only in different classes of stocks and bonds but in commodities and other assets (as well as a combinations of two or more of these forms of asset).

Pooled funds have lower fees than funds managed by a broker, because they do not have a paid manager looking after an individual investor's money. At the same time, many believe that they offer better returns than bank savings accounts. The returns, however, may vary greatly, depending in large part on the riskiness of the investments that compose the fund.

Hedge funds are a special category of CIV that often engages in highly speculative investments, promising greater earnings potential than most other funds, along with higher risk.

*The term "mutual fund" is most appropriately applied to CIVs that are regulated under the Investment Company Act of 1940 and are open to the general public. This act was updated by the Dodd-Frank Act of 2010, discussed in Chapter 30.

Because they carry greater risk, hedge funds are only permitted to do business with particular (high net worth) individuals and institutions. Hedge funds are not necessarily commingled; though it is unusual, a hedge fund can be created by a single very large investor.

pension fund: a fund with the exclusive purpose of paying retirement benefits to employees

Pension funds are another type of CIV that accumulate savings from workers, sometimes including a matching contribution from employers, usually over a long period, to be disbursed as benefits in retirement. Access to the funds before retirement is highly restricted, with significant penalties for early withdrawals. To encourage workers to participate (thereby voluntarily deferring a percentage of their pay that they could otherwise use for current consumption), such funds are granted generous tax breaks, both through reducing taxable income by the amount of the employee's contribution, and by deferring taxes on earnings. Nearly 100 percent of retirement fund dollars are invested in some form of pooled fund. The availability of and extent of choice among funds offered to workers depend on the terms of the specific company or government pension plan.

Some of the largest investors in the world are pension funds that pool the retirement and health savings accounts of workers in the public sector. For example, the California Public Employees Retirement System (CalPERS) had about $248.8 billion in investments as of December 2012. CalPERS' income comes from returns on its investments and from the health-care and pension plans of more than a million workers and their employers, who are government agencies at the state or local level, as well as public schools. CalPERS provides health-care benefits to about 1.6 million beneficiaries and their families, and retirement benefits to about 553,000 individuals.

insurance company: a company that pays to cover all or part of the cost of specific risks against which individuals and companies chose to insure themselves

Another example of a nonbank financial institution is an **insurance company**. You might not think of insurance companies as similar to banks, but over time they have come to resemble them in some ways. The principal difference is that instead of making a deposit with an insurance company, you pay it a premium (monthly, quarterly, or annually) that is meant to protect you against a particular risk. The company, however, must have sufficient funds available to pay to beneficiaries that have the bad fortune (fire, flood, theft, accident, ill health, etc.) against which they had been insured. It must therefore earn a return sufficient to cover the cost of these payouts. In this way, an insurance company resembles a bank: It holds a pool of money that it lends to governments and companies and sometimes even invests in stocks or other riskier investments. The huge insurance company American International Group (AIG), for example, put billions into risky investments and had to seek a government bailout during the financial crisis of 2007–8 (discussed further in Chapter 30).

securities broker: an agent responsible for finding a buyer for sellers of different securities, thereby offering enhanced liquidity to the seller

Brokerage services also fall into the category of nonbank financial institutions. **Securities brokers**, for example, keep an inventory of different financial assets—mostly stocks and bonds—that result from playing the role of middleman in transactions between buyers and sellers. They earn a commission, a percentage of the transaction, for the service of linking the buyer and the seller. Their service provides another option for customers who might otherwise put all their savings in a bank account. From the customer's point of view, funds invested with a broker are very liquid—in other words, a broker can easily convert a stock or bond into cash for a client. But since the broker is earning his own fees based on what products the client buys, questions have recently been raised about whom the broker is most likely to be serving: the buyer or the seller? The sellers are apt to be large organizations with close, sometimes financially rewarding, relationships to the broker. In some instances, brokers have encouraged the purchase of stocks or other assets that they knew were unlikely to offer the advertised return because they stood to gain from the transaction.

mortgage broker: an agent who assists in identifying a lender for prospective homeowners looking to borrow money for their purchase

Mortgage brokers perform a similar function, except that their role is specific to real estate purchases. Most homebuyers lack sufficient funds to buy a property outright, so they must borrow a portion of the sale price. The mortgage broker earns a fee for helping the homebuyer and a lender find each other. Traditionally, banks held home mortgages for their duration, satisfied with the interest income that they provided. More recently, many banks more often than not will "flip" the mortgage—that is, sell it to another financial interest. Why banks have been doing this, and what the buyer of the mortgage does with it, are subjects for Chapter 30.

These different examples of institutions engaged in nonbanking finance represent an industry that has been growing in size and importance relative to banking. Their activities do not directly affect the money supply unless it is very broadly defined, because loans from these entities, unlike transactions using bank accounts, are not liquid (and are therefore usually classified as "nonmoney assets"). Nevertheless, as we will see in chapters to follow, they play a critical role in the national economy, as well as in the conduct of monetary policy (discussed in Chapter 27).

All nonbank financial institutions offer customers alternatives, often much more attractive than traditional bank savings. And they exemplify the manner in which the role of money has, over time, shifted from being a mere facilitator of real economic activity to playing an active and essential part in the real economy, with profound economic implications and consequences. We explore the phenomenon in much greater detail in the coming chapters.

4.3 Financialization and Financial Bubbles

By almost any measure, the U.S economy is more dependent than ever on finance. Total financial assets were less than four times GDP in 1970; today they are more than ten times GDP. In 2009, the total value of financial transactions was *73 times* GDP, primarily a result of rapid growth in high-frequency trading, which permits speculators to buy and then quickly sell large quantities of assets. That the economy depends so much on finance does not necessarily pose a problem in itself. Only when financial investment behavior ceases to be prudent do we run into complications. When economies grow on the basis of mass investment in assets with questionable foundations, yet rise in price, the growth is unstable and destined to be of short duration. Such irrational speculative price rises are called bubbles.

Possibly the most famous historical example of a speculative bubble is the Dutch tulip frenzy (called a tulipomania) in the early 1600s. Different tulip types had different values, and since no one knew which type would bloom from a given tulip bulb, mass speculation ensued. Initially only the wealthy Dutch were buying them, but eventually the rest of the population caught the fever. Because everyone was buying tulips, their price rose rapidly, until the peak in March 1637, some select bulbs sold for several times the yearly income of a skilled craftsman. Shortly thereafter, however, confidence in their value vanished. Almost overnight, the tulip market crashed, and many speculators were ruined.

Almost three centuries later, the U.S. stock market also experienced a speculative bubble. Many at the time believed that the rapid increase in stock prices during the 1920s was entirely justified, attributing it to a "new reality" evidenced in the establishment of the Federal Reserve in 1913 along with government policies to extend free trade, fight inflation, and relax of antitrust laws. But what was really driving the bubble was the same factor underlying the Dutch tulip craze—the "herd instinct" that causes people to follow what everyone else is doing and to believe what everyone else believes. In the 1920s it seemed as if everyone was buying stocks. This drove up share prices, in turn making stocks much more attractive. The period was also characterized by heavy borrowing, especially by the U.S. middle class. Toward the end of the 1920s, a substantial share of consumer debt was taken on in order to buy stock shares (instead of consumer goods). In October 1929 the stock market crashed, and the Great Depression followed.

In recent years, many other bubbles have developed, such as in East Asia in 1997, in Russia in 1998, in Argentina in 1999, and in Iceland in 2008 as well as the recent "dot-com" and housing bubbles in the United States. At the root of all of them is a widespread belief in the value of an asset or assets that is reinforced by speculative borrowing. Bubbles are characterized by a rapid increase in prices that are not generally accompanied by an equally rapid improvement in economic conditions. In other words, a defining feature of such bubbles is that there is seldom any economic basis for them. The buying begets more buying, and the appreciation in the asset values is fleeting. Despite having so much experience with bubbles, why do we fail to learn from past mistakes?

Speculative bubbles form for two reasons: one psychological and one economic. The psychological explanation has to do with the faith or "blind optimism" that people exhibit, even when confronted with evidence to the contrary. As discussed in Chapter 8, and contrary to traditional economic theory, people are not always rational. One of the mistakes commonly made is extrapolating values over time. In other words, if home prices in New York City have risen 30 percent in the past year, some might rush to buy property in New York, believing that the trend will continue. Another common mistake, as we have noted, is the tendency to follow the herd. Even someone who doubts that prices could continue to increase might find it difficult to resist buying an asset when everyone he knows has already done so (and has already made money!). The same phenomenon is at play among money managers. Those who take a conservative or contrarian position during a bubble risk performing worse than nearly everyone else. This accounts for the tendency of fund managers to "follow the herd" in the investment advice given to clients.

The main economic element relating to bubbles is the presence of excess liquidity. As we will see in Chapter 27, when interest rates in general are low, borrowing becomes more attractive. If interest rates are low, there is less incentive to save money in a bank. In such instances, investors tend, instead, to borrow from banks and invest the leveraged capital in financial assets such as stocks or real estate, in the hope of reaping returns that are higher than they could obtain from bank savings. As we have seen, such behavior multiplied throughout the macro-economy drives up asset prices on the strength of greater demand for them, leading to the inflation of a financial bubble. Excessive liquidity was a major factor in the housing bubble of the 2000s (discussed in detail in Chapter 30).

4.4 The International Sector

The monetary systems of other countries both resemble and differ from that of the United States. Like the United States, countries such as Japan and a number of members of the European Union possess currencies (the yen and the euro) that are "internationally tradable." What this means is that other countries regard these currencies as inherently valuable, and so they are willing to accept them as payment for traded goods and cross-border investments. Most countries, however, operate with a currency that is suitable as a medium of exchange for domestic purposes but is not desired as a store of value for people in other countries. Indeed, many of the wealthy in such countries prefer to hold their wealth in assets denominated in dollars, euros, or yen.

International links between countries also provide another asset class (in addition to stocks, bonds, and the like), namely, foreign currency. Today, investors in some countries hold a share of their assets in foreign currency (mostly the strong currencies listed above) as a store of value, because foreign currency cannot be used as a medium of exchange in their own country. Some are motivated by the security offered by a stable currency like the yen or the dollar, while others like to speculate on changes in the value of a currency, not unlike what many players do in the stock market.

Indeed, the financial system itself has become globalized. Although international trade has increased in the past four decades, the rapid expansion in cross-border financial flows is even more impressive. As we will see in Chapter 29, financial flows and trade are closely related. To put it as simply as possible, countries with a trade deficit must borrow from countries with trade surpluses. And some countries that persistently run a deficit get to the point where they must borrow from other countries not only to continue to purchase imports but also to service (i.e., pay interest on) their debt.

When you hear economists or reporters speak about "global imbalances," they are referring to a world that is increasingly polarized; deficit countries come to depend on borrowing from surplus countries in order to support their appetite for imports, and surplus countries rely upon the deficit countries to continue purchasing their exports in order to boost their domestic economies and employment. There is little doubt, for example, that other countries' demand over the years for South Korean exports has lifted that country into the group of the world's prosperous countries; other Asian countries—most notably China—have been trying to emulate that success. But basic arithmetic prohibits *every* country from exporting its way to growth (since everyone's exports must be someone else's imports), and the debt that finances the purchases made by the deficit countries only mounts as global imbalances become greater.

These imbalances play an important part in the growing "financialization" of the global economy. The implications for growth, employment, inflation, and sustainability are potentially huge. We look into this in much greater detail in the chapters that follow.

Discussion Questions

1. What is the difference between the real, monetary, and financial economies? In what way are they related to each other? Should growth in one imply growth in the others?
2. Do you think that it is a good idea to allow commercial banks to invest in stocks? In real estate? In junk bonds? Explain.

Review Questions

1. Describe three scenarios that could describe economies in very different situations, with regard to their banking systems and price (in)stability.
2. Describe the three roles played by money.
3. Describe at least three different types of money.
4. Describe at least two measures of money.
5. Draw up and explain the components of a balance sheet for a private bank.
6. What characteristics are needed to make commodity money effective?
7. What is meant by leverage? What are its advantages, and its dangers?
8. What are "pooled funds"? Describe two different kinds of pooled funds. What is the primary advantage of the pooling process?
9. What is a financial bubble? Give some examples, and explain some of th causes of financial bubbles.
10. What does it mean to say that foreign currency can be a store of value but not a medium of exchange?

Exercises

1. Search for the "World Economic Outlook Database" on the internet and locate the most recent version. Use this database to select inflation data (units of percentage change) for Germany, Japan, and the United States for the period 1990 to 2010. Construct a table of annual inflation rates for these countries. Now construct a graph using annual inflation rates on the vertical axis and the year on the horizontal axis. Plot the annual inflation rates from your table in three separate lines on the same graph. How would you compare the experiences of these three countries based on your graph?
2. Use FRED (http://research.stlouisfed.org/fred2/categories), which stands for Federal Reserve Economic Database, "Money, Banking, and Finance," to locate monetary data for M1 money and M2 money (monthly data of each stock, seasonally adjusted). How do the two series relate in size? How do the changes in the two series compare to one another? Does your understanding of the definitions of M1 and M2 help you make sense of what you observe?
3. Determine whether each of the following belongs on the asset side or the liability side of the balance sheet identified in parentheses.
   a. $20,000 loan for a new automobile (balance sheet for an individual)
   b. 10-year government bonds (balance sheet for a bank)
   c. $1,000 checking account (balance sheet for a bank)
   d. $500 in Federal Reserve notes—also known as cash! (balance sheet for an individual)
   e. $10,000 student loan (balance sheet for a bank)

4. Assume a required reserve of 0.10 to complete the following:

Assets		Liabilities	
Reserves	$800,000	Deposits	$2,000,000
Loans	$1,000,000		
Bonds	$400,000		
Total	$2,000,000	Total	$2,000,000

   a. Calculate the required reserves for this bank.
   b. Calculate the initial excess reserves for this bank. What can the bank do with these excess reserves?

5. Assume a required reserve of 0.20 to complete the following:

Assets		Liabilities	
Reserves	$3,000,000	Deposits	$11,500,000
Loans	$6,000,000		
Bonds	$2,500,000		
Total	$11,500,000	Total	$11,500,000

   a. Calculate the required reserves for this bank.
   b. Calculate the initial excess reserves for this bank.

6. State whether the following statements are true or false. If false, also write a corrected statement.
   a. Inflation erodes the value of savings.
   b. Inflation creates "menu costs."
   c. Inflation reduces uncertainty.
   d. Inflation hurts people on fixed incomes.
   e. Inflation redistributes wealth from debtors to creditors.

7. Match each concept in Column A with a definition or example in Column B.

Column A	Column B
a. Excess reserves	1. The ease of use of an asset as a medium of exchange
b. Barter	2. A measure of the money supply that includes currency, checkable deposits, and traveler's checks
c. Deflation	3. An institution such as a bank, savings and loan association, or life insurance company that accepts funds from savers and makes loans to borrowers
d. Required reserves	4. A good used as money that is also valuable in itself
e. Liquidity	5. When the aggregate price level falls
f. Commodity money	6. A medium of exchange that is accepted as money accepted because the government says it has value
g. Fiat money	7. A measure of the money supply that includes all of M1 plus savings deposits, small certificates of deposit, and retail money market funds
h. M1 money	8. Exchange of goods, services, or assets directly for other goods, services, or assets, without the use of money
i. M2 money	9. The portion of bank reserves that banks *must* keep on reserve
j. Financial intermediary	10. The portion of bank reserves that banks are permitted to lend to their customers

27 The Federal Reserve and Monetary Policy

In the wake of the financial crisis of 2007–8, a lot of attention focused on monetary policies, including actions by the Federal Reserve (the Fed) in the United States and the European Central Bank (ECB). The Fed took extraordinary measures to keep U.S. interest rates very low, in an effort to stimulate the economy. The ECB struggled with debt crises in which some of its member states, such as Spain, Portugal, Italy, and especially Greece, needed central bank support to keep up with payments to their creditors.

Regulating the monetary system of a national economy by influencing the actions of banks and other financial institutions seems to be a daunting task for *one* country, never mind all the countries participating in the eurozone. The United States has the good fortune to have a central bank—the Federal Reserve—that needs to tend to the monetary needs of only one economy. As this chapter shows, however, managing monetary policy in even one country is not without its challenges and controversies. In this chapter, we examine the history, structure, and policy-making of the Federal Reserve System, which also gives us a basis for understanding the operation of other central banks.

1. The Federal Reserve System

In 1907, the U.S. economy experienced a bank panic, in which depositors lost trust in banks, tried to withdraw their deposits all at once, and as a result caused many banks to fail. In response, Congress enacted legislation creating the Federal Reserve System in 1913. The Fed is a rather odd organization in that it is not exactly part of the government, yet not entirely separate from it either. It is overseen by a board of governors whose seven members are nominated by the president and approved by the Senate and who serve nonrenewable fourteen-year terms. One member of the board is chosen by the president to serve as chair for a four-year term (though he or she may serve consecutive terms within the 14-year period on the Board if renominated by the president). The long terms of service are intended to help insulate the Fed from short-term political pressures.

The Fed performs a number of important functions. As noted in Chapter 26, it serves as a "banker's bank" by holding deposits made by private banks. One of the Fed's important day-to-day functions involves using these deposits to clear checks that draw funds from one bank and deposit them in another. For example, if you give a check to a friend, who then deposits it in her bank, the check goes to a Fed clearinghouse. Your bank's account at the Fed is debited by the amount of the check, while your friend's bank's account at the Fed is credited with the funds.

If a bank is in need of cash to hold in its vault, it can buy currency from the Fed, using the funds in its Fed account as payment. As we have seen, the Fed orders banks to keep a certain percentage of their deposits as required reserves, in the form of either vault cash or in such deposits at the Fed. Currently, banks are required to keep an amount equal to

10 percent of their checkable deposits as reserves. If it wishes, a bank may keep reserves in excess of the required amount, although if it does it may forgo profitable earnings opportunities.

Another of the Fed's important tasks is to attempt to stabilize the rate of exchange between domestic and foreign currencies. It does this by buying or selling dollars in exchange for foreign currencies, a process that is detailed in Chapter 29. In addition, the Fed, along with other organizations such as the Federal Deposit Insurance Corporation (FDIC), regulates banks, attempting to ensure that they operate as much as possible without error or fraud. Because the FDIC guarantees the value of many accounts, and the Fed is willing to make emergency loans to banks that find themselves short of liquidity, the sorts of crises in depositor confidence that led to bank runs in the past are now far less likely. (Recall from Chapter 26 that "liquidity" refers to availability of cash.)

In terms of structure, the Federal Reserve System consists of the board of governors based in Washington, DC, and twelve regional Federal Reserve Banks based in Atlanta, Boston, Chicago, Cleveland, Dallas, Kansas City (MO), Minneapolis, New York, Philadelphia, Richmond (VA), St. Louis, and San Francisco. The regional Fed banks also have their own branches in many other cities, such as Baltimore, Los Angeles, Miami, and Pittsburgh.

The structure of the European Central Bank (ECB) is somewhat similar to that of the Fed in the United States, the main difference being that it operates across countries. While the ECB has headquarters in Frankfurt, Germany, each of the seventeen member countries also retains its own national central bank.*

The Fed keeps close track of the economy and tries to sense whether some adjustment in the money supply or in interest rates might be necessary to support aggregate demand or to counteract undesirable changes in the inflation rate. The Fed has the ability to choose "targets" for the rate of growth of the money supply or for the level of interest rates. As we will see, the two are related, although in recent years focus has generally been on the interest rate. We examine the macroeconomic consequences of Fed actions later in this chapter, but for right now we concentrate on the mechanics of *how* the Fed influences the money supply and interest rates.

Discussion Questions

1. What is the Federal Reserve System? What event or events caused it to be created? Where are its banks found?
2. Is the Federal Reserve truly an independent bank or is it part of the government? What are its principal functions?

2. MONETARY POLICY

2.1 HOW THE FED CREATES MONEY AND CREDIT

open market operations: sales or purchases of government bonds by the Fed

As we saw in Chapter 26, increasing the amount of reserves that a bank holds indirectly increases the money supply by permitting banks to lend more money. The additional loans increase the number of transaction accounts, adding to the overall supply of money. Each of the means that the Fed has at its disposal targets the level of bank reserves. The most commonly used tool is **open market operations**. In open market operations, the Federal Reserve Bank of New York changes the level of bank reserves by buying or selling government bonds. Such

*The European Central Bank operates in the 17 member countries of the European Union (as of 2013) that have adopted the euro as their currency. The remaining EU countries either have chosen not to join the euro or do not meet the criteria for joining.

Federal Open Market Committee (FOMC): the committee that oversees open market operations. It is composed of the Fed Board of Governors and 5 of the 12 regional Fed presidents

operations are directed by the **Federal Open Market Committee (FOMC)**, which is composed of the Board of Governors of the Fed and 5 of the 12 regional Fed bank presidents.* Let's see what happens when the FOMC undertakes a purchase of government bonds on the open market.

A simplified balance sheet for the Fed is shown in Table 27.1. Because currency is issued by the Fed, currency in circulation is the Fed's major liability. You will recall from Chapter 26 that a liability refers to anything that someone owes to anyone else. Currency is technically a liability to the Fed because it is legally redeemable for equivalent value. Formerly, this meant that the U.S dollar was backed by its value in gold or silver. Today, the best that one could do is get new currency for old currency.

Table 27.1 **A Simplified Balance Sheet of the Federal Reserve**

Assets		Liabilities	
Government bonds	$1200 billion	Currency in circulation	$1100 billion
		Bank reserves	$100 billion

The Fed's other major liability is the reserves held by private banks. Recall that these consist of vault cash plus deposits that the banks have at the Fed. Just as deposits made by individuals at banks are the liabilities of the banks, deposits made by banks at the Fed are liabilities of the Fed. The Fed holds various assets, but the most important one for our story is its stock of government bonds.

When the Fed makes an open market purchase of bonds, its holdings of bonds increase. It generally makes such purchases from a commercial bank, so it pays for the purchase by crediting the bank's account with the Fed by the amount of the purchase.

What does it pay *with?* Unlike any other actor in the economy, the Fed can create funds with the proverbial "stroke of a pen" or, these days, adjusting an entry in a computer database at the New York office. It simply declares that the bank's reserves are now higher by the amount of the bond purchase. Just as the Fed can authorize production of new currency by the Bureau of Engraving and Printing, it is also empowered to create new bank reserves, which in turn expand the money supply by permitting banks to make more loans. These new loans will end up as deposits elsewhere in the banking system—i.e., new money.

monetary base (or high-powered money): the sum of total currency plus bank reserves

When the Fed makes an open market purchase, it increases something called the **monetary base (or high-powered money)**. This is defined as the sum of total currency in circulation plus bank reserves. We noted in Chapter 26 that dollar bills in circulation are "fiat" money, whose value depends on a government declaration that they are money. The monetary base, similarly, is a form of fiat money that the Fed directly controls.

Suppose that the Fed buys $10 million worth of government bonds from ABC Bank. The changes in the Fed's balance sheet and the balance sheet of ABC Bank are shown in Table 27.2. The Fed increases both its holdings of assets and liabilities by $10 million—the bonds being the asset, and bank reserves the liability. ABC Bank changes only the mix of assets it holds, now holding less in bonds and more in reserves. Note that both the Fed and ABC Bank balance sheets still balance. If total assets equaled total liabilities before the change, they will still be equal after the open market purchase.

So far in our story, reserves have risen by $10 million, but the supply of money in circulation (as measured by M1 or other measures) *has not changed.* But if ABC Bank sees opportunities to make profitable loans, it will not let its new $10 million in reserves just sit at the Fed. If it just met its reserve requirement before the bond purchase, then all of this new $10 million is *excess* reserves. It can use this $10 million to make $10 million in new loans. This movement of $10 million from reserves to new loans is shown in Table 27.3(a).

*The president of the Federal Reserve of New York is a permanent member of the FOMC. Presidents from the other 11 regional Fed banks rotate in and out of the other four positions.

Table 27.2 **An Open Market Purchase of Government Bonds by the Fed**

(a) Change in the Fed Balance Sheet

Assets		Liabilities	
Government bonds:	+$10 million	Bank reserves	+$10 million

(b) Change in ABC Bank's Balance Sheet

Assets		Liabilities	
Government bonds	–$10 million		
Reserves	+$10 million		

Table 27.3 **A Loan by ABC Bank Becomes a Deposit in XYZ Bank**

(a) Next Change in the ABC Bank's Balance Sheet

Assets		Liabilities	
Loans:	+$10 million		
Reserves:	–$10 million		

(b) Change in XYZ Bank's Balance Sheet

Assets		Liabilities	
Reserves:	+$10 million	Deposits:	+$10 million

Suppose that ABC Bank makes a $10 million loan to Jane's Construction, and then, after obtaining the loan in the form of a check, Jane's Construction deposits the entire amount of the funds at XYZ Bank. (We assume a different bank, since in general recipients of loans do not have to deposit them in the originating bank. This also allows us to keep track of changes in balance sheets more easily.) The changes in the balance sheets of XYZ Bank are shown in Table 27.3(b). Because the way that the Fed clears checks is by increasing or decreasing the deposits that it holds for banks, the initial impact on XYZ Bank of the deposit of the check by Jane's Construction is a $10 million increase in both its checkable deposits and its reserves at the Fed.

Note, first, that the money supply *has* now increased. Checkable deposits are part of M1, and there are now $10 million more in total deposits in the economy than there were before. Through an open market purchase of bonds paid for by a "stroke of the pen," the Fed has brought new money into being.

Second, note that XYZ Bank now has excess reserves. If required reserves are 10 percent of deposits, it can lend out much of the $10 million in new funds that it has received—$9 million—while keeping only 10 percent ($1 million) as reserves. (Note that ABC Bank was able to lend out the entire $10 million that it received from the Fed. It did not have to keep 10 percent as reserve, because there was no corresponding increase in deposits at ABC—they obtained the $10 million by selling bonds.)

These new loans will, in turn, become new deposits in the banking system (they could return to ABC or XYZ bank, but more likely will end up in other banks). Then M1 will have increased by the initial 10 million, plus the second-round $9 million—already an increase totaling $19 million, which is quite a bit larger than the initial $10 million increase.

Now, of course, the banks that receive the $9 million in deposits resulting from XYZ Bank's loans will find that they have excess reserves and will also be able to make new loans, and the process will continue. Where will it all end? If each bank that receives new funds lends out as much as it can (given the 10 percent reserve requirement), the total amount of new money will eventually be \$100 million*. The logic is similar to the government spending multiplier in fiscal policy. Just as respending by consumers multiplies the original amount of government spending, so the creation of new loans by banks multiplies the original creation of new reserves.

money multiplier: as the ratio of the money supply to the monetary base, it tells by how much the money supply will change for a given change in high-powered money

The story is actually somewhat more complicated than this because sometimes banks hold excess reserves, and often people who take out loans want to hold some of the funds in cash or in types of deposits that are not part of M1. So not all high-powered money creation will translate directly into new deposits and loans, and monetary expansion will not be quite as dramatic as in the example above. Economists define the **money multiplier** as the ratio of the money supply to the monetary base,

$$money\ multiplier = \frac{money\ supply}{monetary\ base}$$

Using M1 as the measure of money, empirical studies have shown the money multiplier in the United States is currently very close to 2. That is, if the Fed acts to increase reserves and currency by \$10 million, the total increase in the money supply would be expected to be around double that:

$$\Delta\ \textbf{money} = \textbf{money multiplier} \times \Delta\ \textbf{monetary base}$$
$$\$20\ million = 2 \times 10\ million$$

With the "stroke of a pen," the Fed open market purchase of government bonds increases the money supply by about twice the value of the initial bond purchase.

Note that, looking at the same story in a slightly different way, the action of the Fed can also be seen as increasing the amount of *credit* extended to private actors in the economy. The Fed, in making an open market purchase of government bonds, in essence takes over a portion of the public debt that was previously held by private institutions. (Recall from Chapter 25 that government bonds are issued by the Treasury to finance federal budget deficits.) The new bank reserves created by the purchase of government bonds allow banks to extend more credit—new loans—to private actors in the economy.

Traditionally, macroeconomists have tended to look at the asset side of the banks' balance sheets and perceive the story outlined above as a matter of increasing deposits and hence increasing the money supply. More recently, some macroeconomists have focused more on the liabilities side of the banks' balance sheets and see this as a story of an expansion of credit. While, in some sense, the two views are just "two sides of the same coin," looking at the money face of monetary policy tends to draw more attention to people's need for liquidity, while looking at the credit face draws more attention to issues of how financial capital is created and distributed within the economy. It is no coincidence that we have these two interpretations; as we explore further in Chapter 30—and have alluded to at the end of Chapter 26—money is itself a form of debt.

2.2 Other Monetary Policy Tools

As we have seen, if the Fed wants to increase the volume of money and private credit circulating in an economy, it can use open market operations. Open market purchases of government bonds increase reserves. Banks will generally then increase their loans, which increases deposits and hence the money supply.

While this is, in fact, what the Fed usually does when it wants to expand the money supply, it also has other tools at its disposal. Another policy that it can implement is to lower the

*This can be calculated by using the formula for an infinite series where x is less than one: $(1 + x + x^2 + x^3 + \ldots + x^n) = 1/(1 - x)$, just as we did in calculating the income/spending multiplier in Chapter 24. In this case $x = 0.9$.

required reserve ratio. This would have the effect of expanding the money supply by allowing banks to make more loans on a smaller base of reserves.

In truth, there is no "single" reserve requirement ratio, as it varies considerably depending on type of deposit and size of bank (based on total deposits). For example, the U.S. reserve requirement is 0 percent for banks with total transactions accounts less than $12.4 million, 3 percent for those between $12.4 million and $79.5 million, and 10 percent for those holding deposits exceeding $79.5 million. The Fed seldom uses the reserve requirement ratio as a monetary tool, however; it last changed the ratio in 1982.

If a bank falls short of having the required amount of reserves on hand, it can borrow funds from the Fed at what is called the "discount window" at a rate of interest traditionally called the **discount rate**. In theory, a reduction in the discount rate should increase the money supply, because this would lower the cost to a bank of being found to be below its required level of reserves. A bank could then be somewhat more aggressive about making loans. In fact, however, since the Fed frowns on (and penalizes) banks that are found to be low on reserves too often, banks tend to prefer to borrow from one another if they need money in the short term (this process is discussed in the following section). In extraordinary circumstances, such as during the financial crisis in 2008, the Fed has taken the opposite approach, of encouraging use of the discount window to promote greater liquidity.

discount rate: the interest rate at which banks can borrow reserves at the Fed discount window

The Fed can cause the money supply (and credit) to contract, as well. If instead of making an open market purchase of government bonds, it makes an open market *sale,* everything in the story we have just told happens in reverse. When the Fed sells bonds, the buyer (usually a commercial bank) must pay the Fed. That means the bank has that much less in its reserve account. Overall, private banks will now hold *more* in government bonds and *less* in reserves. (Of course, banks are not forced to buy bonds. However, the Fed can "flood the market" with bond offerings sufficient to lower the price to a level so attractive that banks would be foolish not to buy.)

If banks hold less in reserves, then they have to tighten up on loans. If they tighten up on loans, then there will be fewer deposits. The money multiplier also works in reverse, so that the original bond sale has a magnified effect in reducing the total money supply.

The Fed can thus increase the money supply by making an open market purchase of bonds, lowering the required reserve ratio, or lowering the discount rate. It can decrease the money supply by making an open market sale of bonds, raising the required reserve ratio, or raising the discount rate. Of these policy tools, however, open market operations are much the most frequently used and most significant in affecting the money supply.

In a growing economy, a central bank would rarely want to shrink the money supply in absolute terms. A growing economy, as measured by GDP, means ever more transactions need to be facilitated by readily available liquid assets and generally growing demand by private economic actors for loans. "Loose" monetary policy, in the case of a real-world growing economy, then, usually means making the money supply grow *faster* than the economy has been growing. "Tight" policy does not mean actually making M1 fall; rather it just means making the money supply grow *slower* than the growth rate of the economy.

In this section, we have discussed the technical question of *how* the Fed or another economy's central bank can change the volume of money and credit in an economy. Now we can move on to the more interesting questions of *why* it may—or may not—want to do so. We introduce these issues by examining two different situations.

- The first case is where inflation can be assumed to be fairly stable, and the main things that policymakers are worried about are output and employment. This case is addressed in the next two sections.
- The second case is where policymakers are primarily worried about inflation. This is addressed in Section 5.

These important base cases are useful for analyzing the situation of certain economies at particular times. The last section of the chapter looks at the more complicated issues of balancing goals related to employment, output, and inflation, and delves into controversies about monetary policies.

Discussion Questions

1. From the description of the Fed and the earlier discussion of money, can you name some things that private banks had to do for themselves before the Federal Reserve System was created? What were some of the problems that resulted?
2. Describe in words how a Fed open market operation can increase the volume of money in the economy.

3. THE THEORY OF MONEY, INTEREST RATES, AND AGGREGATE DEMAND

Our discussion up to this point has focused on the volume of money and credit in the economy. In an economy that is experiencing fairly low inflation and that has a healthy banking system, most of the concern with the money supply is really a concern about interest rates, the availability of credit, and their consequences for aggregate demand. In contemporary discussions of the Fed's monetary policy, the focus is almost always on interest rates. How does the Fed affect interest rates, and how do changing interest rates affect the economy?

3.1 THE FEDERAL FUNDS RATE AND OTHER INTEREST RATES

federal funds rate: the interest rate determined in the private market for overnight loans of reserves among banks

In recent years, when changes in monetary policy have been announced by leaders of the Fed or discussed in the financial pages of the newspaper, attention usually focuses on what is called the **federal funds rate**. This is the going rate of interest determined on a private market of interbank loans. If a bank finds that it has more reserves than it needs to meet its reserve requirements, it offers funds on the "federal funds" market, usually just overnight. If another bank is short on reserves, it borrows on that market and pays back the next day.

Although a quick reading of reports in the media often make it sound as though the Fed directly controls the federal funds rate (for example, headlines may read "Fed Announces Cut in Federal Funds Rate of 0.25 Percent"), this in not, in fact, the case. The Fed announces desired *target* or *benchmark* levels for the federal funds rate and then acts on bank reserves to try to achieve that target. Because the Fed is generally quite effective at this, the difference between the (official) target federal funds rate and the (market-determined) actual federal funds rate is usually small.

A simplified model of the federal funds market is portrayed in Figure 27.1a. The quantity of funds is on the horizontal axis, and the federal funds rate—the price of borrowing on this market—is on the vertical axis. (Note that this is just a specific variant of the sort of "market for loanable funds" discussed in Chapter 24.) The actors on both sides of this market are banks.

The supply curve for federal funds slopes upward, because higher returns on this market mean that banks with excess reserves will be more likely to lend them here, rather than finding other ways to lend them out. The demand curve for federal funds slopes downward, because the lower the interest rate, the more willing banks are to borrow. Figure 27.1a portrays a situation in which the federal funds rate at which the market clears is 6 percent. (Interest rates are generally stated in annualized terms—what borrowers would pay if they held the loan for a year—no matter how long the loan is actually held.)

The Fed undertakes open market operations with the goal of pushing the going rate for loans in that market to the level of its choosing. Recall that when the Fed makes an open market purchase, it increases the quantity of reserves that banks hold. All else being equal, this increases the amount of reserves available for private lending in the federal funds market. In Figure 27.1b, this is shown as the supply curve for federal funds shifting to the right. In this example the federal funds rate falls to 5 percent.

Figure 27.1a **The Market for Federal Funds**

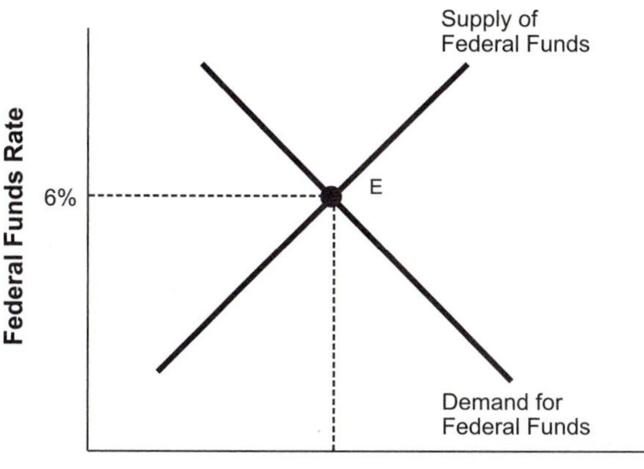

The supply and demand for available funds determine the Federal Funds Rate.

Figure 27.1b **An Open Market Purchase Lowers the Federal Funds Rate**

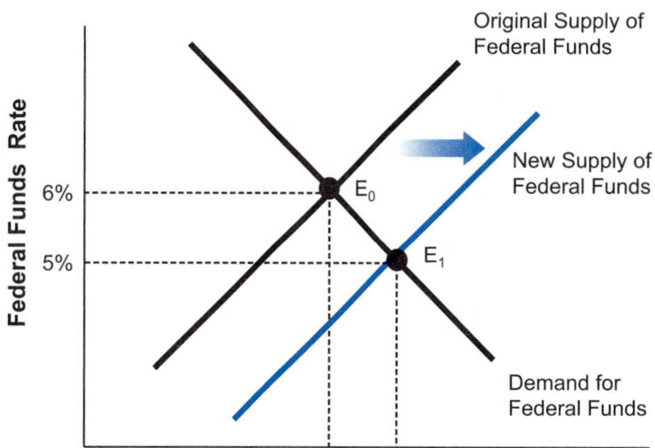

When the Federal reserve makes an open market purchase of government bonds, it increases the supply of reserves that can be lent on the federal funds market, lowering the federal funds rate.

Since 1995, the Fed has explicitly announced its targets for the federal funds rate and then has taken the necessary steps to keep the actual rate as close as possible to the target rate. Figure 27.2 shows how the Fed reacts to a shift in the demand for federal funds. A rise in demand for federal funds is shown by shift A. If the Fed took no action in response to this shift, the increase in demand would cause the interest rate to rise. The Fed counteracts this upward pressure by putting more reserves into the system via open market purchases, shifting the supply curve outward (shift B). The effect is to virtually fix this important interest rate. Conversely, the Fed would meet a decrease in the demand for federal funds with open market sales.

prime rate: the interest rate that banks charge their most creditworthy commercial borrowers

Because financial markets in a sophisticated economy tend to be closely interlinked, a drop in the interest rate in one major market tends to carry over into other markets. When banks have to pay more to borrow reserves, they tend to charge more to their own customers. Figure 27.3 shows how the **prime rate**—the rate that banks charge their most creditworthy commercial customers—closely follows the federal funds rate. Banks have generally kept their prime rate at the federal funds rate plus three percentage points.

Figure 27.2 **Maintaining the Federal Funds Target Rate**

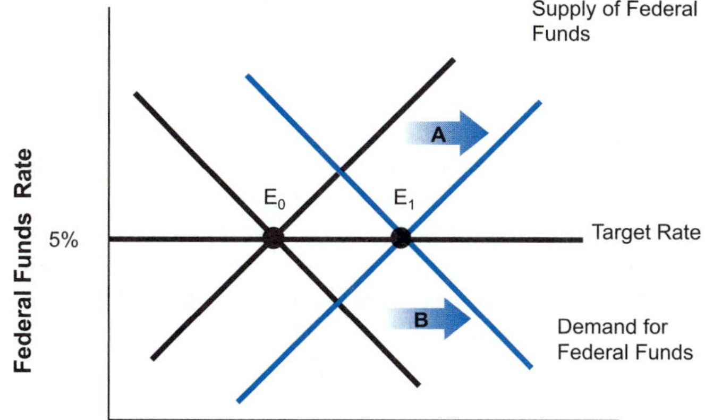

If the Federal Reserve sees the demand for reserves rising (shift A), it supplies more reserves to banks and thus to the federal funds market (shift B). It does the opposite if it sees demand falling. The result is a rate that is virtually fixed at the level targeted by the Federal Reserve.

Figure 27.3 **The Federal Fund and Prime Rates**

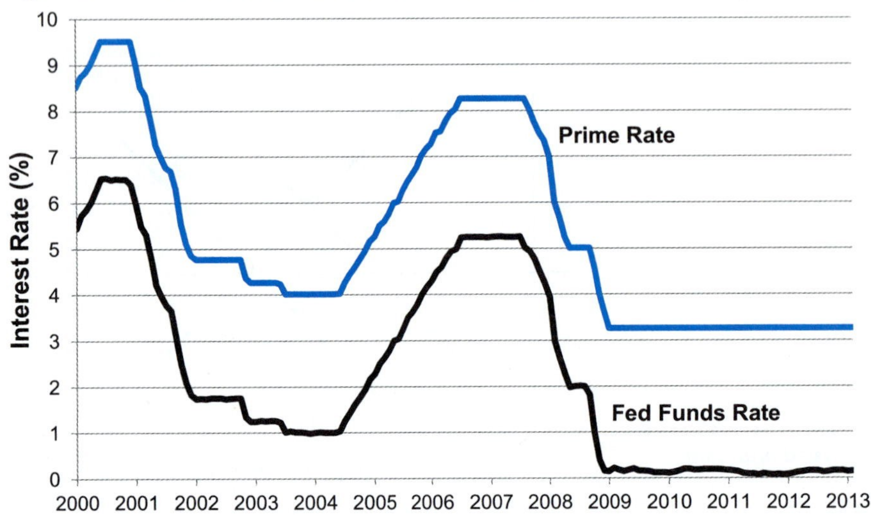

A number of other interest rates in the economy, including the prime rate charged by banks to commercial borrowers, tend to follow the Federal Funds Rate.

Source: Federal Reserve Board, monthly data.

The rate that you, as an individual, will be charged by a bank on a loan will generally be higher than the prime rate, and the interest rate that you receive on your deposits will always be lower than the prime rate (so that the bank can make a profit). Nevertheless, consumer rates also tend to rise or fall with changes in the federal funds rate.

As a general rule, an expansionary monetary policy expands credit and lowers interest rates throughout the economy. Conversely, contractionary monetary policy tends to shrink the volume of credit and raise interest rates throughout the economy.* Thus central bank monetary policy affects businesses and individuals throughout the economy.

3.2 INTEREST RATES AND INVESTMENT

Economists are particularly interested in interest rates because of their effect on investment. To the extent that individuals or businesses make investments using borrowed funds, higher interest rates make investing more expensive, and, hence, less attractive. Residential investment, in particular, has historically been especially sensitive to variations in interest rates. Traditionally, investment in homes has been financed by fifteen- or thirty-year mortgages. A small change in the interest rate can add up, over time, to a very big difference in the total cost of buying a house.

The case for interest rate effects on intended business investment in structures, equipment, and inventories (sometimes referred to as "nonresidential investment") is a bit more mixed. We saw in Chapter 24 that Keynes did not think that changes in the interest rate would be sufficient to get the economy out of the Great Depression. Investor pessimism during that period was very deep. Trying to encourage businesses to invest when they see no prospect of selling more of their goods has been referred to as attempting to "push on a string."

accelerator principle: the idea that high GDP growth leads to increasing investment, and low or negative GDP growth leads to declining investment

The idea that business fixed investment primarily responds to changes in sales much more than to changes in interest rates has been called the **accelerator principle**. If businesses see their sales rising, they may need to expand their capacity—that is, invest in new equipment and structures—in order to keep up with demand for their product. Since the best overall indicator of expanded sales is a rising GDP, this principle says that the best predictor of investment growth is GDP growth. Conversely, a small decline—or even just slowing down—of demand

*Things get more complicated when we consider the duration of loans and the difference between short and long term interest rates. We address this issue in the Appendix.

may lead to a disproportionate drying up of intended investment, as firms come to fear being caught with excess capacity. To the extent the accelerator principle is in force, changes in the interest rate may have only a relatively minor effect on levels of investment.

Given a particular level of optimism or pessimism, however, firms can be expected to pay at least some attention to interest rates in deciding how much to invest. Higher interest rates tend to limit the amount of investment by firms that may need to borrow money to invest. Using the string analogy, it is easier to pull on a string than to push it—tighter monetary policy is likely to restrain overall investment. Combining this logical assumption with the empirically observed sensitivity of residential investment to interest rates, our simple model of macroeconomic stabilization says that, *all else being equal,* lower interest rates will lead to higher intended investment spending (and vice versa for higher interest rates). Intended investment is inversely related to the interest rate, *r,* as shown in Figure 27.4.

Changes in investor confidence, related to actual spending (via the accelerator principle) or to expected levels of spending, can be portrayed as shifting this intended investment curve. An increase in investor confidence, for example, shifts the curve to the right (from I_1 to I_1') as shown in Figure 27.5. At any given interest rate, firms now want to invest more (I** rather than I*). A decrease in investor confidence shifts the curve to the left.

Figure 27.4 **The Intended Investment Schedule**

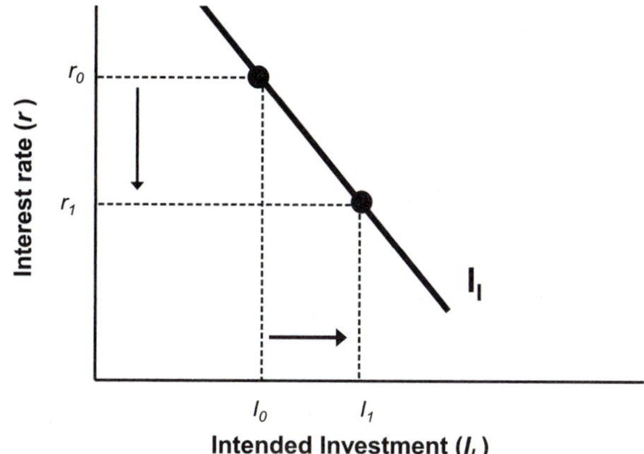

All else equal, if the interest rate falls (from r_0 to r_1), intended investment should rise (from I_0 to I_1).

Figure 27.5 **An Increase in Investor Confidence**

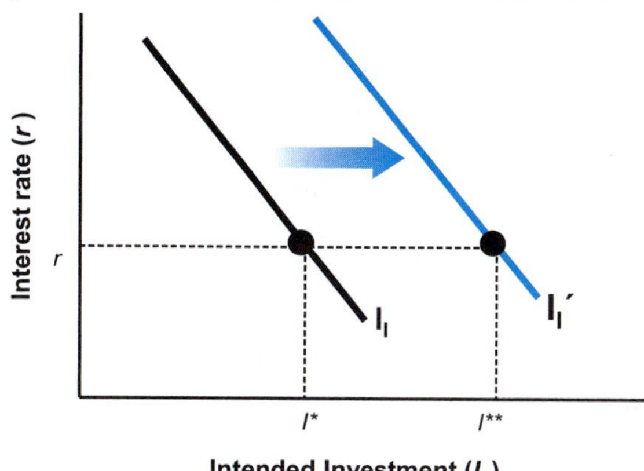

If firms become more confident about future sales, and want to increase their capacity, the intended investment schedule shifts to the right.

3.3 Monetary Policy and Aggregate Demand

Our basic model of aggregate demand, developed in Chapters 24 and 25, can now be expanded to include the effect of monetary policy. In an economy with low inflation and a stable banking system, expansionary monetary policy should tend to lower interest rates (Figures 27.1b and 27.3) and raise intended investment (Figure 27.4). Because intended investment spending, I_I is part of aggregate demand:

$$AD = C + I_I + G + NX$$

this increase in investment should shift the *AD* schedule upward and raise the equilibrium levels of aggregate demand, income, and output, as shown in Figure 27.6.

The chain of causation can be summarized as:

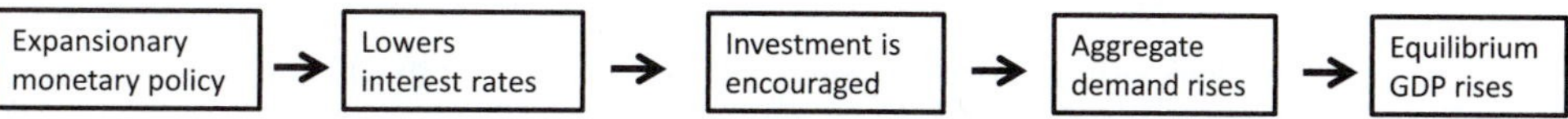

Figure 27.6 **Expansionary Monetary Policy and the AD Curve**

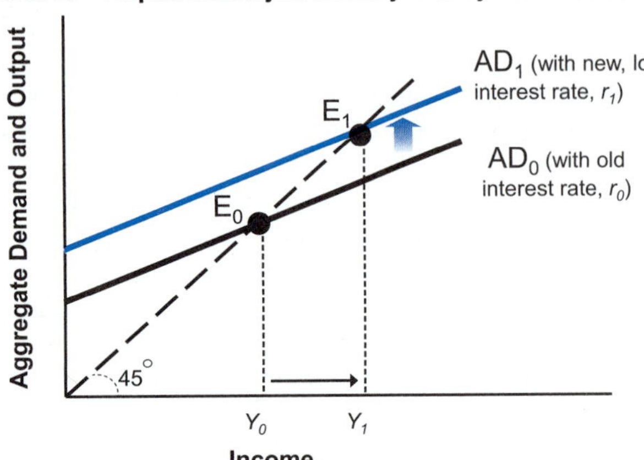

In this model, expansionary monetary policy lowers interest rates, raises investment spending, and raises aggregate demand, income, and output.

If the economy is headed toward a recession, then monetary policy that is relatively loose, increasing the money supply in order to help maintain output, can have a desirable stabilizing effect. Sometimes such an **expansionary monetary policy** is called an **accommodating monetary policy**, especially (though not exclusively) when the Fed is reacting to a specific economic event that might otherwise tend to send the economy into recession.

expansionary monetary policy: the use of monetary policy tools to increase the money supply, lower interest rates, and stimulate a higher level of economic activity

Contractionary monetary policy, however, would be prescribed if the economy seems to be heading towards inflation. In that case, the Fed seeks to slow growth and "cool down" the economy. In the aggregate demand model, a decrease in the money supply will raise interest rates, lower intended investment, shift the *AD* schedule downward, and lower the equilibrium levels of aggregate demand, income, and output.*

Discussion Questions

1. What sorts of interest rates are relevant to your own economic activities?? Do you think that Fed policies affect their levels?
2. Is it always true that an increase in the money supply leads to an increase in investment and aggregate demand? Why or why not?

4. MONETARY POLICIES IN PRACTICE

4.1 THE FED AND INVESTMENT, 2000–2012

accommodating monetary policy: loose or expansionary monetary policy intended to counteract recessionary tendencies in the economy

contractionary monetary policy: the use of monetary policy tools to limit the money supply, raise interest rates, and encourage a leveling off or reduction in economic activity

The effect of Fed policy on investment can be illustrated with several recent historical examples. In late 2000, the federal funds rate stood at 6.5 percent. But there were signs that the economy might be heading into recession: The "dot-com" stock market bubble had burst, and policymakers were worried that the pattern of enthusiastic investment and consumer spending that had fueled GDP growth in the 1990s might be coming to an end. Orders for goods had slowed down. Inventories had built up. In January 2001 the Fed, publicly expressing concern about the weakness of the economy, took action to lower the federal funds rate by half a percentage point. Then, the next month, it lowered it again. Throughout the period 2001–3, it steadily pushed interest rates down, as shown in Figure 27.7. The federal funds rate reached a low of 1 percent in early 2004.

What was the consequence for investment and aggregate demand? The bottom half of Figure 27.7 shows the data for residential and nonresidential private fixed (i.e., noninventory) investment. Nonresidential fixed investment—business investment in equipment and

*In Chapter 29, we look at how monetary policy can also change *AD* by affecting international capital flows, the relative values of national currencies, and net exports.

Figure 27.7 **Monetary Policy and Investment, 2000–2012**

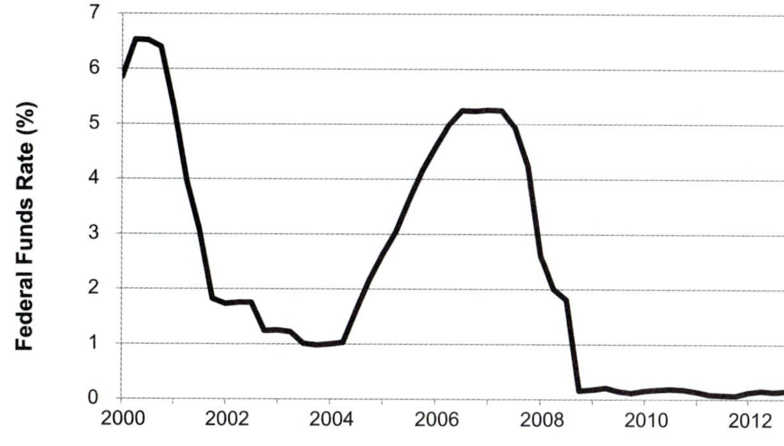

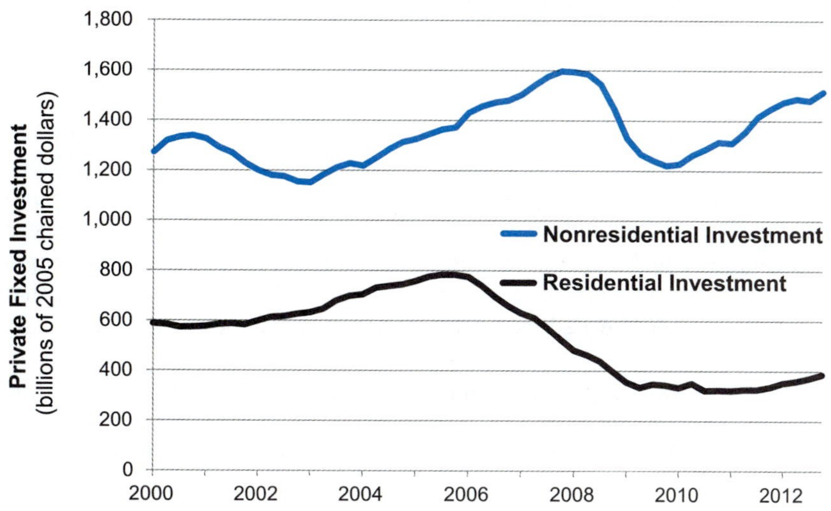

In 2001–3 and from 2007 on, interest rate cuts helped spur residential and non-residential investment, although the response after the Great Recession was slow.

Source: Federal Reserve and Bureau of Economic Analysis, 2013.

structures—might seem to move in the direction *opposite* of that predicted by the theory of investment presented earlier (Figure 27.4). As interest rates steadily fell through 2001 and most of 2002, this kind of investment *fell.*

But recall that the theory said that "all else being equal" a lower interest rate should lead to higher intended investment—and all else was *not* equal during this period. Businesses had too much capacity and inventory and were pessimistic about sales. In terms of the model, Figure 27.8 shows this pessimism shifting the intended investment schedule to the left, from I_1 to I_1'. The lower interest rates due to Fed action may have kept investors from cutting back even more, but the lower rates were not enough to prevent the downturn in nonresidential (and overall) investment, shown on the graph as a shift from I* to I**.

Residential investment, however, shows what many consider a success story for monetary policy during this period. While fixed business investment fell markedly, investment in housing did not fall, but in fact increased steadily (as shown in Figure 27.7). Even though the economy in general was in recession for much of 2001, and investment overall was in a slump, housing investment grew over this period. By November 2002, nonresidential investment had also started growing again.

By May 2004, the Fed believed that the recovery was well under way and would continue. It returned to focusing on its other main macroeconomic goal: controlling inflation. For the

Figure 27.8 **Expansionary Monetary Policy in an Environment of Pessimism**

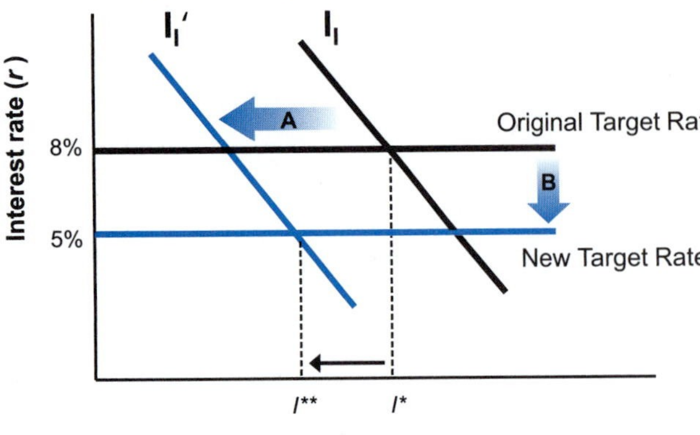

If investors become pessimistic (shift A), the level of intended investment can still fall, even though Fed actions lower the interest rate (shift B). The net effect is that intended investment falls from I_I* to I_I**

next three years, the Fed steadily increased the federal funds rate in an attempt to keep the economy from "overheating." But in late 2007, the Fed again switched to an expansionary stance, largely due to problems that had developed in the housing market.

As you can see in Figure 27.7(b), residential investment went into a slump in 2006, due to overbuilding in the earlier period. Problems in the financing of home mortgages also created a crisis in the credit markets. As we discuss in Chapter 30, during the 2004–7 period banks had aggressively moved into the marketing of "subprime" mortgages (loans given to people whose incomes or credit histories ordinarily would not be good enough to qualify them for mortgages). When borrowers found it impossible to pay back these loans, the value of mortages held by banks and other investors fell drastically, creating a financial crisis and pushing the economy towards recession. Fearing a domino effect that would lead to a severe recession, the Fed took steps to make more money available—an expansionary monetary policy.

As a clear indicator of the Fed's aggressive attempt to forestall recession, it allowed the federal funds rate to sink to historic lows, and far more quickly than during the previous rate reduction. The rate sank from 5.26 percent in mid-2007 to scarcely above 0 (0.16 percent) by the end of 2008. For the next five years, the fed funds rate remained at extraordinarily low levels—in late 2013 it stood at 0.09 percent. Unfortunately, in spite of all the Fed's efforts, the economy fell into recession, and economic recovery was very slow. As of 2013, the Fed's policy remained to keep rates at rock-bottom levels.

Since even a near-zero federal funds rate was insufficient to promote the lending required to kick start the economy, the Fed resorted to an unusual approach known as **quantitative easing (QE)**. Instead of following its regular open market program of government bond purchases, under QE the Fed buys other diverse financial assets (mostly bonds, but many with terms longer than usual) from banks and nonbank institutions alike. The main objective here is not an interest rate target but, rather, to flood the economy with more money, in hopes of provoking the necessary spending to create an economic stimulus (see Box 27.1).

quantitative easing (QE): the purchase of financial assets including long-term bonds by the Fed, creating more monetary reserves and expanding the money supply

As of 2013, three rounds of quantitative easing, referred to as QE1, QE2, and QE3, had taken place. Analyses of the effectiveness of the Fed's policy are varied. On the one hand, there is wide agreement that Fed support was needed to respond to the worst recession since the Great Depression of the 1930s. Although it took time, the economy did start to recover, and it appears that low interest rates and quantitative easing played an important role in this, especially in promoting a housing market recovery through low interest rates for mortgages. But some critics warned that such a massive program of monetary expansion could have undesired effects, such as fueling further financial bubbles or causing inflation to rise. To evaluate these concerns, we need to look a little further into monetary theory.

Box 27.1 Fed Chairman Defends Stimulus Program

In testimony to Congress in February 2013, the Federal Reserve chairman, Ben Bernanke, played down concerns about the Fed's economic stimulus campaign, describing it as necessary and effective.

In response to the economic crisis, the Fed has acquired nearly $3 trillion in Treasury and mortgage-backed securities, and under the QE3 program of "quantitative easing" it plans to expand its holding by $85 billion a month until economic growth picks up and the labor market improves. The Fed also intends to hold short-term interest rates near zero at least until the unemployment rate falls below 6.5 percent.

Mr. Bernanke tried to soothe concerns that the Fed's policies might encourage excessive risk-taking by investors, or lead to renewed inflation. Mr. Bernanke indicated that the Fed took these concerns very seriously, and had expanded its efforts to monitor financial markets. But he also pointed out that inflation under his chairmanship had been the lowest in the period since World War II.

"We do not see the potential costs of increased risk-taking in some financial markets as outweighing the benefits of promoting a stronger economic recovery and more rapid job creation," said Mr. Bernanke.

In July 2013, Mr. Bernanke reiterated that "with unemployment still high and declining only gradually, and with inflation running below the Committee's longer-run objective, a highly accommodative monetary policy will remain appropriate for the foreseeable future."

As of late 2013, predictions by critics that the Fed's policies would lead to runaway inflation had not come to pass. Inflation remained at historically low levels, and inflationary expectations were only a little over 1 percent. At the same time, there was a steady, but slow, decline in unemployment, and a modest revival in consumer confidence.

Sources: Binyamin Appelbaum, "Fed Defends Stimulus in Testimony to Senate," *New York Times*, February 26, 2013; Testimony, Chairman Ben S. Bernanke, *Semiannual Monetary Policy Report to the Congress*, July 13, 2013; Floyd Norris, "Predictions on Fed Strategy that did not Come to Pass," *New York Times*, June 29, 2013.

4.2 The Liquidity Trap and Credit Rationing

As noted above, the federal funds rate hovered just over 0 percent from 2008 through 2013.* This represented perhaps the most expansionary monetary policy in U.S. history. Insofar as recovery was very slow, there was a strong case for continued loosening. But remember our earlier analogy of pushing on a string. As the Fed continues to add to the monetary base and expand the money supply, there is a possibility that it will just create more "slack in the string"—the money will not find its way into useful investment and job creation.

liquidity trap: a situation in which interest rates are so low that the central bank finds it impossible to reduce them further

In the 1930s, Keynes introduced the term **liquidity trap** for a situation in which it is impossible for a central bank to drive interest rates down any lower. In the past few years, the United States appears to have hit this monetary policy wall.

The way a liquidity trap works is that as the Fed creates money, banks, individuals, and business firms simply hold onto the money, rather than using it in ways that increase aggregate demand. Recall that, for expansionary monetary policy to work in the predicted way, banks have to respond to increases in their reserves by making new loans. But what if banks do not find many of their customers creditworthy or their usual customers are not very interested in taking out new loans? Low interest rates may not translate into new credit and new investment, if bankers are not willing to make new loans. Instead, the banks may hold the money as excess reserves to protect themselves against problems with bad loans or other financial demands. This problem repeatedly frustrated the Fed's attempts to spark a recovery from the 2007 crisis.

credit rationing: when banks deny loans to some potential borrowers, in the interest of maintaining their own profitability

Instead of using extra funds to make more loans, banks may tend to engage in **credit rationing** in order to ensure their own profitability. This means that they will lend to the customers whom they deem most creditworthy, using restrictive standards to decide who merits getting a loan. If this happens, some firms and individuals will get the funds that they

* As this text went to press in 2013, the Fed projected continuing to hold rates low through at least the end of 2014.

need, while others—and particularly smaller firms and lower-income individuals—may be frozen out. In this case, monetary policy may have significant distributional effects: in the simplest terms, making the rich richer, and the poor poorer.

The possibility of a liquidity trap or of reluctance among bankers and investors to lend and borrow means that the Fed faces limitations in its ability to stimulate a sluggish economy (see Box 27.1). This does not necessarily mean that the Fed's efforts are fruitless. As of late 2013, evidence indicated that the Fed's purchases of existing mortgages from banks had freed up banks to create new mortgages, improving the situation in the housing market. But at the same time the creation of so much new money raises concerns that some of the money might go to the wrong places, creating inflation in asset and goods prices. As of late 2013, this had not occurred. But concern about future inflation suggests that we should take a further look at monetary policy responses to inflation.

Discussion Questions

1. What is quantitative easing? How is it different from open market operations? Has the Fed had favorable results with it since the 2007 financial crisis?
2. Explain the liquidity trap. Do you think that the theory accurately describes the events after the Great Recession?

5. THE THEORY OF MONEY, PRICES, AND INFLATION

Section 4 laid out a description of the Fed's roles and activities that derives from an assumption of an economy in which inflation is low and steady, so that the main thing the Fed has to worry about is helping to stabilize the levels of investment, aggregate demand, and output. Now let's switch to the opposite extreme. Suppose that the central bank's main worry is controlling inflation. Some different analyses will be helpful in understanding this case.

5.1 THE QUANTITY EQUATION

quantity equation: $M \times V = P \times Y$ where M is the money supply, V is the velocity of money, P is the price level, and Y is real output.

One way of thinking about the relationship between the real economy, money, and prices is based on what economists call the **quantity equation**:

$$M \times V = P \times Y$$

In this equation, Y is, as usual, real output or GDP. P indicates the price level as measured by a price index, for example the GDP deflator discussed in Chapter 20. The multiplication of these two variables means that the right-hand side of the equation represents nominal output (if necessary, review Chapter 20 for an explanation of the difference between nominal and real output).

On the left-hand side, M measures the level of money balances, such as the M1 measure discussed above. V, the only really new variable here, represents the velocity of money. The **velocity of money** is the number of times that a dollar changes hands in a year, in order to support the level of output and exchange represented by nominal GDP. In other words, since the money in circulation is insufficient to "purchase" everything entailed by GDP, velocity represents how often, on average, each dollar changes hands in order for there to be sufficient funds to purchase all the goods and services produced in the economy. (Remember that we are talking both about cash and bank deposits—so "changing hands" could be literal, as when you pay for a pizza with cash, or virtual, as when a bank clears a check on one account, making the funds available to another account holder.)

velocity of money: the number of times that a dollar would have to change hands during a year to support nominal GDP, calculated as $V = (P \times Y)/M$

Since nominal GDP and M1 are observable, velocity can be calculated as the ratio of the two,

$$V = \frac{P \times Y}{M}$$

For the quantity equation to become the basis for a *theory,* rather than merely represent definitions of variables, an assumption needs to be made about velocity. Supporters of different economic theories all have subscribed to the irrefutable arithmetic of the quantity equation. Where they have differed is over assumptions regarding the behavior of one or more of the variables.

quantity theory of money: the theory that money supply is directly related to nominal GDP, according to the equation $M \times \bar{V} = P \times Y$

Two theories we discuss below—classical and monetarist—assume that velocity is constant—changing very little, if at all, with changing conditions in the economy. If this is true, then the level of the money supply and the level of nominal GDP should be tightly related. We denote this assumption that velocity is constant by putting a bar over V. The **quantity theory of money**, then, is characterized by the relation

$$M \times \bar{V} = P \times Y$$

where $\bar{V}$ is read "V-bar." More Keynesian-oriented theories, however, while they may make use of the quantity equation, do not assume that velocity is constant. Their analyses are not based on the quantity theory.

5.2 COMPETING THEORIES

Classical monetary theory is based on the quantity theory of money, plus the assumption that output is always constant at its full-employment level.* That is,

$$M \times V = P \times Y^*$$

where Y^*, as usual, denotes full-employment output. In this case—in contrast to the aggregate demand model described in Section 4—changes in the money supply can have *no* effect on the level of output. The inability of changes in the money supply to affect real output is called **monetary neutrality**. The only variable on the left-hand side that is not constant is the money supply, while the only variable on the right-hand side that is not constant is the price level. Thus, all that a change in the money supply can do is change prices. Rather than an increase in the money supply increasing output, in this model an increase in the money supply has no effect other than to cause inflation.

monetary neutrality: the idea that changes in the money supply may affect only prices, while leaving output unchanged

Classical economists, then, tend to see no need for discretionary monetary policy. On the contrary, they consider it counterproductive. In the case of an economy that is not growing, classical theory would prescribe a stable money supply level to avoid unnecessary changes in prices. In a growing economy, classical theory says that the money supply should grow at the same rate as real GDP in order to keep prices stable. If we assume that the rate of real GDP growth is fairly constant, then the money supply should just grow at a fixed rate, say 3 percent per year. A central bank that enforces this is said to be following a **money supply rule**.

money supply rule: committing to letting the money supply grow at a fixed rate per year

Another famous theory based on the quantity equation is **monetarism**, propounded by Milton Friedman and Anna Jacobson Schwartz in their book *A Monetary History of the United States, 1867–1960,* published in 1963. While Keynes had argued that insufficient investment and aggregate demand caused the Great Depression, Friedman and Schwartz argued that it was caused by a severe contraction in the money supply.

monetarism: a theory associated with Milton Friedman, which claims that macroeconomic objectives are best met by having the money supply grow at a steady rate

Friedman had earlier propounded the quantity theory of money and has become known for his saying that "inflation is always and everywhere a monetary phenomenon." But unlike the pure classical theorists, he thought that *bad* monetary policy could have, at least temporarily, *bad* effects on the real economy. During the early years of the Great Depression, he and

*We simplify here, but to be precise, the classical view is that the economy will always *tend* toward full employment equilibrium in the long run. Please review Chapter 24 for a comparison between the classical and Keynesian views on this point.

Schwartz pointed out, both the money supply and the level of nominal GDP fell sharply. This empirical observation can be seen as consistent with the quantity theory of money:

$$\underset{\downarrow}{M} \times \underset{\substack{\textit{no}\\ \textit{change}}}{\bar{V}} = \underset{\downarrow}{P} \times \underset{\downarrow}{Y}$$

They argued that the contraction in the money supply caused the reductions in both the price level and real GDP—an assertion that remains controversial. Because of his belief in the potential for bad monetary policy to cause harm, Friedman was one of the most vocal proponents of the idea that central banks should simply follow a fixed rule of having the money supply grow at a steady rate. In this regard, he and most classical theorists would have been in agreement.

The quantity equation can also be used to shed light on the problem of very high inflation, described early in Chapter 26. Suppose that the level of output in an economy is stagnant or growing only very slowly. But at the same time suppose that the central bank is causing the money supply to grow very quickly. If people come to expect high inflation, money may become a "hot potato"—people want to hold it for as short a time as possible because it loses value so quickly. They will try to turn money into non-inflating assets—real estate, hard currency, jewelry, or barterable goods—as quickly as they can. This means that the velocity of money also increases. A situation of hyperinflation in a stagnant economy can be illustrated as:

$$\underset{\uparrow}{M} \times \underset{\uparrow}{V} = \underset{\uparrow}{P} \times \underset{\substack{\textit{no}\\ \textit{change}}}{\bar{Y}}$$

where the bar over Y indicates that output is stuck at a level below full employment. With output stagnant, and both money supply and velocity increasing, inflation must result.

While we imagined a printing press in the government's basement in our earlier story about hyperinflation in Chapter 26, a sophisticated economy can also essentially "run the printing presses" if the agency that issues government debt and the central bank work together. For example, suppose that the U.S. Treasury issues new debt, and the Fed immediately buys the same amount of new debt and injects new money into the economy. The effect is the same as if the Fed had just printed new currency, except that the increase in bank reserves is in the form of "a stroke of the pen" instead of freshly printed paper. This is called **monetizing the deficit**. In the United States, however, the Fed does not automatically buy new government debt. It may, as an accommodating move, monetize some deficit spending by the government in order to help the economy out of a recession, but it is not obliged to do so.

monetizing the deficit: when a central bank buys government debt as it is issued (equivalent to "running the printing presses")

Even in less extreme cases, a "loose money" policy can lead to inflation. For example, suppose that the economy is functioning relatively normally, but output has reached its full-employment level (Y^*). If monetary policy continues to be expansionary, inflation is likely to result. (This is discussed more in Chapter 28.)

Discussion Questions

1. What is the difference between the quantity *theory* of money and the quantity *equation?*
2. Has inflation been reported to be a problem in any recent news reports? Check recent inflation data at www.usinflationcalculator.com. How do you think this is related to recent Fed monetary policy?

6. Complications and Policy Controversies

In the real world, central banks generally have to be concerned about output and inflation, as well as banking regulation and stability, all at the same time. When the goals include *both* stabilization of prices and of output, how does this complicate the analysis, and what does this mean for policy?

6.1 THE FED'S DILEMMA

As we saw in Section 3, the Fed tries to get the economy out of a recession through expansionary monetary policy—policies that increase the money supply, lower interest rates, stimulate investment, and thus increase aggregate demand. But if it goes about increasing the money supply too vigorously or at the wrong time (such as when the economy is already nearing full employment), then it can cause inflation to rise (as we saw in Section 4). If inflation is "heating up," then the Fed should use contractionary monetary policy—reining in the money supply, raising interest rates, and discouraging investment in the interest of "cooling off" aggregate demand and economic activity.

This may seem very straightforward, but policy-making can have many complications. For one thing, there is the controversial question of what exactly the "full-employment" level of employment is at any given time. Suppose, for example, that the Fed starts to get nervous about inflation too early in an economic upswing. Perhaps the unemployment rate could have fallen to, say, 4 percent, with little increase in inflation, if the recovery had been allowed to continue, but the Fed switches into inflation-fighting mode at an unemployment rate of, say, 6 percent. By halting the recovery too early, the Fed may end up being blamed for causing unnecessary suffering. But if conditions in the economy are such that letting unemployment fall to 4 percent would cause a large rise in inflation, then if the Fed lets the recovery continue, it will instead end up being blamed for inflation.

There is also considerable controversy over what rates of inflation can be considered acceptable. Some economists find only inflation rates from 0 percent to 2 percent acceptable; others do not see an urgent need for monetary control unless inflation is 5 percent or higher. There is a continuing debate among economists and policymakers over the proper weight to give to GDP growth goals versus price stabilization goals (see Box 27.2).

Another practical problem is that monetary authorities have to pay attention to issues of timing. In Chapter 25 we discussed the "inside lags" of decision making and implementation as well as the "outside lag" of an enacted policy having an effect on aggregate demand. In the case of fiscal policy, the "inside lags" tend to be rather long, as Congress and the President try to agree on a budget, but the "outside lag" is relatively short. For monetary policy, the case tends to be reversed. The Federal Open Market Committee is scheduled to meet eight times a year and may schedule extra meetings. A monetary policy decision only requires

BOX 27.2 RAISING INFLATION TARGETS IN JAPAN

"Japan's new Prime Minister Shinzo Abe declared a 'monetary regime change' as the central bank bowed to government pressure, setting a 2 percent inflation target aimed at helping the country emerge from its prolonged bout of deflation . . . Some economists believe a moderate amount of inflation is grease that can make the wheels of the economy spin faster" (Associated Press, January 22, 2013). Japan has been stuck in a deflationary pattern for decades, as the central bank has had trouble even achieving its 1 percent inflation target.

In August 2013, Bank of Japan Governor Haruhiko Kuroda pledged to continue easing until the 2 percent inflation target is reached. The Bank will conduct open market operations to increase the monetary base from 60 to 70 trillion yen, boosting its purchases of Japanese government bonds to total 50 trillion yen per year to lower interest rates and promote lending.

In a speech to the Kyoto Chamber of Commerce and Industry, Deputy Bank Governor Kikuo Iwata said that it will take time to see the effects of monetary easing in the real economy. He predicted that prices and wages would rise, together with an increase in household income and capital expenditure. The Bank was widely expected to take additional financial easing measures in 2014, reflecting concern that it was not doing enough to achieve its goal in two years.

Sources: "Bank of Japan Sets 2% Inflation Target," *Associated Press*, January 22, 2013; "Japanese Central Bank in Fresh Bid to Spur Inflation," *Associated Press*, April 4, 2013; "BoJ will Continue Easing Until Inflation Reaches 2%," RTT News www.rttnews.com August 28, 2013; "BoJ Beat: Watchers Expect Fresh Easing Next Year," *Wall Street Journal*, September 3, 2013.

discussion and agreement among the FOMC's twelve members, unlike the much more extensive discussions required to get a tax or spending change through Congress. Hence decisions about monetary policy can generally be made more quickly than decisions about fiscal policy. But monetary policy only has an effect on aggregate demand as people change their plans—often their very long-term plans—about investment and spending. So the "outside lag" is generally thought to be longer. There is a danger that the effects of a policy intended to counteract a recession may not be felt until the next boom, or the effects of policies intended to counteract a boom might not be felt until the next recession, exacerbating the business cycle instead of flattening it out.

Lastly, it is not always the case that an economy suffers from *either* recession *or* high inflation. Sometimes, it suffers from both at the same time. Because one problem seems to require expansionary policies while the other calls for contractionary ones, in this case the dilemma facing the Fed is especially acute. We take up this topic in Chapter 28.

6.2 Rules Versus Activism

Given all these caveats about monetary policy, you might think that the Fed would do better just to follow a money supply growth rule as suggested by the quantity theory of money. Indeed, a number of classical macroeconomists make just this argument.

But the quantity theory has its problems. For one thing, the velocity of money is not as constant as the theory assumes. Because financial markets have many linkages, people's desire to hold some of their assets as money, as opposed to another asset, can cause wide swings in velocity. For example, when interest-bearing checking accounts became very popular in the 1980s, M1 grew quickly as people shifted assets from other forms to this new, highly liquid, *and* interest-bearing form. Because V is the ratio of nominal GDP to money balances, the sudden rise in the denominator of this ratio caused the velocity of M1 to fall sharply. Likewise, when the stock market takes a dive, it is common for many people to seek the relative security of money and near-money assets, driving M1 up and velocity down.

Other changes in velocity are harder to explain. Partly this is because people need liquidity not only to facilitate transactions related to GDP—that is, domestic newly produced goods and services—but also to facilitate transactions related to used goods, purchases and sales of assets, and foreign dealings. Financial market innovations, shocks to asset markets, and many other developments in the economy can affect velocity. The more unpredictable velocity is, the harder it is to make policy based on the assumption of a stable relationship between money supply and nominal GDP.

Nor is it true that output is always at its full-employment level, as we saw when looking at unemployment rates in Chapter 23 and at business cycles in Chapter 24. In addition, changes in prices can have causes other than monetary policy, such as when oil prices rise due to shortages or military conflict, and drive up other prices throughout the economy.

As a result, many macroeconomists argue for a more flexible and activist monetary policy stance. Rather than having the Fed locked onto a particular rule, they suggest that the Fed keep an eye on inflation but also remain flexible, so that it can respond to new developments, including financial market changes, price shocks, and threats of recession.

In Chapter 28, we bring together monetary policy, fiscal policy, and the twin goals of output and price stabilization. We also take into account some of the effects that world events, and policy responses to them, have had on the U.S. economy over the past several decades.

Discussion Questions

1. What are some arguments in favor of having the Fed follow a money supply rule? What are some arguments against it?
2. How does the issue of time lags affect fiscal and monetary policy?

REVIEW QUESTIONS

1. Draw up and explain the components of the balance sheet of the Federal Reserve.
2. Show what happens to the Fed's balance sheet and the balance sheet of a bank, when the bank sells bonds to the Fed.
3. Describe how a Fed open market purchase leads to a sequence of loans and deposits and thus a multiplier effect.
4. Describe two tools the Fed can use to affect the money supply, other than open market operations.
5. Describe how a Fed open market purchase changes the federal funds rate.
6. How is investment related to the interest rate? What other factors affect investment? Use a graphical analysis to show these relationships.
7. Show the effects of an expansionary monetary policy in a Keynesian cross diagram.
8. Describe how Fed policy operated during the 2000–2012 period.
9. What is the quantity equation? What is the quantity theory of money?
10. What is monetarism?
11. Discuss how monetary expansion can lead to high inflation, using the quantity equation.
12. What are some of the problems with using a monetary rule?

EXERCISES

1. Suppose that the Fed makes an open market purchase of $200,000 in bonds from QRS Bank.
   a. Show how this affects the Fed balance sheet.
   b. Show how this affects the balance sheet of QRS Bank.
   c. Assume that QRS Bank lends out as much as it can, based on this changed situation. What does its balance sheet look like after it makes the loans?
   d. Assume that all the proceeds from those loans are deposited in TUV Bank. What is the effect on TUV Bank's balance sheet?
   e. Assume that the required reserve ratio is 10 percent. What new opportunity does TUV Bank now face? What is it likely to do?
2. Suppose that the Fed makes an open market *sale* of $15 million in bonds to HIJ Bank.
   a. What is the effect on the Fed's balance sheet?
   b. What is the initial effect on HIJ Bank's balance sheet?
   c. Show in a graph the effect on the market for federal funds. (No numbers are necessary, for this or later sections of this exercise.)
   d. Assuming that the level of business confidence remains unchanged, show on a graph how this open market sale will change the level of intended investment.
   e. What is the effect on aggregate demand and output? Show on a carefully labeled graph.
   f. What is the effect on equilibrium consumption and saving? (You may need to refer back to Chapter 24 to answer this.)
3. Suppose that investor confidence falls, and the Fed is aware of this fact. Using the model presented in this chapter, show (a)–(c) below graphically:
   a. How a fall in investor confidence affects the schedule for intended investment.
   b. What the Fed could do, influencing the federal funds market, to try to counteract this fall in investor confidence.
   c. The effect on *AD* and output if the Fed is able to *perfectly* counteract the fall in business confidence.
   d. Is the Fed likely to be as accurate as assumed in part (c)? Why, or why not?
4. Suppose that the level of nominal GDP in Estilvania is $30 billion and the level of the money supply is $10 billion.
   a. What is the velocity of money in Estilvania?
   b. Suppose that the money supply increases to $15 billion and nominal GDP rises to $45 billion. What has happened to velocity?
   c. Suppose that the money supply increases to $15 billion and nominal GDP rises to $40 billion. What has happened to velocity?
   d. Suppose that the money supply decreases to $8 billion and, as a result, both the price level and real GDP fall, leading to a decrease in nominal GDP to $26 billion. What has happened to velocity?

5. Match each concept in Column A with the best definition or example in Column B.

Column A	Column B
a. Expansionary monetary policy	1. The idea that changes in the money supply affect only prices, not output
b. Fiat money	2. Residential investment
c. Accelerator principle	3. Standardization
d. Monetary neutrality	4. A dollar coin made of minerals worth $.10
e. Velocity	5. The ease with which an asset can be used in trade
f. Liquidity	6. Federal Reserve open market sale of bonds
g. Commodity money	7. A silver coin
h. A good property for money to have	8. A silver certificate
i. A piece of paper representing a claim on something of value	9. Vault cash and bank deposits at the Federal Reserve
j. Bank reserves	10. Currency in circulation, checkable deposits, and travelers checks
k. M1	11. The number of times that a unit of money changes hands in a year
l. Very sensitive to interest rates	12. Relates investment to GDP growth
m. Contractionary monetary policy	13. The Federal Reserve lowers the discount rate

6. The chair of the Federal Reserve semiannually gives testimony before Congress about the state of monetary policy. Find the most recent such testimony at www.federalreserve.gov/newsevents.htm. What does the Fed chair identify as the most significant issues facing the economy? How is the Fed proposing to deal with them?
7. (Appendix A1) Suppose that you have a bond with a face value of $200 and coupon amount of $10 that matures one year from now.
   a. If the going interest rate is 3 percent, how much can you sell it for today?
   b. If the going interest rate is 8 percent, how much can you sell it for today?
   c. What does this illustrate about bond prices and interest rates?
8. (Appendix A2) Suppose that the nominal prime interest rate for a one-year loan is currently 6 percent.
   a. If inflation is 1 percent per year, what is the current real interest rate?
   b. Suppose that many people believe that the inflation rate is going to rise in the future—probably up to 2 percent to 3 percent or more within a few years. You want to borrow a sum of money for ten years and are faced with deciding between
      1) a series of short-term, one-year loans. The interest rate on this year's loan would be 6 percent, while future nominal interest rates are unknown.
      2) A ten-year fixed-rate loan on which you would pay a constant 6.25 percent per year.

      If you agree with most people and expect inflation to rise, which borrowing strategy do you expect might give you the better deal? Why? Explain your reasoning.

APPENDIX

A1. BOND PRICES AND INTEREST RATES

bond: a financial instrument that pays a fixed amount each year (the coupon amount) as well as repaying the amount of principal (the face value) on a particular date (the maturity date).

The process by which monetary policy influences interest rates can be explained by examining the market for federal funds, as was seen in the body of this chapter. Alternatively, it can also be explained by looking at the market for government bonds.

A **bond** represents debt, but, as a particular kind of financial instrument, bonds have some characteristics worth mentioning. When the government (or a business) borrows by selling a bond it makes promises. It promises to pay the bondholder a fixed amount of money each year for a period of time and then, at the end of this time, to repay the principal of the loan. The fixed amount paid per year is called the *coupon amount*. The date that the principal will be repaid is called the *maturity date*. The amount of principal that will be repaid is called the *face value* of the bond.

So far, it seems simple enough—a $100 bond at 5 percent, for example, specifies that its issuer will pay you $5 a year for ten years and then pay you $100 at the end of ten years. What makes bond markets more complicated, though, is that bonds are often sold and resold, changing hands many times before they mature. During the period to maturity, many factors affecting the value of the bond may change, and so the *bond price*—the price at which bondholders are willing to buy and sell existing bonds—may change.

For example, suppose that you bought the bond just described at its face value of $100. The *bond yield to maturity*, or annual rate of return if you hold a bond until it matures, would obviously be 5 percent ($5 annually is 5 percent of the $100 bond price). Suppose that after a couple of years you want to sell your bond (perhaps you need the cash), but meanwhile the rate of return on alternative (and equally safe) investments has risen to 10 percent. People will not be interested in buying your bond at a price of $100, because they would get only a 5 percent return on it, whereas they could get a 10 percent return by investing their $100 elsewhere. To sell your bond you will need to drop the price that you demand until your bond looks as attractive as other investments—that is, until the $5 per year represents a 10 percent yield to maturity.

Conversely, if the return on alternative investments has fallen, say to 2 percent, the $5 per year on your bond looks pretty good, and you will be able to sell it for *more than* $100. Bond prices and bond yields are thus inversely related.*

The U.S. Treasury issues a variety of different kinds of bonds. Treasury bills have a zero coupon amount and mature in one year or less. Because the holder receives no coupons, they are sold at a discount from their face value. Other Treasury bonds pay a coupon amount every six months and have maturities that range from two to thirty years. In the real economy, then, there are many different "government bond" prices—and interest rates. It is only for the sake of simplicity of modeling that we assume only one type of bond and one interest rate.

Although many people and organizations buy and sell government bonds on what is called the "secondary market" (the "primary market" being the Treasury's initial offering of the bonds), the Fed is a major player. Its actions in the market for government bonds are large enough to have discernible effects on the whole market. Expansionary policies tend to raise bond prices and lower bond yields and interest rates; contractionary policies do the opposite.

A simplified (secondary) bond market is shown in Figure 27.9(a). The price of bonds (and the corresponding nominal interest rate) is on the vertical axis and the quantity on the horizontal. The supply curve, in this case, is determined by the willingness of people to sell bonds—that is, to exchange their government debt for cash, which means, in effect, to *stop* lending to the government. The demand curve is determined by people's willingness to buy bonds—that is, to lend to the government. The effect of a Fed open market purchase of bonds is illustrated in Figure 27.9(b). A sizable Fed *purchase* shifts the demand curve for government bonds to the right. As a result, the price of bonds rises. Because bond prices and interest rates are inversely related, the rise in the price of bonds means that the going interest rate on them falls.**

---

*If the bond has one year left to maturity, for example, its value one year from now is $105. We can use the formula [Value next year] / (1 + interest rate) = [Value now] to find out what you could get by selling the bond today. If the interest rate on alternative investments is 10 percent, then $105/(1 + .10) ≈ $95.45. The lower the bond price, the higher the bond yield, and vice versa. Conversely, if the return on alternative investments has fallen, say to 2 percent, the $5 per year on your bond looks pretty good, and you will be able to sell it for *more than* $100. If the interest rate is 2 percent, then $105/(1 + .02) ≈ $102.94.

**The exact relationship depends on the time to maturity of the bond. The longer this time, the greater the impact of an interest rate change on the bond price.

Figure 27.9 **The Market for Government Bonds**

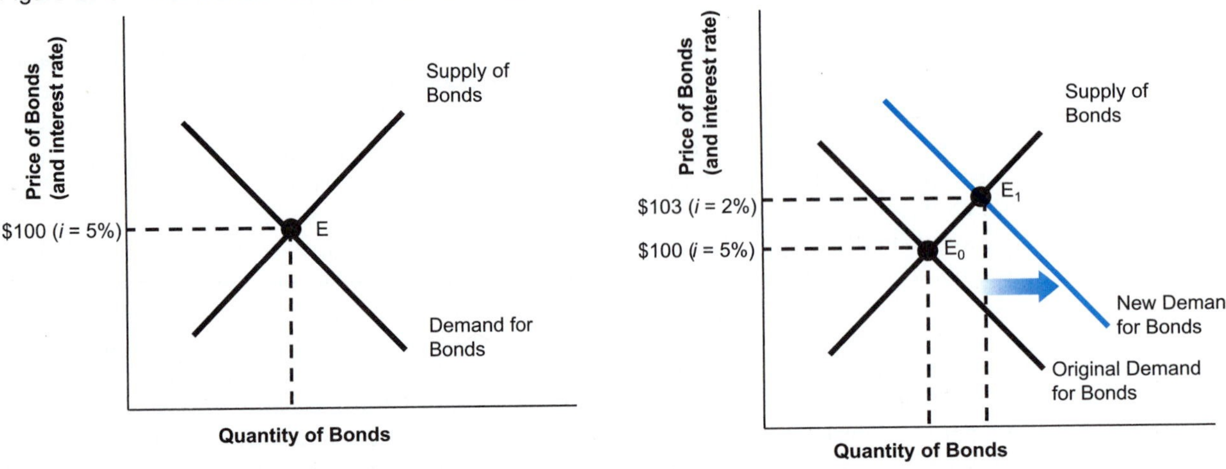

When the Federal Reserve undertakes an open market purchase, it shifts out the demand curve for government bonds. This raises the price of bonds, lowering their interest rate.

Figure 27.10 **The Federal Funds and Three-Month Treasury Bill Rates, 2000–2012**

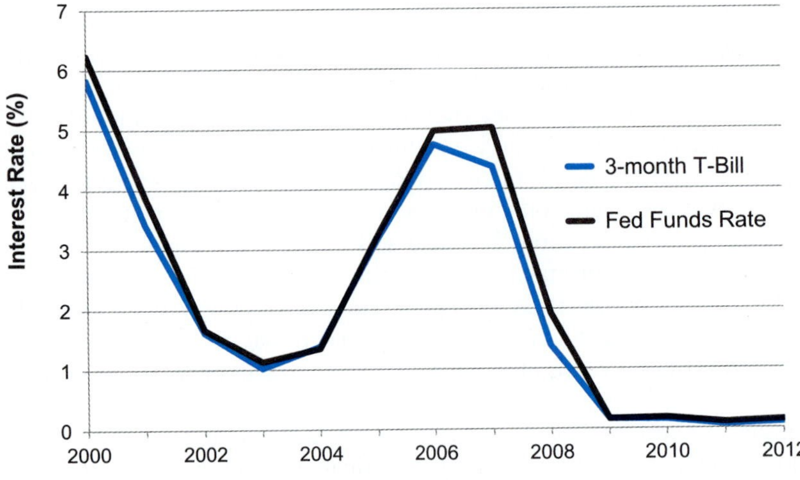

The market for federal funds and the market for short-term Treasury bills are closely related.

Source: Federal Reserve Board, monthly data.

Although this explanation focuses on the market for government bonds, it is actually parallel to the earlier discussion of the Fed and the market for federal funds. The interest rate for three-month Treasury bills and the federal funds rate are graphed together in Figure 27.10 and they track each other closely. The bottom line of this story is the same as that given by the model of federal funds used in this chapter: A Fed open market purchase drives down interest rates.

A2. Short Versus Long-Run and Real Versus Nominal Interest Rates

In the model of interest rates and aggregate demand discussed in Section 3 of the text, we assumed that the Fed, through open market operations, could change the interest rate that influences investment spending. In Figure 27.8 we used the symbol *r* to denote a generalized interest rate. In real life, however, many different interest rates have to be taken into account.

Here we present some basic facts about short-run vs. long-run and real vs. nominal interest rates. We also note the difference between the Fed's focus on the short-term, nominal interest rate and the interest rate that investors often consider the most relevant: that is, the long-term, real interest rate.

In Section 4.1 we discussed the federal funds rate as the principal interest rate targeted by the Fed. This is a short-term, nominal interest rate. It is short term, because while this rate is quoted in annualized terms (that is, what borrowers would pay if they kept the loan for a year), the loans are actually made on one day and paid back the next. The Fed uses a portfolio of government securities with various maturity dates in its open market operations, but many of them have maturity dates of three years or less. The federal funds rate—like any interest rate that you normally see quoted—is a *nominal* interest rate, not adjusted for inflation. The interest rates determined in markets for loanable funds are always nominal rates.

But if you are considering undertaking a substantial business investment project or buying a house, the interest rate that you should be taking into account, if you are a rational decision maker, is the *real* interest rate over the life of the business loan or mortgage. The **real interest rate** is:

real interest rate: nominal interest rate minus inflation, $r = i - \pi$

$$r = i - \pi$$

where r is the real interest rate, i is the nominal interest rate, and π is the rate of inflation.

For example, suppose that you borrow $100 for one year at a nominal rate of 6 percent. You will pay back $106 at the end of the year. If the inflation rate is 0, then the purchasing power of the amount that you pay back at the end of the year is actually $6 more than the amount you borrowed. However, if inflation is 4 percent during the year, the $106 that you pay back is in "cheaper" dollars (dollars that can buy less) than the dollars that you borrowed. The real interest rate on your borrowing will be only 2 percent. The higher the inflation rate, the better the deal is for a borrower at any given nominal rate (and the worse it is for the lender).

If inflation is fairly low and steady—as we assumed in the aggregate demand model—then this difference between real and nominal interest rates is not of crucial importance. If inflation is steady at, say, 2 percent, then both lenders and borrowers mentally subtract 2 percent to calculate the real rate that corresponds to any nominal rate. If the Fed lowers the prime rate from 8 percent to 5 percent, for example, then it correspondingly lowers the real rate from 6 percent to 3 percent.

In recent decades, inflation has been fairly low, usually between 1 and 3 percent. But inflation is not always so predictable. When inflation is high or variable, it is very important to realize that investors' decisions are in reality influenced by the **expected real interest rate**, r_e:

expected real interest rate: the nominal interest rate minus expected inflation, $r_e = i - \pi_e$

$$r_e = i - \pi_e$$

where i is the nominal rate the borrower agrees to pay and π^e is the *expected* inflation rate.

The actual real interest rate (r) can be known only with hindsight. That is, only *after* information on inflation has come for last month or last year, can you calculate what the real interest rate *was* in that period. But you never know with certainty what the real interest rate is right now or what it will be next year. The more changeable inflation is, the harder it is to form reliable expectations about real interest rates.

Since investors are usually interested in long-run, real interest rates, while the Fed controls primarily short-run, nominal interest rates, the impacts of various Fed policies on the economy may not be as straightforward as our basic models imply.

28 Aggregate Supply, Aggregate Demand, and Inflation: Putting It All Together

If you read the financial pages in any newspaper (or sometimes the front pages if economic issues are pressing), you will see discussion about government budgets and deficits, interest rate changes, and how these affect unemployment and inflation. You may also see news about changes in the availability of certain crucial resources—particularly energy resources—and about how the impact of such changes in resource supplies spread throughout the country's economy. How does economic theory help to make sense of it all?

In Chapter 24, we started to build a model of business cycles, focusing at first on the downturn side of the cycle and the problem of unemployment. In Chapters 25, 26, and 27, we explained economic theories concerning fiscal and monetary policy. So far, our models have focused on the "demand side," illustrated by shifts of the aggregate demand (*AD*) curve. In this chapter, we complete the demand-side story so that it includes explicit attention to the potential problem of inflation. Then we move on to the issue of the actual productive capacity of the economy, or "supply-side" issues. Finally, we will arrive at a model that we can use to "put it all together."

1. Aggregate Demand and Inflation

The *AD* curve in the Keynesian model used in the previous three chapters was graphed with income on the horizontal axis and output on the vertical axis. We mentioned that if output is above its full-employment level, there may be a threat of rising inflation, but nothing in the figures incorporated this idea. The graphs that we used all measured income, output, and aggregate demand without considering changes in price levels. It is time now to remedy that omission.

1.1 A New View of the Aggregate Demand (*AD*) Curve

We can develop a different approach to aggregate demand by viewing it in a graphical format that compares output to inflation. In this approach, the *AD* curve shows the effect of inflation on the macroeconomic equilibrium level. To show this graphically, we put inflation on the vertical axis, and output (Y) on the horizontal axis.* This is shown in Figure 28.1. The *AD* curve shown here differs from the Keynesian *AD* curve, since it takes into account price changes, but the points on this new curve all correspond to points where the Keynesian *AD* curve crosses the 45° line.

This view of aggregate demand assumes that higher inflation rates will tend to reduce total demand, for several reasons:

*Some versions of the *AD* curve use "price level" rather than inflation on the vertical axis. The authors of this text believe that using inflation better represents the reality of an economic system in which prices are rarely constant.

Figure 28.1 **The Aggregate Demand curve**

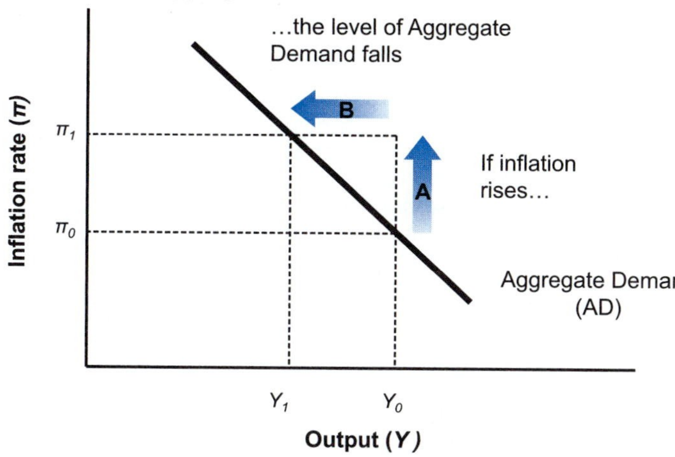

This analysis shows the impact of different inflation levels on Aggregate Demand.

real wealth effect: the tendency of consumers to increase or decrease their consumption based on their perceived level of wealth

real money supply: the nominal money supply divided by the general price level (as measured by a price index), expressed as *M/P*

- When inflation rises, it reduces the value of money assets. Even if this does not reach the level of hyperinflation discussed in Chapter 26, it hurts savers and people who have money balances. This **real wealth effect** tends to reduce their consumption, lowering total demand.
- Inflation also lowers the **real money supply**, defined as *M/P,* where *M* is the nominal money supply and *P* is the general price level. This has an effect similar to contractionary monetary policy, raising interest rates and discouraging investment.
- Inflation hurts net exports by making domestically produced goods more expensive for foreigners and imports more attractive for domestic consumers. This decreases aggregate demand by decreasing net exports.*
- The Federal Reserve generally responds to higher inflation by raising interest rates, as discussed in Chapter 27. This also tends to lower investment and total demand.

1.2 SHIFTS OF THE *AD* CURVE: SPENDING AND TAXATION

The downward slope of the *AD* curve shown in Figure 28.1 is based on the impacts of inflation on aggregate demand. What determines the position of the curve? As discussed in our original Keynesian *AD* analysis, the position of the *AD* depends on specific levels of government spending, taxation, autonomous consumption, autonomous investment, and net exports.** Changes in these variables will cause the curve to shift.

For example, if the government were to undertake expansionary fiscal policy, this would shift the *AD* curve to the right, as illustrated in Figure 28.2. At any level of inflation, there would now be aggregate demand sufficient to support a higher level of output. Alternatively, if output remained constant, there would be higher levels of inflation.

An increase in autonomous consumption or investment would have a similar effect, as would an increase in net exports. Recall that autonomous consumption is the part of household spending that does not depend on income, and autonomous investment is the part of business spending that does not depend on the interest rate. These are often used to represent consumer and business "confidence." Thus an increase in consumer or investor confidence could also cause the rightward shift in Figure 28.2. Conversely, of course, contractionary fiscal policy, reductions in consumer or investment confidence, or reduction in net exports would shift the *AD* curve to the left.

---

*As defined in Chapter 20, and discussed further in Chapter 29, net exports are exports minus imports, and represent a net addition to aggregate demand and GDP levels.

**The specific role of net exports will be discussed further in Chapter 29.

Figure 28.2 **The Effect of Expansionary Fiscal Policy or Increased Confidence on the AD curve**

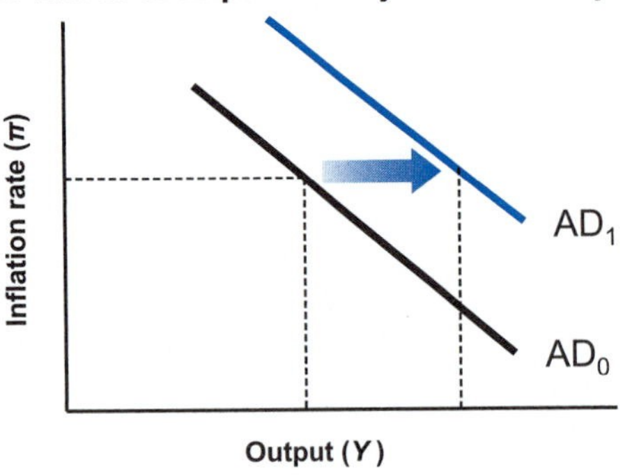

1.3 SHIFTS OF THE *AD* CURVE: MONETARY POLICY

As we have noted, the Federal Reserve usually responds to higher inflation by increasing interest rates, and this is reflected in the slope of the *AD* curve. This kind of policy response, which aims to keep inflation near a target level, is a rather passive sort of monetary policy. A more active form of Fed intervention occurs when the Fed's leaders decide to change policy more fundamentally—either by changing their inflation target or by shifting their focus to fighting unemployment.

For example, in a severe recession the Fed might decide that the economy requires additional stimulus. If the Fed instituted significant expansionary monetary policies, driving interest rates down (as it did, for example, starting in 2007), this would, in theory, have the effect of boosting investment and shifting the *AD* curve to the right. Alternatively, if the Fed decided that its policies on inflation have been too lax, it could tighten monetary policy sharply (this happened, for example, in 1982 in response to severe continuing inflation). This would have the effect of shifting the *AD* curve to the left.

To summarize:

- The *AD* curve indicates levels of equilibrium GDP at different possible rates of inflation.
- The *AD* curve can be shifted by changes in levels of autonomous consumer spending, autonomous investment, fiscal policy, net exports, or by major changes in monetary policy.

Discussion Questions

1. "The negative slope of the *AD* curve means that higher levels of output will lead to lower levels of inflation." Is this statement correct or not? Discuss.
2. Does the Fed always want the inflation rate to be as low as possible? Why or why not?

2. CAPACITY AND THE AGGREGATE SUPPLY CURVE

As we have noted in earlier chapters, increases in *AD* can push output up toward the full-employment level. But what happens when output reaches—or maybe even exceeds—the full-employment level? In a graph such as Figure 28.2, for example, there is nothing in the model that seems to prevent expansionary policies from just shifting the *AD* curve, and output, up and up and up.

Obviously, this cannot be true in the real world. At any given time, there are only certain quantities of labor, capital, energy, and other material resources available for use. The U.S. labor force, for example, comprises just over 150 million people. The United States simply cannot, then, produce an output level that would require the work of 200 million people. This is a *hard capacity constraint:* What happens as an economy approaches maximum capacity can be modeled using the aggregate supply (*AS*) curve. The *AS* curve shows combinations of output and inflation that can, in fact, occur within an economy, given the reality of capacity constraints.

2.1 THE AGGREGATE SUPPLY (AS) CURVE

maximum capacity output: the level of output an economy would produce if every resource in the economy were fully utilized

wage-price spiral: when high demand for labor and other resources creates upward pressure on wages, which in turn leads to upward pressure on prices and, as a result, further upward pressure on wages

wage and price controls: government regulations setting limits on wages and prices or on the rates at which they are permitted to increase

Figure 28.3 shows how aggregate supply is related to the rate of inflation. Starting from the right, at high output levels, we can identify four important, distinct regions of the diagram.

First, the vertical **maximum capacity output** line indicates the hard limit on a macroeconomy's output. Even if every last resource in the economy were put into use, with everybody working flat out to produce the most they could, the economy could not produce to the right of the maximum capacity line.

Just below the maximum capacity level of output, the *AS* curve has a very steep, positive slope. This indicates that, as an economy closely approaches its maximum capacity, it is likely to experience a substantial increase in inflation. If many employers are all trying to hire many workers and buy a lot of machinery, energy, and materials all at once, workers' wages and resource prices will tend to be bid upward. But then, to cover their labor and other costs, producers will need to raise the prices that they charge for their own goods. Then, in turn, if workers find that the purchasing power of their wages is being eroded by rising inflation, they will demand higher wages . . . which leads to higher prices, and so on. The result is a phenomenon called a **wage-price spiral**, in which pressure to produce very high levels of output leads to a steep rise in self-reinforcing inflation.

In the real world, such steep increases in inflation are usually the result of dramatic pressures on producers, such as often occur during a national mobilization for war. During World War II, for example, the U.S. government pushed the economy very close to its maximum capacity—placing big orders for munitions and other supplies for the front, mobilizing the necessary resources by encouraging women to enter the paid labor force, encouraging the recycling of materials on an unprecedented scale, encouraging the planting of backyard gardens to increase food production, and in general pushing people's productive efforts far beyond their usual peacetime levels. As a result, unemployment plummeted. The government, knowing that such pressures could lead to sharply rising inflation (as shown in the wage-price spiral region of Figure 28.3), kept inflation from getting out of hand by instituting **wage and price controls**—direct regulations telling firms what they could and could not do in the way of price or wage increases.

The shaded area to the left of the wage-price spiral region in Figure 28.3 indicates, as it did in the national income equilibrium graphs in Chapters 24 and 25, a range of full-employment levels of output. While it is controversial to say exactly where that level may be, it can be thought of as an output level high enough that unemployment is not considered a national problem. And because it must be low enough to allow for at least a small measurable level of transitory unemployment, the *full-employment* level of output is slightly lower than the *maximum capacity* level of output.

Figure 28.3 **The Aggregate Supply curve**

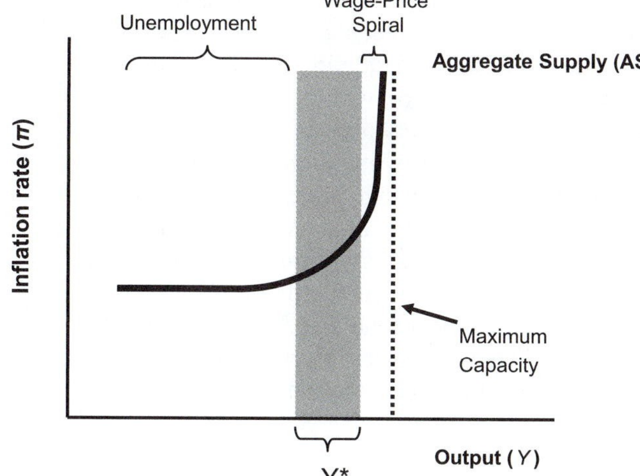

As the economy approaches its maximum capacity, inflation levels tend to rise as excessive demand for workers, goods and services, and production inputs pushes up wages and prices.

Within the full-employment range, Figure 28.3 shows a gently rising *AS* relationship. This is because, even well before an economy approaches the absolute maximum capacity given *all* its resources, producers may tend to run into "bottlenecks" in the supply of *some* resources. Agricultural workers may be plentiful, for example, but professional and technical workers may be in short supply. Or fuel oil may be plentiful, but there may be a shortage of natural gas. Shortages in the markets for particular kinds of labor and other inputs may lead to an acceleration of inflation in some sectors of the economy. Because the measured inflation rate represents an average for the economy as a whole, some aggregate increase in inflation may be observed.

This sort of increase in inflation that comes with high (but not extremely high) production is what economists expect to happen when the economy nears a business cycle "peak." Note, however, that the *AS* curve has been drawn as nearly flat in part of the Y^* range, indicating that combinations of full employment and stable inflation may also be possible.

When the economy is in recession or recovering slowly from a recession, output is below its full-employment level. The flat *AS* line shown in Figure 28.3 for this region indicates that, under these conditions, there is assumed to be no tendency for inflation to rise. Because a considerable amount of labor and other resources are unemployed, there is no pressure for higher wages or prices. It is also likely that because wages and prices tend to be slow in adjusting downward, inflation will not fall either—at least not right away.

2.2 SHIFTS OF THE *AS* CURVE: INFLATIONARY EXPECTATIONS

When people have experienced inflation, they come to expect it. They then tend to build the level of inflation that they expect into the various contracts into which they enter. If a business expects 5 percent inflation over the coming year, for example, it will add 5 percent to the selling price that it quotes for a product to be delivered a year into the future, just to stay even. If workers also expect 5 percent inflation, they will try to get a 5 percent cost of living allowance (COLA), just to stay even. A depositor who expects 5 percent inflation and wants a 4 percent real rate of return will be satisfied only with a 9 percent nominal rate of return.

In this way, an expected rate of inflation can start to become institutionally "built in" to an economy. As a first approximation, it is reasonable to assume that people expect something like the level of inflation that they have recently experienced (an assumption that economists call "adaptive expectations"). Thus inflation can be, to some degree, self-fulfilling.

Because different contracts come up for renegotiation at different times of the year, the process of building in particular inflationary expectations will take place only over time. Because of the time that it takes for prices and wages to adjust, we need to make a distinction between short-run and medium-run aggregate supply responses.

The *AS* curve in Figure 28.3 was drawn for a particular level of expected inflation in the *short run.* Before people have caught on to the fact that the inflation rate might be changing, their expectations of inflation will continue to reflect their recent experience. The rate of inflation at which the *AS* curve becomes horizontal is the expected inflation rate. In this model, an economy in recession, or on the horizontal part of the *AS* curve, will tend in the short run to roll along at pretty much the same inflation rate as it has experienced in the past. Only tight labor and resource markets caused by a boom will tend to increase inflation, which will come as a surprise to people and will not immediately translate into a change in expectations. For the purposes of this model, you might think of the short run as a period of some weeks or months.

Over an unspecified longer period of time—the *medium run*—however, a rise in inflation due to tight markets tends to increase people's expectation of inflation.* If they expect 3 percent inflation but experience 5 percent inflation, the next time that they renegotiate contracts they may build in a 5 percent rate. Figure 28.4 shows how the *AS* curve shifts upward as people's expectation of inflation rises. Note that the maximum capacity of the economy has not changed—

*As distinguished from the *long run,* discussed in the Appendix.

Figure 28.4 **The Effect of an Increase in Inflationary Expectations on the Aggregate Supply curve**

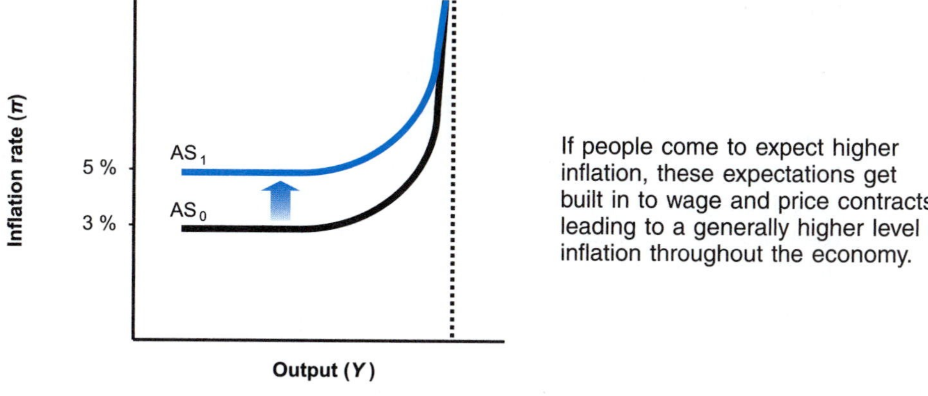

nothing has happened that would affect the physical capacity of the economy to produce. All that has happened is that now, at any output level, people's expectation of inflation is higher.

Similarly, if people experience very loose markets for their labor or products, over the medium run the expected inflation rate may start to come down. Employers may find that they can still get workers if they offer lower COLAs in the new contracts or even force workers to take pay cuts. Producers may raise their prices less this year than last year or cut prices, because they are having trouble selling in a slow market. When people start to observe wage and price inflation tapering off in some sectors of the economy, they may change their expectations about inflation. As people react to the sluggish aggregate demand that occurs during a recession, they will tend, over time, to lessen their expectations about wage and price increases. The graph for this would be similar to Figure 28.4, but would show the *AS* curve shifting downward instead of upward.

2.3 SHIFTS OF THE *AS* CURVE: SUPPLY SHOCKS

supply shock: a change in the productive capacity of an economy

The *AS* curve also shifts when the capacity of the economy changes. A **supply shock** is something that changes the ability of an economy to produce goods and services. Supply shocks can be beneficial, as when there is a bumper crop in agriculture or a new invention allows more goods or services to be made using a smaller quantity of resources. Increases in labor productivity also allow an economy to produce more goods and services.

In such cases, the real capacity of the economy expands, as shown in Figure 28.5. The line indicating maximum capacity shifts to the right, showing that the economy can produce more than before. We model the beneficial supply shock as moving the *AS* curve both to the right and downward. It moves to the right because capacity has increased. It moves downward because beneficial supply shocks are often accompanied by decreases in prices. As computer

Figure 28.5 **A Beneficial Supply Shock: Expansion of Output Capacity**

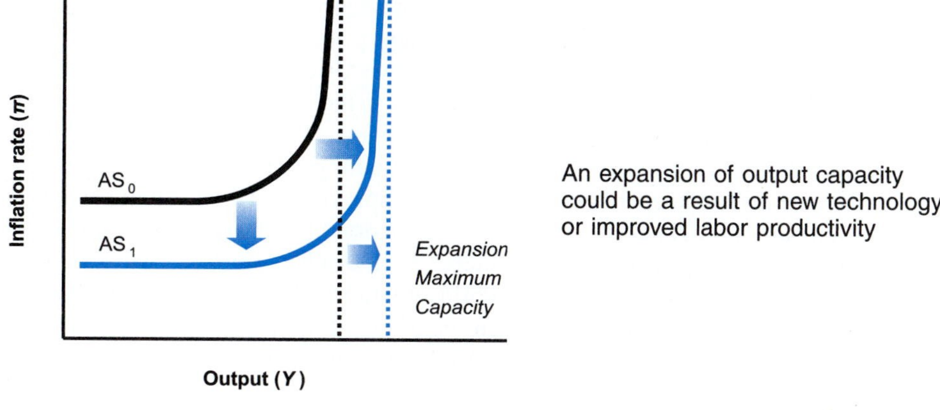

technology has improved, for example, the price of any given amount of computing power has dropped rapidly. To the extent that computers play a significant role in the economy, this tends to undermine inflation.

Supply shocks can also be adverse. In fact, economists were first forced to start theorizing about supply shocks when the oil embargo during the 1970s resulted in steeply rising oil prices. Natural occurrences, such as hurricanes or droughts, and human-caused situations, such as wars, that destroy capital goods and lives are other examples of adverse supply shocks. They reduce the economy's capacity to produce and, by concentrating demand on the limited supplies of resources that remain, tend to lead to higher inflation. Adverse supply shocks would be illustrated in a graph such as Figure 28.5, but with the direction of all the movements reversed.

Discussion Questions

1. Describe in words how the *AS* curve differs from the *AD* curve. What does each represent? What explains their slopes?
2. Do you get "cost of living" raises at your job or know people who do? Why does this practice have important macroeconomic consequences?

3. PUTTING THE AS/AD MODEL TO WORK

Economists invented the *AS/AD* model to illustrate three points about the macroeconomy:

1. Fiscal and monetary policies affect output and inflation:
   - *Expansionary fiscal and monetary policies* tend to push the economy toward higher output. If the economy is approaching its maximum capacity, they will also cause inflation to rise.
   - *Contractionary fiscal and monetary policies* tend to push the economy toward lower output. Inflation is unlikely to fall quickly, but a persistent recession will tend to lower inflation over the long term.
2. *Supply shocks* may also have significant effects:
   - Adverse supply shocks lower output and raise inflation.
   - Beneficial supply shocks raise output and lower inflation.
3. *Investor and consumer confidence and expectations* also have important effects on output and inflation.

Bearing these principles in mind, we will see how this model helps to explain some major macroeconomic events.

3.1 AN ECONOMY IN RECESSION

In Figure 28.6, we bring together the *AS* and *AD* curves for the first time. The (short-run) equilibrium of the economy is shown as point E_0, at the intersection of the two curves. Depending on how we place the curves in the figure, we could illustrate an economy that is in a recession, at full employment, or in a wage-price spiral. (We temporarily omit the maximum capacity line, but we reintroduce it when we discuss inflation.)

In this specific case, the fact that E_0 is to the left of the full-employment range of output indicates that the economy is in a recession. Private spending, as determined in part by investor and consumer confidence, along with government and foreign sector spending, are not enough to keep the economy at full employment. The fact that the curves intersect on the flat part of the *AS* curve indicates that inflation (in the short run) is stable. So in this situation unemployment is the major problem. What can be done?

Figure 28.6 models the real-world situation of the U.S. economy in the 2007–9 recession. Unemployment rose to 10 percent in 2009, but inflation was very low. In this situation, the administration of President Barack Obama called for a major fiscal stimulus program, which

Figure 28.6 **Aggregate Demand and Supply Equilibrium in Recession**

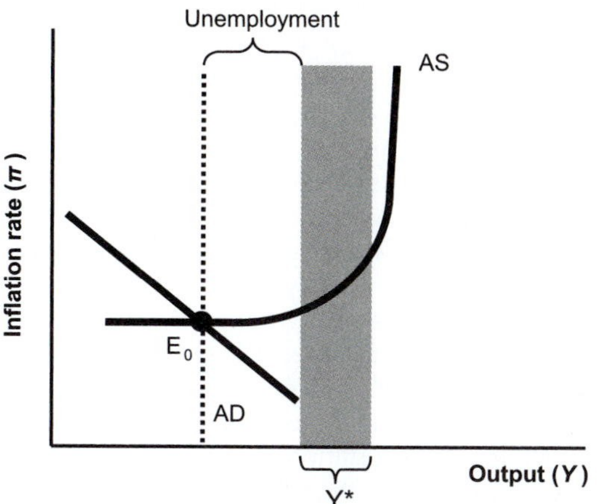

The position of the AD curve indicates a low level of aggregate demand, leading to an economy with unemployment at equilibrium E_0. At this point on the AS curve, inflationary pressures are low.

Figure 28.7 **Expansionary Fiscal Policy in Response to a Recession**

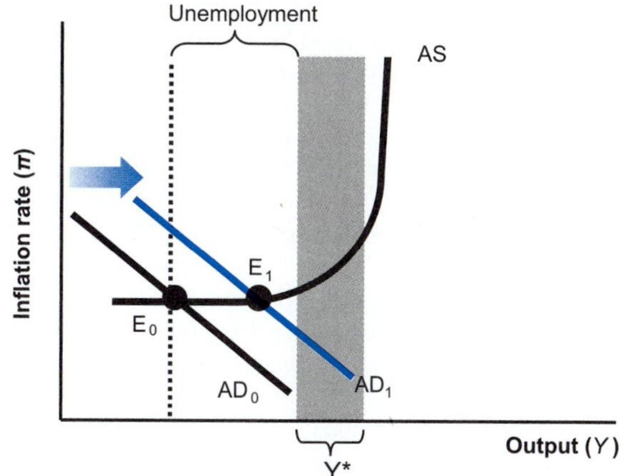

An expansion of government spending, as well as a program of tax cuts, shifts the AD curve to the right. This reduces unemployment, but since the economy is in the flat portion of the AS curve at equilibrium E_1, it has little effect on inflation.

was approved by Congress in early 2009. The goal of the stimulus program, which included $800 billion in increased government spending and tax cuts, was to promote employment both through its direct impact and multiplier effects expanding private spending and employment. This effect is shown in Figure 28.7 as a rightward shift of the *AD* curve.

As noted in Chapter 25 (Box 25.1), the stimulus plan was responsible for adding millions of jobs to the economy. While economists are not in agreement about how large the multiplier effects of the program were, many argue that without the program, the economy would have continued to plunge deeper into recession.[1] The effects, however, were not large enough to bring the economy back to full employment. This is reflected in Figure 28.7 as an *AD* shift that moves output toward, but not into, the full-employment zone.

How about the effect of this expansionary program on inflation? As the *AS/AD* model would lead us to expect, inflation did not rise because the economy did not move beyond the flat portion of the *AS* curve. Some economists and political commentators warned that such a high level of government spending and deficits would certainly cause serious inflation—but as of late 2013, four years after the initiation of the stimulus program, inflation remained low (See Box 28.1).

Given continued unemployment and low inflation, would more macroeconomic stimulus make sense? Some economists argued that it would, but proposals for further fiscal stimulus were not acted on by Congress, largely out of fear that deficits were already too high (for more on this debate, see Chapter 31). So the Federal Reserve stepped in with the further monetary stimulus known as "quantitative easing" (as discussed in Chapter 27). The hope was that a combination of this monetary expansion plus recovering confidence on the part of consumers and businesses could lead to a more complete recovery.

This goal (not yet reached as of late 2013) is shown in Figure 28.8. Here we see that a larger *AD* shift brings the economy back into the full-employment zone. At this point, the model predicts that there could be at least a slight increase in inflation. Detection of such rising inflation would signal the Fed to cut back on its monetary expansion. Provided any inflation effect remained small, the overall effort could be judged a success.

As we see later in this chapter, not all economists agree with this analysis. Some classical economists argue that inflation has merely been delayed but will eventually cause major problems and perhaps force a return to recession. We will look into the theoretical issues involved later (without providing any definite judgment on the debate).

BOX 28.1 WHAT HAPPENED TO INFLATION?

As of mid-2013, inflation in the United States remained sluggish. Prices rose at the slowest pace in at least half a century, up just 1.1 percent over the previous year as of May 2013, according to the Bureau of Economic Analysis. "Inflation has been quiet, and perhaps more important from a central bank perspective, inflationary expectations remain subdued" (Norris, 2013).

> Slow inflation may sound like a good thing, but it's not . . . Economic research suggests that inflation is best in moderation. Price increases lead to wage increases, which make it easier to repay existing debts, like mortgages, and more attractive to incur new debts, like borrowing to start a company. Inflation also functions as a kind of economic WD-40, easing shifts in the allocation of resources. It is easier for struggling companies and industries to adjust by withholding cost-of-living increases than by seeking to impose wage cuts. Perhaps most importantly, moderate inflation keeps the economy at a safe distance from deflation, or general price declines, which can freeze activity as would-be buyers wait for lower prices. (Appelbaum, 2013)

According to Federal Reserve Chairman Ben Bernanke, "We are certainly determined to keep inflation near its objective, not only avoiding inflation that's too high, but we also want to avoid inflation that's too low." According to economist Paul Krugman, the current low inflation results from persistent weakness in the economy, and the need is not for anti-inflationary policy, but for more economic stimulus to fight unemployment. Predictions that stimulus policies by the federal government and the Federal Reserve would lead to runaway inflation have been proved wrong by the course of events (Norris, 2013). While some continue to warn of future inflation, Krugman argues that the reality of continuing unemployment imposes immediate, and lasting, costs on the economy, and therefore represents the more urgent problem to address.

Sources: Binyamin Appelbaum, "Yes, We Have No Inflation," *New York Times*, June 27, 2013; Floyd Norris, "Predictions on Fed Strategy that Did Not Come to Pass," *New York Times*, June 29, 2013; Paul Krugman, "Not Enough Inflation," *New York Times*, May 2, 2013.

Figure 28.8 **A Greater Expansion of Aggregate Demand**

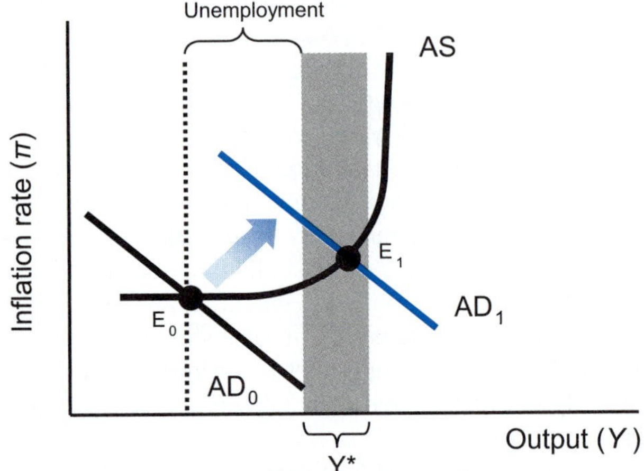

If Aggregate Demand increases by a larger amount, it can bring the economy back into the full employment zone. At equilibrium point E_1 the AS/AD model indicates the possibility of a slightly higher inflation level.

We do know, however, that there have been other times in recent economic history when inflation has been a major problem. What does the *AS/AD* model indicate about policy in such periods? We explore this topic next.

3.2 AN OVERHEATED ECONOMY

Problems with inflation were a major issue in the United States starting in the late 1960s. High government spending, in particular spending on the Vietnam war, meant that fiscal policy was excessively expansionary. Monetary policy during this period tended to accommodate the fiscal expansion. Although unemployment was very low as a result, the economy started to "overheat," causing inflation to rise.

Figure 28.9 **Excessively High Aggregate Demand Causes Inflation**

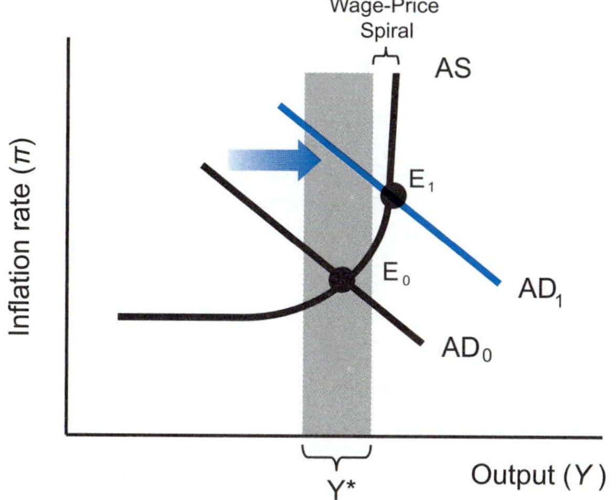

Expansionary policy causes the economy to "heat up." In the short run, people respond by increasing output, but tight markets for labor and other resources cause inflation to rise as well at equilibrium point *E1*.

Figure 28.10 **The Phillips Curve in the 1960s**

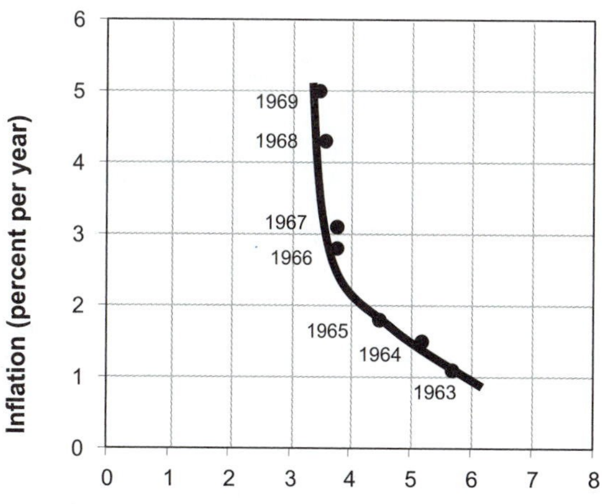

In the 1960s economist A.W. Phillips identified an inverse relationship between inflation and unemployment. While this basic relationship still holds true, events of the 1970s and later showed that inflation can be much more variable than the simple Phillips principle implies.

This period of history is modeled in Figure 28.9. The *AD* curve moves further to the right due to the increases in government spending. It shifts from AD_0, which at E_0 corresponds to a full-employment equilibrium, to AD_1, which crosses the *AS* curve in the wage-price spiral range. The economy became overheated, moving beyond full employment to E_1.

The tradeoff between unemployment and inflation in the 1960s established a pattern that became known as the Phillips curve, after the economist who first identified it. The 1960s Phillips curve is shown in Figure 28.10. As you can see, the shape of the upward-sloping portion of the *AS* curve is essentially a mirror image of the Phillips curve. This is no coincidence. The models that economists developed during the 1960s grew out of observing such a pattern of unemployment and inflation rates and trying to explain why it occurred. The Phillips curve relationship seemed to suggest that policymakers could continue to "trade off" inflation and unemployment—that they could, by use of appropriate fiscal and monetary policies, choose to settle the economy at any point along the curve. Policymakers could push up inflation to keep unemployment low or perhaps sacrifice some employment to push down inflation—or so it was thought at the time.

3.3 Stagflation

stagflation: a combination of rising inflation and economic stagnation

The developments of the early 1970s came as a shock to Phillips-curve–minded economists and policymakers. From 1969 to 1970, unemployment and inflation *both* rose, and both stayed fairly high through the 1970–73 period. This combination of economic stagnation (recession) and high inflation came to be known as **stagflation**.

What happened? In 1968, worried about rising inflation, President Lyndon Johnson persuaded Congress to enact an income tax surcharge. In our model, we show this contractionary fiscal policy as a leftward shift of the *AD* curve in Figure 28.11.

This policy move is widely considered to have been "too little, too late" to curb consumer and investor spending. By the time the economy started to cool off, inflationary expectations had become firmly implanted. Having recently experienced a wage-price spiral, people had built expectations of higher inflation into their wage and price contracts. As Karl Otto Pohl, former president of the Bundesbank, the German central bank, once commented, inflation

Figure 28.11 **Rising Inflationary Expectations and Contractionary Fiscal Policy**

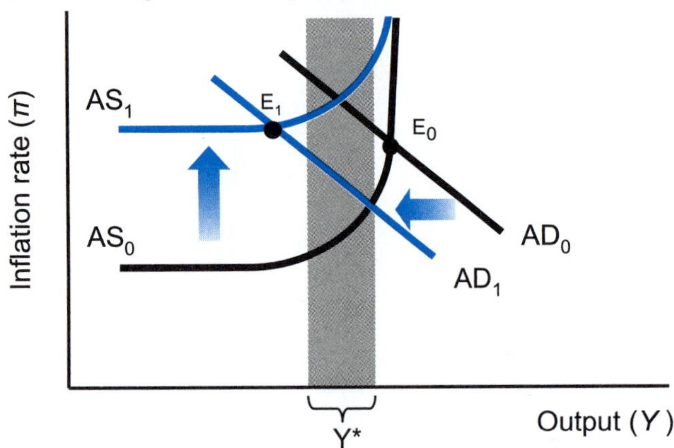

Once inflationary expectations increase, they become difficult to reverse. Contractionary fiscal policy raises unemployment at equilibrium point *E1*, but lowers inflation only slightly.

is like toothpaste—once you squeeze it out of the tube, you cannot get it back in. Although the fiscal cutbacks contributed to falling GDP and rising unemployment, they did not bring down inflation due to this institutional "ratcheting up" of inflationary expectations.

The increase in inflationary expectations is represented by an upward shift of the *AS* curve. In Figure 28.11, the combination of the contractionary fiscal policy and the rise in inflationary expectations is shown as moving the economy from an overheated boom point of E_0 to a recessionary, high inflation point of E_1. This is exactly what happened to the U.S. economy in the early 1970s.

The situation became worse later in the decade. In 1973–74, the member countries of the Organization of Petroleum Exporting Countries (OPEC) cut production, greatly increased the price at which they sold their oil, and even temporarily stopped shipping oil to certain countries. The price of oil, a key input into many production processes, suddenly quadrupled. What effect did this have on the macroeconomy?

The impact of the oil price shock is shown in Figure 28.12. The economy starts off in a recession at point E_0, which is substantially to the left of the initial maximum capacity line. The cut in foreign oil production meant that the United States (and many other oil-importing countries) now suffered from a reduced capacity to produce goods, which is shown in Figure 28.12 by the maximum capacity line and *AS* curves shifting to the left. Even if labor resources were fully employed, an economy with reduced access to other inputs would not be able to produce as much. At the same time, the rise in oil prices had an immediate and direct effect on inflation, shifting the *AS* curve up as well, as also shown in Figure 28.12. Both inflation and unemployment got worse.

Figure 28.12 **The Effect of the Oil Price Shock of the 1970s**

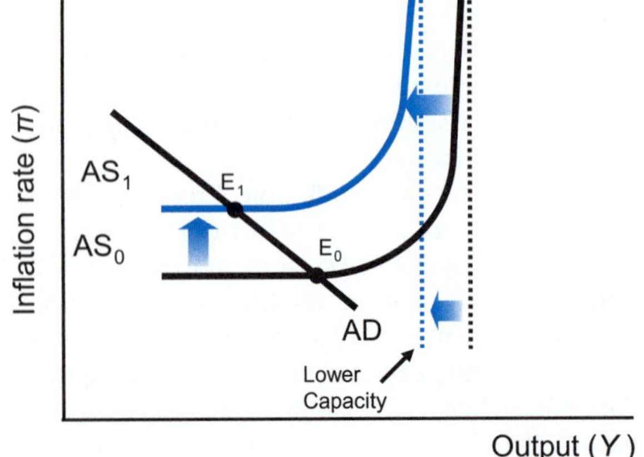

A drastic increase in the price of a key resource reduces the economy's total capacity and shifts the *AS* curve up and to the left. Both inflation and unemployment get worse at equilibrium point E_1.

3.4 A Hard Line Against Inflation

This was still not the end of the inflationary story of the 1970s. Although oil prices held steady and inflation moderated during the period 1975–78, oil prices jumped again in 1979 and 1980. In 1979, the price of oil was *ten* times higher than it had been in 1973. The overall inflation rate in the United States was more than 9 percent in 1979—and exceeded 10 percent (measured at an annual rate) during some months.

The high rates of inflation experienced in the late 1970s were very damaging to the economy. As we noted in Chapter 26, high rates of inflation can wipe out the value of people's savings and make it very difficult for households and business to plan, save, and invest. Because unemployment was also high, as shown in Figure 28.12, it was difficult to see how consumers and businesses could ever recover confidence while inflation seemed out of control.

Even though the economy was already in a recession, and the unemployment rate was above 7 percent, the Federal Reserve, under the chairmanship of Paul Volcker, took deliberate and drastic action to bring the long-term inflation rate down, by implementing very contractionary monetary policies. The effects of these "tight money" policies during the early 1980s can be seen in Figure 28.13.

As discussed earlier, contractionary monetary policy shifts the *AD* curve to the left. The *AS/AD* model predicts that the immediate effect of this policy will be to send the economy even deeper into a recession, with output falling even farther below its full-employment level, as shown by equilibrium point E_1. But there is a further effect, on inflationary expectations.

This contractionary policy was accompanied by many stories in the media about how Volcker was really committed to bringing down inflation, no matter the cost. Because people found this commitment credible, their expectations of inflation also came down. The effect of this decrease in inflationary expectations is shown as a downward shift in the *AS* curve to AS_1, showing a reduction in inflation. Such a recession with falling inflation is, in fact, what happened during the Volker contraction. By 1983, the inflation rate had fallen to 4 percent, but at a significant human and economic cost. Unemployment during 1982 and 1983 rose to nearly 10 percent. But in the years that followed, the economy recovered and employment increased, as shown by equilibrium point E_2.

The experience of the 1980s showed that after inflationary expectations become established, they can be reduced only by policies that cause major economic pain. This has led future policymakers to be very wary of encouraging any new inflationary wage-price spiral. Changes in the global economy in the 1990s, however, made achieving low-inflation goals significantly easier, as discussed in the next section.

Figure 28.13 **The Effects of The Fed's "Tight Money" Policies in the 1980s**

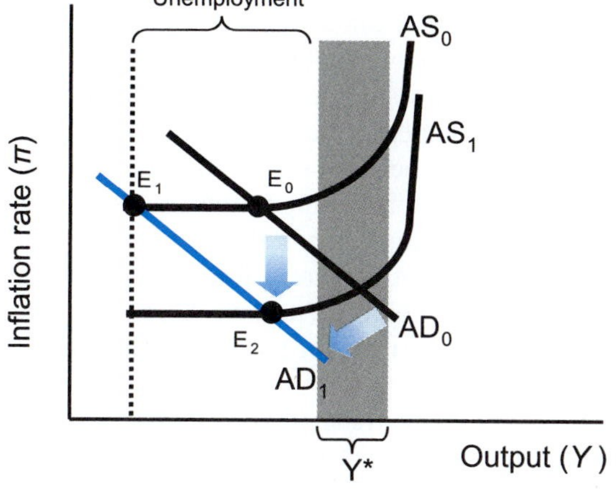

A very restrictive monetary policy drives the *AD* curve sharply to the left, pushing unemployment to very high levels. But a resulting decrease in inflationary expectations shown in aggregate supply curve AS_1 lowers inflation and allows the economy to recover to equilibrium point E_2.

3.5 TECHNOLOGY AND GLOBALIZATION

Following the substantial recession and disinflation of the early 1980s, output began to recover again. Fluctuations in unemployment and inflation continued, though within narrower bands than during the earlier years. From 1984 to 2004, unemployment varied from 4 percent to about 8 percent and inflation from 1 percent to about 6 percent; since 1992 inflation has never risen above 4 percent, and briefly fell to zero following the Great Recession (raising concerns about the opposite problem of deflation, as discussed in Chapter 26). Unemployment was low throughout the 1990s, but peaked again at 10% in 2010 following the Great Recession, and then declined only slowly (see Figures 28.14 and 28.15).

Figure 28.14 **Unemployment trends 1960–present** (Percentage of Labor Force)

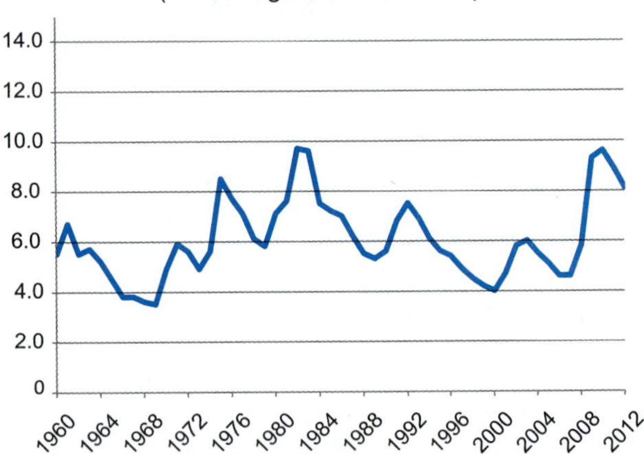

Unemployment peaked in 1982, and again in 2010. Since 2010 unemployment has declined slowly, and was just above 7% at the end of 2013.

Source: Bureau of Labor Statistics, *Current Population Survey*, 2013.

Figure 28.15 **Inflation trends 1960–present**

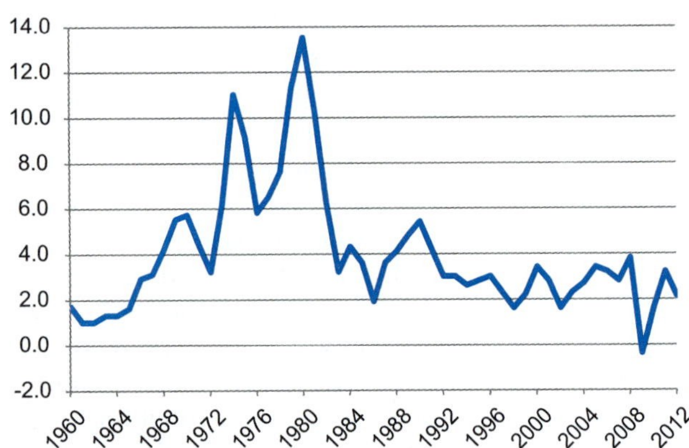

After peaking in 1980, inflation fell throughout the 1980s and 1990s, and has remained low. Following the Great Recession it fell briefly to zero, raising concerns about possible deflation. By 2011 it had returned to about 2%, historically a relatively low level.

Source: Bureau of Labor Statistics, Consumer Price Index (CPI-U), 2013.

We can use our AS/AD analysis to focus on one more period: the expansion of the 1990s. From 1992 to 1998, unemployment rates and inflation rates steadily fell, as shown in Figures 28.14 and 28.15. In 1998, unemployment was 4.4 percent, the lowest it had been since 1965. Inflation was 1.6 percent, lower than it had been in more than 10 years. This was clearly the best macroeconomic performance in decades. Unemployment continued to fall for another two years, reaching 3.9 percent in 2000.

What caused this sustained recovery? Significant advances in innovation—in particular enormous leaps in information technology, including the advent of widespread use of the Internet and information systems for business supplies, deliveries, and product design—provided a major impetus for this period of superior macroeconomic performance. This can be modeled as a period of beneficial supply shocks, as shown in Figure 28.16.

Many economists also point to increasing global competitiveness as a factor in the rising productivity of this period. Competition from foreign firms, they argue, made U.S. firms work harder to become efficient. Meanwhile, competition from foreign workers and anti-union government policies weakened the power of domestic unions. This helped keep wage and price inflation low (though it also had consequences for the U.S. distribution of income, as described in Chapters 10 and 11).

The strong performance of the macroeconomy in the 1990s inspired economic optimism. A number of commentators wondered whether we were entering a "new economy" in which business cycles would become a thing of the past. Events after 2000 proved otherwise. In 2001–2 the stock

Figure 28.16 **The Effects of Technological Innovation and Increased Efficiency**

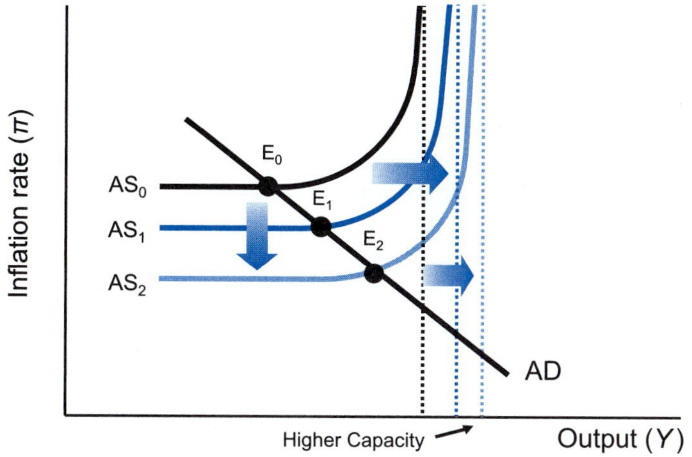

Beneficial supply shocks such as improved technology move the AS curve and the economy's maximum capacity to the right, also tending to raise employment and output while lowering inflation levels, as seen in the shifts from E_0 to E_1 to E_2.

market crashed, as the "dot-com" speculative bubble burst. About a year later, the economy slid into recession. Expansionary fiscal and monetary policies, including tax rate cuts and low interest rates, helped to promote a recovery from that recession. But in 2007, another even more significant speculative bubble in housing collapsed, leading rapidly to the most severe recession since the 1930s—often referred to as the Great Recession because of its length and severity. The housing bubble and the Great Recession are discussed in much greater detail in Chapter 30.

This brings us back to the first application that we discussed for *AS/AD* analysis—policies to recover from recession. It seems that we have not entered a new, business-cycle–free, "recession-proof" economic optimum. Instead, we have relived some of the recessionary problems of previous decades. Although the real productivity gains made during the 1990s did not go away, and the effects of that part of the expansion persist to this day, the kinds of economic fluctuation and policy response that we have tried to model with *AS/AD* analysis clearly remain of prime importance to macroeconomics (see Box 28.2).

BOX 28.2 SOFT JOBS DATA POSES DILEMMA FOR FED

A disappointing jobs report in September 2013 raised questions about whether the Federal Reserve should continue with its stimulus program, or "taper" its efforts. While the economy continued to add jobs, the rate of growth was slow, and the proportion of Americans either working or looking for work fell to its lowest level since 1978. There were a few bright spots in the report, including a slight increase in the number of hours worked and a 5-cent gain in hourly wages for private sector workers. Over the previous year, average hourly earnings have risen by 52 cents, or 2.2 percent, before adjusting for inflation of about 1.6 percent.

> "If you had a more optimistic view of the economy, which I think the Fed does, this should give you some pause," said Joshua Shapiro, chief United States economist at MFR economic consultants. "It's been a real struggle here in the labor market."
>
> Still, some economists said they believed that Fed governors would find enough bright spots in the report to justify scaling back their monthly purchases of long-term Treasury bonds and mortgage-backed securities—measures that help push down long-term interest rates—after their next meeting. "There's just barely enough in that report and other forward-looking indicators to give Fed governors the confidence they need to taper," said Ian Shepardson, chief economist at Pantheon Macroeconomics.

Despite the lukewarm jobs growth, the jobless rate edged closer to the 7 percent level that the Fed had identified as their target for ending asset purchases. Some economists suggested that the Fed governors might taper bond purchases more slowly, and combine this with other measures aimed to maintain employment growth, such as continuing to hold short-term interest rates near zero for an extended period.

Source: Catherine Rampell, "Soft Jobs Data Not Expected to Deter Fed," *New York Times*, September 6, 2013.

Discussion Questions

1. Under what circumstances can aggregate demand be increased without leading to problems with inflation? Under what circumstances is an increase in aggregate demand likely to cause inflation?
2. Stagflation—a combination of unemployment and inflation—seems to be the worst of both worlds. What policies were used to respond to the stagflation of the late 1970s and early 1980s? What factors led to improving economic conditions in the later 1980s and the 1990s?

4. COMPETING THEORIES

The *AS/AD* model has given us insight into some of the major macroeconomic fluctuations of the past several decades. But there remains much room for controversy. Was it necessary to enact expansionary fiscal policy in order to get the economy out of the 2007–8 recession? Was it a good idea for the Federal Reserve to lower interest rates to near zero in 2007–13 to try to promote recovery? Economists differ greatly in their views on these issues, and their theoretical backgrounds tend to inform their answers to these and other more contemporary questions.

Here we review the ways in which classical and Keynesian economics address these questions. Additional theories—some of which take positions between these two poles—are reviewed in the Appendix to this chapter.

4.1 CLASSICAL MACROECONOMICS

As discussed in previous chapters, economists with ties to the classical school tend to believe in the self-adjusting properties of a free-market system. In the classical view, labor markets clear at an equilibrium wage (Chapter 23). Classical markets for loanable funds cause savings and investment to be equal at an equilibrium interest rate (Chapter 24). In theory, then, a smoothly functioning economy should never be at anything other than full employment.

In terms of the *AS/AD* model, the classical theory implies an *AS* curve that is quite different from the one that we have been working with, as shown in Figure 28.17. In such an economy, output would always be at its full-employment level (now shown as a distinct value, rather than a range). The *AD* level would determine the inflation rate, but nothing else.

The rationale for this vertical *AS* curve is as follows. At the full-employment level, people are making their optimizing choices about how much to work, consume, and so on. If for some reason the economy were to produce at less than the full-employment level, the unemployed workers would bid down wages and full employment would be restored. If the economy were to produce at more than its full-employment level, wages would be

Figure 28.17 **The Classical View of AS/AD**

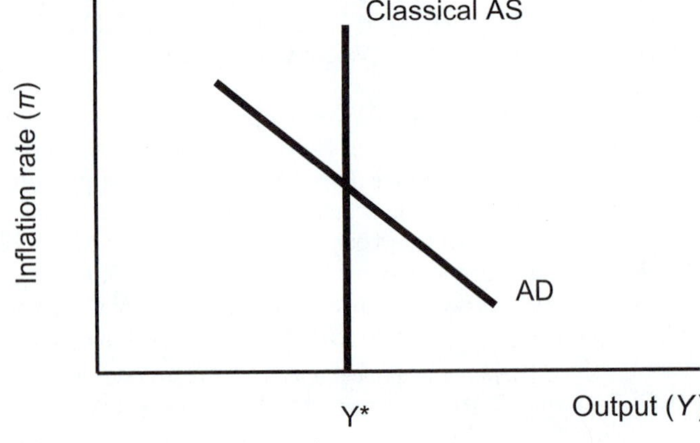

The vertical AS curve represents the classical view that the economy will tend to return to full employment automatically.

bid up, and employment would drop back to its full-employment level. Such processes are assumed to work so quickly and smoothly that the economy will return to full employment fairly quickly.

What, according to the classical model, is the effect of aggregate demand management policies? As we can see in Figure 28.17, expansionary fiscal or monetary policy can have no effect on the output level. Classical economists believe that increased government spending just "crowds out" private spending (as discussed in Chapter 25), in particular spending on investment. Because the economy is already at its full-employment level of Y^*, more spending by government just means less spending by consumers and businesses.

Similarly, in the classical view, monetary expansions are believed to lead only to increased inflation. As we saw in our discussion of classical monetary theory in Chapter 27, the classical prescription is that the central bank should just choose a certain growth rate of the money supply or level of the interest rate to support and stick to it, without concerning itself about unemployment and output. Classical theory tends to support politically conservative policies that emphasize small government and strict rules on monetary policy. Classical economists would tend to say that the fiscal expansionary policies put into place in 2009 were unnecessary for the purposes of macroeconomic stabilization but that the Volcker contraction of the early 1980s was a good idea.

4.2 Keynesian Macroeconomics

The original Keynesian belief was that market economies are inherently unstable. The Keynesian notion of the influence of "animal spirits" on investment refers to the tendency of private decision-makers to become overly optimistic and create booms in investing and production. And the higher the boom, the deeper the crash. Firms that have overextended and overproduced during an upswing need time to regroup, sell off inventory, and so on, before they will be ready to go on the upswing again. Households that have overextended and overspent during a boom also need to regroup and perhaps pay down debt, before they will be willing to restart an optimistic spending bandwagon.

This view of perpetual business cycles is a fundamentally different worldview from those that presume an automatic "settling down" of the economy at a full-employment equilibrium. Keynes did *not* believe that macroeconomic phenomena could be explained by assuming rational, optimizing behavior by individuals and then extrapolating from models of individual markets to the macroeconomy. Modern Keynesians argue that this inherent tendency toward market instability requires active government intervention and that the alternative—simply waiting for the market to correct itself—risks major economic damage and long-term depression.

It is important to note that Keynesians do not only favor expansionary fiscal and monetary policies. They believe that they are needed in case of recession, but under different circumstances, such as the inflationary periods that we have discussed, contractionary policy may be called for. Keynesians thus find the kind of analysis that we have presented in this chapter very useful for determining what type of policy is needed in different circumstances. The traditional model of Keynesian business cycles must be modified to deal with new events such as supply shocks (discussed above) and sustainability issues (discussed in Chapter 33). These require models that are flexible enough to address new issues as they arise. Such models are best built on the understanding that economies are subject to a variety of forces, many of which can swamp the market equilibrium logic that would be expected to lead to a classical situation of full-employment equilibrium.

In the modern era, the debate between economists who favor classical approaches and those who argue for Keynesian analysis has continued. The Great Recession and its aftermath have provided new fodder for these arguments about economic analysis and policy (see Box 28.3).

Box 28.3 Classical and Keynesian Views of Recession and Recovery

The Great Recession of 2007–9 and its aftermath—a very slow recovery that was still in progress as of 2014, five years after the formal end of the recession—have provided a new arena for the long-running debate between classical and Keynesian views in economics.

Two major responses to the recession—the U.S. fiscal stimulus program of 2009–11 and the Federal Reserve policies of ultralow interest rates and "quantitative easing" to expand the money supply—are right out of the Keynesian playbook of expansionary fiscal and monetary policy. At the same time, policies of "austerity" (drastic spending cutbacks) implemented in many European countries reflect the classical perspective that excessive government spending is a problem, not a solution, and that budget deficits need to be eliminated. Thus the discussion has focused on the relative success or failure of these policies.

Keynesians argued that the stimulative fiscal and monetary policies implemented in the United States prevented a much worse recession, saving or creating millions of jobs (Blinder and Zandi, 2010) and putting the country on a (slow) road to recovery. They believed that the results, in terms of employment creation, were limited mainly because the stimulus was not large enough and that the stimulus was essentially reversed after the 2010 Republican congressional victories. Although Keynesians generally supported the Fed's expansionary policies, they suggested that they are subject to the "liquidity trap" identified by Keynes—the tendency of banks and individuals to hold on to money in bad times, limiting the effectiveness of expansionary monetary policy (Krugman, 2011, 2013). Meanwhile, they pointed to the deepening recession in Europe as proof that the "classical medicine" of budget austerity was counterproductive.

Classical economists, by contrast, saw the government efforts at economic stimulation as a failure, one that would saddle the country with an increased burden of debt. According to Allan Meltzer (2011),

> U.S. fiscal and monetary policies are mainly directed at getting a near-term result. The estimated cost of new jobs in President Obama's jobs bill is at least $200,000 per job . . . once the subsidies end, the jobs disappear—but the bonds that financed them remain and must be serviced. Perhaps that's why estimates of the additional spending generated by Keynesian stimulus—the "multiplier effect" have failed to live up to expectations.

As of 2014, the U.S. economy was performing much better than most European economies, which were still well below their production levels of 2007, with unemployment rates reaching Great Depression levels of over 25 percent. Predictions by classical economists of the beneficial effects of budget austerity in Europe, and of accelerating inflation in the United States, had not come true (Morris, 2013). U.S. budget deficits were falling (in June 2013, the federal government even briefly ran a surplus)—something that Keynesians attributed to the success of their policies, while classical economists pointed to budget cuts imposed as part of the "debt ceiling" deal of 2011 (discussed further in Chapter 31).

Does this situation amount to a vindication of Keynesian policies or merely a temporary and partial success that will look different in a long-term perspective? Will the United States end up crippled by debt, or will economic recovery make debt management much easier? Will European economies rebound based on conservative budget policies, or will these countries eventually turn to more expansionary approaches? The economic argument will continue, and new policies and new data will be grist to the mill of continued economic debate.

Sources: Alan S. Blinder and Mark Zandi, "How the Great Recession Was Brought to an End," 2010, www.economy.com/mark-zandi/documents/End-of-Great-Recession.pdf; Paul Krugman, "Keynes Was Right," *New York Times,* December 29, 2011, and "Deficit Hawks Down," *New York Times,* January 25, 2013; Allan H. Meltzer, "Four Reasons Keynesians Keep Getting It Wrong," *Wall Street Journal,* October 28, 2011; Harvey Morris, "Europe Urged to Make a U-Turn on Austerity," *International Herald Tribune,* April 10, 2013.

Discussion Questions

1. What is the effect of expansionary fiscal and monetary policies in the classical model?
2. Which do you think gives a better description of economic realities: classical or Keynesian macroeconomic theory? Explain.

REVIEW QUESTIONS

1. What does the *AD* curve represent, and why does it slope downward?
2. What shifts the *AD* curve?
3. What does the *AS* curve represent, and why does it have the shape that it has?
4. What shifts the *AS* curve?
5. Describe, using the *AS/AD* model, a combination of events that might cause an economy to suffer from "stagflation."
6. Describe, using the *AS/AD* model, the impact of an adverse supply shock.
7. Describe, using the *AS/AD* model, how Federal Reserve policy might bring down inflation over time.
8. Describe, using the *AS/AD* model, the effects of a series of positive supply shocks.
9. What does the *AS* curve look like in the classical model, and why?
10. What underlying dynamic did Keynes believe is behind the business cycle? Illustrate with an ASIAD graph.

EXERCISES

1. For each of the following, indicate which curve in the *AS/AD* model shifts (initially), and in which direction(s):
   a. A beneficial supply shock
   b. An increase in government spending
   c. A monetary contraction designed to lower the long-run inflation rate
   d. An increase in taxes
   e. An adverse supply shock
   f. A fall in people's expectations of inflation
   g. A decrease in consumer confidence
2. Suppose the inflation rate in an economy is observed to be falling. Sketching an *AS/AD* model for each case, determine which of the following phenomena could be the cause. (There may be more than one.)
   a. The federal government gives households a substantial tax cut
   b. Agricultural harvests are particularly good this year
   c. Businesses are confident about the future and are buying more equipment
   d. The Fed is trying to move the economy toward a lower long-run inflation rate
3. Suppose that an economy is currently experiencing full employment, and inflation is only slightly higher than had been expected.
   a. Draw and carefully label an *AS/AD* diagram that illustrates this case. Label the point representing the state of this economy $E_{(a)}$.
   b. Suppose that investors' confidence is actually only in the middle of an upswing. As investor confidence continues to rise, what happens to inflation and output? Add a new curve to your graph to illustrate this, as well as explaining in words. Label the point illustrating the new situation of the economy $E_{(b)}$.
   c. What sort of tax policy might a government enact to try to counteract an excessive upswing in investor confidence? Assuming this policy is effective, illustrate on your graph the effect of this policy, labeling the result $E_{(c)}$.
4. Suppose that an economy is in a deep recession.
   a. Draw and carefully label an *AS/AD* diagram that illustrates this case. Label the point representing the state of this economy E_0.
   b. If no policy action is taken, what will happen to the economy over time? Show on your graph, labeling some new possible equilibrium points E_1, E_2, and E_3. (Think about which curve shifts over time, and why, when the economy stagnates. Assume that no changes occur in investor or consumer confidence or in the economy's maximum capacity output level.)
   c. Suppose that the changes you outlined in (b) occurred very rapidly and dramatically. Is government policy necessary to get the economy out of the recession?
   d. Write a few sentences relating the above analysis to the dispute between classical and Keynesian macroeconomists.
5. Check recent inflation rates in Figure 28.15 and at http://usinflation.org/us-inflation-rate/ What do you think explains the recent pattern of inflation? How does this relate to AS/AD analysis, and to the debate among different schools of thought, as discussed in Box 28.3?
6. Empirical data on the macroeconomy can be found in the *Economic Report of the President.* Go to www.gpoaccess.gov/eop/ and download statistical tables for the "civilian unemployment rate" and "price indexes for gross domestic product." Jot down data on the *seasonally adjusted* unem-

ployment rate and the *percent change in the GDP implicit price deflator* for recent periods. Plot a few points on a graph to show how the economy has performed recently. (Sometimes data is presented for months or calendar quarters, rather than for years. For the purposes of this exercise, you may simply average the numbers within a year to get a number for the year.)

7. Match each concept in Column A with a definition or example in Column B.

Column A	Column B
a. Aggregate supply	1. A rightward shift in the *AD* curve
b. Real wealth effect	2. A suggested relationship between inflation and unemployment
c. Increase in autonomous consumption	3. People's feelings about prices, based on experience or observation
d. Maximum capacity output	4. The economy's total production in relation to inflation
e. Beneficial supply shock	5. A sudden shortage of a key resource
f. Reduction in autonomous investment	6. A self-reinforcing tendency of wages and prices to rise
g. Aggregate demand	7. Increased (or decreased) spending as a result of feeling wealthier (or poorer)
h. Inflationary expectations	8. Government regulations to prevent wages and prices rising
i. Phillips curve	9. The economy's total production if all resources are fully utilized
j. Wage-price spiral	10. A burst of technological progress
k. Wage and price controls	11. Total spending on goods and services in an economy
l. Vertical *AS* curve	12. A leftward shift in the *AD* curve
m. Adverse supply shock	13. Represents the classical model of an economy at full employment

NOTE

1. Congressional Budget Office, *Estimated Impact of the American Recovery and Reinvestment Act on Employment and Output from October 2012 through December 2012*, 2012; "Congressional Budget Office Defends Stimulus," *Washington Post*, June 6, 2012; Alan S. Blinder and Mark Zandi, "How the Great Recession Was Brought to an End," www.economy.com/mark-zandi/documents/End-of-Great-Recession.pdf, 2010.

APPENDIX: MORE SCHOOLS OF MACROECONOMICS

A1. NEW CLASSICAL ECONOMICS

In the simple classical model presented above, the economy is nearly always at or close to full employment. Faced with the empirical evidence of widely fluctuating output and unemployment rates, some modern-day economists—often called "new classical" economists—have come up with a number of theories that seek to explain how classical theory can be consistent with the observed fluctuations.

real business cycle theory: the theory that changes in employment levels are caused by changes in technological capacities or people's preferences concerning work

At one extreme, some economists have sought to redefine full employment to mean pretty much whatever level of employment currently exists. Assuming that people make optimizing choices and markets work smoothly, one might observe employment levels rise and fall if, for example, technological capacities or people's preferences for work versus leisure shift over time. Some new classical economists, who have worked on what is called **real business cycle theory**, have suggested that "intertemporal substitution of leisure" (i.e., essentially, people voluntarily taking more time off during recessions) could be at the root of the lower employment levels observed during some historical periods.

rational expectations theory: the theory that people's expectations about Federal Reserve policy cause predictable monetary policies to be ineffective in changing output levels

Economists of the **rational expectations** school (which originated during the 1970s and 1980s) proposed a theory as to why monetary policy only affects the inflation rate and not output. The basic idea is that people have perfect foresight (i.e., they are perfectly rational), so their decisions already factor in the effects of predictable Fed policy, rendering it ineffective. This model can be explained by using the *AS/AD* model with a classical-type vertical *AS* (as shown in Figure 28.17). This vertical *AS* is interpreted to be the real supply curve for the economy, while in the short term the ordinary, curved *AS* reflects people's inflationary expectations.

Figure 28.18 shows the effects of an expansionary monetary policy in this classical world. Starting at E_0, the Fed acts to shift the *AD* curve to the right by expanding the money supply, from AD_0 to AD_1. Economists of the rational expectations school predict that actors in the private economy will anticipate this expansionary move by the Fed and interpret it to mean that higher inflation is likely. As a result, they immediately raise their inflationary expectations. This rise in expected inflation, shown by the upward shift of the standard *AS* curve from AS_0 to AS_1, cancels out the expansionary effects of the policy. Output will not change, and the economy stays on the classical *AS* curve—but at a higher level of inflation. Possibly a very unexpected move by the Fed might have a temporary effect on output, but as soon as people understand what policies the Fed is carrying out, the policies will become ineffective due to changes in expectations.

Other new classical economists accept that unemployment is real and very painful to those whom it affects. However, they see aggregate demand policies as useless for addressing it. Rather, they claim that unemployment is caused by imperfections in labor markets (the "classical unemployment" described in Chapter 23). To reduce unemployment, new classical economists prescribe getting rid of government regulations (such as rigorous safety standards or minimum wages) that limit how firms can do business, restricting union activity, or cutting back on government social welfare policies that make it attractive (according to the new classical economists) to stay out of work. Market pressures, they believe, will be enough on their own to support full employment—if given free rein.

Figure 28.18 **A New Classical View of Economic Fluctuations**

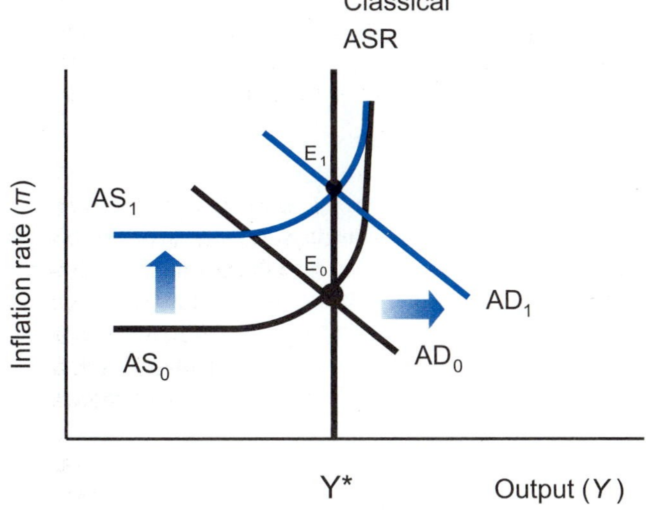

"New Classical" economists suggest that an expansionary move by the Fed, shifting the AD curve to the right, will be accompanied by an increase in inflationary expectations, shifting the AS curve up. The net effect, at E_1, is an increase in inflation with no change in equilibrium output.

A2. THE NEOCLASSICAL SYNTHESIS AND NEW KEYNESIAN MACROECONOMICS

neoclassical synthesis: A combination of classical and Keynesian perspectives

Somewhere in the middle ground is what has been called the "classical-Keynesian synthesis" or **neoclassical synthesis**. (It is a bit confusing that the terms "neoclassical" and "new classical" sound so similar, but they represent two different approaches). In this way of looking at the world, Keynesian theory, which allows for output to vary from its full-employment level, is considered a reasonably good description of how things work in the short and medium run. However, this view holds that, for the reasons set out in the classical model, the economy will tend to return to full employment in the long run.

You may have noticed that in the exposition of the *AS/AD* model above, we talked about the short run and the medium run, but did not mention the long run. This is because in more decidedly Keynesian thought (to be discussed below), the economy is really a succession of short and medium runs. Shocks to the economy are so frequent and so pronounced, and price and wage adjustments (especially downward ones) so slow, that the economy never has a chance to "settle down" at a long-run equilibrium.

In the neoclassical synthesis, however, it is assumed that the economy, if left to its own devices for long enough, would settle back at full employment, due to the (eventual) success of classical wage and price adjustments. Models built on this basis would use an analysis much like that presented in the *AS/AD* model used in the body of this chapter but add a vertical *AS* curve such as that shown in Figures 28.17 and 28.18, labeling it "long-run aggregate supply."

New Keynesian macroeconomics: a school of thought that bases its analysis on micro-level market behavior, but which justifies activist macroeconomic policies by assuming that markets have "imperfections" that can create or prolong recessions

To the extent that neoclassical economists and some Keynesians agree on this model, then, debates come down to a question of how long it takes to get to the long run. More classically-oriented economists tend to emphasize that excessive unemployment is merely temporary and believe that (at least if government stays out of the way) the long run comes fairly soon. Some Keynesian economists, often called **New Keynesians**, have accepted the challenge from classical economists to present all their analysis in terms of the workings of markets, individual optimizing behavior, and possible "imperfections" in markets. They have built up theories (such as efficiency wage theory, discussed in Chapter 23) to explain why wages do not just fall during a recession to create a full employment equilibrium. They tend to work within the neoclassical synthesis, but claim that due to institutional factors the long run may be a long, long way away. They believe that government action, then, is often justified.

A3. POST-KEYNESIAN MACROECONOMICS

post-Keynesian macroeconomics: a school of thought that stresses the importance of history and uncertainty in determining macroeconomic outcomes

Post-Keynesian economists base their analyses on some of the more radical implications of the original Keynesian theory.* They believe that modern economies are basically unstable and do not accept the idea of a long-run equilibrium at full employment. They stress the view that history matters in determining where the economy is today. They also believe that the future, although it will depend to some extent on the actions we take now, is fundamentally unpredictable, due to the often surprising nature of economic evolution and world events.

For example, one post-Keynesian argument is that high unemployment, like high inflation, may also be "toothpaste" that is very difficult to get back into the tube. When people are unemployed for a long time, they tend to lose work skills, lose work habits, and may get demoralized. If this is true, then government action to counter unemployment is even more needed, since high unemployment now may tend to lead to high unemployment in the future, even if the demand situation recovers. (Economists refer to this idea that future levels of

*Again, the similarity between the terms "New Keynesian" and "post-Keynesian" can be confusing, but there is a difference in the theoretical perspectives, as noted.

unemployment—or any other economic variable—may depend on past levels as "hysteresis" or "path dependence.")

In addition, long periods of high unemployment mean a permanent loss of output and investment—making the economy weaker in the long term. For these reasons, it is essential for the government to act to maintain full, or close-to-full, employment. Post-Keynesian economists would say that the fiscal expansionary policies put into place in 2009 were a good idea, because they do not believe that an economy left to its own devices will naturally return to full employment, even "in the long run."

29 The Global Economy and Policy

Do you know how many Philippine pesos, South African rand, or Peruvian nuevos soles you can get for a U.S. dollar? No? If you traveled to one of these countries, you might be surprised to find out that the average person on the street in any city can often easily quote you the going exchange rate between their currency and the U.S. dollar. People in smaller economies have always been very vulnerable to international economic conditions and hence make it a habit to stay current on the rate.

In contrast, because the United States has a large economy and its currency currently dominates the world financial system, people living in the United States have historically tended to be relatively unaware of global economic conditions. In recent years, that has changed. Now international trade and global borrowing and lending have significantly increased in importance, for the United States as well as globally.

The financial crisis of 2007–8 led to a world economic downturn, drawing attention to the degree to which economies are interdependent. Recovery in the United States, for example, was slowed by bad economic conditions in Europe. Much attention has also focused on the large U.S.–China trade imbalance, with efforts by the United States to get the Chinese government to allow an increase in the value of their currency in order to improve the U.S. balance of trade with China. There is concern that the large U.S. trade deficit means that the United States owes too much money to China and that this will cause economic problems in the future. How can we evaluate such international economic issues?

1. Macroeconomics in a Global Context

In earlier chapters, our macro model has generally limited its scope to the three main economic sectors: households, businesses, and the government. We have seen how each of these—through consumption, investment, and government spending—contributes to aggregate demand. It is now time to open things up a bit and introduce the foreign sector. Doing so will provide insight into how national economies are linked together and the opportunities and problems that this linkage creates.

1.1 Global Connections

An economy with no international linkages is called a *closed economy,* while one that participates in the global economy is called an *open economy.* The economic linkages among countries can take many forms, including:

- international *trade flows,* when goods and services that have been created in one country are sold in another

- international *income flows,* when capital incomes (profit, rent, and interest), labor incomes, or transfer payments go from one country to another
- international *transactions in assets,* when people trade in financial assets such as foreign bonds or currencies, or make investments in real foreign assets such as businesses or real estate
- international *flows of people,* as people migrate from one country to another, either temporarily or permanently
- international flows of *technological knowledge, cultural products,* and other intangibles, which can profoundly influence patterns of production and consumption, as well as tastes and lifestyles
- international sharing of, and impact on, *common environmental resources,* such as deep-sea fisheries and global climate patterns
- the institutional environment created by international monetary institutions, international trade agreements, international military and aid arrangements, and banks, corporations, and other private entities that operate at an international scale.

Any one of these forms of interaction may be crucially important for understanding the macroeconomic experience of specific countries at specific times. Mexico and Turkey, for example, receive significant flows of income from remittances sent home by citizens working abroad. Biological hazards, such as diseases or insects that threaten human health or agriculture, can travel along with people and goods. Trade in "intellectual property," such as technology patents and music copyrights, is currently an issue of hot dispute.

Thoroughly describing the international economic system is too large a project for one textbook. This chapter looks at how trade in goods and services affects aggregate demand as well as how it corresponds to a country's international finances. We look at how trade and finance influence the exchange rate of a country's currency. As we will see, these international issues can all affect living standards and macroeconomic stabilization. Later chapters look in more detail at issues of growth and sustainability.

1.2 Major Policy Tools

trade ban: a law preventing the import or export of goods or services

trade quota: a restriction on the quantity of a good that can be imported or exported

tariffs: taxes on imports or exports

We say that a country's economy is "open" if it exports and imports large amounts relative to its GDP and "closed" if it exports and imports relatively small amounts. Governments can try to control the degree of openness or "closedness" of their economy through a variety of policy tools. The most drastic way to "close" an economy is to institute a **trade ban**. In theory a country could prohibit all international trade, but this hardly ever happens. More often countries make trade in selected goods illegal or ban trade with particular countries (such as the U.S. ban on trade with Cuba). Inspections at the country's borders or at hubs of transportation, such as airports, are used to enforce a ban.

A less drastic measure is a **trade quota**, which does not eliminate trade but sets limits on the quantity of a good that can be imported or exported. A quota on imports, by restricting supply, generally raises the price that can be charged for the good within the country. An import quota helps domestic producers by shielding them from lower-price competition. It hurts foreign producers because it limits what they can sell in the domestic market. Some foreign producers may, however, get some benefit in the form of additional revenues from the artificially higher price.

A third sort of policy—which has been used often throughout history—is a **tariff** (or "duty"). Tariffs are taxes charged on imports or exports.* Tariffs, like quotas, can reduce trade because they make internationally traded goods more costly to buy or sell. Like quotas, import tariffs benefit domestic producers while raising prices to consumers. Unlike quotas, however, import tariffs provide monetary benefit to the government that imposes them. Also

*Often misunderstood, tariffs are taxes paid to the government of the importing country *by the importing company or entity,* not by the exporting country.

unlike quotas, tariffs do not give foreign producers an opportunity to increase prices—in fact, foreign producers may be forced to lower prices in order to remain competitive with domestic producers that do not pay the tariff.

non-tariff barriers to trade: use of licensing or other requirements to limit the volume of trade

trade-related subsidies: payments given by governments to producers to encourage more production, either for export or as a substitute for imports

import substitution: the policy of subsidizing domestic producers to make products that can be used in place of imported goods

capital controls: the regulation or taxation of international transactions involving assets

domestic content requirement: laws requiring traded goods to contain a certain percentage of goods produced by domestic companies

foreign trade zone: a designated area of a country within which foreign-owned manufacturers can operate free of many taxes, tariffs, and regulations

migration controls: restrictions on the flow of people into and out of a country

There are also various **non-tariff barriers to trade** that can be imposed. These include the use of specific licensing requirements, standards, or regulations on imported goods, which permit trade but may limit its extent.

The last important major category of trade-related policies—**trade-related subsidies**—may be used to either expand or contract trade. Export subsidies, paid to domestic producers when they market their products abroad, are motivated by a desire to *increase* the flow of exports. Countries can also use subsidies to promote a policy of **import substitution**, by giving domestic producers extra payments to encourage the production of certain goods for domestic markets, with a goal of *reducing* the quantity of imports.

Government policies can also influence international capital transactions (financial flows). Central banks often participate in foreign exchange markets with policy goals in mind, buying or selling foreign currencies, as discussed in detail later in this chapter. Countries sometimes institute **capital controls**, which are restrictions or taxes on transactions in financial assets such as currency, stocks, or bonds, or on foreign ownership of domestic assets such as businesses or land. Restrictions on how much currency a person can take out of a country, for example, are one type of capital control. Such controls are usually instituted to try to prevent sudden, destabilizing swings in the movement of financial capital.

Countries may also regulate the form that foreign business investments can take. Some have required that all business ventures be at least partially owned by domestic investors. Some have required that all traded manufactured goods include at least a given percentage of parts produced by domestic companies. Countries that have adopted such **domestic content requirements** include China, Indonesia, Mexico, and the Philippines. Sometimes such controls are related to a development strategy, while in other cases they simply reflect a desire to avoid excessive foreign control of domestic economic affairs.

Some trade policies are enacted to try to attract foreign investment, for example, by giving foreign companies tax breaks and other incentives. A popular form of this is the **foreign trade zone**, a designated area of the country within which many tax, tariff, and perhaps regulatory policies that usually apply to manufacturing are suspended. By attracting foreign investment, countries may hope to increase employment or gain access to important technologies. A well-known example is the *maquiladora* policy in Mexico under which manufacturing plants can import components and produce goods for export free of tariffs.

Migration controls are another important aspect of international policy. Countries generally impose restrictions on people who visit or move to their territory, and a few also impose tight regulations on people when leaving the country. Although beliefs about race, national culture, and population size are often the most obvious concerns behind the shaping of these controls, economic interests also play a role. For example, policies may be affected by concerns about the skill composition of the domestic labor force or the desire to receive remittances from out-migrants.

Countries do not necessarily choose sets of policies that consistently lead toward openness or consistently toward "closedness." Often there is a mix—policies are chosen for a wide variety of reasons and can even be at cross purposes. Nor do countries choose their policies in a vacuum. Policymakers need to take into account reactions to their policies by foreign governments. Increasingly, they also need to pay attention to whether their policies are in compliance with international agreements.

1.3 Patterns of Trade and Finance

International trade has grown immensely in recent years. Sometimes the sum of a country's imports and exports of goods and services, expressed as a percentage of GDP, is used as a

Figure 29.1 **Trade Expressed as a Percentage of Production, World and United States, 1960–2010**

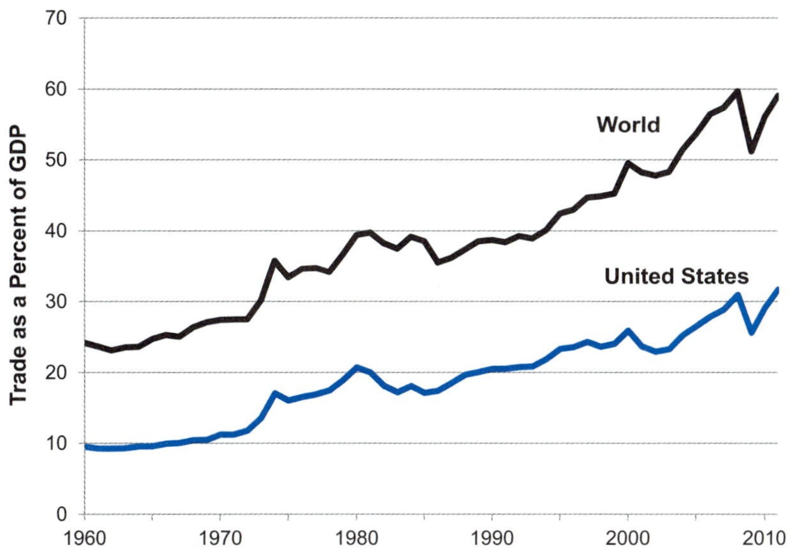

The worldwide volume of trade, including both imports and exports, expressed as a percentage of global GDP, has been increasing over the past four decades. While the United States remains less "open" than many economies, trade has become more important here as well.

Source: World Development Indicators, World Bank, 2012.

Note: Since this measure includes both imports and exports, it does not mean that over 50% of all produced goods and services in the world are traded—it counts the same goods both as exports from one country and imports to another.

measure of an economy's "openness." Growth in trade according to this measure is shown for 1960–2011 in Figure 29.1. Although trade still remains relatively less important in the United States than in many other countries, its importance has been increasing here as well.

Why has trade grown over time? The first reason is improvements in transportation technology. The costs and time lags involved in shipping products by air, for example, are far less now than in 1950. Fruit from Chile and flowers from Colombia are now flown into the United States every day—and are still fresh when they arrive. The second reason for increased trade is advances in telecommunications. The infrastructure for phone, fax, and electronic communication has improved dramatically. Better telecommunications make it possible for many kinds of services, such as customer support and many technical functions, to be directly imported from, for example, call centers in India. The third reason is that many governments have, over time, lowered their tariffs and other barriers to trade. The **World Trade Organization,** with 149 member countries, conducts negotiations aimed at lowering trade barriers, and mediates trade disputes between countries.

World Trade Organization: An international organization that conducts negotiations aimed at lowering trade barriers, and mediates trade disputes between countries.

Figure 29.2 shows the volume of exports that the United States sells to the top eight buyers of its goods and the volume of its imports that come from the top eight countries that sell to it. Historically, the closest neighbors of the United States—Canada and Mexico—have been very important trading partners. Germany, the United Kingdom, and Japan, not surprisingly, have also been leading trade partners. The growing importance of South Korea and Brazil is a more recent phenomenon that can be attributed mostly to their rapid development. The presence of Saudi Arabia among the top eight sellers to the U.S. (as of 2012) was due almost entirely to petroleum imports.

The biggest development in recent years has been the emergence of China as a major source of U.S. imports. Until about 1980, U.S. trade with China was negligible. Since then, U.S. importation of Chinese products—especially electronics (including computers and televisions) as well as clothing, toys, and furniture—has boomed. Although China buys some U.S. goods, including agricultural products and aircraft, the value of U.S. imports from China far exceeds the value of U.S. exports to China.

Figure 29.2 **Top Purchasers of Goods from the United States and Suppliers of Goods to the United States, 2012**

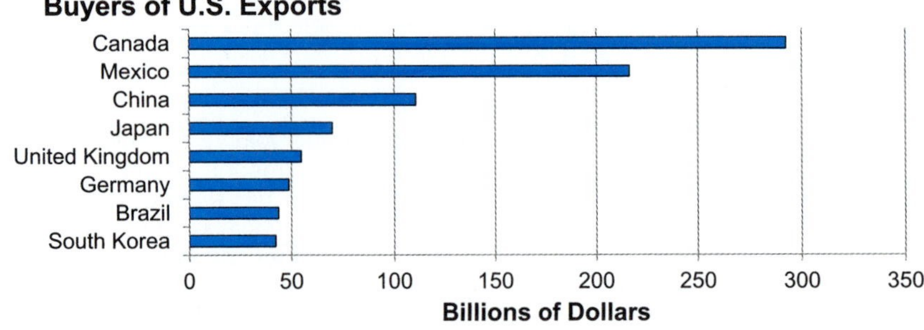

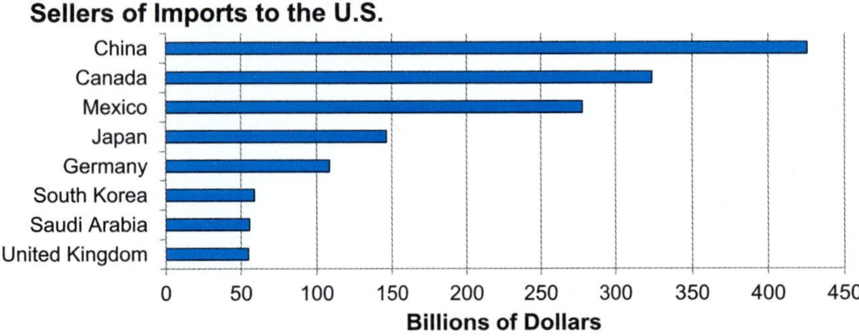

The United States' neighbors, Canada and Mexico, have long been among its major trading partners. But China has been an increasingly important source of merchandise imports.

Source: U.S. Census Bureau, Foreign Trade Statistics, Top Trading Partners, 2012.

The volume of global financial transactions has also exploded in recent years. For example, foreign exchange flows in 2013 averaged about $5.3 trillion—*per day!* This daily figure equates to more than $700 per person on earth. The volume in mid-2013 was almost four times the amount in 2001.[1]

Discussion Questions

1. How do international linkages affect your own life? Can you give examples of the sorts of linkages listed in Section 1.1 that have had direct effects on you or your family?
2. Production of apparel has been widely globalized in recent years. Before going to class, check the labels on a number of items of clothing that you own. Which countries are represented?

2. THE TRADE BALANCE: COMPLETING THE PICTURE

trade deficit: an excess of imports over exports, causing net exports to be negative

How does trade affect the economy? It is certainly an important factor. Consumers who go to any U.S. shopping mall cannot help but notice that a large proportion of the goods are imported. Many U.S. jobs are in industries that depend on export markets. We often hear concern expressed about the **trade deficit**. In 2012, the U.S. trade deficit equaled about 3.4 percent of GDP. This means that people in the United States were spending much more on foreign goods and services (importing) than the United States was selling to foreign buyers (exporting). In other words, U.S. net exports (exports minus imports) were negative. In other countries, such as China, the situation is reversed—they are large net exporters. Were it not for the United States, however, China also would be a sizable net importer, because its total trade surplus in 2012 was less than one-third of its surplus just with the United States (known as a bilateral surplus, equal to $315 billion in 2012).[2]

2.1 THE CIRCULAR FLOW REVISITED

Our trade balance is related to the circular flow discussed in earlier chapters. In this section, we look at the impact of our exports and imports on aggregate demand and GDP. We can introduce trade into our macroeconomic model by adding net exports (*NX*) into the equation for aggregate demand:

$$AD = C + I_I + G + NX$$

As discussed in Chapter 20, net exports (*NX*) equals exports minus imports ($X - IM$). Exports, like intended investment (I_I) and government spending (*G*), represent a positive contribution to aggregate demand. More exports means more demand for domestically produced goods and services. Imports, however, are a negative in the equation. That means they represent a *leakage* from U.S. aggregate demand—a portion of income that is not spent on U.S. goods and services.

Negative net exports (when $X < IM$) therefore represent a net subtraction from demand for the output of U.S. businesses and a net leakage from the circular flow. A decrease in exports (or increase in imports) tends to reduce the circular flow of domestic income, spending, and output—unless injections such as intended investment and government spending counteract this contraction. An increase in net exports, on the other hand, encourages a rise in GDP and employment. For example, an increase in U.S. purchases of foreign cars and a decrease in purchases of domestic cars would lower aggregate demand in the United States (and raise it in other car-exporting countries). But an increase in foreign sales by the U.S. computer software industry would raise U.S. aggregate demand and employment.

Adding exports and imports completes our basic macroeconomic model. We started with a very simple economy, with just consumers and businesses, then added government spending, taxes, and the international sector. We now have a more complex model, with three leakages (saving, taxes, and imports) and three injections (intended investment, government spending, and exports). Imports are considered leakages because, like saving and taxes, they draw funds away from the domestic income-spending flow. Exports, like intended investment and government spending, add funds to the flow. We can modify our original circular flow diagram to show all these flows (Figure 29.3).

Figure 29.3 **Leakages and Injections in a Complete Macroeconomic Model**

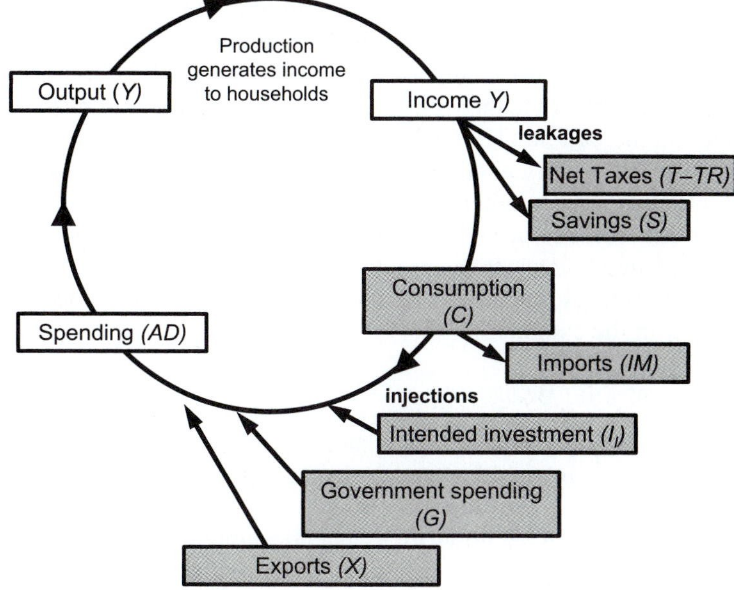

Leakages from the circular flow include taxes, saving, and imports. Injections include intended investment, government spending, and exports. The level of macroeconomic equilibrium will depend on the balance of all these flows as well as consumption levels.

Macroeconomic equilibrium involves balancing the three types of leakage with the three types of injection. A change in any one will alter the equilibrium level of output. The model that we have constructed allows us to understand how all these factors are related to levels of income and employment. We put it to use shortly to explain how saving and investment are linked to the global economy. But first we look at the multiplier effects of exports and imports.

2.2 Effects on the Multiplier

The multiplier effect for an increase in exports is essentially the same as that for an increase in I_I or G. Using the same model as in Chapter 25 (with a multiplier of 5), an increase of exports of 40, for example, leads to an increase of 200 in economic equilibrium.

$$\Delta Y = mult\ \Delta X$$

We can use exactly the same logic for a lump-sum increase in imports—the effect on equilibrium income just goes in the opposite direction. An increase in imports of 40 would lower the equilibrium level of income by 200, and a decrease in imports of 40 would raise the equilibrium by 200.

The multiplier logic becomes a little more complicated, however, when we consider how import levels are determined. In general, when people receive more income in an economy that is open to trade, they spend some of it on domestically produced goods and some on imports. The proportion spent on imports, as we noted above, is a "leakage" that does not add to domestic demand. If we want to account for this fully, we need to modify our multiplier logic. The effect is similar to that of a proportional tax on consumption: It tends to flatten the aggregate demand curve, for the same reason. When people receive additional income, a portion of it "leaks" away into imports. This portion does not stimulate the domestic economy, so multiplier effects are smaller and the economic response a bit less dynamic. Multipliers in the neighborhood of four or five seldom are observed in the real world, because *mpc* is affected not only by our marginal propensity to save but also by the rate of taxation and our marginal propensity to import. For a full treatment of this effect, see Appendix A1.

In an open economy, a portion of any aggregate demand increase goes to stimulate *someone else's economy* via imports. Thus U.S. consumers who buy imported goods from Canada are creating jobs and income in Canada, not the United States. Does this mean that imports are bad for the United States? Not necessarily. Two other factors are important to consider.

The first is that U.S. consumers and U.S. industry benefit from cheaper imported goods and services, raw materials, and other industrial inputs. The second is that at least some of the money spent on imports is likely to return to the United States as demand for exports, which, as we have seen, stimulates an increase in GDP and employment. More generally, the U.S. economy, and overall quality of life in the United States, improves when other countries have healthier economies and diminishes when other countries are suffering economic setbacks. A prosperous world is a happier world for all. Thus, in the largest sense, if China or Canada benefits from exporting to the United States, to some extent this benefits everyone. Problems can arise, however, when trade deficits (negative net exports) are too large for too long. We explore this issue further later in the chapter.

2.3 Balance Between Savings, Investment, and Net Borrowing

We can use our macro model to demonstrate that saving and investment are related not only to net exports but also to foreign lending and borrowing. Understanding this link is critical to making sense of much that happens in the global economy.

We start with the usual equation breaking down GDP into consumption, investment, and government spending. In addition, we follow the convention—seen earlier in Chapter 20—of breaking government spending down into "government consumption" and "government investment," which results in the following equation:

$$GDP = \textit{Personal consumption} + \textit{private investment} + \textit{government consumption} + \textit{government investment} + \textit{net exports}$$

or

$$GDP = C + I_I + G_C + G_I + NX$$

Rearranging, we obtain

$$GDP - C - G_C = I_I + G_I + NX$$

Because saving is what is left over from income after spending on consumption (the left-hand side of the equation above), if we combine private and government savings into a single term S_{total} and private and government investment into a single term I_{total}, we get:

$$S_{total} = I_{total} + NX$$

or:

$$\textit{Total saving} = \textit{Total investment} + \textit{net exports}$$

Thinking about these quantities in terms of valuable goods and services, this important identity says, intuitively, that goods and services that are produced in our domestic economy in excess of what we currently use for consumption can become investment goods—additions to our stock of manufactured assets (including replacement of depreciated assets)—or can be sold to foreign countries (in excess of the value of what we import from them).

Another way of understanding this is in terms of macroeconomic equilibrium. If, say, total domestic saving exceeded investment, a net leakage from the circular flow would occur. In order to obtain an equilibrium, this leakage would need to be offset by a trade surplus (an excess of exports over imports, creating a net injection). If total investment exceeded saving, the opposite would result—that is, there would be a trade deficit. In this case, the net leakage from an excess of imports over exports would balance the net injection caused by investment exceeding savings.

Yet another way to look at the relation of saving, investment, and trade is to think of how the various sectors *finance* their purchases of goods and services. In a contemporary economy, goods are rarely traded for goods; rather, money is used as a means of exchange. So, corresponding to any flow of goods and services transacted in exchanges, there is an equivalent flow of monetary funds.

Consider, for a moment, a closed economy. In this case the last equation would reduce to:

$$S_{total} = I_{total}$$

This says that, in a closed economy, the total amount that is not spent on consumption goods is available for spending on investment goods. How does financial saving get turned into tangible investments?

In the national accounts, it is primarily businesses and the government that are counted as investing. They finance their investment expenditures either from their own savings or by borrowing someone else's savings. Household savings, in the form of income not spent on consumption, can be made available for investment by the other sectors—as when the funds in a household's bank deposit are lent to a business or a household buys a government bond. The "saving = investment" identity tells us that at an aggregate national level in a closed economy, only what the country as a whole saves out of current income can be available to finance investment for the future.

When we consider an open economy, things get more complicated. Now the country as a whole can also borrow from, or lend to, the foreign sector, and the relevant identity, as noted above, is:

$$S_{\text{total}} = I_{\text{total}} + NX$$

If net exports are positive, we sell more goods abroad than we buy. How would people abroad pay for all our goods, if the value of what we sell to them exceeds the value of what they sell to us? They are not earning enough from their sales to pay us! The main way for them to finance their purchases of our goods is by borrowing from us. They would need to borrow the amount by which our exports to them exceed our imports from them. So the identity can be (approximately) rewritten as:

$$S_{\text{total}} = I_{\text{total}} + \textit{net foreign lending}$$

That is, if we had extra savings, above and beyond what is being used for domestic investment, we could lend it to foreigners so that they could buy our goods. The equation above is only approximate, because foreigners can also get more goods and services from us than they sell to us by receiving our goods as gifts, paying for them out of transfer income, or selling us their assets, such as land or businesses, in return. We discuss these possibilities in greater detail in the next section.

In recent years, however, the United States has tended to have net exports that are negative—we tend to buy more from foreign countries than we sell. This means that *we* need to borrow from *them.* The following identity means exactly the same thing as the last one, but is easier to use to represent the recent U.S. situation:

$$S_{\text{total}} = I_{\text{total}} - \textit{net foreign borrowing}$$

When we are in a situation of borrowing from abroad, then the amount we are really "putting away for the future"—that is, saving—is less than what we would assume if we looked only at what we are investing. Although we may be investing domestically, if we are using "net foreign borrowing" to obtain investment funds, we are also creating future indebtedness to other countries by borrowing from them.

Should we worry that our country has to borrow from foreigners? As in the case of your personal finances, it makes a difference what the purpose of the borrowing is. If the borrowing financed the purchase of productive new private or government investment goods, then it might be a way of actually improving the country's outlook for the future. As mentioned in Chapter 19, for many decades international authorities encouraged poor countries to borrow heavily for development projects, using exactly this reasoning.

But if the funds borrowed went largely into investments that did not pay off financially or if the borrowing only financed a high level of consumption, there would be reason to worry. A country that borrows a lot may be in trouble when it comes time to pay back its loans. In recent years, many poor countries have found themselves unable to pay the *interest* on the enormous foreign debts that they have built up over the years—much less repay the principal. In the case of the United States, the country's creditworthiness has not been seriously questioned, and to date paying interest and principal on foreign debt (known as "servicing" the debt) has never posed problems. However, as discussed further in Chapter 31, a high level of international indebtedness has potential costs over the long term.

Discussion Questions

1. What will be the likely effect of increased imports on U.S. GDP? Do imported goods undercut employment in the United States? What other developments in the economy might counteract this effect?
2. Savings, imports, and taxes are all considered "leakages" from aggregate demand. Are they bad for the economy? Or is there an important function for each? How are their levels related to equilibrium GDP, income, and employment?

3. INTERNATIONAL FINANCE

In addition to trade in goods, countries are also linked through exchange of currencies, flows of income, and purchases and sales of real and financial assets across national borders. As we consider how international finance is related to trade and to domestic macroeconomic policies, the realization that "everything is linked to everything else" can become overwhelming. Most topics that we have discussed earlier in this book—such as supply and demand, interest rates, inflation, aggregate demand, and the Fed—will come back into play. In order to ease into the topic, we focus on relatively simple concepts and models, starting with the difference between purchasing power parity and currency exchange rates.

3.1 PURCHASING POWER PARITY

purchasing power parity (PPP): the theory that exchange rates should reflect differences in purchasing power among countries

exchange rate: the number of units of one currency that can be exchanged for one unit of another currency

Purchasing power parity (PPP) refers to the notion that, under certain idealized conditions, the **exchange rate** between the currencies of two countries should be such that the purchasing power of currencies is equalized. Consider, for example, the exchange rate between U.S. dollars ($) and euros (€). As of mid-2013, $1 was worth about €0.75. Equivalently, we could say that one euro was worth $1.33. The two rates are inverses of one another. When we cite "the exchange rate" for the dollar in terms of a foreign currency, what we mean is the number of units of the foreign currency that you can get in exchange for a dollar.

If currencies could be traded freely against one another, if goods were freely traded and totally across countries, and if transportation costs were not important, then there would be a strong logic to the theory of purchasing power parity. Suppose that a winter jacket costs $200 in New York. If you lived in the United States and changed $200 into euros, the theory of PPP says that the number of euros you would receive in exchange for your dollars should be exactly enough for you to buy the identical winter jacket in Paris. If, indeed, the jacket costs €150 (= $200 × 0.75 euros per dollar) in Paris, PPP holds. If economies really were as smoothly integrated as we are assuming in our idealized world, an item (whether a winter jacket or an hour of labor services) should cost the same, no matter where you are.

If this were *not* true, there should be pressures leading toward change. For example, suppose that the jacket costs $200 in New York and €150 in Paris, but the exchange rate is higher, at €1 : US$1. Why would anyone buy a jacket in New York, if by changing their money into euros they could order it from Paris and save $50? For jackets to be sold in both locations—in this idealized world—the price in New York would have to be bid down, the price in Paris would have to be bid up, or the exchange rate would have to fall.

Of course, in the real world, national economies are not nearly as integrated as this theory assumes. Transportation costs do matter; there are many varieties of goods; markets for goods and services do not work as quickly, smoothly, and rationally as sometimes assumed; and exchange rates are often "managed" (see Section 4.3). Any of these factors can mean that converting monetary amounts from one country to another using the prevailing exchange rates may be misleading. The fact that the price of a jacket is higher in Paris than in New York might, for example, reflect a higher general cost of living in Paris.

Sometimes, we see comparisons of international income levels expressed "in PPP terms." Rather than simply using current exchange rates to convert all the various income levels into

purchasing power parity (PPP) adjustments: adjustments to international income statistics to take into account the differences in the cost of living across countries

a common currency, **PPP adjustments** try to take into account the fact that the cost of living varies among countries. For example, converting Mexican average per capita income figure from pesos to dollars would probably understate the living standard of the average Mexican. Even though the conversion is "correct"—in the sense that there exists a peso–dollar exchange rate that can easily be used for such an adjustment—many of the goods and services in Mexico are probably much less expensive than in the United States. So the dollar equivalent of what the average Mexican earns each year goes much further in Mexico.

The "Big Mac Index" published every year by *The Economist* is a somewhat lighthearted attempt to determine how much exchange rates and the price of goods vary from PPP predictions, by comparing the prices (converted into dollars using market exchange rates) of a McDonald's hamburger across various countries. More sophisticated analysis uses a larger "basket" of goods to make such comparisons and estimate appropriate PPP adjustments.

3.2 Currency Exchange Rates

What makes exchange rates go up and down? Currencies are traded against each other all over the world, as people offer to buy and sell. The supply-and-demand model explained in Chapter 4 can be applied to foreign exchange markets, once we realize that an exchange rate is really just another kind of price.

Figure 29.4 shows an idealized foreign exchange market in which U.S. dollars are traded for euros. The quantity of dollars traded is given on the horizontal axis, and the "price" of a dollar is given on the vertical axis, in terms of the number of euros it takes to buy a dollar.

In a well-behaved foreign exchange market, domestic residents largely determine the supply curve of dollars, by deciding how many dollars they are willing to offer in order to buy foreign-produced goods and services and foreign assets. Because foreign-produced goods, services, and foreign assets must be paid for in the currency of the country from which they will be purchased, dollars must be traded in the foreign exchange market. Professional currency traders and banks usually do the actual trading. The more euros that U.S. residents can get for their dollars, the cheaper that European items are to them, and the more they will want to buy from Europe rather than from domestic producers. Thus, the higher the exchange rate, the more dollars they will offer on the market. The supply curve slopes upward.

It is residents of other countries who largely determine the demand curve for dollars. They may want to buy goods and services from the United States or to invest in U.S. bonds or businesses. To make these purchases, they must acquire dollars. The more euros, or other currencies, they have to *pay* to get a dollar, the more likely they are to go somewhere other

Figure 29.4 **A Foreign Exchange Market for Dollars**

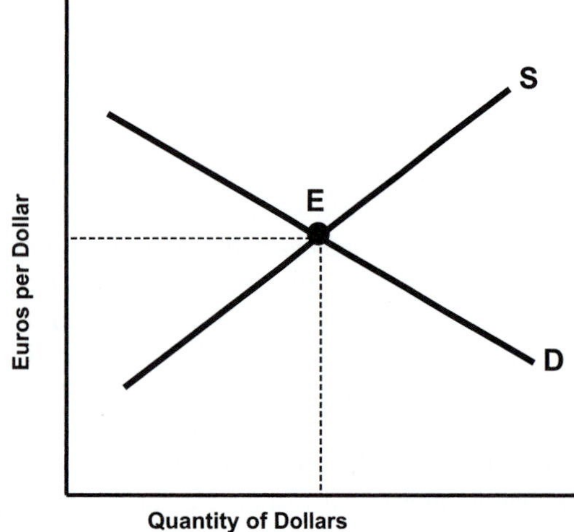

When currencies are traded against each other on a market, the "price" is the exchange rate, that is, the number of units of the other currency that are required to buy a unit of the currency in question.

than the United States for what they want and the lower will be the quantity of dollars that they demand. But if the U.S. dollar is relatively cheap in terms of euros, they will want to demand more dollars. So the demand curve slopes downward. Market equilibrium is established at point E.

currency depreciation: when a currency becomes less valuable, for example, due to a decrease in demand for a country's exports or an increase in its demand for imports

When the exchange rate falls, we say that the currency has **depreciated**. Suppose, for example, that a European technology firm comes out with a new device for listening to music that everyone wants to buy. In their desire to obtain euros to buy the good, people in the United States will offer more dollars on the foreign exchange market, shifting the supply curve to the right. Excess supply will, as in any other market, cause the price to fall, as shown in Figure 29.5. Commentators may say that the dollar is now "weaker" against the euro. (Conversely, of course, the euro is now "stronger" against the dollar.)

currency appreciation: when a currency becomes more valuable, for example, when increased demand for a country's exports causes an increase in demand for its currency

But an increase in demand for U.S. products or assets would lead to an **appreciation** of the dollar. For example, if investors became eager to buy U.S. real estate, the demand curve for dollars would shift outward and the dollar would appreciate—that is, gain in value. A currency may appreciate or depreciate relative to a specific currency, or it may appreciate or depreciate generally—that is, in relation to all or most other currencies.

Which factors are most responsible for the depreciation or appreciation of a country's currency? The first potentially important factor is relative prices. If prices in general rose more rapidly in the United States than in, say, Japan (meaning that inflation is lower in Japan), the Japanese would be less interested in purchasing U.S. goods, *ceteris paribus,* and we would be more interested in purchasing theirs. What this means in terms of the foreign exchange market is that the United States would supply more dollars (in order to obtain yen to make purchases from Japan), and the Japanese would demand fewer dollars to purchase our higher-priced goods.

A rightward shift in supply coupled with a leftward shift in demand unambiguously lowers the yen "price" of the dollar, meaning that the dollar would depreciate relative to the yen (and the yen would appreciate relative to the dollar). Note that, in this example, the dollar would not depreciate with respect to all other currencies—it would merely depreciate relative to the yen.

The second factor influencing exchange rates may be a country's GDP growth rate relative to that of its trading partners. If, for example, the United States experienced rapid growth in employment and output, it would generally mean that imports (as well as consumption, investment, government spending, and exports) also increase relatively rapidly. This would lead the United States to demand more foreign currencies (to purchase imports) relative to

Figure 29.5 **A Supply Shift in a Foreign Exchange Market**

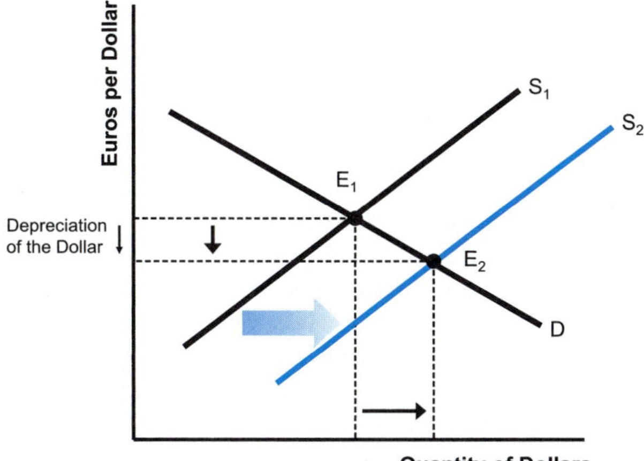

When people become more eager to sell a currency, this causes it to lose value, that is, to depreciate.

the foreign demand for our dollars. Our greater demand for foreign currencies (and supplied more dollars to purchase them) would cause the dollar to depreciate.

One might conclude from this discussion that countries that consistently import more than they export should have a persistently weak currency. The United States has, in fact, imported significantly more than it has exported for many years. Yet the value of the dollar not only has not collapsed but remains one of the most stable currencies.

How is this possible? Some economists highlight interest rates as a third key factor in determining exchange rates. If the interest rate on, say, the six-month U.S. Treasury bill were higher than the rate on comparable investments in other countries, the United States might attract flows of money from foreign investors seeking to exploit the interest rate differential. Because Treasury bills are denominated in dollars, the foreign money would be seeking to buy dollars, raising dollar demand. The result would be an appreciation in the value of the dollar. As a general rule, then, higher relative interest rates have a tendency to raise demand for the domestic currency and hence lead to a currency appreciation.

Yet it would be misleading to attribute dollar stability solely, or possibly even at all, to higher interest rates. For example, most countries set interest rates lower in the wake of the 2007–8 financial crisis, and the United States, as we saw in Chapter 27, has been no exception to this trend. There is a more general foreign appetite for U.S. assets, such as government bonds, that explains the steady and reliable demand for dollars. It is a country's investment attractiveness (or lack thereof) that influences its currency exchange rate; the prevailing interest rate is merely one variable in what makes the country attractive to investors.

In addition to currency needs for trade and investment, many traders buy and sell currency for speculative reasons. As discussed in Chapter 19, sometimes people buy something not because they need it (e.g., in this case, for facilitating a trade in real items), but because they are betting that its price will go up or down in the future. Speculative buying and selling of currencies often plays a large role in foreign exchange markets.

Unfortunately, because the ability of a country to participate in global trade critically depends on its exchange rate, such "bets" have the potential to produce real economic effects that are not always beneficial. As the role of speculation grows in importance relative to other factors that influence exchange rates, the ability of financial decisions to affect entire economies—especially small, relatively vulnerable economies—only increases. The relationship between speculation and finance, on the one hand, and the "real" economy, on the other, is discussed in Chapters 22 and 26 and is explained further in Chapter 30.

As noted above, different countries experience different levels of domestic inflation. To clarify, "inflation" refers to when a currency weakens in terms of domestic purchasing power (higher prices mean that the currency is worth relatively less) while "depreciation" is the weakening of currency in relation to other currencies (a reduction of its exchange rates). As you might expect, the two concepts are related, and what really matters for trade is the **real exchange rate** between currencies. A country with high inflation, for example, will generally experience a steady depreciation of its nominal (money value) exchange rate against the currencies of lower-inflation countries, even without any changes in demand for its items. Foreigners are willing to purchase the country's products at the higher prices resulting from inflation only if they receive more currency units per unit of foreign exchange that they offer, such that the real price remains the same.

real exchange rate: the exchange rate between two currencies, adjusted for inflation in each country

foreign exchange: the class of currencies that is broadly acceptable by foreigners in commercial or investment transactions. Generally limited to three currencies—the dollar, the euro, and the yen.

Most foreign exchange transactions are made in "strong" currencies or currencies that other countries would generally not hesitate to accept as payment for goods and services or for some investments. The U.S. dollar tops the list, but the euro and the yen also qualify and probably the British pound as well. Beyond this, the Swiss franc, famed for its remarkable stability, is also considered to be a member of this exclusive club. But the dollar, the euro, and the yen stand out as the top three. These currencies are often referred to as **foreign exchange** due to their general acceptability for foreign transactions.

Weak economies seldom if ever accept one another's currencies, and sometimes not even *their own* currency, as payment for goods, services, or assets. As will become clear, it benefits them to be paid in strong currencies. Thus the overwhelming majority of global currency trades are in dollars, euros, or yen.

3.3 The Balance of Payments

balance of payments (BOP) account: the national account that tracks inflows and outflows arising from international trade, earnings, transfers, and transactions in assets

current account (in the BOP account): the national account that tracks inflows and outflows arising from international trade, earnings, and transfers

trade account (part of the current account): the portion of the current account that tracks inflows and outflows arising exclusively from international trade in goods and services

The flows of foreign exchange payments into and out of a country are summed up in its **balance of payments (BOP) account**. Table 29.1 shows the BOP account for the United States in 2011. The top part of the table tallies the **current account**, which tracks flows arising from trade in goods and services, earnings, and transfers. The **trade account** (not shown separately in Table 29.1) refers exclusively to the portion of the current account related to exports and imports.

Various kinds of transactions lead to payments flowing into this country (and to a demand for dollars in the foreign exchange market). When we export goods, we receive payments in return. So the first entry under current account inflows is the $1.497 trillion that the United States earned from exports of goods. Exports of services (such as travel, financial, or intellectual property) also bring in inflows, as do incomes earned abroad (as profits or interest) by U.S. residents. All told, inflows into the United States from exports and incomes totaled more than $2.8 trillion in 2011.

Other transactions lead to payments going abroad (and to a supply of dollars to the foreign exchange market). When we import goods and services, we need to make payments to foreign residents. Foreign residents can take home incomes earned in the United States. The BOP account also includes a line for net transfers abroad. The account consists of monies paid out in government foreign aid programs as well as remittances—money sent home to families

Table 29.1 **U.S. Balance of Payments Account** (2011, billions of dollars)

Current account	
Inflows:	
Payments for exports of goods	1,497
Payments for exports of services	606
Income receipts	745
Total	2,848
Outflows:	
Payments for imports of goods	–2,236
Payments for imports of services	–427
Income payments	–518
Net transfers	–133
Total	–3,314
Balance on current account (= inflows – outflows)	**–466**
Capital account	
Outflows (e.g., U.S. lending, portfolio investment, or FDI abroad)	–430
Inflows (e.g., U.S. borrowing from abroad, and portfolio investment or FDI into the United States)*	1,001
Balance on capital account (= inflows – outflows)	**571**
Official reserve account	**–16**
Statistical discrepancy	**–89**
Balance of payments	**0**

Source: U.S. Bureau of Economic Analysis, U.S. International Transactions Accounts Data, table 1, with rearrangements and simplifications by authors.

*Also includes the net value of financial derivatives (financial instruments whose values are linked to an underlying asset, interest rate, or index, such as futures or options).

from the host country by foreign workers. All told, outflows of payments from the United States totaled just over $3.3 trillion in 2011.

The balance on the current account is measured as inflows minus outflows. Because outflows exceeded inflows on the current account in 2011, the United States had a current account deficit. As you can see from Table 29.1, imports of goods exceeded exports, meaning that the United States had a negative trade balance, or trade deficit. Moreover, because income flows and transfers were relatively balanced, it was the trade deficit that largely accounted for the current account deficit of $466 billion. In fact, as you can see in Figure 29.6, the United States has had trade deficits fairly steadily since about 1980, with the gap between imports and exports widening to about 6 percent of GDP in some years, but recently narrowing to about 3 percent.

capital account (in the BOP account): the account that tracks flows arising from international transactions in assets

How can a country steadily import more than it exports? If you, personally, wanted to buy something that costs more than you have the income to pay for, you might take out a loan or perhaps sell something that you own, such as your bicycle or your car. Likewise, countries can finance a trade deficit by borrowing or by selling assets. These are the sorts of transactions listed in the **capital account**.

portfolio investment: investment in stocks or bonds of a foreign country or company

foreign direct investment (FDI): investment in a business in a foreign country

To the extent the United States *lends* abroad (e.g., when the government extends loans to other countries, foreigners borrow from U.S. banks, or people in the United States buy foreign bonds), capital *outflows* are generated. This terminology may be confusing. Think about capital flows as going *in the direction of* the country that ends up with "the cash" or the power to purchase goods, and *away from* the country that "buys something." In the case of a loan, the borrower received "the cash," while the creditor "buys" a bond or other security representing a promise to repay; thus a loan is an outflow from the lender and an *inflow* from the perspective of the borrower. Similarly, if a U.S. firm engaged in **portfolio investment**—investment in the stocks or bonds of a foreign country or company—or **foreign direct investment (FDI)**—the buying of all or part of a business in another country—it is the people abroad who would end up with "the cash," while the U.S. company would receive the asset. This is also counted as an outflow. From Table 29.1, we can see that the United States had $430 billion in capital outflows during 2011.

Figure 29.6 **U.S. Imports and Exports of Goods and Services, 1960–2012**

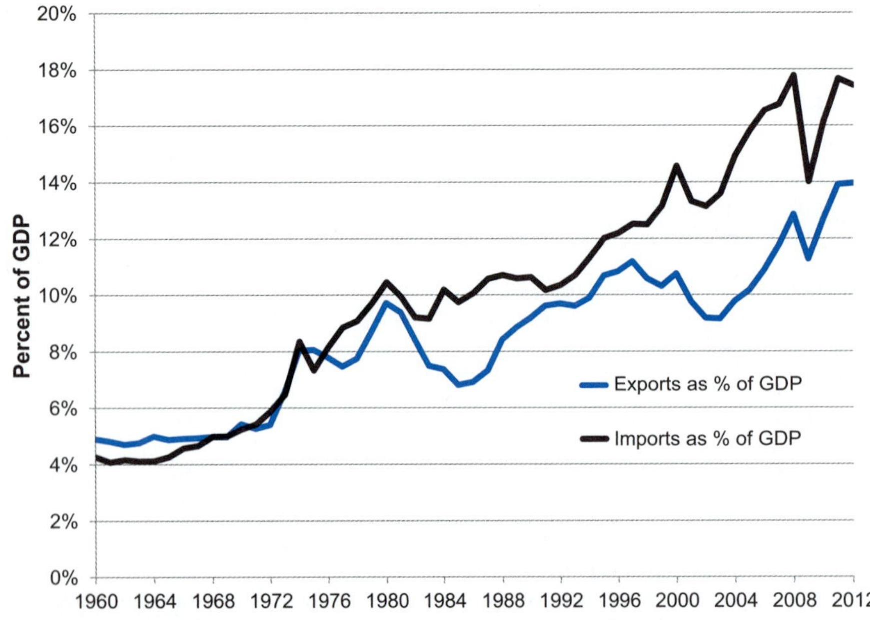

In 1960 imports and exports were each between 4 and 5 percent of GDP. Since then, however, trade—and trade deficits—have increased. In 2012 the United States imported goods and services with a value equal to 17.4 percent of GDP, while exports were equivalent to 14 percent of GDP, creating a trade deficit of 3.4 percent of GDP.

Source: BEA NIPA Tables 4.1 and 1.1.5.

capital flight: rapid movement of capital assets out of a country

Capital outflows can have widely differing meanings and impacts, depending on where they occur. Weak, unstable economies are much more vulnerable to a specific kind of movement known as **capital flight**, which occurs when investors fear investment losses and rush to move their assets to "safer" countries (mostly the United States, the member countries of the European Union, and Japan). Capital flight may represent Wall Street investors rushing to take their money out of a weak country—as happened with South Korea, Indonesia, and the Philippines during the East Asian financial crisis of 1997—or the wealthy elite seeking to take money out of their own country. In either case, capital flight has the potential to destabilize economies by making foreign exchange scarce, and governments will often go to great lengths to try to stop it (see Box 29.1).

A country receives capital *inflows* when it borrows from foreigners or when foreigners purchase assets there. In the case of the United States, many people abroad buy U.S. government bonds, because they are considered a very secure investment. For similar reasons, many also put funds into bank accounts here. These are both capital *inflows*—the sellers of the U.S. securities and the U.S. banks receive "the cash." Likewise, if a foreign multinational bought an interest in a U.S. publishing company, it would be a capital *inflow.* In 2011, the United States received just about $1 trillion in capital inflows.

As with the current account, the balance on the capital account is measured as inflows minus outflows. Thus, the United States had a $571 billion capital account surplus in 2011. It was the willingness of foreigners to buy U.S. securities (and other assets) that financed the deficit in the current account. Many commentators worry that the United States is putting itself in a vulnerable position by relying on borrowing to "spend beyond its means" on imports. Notice that *present-day capital inflows* create the obligation to pay *future income outflows:* The interest due in the future on U.S. government bonds sold abroad this year, and future profits made by firms located in the United States that were bought by foreign parties this year, will become part of "income payments" in the outflows section of the current account, in years to come.

official reserve account: the account reflecting the foreign exchange market operations of a country's central bank

Next comes what is known as the **official reserve account**. It represents the foreign exchange market operations of the country's central bank (in the United States, the Federal Reserve). Why the central bank? Here it is probably more helpful to imagine a somewhat smaller, less-developed country—say, Indonesia. Like any other country these days, it must import some goods and services from other countries. How can it pay for the imports? Its currency, the rupiah, will not do. Most exporters have no faith in the value of the rupiah and will insist on being paid in foreign exchange—that is, dollars, euros, or yen. This presents a problem for Indonesia, because it cannot produce its own dollars. It can, however, obtain them.

Box 29.1 Argentines Turn Cash into Condos in Miami

In 2012, brokers selling Miami real estate found that some of their best clients were from Argentina. Argentines were rushing to move their money out of their country and into real estate in Miami and New York. A weakening Argentinian peso and 25 percent inflation led many affluent Argentines to move their money into American real estate by expensive, even sometimes illegal means.

Capital outflow from Argentina nearly doubled from $11.4 billion to $21.5 billion between 2010 and 2011. The Argentine government has instituted capital controls to try to stop the outflow, requiring special permits to convert pesos into dollars. Trained dogs are even used to sniff out dollars at ports, airports, and border crossings. Some Argentines are willing to pay a black-market premium of up to 40 percent to convert their money into dollars.

The government controls appear to be having success. Capital flight from Argentina fell to $3.57 billion in the first half of 2012, from $11.7 billion in the second half of 2011.

Source: Charles Newbery, "Argentines Turn Cash into Condos in Miami," *New York Times,* September 13, 2012.

For example, when Indonesia exports, say, coffee, it can insist on being paid not in rupiah but in foreign exchange such as dollars. In this way, it has a strong currency available to pay for its imports. It works the same way with the capital account. Indonesia has creditors to whom it owes interest every year (which is reflected in the income section of the current account) that require payment in foreign exchange. Yet Indonesia obtains this foreign exchange not only by exporting coffee and other products but also by attracting foreign capital, which it also insists take the form of dollars, euros, or yen.

Bank Indonesia, the country's central bank, holds reserves of foreign currency, so that it can make up for a balance of payments deficit if necessary. Of course, it cannot do so indefinitely. If the central bank runs short of foreign exchange reserves, the country will have to cut back on imports. But in the short term the central bank can supply foreign exchange to cover a balance of payments deficit or acquire foreign exchange if there is a balance of payments surplus. If the central bank supplies foreign exchange, it is recorded as a positive item in the official reserve accounts; if it acquires foreign exchange, it is recorded as a negative item.

In some versions of the BOP, the official reserve account is lumped with the capital account.* When this is done, the total inflows and outflows from the current and capital accounts always "balance." When treated separately, the official reserve account, as we have seen, offsets the discrepancy between current and capital accounts. The United States reduced its official reserve account by $16 billion in 2011, which means that the Fed's holdings of these assets increased by this amount. If this is confusing, think of it as the negative sign signifying that the Fed removed $16 billion in reserve assets (mostly foreign exchange) from the U.S. economy.

One additional caveat is the statistical discrepancy. It represents an inability of the BEA to make the accounts balance precisely, given problems in the quality of the data, and some small items in the accounts that we do not get into here. Allowing for this discrepancy, the balances in the current account, the capital account, and the official reserve account *must* add up to zero (the "balance of payments"). The difference between the current and capital accounts *must* be "balanced" by a flow of foreign exchange to or from the central bank. Any gap can be fully attributed to measurement error, which is what the statistical discrepancy reflects.

4. MACROECONOMICS IN AN OPEN ECONOMY

In earlier chapters, our discussion of how fiscal and monetary policy can be used to influence aggregate demand was limited to a "closed" economy. We are now ready to consider a more complete picture of the effects of such policies. The bottom line of what is laid out in sections 4.1 and 4.2 is simple to state: The intended effects of monetary policy are strengthened, or amplified, by interactions with the foreign sector; while trade with foreign partners may either strengthen or weaken fiscal policy actions. The reasons why this is so are, however, rather complex. The value of working through them, as we shall do, is that it is a way of showing in action some of the principles of macroeconomic supply and demand that have been laid out thus far.

4.1 FISCAL POLICY

Recall from our earlier concept of a macroeconomic equilibrium that, for equilibrium to be present, injections must equal leakages. We know from Chapter 25 that a budget deficit is a net injection because government spending (injection) is greater than tax revenue (leakage). If we assume that private savings and investment are in balance, a government budget

*In recent years, for example, the International Monetary Fund has resorted to calling the capital account the "financial account," with the latter calculated to include the official reserve account. We prefer to present the traditional approach to the BOP, finding it more transparent about whether a country is truly in surplus or in deficit.

deficit requires a net leakage from the foreign sector for macroeconomic equilibrium to be achieved—that is, imports must exceed exports (again, disregarding for now the transfers and net income).

In other words, a government's budget balance is correlated with the country's trade balance—a government deficit, not financed from domestic savings, implies a trade deficit. But what is the economic mechanism by which they are related? A country's budget balance can influence its trade balance through at least two separate channels, each related to the exchange rate of its currency.

First, we have seen that deficit spending has the potential, in economies at or near full employment, to cause crowding out. This tends to lead to higher interest rates. In an open economy, the higher rates are likely to attract more foreign investment in the form of bond purchases. If foreigners demand more U.S. bonds as a result of the higher interest rates that they offer, the demand for dollars increases (because U.S. bonds are all denominated in U.S. dollars). The resulting increase in demand for dollars, *ceteris paribus,* leads to an appreciation of the dollar compared to other currencies.

We have also seen that a stronger currency makes a country's goods relatively more expensive in the global markets. In other words, if the U.S. dollar appreciated, we would expect the United States to be able to export less than before. At the same time, imports would increase because a stronger dollar makes other countries' goods (denominated in their currencies) appear cheaper. Through this sequence, an increase in the budget deficit might increase the size of the trade deficit.

Notice, however, that while both deficits grow, the economic effect of the rising trade deficit is to offset the expansionary effect of the budget deficit. Imports (leakage from the circular flow) increase while exports (injection) decrease. Because we do not know the magnitude of each of these changes, we are *not* saying that the open economy effect cancels out the original effect of the fiscal stimulus. What we can say is that it probably dampens its effect somewhat.

The other channel is a more direct consequence of the fiscal expansion. Deficit spending boosts aggregate demand, increasing spending and generating greater employment and more income. Yet, as the economy grows, *all* spending grows, including spending on imports. The greater demand for imports increases the global supply of dollars, as U.S. citizens demand more foreign currency to purchase imports. This causes the dollar to depreciate, reversing the process, because a weaker dollar results in more exports and less imports.

Depreciation of the dollar will tend to narrow the trade deficit, resulting in a net injection to the circular flow and *reinforcing* the initial fiscal stimulus. Since the two effects we have described go in opposite directions, we cannot say anything specific about the magnitude of the changes, nor can we say overall whether the "open economy" on balance reinforces or countervails the domestic fiscal policy. But we can say that the effect of deficit spending is complicated by consideration of foreign sector effects.

4.2 MONETARY POLICY

In Chapter 27 we discussed monetary policy in a closed economy. In an open economy, monetary policy is more effective in changing aggregate demand, because, unlike fiscal policy, its global effects unambiguously reinforce the domestic policy.

Suppose that the Fed believes the U.S. economy needs a boost and lowers interest rates in an attempt to stimulate aggregate demand. As we saw in Chapter 27, the decrease in interest rates should encourage investment spending. But in an open economy, the fall in interest rates should also increase net exports, another component of aggregate demand.

This is because a reduction in U.S. interest rates is likely to drive away some foreign financial capital. If interest rates here fell, people abroad would be less inclined to buy U.S. government bonds or put their money in U.S. bank accounts. As they sent their financial capital elsewhere, the demand for U.S. dollars would decrease. This would be portrayed as a leftward shift of the demand curve in the foreign exchange market. As discussed above (refer to Figure 29.4) a decrease in the demand for dollars would cause the dollar to depreciate.

A depreciation in the dollar means that a dollar now buys fewer units of foreign exchange, which, you will recall, discourages spending on imports. Meanwhile, the fact that a dollar can be purchased for fewer units of foreign exchange means that U.S. exports become "cheap" for foreign buyers. Exports should increase. Because it is demand for U.S.-produced goods and services minus imports that enters into aggregate demand, the latter rises. Thus, both an increase in exports and a decrease in imports have the effect of raising aggregate demand.

The openness of the economy can be thought of as adding an extra loop to the chain of causation discussed in Chapter 27, as illustrated below:

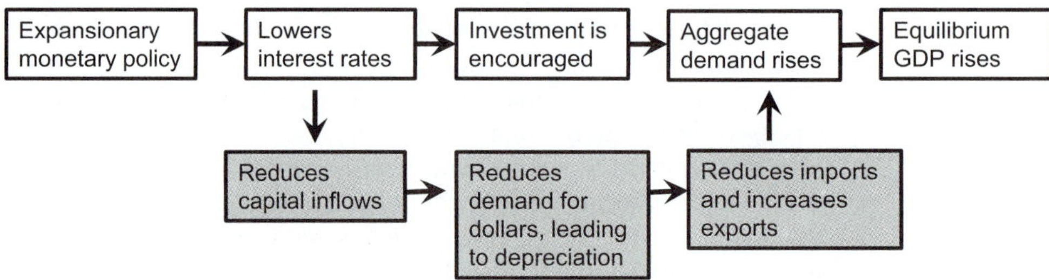

Yet this is not the end of the story. Just as in the earlier case of deficit spending, an increase in aggregate demand tends to produce an increase in imports. As we have seen, this leads to dollar depreciation, as U.S. citizens trade dollars for other currencies so that they can purchase imported products.

Here, also, the effect is to reinforce the initial domestic stimulus, since a weaker dollar tends to narrow the trade deficit that, as we have seen, increases aggregate demand, *ceteris paribus.* So in contrast to the fiscal policy case, where "opening up" the economy produces ambiguous effects in relation to a domestic fiscal stimulus, for monetary policy the international trade consequences clearly reinforce the domestic policy. A monetary stimulus, in other words, is amplified in an open economy. We should note that a monetary contraction would *also* be magnified; the same causal mechanisms would be in effect, only in reverse.

4.3 MANAGED VERSUS FLEXIBLE FOREIGN EXCHANGE

flexible (floating) exchange rate system: a system in which exchange rates are determined by the forces of supply and demand

So far, we have assumed that exchange rates are determined by market forces, as modeled in Figure 29.5. In a **flexible** or **floating exchange rate system**, countries allow their exchange rates to be determined by the forces of supply and demand. But this is not always the case.

Flexible exchange rates can create significant uncertainties in an economy. A manufacturer may negotiate the future delivery of an imported component, for example, only to find that exchange rate changes make it much more expensive than expected to complete the deal. Foreign exchange markets can also be susceptible to wild swings from speculation. A mere rumor of political upheaval in a country, for example, can sometimes create a rush of capital outflows as people try to move their financial assets into foreign banks, causing a precipitous drop in the exchange rate. Or an inability to obtain short-term foreign loans may send an economy into crisis—and its exchange rate swinging—even if over a longer period the economy would be considered financially sound. It can be hard to maintain normal economic activities when exchange rates fluctuate wildly.

fixed exchange rate system: a system in which currencies are traded at fixed ratios

Many countries have tried to control the value of their currencies in order to create a more predictable environment for foreign trade. The strictest kind of control is a **fixed exchange rate system**. In this case, a group of countries commits to keeping their currencies trading at

Bretton Woods system: a system of fixed exchange rates established after World War II, lasting until 1972.

fixed ratios over time. Starting in 1944, many countries, including the United States, had fixed exchange rates under what is known as the **Bretton Woods system** (named after the international monetary conference in Bretton Woods, New Hampshire that created a post-war financial order including the Intentional Monetary Fund and the World Bank).

The exchange rates in such a system, however, do not usually remain perfectly fixed. For one thing, it is impossible to literally fix an exchange rate, because the central bank would need to have perfect (and *continuously* perfect) information about all trades. What the countries that participated in the Bretton Woods conference did—and countries today that fix their currency generally do—is set a "band" or range around a "target rate" and allow the "fixed" rate to fluctuate within this band. In the case of the countries that were part of the Bretton Woods system, the band was very narrow—on the order of plus or minus 1 percentage point.

devaluation: lowering an exchange rate within a fixed exchange rate system

revaluation: raising an exchange rate within a fixed exchange rate system

Over the long term, the target rate within the band can change, at the government's discretion. When a government lowers the level at which it fixes its exchange rate, what is called a **devaluation** occurs, and when it raises it, a **revaluation** takes place. But the system can be undermined if there are too many changes, and when key currencies such as the dollar come under too much selling pressure a fixed exchange rate system can break up. This is what happened to the Bretton Woods system in 1972. The U.S. dollar had been the linchpin of the system, and had been convertible to gold. When the United States suffered large currency outflows, the U.S. eliminated gold convertibility and allowed the currency to float, which was quickly followed by other major countries floating their currencies also.

After the Bretton Woods system ended, many countries moved to a "floating" system, while others tried to exert some management over their currencies. Such management is performed by trying to maintain certain target exchange rates, by "pegging" the currency to a particular foreign currency or by letting it "float" but only within certain bounds (something like the Bretton Woods system, only with a much wider band).

How does a country keep its exchange rate fixed, or at least within bounds? A government has at its disposal two main tools. The first is imposing capital controls. For example, a country that wants to limit foreign exchange trading may require that importers apply for licenses to deal in foreign exchange or impose quotas on how much they can obtain. By only allowing highly regulated transactions, it can control the prices at which exchange transactions are made.

foreign exchange market intervention: an action by central banks to buy or sell foreign exchange reserves in order to keep exchange rates at desired levels

The second is **foreign exchange market intervention**. As we saw earlier in our discussion of official reserve accounts, central banks have the power to intervene in foreign exchange markets. They may do this under a floating exchange rate regime, with the object of raising or lowering the rate, or to build up or lower their holdings of foreign exchange. When a country is committed to a fixed exchange rate, it is the responsibility of the central bank to respond to upward or downward pressures on the rate with appropriate intervention in order to keep the rate at the prescribed level.

To see how intervention works, consider Figure 29.7. Suppose that the government would like to keep the exchange rate of its domestic currency at (or above) the level e^*, but market pressures are represented by the curves S_{market} and D_{market}. At the exchange rate e^*, there is an excess supply (surplus) of domestic currency, and so there is pressure on the exchange rate to fall. The central bank must artificially create more demand for the domestic currency, as shown by demand curve $D_{with\ intervention}$. It does this by going into the market and exchanging foreign currency for domestic currency—essentially "soaking up" the surplus domestic currency.

balance of payments crisis: when a country gets precariously close to running out of foreign exchange and is therefore unable to purchase imports or service its existing debt

The problem is that the central bank can do this only as long as it has sufficient reserves of foreign exchange on hand. If it ran out of foreign exchange, it would be unable to support the currency and be forced to devalue. This is, in fact, fairly common among countries with deficits in their BOP, and in some cases leads to a **balance of payments crisis**.

Is devaluation a bad thing? The answer to this question is complex. Devaluation is generally thought to be good for exporters, because it makes the country's goods cheaper abroad. But it also means that people in the country will find that imports are now more expensive. And

Figure 29.7 **Foreign Exchange Intervention**

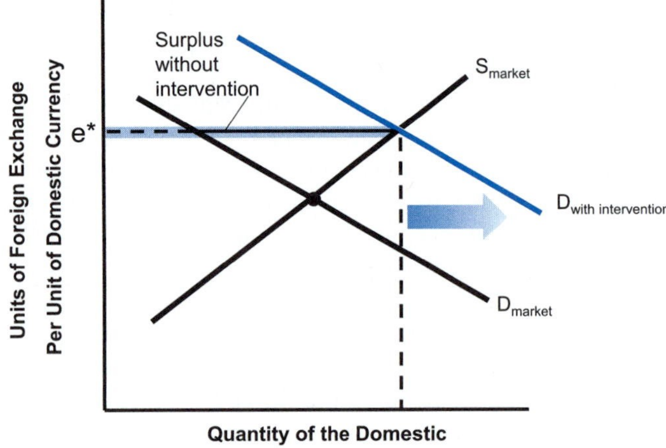

In order to keep the exchange rate at the target level e*, the central bank has to buy up the surplus of domestic currency, using in payment its reserves of foreign exchange.

sometimes devaluation is taken as a sign of instability or poor policy in a country or leads to international runs of speculation or competitive devaluation.

Imagine, for example, an investor who is considering investing $100 million in Bolivian government bonds. If it seemed likely that the country's currency—the sucre—would at some point be devalued, the best strategy would be to avoid investing in Bolivia. If the exchange rate today were 5,000 sucres to the dollar, the investor could purchase 500 billion sucres worth of bonds with $100 million. But if the currency were in fact later devalued—to the point where 10,000 sucres would be needed to purchase a dollar—the investment would subsequently only be worth $50 million if the investor decided to sell the bonds and convert back to dollars. Because of the potential problems resulting from currency devaluation, many economists have grown cautious about recommending devaluation as a cure for international imbalances.

In contrast, a country can keep its exchange rate *lower* than market forces would dictate by supplying a lot of its domestic currency on the market and amassing large amounts of foreign reserves. Recently, China has used this tactic, keeping the value of its currency, the renminbi artificially low to stimulate exports. (The value of renminbi is often cited in terms of its most common unit, the yuan). China has, in the process, become a large holder of U.S. dollars as well as other currencies. China has been under pressure from many countries to revalue the renminbi (see Box 29.2).

One complication with fixed exchange rates is that they make it impossible for a country to conduct independent monetary policy. The reason is that intervention by its central bank on money markets to buy and sell its currency for foreign exchange reasons necessarily affects the country's domestic money supply, and vice versa. A country can set its exchange rate *or* its interest rate, but not both. If it keeps its exchange rate fixed relative to another currency, the interest rates in the two countries will tend to move together.

The adoption of the euro by some member countries of the European Union (EU) is a dramatic recent example of fixed exchange rates—taken a step further. In 1999 eleven member countries established fixed exchange rates between their national currencies and the euro—although, at that time, the euro was just an accounting notation. In 2002, euro banknotes and coins were put into circulation and national currencies were withdrawn. The countries that have adopted the euro have given up having separate monetary policies, putting the European Central Bank in control of monetary policy-making for the group as a whole. Because of this, and the fact that different countries often have different objectives and requirements, monetary policy is often more complicated in the eurozone than in individual countries (see Box 29.3). At latest count, the EU has 27 members, of which 17 participate in the euro.

Box 29.2 United States Pressures China to Revalue Its Currency

For some time, the United States has put pressure on China to revalue its currency. In May 2012, The U.S. Treasury Department said that China had made progress in allowing its currency to rise against the dollar. This finding averted a formal charge of currency manipulation and a likely trade dispute. But the Treasury still considered China's currency, the renminbi, to be undervalued, meaning that it needed to appreciate further against the dollar.

> The renminbi gained 8 percent against the dollar between 2010 and 2012. A currency with a lower value gives China a trade advantage by making its exports cheaper and imports from the United States more expensive. Some American manufacturers have urged the administration to take punitive steps to force China to allow the renminbi to trade freely. The renminbi now trades within a narrow range against the dollar.

The U.S. trade deficit with China was $315 billion in 2012. The continuing trade deficit means that the issue of currency valuation will continue to be a point of dispute between the two countries, with some U.S. legislators urging stronger action to force China to revalue.

Source: Associated Press, "Citing Gains, United States Doesn't Call China Currency Manipulator," May 25, 2012.

Box 29.3 European Central Bank Grapples with Interest Rates and Euro Value

February 7, 2013—Mario Draghi, the president of the European Central Bank, cited the rising value of the euro as a possible threat to the region's economic recovery. His comments immediately sent the euro down sharply against the dollar and yen. While the ECB President denied trying to influence the value of the euro, he implied that the Bank could take action if the euro rose too much.

> "The exchange rate is not a policy target, but it is important for growth and price stability," Mr. Draghi said at a news conference after the regular monthly policy meeting of the ECB's Governing Council, in which the central bank left its main interest rate at 0.75 percent, as expected.
>
> Mr. Draghi, during the news conference, was careful to avoid any explicit threat to take action to push down the euro or to criticize any other countries. He said the euro's current value was not far from its historical norm. But he noted that economic policy by other countries, none of which he identified, could affect exchange rates.
>
> Recovery in the Eurozone could be threatened by the rising value of the euro, which could hurt European exports by making them more expensive for foreign buyers. In recent weeks, the euro has risen substantially against the dollar, to its highest levels in a year.
>
> A stronger euro means that products ranging from cars to wine become more expensive abroad, putting European producers at a disadvantage against foreign competitors. But there are also positive effects. Imports, particularly oil, become less expensive for Europeans, which helps stimulate the economy.

Source: Jack Ewing, "ECB President's Comments Send Euro Lower," *New York Times,* February 7, 2013.

5. International Financial Institutions

World Bank: an international agency charged with promoting economic development, through loans and other programs

The Bretton Woods system of fixed exchange rates was only one aspect of the international financial structure established in the 1940s. Also formed during this period were the International Bank for Reconstruction and Development (IBRD), later expanded into the **World Bank**, with the goal of promoting economic development through loans and programs aimed at poorer countries, and the **International Monetary Fund (IMF),** established to oversee international financial arrangements. Although fixed exchange rates have been abandoned, the World Bank and the IMF continue—with considerable controversy—to play significant roles in international affairs.

International Monetary Fund (IMF): an international agency charged with overseeing international finance, including exchange rates, international payments, and balance of payments management

The IMF was charged with overseeing exchange rates, international payments, and balance of payments management and with giving advice to countries about their financial affairs. The IMF has a complicated governance structure based on voting shares allocated to member countries, but in fact its policy-making has historically been dominated by the United States and certain countries in Europe. The appointed members of its executive board represent the United States, the United Kingdom, Germany, France, and Japan. The IMF recently restructured its voting system to give China, South Korea, Turkey, and Mexico slightly larger shares. Both the World Bank and IMF have their headquarters in Washington, DC.

When a country is in financial trouble—for example, when it is unable to pay the interest that it owes on its foreign debts or is experiencing wild swings in its exchange rate—the IMF (in conjunction with the World Bank, if the country is poor) often advises the government on how to remedy the problem. The IMF has tended to encourage low- and middle-income countries with debt problems to remove their barriers to trade and capital flows, arguing that such liberalization promotes economic growth. The countries are also advised to minimize the size of their government and its expenditures, as a way to reduce the need for borrowing. They are told to keep their inflation rates down and are often advised about their exchange rate policies as well.

Washington Consensus: specific economic policy prescriptions used by the IMF and World Bank with a goal of helping developing countries to avoid crisis and maintain stability. They include openness to trade and investment (liberalization), privatization, budget austerity, and deregulation.

The policy prescriptions of trade liberalization, privatization, deregulation, and small government became known during the 1980s and 1990s as the **Washington Consensus** (described in more detail in Chapter 32). The policies have also become the source of much controversy, as many economists have come to believe that rigid, "one-size-fits-all" application of such policies often works against, rather than for, human welfare and international stability (see Box 29.4).

Although the lending power of the IMF gives it considerable say in the affairs of many countries—for better or worse—the powers of any international organization are limited, especially with regard to the countries that are larger and more powerful. For example, many commentators worry about issues such as the undervalued Chinese renminbi/yuan, or the volume of foreign debt being taken on by the United States, but there is currently no international institution with the power to force China or the United States to change their policies. The IMF was also unable to prevent the rapid development of global financial crisis in 2008–9, although it played a role in putting together bailout packages for some countries after the crisis.

Many observers are currently calling for reforms in the international financial system and perhaps for new international institutions. Dissatisfaction over the IMF prescriptions for liberalization has caused some changes within the organization itself. But some argue that these changes are not sufficient and that more radical changes are necessary. Suggestions include greater regulation of international banking, substantial reforms and increased transparency in multinational corporate governance, restrictions on short-term capital flows, a tax on speculative transactions in foreign exchange (see Chapter 30), and establishment of an international bankruptcy court.

Discussion Questions

1. To check your understanding of international linkages, consider the following hypothetical scenario. Suppose that people overseas become less interested in buying U.S. government bonds (perhaps because they start to think of them as less secure). What would be the effect on:
   a. The BOP financial account?
   b. The supply or demand for U.S. dollars?
   c. The value of the U.S. dollar?
   d. The BOP current account?
2. Have international trade or financial imbalances, or actions of the IMF, been in the news lately? What are the current controversies?

BOX 29.4 THE IMF AND THE ARGENTINE DEFAULT

In December 2001, the Argentine government announced a moratorium on payments on its $155 billion in public foreign debt. This default—the largest by a sovereign nation in history—rocked the international financial world. Was there more that the IMF could have done to prevent this? Or might IMF advice have been part of the reason that the default occurred?

In 1991 Argentina had pegged its currency to the U.S. dollar, as a way of bringing hyperinflation to a halt. The IMF, believing that this would lead to more discipline in Argentine policy-making, approved the peg. But with the dollar strong against the currencies of Europe and Brazil, Argentina's major trading partners, the peg made Argentina's exports expensive. This discouraged Argentine industry and encouraged the purchase of imports. Trade deficits resulted, financed by borrowing from abroad. Unemployment rose.

The IMF advised the Argentine government to address its financial issues by cutting back on government expenditures and privatizing its social security program. The country's leaders complied, even though the economy was in a downturn. The IMF encouraged Argentina to institute free trade policies, though major markets in the United States and Europe remained closed to its exports. Meanwhile, financial crises in Asia, Mexico, and Brazil made investors more nervous about lending to middle-income countries. The fact that the Argentine economy was visibly struggling caused foreign lenders to demand higher interest rates to compensate them for the risk of default. This in turn made the debt even harder to bear, in a vicious circle.

In December 2001, the situation reached a crisis. With official unemployment nearing 20 percent, people demonstrated in the street, which led the government to fall. Unable to make its debt payments, the interim government announced the default. The Argentine economy continued in a downward slide well into 2002.

Some commentators have blamed the default on corruption and mismanagement by the Argentine government and suggested that the crisis might have been avoided if the government had cut its expenditures even *more*. Others, observing that the government budget deficit was actually of a quite reasonable size (less than 3 percent of GDP), believe that inappropriate IMF advice is at least as much to blame. Basic principles of macroeconomics say that a government should raise—not lower—spending during a recession, but the IMF policies went in the opposite direction, pushing the economy into a downward spiral. According to this view, given IMF advice, default was only a matter of time.

Source: Joseph E. Stiglitz, "Argentina, Shortchanged: Why the Nation That Followed the Rules Fell to Pieces," *Washington Post,* May 12, 2002, and other news sources.

REVIEW QUESTIONS

1. In what seven ways are economies connected internationally?
2. List four policies related to international trade.
3. List two policies related to international capital transactions.
4. Briefly describe the recent history of United States and world trade, and list the major U.S. trading partners.
5. What are some international organizations and agreements dealing with trade relations?
6. List six reasons why countries often limit trade.
7. What is the theory of "purchasing power parity"?
8. Who creates the supply of a currency on the foreign exchange market? Who creates the demand?
9. Draw a carefully labeled graph illustrating a depreciation of the dollar against the euro.
10. What are the two accounts in the balance of payment account, and what do they reflect?
11. How and why is an imbalance (surplus or deficit) in the current account related to an imbalance in the capital account?
12. Does having an open economy make monetary policy stronger or weaker? Why?
13. What is the effect of an open economy on fiscal policy?
14. Distinguish between floating and fixed exchange rate systems.
15. How and why might a central bank "intervene" on a foreign exchange market?
16. What is the "Washington Consensus"?
17. What reforms have been suggested for the international financial system?

EXERCISES

1. Singapore is a natural-resource-poor country that has built its economy on the basis of massive imports of commodities and raw materials and similarly massive exports of refined and manufactured goods and services. In Singapore, exports are 178 percent of GDP! But how can a country export *more* than its GDP? (Hint: Remember that imports are subtracted to obtain the measure of *net exports* that is part of GDP.)
2. Classify each of the following as a *trade flow, income flow,* or *asset transaction:*
   a. A U.S. software company sells its products to European consumers
   b. A Saudi investor buys real estate in Europe
   c. A U.S. retailer imports Chinese-made appliances
   d. A worker in the UK sends some of her wages back to her family in India
   e. A Mexican manufacturer pays interest on a loan from a Canadian bank
3. Suppose that, due to rising interest rates in the United States, the Japanese increase their purchases of U.S. securities.
   a. Illustrate in a carefully labeled supply-and-demand diagram how this would affect the foreign exchange market and the exchange rate expressed in terms of yen per dollar.
   b. Is this an appreciation or depreciation of the dollar?
   c. Would we say that *the yen* is now "stronger"? Or "weaker"?
   d. If the rise in interest rates was due to a deliberate Fed policy, does this international connection make such policy more, or less, effective? Explain in a few sentences.
4. Determine, for each of the following, whether it would appear in the *current account* or *financial account* section of the U.S. balance of payments accounts and whether it would represent an *inflow* or an *outflow.*
   a. Payments are received for U.S.-made airplanes sold to Thailand
   b. A resident of Nigeria buys a U.S. government savings bond
   c. A U.S. company invests in a branch in Australia
   d. A Japanese company takes home its profits earned in the United States
   e. The U.S. government pays interest to a bondholder in Canada
5. Match each concept in Column A with a definition or example in Column B.

Column A	Column B
a. Tariff	1. Makes international incomes comparable, by accounting for differences in the cost of living
b. Current account	2. A rise in the value of a currency in a floating exchange rate system
c. Currency appreciation	3. An organization charged with providing loans for development
d. Purchasing power parity adjustment	4. Investing in a foreign business
e. Balance of payments crisis	5. Tracks flows arising from trade, earnings, and transfers
f. Quota	6. A tax put on an internationally traded item
g. Non-tariff barriers to trade	7. When a country runs short of foreign exchange
h. World Bank	8. A rise in the value of a currency, under a fixed exchange rate system
i. International Monetary Fund	9. Using measures such as standards and licensing to restrict trade
j. Capital controls	10. When a central bank buys or sells foreign exchange
k. Revaluation	11. A fall in the value of a currency under a floating exchange rate system
l. Foreign Direct Investment	12. Putting a quantity limit on imports or exports
m. Currency depreciation	13. Government intervention to reduce or eliminate international capital flows
n. Foreign exchange market intervention	14. An organization charged with overseeing international finance

Notes

1. Bank for International Settlements, *Triennial Central Bank Survey*, September 2013.
2. U.S. Census Bureau, *U.S. Trade in Goods with China.* www.census.gov/foreign-trade/balance/c5700.html.

Appendix: An Algebraic Approach to the Multiplier, in a Model with Trade

Just as we modified the multiplier in the appendix to Chapter 25 to take account of the impact of taxes, we can now go a step further to consider the effect of trade. Suppose that, in addition to consumption's depending on income, imports depend on income according to the equation $IM = mpim\, Y$, where *mpim* is the marginal propensity to import (the proportion of additional income spent on imports). The *mpim* is a fraction. Starting with the equation for aggregate demand with a proportional tax that we had derived in the appendix to Chapter 25, we can get an equation for aggregate demand in an economy including trade, as follows:

$$\begin{aligned} AD &= C + I_I + G + X - IM \\ &= \bar{C} + mpc\,(Y - tY + TR) + I_I + G + X - mpim\,Y \\ &= (\bar{C} + mpcTR + I_I + G + X) + [mpc(1 - t) - mpim]\,Y \end{aligned}$$

The *AD* curve now has the intercept given by the first term in parentheses. Changes in exports shift the curve upward or downward. The new slope is given by the term in brackets. The slope is flatter, due to the subtraction of *mpim.*

Solving for *Y* (using the same method as in the appendix to Chapter 25—but leaving out some of the intermediate steps) yields:

$$Y - mpc\,(1 - t)\,Y + mpim\,Y = C + mpc\,TR + I_I + G + X$$

$$Y = \left[\frac{1}{1 - mpc\,(1 - t) + mpim}\right]\left(\bar{C} + mpc\,TR + I_I + G + X\right)$$

The term in brackets is a new multiplier that includes both proportional taxes and imports that depend on domestic income. This multiplier here is even smaller than the previous two. For example, if $mpc = .8$, $t = .2$, and $mpim = .1$, the new multiplier is $1/(1 - .64 + .1)$ or $1/(0.46)$ or approximately 2.2. This is because any increase in *Y* now "leaks" not only into saving and taxes but also into increases in imports (which takes away from demand for domestic products).

PART VIII

Macroeconomic Issues and Applications

30 The Financial Crisis and the Great Recession

The financial crisis that commenced in 2007 and its aftermath have been widely referred to as the "Great Recession"—and with good reason. From its beginning until its nadir in 2009, it was responsible for the destruction of nearly $20 trillion worth of financial assets owned by U.S. households. During this time, the U.S. unemployment rate rose from 4.7 percent to 10 percent (not counting the discouraged and marginally attached workers discussed in Chapter 23). By 2010, college graduates fortunate enough to find a job were, on average, earning 17.5 percent less than their counterparts before the crisis—and experts were predicting that such a decline in earnings would persist for more than a decade.

The crisis also spread beyond U.S. borders. As consumption and income declined in the United States, many countries experienced a significant reduction in exports as well as a decline in the investments that they held in the United States. As a result, global GDP declined by 2 percent in 2009. It has been estimated that between 50 million and 100 million people around the world either fell into, or were prevented from escaping, extreme poverty due to the crisis. Why did this happen? Why were its effects so long-lasting? What lessons can be learned for the future? These are complicated questions to which this chapter provides some answers.

1. Prelude to a Crisis

In retrospect, perhaps it is not difficult to see that something "big" was going to happen. Economic conditions were unusual. The federal funds rate, and interest rates in general, were at historic lows. The extremely low mortgage rates were particularly important, because they motivated an unprecedented rush to buy real estate. Even people who ordinarily would have little hope of obtaining a mortgage got in on the action. As record numbers of consumers bought homes and investment properties, housing prices surged. Most people—realtors in particular—did not appear to think that house prices could ever go down again.

1.1 The Housing Bubble

The housing bubble was an archetypal bubble. Like others before it, this bubble began innocently enough, with an increase in demand for real estate. As we learned in Chapter 4, an increase in market demand tends to increase prices, and the housing market proved no exception. Unfortunately, the increase in home prices fed a speculative frenzy, and millions rushed to buy, believing that prices could only go in one direction—up! The buyers included not only would-be homeowners, but also speculators who were buying simply with an interest in "flipping" the property (reselling at a higher price). The naive view exhibited by so many is characteristic of earlier bubbles, during which the lessons of the past were ignored.

To obtain a sense of the magnitude of the housing bubble, consider that average real home prices—that is, adjusting for inflation—were only 2 percent higher in 1997 than a century

Figure 30.1 **Historical Housing Prices**

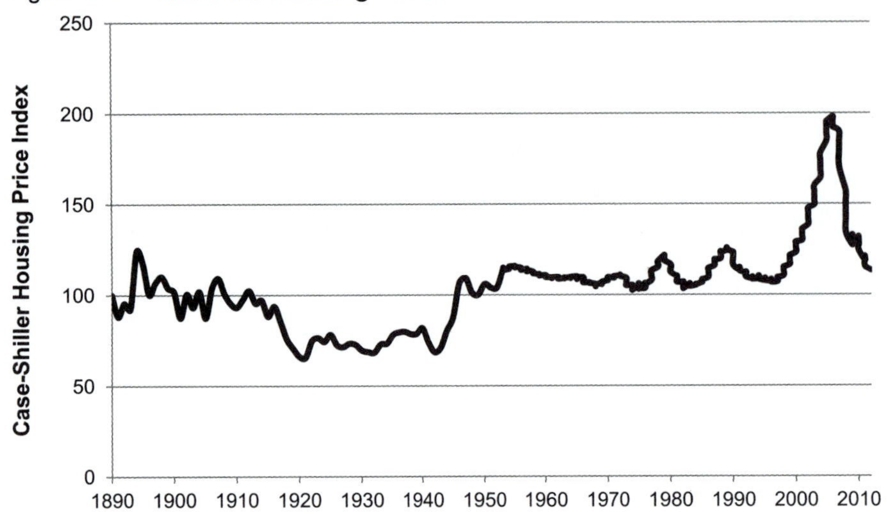

This graph shows the real (inflation-adjusted) cost of housing over the long term, with an index of 100 representing the average cost over the twentieth century. The graph shows fluctuation in real housing prices, with dips around 25 percent below average in the 1920s and '30s, upward spikes of only about 25 percent in later parts of the twentieth century, and then a spike that nearly doubled average house prices in the early years of the twenty-first century.

Source: Shiller dataset. www.econ.yale.edu/~shiller/data.htm.

earlier (Figure 30.1). But prices skyrocketed starting in the late 1990s, and by the time they peaked in 2006 the average price of a house was nearly *twice* the long-term average price in the previous century. And the subsequent collapse was such that a mere six years later, prices had reverted to their long-term trend.

What fed the speculative flurry that gave rise to such a massive bubble? In part, it was the bubble immediately preceding it—the "dot-com" bubble in technology stocks (discussed in Chapter 19). Even after a bubble bursts—and the dot-com bubble deflated from 2000 to 2003—there are winners as well as losers. Many beneficiaries of the dot-com bubble perceived themselves as considerably better off than a few years earlier and spent their newfound wealth on, among other things, bigger and more expensive houses. Demand for houses persisted, and even grew, despite continually increasing prices that, perversely, only confirmed expectations of continually rising prices. The result was an upward spiral of self-fulfilling speculative price hikes.

Another major factor was the unprecedented access to credit in the form of mortgages. During the mid-1990s, U.S. households borrowed an annual average of approximately $200 billion in the form of mortgages for home purchases. The figure rose abruptly to $500 billion for the period 1998–2002 and to $1 trillion from 2003 to 2006. While widespread access to credit is arguably critical for a vibrant economy, an exceedingly rapid increase in borrowing has, throughout history, been among the most consistent determinants of financial crises. By inflating bubbles, credit booms have invariably led to financial busts.

The key Federal Reserve interest rates—particularly the federal funds rate—are decisive in regulating credit availability. We saw in Chapter 27 how the Fed uses monetary policy to control interest rates; the critical point to remember in this context is that changes in the Fed's key rates percolate through the economy, because banks that can borrow at lower rates will also lend at lower rates and vice-versa. The 2001 recession that followed the collapse of the dot-com bubble prompted the Fed, led by Chairman Alan Greenspan, to lower the target federal funds rate from 6 percent to 1.75 percent. The Fed kept the rate low and in the summer of 2003 lowered it still further—to 1 percent, its lowest level in 50 years. The low federal funds rate in turn led to rate reductions across the board, including the rates for loans and home mortgages. These reductions fueled the borrowing binge that caused real estate prices to spiral upward (Figure 30.2).

Mortgage rates hit a 50-year low of just over 5 percent in 2003, and borrowing to finance home purchases consequently skyrocketed. There was also a second, less well understood, channel

Figure 30.2 **Housing Bubble and Credit Access**

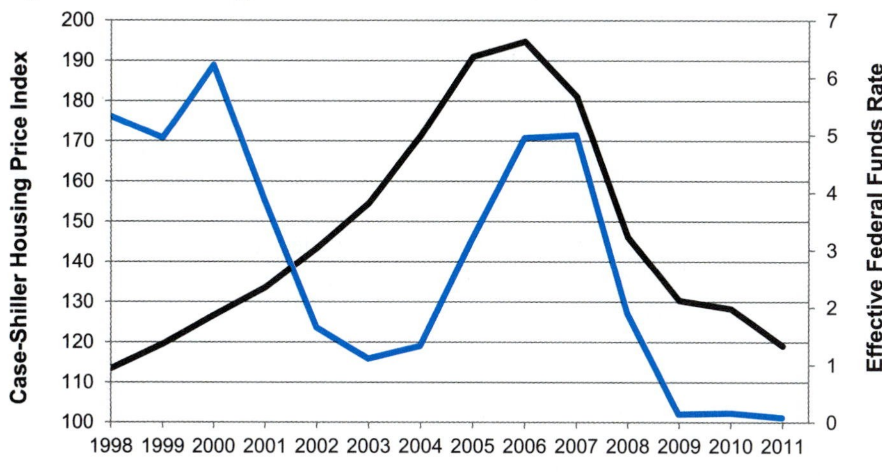

The effective federal funds rate, shown on the right hand vertical axis, plummeted from 2000 until 2004. Although it then began to move back up, the momentum of the housing bubble continued until a softening in housing prices began to be apparent in 2006.

Sources: Federal Reserve (www.newyorkfed.org/markets/statistics/dlyrates/fedrate.html/ and www.federalreserve.gov/releases/h15/data.html); Shiller dataset, www.econ.yale.edu/~shiller/data/ie_data.xls.

through which low rates contributed to the housing bubble. To understand it, you must keep in mind that while low interest rates are attractive to borrowers, they are decidedly unattractive to lenders. Here we are speaking not so much of the commercial banks that are extending mortgages to their customers—because the rate they charge, however low, is always considerably higher than the rate that they must pay to depositors—as of other financial institutions (such as investment banks) or high-net-worth individuals who are seeking higher returns on their money. With the repeal of the Glass-Steagall Act provision separating commercial and investment banking, many more financial players were now able to participate in the mortgage market.

In this period, U.S. Treasury bonds of all types were paying very low rates, and stocks were still not performing well on account of the bursting of the dot-com bubble. Financial investors who had grown accustomed to the much higher returns on their money that were available in previous decades were struggling to find more profitable ways to invest their money. Meanwhile, a rapidly growing number of prospective homebuyers were seeking mortgages at favorable rates. Traditionally, home mortgages involved only the borrower, on one side, and the bank that provided the funds, on the other. But this was to change, as investment banks now saw a unique opportunity to meet both investor and homebuyer interests with a single financial product: a mortgage-backed security (MBS).

mortgage-backed security (MBS): a security composed of a bundle of many home mortgages issued by independent banks

A **mortgage-backed security** is a bundle of independently issued home mortgages that an investor may buy in order to obtain a share of the mortgage interest payments; you could think of it as something like a mutual fund, but containing mortgages instead of stocks or government bonds. The investor also takes on the default risk from the individual mortgages that make up the MBS—that is, the risk that the homebuyers might not be able to make their mortgage payments. This risk varies from case to case, and here is where matters become a bit more complex.

Each MBS is divided into tiers or tranches, with the "senior" tranche the first to be paid in the event of mortgage defaults (hence, the safest). The "lowest tranche" is the riskiest but is correspondingly paid a higher return. Essentially, MBSs are a kind of derivative, constructed by mathematically proficient analysts who are paid to calculate the appropriate risk-return balance for each of the individual tranches.*

*As noted in Chapter 22, derivatives are a financial instrument whose value is "derived" from the value of another, underlying asset. In this case the underlying asset is the original home mortgage.

Following the advent of MBSs in the 1990s, banks increasingly acted as intermediaries that made housing loans and then bundled the mortgages together to be sold for a fee to investors. In the early 2000s, MBSs offered more attractive rates of return to investors than many types of bonds, both because of the Fed's continued low interest rates and the fact that mortgages generally pay higher interest rates than most other types of loans. Private investment banks were selling large quantities of MBSs, and the share of residential mortgages that were bundled into MBSs grew from 50 percent in 1995 to more than 80 percent by 2008.

collateralized debt obligation: an investment product that packages together numerous assets including mortgage-backed securities

But financial institutions then went even further. They developed another type of security known as a **collateralized debt obligation** (CDO), which is an even more complex investment product. It packages together a variety of loans, including, especially, MBSs—thus making it a "bundle of bundles" of mortgages. As in the case of MBSs, a hierarchy of tranches is available, each carrying a calculated risk-return balance. The complexity of the bundling that was involved meant that even the analysts entrusted with the construction of CDOs did not always fully understand them, and certainly the investors who bought them, and many of the financial executives who approved their use, had little idea of the risks involved.

credit default swap: a security that is effectively an insurance policy against defaults related to MBSs and CDOs

After packaging mortgages into MBSs, and MBSs into CDOs, investment banks also sought to insure the most senior tranches of each of them against default risk. Companies such as American International Group (AIG) sold what are known as **credit default swaps** (CDSs), which are a form of insurance policy against defaults related to MBSs or CDOs. In such an arrangement, the buyer of the CDS (usually an investment bank) pays a fee to the seller (an insurance company), which agrees to cover losses in case of a default.

During the early 2000s, it became an increasingly common practice to sell CDSs to insure the top tranches of MBSs and CDOs. Anyone can enter the market to buy a CDS; when one buys the CDS without owning the debt or mortgage that it insures, it is known as a "naked" CDS. Critics have argued that naked CDSs should be banned—likening them to buying fire insurance on your neighbor's home—because the owner of the CDS in this case would gain if the investment defaults on its payments. The European Parliament indeed saw it this way when, in 2011, it banned naked CDSs on European government debt.

To feed the escalating demand for higher returns, investment banks started offering MBSs and CDOs, with the risk to be insured by CDSs. Yet in order to satisfy demand for the new products, it was important to maintain a large nationwide pool of home mortgages. And here a problem emerged. Despite the historically low interest rates and unprecedented access to credit, it seemed that new loans could not be issued quickly enough to fulfill investor demand for the new bundled securities. In order to persuade even more people to become homeowners, banks needed not only to continue offering low rates but also to relax some of their lending criteria. This was to be a critical factor in the subprime crisis.

1.2 THE SUBPRIME CRISIS

Although unbridled optimism about home prices and cheap credit contributed their fair share to the housing bubble, the expansion and deflation of the bubble could not have been so dramatic or damaging in the absence of an extraordinary buildup of risky lending. A new kind of loan, the **subprime mortgage**, became common.

subprime mortgage: a mortgage given to someone with poor credit

Banks typically classify subprime borrowers as individuals who may have difficulty repaying the loan due to a high level of debt, relatively low income, or a poor credit record. Historically, banks have either turned down the subprime borrower or charged him/her a higher interest rate to compensate for the increased lending risk.

During the housing bubble, both restrictions were relaxed: The criteria for mortgage eligibility were loosened, and the interest rate charged to subprime borrowers was lowered. The number of subprime mortgages soared. In 2002, less than 10 percent of U.S. mortgages were subprime; a mere three years later, approximately 25 percent were. While the housing bubble was inflating, many commentators exulted that homeownership was becoming a reality for many for whom it had previously been only a dream. The argument lost credibility several years later, however, when the housing bubble burst. Subprime credit evaporated, and countless borrowers, unable to keep up with their mortgage payments, faced foreclosure.

Evidence supports the claim that the explosion of subprime lending intensified both the rise and the fall of the entire housing bubble. As noted above, mortgage borrowing doubled from an annual average of $500 billion from 1998 to 2002 to $1 trillion in the 2003–6 period. The rapid increase can be attributed largely to the proliferation of subprime lending. When housing prices finally started turning downward in 2006, continuing mortgage payments became especially difficult for subprime borrowers. The resulting wave of subprime foreclosures hastened the downward spiral of prices, because they created a glut in housing supply. Meanwhile, a widespread tightening of credit led to a drop in demand. An increase in supply coupled with a drop in demand is a recipe for lower prices, and that is precisely what was observed after the bubble burst.

Discussion Questions

1. People often refer to the housing "bubble" and even the housing "crisis." Is an increase in the average price of homes not a good thing? What if prices are rising more rapidly than in the past? Explain.
2. Would you prefer interest rates in the economy to be high or low? On what does it depend? Who benefitted from low interest rates during the inflation of the housing bubble? How did the low interest rates create problems?

2. ECONOMIC IMPACTS OF THE CRISIS

In Chapters 22 and 26, we discussed the relationship between the financial and the "real" economies. The financial crisis clearly demonstrated the importance of this relationship. The disappearance of immense financial wealth in the immediate aftermath of the crisis spilled over into the real economy. As people had less wealth, they were apt to spend less. (This is what we identified as the "wealth effect" in Chapter 28.) Even those who preferred to continue spending often found that banks were suddenly much more reluctant to lend them money. Less spending resulted in sharply lower output and a weaker labor market, as our circular flow analysis suggests. (As noted in Chapter 28, Keynesian economists argue that, were it not for an active government policy and the existing social safety net, things could have been much worse.)

2.1 UNEMPLOYMENT AND THE VICIOUS RECESSIONARY SPIRAL

As a consequence of the crisis, the U.S. economy lost nearly 9 million jobs from 2007 to 2009. Over a particular eight-month period spanning 2008 and 2009, the *average* U.S. household lost nearly $100,000 from its property and retirement portfolio values combined. Approximately 11 million homebuyers faced foreclosure from 2008 to mid-2012, accounting for about one of every four mortgages in the United States. Tens of millions were made poorer, if not "officially" poor. Clearly, the massive loss of speculative financial wealth on Wall Street (much of it related to depressed MBS and CDO values) translated to a comparable loss of *real* wealth on "Main Street." The financial crisis had turned into a broad-based economic crisis.

Although many families experienced hardship, certain groups were affected disproportionately. Young people, for example, suffered a heavy impact from the unemployment crisis. Each year brought a new wave of recent graduates into the workforce, adding to the masses of young people already facing dismal job prospects. Certain industries, such as construction and manufacturing, were hit particularly hard. Construction unemployment rates nearly tripled from 2007 to 2010, while manufacturing unemployment jumped from 4.3 percent in 2007 to 12.1 percent in 2009.

The economic impact of the financial crisis persisted for an unusually long period. The unemployment rate remained above 7 percent through late 2013 (see Box 30.1). Why was this? As we saw in earlier chapters, the circular flow economy can, in difficult times, produce a vicious cycle. Unemployed workers generally have less income to spend. Families facing income losses and needing financial assistance can ordinarily borrow money—but after the financial crisis of 2007–8, banks and financial institutions introduced tougher standards for credit card loans and **home equity loans,** in which an equity stake in a home is posted as collateral. This led to a "credit crunch" in which families and business were unable to obtain loans.

home equity loan: a loan that permits a borrower to offer his or her home (or their equity stake in it) as collateral in case of failure to repay the loan

Many families were therefore compelled to cut their spending further; in the period from 2008 to 2011, U.S. consumers on average reported spending $175 per month less than they would have in the absence of a recession. Many employers, suddenly facing lower profits, fired workers, contributing to a vicious unemployment cycle. While the values of MBSs and other newfangled securities seemed to plunge overnight, it took longer for the ensuing credit contraction to affect business bottom lines, employment decisions, and consumer spending. Thus the crisis that began in 2007 led to a recession and very slow recovery that lasted more than five years.

BOX 30.1 THE COSTS OF LONG-TERM UNEMPLOYMENT

The long-term unemployment that followed the Great Recession was unprecedented since the 1930s, and has exacted a huge human and economic cost.

> Long-term unemployment is experienced disproportionately by the young, the old, the less educated, and African-American and Latino workers. While older workers are less likely to be laid off than younger workers, they are about half as likely to be rehired. [As a result] the number of unemployed people between ages 50 and 65 has more than doubled.
>
> The result is nothing short of a national emergency. Millions of workers have been disconnected from the work force, and possibly even from society. If they are not reconnected, the costs to them and to society will be grim. (Baker and Hassett, 2012)

Research indicates a 50 to 100 percent increase in death rates for older male workers in the years following a job loss. One reason for this higher mortality is suicide. The longer the period of unemployment, the higher the risk of suicide. Joblessness is also linked to higher rates of serious disease and higher probability of divorce. Effects last into the next generation; children whose fathers lose a job have lower annual earning as adults than those whose fathers do not experience unemployment.

In the aftermath of the Great Recession, a slow recovery has seen lower job gains for men than women. By 2013, women's total private sector employment was slightly higher than before the recession, but jobs for men still lagged 3 percentage points below their previous levels.

Work-sharing programs that encourage companies to cut hours rather than payrolls, as well as retraining and re-employment programs, could help to mitigate the cost of long-term unemployment. Unfortunately, many state governments have taken the opposite approach, cutting aid to the unemployed. In 2013 North Carolina, with one of the highest jobless rates in the nation, cut both the duration and amount of unemployment benefits. According to economist Paul Krugman, this is "counterproductive as well as cruel—it will lead to lower spending, worsening the economic situation, and destroying more jobs."

Sources: Dean Baker and Kevin Hassett, "The Human Disaster of Unemployment," *New York Times*, May 13, 2012; Floyd Norris, "Gender Gaps Appear as Employment Recovers from the Recession," *New York Times*, July 13, 2013; Paul Krugman, "War on the Unemployed," *New York Times*, June 20, 2013.

Modern economies are, in a certain sense, more vulnerable to events in finance than they were in the past. Due in large part to the proliferation of mutual funds and their increased availability in employee retirement accounts, a higher percentage of the population than ever before have a financial stake in the stock and bond markets.

Today, even if financial instability is mostly speculative in nature and does not have a direct economic cause, it produces very real economic effects because consumers who feel poorer spend less money, potentially triggering a downturn characterized by reduced economic output and high unemployment. As we saw in Chapter 28, a leftward shift in the *AD* curve during the financial crisis decreased GDP and produced widespread fears of deflation.

Income and wealth inequality, already severe before the crisis, only intensified after it. While the wealthiest members of society lost the most in dollar terms (although much of it was recovered by 2010), the lower and middle classes, on average, lost a far greater share of their existing wealth. From mid-2007 to early 2009, U.S. families lost $10.9 trillion in financial investments related to stocks and bonds, amounting to an average loss of nearly $100,000 per household. More than half of U.S. households held retirement accounts whose value plummeted during the crisis, wrecking the retirement plans of millions of middle-class families. From 2007 through 2010, the median household lost nearly 40 percent of owned wealth, effectively undoing 18 years of wealth accumulation. And the poorest 25 percent suffered the most; their average household net worth fell to zero.

2.2 The Great Depression and the Great Recession Compared

Calling the period after the financial crisis the "Great Recession" invites comparison with the other "great" economic downturn of the past century, the Great Depression. What makes the Great Recession different from previous recessions is the duration of the downturn. During most of the twentieth century, after about 1940, a recession was an almost predictable business cycle downturn followed, after a few quarters, by a solid economic recovery. Although the NBER declared the latest recession "officially" over by 2009, the slow pace of recovery in the job market, continued foreclosures, and a continued sense of despondency among the general public made many feel that the "recession" continued much longer. Even after 2009, most of the damaging effects of recession lingered, especially for the long-term unemployed and for new entrants into the labor market.*

Are the current downturn and the Great Depression comparable? Followers of historical trends point out that both downturns were preceded by a period of apparent economic strength. Those who remember the dot-com bubble that preceded the one in housing may not know that Americans experienced a similar asset bubble during the 1920s. Many banks were starting to diversify their services, moving into real estate and other relatively risky investments, potentially contributing to the bubble. Not unlike the more recent period, in the 1920s people were feeling optimistic and were therefore spending, many immoderately, driving prices up. Average annual economic growth during the 1920s is estimated to have been more than 4 percent, so things were looking good. Yet, as also occurred before the current downturn, the rapidly inflating asset bubble in the 1920s, most manifest in the main stock indexes like the Dow Jones Industrials (not in housing), inevitably collapsed.

In terms of possible factors that caused each economic downturn, the two episodes may have been more similar than different. But in terms of economic consequences, the differences are noteworthy, and the principal reason relates to government regulation, automatic stabilizers, and discretionary fiscal and monetary policy. For example, thousands of banks failed in the early years of the Great Depression, causing millions of depositors to lose their savings. In contrast, there was not a single such case in the aftermath of the recent crisis. Some banks

*Remember from Chapter 24 that a recession technically ends as soon as GDP stops falling and starts rising again, but that unemployment may continue to rise for some time after this.

did fail (though far fewer than in the 1930s), but depositors' accounts were protected by the Federal Deposit Insurance Corporation (FDIC). In response to the crisis, the insurance limit for deposits was raised from $100,000 to $250,000, helping to prevent any depositor panic.

The existence of a government-financed "social safety net" also made a major difference. Not only was the unemployment rate at the nadir of the financial crisis much lower than during the depths of the Great Depression (10 percent compared to 25 percent), but the unemployed were eligible for "extended benefits" of up to 99 weeks during the worst period of the recession (reduced to 73 weeks in 2012). There was no unemployment insurance during the Great Depression, nor did food stamps exist.

Such benefits enabled many of those involuntarily jobless to function during the worst part of the recent downturn, keeping consumption levels, and the broader economy, more or less stable despite the slow job recovery. The absence of such basic government support during the 1930s consigned millions to misery and prolonged the depression. In addition to the existence of automatic stabilizers, such as unemployment and food stamps, aggressive expansionary fiscal and monetary policies were put in place by the federal government and the Fed, starting in late 2008 (discussed in detail below).

Broad statistics support the conclusion that, for all the difficulties caused by the Great Recession, they were significantly less than those during the Great Depression. The U.S. economy, for example, moved into its recovery phase a mere year and a half after the financial collapse; during the Great Depression it took almost four years. Because of the social safety net that is in place now, consumption remained relatively stable, and deflation was averted (average prices actually rose nearly 2 percent from 2007 to 2009). In contrast, during the early years of the Great Depression, prices declined by more than 25 percent. And while the Dow Jones Industrials average lost slightly more than half its peak value in late 2008, it lost nearly 90 percent of its value after the market collapsed in 1929.

The principal difference, then, between the two periods is the existence of a social safety net, government regulations to protect ordinary Americans, and activist macroeconomic policy. It is no coincidence that programs such as Social Security, food stamps, and unemployment insurance were introduced in the 1930s under the administration of Franklin D. Roosevelt. For all the anxiety over deregulation and the reduction in the social safety net over the past three decades, the financial crisis laid bare the importance of a government presence in the economy. Government programs, first instituted in the 1930s, kept the current downturn from becoming far worse.

Discussion Questions

1. Do you think changes in the value of "paper assets" like stocks and bonds, or even of homes, should have real economic effects? Why? Why do you think that employment suffered from the disappearance of so much financial wealth following the financial crisis?
2. Do you think that the Great Recession is nearly as bad as the Great Depression was? In what ways is it similar to it? In what ways was it different? Do you know any stories of family members who lived through the Great Depression?

3. UNDERLYING CAUSES OF THE FINANCIAL CRISIS

Many factors were behind the Great Recession. We have reviewed the fact that many unqualified borrowers were permitted—often actively encouraged—to buy homes that they could not afford. Other factors include the determination of large banks and the "titans" of finance to maintain high returns for their loans and investments, in the process downplaying that risks were often, in the end, borne by others. Their ability to do so was greatly increased by a trend towards deregulation of industries, including finance. Economic globalization also provided fuel for the crisis, and allowed it to spread more rapidly. These factors combined to produce other effects on the character of the macroeconomy. These other effects range from growing inequality among the U.S. population, to the structure and functioning of large economic institutions, to global trends and issues.

3.1 Inequality

In the three decades before the 2007 crisis, the income gap between rich and poor members of the U.S. population widened to levels not seen since the 1920s. During the last two decades of the twentieth century, rising income inequality was mostly due not to real income declines for the poor and middle classes but to relative gains for the wealthy. The low and middle-income groups were gaining in absolute terms; the problem was merely to keep pace with the rich. But starting around 1999, things changed. The median U.S. household income began a real decline, signifying that the low and middle classes were now losing in absolute terms as well. The majority of U.S. families now faced difficulty even maintaining their customary level of consumption.

Policymakers could address the growing disconnect between rising consumption expectations by the low- and middle-income groups and their decreasing real incomes in three ways. The first was the "laissez-faire" option of doing nothing and hoping that market forces would, over time, diminish income inequality. The second option was to alter the tax and spending mix in a way that some income could be either directly or indirectly channeled toward the relatively poor. The third option was to encourage credit expansion and set lower interest rate targets, in the hope that families who did not otherwise possess sufficient income to meet their spending needs might borrow to make up the difference. In practice, policymakers rejected the second option of redistributing income in favor of a combination of the first and third options: do nothing about growing inequality, but facilitate greater borrowing on the part of middle-class and low-income families.

Countless U.S. families—subprime or otherwise—exploited the opportunity to take out home equity loans on generous terms. The trend had broad bipartisan support; indeed, many policymakers greeted it with optimism rather than skepticism. It seemed to be a clever way of addressing the economy's need for sustained consumer spending while avoiding the thornier issue of inequality or unpopular government action.

In the years preceding the crisis, the approach appeared to bear fruit. Consumption continued to increase despite declining incomes. Expectation of continued appreciation in their home's value doubtless encouraged families to spend more money than they had. But the numbers contained what should have been a warning. In 1980, for example, U.S. households held an average debt level equal to about 60 percent of disposable income; in 2007 this figure exceeded 130 percent. As a result, there was a sharp increase in the number of families who found themselves unable to continue paying their mortgages. For the many thousands whose home values dropped in the subsequent collapse, it often became more economically practical to default and face foreclosure than to continue to pay, because the monthly payments would continue to reflect the original, and often much higher, value of the home.

Lower interest rates during these years undoubtedly fueled the credit expansion. But household indebtedness might have ballooned even without such stimulus. A widespread perception of falling living standards, largely a consequence of income inequality, was probably sufficient to provoke a rapid increase in demand for loans.

3.2 Bank Size and Deregulation

Many believe that the immense size of some of the leading U.S. banks was one of the causes of the financial crisis. There is little question that banks have gotten much bigger and that banking sector assets have become more concentrated. Since around 1980, the steadily increasing frequency of bank mergers has led to a growing number of large banks. From 1984 to 2007, the number of banks with more than $10 billion in assets increased fivefold, from 24 to 119, and the share of banking sector assets held by large banks increased from 28 to more than 75 percent (Figure 30.3). The consolidation continues to this day. In 2012, the 19 largest banks held more than 60 percent of the assets of the sector, and the six largest of them held assets equal to two-thirds of U.S. GDP.

Figure 30.3 **Increasing Bank Size**

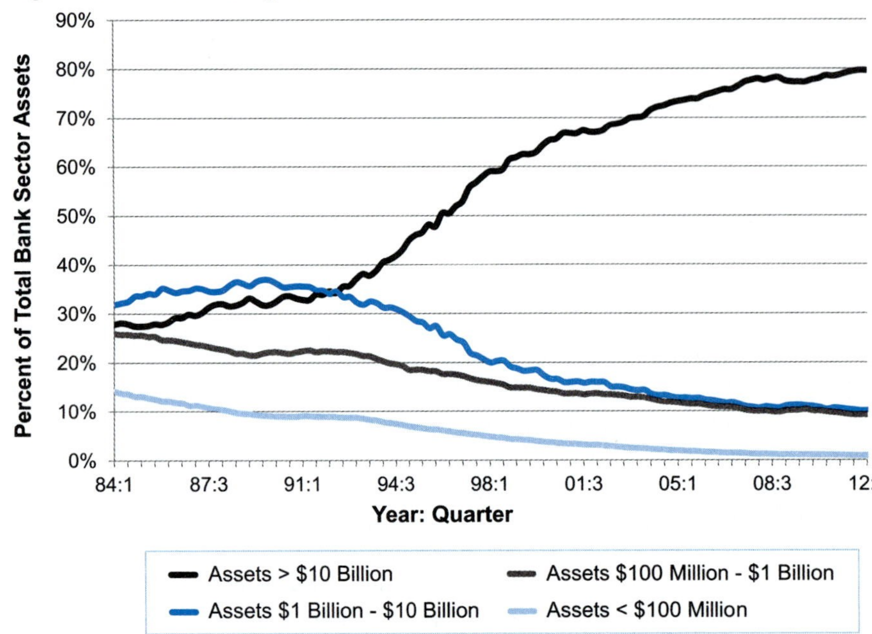

This graph shows the proportion of bank assets held by banks of different sizes. Over a 16-year period, while medium-sized banks gradually declined in proportion of assets held, smaller banks lost ground even faster. The proportion of banks in the largest size category rose from below 30 percent to nearly 80 percent.

Source: Federal Deposit Insurance Corporation (www2.fdic.gov/qbp/); www.fdic.gov/bank/statistical/stats/2012dec/industry.html.

Both geographic and sectoral factors contributed to the consolidation. Before the 1980s, most states had strict regulations forbidding out-of-state banks from owning subsidiary banks within their borders. The point was to impede excessive bank growth. But, beginning in 1980, with the Reagan administration's promotion of a deregulatory agenda, this began to change. More states allowed their banks to merge with banks from outside the state. In 1994, Congress passed the Riegle-Neal Banking and Branching Efficiency Act, which effectively sanctioned and strengthened the deregulatory trend already in motion for more than a decade.

Another important factor was the sectoral changes that banking deregulation permitted. Ever since the Great Depression, customer bank accounts had been protected by the Glass-Steagall Act (see Chapter 26), which separated commercial and investment banking activities, essentially preventing commercial banks from engaging in risky investments and investment banks from holding deposits. The separation between the two was gradually eroded through the 1980s and 1990s, with the Fed becoming increasingly lenient about which activities were permitted for commercial banks. In 1999 the Financial Services Modernization Act (FSMA) effectively overturned Glass-Steagall, allowing large financial companies to engage in commercial and investment banking as well as insurance. This act, perhaps more than any other piece of legislation, contributed to the increase in the number of "megabanks," notable among them being Citigroup, the largest financial company in the world.

Among other important deregulatory policies were the gradual loosening of restrictions on capital across borders, a congressional ban on the regulation of credit default swaps, an agreement to allow banks to measure the riskiness of their own products, and increases in the amount of leverage permitted to investment banks. Allowing banks greater leverage meant that they could borrow huge sums at low rates of interest and invest the borrowed funds in the shaky bond products discussed earlier. Deregulation thus magnified the ultimate effects of the crisis.

At the time many argued that the financial deregulation trend augured well, claiming that large banks are less prone to risk than small ones and therefore have less of a destabilizing effect on the economy. A large bank would, for instance, lend to borrowers who are more geographically dispersed, thereby making it less vulnerable to locally concentrated defaults. Also, according to this argument, a large bank faces less risk because it possesses a greater diversity of income sources (e.g., stocks and real estate, in addition to loans) than a traditional small bank. Supporters also made so-called **economies of scale** arguments, stating that a larger size would allow a bank to operate more efficiently by allowing it to cut costs in many areas. On the other side were those who argued that, insofar as such claims were true, it meant that only large banks were free to take on offsetting degrees of high risk elsewhere by, for example, leveraging highly in order to invest vast sums in potentially risky assets. Empirical studies have generally supported the latter claim. In 2013, megabank JPMorgan Chase agreed to pay a $13 billion settlement resulting from the bank's questionable mortgage practices leading up to the financial crisis.

economies of scale: benefits that occur when the long run average cost of production falls as the size of the enterprise increases

The principal argument against excessively large banks is related to what is known as "too big to fail." **"Too big to fail"** does not mean that it is impossible for a large bank to fail; as the financial crisis made painfully obvious, it is all too possible. What it means is that it is possible for an enterprise to grow to such a size that its subsequent failure would harm not only the shareholders but also the public at large.

"too big to fail": when a company grows so large that its failure would cause widespread economic harm in terms of lost jobs and diminished asset values

Large banks count many other large companies among their creditors, so the failure and eventual bankruptcy of any one of them could cause a "domino effect," in which the inability of one bank to pay other creditors could jeopardize the financial standing of others, with potentially catastrophic spillover effects. It was such a fear that prompted federal regulators to "bail out" large financial companies like Citigroup, Bank of America, and AIG (via grants, loans, or assisted mergers). Although many people did not like the idea of the U.S. government's granting so much assistance to failed banks—which had failed due mostly to recklessness, not poor fortune—it was generally agreed that the alternative—a potential economic collapse—was much worse.

Despite agreeing with the decision, many banking industry critics point out that we would not have faced the problem in the first place if banks had not been permitted to grow "too big." They argue that after banks (or companies in any sector of our economy) become aware that they are "too big," they have an incentive to take on greater risks, anticipating that they will lose very little regardless of the outcome of their ventures. If the ventures fail to pay off, the large banks would be first in line for government assistance in the form of a bailout. The creation of such perverse incentives is what economists refer to as **moral hazard**.

moral hazard: the creation of perverse incentives that encourage excessive risk taking because of protections against losses from that risk

The moral hazard created by "too big to fail" in effect divorced the public's interests from those of the banks, creating a situation in which the pensions or portfolios owned by many millions of households suffered large losses while major banks were bailed out. In 2008, Congress passed the Troubled Asset Relief Program (TARP), which authorized the U.S. Treasury to spend as much as $700 billion in loans, stock purchases, and asset buyouts for insolvent banks, in addition to earlier loans provided by the Fed. This served mostly to assist the "too big" banks; for example, the Treasury spent $220 billion to purchase stock from the 19 largest financial companies but only $41 billion for all other banks.

In its defense, the Treasury pointed out in 2012 that not only had 94 percent of its TARP investments been repaid but that the value of those investments had increased by $19 billion. Nevertheless, taxpayer money had been used to shoulder $700 billion worth of risk. Although the TARP investments turned out favorably this time, the fact that it was even needed vividly illustrates the dangers of a banking sector that is "too big to fail."

3.3 MISGUIDED CORPORATE INCENTIVE STRUCTURE

Although the existence of "megabanks" encouraged financial risk taking, bank managers were facing a changing payment structure that would similarly distort their incentives. Before the 1990s, compensation for bank chief executive officers (CEOs) was mostly unrelated to company fortunes. That is, they were generally paid a salary that would grow at a rate comparable to that of many other employees. If the company performed especially poorly, the CEO might lose his/her job, but otherwise the CEO's salary remained unaffected by company performance.

More recent views, including those taught in business schools, increasingly supported the idea that executive compensation packages should include performance incentives. CEO pay started to come more in the form of stock options, and bonuses were more frequently tied to the company stock value. The rationale for the changes was that they would give CEOs a greater incentive to take steps that would ensure a good return for the company shareholders. Many believed that rapid growth in the stock value would be a reflection of the CEO's ability and understanding of risk.

The new pay structure, however, generated unexpected problems. If CEOs were to be evaluated primarily on the basis of company stock price, they would be motivated to focus on short-term gains in this area, ignoring long-term risks. They would be compensated handsomely—in terms of both the number of stock options and bonus size—if the stock price went up, even if the increase was not sustainable. The CEO might well have left the company before the long-run damage became evident. In the case of the housing bubble, any self-interested CEO could have profited even if he suspected that the rapid increase in home prices could not last. The new pay structure created an incentive for gambling on risky mortgages. It became apparent only later that such an incentive-based pay structure was another example of moral hazard (see Box 30.2).

From 2000 to 2007, the period during which the housing bubble was inflating, Lehman Brothers (which was to be the sole "megabank" to be allowed to fail during the crisis) and Bear Stearns (which also went out of business but was taken over by Bank of America

BOX 30.2 CEO PAY AND TAX LOOPHOLES

According to a 2012 report by the Institute for Policy Studies (IPS), various current tax provisions encourage excessive CEO pay. According to the report:

> The four most direct tax subsidies for excessive executive pay cost taxpayers an estimated $14.4 billion per year—$46 for every American man, woman, and child. That amount could also cover the annual cost of hiring 211,732 elementary-school teachers, or provide Pell Grants of $5,500 to 2,591,021 college students.

The largest of these tax provisions relates to a company's ability to claim a tax deduction for executive pay. A 1993 law limits this deduction to $1 million annually for direct compensation, but there are no deductibility limits placed on "performance-based" pay in the form of stock options. In 2011 Larry Ellison, the CEO of Oracle, received more than $76 million in performance-based pay, and the company did not have to pay any federal taxes on this amount.

Representative Barbara Lee, Democrat of California, has introduced legislation, the Income Equity Act (HR 382), that would limit a company's ability to deduct CEO pay to 25 times the salary of the company's lowest-paid worker. Her bill would not limit the amount that a company could pay its CEO, just the amount that would be tax deductible. The bill "would encourage corporations to raise pay at the bottom of the corporate pay ladder. The greater the pay for a company's lowest-paid worker, the higher the tax-deductible pay for the company's highest-paid executives."

Source: Sarah Anderson, Chuck Collins, Scott Klinger, and Sam Pizzigati, "The CEO Hands in Uncle Sam's Pocket, Executive Excess 2012, 19th Annual Executive Pay Survey," IPS, August 16, 2012.

under pressure from the Fed, thereby technically avoiding bankruptcy) paid their CEOs $61 million and $87 million respectively in bonuses, with both citing unprecedented increases in their stock price as justification. These CEOs also earned $461 million and $289 million respectively from exercising their stock options during this time. During this period, the companies were engaging in the unsustainable borrowing that would lead to their collapse. By the time the game was up in 2007, and the share prices plummeted, the CEOs had already become immensely wealthy and were under no obligation to return the funds.

It may not be self-evident *why* shareholders would allow for such a skewed incentive structure if it actually threatened their share values. Could it be that the inherent moral hazard in such a pay structure did not occur to anyone? It is highly unlikely. The fact is that shareholders in major companies do not actually possess much influence over CEOs. The boards of directors of companies have historically acted, in theory at least, on behalf of shareholders. And one "action" is determining CEO compensation.

In practice, and especially in recent years, company boards tend to be more aligned with CEO interests than with those of the shareholders whom they are presumed to represent. In some companies, CEOs hold sway over board members' compensation and re-election prospects, generating an incentive for "mutual favors." Moreover, many bank CEOs sit on the boards of other banks, providing ample opportunity for board members to cater to CEO interests, and vice versa. Therefore it should be no surprise that some CEOs were allowed to profit greatly from short-term growth, to the cost of not only shareholders but also the population at large.

3.4 Globalization and Long-Term Economic Trends

Events originating outside the United States also contributed to the financial crisis. First, the progressive globalization of labor markets took its toll on U.S. workers. Beginning around the late 1960s, the United States started to rely more on foreign countries (e.g., China and Mexico) for production of consumer goods, because these countries, which pay a far lower average wage, could produce them at a lower price. We noted in Chapter 22 that the U.S. manufacturing sector has been in decline from about this time, and in Chapter 23 that real wages in the United States have failed to keep up with gains in productivity since the 1970s. This trend was facilitated by a gradual weakening of labor unions. In the mid-1960s, about one-third of all employees were in a labor union; today only about 12 percent of public sector workers are, and 7 percent in the private sector.

While globalization also brought significant advantages to the United States (as noted in Chapters 28 and 29), the distribution of the gains and losses tended to reinforce the growing pattern of inequality discussed above. This put pressure on struggling middle-class and low-income families to take on more debt. As we have outlined, easy credit access made going into debt a seemingly attractive option, and as long as house prices were rising, the illusion of increasing wealth encouraged taking on large mortgages. Household debt outstanding, mostly mortgage or credit card debt, rose to 98 percent of GDP by 2007. This allowed American families to live beyond their means, until the 2008 crisis forced massive retrenchment.

Another factor was the persistent U.S. current account deficits. Although the United States did not consistently import more than it exported until the mid-1980s, from then on the current account grew ever more unbalanced. The deficit increased from about 1 percent of GDP in 1990 to 6 percent in 2006, causing a massive inflow of foreign money that, as we saw in Chapter 29, is necessary to keep international financial flows "in balance." The flood of foreign money was invested in a variety of U.S. assets, intensifying the asset price inflation that was already occurring. Some of it was used to purchase Treasury bonds, but much of it financed borrowing by U.S. homeowners or was directly invested in stocks, MBSs, and CDOs.

One major consequence of the foreign savings inflow was that it reinforced the lowering of interest rates. Recalling the classical model of the loanable funds market first discussed in

Chapter 24, the inflow substantially increased supply (a rightward shift of the supply curve), thereby leading to a reduction in the interest rate. We have already seen that low interest rates can potentially induce an increase in the level of real domestic investment, which historically leads to healthy economic growth and domestic employment. But lower interest rates can also play a decisive role in inflating bubbles by fueling consumption and provoking excessive leveraging for purposes of financial speculation. In the case of the foreign inflows resulting from U.S. current account deficits, it is not possible to know whether they would have been sufficient, on their own, to produce a financial bubble in the United States, but we do know that they played an important role.

By the time the housing bubble was close to bursting, the financial sector had been deregulated to an extent not seen since before the Great Depression. Globalization only served to reinforce the inflation of the bubble. Movement of capital by investment banks and hedge funds across borders is only lightly regulated. So the problems discussed earlier, in which there was inadequate oversight of bank investments and loans—and of the management of risk—were magnified because there was no such oversight at all when it came to capital investments from overseas. Because foreign investors were parking their excess funds in the U.S. financial system (recall that they had these funds in no small part as a result of years of trade surpluses with the United States), investment banks and hedge funds possessed more capital with which to take on more risk and more debt (with historically low interest rates serving as another incentive), in order to multiply their returns.

How did finance come to play such an important role in the economy? One possible explanation is that the steady decline in U.S. manufacturing made it increasingly difficult to obtain an attractive return on investments in companies that were manufacturing real products. This downward trend may, at least in part, explain the proliferation of arcane financial products, as discussed earlier. Because expected returns in industry were relatively low, many financial investments seemed to promise attractive returns (if only in the short run). As we have seen, bubbles are inflated when investors desperate for high returns sink their money into assets with highly questionable foundations, causing their price to rise rapidly, which in turn draws in further investors.

Discussion Questions

1. Have you seen anything in the news in recent weeks about the regulation of banking and finance? Do you think, in general, that it is a good idea to allow banks and financial institutions to conduct their business with minimal government interference? Why or why not?
2. Did the financial crisis mostly have to do with banks? Homebuyers? International economics? What do you think is the most important factor that explains it?

4. REMEDIES AND IDEAS FOR AVERTING FUTURE CRISES

The financial crisis called for both short- and long-term responses. Many believe that it was critical, in the short term, to restore at least some semblance of stability to the financial system, lest it collapse and bring the broader economy down with it. This urgent need prompted the government to act, by bailing out the institutions deemed most systemically important to the health of the economy and by instituting a "stimulus" program of federal spending. The Fed joined in as well, actively purchasing not only Treasury bonds but also securities such as MBSs through its "quantitative easing" program (as discussed in Chapter 27).

After the worst had been averted, attention turned to the long-term question—how to prevent future financial crises. This is a more difficult issue. One possible solution is to reverse, at least partially, some of the financial deregulation that helped lead to the crisis. Many have supported calls for more regulation of the financial sector, and some reforms have been implemented, although there has been opposition both from some who think that they go too far and from others who believe that they do not go far enough.

4.1 FISCAL AND MONETARY RESPONSES

After the emergency measures taken to forestall a complete economic collapse in late 2008, there remained the task of stimulating the economy, especially with the goal of creating rapid job growth. To this end, Congress passed the American Recovery and Reinvestment Act (ARRA), an $831 billion government-spending bill. Whether the amount was big enough or too big remains an open question. But independent analysts estimate that ARRA created between 1.5 million and 7.9 million new jobs from 2009 to 2012. Nevertheless, employment growth remained lackluster through 2013, with the unemployment rate remaining above 7 percent.

Moreover, as we have seen, when the government ramps up spending without a corresponding tax increase, the result is a swelling deficit, increasing the overall national debt. Some critics contend that this policy will lead to even greater problems in the long term (we review the issue of deficits and debt in Chapter 31). But one indisputable consequence of the crisis, and the bill that followed, is that Keynesian economics once again became an important influence in U.S. policy-making.

While the federal government was rapidly boosting spending, many state and local governments were doing the precise opposite. The drop in household income resulting from mass layoffs and stagnant wages meant that state and local governments could collect less tax revenue, resulting in the sharpest drop in state tax revenue in U.S. history. State budget deficits ballooned, peaking at a total of $191 billion in 2010 and remaining high at $55 billion even for fiscal year 2013.

You may recall from Chapter 25 that while the federal deficit often seeks to stabilize the macroeconomy by pursuing countercyclical policy (i.e., deficit spending when times are bad, budget balance or surplus* when the economy recovers), states and municipalities—mostly because they are not empowered to create their own money—do the exact opposite. States did receive federal assistance as part of ARRA, but it covered only about 40 percent of their budget shortfalls from 2009 to 2011. To make up the rest, by 2012 46 states had cut spending on services while 30 states had increased taxes. Although fiscally prudent, both policies countervail economic recovery efforts, and some analysts estimate that these "anti-Keynesian" state policies have cost U.S. workers more than 4 million jobs from 2009 to 2012, undercutting the reported job gains from the federal stimulus program.

In the area of monetary policy, the Fed embarked on a stimulus plan that is unprecedented in nature. Immediately after the collapse of Lehman Brothers in 2008, the Fed purchased billions of dollars' worth of shaky assets, including mortgage-backed securities that had lost the majority of their value. The result was that the assets on its balance sheet jumped from about $950 billion in 2007 to more than $2.5 trillion in 2008.**

As discussed in Chapter 27, Fed purchases of securities effectively increase the money supply, because holding more reserves enables banks to offer more loans to the public. The principal difference between quantitative easing and open market operations is that while the latter involves the purchase of government Treasury bonds, the former means that the Fed is buying distressed assets. As of early 2013, the Fed's asset holdings approached $3 trillion, with a significant fraction uncharacteristically invested in assets of questionable value. In the fall of 2012, Fed chair Ben Bernanke announced the third round of quantitative easing (dubbed QE3), through which the Fed committed to purchasing $40 billion in MBSs per month.

These expansionary monetary policies had a major effect in promoting economic recovery, including in the housing market (see Box 30.3). But employing monetary policy to stimulate the economy has limitations; as noted earlier, one could flood the economy with money, but if consumers and businesses remain pessimistic, the existence of more money does not necessarily lead to increases in consumption or investment. Despite the Fed's very

---

*Or at least smaller deficits, facilitated by rising tax revenues.

**In "quantitative easing," the Fed purchases MBSs from banks and credits them with fresh reserves.

Box 30.3 Housing Prices Headed Back Up

Although Figure 30.1 shows housing prices declining from their 2006 peak, more recent data indicate that housing prices are headed back up. Over the 12 months from March 2012 to February 2013, the Case-Shiller index of housing prices was up 9.3 percent. That was the biggest 12-month gain in the index since May 2006, shortly after the index indicated record-high home prices.

> The index showed a 12-month decline in prices almost every month over a five-year period through May 2012. But every month since then has shown a gain in home prices, and each month's gain has been stronger than the one that came before. "Despite some recent mixed economic reports for March, housing continues to be one of the brighter spots in the economy," said David Blitzer, chairman of the index committee at S&P Dow Jones Indices.

While rising housing prices are a sign of an economic recovery, some economists worry that the recent rapid rise in home prices could be problematic. Stan Humphries, chief economist for real estate Web site Zillow, said that "regardless what data you look at, home values are clearly rising at an unsustainable pace."

Mike Larson, real estate analyst at Weiss Research, said he's concerned that much of the increase is being driven by investors flooding into some markets to buy homes in order to rent them out, outbidding the potential homeowners who want to live in a home. "Prices are not at bubblicious levels, but you're talking about a trend that can be destabilizing," he said.

The biggest increase in housing prices was in Phoenix, AZ, a city particularly hard-hit during the financial crisis, where prices increased by 23 percent. Some neighborhoods in the city saw housing prices rise by 40 percent. According to Dean Baker, codirector of the Center for Economic and Policy Research, these dramatic price increases were being driven by speculators. He noted that in the housing markets most hurt by the bursting of the housing bubble, there was a danger that new bubbles will form. "The end of this round of speculation is not likely to be much prettier for the areas affected than the end of the last round," he said.

Source: Chris Isidore, "Home Price Rise Continues to Pick up Speed," CNN Money, April 30, 2013. http://money.cnn.com/2013/04/30/news/economy/home-prices/index.html

expansionary policies, banks remain fairly reluctant to lend their excess reserves, except to their most creditworthy borrowers.

In addition, some fear that the Fed, through its efforts, is inadvertently inflating a new bubble. Wall Street, for example, appears ebullient at the efforts of both the fiscal and monetary authorities to reverse the economic decline; stock indexes rose to record levels in 2013. At the same time, there was a rush into "junk bonds"—corporate bonds considered at moderate to high risk of default—because of their relatively high interest rates. And we should not forget that sustained low interest rates are always an invitation for speculators to leverage their investment positions inexpensively, as some have returned to doing.

4.2 The Dodd-Frank Bill

The deregulation that preceded the financial crisis had been developed over many decades. Starting in the 1980s, many government regulations that had been in place for decades were eliminated. The premise for deregulation was the belief that companies would benefit from less government intrusion in their affairs and that the broader economy would gain from an improvement in investment incentives. As we have noted, important deregulatory legislation, such as the Financial Services Modernization Act—which effectively overturned Glass-Steagall—were adopted, generally with bipartisan support, during the 1990s and 2000s.

But in late 2008 the political atmosphere changed rather abruptly. Suddenly, a clamor arose for regulatory reform to protect Americans from the recklessness of the financial sector, which only intensified after the first recipients of government assistance were revealed to be the financial companies themselves. The principal change arising from the call for reform was the 2010 Dodd-Frank Wall Street Reform and Consumer Protection Act (Dodd-Frank), cosponsored by Senator Chris Dodd (D-CT) and Representative Barney Frank (D-MA), which seeks to address many of the causes of the financial crisis.

First, Dodd-Frank addresses the deteriorating lending standards that encouraged subprime loans and pumped air into the housing bubble. The legislation requires that financial companies that seek to lend money to prospective homeowners use minimum criteria (related to, e.g., credit history and income and debt levels) to determine whether the candidate for a mortgage can reasonably be expected to repay.

The law also seeks to put a halt to so-called predatory lending, which was increasingly common in the last years of the housing bubble. Predatory lending describes the practice in which financial companies target individuals whom they *know* are unlikely to repay a mortgage. Dodd-Frank creates a new Consumer Financial Protection Bureau (www.consumerfinance.gov/) that protects vulnerable borrowers but also monitors loosely regulated lenders known for predatory practices. In July 2013, the Bureau became fully operational with the appointment of a permanent director.

Another key feature of Dodd-Frank is that it directly confronts the moral hazard inherent in the financial system and its pay structure. In order to reduce the extent to which commercial banks transfer risk to investment banks through the use of MBSs and other securities, the legislation requires commercial banks to be exposed to a minimum amount of the mortgage default risk. Dodd-Frank, moreover, puts restrictions on CDSs, requiring companies that seek to insure senior tranches of MBSs or CDOs to post more collateral to back up their value.

In addressing corporate pay structure, Dodd-Frank calls for the Securities and Exchange Commission to ensure that corporate board members who determine CEO compensation do not have private interests in the company that might give them an incentive to favor higher CEO pay over broad shareholder interests.

Dodd-Frank also takes on ratings agencies like Moody's and Standard and Poor's, the companies that rate a great variety of debt and debt-related securities to give investors a clear picture of the riskiness of the asset. The new legislation requires the agencies to disclose the method used to rate each security, in hopes of increasing transparency for investors. It partially addresses conflict of interest concerns stemming from the fact that the agencies are regularly paid by the banks that they rate, possibly creating an incentive to understate the risk of certain securities. Nevertheless, Dodd-Frank does not prohibit ratings agencies from being paid by the firms that they rate.

The legislation also limits the amount of leverage permitted to large financial firms. As noted earlier, the instability leading to the crisis was magnified by the fact that firms were allowed to borrow amounts so high that they intensified the artificial rise in asset prices.

Perhaps most important, the Dodd-Frank bill takes on the issue of "too big to fail." It uses the designation "systemically important" for financial companies that hold assets in excess of $50 billion (of which there are currently almost 40) and subjects them to Fed-imposed restrictions on their activities that are more stringent than those faced by smaller firms. The law also seeks to restrict further growth. For example, it forbids any merger that allows a single firm to hold more than 10 percent of the liabilities of the entire financial sector.

4.3 Beyond Dodd-Frank

Like most historic pieces of legislation, the Dodd-Frank bill has received no shortage of criticism. A familiar argument against it is one that is commonly heard about regulation in general: that the bill creates significant costs for financial firms, slowing down business and job creation. Another point of criticism is that the legislation is too complex, perhaps even contradictory.

A third argument made against Dodd-Frank is that it has been "watered down" to a great extent by intense lobbying efforts by the financial industry itself—suggesting, in effect, that the regulators are under the influence of the regulated. One salient example supporting this claim is the fact that, in 2012, regulators decided that new CDS regulations would not apply to firms that sell less than $8 billion in CDSs per year. Because of this change, which was a direct result of pressure from the finance lobby, the overwhelming majority of companies are exempt from CDS regulations.

As of late 2013, only 40 percent of the rules provided for in Dodd-Frank had been adopted in final form. In the process, a number of them had been watered down or eliminated due to pressure from the financial industry. Dodd-Frank also encountered problems globally, as foreign countries protested aspects that affected their financial companies.

Opposition to Dodd-Frank is not, however, limited to Wall Street. Although much of the public favors reform and greater regulation of the financial industry, many remain opposed to or at least highly skeptical of Dodd-Frank. Polls indicate that nearly half the U.S. population believes that the legislation would do more to protect the financial industry than consumers.

In order to go beyond Dodd-Frank, we must ask not merely how to regulate finance, but also how to redirect finance to the goal of increasing overall benefits to society. One obvious way would be to reverse course in the direction of smaller and more specialized banks, along the lines of the Glass-Steagall Act. Free market principles align with the idea that banks should be "small enough to fail." In other words, market competition should weed out the weak or inferior banks, and in the process the banking system would be made more robust.

A system based on small banks would highlight the important economic role that they already play. Despite holding barely 10 percent of total banking sector assets, small banks provide more than one-third of all small business loans in the United States. This is a critically important service, because small businesses have created over two-thirds of new jobs in the United States since the early 1990s.

Such a change, in effect a return to traditional banking, would require addressing the heavy influence in government that is arguably responsible for the deregulation in the first place: the veritable "revolving door" through which some of the "big players" in finance subsequently take on important government posts, and vice-versa. Attempts to block this door have included proposed requirements that individuals must wait a significant number of years between the time that they leave a government position in which they can affect legislation on industry sectors and when they begin to work in those sectors.

Another means of redirecting finance to serve society would be to ask investors to pay a modest tax each time that they complete a financial transaction. Keynes proposed such a tax in 1936—at a time when the role of finance vis-à-vis the real economy was minuscule compared to today—as a way of discouraging the short-term speculation that makes the price of company stock highly volatile. Decades later, another prominent economist, the Nobel laureate James Tobin, also argued that financial transactions, particularly currency trades, should be taxed. His idea was that each transaction be taxed at a low rate, but that speculators would end up paying much more than long-term investors because they buy and sell securities much more frequently. Today, the term "Tobin tax" is used to refer to any proposed financial transaction tax.

Studies estimate that a financial transactions tax of a fraction of a percentage point would generate billions of dollars in revenue. The European Commission has adopted a tax on all stock, bond, and derivative trading in the European Union beginning in 2014, and Canada has passed legislation that proposes to implement a Tobin tax if enough other countries agree to participate.

In future, the financial sector will continue to be the focus of an extensive debate about regulation, transparency, and the political power of large financial institutions. Economic theory cannot provide definitive answers to these questions, but as this chapter has shown, many of the macroeconomic analyses that we have developed are very relevant to understanding and evaluating these issues.

Discussion Questions

1. What is "quantitative easing"? Can you think of anything you learned earlier in the book to which it is related? What do you think are the main advantages and disadvantages of such a policy?
2. What would you think about a proposal to tax financial transactions? Would you prefer it to an income or a sales tax? Why or why not?

REVIEW QUESTIONS

1. What was the nature of the housing bubble experienced in the early to mid-2000s? What were its main causes?
2. What is "subprime" lending? How did it contribute to the bubble and the subsequent financial crisis?
3. How can a collapse of the U.S housing market and weakness in the banking system cause an economic recession and unemployment?
4. How is the recent economic downturn similar to the Great Depression? How is it different?
5. What are mortgage-backed securities? Collateralized debt obligations? Credit default swaps? Are these "investments" in the traditional sense?
6. Did social inequality play a part in inflating the bubble that led to the 2007 financial crisis? If so, how?
7. What is financial deregulation? How important is it in explaining the financial crisis?
8. Explain "too big to fail" and why it is a potential economic problem in any economic setting. How is "too big to fail" related to moral hazard?
9. Are short-term individual incentives for corporate officers consistent or in conflict with long-run interests of their companies and the economy as a whole?
10. In what ways did globalization contribute to the financial crisis?
11. What have been the principal fiscal and monetary responses to the recession to date? What have been the results thus far?
12. What is the purpose of the Dodd-Frank bill? What are its main provisions? Has it been favorably received?
13. What is the Tobin tax? What would be its effect on financial transactions?

EXERCISES

1. For this exercise you need to locate housing price index data for specific states. Begin at the Federal Housing Finance Agency website (www.fhfa.gov) and select the "State HPI Data" link from the "House Price Index" tab. Select various states to get a better understanding of how the housing market in the U.S. has evolved over the past twenty years (you may want to repeat the three state comparison multiple times to get a larger sense of the experiences of different states, but make sure that at some point you look at states like Nevada and/or Florida and that you spend some time thinking about what the numbers mean). Now write a short summary of what you've learned. Make sure that you incorporate some specific data into your summary.
2. How does the Great Recession compare to recent economic downturns? To explore this question in further detail, begin at the National Bureau of Economic Research website (www.nber.org).
   a. Select "Business Cycle Dates" from the "Data" tab at the NBER site and then record the starting dates (peaks) and ending dates (troughs) for the last four recessions. Assemble these dates in a table.
   b. Now gather some macroeconomic data. You can do this at the Federal Reserve Economic Database (http://research.stlouisfed.org/fred2/). Us-

ing the "National Income & Product Accounts" under the "National Accounts" tab within "Categories," locate Real Gross Domestic Product data for each peak and each trough in your table. Record these numbers in a new table. Calculate the percentage change in Real GDP from peak to trough for each of the last four recessions. Report these results in your new table.

c. Return to the categories page at the FRED website. Select the "Current Population Survey (Household Survey)" link under the "Population, Employment, & Labor Markets" category. Select the "unemployment rate" series and record the numbers for each peak and each trough for each of the last four recessions. Organize these data in a table.

d. Review your tables and calculations. Write a concise summary comparing the Great Recession to the previous three recessions. Make sure that you incorporate specific numbers into your summary.

3. The chapter identifies a series of contributing factors in its exploration of the underlying causes of the financial crisis. Identify the major factors and state which you think were most important.
4. What is the meaning of moral hazard? Give some examples of moral hazard, as discussed in the text, or others that you can think of.
5. Match each concept in Column A with a definition or example in Column B.

Column A	Column B
a. Mortgage-backed security	1. When a company grows so large that its failure would cause widespread economic harm in terms of lost jobs and diminished asset values
b. Collateralized debt obligation	2. A loan that permits a borrower to offer his or her home (or their equity stake in it) as collateral in case of failure to repay the loan
c. Credit default swap	3. A security that is effectively an insurance policy against defaults related to MBSs and CDOs
d. Sub-prime buyer	4. A would-be home-buyer whose credit-worthiness is suspect because he or she already has a high level of debt, and/or a low income, and/or a poor credit record
e. Home equity loan	5. Benefits that occur when the long run average cost of production falls as the size of the enterprise increases
f. "Laissez-faire"	6. The Fed purchases MBSs from banks, and credits them with fresh reserves
g. Economies of scale	7. An investment product that packages together numerous assets, including MBSs
h. Too-big-to-fail	8. Doing nothing
i. Moral hazard	9. A security composed of a bundle of many home mortgages issued by independent banks
j. "Quantitative easing"	10. The lack of any incentive to guard against a risk when you are protected against it

31 Deficits and Debt

You may have seen the national debt clock in New York City that continually shows how much our debt is increasing by the second. The total amount of the debt, which exceeds $16 trillion, seems very large. But what does it mean? To whom do we owe all this money? Is it a serious problem? Should we care about government debt when the economy has yet to recover from the financial crisis? Is it possible for the United States to stop borrowing? This chapter goes into detail in answering these questions and even considers some possible ways to reverse the trend. But first we provide some historical context to the notion of a national debt.

1. Deficits and the National Debt

Perhaps because the two terms sound so much alike, many people confuse the government's deficit with the *government debt.* But the two "D words" are very different. The deficit totaled $1.1 trillion in fiscal 2012, while total federal debt exceeded $16 trillion at the end of fiscal 2012. The reason the second number is much larger than the first is that the debt represents deficits accumulated over many years. In economists' terms, we can say that the government deficit is a *flow variable* while its debt is a *stock variable.* (See Chapter 1 for this distinction.)

The government's debt rises when the government runs a deficit and falls when it runs a surplus.* Figure 31.1 shows some recent data on the government's debt, measured as a percentage of GDP. The two lines on the graph indicate the total government debt and the part of government debt held by the public (as opposed to debt held by government agencies). After hitting a high of more than 100 percent of GDP during World War II, the debt generally declined as a percentage of GDP until 1980. It rose somewhat before 1996, then fell until 2000. Since 2000 the debt has risen, with a particularly sharp increase in the years following the 2007–9 recession.

What is the impact on the economy of government debt? One commonly expressed view of the government's debt is that it represents a burden on future generations of citizens. There is some truth to this assertion, but it is also somewhat misleading. It implicitly compares the government's debt to the debt of a private citizen. Certainly, if you personally accumulated a huge debt, it would not be a good thing for your financial future. But government debt is different in some important ways.

First, about half of government debt is, directly or indirectly, owed to U.S. citizens. When people own Treasury bills (T-bills), Treasury notes, or Treasury bonds, they own government

*Although the arithmetic requires that the debt rise when the government is in deficit—because the only way to finance a deficit is to borrow money—in the case of a surplus it is possible for the government to hold some funds in reserve, for example, to finance future expenditures. It is usually the case, however, that governments will use some or all of a surplus to reduce existing debt.

IOUs. From their point of view, the government debt is an asset, a form of wealth. If your grandmother gives you a U.S. Savings Bond, she is giving you a benefit, not a burden. These assets are some of the safest ones that you can own.

Second, government debt does not have to be paid off. Old debt can be "rolled over," that is, replaced by new debt. Provided that the size of the debt does not grow too quickly, the government's credit is good—there will always be people interested in buying and holding government bonds. Most economists use the rule of thumb that as long as the rate of increase in government's debt is not significantly greater than that of GDP for several years in a row, it does not represent a severe problem for the economy. As Figure 31.1 shows, following the 2007–9 recession, persistently large deficits have caused the debt to rise much more rapidly than GDP in recent years. Nonetheless, the debt is still at a lower level relative to GDP than it was immediately after World War II, which was followed by nearly two decades of relative economic prosperity.

Figure 31.1 **U.S. National Debt as a Percentage of GDP**

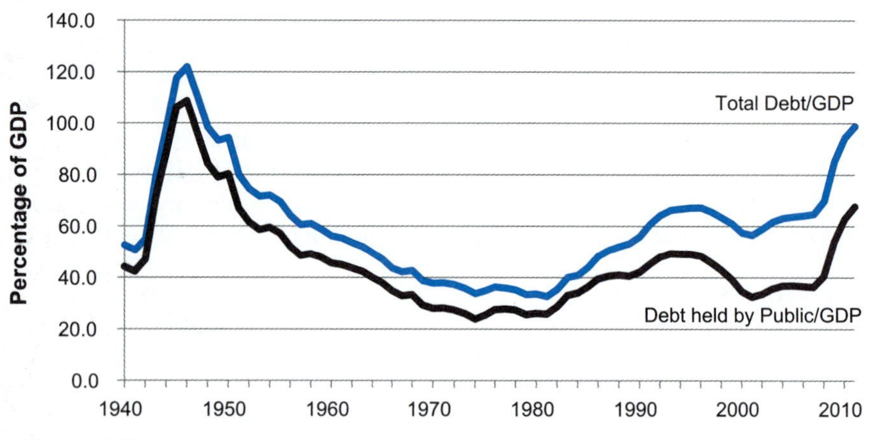

Total U.S. national debt, including debt held by the Federal Reserve Bank, has risen to about 100 percent of GDP, while debt held by the public is about 70 percent of GDP.

Source: Whitehouse.gov

Third, the U.S. government pays interest in U.S. dollars. A country such as Argentina that owes money to other countries and must pay interest in a foreign currency (the U.S. dollar) can get into big trouble and go bankrupt. But it is much easier to manage a debt that is denominated in your own currency. Even if some of the debt is owed to foreigners, the United States does not have to obtain foreign currency to pay it. And so long as foreigners are willing to continue holding U.S. government bonds, it will not be necessary to pay it at all—instead, the debt can be rolled over as new bonds replace old ones.

But this should not encourage us to believe that government debt is never a concern. Rising debt creates several significant problems. First, interest must be paid on the debt. This means that a larger share of future budgets must be devoted to paying interest, leaving less for other needs. It is also true that the largest holders of government bonds tend to be wealthier people, so most of the interest paid by the government goes to better-off individuals. If this payment is not counteracted by changes in the tax system, it encourages growing income inequality. It also creates a problem of generational equity—future taxpayers will have to pay more interest because of government borrowing today. It is a burden on future generations in that debt finance detracts from other important functions that the government could be performing.

A second problem is that in recent years an increasing proportion of the debt has been borrowed from governments, corporations, and individuals in foreign countries (Figure 31.2). The interest payments on this portion of the debt must be made to those outside the country. That means that the United States must earn enough income from exports and other sources to pay not only for imports but also for interest payments to the rest of the world. Alternatively,

Figure 31.2 **Domestic and Foreign Holdings of U.S. Debt**

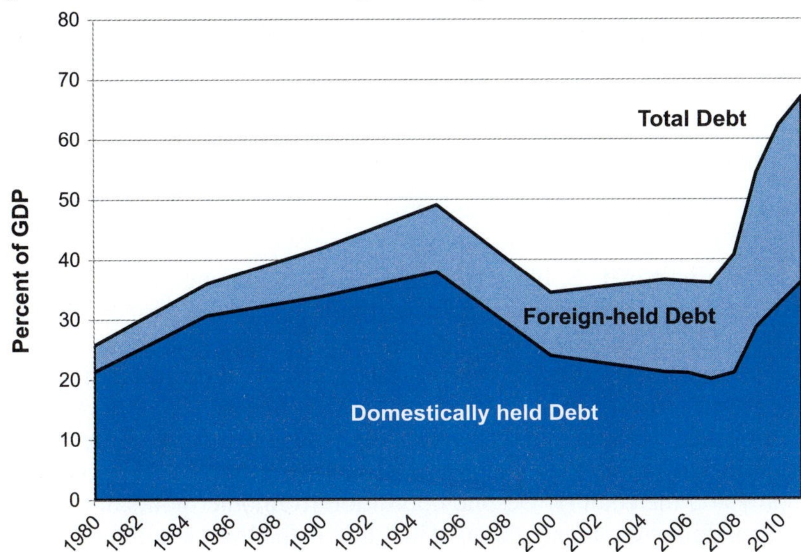

The proportion of the U.S. national debt held by foreign individuals, corporations, and governments has risen in recent years.

Source: White House Office of Management and Budget, Economic and Budget Analyses, Table 6–7.

the country could borrow more, but it is best to avoid this solution, since it would just make the overall foreign debt problem larger in the long run.

Large foreign holdings of debt also pose another problem—what if those foreign debt holders decided to sell the U.S. bonds that they own? In that case, the government might have trouble finding enough people who are willing to hold government bonds (that is, lend money to the government). This could cause interest rates to rise sharply, which in turn would push the government budget further into deficit.

The question "Is government debt worth it?" can be answered only if we consider what that debt is used to finance. In this respect, an analogy to personal or business debt is appropriate. Most people—including economists—do not reject consumer and corporate debt. Rather, our judgment about debt depends on the benefits received.

For example, if debt is accumulated for gambling, it is a bad idea. If the bet does not pay off, then it is very difficult to pay the interest on the debt (not to mention the principal). But if the government borrows to pay for intelligently planned investment, it can be very beneficial. If the investment leads to economic growth, the government's ability to collect tax revenue is enhanced. This kind of borrowing can pay for itself, as long as the investment is not for wasteful "pork barrel" spending, poorly planned or unnecessary projects, and so on. Recalling our earlier discussion of the opportunity cost of government borrowing at full employment, the interest-generating capacity of the proposed project is certainly an important—though not the only—consideration.

Even if the debt finances current spending, it can be justifiable if it is seen as necessary to maintain or protect valuable aspects of life. Most people would not be opposed to borrowing to pay for cleanup after a natural disaster (e.g., in January 2013 Congress appropriated $60 billion in relief funds for Hurricane Sandy relief) or to contain a deadly pandemic. How about for military spending? Opinions differ about whether particular defense expenditures are necessary to maintain or protect valuable aspects of life. But wasteful spending, or spending on unwise defense policies, constitutes a drag on more productive economic activity (as suggested by the production-possibilities curve "guns-versus-butter" analysis introduced in Chapter 1).

The management of debt involves standard principles of wise stewardship of finances. When we apply them to government deficits and debt, we need to weigh the economic benefits of different spending and tax policies.

Discussion Questions

1. What is the difference between the deficit and the national debt? How are they related?
2. "The national debt is a huge burden on our economy." How would you evaluate this statement?

2. THE U.S. NATIONAL DEBT: A HISTORICAL PERSPECTIVE

2.1 TWO CENTURIES OF DEFICITS AND DEBT

Deficit financing has been part of U.S. history from the very beginning. The Continental Congress put the country into debt in order to continue its fight for independence from Great Britain. As is done today, Congress issued bonds in order to finance the country's war effort. There was considerable controversy after the war regarding the role of the new federal government in absorbing the debts incurred by individual states. Alexander Hamilton, secretary of the Treasury under George Washington, was prominent among those who believed that, by introducing greater flexibility into the money supply, a national debt had the potential to strengthen the economy and the country. Despite opposition from other political leaders—John Adams and Thomas Jefferson among them—Hamilton helped set in motion a process through which the federal government regularly relied on debt to finance its operations.

After the United States became independent from Great Britain, its federal government generally repaid its debts fairly quickly. The War of 1812, however, proved very costly, and the national debt approached 15 percent of national income by 1816. In the nineteenth and early twentieth centuries, it was mostly wars that depleted the government's finances. The Civil War was especially costly—the debt approached 40 percent of total national income at its peak—but the Mexican-American and Spanish-American wars also added to the national debt. By 1900 it had fallen below 5 percent of total GDP, but the budget deficits during World War I again pushed the national debt beyond 40 percent of GDP.

In terms of its effect on government finances, the Great Depression of the 1930s was truly a watershed. The economic crisis ultimately led to President Franklin D. Roosevelt's New Deal social programs. From that point on, federal spending on social programs—in addition to continued military spending—has figured prominently in the total debt figures. Consequently, since 1931 the U.S. federal budget has been in surplus only seven years, compared with the years from independence until then, during which surpluses were seen twice as frequently as deficits. National debt in relation to income rose significantly during the 1930s, but it was World War II that had an even greater impact. Because consumer goods were rationed, savings accumulated, and people used them to purchase U.S. war bonds (a form of debt), which helped finance U.S. participation in World War II. After the war, the national debt totaled an unprecedented 122 percent of GDP (Figure 31.1).

2.2 "SUPPLY-SIDE" ECONOMICS

After World War II, as noted, the debt generally declined as a percentage of GDP until 1980. The national debt was just over $900 billion in 1981, but rose by nearly $2 trillion during the next eight years. In other words, over those eight years the country incurred twice as much debt as it had in its first 200 years! How did this happen?

Ronald Reagan's 1980 presidential campaign leaned heavily on the principles of "supply-side" economics, which promised that offering more benefits and incentives to the individuals and groups that held the most wealth and productive capital would stimulate rapid investment growth and job creation. According to this principle, tax cuts would pay for themselves through greater revenues from an expanded economy.

The major policy experiment with supply-side economics was the Economic Recovery Act (ERA, 1981), which cut income and corporate tax rates, substantially reducing government revenues. At the same time, military spending increased in the 1980s. Consequently, the annual budget deficit, which had been 2.7 percent of GDP in 1980, grew to an annual average of 4 percent during the Reagan presidency. True, a portion of the increase was due to cyclical factors, specifically an unusually deep recession in 1981–82. Most of it, however, resulted from the failure of supply-side economics to produce the revenue growth that was needed to make up for the tax cut.

2.3 1989 to the Present

In absolute terms, the national debt continued to grow after Reagan left office, despite the fact that by then public awareness of the government's fiscal problems had grown. In an attempt to address the persistent deficits, President George H.W. Bush raised tax rates slightly and signed a bill in 1990 requiring that all spending increases be matched by either decreases in spending in other areas or tax increases, in a system known as PAYGO ("pay as you go"). Despite the introduction of that system, another recession (1990–91) and the first Iraq war kept deficits in the range of 4 percent of GDP annually. It also did not help matters that sizable sums had to be used to bail out many savings and loan banks that collapsed due to losses from risky and ill-conceived real estate investments (a precursor of the real estate bubble of the twenty-first century). In 1992 the national debt was $4 trillion.

Bush's PAYGO policy was continued under the administration of Bill Clinton. Congress again raised income tax rates, and the end of the cold war allowed the federal government to lower military expenditures (relative to GDP, although not in absolute terms), a side benefit often referred to as a "peace dividend." At the same time, the economy emerged from recession and began a period of sustained growth. The resulting movement from the trough to the peak of the business cycle from 1992 to 2000 generated surpluses in the overall federal budget from 1998 to 2001, a feat that had not been achieved since 1969. This period of budget surpluses, however, was short-lived.

During the presidency of George W. Bush (2001–9), a combination of recession, tax rate cuts, and increased military expenditures pushed the budget back into deficit and caused the debt to increase further. By 2008 the debt totaled almost 70 percent of GDP.

The first Obama administration (2008–12) was spent dealing with the worst recession since the 1930s. During this period, annual deficits averaged 8.7 percent of GDP, and the national debt rose to just over 100 percent of GDP, as the government deployed a $787 billion fiscal policy package to keep the 2007–9 recession from turning into a full-fledged depression. Tax revenue fell sharply, from $2.5 trillion in 2008 to $2.1 trillion in 2009. As is normal in a recession, expenditures increased due to automatic stabilizers (see Chapter 25). The combination of these factors with continued military expenses in Iraq and Afghanistan led to record deficits of more than $1 trillion. In 2012 the deficit began to decline, with further declines projected, but the national debt overall increased to more than $16 billion.

Discussion Questions

1. Has the U.S. federal government ever had a budget surplus? When was the last time? Was there ever a time that the government was not in debt?
2. What causes budget deficits? Are budget deficits necessarily a bad thing?

3. The Debt and Its Links to Finance

3.1 Taxonomy of Debt Types

In the popular press, one encounters different estimates of the country's debt, which can vary considerably. By some estimates, U.S. total debt now approximates 350 percent of GDP. Some confusion has been caused by differing terminology relating to the debt, so it may be helpful to distinguish between different categories.

gross federal debt: total amount owed by the federal government to all claimants, including foreigners, the public in the United States, and other government accounts

public debt: the gross federal debt minus the debt owed to other government accounts such as Social Security and Medicare

Usually, the term "national debt" refers to the **gross federal debt**, which is actually the total debt outstanding for the federal government (Table 31.1) and is the debt to which we have referred until now. It is not, however, the same as the **public debt**. The gross federal debt includes money that the federal government "borrows" from other government accounts. Prominent examples include Social Security and Medicare, which, as noted earlier, are classified as "off budget." Basically, when the government collects more in tax revenue for these programs than it pays out, it realizes an off-budget surplus. It is then in a position to "borrow" the surplus, or at least a portion of it, as an alternative to borrowing money from the public. So it is the public debt, not the gross federal debt, that is a direct consequence of federal budget deficits.

Table 31.1 **Debt Taxonomy**

	Debt type	Description
Government	Gross federal debt	Generally synonymous with the national debt; refers to the total amount of money owed by the federal government to all claimants
	Public debt	Gross federal debt minus debt held in government accounts
	Debt held by public	Public debt minus the debt held by the Federal Reserve
	Internal debt	The share of the gross federal debt owned by domestic individuals or groups
	External debt	The share of the gross federal debt owned by foreign individuals or groups
	State and local debt	The total value of all state and local bonds outstanding
Private	Households and not-for-profits	Includes mortgage debt, credit card debt, and bank loans
	Financial sector	Total of all corporate debt for financial industry
	Nonfinancial business	All corporate debt and bank borrowing for nonfinancial business

debt held by the public: the gross federal debt minus the debt owed to other government accounts and also minus the portion that is held by the Federal Reserve

internal debt: the portion of the gross federal debt that is owed to individuals or groups within the country

external debt: the portion of the gross federal debt that is owed to foreign individuals or groups

Recall that the Federal Reserve is an active participant in the market for U.S. bonds, as it buys and sells them to conduct its open market operations in hopes of influencing interest rates. So the Fed also holds a significant share of the federal debt. Its share is also a part of the public debt. The difference between the public debt and the **debt held by the public** (this terminology is unfortunately confusing, but we need to learn it!) is the debt held by the Fed.

One final distinction is between the **internal debt** and the **external debt**. The internal debt refers to the portion of the gross federal debt that is owned by individuals or groups within the country, and the external debt represents the portion held by foreigners or foreign groups.

Like the federal government, state and municipal governments also often rely on borrowing to fund their operations. They issue a variety of bond instruments to acquire funds from the public, which in a sense add to the country's total indebtedness. This is also a point of frequent confusion. In its common usage, the term "national debt" usually refers only to the federal portion of the debt. This seems reasonable, because it is the debt that is directly related to fiscal policy and how it affects the national economy. Yet if we speak of the total debt of the country, it appears misleading to exclude the state and local debt. And the picture becomes even more complicated, because to get a complete accounting of debt we should include all household debt (e.g., mortgage and credit card), financial sector debt, and the debt of nonfinancial business, which includes both bank loans outstanding and corporate bonds issued to finance private debt.

Figure 31.3 **Total U.S. Indebtedness as a Percentage of GDP**

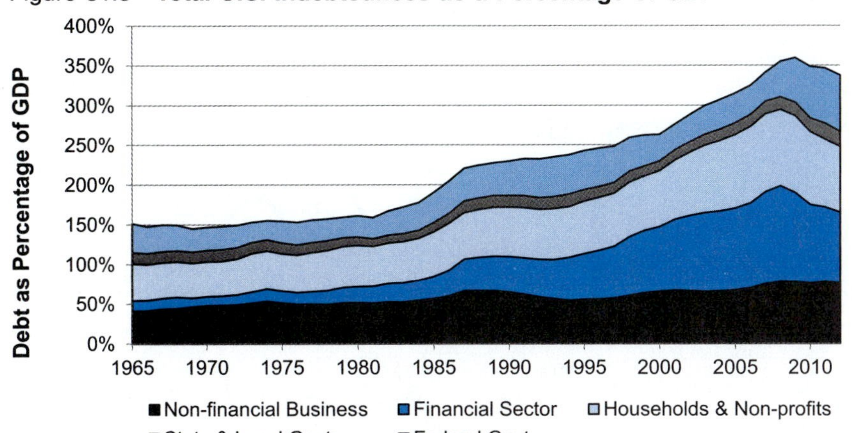

Here the federal debt is only a subset of the total, and one that has not increased substantially over the years. The household sector debt has grown much more rapidly, and that of the financial sector most rapidly of all.

If we add all the categories to represent the total indebtedness of the whole country, we find that, as of 2011, it did indeed exceed 350 percent of GDP and is much more than double what it was in the early 1970s (Figure 31.3). Such an inclusive debt concept is not of great significance in ordinary times, but during the run-up to the Great Recession, it should have been setting off alarm bells, as it meant that the country as a whole had used up much of the leeway in terms of borrowing capacity that could have been drawn on to get out of a recession. Note that since the Great Recession, total debt has fallen as the economic downturn forced households and businesses to reduce their debt levels.

3.2 FEDERAL GOVERNMENT BORROWING: POTENTIAL PROBLEMS

In earlier chapters, we saw that when the government borrows money, it issues bonds on which it must pay interest. The interest payments form part of the annual federal budget. Figure 31.4 shows how these payments as a percentage of federal spending have varied over time. Note that interest payments accounted for a much greater portion of the budget during the 1980s and 1990s than they do now. Considering that federal debt as a percentage of GDP has risen quite rapidly over the past decade, how can this be? The answer is that the unusually low interest rates that have prevailed over the same period make this possible.

We have seen in earlier chapters that a weak economy tends to induce lower interest rates, both naturally and as a consequence of policy measures. If interest rates are lower throughout the economy, the Treasury can issue new debt (e.g., Treasury bonds) at a low interest rate. When it does so, it is effectively reducing the portion of the federal budget that must be set aside for debt service. The phenomenon is not unlike the low monthly payments a homeowner makes after obtaining a mortgage with a very low interest rate. The major difference to keep in mind is that, unlike a household, the federal government has the ability to print money if need be to pay off its debt.

As of January 2013, the interest rate on a 10-year Treasury bond was 1.86 percent (see Figure 31.5). But during 2013 rates started rising, and in September 2013 had reached 2.92 percent. One might think that at the historically low interest rates prevailing from 2009 to 2012, borrowing was especially cheap, making it a good time for the government to run a budget deficit and accumulate debt. The argument for adding to federal debt seems even stronger if the government spends on programs that produce a high multiplier effect (Chapter 25). With low interest rates, the gain from the multiplier effect (in terms of the increase in aggregate demand) is potentially larger than the loss (adding to debt burden), making the net gain positive.

However, it may be counterproductive to allow the debt to grow if it is to finance "low-multiplier" activities. An example is tax cuts for the wealthy, which, as we saw in Chapter

Figure 31.4 **Interest Payments as Percentage of Total Federal Outlays**

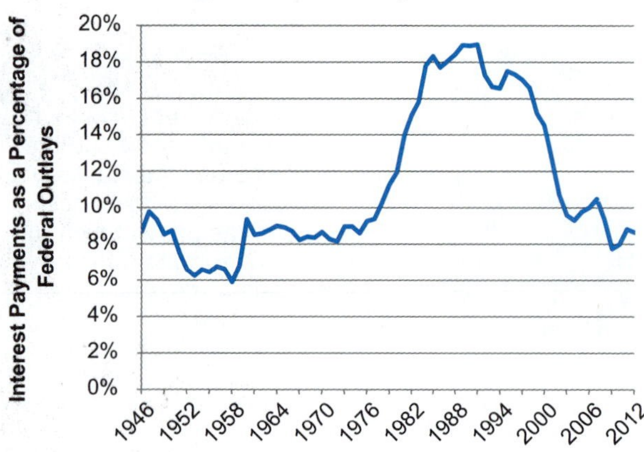

Source: BEA.gov

Despite increasing debt levels, interest payments on the debt have fallen as a percentage of total federal outlays due to unusually low interest rates.

Figure 31.5 **The Interest Rate on 10-Year Treasury Bonds**

Source: St. Louis Federal Reserve Bank.

Interest rates on 10-year Treasury bonds have fallen steadily, and by the end of 2012 were slightly below 2%. They rose somewhat during 2013 (data for 2013 not included here).

25, do not produce as much "bang for the buck" as tax cuts for the poor or new spending on constructive activities. A useful way of understanding the problem is to imagine the federal government as a private business. Would a business borrow money at an interest rate higher than its expected rate of return? Here, the situation is similar, only a bit more complicated; the government needs to assess the projected "social return" of its expenditures.

Another concern with mounting debt is that, if sufficiently large, lenders might start to doubt the borrowers' ability to repay. If the doubt were severe and widespread, it could affect the bond market and, indirectly, the national economy. Risk-averse investors would sell their bonds, driving bond prices down. When bond prices go down, bond yields (interest rates) go up (as noted in the Appendix to Chapter 27), because the amount that the government has to pay in interest on the bond becomes higher relative to the value of the bond.

The greater the unease over the borrower's ability to pay, the higher the interest rate that the borrower must offer in order to attract lenders. In the summer of 2011, Standard and Poor's, one of the major ratings agencies, downgraded U.S. government debt from AAA to AA+. Fortunately for the United States, even with this downgrade, its debt remained very much in demand.

A third potential problem with too much debt concerns exactly how it gets repaid. An indebted country must repay the principal on its debt and service it with interest payments. To do so, it must either engage in new borrowing, raise tax revenues, or **monetize the debt**. We have seen that increasing tax rates has the potential to reduce consumption and investment, hurting GDP growth and employment. But it is also possible to finance a federal budget deficit with bonds that are purchased by the Fed. As we saw in Chapter 27, this amounts to an expansionary monetary policy.

monetizing the debt/monetizing the deficit: when a central bank buys government debt as it is issued (equivalent to "running the printing presses")

A policy of monetizing the debt risks causing inflation, especially if the increase in the money supply is sufficiently large. If such inflation does occur, the bond markets might then demand higher interest rates on new debt to compensate for the anticipated loss from inflation. How serious is this danger? Some economists believe that a mild to moderate increase in inflation is not necessarily a problem, especially if it occurs in a depressed economy facing a looming threat of deflation. As we saw in Chapter 26, deflation would in most circumstances be more dangerous than inflation, while mild inflation has historically been associated with economic recoveries and gains in domestic employment. Severe inflation, however, would be very damaging to the economy, and other economists point to this as a possible result of increasing government debt.

Discussion Questions

1. How many different "types" of debt can you think of? Which one do people usually mean when they speak about the "national debt"?
2. What are some potential problems with excessive federal debt? How can the debt be managed or repaid?

4. Political Economy of the Debt

4.1 Who Owns the Debt?

We have already seen that when the federal government goes into debt, it sells government bonds. But who buys these bonds? It might surprise you to see how ownership of the gross federal debt is divided up. For example, due in large part to the recent and ongoing financial crisis, the Fed has increased its holdings of government bonds, so its share of the total debt was 9.6 percent as of 2012 (Figure 31.6). Meanwhile, the amount owed to the Social Security fund accounts for 16.4 percent of the debt. As noted above in the discussion of the public debt, one thing the federal government may do when it possesses inadequate funds to pursue its objectives is skim off some of the surplus—if one exists—from the Social Security trust fund. It must then issue the fund an IOU in the form of a bond.

Social security is by far the largest of the government accounts that hold federal debt. Among the many other funds, the principal ones are the funds for federal employee retirement, federal hospital insurance, and federal disability insurance. These and all the others collectively account for another 14.8 percent of federal debt. State and local governments, perhaps surprisingly, account for another 4.3 percent. States and municipalities will often use their budget surpluses to buy federal debt, because it is considered mostly risk free.

Figure 31.6 **Ownership of Gross Federal Debt**

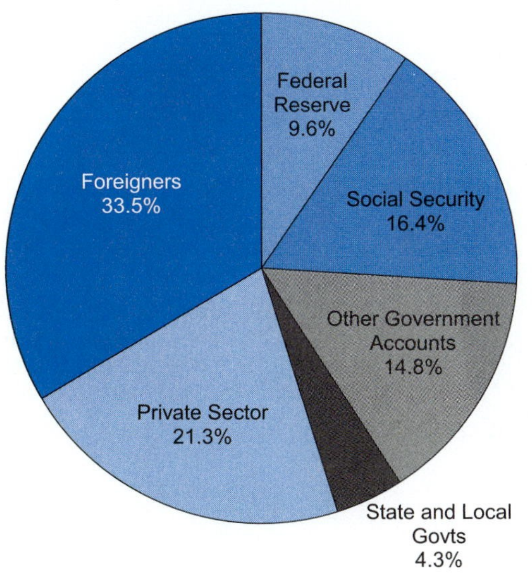

About a third of gross federal debt is held by government agencies, another third by foreign bondholders, and the rest by U.S. individuals, institutions, and state and local governments.

Source: Treasury Department, 2013, *Federal Debt*, Tables FD-1, FD-2, FD-3; *Ownership of Federal Securities*, Tables OFS-1, OFS-2.

The domestic private sector owns a bit more than a fifth (21.3 percent) of the federal debt in the form of bonds, which are found in a variety of locations: banks, pension plans, insurance companies, mutual funds, and others, including households. Finally, as of 2012, foreigners owned just over one-third (33.5 percent) of all federal debt, totaling $5.5 trillion. This is the U.S. external debt; in absolute terms, it is by far the largest external debt of any country, but not when considered relative to GDP, as discussed below.

In 2013, China and Japan together owned more than 42 percent of the external U.S. debt (Figure 31.7), a reflection of the huge trade surpluses that the two countries have had with the United States for several decades. As we saw in Chapter 29, when China and Japan export more to the United States than they import from us, they acquire a surplus of U.S. dollars, which they then use to buy U.S. federal debt. Why do they choose to hold U.S. government debt? For the same reason that domestic investors, state and local governments, and the Social Security trust fund trustees do: Federal debt is widely perceived as returning risk-free income.

Four countries—Brazil, Taiwan, Switzerland, and Belgium—accounted for another 14 percent of the U.S. external debt; major oil-exporting countries had 4.6 percent, and another 5.2 percent were held in Caribbean offshore banking centers. Finally, the remaining countries (approximately 190) collectively owned 33.9 percent of the U.S. external debt as of 2013.

Although in absolute terms the U.S. debt is by far the highest in the world, it is a very different story if we look at total debt in relation to GDP. Japan's ratio of debt to GDP has risen since its economic slowdown started in the 1990s and is currently 214.1 percent of GDP (Figure 31.8). Nevertheless, Japanese bonds are still bought and traded on the secondary market, which may be a testament to the widespread belief in the stability of the Japanese economy. This is in stark contrast to Greece, which has had to raise its bond rates substantially to attract continued investors, even though its debt to GDP ratio (168 percent) is still significantly below Japan's. Italy's ratio, at 122.7 percent, also surpasses that of the United States.

Among the countries listed, only in the UK does the *rate of increase* in the debt:GDP ratio since 2006 surpass that of the United States, whose ratio increased from 66.4 percent to 108.6 percent from 2006 to 2012, impelled by tax cuts and the financial crisis. Still, the U.S. situation continues to resemble Japan's, in that growing indebtedness has not noticeably altered investor confidence, allowing the U.S. bond yields to remain fairly low.

Figure 31.7 **Foreign Holders of Gross Federal Debt**

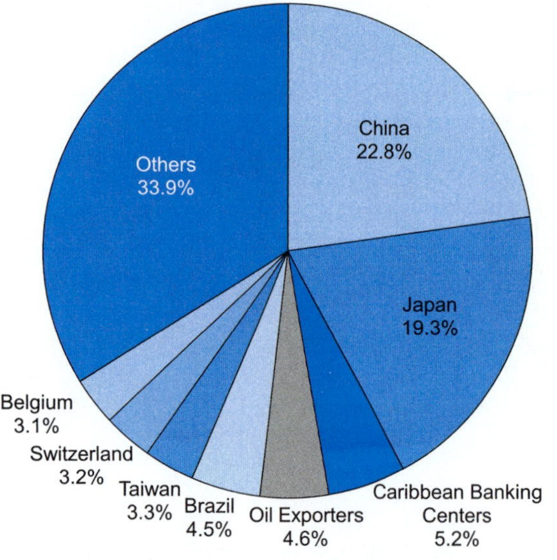

The largest foreign holders of U.S. debt are China and Japan, as a result of their long-running trade surpluses with the United States.

Source: Treasury Department, 2013, *Major Foreign Holders of Treasury Securities*.

Figure 31.8 **Debt-GDP Ratios, an International Comparison**

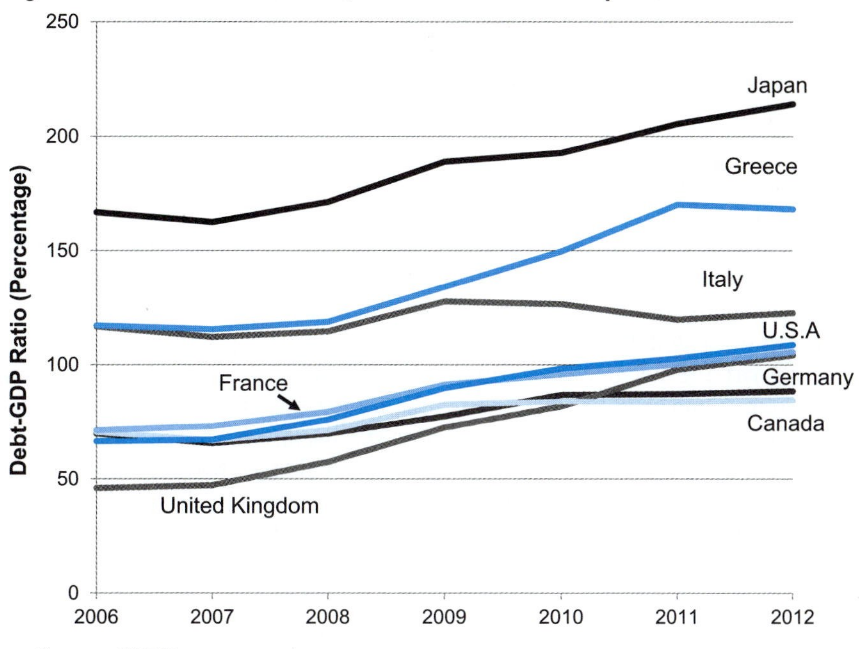

Japan's ratio of debt to GDP is over 200%, but this has not caused economic crisis. Greece, with a much smaller economy, has suffered severely in trying to get its ratio of debt to GDP, now over 150%, under control. Debt to GDP ratios have risen in the US and major European countries since 2006.

Source: OECD, www.oecd.org

4.2 The Balanced Budget Debate

If balancing the budget were legally required, the United States would never have accumulated the debt that it has. Hoping to avoid uncontrolled debt dependence, many in the past have advocated legislation requiring that the budget be balanced. Some have even recommended an amendment to the Constitution requiring a balanced federal budget, but the majority in Congress has always viewed the idea as too extreme.

Most states have a balanced budget requirement that forces them to cut services and government employees during a recession. The federal government often provides aid to allow states to minimize cost cutting, in an attempt to prevent the economy from weakening further. States have no other recourse because, unlike the federal government, they are unable to create additional funds. In large part, this explains why, as we discussed in Chapter 25, states (as well as municipalities) practice "procyclical" instead of countercyclical policy.

A balanced budget amendment would effectively make the federal government little different from the states. Proponents argue that such a law would prevent the federal government from imprudently running deficits, potentially causing inflation, in good economic times. But there is a very serious downside, in that such an amendment would make the federal government powerless to use countercyclical policy to fight recessions.

In 1985, Congress passed the Balanced Budget and Emergency Deficit Control Act, more popularly known as the Gramm-Rudman-Hollings act (named after the senators who sponsored it). It required that a limit be set on the annual deficit and that the limit be reduced until a balanced budget was achieved in 1991. While less stringent than a constitutional requirement, the **deficit ceiling** was nevertheless strict. Not meeting it would require spending to be reduced automatically to the point where the deficit was no higher than the prescribed limit for that year. It proved too much for Congress—and even for the Supreme Court, which found the automatic reduction provision unconstitutional.

deficit ceiling: a congressionally mandated limit on the size of the federal budget deficit

debt ceiling: a congressionally mandated limit on the size of the gross federal debt

In 2011 and again in 2013, the Obama administration faced a potential crisis over the near breaching of what is known as the U.S. **debt ceiling**. (This is different from a deficit ceiling. According to rules set by Congress, a vote of Congress is required to increase the debt beyond a set amount, called the debt ceiling.) As the debt approached the mandated ceiling, the United States faced the prospect of not being able to borrow fresh funds to pay bonds that were coming due for payment. The risk of such a default would be a decline in the perceived creditworthiness of the United States and, as noted earlier, in 2011 Standard and Poor's lowered the grade of U.S. Treasury bonds from AAA to AA+, the first time in history that this had happened.

Following heated and partisan negotiations, Congress and the president struck a deal in 2011, allowing the debt ceiling to be raised (by a trillion dollars or so) and granting the federal government temporary access to more loans. The terms of the deal were that if the government failed to come to a long-term agreement by the end of 2012, the country would fall off a "fiscal cliff," meaning that $607 billion of tax rate increases and spending cuts would be implemented almost immediately.

Completely falling off the fiscal cliff undoubtedly would have contributed to debt reduction, but tax increases and spending cuts of the magnitude imposed by the terms of the 2011 agreement would have created serious dangers for a still-weak national economy. Even under normal conditions, there are strong arguments against a balanced budget requirement, but in early 2013 reducing deficits rapidly could have been especially harmful. From a Keynesian point of view (as noted in Chapters 25 and 28), a period of anemic job growth is a time to pursue countercyclical policy, using deficits to stimulate the economy and create jobs; it makes better sense to wait for a healthier economy before undertaking further deficit reduction.

Obama and Congress debated until the last few hours of 2012 before reaching an agreement in January 2013 to temporarily avoid the "cliff." They agreed, among other things, to restore payroll taxes back to 6.2 percent of income (they had been lowered in 2010 to 4.2 percent as part of a temporary tax holiday) and to raise the marginal tax rate on individuals earning more than $400,000 and households earning more than $450,000 from 35 to 39.6 percent. These tax rate increases were considerably less than those implied by the "cliff." But on the spending side, $85 billion in across-the-board spending cuts, known as the "sequester," did go into effect two months later.

In October 2013, another bitter conflict over the debt ceiling ended with an agreement just one day before the Treasury would have run out of funds to pay off bonds and meet other obligations such as Social Security payments, following a 16-day shutdown of the Federal government. Once again, the President and Congress agreed to negotiate over long-term debt reduction plans.

In the wake of the 2013 government shutdown, it was apparent that the crisis resulted in significant economic costs and a setback to the pace of recovery. Standard and Poor's estimated that the shutdown had cost had cost $24 billion, or $1.5 billion per day, and slowed the country's economic growth by an annualized 0.6 percent for the fourth quarter of 2013. Fighting over the debt appeared to be more damaging than the debt itself.

In the long run, of course, it is important to keep debt levels under control, but it is a mistake to presume that the federal government should maintain zero debt. The ability to use deficits at appropriate times to generate a fiscal stimulus is what sets the federal government apart from the states and cities and possibly protects a weak economy from sinking deeper.

4.3 Imposed Austerity: The Case of the European Union

In recent years, the member countries of the European Union (EU) have been confronting issues similar to those in the United States, but their response has been quite different. In a number of EU countries, as in much of the rest of the world, a financial collapse followed the bursting of real estate bubbles in the U.S. and many other countries. The sudden end to a global spree of excessive bank leverage and speculation forced many economies into recession.

Governments, faced with the choice of complete financial collapse or the bailout of banks with public money, chose the latter. Recessions in countries like Greece, Spain, and Portugal caused government revenues to fall and expenditures to rise, increasing deficit and debt levels. While the overall situation in Europe may seem strikingly similar to that of the United States, there is an important difference. In Europe, much of the crisis focuses on what is called **sovereign debt**—that is, government debt, especially government debt in a currency that the government does not control.

sovereign debt: government debt, especially debt denominated in a currency that the government does not control

Seventeen countries within the European Union have adopted the euro as their currency. In order to participate in the euro currency, EU member countries must meet certain **convergence criteria**. One criterion concerns government finances and requires both that a country's annual deficit not exceed 3 percent of GDP and that its national debt not exceed 60 percent of GDP.* After the country is accepted into the eurozone (countries that have adopted the euro as the national currency), the restriction is relaxed somewhat under circumstances of extreme economic difficulty (which explains, for example, how Greece, Italy, and others can have a debt: GDP ratio much higher than 60 percent), but countries must then demonstrate that they are making progress toward once again achieving the target amounts.

convergence criteria: the requirements that EU member countries must satisfy as a condition of participating in the eurozone

Table 31.2 shows deficit and debt figures for Portugal, Italy, Ireland, Greece, and Spain. Although all are still far from satisfying the convergence criteria (Italy meets the deficit criterion but not the debt criterion), only for Greece have leading experts even discussed possible expulsion from the eurozone. But this does not mean that governments have not taken action to reduce these numbers.

Authorities in the European Union insisted on a policy of **austerity** for deeply indebted countries. Austerity policy required these countries to reduce expenditures or raise taxes to balance their budgets. Unfortunately, such policies have worsened recessionary conditions, pushing unemployment rates in some of the worst-hit countries to Great Depression levels.

austerity: a policy of deficit cutting that reduces public expenditures or raises taxes to balance the budget

Greece, Spain, and, to a lesser degree, Portugal have experienced considerable social unrest in recent years. There is widespread resentment of governments that are willing to bail out investors in the financial industry but then ask the public to accept higher taxes and spending cuts to pay for them. The populations of these countries include millions of retirees who see grave threats to the government pensions on which they rely for income support in their old age.

Since countries that are members of the eurozone do not have their own currencies, they cannot conduct expansionary monetary policy, and under austerity rules they must implement contractionary fiscal policy. The combination renders them unable to use economic policy to promote recovery. Their ability to borrow is also constrained, since too much borrowing could drive the interest rates on their debt to unsustainable levels.

Table 31.2 **EU Deficit and Debt Levels in 2012 (percentage of GDP)**

	Deficit	Debt
Portugal	–4.6	124.3
Italy	–1.7	122.7
Ireland	–8.4	121.6
Greece	–7.4	168.0
Spain	–5.4	87.9

Source: OECD, www.oecd.org.

*The other three, which need not concern us here, are (1) an inflation rate no more than 1.5 percent higher than the average in the three best-performing EU members; (2) not having devalued domestic currency for at least two years; and (3) long-term interest rate no higher than 2 percent above that in the three best EU inflation performers.

The United States does not confront the same problems, for two reasons. The first is that, at least up to the present, its bond yields are not nearly as sensitive to its escalating debt as are yields in other countries. The issue is related to the U.S. position in the global economy, which, as noted in Chapter 29, has much to do with the historic prestige and strength of the U.S. dollar. The U.S. dominance in this regard may change in the future, but as of now the United States enjoys the advantages of having a "safe haven" currency.

The second reason is that the Fed is far more flexible than its EU counterpart, the European Central Bank (ECB). The ECB's singular agenda is controlling inflation, and it does not consider the fiscal conditions in individual countries. The Fed, in contrast, has a dual mandate to address both inflation and unemployment, providing more flexibility to address short-term economic problems.* As we have seen since the financial crisis, the United States has the ability to employ countercyclical fiscal policy and use monetary policy such as lower interest rates and quantitative easing to try to spur economic activity. The EU, however, has favored policies of austerity, which have worsened recessionary conditions but have done little to reduce overall debt levels (see Box 31.1).

Discussion Questions

1. Should there be a balanced budget amendment to the Constitution? What problems might such an amendment create?
2. What is the difference between austerity and stimulus? Which tack does the European Union follow? How is it different from what the United States has done? Which do you think is a better approach?

BOX 31.1 EUROPE PRESSURED TO RECONSIDER AUSTERITY POLICIES

In 2013, unemployment surpassed Great Depression-era levels in Southern Europe, and was rising even in the less hard-hit economies of the north. The jobless rate in the 17 countries of the Eurozone topped 12 percent in mid-2013. Influential voices warned that European policies of austerity were failing, worsening recession while not helping deficit and debt problems.

> After years of insisting that the primary cure for Europe's malaise is to slash spending, the champions of austerity, most notably Chancellor Angela Merkel of Germany, find themselves under intensified pressure to back off unpopular remedies and find some way to restore faltering growth to the world's largest economic bloc.
>
> Mounting doubts among ordinary Europeans and even the International Monetary Fund have forced senior officials in Brussels [official seat of the European Union] to acknowledge that a move away from what critics see as a fixation on debt and deficits toward more growth-friendly policies is necessary. "There has been a clear shift in thinking," said Guntram Wolff, an economist with the European Commission.
>
> Hints of a new approach in Europe are likely to be greeted as good news by the Obama administration, which has urged healthy European economies to stimulate growth with increased spending and more relaxed monetary policy. The American economy, where government spending has not been reduced as drastically, looks relatively robust in comparison with Europe. (Higgins, 2013)

Sources: Andrew Higgins, "Europe Facing More Pressure to Reconsider Cuts as a Cure," *New York Times*, April 26, 2013; Harvey Morris, "Europe Urged to Make a U-Turn on Austerity," *International Herald Tribune*, April 10, 2013; "Joblessness Edges Higher To Hit a Eurozone Record," *New York Times*, Tuesday, July 2, 2013.

*The "dual mandate" results from amendments to the Federal Reserve Act in 1977. Prior to 1977, the Fed did not have a history of pursuing job growth and had a reputation primarily as an inflation fighter.

5. Deficit Projections and Potential Policy Responses

5.1 Deficit Projections

The U.S. annual federal deficit declined from a peak of 10 percent of GDP in 2009 to 7 percent of GDP in fiscal 2012, and appeared on track to decline further, to around 4 percent of GDP in fiscal 2013.[1] The Congressional Budget Office (CBO), which provides nonpartisan economic analysis for Congress, projects that the deficit will continue to decline as a percentage of GDP for a couple of years but then start to increase again after 2015 (Figure 31.9).[2] Although the annual federal deficit averaged 3.1 percent of GDP from 1973 to 2012, the deficit is projected to grow to 3.8 percent of GDP in 2023 and continue on an upward trajectory after that (see Box 31.2).

Figure 31.9 **Projected Annual Deficit as a Percent of GDP**

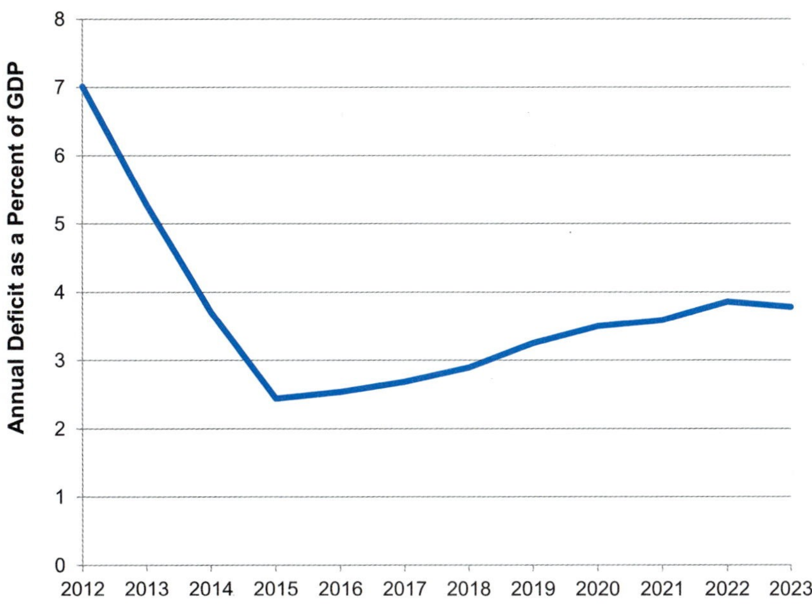

The annual federal deficit is expected to decline through 2015 as the economy improves, but over the longer term deficits are expected to rise due to the effects of an aging population, higher health-care costs and subsidies, and rising interest payments on the national debt.

Source: Congressional Budget Office, *Updated Budget Projections*, 2013.

Similarly, the federal debt held by the public is projected to decrease to 73 percent of GDP in 2018 but then slowly increase to 77 percent of GDP by 2023. The CBO analysis, which assumes no major changes in federal law, identifies four main reasons deficits are projected to remain at relatively high levels even as the economy stabilizes:

1. the demographic pressures of an aging population
2. an increase in health-care costs
3. an increase in federal subsidies for health care
4. an increase in interest payments on the federal debt

Note that the first three factors are closely related and suggest that a focus on health care should be an important component of any significant long-term budgetary reforms in the United States. The CBO explains:

> The aging of the baby-boom generation portends a significant and sustained increase in coming years in the share of the population that will receive benefits from Social Security and Medicare and long-term care services financed through Medicaid. Moreover, per capita spending on health care is likely to continue to grow faster than per capita spending on other goods and services for many years. . . . Without significant changes in the laws

governing Social Security, Medicare, and Medicaid, those factors will boost federal outlays as a percentage of GDP well above the average of the past several decades—a conclusion that applies under any plausible assumptions about future trends in demographics, economic conditions, and health care costs. Unless the laws governing those programs are changed—or the increased spending is accompanied by sufficiently lower spending on other programs, sufficiently higher revenues, or a combination of the two—deficits will be much larger in the future than they have tended to be in the past.[3]

5.2 Policy Choices

The principle that the United States requires long-term budgetary reform is widely accepted. As implied in the CBO quotation above, the basic math dictates that the choices for reform are limited to three basic options:

1. revenue (i.e., tax) increases
2. spending decreases
3. some combination of revenue increases and spending decreases

Few economists or politicians advocate tax increases alone as a solution to reduce the federal deficit. Thus most of the debate concerns whether budgetary reforms should include only spending cuts or whether tax revenues also need to be increased. So far, both spending cuts and tax increases have been pursued.

Box 31.2 Declining Budget Deficits

According to a report issued by the Congressional Budget Office (CBO) in May 2013, the federal deficit fell by 32 percent over the period October 2012—April 2013 compared to the same period in the previous year. The CBO noted:

> The federal government ran a budget deficit of $489 billion in the first seven months of fiscal year 2013, according to CBO's estimates. That amount is $231 billion less than the shortfall recorded during the same period last year, primarily because revenue collections have been much greater than they were at this point in 2012. In contrast, federal spending so far this year has been slightly lower than what it was last year at this time.

And the CBO projected a continuation of the trend of shrinking deficits:

> If the current laws that govern federal spending and taxes do not change, the budget deficit will shrink this year to $642 billion, the smallest shortfall since 2008. Relative to the size of the economy, the deficit this year—at 4.0 percent of gross domestic product (GDP)—will be less than half as large as the shortfall in 2009, which was 10.1 percent of GDP.

Tax receipts increased for several reasons, including:

- rising wages as the economy recovers
- the expiration of a payroll tax cut
- the implementation of higher tax rates on high-income earners
- an increase in corporate taxes due to higher profits

The reasons federal spending decreased included:

- decreasing payments for unemployment benefits
- a 5 percent decrease in defense spending
- decreased spending for housing assistance, energy programs, and international assistance

Spending on some programs increased, including Social Security and Medicare. Spending by the Federal Emergency Management Agency increased due to Hurricane Sandy, and spending by the Department of Agriculture increased as a result of drought conditions.

In longer-range projections, budget deficits were projected to fall even further, to about 2.1 percent of GDP in 2015. However, deficits were projected to increase again in the coming decade, reaching 3.5 percent of GDP in 2023, due to an aging population, rising health care costs, an expansion of federal subsidies for health insurance, and growing interest payments on federal debt.

Sources: Congressional Budget Office, Monthly Budget Review for April 2013, and *Updated Budget Projections,* May 2013.

Federal spending declined from a peak of 25.2 percent of GDP in 2009 to 22.8 percent in 2012, with further minor declines projected through 2017. Federal revenues increased from a low of 15.1 percent of GDP in 2009 to 15.8 percent in 2012 and are expected to continue growing for a few more years. Some of the change in both spending and revenues relates to improving economic conditions, but federal legislation has also been enacted to reduce budget deficits.

As mentioned earlier, in January 2013 Congress agreed to increase tax rates on the wealthiest households (individuals making more than $400,000 per year and couples making more than $450,000). At the same time, the 2010 provision that had temporarily reduced payroll taxes by two percentage points for all workers was allowed to expire. So while the richest households faced the largest tax increases, federal taxes rose for about 77 percent of American households in 2013.

The January 2013 legislation reduced current deficits but did not address the fundamental long-term budgetary imbalance of the federal government. We next consider two proposals for budgetary reform.

5.3 Budgetary Reforms: The Simpson-Bowles Plan

In early 2010, President Obama appointed an 18-member bipartisan commission to develop specific recommendations for deficit reduction. Known as the National Commission on Fiscal Responsibility and Reform (NCFRR), it was led by Republican Alan Simpson (a former senator) and Democrat Erskine Bowles. Their recommendations are commonly known as the Simpson-Bowles Plan.* The plan called for a cumulative (not annual) deficit reduction of almost $4 trillion from 2012 to 2020 and eliminating the deficit entirely by 2035. The plan also projected that the debt held by the public would be reduced to 40 percent of its current level by 2035. Some key elements of this plan include:

1. Reducing discretionary spending by a cumulative $1.7 trillion, including both defense and nondefense cuts. The report suggests spending caps, a three-year freeze on congressional pay, eliminating Congressional "earmarked" spending for specific local projects, and a reduction in the federal workforce.
2. Adding about $1 trillion in cumulative revenues. While the report actually recommends reducing marginal tax rates, it more than offsets that by eliminating more than 150 tax deduction provisions. For example, under current law, a taxpayer can deduct the interest paid on the mortgage for a second home—the plan would eliminate this deduction. The plan advocates that the overall progressivity of the federal tax system should be maintained or increased, rather than imposing an additional burden on low-income households, and also recommends an increase in the gasoline tax of 15 cents per gallon.
3. Creating about $340 billion in cumulative savings from reductions in health-care costs, through various reforms to Medicare and Medicaid.
4. Realizing about $240 billion in cumulative savings from Social Security reforms. The plan recommends gradually increasing the full retirement age from 67 to 69 by 2075, slowing the growth of benefits to middle- and high-income individuals, and raising the cap on income subject to Social Security taxes (the cap was $113,700 as of 2013; increasing the cap would mean that wealthier individuals would pay more social security tax).

After being drafted, the Simpson-Bowles Plan first needed to be approved by 14 members of the full 18-member NCFRR. However, the plan received only 11 votes (support for the plan was split essentially equally among Republicans and Democrats). Thus the plan was not

*The plan is detailed in NCFRR, "The Moment of Truth: Report of the National Commission on Fiscal Responsibility and Reform," December 2010.

put to a vote in Congress. Despite this failure, both Simpson and Bowles have continued to advocate for their plan, making slight changes to it. In February 2013, they wrote:

> The failure to get our debt under control, reform our Tax Code and put our entitlement programs on a fiscally sustainable course is robbing us of the ability to invest in our future and will leave us without the resources we need to meet other challenges facing our nation. And moving forward will be out of our reach as long as we continue to "pass the buck" on the debt crisis. It is critical that leaders in both parties come together in an honest and meaningful way to put our fiscal house in order if they have any hope of addressing the other challenges and opportunities that we face as a nation. . . . If both sides move as one beyond their comfort zone on health and tax reform, those changes could be combined with the other spending cuts discussed in the negotiations last December [2012] to produce a package large enough to stabilize and begin to reduce our debt as a share of the economy.[6]

5.4 Budgetary Reforms: Congressional Budget Office

As a nonpartisan organization, the CBO does not provide specific recommendations. Instead, it aims to analyze the implications of various policy options from an objective point of view. Based on a 2011 analysis, the CBO considers three potential policy objectives:

1. *Balance the federal budget by 2020:* This would require $1 trillion in total annual budgetary reforms by 2020 (i.e., a combination of spending reductions and revenue increases).
2. *Limit debt to 75 percent of GDP in 2020:* This would require $500 billion in total annual budgetary reforms.
3. *A midway objective that would "keep future deficits stable at a relatively small percentage of GDP":* This would require $750 billion in total annual budgetary reforms.

The CBO notes that even the most modest of these proposals (#2) would require substantial policy adjustment:

> Very few policy changes, taken individually, can shrink the deficit enough to achieve any of those objectives. Ultimately, significant deficit reduction is likely to require a combination of policies, many of which may stand in stark contrast to policies now in place. . . . [A] wide gap exists between the future cost of the services that the public has become accustomed to receiving from the federal government—especially in the form of benefits for older people—and the tax revenues that the public has been sending to the government to pay for those services.[4]

The CBO analysis considers three categories of budgetary reforms:

1. *Reduce mandatory spending:* This primarily includes spending on programs such as Social Security, Medicare, and Medicaid.
2. *Reduce discretionary spending:* This includes spending on national defense, education, highways, scientific research, and the environment.
3. *Increase revenues:* This includes letting some existing tax cuts expire, as well instituting new taxes.

The CBO considered nearly 70 potential budgetary changes. For each change, it estimated the budgetary savings that would accrue in 2020 (see Table 31.3).

One implication of the CBO's estimates is that there is no "magic bullet" that can resolve the country's budgetary imbalance. Even the most significant action, letting all 2001, 2003, and

Table 31.3 **Selected Budgetary Reforms, Congressional Budget Office**

Budgetary Reform	Potential Budget Savings in 2020 (billions)
Reductions in Mandatory Spending	
Raise the age of Medicare eligibility to 67	$30
Raise the full retirement age for Social Security	$30
Link Social Security payments to average prices rather than average earnings	$30
Limit malpractice torts	$10
Increase the interest rates charged on student loans	$10
Reductions in Discretionary Spending	
Allow the sequestration budget cuts to reduce military spending*	$75
Allow the sequestration budget cuts to reduce nonmilitary spending	$70
Limit highway funding to expected highway revenues	$11
Reduce funding for the National Institutes of Health	$4
Reduce Department of Energy funding for energy research	$4
Eliminate certain education programs	$2
Revenue Increases	
Allow all 2001, 2003, and 2009 tax cuts to expire as scheduled	$550
Limit tax deductions to 15 percent of income	$150
Institute a tax on greenhouse gas emissions	$140
Eliminate the tax deduction for state and local income	$110
Increase the earnings subject to Social Security taxes	$60
Gradually eliminate the mortgage interest deduction	$50
Increase the motor fuels excise tax by 25 cents per gallon	$30

Source: CBO, *Reducing the Deficit: Spending and Revenue Options,* 2011.

*The "sequestration" budget cuts refer to the Budget Control Act of 2011. Sequestration came into force in 2013.

2009 tax cuts expire, satisfies only the least stringent policy objective listed above. Another implication is that spending cuts alone will not be sufficient to balance the federal budget. Even if all 47 budget cuts considered by the CBO were enacted, including the politically unpopular sequestration cuts, total budgetary savings would be only about $900 billion while $1 trillion in savings would be required to balance the budget.

Revenue increases offer larger total budgetary savings (nearly $2 trillion for all 20 options considered by the CBO), but many of these options are rather unpopular, including letting existing tax cuts expire for all income levels and eliminating various tax deductions. Note that a tax on greenhouse gas emissions, starting at $20 per ton of carbon dioxide and increasing by 5.6 percent per year, could generate $140 billion in additional revenues.[5]

The various budgetary reforms analyzed by the CBO would differ in terms of their impact on the economy and the distribution of the burden. For example, the CBO notes that reducing investment on things like infrastructure and education would decrease future economic production. Increasing the retirement age for Social Security would disproportionately harm lower-income individuals, as they rely more heavily on Social Security benefits.

5.5 Debt and Deficits in Context

The analyses by the CBO and Simpson-Bowles indicate that significant budgetary policy changes are needed to address a long-term structural fiscal imbalance in the United States. In both analyses, most of the policy options are phased in gradually to reduce the likelihood of economic disruptions.

The debate over debts and deficits should be placed in a larger macroeconomic context as well as a social and environmental context. For example, proposals to balance the federal budget by "broadening the tax base" may imply increasing economic inequality, already at historically high levels. Given the strong negative impacts of wide inequalities on the social and economic health of a society, it makes sense that major federal policies, regarding both spending and taxing, should emphasize reducing inequality. As shown in Table 31.3, some possibilities for generating additional revenues also address environmental concerns. A carbon tax on gasoline or, more broadly, on greenhouse gas emissions would not only reduce budget deficits but also internalize the negative externalities associated with burning fossil fuels and increase overall economic efficiency.

Recent budgetary impasses also reflect a change from earlier generations, when policies were frequently adjusted, often with bipartisan support, to address national needs. Consider that Social Security tax rates were raised more than 20 times between 1937 and 1990 as the program's needs increased. More recent strong opposition to raising those taxes stands in contrast to this historical context. Although the budgetary challenge facing the United States may not be its most pressing policy priority, relative to other priorities such as job generation and climate change, it will clearly require some difficult choices. But the problem is solvable, as long as policymakers are willing to compromise and take a long-term perspective.

Discussion Questions

1. Do you think that we can reduce deficits while also avoiding an increase in tax rates? Why would political leaders consider tax hikes? Should everyone experience the same increase?
2. Are there tax policies that can reduce the deficit while also addressing environmental problems?

REVIEW QUESTIONS

1. What is the difference between the national debt and a deficit?
2. What years were debt/GDP levels the highest in the United States? What years were the lowest?
3. What was the role of the national debt in the early period of U.S. history? What was Hamilton's vision for the U.S national debt?
4. How did the national debt picture change with the New Deal and World War II?
5. What factors contributed to the federal surplus during the Clinton administration, and why did it turn into a deficit in the following Bush administration?
6. Summarize some of the potential problems with government debt.
7. What does it mean to monetize the debt?
8. How do European policies of austerity differ from U.S. policies reading debt and deficits?
9. According to the Simpson-Bowles plan, what are six broad ideas for cutting deficits over the next 10 years?
10. According to the Congressional Budget Office, what are some possible budgetary reforms that could reduce the deficit?
11. What are the pros and cons of a balanced budget amendment?

EXERCISES

1. Go to Federal Reserve Economic Database (http://research.stlouisfed.org/fred2/) and look in categories/national accounts for recent data on the U.S. national debt as a percent of GDP and recent figures on budget deficits. What does this tell you about recent trends? Compare the period 1990–2007 to more recent years. Do the figures indicate that we may be returning to a more "normal" situation regarding debt and deficits?
2. Search the internet and locate relatively recent debt / GDP data for European countries. Construct a table of Eurozone members and their debt / GDP ratios based on your search. Review the convergence criteria for participation in the Eurozone presented in the chapter. Don't forget to document your source(s)! What did you discover in this exercise? Explain your answer.
3. The chapter identifies and explains several reasons why it is inappropriate to compare the government

debt to the debt of a private citizen. Which of these explanations are consistent with the presentation in the chapter?

a. Governments have the ability to "roll over" their debt more or less endlessly.
b. Governments cannot default on their debt obligations.
c. A significant portion of the government debt is owed to U.S.citizens.
d. The U.S. government pays interest on its debt in dollars that it prints.
e. Government debt is always used to finance investment.

4. The chapter identifies and explains several reasons why we are likely to observe relatively high deficits in the U.S. even as the economy stabilizes. Which of these explanations is consistent with the chapter's presentation?
   a. Health care costs are expected to continue to increase.
   b. Young adults are having too many children and that creates demographic pressures.
   c. Federal subsidies of health care are expected to grow.
   d. The rising costs of higher education will contribute to deficits.
   e. Interest payments on the debt will likely increase in the future.
5. The chapter is very clear that it's dangerous to assume that, "government debt is never a concern." Which of the following are reasons articulated in the chapter for why debt can be a concern?
   a. Foreign holders of U.S. debt may decide to sell their bonds.
   b. A larger share of future budgets must be devoted to interest payments.
   c. It is always unwise for governments to get into debt
   d. Interest payments to high income individuals could exacerbate income inequality.
   e. Deficit spending during a recession will only make the economic downturn worse.
6. Match each concept in Column A with a definition or example in Column B.

Column A	Column B
a. Debt	1. The portion of the gross federal debt that is owed to individuals or groups within the country
b. Deficit	2. A congressionally mandated limit on the size of the federal debt
c. Gross federal debt	3. The portion of the gross federal debt that is owed to foreign individuals or groups
d. Public debt	4. A stock variable that represents the accumulation of deficits over many years
e. Internal debt	5. The gross federal debt minus the debt owed to other government accounts such as Social Security and Medicare
f. External debt	6. A policy of deficit cutting that reduces public expenditures and/or raises taxes to balance the budget
g. Monetizing the debt	7. A flow variable that measures the excess of spending over revenue collections
h. Debt ceiling	8. The requirements that EU countries must satisfy as a condition for participating in the Eurozone
i. Austerity	9. The purchase of new debt from the Treasury Department by the Federal Reserve
j. Convergence criteria	10. Total amount owed by the federal government to all claimants, including foreigners, the public in the United States, and other government accounts

NOTES

1. Office of Management and Budget, "The President's Budget for Fiscal Year 2013," Historical Table 1.2.
2. Congressional Budget Office, "The Budget and Economic Outlook: Fiscal Years 2013 to 2023," February 5, 2013.
3. CBO, "Choices for Deficit Reduction," November 2012.
4. Ibid., p. 2.
5. See CBO, "Reducing the Deficit: Spending and Revenue Options," March 2011, for details.
6. Erskine Bowles and Alan Simpson, "Memo to Congress, White House: Get Serious on Debt," Politico, February 14, 2013. www.politico.com/story/2013/02/memo-to-congress-white-house-get-serious-on-debt-87678.html.

32 How Economies Grow and Develop

What do people mean by economic development? How do the economic status of countries and the well-being of their people change over time? Most of the macroeconomic theory that we have presented relates to advanced economies such as that of the United States. But if we think back 100 years, the United States was a very different place than it is today. Most transportation was still horse drawn, with only a few cars operating on a poor-quality road system. Most rural areas did not have electricity or telephone service. In 1900, real per capita income in the nation was about $5,000 (measured in 2000 dollars). During the twentieth century, real per capita income in the United States rose about sevenfold, to more than $35,000.

The median income in the world today is about equal to that of the United States in the early 1900s. Although billions of people still live in severe poverty, some formerly poor countries—such as South Korea, China, and India—are rapidly developing. Many others have experienced little economic progress. It is both interesting and important to evaluate how economies grow, how the growth process differs in different cases, and why some countries are very successful at promoting rapid growth, while others seem to be "stuck" at a low level of income.

As we will see in what follows, *economic growth* and *economic development* are not always the same thing, and the differences become more pronounced at higher levels of income. One important theme in this chapter is that, contrary to some earlier theories, there is nothing "automatic" about poor countries becoming developed. Another is that even rapid and sustained GDP growth may not be sufficient to ensure broad-based well-being improvement.

1. Development and Economic Growth

Economic development is an idea that became formalized in the mid-twentieth century, as the colonial empires began to break down and the more industrialized countries gradually took on a changed set of attitudes toward the parts of the world that had not experienced industrialization.* The economic relations between colonies and their rulers had been dominated by the desire of the ruling countries to enrich themselves, first, through extraction of raw materials, and, second, through the creation of markets for goods that they wished to export. By the mid-twentieth century, resistance to imperial domination and strong movements for independence had made it impossible for the ruling countries to maintain their control. The emergence of many new independent countries required a change in attitude.

On the economic side, it was recognized that countries make better trading partners if they can escape from poverty. On the moral side was the recognition that, considering the

*In the first half of the twentieth century, a number of Western countries, including Britain, France, the Netherlands, and Spain, were colonial powers, exerting control over many colonies in Africa, Asia, and South America. Japan was also a colonial power, ruling South Korea and, at various times, parts of China. Most of the colonies had become independent countries by the 1960s.

improvement in living conditions that had accompanied industrialization for the richer countries, it was only right that the "underdeveloped" countries should have a chance to develop their economies and to gain greater wealth and well-being. Some theorists of "neo-colonialism" have argued that the former colonial powers continued to use political and economic power to maintain their dominant position. Nonetheless, newly independent countries were determined to promote economic progress, and the economic theory of development emerged with the purpose of helping to achieve this goal.

The idea of development initially focused on the question: How can poor countries most rapidly follow in the steps of the rich ones? The answers to this question are the subject of a large part of this chapter. We focus especially on the countries where there is a clear need for increased economic development to satisfy people's basic needs for food, shelter, health care, and education. But it is also worth noting that the term "development" can be used for *all* kinds of positive economic change and, thus, could also be applied to the countries that have successfully achieved greater wealth and industrialization. That is an issue to which we return in Chapter 33, where we will take a look at the changes that will be required both in wealthier countries and in rapidly developing countries such as China, if the global economy is to achieve a sustainable balance with its ecological context.

1.1 STANDARD ECONOMIC GROWTH THEORY

As we noted in Chapter 21, there are many criticisms of the use of GDP as a measure of economic progress. Standard models of economic growth, however, are all based on this measure, and we begin by reviewing some of these models.

The simplest definition of economic growth is an increase in real GDP (i.e., GDP adjusted for inflation). The growth rate of real GDP is the percentage change in real GDP from one year to the next. Using what we learned in Chapter 20, we can express the rate of growth in, for example, the period 2011–12, as follows:

$$\textit{growth rate of real GDP} = \frac{\textit{Real GDP}_{2012} - \textit{Real GDP}_{2011}}{\textit{Real GDP}_{2011}} \times 100$$

For example, U.S. real GDP in 2011 (in chained 2005 dollars) was \$13.44 trillion and in 2012 it was \$13.67 trillion. Thus the growth rate of real U.S. GDP from 2011 to 2012 was

$$= \frac{13.67 - 13.44}{13.44} \times 100 = \frac{.23}{12.44} \times 100 = 2.9 \text{ percent}$$

For purposes of evaluating how economic growth is related to economic development, it is often helpful to focus on the growth rate of GDP *per capita*—that is, output *per person*—rather than simply on overall output. Mathematically, GDP per capita is expressed as:

$$\textit{GDP per capita} = \textit{GDP} / \textit{population}$$

The growth rates of GDP, population, and GDP per capita are related in the following way (where the sign ≈ means "approximately equals"):

$$\textit{Growth rate of GDP} \approx \textit{Growth rate of population} + \textit{growth rate of GDP per capita}$$

or:

$$\textit{Growth rate of GDP per capita} \approx \textit{Growth rate of GDP} - \textit{growth rate of population}$$

Figure 32.1 **Economic Growth in the AS/AD Model**

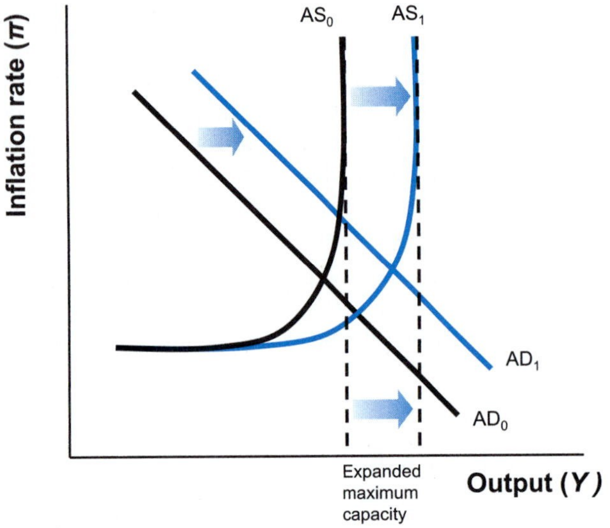

Economic growth increases the maximum capacity of the economy. It involves both supply-side and demand-side expansions, and does not necessarily involve a change in the rate of inflation.

Thus, for example, an economy that has a GDP growth rate of 4 percent and a population growth rate of 2 percent would have a per capita GDP growth rate of approximately 2 percent. The per capita GDP growth rate is especially important because it indicates the actual increase in average income being experienced by the people of the country. If a country had a 2 percent GDP growth rate, but a 3 percent population growth rate, its per capita GDP growth rate would actually be negative, at –1 percent. The people would on average be getting poorer each year, even though the overall economy is growing. Thus for people's incomes on average to increase over time, the GDP growth rate must exceed the rate of population growth.

In terms of the aggregate supply and demand graphs that we used in Chapter 28, economic growth can be shown as a rightward shift of the aggregate supply (*AS*), increasing the economy's maximum capacity (Figure 32.1). If this kind of increase in aggregate supply took place without any shift in aggregate demand (*AD*), its effects would include growth in output and a declining rate of inflation. In practice, however, economic growth is almost always accompanied by, and is often caused at least in part by, an increase in aggregate demand. Thus a more typical pattern for economic growth would be for *both* the *AD* and *AS* curves to shift to the right, as shown in Figure 32.1. In this case, output clearly rises, but the effect on inflation is ambiguous.

What causes economic output to increase? One way that output could increase is if there is an expansion in the inputs used to produce it. Recall that in Chapters 1 and 15 we outlined five kinds of capital. Land and natural resources are *natural capital.* The stock of productive resources that have been produced by people is called *manufactured capital.* All the skills and knowledge possessed by humans are *human capital,* while *social* and *financial* capital both refer to institutional arrangements that make production possible.

Capital expansion is related to the production-possibilities frontier (PPF) that we first saw in Chapter 1. Recall that any point "outside" the PPF is unattainable—impossible to achieve with the *present* endowment of inputs and available technology. So another way of seeing GDP growth is in relation to the capital expansion required to "shift" the PPF outward, to where previously unattainable combinations of, say, guns and butter become possible. Such an outward shift could require an increase in any one of the capital types: for example, if all the material and technological resources are in place but are being used inefficiently, an outward shift could be achieved through an increase in social capital that allows better coordination and cooperation among workers and managers.

Economists sometimes think about output as being generated according to a "production function," which is a mathematical relation between various inputs and the level of output. In the most general sense, we might say that the output of an economy should be expressed as a function of flows from *all* the different types of capital that make production possible. The inputs to the production function are commonly referred to as **factors of production**. In the production functions most commonly used by economists, the factors that are emphasized are manufactured capital and labor. Sometimes, but not always, natural resources are also included.

factors of production: the essential inputs for economic activity, including labor, capital, and natural resources

Technology is the other important variable that influences economic output. We say that a point outside the PPF is unattainable "given available factors of production (i.e., inputs) and the present state of technology." In other words, it matters not only how many of the different factors we possess but also how productive on average each is—and productivity depends crucially on the level of technology.

In their production functions, economists often include a term that captures **total factor productivity**, which includes all contributions to total production not already reflected in the input levels. "Total factor productivity" has often been interpreted as reflecting the way in which technological innovation allows inputs such as capital and labor to be used in more effective and valuable ways. For example, the development of word-processing software greatly increased efficiency compared to the use of typewriters. Typewriters, which seem antique to us today, were themselves a huge productive advance over clerical work using pen and paper. This process of improved technological methods has resulted in an increase in labor productivity—more output can now be produced with fewer inputs. The input most often measured in productivity statistics is labor-hours; however, total factor productivity also takes into account natural capital, machinery, and any other relevant inputs.

total factor productivity: a measure of the productivity of all factors of production. It represents contributions to output from all sources, not just quantities of manufactured capital and labor.

1.2 Historical Overview and Twentieth-Century Theory

The **Industrial Revolution**, a process of rapid social, technological, and economic change, which began in Britain and Western Europe, dramatically changed the nature of economic production. Although, as we discuss later, the applicability of this model to current development issues has been subject to criticism, its strong influence on standard views of economic growth makes it an important starting point for understanding development.

Industrial Revolution: a process of social, technological, and economic change, beginning in Western Europe in the eighteenth century, that developed and applied new methods of production and work organization resulting in a great increase in output per worker

Several elements were critical in creating the Industrial Revolution. First, new agricultural techniques, along with new kinds of tools and machines, made agriculture more productive. Because farmers became more productive, fewer were needed to produce the necessary food, and many migrated to the growing urban areas. Second, the invention and application of technologies using fossil-fuel energy (especially coal) contributed not only to the productivity gains in agriculture but to growth in the number of factory jobs and the development of transportation networks. Third, Britain's increasing reliance on other countries, including its extensive network of colonies, for supplies of raw materials and as markets for its goods, was critical in the development of its industrial sector. Britain imported cotton fiber from India, for example. It discouraged the further development of cotton manufacturing within India by putting high import tariffs on Indian-made cloth, while requiring that India let in British-made cloth tariff-free.

While the Industrial Revolution began in Britain, by the nineteenth and early twentieth centuries it was well along in much of Western Europe and other "early industrializing" countries, such as the United States, Canada, and Australia. It is important not just as a historical episode but because the pattern of economic development that it established has become, in many people's minds, the model for how development should proceed worldwide. The vocabulary of referring to rich countries as "developed" and poorer countries as "developing," for example, involves an implicit assumption that poorer countries are on a path of industrialization, on the road to perhaps eventually "catching up" to rich countries' lifestyles and levels of wealth.

Starting in the early 1950s, a number of economists began to develop theories on how economies develop. The economic historian W.W. Rostow, for example, advanced the thesis that progress from "underdevelopment" to development invariably went through five stages. The first he referred to as "traditional, agrarian society," meaning not only an economy based on farming but also one that was stagnant—that is, not in an active process of development. The second stage, "preconditions for takeoff," is similar to the first, with the important exception that the country now possesses a critical mass of entrepreneurs and educated people, signifying the country's *potential* for development. Although he did not use these terms, for Rostow "human capital" was indispensable for development, and "natural capital" (which even the least developed countries possess), while important, was insufficient.

The third stage was "takeoff" (into self-sustaining growth). At this point, the country realizes its development "potential" by achieving a sufficiently high level of *savings* to finance the *investment*—specifically, manufactured capital accumulation—necessary for growth. From there, growth and development was expected to sustain itself. The fourth stage is the "drive to maturity," and the final stage, where the rich countries currently find themselves, is the "age of high mass consumption."

The main conclusion from Rostow's theory is that after the necessary "preconditions" (education and entrepreneurship) are present, investment in manufactured capital and technology is sufficient to propel a country to a high living standard. A very similar conclusion was reached by the more mathematical Harrod-Domar model, named after the economists Roy Harrod and Evsey Domar.

An important corollary to Rostow's theory is that if domestic savings were insufficient to enable a country to reach the "takeoff" stage, "foreign saving" should help compensate for the shortfall. This could come from private investment, assuming that countries had stable enough conditions to attract foreign investors. The theory also supported the then-widespread view that countries like the United States should provide foreign aid to developing countries in need, to help them raise their living standard (and also given the reality of the cold war, to lure them into their "sphere of influence"). Yet as we will see, success in this effort was far from universal. The failure of aid to stimulate sustained growth in many countries caused a great deal of frustration among policymakers.

By the 1980s, the idea that countries should engage in "structural reforms" as a precondition for being granted aid gained ground. Multilateral institutions such as the International Monetary Fund (IMF) and the World Bank, which provided loans for development or to assist countries in financial difficulties, began to insist that *all* recipient governments undertake a broad swath of policy changes to qualify for further loans. The set of favored policies came to be known as the "Washington Consensus." The main principles of the Washington Consensus were:

- *Fiscal discipline.* Developing countries were urged to end fiscal deficits and balance government budgets by developing reliable sources of tax revenue and limiting spending.
- *Market liberalization and privatization.* Abolition of government-controlled industries, price controls, and other forms of intervention in domestic markets were seen as essential to promoting growth.
- *Trade liberalization and openness to foreign investment.* Countries were pressured to remove tariffs and other barriers to trade, as well as capital controls and other restrictions on foreign investment flows.

Loans from the World Bank, the IMF, and other institutions were made conditional on moving toward making such "structural reforms" or "structural adjustments" in a country's economy. The slogan "stabilize, privatize, and liberalize" governed the thinking of development policymakers. The implicit promise was that if these policies were followed, the conditions for rapid growth would be created. As in Rostow's theory, the emphasis was

Table 32.1 **Per Capita Annual Real GDP Growth in Select Latin American Countries, 1980–2010** (%)

Bolivia	0.5
Brazil	1.0
Chile	3.2
Colombia	1.6
Ecuador	0.8
Mexico	0.7
Peru	1.1
Venezuela	–0.2
Middle Income	3.5

Source: World Bank, World Development Indicators Database, 2013.

on making developing economies "safe" for foreign investment; also, the presumption was that the same guidelines applied to every developing country. A new element that arrived with the Washington Consensus was a set of limitations on the autonomy of developing country governments.

Recent growth performances seriously call into question the validity of these policy prescriptions. The region of the world most influenced by the Washington Consensus has been Latin America, and, as can be seen in Table 32.1, its growth rates over the past three decades compare rather unfavorably to the average growth rate for middle-income countries as a whole (with few exceptions, Latin American countries are in the "middle-income" category). Only Chile, which had 3.2 percent growth from 1980 to 2010, comes close to the global average for middle-income countries. All the other listed countries (with the possible exception of Colombia) grew anemically. The entire Latin America and Caribbean region grew only 0.9 percent on average.

The poor performance of this region of the world is, to date, the strongest indictment of the Washington Consensus. As we will see, however, even where growth in other regions has been stronger, it was quite imbalanced. One of the challenges in development economics is to address the growing inequality that results—both within and among countries.

Discussion Questions

1. How, according to twentieth-century theory, can a country achieve GDP growth? How is growth related to the capital endowments—and which kinds of capital are most important?
2. What, according to Rostow, are the five "stages of growth" through which all countries must pass in order to become developed? Do you think this theory fits with the actual experience of development? Can you name a country at each stage?

2. Country Growth Experiences

The Rostow and Harrod-Domar models were largely based on the phenomenal economic growth record of the industrialized countries. This section briefly reviews that record and then compares more recent growth rates of different countries.

2.1 Growth Comparisons Across Countries

During the twentieth century, real income in the United States rose about sevenfold, and world per capita economic output grew about fivefold. Most of this growth came in the second half of the twentieth century. Figure 32.2 shows the record of global growth since 1971. Gross world product went up by a factor of 3.5 during this period (in inflation-adjusted terms). This was accompanied by a more than doubling in the use of energy, primarily fossil fuels.

Figure 32.2 **World Economic Growth, 1971–2011**

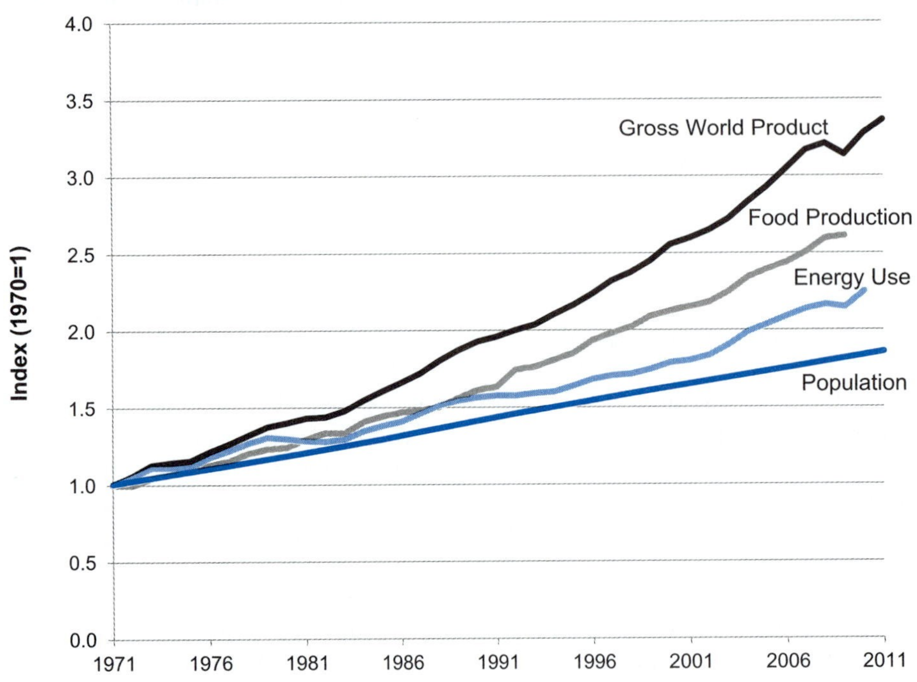

All series are shown using an index of 1 for 1971 levels. During the period 1971–2011, population nearly doubled, energy use more than doubled, food production increased 160 percent, and gross world product increased by 240 percent.

Source: World Bank, World Development Indicators Database, 2013.

Even though world population nearly doubled over the period 1971–2011, food production and living standards grew more rapidly than population, leading to a steady increase in per capita income.

This economic growth has been very unevenly distributed among countries, as well as among people within countries. Table 32.2 shows the per capita national incomes and rates of economic growth for selected countries and income category groups during the period 1990–2011. The table gives national income in purchasing power parity (PPP) terms, comparing countries based on the relative buying power of incomes.

As Table 32.2 shows, the record is highly variable, with some countries achieving less than 1 percent annual per capita economic growth, and others achieving more than 4 percent, with China in the lead at a sizzling 9.5 percent. Some already poor countries, such as Haiti and the Democratic Republic of Congo, are growing even poorer. While the table indicates that the middle-income countries are the fastest-growing group, this is largely a result of high growth rates in China and India, which together account for more than half the population of all middle-income countries.

What accounts for the striking differences in economic fortunes across countries? And can we expect such differences to increase or decrease?

Economies such as those of the United States, Europe, and Japan have benefited from many decades of economic growth. Such growth has not been uniform; periods of expansion have alternated with periods of slowdown or recession. (The Japanese economy, for example, has grown very slowly in recent years.) But overall, GDP in these countries has increased due to a combination of factors including growth in aggregate demand and—as discussed earlier—labor productivity, technological innovation, and investment in manufactured capital.

In addition, successful economic growth has often resulted from taking advantage of trade opportunities. Although industrialized countries have generally benefited from openness to trade, they have also typically used protectionism—tariffs and quotas to limit trade—to foster

Table 32.2 **Income, Growth, and Population Comparisons, Selected Countries and Country Groups**

Country or Category	GDP per capita, 2011 (PPP, 2005, US$)	Percent growth in GDP per capita (PPP, annual average, 1990–2011)	Percent of world population (2011)
High Income	33,566	1.5	16.3
Hong Kong	44,640	3.0	0.1
United States	42,486	1.4	4.5
Japan	30,660	0.7	1.8
France	29,819	1.0	0.9
South Korea	27,541	4.3	0.7
Middle Income	6,245	3.5	72.0
Russia	14,821	0.8	2.0
Turkey	13,468	2.5	0.8
Brazil	10,279	1.7	2.8
China	7,418	9.5	19.3
India	3,203	4.7	17.8
Low Income	1,182	1.9	11.7
Bangladesh	1,569	3.6	2.2
Nepal	1,106	2.1	0.3
Haiti*	1,034	−1.4	0.1
Ethiopia	979	2.8	1.2
Congo, DR	329	−3.0	1.0

Source: World Bank, World Development Indicators Database, 2013.
*Data for Haiti growth rate is for 1991–2011.

the development of important domestic industries. Critics such as economist Ha-Joon Chang claim that such countries have "kicked away" the (protectionist) ladder that they have used to ascend to higher living standards and now insist that poor countries seeking to develop their economies follow "free trade" rules and not use tariffs or quotas to protect their industries.

virtuous cycles (in development): self-reinforcing patterns of high savings, investment, productivity growth, and economic expansion

Japan and other "Asian Tigers" (South Korea, Hong Kong, Taiwan, and Singapore), starting in the mid-twentieth century, demonstrated a pattern of **virtuous cycles** in which high savings and investment lead to greater productivity, a competitive export industry, and growth of domestic industries. The resulting financial capital is then invested in machines, tools, factories, and other equipment that can further enhance productivity—and the cycle begins again. In addition, as the economy grows, more resources are available to invest in the development of health-care and educational systems. It sounds simple and obvious—yet many countries have had great trouble in achieving such virtuous cycles.

One factor that appears to be essential in almost every case for promoting growth and development is human capital. While the U.S. savings rate is low, American investment in human capital is relatively high. For example, only Sweden, Korea, and Finland have college enrollments beyond high school that are higher than those in the United States. The Asian Tigers have also benefited from generally excellent educational systems, along with industrial structure that (especially in Japan) motivated workers with good employment benefits linked to company profitability.

Early theories of development such as Rostow's assumed that the lessons from industrialized economies simply needed to be applied to countries at lower levels of income, so that they could follow a similar path of economic growth. But the global record of uneven development and inequality makes the picture significantly more complex. For example, the global distribution of per capita GDP across countries is shown in Figure 32.3, where each country's per capita GDP in 2011 has been translated into real 2005 U.S. dollars and adjusted for PPP, for the sake of comparability. The United States, along with Canada, most of Europe, Australia, Japan, and a few other countries, enjoys a per capita GDP of more than $25,000.

Figure 32.3 **GDP per Capita in 2011 (in constant 2005 PPP $ per person)**

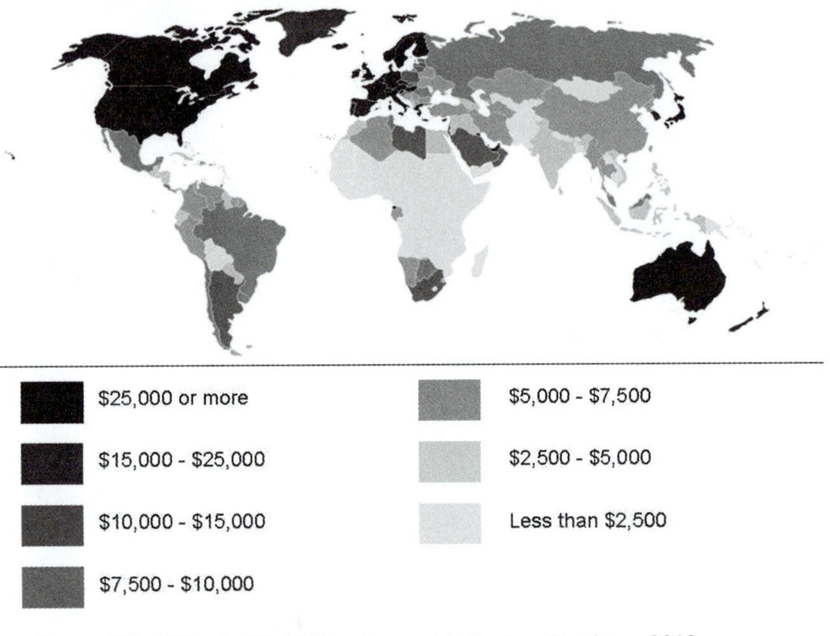

Income per person is highest in the industrialized countries of North America and Europe, along with Japan, Australia, and New Zealand. Income per person is lowest in many African and Asian countries.

Source: World Bank, World Development Indicators Database, 2012.

The poorest countries on earth tend to be in Africa and Asia, where income per capita can be below—sometimes much below—$2,500.

Traditionally, many economists have taken an optimistic view concerning the future of global income inequality. They have argued that a given increase in the manufactured capital stock should lead to a greater increase in output in a country that is capital-poor than in a country that is already capital-rich. Therefore, as developing countries build up their capital stocks, it is just a matter of time until "less developed" countries catch up with the countries that have already "developed." The idea that poorer countries or regions are on a path to "catch up" is often referred to as **convergence**. Describing low-income countries as "developing" assumes that they are on a one-way path toward greater industrialization, labor productivity, and integration into the global economy.

convergence (in reference to economic growth): the idea that underlying economic forces will cause poorer countries and regions to "catch up" with richer ones

Is it true that "developing" countries are, in general, catching up with the "developed" countries? Some studies of GDP per capita growth rates, using data such as that in Table 32.2, emphasize that even the low-income countries have grown more rapidly, on average, than the high-income ones. However, this has largely been due to the strong growth rates experienced by more populous countries (as noted above, the rapid growth of China and India significantly raise the average for the middle-income group of countries). If we look at every country individually, the conclusion on convergence appears more ambiguous.

The evidence suggests that while some developing countries are on a path to catch up with the richer ones in GDP terms, others are not. In fact, if we count each country equally, the average annual growth rate of real GDP per capita (PPP) in 1990–2011 was 0.3 percent in the low-income countries, 1.9 percent in the middle-income countries, and 2.1 percent in the high-income countries—suggesting further divergence rather than convergence. It is also true that if a rich country and a poor one are experiencing the same *percentage* growth rate, this adds a great deal more income in the rich country than in the poor one. Thus in absolute terms the gap between them grows wider unless the poor country has a much higher growth rate.

In spite of all this, when GDP per capita of certain developing countries is expressed as a proportion of average GDP per capita in the high-income countries, some countries do appear

Figures 32.4a and 32.4b **Per Capita GDP Expressed as a Percentage of per-Capita GDP in High-Income Countries**

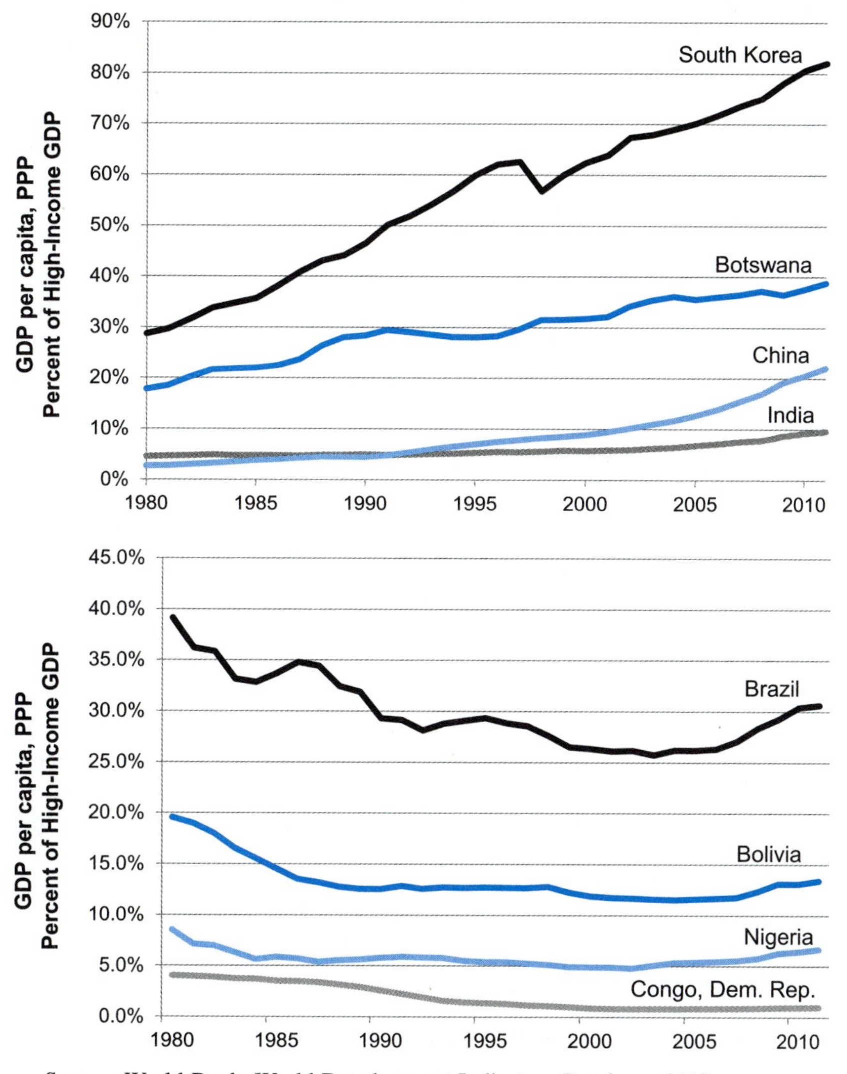

If poor countries are "converging" or "catching up" to rich countries, their incomes should be rising when expressed as a percentage of rich country incomes. This has happened for South Korea, China, and Botswana, and also for India, but much more slowly. Brazil, Bolivia, Nigeria, and the Democratic Republic of the Congo, in contrast, all fell farther behind over the period 1980–2005.

Source: World Bank, World Development Indicators Database, 2013.

to be "catching up" (Figure 32.4a). South Korea, for example, is well on its way to joining the ranks of the rich countries, as its per capita GDP rose from about 30 percent of rich-country GDP in 1980 to more than 80 percent today. Botswana's per capita income also rose considerably over this period, from 20 percent of rich-country GDP to 40 percent. Although at a lower level, the rise in China's per capita GDP has been the most rapid, from less than 3 percent of rich-country GDP to more than 20 percent. Finally, India is also "catching up," albeit somewhat more slowly and from a lower starting point.

Other developing countries exhibit trends such as those seen in Figure 32.4b. Brazil, often touted as one of the most important "newly industrializing countries" (NICs), experienced a per capita income drop in relation to the average in rich countries over the period 1980–2005, but has rebounded somewhat since 2005. Bolivia, Nigeria, and the Democratic Republic of Congo, among many other countries, suffered losses as well, the latter two from a very low starting point, and have had weaker recoveries since 2005 (virtually none for D.R. Congo). A consistent pattern among the countries "falling behind" is a particularly sharp drop in the 1980s, followed by more or less of a leveling off after 2000.

One encouraging fact is that since 2000 there has been significantly more progress toward convergence, driven mainly by rapid growth in China and India but occurring in other countries also. According to one recent study, "the last decade witnessed a sharp reversal from a pattern of divergence to convergence—particularly for a set of large middle-income countries."[1] But even if convergence is sustained, global inequalities will continue for a long time. The United Nations notes that were "high income countries to stop growing today and Latin America and sub-Saharan Africa to continue on their current growth trajectories, it would take Latin America until 2177 and Africa until 2236 to catch up."[2]

How rapidly are countries growing now? Figure 32.5 summarizes a wealth of information about economic growth across countries since 1980. The horizontal axis measures GDP per capita in 2011, in constant chained 2005, PPP-adjusted dollars. The size of the spheres is proportional to the population of the country represented, so that the United States is a medium-size sphere, while China and India—together, home to nearly 40 percent of the world's population—are represented by very large spheres. Spheres on the right represent the United States and other industrialized countries, and spheres on the left represent poorer countries.

The vertical axis measures average annual real GDP per capita growth rates from 1980 to 2011. Thus more rapidly growing countries, including China, India, and South Korea, are high on the graph, while slower-growing countries are represented by spheres closer to the horizontal axis. Some countries have experienced negative growth—that is, their levels of income per person have actually fallen in recent years after adjusting for inflation. High-income countries have generally experienced moderate, positive average growth rates (on the order of 1 percent to 2 percent), while growth rates diverge much more as one moves down the income scale. For developing countries, average growth rates diverge dramatically (ranging from 10 percent for China down to –3 percent for D.R. Congo).

China and India represent the "good news" side of the development story. Although many people in these countries remain very poor, at least the trend is going in the right direction. Because of strong growth in these two very populous countries, a large number of people have been lifted out of poverty in recent decades.

The countries of sub-Saharan Africa, which have been hit particularly hard by AIDS and war, account for a substantial proportion of the very low and negative growth rates (e.g., Côte d'Ivoire and D.R. Congo). This is the very "bad news" side of the contemporary development. Far from "developing," such countries have actually become poorer in recent decades.

Figure 32.5 **Growth and Income Relationship with Area Proportional to Population**

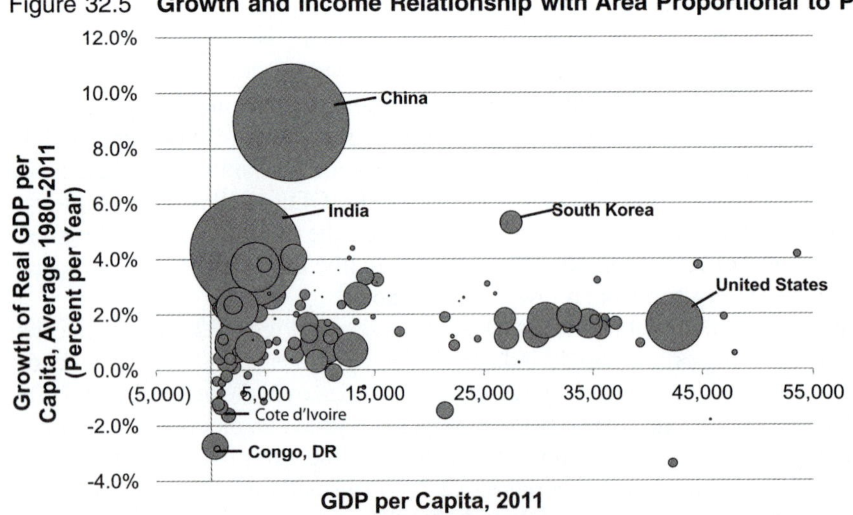

Each circle represents a country. The size of the circle corresponds to the size of the country's population. The location of the circle shows GDP and GDP growth rate.

Source: World Bank, World Development Indicators Database, 2013.

2.2 THE VARIETY OF SOURCES OF ECONOMIC GROWTH

What accounts for the striking differences in economic fortunes across countries? If there were just one simple story about how economic growth occurs, economic analysis would be much easier. In fact, however, one can point to a great variety of factors, all of which may play a role in development. But their significance—and even the direction of their effect, positive or negative—may vary greatly from country to country. For this reason, it is impossible to make all-encompassing statements about why many developing countries have failed to achieve sustained growth. The following observations summarize a range of reasons for growth; their relevance varies from one situation to another.

Natural Resources

Often, one of the first things that students of development think of is the role of natural resources. Indeed, large expanses of arable land, rich mineral and energy resources, good natural port facilities, and a healthy climate may make it easier for a country to prosper, while a poor natural endowment, such as a climate that makes a country prone to malaria or drought, can be a serious drag on development. But the historical record includes some surprises. Hong Kong and Singapore have prosperous trade-based economies, even though they have scant domestic resources, with little land or energy of their own.

In fact, the overexploitation of natural resources can lead both to environmental degradation and to economic distortion. Countries such as Nigeria have found that oil reserves, seemingly a source of wealth, can easily be misappropriated with very damaging effects on development. Misdirected oil revenues can lead to massive corruption and waste. Other sectors of the economy are starved of investment and resources, as available resources go primarily toward oil production. And because oil is an exhaustible resource, the country can eventually run out of oil and find itself worse off than before. Nigeria's experience is symbolic of what many have referred to as the "resource curse" (the idea that countries endowed with abundant natural resources often do worse than countries with fewer resources).

Savings and Investment

Investment in manufactured capital requires financial capital that, as we have seen, comes from savings. Yet investment in industrial manufactured capital is not the only important kind of investment. Investments in agriculture, through improvement of seeds, irrigation, and the like, are also essential to growth. Countries can also invest in human capital by improving their country's systems of education and health care. Workers who are skilled and healthy are more able to be productive. Many economists stress that education in science and technology, in particular, is likely to have significant effects on growth.

Additions to capital, however, do not automatically lead to growth. Technologies that are highly automated or "**capital intensive**" may sometimes be inappropriate in countries with an abundance of potential laborers. In such countries, more appropriate investments might be made in technologies that make greater use of its abundant potential workers—in other words, technologies that are more "**labor intensive**."

capital intensive: a process or procedure that makes use of more capital relative to other inputs such as labor

labor intensive: a process or procedure that makes use of more labor relative to other inputs such as capital

This claim is not without some controversy, because goods produced under labor-intensive processes tend to be less sophisticated and high tech and therefore promise less export revenue than other products made with modern equipment. Indeed, one of the conflicts regularly confronted by developing countries is the need to balance economic diversification (especially into "higher-end" products) with the need to provide employment opportunities for its population. There is also a significant tension between the motivations to provide more sophisticated products for export vs. products that will be of more use to people in the country. In extreme cases, countries export food that their people cannot afford to buy for themselves.

Allocation of Investment

According to market theory, investors should be attracted to the most profitable opportunities. But market allocation of investment alone may ignore social priorities and will not necessarily contribute much to the development of infrastructure (things like roads, ports, railroads, and electronic networks). These and other important public goods such as environmental quality and water supplies require a public role in directing investment.*

industrial policy: a set of government policies designed to enhance a country's ability to compete globally

infant industry: an industry that is not yet globally competitive, but receives government support with the expectation that it may become so

In addition to investing in public goods, governments have often played a role in planning other industrial investments. Known as **industrial policy**, this approach can involve promoting particular industries, using tariffs, subsidies, and other economic tools as needed, even when this implies active government modification of market outcomes. These tools may be applied to protect or subsidize industries that are not yet competitive, in the hope that they may become so over time; this is sometimes referred to as an **infant industry** policy.

Virtually all currently high-income countries used such policies in earlier stages of growth. Britain and the United States consciously formulated tariff policies to encourage domestic industries. Similar industrial policies employed by Japan and the Asian Tigers (Hong Kong, Singapore, South Korea, and Taiwan) were essential to their rapid development between the 1960s and 1990s. Ironically, Western countries that aggressively used industrial policies in earlier stages of development now often preach free trade and fiscal reform to others. As noted earlier, this has led to charges of hypocrisy with regard to developed countries that seem to want to "kick away the ladder" for later industrializers.

Foreign Sources of Financial Capital

bilateral development assistance: aid (or loans) given by one country to another to promote development

multilateral development assistance: aid or loans provided with the announced intention of promoting development by the World Bank, regional development banks, or UN agencies such as the United Nations Development Programme (UNDP)

If a country is not able to finance the investments it needs for development out of its own domestic savings, it generally seeks grants, loans, or investments from abroad. The sources of foreign capital for development can be either public or private. Public aid for development can take the form of either bilateral assistance or multilateral assistance. **Bilateral development assistance** consists of grants or loans made by a rich country's government to a poorer country. Many developing countries also receive **multilateral development assistance** from institutions such as the World Bank and regional development banks such as the Inter-American Development Bank and UN agencies such as the United Nations Development Programme (UNDP). Countries may also borrow from the IMF, particularly during times of crisis.

Private foreign investment is carried out by private companies or individuals. Foreign direct investment (FDI) occurs when a company or individual acquires or creates assets for its own business operations (e.g., a German company building a factory to produce televisions in Mexico). FDI may or may not actually increase the capital stock in the recipient country, because it can include acquisitions of existing capital. Private flows also include loans from private banks. From 2000 to 2010, private flows of investment to developing countries increased dramatically, from $200 billion to more than $1 trillion, but have since leveled off at about $700–800 billion.[3]

The empirical evidence concerning the contribution of public and private foreign capital to economic growth is mixed. Some of the countries that are still among the poorest have also been the heaviest recipients of concessional aid (meaning aid without any requirements for repayment). In some cases, aid went to corrupt leaders who spent it on their own luxurious lifestyles rather than on benefits for their people. Many poor countries are now highly indebted and spend more on debt service (payment of principal and interest) than on health care for their population.

Foreign investment can sometimes play an essential role in spurring development, but welcoming foreign businesses also can have a downside. When a large, powerful transnational corporation moves into a developing country, it may "crowd out" local initiatives, by

*See the definitions of infrastructure and public goods in Chapters 2 and 3.

competing with them for finance, inputs, or markets, sometimes in effect replacing a viable, though small-scale, local business sector with an international corporation producing for international sales. It may also be disruptive politically or culturally. Some of the most oppressive actions in development history (such as peasants being forced off their land or union organizers repressed with violence) have come about through alliances between large transnational corporations and corrupt governments.

Domestic Demand vs. Export Orientation

Because there would be little point in increasing production if what is made cannot find a market, the level of aggregate demand in an economy is also of great importance for growth. One reason that developing countries sometimes fail to achieve sustained growth is that, while production for export is emphasized, not enough is done to develop domestic markets. There are counterexamples to this statement: countries such as Japan and South Korea broke into the ranks of more advanced economies by developing powerful export industries, and China is now following this same path. But export dependence can become a trap that stifles economic development when countries depend on exporting products for which world demand is limited. Producers of agricultural exports, in particular, often suffer when world **terms of trade** turn against them, so that the value of what they can sell on the world market drops relative to the value of what they want to import.

terms of trade: the price of exports relative to imports

Financial, Legal, and Regulatory Institutions

Recently, policymakers have gained a greater appreciation of the role played by financial, legal, and regulatory institutions (which fit into the category of social capital) in encouraging—or discouraging—growth. Very poor countries sometimes have banking and legal systems that do not reach very far into rural areas and provide credit only for the well-connected or well-to-do, making it difficult for small businesses and entrepreneurs to finance new or growing enterprises. The experience of Russia, where GDP fell more than 40 percent during its emergence from communism in the 1990s, highlighted the need for markets to be based in a good institutional framework.

Countries that have been successful in maintaining growth generally have effective systems of property rights and contract enforcement, which allow entrepreneurs to benefit from their investments, as well as effective corporate and bank regulation. Even in the case of property rights, however, the conventional wisdom does not always hold. China and Vietnam, for example, have been able to attract significant amounts of investment, even though, being at least nominally still communist countries, they do not have systems of private property rights. Nevertheless, they are able to assure firms that they will benefit from their investments by other means.

Some developing countries suffer from severe corruption, internal conflict, and other factors that make it difficult for effective institutions to take root. Political instability leads to economic inefficiency, difficulty in attracting foreign investment, and slow or no growth. This, in turn, means that less saving is available for future investment, reinforcing the problems. Breaking this vicious cycle is essential for development but can be very difficult to do.

2.3 Different Kinds of Economies

The previous section focused on the importance of investment—whether in agriculture or industrialization, in human and social capital, or in technology, infrastructure, or other physical capital. This raises the question: Who decides what are the most important investments to make? Should investment decisions be left to private markets or controlled by the government or some combination of the two? Historical experience offers a number of models.

The most extreme form of government control, represented by the experience of the Soviet Union from 1917 to 1989 and often referred to as a "command economy," has generally been discredited as an economic model. Its achievements in areas such as military production and some public goods (such as the Moscow subway system and elements of public education) came at a terrible human cost. Comparisons of Communist North Korea and East Germany with market-oriented South Korea and West Germany showed starkly that markets had a far better chance of achieving a more humane kind of development.

However, these alternatives are not, in fact, the only possibilities. Indeed, there are not only differences between market and command economies, but within each of these categories there is more than one alternative—and relative development successes or failures do not all fall neatly into one place. We can categorize economic organizations according to *forms of ownership,* making a basic distinction between capitalist vs. socialist economies. Then we may further subdivide each of these.

laissez-faire capitalism: a national system characterized by private corporate ownership and a great reliance on exchange as a mode of coordination (with relatively little coordination by public administration)

administrative capitalism: a national system characterized by private corporate ownership and a substantial reliance on public administration (as well as exchange) as a mode of coordination

administrative socialism: a national system in which state ownership predominates and activity is coordinated primarily by public administration (command)

market socialism: a national system in which state ownership predominates but much economic activity is coordinated through markets

Capitalism is a system characterized by predominantly *private ownership* of productive assets; owners may be either private individuals or businesses. Under **laissez-faire capitalism,** the role of the state is supposed to be relatively small; at least in theory, it is confined to maintaining a legal-institutional environment conducive to corporate ownership and market exchange. The United States and the United Kingdom are the two advanced countries that lie closest to this end of the spectrum. In contrast, **administrative capitalism** involves a more substantial amount of state activity alongside market-coordinated activity. Japan, France, and the Scandinavian countries fit this description. Canada, Australia, and New Zealand have tended to be somewhere in the middle, between these two varieties of capitalism.

Socialism is a system that relies much more on *public ownership,* where the owners may be either government or various kinds of cooperatives. The former Soviet Union and North Korea exemplify **administrative socialism**, which centralizes a very large proportion of economic power in the government. In contrast, China and Vietnam have been experimenting with a hybrid—**market socialism**—that keeps *political* power centralized with state ownership predominating, but releases a growing amount of *economic* decision-making power to market forces.

Which of these systems is most conducive to development? And what kind of development? To compare the success of various types of economies, review some of the data presented in Chapter 0. How do the laissez-faire economies of the United States and United Kingdom perform compared to the administrative capitalist economics of Japan, France, and the Scandinavian countries? Or to the market socialism of China or Vietnam?

Consider the clearly economic categories (2 through 7 in Chapter 0): recent growth rate of GDP per capita; net national savings; government debt; labor productivity; average annual hours worked; and unemployment rate. Or what about the more well-being-related categories of income inequality: Internet users; educational performance; life expectancy; and subjective well-being—how do the different types of economies compare in these respects? Finally, consider the last two categories (CO_2 emissions per capita and local air quality), which say something about the hidden environmental and health costs of high levels of production and consumption.

Clearly, there is not a single winner. The United States does relatively well in some areas: It is among the world's richest countries and has very high labor productivity and currently low inflation. It performs poorly on some other measures. The U.S. savings rate is near the bottom. Especially when compared to other developed countries, U.S. educational performance is mediocre, life expectancy is somewhat shorter, and inequality is relatively high.

If you look at the ranking of the countries whose economies are described as administrative capitalism (for example, Japan and the Scandinavian countries), you will find a different pattern—one that, to some people, looks appealing in terms of greater equality as well as health and educational measures.* And China, the nearly unique exemplar of market socialism, is virtually in a class by itself. Its extraordinarily high savings and GDP growth rates make

*If you want to look into this further, you can go to the Web site www.gdae.org/macro/, which provides figures for all countries for which there are reliable statistics, not just those that are presented in Chapter 0.

it the winner among major countries in those categories. Its debt is low and its trade balance positive. But its income inequality, which used to be very low, has climbed to equal that of the United States. While China has a developing middle class, it still has many extremely poor people. On the environmental front, as is well known, it has become a major emitter not only of greenhouse gases but also of other harmful pollutants.

The debate on development continues. As the experience of the twentieth century reveals, there is nothing "automatic" about achieving sustained growth and a high standard of living. Undoubtedly, a combination of market and government-led policies will be used as countries continue to strive to develop. The unsettled question is how to determine the combination that will work best for a particular country and how best to promote a combination of goals that include economic development and social well-being. The fact that each country is unique and therefore requires a unique "playbook" of strategies makes the task of development economists all the more challenging.

Discussion Questions

1. Do you think that the economic challenges faced by developing countries today are the same as those faced by industrialized countries when they were starting out? If not, how are they different?
2. Think of a poor country that you know a little about—even if what you know is just where it is on a world map and who its neighbors are. Considering the varieties of sources of economic growth, where would you propose starting to design a development plan for that country?

3. UNDERSTANDING POVERTY

From the early days of development economics, the eradication of poverty has always been a goal—sometimes the primary goal, at other times taking second or third place to other goals, but always an important consideration. However, the understanding of poverty is not as obvious as might at first appear. This section uses the lens of measurement to show how different groups have tried to understand the issue.

3.1 GDP GROWTH AND POVERTY REDUCTION

There is a close relationship between the goals that we set ourselves and the metrics that we use to assess where we are and how well we are progressing toward our goals. Joining a growing (new) consensus, the IMF and World Bank have replaced their focus on "structural adjustment" with an emphasis on "poverty-reduction" policies that are intended to give countries more voice in creating their own development solutions.* To reach such a goal, the first requirement is to define and measure the thing that we want to change.

As noted earlier, the simplest way of defining poverty is according to average income, or GDP per capita. Yet averages hide a great deal. An average GDP per capita of $9,000 could exist in a country where most people are able to cover their basic needs for nutrition, basic health care, and shelter, along with some access to education and communications. Alternatively, most of the people in such a country could be living in dire poverty, with a small percentage being quite rich, leading to the same *average* GPD per capita of $9,000. We must therefore consider some other poverty measures, as additional ways of understanding where economic growth is most needed and what role it plays in the larger topic of development.

poverty line: the income threshold below which members of a population are classified as poor

One common approach is to define poverty as the percentage of the population below what is known as the **poverty line**. One international poverty line that is often used as a minimum

*See www.imf.org/external/np/exr/facts/prsp.htm and www.worldbank.org/en/topic/poverty

Table 32.3 **Growth Rates and Changes in Poverty Rates, Select Countries**

	Period	Annual growth rate in per capita GDP, %	Poverty rate at beginning of period, %	Poverty rate at end of period, %
Bangladesh	1984–2010	2.9	60.6	43.3
Brazil	1981–2009	1.1	13.6	6.1
China	1981–2009	9.1	84.0	11.8
Egypt	1991–2008	2.9	4.5	1.7
Ethiopia	1982–2011	1.8	66.2	30.7
India	1978–2010	3.9	65.9	32.7
Indonesia	1984–2010	3.6	62.8	18.1
Mexico	1984–2010	0.8	12.8	0.7
Nigeria	1986–2010	2.3	53.9	68.0
Philippines	1985–2009	1.6	34.9	18.4
South Africa	1993–2009	1.5	24.3	13.8
Thailand	1981–2010	4.2	22.0	0.4

Source: World Bank, World Development Indicators Database, 2013.
Note: The poverty rate is based on a poverty line of $1.25 per day.

standard to escape extreme poverty is $1.25 per day. According to this measure, many developing countries experiencing at least modest growth rates have succeeded in reducing the incidence of poverty in their countries. For example, from 1984 to 2010, Mexico had an average annual growth rate in per capita GDP of only 0.8 percent, yet this was sufficient to reduce its poverty rate from 12.8 to less than 1 percent (Table 32.3). And Brazil more than halved its poverty rate from 1981 to 2009 despite a growth rate of only 1.1 percent. Of the countries shown, Nigeria is the only one experiencing growth and an *increase* in poverty.

In comparing countries, it is necessary to use a universal standard, such as the $1.25-per-day threshold on which the poverty rates shown in the table are based. Almost all countries also have their own (national) poverty line—the threshold for the United States, for example, is about $20,000 per year for a family of four—and calculate their national poverty rate based on it. While not useful for comparing across countries, the advantage of a national poverty line is that it allows a country to define poverty according to its own standard of living. An income that classified someone as poor in the United States would almost certainly not be considered living at the poverty level in India. The international standard of $1.25 per day may help in classifying poor countries, but would be useless for rich countries, where the poverty rate using this standard would be nearly zero.

Both approaches are typically referred to as "headcount" measures, since they simply require the "counting" of people who fall below the poverty line. But many find that measuring poverty based exclusively on income reflects only a small part of the poverty picture. In what follows, we consider a more broad-based measure of poverty.

3.2 The Multidimensional Poverty Index

Amartya Sen, a Nobel prize–winning economist, has argued that basing poverty on income deficiencies is exceedingly narrow and often does not provide an accurate picture of how poor a population may be. He has proposed that one's **capabilities**—that is, the opportunities that people have to be well-nourished, decently housed, have access to education, and in many other ways live lives that they find worthwhile—are more important than a simple income measure. Sen emphasizes the goal of enlarging people's choices, which depends fundamentally on building their capabilities.

capabilities: the opportunities that people have to pursue important aspects of well-being, such as being healthy and having access to education

The Multidimensional Poverty Index (MPI), based on Sen's work, was developed in 2010 by the Oxford Poverty and Human Development Initiative for the United Nations Development Programme's *Human Development Report*. The MPI considers several elements that are critical for a decent life, in the areas of physical living standards, education, and health, as outlined in a study by Oxford University (see Box 32.1). Although the 10 items on the list are not the only essentials, they are good proxies; people who do not have these can reasonably be considered deprived, or poor.

The study found that a total of 1.6 billion people are living in multidimensional poverty. This is more than 30 percent of the people living in the 104 countries surveyed. Among these, South Asia leads the world in poverty, with between 52 percent and 62 percent of those defined in the MPI as being in the world's bottom billion.* About 40 percent of the total are in India. Most of the rest live in sub-Saharan Africa, which is home to between 33 percent and 39 percent of the poorest billion. Of the 104 countries in the survey, only four—Belarus, Hungary, Slovenia, and Slovakia—were not home to any of the poorest billion people. Surprisingly, 41,000 of the poorest billion people live in countries defined, in this study, as high income: Croatia, Estonia, United Arab Emirates, Trinidad and Tobago, and the Czech Republic.

Box 32.1 How the MPI Definition of Poverty Is Constructed

A person is identified as multidimensionally poor if he or she is deprived in one third or more of the following weighted indicators:

Education (each indicator is weighted equally at 1/6)

- *Years of Schooling:* deprived if no household member has completed five years of schooling
- *School Attendance:* deprived if any school-age child is not attending school in years 1 to 8

Health (each indicator is weighted equally at 1/6)

- *Child Mortality:* deprived if any child in the family has died
- *Nutrition:* deprived if any adult or child for whom there is nutritional information is malnourished

Living standards (each indicator is weighted equally at 1/18)

- *Electricity:* deprived if the household has no electricity
- *Drinking Water:* deprived if the household lacks access to clean drinking water or clean water is more than a 30-minute walk from home, round-trip
- *Sanitation:* deprived if the household does not have adequate sanitation or their toilet is shared
- *Flooring:* deprived if the household has a dirt, sand, or dung floor
- *Cooking Fuel:* deprived if the household cooks with wood, charcoal, or dung
- *Assets:* deprived if the household does not own more than one of: radio, TV, telephone, bike, motorbike, or refrigerator; and does not own a car or tractor

Technical note: The MPI is the product of two components: (1) Incidence, the percentage of people who are disadvantaged (or the headcount ratio, H); and (2) Intensity of people's deprivation, the average share of dimensions in which disadvantaged people are deprived (A). Thus *MPI = HxA*.

Source: Sabina Alkire, José Manuel Roche and Suman Seth, Oxford Poverty & Human Development Initiative, Multidimensional Poverty Index 2013, www.ophi.org.uk, March 2013.

It is interesting to compare the results of the MPI study with the "less than $1.25 a day" (income-poor) approach. In some countries, there are large discrepancies between the percentage of the population that is "MPI poor" and the percentage that is income poor. At one end of the scale are the countries that are the least poor in MPI terms. Three of these—Ecuador, Macedonia, and Georgia—are nevertheless identified as having between 10 percent and 20 percent of their population earning less than $1.25 a day.

*The imprecision is due to three alternative regional divisions used: national, subnational, and individual.

The two largest discrepancies in the middle group are China, with nearly 30 percent below $1.25, but only a little over 10 percent MPI poor; and Swaziland, with over 40 percent income poor, but about 20 percent MPI poor.

As we survey the poorest countries (on both scales), which are mostly in Africa, we find that the proportions of the population suffering from MPI deprivation tend to be greater than the proportions living below $1.25 a day. Exceptions include Nigeria, with more than 50 percent MPI poor but nearly 70 percent income poor, and Madagascar, with nearly 70 percent MPI poor but more than 80 percent income poor.

Such discrepancies reveal the potential limitations in relying exclusively on income-based poverty measures. Clearly, based on the Oxford study, being above the income poverty line is neither necessary nor sufficient for escaping multidimensional deprivation. If income is a means to an end, and the "ends" include the health, education, and physical living standards criteria outlined in the MPI report, then multidimensional poverty may be more relevant than income poverty in the assessment of deprivation within countries. As we see in the following section, this "multidimensionality" is also present in any evaluation of a country's progress in achieving development.

3.3 Human Development and the Millennium Development Goals

There are alternatives to measuring development primarily in terms of GDP. Bearing in mind the "capabilities" approach and multidimensional approaches to defining poverty, some have argued that development should be geared primarily to meeting basic needs for food, shelter, and health care. The **human development** approach includes attention to such basic needs but goes further to encompass other dimensions of a worthwhile life.

human development: an approach to development that stresses the provision of basic needs such as food, shelter, and health care

Recent UNDP reports have, for example, examined how widespread, socially accepted domestic violence limits the human development of women in many regions and how human development may be limited by political oppression along ethnic or other lines. Such issues affect countries with high material standards of living, as well as those still unable to supply basic goods.

In September 2000, the member states of the United Nations unanimously declared their intention to try to reach a set of development objectives called the **Millennium Development Goals (MDGs)**. These goals focus on improvements in the life of the very poorest people in the world, emphasizing food security, education, gender equity, and health care (see Box 32.2). The MDGs include mention of environmental sustainability (discussed in Chapter 33). Most of the goals set a deadline of 2015 for achievement.

Millennium Development Goals (MDGs): a set of goals declared by the United Nations in 2000, emphasizing eradication of extreme poverty; promotion of education, gender equity, and health; environmental sustainability; and partnership between rich and poor countries

Each of the eight main *goals,* such as "reduce child mortality," is accompanied by one or more specific *targets,* such as "reduce the under-five mortality rate by two-thirds between 1990 and 2015." These targets, in turn, may relate to a number of policy actions, such as increasing education for mothers, vaccinating against measles, and distributing malaria-fighting mosquito nets. The eighth goal, "develop a global partnership for development," points to some policies that the richer countries should enact. They include eliminating tariff barriers to poor countries' products, canceling or restructuring debts, increasing foreign aid, easing the flow of essential drugs, and sharing technology.

As a high-profile, specific commitment of UN members, the MDG declaration has served to increase the global attention paid to the promotion of human development. Some have nevertheless criticized the MDGs, believing that the goals do not go far enough in addressing inequalities and injustices between rich and poor countries. And although the MDGs are a noble statement of intent, the follow-through on them since their declaration in 2000 has had mixed results.

For example, while the UN claims that the first MDG of halving the proportion of people living on less than $1.25 a day was met three years before the target date, progress has been very uneven. While regions such as North Africa and East Asia have seen considerable gains,

Box 32.2 The Millennium Development Goals

1. Eradicate extreme poverty and hunger—Halve, between 1990 and 2015, the proportion of people whose income is less than $1 a day or who suffer from hunger
2. Achieve universal primary education—Ensure that, by 2015, children everywhere, boys and girls alike, will be able to complete a full course of primary schooling
3. Promote gender equality and empower women—Eliminate gender disparity in all levels of education no later than 2015
4. Reduce child mortality—Reduce by two-thirds, between 1990 and 2015, the under-five mortality rate
5. Improve maternal health—Reduce by three-quarters, between 1990 and 2015, the maternal mortality ratio
6. Combat HIV/AIDS, malaria, and other diseases—By 2015 have halted and begun to reverse the spread of HIV/AIDS, malaria, and other major diseases
7. Ensure environmental sustainability—Integrate the principles of sustainable development into country policies and programs and reverse the loss of environmental resources. Halve, by 2015, the proportion of people without sustainable access to safe drinking water and basic sanitation. Have achieved, by 2020, a significant improvement in the lives of at least 100 million slum dwellers
8. Develop a global partnership for development—Including fair trade, debt relief, and access to health and information technology

Source: United Nations Development Programme, www.undp.org/content/undp/en/home/mdgoverview/

conditions in Oceania (Pacific islands) and parts of sub-Saharan Africa have deteriorated (see Figure 32.5 and Table 32.3). In fact, were it not for poverty reduction in two countries—China and India—the picture would look far less optimistic.

According to the UN's *Millennium Development Goals Report 2013*, "big gains have been made in health. Between 2000 and 2010, mortality rates from malaria fell by more than 25 percent globally, and an estimated 1.1 million deaths were averted. Death rates from tuberculosis could be halved by 2015, compared to 1990 levels."[4] While new HIV/AIDS infections are declining, an estimated 34 million people were living with HIV in 2011. 8 million people in developing regions were receiving antiretroviral therapy, and the price of anti-HIV drugs has been brought down.

While there has been progress in reducing child and maternal mortality rates, improving school enrollments, and expanding access to sanitation, the U.N. report notes that 57 million children still do not have access to primary education, and 2.5 billion people still lack improved sanitation facilities. According to the report, "progress towards the eight MDGs has been uneven not only among regions and countries, but also between population groups within countries."

Debts are being cancelled for nineteen of the very poorest highly indebted countries, but they remain a burden for many others. Only five countries (all European) have met the UN target for offering international aid of at least 0.7 percent of GDP; overall, net aid disbursements have declined, especially for the least developed countries. The Doha round of World Trade Organization negotiations, intended to achieve reforms that would help developing countries, remains stalled after more than ten years.

Little progress has been made in opening up rich country markets to the products of poorer countries. The spread of some kinds of technology (particularly cell phones) has been rapid in some areas, but a technological gulf between rich and poor countries persists. In short, while there has been progress in certain areas, it is not clear that poor countries as a whole are "converging" to the levels of human development enjoyed in the industrialized world. For many countries, it seems that the opposite is true.

In addition to inadequate funding, another reason for limited success in achieving the MDGs may be a degree of incompatibility between its goals and the macroeconomic strategies employed by donor countries and multinational agencies, such as the IMF and the World Bank. The MDGs were derived from the UN work in defining and assessing human development. While, as noted above, the World Bank and IMF have recently shifted their focus to incorporate poverty reduction, for much of the last several decades development efforts were still dominated by the "neoliberal" Washington Consensus (discussed above).*

The neoliberal strategy was poorly suited to achieving the MDGs because, in effect, it has different goals (see Box 32.3). It does not concern itself with issues that are central to the UN concept of human development, such as care for children and the aged, inequality in general, or gender equity, including intra-household distribution of income and assets.**

Box 32.3 Comparison of Neoliberal and United Nations Approaches to Development

Multilateral agencies in charge of development have often acted at cross purposes, with public statements of goals coming from the United Nations but implementation carried out by agencies with a "neoliberal" orientation towards development. Some of the differences were summarized in a UN Briefing Note written by advocates of the human development approach:

> The human development approach emphasizes three areas of concern. First, it underlines the need for the inclusion of a broader group of governmental and nongovernmental actors in decision-making processes. In government, policy-making cannot be left to economic and financial decision makers alone. Other ministries or departments, particularly those concerned with nutrition, health, and education, need to be a part of the process. Outside government, local communities need to be included to ensure a human focus and a clear understanding of available options.
>
> Second, the human development approach broadens the scope of indicators used to monitor development. In place of neoliberalism's sharp focus on economic and financial indicators as a means to human ends, human development relies on a wider range of human and social indicators that are given primary place as ends in themselves. Thus special importance is given to indicators that track the human situation: life expectancy, nutritional status, and ultimately of well-being and happiness. In this regard, human development is similar to the basic needs approach of the 1970s.
>
> Third, there are differences in the two approaches that reflect different attitudes toward international policy. The urgency of human development needs requires stronger international action and more rapid and flexible support, financially in access to markets and in other forms such as peace operations. Moreover, the values and principles at the heart of the human development approach extend far beyond neoliberalism's preoccupation with economic efficiency and include human rights, justice, and human solidarity.

Source: Richard Jolly, Louis Emmerij, and Thomas G. Weiss, *UN Intellectual History Project Briefing Note Number 8*, July 2009, http://hdr.undp.org/en/media/Jolly%20HDR%20note%20%20UN%20Intellectual%20History%20Project%208HumDev.pdf, accessed April 2, 2013.

Discussion Questions

1. Do you think the categories in the Multidimensional Index of Poverty do a good job of reflecting who is truly poor? If you were asked to add one item to this list, what would it be?
2. Do you think the Millennium Development Goals realistic or achievable? What does the mixed success in achieving them so far say about current development policies?

*"Neoliberal" here refers to market-oriented development theory. It is derived from an older sense of the word "liberal," meaning freeing markets from government controls. This can be confusing since "liberal" in politics today often means using government action to help the poor.

**"Intra-household distribution" refers to the role of women in managing household income and assets. Often control over income and assets remains in the hands of men, while women are required to do most of the household labor.

4. INEQUALITY

We have discussed the issue of inequality *between* countries. Also important is the level of inequality *within* countries. As we have seen, many countries have very high levels of inequality (as measured by the Gini coefficent, discussed in Chapter 11), meaning that the poorest 40 percent of the population receive a meager share of national income, while in other countries the "pie" is more equally shared. Apart from any potential ethical issues, inequality within countries should concern us if it significantly influences a given country's prospects of achieving sustained growth and development.

4.1 GROWTH, INEQUALITY, AND THE KUZNETS CURVE

Although economic growth and poverty reduction have most often been the primary goals of development, there have also been many thinkers—in philosophy as well as in economics and other social sciences and humanities—who have placed equality, equity, or fairness high on their list of end goals: objects worth achieving for their own sake. Yet not everyone considers such matters paramount, especially economists. For some, equality is regarded as an intermediate goal—something worth achieving if it leads to other desirable outcomes. And some have argued that *in*equality may have a role to play at least at some stages in efforts toward economic development.

Although we saw in Chapter 11 that the extent of income inequality within countries is highly variable, it turns out that world income inequality is more extreme than in any individual country. In Figure 32.6, the world's population is organized into successive income quintiles, each representing 20 percent of the world's population. Thus the bottom quintile represents the poorest 20 percent of humanity, the next quintile represents the second-poorest 20 percent, and so on. The area associated with each quintile is in proportion to how much of the world's income they receive. Remarkably, 82.8 percent of the world's income goes to the richest 20 percent. Meanwhile, the poorest 40 percent receive only 3.1 percent of the world's income. This outcome is a product of *both* growing income inequality within many countries and growing inequality between countries (e.g., poor countries "falling behind").

Figure 32.6. **The Unequal Distribution of the World's Income, 2007**

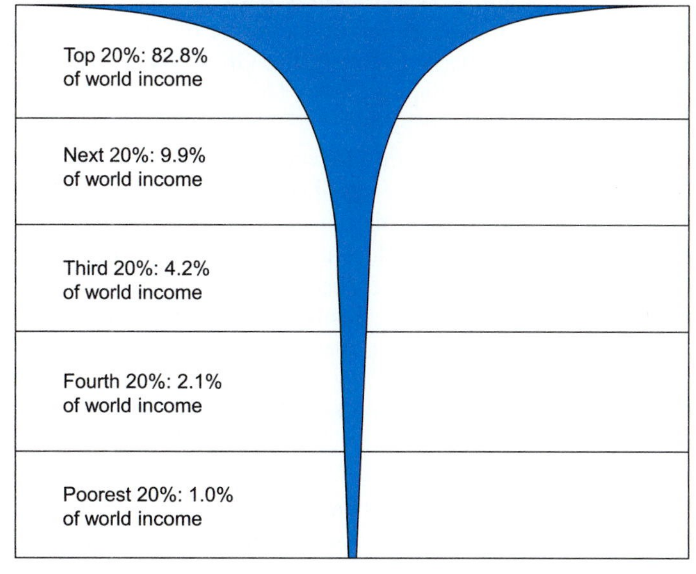

The "champagne glass" shape of the world's income distribution is based on over 80 percent of the world's income going to the top 20 percent of the world's population, while the poorest 20 percent get only 1 percent of total income.

Source: I. Ortiz and M. Cummings, "Global Inequality: Beyond the Bottom Billion," UNICEF Social and Economic Policy Working Paper, April 2011.

Kuznets curve hypothesis: the theory that economic inequality first increases during the initial stages of economic development but then eventually decreases with further economic growth

Early in the history of development theory, Simon Kuznets (the same economist who initiated work on National Income and Product Accounts, as discussed in Chapter 20) discussed the issue of inequality in a famous paper.[5] He proposed that during the initial stages of economic growth, inequality would increase as investment opportunities created a wealthy class, while an influx of rural laborers into cities would keep wages low. Eventually, according to Kuznets, further industrialization would lead to democratization, widespread increases in education, and safety-net policies that would lead to lower inequality. This **Kuznets curve hypothesis** suggests an inverted-U relationship between economic growth and inequality—inequality would first rise, then fall, with economic growth.

Some countries' development paths roughly correspond to the Kuznets curve hypothesis, especially the early industrializers, such as England, France, Sweden, and Germany—however, the evidence is more mixed when we consider a broader range of countries. Some countries, such as Norway, Japan, and South Korea, have experienced economic growth with a continual decrease in economic inequality. And as we have seen in earlier chapters, economic growth in the United States since the 1970s has been associated with an increase in inequality, which also contradicts the basic Kuznets curve hypothesis.[6]

Although the Kuznets curve hypothesis looks primarily at the influence of economic growth on inequality, we can also look at the relationship in the opposite direction—how the level of inequality influences economic growth. Here the evidence is also mixed: Some studies find that countries that are highly unequal at the start of development have a difficult time achieving rapid growth, and others support the view that inequality correlates positively with growth. The latter conclusion conforms to a view sometimes associated with traditional economics: that the existence of economic inequality creates an incentive for hard work, thereby helping the economy grow. In other words, if the economic outcomes in a society were too equal, there would be little reason to seek to improve one's economic situation.

More recently, however, economists have debated whether the high level of inequality in the United States is slowing the recovery from the Great Recession. Nobel prize–winning economist Joseph Stiglitz, for example, argues that in the recent case of the United States, high inequality impedes economic recovery. He claims that the U.S. middle class is now weaker than in the past and is therefore unable to fuel a recovery adequately with consumer spending. A weakened middle class is also less likely to invest sufficiently in education or start enough new businesses.

According to research by the IMF, inequality is associated with greater economic instability.[7] It may be no coincidence that the most significant economic downturns in the United States over the past 100 years, the Great Depression and the Great Recession, both occurred during peaks of inequality. As we saw in Chapter 11, the United States is the most economically unequal among the industrialized countries.

Others, such as Paul Krugman (another Nobel prize–winning economist), believe that it is not income inequality per se that impedes economic recovery. The problem is that extreme income inequality gives rise to *political* inequality, and this is what can impede recoveries. Krugman suggests that the slow economic recovery is due mostly to political problems. According to this view, wealthy individuals and powerful corporations in the United States, interested in their own economic welfare and wielding significant political power, can effectively prevent the policies that would promote a broad-based economic recovery (see Box 32.4 and Figure 32.7).

According to a recent OECD report,[8] such policies for broad-based recovery should include:

1. *Promoting education:* policies that increase high school and college graduation rates as well as policies that promote equal access to education, reduce inequality, and increase long-term economic growth.

Box 32.4 A United States Recovery for the 1 Percent

As the U.S. economy gradually recovered from the impact of the Great Recession of 2007–9, a disproportionate share of the economic gains went to the wealthiest Americans. While incomes for typical American households remained flat and the percentage in poverty did not decline, those who were already wealthy improved their position further.

> From 2009 to 2012, average real income per family grew modestly by 6.0%. However, the gains were very uneven. Top 1% incomes grew by 31.4%, while bottom 99% income grew by only 0.4% from 2009 to 2012. Hence, the top 1% captured 95% of the income gains in the first three years of the recovery. (Saez, 2013)

As a result, overall U.S. inequality increased to record levels. This raised questions about the durability of the recovery, since an economically healthy middle class is important for maintaining a stable level of aggregate demand. Economist Paul Krugman suggests that the rich, comfortable with a situation that "has been dismal for workers but not at all bad for the wealthy," oppose the kinds of policies that would favor more distribution of income to the middle class and low income families (Krugman, 2013). Historically, periods of high inequality in U.S. history, during the 1920s and recently, have been associated with the economic instability of the Great depression and the Great Recession (see Figure 32.7).

> The pay gap between the richest 1 percent and the rest of America widened [in 2012], making a record. The top 1 percent of U.S. earners collected 19.3 percent of household income in 2012, their largest share in Internal Revenue Service figures going back a century. (Wiseman, 2013)

> The top 10 percent of earners took more than half of the country's total income in 2012, according to an updated study by economist Emmanuel Saez and Thomas Piketty. . . . The economy remains depressed for most wage-earning families. With sustained, relatively high rates of unemployment, businesses are under no pressure to raise their employees' incomes because both workers and employers know that many people without jobs would be willing to work for less. The share of Americans working or looking for work is at its lowest in 35 years. (Lowrey, 2013)

Sources: Emmanuel Saez, "Striking it Richer: The Evolution of Top Incomes in the United States, University of California Economic Department discussion paper, September 2013; Paul Krugman, "The 1 Percent's Solution," *New York Times*, April 26, 2013; Paul Wiseman, "Top 1% Took Record Share of U.S. Income in 2012," *Associated Press*, September 10, 2013; Annie Lowrey, "The Rich Get Richer Through the Recovery," *New York Times*, September 10, 2013, http://economix.blogs.nytimes.com/2013/09/10/the-rich-get-richer-through-the-recovery/

Figure 32.7 **Shares of U.S. Income Going to Top 10 Percent and Top 1 Percent, 1917–2012**

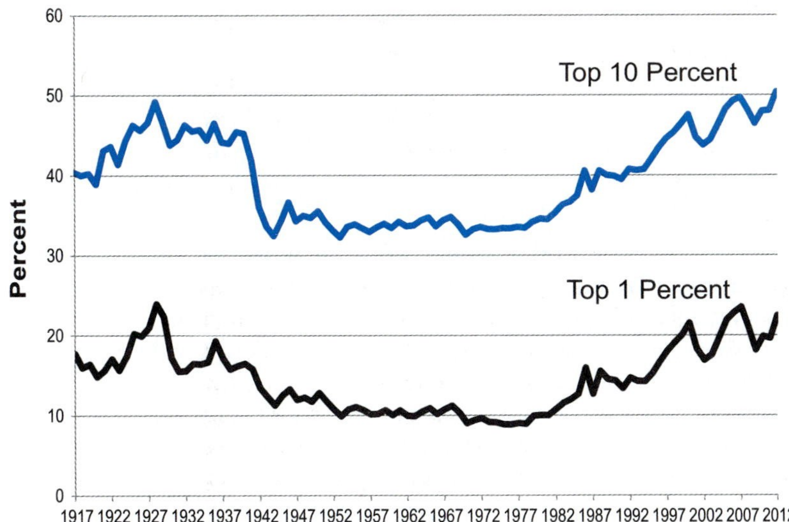

The share of U.S. income going to the top 10 percent of families exceeded 50 percent in 2012, for the first time in the nation's history. The top 1 percent increased their share to nearly 20 percent. Similar levels of concentration were seen in the 1920s, but for many decades in between, the United States was characterized by less inequality, with lower shares for the top income earners.

Source: Thomas Piketty and Emmanuel Saez, U.S. incomes series, http://elsa.berkeley.edu/~saez/TabFig2012prel.xls
Note: Top 1 percent share includes capital gains.

2. *Well-designed labor market policies and institutions:* For example, as long as the minimum wage is not too high to reduce overall employment significantly, it can reduce wage inequality. Strong unions can also reduce wage inequality.
3. *Immigration and discrimination policies:* Policies that promote the integration of immigrants and that prohibit all forms of discrimination reduce inequality and can increase growth.
4. *Tax policies:* Eliminating tax loopholes that benefit primarily high-income households, such as the mortgage interest deduction, would increase the overall progressivity of the tax system and allow for a reduction in marginal tax rates, which increase the incentive for working.

The OECD report notes that some policies to promote economic growth are likely to increase inequality, such as shifting from taxation of income to taxation of consumption, using a sales tax or value-added tax (VAT)*. Thus the challenge becomes one of identifying policies that offer "win-win" outcomes—that is, those that promote both GDP growth and a reduction in the degree of income inequality.

Up to what point should inequality be reduced? Just as no one would be likely to advocate the extreme position of "the more inequality the better," few would support the idea of attempting to achieve perfectly equal income distribution throughout a society. Yet there is widespread concern that inequality has become excessive in many countries. High inequality exists in many developing countries but has also become increasingly evident in the United States. As noted, the evidence remains inconclusive regarding its effect on growth. But when we broaden our scope to consider the well-being aspects of development, instead of just economic growth, the negative effects of inequality become more apparent.

4.2 Recent Studies of Inequality

Even if the relationship between income inequality and GDP growth remains somewhat ambiguous, the same is not true for the relationship between inequality and broad-based well-being. Countries that are more unequal in terms of income generally perform more poorly on many well-being indicators.

One way in which inequality affects people is in its impact on population health. Figure 32.8 plots one proxy for health—average life expectancies—against GDP per capita, with spheres, as before, proportional to the population of the country represented. A curve is drawn to fit the general pattern made by the data points. Looking at the far left-hand side of the figure, it is clear that living in a very poor country, such as Nigeria, dramatically increases the chance that one will die prematurely, compared with living in a country with somewhat higher GDP/capita, such as India or China. On the left-hand portion of the graph, we can see that substantial inequality *between* countries plays an important role in determining longevity.

In the middle section of the graph, moving from left to right, we see countries such as Mexico, which has achieved a life expectancy fairly close to those of the richest countries, even though its average income per capita is not even half as high. But South Africa lies far below the line, reflecting a case in which inequality makes it difficult to translate a moderate *average* level of income into well-being and longevity.

Looking at the spheres representing Western Europe, Japan, and the United States at the right-hand side of the figure, we see that the positive relationship between income and life expectancy essentially disappears. At high incomes, in fact, inequality within countries—not

*A value-added tax, or VAT, is imposed on the net value added in an industry (revenues minus costs of intermediate inputs). The concept of value added was discussed in Chapter 20.

Figure 32.8 **The Relation Between Life Expectancy and Income, with Area Proportional to Population**

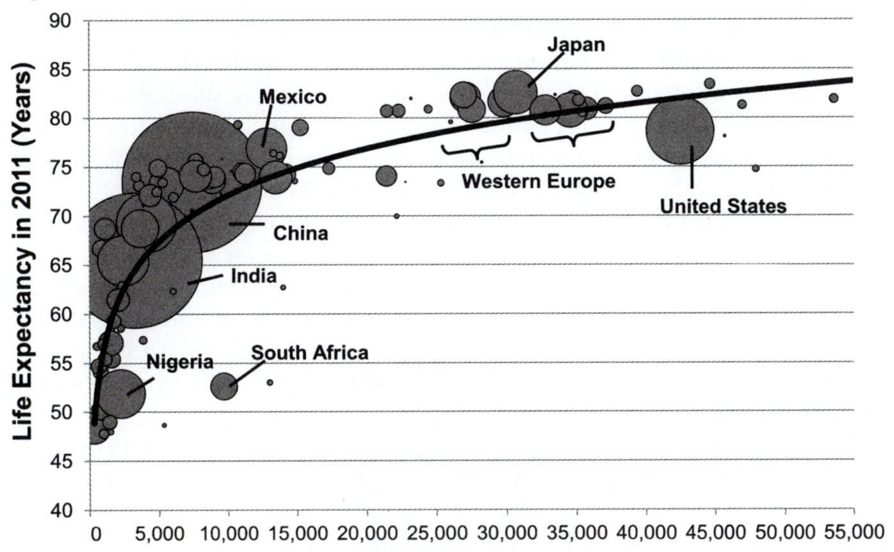

At very low levels of income per head, increases in per capita income are associated with steep increases in life expectancy. After a middle-income level of per capita GDP is reached, however, increases in income are associated with much more modest increases in life expectancy, and at high incomes the relationship flattens out.

Source: World Bank, World Development Indicators Database, 2013.

income per capita—may be an important factor in determining health and life expectancy. For example, according to a recent study, despite the fact that the average U.S. citizen can expect to live about 77 years on average—which is considerably better than the global average of about 70 years—U.S. life expectancy is lower than most other (generally more equal) industrialized countries, which are in the 78- to 82-year range. Infant mortality also appears to be higher in countries with greater inequality.[9] The authors of this study argue that inequality is positively associated with a range of negative social outcomes, including mental health and incidence of violence.

Another recent study emphasizes the enormous inequality *between* countries in outcomes other than income:

> The differences in life expectancy between countries dwarf those between different groups within countries. (This is true for income inequality, too.) There is an eight-year difference in life expectancy between Japanese women (86.1 years) and Japanese men (78.0 years), but both Japanese men and women can expect to live almost twice as long as a newborn in the countries with the lowest life expectancy in sub-Saharan Africa (Zambia, Angola, and Swaziland).
>
> Infant mortality rates—which are the main drivers of differences in life expectancy between rich and poor countries—vary from 3 per 1,000 in Iceland and Singapore to more than 150 per 1,000 in Sierra Leone, Afghanistan, and Angola. In 1990, more than a quarter of children in Mali did not live to see their fifth birthdays, a marked improvement over 1960, when around half died in childhood—or put even more starkly, when median life expectancy at birth was only five years.[10]

Thus it seems clear that a special focus of development should be on increasing incomes for the poorest and eliminating the kinds of inequality that lead to major human suffering. These goals needs to be balanced with the more general objectives of development discussed above in Sections 1 and 2.

4.3 Economic Development and Human Development

Over the past century, the world has seen dramatic economic growth, but the benefits of this growth have been unevenly distributed. Some developing countries, such as India and China, have experienced rapid growth rates.* Others, such as most countries in sub-Saharan Africa and some countries in Latin America and Central Asia, are still struggling with low, or even negative, growth rates. In terms of living standards and well-being, much of the world's population has been left out of the significant progress that appears in aggregate statistics. In the future, further development is clearly essential but simple models of economic growth may fail to capture important elements of the development challenge (see Box 32.5).

A growing number of development economists recognize the need to rethink development more in the direction of broad-based human development, with increased emphasis on inequality at all levels of development. For those suffering material deprivation, GDP growth is often, but not always or only, the first solution and policies to achieve GDP growth should be balanced with promotion of human development goals.

There is another important reason for a shift in paradigms regarding economic development. We cannot assume that indefinite GDP growth will in the long term be *ecologically sustainable.* This is the focus of Chapter 33, in which we consider some of the issues relating to the environmental and resource limits that we face in the twenty-first century.

Box 32.5 Comparing India and China in Human Development

Both India and China have experienced rapid economic growth since 2000, but there are significant differences in their human development levels. Nobel Prize winner Amartya Sen, who originated the "capabilities" approach to development, comments that the most significant gap between China and India is not in growth rates but in the provision of essential public services:

> Inequality is high in both countries, but China has done far more than India to raise life expectancy, expand general education, and secure health care for its people. India has elite schools of varying degrees of excellence for the privileged, but among all Indians 7 or older, nearly one in five males and one in every three females are illiterate. And most schools are of low quality; less than half the children can divide 20 by 5, even after four years of schooling. . . . The poor have to rely on low-quality—and sometimes exploitative—private medical care, because there isn't enough decent public care. . . .
>
> India's underperformance can be traced to a failure to learn from the examples of so-called Asian economic development, in which rapid expansion of human capability is both a goal in itself and an integral element in achieving rapid growth.

Despite a lack of democratic process in China, its leaders have placed a priority on eliminating hunger, illiteracy, and medical neglect. According to Sen, if India is to match China's economic record, it needs a "better-educated and healthier labor force at all levels of society," as well as "more knowledge and public discussion about the nature and huge extent of inequality and its damaging consequences for economic growth."

Source: Amartya Sen, "Why India Trails China," *New York Times,* Op-Ed, June 19, 2013.

Discussion Questions

1. How important to you are your income goals, relative to your other goals? A recent survey, for example, asked respondents to say whether each of the following was absolutely

*Both China and India experienced extremely high growth rates of up to 10% per year or more during the decade 2000–2010, although growth rates in both countries have recently slowed somewhat. See http://data.worldbank.org/indicator/NY.GDP.MKTP.KD.ZG

necessary, very important, somewhat important, not very important, or not at all important "for you to consider your life as a success." How would you answer?

Earning a lot of money	Having an interesting job
Seeing a lot of the world	Helping other people who are in need
Becoming well-educated	Living a long time
Having a good marriage	Having good friends
Having a good relationship with your children	Having strong religious faith

2. How would you balance the issue of human development with the issue of economic growth? Is growth essential for human development? Could the answer differ for different countries? What kinds of policies do you think are best for promoting human development?

REVIEW QUESTIONS

1. Which two variables can be added together to obtain the growth rate of GDP in a country?
2. How can economic growth be represented using the *AS/AD* graphs discussed in Chapter 28?
3. What was the Industrial Revolution? What factors were essential in creating the Industrial Revolution?
4. How evenly has economic growth been distributed among different countries in recent decades?
5. What factors are generally considered responsible for GDP growth in developed countries? Have the factors responsible for growth been the same in all developed countries?
6. About how much of the world's income goes to the richest 20 percent? How much goes to the world's poorest 40 percent?
7. What is the concept of convergence in economic growth?
8. What is the evidence for and against economic convergence?
9. How can investment be used to promote economic development?
10. Is an abundance of natural capital a prerequisite for economic development?
11. How can export development both promote and threaten economic growth?
12. In what different methods can foreign capital be provided to promote economic development?
13. What has been the most significant source of foreign capital for economic development in recent years?
14. What are the main principles of the Washington Consensus?
15. What is the evidence regarding the performance of the Washington Consensus recommendations?

EXERCISES

1. Suppose the real GDP of Macroland is $1.367 trillion in Year 1 and $1.428 trillion in Year 2. Also, assume that population in Macroland grew from 128 million in Year 1 to 131 million in Year 2.

   a. What is the growth rate of real GDP in Macroland during this period?
   b. What is the growth rate of real GDP per capita in Macroland?
   c. What is real GDP per capita in Macroland in Year 2?

2. Suppose we know that the growth rate of output per worker in Macroland is 1.7 percent per year and the growth rate of total factor productivity is 0.8 percent per year. Using the growth accounting equation, calculate the growth rate of manufactured capital per worker in Macroland.
3. Using the data for each country in Table 32.1, create a graph similar to Figure 29.6 showing real GDP per capita in 2005 on the horizontal axis and the rate of real GDP per capita growth for 1990–2005 on the vertical axis. (You don't need to include the three country income groups.) Draw each data point as a sphere approximately equal to the population of the country. Does your graph support economic convergence? Explain.

4. Match each concept in Column A with a definition or example in Column B:

Column A	Column B
a. Factors of production	1. Nigeria
b. A country that has shown significant economic convergence in recent decades	2. Development assistance from one country to another
c. Foreign direct investment	3. 3.1 percent
d. The percentage of global income going to the top 20 percent of the world's population	4. Singapore
e. Fiscal discipline	5. A characteristic of the Industrial Revolution
f. An example of a country that has grown despite a low savings rate	6. Income inequality first increases, then decreases, with development
g. Total factor productivity	7. The effect of technology on the productivity of capital and labor
h. The percentage of global income going to the bottom 40 percent of the world's population	8. A structural reform under the Washington Consensus
i. Bilateral development assistance	9. 2 percent
j. A country that has grown despite a lack of natural resources	10. China
k. High savings and investment rates	11. 82.8 percent
l. Growth in GDP per capita if population grows by 2 percent and GDP grows by 4 percent	12. A common factor in the economic development of the "Asian Tigers"
m. A country that has not shown economic convergence in recent decades	13. United States
n. The use of technologies employing fossil fuel energy, especially coal	14. Labor, capital, and natural resources
o. Kuznets curve hypothesis	15. A European company purchases a factory in an African country

NOTES

1. Justin Yifu Lin and David Rosenblatt, "Shifting Patterns of Economic Growth and Rethinking Development," *Journal of Economic Policy Reform,* 15:3 (2012): 171–194.

2. United Nations Development Programme (UNDP), *Human Development Report 2005: International Cooperation at a Crossroads,* 2006, p. 37.

3. "Capital Flows to Developing Countries," *The Economist,* June 16, 2012.

4. United Nations, *The Millennium Development Goals Report 2013* (New York: United Nations, 2013). www.un.org/millenniumgoals/pdf/report-2013/mdg-report-2013-english.pdf.

5. Simon Kuznets, "Economic Growth and Income Inequality," *American Economic Review* 45 (1955): 1–28.

6. See Thomas Piketty, *Capital in the Twenty-First Century* (Cambridge, MA: Harvard University Press, 2014).

7. www.imf.org/external/pubs/ft/survey/so/2011/INT101111A.htm.

8. www.oecd.org/employment/job-richgrowthessentialforg20recoverysayoecdandilo.htm.

9. Richard Wilkinson and Kate Pickett, *The Spirit Level* (New York: Bloomsbury Press, 2010).

10. Angus Deaton, "What Does the Empirical Evidence Tell Us About the Injustice of Health Inequalities?" Center for Health and Wellbeing, Princeton University, November 2011.

33 Growth and Sustainability in the Twenty-First Century

What will the world be like in 2050 or 2100? Will the world situation be characterized as one of widespread material affluence and social peace? Or will the gap between the "haves" and the "have-nots" be even bigger and the planet afflicted by widespread social conflict and environmental damage? Of course, no one can foresee the future. But we can at least consider how some especially pressing social and environmental challenges will affect the macroeconomics of the future.

1. Macroeconomic Goals: Looking Forward

As we have seen throughout this text, macroeconomics is, at its base, concerned with human well-being. The goals of macroeconomic institutions and policies are (as described in Chapter 1) the achievement of good living standards; stability and security; and financial, social, and ecological sustainability.

Much of traditional macroeconomics, as we have seen, tends to focus on the stability and growth rate of real GDP. To the extent that growth in GDP leads to growth in well-being, this is a sensible strategy. But as we saw in Chapter 21 on alternative national accounts, GDP does not measure or report on many important issues of well-being such as environmental deterioration, unpaid home production, and inequality in the distribution of wealth and income. GDP rises when there is increased production of goods that are damaging to society or the environment or that simply make up for damage already done. A narrow focus on stability and growth in GDP also ignores changes in the conditions of work, stresses imposed on families, and developments in the social and financial infrastructure of an economy.

Some people believe that continued GDP growth and technological innovation will solve the social and environmental problems of the present and future. Others, however, believe that many of the social problems of today—including environmental degradation, growing inequality, and inadequacies in health care, child care, and education—can be traced to the fact that existing forms of economic growth and development have in some ways worked against "true" or sustainable well-being.

In Chapter 32, we examined concepts of human development, based on a broader perspective suggesting that economic growth alone is not sufficient—though it is often necessary—for fostering and maintaining human well-being. In this chapter, we look at a second challenge to standard economic growth, relating to the impacts of economic growth on the environment and the extent to which finite planetary limits might make unlimited GDP growth infeasible.

2. Macroeconomics and Ecological Sustainability

In Chapter 32, we noted that world economic production has more than tripled since the early 1970s. Further economic growth is clearly desirable in developing countries to improve the well-being of more than a billion people who are now living in desperate poverty. Continued economic growth has been a principal policy objective in industrialized countries.

But as the twenty-first century proceeds, we must consider whether it is possible, or even desirable, to continue along the economic growth trajectory of the twentieth century. Economic growth has been accompanied by an increasing demand for natural resources, as well as increases in waste, pollution, and ecosystem damages. Many ecologists warn us that the current scale of human impact on the natural world is already unsustainable. Yet the ecological implications of a further doubling, quadrupling, or more, of human economic activity is an issue that, to date, has received little attention from macroeconomists.*

In this section, we consider the implications of current environmental issues for economic growth and development. First, we present an overview of some of the most pressing global environmental problems. Then we explore the relationship between economic growth and environmental quality and discuss policies to promote ecologically sustainable development.

2.1 Major Environmental Issues

A number of environmental issues are closely related to economic growth, including:

Global Population

Economic and technological growth since the Industrial Revolution has fostered a dramatic increase in world population. Global population was approximately 1 billion in 1800, increased to 2 billion around 1930 and 3 billion in 1960. In 2000, it increased to 6 billion, and in 2011 it passed 7 billion. Human population growth contributes to increases in many environmental pressures, including those related to food production. Although so far intensification of food production has kept pace with population growth, it has led to significant costs in terms of land degradation, pollution from fertilizers and pesticides, and overtaxing of water supplies.

Global population growth rates are currently declining, and many projections indicate that the human population will peak sometime in the twenty-first century (see Appendix). A stable or declining global population would eventually ease environmental pressures, but a substantial population increase is still predicted in the coming decades. Medium-range projections by the United Nations show a global population of 9.2 billion people in 2050, with almost all future population growth occurring in developing countries.

Resource Depletion

As noted in Chapters 22 and 32, depletion of important renewable and nonrenewable resources has accompanied economic growth. Many of the world's fisheries are in decline due to overfishing. Tropical forests are being lost at a rapid rate. Nearly a billion people live in countries where usable water is in scarce supply and water sources continue to be overdrawn and polluted. Stocks of key mineral resources, such as aluminum and copper, are for the most part not close to exhaustion, but high-quality reserves are being depleted, and recovery of lower-quality reserves tends to involve higher energy and environmental costs.

Probably no other natural resource has been more critical for modern economic growth than fossil fuels. These fuels (oil, coal, and natural gas) currently provide more than 80 percent of global energy supplies. The U.S. Department of Energy projects that global demand for fossil-fuel energy will increase approximately 60 percent between 2006 and 2030. However, many estimates suggest that global production of conventional oil, the most-used energy source, will peak within the next few decades. While "unconventional" sources of oil and gas, such as shale oil and natural gas obtained through hydraulic fracturing or "fracking,"

*At a GDP growth rate of 3 percent, a doubling of GDP takes about 24 years. A quadrupling would take 48 years.

may expand supplies, these sources are likely to be more expensive and come at higher environmental cost. All of these fuels contribute to CO_2 emissions that cause global climate change (discussed in detail below). Given the current dependence on fossil fuels, limitations on their use, for economic or environmental reasons, could challenge both the potential for industrialized countries to maintain their living standards and for developing countries to reduce poverty.

Pollution and Wastes

As discussed in Chapter 21, damage from pollution is not reflected in traditional national accounting measures, even though it clearly reduces welfare. Industrial countries generate the vast majority of the world's pollution and waste. Although rich countries are home to only about one-sixth of the world's population, they generate about two-thirds of global industrial wastes by volume. But pollution also jeopardizes economic development in poorer countries. For example, a 2006 "Green GDP" estimate for China indicated that environmental costs amounted to between 3 percent and 10 percent of China's GDP. A 2007 estimate by the World Bank and China's State Environmental protection Agency put air and water pollution costs alone at 5.8 percent of GDP.[1]

In some cases, toxic wastes are exported from industrialized countries to low-income countries that need the income they earn as compensation for accepting wastes but are ill equipped to receive and process them. Rapid future development will mean that pollution and waste management problems, both domestic and trade-related, are likely to grow, despite efforts to control them with environmental regulations.

2.2 THE RACE BETWEEN TECHNOLOGY AND RESOURCE DEPLETION

In the history of economic development, when one resource became scarce, another has been found to replace it. Thus, as wood and whale oil became scarce as energy sources, fossil fuels were discovered and developed to take their place. Another example is the development of a variety of plastics that have replaced metal or wood inputs in countless products. Even when resources are abundant, there may be substitutes (or potential substitutes) that can be used more inexpensively. Much of the story of economic growth is associated with productivity gains from being able to produce goods and services with progressively cheaper resources.

Yet there is some debate about possible limits to such a process. Some "technological optimists" believe that human ingenuity is virtually limitless and that humans will always be capable of finding economic substitutes for existing resources, as they grow scarcer. But do substitutes exist for *all* resources? And are some resources more essential than others?

There is no substitute for potable fresh water, which is absolutely essential for humans and many other species. Even where a resource is not essential and substitutes are conceivable, it may be necessary to contend with the difficulty of obtaining the substitutes and the associated costs in terms of money or energy.

The minerals sector is an example of a significant area in which costs have recently been rising. Mineral prices increased significantly from 2000 to 2012, and growing demand from developing economies suggests that they may continue to rise over the medium to long term.

Copper is one important mineral for which technology had seemed for a long time to be winning the race against resource depletion. Plastic has replaced copper in many uses, such as plumbing, and plastic fiber-optic cables (as well as wireless technologies) have displaced copper wires for long-distance information transmission. Yet global demand for copper continues to grow, and copper prices tripled between 2000 and 2012. Copper in the ground remains in reasonably plentiful supply, but what is left to mine is of lower quality than what has already been taken. This is economically and ecologically important because when ore quality drops, more energy is typically required to extract and refine it. And generally the more energy-intensive the extraction of the mineral is, the more adverse the environmental impacts (e.g., pollution) that are produced.

Another important example is phosphorus, which is a critical input in the fertilizer used in the mass production of food. It has no known substitutes and there are no synthetic ways of creating it. Researchers are therefore focusing on methods of reducing dependence on the element or looking for ways of reusing it, conserving it at the point of use, or recycling it from plant and animal wastes.

2.3 A Biological Example: Fish Stocks

Unlike minerals, fish are a renewable or reproducible resource. Yet renewable does not mean inexhaustible: It is quite possible for us to run out of fish in the wild if we harvest them more rapidly than they are able to reproduce.

Many deep-sea fish (e.g., Atlantic halibut, bluefin tuna, and cod) are seriously depleted. If the danger is recognized early enough, and steps are taken to reduce fishing activity sufficiently in areas where they spawn, fish populations can often recover. Canada imposed an indefinite moratorium on cod fishing in 1992, and the Magnuson-Stevens Fishery Conservation and Management Act, passed in the United States in 1996, limited the allowable catch for dozens of species. About half of them are recovering, but many species, including cod and flounder, are still in danger. Many other species around the world suffer from overfishing as well as habitat destruction. According to the United Nations Food and Agriculture Organization, 80 percent of the world's marine fish stocks are fully exploited or overexploited.[2]

Ironically, technological change has contributed to the decline. The introduction of bigger boats, sonar technology for finding fish, and large-scale "drift nets" have all increased depletion rates. Increasing scarcity has raised the market price for most wild-caught fish, generating incentives to expand aquaculture (fish farming). But there are also adverse ecological impacts from aquaculture, especially with the farming of saltwater species, such as shrimp and salmon. Five pounds of wild-caught fish are used as feedstock in the production of each pound of farmed salmon, while shrimp farming has led to widespread destruction of coastal mangrove forests.

Discussion Questions

1. Are you concerned about the future impacts of population growth and resource and environmental impacts? Do you think there should be some limits to population and/or economic growth?
2. Do you consider yourself a "technological optimist"? Do you believe that natural resource constraints represent a serious threat to economic production in the future? If so, which resources do you think we should be most concerned about?

3. Climate Change

The resource and environmental issues discussed above all pose serious problems. But perhaps the primary environmental challenge of the twenty-first century is global climate change. Global climate change combines issues of resource use and environmental impact, and is strongly related to economic growth.

3.1 Greenhouse Emissions and Global Temperature Change

Recent research, summarized in a 2007 report by the Intergovernmental Panel on Climate Change (IPCC), has virtually eliminated any doubts that human activities are affecting the earth's climate.[3] Emissions of various greenhouse gases, particularly CO_2, trap heat near the earth's surface, leading not only to a general warming trend but to sea-level rise, ecological disruption, and an increase in severe weather events, such as hurricanes, floods, and droughts.

Figure 33.1 **Global Temperature Trends, 1900–2100**

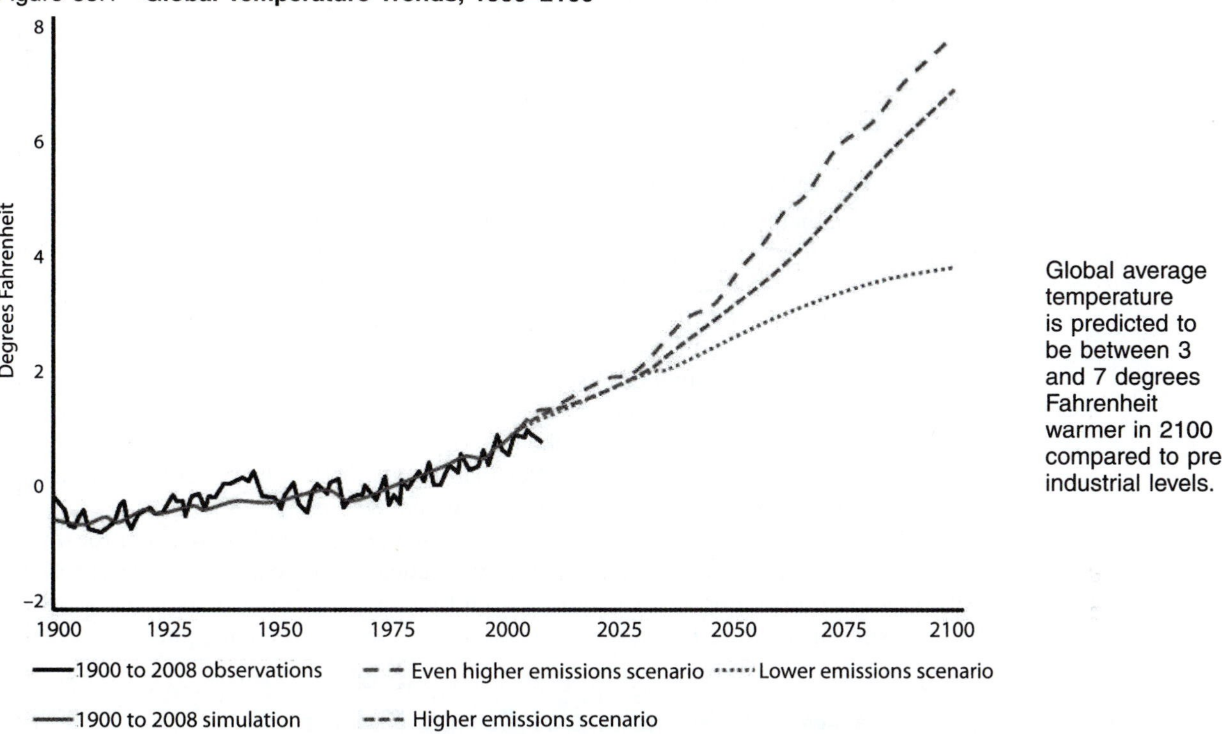

Source: U.S. Global Change Research Program. www.globalchange.gov

Greenhouse gases persist for decades or more in the earth's atmosphere. In addition, there is a lag between the time a gas is emitted and the time when its effects are fully realized. Thus, even if annual emissions of greenhouse gases were immediately stabilized at current levels, the concentration of these gases in the atmosphere would continue to rise, with effects such as sea-level rise continuing for centuries. Global emissions of greenhouse gases will eventually need to be reduced significantly—as much as 80 or 90 percent lower than current levels by 2050—if we are to avoid the most dangerous effects of climate change. But, rather than declining, emissions of the major greenhouse gases are rising rapidly, primarily driven by fossil-fuel–based economic growth.

According to the U.S. Energy Information Administration, global emissions of CO_2 rose by 35 percent between 2000 and 2011. Estimated U.S. emissions actually *declined* by 6 percent over the same period, partly as a result of the 2007–9 recession and partly due to a shift to less–carbon-intensive natural gas. While U.S. emissions per person remain far higher than those in developing countries such as China and India, rapid growth in these countries accounts for a steady rise in emissions, which can be expected to continue for years to come.

Predicting the precise effects of climate change is subject to substantial uncertainty. The IPCC report summarizes the predictions of various climate change models. They reported a range in which the average global temperature was expected to be between 1.1° and 6.4° C (2.0 ° and 11.5° F) warmer in 2100 compared to preindustrial levels, with the most likely range being between 1.8° C and 4° C (3° F to 7° F). This range of possible temperature increases is shown in Figure 33.1.

The likely effects of a 2° C increase in global average temperature (towards the lower end of the projected range) include:

- A 20–30 percent decrease in water supplies in already vulnerable regions such as southern Africa and the Mediterranean;

- Significant declines in crop yields in tropical regions;
- 40–60 million more people exposed to malaria in Africa;
- As many as 10 million more people affected by coastal flooding each year, with major low-lying areas swamped and coastal cities endangered;
- 15–40 percent of species in danger of extinction.

A report sponsored by the British government in 2006 finds that, under a "business-as-usual" (BAU) scenario, there is at least a 50 percent chance of an average temperature increase of more than 5°C (9°F) by the early twenty-second century. Climate change of this magnitude could lead to catastrophic effects such as the irreversible melting of the Greenland ice sheet, the collapse of the Amazon forest, and flooding of major cities including London and New York (see Box 33.1).

This report specifically examined the economics of climate change. It estimates the costs of climate change in the twenty-first century as between 5 percent and 20 percent of global GDP, while the most severe effects of climate change could be avoided at a cost of approximately 1 percent of GDP. Thus, the report concludes that it appears that the benefits of immediate action to minimize climate change significantly exceed the costs (see Box 33.1).

Although the most dangerous impacts of climate change are not likely to occur for several decades or more, the actions taken in the next few decades will almost surely have a profound effect on those ultimate impacts. Delaying action for even a decade would lead to a greater risk of catastrophic effects. This has significant implications for global equity. The impacts

BOX 33.1 THE STERN REVIEW—THE ECONOMICS OF CLIMATE CHANGE

Published in October 2006, the British government report written by former World Bank chief economist Nicholas Stern presents an urgent case for strong and immediate action to respond to the threat of global climate change. According to this report:

> The scientific evidence is now overwhelming: climate change presents very serious global risks, and it demands an urgent global response. . . . Under a BAU [business as usual] scenario, the stock of greenhouse gases could more than treble by the end of the century, giving at least a 50 percent risk of exceeding 5°C global average temperature change during the following decades. This would take humans into unknown territory. An illustration of the scale of such an increase is that we are now only around 5°C warmer than in the last ice age. Such changes would transform the physical geography of the world. A radical change in the physical geography of the world must have powerful implications for the human geography—where people live, and how they live their lives.
>
> The evidence gathered by the Review leads to a simple conclusion: *the benefits of strong, early action considerably outweigh the costs.* The evidence shows that ignoring climate change will eventually damage economic growth. Our actions over the coming few decades could create risks of major disruption to economic and social activity, later in this century and in the next, on a scale similar to those associated with the great wars and the economic depression of the first half of the twentieth century. And it will be difficult or impossible to reverse these changes. Tackling climate change is the pro-growth strategy for the longer term, and it can be done in a way that does not cap the aspirations for growth of rich or poor countries. The earlier effective action is taken, the less costly it will be.
>
> In summary, analyses that take into account the full ranges of both impacts and possible outcomes—that is, that employ the basic economics of risk—suggest that BAU climate change will reduce welfare by an amount equivalent to a reduction in consumption per head of between 5 and 20 percent. Taking account of the increasing scientific evidence of greater risks, of aversion to the possibilities of catastrophe, and of a broader approach to the consequences than implied by narrow output measures, the appropriate estimate is likely to be in the upper part of this range. . . . It is still possible to avoid the worst impacts of climate change; but it requires strong and urgent collective action. Delay would be costly and dangerous.

Source: Excerpted from the Stern Review, available at http://webarchive.nationalarchives.gov.uk/20130129110402/http://www.hm-treasury.gov.uk/sternreview_summary.htm (emphasis added).

of climate change—including coastal flooding, agricultural yield reductions, spreading of tropical diseases, and water shortages—are poised to fall disproportionately on the developing countries. While the rich countries would, to some extent, be able to adapt to many of the effects of climate change, most developing countries lack the financial and technical resources to do so. The 2007 IPCC report notes that climate change is likely to exacerbate global inequalities and impede economic development in poorer countries.

3.2 National and Global Responses to the Climate Challenge

Because many modern environmental problems are global in scope, they require a coordinated international response. The challenge of global climate change presents an illustration of how difficult this can be in practice. The Kyoto Protocol, drafted in 1997, committed industrialized countries to reduce their greenhouse gas emissions by an average of 5 percent below their 1990 emissions in time for the period 2008–2012. But it was not until 2005 that enough countries ratified the treaty to enable it to enter into force. The United States, the world's largest emitter of greenhouse gases, refused to ratify the treaty on the grounds that it would hurt the U.S. economy and because it does not bind developing countries to any emissions targets. Many of the countries that had ratified the treaty, moreover, did not meet their emissions targets.

International negotiations have tried to draft a "roadmap" for a new treaty to succeed the Kyoto Protocol since it expired in 2012. But although negotiators generally agree that "deep cuts" in greenhouse gas emissions are necessary, they have failed to agree on firm emissions targets or to decide on how to allocate responsibility between developing and industrialized countries.

The best hope for avoiding the worst impacts of climate change is to replace fossil-fuel energy sources with plentiful, less ecologically destructive resources, such as wind and solar power. There is also great potential to reduce energy demand through greater efficiency. Currently, technological progress reduces energy use per unit GDP by about 2 percent per year in the United States and other advanced countries. But combined with an economic growth rate of about 3 percent per year, this still results in about a 1 percent per year increase in energy use. Doubling the rate of energy efficiency gain would mean a 1 percent *decrease* in energy use per year—making it much easier to achieve carbon emissions reduction targets.

Opportunities for reducing emissions are described in the *2013 Annual Energy Outlook* report of the U.S. Energy Information Administration. The Extended Policies case in this report shows that the United States could avoid an increase in greenhouse gas emissions between 2013 and 2040 by continuing a number of current policies, including the production tax credit for wind, geothermal, biomass, and hydroelectric power and the investment tax credit for solar and by updating and strengthening a number of other policies, including the fuel-economy standards for new cars and appliance efficiency standards. These policy extensions and updates would reduce projected greenhouse gas emissions by an estimated 6 percent by 2040.

3.3 The Cost of Responding Versus the Cost of Inaction

A report from the World Economic Forum in Davos, Switzerland, has estimated that $700 billion in public and private investments will be needed each year to shift the global economy away from its dependence on fossil fuels. There is growing interest in the idea of using a tax on carbon-based energy to raise some of these funds. The Tax Policy Center has reported that estimates of income from such a tax in the United States could range from 0.5 percent of the country's GDP (for a tax of $15 per ton of CO_2) to 0.8 percent of GDP (for a tax of $31 per ton of CO_2). A tax of $31 per ton would translate to an extra 30 cents per gallon of gas. The revenue raised would be about $120 million per year.[4] (By comparison, the Swiss economy is performing well even with an effective carbon tax rate of more than $140 per ton.)

Revenues raised by such a tax could be used to fund the transition to renewable energy. In addition a carbon tax would encourage people and businesses to use less energy, with reductions concentrated in the energy sources that produce the most carbon (and therefore would be most heavily taxed): coal first, then petroleum, then natural gas—the latter being only half as carbon-intensive as coal but still a significant contributor to climate change.

The most serious disadvantage to a carbon tax is that it would fall more heavily on the poor. The Congressional Budget Office estimates that the poorest fifth of Americans spend 21.4 percent of their income on gas and utilities, while the richest 20 percent spend only 6.8 percent. There are, however, several ways to respond to this, the most straightforward being a direct rebate of some of the tax revenues for those most in need.

Some of the money raised through energy taxes could be used for disaster preparedness and relief. Climate change is already leading to higher cost from natural disasters. The drought of 2012 in the Southern and Western United States, considered by many analysts to be a result of climate change, cost about $35 billion. The same year, Hurricane Sandy was responsible for at least $65 billion in damage. In 2013, severe flooding in Colorado required evacuation of thousands and caused billions in damage. While no single climate event can be definitely linked to climate change, greater flooding, drought, and more intense hurricanes are predicted effects of climate change.

Although a large-scale energy transition away from fossil fuels would have significant costs, they may be quite modest on a macroeconomic scale and should be balanced against the growing costs likely to be caused by climate change, including extreme weather, agricultural output losses, and possible effects of famine, armed conflict, and mass migration if large areas are affected by sea-level rise or desertification. At the same time, looked at from the point of view of Keynesian macroeconomic analysis, the policies and actions suggested for preventing further climate change could bring potentially large economic benefits in terms of employment creation.

Discussion Questions

1. How do you think we should evaluate the economic impacts of climate change? Check the short executive summary of the Stern Review on the Economics of Climate Change (see Box 33.1). Do you agree with the conclusions of the Report?
2. What do you think should be done by the United States in response to global climate change? Can you think of specific policies that would reduce carbon emissions without resulting in significant economic disruption?

4. ECONOMIC GROWTH AND THE ENVIRONMENT

4.1 THE ENVIRONMENTAL KUZNETS CURVE HYPOTHESIS

Some researchers have suggested that, in the long run, economic development reduces per capita environmental damages. The logic behind this assertion is that sufficient wealth and technology allow countries to adopt clean production methods and move to a service-based economy. Further, environmental quality is generally considered a "normal good," meaning that people will demand more of it as they become wealthier.

The environmental Kuznets curve (EKC) hypothesis posits an inverted U-shaped relationship between economic development and environmental damages.* It states that

*This hypothesis was not devised by Simon Kuznets but is similar to his hypothesis, discussed in Chapter 32, that inequality first increases, then decreases with growing national wealth.

Figure 33.2 **Environmental Kuznets Curve for Sulfur Dioxide Emissions**

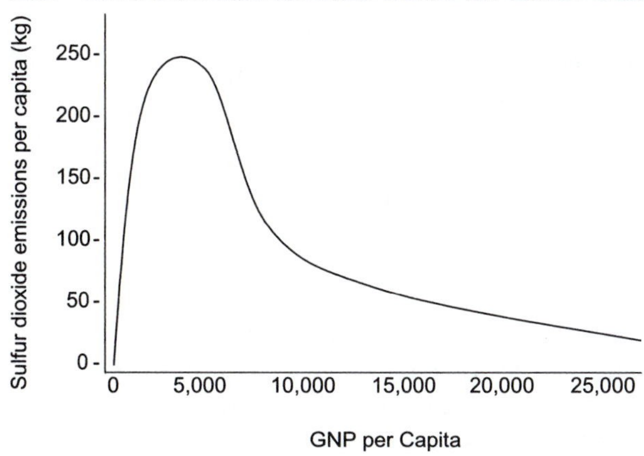

The empirical relationship between sulfur dioxide emissions and the level of economic development in a country supports the EKC hypothesis.

Source: T. Panayotou, "Empirical Tests and Policy Analysis of Environmental Degradation at Different Levels of Development," International Labour Office Working Paper, 1993.

environmental damage per capita increases in the early stages of economic development, reaches a maximum, and then diminishes as a country attains higher levels of income. If the evidence supported this hypothesis, it would imply that economic growth would eventually promote a cleaner environment.

Does this principle really work? The EKC relationship does seem to hold for some pollutants. Figure 33.2 shows the findings of a study that estimated the relationship between per capita sulfur dioxide emissions (the primary cause of "acid rain") and a country's per capita income. Sulfur dioxide emissions per capita appear to peak at an income level of around $5,000 and decline as incomes rise further. Studies of some other pollutants, mostly air pollutants, have also given limited support to the EKC hypothesis.

However, the EKC relationship does not appear to hold for many other environmental problems. Studies of municipal waste and energy use find that environmental impacts generally continue to rise as incomes rise. Perhaps most importantly, CO_2 emissions show a positive relationship with average income, as shown by the upward-sloping trend line in Figure 33.3, with

Figure 33.3 **Carbon Dioxide Emissions vs. GDP per Capita, 2009**

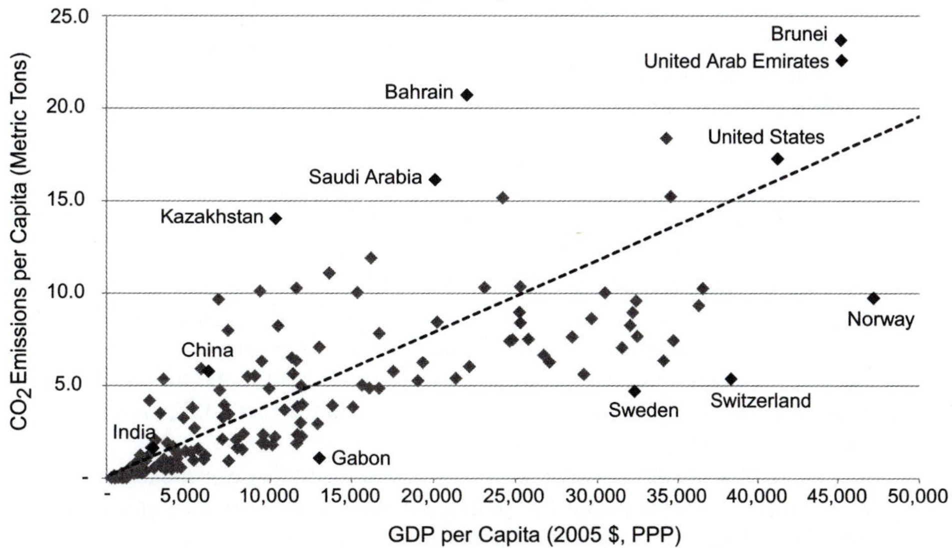

Carbon dioxide emissions per capita tend to increase with higher levels of economic development in a country.

Source: World Bank, World Development Indicators Database, 2013.

no apparent turning point. This means that carbon emissions can be generally expected to increase as economies grow, unless current dependence on fossil-fuel energy is dramatically altered.

Thus, contrary to the EKC hypothesis, economic growth appears unlikely to provide a guaranteed path to environmental sustainability. The relationship between growth and the environment is, in reality, more complex. Average income is not the only relevant factor in determining environmental impacts; the distribution of resources also plays a key role. Sustainable development needs to include reducing economic inequalities along with preserving the environment.

Some environmental damage, such as soil erosion and deforestation, may occur because poor people engage in unsustainable practices simply to survive. Programs to eliminate poverty in developing countries can provide people with choices that are less environmentally destructive. Meanwhile, environmental degradation typically hits the poorest people the hardest, because many rely heavily on the natural environment for their subsistence.

Policies that improve the environment can thus also serve to reduce poverty and economic inequality. The objectives of human development and environmental protection are actually interlinked. The promotion of human development in poor countries can improve environmental quality while policies to improve the environment can also reduce economic disparities. This suggests the need for a coordinated policy response that considers the linkages between human development and the environment.

4.2 Policies for Sustainable Development

Much of macroeconomic theory and policy is currently oriented toward promoting continuous economic growth. What kind of policies would be required to promote ecological sustainability? How can these policies be designed to such that they also maintain well-being and promote human development, especially in developing countries?

Some ecologically oriented economists view "sustainable growth" as a contradiction in terms. They point out that no system can grow without limit. Yet it seems that some kinds of economic growth are essential. For the large number of people in the world who cannot satisfy their basic needs, for example, an increase in consumption of food, housing, and other goods is clearly required. For those who have already achieved a high level of material consumption, there are possibilities for continued improvements in well-being through expanded educational and cultural services that do not necessarily have a large negative environmental impact. But there is nothing in standard macroeconomics to guarantee that economic growth will be either equitable or environmentally benign. Specific policies for sustainable development are therefore needed.

What might such policies involve? There are numerous possibilities, including:

Green Taxes

"Green" taxes make it more expensive to undertake activities that deplete important natural resources or contribute to environmental degradation. They discourage energy- and material-intensive economic activities, while favoring the provision of services and labor-intensive industries. One example of a green tax, as discussed above, is a tax on the carbon content of energy supplies, favoring renewables and efficiency over carbon-based fuels. All countries have implemented environmentally based taxes to some extent. As shown in Figure 33.4, environmental taxes in industrial countries can range from 3.5 percent to over 10 percent of total tax revenues.

Green taxes are strongly supported by economic theory as a means of internalizing negative externalities such as pollution. When a negative externality such as pollution exists, an unregulated market will result in an inefficient allocation (as discussed in Chapter 13). Because all taxes, in addition to raising revenue, discourage the "taxed" activity, it is economically desirable to discourage "bads" such as environmental pollution and natural resource depletion

Figure 33.4 **Environmentally Based Taxes as a Share of Total Tax Revenue, Select Industrialized Countries, 2006**

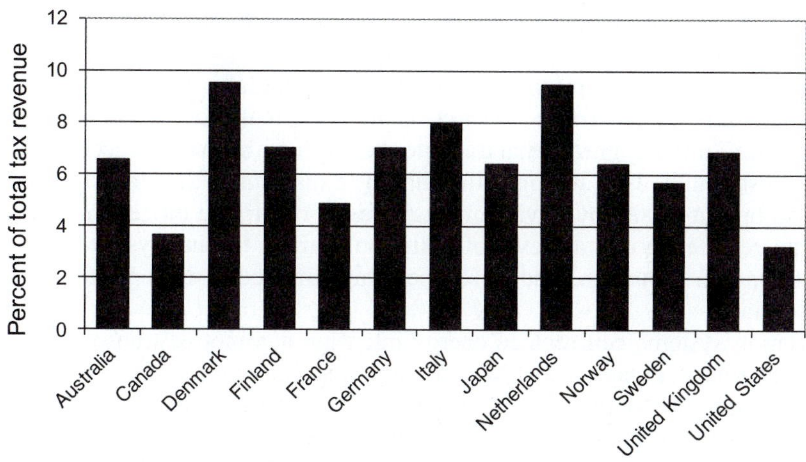

Environmentally based taxes account for about 10 percent of total tax revenue in Denmark and the Netherlands, but only about 3 percent of total revenue in the United States.

Source: OECD, OECD/EEA Instruments Database, 2007.

by placing taxes on them, rather than on positive economic activities like investment and the earning of income.

Two common objections to green taxes frequently arise. First, it is likely that green taxes would fall disproportionately on lower-income households. But as noted earlier, a rebate or credit to these households could be implemented to avoid making a green tax regressive. The other criticism is that green taxes are politically unpopular—no one wants higher taxes. Increases in green taxes can be offset, however, by reductions in other taxes (such as income taxes) so that the tax burden on a typical household remains unchanged. Also, households and businesses would have the option to lower the amount of green taxes they pay by undertaking energy conservation measures and other environmentally friendly practices, which is not the case with other income or business taxes.

Eliminating Subsidies

Agricultural and energy subsidies that encourage the overuse of energy, fertilizer, pesticides, and irrigation water could be reduced or eliminated. This would reduce government expenditures, and the money saved could be used to lower taxes or to promote more sustainable agricultural systems that rely on the recycling of nutrients, crop diversification, the use of natural pest controls, and minimizing the use of artificial chemicals and fertilizer. Such systems also tend to be more labor-intensive, so they also have the potential to boost employment.

Recycling and Renewable Energy

Policies such as deposit/refund systems or targeted subsidies can be used to promote greater recycling of materials and the use of renewable energy. Through research and development grants, subsidies, and tax breaks, governments can support the expansion of energy from solar power, wind, and geothermal heat. Strategic public investment in new technologies such as fuel cells and high-efficiency industrial systems can eventually make these technologies cost-competitive.

Tradable Permits

Tradable permit systems (often called "cap-and-trade") can set an overall limit on pollution by offering a limited number of permits allowing the emission of specific quantities and types of pollution. These plans are based on the principle that a process of pollution reduction may be most efficiently achieved by allowing businesses to choose between finding low-cost ways to reduce their emissions and paying to buy permits. After the permits are distributed to firms, they can then buy them from or sell them to other firms. Pollution reduction will occur first where it can be done most economically.

This efficiency characteristic makes tradable permit systems popular among economists. Although environmentalists have sometimes objected, on principle, to the idea of government issuing "permits to pollute," it is recognized that tradable permits have been used successfully in several instances, most notably in reducing sulfur dioxide emissions in the United States. Such permits can also be purchased by environmental groups or private citizens in order to retire them and thus reduce the overall level of pollution. Carbon trading systems apply the same principle to carbon reduction, and have been implemented in Europe, the U.S. Northeast, and California.

Efficient transportation systems can replace energy-intensive automotive transport with high-speed trains, public transit, greater use of bicycles, and redesign of cities and suburbs to minimize transportation needs. In countries such as the United States, where automobile-centered systems are already extensively developed, the use of highly fuel-efficient cars can reduce fuel needs; in some developing countries, automobile dependence might be avoided altogether.

Debt-for-Nature Swaps

Debt-for-nature swaps work by forgiving the debt of developing countries in exchange for agreements to protect nature reserves or pursue environmentally friendly policies. For example, in 2002 the United States canceled $5.5 million in debt owed to it by Peru in return for Peru's agreement to conserve 10 rainforest areas covering more than 27.5 million acres. This innovative form of international fiscal policy was authorized by the Tropical Forest Conservation Act of 1998.

4.3 SUSTAINABILITY AND CONSUMPTION

As discussed earlier, global inequalities currently mean that many people in the world have too little to live on, while others consume at high levels. Some theorists have suggested replacing the goal of ever-increasing consumption with the goal of *sufficiency.* This idea can be developed at two levels. At the individual level is the question of the amount of consumption that is sufficient to support human well-being. At the macro or global level is the question of what kinds and amounts of consumption can be sustained, by humanity as a whole, without destructive environmental consequences. Note that the second question includes two different issues: the *kinds* of consumption and the aggregate *quantities* consumed.

Alan Durning, the author of *How Much Is Enough: The Consumer Society and the Future of the Earth,* has proposed dividing the global population into three groups classified according to their consumption levels and environmental impacts.[5] Table 33.1 presents a similar classification using updated data. We see that energy use, carbon emissions, and vehicle use are all much lower for those in the global lower-income class than in the rest of the world. Although these households are often forced to undertake ecologically unsustainable actions simply to survive, their overall impact on global environmental problems is relatively minor.

The global "middle class" uses more resources than the poor, but its lifestyle is still relatively environmentally sustainable. Those in this class rely primarily on bicycles and public transportation, eat a grain-based diet, and use a moderate amount of energy. Durning suggests that the entire world population could live at this level of affluence without exceeding the ecological capacity of the planet.

The global upper-income class relies on private vehicles and air transportation, eats a diet including daily consumption of meat, and uses a significantly higher amount of energy than the other classes. The rest of the world could not possibly emulate the lifestyle of this class without exceeding the capacity of the global environment.

Table 33.1 **Global Population Classification by Income and Environmental Impacts, 2013**

	Global lower-income	Global middle-income	Global high-income
Population (millions)	817	5,022	1,135
Average income per capita (U.S. dollars)	571	4,148	39,860
Energy use per capita (kg oil equivalent)	363	1,310	5,000
Electricity power consumption per capita (kWh)	242	1,823	9,415
Carbon dioxide emissions per capita (metric tons)	0.3	3.5	11.4
Passenger cars per 1,000 population	10	60	620

Each of the three groups defined here needs to approach environmental sustainability with different objectives.

• For the lower-income group, the focus must be on improving material living standards and expanding options while taking advantage of environmentally friendly technologies.

• The challenge for the middle-income group is to keep overall environmental impacts per capita relatively stable by pursuing a development path that avoids a reliance on fossil fuels, disposable products, and ever-increasing levels of material consumption.

• Finally, the high-income group must find a way to reduce environmental impacts per capita through technological improvements, intelligently designed policies, and changes in lifestyle aspirations.

Source: World Bank, *Little Green Data Book 2013; World Development Indicators 2013.*

The problem may not be as irresolvable as it appears. In addition to the question of what is possible—that is, ecologically sustainable—we need to ask what is *desirable.* In rich countries, it has become increasingly important to recognize that "too much" can be just as much of a problem as "too little." Increasing consumption may bring little benefit and can actually be worse for individuals, who may suffer ill health from overeating, sedentary lifestyle and reliance on automobiles, and, according to some social scientists, spiritual malaise from exclusive or excessive attention to material things. At high income levels, other dimensions of human development, such as freedom from violence, closer and more peaceful families and communities, a satisfying work life or volunteer opportunities, cultural activities, and investments in the productive and creative capacities of the next generation may be more important than having more marketed goods and services. To the extent that we trade material consumption for these other objectives, sustainability becomes less of a challenge.

Moreover, a large portion of every country's social and individual well-being depends on the maintenance of homes and families, including care of sick and elderly people, along with other productive activities that take place in homes and communities but are not bought and sold in formal markets (as discussed in Chapters 2 and 21). Many adults today feel squeezed between the demands of conventional, forty hours (or more) per week of paid employment and the time requirements of their families. As we saw in Chapter 10, full-time employment in Europe requires the equivalent of five fewer weeks of work per year, on average, than full-time employment in the United States. Europeans have in effect chosen to translate part of their increased labor productivity into increased leisure, instead of using it all to increase earnings and consumption. As shown in Figure 33.5, there is a tradeoff between leisure time and money earned, with one the opportunity cost for the other; where a country situates itself on the "consumption-possibilities frontier" depends on the culture and the prevailing attitudes toward work.

Economic practices that make people "rich" as consumers but "poor" as family and community members are not consistent with the human development goal of having the freedom to live a valuable life. They are also not ecologically sustainable in the long run, at least if every human on earth aspires to the highest levels of consumption. Fortunately, it is growing increasingly apparent that scaling back in the area of material consumption not only is good for the natural environment but also—at least beyond a certain level of income—can enhance our overall well-being.

Figure 33.5 **A Consumption Possibilities Frontier**

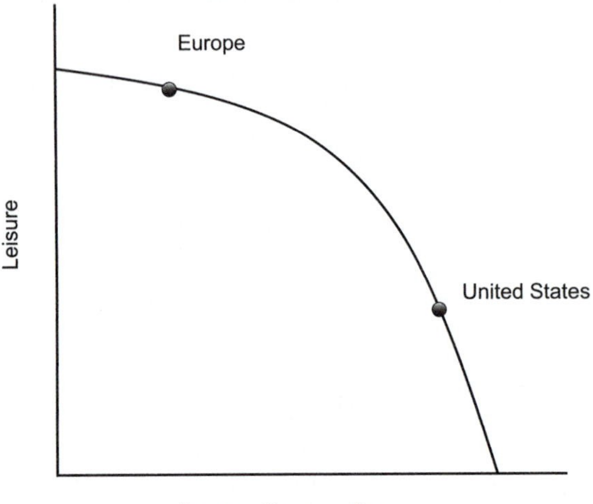

The diagram illustrates the tradeoff between consumption and leisure time. Europeans on average live at a lower material standard than people in the United States, because they do not work as many hours, hence earn less income. On the plus side, they enjoy more leisure time, which Americans sacrifice in order to be able to consume more.

4.4 Sustainability and Investment

throughput: the flow of raw materials and energy through the economy, leading to outputs of waste

If an ecological perspective implies limits on consumption, what happens to investment? As we have seen earlier in this book, investment spending has often been crucially important for aggregate demand and employment. Yet additional investments in traditional kinds of plant and equipment, which rely heavily on fossil fuels, may work against environmental sustainability. This dilemma can be resolved only by forms of investment that improve well-being but do not increase what has been called **throughput**—the use of raw materials and energy as inputs, resulting in the creation of wastes as system outputs. The social and environmental challenges that have been outlined in this chapter suggest the need for large investment expenditures, many of which are not directly related to increasing material consumption. Rather than being a burden or threat, such investment expenditures may be the solution to maintaining employment with limited consumption.

As we saw in Chapter 32, many countries in the past used industrial policies successfully, to push an economy from one phase to another. The United States could not have gone from a mostly agrarian economy to an industrial one without government assistance in developing transportation and communication systems. Japan's government carefully selected a sequence of industries to support, going from low-tech and labor-intensive to high-tech and information-intensive. All of the successful European, Asian, and North American economies have depended on essential support from national investments in education and public health. Many such investments are "public goods" (as discussed in Chapter 2) because, although they provide widespread benefits, it is hard to collect payment from the people who benefit from them; hence, if they are to occur, they must be supported through national action.

A similar set of strategic investments, focused on areas such as alternative energy, public transportation, sustainable agriculture, education, and health services could move countries toward a more environmentally sustainable economy. Such investments contribute to economically and environmentally positive development but may not pay the kind of return that would encourage private companies to undertake them. Yet with such strategic investments in place, the private sector can be relied on for much of the follow-through—much as, in the past, the U.S. government provided interstate highways, while the private sector supplied cars and trucks.

It is also important to remember that, as discussed in Chapter 21, "investments" should really refer to much more than just factories and equipment. Environmental policy is concerned with protecting, or avoiding *dis*investment in, the global commons—the oceans,

Box 33.2 Discounting the Future

In economic theory, future costs and benefits are often evaluated with a technique called discounting. The theory behind discounting is that a dollar today is worth more than a dollar tomorrow—even after correcting for inflation. The discount rate, sometimes referred to as the "time discount rate," is the annual rate at which dollar values are considered to change over time (this is a different, broader use of the term than the Federal Reserve's discount rate offered to member banks, discussed in Chapter 26). Use of a discount rate often depends on the assumption that people of the future will be better off than people today—therefore, a dollar is worth more to us now than it will be to our great-grandchildren, even after accounting for possible inflation. For most commercial and financial calculations, the use of a discount rate makes sense. However, its application to social and environmental costs and benefits is more complicated.

To illustrate the impact of discount rate calculations, at an 8 percent discount rate, $1.00 today becomes worth $1.08 next year and ($1.00) (1.08^{10}) = $2.16 ten years from now. Similarly, $1.00 to be received ten years from now is worth only ($1.00)/($1.08^{10}$) = $0.46 today.

For longer periods, the impact of discounting becomes much more dramatic. The present value of $1,000 fifty years from now is only $87.20 at a 5 percent discount rate, and the value of $1,000 one hundred years from now is only $7.60. At a 10 percent discount rate, the value of $1,000 one hundred years from now is only 7 cents! This would mean that, applying a discount rate of 10 percent, it is not worth spending more than 7 cents today to avoid $1,000 worth of damages one hundred years from now. This has led to a serious criticism of the discounting approach. How can we justify a technique that might implicitly consider serious damages to future generations less important than moderate costs today?

Discounting is essential if we are considering the economics of, for example, taking out a mortgage to buy a house or a loan to finance a business investment. The benefits of being able to own and live in the house starting today may well outweigh the future costs of paying interest on the mortgage over the next twenty years. Similarly, the income generated by the business investment can be compared to the annual payments on the loan—if the rate of return on the investment exceeds the discount rate, it brings net benefits.

In such cases, it makes sense to use the commercial discount rate, determined in current markets, to compare present and future costs and benefits. But can we say that a GDP gain today, or in the near future, outweighs major damage in the next generation? How should we evaluate broader environmental impacts that will continue over long periods?

We can try to resolve the problem by defining a **social discount rate**—a rate that attempts to reflect the appropriate social valuation of future costs and benefits. Estimates of social discount rates vary but are usually significantly lower than commercial discount rates and include a rate of zero. But, of course, private market actors such as corporations will base their decisions on the current market rate of interest, not a social discount rate. Public investments, by contrast, can be based on a judgment that the appropriate social discount rate is lower—which means that the future should be weighted more heavily. This might justify, for example, more investments in energy efficiency and carbon-free energy sources today, to avoid damages from climate change that are likely to occur in future decades.

social discount rate: a discount rate that reflects social rather than market valuation of future costs and benefits; usually lower than the market discount rate

the atmosphere, the world's store of living species, and other aspects of natural and social capital that greatly affect the possibilities and the quality of life for present and future human generations.

This kind of long-term investment requires a more future-oriented perspective than is used for most business investments. The use of market discount rates (see Box 33.2) tends to limit the planning horizons of most businesses and individuals to about twenty to thirty years. But long-term sustainability demands a generational perspective, because many of the most severe impacts of problems such as global climate change will take decades, or even centuries, to unfold.

Discussion Questions

1. How do you think your environmental impacts compare with those of the average person in the world?
2. Does reducing environmental impacts require sacrifice, or can it be done in ways that increase overall well-being?

5. ARE STABILIZATION AND SUSTAINABILITY IN CONFLICT?

Earlier chapters have emphasized that a high level of aggregate demand is necessary to support a high output level, keeping income levels up and unemployment down. Is this goal in conflict with the goal of environmental sustainability? In some ways, it appears that it is, given the evidence that we have reviewed on how environmental problems increase with higher consumption. But there may be ways to reconcile the goals of higher living standards, full employment, and environmental sustainability. To do so, we have to re-examine some of our assumptions about economic growth.

5.1 WHAT DO WE REALLY WANT FROM EMPLOYMENT?

The macroeconomic models that we have developed starting in Chapter 24 have implicitly assumed that more employment is better. There is no doubt that needing a job and not being able to find one can be very tough on the unemployed. In addition to the lack of income—which can cause severe hardship and poverty for a worker and his or her family—unemployment can also have serious psychological repercussions. People often feel demoralized and depressed when they find that they are not wanted. Studies of the effects on health and mortality of business cycle swings show that suicide rates rise during economic downturns (see Chapter 30, Box 30.1). Clearly, a humane society should want to keep such suffering at a minimum, to the extent possible.

Rather than just thinking about "employment" and "unemployment," perhaps macroeconomists should be thinking more about the *quality, types,* and *intensity* of employment that an economy offers and what these mean for people's well-being. Being pushed out of the wage-earning system is clearly injurious to the involuntarily unemployed, and being deprived of sufficient income is very tough on the working poor. But the solution need not mean that everyone should always work 40 or more hours a week.

As discussed in Chapter 23, people also benefit from hours that they spend away from paid employment; this time provides opportunities to do unpaid work, including family care, and also to pursue leisure activities. It may be possible to keep employment *levels* high while reducing material and energy throughput, if we, as a society, think creatively enough about what sorts of, as well as *how much,* employment we really want.

The Dutch government, for example, responded to an economic downturn in the 1980s by stabilizing wages and allowing work hours to decline in order to reduce the unemployment rate. The idea, in other words, was to "share" available work hours among more people. New government employees were hired for four instead of five days per week. Other sectors soon followed, and eventually even Dutch banks adopted 80 percent schedules and a four-day workweek. In July 2000, the country passed the Working Hours Adjustment Act, landmark legislation that granted employees the right to reduce their weekly hours (even below 80 percent in many cases) without losing their job or suffering a reduction in hourly pay or employment benefits.[6]

In the same year, the French government reduced the standard workweek from 39 hours to 35 hours. Both the Dutch and French policies were motivated primarily by the desire to reduce the unemployment rate, but they also served to enhance workers' quality of life by affording them more leisure time. Because more leisure time and lower earnings on average leads to less consumption (and less throughput), both policy initiatives are examples of innovative macroeconomic policy that takes into account both stabilization and sustainability concerns.

5.2 WHAT DO WE REALLY WANT FROM PRODUCTION?

The model that we developed in earlier chapters works only with the *level* of output, *Y,* and says nothing about the *composition* of output. From a sustainability perspective, however, the composition of output makes a very big difference. Some things that we benefit from and enjoy require relatively little use of material and energy inputs. Eating locally grown produce, taking a bike ride with friends, or engaging in educational and cultural activities, for example, puts little stress on the natural environment. Other activities, such as heating and furnishing a very large house, driving an SUV, or maintaining a perfect lawn using chemical fertilizer, have more negative impacts. Shifting away from producing goods and services that are most damaging to ecological systems and toward producing goods and services that are less destructive—or even environmentally beneficial—could allow an economy to maintain consumption, investment, and employment in a less environmentally damaging way.

Another important macroeconomic issue relates to population stabilization. As discussed further in the Appendix to this chapter, the United States and many other countries in the world are already experiencing a growing ratio of retirees to active workers. Many elderly people need extra medical care and personal care. This suggests that while an economy may need to release some workers from high-throughput jobs for sustainability reasons, there will also be an increased demand for workers in medical and social services.

Similarly, while some opportunities for investment would no longer be available in a more sustainable economy, many more would open up. Investments in energy-saving infrastructure for transportation, in wetland restoration, and in conversion of residential and commercial buildings to more environmentally friendly patterns of energy and chemical use, for example, would create additional employment opportunities. While employment might decline in fossil-fuel and high-polluting industries, these possibilities for expanded job creation suggest that pursuing sustainability goals need not conflict with the goal of full employment.

The problems of transitioning to a more sustainable macroeconomy should not be minimized. People who build SUVs today, for example, cannot simply start building solar panels tomorrow—changes in human and manufactured capital must take place first. But neither should these problems be enlarged out of proportion. Scientific evidence suggests that a conversion to a less resource-intensive economy is not a matter of *if* but, rather, a matter of *when* and *how*. And the longer the conversion is put off, the more difficult it is likely to be.

5.3 Sustainability at the Local Level

Sustainable development does not depend only on national policies; it can also be developed from the bottom up, starting at the local level. Important aspects of local sustainability include*:

Democratization of Ownership

About 130 million Americans—40 percent of the population—are members of some form of one-person, one-vote cooperative. A program initiated by the federal government in the 1980s has resulted in about 11,000 employee stock ownership plans (ESOPs), involving 10.3 million people, in virtually every sector, and some are very large and sophisticated. Three million more individuals are involved in worker-owned companies of this kind than are members of unions in the private sector.

In addition, thousands of "social enterprises" use democratized ownership both for profitable production and to achieve a broader social purpose. By far, the most common social enterprise is the Community Development Corporation (CDC), numbering nearly 5,000 in U.S. cities. For the most part, CDCs serve as low-income housing developers and incubators for small businesses.

Another form of democratized ownership involves a growing number of "land trusts"—essentially nonprofit corporations that own housing and promote both conservation and low-

---

*Many of the examples cited are drawn from Gar Alperovitz, *What Then Must We Do?* (White River Junction, VT: Chelsea Green, 2013).

and moderate-income housing. Democratized ownership also takes the form of publicly run services and enterprises in local communities. More than two thousand publicly owned electric utilities are in operation, providing electricity at lower cost to the consumer. About 25 percent of electricity in the United States is supplied by locally owned public utilities and cooperatives.

In the financial sector, co-ops take the form of credit unions—essentially democratized, one-person, one-vote banks. More than 95 million Americans are involved; assets total approximately $1 trillion. Following the financial failures of 2008, campaigns to "move your money" shifted hundreds of millions, if not billions of dollars from Wall Street and large banks to credit unions and smaller banks.

"Greening" Communities

In many cases, worker-owned companies have emphasized "green" design. In Kansas City, Missouri, a municipal "Green Impact Zone" has brought together public and private resources to transform a decaying neighborhood into a sustainable urban community. The effort includes school improvements, weatherization, job training and placement programs, business development (initially targeted at improving energy efficiency), renewable energy and water conservation programs, installation of a smart grid by Kansas City Power and Light, and new programs to develop housing on abandoned lots.

In Austin, Texas, another green municipal development initiative is working to build a regional economy that emphasizes green business leadership, clean technology, new jobs, and expanding opportunity. The city supports local companies that "green" their operations, and aims to make the city's operations completely carbon-neutral (i.e., with net zero carbon emissions) by 2020—including reducing greenhouse gas emissions by switching to renewable energy, replacing inefficient lighting, and replacing vehicle fleets, plus conservation programs covering water, air quality, waste reduction and recycling, and green gardening.

These examples suggest that a different economic model of local development can combine democratization and ecological sustainability. It is worth considering whether such initiatives can be "scaled up" to the macroeconomic level, a question that we address in the next section.

5.4 MACROECONOMIC POLICIES FOR STABILIZATION AND SUSTAINABILITY

In Chapter 25, we saw how government spending and taxing policies can contribute to stabilization, and in Chapters 26 and 27, we looked at issues of money and credit. A society committed to both stabilization and sustainability could find ways to use these standard macroeconomic tools to work toward both goals.

Some economic policies aimed at promoting sustainability might actually represent a return to well-known Keynesian-style policies but with a new ecological twist—a strong emphasis on government and private investment in green technologies and a tax structure that shifts the tax burden from income, labor, and capital to the use of fossil fuels and resources.

As discussed in Chapter 28, the stimulus plan proposed by the Obama administration in 2009 and adopted by Congress was a classic Keynesian expansionary policy. About 10 percent of the stimulus specifically targeted environmental objectives (see Box 33.3). Such "green Keynesian" policies could be widely adopted and expanded to promote the transition to a more sustainable economic system.

steady-state economy: an economy with no increase in population, or in the rate of use of raw materials and energy

Some ecologically oriented economists have suggested that, rather than growing indefinitely on an exponential path—say of 4 percent GDP growth per year—national and global economic systems must follow what is called a logistic pattern, in which growth is eventually limited, at least in terms of resource consumption. This would lead to what is called a **steady-state economy**, in which population and economic output are stabilized (see Figure 33.6).

Figure 33.6 **Growth Reaching a Steady-State**

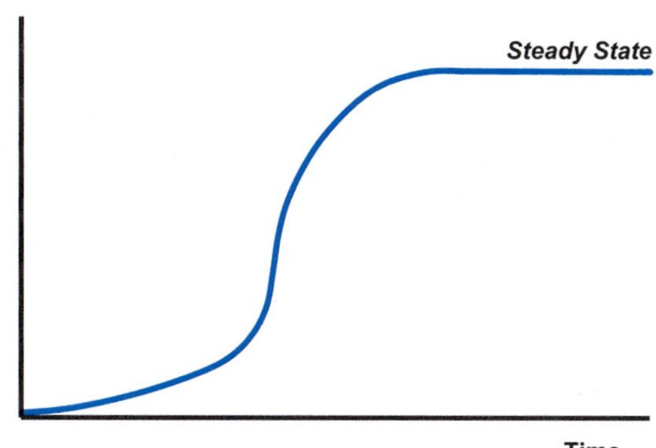

After starting with an exponential growth pattern, an economy adapting to a steady-state reduces its rate of growth in what is called a logistical pattern, approaching a maximum level at which economic activity stabilizes.

Box 33.3 "Green" Keynesian Policies in the United States

The $787 billion stimulus package adopted by the U.S. Congress in 2009 to promote recovery from the 2007–9 recession contained about $71 billion for "green" investments, plus $20 billion in "green" tax incentives, including:

- Energy efficiency in Federal buildings and Department of Defense facilities—$8.7 billion
- Smart-grid infrastructure investment—$11 billion
- Energy and conservation grants to state and local governments—$6.3 billion
- Weatherization assistance—$5 billion
- Energy efficiency and renewable energy research—$2.5 billion
- Advanced battery manufacturing—$2 billion
- Loan guarantees for wind and solar projects—$6 billion
- Public transit and high-speed rail—$17.7 billion
- Environmental cleanup—$14.6 billion
- Environmental research—$6.6 billion

The double benefit of such policies is that they promote employment and also advance a transition to a more environmentally sustainable economy. It is easily possible to envision much larger programs of this nature. For example, the stimulus program included $5 billion for weatherization programs. A major nationwide program for energy efficiency retrofit in houses and commercial buildings could easily be ten times as large. The stimulus program temporarily quadrupled U.S. spending on energy and environmental research and development; a permanent increase of this magnitude would have enormous long-term benefits in promoting a transition to efficiency and renewables.

Source: Jonathan M. Harris, "Green Keynesianism: Beyond Standard Growth Paradigms," in Robert B. Richardson ed., *Building a Green Economy: Perspectives from Ecological Economics* (East Lansing, MI: Michigan State University Press, 2013).

These environmental limits on growth would apply to resource and energy consumption; at the same time, activities that do not involve resource consumption, which are environmentally neutral or environmentally friendly, could continue to grow. Such activities could include services, arts, communication, and education. After basic needs are met and reasonable levels of consumption achieved, the concept of sustainable development implies that economic development should be increasingly oriented toward this kind of inherently "sustainable" activities.

One model of a transition to a steady-state economy has been presented by the Canadian economist Peter Victor. An economic model called "LOWGROW," when applied to the Canadian economy, models "socio-eco-environmental" paths that offer attractive social and environmental outcomes without requiring economic growth.[7] In the scenario presented in Figure 33.7, the Canadian government is assumed to introduce a tax on greenhouse gas (GHG) emissions, creating incentives to switch from high GHG sources of energy to lower ones, making energy

Figure 33.7 **A No-Growth Scenario for the Canadian Economy**

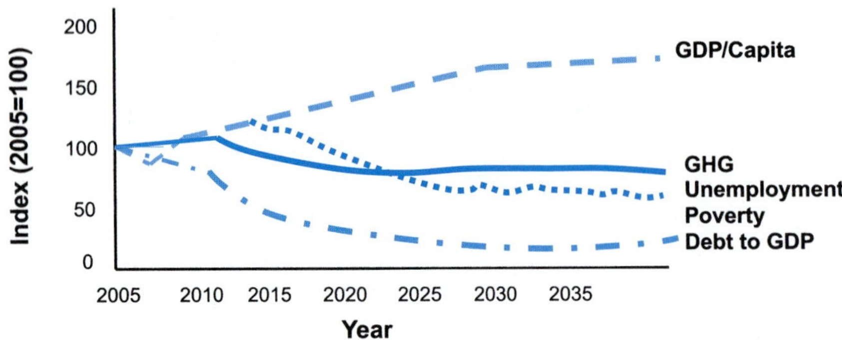

Even though projected GDP/capita stops growing in this macroeconomic model, well-being continues to increase, with declining unemployment, poverty, and debt, and improved environmental conditions.

Source: Adapted from Peter Victor, *Managing Without Growth: Slower by Deisgn, not Disaster.* Northampton, MA: Edward Elgar, 2008, p. 182.

in general more expensive and encouraging conservation and efficiency. The revenues from the GHG tax are used to reduce other taxes, so that the net effect on revenues is zero.

In this scenario, GDP per capita stabilizes after 2025, and GHG emissions decrease by 22 percent by 2035. Poverty levels as well as unemployment decrease significantly, and fiscal balance is reached, with a steady decrease in the debt to GDP ratio. A shorter workweek allows for full employment, with less growth in material consumption but more spending on health care and education. Such models show that slower growth leading to no growth can be consistent with full employment, virtual elimination of poverty, more leisure, considerable reduction in GHG emissions, and fiscal balance.

Discussion Questions

1. Cutting the length of the standard full-time workweek could be one way to keep people employed while cutting down on the "throughput" of materials and energy. Can you think of other policies that might also have this effect?
2. Do you think that an economic system can prosper without growth? Can we distinguish among growth in GDP, growth in employment, and growth in well-being? To what extent do these necessarily go together, and to what extent can improvements in employment and well-being be separated from GDP growth?

6. CONCLUDING THOUGHTS

Throughout the twentieth century, the main objective of macroeconomics was steady, strong economic growth. Considering the challenges that we face in the twenty-first century, macroeconomics itself will need to adapt to new realities. Employment, price stability, and GDP growth will continue to be issues of great importance—not as ends in themselves, however, but as the means to the broader goals of human development and sustainability. Keeping the ultimate well-being goals in mind, macroeconomics must look beyond the experience of the past and ask new questions.

A fundamental question confronting macroeconomics in the twenty-first century is how the majority of people in the world, currently at relatively low standards of living, can improve their well-being. The issues of "human development" discussed in Chapter 32 involve a combination of traditional economic growth and new approaches more oriented toward dealing with problems of poverty, inequality, and ecological sustainability.

Economic analysis needs to take into account the need for technologies that can provide energy and materials for human consumption in ways that are ecologically sound, and that help to remedy past damages (Box 33.4). The transition to a more sustainable economy will have economic costs, but also significant benefits, such as increased employment and

Box 33.4 Technologies for a Sustainable Economy

Technological progress can reduce the need for resource inputs and mitigate or eliminate environmental impacts. For a new technology to be adopted in the marketplace, it must be cost-effective. Recent developments have encouraged hope that some environmentally sound technologies are, or may soon become, competitive with more energy and resource-intensive and fossil-fuel based technologies.

- Renewable power sources have steadily declined in cost. Land-based wind power is now fully competitive with coal and nuclear power (Ailworth, 2013). While solar and offshore wind power remain more expensive than conventional power, their costs have declined also. Technologies such as solar roof tiles make it possible for buildings to generate much or all of their own power, thus adding to the asset value of the building.
- The American Council for an Energy Efficient Economy estimates that only 14 percent of energy used in the U.S. economy was converted to useful work, leaving enormous potential for efficiency improvement. Their website www.aceee.org lists technologies and policies that can achieve much greater energy efficiency.
- Engineers at Lockheed Martin are creating a better way to desalinate water to meet the growing global demand for potable water by using filters embedded with sheets of graphene, which are 500 times thinner than others, taking much less energy to push water through them to remove salt.
- Rentricity is a New York–based company that uses water pressure in municipal pipes to create electricity. Using this otherwise untapped resource for energy also reduces costs for water utility companies.
- The Disappearing Packaging project includes printing packaging information on the surface of products using ink that washes off, tear-off tea bags and laundry detergent pods (eliminating the need for outer packaging), and a garbage bag that does double duty as packaging. The goal is a dramatic reduction in the 140 billion pounds of packaging that are dumped as waste every year in the United States.

Sources: Erin Ailworth, "Massachusetts Utilities Go for Wind Power," *Boston Globe*, September 23, 2013; John A. Laitner, "Linking Energy Efficiency to Economic Productivity," American Council for an Energy-Efficient Economy http://www.aceee.org/research-report/e13f; Rachel Feltman, "Lockheed's Better, Faster Way to Desalinate Water," *Popular Mechanics* March 14, 2013; Rentricity and Disappearing Package examples (and others) from www.dmass.net.

improved quality of life. Another set of essential questions relates to how macroeconomics can be reformed to take into account the distant future. A first step in this direction must be recognizing that in important areas it is inappropriate to discount the future (see Box 33.2). When our great-great-grandchildren are alive, their lives and well-being will be as important to them as ours are to us. (This perspective, though often neglected in economics, is not new and was emphasized by John Maynard Keynes in the 1930s—see Box 33.5.)

The macroeconomics of the twenty-first century must be truly global. The social problems of poverty reduction, as well as major environmental problems such as global climate change, can be partly addressed at the national level, but the roles of international trade and global institutions are critical. Our earlier analyses of national income, fiscal and monetary policy, unemployment and inflation, and other macroeconomic issues, remain relevant, but must be placed in the context of global developmental and environmental challenges.

Discussion Questions

1. Are you optimistic or pessimistic about the future when it comes to reducing global inequalities? Do you believe that the world will be less or more unequal in fifty years? What about environmental problems—do you think they will grow better or worse in your lifetime?
2. Do you agree with Keynes's belief that industrialized countries will soon reach a point where needs will be "satisfied in the sense that we prefer to devote our further energies to noneconomic purposes"? Do you think that we are any closer to this point than 1930, when Keynes wrote his essay? Do you see any evidence that this is starting to occur?

BOX 33.5 ECONOMIC POSSIBILITIES FOR OUR GRANDCHILDREN

What can we reasonably expect the level of our economic life to be a hundred years hence? What are the economic possibilities for our grandchildren? John Maynard Keynes thought that:

> a point may soon be reached, much sooner perhaps than we are all of us aware of, when these needs are satisfied in the sense that we prefer to devote our further energies to non-economic purposes. . . . I draw the conclusion that, assuming no important wars and no important increase in population, the economic problem may be solved, or be at least within sight of solution, within a hundred years. This means that the economic problem is not—if we look into the future—the permanent problem of the human race.
>
> Thus for the first time since his creation man will be faced with his real, his permanent problem—how to use his freedom from pressing economic cares, how to occupy the leisure, which science and compound interest will have won for him, to live wisely and agreeably and well.
>
> When the accumulation of wealth is no longer of high social importance, there will be great changes in the code of morals. . . . The love of money as a possession—as distinguished from the love of money as a means to the enjoyments and realities of life—will be recognized for what it is, a somewhat disgusting morbidity, one of those semi-criminal, semi-pathological propensities which one hands over with a shudder to the specialists in mental disease. All kinds of social customs and economic practices, affecting the distribution of wealth and of economic rewards and penalties, which we now maintain at all costs, however distasteful and unjust they may be in themselves, because they are tremendously useful in promoting the accumulation of capital, we shall then be free, at last, to discard.
>
> Of course there will still be many people with intense, unsatisfied purposiveness who will blindly pursue wealth—unless they can find some plausible substitute. But the rest of us will no longer be under any obligation to applaud and encourage them.

Source: John Maynard Keynes, "Economic Possibilities for Our Grandchildren," *Essays in Persuasion*. New York: Classic House Books, 2009 [original publication 1930].

REVIEW QUESTIONS

1. What are some of the environmental issues related to economic growth?
2. What are some of the projected effects of future climate change?
3. What is the environmental Kuznets curve (EKC) hypothesis? What is the evidence regarding this hypothesis?
4. What are "green" taxes?
5. What are tradable permit systems?
6. What is a debt-for-nature swap?
7. What is the idea of sufficiency?
8. How do environmental impacts differ across the three global income classes?
9. What are some examples of local sustainability?
10. What are "green Keynesian" policies? Give some examples.
11. What is a steady-state economy?

EXERCISES

1. Issues of environmental sustainability can sometimes be a bit abstract. This exercise is designed then to an individual level. Start at http://www.myfootprint.org/ and familiarize yourself with the notion of "ecological footprints," then take the quiz to discover what your personal footprint looks like. What did you learn that was new information to you? What specifically can you do about this new information?
2. Begin at the website of the Global Footprints Network (www.footprintnetwork.org) and locate the "Footprint for Nations" under Footprint Basics. Access (or download) the 2010 Data Tables (in Excel format) and familiarize yourself with these 2007 data to complete the following:
   a. What was the per capita ecological footprint of consumption for the United States?
   b. What was the per capita biocapacity in the United States?

c. Explain the meaning of the two numbers you just located. What are the implications?

d. Search through the database to locate the nations that had a larger footprint than the United States in 2007. Identify these nations and their footprints in a table.

e. Study the income and continent category summaries in the database. What conclusions can you draw from these summaries? Explain your answer.

3. Match each concept in Column A with a definition or example in Column B:

Column A	Column B
a. "Green" taxes	1. Opportunity for developing countries to protect nature reserves or pursue environmentally friendly policies
b. Tradable permit systems	2. An inverted U-shaped relationship between economic development and environmental damages
c. Debt-for-nature swaps	3. A situation where population and the use of raw materials and energy have stabilized
d. Throughput	4. Based on the principle that a process of pollution reduction may be most efficiently achieved if businesses have choices
e. Social discount rate	5. Designed to discourage pollution and natural resource depletion by making them more expensive
f. Environmental Kuznets Curve	6. Reflects social rather than market valuation of future costs and benefits;
g. Steady-state economy	7. The flow of raw materials and energy into the economic system, and the flow of wastes from the system

Notes

1. World Bank and State Environmental Protection Agency, People's Republic of China, *Cost of Pollution in China*. Washington, D.C.: World Bank, 2007.

2. Food and Agriculture Organization of the United Nations (FAO), *Review of the State of World Marine Fishery Resources*. Rome, Italy: FAO, 2012.

3. Intergovernmental Panel on Climate Change, *Climate Change 2007: The Physical Science Basis*. Cambridge, UK, and New York: Cambridge University Press, 2007.

4. Samuel Brown, William G. Gale, and Fernando Saltiel, *Carbon Taxes as Part of the Fiscal Solution*. Urban Institute and Brookings Institution Tax Policy Center. http://taxpolicycenter.org/

5. Alan Durning, *How Much Is Enough: The Consumer Society and the Future of the Earth*. New York: Norton, 1992.

6. See http://blogs.worldwatch.org/sustainableprosperity/the-80-percent-solution/

7. Peter Victor, *Managing Without Growth: Slower by Design, not Disaster*. Northampton, MA: Edward Elgar, 2008.

Appendix: Demographic Challenges

One of the important issues in the area of human development and environmental sustainability is the question of *how many* people we need to be concerned about. In 1700, the human population was about 600 million. In 1927, it was 2 billion. Currently, more than 7 billion people live on this planet. Will national and global populations continue to grow, level off, or even shrink? What are the macroeconomic challenges presented by likely demographic changes in the coming century?

The relationship between demographic and economic issues is multifaceted. On the one hand, growth in the size of economies is often associated with population growth, because a growing population means more workers and hence greater ability to produce. On the other hand, human well-being can be endangered when population growth outpaces available resources, including environmental resources. If the production of needed goods and services cannot keep pace with population, lower standards of living can result. In addition to the question of population size, issues about the composition of a population, when considered according to characteristics such as age, can also be important in explaining economic change. After introducing some basic concepts in demography (the study of populations), this appendix examines the macroeconomic challenges posed by continued growth in global populations and the dramatic aging of populations in many countries.

birthrate: the annual number of births per 1,000 population

fertility rate: the average number of births per woman of reproductive age

A1. Basic Demographic Terms and History

Although the terms "birthrate" and "fertility rate" may seem as if they should mean the same thing, in the field of demography they have different meanings. The **birthrate** is the annual number of births per 1,000 *people* in a population. The **fertility rate**, refers to the average number of births *per woman of reproductive age* in a population. The birthrate in any country will depend on two things: first, the proportion of people in the country who are women of reproductive age, and, second, the rate of fertility among these women. Similarly, the **death rate** is the annual number of deaths per 1,000 people, while a **mortality rate** refers to deaths within a specific group.

death rate: the annual number of deaths per 1,000 population

mortality rate: the average number of deaths among a specific group

If the fertility rate is equal to what is called the **replacement fertility rate**, then the next generation will be the same size as the current one—women will, on average, produce just enough children to replace themselves and one other adult. Currently, the replacement fertility rate for industrialized countries is about 2.1 children per woman. (It is slightly higher than 2 because slightly more males than females are born, and some female children will die before reaching reproductive age.) In countries with higher mortality rates or larger ratios of men to women, the replacement fertility rate is somewhat higher.

replacement fertility rate: the fertility rate required for each generation to be replaced by a subsequent generation of the same size

It might seem that a country with fertility rates that are exactly equal to the replacement rate should have a stable population. However, this is not necessarily so, due to a phenomenon called **population momentum**. Recall that the birthrate depends not only on the fertility rate but also on the size of the childbearing population. Suppose that a country has relatively few older people and large numbers of people of childbearing age. Its population will continue to grow even with a replacement fertility rate because the birthrate will be high (reflecting the size of the childbearing group), while the death rate will be low (because only a small proportion of the population will be reaching the end of life). Only when birthrates and death rates are equal does a population stabilize.

population momentum: the trend in population size that results from its age profile, in particular the number of women who are of childbearing age or younger

In the past two hundred to three hundred years, the industrialized countries have experienced a **demographic transition** from a combination of high birthrates and death rates to a combination of low birthrates and death rates. But this transition has not been smooth. Table 33.2 outlines the four—or perhaps five—stages of demographic transition.

demographic transition: the change over time from a combination of high birth and death rates to a combination of low birth and death rates

In the first stage, women spend a great deal of time and effort in bearing and raising children, at much risk to their own health, only to see many of their children die young. Thus moving away from the first stage is an important goal of human development. Populations in the third and fourth stage have moved past the highest birth and death rates, making a higher quality of life possible.

Although birth and death rates are crucially important for explaining population trends in any country, for some countries the net migration rate is also important. The **net migration rate** is the number of people gained by migration (calculated as the number of people who move into an area minus the number of people who moved out of the area) over a year, usually expressed per 1,000 people.

net migration rate: the net gain in population from migration, per 1,000 population

Table 33.2 **Stages of Demographic Transition**

First Stage	Both birth and death rates are high. On average, the number of children that survive in each family is just enough to keep the population stable or growing very slowly.
Second Stage	Death rates are reduced, while birthrates stay high, so parents are typically survived by significantly more than the two children required to replace them. From the eighteenth to the twentieth centuries, this second stage developed in industrializing countries due to the nutritional advances that followed increased agricultural productivity, and (especially after about 1850) better medical care and sanitation.
Third Stage	Birthrates start declining, but are still higher than death rates. The increased availability of contraception and improvements in female education contribute to this stage. In the third stage, fertility rates are initially above replacement level but will eventually drop to or possibly below replacement level. Population growth slows down, though it continues to grow because of the number of women of childbearing age.
Fourth Stage	Birthrates and death rates equalize at a low rate. Population growth is zero—but the population is considerably larger than it was when the process began.
Fifth Stage	Birthrates are lower than death rates. When the demographic transition was first conceptualized, the process was expected to stop at the fourth stage. In fact, however, some countries may move fairly rapidly from above- to below-replacement birthrates, passing through the fourth stage of equal birth and death rates. Population actually declines.

A2. Global Population Patterns and Policies

The industrialized countries are generally in the third or fourth stage of the demographic transition. The fertility rate in the United States is near 2.1, while most other industrialized countries have fertility rates well below 2. Italy was one of the first countries to be recognized as having a below-replacement birthrate, entering the third stage in about 1960. Its population, nevertheless, continued to increase, from 50 million to about 57 million now (due to population momentum). Given current trends, Italy's fifth stage is about to begin; unless fertility rates rebound, the population is predicted to sink to 54 million in 2025 and 38 million in 2050—a 33 percent decline from the peak. Germany and Japan are other countries where population decline has just begun. Government policies in such countries now often seek to increase births (see Box 33.6).

Throughout most of the world, populations are still growing. Many governments and international agencies working in poorer countries have tried to bring down fertility rates, in order to ease the stress that a quickly growing population puts on resources and productive

Box 33.6 Shrinking Italy

Although many environmentalists fret about overpopulation, Italians are fretting over the opposite. Despite the stereotype of its massive Catholic clans, Italy actually has one of the lowest birthrates in the world, a population set to shrink by a third by 2050, and the world's highest percentage of population aged 65 or older (21 percent in 2013). The country wants babies. Badly. [In 2004] the Italian government offered a $1,300 one-time payment to couples who had a second child. The rural village of Laviano, fearful of disappearing altogether, is offering $14,000 for every baby produced. Studies show, however, that while cash payments may accelerate breeding schedules, they don't persuade tot-averse citizens to procreate. Some activists say what's really needed is more public-policy support for working mothers. If serious steps aren't taken, says Franca Biglio, mayor of Marsaglia (population 400), "Our bella Italia will become a deserted wilderness."

Source: Tracy Wilkinson, "Mayor of Shrinking Italian Town Pays Women to Give Birth," *Los Angeles Times,* February 13, 2005; Population Resource Bureau, *World Population Data Sheet 2013.* www.prb.org.

capacities. These programs have often been successful, at least to a degree, and some population policies simultaneously serve other human development ends.

Increasing women's access to health services and education has often played a crucial role, not only delivering knowledge about family planning but also giving women the power to play a greater role in household decisions. Other policies, such as China's long-time policy of penalizing families with more than one child, are more coercive. Forced sterilizations, forced abortions, and infanticide (especially of girls, in cultures that prize boys) are the darker side of a compulsory approach to population control.

Population trends in China and India are especially noteworthy, because together they are home to nearly 40 percent of the world's population. Even though China has put downward pressure on population with its one-child policy and had a fertility rate estimated at 1.64 in 2010, its population is still growing due to population momentum. The UN projections suggest that its population will continue to grow until 2030, peaking at 1.45 billion. India currently has a smaller population than China, and its fertility rate has fallen by half since the 1960s. But with a current fertility rate of 2.73, India is expected to displace China as the world's most populous country within the next 50 years. Populations are also still growing in most middle-income countries, though their fertility rates vary, some above and others below replacement.

Sub-Saharan Africa has had some of the world's highest fertility rates in modern times—as many as seven children per woman in some countries. Tragically, however, the HIV/AIDS pandemic has drastically increased mortality rates in many of these countries. The population story in the Russian Federation is also rather grim. Suffering from the special conditions of a poorly managed transition from socialism to a market economy, it has experienced both high death rates and low birthrates. Its population, which reached a high of 148 million in 1990, had fallen to 143 million by 2013 (although birth rates have recently started to rise).

On the global scale, projections about population made by the United Nations Population Division forecast world population rising from its current level of 7 billion to 9 billion by 2050. Most of the additional people will live in the less industrialized parts of the world. The projections assume that life expectancy will increase except where a population is affected by HIV/AIDS.

The UN projections, however, do not take into account the consequences of environmental degradation. Whether the resources of the world will be able to continue to support such a growing population remains to be seen. If population ceases to grow in this century, will it be because of individual choices and human development–oriented policies, such as increasing people's power to control their family size? Or because of coercive polices or high death rates due to flood, famine, and disease? Macroeconomic policies concerning resource use, development, and international economic relations hold part of the key to these important questions.

A3. The Issue of Aging Populations

To those who have been concerned about the ecological, economic, and social impacts of rapid population growth or excessively high population density, stabilizing populations are good news. But there are also significant threats and challenges inherent in the fourth and fifth stages of the demographic transition. The most obvious problems arise from the fact that rapidly falling birthrates lead to changes in the age structure of a population.

A convenient way to visualize the age structure of a population is to chart the numbers of men and women in different age categories, as shown in Figure 33.8 for the case of the United States. Such figures are sometimes called "population pyramids," because in populations with sizable, steady birthrates and regular, steady death rates among the elderly, they take on the triangular shape shown in Figure 33.8(a), representing the U.S. population in 1900.

Although fertility rates fell in the United States in the twentieth century, this fall was not steady. Fertility was particularly low during the Great Depression and then rebounded in part after World War II. People born between 1946 and 1964 are thus said to belong to the "baby boom" generation. Then, after the "baby boom" came the "baby bust" and a transition to a substantially lower fertility rate. As a result, the "pyramid" by 2000 did not look so triangular anymore. At the turn of the twenty-first century, a high proportion of people were in their prime working years, with relatively small numbers of the elderly and children, as shown in Figure 33.8(b).

As the bulge created by middle-aged baby boomers moves farther up the pyramid over the coming decades, the proportion of the population in retirement years will rise. (The first baby

Figure 33.8 **Population by Age and Sex, United States, 1900, 2000, and 2040 (projected)**

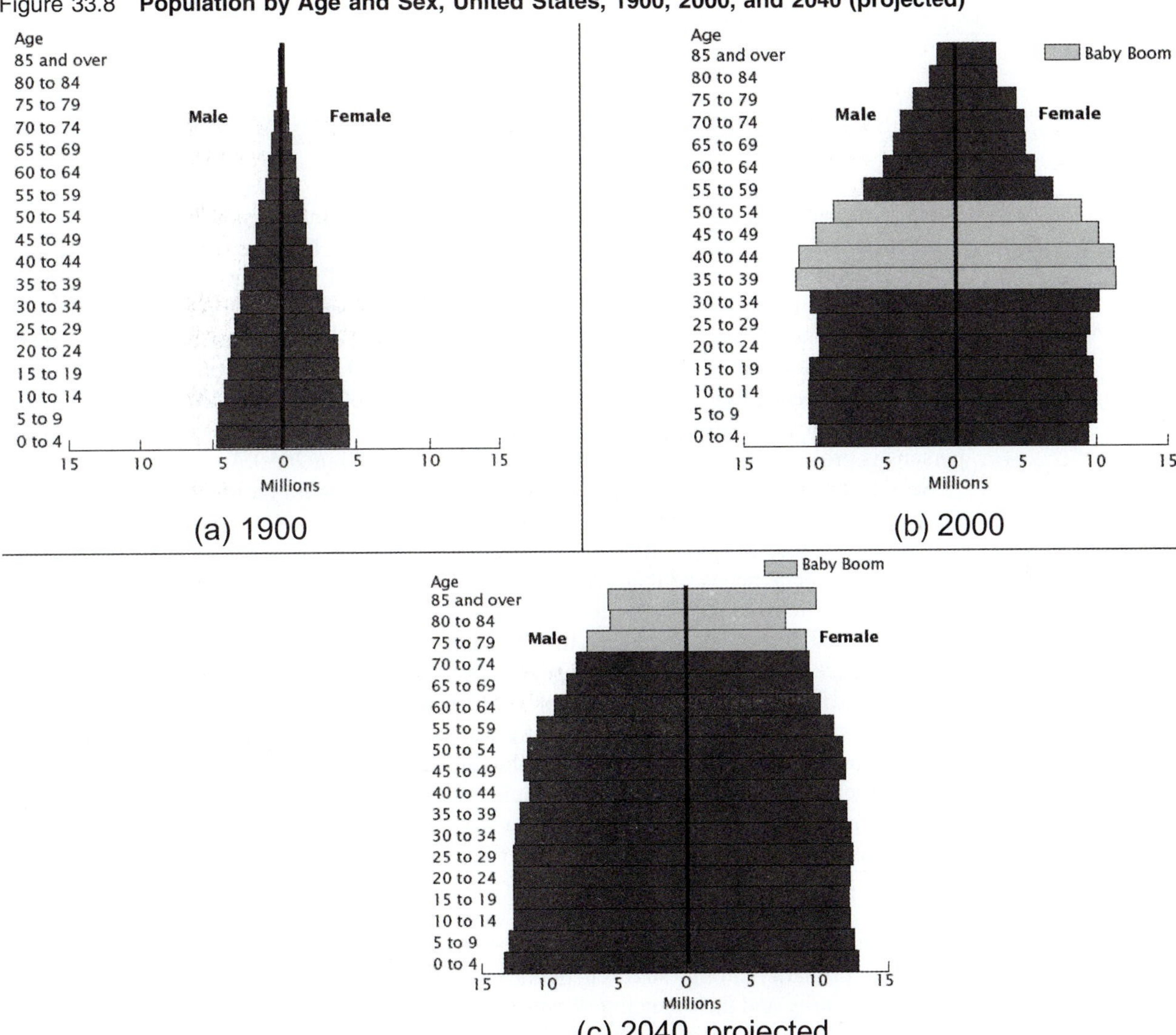

In 1900, the "population pyramid" shows a small elderly population, a larger middle-aged population, and an even larger population of children. By 2000, falling birth rates made the middle tiers of the "pyramid" bulge outward. The proportion of older people in the population is forecast to be much higher in future decades.

Source: Wan Wan He, Manisha Sengupta, Victoria A. Velkoff, and Kimberly A. DeBarros, U.S. Census Bureau, Current Population Reports, P23–209, "65+ in the United States: 2005," U.S. Government Printing Office, Washington, DC, 2005.

Figure 33.9 **Old-Age Dependency Ratios, 1950–2050**

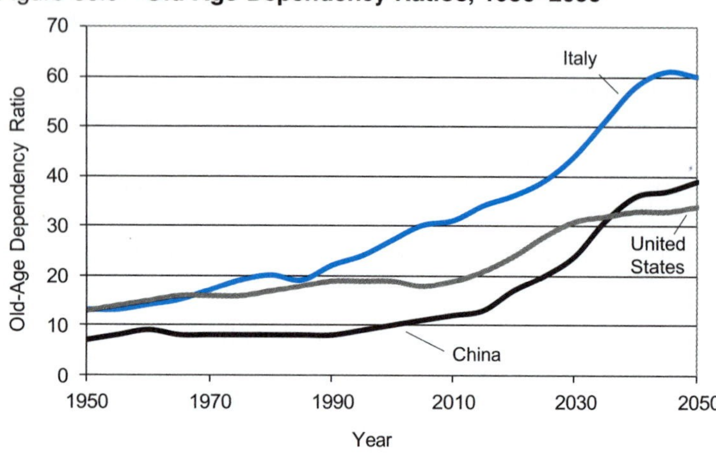

Countries with sharp declines in birth rates can expect to have a rising ratio of older people to working-age people over the next several decades.

Source: United Nations, *World Population Prospects: The 2006 Revision,* Population Database. Figure based on medium-variant projections.

boomers turned 65 in 2011.) Government projections suggest that the age structure of the U.S. population will look like Figure 33.8(c) in 2040—much more like a rectangle than a triangle.

Other countries that have experienced a "baby bust" will face a similarly top-heavy age structure. This means that there will be fewer people of working age to support people who have retired. The **old-age dependency ratio** is often defined as the number of people age 65 and over for each hundred people age 15–64. Figure 33.9 shows the projected rises in the old-age dependency ratio for three of the countries that we have discussed: China, Italy, and the United States. In Italy, for example, the number of older people per 100 working-age persons is projected to rise from about 30 now to nearly 70 in 2050.

old-age dependency ratio: the number of retirees relative to the number of active workers

Such a changing age structure has a number of implications for national macroeconomics:

- First, each future worker will have considerably more retired people dependent on his or her services. The needs of the elderly for health and social services may lead to a further sectoral shift toward service-sector employment. In some countries, the need for workers may be filled, in part, by increased immigration.
- Second, there are implications for savings rates. With more people drawing down their retirement savings and fewer people in the process of building up their savings in preparation for retirement, one can expect national savings to be depressed. This may boost consumption and aggregate demand but may also cause a lack of loanable funds needed for investment purposes.
- Third, there are implications for government budgets. An aging population means fewer people paying taxes, at the same time that more people become reliant on public retirement programs and publicly provided social services and medical care. Such strains on public finances may lead to higher taxes or lower benefits or cuts in other areas.

In countries such as the United States, which has a long history of retirement support, the effect may be felt primarily through strains in public budgets—as current controversies over the future of Social Security and the financing of prescription drugs for the elderly already demonstrate. The aging of the population may be felt even more acutely in China, where pensions, medical care, and other support for the elderly are looming as possibly the leading social crisis.

A.4 Demographic Challenges Ahead

The population pyramids shown in Figure 33.8 can be used, with a little assistance from your imagination, to illustrate another, very important point. Figure 33.8(a) showed the

United States in 1900; it can also serve as a generalized picture of any country that has a growing population impelled by fertility rates above replacement. More than half the world's population—about 3.5 billion people—fit this picture. At the same time, Figure 33.8(c) is a reasonably good picture of the squared-off "pyramids" that will, in the foreseeable future, characterize nearly all the rich countries of the world: Western Europe, Japan, and a few other highly industrialized countries.

As the developing countries gradually stabilize, their population "pyramids" will fill out just as those for the United States did over the past century, representing the additional 2 billion people in the UN's population projections for 2050. These population images and the underlying realities, including growing inequalities of living standards, will be of great global significance for at least the next 50 years.

Although there is no certainty that inequalities between rich and poor will diminish in the foreseeable future, by midcentury there will be some important factors to add to the situation just described. China's population (as noted earlier) will have begun to decline by 2050. It also seems likely that India's declining fertility rate will not stop when it reaches 2.1, but will continue to fall, so that sometime in the second half of the twenty-first century India will join China in a new category of countries that, even if not yet rich, have nevertheless reversed the long growth trend of the second stage of the demographic transition.

With China and India, and a number of other countries as well, eventually joining the list of countries with below-replacement fertility, it seems likely that within this century we will see a stabilization of the global human population. It is also possible that, beyond stabilization, the shrinking of populations will continue in the richer countries and spread to others as well. In terms of resource demands, pollution generation, and pressure on the earth's ecological capacity, stabilization of population is desirable. However, significant changes will be required in how people conceptualize and pursue their goals if a shift toward smaller populations is to be felt as positive rather than severely negative.

Macroeconomic theory has a significant role to play in helping to understand and plan for these changes, including the need to revise expectations, behaviors, policies, and theories to assist populations in adapting to a changing age profile. This has potentially large implications for medical care and other services, GDP, policy, and culture. One important challenge is discovering how the elderly can be more of a resource than a drain; this is desirable from an economic point of view as well as in terms of the psychological well-being (sense of meaning and purpose in life) of the elderly.

An overriding concern in the first half of the twenty-first century must be the need to provide food, energy, education, and productive work for a likely sizable increase in the number of people on earth—with virtually all of that increase occurring in areas where economic as well as social, cultural, and political systems are already hard pressed to adapt to past and present population growth.

The record of the past three hundred years is one of astonishing achievement, in which the total human population has multiplied more than tenfold, with more than half of those now alive enjoying a level of material consumption that would have been considered great riches in any previous era. But the number now living in extreme poverty is greater than the entire human population at the beginning of the demographic transition. And the natural capital on which humanity can draw is now significantly degraded. The moral of the demographic story is sobering: It is the need to find ways to provide better lives for more people, with limited natural resources.

Glossary

absolute deprivation: severe deprivation of basic human needs (9)

abundance: resources are abundant to the extent that they exist in plentiful supply for meeting various goals (1)

accelerator principle: the idea that high GDP growth leads to increasing investment, and low or negative GDP growth leads to declining investment (27)

accommodating monetary policy: loose or expansionary monetary policy intended to counteract recessionary tendencies in the economy (27)

accounting costs: actual monetary costs paid by a producer as well as estimated reduction in the value of the producer's capital stock (16)

accounting profits: the difference between total revenues and accounting costs (17)

accurate: describes something that is correct (even if only in a general way) (4)

administrative capitalism: a national system characterized by private corporate ownership and a substantial reliance on public administration (as well as exchange) as a mode of coordination (32)

administrative obstacles: use of environmental, health, or safety regulations to prevent imports from other countries under the pretext of upholding higher standards (7)

administrative socialism: a national system in which state ownership predominates and activity is coordinated primarily by public administration (command) (32)

adverse selection: a system that favors the weaker members of a given population, generally to the detriment of the system itself (18)

aggregate (or market) benefits: the benefits to all consumers in a market (6)

aggregate demand (AD): the total demand for all goods and services in a national economy. In a simple model without government or foreign trade, what households and firms *intend* to spend on consumption and investment: $AD = C + II$ (19, 24)

altruistic behavior: actions focused on the well-being of others, with no thought about oneself (8)

anchoring effect: overreliance on a piece of information that may or may not be relevant as a reference point when making a decision (8)

appropriation (of federal funds): Congressional approval of funds for a particular purpose (25)

artificially scarce good: a good that is excludable but nonrival (14)

aspirational group: the group to which an individual aspires to belong (9)

assets: property owned by an individual or company (1, 19)

auction market: a market in which an item is sold to the highest bidder (3)

austerity: a policy of deficit cutting that reduces public expenditures or raises taxes to balance the budget (31)

automatic stabilizers: tax and spending institutions that tend to increase government revenues and lower government spending during economic expansions but lower revenues and raise government spending during economic recessions (25)

availability heuristic: placing undue importance on particular information because it is readily available or vivid (8)

average cost (or average total cost): cost per unit of output, computed as total cost divided by the quantity of output produced (16)

average variable cost (AVC): total variable cost divided by the quantity produced (16)

backward-bending individual paid labor supply curve: a pattern that arises because, beyond some level of wages, income effects may outweigh substitution effects in determining individuals' decisions about how much to work (10)

balance of payments (BOP) account: the national account that tracks inflows and outflows arising from international trade, earnings, transfers, and transactions in assets (29)

balance of payments crisis: when a country gets precariously close to running out of foreign exchange and is therefore unable to purchase imports or service its existing debt (29)

balanced budget multiplier: the impact on equilibrium output of simultaneous increases of equal size in government spending and taxes (25)

bank reserves: funds not lent out or invested by a private bank but kept as vault cash or on deposit at the Federal Reserve (26)

bargaining: an activity in which a single buyer and a single seller negotiate the terms of their exchange (3)

barriers to entry: economic, legal, or deliberate obstacles that keep new sellers from entering a market (18)

barter: exchange of goods, services, or assets directly for other goods, services, or assets, without the use of money (26)

base year (in the constant-dollar method of estimating GDP): the year whose prices are chosen for evaluating production in all years. Normally real and nominal GDP are equal only in the base year (20)

basic neoclassical (traditional microeconomic) model: a model that portrays the economy as a collection of profit-maximizing firms and utility-maximizing households interacting in perfectly competitive markets (2)

behavioral economics: a subfield of microeconomics that studies how individuals and organizations make economic decisions (8)

behavioral equation: in contrast to an accounting identity, a behavioral equation reflects a theory about the behavior of one or more economic agents or sectors. The variables in the equation may or may not be observable (24)

bilateral development assistance: aid (or loans) given by one country to another to promote development (32)

bilateral monopoly: the situation in which there is only one buyer confronting only one seller (10)

birthrate: the annual number of births per 1,000 population (33, Appendix)

bond: a financial instrument that pays a fixed amount every year (the coupon amount), as well as repaying the amount of principal (the face value) on a particular date (the maturity date) (27)

bounded rationality: the hypothesis that people make choices among a somewhat arbitrary subset of all possible options due to limits on information, time, or cognitive abilities (8)

Bretton Woods system: a system of fixed exchange rates established after World War II, lasting until 1972 (29)

budget deficit: an excess of total government outlays over total government tax revenues (25)

budget line: a line showing the possible combinations of two goods that a consumer can purchase (9)

budget surplus: an excess of total government tax revenues over total government outlays (25)

Bureau of Economic Analysis (BEA): the agency in the United States in charge of compiling and publishing the national accounts (20)

Bureau of Labor Statistics (BLS): In the United States, the government agency that compiles and publishes employment and unemployment statistics (23)

business (trade) cycle: recurrent fluctuations in the level of national production, with alternating periods of recession and boom (19)

business sphere: firms that produce goods and services for profitable sale (2)

capabilities: the opportunities that people have to pursue important aspects of well-being, such as being healthy and having access to education (32)

capital: any resource that is valued for its potential economic contributions (15)

capital account (in the balance of payments account): the account that tracks flows arising from international transactions in assets (29)

capital controls: the regulation or taxation of international transactions involving assets (29)

capital flight: rapid movement of capital assets out of a country (29)

capital gains: increase in the value of an asset at the time it is sold compared to the price at which it was originally purchased by the same owner (11)

capital income: rents, profits, and interest (11)

capital stock: a quantity of any resource that is valued for its potential economic contributions (1)

capital-intensive production: production using methods that involve a high ratio of capital to labor (7, 32)

ceteris paribus: a Latin phrase that means "other things equal" or "all else constant" (4)

chain-type quantity index: an index comparing real production in the current year to the reference year, calculated using a series of year-to-year Fisher quantity indexes (20, Appendix)

change in demand: a shift of the entire demand curve in response to something changing other than price (4)

change in the quantity demanded: movement along a demand curve in response to a price change (4)

change in the quantity supplied: movement along a supply curve in response to a price change (4)

change in supply: a shift of the entire supply curve in response to something changing other than price (4)

circular flow diagram: a graphical picture of an economy consisting of households and firms that are engaging in exchange (2)

classical economics: the school of economics, originating in the eighteenth century, that stressed issues of growth and distribution, based on an image of smoothly functioning markets (8, 19)

climate change: long-term changes in global climate, including warmer temperatures, changing precipitation patterns, more extreme weather events, and rising sea levels (14)

closed economy: an economy with no foreign sector (20)

collateralized debt obligation: an investment product that packages together numerous assets including mortgage-backed securities (30)

collective investment vehicle or pooled fund: an investment vehicle that pools investments from many different sources, making investment decisions for them all as a group (26)

collusion: cooperation among potential rivals to gain market power as a group (18)

commodity market: a market for a raw material (3)

commodity money: a good used as money that is also valuable in itself (26)

common good: the general well-being of society, including one's own well-being (8)

common property resource: a resource that is nonexcludable and rival (14)

comparative advantage: the ability to produce some good or service at a lower opportunity cost than other producers (7)

compensating wage differentials: the theory that, all else being equal, workers will demand higher wages for jobs with unappealing characteristics, and be willing to accept lower wages for jobs with better characteristics (10)

complementary good: a good that is used along with another good (4)

congestion: the point at which the demand for a nonrival good results in a diminished benefit to each user, and thus it becomes rival (14)

constant marginal costs: the situation in which the cost of producing one additional unit of output stays the same as more output is produced (16)

constant marginal returns: a situation in which each successive unit of a variable input produces the same marginal product (16)

constant returns to scale: situations in which the long-run average cost of production stays the same as the size of the enterprise increases (16)

consumer durable goods: consumer purchases that are expected to last longer than three years. These are generally items of equipment, such as vehicles and appliances, used by households to produce goods and services for their own use (20)

consumer price index (CPI): an index measuring changes in the prices of goods and services bought by households (20)

consumer society: a society in which a large part of people's sense of identity and meaning is found through the purchase and use of consumer goods and services (9)

consumer sovereignty: the idea that consumers' needs and wants determine the shape of all economic activities (9)

consumer surplus: the net benefits obtained from a purchase, equal to the difference between a consumer's maximum willingness to pay and the price (6)

consumerism: having one's sense of identity and meaning defined largely through the purchase and use of consumer goods and services (9)

consumption: the final use of a good or service to satisfy current wants (1)

contingent ranking: a stated preference method in which respondents are asked to rank various hypothetical scenarios (13)

contingent valuation: a stated preference method where survey respondents are asked about their willingness to pay for a hypothetical outcome (13)

contractionary fiscal policy: reductions in government spending or transfer payments or increases in taxes, leading to a lower level of economic activity (25)

contractionary monetary policy: the use of monetary policy tools to limit the money supply, raise interest rates, and encourage a leveling off or reduction in economic activity (27)

convergence (in reference to economic growth): the idea that underlying economic forces will cause poorer countries and regions to "catch up" with richer ones (32)

convergence criteria: the requirements that EU member countries must satisfy as a condition of participating in the eurozone (31)

core sphere: the economic activities of households, families, and communities (2)

cost of illness method: a nonmarket valuation technique that estimates the direct and indirect costs associated with illnesses with environmental causes (13)

cost-benefit analysis: a technique to analyze a policy or project proposal in which all costs and benefits are converted to monetary estimates, if possible, to determine the net social value (13)

countercyclical policy: fiscal policy in which taxes are lowered and expenditure is raised when the economy is weak, and the opposite occurs when the economy is strong (25)

credit default swap: a security that is effectively an insurance policy against defaults related to MBSs and CDOs (30)

credit rationing: when banks deny loans to some potential borrowers, in the interest of maintaining their own profitability (27)

crowding in: the process in which government spending leads to more favorable expectations for the economy, thereby inducing investment (25)

crowding out: a reduction in the availability of private capital resulting from federal government borrowing to finance budget deficits (25)

currency appreciation: when a currency becomes more valuable, for example, when increased demand for a country's exports causes an increase in demand for its currency (29)

currency depreciation: when a currency becomes less valuable, for example, due to a decrease in demand for a country's exports or an increase in its demand for imports (29)

current account (in the balance of payments account): the national account that tracks inflows and outflows arising from international trade, earnings, and transfers (29)

cyclical deficit (surplus): the portion of the deficit (or surplus) that is caused by fluctuations in the business cycle (25)

cyclical unemployment: unemployment caused by a drop in aggregate demand (23)

damage-cost approach: assigning a monetary value to an environmental service that is equal to the actual damage done when the service is withdrawn (21)

deadweight loss: a reduction in social welfare as a result of a market regulation (6)

death rate: the annual number of deaths per 1,000 population (33, Appendix)

debt ceiling: a congressionally mandated limit on the size of the gross federal debt (31)

debt finance: borrowing others' funds to make productive investments (15)

debt held by the public: the gross federal debt minus the debt owed to other government accounts and also minus the portion that is held by the Federal Reserve (31)

decreasing marginal costs: the situation in which the cost of producing one additional unit of output falls as more output is produced (16)

defensive expenditures: money spent to counteract economic activities that have caused harm to human or environmental health (21)

defensive expenditures approach: a nonmarket valuation technique that obtains benefit estimates based on the cost of actions that people take to avoid environmental harm (13)

deficit ceiling: a congressionally mandated limit on the size of the federal budget deficit (31)

deficit spending: government spending in excess of tax revenues collected (25)

deflation: when the aggregate price level falls (26)

demand: the willingness and ability of purchasers to buy goods or services (3)

demand curve: a curve indicating the quantities that buyers are willing to purchase at various prices (4)

demand schedule: a table showing the relationship between price and the quantity demanded (4)

demographic transition: the change over time from a combination of high birth and death rates to a combination of low birth and death rates (33, Appendix)

dependency needs: the need to receive care, shelter, or food from others when unable to provide these for oneself (9)

depreciation: decrease in the usefulness (the quality or quantity) of a stock of capital due to wear and tear or obsolescence (15, 20)

devaluation: lowering an exchange rate within a fixed exchange rate system (29)

diminishing marginal returns: a situation in which each successive unit of a variable input produces a smaller marginal product (16)

diminishing marginal utility: the tendency for additional units of consumption to add less to utility than did previous units of consumption (9)

discount rate: the annual percentage rate at which future costs and benefits are discounted relative to current costs and benefits (13)

discount rate (in finance): the interest rate at which banks can borrow reserves at the Fed discount window (27)

discounting: an approach in which costs and benefits that occur in the future are assigned less weight (i.e., discounted) relative to current costs and benefits (13)

discouraged workers: people who want employment but have given up looking because they believe that there are no jobs available for them (23)

discretionary fiscal policy: changes in government spending and taxation resulting from deliberate policy decisions (25)

diseconomies of scale: situations in which the long-run average cost of production rises as the size of the enterprise increases (16)

disposable income: income remaining for consumption or saving after subtracting taxes and adding transfer payments (25)

distribution: the allocation of products and resources among people (3)

division of labor: an approach to production in which a process is broken down into smaller tasks, with each worker assigned only one or a few tasks (19)

domestic content requirement: laws requiring traded goods to contain a certain percentage of goods produced by domestic companies (29)

double auction: an auction in which both the buyers and sellers state prices at which they are willing to make transactions (3)

dual labor markets: a situation in which *primary* workers enjoy high wages, opportunities for advancement, and job security, while *secondary* workers are hired with low wages, no opportunities for advancement, and no job security (10)

dumping: selling products at prices that are below the cost of production (7)

duopoly: a market with only two sellers (18)

Dutch auction: an auction in which the opening price is set high and then drops until someone buys (3)

dynamic analysis: analysis that takes into account the passage of time (3)

ecolabeling: product labels that provide information about environmental impacts, or indicate certification (9)

ecological footprint: an estimate of how much land area a human society requires to provide all that the society takes from nature and to absorb its waste and pollution (9)

economic actor (economic agent): an individual or organization involved in the economic activities of resource maintenance or the production, distribution, or consumption of goods and services (1)

economic cost: the total cost of production, including both accounting and opportunity costs (16)

economic development: the process of moving from a situation of poverty and deprivation to a situation of increased production and plenty, through investments and changes in the organization of work (19)

economic efficiency: the use of resources, or inputs, such that they yield the highest possible value of output or the production of a given output using the lowest possible value of inputs (1)

economic growth: increases in the level of marketed production in a country or region (19)

economic liability: anything that one economic actor owes to another (26)

economic mobility: the potential for an individual or household to change its economic conditions (for better or worse) over time (11)

economic profits: the difference between total revenues and economic costs (17)

economics: the study of how people manage their resources to meet their needs and enhance their well-being (1)

economies of scale: benefits resulting from situations in which the long-run average cost of production falls as the size of the enterprise increases (7, 30)

ecosystem services: tangible benefits that humans obtain from natural processes, such as nutrient recycling, flood control, and pollination (13)

effective tax rate: one's taxes expressed as a percentage of total income (12)

efficiency: the use of resources in a way that does not waste any inputs. Inputs are used in such a way that they yield the highest possible value of output, or a given output is produced using the lowest possible value of inputs (2)

efficiency wage theory: the theory that an employer can motivate workers to put forth more effort by paying them somewhat more than they could get elsewhere (10, 23)

elasticity: a measure of the responsiveness of an economic actor to changes in market factors, including price and income (5)

empirical investigation: observation and recording of the specific phenomena of concern (2)

employed person (Bureau of Labor Statistics household survey definition): a person who did any work for pay or profit during the week before he or she is surveyed by the BLS or who worked for fifteen hours or more in a family business (23)

employee morale: the attitude of workers toward their work and their employer (10)

employer-specific human capital: knowledge and skills that have been gained on a particular job and are useful only as long as a worker remains with the same employer (10)

environmentally adjusted net domestic product (EDP): GDP less depreciation of both manufactured and natural capital (21)

equity finance: an economic actor's use of its own funds to make productive investments (15)

estate taxes: taxes on the transfers of large estates to beneficiaries (12)

excess reserves: the portion of bank reserves that banks are permitted to lend to their customers (26)

exchange: the trading of one thing for another (1)

exchange rate: the number of units of one currency that can be exchanged for one unit of another currency (29)

exchange value: value that corresponds to the value of goods or services for which the item can be exchanged (26)

excise tax: a per-unit tax on a good or service (12)

excludable good: a good whose consumption by others can be prevented by its owner(s) (14)

exclusionary practices: when a firm gets its suppliers or distributors to agree not to provide goods or services to potential competitors (18)

expansionary fiscal policy: the use of government spending, transfer payments, or tax cuts to stimulate a higher level of economic activity (25)

expansionary monetary policy: the use of monetary policy tools to increase the money supply, lower interest rates, and stimulate a higher level of economic activity (27)

expected real interest rate: the nominal interest rate minus expected inflation, $re = i - \varpi e$ (27, Appendix)

explicit contract: a formal, often written agreement that states the terms of an exchange and may be enforceable through a legal system (3)

external debt: the portion of the gross federal debt that is owed to foreign individuals or groups (31)

externalities: side effects or unintended consequences, either positive or negative, that affect persons or entities such as the environment that are not among the economic actors directly involved in the economic activity that caused the effect (see also **negative externalities and positive externalities**) (1, 13)

factor markets: markets for the services of land, labor, and capital (2)

factor-price equalization: the theory that trade should eventually lead to returns to factors of production that are equal across countries (7)

factors of production: the essential inputs for economic activity, including labor, capital, and natural resources (32)

federal funds rate: the interest rate determined in the private market for overnight loans of reserves among banks (27)

Federal Open Market Committee (FOMC): the committee that oversees open market operations. It is composed of the Fed Board of Governors and five of the twelve regional Fed presidents (27)

fertility rate: the average number of births per woman of reproductive age (33, Appendix)

fiat money: a medium of exchange that is used as money because a government says it has value, and that is accepted by the people using it (26)

final goal: a goal that requires no further justification; it is an end in itself (1)

final good: a good that is ready for use, needing no further processing (20)

financial assets: a variety of holdings in which wealth can be invested with an expectation of future return (22)

financial capital: funds of purchasing power available to purchase goods and services or facilitate economic activity (1, 15)

financial institution: any institution that collects money and holds it as financial assets (22)

financial intermediary: an institution such as a bank, savings and loan association, or life insurance company that accepts funds from savers and makes loans to borrowers (26)

financial market: a market for loans, equity finance, and financial assets (3)

financialization: a process in which the financial sector of the economy is increasingly able to generate and circulate profits that are not closely related to the real economy (22)

fiscal policy: government spending and tax policy, involving the manipulation of levels of government spending and taxation to raise or lower the level of aggregate demand (19, 25)

Fisher quantity index: an index that measures production in one year relative to an adjacent year by using an average of the ratios that would be found by using first one year, and then the other, as the source of prices at which production is valued (20, Appendix)

fixed assets: equipment owned by businesses and governments; structures; residences; and software (20)

fixed costs (or sunk costs): production costs that cannot be adjusted quickly and that must be paid even if no production occurs (16)

fixed exchange rate system: a system in which currencies are traded at fixed ratios (29)

fixed input: a production input that is fixed in quantity, regardless of the level of production (16)

fixed manufactured capital: manufactured goods that yield a flow of productive services over an extended period (15)

flexible (floating) exchange rate system: a system in which exchange rates are determined by the forces of supply and demand (29)

flow: something whose quantity can be measured over a period of time (3, 15)

foreign direct investment (FDI): investment in a business in a foreign country (29)

foreign exchange: the class of currencies that is broadly acceptable by foreigners in commercial or investment transactions. Generally limited to three currencies—the dollar, the euro, and the yen (29)

foreign exchange market intervention: an action by central banks to buy or sell foreign exchange reserves in order to keep exchange rates at desired levels (29)

foreign trade zone: a designated area of a country within which foreign-owned manufacturers can operate free of many taxes, tariffs, and regulations (29)

fractional reserve system: a banking system in which banks are required to keep only a fraction of the total value of their deposits on reserve (26)

framing: changing the way a particular decision is presented to people in order to influence their behavior (8)

free riders: those who obtain the benefits of a public good without paying anything for it (14)

free trade: exchange in international markets that is not regulated or restricted by government actions (7)

frictional unemployment: unemployment that arises as people are in transition between jobs (23)

"full-employment output" (Y^*): for modeling purposes, a level of output that is assumed to correspond to a case of no excessive or burdensome unemployment, but the likely existence of at least some transitory unemployment (24)

GDP deflator (implicit price deflator): a price index created by dividing nominal GDP by real GDP (20, Appendix)

general human capital: knowledge and skills that workers can take with them as they move from one employer to another (10)

gift taxes: taxes on the transfer of large gifts to beneficiaries (12)

Gini ratio (or Gini coefficient): a measure of inequality, based on the Lorenz curve, that goes from 0 (absolute equality) up to 1 (absolute inequality). Greater inequality shows up as a larger area between the Lorenz curve and the diagonal line of absolute equality (11)

global economy: the system of economic rules, norms, and interactions by which economic actors and actions in different parts of the world are connected to one another (19)

global public good: a public good available to the entire population of the planet (14)

globalization: the extension of free trade and communications across the entire world, leading to a great increase in the volume of traded goods and services, and in expanded interconnections among different regions (7)

government bond: an interest-bearing security constituting a promise to pay at a specified future time (25)

government outlays: total government expenditures, including spending on goods and services and transfer payments (25)

government spending (G): the component of GDP that represents spending on goods and services by federal, state, and local governments (25)

green consumerism: making consumption decisions at least partly on the basis of environmental criteria (9)

greenhouse gases: gases such as carbon dioxide and methane whose atmospheric concentrations influence global climate by trapping solar radiation (14)

gross domestic product (GDP) (BEA definition): a measure of the total market value of final goods and services newly produced within a country's borders over a period of time (usually one year) (20)

gross federal debt: total amount owed by the federal government to all claimants, including foreigners, the public in the United States, and other government accounts (31)

gross investment: all flows into the capital stock over a period of time (20)

hedge fund: a type of pooled fund that often engages in highly speculative investments and to which access is generally restricted to wealthy clients (26)

historical investigation: study of past events (2)

home equity loan: a loan that permits a borrower to offer his or her home (or their equity stake in it) as collateral in case of failure to repay the loan (30)

human capital: people's capacity for engaging in productive activities, including individual knowledge and skills (1, 15)

human development: an approach to development that stresses the provision of basic needs such as food, shelter, and health care (32)

identity (accounting identity): an equation in which the two sides are equal by definition (20)

implicit contract: an informal agreement about the terms of a market exchange, based on verbal discussions or on traditions and normal expectations (3)

import substitution: a policy undertaken by governments seeking to reduce reliance on imports and encourage domestic industry, including subsidizing domestic producers to make products that can be used in place of imported goods as well as protectionist policies (7, 29)

imputation: a procedure in which values are assigned for a category of products, usually using values of related products or inputs (20)

inadequacy: a situation in which there is not enough of a good or service, provided at prices people can afford, to meet minimal requirements for human well-being (4)

income effect of a price change: the tendency of a price increase to reduce the quantity demanded of normal goods (and to increase the quantity demanded of any inferior goods) (5)

income elasticity of demand: a measure of the responsiveness of demand to changes in income, holding price constant (5)

increasing marginal costs: the situation in which the cost of producing one additional unit of output rises as more output is produced (16)

increasing marginal returns: a situation in which each successive unit of a variable input produces a larger marginal product (16)

index number: a figure that measures the change in magnitude of a variable, such as a quantity or price, compared to another period (20)

indifference curve: a curve consisting of points representing combinations of various quantities of two goods, such that every such combination gives the consumer the same level of utility (9)

individual demand: the demand of one particular buyer (4)

individual supply: the supply of one particular seller (4)

individual transferable quota (ITQ): tradable rights to access or harvest a common property resource, such as the right to harvest a particular quantity of fish (14)

industrial concentration ratio: the share of production, sales, or revenues attributable to the largest firms in an industry (18)

industrial policy: a set of government policies designed to enhance a country's ability to compete globally (32)

Industrial Revolution: a process of social, technological, and economic change, beginning in Western Europe in the eighteenth century, that developed and applied new methods of production and work organization resulting in a great increase in output per worker (32)

infant industry: an industry that is not yet globally competitive, but receives government support with the expectation that it may become so (7, 32)

inferior goods: goods for which demand decreases when incomes rise and increases when incomes fall (5)

inflation: a rise in the general level of prices (19)

informal sphere: businesses operating outside government oversight and regulation. In less industrialized countries, it may constitute the majority of economic activity (2)

in-kind transfers: transfers of goods or services (1)

input substitution: increasing the use of some inputs, and decreasing that of others, while producing the same good or service (16)

inputs: resources that go into production (1, 16)

institutions: ways of structuring human activities based on customs, habits, and laws (3)

insurance company: a company that pays to cover all or part of the cost of specific risks against which individuals and companies chose to insure themselves (26)

intangible capital: resources that cannot be seen or touched (15)

interest: the charge for borrowing money (15)

intermediate goal: a goal that is desirable because its achievement will bring you closer to your final goal(s) (1)

intermediate good: a good that will undergo further processing (20)

intermediate goods market: a market for an unfinished product (3)

internal debt: the portion of the gross federal debt that is owed to individuals or groups within the country (31)

internalizing negative externalities: bringing external costs into the market (for example, by instituting a Pigovian tax at a level equal to the externality damage), thus making market participants pay the true social cost of their actions (13)

International Monetary Fund (IMF): an international agency charged with overseeing international finance, including exchange rates, international payments, and balance of payments management (29)

intrinsic value: the value of something in an ecological or ethical sense, apart from any economic value based on willingness to pay; value related to the tangible or physical properties of the object (1, 26)

inventories: stocks of raw materials or manufactured goods being stored until they can be used or sold (15, 20)

investment: actions taken to increase the quantity or quality of a resource over time (1, 15)

Keynesian economics: the school of thought, named after John Maynard Keynes, that argued for the active use of fiscal policy to keep aggregate demand high and employment rates up (19)

Kuznets curve hypothesis: the theory that economic inequality first increases during the initial stages of economic development but then eventually decreases with further economic growth (32)

labor force (BLS definition): people who are employed or unemployed (23)

labor force participation (LFP) rate: the percentage of the adult, noninstitutionalized population that is either working at a paid job or seeking paid work; the labor force as a percentage of the civilian noninstitutional population (10, 23)

labor income: payment to workers, including wages, salaries, and fringe benefits (11)

labor intensive: a process or procedure that makes use of more labor relative to other inputs such as capital (32)

labor market: a market in which employers interact with people who wish to work (3)

labor market discrimination: a condition that exists when, among similarly qualified people, some are treated disadvantageously in employment on the basis of race, gender, age, sexual preference, physical appearance, or disability (10)

labor productivity: the market value of the output that results from a given amount of labor (19, 23).

labor unions: legally recognized organizations that collectively bargain for their members (workers) regarding wages, benefits, and working conditions (10)

labor-intensive production: production using methods that involve a high ratio of labor to capital (7)

laissez-faire: the view that government intervention in markets should be limited to what is absolutely necessary. The term is French and means "leave alone" (6)

laissez-faire capitalism: a national system characterized by private corporate ownership and a great reliance on exchange as a mode of coordination (with relatively little coordination by public administration) (32)

laissez-faire economy: an economy with little government regulation (3)

leverage: the use of debt to increase the potential rate of return of one's investment (at greater risk) (26)

limiting factor: a fixed input that creates a constraint to increasing production (16)

liquidity: the ease of use of an asset as a medium of exchange (26)

liquidity trap: a situation in which interest rates are so low that the central bank finds it impossible to reduce them further (27)

living standard (or lifestyle) goals: goals related to satisfying basic needs and getting pleasure through the use of goods and services (9)

living standards growth: improvements in people's diet, housing, medical care, education, working conditions, and access to transportation, communication, entertainment, and other amenities (19)

loan: money borrowed for temporary use, on the condition that it be repaid, usually with interest (15)

local monopoly: a monopoly limited to a specific geographic area (18)

long run (in terms of production processes): a period in which all production inputs can be varied in quantity (16)

long-run average cost: the cost of production per unit of output when all inputs can be varied in quantity (16)

long-run elasticity: a measure of the response to a price change after economic actors have had time to make adjustments (5)

Lorenz curve: a line used to portray an income distribution, drawn on a graph with percentiles of households on the horizontal axis and the cumulative percentage of income on the vertical axis (11)

lower-bound estimate: an estimate that represents the minimum potential value of something. The actual value is thus greater than or equal to the lower-bound estimate (13)

M1: a measure of the money supply that includes currency, checkable deposits, and travelers checks (26)

M2: a measure of the money supply that includes all of M1 plus savings deposits, small certificates of deposit, and retail money market funds (26)

macroeconomics: the subfield of economics that focuses on the economy as a whole (1, 19)

macroeconomy: an economic system whose boundaries are normally understood to be the boundaries of a country (19)

maintenance-cost approach: assigning a monetary value to an environmental service that is equal to what it would cost to maintain the same standard of services using an alternative method (21)

manufactured (or produced) capital: physical assets generated by applying human productive activities to natural capital (1, 15)

manufacturing productivity: an index of the value of the goods produced per hour of labor in the manufacturing sector (22)

marginal analysis: analysis based on incremental changes, comparing marginal benefits to marginal costs (16)

marginal benefit (for consumers): the benefit of consuming one additional unit of something (6)

marginal benefits curve: a curve showing the additional benefit from each unit consumed. Another name for a demand curve, as applied to welfare economics (6)

marginal change: a change of one unit (either an increase or a decrease) (6)

marginal cost: the cost of producing one additional unit of something (6)

marginal factor cost of labor (MFCL): the amount that a unit of additional labor adds to the firm's wage costs (10)

marginal physical product of labor (MPPL): the amount that a unit of additional labor contributes to the physical product of a firm (10)

marginal product: the additional quantity of output produced by increasing the level of a variable input by one, holding all other inputs constant (16)

marginal propensity to consume: the number of additional dollars of consumption for every additional dollar of income (typically a fraction between zero and one) (12, 24)

marginal propensity to save: the number of additional dollars saved for each additional dollar of income (typically a fraction between zero and one) (24)

marginal rate of substitution: how much of one good the consumer is willing to give up to get more of another (9)

marginal revenue: the additional revenue obtained by selling one more unit. In a perfectly competitive market, marginal revenue equals price (17)

marginal revenue product of labor (MRPL): the amount that a unit of additional labor contributes to the revenues of the firm (10)

marginal tax rate: the tax rate applicable to an additional dollar of income (12)

marginally attached workers: people who want employment and have looked for work in the past twelve months but not in the past four weeks (23)

market (first meaning): a place (physical or virtual) where there is a reasonable expectation of finding both buyers and sellers for the same product or service (3)

market (second meaning): an institution that facilitates economic interactions among buyers and sellers (3)

market (third meaning): an economic system (a "market economy") that relies on market institutions to conduct many economic activities (3)

market consumer surplus: the difference between aggregate costs and aggregate benefits, or net benefits obtained by all consumers in a market. On a supply-and-demand graph, it is equal to the area under a demand curve but above the price (6)

market (or aggregate) demand: the demand from all buyers in a particular market (4)

market disequilibrium: a situation of either shortage or surplus (4)

market equilibrium (market-clearing equilibrium): a situation in which the quantity supplied equals the quantity demanded, and thus there is no pressure for changes in price or quantity bought or sold (4)

market failure: a situation in which markets yield inefficient or inappropriate outcomes; alternatively, where unregulated markets fail to produce the socially efficient outcome (3, 6)

market power: the ability to control, or at least affect, the terms and conditions of a market exchange (3, 17)

market price: the prevailing price for a specific good or service at a particular time in a given market (4)

market producer surplus: the net benefit (profits) obtained by all producers in a market. On a supply-and-demand graph, it is the area below price but above the supply curve (6)

market quantity sold: the number of "units" of a specific good or service sold in a given market during a particular period (4)

market socialism: a national system in which state ownership predominates but much economic activity is coordinated through markets (32)

market (or aggregate) supply: the supply from all sellers in a particular market (4)

market value: the maximum amount that economic actors are willing and able to pay for a good or service (i.e., effective demand) (4)

market-based approaches (to pollution regulation): policies that create an economic incentive for firms to reduce pollution without mandating that firms take any specific actions (13)

markup (or cost-plus) pricing: a method of setting prices in which the seller adds a fixed percentage amount to his or her costs of production (4)

maximum capacity output: the level of output an economy would produce if every resource in the economy were fully utilized (28)

maximum efficient scale: the highest quantity of output at which a firm achieves its minimum per-unit production costs (16)

maximum willingness to pay (WTP): the maximum amount that a rational consumer will pay for a particular product. In welfare economics, consumers' maximum WTP represents the total benefits that they expect to obtain from a product, expressed in monetary terms (6)

means-tested programs: programs designed to transfer income to recipients based on need (11)

meliorating: starting from the present level of well-being and continuously attempting to do better (8)

menu costs: the costs to a supplier of changing prices listed on order forms, brochures, menus, and the like (19)

microeconomics: the subfield of economics that focuses on activities that take place within and among the major economic organizations of a society (1)

migration controls: restrictions on the flow of people into and out of a country (29)

Millennium Development Goals (MDGs): A set of goals declared by the United Nations in 2000, emphasizing eradication of extreme poverty; promotion of education, gender equity, and health; environmental sustainability; and partnership between rich and poor countries (32)

minimum efficient scale: the lowest quantity of output at which a firm achieves it minimum per-unit production costs (16)

model: an analytical tool that highlights some aspects of reality while ignoring others (2)

monetarism: a theory associated with Milton Friedman, which claims that macroeconomic objectives are best met by having the money supply grow at a steady rate (see also **monetarist economics**) (27)

monetarist economics: the school of economic thought that focused on the effects of monetary policy and argued that governments should aim for steadiness in the money supply rather than play an active role (19)

monetary base (or high-powered money): the sum of total currency plus bank reserves (27)

monetary neutrality: the idea that changes in the money supply may affect only prices, while leaving output unchanged (27)

monetary policy: the use of tools controlled by the government, such as banking regulations and the issuance of currency, to affect the levels of money supply, interest rates, and credit (1, 26)

monetizing the debt/monetizing the deficit: when a central bank buys government debt as it is issued (equivalent to "running the printing presses"). In the United States, the purchase of new debt from the Treasury by the Federal Reserve (27, 31)

money: a medium of exchange that is widely accepted, durable as a store of value, has minimal handling and storage costs, and serves as a unit of account (3)

money multiplier: as the ratio of the money supply to the monetary base, it tells by how much the money supply will change for a given change in high-powered money (27)

money supply rule: committing to letting the money supply grow at a fixed rate per year (27)

monopolistic competition: the situation in which there are many sellers, but they sell slightly different things (18)

monopsony: a situation in which there is only one buyer but many sellers. This situation occurs in a labor market in which there are many potential workers but only one employer (10)

moral hazard: the creation of perverse incentives that encourage excessive risk taking because of protections against losses from that risk (30)

mortality rate: the average number of deaths among a specific group (33, Appendix)

mortgage broker: an agent who assists in identifying a lender for prospective homeowners looking to borrow money for their purchase (26)

mortgage-backed security (MBS): a security composed of a bundle of many home mortgages issued by independent banks (30)

multilateral development assistance: aid or loans provided with the announced intention of promoting development by the World Bank, regional development banks, or UN agencies such as the United Nations Development Programme (UNDP) (32)

national accounting conventions: habits or agreements, adopted by government agencies in order to make national accounts as standardized and comparable across different countries and periods as possible (20)

national income (NI): a measure of all domestic incomes earned in production (20)

National Income and Product Accounts (NIPA): a set of statistics compiled by the BEA concerning production, income, spending, prices, and employment (20)

natural capital: physical assets provided by nature (1, 15)

natural monopoly: a monopoly that arises because the minimum efficient scale of the producing unit is large relative to the total market demand (18)

negative externalities: harmful side effects, or unintended consequences, of economic activity that affect those who are not directly involved in the activity (1)

negative (or inverse) relationship: the relationship between two variables if an increase in one variable is associated with an decrease in the other variable (or vice versa) (2)

neoclassical model: a model that portrays the economy as a collection of profit-maximizing firms and utility-maximizing households interacting through perfectly competitive markets (8)

neoclassical synthesis: A combination of classical and Keynesian perspectives (28, Appendix)

net benefits: benefits minus any costs. Consumer surplus is a measure of net benefits because it is equal to the difference between the maximum willingness to pay and price (6)

net exports: the value of exports less the value of imports (20)

net investment: gross investment minus an adjustment for depreciation of the capital stock (, 20)

net migration rate: the net gain in population from migration, per 1,000 population (33, Appendix)

net national product (NNP): a measure of national production in excess of that needed to replace worn-out manufactured capital, calculated by subtracting depreciation from GDP (20)

net taxes: taxes minus transfer payments (25)

network externality (in production): a situation in which a particular technology or production process is more likely to be adopted because other economic actors have already adopted it (17)

New Keynesian macroeconomics: a school of thought that bases its analysis on micro-level market behavior, but which justifies activist macroeconomic policies by assuming that markets have "imperfections" that can create or prolong recessions (28, Appendix)

nominal (current dollar) GDP: gross domestic product expressed in terms of current prices (20)

nonbank financial institution: a financial institution that performs a number of services similar to those offered by banks but that is not a licensed bank and is not subject to banking regulations (26)

nonexcludable good: a good whose benefits are freely available to all users (14)

nonmarket valuation techniques: economic valuation methods that obtain estimates for goods and services not directly traded in markets (13)

nonprice competition: competition through activities other than setting prices, such as advertising and location (18)

nonprice determinants of demand: any factor that affects the quantity demanded, other than the price of the good or service being demanded (4)

nonprice determinants of supply: any factor that affects the quantity supplied, other than the price of the good or service offered for sale (4)

nonrenewable resource: a resource that cannot be reproduced on a human time-scale, so that its stock diminishes with use over time (15)

nonrival good: a good that can be consumed by more than one person at a time. The marginal cost of providing a nonrival good to an additional person is zero (14)

non-tariff barriers to trade: use of licensing or other requirements to limit the volume of trade (29)

nonuse benefits: nontangible welfare benefits that people derive from ecosystems without physical interaction (i.e., psychological benefits) (13)

normal goods: goods for which demand increases when incomes rise and decreases when incomes fall (5)

normative questions: questions about how things should be (1)

"not in the labor force" (Bureau of Labor Statistics definition): the classification given to people who are neither "employed" nor "unemployed" (23)

occupational segregation: the tendency of men and women to be employed in different occupations (10)

off-budget expenditures: government-funded programs that are exempted from the normal budgeting process because the taxes that fund them cannot be used for budgetary items that are subject to congressional appropriations (25)

official reserve account: the account reflecting the foreign exchange market operations of a country's central bank (29)

Okun's "law": an empirical inverse relationship between the unemployment rate and real GDP growth (24)

old-age dependency ratio: the number of retirees relative to the number of active workers (33, Appendix)

oligopoly: the situation in which there are so few sellers that each needs to watch what the others are doing (18)

oligopsony: the case of a relatively small number of buyers (10)

on-budget expenditures: all federal expenditures that rely on general tax revenue subject to congressional approval each year (25)

open auction: an auction in which the opening price is set low and then buyers bid it up (3)

open economy: an economy with a foreign sector (20)

open market operations: sales or purchases of government bonds by the Fed (27)

opportunity cost: the value of the best alternative that is forgone when a choice is made (1)

opportunity-cost method (for estimating the value of household production): valuing hours at the amount that the unpaid worker could have earned at a paid job (21)

optimizing behavior: behavior that achieves an optimal (best possible) outcome (8)

output sectors: divisions of a macroeconomy based on what is being produced (22)

outputs: the goods and services that result from production (1, 16)

path dependence: a condition that exists when economic developments depend on initial conditions and past events—that is, when "history matters" (17)

payoff matrix: a table used in game theory to illustrate possible outcomes for each of two players, depending on the strategy that each chooses (18)

pension fund: a fund with the exclusive purpose of paying retirement benefits to employees (26)

perfect competition: a market for the exchange of identical units of a good or service, in which there are numerous small sellers and buyers, all of whom have perfect information (17)

perfectly competitive market equilibrium: the market equilibrium in a perfectly competitive market in which the economic profits of each individual seller are zero, and there is no incentive for entry or exit (17)

perfectly inelastic demand: the quantity demanded does not change at all when price changes. The elasticity value is 0 (5)

physical capital: resources that are tangible (i.e., can be touched or seen) (15)

physical infrastructure: roads, ports, railroads, warehouses, and other tangible structures that provide the foundation for economic activity (3)

Pigovian tax: a tax levied on a product to reduce or eliminate the negative externality associated with its production (13)

pollution standards: policies that control pollution by setting allowable pollution standards or controlling the uses of a product or process (13)

population momentum: the trend in population size that results from its age profile, in particular the number of women who are of childbearing age or younger (33, Appendix)

portfolio investment: the purchase of financial assets such as stocks and bonds; in international finance, investment in stocks or bonds of a foreign country (26, 29)

positive externalities: beneficial side effects, or unintended consequences, of economic activity that accrue to those who are not among the economic actors directly involved in the activity (1)

positive questions: questions about how things are (1)

positive (or direct) relationship: the relationship between two variables if an increase in one variable is associated with an increase in the other variable (2)

posted prices: prices set by a seller (3)

post-Keynesian macroeconomics: a school of thought that stresses the importance of history and uncertainty in determining macroeconomic outcomes (28, Appendix)

poverty line: the income threshold below which members of a population are classified as poor (32)

precautionary principle: the principle that we should err on the side of caution when dealing with natural systems or human health, especially when there is a low-probability risk of a catastrophic outcome (13, 19)

precise: describes something that is exact (though it may be unrealistic) (4)

predatory pricing: a powerful seller's temporary pricing of its goods or services below cost, in order to drive weaker competitors out of business (18)

present value: the current value of a future cost or benefit, obtained by discounting (13)

price ceiling: a regulation that specifies a maximum price for a particular product (6)

price discrimination: a seller's charging different prices to different buyers, depending on their ability and willingness to pay (18)

price elasticity: a measure of the sensitivity or responsiveness of quantity supplied or demanded to changes in price (5)

price elasticity of demand: a measure of the responsiveness of quantity demanded to changes in price (5)

price elasticity of supply: a measure of the responsiveness of quantity supplied to changes in price (5)

price fixing: a form of collusion in which a group of sellers implicitly agrees to maintain a common price (18)

price floor: a regulation that specifies a minimum price for a particular product (6)

price leadership: a form of collusion in which many sellers follow the price changes instituted by one particular seller (18)

price maker: a seller that can set the selling price, constrained only by demand conditions (18)

price taker: a seller that has no market power to set price. Price is determined solely by the interaction of market supply and market demand (17)

price war: a situation in which a firm cuts prices in order to try to undercut its rivals, and the rivals react by cutting prices even more (18)

price-elastic demand: a relationship between price and quantity demanded characterized by relatively strong responses of buyers to price changes (5)

price-elastic demand (technical definition): the percentage change in the quantity demanded is larger than the percentage change in price. The elasticity value is more than 1 (5)

price-inelastic demand: a relationship between price and quantity demanded characterized by relatively weak responses of buyers to price changes (5)

price-inelastic demand (technical definition): the percentage change in the quantity demanded is smaller than the percentage change in price. The elasticity value is less than 1 (5)

primary sector: the sector of the economy that involves the harvesting and extraction of natural resources and simple processing of these raw materials into products that are generally sold to manufacturers as inputs (22)

prime rate: the interest rate that banks charge their most creditworthy commercial borrowers (27)

principal: the original amount of money borrowed (15)

private good: a good that is excludable and rival (14)

private property: ownership of assets by nongovernment economic actors (3)

procyclical policy: fiscal policy in which taxes are lowered and expenditure is raised when the economy is strong, and the opposite is done when the economy is weak (25)

producer surplus: the net benefits that producers receive from selling products, equal to the difference between the selling price and the marginal costs (6)

product markets: markets for newly produced goods and services (2)

production: the conversion of resources into goods and services (1)

production function: an equation or graph that represents a relationship between types and quantities of inputs and the quantity of output (16)

production-possibilities frontier (PPF): a curve showing the maximum amounts of two outputs that society could produce from given resources, over a given period (1)

profit maximization (under perfect competition): a seller should increase production up to the point where $MR = MC$. As $MR = P$ under perfect competition, we can also define the profit maximizing solution by setting $P = MC$ (17)

progressive tax: a tax in which the percentage of one's income that is paid in taxes tends to increase with increasing income levels (12)

proportional tax: a tax in which all taxpayers pay the same tax rate, regardless of income (12)

public debt: the gross federal debt minus the debt owed to other government accounts such as Social Security and Medicare (31)

public good: a good whose benefits are freely available to anyone, and whose use by one person does not diminish its usefulness to others; a good that is nonexcludable and nonrival (2, 14)

public purpose sphere: governments as well as other organizations that seek to enhance well-being without making a profit (2)

purchasing power parity (PPP): the theory that exchange rates should reflect differences in purchasing power among countries (29)

purchasing power parity (PPP) adjustments: adjustments to international income statistics to take into account the differences in the cost of living across countries (29)

pure monopoly: the situation in which there is only one seller (18)

quantitative easing (QE): the purchase of financial assets including long-term bonds by the Fed, creating more monetary reserves and expanding the money supply (27)

quantity adjustments: a response by suppliers in which they react to unexpectedly low sales of their good primarily by reducing production levels rather than by reducing the price and to unexpectedly high sales by increasing production rather than raising the price (19)

quantity equation: $M \times V = P \times Y$, where M is the money supply, V is the velocity of money, P is the price level, and Y is real output (27)

quantity index: an index measuring changes in levels of quantities produced (20)

quantity theory of money: the theory that money supply is directly related to nominal GDP, according to the equation $M \times \bar{V} = P \times Y$ (27)

race to the bottom: a situation in which countries or regions compete in providing low-cost business environments, resulting in deterioration in labor, environmental, or safety standards (7)

rational expectations theory: the theory that people's expectations about Federal Reserve policy cause predictable monetary policies to be ineffective in changing output levels (28, Appendix)

rationality axiom: the statement that "rational economic man maximizes his utility (or self-interest)" (8)

real business cycle theory: the theory that changes in employment levels are caused by changes in technological capacities or people's preferences concerning work (28, Appendix)

real exchange rate: the exchange rate between two currencies, adjusted for inflation in each country (29)

real GDP: a measure of gross domestic product that seeks to reflect the actual value of goods and services produced, by removing the effect of changes in prices (20)

real interest rate: nominal interest rate minus inflation, $r = i - \varpi$ (27, Appendix)

real money supply: the nominal money supply divided by the general price level (as measured by a price index), expressed as M/P (28)

real wealth effect: the tendency of consumers to increase or decrease their consumption based on their perceived level of wealth (28)

recession: a downturn in economic activity, usually defined as lasting for two consecutive calendar quarters or more, now "officially" determined by the National Bureau of Economic Research (19, 23)

reference group: the group to which an individual compares himself or herself (9)

regressive tax: a tax in which the percentage of one's income paid in taxes tends to decrease with increasing income levels (12)

regulated monopoly: a monopoly run under government supervision (18)

regulation: setting standards or laws to govern behavior (2)

relative deprivation: the feeling of lack that comes from comparing oneself with someone who has more (9)

renewable resource: a resource that regenerates through short-term natural processes (15)

rent: payments for the direct or indirect use of any capital assets (11)

replacement cost methods: nonmarket valuation techniques that estimate the value of ecosystem services based on the cost of actions that provide substitute services (13)

replacement fertility rate: the fertility rate required for each generation to be replaced by a subsequent generation of the same size (33, Appendix)

replacement-cost method (for estimating the value of household production): valuing hours at the amount it would be necessary to pay someone to do the work (21)

required reserves: the portion of bank reserves that banks *must* keep on reserve (26)

resale market: a market for an item that has been previously owned (2)

resource maintenance: preserving or improving the resources that contribute to the enhancement of well-being, including natural, manufactured, human, and social resources (1)

restorative development: economic progress that restores economic, financial, social, or ecological systems that have been degraded and are no longer adequately supportive of human well-being in the present and the future (19)

retail markets: markets where goods and services are purchased by consumers from businesses, generally in small quantities (3)

revaluation: raising an exchange rate within a fixed exchange rate system (29)

revealed preference methods: valuation techniques that infer the value of nonmarket goods and services based on people's decisions in related markets (13)

revenue-neutral (taxes): offsetting any tax increases with decreases in other taxes such that overall tax collections remain constant (13)

rival good: a good that can only be consumed by only one person at a time (14)

rule of 72: a shorthand calculation that states that dividing 72 by an annual growth rate yields approximately the number of years it will take for an amount to double (20)

satellite accounts: additional or parallel accounting systems that provide measures of social and environmental factors in physical terms, without necessarily including monetary valuation (21)

satisfice: to choose an outcome that would be satisfactory and then seek an option that at least reaches that standard (8)

saving: refraining from consumption in the current period (1)

Say's Law: the classical belief that "supply creates its own demand" (1)

scarcity: the concept that resources are not sufficient to allow all goals to be accomplished at once (1)

screening methods: approaches used by employers to limit their job search to specific candidates (10)

sealed-bid auction: an auction in which bids are given privately to the auctioneer (3)

secondary sector: the sector of the economy that involves converting the outputs of the primary sector into products suitable for use or consumption. It includes manufacturing, construction, and utilities (22)

securities broker: an agent responsible for finding a buyer for sellers of different securities, thereby offering enhanced liquidity to the seller (26)

short run (in terms of production processes): a period in which at least one production input has a fixed quantity (16)

shortage: a situation in which the quantity demanded at a particular price exceeds the quantity that sellers are willing to supply (4)

short-run elasticity: a measure of the relatively immediate responsiveness to a price change (5)

signaling theory: a theory of the value of an education that suggests that an educational credential *signals* to an employer that a potential worker has desired character traits and work habits (10)

skill-biased technical change: the theory that relative wage gains will be the greatest for those workers that who possess the education and skills to use modern technologies (23)

social capital: the institutions and the stock of trust, mutual understanding, shared values, and socially held knowledge that facilitates the social coordination of economic activity (1, 15)

social discount rate: a discount rate that reflects social rather than market valuation of future costs and benefits; usually lower than the market discount rate (33)

social efficiency (in welfare economics): an allocation of resources that maximizes the net benefits to society (6)

social insurance taxes: taxes used to fund social insurance programs such as Social Security, Medicare, and Medicaid (12)

social organization: the ways in which human productive activities are structured and coordinated (15)

social value: the extent to which an outcome moves us toward our final goals (4)

social welfare: total benefits to society minus total costs, or total net benefits (6)

sovereign debt: government debt, especially debt denominated in a currency that the government does not control (31)

specialization: in production, a system of organization in which each worker performs only one type of task (19)

speculation: buying and selling assets with the expectation of profiting from appreciation or depreciation in their value (19)

speculative bubble: the situation that occurs when mutually reinforcing investor optimism raises the value of an asset far above what can be justified by fundamental value (19)

stagflation: a combination of rising inflation and economic stagnation (28)

stated preference methods: nonmarket valuation techniques that directly ask survey respondents about their preferences in a hypothetical scenario (13)

static analysis: analysis that does not take into account the passage of time (3)

steady-state economy: an economy with no increase in population, or in the rate of use of raw materials and energy (33)

"sticky wage" theories: theories about why wages stay at above-equilibrium levels, despite the existence of a labor surplus (23)

stock: something whose quantity can be measured at a point in time (1, 15)

stock-flow diagram: a diagram that shows how a stock changes over time, as flows add to it or subtract from it (1, 15)

structural deficit (surplus): the portion of the deficit (or surplus) that results from tax and spending policy dictated by the president and Congress at their discretion (25)

structural unemployment: unemployment that arises because people's skills, experience, education, or location do not match what employers need (23)

subjective well-being (SWB): a measure of welfare based on survey questions asking people about their own degree of life satisfaction (9, 21)

subprime mortgage: a mortgage given to someone with poor credit (19, 30)

subsidy: a per-unit payment to producers to lower production costs and encourage greater production (13)

substitutability: the possibility of using one resource instead of another (15)

substitute good: a good that can be used in place of another good (4)

substitution effect of a price change: the tendency of a price increase for a particular good to reduce the quantity demanded of that good, as buyers turn to relatively cheaper substitutes (5)

sunk cost: an expenditure that was incurred or committed to in the past and is irreversible in the short run (17)

supply: the willingness of producers and merchandisers to provide goods and services (4)

supply curve: a curve indicating the quantities that sellers are willing to supply at various prices (4)

supply schedule: a table showing the relationship between price and quantity supplied (4)

supply shock: a change in the productive capacity of an economy (28)

supply-side economics: an economic theory that emphasizes policies to stimulate production, such as lower taxes. The theory predicts that lower marginal tax rates stimulate greater economic effort, saving, and investment, thereby increasing overall economic output and tax revenues (12, 25)

surplus: a situation in which the quantity that sellers are prepared to sell at a particular price exceeds the quantity that buyers are willing to buy at that price (4)

sustainable socioeconomic system: one that maintains its resources such that at least the same level of social well-being can be maintained over time (15)

tacit collusion: collusion that takes place without creation of a cartel (18)

tariffs: taxes (or duties) charged by national governments to the importers of goods from other countries; tariffs can also be placed on exports (7, 29)

tax incidence analysis: the study of who bears the ultimate burden of a tax (12)

tax multiplier: the impact of a change in a lump sum tax on economic equilibrium, expressed mathematically as $\Delta Y/\Delta \times \bar{T}(mult)(mpc)$ (25)

taxable income: the portion of one's income that is subject to taxation after deductions and exemptions (12)

technological progress: the development of new methods of converting inputs (resources) into outputs (products or services) (1)

technological unemployment: unemployment caused by reduced demand for workers because technology has increased the productivity of those who have jobs, effectively reducing the demand for workers (23)

terms of trade: the price of exports relative to imports (32)

tertiary sector: the sector of the economy that involves the provision of services rather than of tangible goods (22)

theoretical investigation: analysis based in abstract thought (1)

theory of market adjustment: the theory that market forces will tend to make shortages and surpluses disappear (4)

third-party effects: impacts of an economic transaction on those not involved in the transaction, such as the health effects of pollution (6)

three major macroeconomic goals: the achievement of good living standards, stability and security, and environmental sustainability (19)

throughput: the flow of raw materials and energy through the economy, leading to outputs of waste (33)

time discount rate: an economic concept describing the relative weighting of present benefits or costs compared to future benefits or costs (8)

time lags: the time that elapses between the formulation of an economic policy and its actual effects on the economy (25)

time-series data: observations of how a numerical variable changes over time (2)

"too big to fail": when a company grows so large that its failure would cause widespread economic harm in terms of lost jobs and diminished asset values (30)

total cost: the sum of fixed and variable costs (16)

total cost curve: a graph showing the relationship between the total cost of production and the level of output (16)

total economic value: the sum of all the benefits for which people are willing to pay, with respect to an ecosystem or natural place (13)

total factor productivity: a measure of the productivity of all factors of production. It represents contributions to output from all sources, not just quantities of manufactured capital and labor (32)

total income: the sum of income that an individual or couple receives from all sources (12)

total product curve: a curve showing the total amount of output produced with different levels of one variable input, holding all other inputs constant (16)

total revenues: the total amount of money received by a seller, equal to price times quantity (17)

tradable pollution permits: a system of pollution regulation in which a government allocates permits that are required in order to produce pollution. After they are allocated, these permits may be traded among firms or other interested parties (13)

trade account (part of the current account): the portion of the current account that tracks inflows and outflows arising exclusively from international trade in goods and services (29)

trade ban: a law preventing the import or export of goods or services (29)

trade deficit: an excess of imports over exports, causing net exports to be negative (29)

trade quota: a nationally imposed restriction on the quantity of a particular good that can be imported from another country (7, 29)

trade-related subsidy: payments given to producers to encourage more production, either for export or as a substitute for imports (7, 29)

tragedy of the commons: a situation in which an unregulated common property resource is seriously degraded due to overuse (14)

transaction costs: the costs of arranging economic activities (3)

transfer: the giving of something with nothing specific expected in return (1)

transfer payments: payments by government to individuals or firms, including Social Security payments, unemployment compensation, interest payments, and subsidies (25)

travel cost models: a revealed preference method used to obtain estimates of the recreation benefits of natural sites based on variations in the travel costs paid by visitors from different regions (13)

triple bottom line: an assessment of the performance of a business according to social and environmental goals as well as making profits (16)

underemployment: working fewer hours than desired or at a job that does not match one's skills (23)

underground market: a market in which illegal goods and services are sold or legal goods and services are sold in an illegal way (3)

unemployed person (BLS definition): a person who is not employed but who is actively seeking a job and is immediately available for work (23)

unemployment: a situation in which people seek a paying job, but cannot obtain one (19)

unemployment rate: the percentage of the labor force made up of people who do not have paid jobs but are immediately available and actively looking for paid jobs (23)

unit-elastic demand: the percentage change in the quantity demanded is exactly equal to the percentage change in price. The elasticity value is 1 (5)

upstream taxes: taxes instituted as close as possible in a production process to the extraction of raw materials (13)

utility: the level of usefulness or satisfaction gained from a particular activity such as consumption of a good or service (2, 9)

utility function (or total utility curve): a curve showing the relation of utility levels to consumption levels (9)

value of a statistical life (VSL): society's willingness to pay to avoid one death, based on the valuation of relatively small changes in mortality risks (13)

value-added: the value of what a producer sells, less the value of the intermediate inputs it uses, except labor. This is equal to the wages paid out by the producer plus its profits (20)

variable costs: production costs that can be adjusted relatively quickly and that do not need to be paid if no production occurs (16)

variable input: a production input whose quantity can be changed relatively quickly, resulting in changes in the level of production (16)

velocity of money: the number of times that a dollar would have to change hands during a year to support nominal GDP, calculated as $V = (P \times Y)/M$ (27)

virtuous cycles (in development): self-reinforcing patterns of high savings, investment, productivity growth, and economic expansion (32)

voluntary simplicity: a conscious decision to live with limited or reduced level of consumption, in order to increase one's quality of life (9)

wage and price controls: government regulations setting limits on wages and prices or on the rates at which they are permitted to increase (28)

wage-price spiral: when high demand for labor and other resources creates upward pressure on wages, which in turn leads to upward pressure on prices and, as a result, further upward pressure on wages (28)

wage-productivity gap: the gap between the growth of labor productivity and the growth of hourly labor compensation (23)

Washington Consensus: Specific economic policy prescriptions used by the IMF and World Bank with a goal of helping developing countries to avoid crisis and maintain stability. They include openness to trade and investment (liberalization), privatization, budget austerity, and deregulation (29)

waste products: outputs that are not used either for consumption or in a further production process (1)

wealth: the net value of all the material and financial assets owned by an individual (1)

welfare economics: the branch of microeconomics that seeks to estimate the social welfare of different scenarios in order to determine how to maximize net social benefits (6)

well-being: a term used broadly to describe a good quality of life (1)

wholesale markets: markets where final goods are purchased by retailers from suppliers, normally in large quantities (3)

willingness-to-pay (WTP) principle: the economic value of something, such as an environmental benefit, is equal to the maximum amount people are willing to pay for it (13)

worker cooperatives: a labor arrangement in which the owners of an enterprise are the workers themselves (10)

World Bank: an international agency charged with promoting economic development, through loans and other programs (29)

World Trade Organization (WTO): an international organization that provides a forum for trade negotiations, creates rules to govern trade, and investigates and makes judgment on trade disputes (7, 29)

Index

Note: Italicized locators indicate figures.

C

D

E

F

G

H

J

K

L

M

N

T

U

V

W

Z

About the Authors

Neva R. Goodwin (PhD, Boston University) is co-director of the Global Development and Environment Institute (GDAE) at Tufts University.

Jonathan M. Harris (Ph.D., Boston University) is director of the Theory and Education Project at GDAE.

Julie A. Nelson (Ph.D., University of Wisconsin, Madison) is Professor of Economics at the University of Massachusetts Boston and Senior Research Fellow at GDAE.

Brian Roach (Ph.D, University of California, Davis) is Senior Research Associate at GDAE.

Mariano Torras (Ph.D., University of Massachusetts, Amherst) is Professor of Economics at Adelphi University and Senior Research Fellow at GDAE.

Contributor **Frank Ackerman** is Senior Economist at Synapse Energy Economics, Cambridge, Massachusetts.

Contributor **Thomas Weisskopf** is Professor of Economics Emeritus at the University of Michigan, Ann Arbor, Michigan.

Contributor **James Devine** is Professor of Economics at Loyola Marymount University, Los Angeles.